The
Fundamentals
of Canadian

INCOME TAX

Fifth Edition

Vern Krishna, QC, FRSC, FCGA

B. Comm., LL.B., MBA, Dip. Law (Cantab), LL.M. (Harvard)
Professor of Common Law, University of Ottawa
Of Counsel: Koskie Minsky (Toronto)

CGA Tax Research Centre
(University of Ottawa)

This publication is designed to provide accurate and authoritative information. It is sold with the understanding that the publisher is not engaged in rendering legal, accounting or other professional advice. If legal advice or other expert assistance is required, the services of a competent professional should be sought. The analysis contained herein represents the opinions of the authors and should in no way be construed as being either official or unofficial policy of any governmental body.

Canadian Cataloguing in Publication Data

Krishna, Vern
    The fundamentals of Canadian income tax

5th ed.
Includes bibliographical references and index.
ISBN 0-459-57455-8

1. Income tax — Law and legislation — Canada.
I. Title.

KE5759.K74 1995   343.7105'2   C95-932203-5
KF6499.ZA3K74 1995

CARSWELL
Thomson Professional Publishing

One Corporate Plaza	Customer Service:
2075 Kennedy Road	Toronto: 1-416-609-3800
Scarborough, Ontario	Elsewhere in Canada: 1-800-387-5164
M1T 3V4	Fax: 1-416-298-5094

To Savitri, Linda, Nicola and Sacha

Preface to the Fifth Edition

The Fifth Edition of Fundamentals of Canadian Income Tax is a comprehensive examination of income tax law for students of law and business, legal practitioners and professional accountants. As with previous editions, I assume that readers come to the subject of income tax law and tax practice with varying backgrounds and limited prior knowledge of the subject. Students are generally, and unnecessarily, apprehensive of tax law. Practitioners prefer to steer clear of the subject, though they do so at their own peril. I have written this work on the assumption that the reader knows little of the subject. I hope that readers are not offended by this assumption. It serves as a useful yardstick in that it allows one to build up from fundamental concepts to a more sophisticated and technical analysis of the law.

The title of this work, "The Fundamentals of Canadian Income Tax", is important. The text focuses on the *fundamental* principles and basic concepts of income tax law. Technical detail is superimposed on these fundamentals only to the extent necessary to an understanding of tax law and practice.

I repeat what I said in the first edition. The *Income Tax Act* is a legislative enactment that must be read in the manner of all statutes: carefully, methodically, and in the context of evolving and shifting doctrines of statutory interpretation, which have undergone radical changes since the publication of the first edition in 1985. We have moved away from the doctrines of strict and literal interpretation towards a purposive approach to statutory construction. Purposive interpretation, which started with *Stubart* in 1984, is now firmly entrenched in Canadian tax law. In addition, we also have the (in)famous General Anti-Avoidance Rule, which takes the doctrine of purposive interpretation one step further: not only should the *Act* be interpreted purposively, but tax arrangements that abuse the underlying policy of the *Act* may be recharacterized by the Revenue. That, indeed, is a formidable power. Thus, it is that much more imperative that we emphasize the principles and underlying concepts in our understanding of the workings of income tax law.

The Fifth Edition is much more than simply an updating of its predecessor. Of course, I updated the text to take into account legislative amendments, judicial decisions and administrative pronouncements since the last edition. It has also been expanded to take into account the shifting emphasis of the economy towards international business. Hence, I include six new chapters on international transactions, immigration and emigration.

There is an extensive bibliography at the end of each chapter for those who wish to pursue particular topics in greater detail. There are also references at the beginning of each chapter to the relevant sections of the Act, Interpretation Bulletins, Advance Rulings, and Information Circulars. These will allow the reader to move into greater levels of detail as individual circumstances warrant.

I received substantial help in the preparation of this edition from my research assistant, Ms. Julie Colden, now of Ogilvy Renault in Ottawa. Ms. Colden did a remarkable job of reviewing the textual material, references and bibliography under extremely tight deadlines. She made valuable suggestions that improved the text and I was grateful for her help throughout this project. Of course, as always, I owe an enormous debt of gratitude to my secretary, Mrs. Fran Russo, who has had to live with many editions of this text. Over the years, we have learned new technology to produce this work and we fully expect further technological improvements will test our ability to adapt as we work through future editions.

Dr. Johnson said that the only end of writing is to enable readers to better enjoy life or better to endure it. I remain sceptical that this edition will, any more than its predecessors, satisfy his first criterion. I am more optimistic, however, that it will allow students to better endure their income tax courses with less anxiety and reduce the research burden on practitioners.

The law in this text is dated as at June 15, 1995 though segments of Bill C-70, which received Royal Assent on June 22, 1995, have also been incorporated as appropriate.

Vern Krishna

Acknowledgement

I wish to acknowledge the assistance and support of The Fellows and Life Fellows of the Foundation of Legal Research in the preparation of this text.

*The art of taxation is so to pluck the goose
that the maximum number of feathers are obtained
with the minimum amount of hissing.*

Jean Colbert (1665)

SUMMARY TABLE OF CONTENTS

SUMMARY TABLE OF CONTENTS

DETAILED TABLE OF CONTENTS

CHAPTER I — INTRODUCTION

CHAPTER II — INTERPRETATION OF TAX LAW

CHAPTER IV — WHAT IS INCOME?

CHAPTER V — INCOME FROM AN OFFICE OR EMPLOYMENT

CHAPTER VII — BUSINESS AND PROPERTY INCOME: INCLUSIONS

CHAPTER VIII — BUSINESS AND PROPERTY INCOME: DEDUCTIONS

CHAPTER IX — CAPITAL GAINS

CHAPTER X — OTHER SOURCES OF INCOME

CHAPTER XII — TAXABLE INCOME

CHAPTER XIII — COMPUTATION OF TAX PAYABLE

CHAPTER XIV — CORPORATIONS AND SHAREHOLDERS: GENERAL

CHAPTER XV — CORPORATE FINANCE

CHAPTER XVI — PRIVATE CORPORATIONS: INVESTMENT INCOME

CHAPTER XVII — PRIVATE CORPORATIONS: BUSINESS INCOME

CHAPTER XVIII — DIVIDENDS AND CAPITAL DISTRIBUTIONS

CHAPTER XIX — TAXATION OF SHAREHOLDERS

CHAPTER XX — REORGANIZATIONS: TRANSFER OF PROPERTY TO A CORPORATION

CHAPTER XXI — NON-ARM'S LENGTH SHARE TRANSFERS

CHAPTER XXII — SHARE-FOR-SHARE EXCHANGES

Table of Contents

CHAPTER XXVI — ADMINISTRATION

CHAPTER XXVII — INTERNATIONAL: GENERAL PRINCIPLES

CHAPTER XXVIII — IMMIGRATION

CHAPTER XXIX — NON-RESIDENTS

CHAPTER XXX — INBOUND INVESTMENTS

CHAPTER XXXI — OUTBOUND INVESTMENTS AND FOREIGN INCOME

CHAPTER XXXII — EMIGRATION

XXXIII — TAX AVOIDANCE

TABLE OF CASES

All references are to page numbers.

Border Chemical Co. v. The Queen (1987), 87 DTC 5391 (F.C.T.D.) 360

Borlands Trustee v. Steel Bros. & Co., [1901] 1 Ch. 279 684

Botkin v. M.N.R., [1989] 2 CTC 2110, 89 DTC 398 (T.C.C.) 391, 1278

Bourdon v. M.N.R., [1984] CTC 2654, 84 DTC 1411 (T.C.C.) 1102

Bowater Power Co. v. M.N.R., [1971] CTC 818, 71 DTC
    5469 (F.C.T.D.) 356

Bowles v. Bank of England, [1913] 1 Ch. 57 . . . . 11, 65

Br. Amer. Tobacco Co. v. I.R.C., [1943] AC 335 (H.L) 1012

Br. Amer. Tobacco Co. v. I.R.C. [1943] 1 All ER 13 (H.L.) 778, 1334

Br. Insulated & Helsby Cables v. Atherton, [1926] AC 205 (H.L.) 356

Br. Launderer's Research Assn. v. Hendon Borough Rating Authority,
    [1949] 1 KB 462 583

Br. Salmson Aero Engines Ltd., I.R.C. v. (1938), 22 Tax Cas. 29 (C.A.) 358

Bradbury v. English Sewing Cotton Co., [1923] AC 744 684

Brady-Browne v. M.N.R., (1969), 69 DTC 797 (T.A.B.) 1148

Branch v. The Queen, [1976] CTC 193, 76 DTC 6112 (Alta. Dist. Ct.) 1370

Brassard v. Smith, [1925] AC 371 (P.C.) 139, 140

Bridges v. Hewitt, [1957] 2 All ER 281 (C.A.) 197

British Guiana Credit Corp. v. Da Silva, [1965] 1 WLR 248 (P.C.) 215

British Thomson - Houston Co. v. Sterling Accessories Ltd., [1924]
    2 Ch. 33 655

British Westinghouse Electric Mfg. Co. v. Underground Electric Rys.
    Co. of London, [1912] AC 673 (H.L.) 314

Broitman v. M.N.R., [1986] 2 CTC 2283, 86 DTC 1711 (T.C.C.) 843

Bronfman Trust v. The Queen, [1987] 1 CTC 117, 87 DTC 5059
    (S.C.C.) 58, 62, 383, 387, 388, 391, 712, 713, 714, 715, 716, 718,
                          1270, 1271, 1274, 1275, 1276, 1278, 1373, 1374

Bronfman, M.N.R. v., [1965] CTC 378, 65 DTC 5235 (Ex. Ct.) 128, 527

Brooks v. M.N.R., [1977] CTC 2048, 77 DTC 38 (T.R.B.) 543, 546

Brown, Dep. A. G. Can. v., [1964] CTC 483, 64 DTC 483
    (S.C.C.) [B.C.] 1144

Brown v. M.N.R. (1950), 1 Tax ABC 373, 50 DTC 156 369

Brown v. Helvering, 91 US 193 (1934) 545

Brown v. The Queen, [1975] CTC 611, 75 DTC 5433 (F.C.T.D.) 591

Brown v. Waterloo Reg. Bd. of Commr. of Police (1982), 37 OR (2d)
    277; revd. 43 OR (2d) 113 (Ont. C.A.) 216

Brumby v. Milner, [1976] 3 All ER 636 (H.L.) 194

Buckerfield's Ltd. v. M.N.R., [1964] CTC 504, 64 DTC 5301
    (Ex. Ct.) 595, 778, 784, 1012, 1333

Bullen v. Wisconsin, 240 USR 625 (1916) 1368

CHAPTER I

INTRODUCTION

> Others may be inspired by the reflection that, if two hundred years ago men revolted on the principle that "Taxation without representation is tyranny", then today men may rise in righteous wrath because taxation with representation, but beyond human comprehension is even worse.
> (Judge Malcolm Wilkey of the U.S. Court of Appeals)

"Tax" is a compulsory contribution levied on individuals, firms or property in order to transfer resources from the private to the public sector.

Usually, although not inevitably, there are two principal reasons in modern industrialized societies for levying taxes: (1) to finance public sector goods and services, and (2) to redistribute income amongst the various segments of a society. The dominance of one or other of these two purposes depends, in large measure, upon the prevailing political philosophy of the society. In addition to public financing and income redistribution, however, the tax system can be, and is, used to implement socio-economic policy.

It is important to note that some levies are in fact taxes despite their being disguised by more attractive nomenclature. Thus, to the extent that the Canada Pension Plan and Unemployment Insurance involve compulsory transfer payments measured in part by reference to income, they are, in effect, income taxes.

1. HISTORICAL BACKGROUND

The federal income tax on business profits was introduced in Canada in 1916 and a tax on personal incomes was introduced in 1917. Both of these taxes were initially espoused as temporary measures to finance the Dominion's needs during the First World War.[1] As history has proven, the tax was not, as the name of its enabling legislation, the *Income War Tax Act*, implied, a temporary tax.

Following the Second World War, the *Income War Tax Act* was replaced with the *Income Tax Act* ("the Act"), effective from January 1, 1949.

The following is a chronological listing of some of the major milestones in Canadian fiscal history up to 1988:

1917	Original federal income tax statute
1940	Rowell-Sirois Royal Commission Report on Dominion Provincial Relations
1942	Federal-provincial wartime fiscal arrangements
1947-48	First major postwar revision of federal-provincial arrangements
1947	Quebec and Ontario re-enter corporate income tax field

---

[1] Prior to the First World War the principal sources of revenue were customs duties and excise taxes.

1949   First major federal income tax revision
1954   Quebec re-enters personal income tax field
1962   Appointment of Royal Commission on Taxation (Carter Commission)
1966   Report of Royal Commission on Taxation in Quebec (Belanger Commission)
1967   Report of Carter Royal Commission
1967   Report of Ontario Committee on Taxation (Smith Committee)
1969   Federal White Paper, "Proposals for Tax Reform"
1970   Senate Committee Report on Federal White Paper
1970   Commons Committee Report on Federal White Paper
1971   1971 Federal Tax Reform Bill
1972   1972 Federal *Income Tax Act* (Bill C-259)
1987   1987 Federal Tax Reform Proposals (White Paper)
1988   1988 Federal *Income Tax Act* (Bill C-139)

The present version of the *Income Tax Act*[2] commenced in 1972. It was enacted after an extended period of analysis and debate commencing with the appointment of a Royal Commission on Taxation (the "Carter Commission") in 1962. The commission reported its findings in 1967 in a seven-volume report, the "Carter Report".[3]

The Carter Report recommended radical change of the tax system. In particular, it recommended taxation on the basis of a "comprehensive tax base" that would include all net gains, gifts, imputed income and accrued gains. It also favoured full taxation of capital gains. Both of these proposals proved to be too radical for the time and were dropped from the 1971 Tax Reform Bill. Since that time, however, selected aspects of the reform proposals have crept into the tax system and we have seen incremental taxation of capital gains.

2. THE 1969 WHITE PAPER

Following the Carter Report, the federal government tabled a White Paper ("Proposals for Tax Reform") in Parliament in November 1969. The purpose of the White Paper was to stimulate public discussion of the proposals for tax reform. Although the White Paper was based in substantial measure on the Carter Report, it modified several important recommendations of the report. Most significantly, the White Paper rejected outright the cornerstone of the comprehensive tax base, the idea that "a buck is a buck is a buck".

The White Paper opted to continue with taxation based upon source and type of income. The White Paper also modified the Carter proposals in respect of the full integration of corporate earnings with shareholder taxation. The rejection of Carter's "a

---

[2] *Income Tax Act*, R.S.C. 1985, c. 1 (5th Supp.) as amended, introduced as Bill C-259 on June 30, 1971 with Royal Assent on December 23, 1971.

[3] Mr. Kenneth Carter was a distinguished accountant practising in Toronto.

buck is a buck" proposal resulted in the Act being much more complicated than it would have been if all types of income were treated alike for tax purposes.

The publication of the White Paper in 1969 was followed by a lengthy and controversial debate on the proposed structure of the federal income tax system. Due to the pervasive public interest in the subject of taxation, "tax reform" moved quickly into the political arena where it immediately fell victim to power politics. Extensive lobbying by various interest groups, including provincial governments, professional associations, lawyers and accountants, eventually had an impact on the tax proposals. The "reformed" *Income Tax Act*, substantially modified and diluted from the Carter Report, was finally enacted and came into force on January 1, 1972.

3. POST-1971 CHANGES

Since 1971, the federal income tax system has been, and continues to be, subjected to substantial change through annual legislative amendments. Some of the amendments address technical and structural deficiencies in the legislation, while others introduce new schemes. The annual enactment of layer upon layer of substantive and technical amendments has made its mark on the system. The income tax law of Canada now functions at a level of technical complexity and legal obscurity that is well beyond the comprehension of most educated people.

For 15 years after the introduction of the 1972 "reform" Act we saw frenzied activity in tax law. There were more and more complicated technical statutory changes, administrative amendments, refinements, finetuning of fiscal policies and the introduction of increasingly generous tax incentives and giveaway programs. During this period we saw the introduction of tax shelters in respect of housing projects, oil and gas drilling funds, Canadian films, deferred income plans, mining flow-through shares, and the notorious scientific research tax credits (SRTCs). The SRTC scheme alone cost the federal treasury in excess of $2 billion in lost revenues during the two years that the program was in existence. The SRTCs were the subject of hundreds of tax schemes (scams), illegal activity and, later, protracted litigation when Revenue Canada attempted to collect illegally foregone taxes from the directors of companies involved in the schemes.

This period also saw the *Income Tax Act* grow by leaps and bounds as each successive government introduced new incentive schemes and tried to plug loopholes in older ones. As it grew, it also became increasingly complicated.

By 1987, most tax lawyers and tax accountants could claim expertise only in limited and narrow segments of the statute. The age of the generalist in tax law passed into history. In that year the Conservative Government tabled another White Paper ("Tax Reform '87"), with the stated purpose of refining the *Income Tax Act* so as to make it fair, competitive, simple, consistent, and reliable.

The White Paper was reviewed by the Standing Committee on Finance and Economic Affairs of the House of Commons (the Blenkarn Committee) which made 81 recommendations for changes to the government's proposals. It was also studied by the Standing Senate Committee on Banking, Trade and Commerce (the "Sinclair Committee") which made 29 recommendations for changes. The Minister of Finance, Michael Wilson, tabled his Notice of Ways and Means Motion to implement the Tax Reform '87 proposals on December 16, 1987. He ignored all but three minor changes recommended by the Parliamentary committees.

The new "re-reformed" Act retains the essential character of its predecessors. The Carter proposal that a "buck is a buck" was rejected once again by the reformers. Although the 1987 changes to the Act moved towards higher taxation of capital gains, they maintained the essence of the earlier tax system, namely, that different types of income are, in effect, taxed at different rates and subject to different rules.

The new proposals did little to simplify the *Income Tax Act*. Indeed, if anything, the 1987 tax reform exercise elevated the statute to a new level of complexity coupled with uncertainty. As W.J. Strain, co-chair of the Joint Committee on Taxation of the Canadian Bar Association and the Canadian Institute of Chartered Accountants, said in addressing the House of Commons Committee on Finance and Economic Affairs:

> For any taxpayer to pick up some of this legislation we are looking at today and understand how these rules are going to impact on him when he sits down to fill out his tax return is almost impossible.

> There is no quick fix to the complexity issue. It is a very long-term problem, but I fear that the Government's priority for tax simplification has fallen down to the bottom of the various objectives set out for tax reform.

4. CONSTITUTIONAL BACKGROUND

(a) Division of Powers

The constitutional authority to impose an income tax is found in the *Constitution Act, 1867*. The federal Parliament has the power under subsection 91(3) to raise money by *any* mode or system of taxation.

The power of the provincial legislatures to impose taxes is restricted by subsection 92(2) to direct taxation within the province for the purpose of raising revenue for provincial purposes.

Neither the Dominion nor a province may delegate to the other its power to legislate on taxation.[4]

Provincial taxing legislation must satisfy three tests:

- the tax must be a *direct* tax;
- the tax must be imposed *within the province*; and
- the tax must be imposed *for the purpose* of raising revenue for provincial purposes.

---

[4] *A.G. N.S. v. A.G. Can.* (1950), 50 DTC 838 (S.C.C.).

The last requirement prevents a province from using its taxing power for colourable purposes. The rationale for limiting provincial legislatures to direct taxation is to contain provincial powers within provincial boundaries. To be sure, this objective is not met to the extent that direct taxes are passed on to persons (for example, consumers) outside the province.

The legal distinction between direct and indirect taxation was formulated by John Stuart Mill in 1848. Thus:[5]

> A direct tax is one which is demanded from the very persons who it is intended or desired should pay it. Indirect taxes are those which are demanded from one person in the expectation and intention that he shall indemnify himself at the expense of another; such as the excise or customs.

Most economists today would take exception to Mill's definition. Indeed, the question as to who actually bears the burden of any tax (the "incidence of taxation") is one of the more controversial economic issues of our time. Nevertheless, Mill's definition is now accepted by the courts as the most useful explanation of direct and indirect taxes for constitutional law purposes.[6]

The constitutionality of a tax is to be determined by its nature and general tendencies at the time of its enactment. Economic recoupment is not the critical factor in distinguishing between direct and indirect taxes. The distinction rests on the general tendency of the tax. As LaForest J. says:[7]

> . . . what is required to constitute an indirect tax is the passing on of the tax itself in a recognizable form, not its recovery by more or less circuitous operation of economic forces.

Federal and provincial taxing powers overlap to the extent that the federal Parliament has the power to raise money by both direct and indirect taxation. Thus, a Canadian resident may be taxed at the federal level and also by the province in which he or she resides.

(b) Administrative Responsibility

Financial affairs falling within the authority of the federal power are administered by the Department of Finance.[8] The administration of the *Income Tax Act* is supervised by the Minister of National Revenue.[9] Thus, Canada, unlike most other countries, has

---

[5] See: *Cotton v. The King*, [1914] AC 176 at 193 (P.C.); see also *Atlantic Smoke Shops Ltd. v. Conlon*, [1943] CTC 294 (P.C.); see generally La Forest J., "The Allocation of Taxing Power under the Canadian Constitution", *Can. Tax Paper No. 45* (Can. Tax. Foundation, 1967).

[6] *Bank of Toronto v. Lambe* (1887), 12 App. Cas. 575 (P.C.).

[7] La Forest, "The Allocation of Taxing Power under the Canadian Constitution", *Can. Tax. Paper No. 45* (Can. Tax. Foundation, 1967), at 81.

[8] *Financial Administration Act*, R.S.C. 1985, c. F-11.

[9] *Department of National Revenue Act*, R.S.C. 1985, c. N-15.

placed the responsibility for enactment of fiscal legislation and its administration in different ministries.[10]

(c) Restraint on Powers

Section 125 of the *Constitution Act, 1867* provides that no lands or property belonging to Canada or any province shall be liable to taxation. The effect of this provision is to provide intergovernmental immunity from taxation in respect of "lands or property" owned by the federal or provincial Crown. The restriction also extends to Crown agents such as Crown corporations.

What is the extent of this protection? The first question to be determined is whether a particular statutory measure is a "taxation" measure or the exercise of regulatory power under some other legislative head, for example, the commerce clause. On its surface, it appears as if section 125 only exempts provincial "lands or property" from federal taxation. The restraint on the federal government has, however, been more broadly interpreted. Section 125 applies not only to provincial lands or property but also to taxes levied on persons and transactions in respect of Crown property. Section 125 overrides the express powers of taxation contained in subsections 91(3) (the federal power) and 92(2) (the provincial power) of the *Constitution Act, 1867*. Thus, section 125 clearly provides a constitutional guarantee of immunity from federal taxation of provincial property.[11] As the Supreme Court of Canada has said:[12]

> This immunity would be illusory if it applied to taxes "on property" but not to a tax on the Crown in respect of a transaction affecting its property or on the transaction itself. The immunity would be illusory since, by the simple device of framing a tax as "*in personam*" rather than "*in rem*" one level of government could with impunity tax away the fruits of property owned by the other. The fundamental constitutional protection framed by section 125 cannot depend on subtle nuances of form.

Hence, once it is determined that the "pith and substance" of a measure is "taxation", section 125 restrains the federal government from imposing the tax on provincial lands, property, Crown agents, and transactions directly involving provincial property. This appears to be the case whether or not the province is involved in commercial activity. In Professor Hogg's words:[13]

> . . . Section 125 probably covers taxation of all property belonging to Canada or a province, regardless of whether the property is acquired for or employed in a commercial activity or a governmental activity. The section is not limited to non-commercial property.

---

[10] The paramountcy doctrine does not apply to this potential for double taxation; see *Forbes v. A.G. Man.*, [1937] AC 260 (P.C.).

[11] *Re Exported Natural Gas Tax*, [1982] 1 SCR 1004 (S.C.C.).

[12] *Id.*, at 1078.

[13] Hogg, *Constitutional Law of Canada*, 2nd ed. (Toronto: Carswell, 1985), at 625.

The determination of whether the substance of legislation constitutes taxation or the exercise of a regulatory power can be a difficult question and, in some cases, produce dubious results.[14]

5. FEDERAL-PROVINCIAL TAX AGREEMENTS

Prior to 1962, the federal government dominated the field of income taxation. With the exception of Ontario and Quebec, the federal government was allowed to occupy the entire field of individual and corporate income taxation in exchange for agreed upon "rental" payments to the provinces. The "rental" payments were compensation to the provinces in exchange for giving up their constitutional rights to levy direct taxes.

The structure of the arrangement between the federal and provincial governments was altered by the *Federal-Provincial Fiscal Arrangements Act (1961)* under which the federal Parliament unilaterally vacated a portion of the income tax field to the provinces. The withdrawal of the federal government allowed the provinces to re-enter the income tax field and impose their own taxes.

The federal government has tax collection agreements with most of the provinces under which the federal government collects the provincial income tax on behalf of the provinces. To facilitate tax collection and assessment, the agreements require the provinces to levy their tax by reference to a taxable base identical to that used for federal income tax purposes. Thus, in most of the provinces, the provincial income tax payable by individuals is calculated as a percentage of their federal tax payable. Provincial corporate taxes are also calculated as a percentage of taxable income as determined for federal purposes.

The system requires, however, that the participating provinces restrict themselves to levying a basic tax upon the amount of the Federal tax and this limits provincial flexibility in raising revenues. Quebec is the only province which administers both its corporate and individual income taxes; Ontario and Alberta collect their own corporate taxes.

The relevant legislation for determining federal-provincial income tax arrangements is the *Federal-Provincial Fiscal Arrangements and Federal Post-secondary Education and Health Contributions Act.*[15] All provinces, other than Quebec, collect their personal income tax revenues by piggybacking the federal tax. Thus, with the exception of individuals living in Quebec, resident individuals pay provincial tax at a rate that is a percentage of their basic federal tax.

For 1994-1995, the rates (ignoring special surtaxes and adjustments) of provincial tax as a percentage of federal tax were as follows:

---

[14] See *British Columbia (A.G.) v. Canada (A.G.)*, [1924] AC 222 (P.C.).

[15] *Federal-Provincial Fiscal Arrangements and Federal Post-secondary Education and Health Contributions Act*, R.S.C. 1985, c. F-8.

Alberta	45.5%
British Columbia	52.5%
Manitoba	52.0%
New Brunswick	64.0%
Newfoundland	69.0%
Nova Scotia	59.5%
Ontario	58.0%
Prince Edward Island	59.5%
Saskatchewan	50.0%
Northwest Territories	45.0%
Yukon	48.0%
Non-residents	52.0%

Residents of Quebec receive an abatement of 16.5 per cent from their basic federal tax, but are required to pay Quebec income tax according to a special scale of rates.

The combined top marginal rates for 1993 and 1994 are as follows:

	1993	1994
Saskatchewan	51.95	52.0
Quebec	52.94	52.9
Manitoba	50.40	50.4
Nova Scotia	50.30	53.8
Prince Edward Island	50.30	50.3
New Brunswick	50.74	51.4
Newfoundland	51.33	51.3
British Columbia	51.12	54.2
Ontario	52.35	53.2
Alberta	46.07	46.1
Yukon	46.55	46.6
Northwest Territories	44.37	44.4

Notwithstanding the substantial increases in federal and provincial tax rates in recent years (approximately 25 per cent between 1980-1991), government debt continues to increase and annual deficits add to the substantial cost of financing the public debt.

TABLE 1
NET GOVERNMENT DEBT

FISCAL Y/E MARCH	FEDERAL GOVERNMENT $ Billions	% CHANGE from previous year	PROVINCIAL GOVERNMENT $ Billions	% CHANGE from previous year	TOTAL $ Billions	% CHANGE from previous year
1981	90.4	—	26.0	—	116.4	—
1982	106.0	17.3	25.0	3.8	131.0	12.5
1983	135.1	27.5	33.3	33.2	168.4	28.5
1984	168.0	24.4	41.5	24.6	209.5	24.4
1985	206.6	23.0	49.7	19.8	256.3	22.3
1986	241.3	16.8	60.7	22.1	302.0	17.8
1987	272.0	12.7	73.4	20.9	345.4	14.4
1988	300.3	10.4	80.8	10.1	381.1	10.3
1989	329.2	9.6	86.5	7.1	415.7	9.1
1990	358.3	8.8	92.1	6.5	450.4	8.3
1991	390.3	8.9	101.7	10.4	492.0	9.2
1992	424.8	8.8	126.5	24.4	551.3	12.1
1993	465.3	9.5	162.1	28.1	627.4	13.8
1994	511.0	9.8	184.0	13.5	695.0	10.8

The net public debt consists of the federal government's total liabilities less its financial assets. In 1993, for example, total liabilities amounted to $504.9 billion, while financial assets were $39.6 billion. Thus, the *net* federal government debt was $465.3 billion.

TABLE 2
GOVERNMENT DEFICITS

FISCAL Y/E MARCH	FEDERAL GOVERNMENT $ Billions	% CHANGE from previous year	PROVINCIAL GOVERNMENT $ Billions	% CHANGE from previous year	TOTAL $ Billions	% CHANGE from previous year
1981	14.7	—	5.7	—	20.4	—
1982	15.6	6.1	5.4	5.3	21.0	2.9
1983	29.0	85.9	10.4	92.6	39.4	87.6
1984	32.9	13.4	8.1	22.1	41.0	4.1
1985	38.6	17.3	8.2	1.2	46.8	14.1
1986	34.6	10.4	10.2	24.4	44.8	4.3
1987	30.8	11.0	12.9	26.5	43.7	2.5
1988	28.2	8.4	7.7	40.3	35.9	17.8
1989	29.0	2.8	5.4	29.9	34.4	4.2
1990	29.0	0.0	4.7	13.0	33.7	2.0
1991	32.1	10.7	9.5	102.1	41.6	23.4
1992	34.5	7.5	22.8	140.0	57.3	37.7
1993	40.5	17.4	24.9	9.2	65.4	14.1
1994	45.7	12.8	20.2	18.9	65.9	0.8

For 1993, the federal government's revenues were $121.4 billion, while budgetary spending was $161.9 billion. This produced a deficit of $40.5 billion which, added to the deficits of previous years of $424.8 billion, brought the net government debt to $465.3 billion. Not coincidentally, the cost of financing the public debt in the same year at $39.4 billion was equal to the budget deficit for the year.

6. THE LEGISLATIVE PROCESS

(a) House of Commons

Legislation in respect of income tax originates in the House of Commons on the recommendation of the Governor General.[16] Income tax legislation may not be introduced in the Senate, nor is it possible for a private member to introduce a tax bill in the House of Commons.

As a matter of parliamentary tradition, the Minister of Finance presents a Budget[17] to the House of Commons, following which a Notice of Ways and Means Motions is tabled to introduce amendments to the *Income Tax Act.* The Budget allows the government of the day an opportunity to review the state of the economy and to announce policies in respect of economic and fiscal programs. Following the Budget, there is a debate in the House. The debate may take no more than six sitting days of the House of Commons.

The parliamentary tradition that tax changes should be announced by the Minister of Finance only in the House of Commons softened somewhat and some Ministers of Finance now simply announce proposed tax changes by press release.

Some time after the Budget debate, the Minister of Finance introduces amending legislation in the form of a Bill to implement the proposals set out in the Notice of Ways and Means Motions. The Bill is given a first reading in the House to make it a public document and is then debated in principle during second reading. Following second reading, income tax bills are debated by the Committee of Ways and Means, which is a committee of the whole House.[18] The Bill may also be considered by specialized committees such as the Committee on Finance, Trade and Economic Affairs, where particular provisions of the Bill may be amended. Following detailed examination of the Bill by the Committee of the Whole House, it is given third reading and sent to the Senate.

---

[16] *Constitution Act, 1867 (U.K.),* c. 3, ss. 53, 54.

[17] "Budget" (contrary to the understanding of the term by accountants who view it as a financial statement) is a derivation from the old French "bougette", meaning "a little bag". In British parliamentary tradition, the "little bag" was replaced by a "little box" (14½" by 10") made for Gladstone in about 1860. This box has been carried by every subsequent Chancellor but one to deliver the Budget.

[18] Unlike bills dealing with non-tax matters, it is the entire House which constitutes the Committee. The public may not make representations directly to the Committee of the Whole House.

(b) Senate

Although the Senate does not have the power to initiate income tax legislation, it does have the constitutional authority to debate tax bills that have been referred to it by the House of Commons. The Senate Committee on Banking, Trade and Commerce is a particularly influential committee whose deliberations may have a substantial impact on such a bill. As a practical matter, with the exception of purely technical changes, the Senate does not amend income tax legislation without the approval of the Cabinet.

(c) Retrospective Effect

Constitutional law and tradition dictate that taxes may only be imposed and collected by an Act of Parliament.[19] There is no legal authority to collect taxes before the Budget imposing the tax is enacted and receives Royal Assent. In fact, federal income taxes are usually collected on the basis of the Notice of Ways and Means Motions, sometimes many months before Parliamentary approval is obtained.[20] For example, some of the 1987 White Paper proposals took effect on June 18, 1987, even though the Notice of Ways and Means was not tabled until December 16, 1987 and the implementing legislation (Bill C-139) was not tabled in the House of Commons until June 30, 1988.

The legislation, when enacted, is made retrospective to the Budget date. This process, in effect, whitewashes any constitutional illegality of collecting taxes prior to their legislation. Canadian taxpayers and their professional advisers have resigned themselves to this practice with dejected pragmatism. Litigation to establish the constitutional illegality of the practice would end in a pyrrhic victory since most budgets have retrospective effect.[21]

7. THE EXECUTIVE PROCESS

The responsibility for fiscal policy and legislation rests with the Minister of Finance. The Department of Finance (specifically, the Tax Policy and Legislation

---

[19] See, e.g., *Bowles v. Bank of England,* [1913] 1 Ch. 57.

[20] For example, there was a 16-month delay between the November 1981 budget speech and its eventual legislative enactment.

[21] See, e.g., *Swanick v. M.N.R.,* [1985] 2 CTC 2352, 85 DTC 630 (T.C.C.) (taxpayer filed return on basis of existing law; Minister assessed return on basis of law enacted 14 months later but made retrospective to earlier period; taxpayer not deprived of property without due process of law); see also *Gustavson Drilling (1964) Ltd. v. M.N.R.,* [1977] 1 SCR 271 (S.C.C.), at 279 *per* Dickson J.:

> First, retrospectivity. The general rule is that statutes are not to be construed as having retrospective operation unless such a construction is expressly or by necessary implication required by the language of the Act. An amending enactment may provide that it shall be deemed to have come into force on a date prior to its enactment or it may provide that it is to be operative with respect to transactions occurring prior to its enactment. In those instances the statute operates retrospectively.

Division) carries most of the burden of advising the Minister on changes to income tax legislation. This Division prepares the substantive tax policy papers and most of the income tax legislation. The Tax Policy and Legislation Division reports through an Assistant Deputy Minister to the Deputy Minister of Finance.

The responsibility for administering the *Income Tax Act* lies with the Department of National Revenue, which also has a division concerned with tax policy. There is a close liaison between the tax policy divisions of the two Departments, particularly on technical and administrative matters.

The Legislative Branch of the Department of Justice is technically responsible for the drafting of income tax legislation. Officials of the Department of Justice are specifically seconded to the Department of Finance for drafting tax legislation. In fact, though not in theory, few lawyers are involved in the drafting of tax legislation. More by accident than by design, most of the income tax amendments are drafted by accountants, many of whom have served with Revenue Canada as auditors.

8. THE JUDICIAL PROCESS

The responsibility for litigating income tax disputes rests primarily with the Department of Justice.

A taxpayer who disagrees with Revenue Canada's assessment of his or her income tax liability may litigate the assessment in the Tax Court of Canada. An appeal or review of a decision of the Tax Court lies with the Federal Court of Appeal and from there to the Supreme Court of Canada.

The Supreme Court of Canada is the ultimate arbiter of income tax matters. Recourse to it is only possible by way of leave to appeal. As a matter of practice, the Supreme Court of Canada rarely grants leave to appeal in income tax matters. For all practical purposes then, the Federal Court of Appeal is the final appellate tribunal in most income tax cases.

The Tax Court of Canada has the sole power to hear appeals under the *Income Tax Act* and certain other statutes. There are, however, two distinct streams of procedure and appeal in the Tax Court: an informal and expeditious procedure for appeals in cases involving less than $14,000 in disputed taxes (or $24,000 of losses); and a more complex and formal procedure for cases involving sums greater than $14,000 in disputed taxes (or $24,000 of losses).

9. TAX SYSTEM OBJECTIVES

The mechanism used to transfer resources from the private to the public sector takes a variety of forms, and the amount to be transferred is determined by reference to alternative bases. Given the variety of alternative transfer mechanisms available, it is desirable to select that mechanism or process that, in addition to financing the public sector, facilitates the attainment of other societal goals. Thus, a good part of tax policy is concerned with the analysis of "societal goals" and the cost of their implementation.

(a) Revenue Needs

A tax system derives revenues by applying tax rates to a taxable base. The formula is straightforward:

$$\text{TAX REVENUE} = \text{TAXABLE BASE} \times \text{RATE}$$

Thus, revenue can be generated by increasing the taxable base or by adjusting the scale of tax rates.

In an *income* tax system the taxable base relies upon a measure of "income". This is primarily a function of accounting. There are, however, numerous other external influences which affect the determination of income for tax purposes or "taxable income". The greater the number of external influences, the more complex the process of income determination.

All tax systems owe their initial existence to societal need for money. Indeed, most modern tax systems had their genesis in financing wars. Thus, it is tempting to infer that the sole objective of an income tax system is the raising of revenue. To be sure, the need for revenue provides the principal impetus to levy an income tax, but this need should not be confused with the rationale and purpose of having an *income* tax. Indeed, if the raising of revenue were the only objective of a tax system, this objective could be satisfied by simpler means. For example, consumption and sales taxes (such as the Goods and Services Tax) could raise the same amount of revenue through a much simpler mechanism than the income tax system.[22]

The personal income tax provides by far the largest share of federal revenues and has grown at the fastest rate. from 40 per cent of total revenues in 1980 to 48 per cent in 1992.

Sources of Federal Revenues (1992)

Source	Per cent of Total Revenues
Personal income tax	48
Sales/Excise taxes	18
UI premiums	14
Other revenues	13
Corporate income Tax	7
Total	100

The personal income tax is also a significant component of provincial revenues.

[22] See, e.g., *Economic Review* 1970-79 (Department of Finance, Canada); W.I. Gillespie, *Incidence of Taxes and Public Expenditure in the Canadian Economy*, a study prepared for the Royal Commission on Taxation (Ottawa: Queen's Printer, 1964), at 66.

Sources of Provincial Revenues (1992)

Source	Per cent of Total
Personal income tax	33
Other*	29
Sales tax	24
Payroll taxes	11
Corporate income tax	3
Total	100

*Royalties, license fees, liquor profits, insurance taxes, etc.

The debate as to the appropriate balance between income and consumption taxes as a revenue source depends upon implicit social and political values. The structural characteristic that is common to taxes based upon consumption is that the burden of these taxes is regressively distributed, i.e., these types of taxes impose a disproportionate burden on lower income groups. For example, although sales taxes are nominally levied at a flat rate, the burden of a sales tax is regressively distributed in relation to income due to the differing consumption patterns of the rich and poor. Stated another way, since lower income taxpayers tend to devote proportionally more of their income on current consumption and less on savings than do higher income taxpayers, a tax calculated by reference to consumption or sales places a proportionately heavier burden on the poorer segments of society. Thus, sales taxes are a useful supplement to, but not a substitute for, broader based income taxes.

Society should be concerned not only with the use of taxes to raise public revenue, but also with the manner in which the tax burden is distributed. Thus, the revenue that a society needs should be raised in a "fair" manner. Unfortunately, while it is relatively easy to get most people to agree, at least in the abstract, on the desirability of fairness in a tax system, translating the concept of "fairness" into an acceptable working formula is a much more difficult task. Here, as elsewhere, it is easier for people to agree on the labels to be attached to tax objectives than to reach consensus regarding their substance.

A "good" tax ought to be equitable, convenient, certain and economical.[23] "Fairness" implies at least two distinct aspects: (1) The technical measure of income should be fair; and (2) The distribution of the tax burden should be equitable. The first aspect is concerned essentially with measurement, the second with distribution of tax incidence.

(b) Equity

Equity has two perspectives: the benefit derived by the taxpayer, and the ability to pay taxes.

---

[23]   Smith, Adam, *The Wealth of Nations* (New York: Random House, 1937), at 777-79.

(i) *The Benefit Principle*

The benefit principle requires that the burden of a tax correspond to the benefits received from government expenditures. This principle accords with a sense of fairness, all the more so where the service provided by the government is non-essential. Thus, it is comparatively easy to accept the imposition of gasoline taxes and special toll charges for users of express highways, so long as the proceeds of these tolls and taxes are expended on highway projects. It is also arguable that taxes levied on the benefit principle promote economic efficiency since consumer prices reflect the full cost of services rendered and, therefore, resources tend to be devoted to services without detracting from a greater value in competing use.[24]

(ii) *Ability to Pay*

An alternative perspective on equity is the relationship of the burden of a tax to the taxpayer's ability to bear it. If ability to bear the burden of tax is accepted as a facsimile of equity in a tax system, then the system should respond in an objective and reliable way to measure a taxpayer's "ability to pay".

A taxpayer's ability to pay can be measured by several means. For example, taxes based on accumulated wealth, inherited wealth, consumption or income each deal with different aspects of ability to pay. But agreement on a particular yardstick of "ability to pay" does not resolve all the difficulties. For example, agreeing that income is a reasonable measure of ability to pay does not answer questions such as: Which types of receipts should be included in income? When should a gain be recognized as income? Should "imputed income" be included in income for tax purposes?

Although there appears to be fairly widespread support for the proposition that a tax system should be fair, and convincing support for the proposition that "income" is a reasonable measure of ability to pay, there is little agreement on which receipts should be included in income, when capital gains should be included and, if included, how they should be taxed. The following examples illustrate some of these problems:

- Assume that two individuals, A and B, each receive $1,000. Taxpayer A acquires his $1,000 as wages in return for services rendered. Taxpayer B acquires her $1,000 in a poker game. In determining the abilities of A and B to bear the burden of tax, should the tax system make a distinction based on the *source* of their incomes? That is, do A and B have differing abilities to pay tax because they derive their receipts from different sources?

---

[24] No attempt is made here to frame the analysis on the distinction between "pure public goods" — such as national defence — and "merit goods" (education, health care, environmental control, parks and recreational facilities) that can be supplied by the private sector but are supplied by the public sector for various reasons. "Merit goods" may be supplied by the public sector for economic reasons or on considerations of overriding societal benefit. It is also usually politically convenient that the public sector provide certain "merit goods".

- Assume that C and D each have $100,000 in cash. C invests her money in 10 per cent government bonds and receives $10,000 interest each year. She pays tax on this interest at a rate of 50 per cent and is left with $5,000 for her personal expenses. She uses the $5,000 to rent a small apartment for her living accommodation. In contrast, D invests his $100,000 to purchase a larger apartment that he occupies and, in doing so, receives approximately $10,000 in rental benefits. In determining the abilities of C and D to bear the burden of tax, should the tax system differentiate between earned interest income and imputed rental income? Would C be better off to lend her landlord $100,000 interest-free and permanently occupy a larger apartment on a rent-free basis?

- Assuming the same facts as above, now suppose that C sells her government bonds for $120,000 and D sells his apartment for $120,000. With C and D each in receipt of a gain of $20,000, do they have differing abilities to pay tax on their profit? Should either gain of $20,000 be excluded from income?

- Assume that E sells some shares for a cash profit of $10,000, pays tax at a rate of 50 per cent on the profit, and is left with $5,000. In contrast, F decides to hold on to an identical investment and keeps a "paper profit" of $10,000. Do these two individuals have a differing ability to bear the burden of tax? Is the difference in ability to pay based on their respective wealth or the cash available to pay tax?

(A) Horizontal and Vertical Equity

There are two very distinct senses in which the term "equity" is used in the context of income tax: horizontal and vertical. "Horizontal equity" means that taxpayers in comparable financial circumstances should be treated equally, whereas "vertical equity" means that the tax burden should fall more heavily on the rich than on the poor.

Although we refer to two different types of equity, horizontal and vertical, the two are not unconnected. We describe a tax system as follows:

TAX REVENUE = TAX BASE x TAX RATE

Horizontal equity is concerned with measuring the size of the tax base. Vertical equity is concerned with the burden imposed by the tax rate.

Since total tax revenue is the product of the tax base and the tax rate, distortion of one of the variables will usually cause a distortion in the other. For example, if it is necessary for a government to raise $2,000 of tax revenue by taxing $10,000 of income at a rate of 20 per cent, exclusion of $1,000 of a particular species of income (for example, gambling profits) from the tax base will, in the long run, result in a higher rate of tax on what is left in the tax base. This is not to suggest that the tax base should not be deliberately eroded under the proper circumstances, but merely to emphasize that the benefit accruing from eroding the tax base should outweigh the resulting sacrifice of horizontal equity. That is, if we are to provide tax preferences to certain groups of taxpayers, there should be corresponding countervailing benefits to society at large.

The second aspect of "ability to pay" is seen in the principle of vertical equity that requires the tax burden to be more heavily borne by the rich than the poor. This principle does not, by itself, provide an answer to the more pragmatic question: How much more than the poor should the rich pay? This is because the principle of vertical equity can be implemented by using either proportional, regressive, or progressive tax rates.

(B) Different Rate Systems

In a proportional rate system all taxable income is taxed at a flat or constant rate, that is, the marginal rate of tax at all levels of income is constant. For example, if three taxpayers A, B and C with taxable incomes of $20,000, $40,000 and $60,000 respectively were taxed at a flat (proportional) rate of 17 per cent, total tax revenue collected would be $20,400.

Taxpayer	Taxable Income	Tax	Average Rate
A	$20,000	$ 3,400	17%
B	$40,000	$ 6,800	17%
C	$60,000	$10,200	17%
		$20,400	

Thus, in a proportional rate system, higher income levels bear a heavier tax burden. In the above example, C pays three times, and B pays twice the total tax paid by A. Sales and consumption taxes (such as the GST) are generally levied as proportional taxes, that is, a single percentage rate is applied to all sales regardless of amount.

A regressive tax rate system levies tax at a declining proportion of rising taxable income, that is, the marginal rate of tax decreases as taxable income increases. The following is a hypothetical regressive rate structure:

Taxable Income	Tax Rate
On the first $10,000	25.0%
On the next $10,000	20.0%
On the next $20,000	15.0%
On the next $20,000	4.5%

Applying these rates to the three taxpayers in the previous illustration would also produce total tax revenue of $20,400.

Taxpayer	Taxable Income	Tax	Average Rate
A	$ 20,000	$ 4,500	22.5%
B	$ 40,000	$ 7,500	18.8%
C	$ 60,000	$ 8,400	14.0%
		$20,400	

Once again, the general principle of vertical equity is satisfied while maintaining a constant level of total revenue.

In a progressive system, such as the Canadian tax system, the rate of tax increases with the level of income. Thus, higher income earners not only pay more tax than lower income earners, they also pay at a higher rate (see Chapter XIII "Computation of Tax Payable").

These examples illustrate some of the available methods of raising revenue. Merely enunciating the principle of vertical equity does not assist us in selecting one alternative over another. Since all three rate systems theoretically satisfy the principle of vertical equity, the selection of one rate system over another requires consideration of other objectives.

Of the three alternatives, we can discard a regressive rate system as being politically unpalatable. While the other two systems, proportional and progressive, are both politically acceptable, they flow from different theoretical premises and are attended by different economic consequences.

Theoretically, a progressive structure can be justified on two arguments. First, it is arguable that the utility of incremental sums of money declines as an individual receives more and more money. Just as an individual who is given a barrel of apples has a lower marginal utility for the second apple than the first, lower for the third than for the second, and so on, so also the marginal utility of money will decline as the individual's income increases. Thus, the theory of diminishing marginal utility suggests that the marginal utility of an incremental $100 is greater at an income level of $2,000 than at $20,000. Stated another way, while the total utility of money increases, it does so at a diminishing rate.

Second, an individual's capacity (though not willingness) to pay tax increases as his or her income rises. Given an increase in capacity to bear a greater burden of tax, some consider it to be "fair" that an individual not only pays more taxes, but does so at a progressive rate. The ultimate acceptance or rejection of this line of reasoning depends upon the value judgements which are brought to bear on the question. As Goode has stated:[25]

> My observation is that the majority of citizens and legislators in the U.S. and other democratic countries accept ability to pay as a guiding principle of taxation and interpret it as justifying progressivity. They talk and act as if they believe that progressive taxation is needed to maintain a proper relation between the sacrifices of individual taxpayers and to give recognition to social priorities in the use of income and wealth.

(c) How Much Progression?

Even if we agree that a progressive rate system is "fairer" than a proportional system, the debate continues. How progressive should the rate schedule be? In economic terms, what is the ideal slope of the marginal rate curve?

---

[25] Goode, Richard B., *The Individual Income Tax* (Washington, D.C.: The Brookings Institution, 1964), at 19.

The Canadian personal tax system is "progressive" in the sense that those with higher incomes pay not only more tax in absolute dollars but also pay at a higher marginal rate. How much more should high income earners pay than lower income earners? At what point does the personal tax become a disincentive for productive work? How do we know when we reach the turning point of marginal tax rates after which they become counterproductive?

Most people agree that an income tax system should be based on a progressive rate structure with the rich paying more than the poor. The difficult question is: How progressive should the rate structure be? Table 3 is an overview of the progressivity built into the rate structure.

TABLE 3

	Percentage Tax Filers	Percentage of Total Income	Percentage Total Tax
1991 Income Class			
Under — $25,000	62	27	11
$25,000 — $50,000	28	40	40
$50,000 — $100,000	9	23	31
$100,000 and over	1	10	18
	100	100	100

The first point to observe is that of the approximately 19 million tax filers in 1991, only 13.7 million actually paid income tax; the remaining 5.3 million individuals were non-taxable. In 1991, 62 per cent of Canadian tax filers with incomes below $25,000 contributed 11 per cent of the total individual tax. In contrast, 1 per cent of the total with incomes $100,000 and over contributed 18 per cent of the total individual tax.

It is clear that the extremities of the population cannot be the primary source of revenues: The bottom extremity is too poor to pay more; the top, which comprises only 1 per cent, is too small a group to make a substantial difference to overall revenues. Hence, it is inevitable that the burden of the individual tax system rests on those earning between $25,000 to $100,000. This segment makes up 37 per cent of tax filers and contributes nearly double that percentage in total tax.

(d) Economic Objectives

The economic objectives of tax policy may be summarized as follows: stabilization of the economy at full employment, price stability and the promotion of economic growth.

A progressive rate structure provides a stabilizing influence by relating marginal rates of tax to the level of economic activity. Hence, in a general business decline when income is falling, taxpayers move into lower marginal tax classes resulting in a reduction of tax collected. Consequently, disposable income is bolstered and consumer expenditures are supported. Conversely, as income increases in periods of economic boom, taxpayers are taxed at higher marginal rates and the resulting increase in taxes causes disposable income to increase at a rate slower than the increase in gross income. This acts as a restraint on consumer expenditures.

Of course, economic stabilization can also be achieved by alternative fiscal measures. For example, personal exemption levels and tax rates can be adjusted in line with economic changes to increase or reduce tax revenues. Such adjustments, however, require political approval that may or may not be attainable. The advantage of a progressive rate system is that the stabilization effects are built-in and, therefore, there is no need for specific fiscal action.

While automatic stabilization is a useful feature of a progressive rate structure, it needs to be supplemented by discretionary action to adjust to changing economic conditions. Discretionary action can be used to stabilize the economy through the manipulation of government spending programs and tax adjustments. For example, given a need to stimulate the economy, a government can either increase public sector spending or stimulate private sector consumption through tax cuts. The ultimate impact of these two alternatives, which are not mutually exclusive, will be different and will depend in part on the magnitude of the multiplier in effect at the particular time.

Example I.1

Assuming an effective tax rate of 25 per cent of each dollar of GNP, a consumption ratio of 80 per cent of additional income received, and a proposal to increase government spending by $10 million, the ultimate impact on GNP is shown below:

MULTIPLIED EFFECT OF $10 MILLION INCREASED GOVERNMENT SPENDING

(1) Addition to GNP	(2) Effective tax at 25%	(3) After tax income 75%	(4) Consumer Spending [(3) × 80%)]
10.00	2.50	7.50	6.00
6.00	1.50	4.50	3.60
3.60	0.90	2.70	2.16
2.16	0.54	1.62	1.30
1.30	0.32	0.98	0.78
0.78	0.20	0.58	0.47
0.47	0.12	0.35	0.28
0.28	0.07	0.21	0.17
0.17	0.04	0.13	0.10
0.10	0.03	0.07	0.06
0.06	0.01	0.05	0.04
0.04	0.01	0.03	0.02
0.02	0.01	0.01	0.01
0.01	0.00	0.01	0.01
0.01	0.00	0.01	0.01
25.00			

In Example I.1, an initial increase of $10 million in public sector spending enhances GNP by $25 million; in economic jargon the multiplier is 2.5.

Alternatively, assume that the government decided to stimulate the economy through a tax cut of $10 million. The ultimate increase in GNP, using the same assumptions as above, would amount to $20 million as shown in Example I.2.

Example I.2

MULTIPLIED EFFECT OF $10 MILLION TAX CUT

(1) Addition to GNP	(2) Effective tax at 25%	(3) After tax income 75%	(4) Consumer Spending [(3) × 80%)]
—	—	10.00	8.00
8.00	2.00	6.00	4.80
4.80	1.20	3.60	2.88
2.88	0.72	2.16	1.73
1.73	0.43	1.30	1.04
1.04	0.26	0.78	0.62
0.62	0.16	0.46	0.37
0.37	0.09	0.28	0.22
0.22	0.06	0.16	0.13
0.13	0.03	0.10	0.08
0.08	0.02	0.06	0.05
0.05	0.01	0.04	0.03
0.03	0.01	0.02	0.02
0.02	0.00	0.02	0.00
20.00			

Using this approach, GNP would increase by $20 million; stated another way, the multiplier is equal to 2.

The particular method selected to stimulate (or depress) the economy at any time will depend on various factors, one of which will be the size of the multiplier. In the above illustration, the increase in government spending has a larger multiplier due to the "first round effect" ($10 million vs. $8 million). The choice of method will be influenced by many considerations such as the efficiency of providing goods and services in the public sector, the desire for long or short-run stabilization, and the speed with which economic correction is required. For example, since changes in individual tax rates produce a very fast response, this method is particularly useful for short-run adjustments.

Complementing its use as an economic stabilizer, the income tax system can also be used to promote economic growth. Thus, the tax system can be used to align total demand with the productive potential of an economy. Also, depending on particular economic and political needs, the tax system can be used to manipulate private demand and investment through the adjustment of depreciation allowances, investment credits, sheltered investments, and tax deferral opportunities.

In addition to its direct impact, it is also important to consider the indirect effect of a tax system on economic activity. For example, what is the effect of taxes on incentives to work and on investment and risk-taking?

The question of whether any tax, and a progressive tax in particular, creates a disincentive to work and a preference for leisure can be examined both theoretically and empirically. Theoretically, the imposition of an income tax results in two opposite "pulls" on behaviour. On the one hand, the price of leisure, measured in terms of wages foregone by not working, declines as a tax increases. Algebraically, the price of leisure (P) may be represented as:

$$P = [W - t(W)]$$

where: W = hourly wage rate;
        t = marginal tax rate.

As the price of leisure falls, its demand increases and there is an incentive for individuals to substitute cheaper goods (leisure) for more expensive goods (work). This substitution effect acts as a disincentive to work.

On the other hand, the effect of an income tax is to reduce an individual's real disposable income (Yd). Hence, algebraically,

$$Yd = h[W - T(W)]$$

where: h = hours worked;
        W = wage rate; and
        T = average tax rate.

As real disposable income falls, there is an incentive to work longer or harder to restore the prior level of disposable income. The incentive will be that much stronger when an individual is locked into a fixed level of contractual obligations, e.g., mortgage payments.

One can make several observations on this theoretical analysis. First, traditional microeconomic analysis is premised on the idea that individuals can choose between work and leisure and, at least implicitly, assumes that an individual can vary his or her hours of work. Where this assumption is unrealistic the analysis obviously fails.

Second, even on a theoretical level, it is impossible to determine *a priori* whether the net effect of the opposite pulls will be to create an incentive or disincentive to work. All that can be said theoretically is that if the substitution effect prevails, creating a net disincentive to work, the disincentive is likely to be greater under a progressive rate system than under a proportional tax.

Third, individuals who are independent enough to vary their working hours may also be able to shift any increase in tax burden to their customers.

Finally, non-monetary and untaxed rewards such as job satisfaction, power, prestige and self-esteem may influence individuals to continue or increase their work effort.

The empirical evidence that is available concerning the influence of taxes on work effort suggests that the net effect is minimal. For example, Break's study based on a sample of 306 self-employed solicitors and accountants (63 per cent of whom faced marginal rates in excess of 50 per cent), concluded that, despite the grumbling, the net effect was "not large enough to be of great economic or sociological significance".[26] A Canadian study based on a sample of both professionals (higher incomes, higher marginal rates, flexibility of hours and more formal education) and non-professionals (hourly rated, less flexibility in hours worked) concluded as follows:[27]

> . . . the work incentives of both professional and non-professional labour in this area are in no way being significantly affected by the present personal income taxation, nor are likely to be in the event of future tax changes.

The fact that the empirical evidence suggests no significant net work disincentive in the total labour supply should not be taken to mean that progressive marginal rates can be ignored in the formulation of tax policy. Since individuals are really concerned with standards of living, whether or not a specific policy or condition acts as a work disincentive depends on whether or not income can be supplemented by other means. While the "income effect" provides an impetus to maintain a standard of living, the standard can also be attained or maintained through the use of tax-free "perks". If this occurs, there is a disincentive to replace the income that is lost through increased tax rates. Thus, excessive loopholes in the taxation of "perks" can lead to a dilution of the "income effect". Finally, in evaluating the empirical evidence it is important to bear in mind that the studies did not consider the ultimate expression of disincentive effects, namely, the "brain drain" to countries levying lower taxes.

The second concern in respect of progressive rate systems is that they inhibit risk-taking and investment and, therefore, impede economic growth. Here also, the influence of a tax system on risk-taking depends upon the opposite pulls of the substitution and income effects. Since a tax reduces the net yield of an investment it inhibits risk-taking. Concurrently, a reduced net yield provides an impetus to take greater risks to restore disposable income. It is impossible to predict, even theoretically, the net outcome of these opposite pulls.

There are several additional factors which should also be considered in evaluating the ultimate effect of progressive taxes on investment. First, a considerable amount of investment is undertaken by corporations that pay tax at an effective rate that is considerably lower than the top individual rates.[28] Second, the possibility of converting what might otherwise be an income gain into a capital gain is a particularly attractive

---

[26] Break, George F., "Income Taxes and Incentives to Work: An Empirical Study" (1957), 47 *Amer. Economic Review* 529; see also Sanders, Thomas A., *Effects of Taxation on Executives* (Boston: Harvard University Graduate School of Business Administration, 1951).

[27] Chatterjee and Robinson, "Effects of Personal Income Tax on Work Effort: A Sample Survey" (1969), 17 *Can. Tax J.* 211 at 219.

[28] *Income Tax Act*, ss. 123, 125 and 125.1.

incentive to investment.[29] Third, incentives in the form of generous depreciation allowances can be used to increase net yields of projects and to encourage investment.

The empirical evidence that does exist appears to confirm the view that replacement of the progressive tax by a flat rate tax would not have an appreciable impact. For example, Goode estimated that replacement of the progressive personal income tax by a flat rate tax on consumption would have increased personal saving by $2.5 million in 1960 in the U.S. On the basis of his study he concluded that "...the possibility of speeding growth by tax revisions that will stimulate savings is unimpressive".[30]

At the corporate level, the economic impact of tax policy is even more obscure. There is no agreement on the fundamental question of who bears the corporate income tax. Thus, although the point of impact of the corporate tax is the corporation itself, it remains uncertain whether the incidence of the tax is shifted back into the factors of production (for example, wages) or forward to consumers in the price of goods and services. The following two excerpts indicate the divergence of views on the question of tax incidence:

> The initial or short run incidence of the corporate income tax seems to be largely on corporations and their stockholders. . . . There seems to be little foundation for the belief that a large part of the corporate tax comes out of wages or is passed on to consumers in the same way that a selective excise (tax) tends to be shifted to buyers.[31]

> . . . [A]n increase in the (corporate) tax is shifted fully through short-run adjustments to prevent a decline in the net rate of return (on corporate investment), and . . . these adjustments are maintained subsequently.[32]

Based on a review of the arguments, Pechman concluded that the evidence was inconclusive and that the ". . . data do not permit a clear determination of the factors affecting price and wage decisions: different authors examining the same set of facts have come to diametrically opposite conclusions".[33]

---

[29] See Butters. J.N., L.E. Thompson and L.L. Bollinger, *Effects of Taxation: Investment by Individuals* (Boston: Harvard University Graduate School of Business, 1953).

[30] Goode, Richard, *The Individual Income Tax* (Washington, D.C.: The Brookings Institution, 1964), at 74.

[31] Goode, Richard, *The Corporation Income Tax* (John Wiley, 1951), at 71-72.

[32] Krzyzaniak. Marian and Richard A. Musgrave, *The Shifting of the Corporation Income Tax* (Baltimore: Johns Hopkins Press, 1963), at 65.

[33] Pechman, Joseph A., *Federal Tax Policy* (Washington, D.C.: The Brookings Institution, 1971), at 114.

10. TAX SYSTEM CHARACTERISTICS

A good tax system should be neutral, efficient, and simple.

(a) Neutrality

A neutral tax is one that does not distort or interfere with market decisions in the efficient allocation of resources. Thus, a progressive tax is neutral if it does not create an incentive toward leisure or promote an anti-work ethic.

It is important, however, in evaluating a tax provision, to remember that certain provisions are deliberately structured to be non-neutral. Since a tax system also implements economic policy, the provisions of a taxing statute may be deliberately non-neutral or "directive" in nature. Indeed, in some cases, non-neutrality may be the very reason for the introduction of a tax amendment. For example, tax rules that permit immediate deductions from income for contributions to registered retirement savings plans (RRSPs) are intended to encourage taxpayers to provide for their own old age security and are, therefore, deliberately non-neutral in that they encourage saving over present consumption. However, since 100 per cent of all capital gains accumulated in these plans are subject to tax upon withdrawal, these plans are biased in favour of debt rather than equity investments. In this sense, RRSPs are non-neutral and may distort the allocation of resources in the capital markets.

A tax system is sometimes used as an instrument of social engineering. It can be used to induce certain behaviours or activities and to discourage others. One of the more innovative uses of the system as an instrument of engineering is Quebec's child incentive program. Concerned with the declining birth rate in the francophone population, Quebec offers parents $3,000 per child for their third and subsequent children.

(b) Efficiency

Efficiency is also a desirable tax attribute. Thus, whenever possible, a tax system should be designed to promote fiscal efficiency, both with respect to compliance by the taxpayer and administration by the government. In evaluating the efficiency of a fiscal system, it should be borne in mind that, to a degree, higher administrative costs purchase equity.

(c) Simplicity

A tax system should be reasonably simple to comprehend and to apply. Hence, tax information should be readily obtainable from financial records, and most ordinary taxpayers should be able to prepare their own individual tax returns. Tax simplicity also promotes fairness by permitting tax administrators to apply the law uniformly across the country. Unfortunately, it appears easier to talk of tax simplification than to do anything about it. As subsequent parts of this text bear witness, the Canadian income tax system moves from one level of complexity to the next with each purported attempt to simplify or amend it.

Although there is universal agreement that the tax system should be simple enough for the average taxpayer to understand, there is little evidence to suggest that simplification of the *Income Tax Act* is a matter of high priority for the Department of Finance. Most commission reports and studies recommending simplification of the tax system are shelved by the Department as "unworkable".

To be sure, the criticism that the tax system is complex can be overstated. The *Income Tax Act* is used to raise and redistribute revenues in a complex economic and legal system and a measure of structural complexity in the fiscal system is inevitable. After all, tax law deals not only with individuals but also with corporations, trusts, partnerships, agency and every possible combination of these institutions and relationships. These are complex structures and relationships and any law proposing to regulate their activities must necessarily be complex.

Complaint about the complexity of tax law is not a new phenomenon. The team of experts who drafted the consolidation to the English income tax laws had this to say on the subject:

> To expect from us codification of the law of income tax which the layman could easily read and understand was a vain hope which only the uninstructed could cherish.

Have we gone so far, then, in pursuing our objectives that tax simplification has become the impossible dream? As the Standing Committee on Finance and Economic Affairs candidly admitted in its Fourth Report (June 19, 1986):

> The Committee also makes extensive recommendations with respect to how the current *Income Tax Act* ought to be rewritten to make it readable. You will know, as do others in this House, that it is virtually impossible for Members of Parliament to understand the *Income Tax Act*. Indeed, senior tax practitioners have indicated they cannot understand the Act themselves.

(d) Declaration of Taxpayer Rights

The role of taxation in history has not been entirely undramatic. The greatest constitutional document in the common law world, the Magna Carta, was precipitated in substantial measure by King John's penchant for increasing feudal taxation without consultation with his lords. The underlying grievances of the Peasant's Revolt of 1381 was a poll-tax on all males and females over the age of 15. The drama of the event is recorded in Hume's *History of England*:

> The first disorder was raised by a blacksmith in a village of Essex. The tax-gatherers came to this man's shop while he was at work; and they demanded payment for his daughter, who he asserted to be below the age assigned by the statute. One of these fellows offered to produce a very indecent proof to the contrary, and at the same time laid hold of the maid: which the father resenting, immediately knocked out the ruffian's brains with his hammer.

The modern tax collector's image has improved somewhat, but not substantially. The tax collectors' proclivity towards oppressive conduct and insensitive behaviour was reflected in the report of the Conservative Task Force on Revenue Canada (1984). Concerning Revenue Canada's tax collection methods, the task force said:

- What we heard disturbed us deeply. We were distressed by the fear with which ordinary Canadians greet a call from the tax department, a fear that is sometimes cultivated by Revenue Canada.

- Another impression that was deeply instilled in us during our tour was that the tax burden is falling disproportionately on Canadians of modest means, as a result of Revenue Canada's actions.

- The complexity of the many provisions affecting lower income Canadians often causes serious resentment. This is also the group that is most likely to be audited by less-experienced employees who may make serious errors. These taxpayers can least afford the costly professional assistance needed to defend their rights.

- As a result of tinkering by successive Ministers of Finance in the past two decades, the *Income Tax Act* has grown from a complex but manageable statute into five pounds of confusing and often unintelligible legislation.

- If the rule of law is to survive, citizens must understand the laws they are expected to obey. When legislation becomes so complicated that few people within the government can claim to understand it fully, public confidence in its fairness breaks down.

- Another factor that undermines the rights of ordinary Canadians is the sweeping powers given to the Department. In some cases, they are even greater than the powers of the police . . . .

Later in the same year, the Conservative Government, by then in power, issued a declaratory statement which was impressively entitled the "Declaration of Taxpayer Rights". The declaration addressed some of the task force's concerns, but it did not have any force of law and was never enacted into legislation. The so-called "presumption of honesty" in the declaration stands in flagrant opposition to the established tax rule that the Minister's assessment is *conclusively* presumed to be correct unless established otherwise by the taxpayer. In other words, the taxpayer carries the burden of proof to show that the Minister's assessment is wrong.[34] The burden is hardly reflective of a presumption of taxpayer honesty.

---

[34] *Johnston v. M.N.R.*, [1948] CTC 195, 3 DTC 1182 (S.C.C.).

Revenue Canada Taxation
Revenu Canada Impôt

Declaration of Taxpayer Rights

FAIR TREATMENT IN ALL DEALINGS WITH NATIONAL REVENUE TAXATION MEANS IMPORTANT RIGHTS TO:

Information

You are entitled to expect that the Government will make every reasonable effort to provide you with access to full, accurate and timely information about the *Income Tax Act*, and your rights under it.

Impartiality

You are entitled to an impartial determination of law and facts by departmental staff who seek to collect only the correct amount of tax, no more and no less.

Courtesy and Consideration

You are entitled to courtesy and considerate treatment from National Revenue Taxation at all times, including when it requests information or arranges interviews and audits.

Presumption of Honesty

You are entitled to be presumed honest unless there is evidence to the contrary.

FAIR TREATMENT UNDER THE CONSTITUTION AND LAWS OF CANADA INCLUDES IMPORTANT RIGHTS TO:

Privacy and Confidentiality

In addition to other constitutional and legal rights, you have a special right that personal and financial information you provide to National Revenue Taxation will be used only for purposes allowed by law.

Independent Review

You are entitled to object to an assessment or reassessment if you think the law has been applied incorrectly. To protect this right, you must file your objection within 90 days of the assessment or reassessment. Filing an objection will start an independent review by departmental appeals officers. If they don't resolve the matter to your satisfaction, they will explain how you can appeal to the courts.

An Impartial Hearing Before Payment

Until you have had an impartial review by the Department or a court, you may withhold amounts disputed in formal objections filed after January 1, 1985. If you appeal to a higher court, you will be able to provide equivalent security instead of paying those disputed amounts.

Certain exceptions, set out in legislation to guarantee these rights, are applicable to frivolous appeals to the courts, or where collection is clearly in jeopardy.

> **YOU ARE ENTITLED TO EVERY BENEFIT ALLOWED BY THE LAW**
>
> You have a right to arrange your affairs in order to pay the minimum tax required by law. You can also expect your government to administer tax law consistently, and to apply it firmly to those who try to avoid paying their lawful share.

(e) Precision

A tax system should also be sufficiently precise to ensure that taxpayers and their advisers can evaluate the consequences of transactions before they are consummated. Complex and imprecise laws cause uncertainty and impede economic activity. In particular, tax provisions that grant discretionary authority to the Minister cause considerable uncertainty for taxpayers. Given the imperfect science of words, however, it is impossible to expect absolute precision from the *Income Tax Act*. The shift towards purposive interpretation of the Act should, however, assist taxpayers in filling in gaps in the legislative language.

11. FUNDAMENTAL CONCEPTS

(a) Tax Base

Before we embark upon a detailed review of the Canadian income tax system, it may be useful to take an overview of some of the fundamental concepts of the system. As already noted, income tax liability is determined by applying a tax rate to a taxable base. The taxable base for federal purposes is "taxable income". For provincial tax purposes, the taxable base is the federal tax payable. Thus, the provincial tax (except in Quebec) piggybacks the federal tax base. Hence, tax base changes in the federal tax system almost invariably have an effect on provincial revenues.

Taxable income derives from a two-step process. First, we determine gross income from which we deduct expenses incurred to earn the income. This process provides us with the taxpayer's "net income". Next, we deduct other expenditures that may not have been incurred to earn income, but which we allow as a deduction for other policy reasons. For example, in the case of individuals, we permit a deduction for certain medical expenses. The residue is the taxpayer's taxable income.

(b) Tax Rates

The federal tax rate is applied to taxable income in order to determine tax payable.

The income tax system utilizes two types of rates: graduated and flat. In a graduated system the rate of tax increases or progresses with increases in taxable income. Hence, we refer to such systems as a "progressive" rate structure. The term "progressive" refers to the slope of the curve when tax rates are plotted on the vertical axis of a graph and taxable income on the horizontal axis.

In contrast, a flat rate is a proportional tax because it is applied at a uniform rate regardless of income level. Thus, a taxpayer's tax liability in a proportional system increases at the same rate as increases in the taxable base.

Graduated rates are applied to individuals and testamentary trusts. Corporations and *inter vivos* trusts are taxable at a flat rate. There are, however, several flat rates for different levels and types of income. Hence, in effect, corporations are also taxable on a graduated rate basis, but the slope and shape of the curve is different from the progressive rate schedule.

The highest rate of tax applicable to a taxpayer's top dollar of income is referred to as his or her "marginal rate". In 1995, the highest federal marginal tax rate is 29 per cent. This rate is reached at a taxable income of $59,180. The marginal rate of tax should be distinguished from the average and effective rates of tax.

The "average rate" of tax is obtained by dividing total tax payable by *taxable income*. It reflects the average of all applicable rates. A taxpayer's "effective rate" of tax is his or her total tax payable divided by net income.

Example I.3

Assume that a taxpayer has $100,000 *net* income and $80,000 *taxable* income.

Using 1995 federal tax rates, the federal tax payable (ignoring surtaxes, etc.) is determined as follows:

On the first	$29,590	@ 17%	=	$ 5,030
On the next	$29,590	@ 26%	=	$ 7,693
On the final	$20,820	@ 29%	=	$ 6,038
	$80,000			$18,761

Then, the taxpayer's

• marginal tax rate is 29 per cent,

• average tax rate is 23 per cent, and

• effective tax rate is 19 per cent.

Each of these rates is meaningful for different purposes. The marginal rate is important in tax planning. It tells the taxpayer how much he or she will save on his or her taxes as a result of a particular tax plan or structure. The effective rate measures the *real* burden of taxes. For example, a high marginal rate of tax with generous personal deductions from net income will produce a low effective rate. The effective rate of tax is a more meaningful figure in international tax comparisons.

(c) Provincial Taxes

In addition to federal taxes, there are also provincial taxes. Provincial taxes are generally applied as a percentage of the federal tax payable. A taxpayer's total tax liability is the aggregate of his or her federal *and* provincial taxes payable.

Provincial rate schedules vary from province to province. Hence, Canadian residents face different tax burdens depending upon their province of residence.

(d) Taxpayers

The income tax system applies to:

- individuals,
- corporations,
- estates and trusts, and
- partnerships

Each individual is a taxpayer in his or her own right and must file a separate tax return in respect of his or her taxable income. Married persons must file separate tax returns. The Canadian tax system does not provide for the filing of "joint returns" for married persons.

Corporations, trusts and estates are also taxpayers in their own right and file separate returns from their owners or beneficiaries.

(e) Taxable Year

Taxpayers generally pay tax on an *annual* basis. But "annual" means different things to different taxpayers. Individuals must file their tax returns on the basis of the calendar year and the return must be filed by April 30 of the year end. For example, an individual must file his or her 1995 income tax return by April 30, 1996.

Corporate taxpayers are required to file their tax returns on a "fiscal year" basis. A fiscal year is any twelve-month period. For example, a corporation may have a fiscal year that runs from July 1, 1995 to June 30, 1996.

12. THE INCOME TAX PROCESS

References:

ITA:

Subs. 150(1)	Tax Returns
S. 152	Assessment of Tax
S. 162	Penalties
S. 165	Objections to Assessments
S. 169	Appeals to Court

BULLETINS, CIRCULARS & RULINGS:

IT-241	August 11, 1975	Reassessments Made After the Four-Year Limit
IT-326R2	February 2, 1990	Returns of Deceased Persons as "Other Persons"
IC 75-7R3	July 9, 1984	Reassessment of a Return of Income
IC 80-7	June 30, 1980	Objections and Appeals
IC 85-1R2	October 23, 1992	Voluntary Disclosures
IC 92-5	November 6, 1992	T1, T2 & T3 Custom Returns

The Canadian income tax system relies on self-assessment of tax liabilities. A taxpayer is required to calculate his or her income tax liability for a taxation year, complete an income tax return and declare the amount of his or her income tax liability.[35]

Corporate taxpayers are required to file income tax returns for each taxation year, whether or not they have income taxable in the year. Returns are to be filed without notice or demand within six months from the end of the corporation's taxation year.[36] The return must be prepared in a prescribed manner and provide certain prescribed information.

In contrast, only individuals who have tax to pay for the taxation year are required to file an income tax return. Individuals who do not have any taxable income in a particular taxation year are not required to file income tax returns for that year. However, an individual may voluntarily file a tax return even if he or she is not liable for tax so as to trigger the start of the limitation period.

Failure to file a return on time and failure to furnish required information renders a taxpayer liable to penalties.[37]

After a taxpayer files an income tax return, Revenue Canada does a "quick assessment" of the return to determine if the liability has been calculated accurately.[38] This assessment is concerned only with obvious mathematical errors and the matching of data supplied by the taxpayer with information Revenue Canada has obtained from other sources. For example, information slips filed by employers are matched with the amount of income declared by employees on their tax returns.

---

[35] Subs. 150(1).

[36] Para. 150(1)(*a*).

[37] Subss. 162(1)–(3); note, however, that persistent failure to file tax returns, even if done intentionally, does not, *by itself*, constitute wilful evasion.

[38] Subs. 152(1). For the meaning of "assessment" see *Pure Spring Co. v. M.N.R.*, [1946] CTC 169 at 198, 2 DTC 844 at 857 (Ex. Ct.); *Dezura v. M.N.R.*, [1974] CTC 375 at 380, 73 DTC 1101 at 1103 (Ex. Ct.).

Revenue Canada issues a "quick assessment" between eight to 15 weeks of filing the return. The most important aspect of the Notice of Assessment is that its issuance commences the running of the three or six-year limitation period within which the Minister may reassess the taxpayer.[39]

For most taxpayers, the "quick assessment" notice is the final communication they will receive from Revenue Canada in respect of a particular year. The Department does, however, have the authority to reassess a taxpayer if it later determines that its initial assessment was based upon incorrect information.

The time period within which the Department can reassess a taxpayer depends upon the facts leading to the reassessment. Where a taxpayer has made a misrepresentation attributable to neglect, carelessness, wilful default, or fraud, the Department is not subject to any limitation period and can reassess the taxpayer at any time.[40] Otherwise, the Department can reassess a taxpayer only within a period of three or, in certain cases, six years from the day that it mailed the taxpayer's initial assessment.[41] The limitation period runs from the date of the mailing of the Notice of Assessment and *not* from the date that the income tax return is filed.

A taxpayer can appeal his or her assessment by filing a Notice of Objection with the Minister.[42] Filing of the Notice of Objection is the first legal step in the resolution of an income tax dispute. An individual must file the Notice in writing no later than:

- one year of the taxpayer's due date for filing his or her return; and

- 90 days from the date of *mailing* of the Notice of Assessment to which it relates.

All other taxpayers are required to file the Notice within 90 days of the mailing of the Notice of Assessment.

Failure to file a Notice of Objection within the limitation period may leave the taxpayer without any legal recourse against the assessment. Although a taxpayer can apply to have the time limit for filing a Notice of Objection extended, it is not easy to persuade the Tax Court to grant an extension.[43] As the Court observed in *Savary Beach Lands Ltd. v. M.N.R.*:[44]

> [t]his Board takes the position that the granting of an extension of time under section 167 will be the exception rather than the rule . . . to simply grant such extensions and imply that all applications —

---

[39] Subs. 152(4).

[40] Subpara. 152(4)(*a*)(i).

[41] Para. 152(4)(*c*).

[42] Subs. 165(1).

[43] Subs. 166.2(5).

[44] *Savary Beach Lands Ltd. v. M.N.R.*, [1972] CTC 2608 at 2609, 72 DTC 1497 (T.R.B.).

where the breach is but a few days — will be granted, is to make a mockery of the period of limitations set down in the Act.

The Minister will do one of three things with the objection to the assessment: confirm the assessment, vary it, or vacate it.[45]

At this stage of the proceedings, it is usual for the taxpayer to meet with departmental officials to discuss the substance of the objection with a view to arriving at an acceptable solution. The taxpayer may adduce additional factual information and present legal arguments in support of his or her objection.

Where the Minister confirms the assessment or does not respond within 90 days, the taxpayer can appeal the assessment to the Tax Court of Canada.[46] The time limit for appeal is 90 days from the day the notice confirming the taxpayer's assessment is *mailed.* There is no limitation period if the Minister does not respond to the taxpayer's Notice of Objection.

A decision of the Tax Court can be appealed to the Federal Court of Appeal.[47] An appeal from the Federal Court of Appeal lies to the Supreme Court of Canada provided that leave to appeal is granted either by the Court of Appeal or the Supreme Court.[48] Leave to appeal is granted only in the following circumstances:

- if the Court of Appeal thinks that the question involved is one that ought to be decided by the Supreme Court; or
- if the Supreme Court is of the view that the issue litigated is one of public importance.

The dollar value of the dispute is not determinative in granting leave to appeal.[49]

13. GENERAL STRUCTURE OF THE ACT

The *Income Tax Act* addresses the following five basic questions:

1. Who is taxable?
2. What is taxable?
3. What is the rate of tax?

---

[45] Subs. 165(3).

[46] S. 169.

[47] *Federal Court Act*, R.S.C. 1985, c. F-7, s. 27.

[48] *Federal Court Act*, s. 31.

[49] See, e.g., *The Queen v. Savage*, [1980] CTC 103, 80 DTC 6066; reversed on other grounds [1981] CTC 332, 81 DTC 5258 *(sub nom. Savage v. The Queen)*; affirmed [1983] CTC 393, 83 DTC 5409 (S.C.C.) (leave to appeal $300 assessment granted).

4. When does tax have to be paid?, and

5. What happens in the event of non-compliance by taxpayers or disputes between the taxpayer and the revenue authorities?

These five questions, which are common to all fiscal legislation, are answered in the Act in a systematic and organized manner.

The Act is divided into Parts and each Part deals with a distinct subject matter. The Parts are divided into Divisions; the Divisions are divided into subdivisions and each subdivision is made up of sections. The sections are subdivided into subsections, which are divided into paragraphs; paragraphs are divided into subparagraphs which, in turn, are divided into clauses and subclauses.

Example I.4

Section 6
Subsection 6(1)
Paragraph 6(1)(*b*)
Subparagraph 6(1)(*b*)(i)
Clause 6(1)(*b*)(i)(A)
Subclause 6(1)(*b*)(i)(A)(I)

The bulk of the provisions are found in Part I. Parts I.1 through XIV deal with special situations and taxes. Parts XV to XVI deal with administration, enforcement and tax evasion. Part XVII is concerned with interpretation and includes most of the general definitions used in the Act.

14. THE *INCOME TAX ACT*

The following is an overview of the *Income Tax Act*:

PART I	Income Tax
Division A	Liability for Tax
Division B	Computation of Income
Subdivision a	Income or Loss from an Office or Employment
Subdivision b	Income or Loss from a Business or Property
Subdivision c	Taxable Capital Gains and Allowable Capital Losses
Subdivision d	Other Sources of Income
Subdivision e	Deductions in Computing Income
Subdivision f	Rules Relating to Computation of Income
Subdivision g	Amounts Not Included in Computing Income
Subdivision h	Corporations Resident in Canada and Their Shareholders
Subdivision i	Shareholders of Corporations Not Resident in Canada
Subdivision j	Partnerships and Their Members
Subdivision k	Trusts and Their Beneficiaries

SELECTED BIBLIOGRAPHY TO CHAPTER I

History

Analysis of the Canadian Tax Reform Bill, 1971 (C.C.H. Can. Ltd., 1971).

Bale, G., "The Individual and Tax Reform in Canada" (1971), 49 *Can. Bar Review* 24.

Bale, G., "The Treasury's Proposals for Tax Reform: A Canadian Perspective", in *Law and Contemporary Problems* (Durnham: Duke University School of Law, 1985), p. 151.

Ballentine, J.G., "Broadening our Approach to Income Tax Reform" (Spring 1986), 5:1 *Amer. Journal of Tax Policy* 1.

Beam, Robert E., and Stanley N. Laiken, "Introduction to Federal Income Taxation in Canada — Commentary and Problems" (CCH Can. Ltd., 1991).

Bittker, B., "A Comprehensive Tax Base as a Goal of Income Tax Reform" (1967), 80 *H.L.R.* 925.

Blum, W.J., "Federal Income Tax Reform — Twenty Questions" (November 1963), 41 *Taxes* 672.

Bossons, John, "Tax Reform and International Competitiveness", in *Proceedings of 39th Tax Conf.* 5:1 (Can. Tax Foundation, 1987).

Bottle, K., "The 1987 White Paper on Tax Reform" (1988), 3 *J. of Law & Soc. Pol.* 66.

Break, G.F., and J.A. Pechman, *Federal Tax Reform: The Impossible Dream* (Washington: 1975).

Brian, J. Arnold, "Once More Into the Breach: Recent Developments in Canadian Tax Reform" (1987), 4:2 *Australian Tax Forum* 197.

Brooks, W. Neil, *The Quest for Tax Reform* (Carswell: Toronto, 1988).

Brown, R.D., "Canadian Tax Reform: Can We Do Better the Second Time Around?", in *Proceedings of 38th Tax Conf.* 3:1 (Can. Tax Foundation, 1986).

Brown, R.D., "The Painful Realities of Tax Reform" (June 1987), 120:6 *CA Magazine* 26.

Brown, R.D., and R.J. Dart, "Tax Reform — An Appraisal" (May 1974), 12:1 *Osgoode Hall L.J.* 527.

Chiorazzi, M., "Tax Reform During President Reagan's First Four Years: A Selective Bibliography", in *Law and Contemporary Problems* (Durnham: Duke University School of Law, 1985), p. 301.

Cohen, Marshall A., and Stephen R. Richardson, "Fifteen Years After Tax Reform: A Retrospective", [1986] *Special Lectures LSUC* 1.

Corn, George, "Tax Reform, February 10, 1988 Budget" (1988), 2 *Can. Current Tax. J.* J-73.

Corn, George, "Tax Reform: Personal Income Tax" (1988), 2 *Can. Current Tax J.* J-633.

Couzin, Robert, "Tax Legislation and Tax Reform in Canada" (1986), 38:3 *The Tax Executive* 201.

Department of Finance, "Tax Reform, 1987: Economic and Fiscal Outlook", *read by Michael H. Wilson, Minister of Finance* (Ottawa: The Department, 1987).

Department of Finance, "Tax Reform, 1987: The White Paper", *read by Michael H. Wilson, Minister of Finance* (Ottawa: The Department, 1987).

Dewling, Alan M., "Tax Planning Strategies for Individuals After Tax Reform", in *Proceedings of 39th Tax Conf.* 26:1 (Can. Tax Foundation, 1987).

Dodge, David A., "New Directions in Canadian Tax Policy" (1989), 41 *Tax Exec.* 111.

Drache, A.B.C., "Introduction to Income Tax Policy Formulation: Canada 1972-76" (1978), 16 *Osgoode Hall L. J.* 1.

Dungan and Wilson, "Macroeconomic Effects of Tax Reform in Canada" (1988), 36 *Can. Tax J.* 110.

Gibson, "Tax Policy for the Long and Short Run" (1963), 11 *Can. Tax J.* 58.

Goodwin, Robert B., "Canadian Tax Reform: Can We Do Better the Second Time Around?", in *Proceedings of 38th Tax Conf.* 3 (Can. Tax Foundation, 1986).

Goodman, W.D., "Tax Reform — The Continuing Challenge" (1978), 16 *Osgoode Hall L. J.* 147.

Grady, Patrick, "Real Effective Corporate Tax Rates in Canada and the United States After Tax Reform" (1989), 37 *Can. Tax J.* 647.

Gravelle, Pierre, "Tax Reform" (1988), 22 *CGA Magazine* 16.

Grove, Jill S., ed., *Canadian Income Tax Law and Policy* (Toronto: Richard De Boo, 1987).

Harris, "Tax Reform in Canada — Stage II" (1970), 24 *Bull. Int'l. Fisc. Doc.* 179.

Harris, "What Should Canada Do with the Carter Report?" (1967), 21 *Bull. Int'l. Fisc. Doc.* 531.

Head, J.G., "The Carter Legacy: An International Perspective" (1987), 4:2 *Australian Tax Forum* 143.

Huggett, Donald R., "Legislation by Decree: Pinpointing the Need for Tax Reform" (1987), 14:8 *Can. Tax News* 85.

Huggett, Donald R., "Nothing Ventured, Nothing Gained" (Federal Budget of February 18, 1987) (1987), 14:9 *Can. Tax News* 92.

Huggett, Donald R., "Once Bitten — Twice Shy" (Analysis of Federal Tax Measures) (1986), 13 *Can. Tax News* 129.

Huggett, Donald R., "Undoing Reform; Reform Legislation; Righteous Wrath" (1988), 16 Can. *Tax News* 1.

"Income Tax Reform" (1988), 15 *Can. Tax News* 10.

Joint Committee on Taxation of the Canadian Bar Association and the Canadian Institute of Chartered Accountants, *Tax Reform Cleanup: An Identification of Significant Deficiencies in Phase One of the Government's Tax Reform* (Toronto: The Committee, March 1989).

Kesselman, Jonathon R., *Role of the Tax Mix in Tax Reform* (Dept. of Economies, University of British Columbia, 1985).

Krever, "The Origin of Federal Income Taxation in Canada" (Winter 1981), *Can. Tax.* 170.

Krishna, Vern, "A Law that Taxes our Understanding" (1986), 10:9 *Can. Law* 10.

Krishna, Vern, "Developments in Income Taxation Law: The 1985-86 Term" (1987), 9 *Supreme Court L.R.* 487.

McLellan, Ray. R., "Tax Reform 1987: An Overview of the Federal Government White Paper of June 18, 1987" (Toronto Legislative Library, Legislative Research Service, Current Issue Paper No. 61, 1987).

Mintz, Jack M., "Tax Reform in 1987: What Lies Ahead for 1988 and Beyond?", in *Proceedings of 39th Tax Conf.* 3:1 (Can. Tax Foundation, 1987).

Moore, Perry, and Beach, *The Financing of Canadian Federation, The First Hundred Years* (Can. Tax Foundation, 1966).

Parizeau, Jacques, "Implications of Tax Reform for Federal-Provincial Relations", in *Proceedings of 39th Tax Conf.* 4:1 (Can. Tax Foundation, 1987).

Perry, David B. and Janet L. Ballantyne, "Tax Reform in the United States and Canada: The Position of State and Provincial Governments" (1986), 34 *Can. Tax J.* 917.

Perry, David B., *Taxation in Canada*, 3rd ed. (Toronto: Can. Tax Foundation, University of Toronto Press, 1961).

Plume, Clifford R., "The Efficacy of Holding Companies in the Light of the Tax Reform Proposals", in *Proceedings of 39th Tax Conf.* 15:1 (Can. Tax Foundation, 1987).

Rotenberg. L.A., "Tax Reform Down on the Farm" (1988), 121:4 *CA Magazine* 34.

Rousseau, Henri-Paul, "La Réforme de la fiscalité au Canada" (mai/juin 1987), 14:3 *Banquier* 32.

Smith, Margaret, *Reform of the Personal Income Tax System* (Library of Parliament, 1987).

Wilson, Michael H., "Meeting the Challenge of Tax Reform", in *Proceedings of 38th Tax Conf.* 2:1 (Can. Tax Foundation, 1986).

Zelenak, Lawrence, "When Good Preferences Go Bad: A Critical Analysis of the Anti-Tax Shelter Provisions of the Tax Reform Act of 1986" (February 1989), 67 *Texas Law Rev.* 499.

Constitutional Authority for Taxation

Hogg, *Constitutional Law of Canada*, 3rd ed. (Toronto: Carswell, 1992).

La Forest, G.V., "The Allocation of Taxing Power under the Canadian Constitution", *Can. Tax Paper No. 45* (Can. Tax Foundation, 1967).

La Forest, G.V., "The Allocation of Taxing Power under the Canadian Constitution", *Can. Tax Paper No. 65* (Can. Tax Foundation, 1981).

Moull, William D., "Intergovernmental Immunity From Taxation: The Unsolved Issues" (1984), 32 *Can. Tax J.* 54.

The Legislative Process

Canadian Tax Foundation Committee on the Budget Process, "The Canadian Budget Process" (1986), 34 *Can. Tax J.* 989.

Shaviro, Daniel, "Beyond Public Choice and Public Interest: A Study of the Legislative Process as Illustrated by Tax Legislation in the 1980's" (November 1990), 139 *U. Pa. L. Rev.* 1-123.

The Executive Process

Edwards, S.E., "Drafting Fiscal Legislation" (1984), 32 *Can. Tax J.* 727.
Jackett, W.R., "Too Much Income Tax Law?", *Can. Tax J.* 54.

The Income Tax Process

Davidson, "The Reorganization of the Legislation Branch of Revenue Canada Taxation" (1978), 26 *Can. Tax J.* 429.
Drache, Arthur B.C., "Income Tax Policy Formulation in Canada, 1972-76" (1978), 16 *Osgoode Hall L.J.* 1.
Thorson, "Formulation, Enactment and Administration of Tax Changes", in *Proceedings of 24th Tax Conf.* 14 (Can. Tax Foundation, 1972).
Thorsteinsson, P., "How to Settle an Income Tax Controversy, through Litigation and Before", *1978 Conference Report* (Can. Tax Foundation, 1979).

Tax System Objectives

"Anatomy of a Tax System", in *Proceedings of 20th Tax Conf.* 7 (Can. Tax Foundation, 1967).
Andrews, W.D., "A Consumption Type or Cash Flow Personal Income Tax" (April 1984), 87:6 *H.L.R.* 1113.
Bale, G., "Temporary Equity in Taxation" (1977), 55 *Can. Bar Rev.* 1.
Ballantyne, Janet L., "The Tax Burden of the Middle-Class Canadian" (1986), 34 *Can. Tax J.* 671-680.
Bird, "Income Redistribution and Ability to Pay", in *Proceedings of 20th Tax Conf.* 242, 256-64 (Can. Tax Foundation, 1967).
Bradford, D.F., "The Case for a Personal Consumption Tax", in *What Would be Taxed: Income or Expenditure?* (Washington: The Brookings Institution, 1980), pp. 75-113.
Bruce, Neil, "Ability to Pay and Comprehensive Income Taxation: Annual or Lifetime Basis?" as found in Brooks, W. Neil, ed., *The Quest for Tax Reform* (Toronto: Carswell, 1988), p. 157.
Chapman, S.J., "The Utility of Income and Progressive Taxation" (1913), 23 *Econ. J.* 25.
Crowe, Ian, "Taxation: Uncertain Incentives" (March 1991), 124 *CA Magazine* 51.
Drache, Arthur B.C., "A Fair Tax System?" (1994), 16 *Can. Taxpayer* 9.
Drache, Arthur B.C., "Unfairness in Taxation" (1993), 15 *Can. Taxpayer* 19.
Hettich, Walter and Stanley Winer, *Economic and Political Foundations of Tax Structure* (Dept. of Economics, Carleton University, 1986).
Howard, R., G. Ruggeri and Van D. Wart, "The Progressivity of Provincial Personal Income Taxes in Canada" (1991), 39 *Can. Tax J.* 288.

Kesselman, Jonathan R., *Rate Structure and Personal Taxation: Flat Rate or Dual Rate?* (Wellington, New Zealand: Victoria University Press for the Institute of Policy Studies, 1990).

McQuaig, Linda, *Behind Closed Doors: How the Rich Won Control of Canada's Tax System and Ended Up Richer* (Markham, Ontario: Penguin Books Canada, 1987).

Salyzyn, Vladimir, "Canadian Income Tax Policy: An Economic Evaluation" (1987), 66 *Can. Bar Rev.* 405.

Salyzyn, Vladimir, *The Economic Analysis of Taxes* (Detselig Enterprises, 1985).

Smith, Roger S., "Flat Rate Tax Potential: A Preliminary Comparison of Three Countries" (1986), 34 *Can. Tax J.* 835.

Whalley, John, *Regression or Progression: The Taxing Question of Incidence Analysis* (Department of Economics, University of Western Ontario, 1984).

System Characteristics

Atkeson, T.C., "Tax Simplification from the Viewpoint of a Professor of Taxation", in *Essays on Taxation* (New York: Tax Foundation Inc., 1974), pp. 93-109.

Audie, Suphan, "Does the Personal Income Tax Discriminate Against Women?" (1981), 1 *Pub. Fin.* 1.

Cassidy, Michael, "Fairness and Efficiency: Can Tax Reform Do the Job?", in *Proceedings of 39th Tax Conf.* 2:1 (Can. Tax Foundation, 1987).

Daly, Michael J., Jack Jung and Thomas Schweitzer, "Toward a Neutral Capital Income Tax System" (1986), 34 *Can. Tax J.* 1331.

Davies, James B., and France St-Hillaire, *Reforming Capital Income Taxation in Canada: Efficiency and Distributional Effects of Alternative Options* (Economic Council of Canada, 1987).

Drache, Arthur B.C., "Flat Taxes Emerging Again" (1993), 15 *Can. Taxpayer* 45.

Eustice, James S., "Tax Complexity and the Tax Practitioner" (Fall 1989), 45 *The Tax Lawyer* 7.

Gillespie, W. Irwin *et al.*, "Tax Incidence in Canada" (1994), 42 *Can. Tax J.* 348.

Howard, R. *et al.*, "The Redistributional Impact of Taxation in Canada" (1994), 42 *Can. Tax J.* 417.

Hugget, Donald R., "E Pluribus Unum (The Single Tax)", 18 *Can. Tax News* 1.

McCaffery, Edward J., "The Holy Grail of Tax Simplification", [1990] 5 *Wis. L. Rev.* 1267.

Mills, Dennis, *The Single Tax — Fair and Simple for All Canadians* (Toronto: Hemlock Press, 1990).

Mills, W.D., "Tax Simplification from the Viewpoint of the Legislator", in *Essays on Taxation* (New York: Tax Foundation Inc., 1974), pp. 74-92.

Peterson, C.R., "Tax Simplification From the Viewpoint of the Tax Attorney", in *Essays on Taxation* (New York: Tax Foundation Inc., 1974), pp. 110-117.

Prebble, John, "Why is Tax Law Incomprehensible?", [1994] *British Tax Rev.* 380.

Roberts, S.I., *et al.*, "Report on Complexity and the Income Tax" (1971-72), 27 *Tax Law Review* 325.

Ruggeri, G.C., *et al.,* "The Redistributional Impact of Taxation in Canada" (1994), 42 *Can. Tax J.* 417.

"Simplification" (Summary of Recommendations of the Commons Standing Committee on Finance and Economic Affairs Report Entitled 'Tax Simplification') (1986), 14 *Can. Tax News* 25.

Sherbaniuk, D.J., "Tax Simplification — Can Anything Be Done About It?", in *Proceedings of 40th Tax Conf.* 3:1 (Can. Tax Foundation, 1988).

Strain, William J., David A. Dodge and Victor Peters, "Tax Simplification: The Elusive Goal", in *Proceedings of 40th Tax Conf.* 4:1 (Can. Tax Foundation, 1988).

Other

Aaron, H.J., ed., *Inflation and the Income Tax* (Washington: The Brookings Institution, 1976).

Allen, R.I.G. and D. Savage, "The Case for Inflation Proofing the Personal Income Tax" (1974), *Br. Tax Rev.* 299.

Alter, Dr. A., "Different Techniques for Adjusting Taxable Income Under Inflationary Conditions" (1986), *Br. Tax Rev.* 347.

Andrew, W.D., "Personal Deductions in an Ideal Income Tax" (December 1972), 86 *H.L.R.* 2:309.

Arnold, B.J., *Timing and Income Taxation: The Principles of Income Measurement for Tax Purposes* (Toronto: Can. Tax Foundation, 1983).

Barry, David B., "The Relative Importance of Personal and Corporation Income Tax" (1986), 34 *Can. Tax J.* 460-67.

Beale, "The Measure for Income Taxation" (1911), 19 *Journal of Political Economy* 655, 661.

Bird, "The Tax Kaleidoscope" (1970), *Can. Tax J.* 444.

Blais, André and François Vaillancourt, *The Political Economy of Taxation: The Corporate Income Tax and the Canadian Manufacturing Industry* (Montreal: Université de Montréal, 1986).

Blum, "Tax Lawyers and Tax Policy" (March 1961), *Taxes* 247.

Bradford, D.F., *Untangling the Income Tax* (Cambridge: Harvard University Press, 1986).

Brean, Donald S., "International Influences on Canadian Tax Policy: The Free Trade Agreement and U.S. Tax Reform", [1988] *Corporate Management Tax Conference* 13:1.

Broadway and Kitchen, "Canadian Tax Policy", *Can. Tax Paper No. 63* (Can. Tax Foundation, 1980).

Broadway and Kitchen, "Canadian Tax Policy", *Can. Tax Paper No. 76* (Can. Tax Foundation, 1984).

Carver, "The Minimum Sacrifice Theory of Taxation" (1904), 19 *Political Science Quarterly* 66.

Colley, G.M., "Is Indexing a Necessary Evil/L'indexation: un mal nécessaire?" (1986), 119:9 *CA Magazine* 52.

Douglas, P.H., "The Problem of Tax Loopholes" (Winter, 1967-68), 37 *Amer. Scholar* 21.

Drache, Arthur B.C., "Towards a New Tax Philosophy" (1993), 15 *Can. Taxpayer* 185.

Dulude, Louise, "Taxation of the Spouses: A Comparison of Canadian, American, British, French and Swedish Law" (1985), 23 *Osgoode Hall L.J.* 67.

Eaton, A.K., "Essays in Taxation", *Can. Tax Paper No. 44* (Can. Tax Foundation, 1966).

Eisenstein, L., "Some Second Thoughts on Tax Ideologies", 20 *Tax Law Rev.* 453.

Goode, R., *The Individual Income Tax* (Washington: The Brookings Institution, 1976).

Groves, N.M., *Tax Philosophers: Two Hundred Years of Thought in Great Britain and the United States* (Madison: 1974).

Haig, R.M., "The Concept of Income — Economic and Legal Aspects", in *Federal Income Tax* (New York: Columbia University Press, 1921), pp. 1-28.

Hellerstein, J.R., *Taxes, Loopholes and Morals* (New York: McGraw Hill, 1963).

Heyding, "Legislation by Formula" (1959), *Can. Tax J.* 366.

Huggett, Donald R., "A Minimum Income Tax", in *Proceedings of 37th Tax Conf.* 10:1 (Can. Tax Foundation, 1985).

Huggett, Donald R., "Dear Mike" (fictitious letter to Minister of Finance Michael Wilson) (1986), 14 *Can. Tax News* 17.

Johnson, Calvin H.,"Why Have Anti-Tax Shelter Legislation? A Response to Professor Zelenak" (February 1989), 67 *Texas Law Rev.* 591.

Jones, R., *The Nature and First Principles of Taxation* (1914).

Kaldor, N., *An Expenditure Tax* (London: George Allen & Unwin Ltd., 1955).

Klein, W.A., *Policy Analysis of the Federal Income Tax Text and Readings* (New York: The Foundation Press, 1976).

Lahey, Kathleen, "The Tax Unit in Income Tax Theory" in *Women, the Law and the Economy* (Toronto: Butterworths, 1985), pp. 277-310.

"More Written Rules for Taxation", in *Proceedings of 14th Tax Conf.* 198 (Can. Tax Foundation, 1960).

Perry, David B., "Government Reliance on Personal Income Taxes in Canada" (1994), 42 *Can. Tax J.* 1145.

Perry, David B., "Individual Tax Burdens in the OECD" (1994), 42 *Can. Tax J.* 288.

Perry, Harvey J., "Taxation in Canada", *Can. Tax Paper No. 74* (Can. Tax Foundation, 1984).

Simons, H.C., *Personal Income Taxation* (Chicago: University of Chicago Press, 1938).

Thirsk and Whalley, "Tax Policy Options in the 1980's", *Can. Tax Paper No. 66* (Can. Tax Foundation, 1982).

Verchere, Bruce, and Jacques Mernier, "Rights and Freedoms in Tax Matters", in *Proceedings of 38th Tax Conf.* 39 (Can. Tax Foundation, 1986).

CHAPTER II

INTERPRETATION OF TAX LAW

The difficulties of so-called interpretation arise when the Legislature has had no meaning at all; when the question which is raised on the statute never occurred to it; when what the judges have to do is, not to determine what the legislature did mean on a point which was present to its mind, but to guess what it would have intended on a point not present to its mind, if the point had been present.

(John Chipman Gray, *Nature and Sources of the Law: Statutes* (1921 ed.))

1. SOURCES OF LAW

(a) The Income Tax Act

The *Income Tax Act* is a statute of the Parliament of Canada and is the primary source of income tax law in Canada.[1] Hence, the general legal principles applicable to the interpretation of statutory instruments also apply to the *Income Tax Act*. There are no special rules for the construction of taxing statutes. As Lord Russell said:[2]

I see no reason why special canons of construction should be applied to any Act of Parliament, and I know of no authority for saying that a taxing Act is to be construed differently from any other Act. The duty of the court is, in my opinion, in all cases the same, whether the Act to be construed relates to taxation or to any other subject, namely to give effect to the intention of the Legislature as that intention is to be gathered from the language employed having regard to the context in connection with which it is employed.

(b) International Tax Treaties

Canada has entered into numerous bilateral international tax treaties. These treaties deal with matters of concern to taxpayers engaged in international transactions. Canada's bilateral treaties are enacted and adopted by Parliament and form part of Canadian domestic law. There are, however, special rules for the interpretation of tax treaties and international conventions. These are discussed in greater detail later in this chapter.

---

[1] *Income Tax Act*, R.S.C. 1985, c. 1 (5th Supp.). Regulations, tax treaties and the Income Tax Application Rules are the other sources.

[2] *A.G. v. Carlton Bank*, [1899] 2 QB 158 at 164, cited by Angers J. in *MacLaren v. M.N.R.*, [1934] Ex. CR 13 (Ex. Ct.); *Canterra Energy Ltd. v. The Queen*, [1987] 1 CTC 89, 87 DTC 5019 (F.C.A.) (general principles of statutory interpretation ". . . are as applicable for guidance in the interpretation of the *Income Tax Act* as for any other statute"). See also C.E.D. (Ont. 3rd) Title 136: Statutes (general legal principles applicable to the interpretation of statutes).

(c) Income Tax Regulations

Income Tax Regulations are passed under the authority of the Act pursuant to authority delegated by Parliament to the federal Cabinet. Thus, regulations can be changed, added to, or deleted by Order-in-Council without parliamentary approval.

The rationale for allowing certain tax rules to be prescribed by regulation is to allow for flexibility in income tax administration. Unlike the Act, regulations can be changed relatively quickly and without the necessity of parliamentary debate. It is important to note, however, that regulations are valid only if they are within the law authorized by the Act. For example, all of the detailed rules pertaining to capital cost allowance are contained in the regulations. The statutory authority for these regulations is paragraph 20(1)(*a*). Without the *specific* statutory authority allowed in paragraph 20(1)(*a*), the regulations dealing with capital cost allowance would be *ultra vires* the Act and without any force of law.

(d) Income Tax Application Rules, 1971 (ITARs)

ITARs are statutory provisions that are intended to facilitate the transition from the "old Act" (that is, the Act as it applied prior to 1972) to the current version of the Act (referred to as the "new Act"). For example, capital gains were not taxed under the "old Act". To provide for an orderly transition from the old to the new system, the Income Tax Application Rules contain detailed rules governing the valuation of capital property as at December 31, 1971. The general effect of these rules is to exempt from tax all capital gains accrued, but not realized, to December 31, 1971. In the absence of such transitional rules, the Act would have the effect of retroactively taxing gains accrued prior to 1972.

2. ADMINISTRATIVE PRONOUNCEMENTS

References:

BULLETINS, CIRCULARS & RULINGS:

IC 70-1	August 25, 1970	Announcement — Information Circulars and Interpretation Bulletins
IC 93-1	August 9, 1993	List of Taxation Forms and Publications Available for the Use by the Public

Revenue Canada, the department charged with the responsibility of administering the *Income Tax Act*, publishes three principal types of administrative pronouncements: Interpretation Bulletins, Information Circulars, and Advance Income Tax Rulings.

(a) Interpretation Bulletins

Interpretation Bulletins (referred to as "ITs") represent Revenue Canada's administrative interpretation of various provisions of the Act. These bulletins, *which do not have the force of law,* serve two purposes. They allow Revenue Canada to communicate with its own work force and field assessors so that they apply and interpret the Act in a uniform manner. They are also a source of information for taxpayers as to Revenue's interpretation of the Act. Thus, although not law, bulletins serve as a useful source of information for taxpayers and, at the very least, provide some insight into Revenue's assessing policy.

Interpretation Bulletins represent the opinion of the Minister of National Revenue, but they do not bind the Minister. A *fortiori* they do not bind the taxpayer. ITs may be introduced in litigation as evidence but only as persuasive authority.[3] They are sometimes introduced as self-serving opinion evidence by Revenue Canada to bolster its case through its own interpretation of the law.

(b) Information Circulars

Reference:

BULLETINS, CIRCULARS & RULINGS:

IC 93-2   August 9, 1993   Index of Information Circulars

Information Circulars (ICs) are also official publications of Revenue Canada. While Interpretation Bulletins deal with substantive income tax law, Information Circulars are generally concerned with administrative and procedural matters such as tax collection, tax avoidance, objections and appeals, elections, and instalment payments, etc.

(c) Advance Rulings

Reference:

BULLETINS, CIRCULARS & RULINGS:

IC 70-6R2   September 28, 1990   Advance Income Tax Rulings

Unlike Interpretation Bulletins and Information Circulars that are issued for general consumption, Advance Rulings are initially issued by Revenue Canada only directly to the taxpayer who applies for the ruling. A ruling is issued only on the basis of the *specific* facts of a *contemplated* transaction as set out in the taxpayer's ruling application.

---

[3] *See Harel v. Dep. Min. of Revenue (Quebec),* [1978] 1 SCR 851 at 859, [1977] CTC 441 at 448, 77 DTC 5438 at 5442; *Nowegijick v. The Queen,* [1983] 1 SCR 29 at 37, [1983] CTC 20 at 24, 83 DTC 5041 at 5044; *The Queen v. Royal Trust Corp. of Can.,* [1983] CTC 159 at 165-66, 83 DTC 5172 at 5177 (F.C.A.); *Mothers Pizza Parlour (London) Ltd. v. The Queen,* [1985] 1 CTC 361 at 367, 85 DTC 5271 at 5275 (F.C.T.D.). All of these cases concern IT-331, paragraph 26, where the view is expressed that "processing" includes the preparation of meals.

(i) Definition

An Advance Ruling is a statement given by the Rulings Division of Revenue Canada to inform a particular taxpayer of how Revenue Canada will interpret specific provisions of the law with respect to a definite transaction which the taxpayer is contemplating. Advance Rulings are official interpretations of the Act and, in a sense, they are similar to formal opinions issued by private tax advisers. The effect, however, of an Advance Income Tax Ruling, goes beyond that of an ordinary tax opinion: The ruling is administratively considered to be binding upon the Department.

(ii) Binding on Department

Advance Income Tax Rulings are not binding on Revenue Canada as a matter of law; they are only binding in the sense that the Department considers itself administratively bound by its own rulings. As a matter of practice, however, Advance Rulings are generally binding upon the Department. The binding character of Advance Rulings is obviously what makes them attractive to taxpayers engaged in commercial transactions. Though this is not entirely a satisfactory position, it appears to work quite well for Canadian taxpayers. Foreign taxpayers may have some difficulty understanding the nuances of this Canadian procedure.

(iii) No Obligation to Issue Ruling

The Department considers the provision of Advance Income Tax Rulings to be an administrative service and there is no legal requirement to issue a ruling. Hence, the Department may refuse an Advance Ruling or, in some circumstances, it may issue a ruling subject to qualifications set out therein.

(iv) Only Proposed Transactions

Rulings are only given in respect of proposed transactions. The purpose of the ruling is to enable a taxpayer to decide on a particular course of action. Thus, they are issued only in respect of proposed transactions that are seriously contemplated and are not of a hypothetical nature. Hence, the name "Advance" Ruling. Rulings are not issued on completed or substantially consummated transactions.

The characterization of a transaction or series of transactions as being either hypothetical, seriously contemplated, or completed depends on the facts and circumstances of each case. Where a transaction is too indefinite and vague, it is considered "hypothetical" and no ruling will be issued. At the other extreme, a transaction that is completed or substantially completed does not qualify for an Advance Ruling. Thus, rulings are issued only in respect of proposed transactions that are seriously contemplated and are not of a hypothetical nature. This policy is premised on the rationale that Revenue Canada does not wish to provide taxpayers with binding rulings for the purpose of allowing them to construct or reconstruct transactions for maximum tax advantage. Rather, the underlying purpose of Advance Rulings is to assist taxpayers in carrying out transactions which are otherwise in process but not completed.

(v) Scope

An Advance Ruling is valid only for the taxpayer to whom it is issued and on whose behalf it was requested. Further, rulings have application only in respect of the transaction specified in the ruling request and to no other transactions. Hence, it is important that all persons who wish to benefit from an Advance Ruling should be made parties to the ruling request. In certain limited cases, rulings may be issued to a group of unnamed persons, for example, subscribers to shares under a prospectus or offering memorandum.

(vi) Revocation

A ruling may be revoked retroactively if a material omission or misrepresentation of relevant facts is brought to light or if the Department deems such a course is warranted upon disclosure of the purpose underlying the transaction(s). The Department's policy on the possibility of revocation is generally sufficient to ensure that taxpayers make full disclosure of all of the relevant facts and purposes underlying proposed transactions. There is no official disclosed record of the number of rulings that have been revoked.

A ruling may also be revoked if it was issued on the basis of an interpretation of law that is subsequently altered as a result of a judicial decision. In this circumstance, however, the revocation would not take effect prior to the date of the relevant decision. The Department also issues a notice advising the taxpayer to whom the ruling was issued of the prospective revocation of the ruling.

(vii) Change in Law

Where the law upon which a ruling was based is statutorily amended, the ruling ceases to be valid from the effective date of the change in the law. In this circumstance, the Department does not notify the taxpayer of the change. No notice of change is given to affected taxpayers because they are presumed to know the law and it would be impractical to give notice to all those who may be adversely affected.

(viii) Excluded Transactions

Revenue Canada does not rule on certain types of transactions. For example, the Department will generally refuse rulings in the following circumstances:

- Where a transaction is the same in character as a completed transaction entered into by the taxpayer in a prior year and the tax effect of the earlier transaction is under discussion with the taxpayer or in dispute. The rationale for this exclusion is that rulings are not given in respect of completed transactions and, as such, should not be given in respect of transactions that are virtually identical to previously completed transactions.

- Where the central issue involves a matter that is before the courts or, if a judgment has been issued, an appeal to a higher court is being considered. The Department cannot interpret the law contrary to decisions of the courts and does not wish to anticipate judicial decisions on outstanding matters.

- Where the major issue is whether a sale or purchase of property should be viewed as on account of an income or capital transaction. Such issues are essentially questions of fact.

3. CONSTITUTIONAL LIMITS

Income and other taxes can only be levied under the authority of specific fiscal legislation. There is no such thing as common law taxation. These principles have been part of Anglo-Saxon legal traditions since the Magna Carta in 1215. The spirit of the Magna Carta, exported to the United States and Canada, is captured in the Fifth Amendment to the U.S. Constitution and section 7 of the *Canadian Charter of Rights and Freedoms*, that states:

> . . . Everyone has the right to life, liberty and security of the person and the right not to be deprived thereof except in accordance with the principles of fundamental justice. . . .

In Canada, the constitutional power to levy taxes is shared by the federal Parliament and provincial Legislatures.[4]

The *Income Tax Act* is subject to the *Canadian Charter of Rights and Freedoms*.[5] Two provisions of the Charter are particularly relevant in the context of income tax law: Equality rights and the right to be secure against unreasonable search and seizure. Section 15 of the Charter reads:

> 15.(1) Every individual is equal before and under the law and has the right to the equal protection and equal benefit of the law without discrimination and, in particular, without discrimination based on race, national or ethnic origin, colour, religion, sex, age or mental or physical disability.
>
> (2) Subsection (1) does not preclude any law, program or activity that has as its object the amelioration of conditions of disadvantaged individuals or groups including those that are disadvantaged because of race, national or ethnic origin, colour, religion, sex, age or mental or physical disability.

Section 8 of the Charter reads:

> Everyone has the right to be secure against unreasonable search or seizure.

A taxpayer whose constitutional rights are violated may apply to a court of competent jurisdiction for relief against the violation. Section 24 of the Charter gives the courts virtually unlimited power to provide relief or remedy for violation of taxpayers' constitutional rights:

> 24.(1) Anyone whose rights or freedoms, as guaranteed by this Charter, have been infringed or denied may apply to a court of competent jurisdiction to obtain such remedy as the court considers appropriate and just in the circumstances.
>
> (2) Where, in proceedings under subsection (1), a court concludes that evidence was obtained in a manner that infringed or denied any rights or freedoms guaranteed by this Charter, the evidence shall

---

[4]   *Constitution Act, 1867*, subss. 91(3) and 92(2).

[5]   *Canadian Charter of Rights and Freedoms, Constitution Act, 1982:* see R.S.C. 1985, App. II (No. 44).

be excluded if it is established that, having regard to all the circumstances, the admission of it in the proceedings would bring the administration of justice into disrepute.

4. THE INTERPRETATION ACT

The proper construction of the *Income Tax Act* is a question of law. The Act is subject to the *Interpretation Act* and must be read according to the rules contained therein.[6]

Section 12 of the *Interpretation Act* reads:

Every enactment is deemed remedial, and shall be given such fair, large and liberal construction and interpretation as best ensures the attainment of its objects.

Thus, the *Income Tax Act* is to be read as a remedial statute and interpreted in such a fair and liberal manner as best ensures the attainment of its objects.[7]

5. GENERAL PRINCIPLES

(a) Ordinary Meaning

As a general rule, clear and unequivocal words used in a statute are to be assigned their ordinary, everyday meaning *unless* the words are specifically assigned different definitions. This is the rule even if the interpretation produces an "unfair" result. For example, the requirement that a deduction for alimony payments be supported by a *written* agreement is strictly enforced even if it produces unforeseen hardship for those who do not reduce their agreement to writing.[8]

The meaning of a word or phrase that is capable of diverse interpretation, however, may depend upon the circumstances of its use. In *Ransom v. Higgs*, Lord Simon said:[9]

The meaning of a word or phrase in an Act of Parliament is a question of law not fact; even though the law may then declare that the word or phrase has no statutory meaning beyond its common acceptance and that is a question of fact whether the circumstances fall within such meaning (*Cozens v. Brutus*

---

[6] *Interpretation Act*, R.S.C. 1985, c. I-21, as amended. Section 3 reads:
  (1) Every provision of this Act applies, unless a contrary intention appears, to every enactment, whether enacted before or after the commencement of this Act.
  (2) The provisions of this Act apply to the interpretation of this Act.
  (3) Nothing in this Act excludes the application to an enactment of a rule of construction applicable thereto and not inconsistent with this Act.

[7] See *Forest v. The Queen* (1979), 80 DTC 6149 (F.C.T.D.) (issue whether benefits "received" by non-residents and withholding tax exigible); *M.R.T. Invts. Ltd. v. The Queen*, [1975] CTC 354, 75 DTC 5224; affirmed [1976] CTC 294, 76 DTC 6158 (F.C.A.) (company carrying on investment activities may be "active business"); *Sussex Peerage Case* (1844), 8 ER 1034 (H.L.), *per* Lord Chief Justice Tindal "...if the words of the statute are in themselves precise and unambiguous, then no more can be necessary than to expound those words in their natural and ordinary sense". See also *Grey v. Pearson* (1857), 10 ER 1216 (H.L.) (estate litigation: "die under 21 and without issue").

[8] *Hodson v. The Queen*, [1988] 1 CTC 2, 88 DTC 6001 (F.C.A.).

[9] *Ransom v. Higgs*, [1974] STC 539 at 561, [1974] 1 WLR 1594 at 1618.

[1973] AC 854). But many words and phrases in English have many shades of meaning and are capable of embracing a great diversity of circumstances. So the interpretation of the language of an Act of Parliament often involves declaring that certain conduct must as a matter of law fall within the statutory language (as was the actual decision in *Edwards v. Bairstow* [1956] AC 14, 36 TC 207); that other conduct must as a matter of law fall outside the statutory language; but that whether yet a third category of conduct falls within the statutory language or outside it depends on the evaluation of such conduct by the tribunal of fact. This last question is often appropriately described as one of "fact and degree".

(b) Definitional Structure

In determining the meaning of a word or phrase one refers first to one of the definition sections of the Act. In the absence of a specific statutory definition, words and phrases are given their ordinary, everyday meaning.

The definitional sections of the Act operate at different levels. Subsection 248(1) is a general definition provision which contains definitions applicable to the entire Act. There are also divisional definitions throughout the statute that apply only to a particular part or division of the Act. For example, the definitions in section 54 apply to subdivision c of Division B and are concerned only with terms used in determining capital gains and losses. Then there are definitions which apply only to a particular section of the Act. For example, the definitions in subsection 125(7) apply specifically to words and phrases used in section 125.

(c) Normal Usage

In determining the meaning of a word, the courts usually prefer a meaning attributed to it in ordinary speech or usage rather than a technical meaning.[10] A word should only be interpreted technically in preference to its ordinary and grammatical meaning if such an interpretation is justified by the statutory context in which it appears.[11] It is, of course, quite possible that a word initially interpreted in its ordinary

---

[10] *Dauphin Plains Credit Union Ltd. v. Xyloid Industries Ltd.*, [1980] CTC 247, 80 DTC 6123 (S.C.C.) (meaning of "liquidation" taken by majority of Court to be wide, usual meaning); *Pfizer Co. v. Dep. M.N.R. (Customs & Excise)*, [1977] 1 SCR 456 (S.C.C.); *Trans-Prairie Pipelines Ltd. v. M.N.R.*, [1970] CTC 537, 70 DTC 6351 (Ex. Ct.) (interest deductible while money employed in business, not for life of loan).

[11] *Canterra Energy Ltd. v. The Queen*, [1987] 1 CTC 89, 87 DTC 5019 (F.C.A.) ("minus" used in its mathematical sense rather than its ordinary and grammatical sense; hence, subtraction could result in a negative number).

sense later develops, through judicial reinterpretation, into a word with an unordinary meaning.[12]

Where a word has more than one ordinary meaning, courts usually prefer the wider, more predominant meaning of the word over a narrow, less common meaning.[13]

(d) Ambiguity

Where words are ambiguous, courts should select that interpretation which best promotes the smooth working of the system[14] and avoid those interpretations which produce absurd, unjust, anomalous or inconvenient results.[15] Courts avoid interpretations resulting in absurd, inconvenient and unjust results, but only where the words used in a statutory provision are *ambiguous*.

Where statutory language is clear and unambiguous, the traditional approach was that courts would apply the language even if the result of such an interpretation is

---

[12] See, e.g., *I.R.C. v. Scottish & Newcastle Breweries Ltd.*, [1982] STC 187 (H.L.), *per* Lord Wilberforce, on the meaning of the word "plant":

> The word "plant" has frequently been used in fiscal and other legislation. It is one of a fairly large category of words as to which no statutory definition is provided ("trade", "office", even "income" are others), so that it is left to the court to interpret them. It naturally happens that as case follows case, and one extension leads to another, the meaning of the word gradually diverges from its natural or dictionary meaning. This is certainly true of "plant". No ordinary man, literate or semi-literate, would think that a horse, a swimming pool, movable partitions or even a dry dock was plant, yet each of these has been held to be so: so why not such equally improbable items as murals or tapestries or chandeliers?

[13] *The Queen v. Continental Air Photo Ltd.*, [1962] CTC 495, 62 DTC 1306 (Ex. Ct.) ("portrait" does not include aerial photography of farms); *M.N.R. v. Ritchie*, [1971] CTC 860, 71 DTC 5503 (F.C.T.D.) (words susceptible both to reasonable and unreasonable interpretation).

[14] *Shannon Realties Ltd. v. Ville de St. Michel*, [1924] AC 185 (P.C.).

[15] *The Queen v. Judge of City of London Court*, [1892] 1 QB 273 (C.A.) (whether amount received from employer for completing course constituted a "prize"). See also *Gill v. Donald Humberstone & Co.*, [1963] 1 WLR 929 (H.L.) (roofer not in "working place" when fell off ladder); *Railton v. Wood* (1890), 15 App. Cas. 363 (P.C.) ("distress for rent" includes holder of bill of sale taking back goods from bailiff); *Fry v. I.R.C.*, [1959] 1 Ch. 86 (C.A.) (estate tax on reversionary interest in possession but not indefeasibly vested); *Arrow Shipping Co. v. Tyne Improvement Commr., The Crystal*, [1894] AC 508 (H.L.) (interpretation of "possession" at time of salvage and destruction of vessel); *The Queen v. Overseers of Tonbridge* (1884), 13 QBD 339 (C.A.) (dispute over jurisdiction to levy rates by opposing burial boards; ordinary meaning conflicted with other Act).

absurd, anomalous or inconvenient. To do otherwise would have the judiciary usurp the function of the Legislature. In Lord Esher's words:[16]

> Now I say that no such rule of construction was ever laid down before. If the words of an Act are clear, you must follow them, even though they lead to a manifest absurdity. The court has nothing to do with the question whether the legislature has committed an absurdity. In my opinion, the rule has always been this — if the words of an Act admit of two interpretations, then they are not clear; and if one interpretation leads to an absurdity, and the other does not, the court will conclude that the legislature did not intend to lead to an absurdity, and will adopt the other interpretation.

The more modern view, however, is towards a purposive approach to statutory interpretation and the avoidance of absurd results.[17]

(e) Context

Even the simplest words are susceptible to misunderstanding and must be read in context.[18] Thus, when Justice Holmes was asked to determine whether an aircraft was a "motor vehicle" for the purposes of a motor vehicle theft statute, he disposed of the question as follows:[19]

> No doubt etymologically it is possible to use the word to signify a conveyance working on land, water or air, and sometimes legislation extends the use in that direction. . . . But in everyday speech "vehicle" calls up the picture of a thing moving on land.

There are three rules of interpretation concerned with statutory context.

---

[16] *The Queen v. Judge of City of London Court*, ante, at 290; see also *The Queen v. Savage*, [1980] CTC 103, 80 DTC 6066, reversed on other grounds [1981] CTC 332, 81 DTC 5258 *(sub nom. Savage v. The Queen)*, affirmed [1983] CTC 393, 83 DTC 5409 (S.C.C.) (whether $500 exemption applicable to "prize" from employer); *Victoria City Corp. v. Bishop of Vancouver Island*, [1921] 2 AC 384 (P.C.) (should exemption for house of worship include land upon which building erected); *I.R.C. v. Hinchy*, [1960] AC 748 (H.L.) (whether fine of "treble the tax" owed should include surtax); *Cartledge v. E. Jopling & Sons*, [1963] AC 758 (H.L.) (statutory limitation period expired before workers aware noxious dust caused injury to lungs); *Mersey Docks & Harbour Bd. v. Henderson Bros.* (1888), 13 App. Cas. 595 (H.L.) (dues in port payable when "trading inwards" or "trading outwards"; interpretation in respect of voyage with several ports); *Clerical, Med. & Gen. Life Ass. Soc. v. Carter* (1889), 22 QBD 444 (C.A.) (interpretation of "profits or gains" and "interest of money"); *Warburton v. Loveland* (1832), 2 Dow & Cl. 480 (H.L.); *Corp. d'Administration et de Placements Ltée v. Castonguay* (1970), 3 NBR (2d) 278 (Q.B.) (two interpretations of *Creditor's Relief Act*, one avoided injustice).

[17] See, for example, *Québec (Communauté urbaine) v. Corporation Notre-Dame de Bon-Secours*, [1994] 3 SCR 3.

[18] As Justice Cardozo explained in *Panama Refining Co. v. Ryan*, 293 U.S. 388, 433 (1935): "The meaning of a statute is to be looked for, not in any single section, but in all the parts together and in their relation to the end in view".

[19] *McBoyle v. U.S.*, 283 U.S. 25, 26 (1931).

Words and phrases are to be interpreted in the context of the statutory provision in which they appear and in the context of the *entire* Act. As Lord Herschell said in *Colquhoun v. Brooks*:[20]

> [i]t is beyond dispute, too, that we are entitled and indeed bound when construing the terms of any provision found in a statute to consider any other parts of the Act which throw light upon the intention of the legislature and which may serve to show that the particular provision ought not to be construed as it would be if considered alone and apart from the rest of the Act.

Second, words and concepts are to be read in the context of the statute in which they appear. Hence, the same word or concept in different statutes will not necessarily bear the same interpretation. For example, an "investment" for the purposes of legislation regulating investment contracts is not necessarily an investment asset for the purpose of determining whether a gain constitutes a capital gain for tax purposes.[21]

Third, a common commercial or financial word should be interpreted in the context of its ordinary commercial or financial usage.[22]

(f) Purposive Interpretation

(i) Background

It used to be the rule that tax statutes were interpreted literally and strictly, even where such interpretation produced hardship or inconvenience. Lord Cairns described the rule of strict interpretation as follows:[23]

> I am not at all sure that, in a case of this kind — a fiscal case — form is not amply sufficient; because, as I understand the principle of all fiscal legislation, it is this: if the person sought to be taxed comes within the letter of the law he must be taxed, however great the hardship may appear to the judicial mind to be. On the other hand, if the Crown, seeking to recover the tax, cannot bring the subject within the letter of the law, the subject is free, however apparently within the spirit of the law the case might

---

[20] *Colquhoun v. Brooks* (1889), 14 App. Cas. 493 at 506 (H.L.); cited with approval by Pratte J. in *The Queen v. Cie Immobilière B.C.N. Ltée*, [1979] CTC 71, 79 DTC 5068 (S.C.C.). See also *Highway Sawmills Ltd. v. M.N.R.*, [1966] CTC 150 at 157-58, 66 DTC 5116 at 5120 (S.C.C.):
> The answer to the question what tax is payable in any given circumstances depends, of course, upon the words of the legislation imposing it. Where the meaning of those words is difficult to ascertain it may be of assistance to consider which of two constructions contended for brings about a result which conforms to the apparent scheme of the legislation.

Can. Sugar Refining Co. v. The Queen, [1898] AC 735 (P.C.), *per* Lord Davey:"Every clause of a statute should be construed with reference to the context and the other clauses of the Act, so as, so far as possible, to make a consistent enactment of the whole statute or series of statutes relating to the subject-matter."; *The Queen v. Cadboro Bay Holdings Ltd.*, [1977] CTC 186, 77 DTC 5115 (F.C.T.D.) ("active business" defined as any quantum of activity giving rise to income); *Noranda Mines Ltd. v. The Queen*, [1982] CTC 226, 82 DTC 6212 (F.C.T.D.) (words claimed to be ineffectual or surplusage).

[21] *First Investors Corp. v. The Queen*, [1987] 1 CTC 285, 87 DTC 5176 (F.C.A.).

[22] *Bank of N.S. v. The Queen*, [1980] CTC 57, 80 DTC 6009; affirmed [1981] CTC 162, 81 DTC 5115 (F.C.A.).

[23] *Partington v. A.G.* (1869), 4 LR 100 (H.L.).

otherwise appear to be. In other words, if there be admissible, in any statute, what is called equitable construction, certainly such a construction is not admissible in a taxing statute where you simply adhere to the words of the statute.

Thus, the Act was interpreted literally, regardless of consequences.[24] As Lord Halsbury said in *Tennant v. Smith*:[25]

In various cases the principle of construction of a taxing Act has been referred to in various forms, but I believe they may be all reduced to this, that inasmuch as you have no right to assume that there is any governing object which a taxing Act is intended to attain other than which it has expressed by making such and such objects the intended subject for taxation, you must see whether a tax is expressly imposed.

Cases, therefore, under the Taxing Acts always resolve themselves into a question of whether or not the words of the Act have reached the alleged subject of taxation.

The rule of strict interpretation had two edges and could cut both for and against the taxpayer. To tax a person, the words of the Act had to unambiguously bring the prospective taxpayer within their scope. The courts would not assume that a transaction fell within the intention or purpose of a provision if the transaction did not clearly come within its express terms. In other words, the Minister was required to bring the taxpayer within the letter of the law. Similarly a taxpayer who came within the letter of the law was subject to tax, no matter how great the hardship that resulted.[26]

---

[24] In *Pryce v. Monmouthshire Canal & Ry. Co.* (1879), 4 App. Cas. 197 at 202-203 (H.L.), the principle was stated as follows:

My Lords, the cases which have decided that Taxing Acts are to be construed with strictness, and that no payment is to be exacted from the subject which is not clearly and unequivocally required by Act of Parliament to be made, probably meant little more than this, that, inasmuch as there was not *a priori* liability in a subject to pay any particular tax, nor any antecedent relationship between the taxpayer and the taxing authority, no reasoning founded upon any supposed relationship of the taxpayer and the taxing authority could be brought to bear upon the construction of the Act, and therefore the taxpayer had a right to stand upon a literal construction of the words used, whatever might be the consequence.

[25] *Tennant v. Smith,* [1892] AC 150 at 154 (H.L.).

[26] *Witthuhn v. M.N.R.* (1957), 3 Tax ABC 33, 57 DTC 174 (T.A.B.) (taxpayer denied deduction for medical expenses because wife not confined to wheelchair but using rocking chair); *Overdyk v. M.N.R.*, [1983] CTC 2361, 83 DTC 307 (T.R.B.) (chair with caster-like wheels mounted under legs qualifying as wheelchair for purposes of medical expense deduction). See generally *Jodrey Estate v. Min of Fin. (N.S.)*, [1980] CTC 437 (S.C.C.); *Royal Bank v. Dep. M.N.R.*, [1982] CTC 183, 81 DTC 5301 (S.C.C.). The reluctance of the courts to interpret legislative language beyond the words used in a provision may be seen in the comments of Chief Justice Thurlow in *The Queen v. B & J Music Ltd.*, [1983] CTC 50 at 51, 83 DTC 5074 at 5075 (F.C.A.), leave to appeal to S.C.C. refused (1983), 50 NR 159:

I accept that view that section 125 affords Canadian-controlled private corporations special tax treatment. That, to my mind, is its purpose but, as I see it, the purpose is to be carried out only to the extent that the language of the section so provides. It is not open to the court to extend the application of what the section provides by reliance on some supposed but unexpressed intendment.

Canadian courts applied the literal, English, approach to statutory construction in their interpretation of fiscal legislation.[27] For reasons that were never clearly articulated in the cases, most Canadian courts ignored section 12 of the *Interpretation Act*, which requires every Act to be interpreted in a fair, large and liberal manner *so as to ensure the attainment of its objects*. This judicial attitude was all the more remarkable because the federal *Interpretation Act*, which was the very first piece of legislation enacted in Canada after Confederation, was enacted 50 years before the *Income Tax Act*.[28]

The doctrine of strict interpretation would have worked well if legislative purpose could always be precisely and accurately captured in statutory language. Then, legislative purpose could be implemented simply by applying the words used in the statute. Experience, however, has taught us that the *Income Tax Act* is just not susceptible to such precise drafting. As long ago as 1936, in an era of comparatively simple tax legislation, an English codification committee realized the futility of attempting to anticipate every situation with comprehensive legislative drafting:[29]

> The imagination which can draw an income tax statute to cover the myriad transactions of a society like ours, capable of producing the necessary revenue without producing a flood of litigation, has not yet revealed itself.

Indeed, one can go further and postulate that a good measure of the complexity of the tax statute is directly attributable to the doctrine of strict interpretation. There is impressionistic evidence to suggest that as the courts applied the doctrine of strict interpretation with increasing stringency, the legislative draftsman responded with ever more complex and comprehensive statutory language in an attempt to provide for, and anticipate, every conceivable factual circumstance and nuance of possible transactions.

---

[27] See generally, McGregor's review of Canadian cases in "Interpretation of Taxing Statutes: Whither Canada?" (1968), 16 *Can. Tax J.* 122, where the author concludes by saying:

> Meanwhile, while there have been two major instances of broad interpretation . . . some instances of judgments which invoke the intention of the legislature and some of interpretation "in context", on the whole, the attitude of the Canadian courts seems still to be traditional in the adoption of strict interpretation.

It warrants emphasis that the English *Interpretation Act* does not contain any provision that is equivalent to s. 12 of its Canadian counterpart.

[28] *Interpretation Act*, 1867 (31 Vict.), c. 1, subs. 7(39) (assented to December 21, 1867) read as follows:

> The Preamble of every such Act as aforesaid shall be deemed a part thereof intended to assist in explaining the purport and object of the Act; — And every Act and every provision or enactment thereof shall be deemed remedial, whether its immediate purport be to direct the doing of any thing which Parliament deems to be for the public good or to prevent or punish the doing of any thing which it deems contrary to the public good, — and shall accordingly receive such fair, large and liberal construction and interpretation as will best ensure the attainment of the object of the Act and of such provision or enactment according to their true intent, meaning and spirit.

[29] *Report of Income Tax Codification Committee*, Cmd. 5131 (England, 1936), at 16-19.

(ii) The Modern Approach

Literal interpretation worked adequately when tax statutes were intended primarily, if not exclusively, to raise revenues. It did not work as well, however, when tax law moved from being solely a revenue raising statute to a multi-purpose instrument that raises revenue *and* promotes socio-economic policies.

In 1984, Canadian tax law made a dramatic shift in interpretational philosophy. In *Stubart Investments Ltd.*, the Supreme Court of Canada rejected six decades of literal interpretation and moved to the purposive approach.[30] Following *Stubart*, the Supreme Court expanded on more specific aspects of interpretative methodology in *Golden*,[31] *Bronfman Trust*[32], *Johns-Manville Canada*,[33] *Antosko*[34] and *Corporation Notre-Dame de Bon-Secours*.[35] These decisions offer a virtual codification of the rules of interpretation of tax law.

The *Income Tax Act* is to be read in context, in its grammatical and ordinary sense, harmoniously with the scheme and object of the Act, and with a view to its legislative intention.[36]

The rationale of the purposive approach is simple. Legislation is enacted for a purpose and, hence, should be interpreted in a manner as best enhances the attainment of that purpose. Justice Frankfurter put the case for purposive interpretation as follows:[37]

---

[30] *Stubart Investments Ltd. v. The Queen*, [1984] 1 SCR 536, [1984] CTC 294, 84 DTC 6305. See also: *Irving Oil Ltd. v. The Queen*, [1988] 1 CTC 263, 88 DTC 6138 (F.C.T.D.); affirmed [1991] 1 CTC 350, 91 DTC 5106 (F.C.A.); *Indalex Ltd. v. The Queen*, [1986] 2 CTC 482, 86 DTC 6039 (F.C.A.); *Consolidated Bathurst Ltd. v. The Queen*, [1985] 1 CTC 142, 85 DTC 5129 (F.C.T.D.); affirmed in part [1987] 1 CTC 55, 87 DTC 5001 (F.C.A.); *Orr v. M.N.R.*, [1989] 2 CTC 2348, 89 DTC 557 (T.C.C.); *Hickman Motors Ltd. v. The Queen*, [1993] 1 CTC 36, 93 DTC 5040 (F.C.T.D.); *Earlscourt Sheet Metal Mechanical Ltd. v. M.N.R.*, [1988] 1 CTC 2045, 88 DTC 1029 (T.C.C.); *Montgomery v. M.N.R.*, [1987] 2 CTC 2023, 87 DTC 355 (T.C.C.); *Vivian v. The Queen*, [1984] CTC 354, 84 DTC 6447 (*sub nom. The Queen v. Parsons*) (F.C.A.); *Bastion Management Ltd. v. M.N.R.*, [1988] 1 CTC 2344, 88 DTC 1245 (T.C.C.), affirmed [1994] 2 CTC 70, 94 DTC 6271 (F.C.T.D.); *Daggett v. M.N.R.*, [1992] 2 CTC 2764, 93 DTC 14; *454538 Ontario Ltd. v. M.N.R.*, [1993] 1 CTC 2746, 93 DTC 427 (T.C.C.); *Goulard v. M.N.R.*, [1992] 1 CTC 2396, 92 DTC 1244 (T.C.C.).

[31] *The Queen v. Golden*, [1986] 1 SCR 209, [1986] 1 CTC 274, 86 DTC 6138.

[32] *Bronfman Trust v. The Queen*, [1987] 1 CTC 117, 87 DTC 5059 (S.C.C.).

[33] *Johns-Manville Can. Inc. v. The Queen*, [1985] 2 SCR 46, [1985] 2 CTC 111, 85 DTC 5373.

[34] *Antosko v. The Queen*, [1994] 2 CTC 25, 94 DTC 6314 (S.C.C.).

[35] *Québec (Communauté urbaine) v. Corp. Notre-Dame de Bon-secours*, [1994] 3 SCR 3.

[36] *Stubart Investments Ltd. v. The Queen*, 1984 1 SCR 536, [1984] 2 CTC 294, 84 DTC 6305.

[37] Frankfurter, Felix, "Some Reflections on the Reading of Statutes" (1947), 47 *Colum. L. Rev.*, No. 4, 527 at 538-39.

> Legislation has an aim: it seeks to obviate some mischief, to supply an inadequacy, to effect a change
> of policy, to formulate a plan of Government. That aim, that policy is not drawn, like nitrogen, out of
> the air; it is evinced in the language of the statute as read in the light of other external manifestations
> of purpose.

Thus, in a sense, the purposive approach is a manifestation of judicial deference to legislative supremacy.

But, purposive interpretation may put a gloss on legislative language that was never contemplated. Faced with clear and unambiguous language, should the courts attempt to extract legislative purpose or interpret the language as written? In *Antosko*,[38] for example, the Supreme Court of Canada adopted a restrictive view of purposive interpretation. Contextual and purposive interpretation should not be used to alter the result of commercial transactions where the words of the Act are clear and plain. The Supreme Court addressed the balance between the judicial and legislative roles as follows:[39]

> In the absence of evidence that the transaction was a sham or an abuse of the provisions of the Act, it
> is not the role of the court to determine whether the transaction in question is one which renders the
> taxpayer deserving of a deduction. If the terms of the section are met, the taxpayer may rely on it, and
> it is the option of Parliament specifically to preclude further reliance in such situations.

And again:[40]

> Where the words of the section are not ambiguous, it is not for this Court to find that the appellants
> should be disentitled to a deduction because they do not deserve a "windfall". . . In the absence of a
> situation of ambiguity, such that the Court must look to the result of a transaction to assist in
> ascertaining the intent of Parliament, a normative assessment of the consequences of the application of
> a given provision is within the ambit of the legislature, not the courts.

Thus, *Antosko* walked the tightrope between strict and literal construction, which might produce absurd results, and pedantic application of the purposive approach in the face of clear and unambiguous legislative language.

The purpose rule is not a substitute for the plain meaning rule. It is used where statutory language is obscure or ambiguous and a court needs assistance in determining legislative intention. Otherwise, unambiguous legislative language is interpreted according to its plain meaning, but not so literally as to produce absurd results.

(g) Not a Penal Statute

The interpretation of tax legislation should follow the ordinary rules of interpretation applicable to any other legislation. The old notion that taxing statutes are, in effect, penal statutes has no place in modern interpretation.

---

[38] *Antosko v. The Queen,* [1994] 2 CTC 25, 94 DTC 6314 (S.C.C.).

[39] *Antosko v. The Queen, ante,* [1994] 2 CTC at 32, 94 DTC at 6320.

[40] *Antosko v. The Queen, ante,* [1994] 2 CTC at 33, 94 DTC at 6321.

(h) Characterization of Expenditures

The characterization in taxation law of an expenditure is, in the final analysis (unless the Act is explicit), one of policy.[41] Since the accurate measurement of annual income is a fundamental policy of the Act, this rule is of particular relevance to the classification of expenditures on account of business, capital, eligible capital and the characterization of losses.

(i) Multi-purpose Statute

The Act should not be read simply as a vehicle for the raising of revenues. It is a multi-purpose statute that also serves other purposes: Social, economic, and cultural. These purposes can be as important to society as the raising of revenues to finance public expenditures. As the Supreme Court said in *Golden*:[42]

> Strict consideration in the historic sense no longer finds a place in the canons of interpretation applicable to taxation statutes in an era such as the present, where taxation serves many purposes in addition to the old and traditional object of raising the cost of government from a somewhat unenthusiastic public.

Hence, tax expenditures should not be considered to be undesirable *per se*, but should be evaluated in the context of the purpose for which they are legislated. To be sure, policy makers should consider the effectiveness of tax expenditures versus budgetary expenditures. But the courts should interpret expenditure provisions in the context of their legislative purpose.

(j) Resolution of Ambiguity

Where the Act is not explicit, reasonable uncertainty or factual ambiguity resulting from the lack of explicitness should be resolved in favour of the taxpayer.[43] This rule applies when a court is compelled to choose between alternatives that are equally valid and *bona fide* interpretations. The presumption in favour of the taxpayer is *residual* in nature and should play only an exceptional part in the interpretation of tax legislation.[44] Thus, every effort must first be made to determine the meaning of the Act. Only when this proves to be impossible, or produces *bona fide* alternative interpretations, is it legitimate to apply the presumption in favour of the taxpayer.

(k) No Interpretive Presumptions

The old rule that exemptions were to be strictly interpreted against the taxpayer and charging provisions strictly against the State no longer applies.

---

[41] *Johns-Manville Canada Inc. v. The Queen*, [1985] 2 SCR 46, [1985] 2 CTC 111, 85 DTC 5373.

[42] *Golden v. The Queen*, [1986] 1 CTC 274 at 277, 86 DTC 6138 at 6140 (S.C.C.).

[43] *Johns-Manville Canada Inc. v. The Queen*, [1985] 2 CTC at 126, 85 DTC 5373 at 5384 (S.C.C.).

[44] *Québec (Communauté urbaine) v. Corporation Notre-Dame de Bon-Secours*, [1994] 3 SCR 3 at 16.

The Supreme Court emphatically rejected any such presumptions in *Corporation Notre-Dame de Bon-Secours*:[45]

> . . . Adhering to the principle that taxation is clearly the rule and exemption the exception no longer corresponds to the reality of present-day tax law.

The purposive approach favours the taxpayer or the revenue authorities depending on the legislative provision in question and *not* on the existence of predetermined presumptions.[46] The underlying purpose of the provision in question determines whether a strict or liberal interpretation is appropriate in the circumstances and whether the Department or the taxpayer should be favoured in the particular interpretation.[47] Hence, incentive provisions should be interpreted to enhance their underlying purpose and anti-avoidance provisions should be read to restrict and circumscribe abusive tax avoidance.

(I) Substance Over Form

Substance should be given precedence over form to the extent that this is consistent with the wording and objective of the statute.[48] This rule, which is one of the chestnuts of judicial interpretation, is easier to state than it is to apply. To be sure, it is entirely relevant to purposive interpretation that tax arrangements and transactions should be looked at from their substantive content as opposed to their form. Thus, one asks:

- What does the transaction or arrangement achieve?

- Does the result fit within the purpose of the statutory provision(s)?

- If it does not fit within the purpose of the provision(s), should the taxpayer be allowed the benefit of the provision or be subject to the avoidance strictures of the Act?

The doctrine of substance over form has been articulated in various ways. The principal difficulty with the doctrine is that, despite its intuitive appeal, it does not offer any objective yardstick by which it may be measured against particular facts. Hence, it is an unpredictable doctrine of varying reach. Lord Tomlin referred to it as the "so-called doctrine" in the *Duke of Westminster*:[49]

> . . . it is said that in revenue cases there is a doctrine that the Court may ignore the legal position and regard what is called "the substance of the matter" . . . This supposed doctrine . . . seems to rest for its

---

[45] *Id.,* at 14.

[46] *Id.,* at 17.

[47] *Id.,* at 14.

[48] *Id.,* at 17.

[49] *C.I.R. v. The Duke of Westminster,* [1936] AC 1 at 3-4 (H.L.).

support upon a misunderstanding of language used in some earlier cases. The sooner this misunderstanding is dispelled, and the supposed doctrine given its quietus, the better it will be for all concerned, for the doctrine seems to involve substituting "the incertain and crooked cord of discretion" for "the golden and straight metwand of the law". Every man is entitled if he can to order his affairs so as that the tax attaching under the appropriate Acts is less than it otherwise would be. . . . This so-called doctrine of "the substance" seems to me to be nothing more than an attempt to make a man pay and notwithstanding that he has so ordered his affairs that the amount of tax sought from him is not legally claimable.

Notwithstanding these reservations, the doctrine has had a pervasive effect in Canadian tax jurisprudence. It was knocked down in *Stubart*, but raised again under the guise of the commercial reality test in *Bronfman Trust*.[50] As Chief Justice Dickson said:[51]

I acknowledge, however, that just as there has been a recent trend away from strict construction of taxation statutes . . . so too has the recent trend in tax cases been towards attempting to ascertain the *true commercial and practical nature of the taxpayer's transaction*. There has been, in this country and elsewhere, movement away from tests based on the form of transactions and towards tests based on what Lord Pearce has referred to as a "common sense appreciation of all the guiding features" of the events in question. . . . This is, I believe, a laudable trend *provided it is consistent* with the text and purposes of the taxation statute. [Emphasis added.]

But what do we mean by the "substance" of a transaction? Do we mean economic or legal substance? Assume, for example, that a taxpayer wants to use a capital asset in his or her business and is faced with three alternatives. The taxpayer can:

• purchase the asset outright and acquire title to it immediately, regardless whether he or she pays for it upon acquisition or over some extended period of time;

• lease the asset for a period of time and pay rent for its use, but without acquiring title in the property; or

• lease the asset over a period of time, with an option to purchase the property for a token amount upon the expiration of the lease.

In each case, the taxpayer makes use of the property in business and is entitled to a write-off of some or all of the cost of the property. In the first case, the taxpayer clearly acquires title and ownership to the property. The cost of the asset is a capital payment which, in the case of depreciable property, for example, would be eligible for capital cost allowance.

In the second case, the taxpayer has no title to the property but merely acquires a user interest in exchange for rental payments. The payments may or may not coincide with the amount deductible as capital cost allowance in the first case. This would depend upon the term of the lease, the cost of financing, and where applicable, statutory restrictions on quantum.

---

[50] *Bronfman Trust v. The Queen*, [1987] 1 CTC 117, 87 DTC 5059 (S.C.C.).

[51] *Bronfman Trust v. The Queen, ante*, [1987] 1 CTC at 128, 87 DTC at 5066-5067.

In the third case, the taxpayer, in economic substance, purchases the property, but with a delayed transmission of title. The economic effect of the transaction is identical to an outright purchase of the property. As a matter of legal substance, however, the taxpayer is merely a lessee of the property during the tenure of the lease and acquires legal title only upon the expiration of the lease. Thus, the legal substance of the transaction is that it is a lease until such time as the purchaser acquires title.

6. RES JUDICATA

The doctrine of *res judicata* applies to income tax law. Thus, a judicial decision determines every right, question, or fact distinctly put in issue by the parties to a dispute and all matters which *ought* to have been brought forward as part of the litigation. Thus, when an issue is litigated between the taxpayer and Revenue Canada (Taxation), the judgment of the court (subject only to appeal) conclusively determines all matters in connection therewith.

The doctrine of *res judicata* in tax law applies only to *the particular taxation year* that was the subject of the dispute. A judicial determination in respect of a particular issue for a particular year does not bind either the taxpayer or Revenue Canada on the same issue in a subsequent taxation year. For example, a decision that a particular property constitutes inventory in one year does not mean that it, or a similar property, cannot be considered capital property in another year.

7. ESTOPPEL

The Crown is not estopped by any representation of fact or statement of law made by its officials. A taxpayer who is misled by a statement made by an official of, or a publication by, Revenue Canada cannot use the misrepresentation to support his or her position.[52] It is, therefore, particularly important for taxpayers who receive "informal advice" from tax officials to assess the advice on the basis of the law.

---

[52] *M.N.R. v. Inland Indust. Ltd.*, [1972] CTC 27, 72 DTC 6013 (S.C.C.) (". . . the Minister cannot be bound by an approval given when the conditions prescribed by the law were not met."); *Wollenberg v. M.N.R.*, [1984] CTC 2043, 84 DTC 1055 (S.C.C.) (estoppel incapable of putting aside or overriding provisions of Act as enacted by Parliament); *Cohen v. The Queen*, [1978] CTC 63, 78 DTC 6099; affirmed [1980] CTC 318, 80 DTC 6250 (F.C.A.) (Minister permitted to renege on earlier arrangement and reassess); *Gauthier v. M.N.R.*, [1978] CTC 2175, 78 DTC 1126 (T.R.B.) (taxpayer followed Minister's advice to her prejudice; Court powerless to remedy situation); *Stickel v. M.N.R.*, [1972] CTC 210, 72 DTC 6178, reversed on other grounds [1973] CTC 202, 73 DTC 5178, affirmed [1974] CTC 416, 74 DTC 6268 (S.C.C.) (interpretation bulletin offered incorrect opinion of tax treaty); *Gibbon v. The Queen*, [1977] CTC 334, 77 DTC 5193 (F.C.T.D.) (Minister's erroneous assessment not to be relied upon). But see *The Queen v. Langille*, [1977] CTC 144, 77 DTC 5068 (F.C.T.D.) (first case in which estoppel successfully invoked against Minister). As a matter of administrative practice, Revenue Canada usually considers itself bound by its advance rulings, but only to each taxpayer to whom a ruling is issued; see IC 70-6R2, "Advance Income Tax Rulings" (September 28, 1990). Revenue Canada can, and has, withdrawn rulings which it has given in error; see TR-91 given to Global Strategy Corp. ("Tax world jolted by Revenue's revocation", *The Financial Post,* Oct. 12, 1985, p. 29).

8. RETROSPECTIVE APPLICATION

Provisions of the *Income Tax Act* that adversely affect taxpayers do not apply retroactively unless such a construction is very clearly dictated by the statutory language. This fundamental principle is not unique to tax law. Mr. Justice Willes said in *Phillips v. Eyre:*[53]

> Retrospective laws are no doubt *prima facie* of questionable policy, and contrary to the general principle that legislation by which the conduct of mankind is to be regulated ought, when introduced for the first time, to deal with future acts, and ought not to change the character of past transactions carried on upon the faith of the then existing law.

Similarly, in *Re Athlumney:*[54]

> Perhaps no rule of construction is more firmly established than this — that a retrospective operation is not to be given to a statute so as to impair an existing right or obligation, otherwise than as regards a matter of procedure, unless that effect cannot be avoided without doing violence to the language of the enactment. If the enactment is expressed in language which is fairly capable of either interpretation, it ought to be construed as prospective only.

The presumption against retrospective application of statutes is, of course, subject to the proviso that the statute itself may deem otherwise. A legislative body can always give retroactive force to statutory provisions despite the presumption:[55]

> The general rule is that statutes are not to be construed as having retrospective operation unless such a construction is expressly or by necessary implication required by the language of the Act. An amending enactment may provide that it shall be deemed to have come into force on a date prior to its enactment or it may provide that it is to be operative with respect to transactions occurring prior to its enactment. In those instances the statute operates retrospectively.

A statutory provision is considered retrospective if it creates new obligations, imposes new duties, or attaches new disabilities in respect of past events and transactions.[56] The courts will not interpret an Act to impair vested rights unless the language of the amending provision is unambiguous and demands such a construction.[57] Conversely,

---

[53] *Phillips v. Eyre* (1870), 6 LR QB 1.

[54] *Re Athlumney*, [1898] 2 QB 547 at 551-2.

[55] *Gustavson Drilling (1964) Ltd. v. M.N.R.*, [1977] 1 SCR 271 at 279, [1976] CTC 1 at 6-7, 75 DTC 5451 at 5454, *per* Dickson J.

[56] *Craies on Statute Law*, 7th ed. (London: Sweet & Maxwell, 1971), at 387.

[57] *Spooner Oils Ltd. v. Turner Valley Gas Conservation Bd.*, [1933] SCR 629 (S.C.C.). Note, however, that no person has a vested right to static continuance of the tax law; see *Gustavson Drilling (1964) Ltd. v. M.N.R.*, [1976] CTC 1 at 9, 75 DTC 5451 at 5456 (S.C.C.), specifically, the comments of Dickson J.: "... No one has a vested right to continuance of the law as it stood in the past; in tax law it is imperative that legislation conform to changing social needs and governmental policy".

the enactment of a statutory provision should not be construed as necessarily changing the law that existed prior to the enactment.[58]

Taxpayers have the right to certainty in commercial transactions, both in respect of legislative changes and administrative interpretation. Retrospective legislation undermines the rule of law.

9. UNCONSTITUTIONAL LAW

Constitutional law and tradition require that taxes may only be imposed and collected under the authority of an Act of Parliament or provincial legislative assembly.[59] Thus, there is no legal authority in Canada to collect taxes before a budget bill is enacted and receives Royal Assent. In contrast, Britain has such an enactment,[60] which allows a resolution adopted by the Committee of Ways and Means the effect of law for a limited period of time.

As a matter of practice, Budget bills stipulate an enactment date (usually the date of the budget speech) for the various motions that are introduced to amend the *Income Tax Act*. The bill, when enacted, is made retrospective to the date specified in the budget.[61] This, in effect, whitewashes any constitutional illegality involved in the premature collection of taxes.

Litigation to challenge the constitutional illegality of premature tax collection would, at best, result in pyrrhic victory since the budget bill would be enacted prior to commencement of the litigation. Once the bill is actually enacted into law, the tax becomes "payable" as of the date set out in the legislation regardless of the date that the legislation receives Royal Assent.

It is arguable that premature tax collection is contrary to the *Canadian Bill of Rights* to the extent that such collection procedures abrogate, breach or infringe the rights and freedoms expressed therein. The more difficult question, however, is whether the courts will do anything about the infringement or abrogation of rights. The Supreme Court of Canada held in *Hydro Electric Comm. of Nepean v. Ont. Hydro* that payment of invalid taxes is not recoverable.[62] This case was decided on the basis that taxes paid

---

[58] See subs. 45(2) of the *Interpretation Act*, R.S.C. 1985, c. I-21:

    45.(2) The amendment of an enactment shall not be deemed to be or to involve a declaration that the law under such enactment was or was considered by Parliament or other body or person by whom the enactment was enacted to have been different from the law as it is under the enactment as amended.

[59] *Bowles v. Bank of England*, [1913] 1 Ch. 57.

[60] *Provisional Collection of Taxes Act*, 1913 (3 & 4 Geo. 5, c. 3).

[61] See, e.g., *Beesley v. M.N.R.*, [1986] 2 CTC 2018, 86 DTC 1498 (T.C.C.) (Parliament constitutionally empowered to enact legislation having retroactive effect).

[62] *Hydro Electric Comm. of Nepean v. Ont. Hydro*, [1982] 1 SCR 347.

by virtue of a regulation held to be *ultra vires* on constitutional grounds are not recoverable. It is possible, however, that a court may take a different view of taxes collected on the basis of a statute that is unconstitutional because it has not been enacted.

10. TERRITORIAL LIMITATIONS

The Act only applies to persons who have some *nexus*, bond or link, whether physical or financial, with Canada.[63] It is a well accepted principle that fiscal statutes are not enforced outside the territorial scope of the country responsible for their legislation. Thus, Canada does not enforce foreign tax laws, and it will not, even indirectly, assist foreign countries in the enforcement of their tax laws in Canadian courts.[64]

11. FRENCH AND ENGLISH VERSIONS

All statutory enactments of the Parliament of Canada must be printed and published in both English and French.[65] The usual practice is to print federal statutes in two columns, one side English and the other side French.

Unless one of the versions produces a result or interpretation that is incompatible with the legal system in that particular part of Canada, the general rule of interpretation is to give preference to the version that, according to the true spirit, intent and meaning of the statute, best ensures the attainment of its objects. Thus, a court will look to see which of the versions fits in with the scheme of the statute as a whole and adopt that interpretation which best suits its objects.[66]

---

[63] See generally *Allied Farm Equipment v. M.N.R.*, [1972] CTC 619, 73 DTC 5036 (F.C.A.). See also: *Lea-Don Can. Ltd. v. M.N.R.*, [1969] CTC 85, 69 DTC 5142; affirmed [1970] CTC 346, 70 DTC 6271 (S.C.C.) (CCA not claimable by non-residents unless carrying on business in Canada).

[64] *Holman v. Johnson* (1775), 98 ER 1120 (should individual with knowledge of smuggling scheme be permitted remedy for non-payment of price); *The Queen of Holland v. Drukker*, [1928] 1 Ch. 877 (whether foreign national (Dutch sovereign) permitted to sue in English Courts for revenue claim against Dutch subject). See also, e.g., *U.S. v. Harden*, [1963] CTC 450, 63 DTC 1276 (S.C.C.), where the United States government sought to circumvent this rule, first by obtaining a judgment in the United States court and then by contending that it was seeking to apply, not the United States tax law, but merely the enforceability of a judgment of the United States courts. This was rejected by the Supreme Court of Canada as an indirect attempt to enforce foreign fiscal legislation.

[65] *Constitution Act, 1867*, s. 133.

[66] See *The Queen v. Cie Immobilière BCN Ltée*, [1979] CTC 71 at 75, 79 DTC 5068 at 5071 (S.C.C.), where Pratte J. rejected the view that the narrower of the two versions should prevail: "...the narrower meaning of one of the two versions should not be preferred where such meaning would clearly run contrary to the intent of the legislation and would consequently tend to defeat rather than assist the attainment of its objects".

12. DEFINITIONS

As already noted, the first and foremost rule of statutory interpretation is that the words used in a statute ought to be given their ordinary, everyday meaning *unless* they are specifically assigned different definitions by the statute in question.

The definitional sections of the Act fall into three broad categories: those which explain the meaning of a word or phrase, those which merely describe, and those which dictate a particular meaning regardless of all other considerations.

Strictly speaking, a definition is a precise statement of the nature of a thing, the meaning of a word, or the character of an event. Used in this sense, a definition begins by saying that a word or phrase "means" something.[67] The use of the word "means" is usually restrictive; it confines the meaning attributable to the word being defined.

There are, however, many so-called "definitions" that do not, in fact, define but broaden the application of a word or phrase so as to "include" something else.[68] Generally speaking, a provision describing a word to "include" something else tends to enlarge the meaning of the word.[69] There are, however, circumstances in which an "includes" definition is so exhaustive as to be virtually transformed into a "means" definition.[70]

The third category of definitions includes those which *impose* a meaning on a word by deeming it to mean something. A deeming clause can cause a word or phrase to connote something entirely different from that which it would have been understood to mean in the absence of the clause.[71] Thus, a deeming provision can artificially import

---

[67] See, e.g., subs. 248(1) ("prescribed"), ("regulation"), ("retiring allowance") and ("share").

[68] See, e.g., subs. 248(1) ("farming"), ("shareholder"), and ("taxpayer").

[69] As Lord Watson observed in *Dilworth v. Stamps Commr.*, [1899] AC 99 at 105-106 (P.C.):

> The word "include" is very generally used in interpretation clauses in order to enlarge the meaning of words or phrases occurring in the body of a statute; and when it is so used these words or phrases must be construed as comprehending, not only such things as they signify according to their natural import, but also those things which the interpretation clause declares that they shall include.

See also *C.B.A. Engineering Ltd. v. M.N.R.*, [1971] CTC 504, 71 DTC 5282; affirmed [1974] CTC 888 (F.C.A.) (whether engineering firm engaged in farming as public-relations move); *Assoc. Corp. of N. Amer. v. The Queen*, [1980] CTC 80, 80 DTC 6049; affirmed [1980] CTC 215, 80 DTC 6140 (F.C.A.) (Minister not permitted to expand meaning of "interest" in tax treaty).

[70] *Dilworth v. Stamps Commr., ante.*

[71] *The Queen v. Sutherland*, [1980] 2 SCR 451 (S.C.C.). See, e.g., para. 251(1)(*a*). A deeming clause is the ultimate manifestation of Parliamentary supremacy and can defy natural law; see, e.g., para. 55(5)(*e*) which deems a person not to be related to his or her brother or sister.

into a word or phrase a meaning that it would not otherwise convey. Thus, a deeming provision can create a statutory fiction. As Beetz J. said:[72]

> . . . as a rule [a deeming provision] implicitly admits that a thing is not what it is deemed to be but decrees that for some particular purpose it shall be taken as if it were that thing although it is not or there is doubt as to whether it is. A deeming provision artificially imports into a word or an expression an additional meaning which they would not otherwise convey beside the normal meaning which they retain where they are used; it plays a function of enlargement analogous to the word "includes" in certain definitions; however "includes" would be logically inappropriate and would sound unreal because of the fictional aspect of the provision.

For example, paragraph 55(5)(*e*) deems a brother and his sister not to be related to each other for certain purposes of the Act.

13. INTERNATIONAL TAX TREATIES

Canada has entered into bilateral tax treaties with several countries. The purpose of these tax treaties is three-fold:

* to avoid double taxation;

* to prevent income tax evasion; and

* to provide certainty in international commercial transactions.

(a) Application of International Law

The subject of treaty interpretation in international law is complex. As McNair said:[73]

> . . . there is no part of the law of treaties which [he] approaches with more trepidation than the question of interpretation.

Tax treaties (like other international treaties) are to be interpreted according to the rules of international law and not according to the rules of statutory interpretation

---

[72] *The Queen v. Verrette*, [1978] 2 SCR 838 at 845 (S.C.C.). See also *M.N.R. v. People's Thrift & Invt. Co.*, [1959] CTC 185, 59 DTC 1129 (Ex. Ct.) (statute interpreted by "parliamentary expansion", i.e., by reference to subsequent amendments); *Birmount Hldg. Ltd. v. The Queen*, [1978] CTC 358, 78 DTC 6254 (F.C.A.) (company carrying on business deemed in law to be resident); *Gillespie v. The Queen*, [1982] CTC 378, 82 DTC 6334 (F.C.A.) (statutory assumption, although incorrect, not open to rebuttal).

[73] A.D. McNair, *The Law of Treaties*, 2nd ed. (Oxford: Oxford Univ. Press, 1961).

applicable to domestic fiscal legislation.[74] The doctrine of strict interpretation of fiscal legislation, now considered defunct in domestic interpretation, was never considered appropriate for treaty interpretation. Thus,[75]

> [t]he accepted principle appears to be that a taxing Act must be construed against either the Crown or the person sought to be charged, with perfect strictness — so far as the intention of Parliament is discoverable. Where a tax convention is involved, however, the situation is different and a liberal interpretation is usual, in the interests of the comity of nations. Tax conventions are negotiated primarily to remedy a subject's tax position by the avoidance of double taxation rather than to make it more burdensome. This fact is indicated in the preamble to the Convention.

(b) Methods of Interpretation

There appear to be at least two distinct differences between the interpretation of international tax treaties and domestic tax legislation. First, since international tax treaties are not written with the same legislative precision as the *Income Tax Act*, it is unreliable to place as great an emphasis on the literal meaning of the words in the treaty. As Addy, J. said in *Gladden Estate*:[76]

> Contrary to an ordinary taxing statute a tax treaty or convention must be given a liberal interpretation with a view to implementing the true intentions of the parties. A literal or legalistic interpretation must be avoided where the basic object of the treaty might be defeated or frustrated insofar as the particular item under consideration is concerned.

A second difference is in the use of extrinsic evidence (such as, preparatory work in the form of committee reports, working papers and government documents). Traditionally, Canadian courts have not readily admitted such extrinsic evidence in the interpretation of the *Income Tax Act*. Although the barriers towards the admission of extrinsic evidence have been lowered in recent years, Canadian courts still approach

---

[74] See, generally, A.D. McNair, *The Law of Treaties*, 2nd ed. (Oxford: Oxford Univ. Press, 1961); D.P. O'Connell, *International Law*, 2nd ed. (London: Stevens, 1970); McDougall, Lasswell & Miller, *The Interpretation of Agreements and World Public Order* (New Haven, CT: Yale Univ. Press, 1967); G.C. Fitzmaurice, "Vae victis, or, Woe to the Negotiators" (1971), 65 *Am. J. Int'l. L.* 358; J.G. Castel, *International Law*, 3rd ed. (Toronto: Butterworths, 1976); J. Van Houtte, *Principles of Interpretation in Internal and International Tax Law* (Int. Bur. of Fisc. Doc., 1968); S.K. Agrawla (Ed.), *Essays on the Law of Treaties* (Essex: Orient Longman Ltd., 1972); T.O. Elias, *The Modern Law of Treaties* (Dobbs Ferry, N.Y.: Oceana Publications, 1974); G.C. Fitzmaurice, "The Law and Procedure in the International Court of Justice; Treaty Interpretation and Certain Other Treaty Points" (1951), 28 *Br. Yr. Bk. of Int'l. L.* 1; I.M. Sinclair, "Treaty Interpretation in the English Courts" (1963), 12 *Int'l and Comp. L.Q.* 508; C.H. Schreuer, "The Interpretation of Treaties by Domestic Courts" (1971), 45 *Br. Yr. Bk. of Int'l. L.* 255; J.L. Brierly, *Law of Nations* (4th ed., Oxford, 1949), at 234 *et. seq.*; *Oppenheim's International Law* (8th ed. by H. Lauterpract, London, 1955) vol. 1, at 950 *et seq.*

[75] *Saunders v. M.N.R.*, 54 DTC 524 at 526 (T.A.B.) cited with approval in *C.P. Ltd. v. The Queen*, [1976] CTC 221, 76 DTC 6120 (F.C.T.D.), *per* Walsh J.: "The parties are in agreement that the terms of a treaty will over-ride an Act and that it should be construed more liberally".

[76] *J.N. Gladden Estate v. The Queen*, [1985] 1 CTC 163 at 166, 85 DTC 5188 at 5191 (F.C.T.D.) (exemption of tax on capital gains of non-residents under the *Canada-U.S. Tax Convention* applies to deemed dispositions upon death).

supplementary materials with caution. Generally speaking, Canadian courts restrict the admission of extrinsic evidence to official statements by the responsible Minister, governmental documents such as the Minister's Technical Notes tabled with the legislation at the time that it is introduced in the House, and Revenue Canada's administrative bulletins and interpretations.

In contrast, extrinsic evidence is readily admissible in the interpretation of international tax treaties. The House of Lords has said in the context of the English rules of statutory interpretation:[77]

> [s]o far as purely domestic legislation is concerned it is well established as a principle of interpretation that, even where the words of a statute are ambiguous or obscure, the proceedings in Parliament during the course of the passage of the Bill may not be resorted to for the purpose of ascertaining what ambiguities or obscure provisions mean. . . . So Hansard can never form part of the "travaux préparatoires" of any Act of Parliament whether it deals with purely domestic legislation or not. . . .
>
> It is, however, otherwise with that growing body of written law in force in the United Kingdom which, although it owes its enforceability within the United Kingdom to its embodiment in or authorization by an Act of Parliament, nevertheless owes its origin and its actual wording to some prior law-making process in which Parliament has not participated, such as the negotiation and preparation of a multinational international convention . . . which Her Majesty's Government wants to ratify on behalf of the United Kingdom but can only do when the provisions of the Convention have been incorporated in our domestic law. . . .
>
> . . .
>
> My Lords, it would seem that courts charged with the duty of interpreting legislation in all the major countries of the world have recourse in greater or less degree to "travaux préparatoires" or "legislative history" (as it is called in the United States) in order to resolve ambiguities or obscurities in the enacting words . . .
>
> . . .
>
> Accordingly, in exercising its interpretative function of ascertaining what it was that the delegates to an international conference agreed upon by their majority vote in favour of the text or an international convention where the text itself is ambiguous or obscure, an English court should have regard to any material which those delegates themselves had thought would be available to clear up any possible ambiguities or obscurities.

O'Connell explains the use of legislative history as follows:[78]

> From a policy point of view resort to travaux preparatoires is unavoidable. A municipal judge operates within an accepted context of social patterns, and is not open to the criticism of favouring a political position represented by one or other party. An international judge, however, is very vulnerable in this respect, and it is a guarantee both to him and to the litigant States of judicial impartiality if his area of discretion is delimited. Instead of devising a construction to a treaty which is open to alternative interpretations, he has the remedy of discovering exactly what the parties meant by examining their minutes of conferences, their correspondence and their rejected drafts. If objectivity is the aim of judicial construction, it is best achieved by this means. Furthermore, a treaty, unlike a municipal contract, often

---

[77] *Fothergill v. Monarch Airlines Ltd.*, [1981] AC 251 at 281-3 (H.L.), *per* Lord Diplock. See also Art. 32, *Vienna Convention*.

[78] D.P. O'Connell, *International Law*, 2nd ed. (London: Stevens, 1970), at 262.

represents a compromise of vital political interests. To interpret it without reference to the struggle for compromise is gravely to over-simplify the problem of treaty application.

For example, the *Revised Technical Explanation: Canada-U.S. Income Tax Convention, 1980* is an official document of the U.S. Treasury Department that sets out its view on the meaning of the Convention. Although Canada has not issued a similar guide to the Convention, it officially accepts the U.S. Treasury Department's technical explanation.[79]

(c) The Vienna Convention

The principles of international treaty interpretation are codified in the *Vienna Convention* that came into force on January 27, 1980. Canada is a signatory to the Convention. Article 26 of the Convention provides that every treaty in force is binding upon the parties to it and must be performed by them in good faith.

(i) Primary Document

The *Vienna Convention* is considered to be one of the primary documents of international law and an authoritative source in the conduct of international relations. The Department of External Affairs in a memorandum (June 4, 1970) set out the position of the Canadian government on the Convention as follows:

> This Convention constitutes a law-making treaty laying down the fundamental principles of contemporary treaty law. Because of the paramount importance of treaties as a source of the international legal obligations binding upon states and the diversity and comprehensiveness of the interlocking network of treaties which today regulate the major part of transactions between states and serve to establish the relationships among them, the Convention must be viewed as virtually the constitutional basis, second in importance only to the U.N. Charter, of the international community of states.

The principles of international law as stated in the *Vienna Convention* are considered as pre-existing principles.[80] As such, the Convention is sometimes applied even to treaties concluded before its enactment. In *Gladden Estate*,[81] for example, the Court referred to Articles 31 and 32 of the *Vienna Convention* in interpreting Article VIII of the 1942 *Canada-U.S. Treaty* although the *Convention* itself only came into force on January 27, 1980.

(ii) Interpretation

The general rules of interpretation in the *Vienna Convention* are contained in Articles 31, 32 and 33.

---

[79] Department of Finance press release, August 16, 1984.

[80] See, for example, *Melford Developments Inc. v. The Queen*, [1982] CTC 330, 82 DTC 6281 (S.C.C.) (guarantee fees paid by Canadian resident to German bank earned in normal banking operations, thus in the nature of industrial and commercial profits rather than interest; not subject to withholding tax).

[81] *J.N. Gladden Estate v. The Queen*, [1985] 1 CTC 163, 85 DTC 5188 (F.C.T.D.).

Article 31

1. A treaty shall be interpreted in good faith in accordance with the ordinary meaning to be given to the terms of the treaty in their context and in the light of its object and purpose.

2. The context for the purpose of this interpretation of a treaty shall comprise, in addition to the text, including its preamble and annexes:

    (a) any agreement relating to the treaty which was made between all the parties in connexion with the conclusion of the treaty;

    (b) any instrument which was made by one or more parties in connexion with the conclusion of the treaty and accepted by the other parties as an instrument related to the treaty.

3. There shall be taken into account, together with the context:

    (a) any subsequent agreement between the parties regarding the interpretation of the treaty or the application of its provisions;

    (b) any subsequent practice in the application of the treaty which establishes the agreement of the parties regarding its interpretation;

    (c) any relevant rules of international law applicable in the relations between the parties.

4. A special meaning shall be given to a term if it is established that the parties so intended.

Article 32

Recourse may be had to supplementary means of interpretation, including the preparatory work of the treaty and the circumstances of its conclusion, in order to confirm the meaning resulting from the application of Article 31, or to determine the meaning when the interpretation according to Article 31:

    (a) leaves the meaning ambiguous or obscure; or

    (b) leads to a result which is manifestly absurd or unreasonable.

Article 33

1. When a treaty has been authenticated in two or more languages, the text is equally authoritative in each language, unless the treaty provides or the parties agree that, in the case of divergence, a particular text shall prevail.

2. A version of the treaty in a language other than one of those in which the text was authenticated shall be considered an authentic text only if the treaty so provides or the parties so agree.

3. The terms of the treaty are presumed to have the same meaning in each authentic text.

4. Except where a particular text prevails in accordance with paragraph 1, when a comparison of the authentic texts discloses a difference of meaning which the application of Articles 31 and 32 does not remove, the meaning which best reconciles the texts, having regard to the object and purpose of the treaty, shall be adopted.

Articles 31 to 33 embody a general expression of the principles of treaty interpretation and customary international law. The principles are expressed in general terms and there is considerable latitude in their application. They are not, however, exhaustive of the rules of interpretation.

Article 31(1) of the Convention states the general rule and a hierarchy for the interpretation of treaties. A treaty shall be interpreted:

- in good faith;

- in accordance with the ordinary meaning to be given to the terms of the treaty in their context; and

- in the light of its object and purpose.

The "ordinary meaning" to be given to the terms must be determined in the light of the object and purpose of the treaty. Typically, Canada's bilateral tax treaties stipulate dual purposes: avoidance of double taxation and prevention of fiscal evasion.

(A) Good Faith

It is a cardinal principle of interpretation that a treaty should be interpreted in good faith and not lead to a result that would be manifestly absurd or unreasonable. This principle is specifically set out in Article 26 of the Convention.

The principle of good faith is not simply an abstract notion in the interpretation of treaties. The principle applies to the entire process of interpretation: examination of the text of the treaty, its context, subsequent practices and implementation.

(B) Ordinary Meaning of Words

The starting point in interpretation is the text of the treaty. The text is considered to be the expression of the intention of the parties.[82]

As with domestic legislation, the general rule of interpretation is that the terms of a treaty are to be interpreted according to the "ordinary meaning" of the words used. But "ordinary meaning" requires more than a simple grammatical analysis of the words used: the meaning of the words must be derived from the context of the text.

The *Young Loan*[83] arbitration illustrates this rule. The arbitration involved the interpretation of an exchange guarantee in an agreement that required, should the rates of exchange of the currencies of issue alter thereafter by 5 per cent or more, the instalments due after the issue date, while still being made in the currency of the country of issue: ". . . shall be calculated on the basis of the least depreciated currency . . .". What did the words ". . . the least depreciated currency" mean in the context of the agreement? Did the phrase cover any general fall in the value of one currency in relation to another or was it confined to the formal devaluation of a currency by governmental acts? The majority, after citing Article 31(1) of the *Vienna Convention*, said:[84]

> The decisive terms to be interpreted are the words *Abwertung*, "depreciation", *dépréciation*. The Tribunal has no doubt that if it were to proceed on terminology alone, and take the words in their ordinary, everyday sense in the language concerned, it is at least not excluded that the German text would provide one answer to the original query, and the French and English texts a different one. In German, the meaning of the term *Abwertung* is relatively clear. In the proper, technical language, it means a reduction in the external value of a currency — in relation to a fixed yardstick e.g. gold — by

---

[82] See, for example, *Crown Forest Industries Ltd. v. The Queen*, [1992] 2 CTC 1 at 7-8, 92 DTC 6305 at 6310 (F.C.T.D.) ("It is the very words as expressed in the Convention to which a liberal interpretation is given. It therefore cannot be an interpretation which is unsupported by those words as so expressed."); affirmed [1994] 1 CTC 174, 94 DTC 6107 (*sub nom. The Queen v. Crown Forest Industries Ltd.*).

[83] *Young Loan Arbitration* (1980), 59 ILR 495.

[84] *Id.*, at 530.

an act of government. . . . In English and French, on the other hand, the terms "depreciation" and *dépréciation*, as they occur in the disputed clause, are normally used to describe the economic phenomenon of depreciation of a currency quite generally, while "formal" devaluation is usually termed "depreciation" or *dépréciation*. . . . Since the vagueness of the terms used in the English and French texts and the possible discrepancy between the German version of the disputed clause on the one hand and the French and English versions on the other cannot be eliminated by textual interpretation, the words to be construed must, under Article 31(1) of the Vienna Convention on the Law of Treaties, be interpreted "in their context". "Context" in this case means both the wording in full of the disputed clause and the body of the [agreement] as a whole.

(C) Special Meaning of Words

Article 31(4) of the *Vienna Convention* provides that "a special meaning shall be given to a term if it is established that the parties so intended". Although this principle may appear to be somewhat obvious and not in need of elaboration, there is some benefit to be derived from a specific statement on the point: The burden of proof lies on the party who invokes the special meaning of the term.[85]

(D) Contextual Interpretation

The text of the *Vienna Convention* must be read in context and as a whole. Article 31(2) defines "context" for the purposes of the interpretation of a treaty to include any agreements relating to it that were made between the parties in connection with the conclusion of the treaty.

Context also includes any instruments made by one or more of the parties in connection with the conclusion of the treaty and accepted by the other as an instrument related to the treaty. Thus, a unilateral document is not regarded as forming part of the context unless it was made in connection with the conclusion of the treaty and was accepted by the other parties to the treaty.

(E) The Preamble

The preamble to a treaty can be helpful in determining its object and purpose. As Judge Fitzmaurice said:[86]

> Although the objects of a treaty may be gathered from its operative clauses taken as a whole, the preamble is the normal place in which to embody, and the natural place in which to look for, an express or explicit general statement of the treaty's objects and purposes. Where these are stated in the preamble, the latter will, to that extent, govern the whole treaty.

Conversely, a treaty should not be interpreted in such a manner as to go beyond its object and purpose as stated in its preamble. In *United States National in Morocco*,[87]

---

[85] Yearbook of the International Law Commission (1966-II) at 222.

[86] Fitzmaurice, Gerald, "The Law and Procedure of the International Court of Justice, 1951-4: Treaty Interpretation and Other Treaty Points" (1957), 33 *B.Y.I.L.* 203 at 228.

[87] *Case concerning rights of nationals of the United States of America in Morocco, Judgment of August 27, 1952*: I.C.J. Reports 1952, p. 176, at 196.

for example, the International Court of Justice referred to the preamble to the Convention in issue in order to ascertain its object and purpose and said:

> In these circumstances, the Court cannot adopt a construction by implication of the provisions of the . . . Convention which would go beyond the scope of its declared purposes and objects.

(F) Subsequent Agreements and Subsequent Practice

The conduct of the parties subsequent to the ratification of the treaty may be an important determinant in its interpretation. Article 31(3) requires that there should be taken into account any subsequent agreement between the parties regarding the interpretation of the treaty and any subsequent practice in the application of the treaty that establishes an agreement of the parties regarding its interpretation. In the *Chamizal* case, for example, the umpire stated:[88]

> On the whole, it appears to be impossible to come to any other conclusion than that the two nations have, by their subsequent treaties and their consistent course of conduct in connection with all cases arising thereunder, put such an authoritative interpretation upon the language of the Treaties of 1848 and 1853 as to preclude them from now contending that the fluvial portion of the boundary created by those treaties is a fixed line boundary.

There must, however, be some established "practice" to look at in the interpretation of the treaty and an isolated incident or transaction is not sufficient to constitute an implicit modification of the terms of the treaty.

(G) Customary International Law

Article 31(3)(c) requires that in the interpretation of a convention there shall be taken into account together with the context:

> Any relevant rules of international law applicable in the relations between the parties.

Thus, treaties must be read not only in their own context, but also in the wider context of general and customary international law.

(H) Intention of Parties

A treaty should be interpreted in accordance with the intentions of the parties at the time of its conclusion. The task is to determine what was the intention of the parties at the relevant time. Should treaty provisions be interpreted in light of the rules of international law in force at the time that the treaty was concluded or according to the rules in force at the time that the treaty is interpreted? There is support for both points of view. There are those who argue that it is logical that treaties should be interpreted according to the state of international law at the time that they are concluded. In the *Island of Palmas* arbitration, for example, Huber said:[89]

> . . . A juridical fact must be appreciated in the light of the law contemporary with it, and not of the law in force at the time when a dispute in regard to it arises or falls to be settled.

---

[88] *The Chamizal Arbitration Between the United States and Mexico* (1911), 5 A.J.I.L. 782 at 805.

[89] *Island of Palmas Case (Netherlands v. U.S.)* (1925), 2 Rep. Int'l. Arb. Awards 829 at 845.

But the evolution and development of international law may also have an influence on the interpretation of terms and expressions used in a treaty. There is some cautious support from the International Court of Justice for the view that treaties should be interpreted in the context of international law as it evolves. In *Legal Consequences for States of the Continued Presence of South Africa in Namibia*,[90] for example, the Court said:

> Mindful as it is of the primary necessity of interpreting an instrument in accordance with the intentions of the parties at the time of its conclusion, the Court is bound to take into account the fact that the concepts embodied . . . were not static, but were by definition evolutionary, as also, therefore, was the concept of the "sacred trust". The parties to the Covenant must consequently be deemed to have accepted them as such. That is why, viewing the institutions of 1919, the Court must take into consideration the changes which have occurred in the supervening half-century, and its interpretation cannot remain unaffected by the subsequent development of law. . . . Moreover, an international instrument has to be interpreted and applied within the framework of the entire legal system prevailing at the time of the interpretation.

(I) Use of Supplementary Materials

Article 32 of the *Vienna Convention* provides that in the interpretation of a treaty, recourse may be had to supplementary means of interpretation, including the preparatory work of the treaty, the circumstances of its conclusion and the historical background against which the treaty was negotiated. This information, generally referred to as the *travaux préparatoires*, should be used only in circumstances when the meaning of a particular provision is ambiguous, obscure or leads to a result that is manifestly absurd or unreasonable. In most cases, the very fact that the disputed provisions are before the tribunal suggests that there is ambiguity or obscurity in the meaning of the provisions.

The use, and the extent of reliance upon, *travaux préparatoires* varies between tribunals. Anglo-Canadian courts have always been more receptive towards the use of supplementary materials and extrinsic evidence in international law than they have been in the interpretation of domestic legislation. As Lord Diplock said in *Fothergill v. Monarch Airlines Ltd.*:[91]

> The primary end of treaty interpretation is to give effect to the intentions of the parties, and not to frustrate them. But as Lauterpacht expresses it, "the eliciting of the intentions of the parties is not normally a task which can be performed exclusively by means of logical or grammatical interpretation". Furthermore, the "intentions" of the parties may never have crystallised or been formulated beyond a certain point. Every lawyer knows that the parties to a contract contemplate only performance: they enter into the transaction with optimism, and do not ordinarily advert to the problems raised by, for example, frustration. The courts pretend that the parties intended what they, the courts, believe they would have intended had they reflected on the matter. It is clear, then, that "intention" is very often a fiction, and even when there was a conscious intention the words designed to be expressive of it may

---

[90] *Legal Consequences for States of the Continued Presence of South Africa in Namibia (South West Africa) notwithstanding Security Council, Resolution 276 (1970), Order No. 2 of 26 January 1971*, I.C.J. Reports 1971, p. 6.

[91] *Fothergill v. Monarch Airlines Ltd.*, [1981] AC 251 at 281-283.

not be particularly helpful for this purpose. The same is true of treaty interpretation with the added difficultly that the parties may never really have wanted to come to agreement and may have deliberately left the area of operation of the treaty opaque.

Anglo-Canadian courts are now increasingly inclined to admit supplementary and extrinsic materials in the interpretation of their domestic fiscal legislation and should be that much more receptive to the introduction of *travaux préparatoires* in dealing with bilateral treaties. Canadian courts in particular are now much more liberal in allowing extrinsic evidence since the Supreme Court's decision in *Stubart*[92] which called for a purposive interpretation of the *Income Tax Act*.

Finally, it is important to note the difference between "supplementary materials" and "agreements" and "instruments". Under Article 31(2)(a) or (b) an "agreement" or "instrument" may be used to determine the ordinary meaning to be given to the terms of the treaty in their context. "Supplementary" works may only be used to confirm the meaning of the words of a treaty as determined by Article 31 or to determine the meaning of terms that may be ambiguous, obscure or lead to an unreasonable or absurd result. Consider, for example, whether the 1984 Technical Explanation of the *Canada-United States Income Tax Convention* (1980) should be considered as supplementary materials or an agreement or instrument for use in interpretation. Given that the Department of Finance has accepted the Technical Explanation, the better view is that it should be regarded as either an agreement or instrument rather than supplementary materials.

(d) Law of the Forum

(i) General

Tax treaties often use terms that have a special meaning in tax laws. Sometimes, the same word may have different meanings in different countries. Undefined terms in a treaty are generally interpreted in accordance with the applicable domestic income tax law.

Most of Canada's tax treaties contain a provision similar to the following:[93]

As regards the application of the Convention by a Contracting State any term not defined therein shall, unless the context otherwise requires, have the meaning which it has under the law of that State concerning the taxes to which the Convention applies.

(ii) Ambulatory Meaning

What happens when it is unclear whether terms used in a treaty have been amended, either expressly or impliedly, by legislation enacted after the ratification of

---

[92] *Stubart Investments Ltd. v. The Queen,* [1984] 1 SCR 536, [1984] CTC 294, 84 DTC 6305.

[93] Based on Article 3(2) of the *Convention of the Organization for Economic Co-operation and Development ("OECD Model Treaty"),* 14 December 1960, [1961] Can. T.S. No. 18; see, *e.g.,* Article III(2), *Canada-United States Income Tax Convention,* September 26, 1980, [1984] Can. T.S. No. 15.

the treaty? Prior to the enactment of the *Income Tax Conventions Interpretation Act*[94], words used in a treaty were considered static — that is, they were interpreted in the context of the income tax law of Canada in effect at the time that the treaty was adopted without regard to subsequent statutory amendments.[95]

The static approach to the interpretation of undefined terms was changed in respect of events and transactions occurring after June 23, 1983. Section 3 of the *Income Tax Conventions Interpretation Act* now provides:

> Notwithstanding the provisions of a convention or the Act giving the convention the force of law in Canada, it is hereby declared that the law of Canada is that, to the extent that a term in the convention is
>
> (a) not defined in the convention,
>
> (b) not fully defined in the convention, or
>
> (c) to be defined by reference to the laws of Canada,
>
> that term has, except to the extent that the context otherwise requires, the meaning it has for the purposes of the *Income Tax Act*, as amended from time to time, and not the meaning it had for the purposes of the *Income Tax Act* on the date the convention was entered into or given the force of law in Canada if, after that date, its meaning for the purposes of the *Income Tax Act* has changed.

Thus, notwithstanding the provisions of any international tax treaty, undefined or incompletely defined terms within a treaty are interpreted in the context of the *Income Tax Act* as amended from time to time.[96] Undefined treaty terms have an "ambulatory" meaning and references to the Act are read as references to the legislation at the relevant time and not as of the time the treaty was implemented.

(e) Model Tax Conventions

Juridical double taxation is the imposition of identical (or comparable) taxes by two countries on the same taxpayer in respect of the same subject matter and for identical time periods. Juridical double taxation can arise frequently because most countries exercise jurisdiction to tax on at least two basis: source of income and residence of the taxpayer. Tax treaties are bilateral conventions negotiated between countries for the primary purpose of resolving juridical double taxation.

The movement to resolve double taxation problems through tax treaties gained momentum after the end of the Second World War. In order to facilitate the negotiation of bilateral tax treaties between countries on a reasonably consistent basis, the Organization for Economic Cooperation and Development (the "OECD") and the United

---

[94] *Income Tax Conventions Interpretation Act*, R.S.C. 1985, c. I-4, as amended.

[95] See, for example, *The Queen v. Melford Devs. Inc.*, [1982] CTC 330, 82 DTC 6281 (S.C.C.) (guarantee fee paid to West German bank in the nature of industrial or commercial profit rather than interest; exempt from non-resident income tax).

[96] *Income Tax Conventions Interpretation Act*, R.S.C. 1985, c. I-4, s. 3.

Nations developed model tax conventions which countries can use as the foundation for their bilateral treaty negotiations. The principal philosophical difference between the two models is the emphasis that each places upon the jurisdiction to tax income at its source.

(i) The OECD

The OECD was created by virtue of a Convention signed in Paris on December 14, 1960 and came into force on September 30, 1961. Pursuant to Article 1 of the Convention, the OECD is committed to promoting policies designed:

- to achieve the highest sustainable economic growth and employment and a rising standard of living in Member countries, while maintaining financial stability, and thus to contribute to the development of the world economy;

- to contribute to sound economic expansion in Member as well as non-member countries in the process of economic development; and

- to contribute to the expansion of world trade on a multi-lateral, non-discriminatory basis in accordance with international obligations.

The following are the 25 Member countries of the OECD:

Australia	Iceland	Portugal
Austria	Ireland	Spain
Belgium	Italy	Sweden
Canada	Japan	Switzerland
Denmark	Luxembourg	Turkey
Finland	Mexico	The United Kingdom
France	New Zealand	The United States
Germany	The Netherlands	
Greece	Norway	

(ii) The OECD Model Tax Convention

The main purpose of the *OECD Model Tax Convention on Income and on Capital* ("*OECD Model Convention*") is to provide a means of uniformly settling the most common problems which arise in the field of international juridical double taxation. Member countries are generally expected to conform to the *Model Convention* when negotiating bilateral tax treaties. Canada is a member of the OECD and follows the *Model Convention* as closely as possible.

The Commentary to the *OECD Model Convention* also plays an important role in treaty interpretation and is used to ascertain the meaning of articles in treaties modelled on it.[97]

---

[97] See, for example, *The Queen v. Crown Forest Industries Ltd.*, [1994] 1 CTC 174, 94 DTC 6107 (F.C.A.).

(A) Historical Background

There was no substantial impetus for the negotiation of double taxation treaties in the 19th century or in the early part of the 20th century. Tax rates were comparatively low and the problems of double taxation were not particularly acute. After the First World War, there was a more concerted effort to study the problem of double taxation. Thus, the League of Nations commenced a project in 1921. The study was long and protracted and it was not until 1943 that the so-called "Mexico draft convention" emerged. The League's Fiscal Committee reviewed the Mexico draft in 1946 and then produced a new draft of its own.

The next move came from the Organization for European Economic Co-operation, which by 1956 had set up its Fiscal Committee. From 1958 to 1961 the Fiscal Committee's various proposals for a series of Model Articles were published with commentaries and discussion. The Organization for European Economic Co-operation was reconstituted in 1960-61 to form the OECD, which published its first complete draft convention in July 1963.

The 1963 *Model Convention* was revised on the basis of the experience gained by Member countries in the application of bilateral conventions and a new Model and related commentary was published in 1977.

The Committee on Fiscal Affairs continued to examine issues directly or indirectly related to the 1977 *Model Convention*. As the world economy grew, so did tax avoidance and evasion. In 1991, recognizing that the *Model Convention* and its commentary had become an ongoing process, the OECD's Committee on Fiscal Affairs decided to adopt an ambulatory approach and provide periodic and more regular updates and amendments. This process lead to the publication of the *Model Convention* in 1992. The 1992 *Model Convention* is not a comprehensive revision of its predecessor but a first step in a revision process that is expected to continue on a periodic basis.

Canada negotiates and patterns its bilateral tax treaties on the basis of the *OECD Model Convention*. Each Canadian bilateral treaty is, however, slightly different and varies from the *Model*.

(B) Structure

The *OECD Model Convention* is divided into seven chapters as follows:

Chapter I: Scope of the Convention
Chapter II: Definitions
Chapter III: Taxation of Income
Chapter IV: Taxation of Capital
Chapter V: Methods for Elimination of Double Taxation
Chapter VI: Special Provisions
Chapter VII: Final Provisions

The *OECD Model Convention* rests on three basic propositions:

1. The country of residence will eliminate double taxation either through a foreign tax credit mechanism or by exempting foreign income from tax;

2. The source country will reduce the scope of its jurisdiction to tax at source; and

3. Where the source country retains the jurisdiction to tax at source, it will reduce the rate at which it levies tax.

These propositions are generally accepted by developed countries as appropriate for treaties amongst themselves.

Developing countries, however, take a different view of tax treaties. They accept the first proposition, namely, that the country of residence should eliminate double taxation either through a foreign tax credit or through exemptions for foreign source income. They have not, however, generally accepted the second proposition, namely, reduction of the source country's jurisdiction to tax. Indeed, some developing countries contend that jurisdiction to tax at source should be exclusive and not shared.

(C) Scope

Bilateral conventions tend to define their scope in terms of the residence of persons within their jurisdiction. Thus, modern conventions typically apply to "residents", rather than to "citizens" or "nationals", of Contracting States. Article 1 of the *OECD Model Convention*, for example, states:

> This Convention shall apply to persons who are residents of one or both of the Contracting States.

Similarly, Article 1 of *Canada-United States Treaty* (1980)[98] states:

> This Convention is generally applicable to persons who are residents of one or both of the Contracting States.

The word "generally" in the *Canada-U.S. Treaty* is used because certain of its provisions apply to persons who are residents of neither Canada nor the United States. For example, the United States reserves the right to tax its citizens.

The term "resident" is defined in the *OECD Model Convention* as "any person who, under the laws of that State, is liable to tax therein by reason of his or her domicile, residence, place of management or any other criterion of a similar nature".[99] It warrants emphasis, however, that international tax treaties are not concerned with the concept of "residence" as interpreted under the domestic laws of Contracting States. The term "resident" is usually a defined term in a treaty and the concept of "resident of a Contacting State" is used only for the purposes of the particular treaty.

---

[98] *Canada-United States Income Tax Convention, ante.*

[99] Article 4, *OECD Model Convention.*

Clearly, the concept of "resident of a Contracting State" is central to the jurisdiction to tax. The concept is used to:

- determine the scope of a convention;

- solve double taxation problems arising as a result of dual residence; and

- solve double taxation problems arising as a consequence of tax being levied on the basis of residence in one state and on the basis of source or *situs* in the other state.

(D) Taxes Covered

A bilateral treaty will specify the taxes that it covers: The *OECD Model Convention* applies to taxes on income and on capital, whether imposed by the Contracting States, its political subdivisions or local authorities.[100]

The *Canada-U.S. Treaty*, for example, applies to taxes on income and on capital imposed on behalf of each Contracting State, irrespective of the manner in which they are levied. These include:[101]

(a) in the case of Canada, the taxes imposed by the Government of Canada under Parts I, XIII and XIV of the *Income Tax Act*; and

(b) in the case of the United States, the Federal income taxes imposed by the *Internal Revenue Code*.

The Treaty also applies to any identical or substantially similar taxes on income and taxes on capital imposed after the date of signature of the Convention in addition to, or in place of, the existing taxes.

Taxes on "income" and on "capital" include taxes on profits and gains derived from the alienation of movable or immovable property, as well as taxes on capital appreciation. The Treaty does not cover estate, gift and generation-skipping transfer taxes, social security taxes or excise taxes on insurance premiums in the United States.

Canada reserves its position on Article 2(1) of the *OECD Model Convention*, which says that the Convention should apply to taxes of political subdivisions or local authorities. For example, the only taxes covered in Article II(2) of the *Canada-U.S. Treaty* are those covered by the federal *Income Tax Act*. State taxes and Canadian provincial taxes are not generally covered by the Treaty. Where, however, state and provincial taxes are imposed in accordance with the provisions of the *Canada-U.S. Treaty*, a foreign tax credit is ensured by Article XXIV(7).

(E) Interpretation of Undefined Terms

Article 3(2) of the *OECD Model* provides as follows:

---

[100] Article 2(1), *OECD Model Convention*.

[101] Article II, *Canada-United States Income Tax Convention, ante*.

As regards the application of the Convention by a Contracting State any term not defined therein shall, unless the context otherwise requires, have the meaning which it has under the law of that State concerning the taxes to which the Convention applies.

This Article is a rule of general interpretation and is unique in international treaty law in the sense that an undefined term can be accorded different meanings according to the domestic law definitions of the contracting parties.

Both Article 3(2) of the *OECD Model Convention* and section 3 of the *Income Tax Conventions Interpretation Act* ("ITCIA") provide that domestic law definitions of undefined terms are to be used unless the context otherwise *requires*. The context of a treaty embodies both its internal and external contexts. Thus, the use of the word "requires" may limit the extent to which domestic amendments subsequent to the signing of a treaty can change the interpretation originally intended by the Contracting States. It is arguable that the State of the income tax law at the time that a treaty is entered into constitutes part of its overall context. Thus, a fairly convincing case should be made before a change in domestic legislation is allowed to substantially emasculate the provisions of a treaty.

Article 3(2) is intended to provide a balance between the need to ensure permanency of contractual commitments undertaken by countries when signing a convention and the need to be able to apply treaties in a convenient and practical way over time. The OECD Commentary states that a country should not be allowed to empty a convention of its substance by later amending in its domestic law the scope of terms not defined in the Convention.[102] If amendments to internal law definitions are so substantial that they could not reasonably have been foreseen by the contracting parties at the time the treaty was concluded, the contextual rules would suggest that amendments to the meaning of undefined terms should not be applied to the interpretation of the Treaty.

Section 3 of the ITCIA also provides that, except to the extent that the context otherwise requires, any amendments to definitions in the *Income Tax Act* must be applied in the interpretation of Canadian tax treaties regardless of the extent to which they depart from the meaning of the definitions in force at the time that the particular treaty was made. Thus, it is quite clear that ITCIA calls for an ambulatory interpretation of undefined and incompletely defined terms. Section 3 should, however, also be carefully interpreted because of the significant exception to its application: it calls for ambulatory interpretation *except to the extent that the context otherwise requires.* Hence, definitional changes should be restricted by contextual interpretation.

14. AIDS TO CONSTRUCTION

Over the years the courts have developed various interpretive aids to assist in the process of statutory interpretation. They have also developed evidentiary rules regarding

---

[102] See paragraph 13 of the Commentary of the *OECD Model Convention.*

the types of documents that may be used to determine the intention or meaning of words used in a statute.

(a) *"Ejusdem Generis"* Rule

General words which follow particular and specific words of the same nature take their meaning from the context of the specific words and are not given their ordinary meaning. As Maxwell said:[103]

> [t]he general expression is to be read as comprehending only things of the same kind as that designated by the preceding particular expressions, unless there is something to show that a wider sense was intended, as where there is a provision specifically accepting certain classes clearly not within the suggested genus.

The *ejusdem generis* rule only applies when it is possible to construct a *genus* out of the specific words or phrases used; it does not apply when the specific words relate to different objects of a widely differing character that do not constitute a class or kind of objects.[104] For example, section 54 defines "listed personal property" of a taxpayer to mean, *inter alia*, a "print, etching, drawing, painting, sculpture, or *other similar work of art*" (emphasis added). According to this rule, the phrase "other similar work of art" is to be interpreted in the context of the class created by the immediately preceding specific words, namely, prints, etchings, drawings, paintings, or sculptures. Works of art that do not resemble those specifically listed in the class are not "listed personal property".

(b) *Expressio Unius, Exclusio Alterius*

Expressio unius, exclusio alterius means that the express mention of one thing implies the exclusion of other items of the same class that are not mentioned. Thus, if the Act specifies one exception to a general rule, other exceptions are excluded. Stated another way, the mention of one or more things of a particular class in a statutory provision may be regarded as silently excluding all other members of the class.[105] The *exclusio* rule is not to be applied where it produces an inconsistent, absurd or unjust result.[106]

---

[103] *Maxwell on Interpretation of Statutes*, 12th ed. (London: Sweet & Maxwell, 1969), at 297.

[104] *Stouffville Assess. Commr. v. Mennonite Home Assn.*, [1973] SCR 189.

[105] *The Queen v. Int. Nickel Co. of Can.*, [1974] CTC 443, 74 DTC 6382; affirmed [1975] CTC 620, 75 DTC 5460 (S.C.C.).

[106] As Lopes L.J. said in *Colquhoun v. Brooks* (1888), 21 QB 52 at 65:
> [i]t is often a valuable servant, but a dangerous master to follow in the construction of statutes or documents. The *exclusio* is often the result of inadvertence or accident, and the maxim ought not to be applied when its application, having regard to the subject-matter to which it is to be applied, leads to inconsistency or injustice.

15. EXTRINSIC EVIDENCE

The traditional approach to statutory interpretation was to exclude extrinsic evidence as an aid in statutory construction ("the exclusionary rule"). Statutory instruments were interpreted within their four corners and, sometimes, in the context of explicit recitals contained therein.[107] Lord Reading explained the exclusion of extrinsic evidence to the House of Lords in the following way:[108]

> Neither the words of the Attorney General nor the words of an ex-Lord Chancellor, spoken in this House, as to the meaning intended to be given to language used in a Bill, have the slightest effect or relevance when the matter comes to be considered by a Court of Law. The one thing which stands out beyond all question is that in a Court of Law you are not allowed to introduce observations made either by the Government or by anybody else, but the Court will only give consideration to the Statute itself. That is elementary, but I think it is necessary to bring it home to your Lordships because I think too much importance can be attached to language which fell from the Attorney General.

English law did not generally permit reference to parliamentary material as an aid to statutory construction ("the exclusionary rule").[109]

The exclusionary rule did not always apply in England but was judge-made around 1769.[110] It did not become an absolute rule until it was adopted as a rule of practice[111] by the House of Lords in 1966. The decision of the House of Lords in

---

[107] See, e.g., *Assam Ry. & Trading Co. v. I.R.C.*, [1935] AC 445 at 458 (H.L.) where the House of Lords observed:

> [i]t is clear that the language of a Minister of the Crown in proposing in Parliament a measure which eventually becomes law is inadmissible and the report of Commissioners is even more removed from value as evidence of intention, because it does not follow that the recommendations were accepted.

Administrative practice and departmental policy were sometimes received as evidence. See, e.g., *Nowegijick v. The Queen*, [1983] CTC 20, 83 DTC (S.C.C.): "Administrative policy and interpretation are not determinative but are entitled to weight and can be an 'important factor' in case of doubt about the meaning of legislation".

[108] 94 H.L. Deb. 232 (5th ser. 1934). See also, Lord Haldane's speech in *Viscountess Rhondda's Claim*, [1922] 2 AC 339 at 383:

> My Lords, the only other point made on the construction of the Act was that this Committee might be entitled to look at what passed while the Bill was still a Bill and in the Committee stage in the House. It was said that there amendments were moved and discussions took place which indicated that the general words of s. 1 were not regarded by your Lordships' House as covering the title to a seat in it. But even assuming that to be certain, I do not think, sitting as we do with the obligation to administer the principles of the law, that we have the least right to look at what happened while the Bill was being discussed in Committee and before the Act was passed. Decisions of the highest authority show that the interpretation of an Act of Parliament must be collected from the words agreed upon by both Houses. The history of previous changes made or discussed cannot be taken to have been known or to have been in view when the Royal assent was given.

[109] See, e.g., *Davis v. Johnson*, [1979] AC 264; *Hadmor Productions Ltd. v. Hamilton*, [1983] 1 AC 191.

[110] *Millar v. Taylor* (1769), 4 Burr 2303.

[111] Judicial Practice Statement by the House of Lords [(Judicial Precedent) [1966] 1 WLR 1234].

Pepper v. Hart[112] to permit the use of parliamentary materials in statutory construction reversed 200 years of English judicial tradition and set a new course for its relationship with Parliament.

The exclusionary rule was justified on various theoretical and pragmatic grounds: cost, utility, constitutional principle and reliability. In *Beswick v. Beswick*, for example, Lord Reid said:[113]

> For purely practical reasons we do not permit debates in either House to be cited: it would add greatly to the time and expense involved in preparing cases involving the construction of a statute if counsel were expected to read all the debates in *Hansard*, and it would often be impracticable for counsel to get access to at least the older reports of debates in Select Committees of the House of Commons; moreover, in a very large proportion of cases such a search, even if practicable, would throw no light on the question before the courts.

Some courts defended the rule on the basis of constitutional principle:[114]

> Legislation in England is passed by Parliament and put in the form of written words. This legislation is given legal effect upon subjects by virtue of judicial decision, and it is the function of the courts to say what the application of the words used to particular cases or individuals is to be. . . . It would be a degradation of that process if the courts were to be merely a reflecting mirror of what some other interpretation agency might say.

Similarly in *Fothergill v. Monarch Airlines Ltd.*:[115]

> The constitutional function performed by courts of justice as interpreters of the written law laid down in Acts of Parliament is often described as ascertaining "the intention of Parliaments"; but what this metaphor, though convenient, omits to take into account is that the court, when acting in its interpretative role, as well as when it is engaged in reviewing the legality of administrative action, is doing so as mediator between the state in the exercise of its legislative power and the private citizen for whom the law made by Parliament constitutes a rule binding upon him and enforceable by the executive power of the state. Elementary justice or . . . the need for legal certainty demands that the rules by which the citizen is to be bound should be ascertainable by him (or, more realistically, by a competent lawyer advising him) by reference to identifiable sources that are publicly accessible.

Others, such as Lord Scarman, were simply skeptical about the value of information derived from parliamentary debates:[116]

> . . . such material is an unreliable guide to the meaning of what is enacted, it promotes confusion, not clarity. The cut and thrust of debate and the pressures of executive responsibility, the essential features of open and responsible government, are not always conducive to a clear and unbiased explanation of the meaning of statutory language. And the volume of Parliamentary and ministerial utterances can confuse by its very size.

---

[112] *Pepper (Inspector of Taxes) v. Hart*, [1992] STC 898 (H.L.).

[113] *Beswick v. Beswick,* [1968] AC 58 at 74.

[114] Per Lord Wilberforce in *Black-Clawson International Ltd. v. Papierwerke A.G.,* [1975] AC 591 at 629.

[115] *Fothergill v. Monarch Airlines Ltd.,* [1981] AC 251 at 259.

[116] *Davis v. Johnson,* [1979] AC 264 at 350.

With fiscal statutes the courts were even more stringent. Not only did the courts confine themselves to the language of the statute, but, as we saw earlier, the language was construed strictly and literally. There was no room, said the judges, for "equitable construction" in tax statutes.[117] Fiscal legislation was read devoid of considerations of policy, purpose and intention. Rowlatt J. stated it succinctly:[118]

> There is no room for intendment in a taxing statute; there is no equity about a tax; there is no presumption about a tax; you read nothing in; you imply nothing, but you look fairly at what is said and at what is said clearly, and that is the tax.

But even when the English courts applied the exclusionary rule, some of their Lordships (speaking in a non-judicial capacity) were prepared to admit the value of Parliamentary debates. As Lord Hailsham L.C. said:[119]

> It really is very difficult to understand what they [the Parliamentary drafters] mean sometimes. I always look at *Hansard*, I always look at the Blue Books, I always look at everything I can in order to see what is meant and as I was a Member of the House of Commons for a long time of course I never let on for an instant that I had read the stuff. I produced it as an argument of my own, as if I had thought of it myself. I only took the trouble because I could not do the work in any other way. As a matter of fact, I should like to let your Lordships into a secret. If you were to go upstairs and you were a fly on the wall in one of those judicial committees that we have up there, where distinguished members of the Bar . . . come to address us, you would be quite surprised how much we read. . . . The idea that we do not read these things is quite rubbish . . . if you think, that they did not discuss what was really meant, you are living in a fool's paradise.

We said earlier that the purposive approach to statutory interpretation requires that the Act be interpreted in such a manner as best enhances the attainment of its purposes. But *how* do we get at the purpose, "object and spirit" or intention of legislation?

Having adopted the purpose approach of statutory construction, the courts should admit all evidence that is relevant to, and useful in, determining legislative intention. The trier of fact can then assess the reliability of, and the weight to be accorded to, the evidence.[120]

No useful purpose is served by setting up *a priori* rules of exclusion. As Justice Frankfurter said:[121]

> Unhappily, there is no table of logarithms for statutory construction. No item of evidence has a fixed or even average weight. One or another may be decisive in one set of circumstances, while of little

---

[117] See, e.g., *Partington v. A.G.* (1869), LR 4 HL 100 (H.L.); *Tennant v. Smith*, [1892] AC 150 (H.L.).

[118] *Cape Brandy Syndicate v. I.R.C.* (1920), 12 Tax Cas. 358 (C.A.).

[119] 418 H.L. Official Report (5th series), Col. 1346, during the debate of Lord Scarman's Bill on the Interpretation of Legislation, March 26, 1982. See also *Davis v. Johnson*, [1978] 1 All E.R. 1132 (H.L.).

[120] *Alta. Inst. on Mental Retardation v. The Queen*, [1987] 2 CTC 70, 87 DTC 5306 (F.C.A.); leave to appeal to S.C.C. refused 87 NR 397. (Court admitted Minister's budget speech and evidence of author through textbook).

[121] Felix Frankfurter, "Some Reflections on the Reading of Statutes" (1947), 47:4 *Colum. L. Rev.* 527 at 543.

value elsewhere. A painstaking, detailed report by a Senate Committee bearing directly on the immediate question may settle the matter. A loose statement even by a chairman of a committee, made impromptu in the heat of debate, less informing in cold type than when heard on the floor, will hardly be accorded the weight of an encyclical.

Identifying the purpose of tax provisions is in itself a complex and uncertain task. It should not be rendered more difficult by excluding relevant evidence.

Unlike most statutes, the *Income Tax Act* is a multi-purpose enactment. To be sure, it is intended to raise an ever increasing amount of revenue for federal and provincial needs. Its reach, however, extends far beyond its revenue raising function. The Act is a tool of social and economic engineering and is used to implement national cultural and political aspirations. Some examples:

Item	Statutory Purpose
Small business deduction	To promote and stimulate capital accumulation for corporations that may not have easy access to the traditional capital markets.
Manufacturing and processing deduction	To stimulate labour intensive sectors of the economy.
Investment tax credit	To stimulate certain sectors of the economy in selected (generally depressed) geographic areas.
Political contribution credit	To provide support for, and encourage Canadians to participate in, the democratic process.
Write-off of CCA certified Canadian films	To promote and stimulate sectors of Canadian cultural industry
Deductions and credits for charitable gifts	To encourage private support for the "public good" which would otherwise be supported from public funds.
Credit for tuition fees	To facilitate post secondary education as part of Canadian social policy.
Denial of CCA on non-Canadian works of art	To encourage economic support of Canadian artists

These examples illustrate the diversity of legislative purpose underlying the many sections of the Act. They also illustrate the need to use extrinsic evidence to determine the purpose of particular provisions.[122]

Some Canadian courts have said that extrinsic evidence may be used even to interpret legislation that is neither ambiguous nor unclear. In *British Columbia Telephone Company*, for example, the Federal Court of Appeal held that it was no longer good law in Canada that precise and unambiguous statutory language must speak for itself.[123] The dictum in *Sussex Peerage*[124] ("If the words of the statute are in themselves precise and unambiguous, then no more can be necessary than to expound those words in their natural and ordinary sense.") is no longer to be considered a statement of the law in Canada.

How can the use of clear and unambiguous statutory language warrant an inquiry into its underlying purpose? If the language is clear and unambiguous, why look behind it to determine the purpose of the legislation? Does the search for purpose in the face of clear and unambiguous statutory language affront the constitutional doctrine that Parliament enacts fiscal legislation and the role of the courts is to interpret it as written?

There are circumstances when extrinsic evidence may reveal the purpose of statutory language even where such language is clear and unambiguous. *Witthuhn*[125] is a classic example: the Tax Appeal Board denied the taxpayer a deduction for medical expenses incurred for his invalid wife who was confined to a rocking chair because the Act only permitted a deduction for people confined to *wheelchairs*. The Board adopted a literal approach to a statutory provision which was clearly intended to provide relief for medical expenses in the particular circumstances. The purpose of the provision would have been quite clear had the Board referred to parliamentary or other extrinsic materials.

In *Spillet*,[126] the Tax Appeal Board carried the absurdity of literal interpretation even further: it denied the taxpayer's claim for a medical expense deduction for equipment to provide life preserving oxygen to his child on the basis that the Act only authorized a deduction for "oxygen" but did not specifically mention the equipment in which the gas was contained!

---

[122] See *Lor-Wes Contracting Ltd. v. The Queen*, [1985] 1 CTC 79, 85 DTC 5310 (F.C.A.) (use of *Hansard* permitted in exposing and examing mischief, evil or condition to which Legislature directing attention); *Edmonton Liquid Gas Ltd. v. The Queen*, [1984] CTC 536, 84 DTC 6526 (F.C.A.) (parliamentary speech by Minister of Finance admitted to adduce object and spirit of statutory provision).

[123] *British Columbia Telephone Company v. Canada*, [1992] 1 CTC 26, 92 DTC 6129 (F.C.A.).

[124] *Sussex Peerage Case* (1844), 8 ER 1034 at 1057.

[125] *Witthun v. M.N.R.* (1959), 57 DTC 174 (T.A.B.).

[126] *Spilltt v. M.N.R.*, [1967] Tax ABC 807, 67 DTC 549.

In both cases, the policy of the statutory provisions would have been better served if the Board had looked at extrinsic evidence despite the obvious clarity of the language. *Witthuhn* obviously involved clear and unambiguous language. *Spillet* reached an absurd result. Both decisions would have benefitted from the use of extrinsic evidence to determine the underlying purpose of the relevant provisions.

How far are the courts willing to go in the use of extrinsic aids to interpret clear and unambiguous language? As Justice MacGuigan said in *British Columbia Telephone Co.*: "The issue as to weight must be squarely faced and honestly answered".[127] The courts will clearly give greater weight to clear words supported by their immediate context than to larger assertions of parliamentary intention, particularly those based on extrinsic evidence. Although this may cause some uncertainty, the benefits to be derived from such an approach clearly outweigh any inconvenience that may result.

The most informative sources of information regarding the legislative purpose of any provision are the briefing notes prepared by the Department of Finance for its Minister. The notes generally describe the "mischief" to be remedied and the statutory solution to address the problem. The briefing notes are also used by the Minister to respond to technical questions raised during Parliamentary debate of the Budget bill. The notes are comprehensive and candid. They are, however, confidential. Unless read into *Hansard*, they are not available for public dissemination.

The briefing notes (in conjunction with other materials) are also used to prepare the Minister's Budget speech and supplementary papers tabled in the House. The speech and supplementary papers are the primary public source of information in respect of government policy on tax legislation. Their introduction, whether by way of argument or evidence, into judicial proceedings, can be useful in eliciting legislative intention. Unfortunately, the Department of Finance, does not support the use of its Technical Notes as an "official interpretation" of legislation that it devises and drafts. For example, in the April 1989 Budget, the Department inserted the following disclaimer to its notes: "These notes are intended for information purposes only and should not be construed as an official interpretation of the provisions they describe".

But the courts are increasingly willing to admit technical notes and other extrinsic evidence. In *Lor-Wes Contracting*,[128] for example, the Federal Court of Appeal

---

[127] *B. C. Telephone Co. v. The Queen*, [1992] 1 CTC 26, 92 DTC 6129 (F.C.A.).

[128] *Lor-Wes Contracting Ltd. v. The Queen*, [1985] 2 CTC 79, 85 DTC 5310 (F.C.A.). See also *Canterra Energy Ltd. v. The Queen*, [1985] 1 CTC 329 at 332, 85 DTC 5245 at 5248 (F.C.T.D.) (". . . the Minister's statement has relevance generally to the issues involved and is admissible", *per* Reed J.), reversed on other grounds [1987] 1 CTC 89, 87 DTC 5019 (F.C.A.); *Alta. Inst. on Mental Retardation v. The Queen*, [1987] 1 CTC 70, 87 DTC 5306, leave to appeal to S.C.C. refused 87 NR 397 (court admitted evidence of author through textbook and Minister's budget speech).

unanimously endorsed admission of the Minister's Budget statement as recorded in *Hansard*. Statements were also admitted in *Vaillancourt*:[129]

> ... in determining the object of the legislation, this Court no longer hesitates to refer to the parliamentary debates when the latter rise above mere partisanship, and in particular in tax matters to refer to the budget speech made by the Minister of Finance.

16. PRESUMPTION AGAINST DOUBLE INCLUSIONS AND DEDUCTIONS

There is a statutory presumption against double inclusion of revenue and double deduction of expenses in calculating income.[130]

---

[129] *Vaillancourt v. Canada*, [1991] 2 CTC 42, 91 DTC 5352 (F.C.A.).

[130] Subs. 4(4).

SELECTED BIBLIOGRAPHY TO CHAPTER II

Statutory Interpretation

Baxt, R., "The New Anti-Avoidance Provisions" N: 9 *Aust. Bus. L. Rev.* 284.

Beaupré, R.M., *Construing Bilingual Legislation in Canada* (Toronto: Butterworths, 1981).

Brockway, David H., "Interpretation of Tax Treaties and Their Relationship to Statutory Law — A U.S. Perspective", in *Proceedings of 35th Tax Conf.* 619 (Can. Tax Foundation, 1983).

Charles, W.H., "Extrinsic Evidence and Statutory Interpretation: Judicial Discretion in Context" (1983), 7 *Dalhousie L.J.* 7.

Corn, George, "Rules of Statutory Interpretation" (1985), 2 *Can. Current Tax* J-95.

Corry, J., "Administrative Law; Interpretation of Statutes" (1939), 1 *U.T.L.J.* 286.

Corry, J., "The Use of Legislative History in the Interpretation of Statutes" (1954), 32 *Can. Bar Rev.* 624.

Couzin, Robert, "What Does It Say in French?" (1985), 33 *Can. Tax J.* 300.

Craies on Statute Law, 7th ed. (Sweet & Maxwell, 1971).

Cross, R., *Statutory Interpretation* (Butterworths, 1976).

Crowe, Ian "Alice in Taxland" (1991), 125 *CGA Magazine* 3213.

Davis, "Legislative History and the Wheat Board Case" (1953), 31 *Can. Bar Rev.* 1. (See also, in this article, the letter from Milner (1953), 31 *Can. Bar Rev.* 228).

Debenham, David Bishop, "The Winds of Taxation" (1986/87), 51 *Sask. Law Rev.* 292.

Driedger, E.A., "A New Approach to Statutory Interpretation" (1951), 29 *Can. Bar Rev.* 838.

Driedger, E.A., *The Construction of Statutes* (Butterworths, 1974).

Driedger, E.A., "Statutes: The Mischievous Literal Golden Rule" (1981), 59 *Can. Bar Rev.* 780.

Driedger, E.A., "Statutory Drafting and Interpretation; Canadian Common Law" (1971), 9 *Co. I. Dr. Comp.* 71.

Edwards, Stanley E., "Drafting Fiscal Legislation" (1984), 32 *Can. Tax J.* 727.

Falesky, Brian A. and Sandra E. Jack, "Is there Substance to 'Substance Over Form' in Canada?" in *Report of Proceedings of 50th Tax Conf.* (Can. Tax Foundation, 1992).

Frankfurter, Felix, "Some Reflections on the Reading of Statutes" (1947), 47:4 *Colum. L. Rev.* 527.

Ghosh, I.J., "The Construction of Fiscal Legislation" [1994] *British Tax Rev.* 126.

Innes, William I., "The Taxation of Indirect Benefits: An Examination of Subsections 56(2), 56(3), 56(4), 245(2), and 245(3) of the Income Tax Act", in *Proceedings of 38th Tax Conf.* (Can. Tax Foundation, 1986).

Kernochan, John M., "Statutory Interpretation: An Outline of Method" (1976), 3 *Dalhousie L.J.* 333.

Kilgour, "The Rule Against the Use of Legislative History: 'Canon of Construction or Counsel of Caution?'" (1952), 30 *Can. Bar Rev.* 769. (See also, in this article, the letters from MacQuarrie (1952), 30 *Can. Bar Rev.* 1087; Milner (1953), 31 *Can. Bar Rev.* 228).

Krishna, Vern, "The Demise of the Strict Interpretation Rule" (1986), 1 *Can. Cur. Tax* J-135.

Krishna, Vern, "Federal Court Relaxes Rules on Deductibility of Fines and Penalties" (1987-88), 2 *Can. Current Tax* J-99.

Krishna, Vern, "Interpreting the Tax Act" (1987), 21 *CGA Magazine* 37.

Krishna, Vern, "New Directions in Tax Interpretation" (1995), 5 *Can. Current Law* 47.

Krishna, Vern, "Supreme Court Restores Balance in Statutory Interpretation" [1994] *Can. Current Tax* J-67.

Krishna, Vern, "The Strict Interpretation Rule" (1987), 21 *CGA Magazine* 33.

Krishna, Vern, "Use of Extrinsic Evidence in Determining the 'Object and Spirit' of Tax Legislation" (1985), 1 *Can. Cur. Tax* C-117.

Landis, "A Note on 'Statutory Interpretation'" (1930), 43 *Harvard L. Rev.* 886.

Levine, Resa E., "Recent Developments in Judicial Interpretation" in *Report of Proceedings of the 50th Tax Conf.* (Can. Tax Foundation, 1992).

Lyman, "The Absurdity and Repugnancy of the Plain Meaning Rule of Interpretation" (1969), 3 *Man. L. J.* 253.

Maxwell, P.B., *Interpretation of Statutes,* 12th ed. (Sweet & Maxwell, 1969).

McCallum, "Legislative Intent" (1966), 75 *Yale L.J.* 754.

McDonnell, T.E., "Statutory Interpretation, 'Acceptable' Tax Planning, Court's Role in Filling In the Gaps in Tax Legislation" (1981), 29 *Can. Tax J.* 188.

McGregor, Gwyneth, "Interpretation of Taxing Statutes: Whither Canada?" (1968), 16 *Can. Tax J.* 122.

McGregor, Gwyneth, "Literal or Liberal? Trends in the Interpretation of Income Tax Law" (1954), 32 *Can. Bar Rev.* 281.

McNab, Charles, "Equity in Income Tax Cases" (1980), 28 *Can. Tax J.* 445.

Minzberg, Samuel, "Income Splitting: Still Alive?", in *Proceedings of 38th Tax Conf.* 35 (Can. Tax Foundation, 1986).

"'Modern' Rules of Statutory Interpretation in the Daily Routine, The" (1990), 44 *DTC* 7005.

Morgan, Vivien, "Stubart: What the Courts Did Next" (1987), 35 *Can. Tax J.* 155.

Nadeau, Claude, "The Interpretation of Taxing Statutes Since Stubart", in *Proceedings of 42nd Tax Conf.* 49:1 (Can. Tax Foundation, 1990).

Nathanson, "The Canadian Charter of Rights and Freedoms, Recent Criminal Prosecution Policy, and the Access to Information Act", in *Proceedings of 35th Tax Conf.* 636 (Can. Tax Foundation, 1983).

Radin, "Statutory Interpretation" (1930), 43 *Harvard L. Rev.* 863.

Rand, Clifford and Allan Stitt, *Understanding the Income Tax Act*, 2nd ed.(Toronto: Carswell, 1991).

Sanagan, "The Construction of Taxing Statutes" (1940), 18 *Can. Bar Rev.* 43.

Schramm, "Taxation, Expenditure Needs and Fiscal Equity" (1968), 16 *Can. Tax J.* 379.

Sherbaniuk, "Retrospectivity", in *Proceedings of 35th Tax Conf.* 727 (Can. Tax Foundation, 1983).

"'Spirit' of the Tax Act, The" (1988), 10 *Can. Taxpayer* 89.

"Spirit of the Law, The: A Practical Example" (1988), 10 *Can. Taxpayer* 110.

Tamaki, "Form and Substance Revisited" (1962), 10 *Can. Tax J.* 179. Wilberforce, E., *On Statute Law* (Stevens, 1881).

Willis, "Statute Interpretation in a Nutshell" (1938), 16 *Can. Bar Rev.* 1.

Treaty Interpretation

Ault, Hugh J., "The Role of the OECD Commentaries in the Interpretation of Tax Treaties" (1994), 4 *Intertax* 144.

Boidman, Nathan, "Interpretation of Tax Treaties in Canada" (1980), 34 *Bull. for Inter. Fisc. Doc.* 388.

Brockway, David H., "Interpretation of Tax Treaties and Their Relationship to Statutory Law — A U.S. Perspective, 1983 Conference Report (*Can. Tax. F.*, 1984) 619.

Coulombe, Gérard, "Certain Policy Aspects of Canadian Tax Treaties", in *1976 Conference Report* (Can. Tax. Foundation, 1977) 290.

Davies, Ward & Beck, "International Tax Treaties", 6 *Ward's Tax Law & Planning* (Carswell), §§ 211-216.

Duval, Marc, "Interprétation des conventions fiscales" (1991), 39 *Can. Tax J.* 1206.

McCart, Janice and Morris, Bernard, "The Income Tax Conventions Interpretation Act — Unilateral Treaty Amendment" (1983), 31 *Can. Tax J.* 1022.

Rosenberg, Mark N., "The Vienna Convention: Uniformity In Interpretation for Gap-Filling — an Analysis and Application" (1992), 20 *Australian Business Law Review* 442.

Tremblay, Richard G., "Crown Forest — Tax Treaty Interpretation Bonanza", [1994] *Can. Current Tax* c-41.

Ward, David A., "Principles to be Applied in Interpreting Tax Treaties", (1977) 25 *Can. Tax J.*, 263.

Ward, David A., "Principles to be Applied in Interpreting Tax Treaties (Updated)" (1980), 34 *Bull. for Inter. Fisc. Doc.* 545.

Ward, David A., "The Income Tax Conventions Interpretation Act", in *1983 Conference Report* (Can. Tax Foundation, 1984) 602.

White, Roger, "Still more on Treaty Interpretation" (1991), 1:2 *British Tax Review* 35.

Wilkie, J.S., "The Canada-United Kingdom Income Tax Convention: Interpretation Issues, Recent Developments and Planning Considerations" (1989), 43 *IBFD Bulletin* 63.

Estoppel

Ainslie, G., "Income Tax Appeals, Administrative and Judicial", *1972 Conference Report* (Can. Tax Foundation, 1973).

Andrews, J., "Estoppel Against Statutes" (1966), 29 *M.L.R.* 1.

Bentley, D., "Estoppel in Public Law: A Reply" (1975), 125 *N.L.J.* 379.

Bowett, D., "Estoppel Before International Tribunals and its Relation to Acquiescence" (1957), 33 *Brit. Yb. Int. L.* 1276.

Dickerson, R., "Estoppel and the Crown", *1977 Conference Report* (Can. Tax Foundation, 1978).

Farrer, F., "A Prerogative Fallacy — That the Crown is Not Bound by Estoppel" (1933), *Law Quarterly Rev.* 511.

Lynn, T., and M. Gerson, "Quasi-Estoppel and Abuse of Discretion as Applied Against the United States in Federal Tax Controversies" (1964), 19 *Tax L. Rev.* 487.

McDonald, P., "Contradictory Government Action: Estoppel of Statutory Authorities" (1979), 17 *Osgoode Hall L.J.* 160.

Quigley, "Estoppel Against the Crown: Selected Problems in the Tax Context", LL.M. Thesis [unpublished], Institute of Comparative Law, McGill University (September 1982).

Rider, Cameron, "Estoppel of the Revenue: A Review of Recent Developments" (1994), 23 *Aust. Tax Rev.* 135

Stikeman, H., *Erosion of Civil Rights under the Income Tax Act — Crown Privilege and Estoppel* (Canadian Bar Association, 1980).

Sources of Law and Information

Davidson, "Advance Rulings and Interpretation Bulletins", in *Proceedings of 35th Tax Conf.* 795 (Can. Tax Foundation, 1983).

Hausman, "Factors Affecting the Canadian Tax Treaty Network Since 1972", in *Proceedings of 35th Tax Conf.* 589 (Can. Tax Foundation, 1983).

Krishna, Vern, "House of Lords Permits Use of Parliamentary Materials in Statutory Construction", [1993] *Can. Current Tax* J-67.

Rand, Clifford, *Understanding the Income Tax Act,* (Toronto: Carswell, 1989).

Rogovin, M., "The Four R's: Regulations, Rulings, Reliance and Retroactivity — A View From Within", *18th Annual Tax Conference,* University of Chicago Law School, reprinted in *Standard Federal Tax Reports* (C.C.H., 1980).

Sherbaniuk, D., "Advance Rulings, Technical Interpretations and Interpretation Bulletins", *Corporate Management Tax Conf.* 86 (Can. Tax Foundation, 1976).

CHAPTER III

WHO IS TAXABLE?

Debt is the Slavery of the Free
(Publius Syrus, First Century, B.C.)

Reference:

ITA:

S. 2   Liability for Tax

1. GENERAL

The first question to be answered in any tax system is: Who is taxable? The answer to this seemingly innocuous question influences the structure of the Act and determines how the tax system establishes its reach over those who come within its scope.

As a general rule, the person who earns income is liable for any tax payable on the income. This rule is modified, however, in certain circumstances where property is transferred between family members.[1]

A tax system can be structured to levy tax on the basis of any one or more of several criteria. For example:

- Citizenship,
- Domicile,
- Residence,
- Source of income, or
- Physical and economic links.

Canada uses "residence" as the primary basis for taxation of income. Source of income is a secondary basis. Canadian residents are taxable on their global income, regardless of where the income is earned or originates. Subject to special tax treaty provisions, non-residents are liable for Canadian tax only on their income earned in Canada.

Canadian residents are subject to federal and provincial tax. "Residence" for tax purposes is not synonymous with physical presence. Rather, the concept of residence refers to the legal and economic *nexus* or link that a person has with Canada. Thus, a person who is physically present in Canada is not necessarily a Canadian resident.

---

[1]   See, *infra*, "Attribution Rules".

Conversely, a person who is physically absent from Canada may be considered to be a Canadian resident for income tax purposes.

The concept of residence for tax purposes is not identical with the concept of residence for immigration purposes. Hence, a Canadian resident for immigration purposes may be non-resident for tax purposes and *vice versa*.

2. INDIVIDUALS

References:

ITA:

S. 114	Part-Year Resident
S. 115	Non-Resident's Taxable Canadian Income
S. 149	Exemptions
S. 250	Deemed Residence

BULLETINS, CIRCULARS & RULINGS:

IT-106R2	February 15, 1991	Crown Corporation Employees Abroad
IT-193SR	September 30, 1985	Taxable Income of Individuals Resident in Canada During Part of a Year
IT-221R2	February 3, 1983	Determination of an Individual's Residence Status
IT-221R2SR	February 20, 1991	Determination of an Individual's Residence Status
IT-298	March 8, 1976	Canada-U.S. Tax Convention — Number of Days "Present" in Canada

FORMS:

NR71	Determination of Residency for Spouses and Dependent Children
NR72	Determination of Residency for Employees Posted Abroad
NR73	Determination of Residency Status (Leaving Canada)
NR74	Determination of Residency Status (Entering Canada)
T626	Overseas Investment Tax Credit

For income tax purposes, individuals are classified into three categories:

1. residents,
2. non-residents, and
3. part-time residents.

The difference between these three categories is important. A resident of Canada is taxable on his or her global income, regardless of where it is earned.[2] A non-resident is subject to Canadian income tax only if he or she is employed in Canada, carries on business in Canada, or disposes of taxable Canadian property.[3] A part-time Canadian resident is subject to tax on his or her global income earned while resident in Canada, but deductions are allocated according to the length of his or her residency in Canada.[4]

Residence may be determined in several ways: by virtue of the common law rules, under the deeming provisions of the Act and, in cases of dual residency, by the provisions of an international tax treaty.

(a) Common Law Residence

Residence at common law is a question of fact.[5] In the absence of a statutory definition of "residence", its dictionary meaning provides a useful starting point: "To dwell permanently or for a considerable time, or to have one's settled or usual abode".

In general terms, an individual's residence is the status arising from his or her *nexus* or link with Canada.[6] An individual's connection or link with Canada can be determined by various factors, such as:

- nationality and background,
- physical presence,
- ownership of property or dwelling in Canada,
- location of family home,
- presence of business interests,
- presence of social interests,
- mode of life and family ties, and
- connection by reason of birth or marriage.

---

[2]   Subs. 2(1). A resident taxpayer is, within limits, entitled to a credit for foreign taxes paid by him or her; see s. 126.

[3]   Subs. 2(3).

[4]   S. 114.

[5]   As Lord Buckmaster observed in *I.R.C. v. Lysaght*, [1928] AC 234 at 247-248 (H.L.):
   . . . it may be true that the word "reside" . . . in other Acts may have special meanings but in the *Income Tax Acts* it is, I think, used in its common sense and it is essentially a question of fact whether a man does or does not comply with its meaning . . . the matter must be a matter of degree. . . .

[6]   *Weymyss v. Weymyss's Trustees*, [1921] Sess. Cas. 30.

(i) General Propositions

In most cases, an individual's residence is determined, not by any single criterion but by the cumulative effect of multiple criteria. The relative weight to be attached to any particular criterion is a question of fact in each case.[7] There are, however, certain generally accepted propositions established in the case law:

- A taxpayer must reside somewhere;[8]

- A taxpayer need not have a fixed place of abode to be resident in the jurisdiction;[9]

- Residence requires more than mere presence within the jurisdiction;[10]

- Residence does not require constant personal presence;[11]

- A taxpayer may have more than one residence;[12]

- The number of days which a taxpayer spends within a particular country is not crucial;[13]

- Residence may be established by presence within Canada even when such presence occurs by virtue of compulsion by the authorities, business necessity or otherwise;[14]

- "Residing" and "ordinarily resident" do not have a special or technical meaning and the question of whether in any year a person is "residing or ordinarily resident in Canada" is a question of fact;[15] and

- Intention and free choice, which are essential elements in domicile, are not necessary to establish residence; residence is quite different from domicile of choice.[16]

---

[7] See, e.g., *MacLean v. M.N.R.*, [1985] CTC 2207, 85 DTC 169 (T.C.C.) (taxpayer resident on the basis of continued connections with Canada despite Revenue Canada's waiver of source deductions).

[8] *Rogers v. I.R.C.* (1897), 1 Tax Cas. 225 (Scot. Ct. of Ex.).

[9] *Reid v. I.R.C.* (1926), 10 Tax Cas. 673 (Scot. Ct. of Sess.).

[10] *Levene v. I.R.C.* (1928), 13 Tax Cas. 486 (H.L.).

[11] *Young, Re* (1875), 1 Tax Cas. 57 (Scot. Ct. of Ex.).

[12] *Lloyd v. Sulley* (1884), 2 Tax Cas. 37 (Scot. Ct. of Ex.).

[13] *Reid v. I.R.C., ante.*

[14] *I.R.C. v. Lysaght*, [1928] AC 234 (H.L.).

[15] *Ibid.*

[16] *Schujahn v. M.N.R.*, [1962] CTC 364, 62 DTC 1225 (Ex. Ct.) (change of domicile depends on will of individual).

"Residing" is not a term of invariable elements, each of which must be present in each case. As Rand J. said in *Thomson v. M.N.R.*:[17]

> . . . [i]t is quite impossible to give it a precise and inclusive definition. It is highly flexible, and its many shades of meaning vary not only in the contexts of different matters, but also in different aspects of the same matter. In one case it is satisfied by certain elements, in another by others, some common, some new.

(ii) Relevant Indicia

The following are some of the relevant indicia in determining an individual's residence:

- Past and present habits of life;
- Regularity and length of visits in the jurisdiction asserting residence;
- Ties within the jurisdiction;
- Ties elsewhere;
- Purposes of stay;
- Ownership of a dwelling in Canada or rental of a dwelling on a long-term basis (for example, a lease for one or more years);
- Residence of spouse, children and other dependent family members in a dwelling maintained by the individual in Canada;
- Memberships with Canadian churches or synagogues, recreational and social clubs, unions and professional organizations;
- Registration and maintenance of automobiles, boats and airplanes in Canada;
- Credit cards issued by Canadian financial institutions and other commercial entities including stores, car rental agencies, etc.;
- Local newspaper subscriptions sent to a Canadian address;
- Rental of Canadian safety deposit box or post office box;
- Subscriptions for life or general insurance including health insurance through a Canadian insurance company;
- Mailing address in Canada;
- Telephone listing in Canada;

---

[17] *Thomson v. M.N.R.*, [1945] CTC 63, 2 DTC 684, affirmed [1946] CTC 51 at 63-64, 2 DTC 812 at 815 (S.C.C.). See also *Beament v. M.N.R.*, [1952] CTC 327, 2 DTC 1183 (S.C.C.) (taxpayer not resident where he was physically absent from Canada, did not maintain any dwelling place in Canada, and maintained matrimonial home in U.K.); *Russell v. M.N.R.*, [1949] CTC 13, 4 DTC 536 (Ex. Ct.) (examination of indicia of residence during active service overseas); *Schujahn v. M.N.R.*, [1962] CTC 364, 62 DTC 1225 (Ex. Ct.) (taxpayer not resident though family remained in Canada for purpose of selling home); *Griffiths v. The Queen*, [1978] CTC 372, 78 DTC 6286 (F.C.T.D.) (established residence was yacht in Caribbean despite spouse, assets and income in Canada).

- Stationery including business cards showing a Canadian address;
- Magazine and other periodical subscriptions sent to a Canadian address;
- Canadian bank accounts other than a non-resident bank account;
- Active securities accounts with Canadian brokers;
- Canadian driver's licence;
- Membership in a Canadian pension plan;
- Frequent visits to Canada for social or business purposes;
- Burial plot in Canada;
- Will prepared in Canada;
- Legal documentation indicating Canadian residence;
- Filing a Canadian income tax return as a Canadian resident;
- Ownership of a Canadian vacation property;
- Active involvement in business activities in Canada;
- Employment in Canada;
- Maintenance or storage in Canada of personal belongings including clothing, furniture, family pets, etc.;
- Obtaining landed immigrant status or appropriate work permits in Canada;
- Severing substantially all ties with former country of residence.

(iii) Revenue Canada's Views

Revenue Canada's views on some of the above criteria are outlined in IT-221R2, "Determination of an Individual's Residence Status" (February 25, 1983).[18] The Department looks quite closely at three factors: Dwelling place, family connections, and personal property and social ties. With regard to the first two factors, for example, the Department states:[19]

> An individual who leaves Canada, but ensures that a dwelling place suitable for year-round occupancy is kept available in Canada for his occupation by maintaining it (vacant or otherwise), by leasing it at non-arm's length, or by leasing it at arm's length with the right to terminate the lease on short notice (less than 3 months) will generally not be considered to have severed his residential ties within Canada.

> If a married individual leaves Canada, but his spouse or dependants remain in Canada, the individual will generally be considered to remain a resident of Canada during his absence. An exception to this may occur where an individual and his spouse are legally separated and the individual has permanently severed all other residential ties within Canada. The residential ties of a single person are frequently of a more tenuous nature and, in the majority of cases, if such a person leaves Canada for 2 years or more and establishes a residence elsewhere, it is likely that he will be a non-resident of Canada during his absence, unless other important ties within Canada indicate that he is not. For example, where a single

---

[18] As revised by Special Release dated February 20, 1991.

[19] IT-221R2, "Determination of an Individual's Residence Status" (February 25, 1983), paras. 7 and 8.

person is supporting someone in a dwelling maintained and occupied by him in Canada and, after his departure, he continues to support that person in the dwelling, he will not be considered to have severed his residential ties within Canada.

Revenue Canada takes the view that, in order to maintain non-resident status, an individual should not maintain substantial social ties and personal property links to Canada. The Department may examine an individual's personal property in Canada and evaluate the reasons for its retention to determine whether the reasons are more consistent with continuing resident status than with non-resident status. The main items considered are:

- Furniture
- Bank accounts
- Professional memberships
- Clothing
- Credit cards
- Medical/hospital insurance
- Automobiles
- Club memberships
- Family allowance benefits

Revenue Canada *presumes* that a Canadian resident who is absent from Canada for less than two years retains resident status while abroad. Similarly, Revenue Canada *presumes* that an individual who is absent from Canada for two or more years is a non-resident of Canada. These are only administrative presumptions which can be rebutted by showing contrary facts. The presumptions do not have any authority in law. For example, an employee who is transferred abroad for a period of 25 months with a guarantee of employment upon return, does not invariably lose Canadian residency for tax purposes; other residential ties with Canada need to be taken into account.

(iv) Multiple Residence

An individual can have more than one residence for tax purposes. An individual may be considered a Canadian resident for Canadian income tax purposes and a resident of some other country under foreign fiscal legislation. Thus, an individual may be liable to double taxation. For example, a Canadian resident who is a citizen of a country that levies tax on the basis of citizenship (e.g., the U.S.) is potentially liable to double taxation, once on the basis of residence and again on the basis of citizenship. The elimination of double taxation is an important reason for participation in international tax treaties and Canada has an extensive international treaty network that provides relief in such circumstances.

(b) Giving Up Residence

To give up Canadian residence a taxpayer should minimize his or her ties with Canada.[20] Revenue Canada looks closely at four factors to determine whether an individual has given up his or her Canadian residence:

1. Permanence and purpose of stay abroad;

2. Residential ties within Canada;

3. Residential ties elsewhere; and

4. Regularity and length of visits to Canada.

For example, at the very least, an individual should:

- sell or lease his or her motor vehicle or dwelling held in Canada;

- cancel any lease in respect of a dwelling in Canada which she or he occupies, or sublease the dwelling for the period of his or her absence;

- cancel bank accounts, club memberships and other similar social and business connections within Canada; and

- maximize the period of his or her physical absence from Canada.

(c) Deemed Residence

An individual is deemed to be a Canadian resident in certain circumstances.[21] An individual cannot, however, be deemed to be resident in Canada by virtue of subsection 250(1) if he or she is already resident in Canada on the basis of the common law factual criteria test.[22]

(i) Sojourners

An individual who sojourns in Canada for 183 days or more in a year is *deemed* to be a resident of Canada *throughout the taxation year.*[23] The days need not be consecutive. The term "day" means a 24-hour period.

The term "sojourn" is not defined in the Act and it is not easy to determine when a person sojourns in a place. To "sojourn" means to stay temporarily as opposed to becoming ordinarily resident. As Estey J. said, "[O]ne sojourns at a place where he

---

[20] See, e.g., *Ferguson v. M.N.R*, [1989] 2 CTC 2387, 89 DTC 634 (T.C.C.) (Canadian in Saudi Arabia for five years considered Canadian resident because he retained Ontario driver's license and union membership and his spouse remained in Canada).

[21] Subs. 250(1).

[22] Special Release to IT-221R2, "Determination of an Individual's Residence Status" (February 20, 1991).

[23] Para. 250(1)(*a*).

unusually, casually or intermittently visits or stays".[24] "Sojourning" is something less than establishing a permanent abode; it is not the length, but the character of the stay which is ultimately determinative of the question.

The fact that an individual is present in Canada for less than 183 days does not, *by itself*, mean that she or he is not a Canadian resident. In other words, while an individual who sojourns in Canada for more than 183 days is *deemed* to be a resident of Canada, individuals who are in Canada for less than 183 days may also be considered residents of Canada under the common law rules.[25] Further, an individual may be considered a Canadian resident for tax purposes even though he or she has only "visitor status" under the immigration rules.[26]

As noted earlier, "sojourning" is to be distinguished from permanent residence. An individual who ceases to be a Canadian resident after 183 days in the year cannot be deemed to be resident in Canada throughout the year by virtue of the sojourning rule. Rather, he or she is a part-time resident for that year.[27] Subsection 250(1) only applies to *sojourners* and not to residents.

(ii) Government Personnel

The following persons are also deemed to be resident in Canada throughout a taxation year:[28]

- Members of the Canadian Forces;
- Members of the diplomatic and quasi-diplomatic services, and officers and servants of the federal or provincial governments if they were resident in

---

[24] *Thomson v. M.N.R.*, [1946] CTC 51 at 70, 2 DTC 812 at 813 (S.C.C.).

[25] This rule is subject to treaty provisions to the contrary. See, e.g., Article XV of the *Canada-United States Income Tax Convention*, 1980 re exemption of employment income where an individual spends less than 183 days in Canada.

[26] *Lee v. M.N.R.*, [1990] 1 CTC 2082, 90 DTC 1014 (T.C.C.) (individual considered resident prior to obtaining landed immigrant status on basis of marriage to Canadian resident and purchase of matrimonial residence).

[27] The Department accepts this position in IT-221R2, "Determination of an Individual's Residence Status" (February 3, 1983), para. 15; but see *Truchon v. M.N.R.* (1970), 70 DTC 1277 (T.A.B.) (incorrectly decided and rule not followed).

[28] Subs. 250(1).

Canada immediately prior to taking up the office or appointment, or if they are in receipt of representation allowances in respect of the year;[29]

- Persons who perform services in a foreign country under a prescribed international development assistance program of the Canadian government, e.g., CIDA programs;

- Members of the overseas Canadian Forces school staff who file returns on the basis of Canadian residence throughout their tour of duty abroad;

- The spouse of any person holding a position referred to in the above categories if the spouse was living with the taxpayer during the taxation year and was resident in Canada in any previous year; and

- A child of a person holding a position referred to in the above categories if the child was wholly dependent upon that person for support.

A person who ceases to hold a position described above is considered to have been resident in Canada for the part of the year during which she or he held that position.[30]

(iii) Prescribed Agencies

Individuals who perform services at any time in the year in a foreign country, under a "prescribed international development assistance program of the Government of Canada", are *deemed* to be resident in Canada during the period of their absence from Canada if they were resident in Canada at any time in the three-month period immediately prior to commencing delivery of service.[31] Thus, there are two conditions to be satisfied before an individual is deemed resident in Canada during a period of absence from Canada:

1. the individual must be working for a *prescribed* international development assistance program, and

2. he or she must have been resident in Canada at some time during the three-month period *immediately* prior to commencing services for the program.

---

[29] In IT-106R2, "Crown Corporation Employees Abroad" (February 15, 1991), para. 2, Revenue Canada describes an "officer or servant" as follows:

The term "officer or servant of Canada" or "officer or servant of a province" includes any officer or employee of a federal or provincial Crown operation or agency if, in the statute under which it is organized or established, its officers and employees are given the status of servants of Her Majesty or are designated as being part of the public service of Canada or the province. If the corporation or agency is designated as an agent of Her Majesty without specific mention being made as to the status of its officers and employees, they will be assumed to be officers or servants of Canada or a province, as the case may be.

[30] Subs. 250(2).

[31] Para. 250(1)(*d*); Reg. 3400. See *Petersen v. M.N.R.*, [1969] Tax ABC 682, 69 DTC 503.

(d) Part-time Residents

Individuals can become residents of Canada or relinquish residence in Canada at any time *during* the calendar year. For example, an individual who is a Canadian resident may, at some time during the year, decide to emigrate from Canada and take up residence elsewhere. Such an individual would be a Canadian resident for part of the year and a non-resident for the remainder of the year subsequent to his or her departure from Canada. As a resident he or she would be taxed on his or her global income earned during the period of his or her residence. As a non-resident, the individual would only be taxable in Canada while employed in or carrying on a business in Canada or disposing of taxable Canadian property, and then only on the income arising from those activities.[32]

A Canadian resident who gives up residence some time during a taxation year may claim deductions for that year on a proportional basis.[33] For example, an individual who becomes a Canadian resident on September 1, 1995 is liable for Canadian tax on his or her global income earned during the period of September 1, 1995 to December 31, 1995. Any personal exemptions would be calculated on the basis of 122/365 (122 being the number of days out of the year spent in Canada) of the annual deductions otherwise available. There are, however, some exemptions that are not available unless the non-resident earns at least 90 per cent of his or her income in Canada.[34]

(e) Departure Tax

An individual is *deemed* to have disposed of his or her property immediately prior to giving up residence in Canada[35] and consequently, he or she may be subject to a "departure tax".

The deeming provision does not apply to any "taxable Canadian property", or any other property which he or she *elects* to have treated as taxable Canadian property, when becoming a non-resident. Instead, the taxpayer will be taxed as a non-resident when he or she actually disposes of the taxable Canadian property at a later date.

Timing can be quite important in deciding in which year any gain or loss arising from a deemed disposition should be included. For example, if a Canadian resident physically leaves Canada on December 31, and arrives at a new destination on January 1, does he or she give up residence on the date of departure or on the date on which he or she assumes the new residence? As noted earlier, since the determination of residence at common law is a question of fact, all contributing circumstances need to

---

[32] Subs. 2(3).

[33] Ss. 114, 118.91.

[34] S. 118.94.

[35] Para. 128.1(4)(*b*).

be examined carefully in order to pin-point the time at which a taxpayer gives up his or her residence.[36]

(f) Becoming a Canadian Resident

An individual who takes up residence in Canada is taxed as a part-year resident in the year of his or her arrival. He or she is taxed as two separate persons in the year of arrival in Canada: As a non-resident person prior to his or her arrival and as a resident after his or her arrival.

(i) Year of Arrival

It is generally more advantageous for an individual to establish residence in Canada rather than be considered a "sojourner" in Canada in the year of arrival. A sojourner is deemed to be a Canadian resident for the entire year and is liable to full Canadian tax on his or her world-wide income.[37] An incoming resident is taxable on his or her world income only after arrival in Canada. Thus, timing is important and can be used to minimize tax by splitting the taxpayer's income between Canada and his or her country of departure.

(ii) Immigration

The requirements of "residence" for immigration purposes are different from those for tax purposes. An individual can establish permanent residence status for immigration purposes without becoming a resident of Canada for tax purposes. "Landed immigrant" status is determined on the basis of selection standards that are quite different from those used to determine residence for tax purposes.

For immigration purposes, a landed immigrant must spend 183 days in Canada in a *12-month period*. For tax purposes, an individual is deemed to be a resident of Canada if he or she spends 183 days or more in Canada in *a calendar year*. Thus, it is possible for an individual to take up landed immigrant status in Canada in a particular year and maintain non-resident status for income tax purposes.

(g) Dual Residence

A taxpayer with international interests may be exposed to taxation in multiple jurisdictions. For example, a Canadian resident who resides more than 183 days in a year in the U.S. and receives dividends from a British corporation carrying on business in Hong Kong is liable for tax on the income in at least two jurisdictions: Canada and the United States. It is obvious that such taxpayers require relief from multiple taxation.

---

[36] See, e.g., *Schujahn v. M.N.R.*, [1962] CTC 365, 62 DTC 1225 (Ex. Ct.) (taxpayer became non-resident months before wife and son sold family home and themselves became non-resident); *Davis v. The Queen*, [1978] CTC 536, 78 DTC 6374; affirmed [1980] CTC 88, 80 DTC 6056 (F.C.A.) (individual ceases to be resident once ship or aircraft leaves Canadian waters or airspace).

[37] Para. 250(1)(*a*); subs. 2(1).

(i) Unilateral Relief

Canada provides a certain amount of unilateral tax relief from double taxation through its foreign tax credit mechanism. Generally, a Canadian resident may deduct an amount equal to the non-business income taxes he or she has paid to a foreign jurisdiction from taxes payable in Canada. The foreign tax credit cannot, however, exceed the amount of Canadian tax that would have been payable on the foreign income had that income been earned in Canada. In other words, the maximum foreign tax credit available to a resident is limited to the maximum tax payable had the income been earned in Canada instead of a foreign country. The foreign tax credit mechanism places the cost of providing relief squarely on the Canadian treasury.

(ii) Bilateral Relief

Canada has bilateral income tax treaties with many countries. These treaties provide relief against double taxation of income. A treaty may, for example, provide that an individual is only taxable on a particular type of income in the country of residence and not in the country in which the income is earned.

How do we resolve problems of multiple "residence" for tax purposes? The usual rule in most of Canada's international tax treaties is that a taxpayer's residence is to be determined by the domestic tax law of his or her treaty country. Thus, Canada determines taxpayer residence by reference to its domestic rules.

(h) OECD Model Convention

Where a taxpayer is found to be a resident of two or more countries, one should refer to the relevant treaty to resolve the conflict. Article 4 of the *OECD Model Convention*, for example, illustrates how multiple residence problems are sometimes resolved.

The *OECD Model Convention* is not concerned with the determination of a taxpayer's residence for the purposes of determining liability for tax under the domestic laws of any of the Contracting States. The determination of residence for domestic fiscal purposes is entirely a matter of local law and statutory rules.

Article 4 of the *Model Convention* states:

1. For the purposes of this Convention, the term "resident of a Contracting State" means any person who, under the laws of that State, is liable to tax therein by reason of his domicile, residence, place of management or any other criterion of a similar nature. But this term does not include any person who is liable to tax in that State in respect only of income from sources in that State or capital situated therein.

2. Where by reason of the provisions of paragraph 1 an individual is a resident of both Contracting States, then his status shall be determined as follows:

(a)   he shall be deemed to be a resident of the State in which he has a permanent home available to him; if he has a permanent home available to him in both States, he shall be deemed to be a resident of the State with which his personal and economic relations are closer (centre of vital interests);

(b)   if the State in which he has his centre of vital interests cannot be determined, or if he has not a permanent home available to him in either State, he shall be deemed to be a resident of the State in which he has an habitual abode;

(c)   if he has an habitual abode in both States or in neither of them, he shall be deemed to be a resident of the State of which he is a national;

(d)   if he is a national of both States or of neither of them, the competent authorities of the Contracting States shall settle the question by mutual agreement.

3.   Where by reason of the provisions of paragraph 1 a person other than an individual is a resident of both Contracting States, then it shall be deemed to be a resident of the State in which its place of effective management is situated.

The tie-breaker rules are intended to determine the degree of attachment that an individual has with a particular country. The attachment criteria are ranked as follows:

- location of permanent home;
- centre of vital interests;
- habitual abode;
- nationality; and
- settlement by mutual agreement.

(i) Permanent Home

A "dual resident individual" is initially deemed to be a resident of the country in which he or she has a permanent home. Permanence implies that the individual must have arranged and retained the home for his or her permanent use, as opposed to temporary use or stays of short duration.

The term "home" includes any form of residential establishment, for example, a house, apartment, or rented furnished rooms. It is the permanence of the home, rather than its size or nature, that provides the measure of the individual's degree of attachment to the country.

(ii) Centre of Vital Interests

Where an individual has a permanent home in both countries of which he or she is considered a resident under domestic law, the country with which he or she has closer personal and economic relations ("centre of vital interests") is considered his or her country of residence.[38]

Personal and economic relations are determined by family and social relations, occupation, political, cultural and other activities, place of business, and the place of administration of property. The OECD Commentary states as follows:[39]

---

[38]   Article 4(2)(b), *OECD Model Convention*.

[39]   Para. 15, *Commentary on Article 4(2)*.

The circumstances must be examined as a whole, but it is nevertheless obvious that considerations based on the personal acts of the individual must receive special attention. If a person who has a home in one State sets up a second in the other State while retaining the first, the fact that he retains the first in the environment where he has always lived, where he has worked, and where he has his family and possessions, can, together with other elements, go to demonstrate that he has retained his centre of vital interests in the first State.

(iii) Habitual Abode

If an individual's centre of vital interests cannot be determined or he or she does not have a permanent home in either country, the individual is considered to be a resident of the country in which he or she has an habitual abode.

Where an individual has a permanent home available to him or her in both countries, an habitual abode in one, rather than in the other, will tip the balance towards the country where he or she stays more frequently. Thus, it may be necessary to look at the individual's stays, not only at his or her permanent home in the country in question, but also at any other place in the same country.

Where, however, an individual does not have a permanent home in either country, all stays in the country should be considered without reference to the reason for the stay. For this purpose, it is necessary to determine whether the individual's residence in each of the two countries is sufficiently "habitual" over a period of time to provide a meaningful answer.

(iv) Nationality

If none of the above criteria are sufficient to break the deadlock, the individual is considered to be a resident of the country of which he or she is a national.

(v) Competent Authorities

Finally, if the problem of dual residence cannot be resolved through the application of any of the above attachment criteria, the matter is referred to the competent authority of each country concerned for resolution.

3. CORPORATIONS

References:

ITA:

S. 253   Definition: Carrying on Business

REGULATION:

900(2)(*b*)   Powers Delegated to Director

A corporation is a legal entity in its own right, a person distinct from its shareholders and, as a person, subject to tax under the Act.[40] As with individuals, Canadian resident corporations are subject to tax on their global income. The residence of a corporation is also determined in one of three ways: at common law, under statutory rules, or by international treaty.

(a) Common Law Rules

(i) Central Management

Common law residence is essentially a question of fact. The central question to be determined in each case is: Where does the corporation's "central management and control" abide?[41] In Lord Loreburn's words:[42]

> . . . In applying the conception of residence to a company, we ought, I think, to proceed as nearly as we can upon the analogy of an individual. A company cannot eat or sleep, but it can keep house and do business. We ought, therefore, to see where it really keeps house and does business. . . . The decision [in *Calcutta Jute Mills v. Nicholson* (1876), 1 Ex. D. 248] involved the principle that a company resides for purposes of income tax where its real business is carried on. [That decision] has been acted upon ever since. I regard that as the true rule, and the real business is carried on where the central management and control actually abides.

Corporate residence is to be distinguished from corporate capacity. Residence is determined by actual central management and control; that is, the test of common law residence is *de facto* control. The capacity of a corporation is governed by its constating documents (*de jure* control) and by the law of the jurisdiction which governs the transaction in question.

(ii) General Propositions

The following propositions apply to corporate residence:

---

[40] Subss. 2(1); 248(1) "person".

[41] *De Beers Consolidated Mines Ltd. v. Howe*, [1906] AC 455 at 458 (H.L.) (central management and control determined through scrutiny of course of business and trading); *Unit Const. Co. v. Bullock*, [1959] 3 All ER 831 (H.L.) (three wholly-owned African subsidiaries of English corporation resident in U.K. because parent corporation exercised *de facto* control of subsidiaries from U.K.). The English common law test of "central management and control" is part of Canadian tax law: see *B.C. Electric Railway v. The Queen*, [1946] CTC 224, 2 DTC 839 (P.C.) (corporation was resident where whole of business carried on, all directors resident, and all shareholders meetings held in Canada). See also *Bedford Overseas Freighters Ltd. v. M.N.R.*, [1970] CTC 69, 70 DTC 6072 (Ex. Ct.) (management and control of business exercised by Canadian directors though instructed by non-resident shareholder owner); *Zehnder & Co. v. M.N.R.*, [1970] CTC 85, 70 DTC 6064 (Ex. Ct.) (management of company and attention to company's interests and affairs exercised in Canada); *Birmount Hldgs. Ltd. v. The Queen*, [1978] CTC 358, 78 DTC 6254 (F.C.A.) (company "keeping house" and "doing business" in Canada; see list of factors considered).

[42] *De Beers Consolidated Mines Ltd. v. Howe, ante,* at 458.

- A corporation can have more than one residence if its central management and control is diversified and located in more than one jurisdiction.[43]

- Central management and control refers to the exercise of power and control by the corporation's board of directors and not to the power of the corporation's shareholders who may install or remove directors. Thus, the residence of its shareholders is irrelevant for the purposes of determining a corporation's residence.[44]

- The residence of a subsidiary corporation, even a wholly-owned subsidiary, is determined independently of its parent corporation. Here too, it is necessary to locate the subsidiary's central management and control.

- A subsidiary corporation may have the same residence as its parent corporation if the parent exercises effective control over the subsidiary's activities and management.[45]

The principles stated to this point are clear and well established in tax jurisprudence. Less certain, however, is the importance to be attached to the residence of corporate directors and the location of board meetings. It appears that the place where the directors meet to exercise *de facto* management and control is more important than the place where the directors themselves reside.

The determination of corporate residence according to the common law test requires a careful examination of all of the circumstances surrounding the management of the corporation. These circumstances include:

- The location of meetings of the directors;

- The degree of independent thought exercised by the directors; and

- The relative degree of influence and power exercised by Canadian directors *vis-à-vis* foreign directors (the "rubber stamp" test).

There is no clear-cut, bright-line test that determines corporate residence in every case. Ultimately, each case depends upon its own facts and an evaluation of where the corporation is effectively controlled.

As a matter of practice, regardless of the location of effective management, Revenue Canada is less likely to challenge the status of foreign corporations incorporated in taxable and high-tax jurisdictions. They are more likely to tax foreign corporations domiciled in low-tax jurisdictions and tax havens. This policy is premised

---

[43] *Swedish Central Ry. Co. v. Thompson*, [1925] AC 495 (H.L.) (company resident in location of registered office and where controlled and managed); *M.N.R. v. Crossley Carpets (Can.) Ltd.*, [1969] 1 Ex. CR 405 (Ex. Ct.) (paramount authority for businesses divided between two countries).

[44] *Gramophone & Typewriter Co. v. Stanley*, [1908] 2 KB 89 (C.A.).

[45] *Unit Construction Co. v. Bullock, ante.*

more on pragmatism than on legal theory: The net overall revenue gain to be derived from asserting Canadian corporate residence is minimal if the corporation claims a full foreign tax credit in respect of its offshore income.

A corporation concerned with maintaining non-resident status should endeavour to locate the following activities outside of Canada:

- Board of directors' meetings;
- Corporate banking;
- Registered head office;
- Residence of directors with signing and decision-making authority; and
- Execution of major business contracts and financing documents.

Where there are several directors, the majority of the directors should be non-Canadian residents and should meet outside of Canada for board meetings. The annual shareholders meeting should also be held outside of Canada and communications between non-resident directors and Canadian corporate officers should be minimized.

(b) Deemed Residence

The Act deems corporations to be resident in Canada if they are incorporated in Canada. For example, any corporation incorporated in Canada after April 26, 1965 is deemed to be resident in Canada regardless of the location of its *de facto* central management and control.[46]

A corporation incorporated in Canada prior to April 27, 1965 is deemed to be resident in Canada *throughout* a taxation year if:[47]

- it actually becomes resident in Canada at any time under the common law rules; or
- it carries on business in Canada during any taxation year.[48]

A corporation is deemed to be resident in Canada *throughout* a taxation year if it is incorporated in Canada.[49] Thus, a corporation incorporated in Canada is by definition also a "Canadian corporation".[50]

---

[46] Para. 250(4)(*a*).

[47] Para. 250(4)(*c*).

[48] This rule only applies to taxation years ending after April 26, 1965. Note the meaning of "carrying on business in Canada" in s. 253.

[49] Para. 250(4)(*a*). This deeming provision only applies to corporations incorporated in Canada after April 26, 1965.

[50] Subs. 89(1) "Canadian corporation".

A corporation that was originally incorporated in Canada but has been granted articles of continuance in another jurisdiction is not considered resident in Canada by virtue of its incorporation from the time that it is continued in the other jurisdiction.[51]

A corporation that was incorporated in Canada before April 9, 1959 is resident in Canada throughout a taxation year if it satisfies certain criteria and was resident in Canada or carried on business in Canada at any time in the taxation year or at any time in any preceding taxation year commencing after 1971.[52]

(c) Dual Residence

Tax treaties can play an important role in determining corporate residence. Generally speaking, a treaty may provide for the resolution of dual residence problems in one of several ways:

- by deeming residence in the country in which the corporation's effective management is situated (the *OECD Model*);
- by deferring the matter to the "competent authorities" of the contracting countries; or
- by deeming the corporation to be resident in the jurisdiction in which it was incorporated (the U.S. Model).

(i) **OECD Model Convention**

Article 4(3) of the *OECD Model Convention* states:

... Where ... a person other than an individual is a resident of both Contracting States, then it shall be deemed to be a resident of the State in which its place of effective management is situated.

Article 4(3) is concerned with corporations and all other bodies of persons, irrespective of whether or not they are legal entities.

Under Canadian law, a corporation is a legal entity in its own right and, for tax purposes, is considered a person and taxpayer separate and apart from its shareholders.[53]

A corporation can be resident in more than one country because of multiple jurisdictional claims on the corporation. For example, a corporation may be considered to be resident in Canada because it was incorporated in Canada and at the same time be resident in another country because its effective management is exercised from that country.

---

[51] Subs. 250(5.1).

[52] Para. 250(4)(*b*).

[53] Subs. 248(1) "person".

The *OECD Model* states that the location of a corporation's formal registration should not be determinative of its tax status. Thus, the *Model Convention* uses the "place of effective management" as the criterion for determining the residence of persons other than individuals. Both Canada and the United States, however, reserve the right to use the place of corporate incorporation or organization as the determinative test for corporate residence.

(ii) Concept of "Permanent Establishment"

The general treaty rule is that corporate profits are taxable in a State if the enterprise carries on business in the State through a "permanent establishment." Hence, although the general domestic rule is that a non-resident is taxable on business income earned in Canada, the international treaty rule which prevails is that a non-resident is taxable in Canada only if it has a permanent establishment in Canada. The existence of a Canadian "permanent establishment" provides a treaty nexus for Canadian taxation of the business of a non-resident corporation.

The term "permanent establishment" is essentially a tax treaty concept and, therefore, must be interpreted in that context. Typically, Canadian tax treaties provide that the term "permanent establishment" means a "...fixed place of business in which the business of the enterprise is wholly or partly carried on".[54] But what does this mean? In *Re Consol. Premium Iron Ores,* the United States Tax Court said:[55]

> The term "permanent establishment", normally interpreted, suggests something more substantial than a license, a letterhead and isolated activities. It implies the existence of an office, staffed and capable of carrying on the day-to-day business of the corporation and its use for such purpose, or it suggests the existence of a plant or facilities equipped to carry on the ordinary routine of such business activity. The descriptive word "permanent" in the characterization "permanent establishment" is vital in analyzing the treaty provisions. . . . It indicates permanence and stability.

In determining whether a corporation has "an office" in a particular place, one looks to the following factors:

- Presence of permanent physical premises,
- Presence of directors or employees,
- Bank accounts and books of accounts,
- Telephone listings, and
- Employees or agents established with the general authority to contract for the taxpayer in that jurisdiction.

Article 5 of the *OECD Model Convention* defines a "permanent establishment" as follows:

---

[54]   Article 5, *OECD Model Convention.*

[55]   *Re Consolidated Premium Iron Ores* (1957), 28 TC 127 at 152; affirmed S. (2d) 230 (6th Circuit, 1959).

1. For the purposes of this Convention, the term "permanent establishment" means a fixed place of business through which the business of an enterprise is wholly or partly carried on.

2. The term "permanent establishment" includes especially:

   (a) a place of management;

   (b) a branch;

   (c) an office;

   (d) a factory;

   (e) a workshop; and

   (f) a mine, an oil or gas well, a quarry or any other place of extraction of natural resources.

3. A building site or construction or installation project constitutes a permanent establishment only if it lasts more than twelve months.

4. Notwithstanding the preceding provisions of this Article, the term "permanent establishment" shall be deemed not to include:

   (a) the use of facilities solely for the purpose of storage, display or delivery of goods or merchandise belonging to the enterprise;

   (b) the maintenance of a stock of goods or merchandise belonging to the enterprise solely for the purpose of storage, display or delivery;

   (c) the maintenance of a stock of goods or merchandise belonging to the enterprise solely for the purpose of processing by another enterprise;

   (d) the maintenance of a fixed place of business solely for the purpose of purchasing goods or merchandise or of collecting information, for the enterprise;

   (e) the maintenance of a fixed place of business solely for the purpose of carrying on, for the enterprise, any other activity of a preparatory or auxiliary character;

   (f) the maintenance of a fixed place of business solely for any combination of activities mentioned in sub-paragraphs (a) to (e) provided that the overall activity of the fixed place of business resulting from this combination is of a preparatory or auxiliary character.

5. Notwithstanding the provisions of paragraphs 1 and 2, where a person — other than an agent of an independent status to whom paragraph 6 applies — is acting on behalf of an enterprise and has, and habitually exercises, in a Contracting State an authority to conclude contracts in the name of the enterprise, that enterprise shall be deemed to have a permanent establishment

in that State in respect of any activities which that person undertakes for the enterprise, unless the activities of such person are limited to those mentioned in paragraph 4 which, if exercises through a fixed place of business, would not make this fixed place of business a permanent establishment under the provisions of that paragraph.

6. An enterprise shall not be deemed to have a permanent establishment in a Contracting State merely because it carries on business in that State through a broker, general commission agent or any other agent of an independent status, provided that such persons are acting in the ordinary course of their business.

7. The fact that a company which is a resident of a Contracting State controls or is controlled by a company which is a resident of the other Contracting State, or which carries on business in that other State (whether through a permanent establishment or otherwise), shall not of itself constitute either company a permanent establishment of the other.

(iii) Canada-U.S. Treaty

Article IV(3) of the *Canada-U.S. Treaty* provides that:

> Where . . . a company is a resident of both Contracting States, then if it was created under the laws in force in a Contracting State, it shall be deemed to be a resident of that State.

A corporation that is considered to be "dually resident" in both Canada and the United States is deemed to be resident in the place where it was incorporated rather than in the location of its effective management. For example, a U.S. corporation that is effectively managed in Canada is a Canadian resident by virtue of the common law test and a U.S. corporation under the statutory test. Article IV(3) breaks the deadlock of dual residence by deeming the corporation to be a U.S. corporation for treaty purposes.

Some jurisdictions allow local incorporation of an entity that is already organized and incorporated under the laws of another country. Under Article IV(3), however, the determative factor is the location of the corporation's original creation.[56]

(iv) Anti-treaty Shopping

The above discussion makes it clear that taxpayers (particularly corporate taxpayers) can arrange their affairs to take advantage of the rules that determine residence by virtue of specific statutory provisions. For example, a corporation may be incorporated (or not incorporated) in a particular jurisdiction in order to locate (or not locate) its residence in that place. This might allow the corporation to reduce its tax by virtue of bilateral tax treaties negotiated by the particular jurisdiction.

There is little doubt that there is increasing concern in the international community that treaties should limit, or at least restrain, tax planning directed solely at tax

---

[56] See *Revised Technical Explanation — Canada-U.S. Income Tax Convention 1980* (U.S. Treasury Department).

avoidance through treaty shopping. There can be little doubt that the trend in international communities is towards placing greater restrictions on the "improper" use of tax treaties. Thus, just as we see domestic statutory restrictions (for example, GAAR[57]) on the application of the *Westminster*[58] principle, so also do we see increasing restrictions appearing in bilateral tax treaties that are intended to curtail what would otherwise be legitimate tax avoidance. Article XXIXA of the *Canada-U.S. Treaty*, for example, limits the benefits of the treaty to "qualifying persons", a phrase that is restrictively defined. The Article also allows the authorities to deny the benefits of the treaty where it is used in an abusive manner.

(A) *OECD Model Convention*

The *OECD Model Convention* considers the improper use of bilateral tax conventions in its commentary on Article I. The commentary states:

> True, taxpayers have the possibility, double tax conventions being left aside, to exploit the differences in tax levels as between States and the tax advantages provided by various country's taxation laws, but it is for the States concerned to adopt provisions in their domestic laws to counter possible manoeuvres. Such States will then wish, in their bilateral double taxation conventions, to preserve the application of provisions of this kind contained in their domestic laws. . . . For example, if a person . . . acted through a legal entity created in a State essentially to obtain treaty benefits which would not be available directly to such person. Another case would be one of an individual having in a Contracting State both his permanent home and all his economic interests, including a substantial participation in a company of that State, and who, essentially in order to sell the participation and escape taxation in that State on the capital gains from the alienation . . . transferred his permanent home to the other Contracting State, where such gains were subject to little or no tax. . . . It may be appropriate for Contracting States to agree in bilateral negotiations that any relief from tax should not apply in certain cases, or to agree that the application of the provisions of domestic laws against tax avoidance should not be affected by the Convention.

The commentary goes on to discuss various approaches which member countries may consider in combatting the problem of tax avoidance through, for example, the use of conduit companies. It suggests that member countries may consider negotiating the use of "look-through" provisions to disallow treaty benefits to corporations that are not owned, directly or indirectly, by residents of the country in which the corporation is a resident. The Commentary suggests the following wording for a "look-through" provision:

> A company which is a resident of a Contracting State shall not be entitled to relief from taxation under this Convention with respect to any item of income, gains or profits unless it is neither owned nor controlled directly or through one or more companies, wherever resident, by persons who are not residents of the first-mentioned State.

The use of such a provision in a Canadian bilateral tax treaty would prevent residents of third party countries from incorporating in Canada in order to take advantage of

---

[57] S. 245.

[58] *C.I.R. v. The Duke of Westminster*, [1936] AC 1 (H.L.) (taxpayer entitled to order affairs so as to minimize tax payable).

Canada's treaty network with other countries. Such anti-treaty shopping provisions have been negotiated by the United States in its treaties with Germany and Mexico.[59]

(B) Canada-Mexico Treaty

Canada has negotiated anti-treaty shopping rules with some countries. Article 27(3) of the *Canada-Mexico Income Tax Convention* (1991), for example, states:[60]

> The Convention shall not apply to any company, trust or partnership that is a resident of a Contracting State and is beneficially owned or controlled directly or indirectly by one or more persons who are not residents of that State, if the amount of the tax imposed on the income or capital of the company, trust or partnership by that State is substantially lower than the amount that would be imposed by the State if all of the shares of the capital stock of the company or all of the interests in the trust or partnership, as the case may be, were beneficially owned by one or more individuals who were residents of that State.

(C) Canada-Barbados Treaty

In other cases, Canada has negotiated that treaty benefits may not apply to specified corporations established in particular jurisdictions. Article XXX(3) of the *Canada-Barbados Income Tax Agreement*,[61] for example, states that it ". . . shall not apply to companies entitled to any special tax benefit under the Barbados *International Business Companies (Exemption from Income Tax Act)* . . . or to companies entitled to any special tax benefits under any similar law enacted by Barbados in addition to or in place of that law".

(D) Canada-U.S. Treaty

Similarly, Article XXIX(6) of the *Canada-U.S. Treaty*[62] denies certain treaty benefits to non-resident-owned investment corporations as defined under section 133 of the *Income Tax Act* or under any similar provision enacted by Canada.

4. TRUSTS

References:

ITA:

Subs. 104(2)   Rules — Trusts

BULLETINS, CIRCULARS & RULINGS:

IT-447	May 30, 1980	Residence of a Trust or Estate
IT-465R	September 19, 1985	Non-Resident Beneficiaries of Trusts

---

[59] See, for example, Article 28 of the *U.S.-Germany Treaty* and Article 17 of the *U.S.-Mexico Treaty*.

[60] Article 27(3), *Canada-Mexico Income Tax Convention*, 8 April 1991, [1992] Can. T.S. No. 15.

[61] *Canada-Barbados Income Tax Agreement*, 22 January 1980, [1980] Can. T.S. No. 29.

[62] *Canada-United States Income Tax Convention*, 26 September 1980, [1984] Can. T.S. No. 15.

A trust is *not* a separate legal entity; it is a legal relationship. For tax purposes, however, a trust is deemed to be an individual.[63] Hence, it is taxable as a person separate and apart from its trustee.

A trust arises where one person (the trustee) is, by law, compelled to hold property for the benefit of some other person (the beneficiary), and the property is held in such a way that the real benefit of the property accrues, not to the trustee, but to the beneficiary. The essence of a trust is that it is a relationship that separates legal title and control of property from its use and enjoyment. The person who controls the property is usually referred to as the trustee; the person for whose use, enjoyment or benefit the property is held is referred to as the beneficiary.

The residence of a trust for tax purposes is a question of fact determined according to the common law rules applicable to individuals. A trust is generally considered to reside where its trustee resides.[64] Where a trust has more than one trustee, it is resident where a majority of its trustees reside, provided that the trust instrument permits majority decisions on all matters within the discretion of the trustees.[65] Canadian courts do not accept the notion that a trust can have a dual residence. In this respect, trusts are quite unlike individuals and corporations that can have dual residences.[66]

The problems of determining the residence of a trust are, however, exacerbated because of the differences between the obligations of trustees and corporate directors. Thus, in the event that a trust has multiple trustees, some of whom are individuals and others corporations, it becomes necessary to determine the residence of each of the trustees according to the common law and applicable statutory rules. For example, an individual trustee's residence may be determined according to the common law tests and the residence of a corporate trustee determined by reference to statutory deeming provisions. The determination of a trust's residence becomes that much more complicated if its trustees are located in different jurisdictions, each with bilateral tax treaties with Canada.

Generally speaking, a trust's residence is determined by the residence of its trustees and not by the residence of its beneficiaries or the residence of its settlor. Furthermore,

---

[63] Subs. 104(2).

[64] *McLeod v. Min. of Customs & Excise*, [1917-27] CTC 290, 1 DTC 85 (S.C.C.) (taxation of accumulated income in hands of trustee); *M.N.R. v. Royal Trust Co.*, [1928-34] CTC 74, 1 DTC 217 (S.C.C.) (trust with non-resident beneficiaries but resident trustee taxable); *M.N.R. v. Holden*, [1928-34] CTC 127, 1 DTC 234; varied on other grounds [1928-34] CTC 129, 1 DTC 243 (P.C.) (trust taxed on undistributed income whether beneficiaries resident or not); *Williams v. Singer*, [1921] 1 AC 65 (H.L.) (trust not taxed on foreign dividends received for non-resident beneficiary); *I.R.C. v. Gull*, [1937] 4 All ER 290 (English charitable trust exempt where one trustee non-resident).

[65] *Thibodeau v. The Queen*, [1978] CTC 539, 78 DTC 6376 (F.C.T.D.); see also IT-447, "Residence of a Trust or Estate" (May 30, 1980).

[66] IT-447, "Residence of a Trust or Estate" (May 30, 1980).

the residence of a trust is not easily determined by the "central management and control" test because trustees cannot delegate any of the authority to co-trustees.

Given the uncertainty associated with determining the residency of a trust, it is crucial that non-resident trusts provide that at least a majority of the trustees are non-residents of Canada. Further, it is probably prudent that all meetings of the trustees are held outside of Canada and that the majority of the trust's assets are invested outside Canada. In the event that a non-resident trust has a "protector", it is preferable that the protector is not a Canadian resident. Further, the protector should not have the unrestricted power to appoint and remove trustees.

5. PARTNERSHIPS

Reference:

ITA:

Subs. 96(1)   General Rules — Partnerships

Partnership is the relationship that subsists between persons carrying on business in common with a view to profit.[67] A partnership is a *relationship* between persons; it is *not* a separate legal entity.

For income tax purposes, partnership income is calculated *as if* the partnership were a separate person.[68] The character of the partnership's income, however, flows through to each partner when it is allocated by the partnership to its partners.

Members of a partnership who are individuals are taxed as individuals. Corporate partners are taxed as corporations. The residence of each partner must be separately determined. The residence of corporate partners is determined according to the rules applicable to corporations.

A "Canadian partnership" is a partnership of which all the members are resident in Canada.[69]

6. NON-RESIDENTS

References:

ITA:

S. 128.1   Deemed Dispositions and Acquisitions on Ceasing or Acquiring Residence

---

[67] *Partnerships Act*, R.S.O. 1990, c. P.5, s. 2.

[68] Para. 96(1)(*a*).

[69] S. 102. Only Canadian partnerships are eligible for certain rollovers; see, e.g., subs. 98(3).

BULLETINS, CIRCULARS & RULINGS:

IT-163R2	September 19, 1985	Election by Non-Resident Individuals on Certain Canadian Source Income
IT-171R2	March 30, 1992	Non-Resident Individuals — Computation of Taxable Income Earned in Canada and Non-refundable Tax Credits
IT-420R3	March 30, 1992	Non-Residents — Income Earned in Canada
IT-465R	September 19, 1985	Non-Resident Beneficiaries of Trusts
IC 77-16R4	May 11, 1992	Non-Resident Income Tax

Canada taxes its residents on their world wide income and non-residents on Canadian source income.

A non-resident person is liable to Canadian tax only if, at any time either in the current year or a previous year, he or she was employed in Canada, carried on business in Canada, or disposed of taxable Canadian property.[70] This rule is subject to overriding provisions in Canadian tax treaties.

An individual is considered to be employed in Canada if he or she performs the duties of an office or employment in Canada, regardless whether or not the employer is resident in Canada.[71] There are, however, certain non-resident persons who are *deemed* to have been employed in Canada in the year.[72]

A non-resident person is considered to be carrying on business in Canada if he or she is engaged in a business activity, solicits orders, or offers anything for sale in Canada.[73] "Business" includes a profession, calling, trade, manufacturer or undertaking of any kind whatever, and an adventure or concern in the nature of trade.[74]

Whether a person is carrying on business in Canada is a question of fact. The following criteria are relevant in answering the question:

---

[70] Subs. 2(3).

[71] Subs. 248(1) ("employment") and ("office"). Only an individual can be an employee or officer.

[72] Subs. 115(2).

[73] S. 253. Canvassing for business may be construed as solicitation for orders, even though it falls short of offering for sale. Thus, solicitation of orders falls somewhere between an invitation to treat and an offer in law; see *Sudden Valley Inc. v. The Queen*, [1976] CTC 297, 76 DTC 6178; affirmed [1976] CTC 775, 76 DTC 6448 (F.C.A.).

[74] Subs. 248(1) ("business"); *Tara Explo. & Dev. Co. v. M.N.R.*, [1970] CTC 557, 70 DTC 6370; affirmed [1972] CTC 328 (*sub nom. M.N.R. v. Tara Explo. & Dev. Co.*) (S.C.C.) (foreign company taxable on incidental Canadian securities but not under tax treaty); *The Queen v. Gurd's Prods. Co.*, [1985] 2 CTC 85, 85 DTC 5314 (F.C.A.), leave to appeal to S.C.C. refused 64 NR 156 (sufficient indicia of business outweighed sham argument that company only pretended to operate from Canada).

- Presence of a physical establishment in Canada;[75]
- Presence of an inventory in Canada, whether in an owned establishment or rented warehouse;
- The location where contracts are executed;[76]
- The location where goods are delivered;
- The location where payment is received; and
- Presence of agents responsible for soliciting orders and offering merchandise for sale.[77]

A non-resident company carrying on business in Canada at any time in a taxation year is required to pay a "branch tax" in addition to Part I tax.[78]

A non-resident person who disposes of "taxable Canadian property" in Canada is liable for tax on a portion of the gains therefrom.[79]

---

[75] *C.I.T. (Bombay) v. Govindram Seksaria*, [1937] ITR 584.

[76] See, generally, *Ross & Co. v. M.N.R.*, [1967] Tax ABC 594, 67 DTC 421 (T.A.B.) (Bahamian corporation taxable on Canadian profits from disposition of shares in Canada through Toronto securities dealer); *Geigy (Can.) Ltd. v. Social Services Tax Commr.*, [1969] CTC 79 (B.C.S.C.) (drugs manufactured and orders received and accepted at Montreal Head Office; only sales promotion in B.C.). A useful summary of the rules is contained in *Crookston Bros. v. Furtado* (1910), 5 Tax Cas. 602 at 615 (Scot.):
> Viewing the matter in the light of authority, I consider that the following propositions may be deduced from the numerous cases which have been decided — In the first place if contracts are concluded by or on behalf of a foreigner, and the goods delivered and payments made, all within the United Kingdom, it seems clear that the foreigner will be held to exercise a trade in this country. Next, I think the result will be the same if the contracts are concluded and deliveries made in this country, although the payments are received abroad.

[77] See *Greenwood v. F.L. Smidth & Co.* (1922), 1 AC 417 (H.L.) (two tests of whether trade carried on are outlined in argument not decision); *Re Procter & Gamble Co.*, [1935-37] CTC 334 (Sask. K.B.) illustrates how the courts will look past words of convenience in a contract; as Taylor J. observed at 336:
> [i]t seems somewhat a refinement of reasoning to suggest that this company is not doing business within the province. The fact is that they find a market for their products and advertise in that market extensively by radio announcements, magazines, and other methods. Their salesmen "push" sales here and take orders or offers to purchase from Saskatchewan purchasers. These orders happen to have on them a printed clause that they are not binding on the company until they are accepted by the head office but the practice is to ship these orders without special acceptance in any case. They thus sell and deliver into Saskatchewan annually about $300,000 of their products. That seems to be doing a pretty good business in Saskatchewan.

[78] S. 219.

[79] Subs. 248(1) ("taxable Canadian property") and para. 115(1)(*b*).

7. EXEMPT PERSONS

Reference:

ITA:

S. 149   Exemptions

REGULATION:

3400   International Development Assistance Programs

Certain persons who might otherwise be considered residents of Canada are specifically exempted from Canadian income tax. These include:[80]

- Persons holding diplomatic and quasi-diplomatic positions in Canada, members of their families and their servants;
- Municipal authorities;
- Municipal or provincial corporations;
- Registered charities;
- Labour organizations;
- Non-profit clubs, societies or associations ("NPOs");[81]
- Prescribed small business investment corporations;[82]
- Registered pension funds and trusts;
- Trusts created for:
- employee profit sharing plans;
- registered supplementary unemployment benefit plans;
- registered retirement savings plans;
- deferred profit sharing plans;
- registered education savings plans;
- retirement compensation arrangements.

These persons are exempt from tax only if they satisfy all of the conditions necessary for attaining exempt status.

---

[80] S. 149. The persons listed in this section are exempt from Part I tax. Subs. 227(14) extends the exemption for taxes under other parts to corporations exempt under s. 149.

[81] An election by an NPO for the purposes of GST legislation does not, in and of itself, adversely affect its tax exempt status for income tax purposes: Technical Interpretation (August 27, 1990), Revenue Canada.

[82] Para. 149(1)(*o.3*); Reg. 5101(1).

8. PROVINCIAL RESIDENCE

References:

REGULATIONS:

2601	Residents of Canada — Income Earned in a Province
2606(2)	Business Income in a Province, Calculation
2606(3)	Business Income in a Province, Definitions

Canadian residents are liable for federal and provincial tax on their world-wide income. The rate of provincial tax is set by the provinces, but the taxable base on which provincial tax is applied is determined under the federal Act.

Except for Quebec, all of the provinces have entered into tax collection agreements with the federal government. These agreements allow the federal government to act on behalf of the provinces to collect their share of individual income taxes.

For provincial income tax purposes, an individual is deemed to have been resident *throughout a taxation year* in the province in which he or she resides on December 31 of that year.[83] This rule is administratively convenient and provides an easy way to allocate taxable income earned in a year to the provinces.

Except for Alberta, Ontario and Quebec, the provinces have also entered into tax collection agreements with the federal government to have corporate tax collected on their behalf.

9. ATTRIBUTION RULES

References:

ITA:

Subs. 56(2)	Indirect Payments
Subs. 56(4.1)	Interest Free or Low Interest Loans
Subs. 56(4.2)	Loans for Value
S. 74.1	Transfers and Loans to Spouse, Minors
S. 74.2	Deemed Gain or Loss
S. 74.5	Transfers for Value
S. 160	Non-Arm's Length Transfer

BULLETINS, CIRCULARS & RULINGS:

IT-335R	September 11, 1989	Indirect Payments

---

[83] *Federal-Provincial Fiscal Arrangements and Federal Post-secondary Education and Health Contributions Act*, R.S.C. 1985, c. F-8, subpara. 10(a)(i).

(a) Purpose

The general rule in income tax law is that the person who receives or earns income is liable for any tax payable on that income. Without more, however, this rule would be an invitation for high income taxpayers to reduce their taxes by shifting their income to lower income family members. For example, an individual with a high marginal tax rate may be tempted to transfer investments to his or her spouse with a lower marginal rate so that any income from investments is taxable to the lower income spouse. There are attribution rules that prevent such blatant forms of income shifting. There is also a general anti-avoidance rule ("GAAR") to control "abusive" forms of tax avoidance.[84]

The attribution rules protect the integrity of the progressive tax rate system as it applies to individuals.[85] The rules are of two types: General rules to prevent income splitting and specific rules which protect the integrity of the general rules.

(b) Indirect Payments

A taxpayer who transfers income or property to another taxpayer may be deemed to have constructively received the diverted income or property.[86] For example, an individual who deposits his or her pay cheque directly into his or her spouse's savings account remains liable for tax on the salary, despite having relinquished actual ownership and control over the property. The taxpayer is considered to retain constructive ownership of the property for tax purposes. The purpose of this rule is to prevent taxpayers from artificially reducing their income by diverting funds to other persons so as to lower their marginal rate of tax.

The doctrine of constructive receipt of income applies to a taxpayer where:[87]

- there is an actual payment or transfer of property to a person,
- at the direction, or with the concurrence, of the taxpayer,
- that is made for the taxpayer's benefit or for the benefit of a person whom the taxpayer wishes to benefit,
- and the payment is of a type that would ordinarily have been included in the taxpayer's income if he or she had received it directly.

---

[84] See Chapter XXVI "Administration".

[85] S. 56, subss. 74.1(1) and (2). Special rules apply in respect of farm property transferred by a farmer to a child if the child disposes of the property before attaining 18 years of age: s. 75.1.

[86] Subs. 56(2); see also IT-335R, "Indirect Payments" (September 11, 1989).

[87] Subs. 56(2).

In these circumstances the transferor is deemed to be in constructive receipt of the diverted payment.[88]

Directors of a corporation who declare a dividend do so in their capacity as directors and fiduciaries. Thus, they are not considered to have constructively received any dividends that they declare on behalf of the corporation.[89] As a general rule, subsection 56(2) does not apply to dividends.[90]

(c) Transfers of Rights to Income

The doctrine of constructive receipt also applies where *rights to receive income* (as opposed to the income itself) are transferred to another individual.[91] The essence of this type of transfer is that the individual transfers the right to all future income but not the ownership of the income-generating property. Thus, the transferee then owns the *right to all future income or revenues* yielded by the property, but does not own the property itself. Any transfer of the property itself would be caught by subsection 56(2).

(d) Interest-free or Low Interest Loans

A taxpayer can also shift his or her tax burden by loaning money at rates lower than the commercial rate of interest. For example, in the simplest case, an individual can make an interest-free loan. Where the purpose of the loan is to reduce or avoid tax

---

[88] *McClurg v. M.N.R.*, [1991] 1 CTC 169, 91 DTC 5001 (S.C.C.) (income not attributed to director of corporation for participating in declaration of corporate dividend); *Boardman v. The Queen*, [1986] 1 CTC 103, 85 DTC 5628 (F.C.T.D.) (shareholder taxable on diversion of corporate assets to settle financial obligations on divorce); *M.N.R. v. Bronfman*, [1965] CTC 378, 65 DTC 5235 (Ex. Ct.) (directors of corporation liable for taxes on account of gifts to relatives in need of financial assistance; combining subss. 15(1) and 56(2)); *Reininger v. M.N.R.*, 58 DTC 608 (corporate loan to wife of principal shareholder taxable to him under subss. 15(2) and 56(2)); *Perrault v. The Queen*, [1978] CTC 395, 78 DTC 6272 (F.C.A.) (waiver of dividend by majority shareholder in favour of minority shareholder was dividend income); *New v. M.N.R.*, [1970] Tax ABC 700, 70 DTC 1415 (T.A.B.) (controlling shareholder in receipt of income for benefit conferred on son through rental of corporate property to son at less than fair market value).

[89] *The Queen v. McClurg*, [1988] 1 CTC 75, 88 DTC 6047 (F.C.A.), *per* Urie J.:

The language of the subsection [56(2)] creating the essential ingredients required in its application, viewed in light of its purpose, is simply not apt, in my opinion, to encompass the acts of a director when he participates in the declaration of a corporate dividend unless it is read in its most literal sense. To do so ignores the existence of the corporate entity. Only the most explicit language, which is not present in subs. 56(2), would justify the notion that a director acting as such could be seen as directing a corporation to divert a transfer or payment for his own benefit or the benefit of another person, absent bad faith, breach of fiduciary duty or acting beyond the powers conferred by the share structure of the corporation, none of which bases have been alleged here.;

affirmed, [1991] 1 CTC 169, 91 DTC 5001 (S.C.C.).

[90] *Neuman v. M.N.R.*, [1994] 1 CTC 354, 94 DTC 6094 (F.C.T.D.) (dividends paid to controlling shareholder's spouse not taxable in his hands despite absence of any "contribution" by spouse).

[91] Subs. 56(4).

and the money is loaned to a non-arm's length person, the borrower's income from the loan is deemed to be the income of the lender.[92] Any income from property substituted for the loan and income from property purchased with the loan is also included in the lender's income.

Example III.1

(i) An individual loans $50,000 to her spouse who earns 10 per cent by depositing the money in a GIC. The $5,000 interest earned is included in her income for the year.

(ii) An individual loans $100,000 to his niece at 5 per cent interest per year. The niece purchases an investment certificate yielding 8 per cent per year. The income from the investment certificate ($8,000) minus the amount paid as interest ($5,000) by the niece is income to the individual.

(e) Transfers/Loans to Spouse

An individual who transfers or loans property, directly or indirectly, to his or her spouse or to a person who becomes his or her spouse after the transfer or loan of property, is taxable on any income from the property or from any property substituted for the transferred property. Any income or loss generated by the transferred or loaned property is attributed to the transferor during his or her lifetime, so long as he or she remains resident in Canada and continues to live with the transferee spouse.[93] Any taxable capital gains and allowable capital losses from dispositions of the transferred or loaned property are also attributed to the transferor.[94] Thus, in both cases, the transferor is deemed to have constructively received the transferred income (loss) or taxable gain (loss).

(f) Transfers/Loans to Persons Under 18 Years of Age

An individual who transfers or loans property to a person under 18 years of age who is the transferor's niece or nephew or does not deal at arm's length with the transferor, is taxable on any income earned on the property.[95] Thus, income and losses realized by the recipient of the transferred property are attributed to the person who transferred or loaned the property.

---

[92] Subs. 56(4.1).

[93] Subs. 74.1(1). *The Queen v. Kieboom*, [1992] 2 CTC 59, 92 DTC 6382 (F.C.A.) (income from taxpayer's gift of non-voting shares to wife and children subject to attribution).

[94] Subs. 74.2(1).

[95] Subs. 74.1(2).

(g) Non-arm's Length Loans

The two rules discussed above (loans and transfers to spouses and to certain persons under 18 years of age) prevent taxpayers from engaging in the more blatant forms of income splitting.

There is, however, an additional rule that is even broader: Income from any property (for example, money) loaned to a non-arm's length borrower may be attributed and taxed to the lender if one of the main purposes of the loan is to reduce or avoid tax, for example, by income splitting.[96] This rule is considerably broader in scope than the more specific attribution rules in that it applies to low cost or interest-free loans to any individual with whom the lender does not deal at arm's length. This rule does not apply to transfers of property; it only applies to loaned property.

Unlike the more specific attribution rules, the non-arm's length rule may be applied only if it is established that the lender loaned the property for the purposes of reducing or avoiding tax on income that would otherwise have been earned on the loaned property. A loan for a purpose other than tax reduction or avoidance (for example, a loan made for altruistic reasons to a relative or friend) is not subject to the attribution rule.

There is no attribution of income if the loan is made at the prescribed rate of interest and the interest is paid to the lender no later than 30 days after the end of the particular taxation year.[97]

(h) Interpretation and Application

The following aspects of the attribution rules warrant particular attention:

- The term "transfer" is interpreted very widely to include any divestiture of property from one person to another and includes gifts. In *Fasken Estate*, for example, the courts said:[98]

  > [t]he word "transfer" is not a form of art and has not a technical meaning. It is not necessary to a transfer of property from a husband to his wife that it should be made in any particular form or that it should be made directly. All that is required is that the husband should so deal with the property as to divest himself of it and vest it in his wife, that is to say, pass the property from himself to her. The means by which he accomplishes this result, whether direct or circuitous may properly be called a transfer.

---

[96]   Subs. 56(4.1).

[97]   Subs. 56(4.2).

[98]   *Fasken Estate v. M.N.R.*, [1948] CTC 265 at 279, 4 DTC 491 at 497 (Ex. Ct.); see also *St. Aubyn v. A.G.*, [1952] AC 15 at 53 (H.L.), per Lord Radcliffe:

> If the word "transfer" is taken in its primary sense, a person makes a transfer of property to another person if he does the act or executes the instrument which divests him of the property and at the same time vests it in that other person.

- Attribution only applies to income and losses from transferred *property* and not to income and losses from a business.[99]

- The attribution rules do not generally apply to sales at fair market value, provided that the vendor is paid for the property.[100]

- Loans, other than loans that bear a commercial rate of interest, are subject to the attribution rules. A loan is considered to bear a commercial rate of interest if the rate charged is at least equal to the prescribed rate or the arm's length market rate.[101]

- In the case of a transfer or loan to a person under the age of 18, income attribution continues until the person reaches 18 years of age.

- Tax liability from the application of the attribution rules is joint and several.[102]

- The income attribution rules only apply to spouses during the period that they are married *and* living together. The rules cease to apply upon divorce or separation by reason of matrimonial breakdown.[103]

- There is no attribution of capital gains and losses following divorce or separation pursuant to matrimonial breakdown,[104] provided that the parties file a joint election precluding attribution. The election must be filed in the year the parties begin to live separate and apart.

---

[99] See *Robins v. M.N.R.*, [1963] CTC 27, 63 DTC 1012 (Ex. Ct.) where Noel J. had this to say about the predecessor sections to s. 74.1:

> Section 21 as well as Sections 22 and 23 are designed to prevent avoidance of tax by transfer of income producing property to persons who are normally in close relationship with the transferor. But what is deemed to be the income of the transferor, and this is clearly stated, is income from property only. Indeed, there is no mention of income from a business such as we have here and, therefore, this section can be of no assistance in determining whether the business profit resulting from a real estate transaction is taxable as income of the appellant or his wife.

See, also, *Wertman v. M.N.R.*, [1964] CTC 252, 64 DTC 5158 (spouses' joint investment in building with funds from community property); *M.N.R. v. Minden*, [1963] CTC 364, 63 DTC 1231 (Ex. Ct.) (lawyer advanced money to spouse for investments without documentation, interest or security). For the distinction between income from business and income from property see Chapter VI "Business and Investment Income: General".

[100] Subs. 74.5(1).

[101] Subs. 74.5(2).

[102] Para. 160(1)(*d*).

[103] Para. 74.5(3)(*a*).

[104] Para. 74.5(3)(*b*).

10. INDIANS

Reference:

BULLETINS, CIRCULARS & RULINGS:

IT-62   August 18, 1972   Indians

Indians are citizens subject to all of the responsibilities of other Canadian citizens except for those responsibilities governed by treaties or the *Indian Act*.[105] Thus, Indians are liable for taxes except when they are specifically exempted from taxation.

(a) Exemption from Tax

The tax status of Indians is determined for the most part by two statutes: The *Indian Act*[106] and the *Income Tax Act*.

The principal provision is section 87 of the *Indian Act* which provides as follows:

> . . . Notwithstanding any other Act of the Parliament of Canada or any Act of the legislature of a province . . . the following property is exempt from taxation, namely:
>
> (a) the interest of an Indian or a band in reserve or surrendered lands; and
>
> (b) the personal property of an Indian or band situated on a reserve;
>
> and no Indian or band is subject to taxation in respect of the ownership, occupation, possession, or use of any property mentioned in paragraph (a) or (b) or is otherwise subject to taxation in respect of any such property. . . .

This exemption is recognized by paragraph 81(1)(*a*) of the *Income Tax Act*, which exempts from taxation "an amount that is declared to be exempt from income tax by any other enactment of the Parliament of Canada".

The exemption from taxation is only available where the following circumstances co-exist:

- the taxpayer claiming the exemption qualifies as an "Indian or a band";
- the property is either an interest in reserve or surrendered lands or is personal property; and
- the property is *situated* on a reserve.

Certain properties are deemed to be situated on a reserve. Subsection 90(1) of the *Indian Act* reads as follows:

> For the purposes of ss. 87 and 89, personal property that was
>
> (a) purchased by Her Majesty with Indian monies or monies appropriated by Parliament for the use and benefit of Indians or bands, or

---

[105] *Nowegijick v. The Queen*, [1983] 1 SCR 29, [1983] CTC 20, 83 DTC 5041.

[106] *Indian Act*, R.S.C. 1985, c. I-5.

(b) given to Indians or to a band under a treaty or agreement between a band and Her Majesty,

shall be deemed always to be situated on a reserve.

The exemption of Indians from taxation is rooted in Canadian political history and has no connection whatsoever to income tax policy. Section 87 of the *Indian Act* is more than sufficient authority for the exemption ("Notwithstanding any other Act of the Parliament of Canada. . . ."). It does not need to be bolstered by section 81 of the *Income Tax Act*.

The purposes of the exemptions from tax are to preserve the entitlement of Indians to their reserve lands and to ensure that property on their lands is not eroded through taxation or seizure.[107] The exemption is a recognition by the Crown, as expressed in the *Royal Proclamation of 1763*, that Indians should not be dispossessed of their property which they hold *qua* Indians. The exemption is intended to shield Indians from non-natives, who might otherwise be included to dispossess Indians of their land base and personal property on their reserves.

Since the exemption is a provision of the *Indian Act*, it should be interpreted in the context of that statute, rather than in terms of tax policy. Hence, the exemption must be read in the light of Canadian history, British colonial philosophy and its intended purposes: The protection of Indian reserve lands and personal property situated on such lands.

(b) "An Indian or a Band"?

The terms, "Indian" and "band", are interpreted according to the meaning given to the words in the *Indian Act*. Section 2 of the *Indian Act* defines an "Indian" as a "person who is registered as an Indian or is entitled to be registered as an Indian". "Band" refers to a body of Indians for whose use, and benefit in common, lands have been set apart as reserves, and moneys have been held or declared to be such on their behalf by order of the federal Cabinet. The determining factor for tax purposes is whether the taxpayer is *"entitled"* to be registered as an Indian and not whether the taxpayer's name appears, correctly or otherwise, on the Band List.[108]

Although section 87 of the *Indian Act* and paragraph 81(1)(*a*) of the *Income Tax Act* appear complementary to each other, the former provision, by its own terms, prevails over any contrary intention that may be expressed or implied in the *Income Tax Act*.[109]

---

[107] *Mitchell v. Peguis Indian Band*, [1990] 2 SCR 85.

[108] *Boadway v. M.N.R.*, [1980] CTC 2382, 80 DTC 1321 (T.R.B.).

[109] *Greyeyes v. The Queen*, [1978] CTC 91, 78 DTC 6043 (F.C.T.D.).

(i) Entitlement to Status and Band Membership

The following individuals are entitled to registered status and band membership:[110]

- Those individuals already on the Indian Register or on a Band List, whether or not they were or are "entitled" legally to have their name on the list;[111]

- Those individuals who were entitled to be "registered Indians" under the *Indian Act* before April 17, 1985, whether or not their name actually appeared on a Band List or the Indian Register;[112]

- Anyone who belongs to a group that is declared by the federal Cabinet after April 17, 1985 to be an Indian Band;[113]

- Women who lost status by marrying a man who was not a registered Indian;[114]

- Children who lost status when their mother was disenfranchised for marrying a man who was not a registered Indian;[115]

- Children caught by the "double-mother rule" because their mother and father's mother were not status Indians before their marriage;[116]

- Children born outside legal marriage whose registration as status Indians was rejected because their mother was status but their father was not, or because they were female children of only one status parent;[117] and

- Anyone born on or after April 17, 1985 both of whose parents are entitled to status and to membership in the same band, whether his or her parents are alive or not.[118]

---

[110] *Indian Act*, R.S.C. 1985, c. I-5.

[111] Para. 6(1)(*a*).

[112] Para. 6(1)(*a*).

[113] Para. 6(1)(*b*).

[114] Para. 6(1)(*cc*).

[115] Para. 6(1)(*cc*).

[116] Para. 6(1)(*cc*).

[117] Para. 6(1)(*c*).

[118] Para. 6(1)(*f*).

(ii) Entitlement to Status but not to Band Membership

The following individuals are entitled to status but not to immediate band membership:[119]

- Any Native person who voluntarily disenfranchised, including wives or dependent, unmarried children who lost status due to a man's voluntary disenfranchisement;[120]

- Anyone who lost status for residing outside the country for more than five years prior to 1951 without consent of an Indian agent;[121]

- Anyone who lost status as a result of becoming a lawyer, doctor, minister or university graduate before 1920;[122]

- Anyone, both of whose parents are entitled to be registered for any reason under the new *Indian Act*, whether his or her parents are alive or not;[123] and

- Anyone who has only one parent who is entitled to status under any of the previous categories, whether that parent is alive or not.[124]

(c) "Reserve"

A "reserve" is defined as a tract of land, legally owned by the federal government but set aside for the use and benefit of a "band of Indians".[125] A band may surrender or release its interest in reserve lands but the surrender may only be made to the government.

The personal property of an Indian person or a band situated on surrendered lands does not qualify for exemption from tax. In certain circumstances, however, Revenue Canada takes the view that "surrendered lands" continue to be a "reserve".[126] It is the *property*, not the *person*, that is required to be situated on a reserve.[127]

---

[119] *Indian Act*, R.S.C. 1985, c. I-5.

[120] Para. 6(1)(*d*).

[121] Subpara. 6(1)(*e*)(i).

[122] Subpara. 6(1)(*e*)(ii).

[123] Para. 6(1)(*f*).

[124] Subs. 6(2).

[125] Subs. 2(1).

[126] IT-62, "Indians" (August 18, 1972), para. 6(m).

[127] *Greyeyes v. The Queen*, [1978] CTC 91, 78 DTC 6043 (F.C.T.D.).

(d) Corporations

The exemption from taxation only applies to an "Indian or a band". A corporate entity does not ordinarily qualify under either of these categories and is not entitled to the benefit of the exemption created by section 87 of the *Indian Act*.

In *Kinookimaw Beach Assn.*,[128] the association claimed exemption from provincial education and hospitalization tax on the basis that it was a corporate entity formed by seven Indian bands for the purposes of developing reserve lands as a resort area. The taxpayer urged the Saskatchewan Court of Appeal to pierce the corporate veil of the association so that it might claim the benefit of tax exempt status under the *Indian Act*. The Court refused to pierce the corporate veil. Culliton C.J.S. said:[129]

> . . . the autonomous and independent existence of the corporate structure must be accepted and respected unless it can be shown that such structure is being deliberately used to defeat the intent and purpose of a particular law, or is intended to or does convey a false picture of independence between one or more corporate entities which, if recognized, would result in the defeat of a just and equitable right.

The association had not been incorporated with an intent to evade the purposes of the taxing statute. In the Court's words:[130]

> In this case no attempt has been made to evade the intent and purpose of the taxing statute through the corporate structure, nor is there any doubt as to the true legal position of the Association as related to the Indian bands. Here the Indian bands decided that the most efficient manner of attaining their objectives was through a corporate structure.

It is ironic that the association was held liable to tax as a corporate entity because it had not been incorporated with an intent to avoid tax. Had the association been created with an intent to avoid taxes, would the Court have been prepared to pierce its corporate veil so that it would not be taxable?

A corporation is a legal entity which exists independently of the character or status of its shareholders. Hence, the status of any or all of its shareholders or the presence of a registered office on or off a reservation has no bearing in law on the status of the corporation.[131] Situating a corporation on the reserve, however, may affect the *situs* of its debts and obligations.

Although a corporation *per se* does not qualify for exemption from tax, a corporation that is owned by an Indian Band that constitutes a municipality is exempt from income tax.[132]

---

[128] *Kinookimaw Beach Assn. v. Sask.*, [1979] 6 WWR 84 (Sask. C.A.).

[129] *Id.*, at 88-89.

[130] *Id.*, at 89.

[131] *Re Stony Plain Indian Reserve No. 135*, [1982] 1 WWR 302 (Alta. C.A.).

[132] *Otineka Development Corporation v. M.N.R.*, [1994] 1 CTC 2424, 94 DTC 1234 (T.C.C.).

(e) Structure of *Indian Act*

The *Indian Act* gives the Indian a choice in respect of his or her tax structure: Situate property on a reserve and protect it from taxation and seizure or locate it off reserve and subject it to the ordinary commercial and tax rules of society at large. Thus, the exemption for Indians comes down to two factors:

1. the determination of income as personal property; and
2. the situs of the property on a reserve.

"Income" is "property",[133] as is "taxable income": "A tax on income is in reality a tax on property itself. If income can be said to be property I cannot think that taxable income is any less so".[134] Taxable income is income subject to specific calculation in order to determine the quantum of tax. Thus, the exemption in section 87 applies to both persons and property.[135]

(f) Situs

The second factor in determining whether an Indian is exempt from tax on a specific source or type of income is the situs of the property or source from which the income is earned. The exemption applies only to property *situated* on a reserve.

In private law, the *situs* of property depends upon the rules of property law and private international law. The private law rules were traditionally also applied to tax law.

In 1992, however, the Supreme Court of Canada, which had earlier begun to move towards purposive interpretation, made a radical shift in the meaning of situs for tax purposes.[136] Situs under the *Indian Act* must be determined according to the purpose of the statute, not the purposes of the conflict of laws.[137]

The situs of tangible property is where it is physically located.[138] Thus, it is always easy to determine the situs of land since that situs is constant and immovable. Similarly, interests in land flow from the land and are considered to be situated where the land is situated.[139] More specifically, all real property, interests and charges in or over Canadian land are classified as immoveables. This rule applies to freehold land,

---

[133] *Bachrach v. Nelson*, 182 NE 909 (S.C. Ill., 1932).

[134] *Nowegijick v. The Queen, ante*, [1983] 1 SCR at 38, [1983] CTC at 25, 83 DTC at 5045.

[135] *Nowegijick v. The Queen, ante.*

[136] *Glenn Williams v. The Queen*, [1992] 1 CTC 225, 92 DTC 6320 (S.C.C.).

[137] *Glenn Williams v. The Queen, ante*, [1992] 1 CTC at 231, 92 DTC at 6325.

[138] *Cammell v. Sewell* (1860), 157 ER 1371 (Ex. Ch.).

[139] *Philipson-Stow v. I.R.C.*, [1960] 3 All ER 814 (H.L.).

leasehold interests, freehold land that is subject to a trust, rent charges, mineral rights, and to the interest of a mortgagee.[140]

The situs of tangible property other than land is more difficult to determine. Since tangible property (other than land) may be movable, its situs may change from time to time. Thus, unlike land, the situs of tangible movable property must be determined as at a particular time. The general rule in respect of tangible property (other than land) is that the property is considered to be situated where it is to be found. Special rules apply in respect of moving objects such as ships and aircraft.

In determining the situs of personal property, however, it is necessary to have regard to the purposes underlying the *Indian Act* and not merely the rules of private law.[141] One should look at all relevant connecting factors in the light of:

- the purpose of the exemption;
- the type of property; and
- the nature of the tax on of the particular type of property.[142]

Thus, the rules of private international law should be applied in the context of the "connecting factors" between the property and the purposes of the *Indian Act*. The principles of tax policy and tax equity have minimal, if any, influence in the determination of situs of property other than land.

(i) Statutory Situs

Section 90 of the *Indian Act* declares that:

(1) For the purposes of sections 87 and 89, personal property that was

    (a) purchased by Her Majesty with Indian moneys or moneys appropriated by Parliament for the use and benefit of Indians or bands, or

    (b) given to Indians or to a band under a treaty or agreement between a band and Her Majesty,

shall be deemed always to be situated on a reserve.

Section 90 creates a statutory situs in respect of "property" which is the subject of certain Crown obligations, whether such obligations were created under a treaty or otherwise. "Treaties and statutes relating to Indians" are liberally interpreted.[143] Thus, it is well accepted that section 90 covers more than personal property transferred to

---

[140] Castel, *Canadian Conflict of Laws* (Toronto: Butterworths, 1986), at 400.

[141] *Glenn Williams v. The Queen*, [1992] 1 CTC 225; 92 DTC 6320 (S.C.C.).

[142] *Glenn Williams v. The Queen*, ante, [1992] 1 CTC at 232, 92 DTC at 6326.

[143] *Nowegijick v. The Queen*, [1983] CTC 20, 83 DTC 5041 (S.C.C.).

Indians pursuant to a treaty or agreement. The section also covers payments and rebates paid by a provincial government or the federal government.[144]

(ii) Intangible Property

The determination of the situs of intangible property is even more complicated than the determination of the situs of tangible property. By definition, intangible property is incorporeal and does not have any physical existence. The situs of intangible property is determined according to special rules with respect to each type or category of property. As a general rule, however, the situs of intangible property is where the property is dealt with by persons who are involved with, and interested in, its existence and management.[145]

(iii) Corporate Shares

Corporate shares are considered to be situated where they can be dealt with effectively.[146] McLeod states the proposition as follows:[147]

> Shares in a limited company are situate where, in the ordinary course of business, they can be dealt with so as to bind the company.

Hence, the situs of shares will vary according to the manner in which the shares can be transferred so as to effectively bind the corporation. The manner in which shares may be transferred is determined by reference to the statute under which the corporation is incorporated. The situs of shares which can be transferred by delivery is determined

---

[144] *Mitchell v. Peguis Indian Band*, [1990] 2 SCR 85 (specific moneys protected by *Indian Act* not subject to garnishment); *Fayerman Bros. v. Peter Ballantyne Indian Band*, [1986] 1 CNLR 6 (Sask. Q.B.) (application to quash garnishment before judgment; money paid constituted personal property and consequently exempt); *Fricke v. Mitchell,* [1986] 1 WWR 544 (B.C.S.C.) (protected moneys deposited in off-reserve bank remained protected from attachment).

[145] *New York Life Ins. Co. v. Pub. Trustee*, [1924] 2 Ch 101 (C.A.).

[146] *Brassard v. Smith*, [1925] AC 371 (P.C.).

[147] McLeod, *The Conflict of Laws* (Calgary: Carswell, 1983), at 189.

according to where the document is situate.[148] In the case of shares that may only be transferred by registration, situs is where the share register is located.[149]

(A) Transfer under the *Canada Business Corporations Act*

The transfer of securities of corporations incorporated under the *Canada Business Corporations Act*[150] ("CBCA") is governed by Part VII of that statute. The terms, "security" and "security certificate" cover corporate shares issued in bearer or registered form.[151] Every security holder is entitled to a certificate or a non-transferable written acknowledgement of his or her right to obtain a certificate.[152]

A corporation is required to maintain a security register in which it records securities issued in registered form.[153] A security is considered to be in registered form if it specifies the name of the person entitled to the security or to the rights that attach to the security, and its transfer is capable of being recorded in a securities register. A security is also considered to be in registered form if it bears a statement to that effect.[154]

A security is considered to be in bearer form if it is payable to the bearer according to its terms and without need of any endorsement.[155] A corporation is required to

---

[148] *Secretary of State of Can. v. U.S. Alien Property Custodian*, [1931] 1 DLR 890 (S.C.C.) (determination of valid custodian of "enemy" property vested in U.S.A. following First World War); *Winans v. A.G.*, [1910] AC 27 (H.L.) (property passing on death subject to estate duty, apart from character or destination of property).

[149] *Erie Beach Co. v. A.G. Ont.*, [1930] 1 DLR 859 (P.C.) (relevant Companies Act determinative of nature of property in shares for purposes of situs of property passing on death); *Brassard v. Smith*, [1925] AC 371 (Quebec succession duties not leviable on bank shares located in Quebec owned by deceased domiciled elsewhere, as shares transferable only in Nova Scotia; *A.G. v. Higgins* (1857), 157 ER 140 (names of executors inserted into register of shareholders in Scotland); *New York Breweries Co. v. A.G.*, [1899] AC 62 (H.L.) (U.K. company paid interest and dividends due to executors of deceased non-resident and transferred shares and debenture into the names of the executors in the company books in U.K.; since the executors had not obtained probate in U.K., company liable as executors *de son tort*; see Halsbury L.C. at 68); *I.R.C. v. Maple & Co. (Paris)*, [1908] AC 22 (H.L.) (property located in France sold from one U.K. company to another by deed executed in France; property "conveyed" and taxable in U.K.); *Baelz v. Pub. Trustee*, [1926] Ch 863 (situs of shares for income tax purposes distinguished from residence of company); *London & South Amer. Invest. Trust v. Br. Tobacco Co. (Australia)*, [1927] 1 Ch 107 (deduction of withholding on shares held by foreign national disputed as not being asset situate in Australia).

[150] *Canada Business Corporations Act* ("CBCA"), R.S.C. 1985, c. 44.

[151] CBCA, subs. 48(2).

[152] CBCA, subs. 48(1).

[153] CBCA, subs. 50(1).

[154] CBCA, subs. 48(4).

[155] CBCA, subs. 48(6).

maintain a central registry of its securities in Canada. It may, however, maintain branch registers outside Canada.[156]

A corporation is under an obligation to register a transfer of its securities if:

- The security is endorsed by the appropriate person;
- Reasonable assurance is given that the endorsement is genuine and effective;
- Applicable laws relating to the collection of taxes have been complied with;
- The transfer is rightful or is to a *bona fide* purchaser; and
- Any fees payable to the corporation in respect of the issuance of new securities following the transfer have been paid.

(B) Multiple Registries

We saw earlier that the situs of shares that may be transferred by registration depends upon the location of the share register. This rule, however, is predicated on the existence of a single share registry. To avoid ambiguities and difficulties that may result from multiple share registers, it is advisable to maintain a single registry at the corporation's registered head office. If the registered head office of the corporation is located on a reserve, the situs of the shares will also be located on that reserve.

The presence of a share registry at a particular location on a reserve is critical to obtaining the benefits of tax exempt status. The presence of share certificates or the domicile of a shareholder in a place is not sufficient to establish situs in that place.[157] Nor is the presence of a corporate head office in a particular place sufficient to locate its shares in that place.[158] But where there are two or more share registers, the domicile of the shareholder may, if it corresponds with the location of one of the registries, be determinative of the situs of these shares.[159]

It is clear from the above that the determination of situs in circumstances where a corporation maintains multiple registries can be quite complicated and give rise to substantial uncertainty. These problems can best be avoided by maintaining a single registry at the corporation's head office, which, if located on a reserve, will permit tax-exempt status.

---

[156] CBCA, subs. 50(3).

[157] *Re Mathews*, [1938] 2 DLR 763 (Ont. Surr. Ct.) (shares which could only be dealt with outside of Ontario situate outside Ontario, see discussion of promissory notes and foreign bonds); *Treasurer of Ont. v. Blonde*, [1941] OR 227 (C.A.) (only necessary to determine that situs not in jurisdiction, not necessary to prove it is somewhere else).

[158] *Re Macfarlane*, [1933] OR 44 (C.A.).

[159] *Williams v. The King*, [1941] 1 DLR 22; affirmed [1942] 3 D.L.R. 1 (P.C.).

(iv) Partnerships

A share in a partnership is situate where the business is carried on. Where the business is carried on in more than one jurisdiction, the situs of the share is the country where the headquarters of the business are located.[160]

The question to be asked in determining partnership situs is: Where is the business of the partnership located?[161] The focus is on the business of the partnership and not necessarily on the partnership itself. The residence of the partners is not the determining factor. As Lord Herschell said in *Laidlay*:[162]

> My Lords, giving the fullest weight to all the arguments based upon the transactions which were to take place in this country and the residents of partners here, it appears to me impossible to hold that they in any way countervail or get rid of the considerations with which I started, and which point to this being an Indian business, and, therefore, a business the partnership property of which is locally situate in India.

The following factors locate a partnership's business:

- The field of operations, that is, the locality in which the business is conducted;

- The location of partnership assets; and

- The location of the partnership's books and records and the keeping of partnership accounts.

The determination as to where a partnership is conducting its business is a question of fact in each case. The partnership agreement may evidence the partners' intentions in respect of the business. Other factors include:

- where the business is conducted;

- where decisions are made;

- where books and records are kept, and

- how the general process of accounting to the partners is undertaken.[163]

Where the partnership business is carried on in more than one location, the situs of the interest is where the headquarters of the business are located.

---

[160] McLeod, *The Conflict of Laws* (Calgary: Carswell, 1983), at 193.

[161] *Laidlay v. Lord Advocate* (1890), 15 App. Cas. 468 (H.L.).

[162] *Id.*, at 488. See alse *Beaver v. Master in Equity of Supreme Court of Victoria*, [1895] AC 251 (P.C.).

[163] See *Commr. of Stamp Duties v. Salting*, [1907] AC 449 (P.C.).

(v) Trusts

The situs of an interest under a trust depends upon the beneficiary's interest in the trust. McLeod states the rule as follows:[164]

> An interest under a trust, where the beneficiary has a beneficial interest in the trust property, is situate where the trust property is located. An interest under a trust, where the beneficiary has no beneficial interest in the trust property but merely a right of action against the trustee, is situate in the trustee's place of business, i.e., where the action may be brought to enforce the trust obligation.

The interest of a beneficiary under a trust is a chose in action, and the situs of that chose is where the trustees reside and administer the trust.[165]

The trustee is the legal owner of trust property and can freely deal with the property. The beneficiary has a right of enjoyment in the property. Under this theory, the beneficiary has only a right of action against the trustees and, therefore, a chose in action. The proprietary interest has its situs where the trustee administers the trust.[166]

There is, however, another theory: In "substance" a beneficiary of a trust has an interest in its property and it is to the property that she or he looks for the benefit under the trust. Thus, under this theory, a trust is considered a conduit for the transfer of proprietary benefits from the property to the beneficiary. Under the "substance" theory, the beneficiary's interest has its situs where the trust property is located.

It is not clear which theory prevails in any particular situation and this uncertainty makes tax planning somewhat difficult. The "substance" theory has tended to prevail in cases involving taxation. In *M.N.R. v. Trans Can. Invt. Corp.*,[167] for example, the Court maintained that the beneficial owner of corporate shares held by a trust had a direct interest in dividends paid on the shares and that the character of the dividend payments did not change through the intervention of the trustee.

The location of a trust may depend upon its place of administration. Once the place of administration is fixed at the time that the trust is created, the law of that place governs administration for the lifetime of the trust.[168] This rule, however, only applies in the absence of power in the trust instrument which authorizes the trustee(s) to change the place of administration. Where, however, the trustees are expressly given the power to change the place of administration, the power is valid and may be used to change the situs of a trust.

The situs of a trust may be changed in several ways:

---

[164] McLeod, *The Conflict of Laws* (Calgary: Carswell, 1983), at 193.

[165] Waters, *Law of Trusts in Canada* (Toronto: Carswell, 1984), at 1135.

[166] *Id.*, at 1137.

[167] *M.N.R. v. Trans. Canada Invt. Corp.*, [1956] SCR 49, [1955] CTC 275, 55 DTC 1191.

[168] *Re Weston's Settlements; Weston v. Weston*, [1968] 3 All ER 338 (C.A.).

- The trust's funds may be transferred from one jurisdiction into another (for example, non-reserve to reserve). In *Re Seale's Marriage Settlement*,[169] for example, the Court allowed a transfer of funds from a British trust to a Canadian trust because the evidence disclosed that this would be financially advantageous to the trust and would also allow the beneficiary better access to the trustees. Thus, financial considerations may be of sufficient significance to warrant a change of situs.

- Situs may also be changed by making use of rules of a particular jurisdiction. For example, the situs of property such as a specialty debt may be changed if the debt is secured by a mortgage on land. In *Toronto Gen. Trusts Corps.*,[170] the situs of property was changed when a trust was set up for bond holders and secured by a mortgage on land. The jurisdiction in which the land was situated required that the mortgage be registered in the jurisdiction in order for it to be considered valid. Thus, a specialty debt, which normally has its situs where the instrument is physically located, had, in effect, its situs changed to the situs of the land.

(vi) Debts

The situs of a debt depends upon the type of debt and the purpose for which situs is being determined.

For the purposes of conflict of laws, a simple debt, being a personal right due from the debtor, is situated where the debtor resides.[171] The place of residence is the place where the creditor is most likely to be able to serve the debtor and the place where the debtor is most likely to have assets available to satisfy the debt. Where the debtor has more than one residence, the creditor may stipulate one of the residences as the place of payment. The stipulated residence is then considered to be the situs of the debt.

A specialty debt — a debt due under seal or from the Crown — is evidenced by a document, usually under seal. For the purposes of conflict of laws, a specialty debt has its situs where the document evidencing the debt is located, whether or not this corresponds to the debtor's residence. Where there is more than one copy of the document, the situs of the debt is considered to be where the original of the document is located.

A mortgage is a particular type of specialty debt that has two separate aspects: It represents an interest in land and is a personal debt. The interest in land dominates over the personal obligation and the situs of a mortgage is where the land on which the

---

[169] *Re Seale's Marriage Settlement*, [1961] 3 All ER 136.

[170] *Toronto General Trust Corp. v. The King*, [1919] AC 679 (P.C.).

[171] See: North, *Private International Law* (11th Ed. 1987); McLeod, *The Conflict of Laws* (Calgary: Carswell, 1983), at 187.

mortgage is granted is located. Since mortgage documents are usually registered in the local land registry office, the mortgage has its situs in the same location as the land.

A debt does not have a situs until such time as it is payable and recoverable.[172]

Where the debtor is a corporation, the residence of the company is determined by the locality of its principal place of business.[173]

Where a corporation carries on business in more than one jurisdiction, the parties may provide where the debt is to be payable.[174] In the absence of an express or implied provision of where the debt is to be payable a debt is situate where, in the ordinary course of business, it would be paid.[175]

The above principles do not necessarily apply to the situs of debts for purposes of the exemption under the *Indian Act*. Residence of the debtor is an important, but not exclusive, connecting factor for the purposes of the *Indian Act*. The weight to be attached to the debtor's residence depends upon the type of debt under consideration. Other factors to be considered include:

- Residence of the creditor;
- Place where debt is to be paid;
- Location of employment if the debt relates to employment; and
- The status of the debtor (e.g., Crown agency).

Thus, the test for tax purposes is flexible and determined by the type of debt and the context in which it arises. Given the purpose of the exemption, the determinative questions are: To what extent is each factor relevant and does taxation of the particular property erode the rationale of the tax exemption for Indians *qua* Indians?[176]

---

[172] *Re Helbert Wagg & Co.'s Claim*, [1956] Ch 323.

[173] *N. Y. Life Ins. Co. v. Pub. Trustee*, [1924] 2 Ch. 101 (C.A.) (payments out of matured insurance policies involving treaty charge; location of debt an issue); *Re Lawton*, [1945] 4 DLR 8 (Man. C.A.) (insurance money paid to estate claimed taxable by two provinces; thorough analysis of situs of insurance money); *Carron Iron Co. v. Maclaren* (1855), 10 ER 961 (H.L.) (issue of duplication of litigation where company domiciled in England and Scotland) .

[174] *N. Y. Life Ins. Co. v. Pub. Trustee, ante*; *Re Russo-Asiatic Bank Re; Russian Bank for Foreign Trade*, [1934] 1 Ch. 720 (assignments of bills of exchange lost in mail; existence of debtor in question where bank liquidated); *Jabhour v. Custodian of Israeli Absentee Property*, [1954] 1 All ER 145 (situs of chose in action where insurance payment made to Absentee Property Custodian; claim made following explosion in future State of Israel).

[175] *The Queen v. Lovitt*, [1912] AC 212 (P.C.).

[176] *Glenn Williams v. The Queen*, [1992] 1 CTC 225, 92 DTC 6320 (S.C.C.).

(vii) Goodwill

The goodwill of a business is situate where the business premises are located. In *I.R.C. v. Muller & Co.'s Margarine Ltd.*,[177] the House of Lords held that goodwill was not something that could exist as a separate entity, distinct from the property with which it was affiliated. "The combination of a suitable shop with the trade done in it, and the goodwill inducing that trade, seem to me to be inseverable"(*per* Lord Brampton).[178]

---

[177] *I.R.C. v. Muller & Co.'s Margarine Ltd.*, [1901] AC 217 (H.L.).

[178] *Id.*, at 231.

SELECTED BIBLIOGRAPHY TO CHAPTER III

General

Bain, James R., "A Matter of Preference" (1994), 127 *CA Magazine* 43.

Baker, Samuel R., "Carrying on Business Through a Branch and Disposing of Taxable Canadian Property", in *Proceedings of 26th Tax Conf.* 84 (Can. Tax Foundation, 1975).

Bale, "The Basis of Taxation", Chapter 2, *Can. Tax.,* Hansen, Krishna and Rendall, eds., (Toronto: Richard De Boo, 1981).

Balogh, L.V., "Taxation of Income Earned Outside Canada" (1981), *Can. Tax.* 579.

Basran, Jasvinder S., "Individual or Family: Beyond Ability to Pay, An Examination of the Appropriate Unit of Tax in Relation to the Broad Goals and Policies of the Canadian Tax System" (1993), 57 *Sask. Law Rev.* 349.

Crago, Joyce M. "The Unit of Taxation: Current Canadian Issues" (1993), 52 *University of Toronto Fac. Law Rev.* 1.

Dalsin, Derek, T., "Canada-U.S. Dual Resident Corporation: Tax Planning Restricted" (1986), 34 *Can. Tax J.* 621.

"Dual Resident Companies" (1987), *Brit. Tax Rev.* 5.

Friesen, Robert A., "Contemporary Issues in Cross-Border Transactions", in *Proceedings of 38th Tax Conf.* 22 (Can. Tax Foundation, 1986).

Goodman, Wolfe D., "Coping with Deemed Realization of Estates and Trusts" in *Proceedings of 42nd Tax Conf.* (Can. Tax Foundation, 1990).

Goodman, Wolfe D., "Income Tax — Attribution of Income — Non-arm's Length Loans" (1988/89), *Estates and Trusts J.* 77.42

Goodman, Wolfe D., "Splitting Income Between a Trust and its Beneficiaires" (1991), 10 *Estates and Trusts J.* 291.

Gray, Kerry, "U.S. Citizens Employed in Canada: An Update" (1986), 34 *Can. Tax J.* 1463.

Hawkesworth, Kathryn B., "Planning for 1993: Proposed Amendments to the Deemed Realization Rules for Trusts" (1992), 40 *Can. Tax J.* 190.

"Income Tax Residence Rules", in *Proceedings of 15th Tax Conf.* 235 (Can. Tax Foundation, 1961).

Innes, William I., "The Taxation of Indirect Benefits: An Examination of Subsections 56(2), 56(3), 56(4), 245(2), and 245(3) of the Income Tax Act", in *Proceedings of 38th Tax Conf.* 42 (Can. Tax Foundation, 1986).

Ireland, Chris, "Tax Time for Trusts" (1991), 124 *CA Magazine* 27.

Johnson, "Relief from Double Taxation" (1986), 26 *U.T. Fac. L. Rev.* London, Jack R., "The Impact of Changing Perceptions of Social Equity on Tax Policy: The Marital Tax Unit" (1988), 26 *Osgoode Hall Law Journal* 287.

McGregor, Gwyneth, "Deemed Residence" (1974), 22 *Can. Tax J.* 381.

McLean, Bruce M., "Sourcing of Business Income", *Corporate Management Tax Conf.* 9:1 (Can. Tax Foundation, 1987).

McQuillan, Peter and James Thomas, *Understanding the Taxation of Partnerships* (Don Mills, Ont.: CCH Canadian, 1991).

Morris, D. Bernard, "Jurisdiction to Tax: An Update", in *Proceedings of 31st Tax Conf.* 414 (Can. Tax Foundation, 1979).

Ouellette, Laurie L., *Estates amd Trusts: Income Tax Aspects* (Vancouver: Certified General Accountants Association of Canada, 1994).

Partnership Taxation (Mississauga, Ont.: Insight Press, 1989).

Perry, Harvey, "Federal Individual Income Tax: Some General Concepts", *Tax Paper No. 89* 31 (Can. Tax Foundation, 1990).

Raphael, Lloyd F., *Canadian Income Tax of Trusts* (Don Mills, Ont.: CCH Canadian, 1993).

Rossiter, James, "The Application of Part XIII Nonresident Withholding Tax to Deemed Payments" (1986), 34 *Can. Tax J.* 511.

Scace, Arthur R.A., "Liability for Tax: Who is Taxed?" (Chapter 1), in *The Income Tax Law of Canada,* 4th ed. 1979, pp. 1-32.

Thirsk, Wayne, "Giving Credit Where Credit is Due: The Choice Between Credits and Deductions Under the Individual Income Tax in Canada" (1980), 28 *Can. Tax J.* 32.

Tiley, John, "The Taxation of Trusts: Comments" in *Equity, Fiduciaries and Trusts* (Toronto: Carswell, 1989), at 317-347

Wakeling, Audrey A., "Tax Planning with Trusts" in *Proceedings of 42nd Tax Conference* (Can. Tax Foundation, 1990), at 35:1.

Working Group Report: Women and Taxation (Toronto: Ontario Fair Tax Commission, 1992).

Yerbury, Paul D., "Dual Resident Companies: Tax Planning for Multinationals" (1987), 15 *I.B.L.* 158.

Residence — Individuals

Brown, "Can You Take It With You? The Departure Tax and All That" (1972), 20 *Can. Tax J.* 470.

Halpern, Jack V., "Residence or Domicile: A State of Mind", (1993), 41 *Can. Tax J.* 129.

Hansen, "Individual Residence", in *Proceedings of 29th Tax Conf.* 682 (Can. Tax Foundation, 1977).

Harris, Gregory H. and Paul R. LeBreux, "Pre-departure Planning: Ceasing Residential Ties with Canada (Part 1)" (1993), 10 *Business and Law Rev.* 73.

Harris, Gregory H. and Paul R. LeBreux, "Pre-departure Planning: Ceasing Residential Ties with Canada (Part 2)" (1994), 11 *Business and Law Rev* 73.

Jackel, Monte A., "Canadian/U.S. Treaty: Dual Status Aliens Torn Between Two Nations" (March 1989), 47 *Advocate* 269.

Koerner, "Income Tax Residence Rules", in *Proceedings of 13th Tax Conf.* 235 (Can. Tax Foundation, 1961).

Lowden, John H. and Donald M. Taniguchi, "Employee Transfers: Moving to or from Canada on Foreign Assignment (Part 1)" (1993), 41 *Can. Tax J.* 576.

Lowden, John H. and Donald M. Taniguchi, "Employee Transfers: Moving to or from Canada on Foreign Assignment (Part 2)" (1993), 41 *Can. Tax J.* 756.

McGregor, "Deemed Residence" (1974), 22 *Can. Tax J.* 381.

McKie, A.B., "Departing — A Sweet Sorrow" (1985), 92 *Can. Bank* 5:52.

Monteith, Maralynne A., "Executive Transfers: The Problem of Foreseeable Return" (1994), 5 *Tax. of Executive Compensation and Retirement* 851.

Morris, "Jurisdiction To Tax: An Update", in *Proceedings of 31st Tax Conf.* 414 (Can. Tax Foundation, 1979).

Perry, Harvey, "Federal Individual Income Tax: Some General Concepts", *Tax Paper No. 89* 31 (Can. Tax Foundation, 1990).

Schwartz, Marlene R., "New Proposed Regulations Regarding Resident Aliens (U.S.)" (1987), 35 *Can. Tax J.* 1533.

Sherbaniuk, D., et al., "Liability for Tax — Residence, Domicile or Citizenship?", in *Proceedings of 15th Tax Conf.* 325 (Can. Tax Foundation, 1963).

Smart, P. St.J., "Ordinarily Resident" (January 1989), 38 *Int. & Comp. L. Q.* 175.

Smith, "What Price Residence?" (1961), 9 *Can. Tax J.* 381.

Suarez, Steve, "Gone but not Forgotten" (1991), 124 *CA Magazine* 32.

Wosner, "Ordinary Residence, The Law and Practice" (1983), *Br. Tax Rev.* 347.

Residence — Corporations

Farnsworth, *The Residence and Domicile of Corporations* (London: Butterworth, 1939).

Flannigan, Robert, "Corporate Residence at Common Law" (1990), 5 *Securities and Corporate Regulation Rev.* 42.

Flatters, Michael J., "Proposed Amendments to Corporate Continuance and Residence" (1993), 41 *Can. Tax J.* 567.

Friesen, Timbrell, *Canadian Taxation of Income Arising in Non-Resident Corporations and Trusts* (Toronto: CCH Canadian Ltd., 1975).

Ilersic, "Tax Havens and Residence" (1982), 30 *Can. Tax J.* 52.

Kaufman, "Fiscal Residence of Corporations in Canada" (1984), 14 *R.D.U.S.* 511.

Lanthier, Allan R., "Corporate Immigration, Emigration and Continuance", [1993] *Corp. Mgmt. Tax Conf.* 4:1.

Pyrcz, "Corporate Residence" (1973), 21 *Can. Tax J.* 374.

Raizenne, Robert, "Corporate Residence, Immigration and Emigration", in *Special Seminar on International Tax Issues 1993* (Scarborough, Ont.: Carswell, 1994).

Richards, Gabrielle M.R., "Exit Tax: Corporate Emigration and Continuance" (1993), 4 *Can. Current Tax* J13.

Sarna, "Federal Continued Corporations and the Deemed-Resident Provisions of subsection 250(4) of the Income Tax Act" (1979), *McGill L.J.* 111.

Thomas, "Associated Corporations; Principal Residence", in *Proceedings of 34th Tax Conf.* 689 (Can. Tax Foundation, 1984).

Ward, "Corporate Residence as a Tax Factor", *Corporate Management Tax Conf.* 3 (Can. Tax Foundation, 1961).

Webb, "Residence; Determination of Type of Income; Foreign Tax Credits", in *Proceedings of 28th Tax Conf.* 503 (Can. Tax Foundation, 1976).

Residence — Trusts

Cooper, "Canadian Resident Inter Vivos Trusts with Nonresident Beneficiaries" (1982), 30 *Can. Tax J.* 422.

Cullity, "Non-Resident Trusts", in *Proceedings of 33rd Tax Conf.* 646 (Can. Tax Foundation, 1983).

Friesen, Timbrell, *Canadian Taxation of Income Arising in Non-Resident Corporations and Trusts* (Toronto: CCH Canadian Ltd., 1975).

Green, "The Residence of Trusts for Income Tax Purposes" (1973), 21 *Can. Tax J.* 217.

Noble, "Some Tax Avoidance Aspects of Non-Resident Trusts" (1979), 5 *Estates Q.* 81.

Sarkari, "Taxation of Non-Resident Trusts" (1974), 22 *Can. Tax J.* 584.

Taxation of Non-Resident Beneficiaries, Audio Archives of Canada, 1984.

Residence — Partnerships

Gansi, D.C., "Unincorporated Business and Investments: The Use of Partnerships", [1986] *Special Lectures (LSUC)* 237.

McQuillan, Peter, *Understanding the Taxation of Partnerships*, 3rd ed. (Don Mills, Ont.: CCH Canadian, 1991).

Witterick, Robert G., "The Partnership as a Modern Business Vehicle", in *Proceedings of 41st Tax Conf.* 21:1 (Can. Tax Foundation, 1989).

Non-Residents

Bacal, Norman and Richard Lewin, "The Taxation in Canada of Nonresident Performing Artists and Behind-the-Camera Personnel" (1986), 34 *Can. Tax J.* 1287.

Balogh, L,V., "Taxation of Non-Residents" (1981), *Can. Taxation* 937.

Cameron, John R., "Sales of Land by Non-residents" (1985/86), 12 *Nova Scotia Law News* 103.

"Canadian Taxation of United States Persons", in *Proceedings of 27th Tax Conf.* 54 (Can. Tax Foundation, 1975).

Friesen, Timbrell, *Canadian Taxation of Income Arising in Non-Resident Corporations and Trusts* (Toronto: CCH Canadian Ltd., 1975).

Hausman, Chown, Tillinghast, "International Aspects — 2", in *Proceedings of 23rd Tax Conf.* 279 (Can. Tax Foundation, 1971).

Huggett, "Non-Residents" (1970), 97 *Can. Chart Acc.* 364.

Lindsay, "Withholding Tax: Compliance Problems of the Canadian Payor", *Corporate Management Tax Conf.* 52 (Can. Tax Foundation, 1976).

Macdonald, "Taxation of Non-Residents", [1964] *Special Lectures LSUC* 69.

Noble, "Some Tax Avoidance Aspects of Non-Resident Trusts" (1979), 5 *Estates Q.* 81.

Peters, V., "Taxation of Non-Resident Investment in Canada", [1986] *Special Lectures (LSUC)* 155.

Sarkari, "Taxation of Non-Resident Trusts" (1974), 22 *Can. Tax J.* 584.

Spence, "The Role of the Permanent Establishment Concept" (1966), 24 *U.T. Fac. of L. Rev.* 82.

Taxation of Non-Resident Beneficiaries, Audio Archives of Canada, 1984.

Wray, Donald, W. and Scott R. Barbard, "Taxation of Non-Resident Athletes and Entertainers Performing in Canada" (1986), 34 *Can. Tax J.* 1150.

Anti-Avoidance Rules

Brahmst, Oliver C., "Beware of the Breadth of Subsection 56(4.1)" (1991), *Can. Current Tax* P-43.

Brahmst, Oliver C., "Developments in Executive Compensation" (1991) 3 *Can. Current Tax* P-43.

Brahmst, Oliver C., "Subsection 56(4.1) — An Update" (1992) 3 *Can. Current Tax* P-47.

Corn, George, "Indirect Payments and Transfers of Rights to Income" (1991), 3 *Can. Current Tax* J-65.

Crawford, William E., "Subsection 56(4.1) and Income-Splitting Trusts", in *Proceedings of 42nd Tax Conf.* 4:57 (Can. Tax Foundation, 1990).

Drache, A.B.C., "Buying Your Student a Home" (1991), 13 *Can. Taxpayer* 115.

Drache, A.B.C., "Employing Your Child" (1991), 13 *Can. Taxpayer* 94.

Drache, A.B.C., "Income-Splitting Loophole Closed" (1992), 14 *Can. Taxpayer* 21.

Drache, A.B.C., "Income-Splitting Needs Advanced Planning" (1991), 13 *Can. Taxpayer* 181.

Drache, A.B.C., "Income-Splitting Through Lending" (1991), 13 *Can. Taxpayer* 174.

Drache, A.B.C., "January Ideal for Income Split" (1995), 17 *Can. Taxpayer* 9.

Drache, A.B.C., "Non-Attributable Gains on Transfer to a Spouse" (1991), 13 *Can. Taxpayer* 95.

Drache, A.B.C., "Setting Income Splitting Targets" (1994), 16 *Can. Taxpayer* 38.
    Drache, A.B.C., "Subsection 56(2) — Another Round to the Taxpayer" (1994), 16 *Can. Taxpayer* 27.

Glover, Paul, "Income Splitting — Further Restrictions" (May-June 1987), 61 *CMA Magazine* 30.

Glover, Paul, "Splitting Income Was a Common Planning Tool" (March-April 1987) 61 *CMA Magazine* 28.

Goodman, Wolfe D., "Income Tax — Attribution of Income — Non-Arm's Length Loans" (1988-89), 9 *Est. & Tru. J.* 77.

Knight & Knight, "Barriers to the Application of the Constructive Receipt Doctrine" (1988), 41 *Tax Exec.* 199.

Krishna, Vern, "Corporate Share Capital Structures and Income Splitting" (August 1991) 3 *Can. Current Tax* C-71.

Krishna, Vern and J. Anthony VanDuzer, "Corporate Share Capital Structures and Income Splitting: McClurg v. Canada" (March 1993) 3 *Can. Bus. L.J.* 335.

McDonnell, T.E., "Tax Avoidance: Splitting Decision" (1991), 39 *Can. Tax J.* 637.

Minzberg, Samuel, "Income Splitting: Still Alive?", in *Proceedings of 38th Tax Conf.* 35:1 (Can. Tax Foundation, 1986).

Noirs, Derrick A., "Provisions That Restrict or Deny Losses and Corporate Attribution", in *Proceedings of 41st Tax Conf.* 14:1 (Can. Tax Foundation, 1989).

Rohde, Richard, "Attribution/Retribution (New Income Splitting Arrangements)" (1986), 14 *Can. Tax News* 37.

Sklar, Murray, "Don't Get Trapped by the New Income Attribution Rules" (January 1987), 120 *CA Magazine* 42.

St.-Onge, Francine, "Tax Strategy — Beneficial Election" (May 1991) 25 *CGA Magazine* 20.

Tardif, Simon J. and Deborah Duncan, "Income Splitting and Estate Freezing After Tax Reform", in *Proceedings of 39th Tax Conf.* 39:1 (Can. Tax Foundation, 1987).

Young, Claire F.L., "The Attribution Rules: Their Uncertain Future in the Light of Current Problems" (1987), 35 *Can. Tax J.* 275.

International Aspects

Arnold, Brian J., "Tax Discrimination Against Aliens, Non-residents and Foreign Activities: Canada, Australia, New Zealand, the United Kingdom and the United States", *Canada Tax Paper No. 90* (Toronto: Canada Tax Foundation, 1991).

Barbeau, "An Introduction to International Tax Planning" (1963), 6 *Can. B.J.* 214.

Bernstein, Jack, "A Guide for the Emigrating Canadian Resident", [1993] *Corp. Mgmt. Tax Conf.* 12:1.

Broadhurst, "Canada-U.S. Tax Treaty (Part I)" (1980), 28 *Can. Tax J.* 799.

Broadhurst, "Canada-U.S. Tax Treaty (Part II)" (1981), 29 *Can. Tax J.* 61.

Broadhurst, "The Canada-U.S. Treaty Protocol" (1983), 31 *Can. Tax J.* 820.

Broadhurst, "Income Tax Treaties" (Parts 1-4) (1978), 26 *Can. Tax J.* 217, 322, 575, 684.

Brown, "Can You Take It With You? The Departure Tax and All That" (1972), 20 *Can. Tax J.* 470.

Brown, "International Tax Planning — What Is It All About?" (1976), 24 *Can. Tax J.* 55.

Coulombe, "Certain Policy Aspects of Canadian Tax Treaties", in *Proceedings of 28th Tax Conf.* 290 (Can. Tax Foundation, 1976).

Drache, A.B.C., "Canadian Residents Working Abroad" (1994), 16 *Can. Taxpayer* 15.

Emes, Bryan R., "Planning for Immigration to Canada from Countries other than the United States", [1993] *Corp. Mgmt. Tax Conf.* 13.

Jones, Avery, "Dual Residence of Individuals: Meaning of Expressions in OECD Model Convention" (1981), *Brit. Tax Rev.* 15.

Hausman, James S., *International Tax Planning* (Faculty of Law, University of Toronto, 1986).

Horne, B.D., "Planning for the Departure Tax" (1991), 3 *Canada's Immigration and Citizenship Bulleting No. 3* 3.

MacKenzie, B. Brian, "The Tax Consequences of Moving Between Canada and the United States" (1990), 48 *The Advocate* 525.

Marshall, J., "The New Canada-United States Income Tax Treaty" (Practising Law Institute: New York, 1984).

Miller, Donald K., "Tax Considerations for U.S. Citizens Moving to Canada", [1993] *Corp. Mgmt. Tax Conf.* 16:1.

Peats, Francisco Alfredo Garcia, "Triangular Cases and Residence as a basis for Alleviating International Double Taxation: Rethinking the Subjective Scope of Double Tax Treaties" (1994), 11 *Intertax* 473.

Perry, David B., "OECD International Tax Comparisons" (1988), 38 *Can. Tax J.* 1320.

Sharpening, Robert H., "Tax Reform Act of 1986: Impact on Canadian Citizens Living or Working in United States" in *Report of Proceedings of 38th Tax Conf.* (Canada Tax Foundation, 1986).

Smith, Carlton, M., "United States Assists Revenue Canada in Obtaining a Client's Name" (1988), 36 *Can. Tax J.* 469.

Suarez, Steve, "Tax Planning for Departure from Canada" (1991), 39 *Can. Tax J.* 1.

Wach, T.S., "Tax Planning for Immigrants: Capital Assets" (1991), 2 *Canada's Immigration and Citizenship Bulletin No. 10* 4.

Indians

Bartlett, Richard H., *Indians and Taxation in Canada* (Saskatoon: Native Law Centre, University of Saskatchewan, 1992).

Drache, A.B.C., "Indians Protest Tax" (1995), 17, *Can. Taxpayer* 10.

Drache, A.B.C., "The Inuit Land Claim Deal" (1992), 14 *Can. Taxpayer* 4.

Drache, A.B.C., "Native Issues Get Attention" (1991), 13 *Can. Taxpayer* 49.

Drache, A.B.C., "Some Indians to Lose Tax-free Status" (1993), 15 *Can. Taxpayer* 22.

Drache, A.B.C., "Tax Court Hands Indian Corporations Bonanza" (1994), 16 *Can. Taxpayer* 35.

Gardner-O'Toole, Elaine, *Aboriginal People and Taxation* (Ottawa: Library of Parliament, Research Branch, 1992).

Morry, Howard L., "Taxation of Aboriginals in Canada" (1992), 21 *Manitoba Law Journal* 426.

Nixon, Blair D. and Dennis F. Sykora, "Taxation and First Nations: Shifting Parameters" (1992), 5 *Canadian Petroleum Tax J.* 49.

Reiter, Robert A., *Tax Manual for Indians* (Edmonton: First Nations Resource Council, 1990).

Strother, Robert C. and Robert A. Brown, "Taxation of Aboriginal People in Canada" in *Report of Proceedings of 42nd Tax Conf.* (Can. Tax Foundation, 1990).

Report, 8317. Planning for the Department and after the Canada's Immigrants and Charitable Religion, No. 99.

MacKenzie, B. Stuart. "The Tax Consequences of Moving Home in Canada and the United States (Toronto: Carswell, 1994).

McGill, G. "The Non-Canada-United States Income Tax Treaty" (Receiving Law Seminar, New York 1993).

Olin, Gerald S. "Tax Consequences of Emigration: Moving to Canada," (1991) Can. Mining Tax Conf. 14:1.

Payne, Franklin. "Helly Garcia, 'Transplant Cases' and Resolution of a basis for Alleviating International Double Taxation: Redistributing the Subjective Scope of Public Tax Issues," (1993) 16 Interim 779.

CHAPTER IV

WHAT IS INCOME?

A word is not a crystal; transparent and unchanged, it is the skin of a living thought and may vary in colour and content according to the circumstances and the time in which it is used.

(Justice Holmes in *Towne v. Eisner*, 245 U.S. 418, 425, 38 S.Ct. 158, 159, 62 L.Ed. 372, 376.)

1. THE MEANING OF "INCOME"

References:

ITA:

S. 2	Liability for Tax
S. 3	Income for Taxation Year
S. 4	Income From a Source — Deductions, Inclusions
S. 152	Assessment

BULLETINS, CIRCULARS & RULINGS:

IT-62	August 18, 1972	Indians
IT-256R	August 27, 1979	Gains from Theft, Defalcation or Embezzlement
IT-334R2	February 21, 1992	Miscellaneous Receipts
IT-365R2	May 8, 1987	Damages, Settlements and Similar Receipts
IT-377R	January 27, 1989	Director's, Executor's or Juror's Fees
IT-420R3	March 30, 1992	Non-Residents — Income Earned in Canada

(a) General

It is useful to commence by emphasizing the obvious: The *Income Tax Act* levies a tax upon *income,* not upon capital, consumption or wealth. The concept of income is the core of the taxable base. The definition of income determines the size and structure of the revenue base and, implicitly, colours the ideology of the tax system. Yet, as we shall see, "income" is not a well understood concept.

The initial step in determining whether a receipt is taxable as *income* is to determine the nature and character of the receipt. If a receipt constitutes "income," it is included in the taxable base *unless,* even though of an income nature, it is excluded by virtue of a specific statutory provision. For example, although salary is usually taxable, the Governor General's salary and allowances are not taxable as income by virtue of the exemption in paragraph 81(1)(*n*).

Figure 1 presents an overview of the Act's characterization of receipts into taxable and non-taxable components.

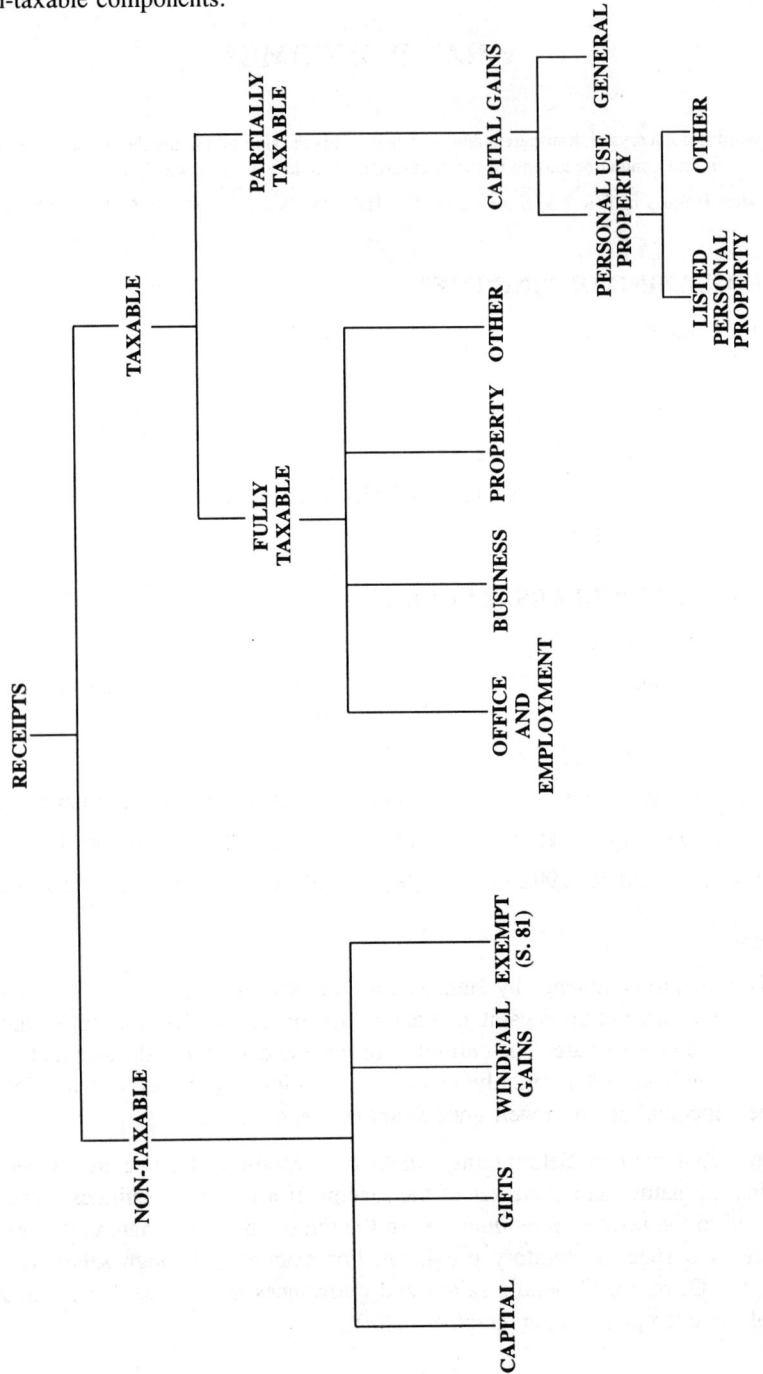

The term "income" is not generically defined in the *Income Tax Act*. Although the Act sometimes speaks of what is included in or excluded from income, it neither identifies nor describes the legal characteristics of income.[1] For example, paragraph 6(1)(*a*) specifies that the value of board and lodging is included in employment income; subsection 7(1) deems certain stock option benefits to be employment income; subsection 6(9) deems imputed interest from an interest-free loan to be income, etc.

The seemingly simple task of identifying and characterizing income in law creates considerable difficulty. For example: assume an employer gives his or her employee $1,000 at Christmas. Is the employee taxable on the $1,000? Does the $1,000 constitute income to the employee? The employee is subject to tax if the $1,000 represents remuneration, but is not taxable if the $1,000 represents a gift, since gifts are not considered income at law. The answer is easy to determine once the line is drawn between remuneration and gifts: The difficulty lies only in drawing the line.

Four questions need to be answered:

1. What is income?

2. What is the source of the income?

3. Whose income is it for tax purposes? and

4. When is the income taxable?

We address the first two questions in this chapter. The remaining questions are answered later.

(b) Dictionary Definitions

We start with the simple question: What is income? The characterization of a receipt as being on account of "income" or on account of something else is always the first step in determining the taxable base and, hence, liability for tax.

Webster's Dictionary defines income as:

> . . . a gain which proceeds from labour, business, property, or capital of any kind, as the produce of a farm, the rent of houses, proceeds of professional business, the profits of commerce, or of occupation, or the interest of money or stock in funds.

The *Oxford Dictionary* describes income as "periodical (usually annual) receipts from one's business, lands, work, investments, etc.".

These definitions, which emphasize the concept of income as an annual or recurring gain derived from labour or capital are useful, but not definitive for tax purposes.

---

[1] See, e.g., paras. 12(1)(*c*) (interest), 12(1)(*j*) (dividends), 12(1)(*m*) (benefits from trusts), and 12(1)(*o*) (royalties).

(c) Income in Economics

Economists have long considered the nature of income and its measurement for tax purposes. The most famous economic definition of income is the Haig-Simons formulation:[2]

> . . . Personal taxable income may be defined as the algebraic sum of (1) the market value of rights exercised in consumption, and (2) the change in the value of the store of property rights between the beginning and end of the period in question.

This definition considers income to be the *value* of goods and services consumed in a time period, adjusted for any increase or decrease in the *value* of assets on hand at the end of the period over the *value* of assets on hand at the beginning of the period. For example, if a taxpayer began the year with assets valued at $1,000, spent $20,000 on personal expenditures during the year and had assets valued at $5,000 at the end of the year, his or her income for the year would be $24,000.

The Haig-Simons formulation of income does not distinguish between sources of income. Net accretion of wealth includes full inclusion of unrealized capital gains, imputed rent on owner-occupied housing, and even increases in human capital resulting from education or acquired skills. The definition does not provide for tax "preferences".

There are other definitions of "income". For example:

> R. Haig, "The Concept of Income," in *The Federal Income Tax* Tax 1, 7 (Columbia University, 1921): "Income is the money value of the net accretion to one's economic power between two points of time."

> C. Plehn, "Income as Recurrent, Consumable Receipts," 14 *Amer. Econ. Rev.* 1, 5 (1924): "Income is essentially wealth available for recurrent consumption, recurrently (or periodically) received. Its three essential characteristics are: receipt, recurrence and expendability."

> W. Hewett, *The Definition of Income and its Application in Federal Taxation*, (1925), pp. 22-23: "Net individual income is the flow of commodities and services accruing to an individual through a period of time and available for disposition after deducting the necessary cost of acquisition."

> R. Posner, *Economic Analysis of Law*, (1973), pp. 231-32: "The broadest definition of income would be all pecuniary and non-pecuniary receipts, including leisure and gifts."

Professor Irving Fisher, of Yale, considered income to be "a flow of benefits during a period of time".[3]

---

[2]   In Haig's language, income is "the increase or accretion in one's power to satisfy his wants in a given period in so far as that power consists of (a) money itself or, (b) anything susceptible of valuation in terms of money". Simons equates personal income with the algebraic sum of consumption and change in net worth. See "The Concept of Income — Economic and Legal Aspects" in R.M. Haig (ed.), *The Federal Income Tax* (New York, 1921).

[3]   Fisher, Irving, *Elementary Principles of Economics* (New York: The MacMillan Company, 1911), at 34.

Professor Ely, of Wisconsin, distinguished between wealth and income:[4] "Wealth refers to the stock of goods on hand at a particular time. Real income, on the other hand, has reference to the satisfaction we derive from the use of material things or personal services during a period of time."

Sir John Hicks, the Oxford economist and Nobel laureate, defined income as the maximum amount that an individual could spend in a period and still expect to be *as well off* at the end of the period as she or he had been at the beginning.

Most of these comprehensive definitions of income were strongly endorsed by the Carter Commission in its thought provoking report on the Canadian tax system:[5]

> We are completely persuaded that taxes should be allocated according to the changes in the economic power of individuals and families. If a man obtains increased command over goods and services for his personal satisfaction, we do not believe it matters, from the point of view of taxation, whether he earned it through working, made it through operating a business, received it because he held property, made it by selling property, or was given it by a relative. Nor do we believe it matters whether the increased command over goods and services was in cash or in kind. Nor do we believe it matters whether the increase in economic power was expected or unexpected, whether it was a unique or recurrent event, whether the man suffered to get the increase in economic power, or it fell in his lap without effort.

Although these notions of income are premised on rational principles, the implementation of abstract concepts such as benefits, utilities, and satisfactions is all but impossible. The concept of income for tax purposes must be one that is capable of being administered on a day-to-day basis. As Professor Taussig, of Harvard, concluded:[6]

> . . . for almost all purposes of economic study, it is best to content ourselves with a statement, and an attempt at measurement, in terms not of utility but of money income. . . . The reason for this rejection of a principle which is in itself sound lies in the conclusion . . . regarding total utility and consumer's surplus: they cannot be measured.

The fundamental theory underlying the Haig-Simons formulation of income is applied in certain circumstances to calculate a taxpayer's income in the absence of adequate accounting records. For example, the Minister can issue an "arbitrary" assessment based on the taxpayer's net worth.[7] A taxpayer's "net worth" in a year is

---

[4] Ely, *Outlines of Economics* (New York: The MacMillan Company, 1908), at 98. See also, Professor Alfred Marshall, of Cambridge, *Elements of Economics of Industry* (London: Macmillan, 1901), at 51: . . . a woman who makes her own clothes, or a man who digs in his own garden or repairs his own house, is earning income just as would the dressmaker, gardener, or carpenter who might be hired to do the work . . . . For scientific purpose, it would be best if the word income when occurring alone should always mean total real income.

[5] *Report of the Royal Commission on Taxation* (Ottawa: Queen's Printer, 1966) (Chair: K.M. Carter), vol. 1, at 9; see also Simons, *Personal Income Taxation: The Definition of Income as a Problem of Fiscal Policy* (Chicago: University of Chicago Press, 1938).

[6] Taussig, *Principles of Economics,* Vol. X (New York: The MacMillan Company, 1916), at 134.

[7] Subs. 152(7).

the difference between his or her wealth at the beginning and end of the year after adjustments for amounts consumed during the year.[8] A "net worth" assessment is, in effect, a modified application of the concept underlying the Haig-Simons formulation of income.

But even a limited application of the Haig-Simons formulation of income as the net accretion of wealth between two points in time has its problems. How, for example, does one measure the "value" of assets at the beginning and end of every fiscal year? In determining whether a taxpayer is "as well off" at the end of a year as at its beginning, does one measure in terms of "real" or nominal dollars? Even assuming that it is possible to track one's expenditures accurately for a given period, periodic valuation of assets would present great difficulties and, in some cases, create considerable uncertainty. It may also involve a considerable expense where, for example, the asset is not publicly traded in an open market.

It would be a grave error, however, to conclude that economic definitions do not influence the statutory scheme for the recognition of income and the timing of inclusions in the taxable base. The taxation of unrealized interest[9] and imputed benefits from low cost loans,[10] for example, are manifestations of the influence of classical economic thought on the legal concept of income.

(d) Income in Law

"Income" as used in the Act is a less comprehensive concept than its equivalent in economics and falls far short of the notion of the "accrual" of all wealth. The legal concept of income differs from the economist's concept in at least two ways: (1) the exclusion of unrealized gains; (2) the rigid classification of income by source.

(i) Realized Gains

We turn now to the question: *When* is income taxable? For most purposes of the Act, "income" refers to realized wealth and does not include mere accrual of wealth. With very few exceptions, income is recognized for tax purposes only when it is realized or crystallized in a market transaction such as a sale, exchange or disposition. In contrast, the economist refers to income as an "accretion" to wealth, whether or not the increased value has been realized in a market transaction.

An example may help clarify this distinction. Assume that an individual purchases shares at a price of $10 per share and that the shares increase in value to $25 per share by the end of the year. Under the Haig-Simons formulation of income, the individual's income for the year is $15 per share. This amount represents the increase in the *value* of the shares and, hence, the increase in wealth. For most tax purposes, however, the

---

[8]   See Chapter VI "Business and Investment Income: General".

[9]   Subs. 12(4).

[10]   Subs. 15(9), s. 80.4.

taxpayer does not report any income until such time as the shares are sold and the gain is actually triggered or realized.[11]

(ii) Source

The economist is not concerned with tax differentials based on the source of income: All accretions of wealth are income, regardless of source.

In contrast, segregation of income by source is the essence of the structure of the Canadian income tax system. There is no concept more fundamental to the Act than that income from each source must be separately calculated according to the rules applicable to that particular source.

Two additional principles warrant attention in this context. Income is an amount that arises or results from profit or *gain*, but does not include the realized value of the *source* of the gain itself.[12] For example, assume that a taxpayer buys goods at a cost of $10 per unit and sells the goods for $30 per unit. The taxpayer's income is $20 per unit, *not* $30. The first $10 from the sale is merely recovery of the capital investment in the goods.

Second, *in the absence of specific statutory rules,* "income" means *net* income determined in accordance with ordinary, commercial principles. In *Dominion Natural Gas,* for example:[13]

> The generally recognized rule as regards trade expenses is that a deduction is permissible when it is justifiable on business and accountancy principles, but this principle is subject to certain specific statutory provisions which prohibit the allowance of certain expenses as deductions in computing the net profit or gain to be assessed. To the extent that ordinary business and accountancy principles are not invaded by the statute, they prevail.

Thus, although the Act does not use an adjective to qualify "income," the term is read as "net income".[14] For example, assume that a taxpayer buys inventory for $10 per unit and pays $1 per unit on account of freight to have the goods delivered to his or her business premises. The inventory then sells for $30 per unit and the taxpayer pays shipping costs of $2 per unit. The taxpayer's *gross* revenue is $30 per unit, but "income" for tax purposes is only $17 per unit.

---

[11] In certain circumstances, the Act deems a disposition even where there has been none. For example, a deceased is *deemed* to have disposed of all his or her property immediately before death: subs. 70(5).

[12] This principle underlies the oft-quoted statement that income is the fruit only and never the tree; see e.g., *Stratton's Independence v. Howbert,* 213 US 399; *Ryall v. Hoare* (1923), 8 Tax Cas. 521. This principle is modified by statutory provisions in certain circumstances; e.g., para. 12(1)(g) taxes as income any amounts paid that are calculated by reference to production, regardless of whether or not the payment actually represents an instalment of the sale price of the property.

[13] *Dominion Natural Gas Co. v. M.N.R.,* [1940-41] CTC 144 at 147-48, 1 DTC 499-81 at 499-83 (Ex. Ct.) reversed on facts [1940-41] CTC 155, 1 DTC 499-133 (S.C.C.).

[14] See Chapter VI "Business and Investment Income: General".

2. INCOME FROM A SOURCE

Section 3 is the anchor for the structure of the Act. It contains the basic rules for determining income for a taxation year for the purposes of Part I of the Act. The section sets out the rigid sequence in which separate sources of income and losses are aggregated in determining income.

One of the hallmarks of the Canadian income tax system is its rigid classification of income and losses by source. Section 3 identifies at least six major categories into which income and losses are classified. Some of the categories (such as capital gains) are further divided into subcategories. The rules in respect of the computation of income and losses from each source are then set out neatly, but not simply, in separate subdivisions of the Act.

The rigid scheme by which income and losses are segregated into separate compartments according to source contributes more than any other single factor to the complexity of the tax system. Taxpayers, understandably, make every effort to reclassify income from high rate sources into income that is either tax exempt or taxed at a lower rate. Indeed, the quintessential characteristic of tax planning is the conversion of income that is taxable at a high rate into income that is tax exempt or tax deferred. The distinction between business income and capital gains, for example, has been the subject of hundreds of litigated cases because of the lower rate of tax levied on capital gains.

Equally troublesome, and sometimes even more subtle, is the distinction between income from a business and income from property.

STRUCTURE OF SECTION 3

<u>Paragraph</u>

3(*a*) Employment income $ +
Business and property income   +
Other income (excluding
          taxable capital gains)   +
                                                              —————
                                                             $

ADD

3(*b*) Taxable capital gains
          (including taxable *net*
          gains from LPP)[15] $ +
Exceeds:
Allowable capital losses
          (other than LPP losses) in excess of allowable
          business investment losses   – +
                                                              —————
                                                             $

EXCEEDS

3(*c*) The remaining subdivision deductions
(negative number is deemed equal to zero)   –
                                                              —————
                                                             $

EXCEEDS

3(*d*) Office and employment losses $ –
Business and property losses
Allowable business investment losses   –
                                                              —————

INCOME FOR THE YEAR $
                                                              —————
(negative number is deemed equal to zero)

Each category of income in section 3 is referred to as "income from a source" and income from each source is calculated separately.[16] For example, employment income is a category of income separate and apart from income from business and income from property which, in turn, are segregated from capital gains. The rules that apply to the computation of income from each of these sources are quite different.

---

[15] Listed personal property.

[16] Subs. 4(1). The source concept was borrowed from the United Kingdom's tax system under which income is taxable if it falls into one of the Schedules of the *Income and Corporation Taxes Act*, 1970 (Eng.), c. 10.

The computation of income from each source typically involves four steps:

- Characterization of a receipt as being on account of income or capital;

- Classification of income receipts by source;

- Application of the computational rules to each source of income; and

- Aggregation of the various sources of income in the sequence set out in section 3.

(a) Sources

The named sources of income are as follows:

- Office;

- Employment;

- Business;

- Property; and

- Capital gains.

It is important to note, however, that apart from these named sources, section 3 specifies that income from *any* other source is also taxable.

(b) And More Sources

Some of the above sources of income are further divided into subcategories. For example, capital gains from listed personal property are treated separately and differently from "ordinary" capital gains; business investment losses are treated differently from ordinary capital losses.[17] Indeed, as we shall see, a good deal of the complexity of the statute is directly attributable to the requirement that income be pigeon-holed into narrow compartments, each with its own set of computational rules and restrictions. This, in turn, requires an elaborate legislative infrastructure to prevent leakage from one compartment into another.

---

[17] S. 54 ("listed personal property") and s. 41, paras. 39(1)(*b*) and (*c*); see Chapter XII "Computation of Taxable Income".

Example IV.1

Assume:

The following data applies to an individual taxpayer. All amounts shown are net of deductions in each category.

Employment income	$30,000
Business (No. 1) income	12,000
Business (No. 2) loss	(6,000)
Property income	6,000
Taxable capital gains (shares)	1,500
Net taxable listed personal property gain	1,500
Allowable capital losses (*including* allowable business investment losses)	(4,900)
Moving expenses	
Allowable business investment losses	(800)
	(4,000)

Then:

Paragraph 3(a)

Employment income	✱ no 'loss' amts.	$30,000
Business income		12,000
Property income		6,000
		48,000

ADD Paragraph 3(b)

Taxable capital gains	$ 1,500	
Taxable *net* LPP gain	1,500	
	3,000	
Exceeds:		
Allowable capital losses in excess of allowable business investment losses ($4,900 – 4,000)	(900)	2,100
		50,100

EXCEEDS Paragraph 3(c)

Moving expenses	(800)
	49,300

EXCEEDS Paragraph 3(d)

Business loss	6,000	
Allowable business investment losses	$ 4,000	(10,000)
Income for the year		**$39,300**

The importance of characterizing income by source cannot be over-emphasized. Some sources of income (for example, business income) are fully taxed; capital gains receive preferential treatment, with either 75 per cent or no portion of such income being taxed because of special exemptions; other sources (for example, windfall gains) are not taxed at all.

(c) Losses

The characterization of losses is equally important: business losses are fully deductible against any source of income; capital losses are only partially deductible from income and then only from taxable capital gains. Similarly, listed personal property losses (a special type of capital loss) are deductible only against gains from listed personal property and not from other types of capital gains, and so on. See Chapter IX "Capital Gains" for a detailed discussion of capital gains.

(d) The U.K. Approach

The idea of segregating income by source was first conceived in the United Kingdom in *Addingtons Act*[18] in 1803: Taxpayers filed separate tax returns for each source of income so that no single official would know the total of each person's income. Thus, the source doctrine (known as the schedule system in the United Kingdom) was originally intended to protect the privacy of taxpayers.

The source doctrine is now used for very different purposes and its rigid structure causes substantial complexity in the tax system. There is, however, an important difference between the English schedular system and the Canadian source doctrine. Under the English *Income and Corporation Taxes Act*,[19] a receipt is not taxable as income unless it comes within one of the named schedules, which are mutually exclusive.[20] Thus, the schedules mark the outside boundaries of the tax net.[21] The position is not as clear under the Canadian *Income Tax Act*.

---

[18]   1803 (43 Geo. III), c. 122.

[19]   *Income and Corporation Taxes Act*, 1970 (Eng.), c. 10.

[20]   S. 1. As Lord Radcliffe said in *Mitchell v. Ross,* [1961] 3 All ER 49 at 55, 40 Tax Cas. 11:
   Before you can assess a profit to tax you must be sure that you have properly identified its source or other description according to the correct Schedule; but once you have done that, it is obligatory that it should be charged, if at all, under that Schedule and strictly in accordance with the Rules that are there laid down for assessments under it. It is a necessary consequence of this conception that the sources of profit in the different Schedules are mutually exclusive.

[21]   There are six schedules, some of which are subdivided into cases. Each schedule deals with a particular type of income.

(e) The Canadian Approach

The named sources (office, employment, business, property and capital gains) are not exhaustive and income can arise from *any* other unnamed source. Hence, income from any source inside or outside Canada is taxable under paragraph 3(*a*) of the Act.[22] This is justifiable both on the basis of the language of the statute and on policy grounds. To the extent that ability to pay is an important value in the tax system, all income accretions to wealth are a measure of that ability and should be taxable regardless of source.

The reach and scope of the source doctrine is, however, far from settled. The Supreme Court's decision in *Fries v. M.N.R.*[23] that strike pay does not constitute income leaves the issue open. Although *Fries* is unequivocal that strike pay is not taxable, the Court did not address the fundamental question: *Why* is strike pay not taxable? Is it because strike pay is not "income" or because it does not have a "source"?

The facts underlying *Fries* were as follows: the taxpayer was an employee of the Saskatchewan Liquor Board and a member of the Saskatchewan Government Employees' Union ("Union"). The taxpayer's bargaining unit, the Public Service Bargaining Unit, went on strike and the taxpayer received strike pay equal in amount to what his normal net take home pay would have been without the strike. The Union's strike fund was formed out of the tax deductible dues contributed by its members. The usual "strike stipend" paid to members on strike was $10 a week. The Union's provincial executive, however, had the sole right to determine the amount to be paid. They generally authorized strike stipend payments of up to 80 per cent of gross pay, but in this case they authorized stipends equal to the full amount of the members' normal take home pay. The employees of the Liquor Board voted in favour of supporting the strike and the members knew that there would be a recommendation that they would be reimbursed their full loss of pay as a result of the strike support.

Although the case was heard by a total of 13 judges in various courts, the Supreme Court adopted the decision of Judge Taylor in the Tax Review Board. The Board excluded strike pay from income because the Act does not *specifically* provide for such taxation. The Board said:[24]

> The board need express no opinion on the principle involved — whether "strike pay" should or should not be taxable even though that principle was vigorously contested by the parties. It is only required that the Board express an opinion on whether the Act as it now stands provides for the taxation of the amount in question as well as it can be identified and described. The Act does not provide for such taxation.

---

[22] *Income Tax Act*, para. 3(*a*) requires income "from a source inside or outside Canada" to be included in income.

[23] *Fries v. M.N.R.*, [1990] 2 CTC 439, 90 DTC 6662 (S.C.C.).

[24] *Fries v. M.N.R.*, [1983] CTC 2124 at 2128, 83 DTC 117 at 121 (T.R.B.).

Section 3, however, specifically includes in a taxpayer's income for a year, income from *any* source inside or outside Canada.

Although it is clear that strike pay is not taxable, the more important question for taxpayers is: What else is not taxable under the *Fries* doctrine? Are there other receipts with characteristics similar to strike pay that may also be non-taxable? If so, what are the necessary characteristics of exempt income? The Supreme Court left these issues for another day.

(f) Dimensions of the Source Concept

There are two different dimensions to the concept of "income from a source": "source" of income may denote either geographic location or type of activity.

The geographical source of income is important in determining the credit available for taxes paid to a foreign jurisdiction[25] and to the application of tax treaties.

The sourcing of income by type of activity determines the tax rate applicable to the particular source.

Income from each source is brought into the computation of net income at different stages and according to a rigid and predetermined formula. There is no room for variation from the formula. The formula is unyielding and absolute. Only positive amounts of income enter into the calculation under paragraph 3(*a*); negative amounts (losses) may only be deducted under paragraph 3(*d*), except for allowable capital losses which are deducted from capital gains under paragraph 3(*b*). In effect, section 3 controls the *type and amount of losses* allowable and the *sequence* in which they may be deducted in computing income in the year. The difference in result between simple mathematical aggregation of income and losses and the calculation of net income by source of activity as required by section 3, is illustrated in Example IV.2.

---

[25] S. 126. See Chapter XIII "Computation of Tax Payable".

Example IV.2

Assume that the following data applies to three corporations:

	Corporation		
	A	**B**	**C**
Business income	$ 1,000	$ 2,000	$ 6,000
Property income	(1,000)	2,000	—
Taxable capital gains	2,000	(2,000)	(4,000)
Aggregate income	2,000	2,000	2,000
Income for tax purposes is:			
Business income	1,000	2,000	6,000
Property income	—	2,000	—
Taxable capital gains	2,000	—	—
	3,000	4,000	6,000
Exceeds:			
Property or business losses	(1,000)	*	*
Income for the year	$ 2,000	$ 4,000	$ 6,000

*Capital losses may only be offset against capital gains.

We have already seen that income from each source must be calculated separately. Thus, a taxpayer is required to compute income as though *each* source of income was his or her *only* source of income. Deductions from income are similarly limited: A deduction may only be taken against a source of income if it may be regarded as applicable to that source.[26]

3. STRUCTURE OF THE ACT

A person may be liable for tax under different Parts of the *Income Tax Act*. For example, residents, and non-residents who are employed or carry on a business in Canada, are taxable under Part I of the Act. Under Part XIII of the Act, non-residents are subject to withholding tax on certain forms of passive income (such as dividends, interest). There are also special taxes imposed under Part IV on certain types of investment income and under Part II.1 on dividend-like payments. We focus our present discussion on Part I of the Act; the other Parts of the Act are discussed later.

---

[26] Subs. 4(1).

A taxpayer's liability for tax under Part I is determined by reference to "taxable income".[27] The applicable tax rate is applied to taxable income to determine the amount of basic federal tax payable. Tax credits and surcharges are then applied to determine the net *federal* tax payable. With the exception of Quebec, provincial taxes are calculated as a percentage of federal taxes.

The general scheme for determining tax payable under Part I is as follows:

TAXATION OF CANADIAN RESIDENTS
Sources of Income
(Division B)

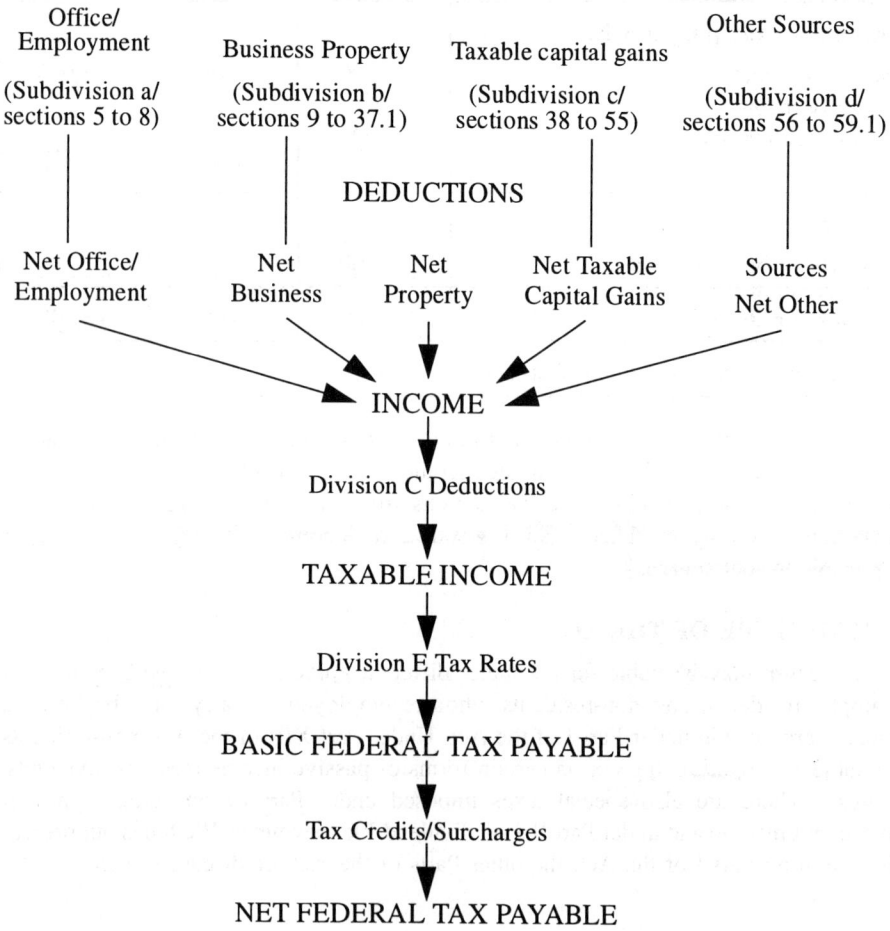

---

[27]   S. 2; Part I, Division C.

4. DEDUCTIONS vs. CREDITS

The Act allows deductions in some cases and allows credits in other cases. The difference between a deduction and a credit is that a deduction from income has the effect of reducing income which reduces the amount of tax payable. A tax credit directly reduces the amount of tax payable without reducing income.

Example IV.3		
Assume:		
A taxpayer with a marginal tax rate of 50 per cent has income of $100,000. The following example illustrates the effect of a $20,000 deduction from income compared to a credit of $20,000 against tax.		
	Deduction from income	**Tax credit**
Income	$ 100,000	$ 100,000
Less: deduction	(20,000)	—
Taxable income	80,000	100,000
Tax at 50%	40,000	50,000
Tax credit	—	(20,000)
Net payable	$ 40,000	$ 30,000

As Example IV. 3 illustrates, other things being equal, a dollar of tax credit is worth more to a taxpayer than a one dollar deduction from income. The reason for this is that, in real terms, a deduction is only worth its face value multiplied by the taxpayer's marginal rate of tax. For instance, a $1,000 deduction to an individual taxed at 25 per cent is equal to a saving of $250.

5. EXCLUSIONS FROM INCOME

References:

ITA:

Subs. 81(1)   Amounts Not Included in Income

BULLETINS, CIRCULARS & RULINGS:

IT-397R   February 23, 1990   Amounts Excluded from Income — Statutory Exemptions and Certain Service or RCMP Pensions, Allowances and Compensation

(a) General

Income for tax purposes is not synonymous with either the economist's or the accountant's understanding of income. It is a far less comprehensive measure of wealth than that contemplated by classical economists. Economists measure income by reference to the accretion of wealth between two points in time. The tax system proceeds on a judicial understanding of what constitutes "income", which is supplemented by numerous *ad hoc* statutory inclusions[28] and exclusions.[29] As Professor Rendall said:[30]

> [t]he fact is that our notions of income have been intuitive rather than logical and that our jurisprudence has developed on a case-by-case basis and has often reflected primarily a gut feeling about the characterization of a particular amount. What this means is that "income", for tax purposes, is not at all a single, consistent, concept.

Similarly, as we shall see in later chapters, income for tax purposes may be quite different from income for accounting purposes and financial statements.

The following are some of the more prominent exclusions from income:

- Gambling gains,
- Gifts and inheritances, and
- Windfall gains.

(b) Gambling Gains

Winnings from casual betting and incidental gambling are not considered income. The exclusion from income has been explained by some judges on the basis of the rationality of the activity that underlies the gambling gain:[31]

> What is a bet? A bet is merely an irrational agreement that one person should pay another person something on the happening of an event. A agrees to pay B something if C's horse runs quicker than D's or if a coin comes down one side up rather than the other side up. There is no relevance at all between the event and the acquisition of property. The event does not really produce it at all. It rests, as I say, on a mere irrational agreement.

It is a dubious proposition whether the exclusion of gambling gains from income can be justified on the basis of any reliable theory. Some courts have said that such gains do not flow from a source. This interpretation, however, ignores the statutory language of section 3 which includes income from any source inside or outside Canada.[32]

The exclusion may be more easily rationalized, however, on the basis of administrative considerations. Gambling gains are excluded from income only where the taxpayer realizes the gain in pursuit of a hobby and is not engaged in the business

---

[28] See, e.g., s. 12.

[29] See, e.g., s. 81.

[30] Rendall, "Defining the Tax Base", in Hansen, Krishna, Rendall eds., *Canadian Taxation* (Toronto: DeBoo, 1981).

[31] *Per* Rowlatt, J., in *Graham v. Green (Insp. of Taxes)*, [1925] 2 KB 37 at 39-40; *M.N.R. v. Morden*, [1961] CTC 484, 61 DTC 1266 (Ex. Ct.).

[32] See, e.g., *Rumack v. M.N.R.*, [1992] 1 CTC 57 at 59, 92 DTC 6142 at 6144 (F.C.A.).

of gambling.[33] Similarly, losses from gambling may not be deducted from income unless the losses are incurred in the conduct of a gambling *business*. The exclusion from income applies only to the capital sum of the gain and not to any income from the invested gain. For example, the exclusion does not extend to "cash for life" lotteries.[34]

(c) Gifts and Inheritances

Gifts and inheritances are also excluded from income for tax purposes. An economist would say that the recipient of a gift enhances his or her financial well-being and, therefore, the value of the gift should be included in income. For tax purposes, however, gifts and inheritances are not taxed.[35]

"Gift" is defined in *Halsbury* as follows:

A gift *inter vivos* may be defined shortly as the transfer of any property from one person to another gratuitously while the donor is alive and not in expectation of death. . . .

Black's Law Dictionary defines a "gift" as:

A voluntary transfer of personal property without consideration. . . .

A parting by owner with property without pecuniary consideration.

The *Shorter Oxford Dictionary* defines "giving" as:

. . . A transfer of property in a thing, voluntarily and without any valuable consideration. . . .

Thus, a "gift" is a voluntary and gratuitous transfer of property from one person to another. It may be subject to a pre-condition but, this apart, it is not revocable or terminable. A transfer of property from one person to another qualifies as a gift only if the transfer is both voluntary and made without any expectation of reward or return. A payment that takes the form of or requires a *quid pro quo* is not a gift.

(d) Windfall Gains

It is difficult to articulate a rational argument as to why "windfall gains" are, or should be, excluded from income. As with gifts and inheritances, windfall gains are an accretion to wealth and enhance the taxpayer's ability to pay. If the policy of the income tax is to impose similar tax burdens on those in similar financial circumstances, there is little merit in distinguishing between increments to wealth on the basis of their

---

[33] See, e.g., *M.N.R. v. Walker*, [1951] CTC 334, 52 DTC 1001 (Ex. Ct.) (gambling winnings taxable when achieved by taxpayer who himself owned and raced horses, had inside information and could not afford to lose).

[34] *Rumack v. M.N.R.*, [1992] 1 CTC 57, 92 DTC 6142 (F.C.A.).

[35] The Carter Commission proposed that, subject to a minimum exemption, gifts and inheritances should be included in the income of the recipient; see *Report of the Royal Commission on Taxation* (Ottawa: Queen's Printer, 1966) (Chair: K.M. Carter), vol. III, chapter 17.

source or expectations of return. Traditionally, however, Canadian courts have not considered windfalls as income for tax purposes.

It is even more difficult to define what constitutes a "windfall gain". The phrase is generally understood to include unexpected or unplanned gains that cannot be linked to one of the usual, identified sources (office, employment, business, property, and capital gains) of income. In fact, the category "windfall gains" represents nothing more than an unarticulated, and probably irrational, bias against taxing certain types of gains. Some courts have said that income can only arise from *expected* returns and "unexpected" gains are windfalls and are not taxable as income.

In *The Queen v. Cranswick*, for example:[36]

> In the absence of a special statutory definition extending the concept of income from a particular source, income from a source will be that which is typically earned by it or which typically flows from it as the expected return. The income which is typically earned by shares of capital stock consists of dividends paid by the company in which the shares are held. The payment in the present case was of an unusual and unexpected kind that one could not set out to earn as income from shares, and it was from a source to which the respondent had no reason to look for income from his shares. I agree with the learned trial judge that it was in the nature of a "windfall".

Windfall gains usually arise from unexpected sources. In addition, windfalls should satisfy the following criteria:

- the gain does not result from a legally enforceable claim,
- payment is not expected, either specifically or customarily,
- there is no foreseeable element of recurrence,
- the payor is not customarily a source of income for the recipient of the gain,
- payment is not given as consideration for services rendered, to garner favour, or anything else provided, and
- the payment is not earned as a result of an activity or pursuit of gain.

None of these criteria or characteristics is conclusive in determining whether a gain represents a "windfall gain" or "income" to a taxpayer. In each case the taxpayer must persuade the authorities that the gain is sufficiently unexpected, unplanned, and unrelated to one of the five named sources of income.[37]

---

[36] *The Queen v. Cranswick*, [1982] CTC 69 at 73, 82 DTC 6073 at 6076 (F.C.A.); leave to appeal to S.C.C. refused 42 NR 35.

[37] *MacEachern v. M.N.R.*, [1977] CTC 2139, 77 DTC 94 (T.R.B.) (proceeds from sale of gold and silver coins found by three deep-sea divers was income from organized activity that was more than a hobby); *Bell v. The Queen*, [1992] 2 CTC 260, 92 DTC 6472 (F.C.A.) (lump sum payment to corporate taxpayer upon termination of exclusive distributorship agents was income); *Johnson & Johnson Inc. v. Canada*, [1994] 1 CTC 244, 94 DTC 6125 (F.C.A.) (unexpected refund was business income and not windfall when looked at in context).

Some examples of "windfall gains" that have been accepted by the courts are: voluntary payments to flood victims,[38] and unexpected money payments to mollify minority shareholders.[39]

A lump-sum inducement payment is not a windfall gain.[40] Inducement payments constitute incentives to induce certain acts, for example, to encourage a lessee to locate in a shopping mall.[41]

6. BARTER TRANSACTIONS

Reference:

BULLETINS, CIRCULARS & RULINGS:

IT-490   July 5, 1982   Barter Transactions

A barter transaction is one in which two or more persons agree to a reciprocal exchange of goods or services without the use of money. In its simplest form, bartering is nothing more nor less than a market transaction where the medium of exchange is goods or services instead of legal tender.[42] A reciprocal exchange of gifts, however, is not a barter.

Payments in kind for goods and services are governed by the same principles applicable to payments in cash. Thus, a payment in kind may be characterized as being on account of income, capital property, eligible capital property, or capital. In each case the source and value of the payment must be identified.

Payments in kind may involve bilateral or multilateral exchanges of property. For example, a lawyer who renders legal services to a farmer may accept a cow in settlement of the account. Alternatively, the lawyer may accept a non-cash credit which can be exchanged in a barter "pool" for other goods and services, e.g., the cow credit may be exchanged for plumbing services. The essence of barter transactions is that they involve an exchange, whether bilateral or multilateral, of goods and services without the use of money.

---

[38] *Federal Farms Ltd. v. M.N.R.*, [1959] CTC 98, 59 DTC 1050 (Ex. Ct.) (voluntary payments to help taxpayer whose farm was flooded during hurricane was gift, not income).

[39] *The Queen v. Cranswick, ante* (majority shareholder paid minority shareholder sum to avoid controversy over reorganization; unexpected and unusual payment was windfall).

[40] Para. 12(1)(x).

[41] *French Shoes Ltd. v. The Queen*, [1986] 2 CTC 132, 86 DTC 6359 (F.C.T.D.) ("...an inducement is not a 'windfall', it is an incentive, a reason for doing something").

[42] IT-490, "Barter Transactions" (July 5, 1982).

Barter transactions give rise to special valuation problems. Should the payment in kind be valued on the basis of its *value in use* to the recipient or its *value in exchange* for the goods or services sold or rendered?

Suppose a lawyer renders legal services for which she would usually charge $2,000 in exchange for a cow that has a market value of $1,600. How much should she include in her income, $2,000 (value of her services) or $1,600 (value of her exchange)? Revenue Canada takes the view that the recipient's income is increased by the price that he or she would "normally have charged" for the goods or services provided,[43] in this example, $2,000. Where, however, the goods or services given up cannot readily be valued but the goods or services rendered can, the value of the latter can be used to set the price of the transaction.

In multilateral barter schemes with restrictions on exchange of barter credits, the value of consideration received may be considerably less than the "theoretical" value of goods and services sold or rendered. Since barter credits are a substitute medium of exchange, it is the value of the medium which should determine the price to be recognized. In effect, a taxpayer who renders services for credits which have a restricted exchange value discounts the price normally charged in a transaction for legal tender.

In *Linett v. M.N.R.*,[44] for example, the taxpayers were partners in a law firm. The firm had an account with a barter exchange known as Tradex. Under the Tradex scheme, member businesses accepted barter credits from other members in exchange for goods and services. The taxpayers accepted Tradex credits in exchange for legal services and, for tax purposes, valued each dollar credit at 55 cents. The Minister assessed on the basis that each dollar credit should be valued at par. The Tax Court held that the Tradex credits were worth less than their face value. The credits had restricted exchange features, were indiscriminately issued for services not rendered, and the scheme was falling apart. Thus, even though the taxpayers billed full value for their legal services, their income was only enhanced by the discounted value of their credits.

7. EXEMPT INCOME

References:

ITA:

S. 126   Foreign Tax Deduction

S. 149   Persons Exempt From Tax

---

[43] *Ibid.*

[44] *Linett v. M.N.R.*, [1985] 2 CTC 2037, 85 DTC 416 (T.C.C.).

In addition to the common law exclusions of certain receipts from income, the Act specifically exempts certain forms of income from tax. Note the distinction between a taxpayer who is exempt from tax[45] and income that is tax exempt. In the former case, a specific recipient is exempt from tax regardless of the nature of the income earned. In the latter case, specific types of income are exempt from tax, regardless of who is receiving it.

The following list illustrates the types of exempt income:

Exempt Income	Statutory Provisions	Comments
amounts declared by any other federal statute to be exempt from income tax[46]	para. 81(1)(a)	
amounts from War Savings Certificates	para. 81(1)(b)	
income of a non-resident earned in Canada from operation of a ship or aircraft in international traffic	para. 81(1)(c)	only if the individual's country of residence grants a similar exemption
pension, payment, allowance or compensation received under *Pension Act, Merchant Navy Veteran and Civilian War-related Benefits Act, Gallantry Awards Order* or section 9 of the *Aeronautics Act*	para. 81(1)(d)	
payments received on account of death or disability incurred in war service from an allied country	para. 81(1)(e)	only if the country grants similar relief with respect to pensions paid in Canada
any payments with respect to death or injury sustained in the 1917 Halifax explosion	para. 81(1)(f)	
compensation paid by Federal Republic of Germany to victims of Nazi persecution	para. 81(1)(g)	if amount in exempt from tax by German law
income or taxable capital gains from property or from disposition of property received as compensation for physical or mental injury	paras. 81(1)(g.1), (g.2); subs. 81(5)	if income or gain is earned or received before taxpayer becomes 21; taxpayer may elect deemed disposition of capital property in the year he or she attains age of 21
receipt of income-tested social assistance payment by taxpayer on behalf of individual other than spouse or relative	para. 81(1)(h)	if individual resides in taxpayer's principal residence

---

[45] S. 149.

[46] See, e.g., *Indian Act*, R.S.C. 1985, c. I-5; *Foreign Missions and International Organizations Act*, S.C. 1991, c. 41; *Visiting Forces Act*, R.S.C. 1985, c. V-2.

Exempt Income	Statutory Provisions	Comments
amount for injury, disability or death under *RCMP Pension Continuation Act* or *RCMP Superannuation Act*	para. 81(1)(*i*)	
certain payments from an employee profit-sharing plan	para. 81(1)(*k*); s. 144	
receipts of a share of a corporation by prospector or grubstaker	para. 81(1)(*l*); s. 35	to extent provided by s. 35
interest accrued, receivable or received by resident corporation on an obligation received as consideration for the disposition before June 18, 1971 of a business of a public utility or service nature	para. 81(1)(*m*)	if the obligation is guaranteed by the government or one of its agencies of the country where the business is carried on
income from the office of Governor General of Canada	para. 81(1)(*n*)	
education assistance payments or refund of payments under an education savings plan	paras. 81(1)(*o*), (*p*); s. 146.1	
amount paid to an individual as prescribed indemnity under provincial law	para. 81(1)(*q*); Pt. LXV. Reg. 6501	
amounts credited to foreign retirement arrangement account	para. 81(1)(*r*)	
allowances paid to an an elected member of assembly for expenses incidental to the duties of office	subs. 81(2)	to extent that allowance is not more than 1/2 of the maximum of the member's salary
allowances paid to elected officers of municipal utilities board commission or corporation; public or separate school board for expenses incidental to the duties of office	subs. 81(3)	to extent that alowance is not more than 1/2 of the officer's salary
amount received by a part-time employee as an allowance or reimbursement of travelling expenses incurred during a period when he had other employment or carried on a business	subs. 81(3.1)	so long as amounts are reasonable and duties are performed at least 80 kms from his or her principal place of employment or business and residence

SAMPLE CALCULATIONS OF INCOME

Problem IV.4

Harry Schmidt is a Canadian resident. The following data applies in respect of his 1995 taxation year.

INCOME:	
Net salary	$ 54,000
Deductions from salary:	
CPP	445
UIC	648
Income tax	8,000
Pension plan (registered)	3,500
Premiums to group health plan	50
Commissions from employment	7,000
Interest on bonds	5,000
Scholarships	1,000
Net rental income	12,000
Taxable capital gain on listed personal property	12,000
Allowable capital loss on listed personal property	13,000
Taxable capital gain	5,500
Allowable capital loss (incl. ABIL)	3,000
Allowable business investment loss (ABIL)	1,500
EXPENSES:	
Safety deposit box fees	$ 80
Alimony payments	6,500
Charitable donations	2,000
Tuition fees	1,500
Accounting fees for preparation of personal tax return	500
Legal fees to purchase rental property	1,500
Income tax instalments	5,000

Calculate Mr. Schmidt's income for 1995 according to section 3.

Solution IV.4

Income determined under section 3:

para. 3(a):

Gross salary	$ 66,643	
Commissions from employment	7,000	
Less: pension contributions	(3,500)	
Net employment income		$ 70,143
Income from property:		
Net rental income	12,000	
Interest on bonds	5,000	
Safety deposit box fees	(80)	
		$ 16,920
Scholarships	1,000	
Less: exempt amount	(500)	500
		$ 87,563

para. 3(b):

Taxable capital gain	5,500	
Taxable gain on LPP	12,000	
Allowable loss on LPP	(13,000)	
Net gain on LPP		0
		5,500
Allowable capital loss	3,000	
Less ABIL	1,500	
		(1,500)
		$ 91,563

para. 3(c):

Alimony payments	(6,500)	
		$ 85,063

para. 3(d):

Allowable business investment loss	(1,500)	
Income		**$ 83,563**

Note: CPP and UIC payments are claimed as tax credits under s. 118.7.

Problem IV.5

Assume:

The following data applies to Alesia Ng:	1995
Employment income (gross)	$68,000
Registered pension plan contributions	3,500
Business income	15,550
Business losses	9,000
Rental income	12,500
Capital gains	3,000
Taxable listed personal property gain	5,000
Taxable listed personal property loss	7,500
Capital losses	13,500
Alimony expenses	5,000
Allowable business investment losses (ABIL)	2,000

Calculate Ms. Ng's income according to the section format.

Solution IV.5

para. 3(a):

Employment income*	$64,500	
Business income	15,550	
Property income	12,500	
		$92,550

para. 3(b):

Taxable capital gains	2,250	
Net LPP gains	0	
Net gains	$ 2,250	
Allowable capital losses exceeds ABIL	8,125	0
		92,550

Exceeds para. 3(c):

Alimony expenses		5,000
		87,550

Exceeds para. 3(d):

Business losses	9,000	
Allowable Business Investment Losses	2,000	
		11,000
Income		$76,550

*Employment income less registered pension plan deduction of $3,500.

SELECTED BIBLIOGRAPHY TO CHAPTER IV

General

Bittker, "Income Tax Reform in Canada: The Report of the Royal Commission on Taxation" (1968), 35 *U. Chi. L. Rev.* 367.

Bossons, "The Value of a Comprehensive Tax Base Reform Goal" (1970), 13 *J. Law & Econ.* 327.

Bruce, Neil, "Ability to Pay and Comprehensive Income Taxation: Annual or Lifetime Basis" in *The Quest for Tax Reform: The Royal Commission on Taxation Twenty Years Later* (Toronto: Carswell, 1988), at 157.

Csordas, Elizabeth A., "Cost or Market Valuation" (1990), 24 *CGA Magazine* 62.

Davies, N.H., "Income-Plus-Wealth: In Search of a Better Tax Base" (Summer 1984), 15 *Rutgers L. J.* 849.

Drache, A.B.C., "Charity Paper Response", (1991) XIII *Can. Taxpayer* 185.

Haig, R.M., ed., *The Federal Income Tax* (New York, 1921).

Knecthel, Ronald C., "Role of Generally Accepted Accounting Principles in Determining Income for Tax Purposes", in *Proceedings of 31st Tax Conf.* 845 (Can. Tax Foundation, 1979).

Koppelman, Stanley A., "Personal Deductions Under an Ideal Income Tax" (1988), 43 *The Tax Lawyer* 679.

Perry, David B., "Selected Statistics on the Evolution of the Personal Income Tax System Since 1970" (1987), 35 *Can. Tax J.* 207.

Perry, Harvey, "Federal Individual Income Tax: Some General Concepts", *Tax Paper No. 89* 42 (Can. Tax Foundation, 1990).

Rendall, "Defining the Tax Base", in Hansen, Krishna, Rendall eds., *Can. Tax.* (Toronto: De Boo, 1981).

Royal Commission on Taxation, Study No. 19B, pp. 88-157 (1957).

Sewell, David, "Towards Longer Time Horizons in Personal Taxation" (1988), 26 *Osgoode Hall Law J.* 235.

Simons, H.C., *Personal Income Taxation* (Chicago: The University of Chicago Press, 1938).

Stepp, James, "The New Accounting for Income Taxes: An Overview of FAS 96" (1988), 40 *Tax Exec.* 299.

Stone, "A Comprehensive Income Tax Base for the U.S.?: Implications of the Report of the Royal Commission on Taxation" (1969), 22 *Nat. Tax J.* 24.

Wealth Tax: Working Group Report (Toronto: Fair Tax Commission, 1993).

Williamson, W. Gordon, "Changes Relating to the Computation of Income", in *Proceedings of 32nd Tax Conf.* 115 (Can. Tax Foundation, 1980).

The Meaning of "Income"

"Accounting vs. Tax Income", in *Proceedings of 16th Tax Conf.* 350 (Can. Tax Foundation, 1962).

Block, Walter, "Comment on McCready and Maloney on Wealth Taxation" (1992), 35 *Can. Public Administration* 542.

Coppola, Sam, "Is 'Safe Income' a Misnomer?" (August 1989), 122 *CA Magazine* 47.

Csordas, Elizabeth A., "Cost or Market Valuation" (1990), 24 *CGA Magazine* 62.

Ellis, J., "Aggregation of Income and Losses from Various Sources" (1981), *Can. Tax.* 443.

Goodison, Don, "Questionable Income" (December 1989), 23 *CGA Magazine* 17.

La Brie, "The Meaning of Income in the Law of Income Tax" (1953), *U.T.L.J.* 81.

Maloney, Maureen A., "The Case Against Wealth Tax: A Reply" (1992), 35 *Can. Public Administration* 539.

McCallum, Thomas J., "Valuation and Income Tax" (April 1991), 25 *CGA Magazine* 24.

Perry, Harvey, "Federal Individual Income Tax: Some General Concepts", *Tax Paper No. 89* 42 (Can. Tax Foundation, 1990).

Thuronyi, Victor, "The Concept of Income" (1990), 46 *Tax L. Rev.* 45.

Income from a Source

"Is Polanyi Taxable on his Nobel Prize Money?" (1987), 9:6 *Can. Taxpayer* 37.

Jones, David P., "The Revenue Side of Calculating Income", in *Proceedings of 33rd Tax Conf.* 902 (Can. Tax Foundation, 1981).

Jones, David P., "Sources of Income", in *Proceedings of 34th Tax Conf.* 911 (Can. Tax Foundation, 1982).

Raich, Robert, "Characterization of Income and Third Party Alimony Receipts", in *Proceedings of 32nd Tax Conf.* 238 (Can. Tax Foundation, 1980).

Thuronyi, Victor, "The Concept of Income" (1990), 46 *Tax Law Rev.* 45.

Exclusions from Income

Barnett, Terry G., "Cash (and Tax?) for Life Lotteries" (1990), 38 *Can. Tax J.* 675.

Comment, "Taxation of Found Property and Other Windfalls" (1953), 20 *U. Chi. L. Rev.* 748.

Drache, A.B.C., "Gambling as a Tax Substitute" (1991), XIII *Can. Taxpayer* 100.

Drache, A.B.C., "Lottery Winner Taxes" (1991), XIV *Can. Taxpayer* 53.

Drache, A.B.C., "Tax-Free Goodies" (1991), XIV *Can. Taxpayer* 68.

Duff, David G., "Taxing Inherited Wealth: A Philosophical Argument" (1993), 6 *Can. J. of Law and Jurisprudence* 3.

Krishna, Vern, "Windfall Gains and Inducement Payments" (1986), 1 *Can. Current Tax* J-163.

Richards, Gabrielle, "Tenant Inducement Payments Revisited" (1991), 3 *Can. Current Tax* J-81

"The Trade or Business Issue: Can a Gambling Loss Properly be Considered a Business Loss?" (Winter 1985), 19 *Suffolk U.L. Rev.* 907.

Vaillancourt & Grignon, "Canadian Lotteries as Taxes: Revenues and Incidence" (1988), 36 *Can. Tax J.* 369.

Barter Transactions

Krishna, Vern, "Payments in Kind and Barter — Inclusion in Income — Valuation" (1985), 1:20 *Can. Current Tax* J-93.

Exempt Income

Drache, A.B.C., "Tax Exempt Expenses for Moonlighting Employees" (1991), XIII *Can. Taxpayer* 159.

CHAPTER V

INCOME FROM AN OFFICE OR EMPLOYMENT

> Classification is the beginning of wisdom.
> Seligman, Double Taxation and International Fiscal Cooperation (1928)

1. GENERAL

We saw in Chapter IV "What is Income?" that income is determined by source and aggregated in a defined manner and in a specified sequence. Determination of income from an office or employment is the first step in the sequence in paragraph 3(*a*).

Only an individual can have income from an office or employment,[1] that must be calculated separately from other sources of income.

There are three questions to be answered in the determination of employment income:

1. Characterization: What is employment income?

2. Timing: When is employment income taxed?

3. Scope: What is included in employment income?

Accurate classification of employment income is important. The taxation of employment income is substantially different from the rules applicable to business income. The determination of employment income is subject to much more control than is the case for business income.

There are four major distinctions between employment income and business income. First, deductions from employment income are strictly controlled; an employee is not entitled to a deduction from employment income *unless* the deduction is specifically authorized.[2] In contrast, deductions from business income are governed by commercial and accounting principles. Business expenses are generally deductible unless specifically prohibited.[3] This difference in the treatment of deductions from employment and business income is in itself sufficient incentive for taxpayers to attempt

---

[1]   Subs. 248(1) ("employment") and ("office").

[2]   Subs. 8(2).

[3]   Subs. 9(1); *Royal Trust Co. v. M.N.R.*, [1957] CTC 32, 57 DTC 1055 (Ex. Ct.) (payment of dues and memberships in community and social clubs on behalf of employees deductible where employees expected to make contacts and generate business); *Dom. Taxicab Assn. v. M.N.R.*, [1954] CTC 34, 54 DTC 1020 (S.C.C.) (fees to company contracting with taxicab owners not deductible; funds contingently received not income); *Bank of N.S. v. The Queen*, [1980] CTC 57, 80 DTC 6009; affirmed [1981] CTC 162, 81 DTC 5115 (F.C.A.) (value of foreign tax credit determined in accordance with ordinary commercial principles, taking weighted rate of exchange at time tax payable).

to characterize their income as business income. It is much easier to deduct expenses against business income than against employment income.

Second, the taxation year for employment income is always the calendar year.[4] Thus, an employee cannot choose his or her fiscal year-end in respect of employment source income. Business income may be calculated on the basis of a fiscal period. This allows an individual considerable flexibility in planning with respect to business income, especially in selecting the first fiscal period of a business.

Third, tax must be withheld from employment income at its source of payment.[5] Withheld taxes are held in trust for the Crown.[6] Business income is not subject to withholding tax at source. Taxpayers who earn business income are required to make instalment payments on account of their tax payable.[7] Unremitted tax instalments are not held in trust.

Fourth, income from an office or employment is generally taxable on a cash or receipt basis.[8] Income from business or property is generally taxable on an accrual basis, that is, when it is earned, regardless of when it is received.[9]

These differences in the taxation of employment and business income are important not only to the taxpayer but also to the government. Tax on employment income is predictable and easily controlled. Withholding of tax at the source of employment and annual reporting on a computerized form (T4) allows Revenue Canada to verify the amount payable at minimal cost and with speed and accuracy.

There are also important non-tax reasons for distinguishing between employment source and business source income. For example, in an employment relationship the employer is responsible for the following:

- Deducting and remitting UIC and CPP deductions at source,
- Paying the employer's share of UIC and CPP premiums,
- Paying assessments pursuant to the *Workers' Compensation Act,*

---

[4]   Subs. 5(1) and para. 249(1)(*b*).

[5]   Para. 153(1)(*a*).

[6]   Subs. 227(4). Failure to withhold tax on employment income renders the employer liable to a civil penalty of 10 per cent plus interest at a prescribed rate (subs. 227(8)) and to criminal penalties (subs. 238(1)). Directors of a corporation who fail to withhold and remit taxes may be personally liable (subs. 227.1(1)).

[7]   Subs. 157(1).

[8]   Subs. 5(1). There is an important exception for "salary deferral arrangements"; see para. 6(1)(*i*), subs. 248(1) ("salary deferral arrangement") and subs. 6(11).

[9]   S. 9. See Chapter VI "Business and Investment Income: General" for a discussion of the cash and accrual methods of reporting income.

- Paying severance, holiday, sick leave, maternity and termination benefits pursuant to employment standards legislation, and
- Paying termination settlements as required by the doctrines of employment law, e.g., wrongful dismissal.

These obligations apply only in employment relationships.

2. THE CHARACTERIZATION OF EMPLOYMENT INCOME

References:

ITA:

S. 5   Basic Rules: Income from Office or Employment

BULLETINS, CIRCULARS & RULINGS:

IT-168R3	May 13, 1991	Athletes and Players Employed by Football, Hockey and Similar Clubs
IT-292	February 23, 1976	Taxation of Elected Officers of Incorporated Municipalities, School Boards, Municipal Commissions and Similar Bodies

(a) Contract of Employment

The distinction between a contract of employment and a contract for services is based on law and fact and depends upon the nature of the relationship between the parties. The difference between these two types of relationship also depends upon the context in which the question arises. In traditional employer-employee (master-servant) relationships, characterization depends on the degree of control and supervision exercised by one person over another in the provision of services.

In a contract for services, one person engages another to perform services in order to achieve a prescribed objective without necessarily specifying the manner in which the objective is to be attained. The person (sometimes referred to as an independent contractor) who offers his or her services does so for a fee, but the recipient of the service does not control how the work is performed.

In an employment relationship (also referred to as a contract of service), the employee is under the direct control and supervision of the employer and is obliged to obey that person's orders. In this situation, the employer controls not only *what* is done by the employee, but also *how* it is done. Hence, a contract of service is sometimes also referred to as a master-servant relationship.

The classic statement on the distinction between a contract of service and a contract for services is found in *Walker*, where Baron Bramwell said:[10]

> It seems to me that the difference between the relations of master and servant and of principal and agent is this: A principal has the right to direct what the agent has to do; but a master has not only that right, but also the right to say how it is to be done.

(i) Substance of Relationship

The distinction between a contract of service and a contract for services must be determined according to the substance of the relationship between the parties and not merely by reference to the form of the documentation that the parties put forward to assert a particular relationship. The following elements determine the nature of a relationship between persons:

- The degree of supervision,
- The method of remuneration,
- Arrangements for holidays,
- Provision of sick leave,
- Opportunities for outside employment,
- Provision of medical coverage,
- Compensation for work related travel, and
- Termination clauses.

(ii) Control Test

At one time, the "control test" was used almost exclusively to determine whether a person retained another as an employee or as an independent contractor. The control test remains important, particularly in traditional relationships, but it has been supplemented by other tests in recent years.

---

[10] *The Queen v. Walker* (1858), 27 LJMC 207 at 207-208; see also *Alexander v. M.N.R.*, [1969] CTC 715 at 724, 70 DTC 6006 at 6010 (Ex. Ct.) (radiologist at hospital permitted to deduct travelling expenses incurred to fulfill duties at other hospitals); *Rosen v. The Queen*, [1976] CTC 462, 76 DTC 6274 (F.C.T.D.) (full-time civil servant and part-time lecturer denied status as independent contractor for lectures; decision emphasized "control test"); *Ladd v. M.N.R.*, [1978] CTC 3071, 78 DTC 1775 (T.R.B.) (taxpayer's inability to replace his services under agreement determined employment status); *Molot v. M.N.R.*, [1977] CTC 2170, 77 DTC 111 (T.R.B.) (no difference in type of control exercised over a part-time lecturer vs. full-time lecturer; taxpayer was employee although only billing three hours a week); *Ready Mixed Concrete (South East) Ltd. v. Min. of Pensions & Nat. Ins.*, [1968] 2 QB 497, [1968] 1 All ER 433 (contract of service exists if: (l) employee provides *own* work and skill, (2) sufficiently subjects self to control by master, and (3) remaining contractual terms consistent with employment).

The degree and extent of control is tested by four criteria:[11]

1. Power to select the person who renders the service;

2. Mode of payment of wages;

3. Control over the method and performance of work; and

4. Right to suspend or dismiss the person engaged to perform the work.

These four facets of the "control test" are useful in characterizing conventional types of employment relationships, particularly relationships involving unskilled and non-technical persons. Indeed, the label of "master-servant", that is sometimes used to describe these types of relationships, speaks to the nature of the relationship between the person providing the services and the person to whom the services are provided.

The test is, however, of limited value in characterizing working relationships between technical persons and skilled professionals. As MacGuigan J. said in *Wiebe Door Services Ltd.*: ". . . The test has broken down completely in relation to highly skilled and professional workers, who possess skills far beyond the ability of their employers to direct".[12] Thus, although the "control test" is useful in characterizing certain employment relationships,[13] it is of marginal value in characterizing relationships involving highly skilled professionals.[14]

(iii) Organization/Integration Test

Characterizing the working relationships of skilled professionals involves more than merely identifying who has the theoretical power to dictate how work is to be performed. In relationships involving skilled persons, the user of services does not usually have the technical expertise or "know how" to dictate how the work is to be carried out. Hence, any power or control that does exist is more illusory than real. The first reason for hiring a professional is so that she or he can instruct management in the

---

[11] See *Gould v. Minister of National Insurance*, [1951] All ER 368 (K.B.) (contract for services of music hall artist contained restrictions and elements of control but only that necessary for proper working of theatre); *Bell v. M.N.R.* (1952), 52 DTC 8 (T.A.B.) (physician to rural villages contracted to provide services; still maintained private practice); *Fainstein v. M.N.R.* (1952), 52 DTC 102 (T.A.B.) (physician and others setting up health departments).

[12] *Wiebe Door Services Ltd. v. M.N.R.*, [1986] 2 CTC 200 at 203, 87 DTC 5025 at 5028 (F.C.A.).

[13] See, e.g., *Hôpital Notre-Dame et Théoret v. Laurent*, [1978] 1 SCR 605 at 613 where Pigeon J. quoted with approval the following passage from *Traité pratique de la responsabilité civile délictuelle* by André Nadeau (translation):

   The essential criterion of employer-employee relations is the right to give orders and instructions to the employee regarding the manner in which to carry out his work.

[14] See, e.g., *Montreal v. Montreal Locomotive Works Ltd.*, [1947] 1 DLR 161 *per* Lord Wright at 169 (P.C.): "In the more complex conditions of modern industry, more complicated tests have often to be applied. . . . Control in itself is not always conclusive."; *Morren v. Swinton & Pendlebury Borough Council*, [1965] 1 WLR 576 *per* Lord Parker at 582 (Q.B.): ". . . clearly superintendence and control cannot be the decisive test when one is dealing with a professional man, or a man of some particular skill and experience".

performance of complex and technical tasks. A professional or skilled person is hired to provide expertise, not to be told how to do his or her job. As Professor J.G. Fleming said:[15]

> Under the pressure of novel situations, the courts have become increasingly aware of the strain on the traditional formulation [i.e. the control test], and most recent cases display a discernable tendency to replace it by something like an "organization" test. Was the alleged servant part of his employer's organization? Was his work subject to co-ordinational control as to "where" and "when" rather than to "how"?

Lord Denning described the test as follows:[16]

> One feature which seems to run through all the instances is that, under a contract of service, a man is employed as part of the business, and his work is done as an integral part of the business; whereas under a contract for services, his work, although done for the business, is not integrated into it but is only accessory to it.

Thus, the question becomes: Is the person an intrinsic part of the organization with employee status or an adjunct to it, a supplier of services on his or her own account? This is sometimes described as the organization or integration test. Here too, however, there is no simple formula or single test to apply to determine the answer. One looks to the whole scheme of operations to elicit the nature of the relationship between the parties.

The "organization test" is also subject to criticism as being impractical and capable of leading to results as absurd as those of the control test. The integration test provides the wrong answer by the very nature of the question that it poses.

As MacGuigan, J. said in *Wiebe Door Services Ltd.*:[17]

> Lord Denning's test may be more difficult to apply, as witness the way in which it has been misused as a magic formula by the Tax Court . . . in several other cases . . . in all of which the effect has been to dictate the answer through the very form of the question, by showing that without the work of the "employees" the "employer" would be out of business. . . . As thus applied, this can never be a fair test, because in a factual relationship of mutual dependency it must always result in an affirmative answer. If the businesses of both parties are so structured as to operate through each other, they could not survive independently without being restructured. But that is a consequence of their surface arrangement and not necessarily expressive of their intrinsic relationship.

Thus, the focus shifted away from narrow, single criterion, magic formula tests towards broader based (some say "common sense") tests which look to multiple and more general criteria.

---

[15] See Fleming, *The Law of Torts*, 2d. ed. (Australia: The Law Book Co. of Australia Pty Ltd., 1961), at 328-29; quoted with approval by Spence J. in *Cooperators Ins. Assn. v. Kearney*, [1965] SCR 106 at 112.

[16] *Stevenson (Stephenson), Jordan & Harrison Ltd. v. MacDonald & Evans*, [1952] 1 TLR 101 at 111 (C.A.). See also: *Cooperators Ins. Assn. v. Kearney*, [1965] SCR 106.

[17] *Wiebe Door Services Ltd. v. M.N.R.*, [1986] 2 CTC 200 at 205, 87 DTC 5025 at 5029 (F.C.A.).

(iv) The Total Relationship Test

Although the control, organization and integration tests should be used in appropriate situations, they are not determinative. They have an overly narrow focus. The better approach is a more broadly based examination of the "total relationship" between the parties,[18] including:

- Control,
- Ownership of assets,
- Chance of profit, and
- Risk of loss.

These are not separate and independent tests. They are merely four aspects of the same test. The question of the nature of the relationship of persons is to be answered upon analysis of "the combined force of the whole scheme of operations".[19]

The total relationship test is flexible and adaptable to different circumstances. Thus, the question and its analysis can be reformulated as follows:[20]

> . . . "Is the person who has engaged himself to perform these services performing them as a person in business on his own account?" If the answer to that question is "yes," then the contract is a contract for services. If the answer is "no" then the contract is a contract of service. No exhaustive list has been compiled and perhaps no exhaustive list can be compiled of considerations which are relevant in determining that question, nor can strict rules be laid down as to the relative weight which the various considerations should carry in particular cases. The most that can be said is that control will no doubt always have to be considered, although it can no longer be regarded as the sole determining factor; and that factors, which may be of importance, are such matters as whether the man performing the services provides his own equipment, whether he hires his own helpers, what degree of financial risk be taken, what degree of responsibility for investment and management he has, and whether and how far he has an opportunity of profiting from sound management in the performance of his task. The application of the general test may be easier in a case where the person who engages himself to perform the services does so in the course of an already established business of his own; but this factor is not decisive, and a person who engages himself to perform services for another may well be an independent contractor even though he has not entered into the contract in the course of an existing business carried on by him.

(b) Revenue Canada's Administrative View

Revenue Canada does not have a general administrative position that is applicable to all circumstances. It has, however, issued IT-525, "Performing Artists" (April 20,

---

[18] See *Montreal v. Montreal Locomotive Works Ltd.*, [1947] 1 DLR 161 at 169-70, *per* Lord Wright.

[19] See, MacGuigan J. in *Wiebe Door Services Ltd. v. M.N.R.*, *ante*, a decision that has since been frequently cited as the "definitive authority" on the question of characterizing employment relationships; see, *Moose Jaw Kinsman Flying Fins Inc. v. M.N.R.*, [1988] 2 CTC 2377, 88 DTC 6099 (F.C.A.).

[20] The Federal Court of Appeal approved this approach by adopting the statement of Cooke J. in *Market Investigations, Ltd. v. Min. of Social Security*, [1968] 3 All ER 732 at 738-39 in *Wiebe Door Services Ltd. v. M.N.R.*, *ante*, [1986] 2 CTC at 206-207, 87 DTC at 5030.

1990) which deals with certain limited aspects of the characterization problem in relation to musicians and other performing artists. Revenue Canada states:[21]

> Many factors must be taken into consideration in establishing whether an individual is an employee or is self-employed. The question to be decided is whether the contract between the parties is a contract of service that exists between an employer and an employee, or is a contract for services, that is, the engagement of a self-employed individual. A contract of service generally exists if the person for whom the services are performed has the right to control the amount, the nature, and the management of the work to be done and the manner of doing it. A contract for services exists when a person is engaged to achieve a defined objective and is given all the freedom required to attain the desired result.

The Department goes on, however, to deal with particular problems created by persons who have special skills and expertise:[22]

> When dealing with persons of particular skills and expertise, such as artists, supervision and control of the manner in which the work is done may not be a critical and decisive factor. However, the determination of whether or not an artist is under a contract of service or a contract for services is a question of fact, and will depend on the nature and the terms of the contract or arrangement (written or oral), its duration, and all the elements that constitute the relationship between the parties.

An artist is considered to be self-employed if she or he:[23]

- has a chance of profit or risk of loss;
- provides instruments and other equipment;
- has a number of engagements with different persons during the course of a year;
- regularly auditions or makes applications for engagements;
- retains the services of an agent on a continuing basis;
- can select or hire employees or helpers, fix their salary, direct them or dismiss them;
- can arrange the time, place, and nature of performances; or
- is entitled to remuneration that is directly related to particular rehearsals and performances. . . .

The fact remains that characterization of relationships requires a delicate balancing operation, weighing the factors which point in one direction and balancing them against those pointing in the other. One cannot expect the operation to be performed with scientific precision.

Although not openly acknowledged, there is a difference in judicial attitudes in characterizing employment relationships in tax law and in other employment related areas. In employment law, there is a trend towards characterizing workers as employees to enable them to derive the benefits of legislation intended to protect the economically

---

[21] IT-525, "Performing Artists" (April 20, 1990), para. 4.

[22] *Id.*, at para. 5.

[23] *Id.*, at para. 8.

dependent and vulnerable. In tax law, the advantage lies with the independent contractor and, hence, one may be inclined to view the relationship from a different perspective.

3. TIMING OF INCLUSIONS

Reference:

BULLETINS, CIRCULARS & RULINGS:

IT-222R   November 22, 1976   Advances to Employees

Employment source income is generally calculated on a cash basis. An individual is required to include salary and wages in income only when he or she actually receives payment.[24] In contrast, income from business and property is calculated on an accrual basis — revenues and expenses are recognized when earned or incurred, rather than when received or expended.

The difference in the timing of recognition of employment income (cash basis) and business income (accrual basis) allows for some flexibility in tax planning. For example, an individual employed by his or her own corporation is taxable only on the salary that he or she is actually paid, but the corporation may deduct the salary payable on an accrual basis.[25] Hence, the corporation may deduct the expense in one year, while the employee does not include the amount in income until he or she actually receives payment. This imbalance between deduction and inclusion allows for some tax deferral. For this reason, the Act specifically limits the deferral advantage inherent in this type of mismatching of income and expenses to a maximum of 180 days after the end of the employer's fiscal period.[26]

4. SCOPE OF INCLUSIONS IN EMPLOYMENT INCOME

References:

ITA:

S. 6   Income from Office or Employment

S. 7   Employee Share Options

Subs. 56(4.1)   Interest Free or Low Interest Loans

S. 80.4   Loans

---

[24] Subs. 5(1); but see *Blenkarn v. M.N.R.* (1963), 32 Tax ABC 321, 63 DTC 581 (T.A.B.) (voluntary deferment of salary due and payable to employee held to be taxable in year amount due, not when actually received); IT-222R "Advances to Employees" (November 22, 1976) (advance on account of salary included in income in year money advanced to employee); *Ferszt v. M.N.R.*, [1978] CTC 2860, 78 DTC 1648 (T.R.B.) ($5,000 advance against commissions included in income). Farming and fishing businesses also permitted to use cash method of accounting; see s. 28.

[25] *Earlscourt Sheet Metal Mech. Ltd. v. M.N.R.*, [1988] 1 CTC 2045, 88 DTC 1029 (T.C.C.).

[26] Subs. 78(4).

S. 80.5   Deemed Interest

S. 81   Exclusions from Income

Para. 87(2)(*k*)   Payments to Employees

BULLETINS, CIRCULARS & RULINGS:

IT-196R2	November 23, 1981	Payments by Employer to Employee
IT-202R2	September 19, 1985	Employees' or Workers' Compensation
IT-266	November 10, 1975	Taxation of Members of Provincial Legislative Assemblies
IT-316	May 10, 1976	Awards for Employees' Suggestions and Inventions
IT-428	April 30, 1979	Wage Loss Replacement Plans
ATR-21	May 8, 1987	Pension Benefit from an Unregistered Pension Plan

(a) Remuneration

An employee is taxable on amounts received by way of salary, wages and other remuneration, *including gratuities*, in the year.[27]

"Remuneration" is compensation for services rendered by virtue of employment and is in the nature of a reward for services, whether past, present or future.[28] Commissions and bonuses paid by reference to an employment contract and payments to third parties on behalf of an employee are considered remuneration. For example, an agreement to pay an individual a salary net of tax renders the individual taxable on an amount equal to the gross equivalent.[29]

---

[27] Note that the definition of "salary or wages" in subs. 248(1) does not apply for the purposes of calculating employment income under s. 5. See *Adam v. M.N.R.*, 85 DTC 667 (T.C.C.) (mere bookkeeping entries not capable of converting salary into something else, e.g., dividends).

[28] Paraphrasing Upjohn J.'s statement in *Hochstrasser v. Mayes*, [1959] Ch. 22 at 33 (C.A.); see *Brumby v. Milner*, [1976] 3 All ER 636 (H.L.); *Tyrer v. Smart (Inspector of Taxes)*, [1979] 1 All ER 321, [1979] STC 34 (H.L.).

[29] *Nicoll v. Austin* (1935), 19 Tax Cas. 531 (employer requested continued residence of director in costly manor, but paid stipend to compensate for expenses); *Jaworski v. Inst. of Polish Engr. in Great Britain Ltd.*, [1951] 1 KB 768, [1950] 2 All ER 1191 (C.A.) (oral contract for foreign national stipulated deductions and taxes borne by "employer"; held to be contract for services).

The expression "other remuneration" is read *ejusdem generis* and in the context of its antecedents in the sentence. Thus, the expression "other remuneration" also implies compensation for services rendered.[30]

(b) Benefits

References:

BULLETINS, CIRCULARS & RULINGS:

| IT-470R | April 8, 1988 | Employee Fringe Benefits |
| IT-470SR | December 11, 1989 | Employee Fringe Benefits |

The income tax treatment of employee benefits is a matter of considerable concern to taxpayers and the government. Approximately 67 per cent of individual income tax returns are filed by employees who contribute approximately 83 per cent of the total federal income tax collected from individuals. Thus, even a small expansion or contraction of the taxable base to include or exclude benefits from income can have a substantial impact on federal and provincial revenues.

If the words "other remuneration" in subsection 5(1) mean compensation for services rendered, they are also broad enough to catch most employee benefits. Nevertheless, for greater certainty, paragraph 6(1)(*a*) requires an employee to include in his or her income the value of any board, lodging or *other benefits of any kind whatever* which he or she receives or enjoys as a consequence of employment.

A taxpayer receives or enjoys a benefit when he or she consumes or uses the benefit or when the right that gives rise to the benefit vests in him or her.[31]

Paragraph 6(1)(*a*) equalizes the tax payable by employees who receive their compensation in cash with the amount payable by those who receive compensation in kind. In the absence of this rule, the tax system would favour employees who barter for non-cash benefits. The result would be a capricious and irrational tax system where tax burdens would be determined more by fortuitous circumstances of bargaining power than by principles of tax equity and fairness.

What, then, constitutes a benefit for tax purposes? There is no single test or determinative criterion which answers the question. The starting point of the analysis is to determine whether the employee has been conferred an economic advantage that is measurable in monetary terms. If there is an advantage, one asks: Does the advantage enure primarily for the benefit of the employee or the employer? If the advantage is primarily for the employee, then it is a taxable benefit unless it is specifically excluded by the Act.

---

[30] *Hale v. Can.*, [1992] 2 CTC 379, 92 DTC 6370 (F.C.A.) (stock option not "remuneration" but benefit valued in proportion to time spent in Canada); *McNeill v. Can.*, [1986] 2 CTC 352, 86 DTC 6477 (F.C.T.D.) (relocation allowance and payments on account of accommodation differentials not included in employee's income).

[31] *Hogg v. The Queen*, [1987] CTC 257, 87 DTC 5447 (F.C.T.D.).

Employee benefits are classified into four broad categories:

1. Benefits taxable under the broad authority of paragraph 6(1)(*a*);
2. Benefits taxable under narrow statutory provisions which have a limited and specific application;[32]
3. Benefits excluded from income by administrative discretion;[33] and
4. Non-taxable benefits specifically excluded from income by the Act.

Thus, there are three questions to be answered:

1. What constitutes a benefit taxable to an employee?
2. When is the benefit taxed?
3. What is the value of the taxable benefit?

The answers to these questions are neither obvious nor consistent.

(i) Taxable Benefits

(A) Capacity in Which Payment is Made

The first question to be determined is whether a payment to an employee is made to him or her *qua* employee or in some other personal capacity. Is the payment to the employee a gift in a personal capacity or compensation by virtue of employment? If the former, the payment is non-taxable because gifts are not taxable in the Canadian tax system. If the latter, the payment is included in income from employment.[34]

---

[32] For example, automobile standby charges under para. 6(1)(*e*), interest-free and low cost loans under subs. 6(9), and stock option benefits under s. 7.

[33] See IT-470R, "Employee Fringe Benefits" (April 8, 1995) and Special Release (December 11, 1989).

[34] See, e.g., *Busby v. The Queen*, [1986] 1 CTC 147, 86 DTC 6018 (F.C.T.D.); *Phaneuf Estate v. The Queen*, [1978] CTC 21 at 27, 78 DTC 6001 at 6005 (F.C.T.D.), *per* Thurlow, A.C.J.:

> Is the payment made "by way of remuneration for his services" or is it "made to him on personal grounds and not by way of payment for his services"? It may be made to an employee but is it made to him as an employee or simply as a person? Another way of stating it is to say is it received in his capacity as employee, but that appears to me to be the same test. To be received in the capacity of employee it must, as I see it, partake of the character of remuneration for services. That is the effect that, as it seems to me, the words "in respect of, in the course of, or by virtue of an office or employment" in paragraph 6(1)(*a*) have.

See also *Seymour v. Reed*, [1927] AC 554 at 559 (H.L.), where Viscount Cave L.C. expressed the question in the following manner:

> [t]he question, therefore, is whether the sum...fell within the description, contained in r. 1 of Sch. E. of "salaries, fees, wages, prerequisites or profits whatsoever therefrom" (i.e., from an office or employment of profit) "for the year of assessment", so as to be liable to income tax under that Schedule. These words and the corresponding expressions contained in the earlier statutes (which were not materially different) have been the subject of judicial interpretation in cases which have been cited to your Lordships and it must now (I think) be taken as settled that they include all payments made to the holder of an office or employment as such, that is to say, by way of remuneration for his services, even though such payments may be voluntary, but that they do not include a mere gift or present (such as a testimonial) which is made to him on personal grounds and not by way of payment for services. The question to be answered is, as Rowlatt, J. put it: "Is it in

Characterization of capacity of receipt can be quite difficult.[35] It is important to distinguish between English and Canadian cases.

The English test, which asks whether a particular payment is for recognition of service or remuneration for work done in employment, is too narrow under the Canadian Act. *Savage*[36] provides the classic scenario. The taxpayer, a clerical employee of a life insurance company, voluntarily took three courses offered by the Life Office Management Association. The courses, which were part of a series of courses leading to the designation "Fellow of the Life Office Management Association", were designed to provide a broad understanding of insurance company operations. Pursuant to the employer's general corporate policy, which was well publicized and known to most employees, the taxpayer was paid $100 for each course that she successfully completed. The payment constituted taxable benefits from employment because they were paid to the taxpayer in her capacity as an employee and for her advantage.[37]

The Supreme Court held that the phrase "in respect of . . . an office or employment" must be read in its widest possible scope:[38]

. . . Our Act contains the stipulation not found in the English statute referred to, "benefits of any kind whatever . . . in respect of, in the course of, or by virtue of an office or employment". The meaning of "benefit of whatever kind" is clearly quite broad.

---

the end a personal gift or is it remuneration?" If the latter, it is subject to the tax; if the former, it is not.

[35] *Ball v. Johnson* (1971), 47 Tax Cas. 155; *Hochstrasser v. Mayes*, [1960] AC 376 (H.L.) (Court must be satisfied that service agreement was *causa causans* and not merely *causa sine qua non* of receipt of benefit); *Bridges v. Hewitt*, [1957] 2 All ER 281 (C.A.).

[36] *The Queen v. Savage*, [1980] CTC 103, 80 DTC 6066 (F.C.T.D.); reversed on other grounds (*sub nom. Savage v. The Queen*), [1981] CTC 332, 81 DTC 5258 (F.C.A.); affirmed [1983] CTC 393, 83 DTC 5409 (S.C.C.).

[37] Dickson, Ritchie, Lamer and Wilson JJ. specifically addressed the question with reference to para. 6(1)(a)); McIntyre J. left the issue open by excluding payment from income under para. 56(1)(n) and not addressing para. 6(1)(a). According to their Lordships (*The Queen v. Savage, ante,* [1983] CTC at 398, 83 DTC at 5413):
[t]he *Hochstrasser* case and *Ball v. Johnson* are of little assistance. The provisions of s. 156 of the Income Tax Act, 1952 of England are not unlike s. 5(1) of the Canadian Income Tax Act but our Act goes further in s. 6(1)(a). In addition to the salary, wages and other remuneration referred to in s. 5(1), s. 6(1)(a) includes in income the value of benefits "of any kind whatever . . . received or enjoyed . . . in respect of in the course of, or by virtue of an office or employment".

[38] *The Queen v. Savage, ante,* [1983] CTC at 399, 83 DTC at 5414. The Court endorses its earlier decision in *Nowegijick v. The Queen,* [1983] CTC 20 at 25, 83 DTC 5041 at 5045:
[t]he words "in respect of" are, in my opinion words of the widest possible scope. They import such meanings as "in relation to", "with reference to" or "in connection with". The phrase "in respect of" is probably the widest of any expression intended to convey some connection between two related subject matters.

Benefits come in all sorts of varieties and guises. Some are obvious, for example, payment of an individual's personal vacation and living expenses by an employer. Others are more subtle, such as the payment of a grievance settlement to a unionized employee,[39] the discharge of a mortgage upon dismissal from employment,[40] or the issuance of stock options by a person other than the employer.[41] Under the *Savage* doctrine *any* material acquisition which confers an economic advantage on an employee in his or her capacity as an employee, and that does not fall within an excluded category (gifts, for example), is a taxable benefit.[42]

(B) For Whose Benefit is the Payment Made?

The second question is whether the payment to the employee is for the benefit of the employee or the employer. A payment incurred primarily for the convenience or advantage of the employer is not taxable as a benefit to the employee. The question is: Who is the *primary* beneficiary of the payment to the employee? For example, where an employee is asked by her employer to take courses so that she is better trained for her job, the cost of the job training is not a benefit to the employee. The line, however, between what constitutes a benefit to the employee and convenience to the employer is not always clear, particularly where there are mutual benefits.[43]

(C) When are Benefits Taxable?

As a general rule, an employee is taxable on benefits in the year he or she receives or enjoys the benefit. The word "enjoy" enlarges the scope of paragraph 6(1)(*a*) beyond actual receipt of the benefit. A benefit is taxable only if it has vested in the employee in the year.[44] Non-vested rights are not taxable as benefits.

There are considerable difficulties involved in determining if and when rights have vested in an employee and, if they have, the present value of benefits payable in the future. For example, it can be difficult to determine whether an employee has "received

---

[39] *Norman v. M.N.R.*, [1987] 2 CTC 2261, 87 DTC 556 (T.C.C.).

[40] *Galanov v. M.N.R.*, [1987] 2 CTC 2353, 87 DTC 647 (T.C.C.).

[41] *Robertson v. The Queen*, [1988] 1 CTC 111, 88 DTC 6071 (F.C.T.D.).

[42] See, *The Queen v. Savage*, [1983] CTC 393 at 399, 83 DTC 5409 at 5414 approving the judgment of Evans, J.A. in *The Queen v. Poynton*, [1972] CTC 411 at 420, 2 DTC 6329 at 6335-56 (F.C.A.):
   I do not believe the language to be restricted to benefits that are related to the office or employment in the sense that they represent a form of remuneration for services rendered. If it is a material acquisition which confers an economic benefit on the taxpayer and does not constitute an exemption, e.g., loan or gift, then it is within the all-embracing definition of s. 3. A gift is a gesture of goodwill and is made without regard to services rendered by the recipient of the gift. For example, if an employer distributes turkeys to all employees at Christmas, the value of the turkey is not considered to be a benefit which must be included in an employee's income.

[43] See, e.g., *Cutmore v. M.N.R.*, [1986] 1 CTC 2230, 86 DTC 1146 (T.C.C.) (employees taxed on fees paid for preparation of personal tax returns despite employer's policy requiring such preparation).

[44] *Hogg v. The Queen*, [1987] 2 CTC 257, 87 DTC 5447 (F.C.T.D.).

or enjoyed" a benefit from a deferred income arrangement such as a pension plan. To circumvent these difficulties, there is a specific and detailed scheme for the taxation of most deferred income plans. For example, employer contributions to an employee's registered pension plan are not taxable upon payment into the plan, but they are taxable when paid out by the plan to the employee.[45]

(D) How Much is Taxable?

Having determined that a particular payment or "perk" is a taxable benefit from employment, the next question is: What is the taxable amount included in income? Should the recipient pay tax on the fair market value of the benefit, the cost of the benefit to the employer, or on the exchange value of the benefit *to the employee?* For example, suppose an airline allows its employees to travel free of charge on its planes on a space-available basis. Should an employee who takes advantage of the facility be taxable on the equivalent of full-fare, advanced booking fare, or standby fare? What if the employee is "bumped up" into first class because that is the only available space on the flight?

There is no rigid formula for the valuation of benefits in every situation. Some benefits are valued at the cost of the benefit to the employer,[46] others are valued according to market prices for similar products,[47] and some benefits are measured by their opportunity cost.[48] Still others (such as MP's subsidized meals, haircuts and shoeshines, and airline tickets for family members, etc.) are simply overlooked administratively as a matter of pragmatic realism.

Obviously, there is considerable scope for disputes between taxpayers and revenue authorities on the value of benefits derived from employment. To reduce the risk of litigation in respect of benefit valuation, the Act prescribes valuation formulae for some

---

[45] Subpara. 6(1)(*a*)(i) and para. 56(1)(*a*).

[46] See, e.g., *Rendell v. Went* (1964), 41 Tax Cas. 654 (H.L.) (assumption by employer of costs of employee's criminal defence taxable benefit equal in value to amount of cost assumed); see also IT-470R, "Employee Fringe Benefits" (April 8, 1988) (cost of subsidized meals).

[47] See, e.g., *Wilkins v. Rogerson* (1961), 39 Tax Cas. 344 (C.A.) (second-hand value, rather than cost, of suits supplied by employer to employees was amount of taxable benefit); *per* Harman L.J.:

> [t]he only controversy was whether he was to pay tax on the cost of the prerequisite to his employer, or on the value of it to him. It appears to me that this prerequisite is a taxable subject-matter because it is money's worth. It is money's worth because it can be turned into money, and when turned into money the taxable subject-matter is the value received. I cannot myself see how it is connected directly with the cost to the employer. . . . The taxpayer has to pay on what he gets. Here he has got a suit. He can realize it only for £5. The advantage to him is therefore, £5. The detriment to his employer has been considerably more, but that seems to me to be irrelevant. The validity of the Court's reasoning is dubious. Had His Lordship asked the question "what is the value in use?" instead of "what is the value in exchange?", he may have arrived at a different conclusion.

[48] *Youngman v. The Queen*, [1986] 2 CTC 475, 86 DTC 6584 (F.C.T.D.) (shareholder benefit under para. 15(1)(*c*) measured by reference to capital cost of house supplied by corporation rather than by reference to its rental value).

of the more contentious situations, such as benefits from automobiles and low cost loans.[49]

(E) Administrative Policy

As a matter of administrative practice, Revenue Canada does not tax a benefit unless the value of the benefit can be readily measured in monetary terms. For example, it will not attribute an amount to an employee who is given free parking on his or her employer's premises provided that such facilities are available to all employees and it is not possible to appraise the value of the benefit. Similar considerations apply to employer-provided child care facilities. The benefit from such services cannot be valued conveniently without substantial administrative costs.

It is important to distinguish, however, between benefits which are excluded from income by virtue of Revenue Canada's administrative policy and benefits excluded from income by the Act. The former category can quickly be expanded or contracted by a shift in political or administrative policy; the latter can only be changed through the legislative process.

(ii) Non-taxable Benefits

While some benefits are excluded from income by administrative discretion, others are specifically excluded by the Act. For example, subparagraph 6(1)(*a*)(i) specifically excludes from employment income any benefits derived from employer contributions to:

- registered pension funds,
- group sickness or accident insurance plans,
- private health services plans,
- supplementary unemployment benefits plans, and
- deferred profit sharing plans.

One of the recurring factors to consider in respect of employment benefits is the timing of inclusions in income. Some benefits are included in the year the benefit is conferred; others are brought into income only in the year the taxpayer actually derives cash from the benefit. This may result in a mismatch between one taxpayer's deduction in respect of a payment, and another taxpayer's receipt of the payment. For example, although employer contributions to registered pension funds are excluded from the employee's income when paid into the fund, the employer is entitled to an immediate deduction for the contribution even though the employee is taxable only when he or she actually receives the pension.[50]

---

[49] See, e.g., subs. 6(2) (formula for automobile benefits), para. 7(1)(*a*) (formula for stock option benefits), s. 80.4 (formula for benefit of low cost loans).

[50] See paras. 56(1)(*a*) (pension benefits), 56(1)(*g*) (supplementary unemployment benefit plans) and 56(1)(*i*) (deferred profit sharing plans).

(c) Allowances

Reference:

BULLETINS, CIRCULARS & RULINGS:

IT-337R2   May 22, 1984   Retiring Allowances

(i) Meaning

An "allowance" is a limited, predetermined sum of money paid to an individual to provide for certain kinds of expenses; its amount is determined in advance and, once paid, it is at the disposal of the recipient who is not required to account for it.

In contrast, a "reimbursement" is a payment to indemnify an individual against actual expenses; it must be accounted for by providing receipts to substantiate the expenditure.[51]

(ii) Tax Treatment

The taxability of allowances is fundamental to the fairness of the tax system. The exclusion of allowances from the taxable base causes problems of tax equity. Most allowances are taxable as income.[52]

There are some, however, which are *specifically* excluded by the Act. For example, salespeople who are employed for the purpose of selling property or negotiating contracts may exclude a reasonable allowance paid for travelling expenses. Similarly, employees (other than salespeople) may exclude a reasonable allowance paid to them to cover travelling expenses, provided that the allowance is calculated by reference to time spent by the employee travelling away from the municipality where she or he ordinarily works. Hence, employees in receipt of a *per diem* travelling allowance are not taxable on that allowance provided that the amount of the allowance is reasonable.

(iii) Personal or Living Expenses

An allowance for personal or living expenses is included in income unless specifically excluded by paragraph 6(1)(*b*). Each of the exclusions in that paragraph requires the taxpayer to satisfy certain conditions.

Paragraph 6(1)(*b*) is only concerned with allowances and not with reimbursements.[53] A reimbursement of a personal or living expense is taxable as a

---

[51] *Gagnon v. The Queen*, [1986] 1 SCR 264, [1986] 1 CTC 410, 85 DTC 6179 ("allowance" linked to spouse's ability to dispose of it for own benefit regardless of restriction that it be applied to particular purpose); *The Queen v. Pascoe*, [1975] CTC 656, 75 DTC 5427 (F.C.A.) (Court defines "allowance" and "payable on periodic basis"; note CTC editorial note at 656).

[52] Para. 6(1)(*b*).

[53] *The Queen v. Paradis*, [1986] 2 CTC 3, 86 DTC 6029 (F.C.T.D.) (lump sum payment for meals taxable as allowance).

benefit under paragrah 6(1)(*a*) if it is paid in respect of, by virtue of, or in the course of, the taxpayer's employment. The purpose of paragraph 6(1)(*a*) is to tax cash and non-cash income equally and fairly. For example, if an employer *reimburses* his or her employee's American Express bills for personal travel and entertainment, the amount reimbursed constitutes an employment benefit.[54] Thus, unless specifically exempted by the Act, it makes little difference whether a payment to an employee constitutes a reimbursement of, or an allowance for, personal or living expenses. Both are taxable, but under different provisions.

(iv) Special Work Sites

Reference:

BULLETINS, CIRCULARS & RULINGS:

IT-91R3　　　　May 22, 1984　　　Employment at Special or Remote Work Sites

In certain fairly narrowly prescribed circumstances, an employee who has to work at a location that is a considerable distance from home may exclude from his or her income any allowance that he or she receives in respect of board or lodging. An employee in receipt of an allowance in respect of transportation to, or board and lodging at, a temporary work assignment at a special work site may exclude the allowance from income if he or she maintains a self-contained domestic establishment as his or her principal residence at another location.[55] Thus, only those employees who actually maintain two residences, one where they regularly live and the other at the temporary work site, can exclude the allowance. Employees who do not maintain an alternate permanent residence but live in various temporary work site residences are not entitled to exclude living allowances from income.

The cost to an employee of commuting to and from a place of employment is considered a personal expense. It follows, then, that commuting expenses are not generally deductible from income. A special rule applies, however, with respect to part-time employees who travel substantial distances to and from their part-time jobs. A part-time employee who receives an allowance for, or reimbursement of, travelling expenses may exclude the amount received from income if:[56]

- she or he is dealing at arm's length with an employer;
- he or she is employed or carrying on business elsewhere throughout the period of part-time employment;

---

[54] See, e.g., *Sheldon v. M.N.R.*, [1988] 2 CTC 2039, 88 DTC 1392 (compensation paid to employee as reimbursement for decrease in resale value of home constituted benefit from employment).

[55] Subs. 6(6).

[56] Subs. 81(3.1).

- the part-time employment is located not less than 80 kilometres from his or her residence and principal place of employment or business; and

- the allowance for, or reimbursement of, travel expenses is reasonable in amount and is not on account of other non-travel-related expenses incurred in the performance of the part-time employment.

This special rule offers part-time employees some assistance in meeting travel expenses associated with their secondary employment relationships.

(d) Advances and Loans

Reference:

BULLETINS, CIRCULARS & RULINGS:

IT-222R   November 22, 1976   Advances to Employees

Employees are taxable on a cash basis on their employment income. An employee who receives an advance against a salary is taxed in the year in which he or she *actually receives* the advance.[57]

An "advance" is a payment to an employee on account of future salary or wages. The employee is not expected to repay the advance, but to work off his or her financial obligation by rendering service to the employer.[58]

In contrast, a loan is not income. Whether a payment is an advance or a loan is a question of fact. Usually, a loan is a debt acknowledged in writing with provision for repayment within some reasonable time. A person who makes a loan expects the loan to be repaid and, usually, will make reasonable efforts to collect the loan when it falls due.

(e) Automobiles

Reference:

BULLETINS, CIRCULARS & RULINGS:

IT-63R4   March 31, 1994   Benefits, Including Standby Charge for an Automobile, from the Personal Use of a Motor Vehicle Supplied by an Employer.

(i) General

As noted earlier, the valuation of certain types of benefits can give rise to difficult problems, that can result in disputes with Revenue Canada. The valuation of automobile benefits is a fertile area for tax disputes. To minimize the potential for litigation in

---

[57] *Randall v. M.N.R.*, [1987] 2 CTC 2265, 87 DTC 553 (T.C.C).

[58] IT-222R, "Advances to Employees" (November 22, 1976).

respect of such benefits, the Act provides a rigid formula to determine the amount included in income.

(ii) Overview of Rules

An employee who is supplied with an automobile by his or her employer is taxable on the benefit derived from personal use of the automobile. The amount included in income as a taxable benefit is determined by reference to two rules. First, the employee is required to include in income any personal *operating costs* of the automobile to the extent that such costs are assumed by the employer.[59] Second, the employee must include a "reasonable standby charge" for the time the automobile *is available* for his or her personal use.[60] The employee may deduct amounts that he or she reimburses his or her employer on account of the employee's personal use of the automobile.

(iii) Meaning of "Automobile"

An automobile is a motor vehicle that is designed (or adapted) primarily to carry individuals and their personal luggage and that has a maximum seating capacity of nine persons, including the driver. The term includes station wagons and vans which are reasonably permanently equipped to carry between three and nine people, including the driver. It also includes vans and pick-up trucks which are designed (or adapted) to carry three or fewer persons, including the driver, and that are not used primarily for the transportation of goods and equipment. Ambulances, taxis and hearses are not considered to be automobiles.

(iv) Standby Charge

(A) General

An employee is taxable on a reasonable standby charge if his or her employer (or any person related to the employer) provides the employee with an automobile for personal use. An employee is also subject to the standby charge where his or her employer, or a person related to the employer, makes an automobile available to a person *related to* the employee.

What constitutes a "reasonable standby charge" is determined by reference to a formula. The word "reasonable" in the phrase "reasonable standby charge" is misleading. The formula is a deeming provision that dictates the *exact* amount to be included in income in the circumstances. The calculation does not leave any room for judgement or discretion.

(B) Basic Formula

Subsection 6(2) sets out the formula according to which the standby charge is determined. The essence of the formula is that the benefit is equal to 2 per cent of the

---

[59] Subpara. 6(1)(a)(iii); IT-63R4, "Benefits, Including Standby Charge for an Automobile, from the Personal Use of a Motor Vehicle Supplied by an Employer" (March 31, 1994).

[60] Para. 6(1)(e).

original cost of the automobile for every 30-day period that it is available to the employee. A different set of rules appies to automobile salespeople.

The benefit from leased automobiles is calculated as two-thirds of the cost of leasing the automobile (excepting any portion related to insurance) for the period that the automobile is made available to the employee. For the purposes of determining the standby charge, the cost of the automobile is its actual cost, regardless that the employer may not be entitled to depreciate the full cost of the car because of the restrictions on depreciation of luxury automobiles.

Subsection 6(2) provides two formulae for the calculation of a "reasonable standby charge". The first formula is in respect of employer-owned automobiles. The standby charge in respect of an employer-owned automobile is equal to:

$$\frac{\text{cost} \times 2\% \times (\text{no. of days available})}{30}$$

Example V.1

Assume:

Cost of automobile	$20,000
Number of days available	365 days
Personal use of automobile	18,000 kms
Expenses reimbursed by employee	NIL

Then, a reasonable standby charge is:

$$\frac{2\% \times 365 \times \$20,000}{30} = \underline{\underline{\$4,867}}$$

(C) Salespeople

The standby charge for automobile salespeople is calculated somewhat differently. The rate applicable is 75 per cent of the rate applicable to all other employees.[61] Also, the charge is calculated by reference to the *average* cost of *all* automobiles purchased by the employer in the year.

(D) Leased Automobiles

The second formula in subsection 6(2) deals with leased automobiles. The standby charge is equal to two-thirds of the monthly lease cost multiplied by the number of months during which the car was *available* to the employee. The standby charge is reduced if actual use of the automobile averages less than 1,000 kilometres per month.

---

[61] Subs. 6(2.1).

(v) Operating Costs

Personal *net* operating costs paid by an employer on behalf of an employee are also included in the employee's income as a benefit. That is, an employee who makes personal use of an automobile supplied by his or her employer is required to include in his or her income the personal benefit derived from any operating costs paid by the employer. The amount of the benefit is calculated on the basis of actual operating costs such as gas, repairs, maintenance and insurance. Thus, the employer must maintain detailed records of the total operating costs incurred for each vehicle and the number of kilometres that each employee drives for personal and business purposes.

Example V.2

Assume the same facts as in Example V.1, except that the employer pays $3,600 towards the employee's *personal* use operating expenses for which the employee reimburses the employer $1,600.

Then:

(i) Benefit under para. 6(1)(a)

Operating costs paid	$ 3,600
Amount reimbursed	(1,600)
Inclusion in income	2,000

(ii) Standby charge as calculated in Example V.1

$$\frac{2\% \times 365 \times \$20,000}{30} = \qquad \$ 4,867$$

Total inclusion in income $ 6,867

To simplify recordkeeping, an employee who uses his or her automobile primarily (that is, more than 50 per cent) for employment purposes, can opt to include an additional one-half of the automobile standby charge in calculated income in lieu of his or her share of operating costs.[62] For example, in the case of an employer-owned automobile, the employee could include 3 per cent, instead of 2 per cent, of the capital cost of the automobile as income.

(vi) Low Personal Use

An employee who makes minimal use of an employer's automobile is entitled to reduce the amount of the standby charge included in income. To obtain the benefit of the reduced standby charge, the employee must file the prescribed form and satisfy two tests: the automobile must be used substantially (interpreted as 90 per cent) for business purposes and the total amount driven for personal use must be less than 12,000

---

[62] Subs. 6(2.2) applicable to 1984 and subsequent years.

kilometres in the year if the automobile has been available for use all year. In these circumstances, the standby charge is reduced by the following fraction:

$$\frac{\text{number of personal-use kilometres}}{1000 \text{ kilometres per month of availability}}$$

(vii) Reimbursement by Employee

Where an employee reimburses an employer for expenses arising from his or her personal use of the automobile, the amount reimbursed is deducted from income. This reduces the amount of the benefit subject to tax. This rule applies both in respect of reimbursements for operating costs and the standby charge. Generally speaking, it is preferable for an employee not to reimburse an employer for personal use of an automobile since the reimbursement is made with after-tax dollars in order to reduce the amount of tax payable.

(viii) Employee-owned Cars

Where an employee uses his or her own car in the course of employment, his or her employer will usually compensate the employee. The nature and amount of compensation determines the tax treatment of the employee. Generally speaking, an amount paid to reimburse an employee for his or her business use of a personally owned car is not included in income. Reimbursement for business use of a car is generally supported by receipts and vouchers.

Where an employee is compensated by means of an allowance, his or her employer may deduct only allowances paid within prescribed amounts. An allowance is generally an amount paid without any need for specific accounting for the amount paid. For example, an employer may compensate an employee by providing $300 per month. Alternatively, the employer may pay $0.25 per business kilometre driven for business purposes.

An employee who receives a reasonable allowance from an employer as compensation for the business use of a personal automobile is not taxable on the amount received. The Act deems certain allowances (for example, an allowance that is calculated by reference to something other than kilometres driven) not to be reasonable. Where an employee is reimbursed for expenses in addition to being paid a per kilometre allowance, the allowance is deemed to be in excess of a "reasonable amount". In these circumstances, the full amount of the unreasonable allowance is taxable to the employee.

(f) Imputed Interest on Low Cost Loans

References:

BULLETINS, CIRCULARS & RULINGS::

IT-222R	November 22, 1976	Advances to Employees
IT-421R2	September 9, 1992	Benefits to Individuals, Corporations and Shareholders from Loans or Debts

(i) General

An individual who obtains a low cost loan or incurs a debt by virtue of employment is taxable on the imputed benefit derived from the loan or debt.[63] The individual may be taxable even if the loan is made by or to some other person, provided that the loan is made *by virtue* of his or her employment. For example, a loan to an individual's spouse is taxable to the individual if it is made by virtue of his or her employment.

(ii) Value

The value of the taxable benefit of a low cost loan is equal to the interest imputed on the loan.[64] Imputed interest is calculated by reference to a prescribed rate of interest. The rate is determined quarterly and is based on the average Treasury Bill rate of the first month during the preceding quarter.[65]

Although the advantage of low cost loans is reduced by their taxability, these types of loans remain an important benefit for employees. This is because the *effective* after-tax cost of these loans is considerably lower than the cost of loans in the commercial market.

Example V.3

Assume:

A taxpayer with a marginal tax rate of 50 per cent receives an interest-free loan of $100,000 from an employer. The imputed interest included in the employee's income is calculated as follows:

Taxable benefit (12%* × $100,000)	$12,000
Tax thereon (50% × $12,000)	$ 6,000
Effective after-tax cost of loan	
($6,000 for $100,000)	6%

*assume prescribed rate of interest

If an individual is subject to the imputed interest rules in respect of a particular loan or debt, he or she remains liable for all taxation years during which the loan or debt is outstanding, regardless of any subsequent change in the relationship of the parties.

---

[63] Subs. 6(9).

[64] S. 80.4.

[65] Reg. 4301.

(iii) Exclusions

The imputed interest rules do not apply if the rate at which an employee borrows from his or her employer is equal to, or greater than, the prevailing commercial rate for parties dealing with each other at arm's length.[66] Thus, an employee who borrows from an employer at a commercial market rate is not subject to imputed interest if the commercial rate increases after the loan is taken out if all of the other terms and conditions offered are no more advantageous than the terms and conditions available in the commercial marketplace. But the inclusion of terms and conditions that are more favourable than those available in comparable commercial loans at the relevant time will trigger the imputed interest benefit if the prescribed rate of interest increases above the rate charged to the employee.

(iv) Deemed Payments

An employee who is deemed to receive imputed interest is also deemed to have paid an equivalent amount pursuant to a legal obligation.[67] Hence, any interest imputed on a loan or indebtedness used for the purpose of earning income (for example, the purchase of shares) is deductible as interest expense.[68]

(v) Forgiveness of Loan

Where an employer forgives a loan to an employee, the principal amount of the loan is included in the employee's income at the time the loan is forgiven. Any amount included in the employee's income as a benefit at the time the loan was granted reduces the amount included in income upon forgiveness of the loan.

Example V.4

Assume:

An individual receives a loan of $150,000 by virtue of her employment. She pays $8,000 interest on the loan and a corporation related to the employer pays $3,000 interest on her behalf. The prescribed rate of interest is 12 per cent and the loan is outstanding throughout the year.

Then:

Prescribed rate × loan amount	
12% × $150,000 =	$18,000
Add amounts paid by third party	3,000
	$21,000
Less amounts paid on loan	
($8,000 + $3,000)	11,000
Taxable benefit	$10,000

---

[66] Subs. 80.4(3).

[67] S. 80.5; see Chapter VIII "Business and Property Income: Deductions".

[68] Subpara. 20(1)(c)(i).

(g) Stock Option Plans

References:

BULLETINS, CIRCULARS & RULINGS:

IT-113R3   November 30, 1987   Benefits to Employees — Stock Options

ATR-15   November 21, 1986   Employee Stock Option Plan

(i) General

Stock options, a popular form of compensation for key employees and senior executives, provide substantial economic benefits. Stock option benefits are taxable as employment income because they are, in effect, an alternative to cash compensation. The stock option rules, however, also serve other economic objectives, such as promoting equity ownership in Canadian corporations and encouraging better employee-employer working relationships.

The common law rule that stock option benefits arose in the year in which the option was granted[69] created considerable uncertainty in determining the value of benefits derived from unexercised options. The Act resolves the uncertainty by specifying both the method of valuation and the time for inclusion of the benefit in income.[70]

There are four questions to be answered in the context of stock options:

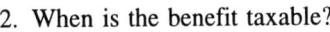

1. Does the benefit from the option derive from employment?

2. When is the benefit taxable?

3. What is the value of the benefit? and

4. How much of the benefit is taxable?

(ii) "By Virtue of Employment"

An individual is taxable on the value of stock option benefits derived by virtue of his or her employment.[71] Subject to tax treaty provisions, non-residents also are taxable on stock options granted in respect of employment in Canada, regardless of where the options are exercised.[72] The benefit is determined by reference to the shares actually acquired pursuant to the stock option plan.[73]

---

[69] See *Abbott v. Philbin*, [1961] AC 352 (H.L.).

[70] S. 7; see generally IT-113R3, "Benefits to Employees — Stock Options" (November 30, 1987).

[71] Subs. 7(5).

[72] *Hale v. The Queen*, [1992] 2 CTC 379, 92 DTC 6370 (F.C.A.).

[73] *Ball v. M.N.R.*, [1992] 2 CTC 2770, 92 DTC 2123 (T.C.C.).

Thus, the first question is: Was the benefit conferred in respect of, in the course of, or by virtue of the employment relationship? Issuance of stock for other considerations (for example, as a gift or in return for guaranteeing a loan) does not give rise to a benefit from employment. Nor is the issuance of stock by virtue of the individual's office (such as a directorship) taxable under these rules.[74]

(iii) Timing

The triggering event for the recognition of stock option benefits is the acquisition of shares at a price less than their value at the time the shares are acquired. The time of acquisition is determined by reference to principles of contractual and corporate law. Contractual principles may be modified by a corporate statute. For example, a federal corporation may not issue shares until they are fully paid for in money or in property.[75] Thus, under federal corporate law, a taxpayer cannot acquire shares in a corporation until he or she has paid for the shares. In some other jurisdictions, however, shares may be purchased and paid for at different times. In these circumstances, shares could be acquired at the time that the contract was completed even though the shares were not paid for until a later date.

(iv) Valuation

Except in special cases (discussed below), the value of a stock option benefit can be determined only at or after the time the stock option is exercised, that is, when the shares are acquired. The value of the benefit is the difference between the cost of the option to the employee, any amount paid for the shares, and the value of the shares at the time they are acquired from the plan.[76] Shares are considered to be acquired when the option is exercised.[77] For example, assume that an individual acquires 100 shares at a cost of $10 per share when the shares have a value of $15 per share. Assume also that the individual pays $1 per share to acquire the option right. In these circumstances the value of the taxable benefit is $400.

"Value" means "fair market value."[78] In the case of publicly traded securities, stock market prices will usually be considered indicative of fair market value. Since listed stock prices inherently reflect the value of minority shareholdings, there is no need to further discount their value for minority interests.

---

[74] *Busby v. The Queen*, [1986] 1 CTC 147, 86 DTC 6018 (F.C.T.D.) (options granted by virtue of taxpayer's "special" relationship with principal shareholder and for guaranteeing corporation's loans not taxable as employment source income).

[75] *Canada Business Corporations Act*, R.S.C. 1985, c. C-44, subs. 25(3); see also *Business Corporations Act*, R.S.O. 1990, c. B.16, subs. 23(3).

[76] Para. 7(1)(*a*).

[77] *Steen v. The Queen*, [1988] 1 CTC 256, 88 DTC 6171 (F.C.A.).

[78] See, e.g., *Steen v. The Queen*, [1986] 2 CTC 394, 86 DTC 6498; affirmed [1988] 1 CTC 256, 88 DTC 6171 (F.C.A.).

The value of shares of private corporations is more difficult to determine. Shares of private corporations are generally valued by reference to estimated future earnings and the adjusted net value of assets. The *pro rata* value of the corporation is then adjusted to reflect a discount for minority interests, lack of market, etc.

(v) Incentive Provisions

There are two special rules in respect of stock option plans. One applies to options issued by Canadian-controlled private corporations ("CCPC") and the other to acquisitions of prescribed equity shares. These rules are incentive provisions intended to stimulate equity participation in Canadian corporations.

(A) Options Issued by CCPCs

Shares acquired from a CCPCs stock plan in an arm's length transaction receive preferential treatment if they are held for at least two years.[79] This is so whether the shares are issued by the employer corporation or by another CCPC with which the employer does not deal at arm's length.

An employee may defer recognition of any benefit that he or she derives from stock options issued by a CCPC until he or she disposes of the shares. Further, upon disposition of the shares, the employee is taxable on only three-quarters of the value of the benefit derived.[80]

Thus, the employee benefits in two ways: first, by deferring any tax liability which would otherwise arise upon acquisition of the shares through an "ordinary" stock option plan; second, by converting what would normally be fully taxable employment source income into income that is, in effect, taxable at a lower rate. The portion of the benefit that is taxable to the employee is not a capital gain but income from employment.

An employee who disposes of shares in a CCPC within two years from the date that he or she acquires them is taxable in the year of disposition on the full value of any benefit derived from their acquisition.[81] An exchange of options or of shares as a consequence of an amalgamation or a share-for-share exchange is not considered to be a disposition for the purposes of the two-year rule.[82]

Shares that are identical properties are deemed to be disposed of in the order they are acquired.[83]

---

[79] Subs. 7(1.1).

[80] See subs. 7(1.1) and para. 110(1)(*d*.1) (full value of benefit being brought into income in same year shares disposed of but employee entitled to *deduction* equal to one-quarter of benefit included in income from employment).

[81] Subpara. 110(1)(*d*.1)(ii).

[82] Subss. 7(1.4) and 7(1.5).

[83] Subs. 7(1.3).

(B) Options for Prescribed Shares

There is also a special rule for stock option plans under which an individual acquires prescribed equity shares in his or her employer's corporation or in a corporation with which the employer does not deal at arm's length: An employee is taxable on only three-quarters of the value of any benefit derived from such a plan. The benefit, however, is taxable on a current basis.

The following conditions must be satisfied in order for a stock option plan to qualify for this special tax treatment:[84]

- The shares must be prescribed[85] at the time of their sale or issuance;
- The employee must purchase the shares for not less than their fair market value at the time the agreement was made; and
- The employee must have been at arm's length with the employer and the issuing corporation at the time the agreement was made.

Non-residents may also claim the benefit of this special treatment.

The purpose of this special rule is to encourage corporate employers to draw their employees into equity ownership. The rationale of the tax incentive is that the mutuality of economic interests that results from employee participation in equity ownership with their employers will increase economic productivity. Thus, only common equity shares are eligible for this special treatment.

(vi) Comparison of Option Plans

The effect of the three different types of stock option plans described above are set out in the following example.

Example V.5
Assume that in 1995 an employee acquires shares in the following circumstances:
Case (A)   General Rules Shares with a fair market value (FMV) of $100 for $76
Case (B)   CCPC Shares with FMV of $100 for $76 from a CCPC and the shares are held for two years
Case (C)   Prescribed Prescribed shares at $76 (FMV at time of agreement) which are sold for $100

---

[84] Para. 110(1)(d).

[85] Reg. 6204.

Then:	(A)	(B)	(C)
	General Rules	CCPC	Prescribed
Acquisition of shares:			
FMV at acquisition	$ 100	—	$ 100
Cost of acquisition	(76) ⟵ N/A		(76)
Stock option benefit	24	—	24
One-quarter deduction	—		(6)
Net inclusion	$ 24		$ 18
Adjusted cost base (ACB) of shares:			
Cost of acquisition	$ 76	—	$ 76
Add:			
stock option benefit	24	—	24
ACB of shares	$ 100		$ 100
Disposition of shares:			
Sale price	$ 100	$ 100	$ 100
ACB	(100) ⟵ (76)		(100)
Capital gain	—	—	—
Stock option benefit	—	24	—
One-quarter deduction *only taxed on 3/4*	—	(6)	—
Net inclusion		$ 18	
Inclusions in income:			
Upon acquisition	24	—	18
Upon disposition	—	18	—
Total	$ 24	$ 18	$ 18

(vii) Disposition of Rights

Where an employee disposes of stock option rights to a person in an arm's length transaction, she or he is deemed to have received a benefit equal to the value of the consideration received for the shares, minus any amount paid to acquire the rights.[86] Similarly, any consideration received for the surrender of stock option rights is taxable as a benefit from a disposition of the rights, presumably also minus amounts paid.[87]

---

[86] Para. 7(1)(b).

[87] *Greiner v. The Queen*, [1984] CTC 92, 84 DTC 6073 (F.C.A.).

(viii) Adjusted Cost Base of Shares

To prevent double taxation of the same amount, the full, and not taxable, value of any benefit included in the employee's income is added base of the shares acquired.[88] Thus, any subsequent gain or loss on the disposition of the shares is calculated by reference to the stepped-up cost base of the shares. For example, where an employee acquires shares at $12 per share when the shares have a market value of $18 per share, the full benefit of $6 is added to the acquisition cost of the shares. Hence, the adjusted cost base of the shares is increased to $18.

(ix) Effect on Employer

Costs associated with a stock option plan are not deductible by the employer corporation because it does not incur any outlay or expense by issuing its shares at less than their market value.[89] It merely foregoes capital proceeds that it would have received had it issued the shares at their fair market value. Hence, unless one of the special incentive provisions in subsection 7(1.1) or paragraph 110(1)(d) applies, it may be advantageous to a corporation that is taxable at full rates to pay its executives a bonus that they can then use to purchase its shares at full, fair market value.

(h) Damages

References:

BULLETINS, CIRCULARS & RULINGS:

IT-337R2	May 22, 1984	Retiring Allowances
IT-365R2	May 8, 1987	Damages, Settlements and Similar Receipts

(i) Wrongful Dismissal

Damages for wrongful dismissal are, in substance and effect, a payment in lieu of notice of termination. Thus, where a contract is terminable on notice, damages for lost earnings are restricted to the amount payable during the period of notice.[90] For tax purposes, damages for wrongful dismissal are considered "retiring allowances"[91] and are taxable as such.[92] This is so whether the damages are paid pursuant to a court order or in settlement of litigation. In either case, the full amount of the payment is included in the taxpayer's income in the year of receipt.

---

[88] Para. 53(1)(j).

[89] Para. 7(3)(b); *The Queen v. Placer Dome Inc.*, [1992] 2 CTC 99, 92 DTC 6402 (F.C.A.).

[90] *British Guiana Credit Corp. v. Da Silva*, [1965] 1 WLR 248 at 259 (P.C.).

[91] Subs. 248(1) ("retiring allowance").

[92] Subpara. 56(1)(a)(ii).

A payment of damages for wrongful dismissal must be reported to Revenue Canada and tax withheld and remitted therefrom at the prescribed rates.[93] Payments to non-residents require withholding tax of 25 per cent of the amount paid.

Where a damage award represents compensation, both for lost earnings during the period for which notice should have been given, and compensation for mental suffering, it might be argued that the mental suffering component is not taxable as a "retiring allowance" since it is not in respect of loss of office or employment.[94] The better view, however, is that the entire award is *in respect of* a loss of office or employment: The earnings component compensates for lack of notice and the mental anguish component compensates for the manner in which the office or employment was lost.[95] Thus, one head of the award goes to time, while the other goes to the method, but both arise from the same cause of action. They are *in respect of* improper loss of office or employment.[96]

(ii) Other Compensation Payments

An amount paid to an employee on account of a contractually agreed settlement (such as a "signing bonus") is included in income regardless of whether the payment is made pursuant to a legal agreement entered into before, during, or immediately after employment.[97]

---

[93] Para. 153(1)(*c*).

[94] *Specht v. The Queen*, [1975] CTC 126, 75 DTC 5069 (F.C.T.D.).

[95] See, for example, the reasoning in *The Queen v. Savage*, [1983] 2 SCR 428, [1983] CTC 393, 83 DTC 5409.

[96] *Young v. M.N.R.*, [1986] 2 CTC 2111, 86 DTC 1567 (T.C.C.). As Linden J. said in *Brown v. Waterloo Reg. Bd. of Commr. of Police* (1982), 37 OR (2d) 277 at 288-89; reversed in part 43 OR (2d) 113 (Ont. C.A.):

> The aim of aggravated damages is to "soothe a plaintiff whose feelings have been wounded by the quality of the defendant's misbehaviour". They are a "balm for mental distress" which is brought about by the wrongful "character of the defendant's wrongdoing". There must be evidence of damage of this type to the plaintiff. Aggravated damages are not meant to punish the defendant. (See Cooper-Stephenson and Saunders, *Personal Injury Damages in Canada* (1981), at p. 55; *Robitaille et al. v. Vancouver Hockey Club Ltd.* (1979), 19 BCLR 158 at 183, *per* Esson J.; varied 124 DLR (3d) 228,16 CCLT 225, 30 BCLR 286 (C.A.).) In sum, though based on the quality of the defendant's conduct, aggravated damages are compensatory in purpose.

> Canadian law seems to have recognized the need for something like aggravated damages in contract law by awarding damages, not only for financial losses, but also for any mental suffering incurred by the plaintiff in appropriate cases. (See *Pilon v. Peugeot Canada Ltd.* (1980), 29 OR (2d) 711, 114 DLR (3d) 378, 12 BLR 227, for example.) The purpose behind allowing such damages is to compensate for hurt feelings, anxiety and stress caused by certain types of contractual breach, where they are in contemplation of the parties. Where the conduct of a defendant which violates a contract is particularly callous, the likelihood of mental suffering would be more foreseeable to him.

[97] Subs. 6(3); *Greiner v. The Queen*, [1984] CTC 92, 84 DTC 6073 (F.C.A.).

(iii) Arbitration Awards and Damages

Arbitration awards paid as damages for breach of a collective agreement are taxable as employment income if paid as compensation for lost wages or other taxable benefits.[98] Although the amount of the award is paid net of deductions (tax, CPP and UIC) to the employee, the gross amount before deductions is included in income.

(i) Salary Deferral Arrangements

(i) Purpose

The general rule is that income from an office or employment is taxed on a cash basis, that is, when the income is actually received by the taxpayer. This rule opens the door to employees to accelerate or defer receipt of employment income to suit their personal circumstances. For example, a taxpayer in a high tax bracket might defer receipt of a portion of his or her annual income from employment until such time as she or he is in a lower tax bracket. The special rules in respect of "salary deferral arrangements" are intended to prevent this type of tax deferral and rate shifting.

The rules in respect of salary deferral arrangements tax employees who are parties to deferred compensation agreements on an accrual basis.[99] At the same time, the employer's deduction in respect of the compensation payment is synchronized with the inclusion of the amount in the employee's income.[100]

(ii) Meaning of "SDA"

A "salary deferral arrangement[101] ("SDA") is a plan or arrangement (whether funded or not) of which one of the main purposes is to permit a taxpayer to postpone tax in respect of salary or wages in a taxation year to a subsequent year. Arrangements that are contingent upon the deferred amount being paid on the occurrence of some event or transaction are considered SDAs unless there is a "substantial risk" that the condition will not be satisfied.

Thus, a salary deferral arrangement requires:

* a plan or arrangement;
* a legal right to defer receipt of salary or wages; and
* an intention to defer receipt for tax reasons.

---

[98] *Vincent v. M.N.R.*, [1988] 2 CTC 2075, 88 DTC 1422 (T.C.C.) (damage award restoring taxpayer to position he would have been in had wages set out in collective agreement for working on day of rest been paid).

[99] See suppara. 6(1)(a)(v), para. 6(1)(i), subss. 6(11)-(14).

[100] Paras. 18(1)(o.1), 20(1)(oo).

[101] Subs. 248(1) "salary deferral arrangement".

(A) Exclusions

The following types of plans are, however, excluded from the meaning of a salary deferral arrangement:

- registered pension funds or plans;
- disability or income maintenance insurance plans with an insurance corporation;
- deferred profit sharing plans;
- employee profit sharing plans;
- employee trusts;
- group sickness or accident insurance plans;
- supplementary unemployment benefit plans;
- vacation pay trusts;
- education or training plans for employees;
- plans for deferring salary or wages of professional athletes;
- plans under which a taxpayer has a right to receive a bonus in respect of services rendered in the taxation year to be paid within three years following the end of the year;
- leave-of-absence arrangements,[102] and
- prescribed plans or arrangements.

A plan is a SDA where tax deferral is *one* of the main purposes of the plan or arrangement. Tax deferral does not have to be the only purpose. Hence, the definition catches plans that are established for multiple reasons if *any* of the reasons happens to be tax deferral. The onus is on the employee to demonstrate that tax deferral was not one of the main purposes of the plan.

(B) Contingent Arrangements

Contingent plans and deferral arrangements with a substantial risk that one of the conditions triggering the contingency will not be satisfied are not considered SDAs. What constitutes a substantial risk of forfeiture sufficient to exclude a plan or arrangement from the definition of SDA? There is a substantial risk of forfeiture if the condition imposes a significant limitation or duty that requires a meaningful effort on the part of the employee to fulfil and the limitation or duty creates a definite and substantial risk that forfeiture may occur. The following types of conditions are not considered sufficient to exempt a plan or arrangement as an SDA:[103]

- Non-competition clauses following retirement or termination;

---

[102] Reg. 6801.

[103] See Department of Finance Technical Notes (Bill C-23) November 7, 1986.

- Restraints on the employee's transferring or encumbering his or her interest in the deferred amount;

- Restraints that make payment contingent on the employee's not being dismissed for cause or the commission of a crime; or

- Receipt of the deferred amount being contingent on the employee's remaining with the employer for a minimum period of time.

(C) Leave of Absence Plans

Certain leave of absence plans are excluded from the definition of salary deferral arrangements. Thus, a leave of absence plan that complies with prescribed conditions may be used to defer tax on income that would otherwise be taxable on a current basis.

An employee may arrange a self-funded leave of absence and defer receipt of up to a maximum of one-third of his or her regular annual salary. Although the tax that would otherwise be payable on the funded salary is deferred, any income earned on the deferred salary remains taxable on a current basis.

The following conditions must be satisfied to qualify a leave of absence plan:[104]

- The arrangement must provide for a leave of absence from employment of not less than six consecutive months (it cannot be used to fund retirement benefits);

- The leave must commence within six years from the beginning of the commencement of the salary deferral;

- The employee must undertake to return to the employer for a further period of employment of at least equal length to that of the leave;

- The amount of salary deferred in any year must not exceed one-third of the employee's regular annual salary; and

- During the leave of absence the employee must not receive any salary, other than the deferred amounts, from his or her employer.

Hence, within the statutory limits, it is possible for an employee to defer tax on a portion of his or her salary for up to six years and to use the accumulated savings to finance a leave of absence from an employer.

---

[104] Reg. 6801.

Example V.6

Ann Smith earns an annual salary of $70,000. She opts to defer 14 per cent of her annual salary in a leave of absence plan. Assuming an investment rate of 10 per cent and a tax rate of 40 per cent (that is, an after-tax return of 6 per cent), Ms. Smith can accumulate $70,510 in six years.

Annual salary	$70,000
Portion deferred (14% × $70,000)	$ 9,800
Monthly deferral (1/12 × $9,800)	$ 816
$816/month compounded at 6% (net of tax for 72 months)	$70,510

(j) Counselling Benefits

Employer-provided counselling services for employees are not taxable as benefits from employment if the counselling is in respect of:[105]

- The employees' physical or mental health;
- Re-employment for employees whose employment has been terminated; or
- Retirement counselling for employees.

These exclusions from employment income are justified on the basis that they facilitate re-employment and mitigate against undue hardship.

(k) Directors' Fees

A director of a corporation holds an "office". Fees received by virtue of a directorship are taxable as income from an office.[106] Where the director's fees are paid directly to a third party or are turned over by the director to a third party (for example, to a partnership of which she or he is a member), the fees are taxable as income of the ultimate recipient and not of the director

(l) Reimbursed Legal Expenses

An employee can deduct any legal expenses incurred in collecting or establishing his or her right to a salary from an employer or former employer.[107] Where an employee is reimbursed for legal expenses incurred in collecting his or her salary, the amount reimbursed is included in employment income.[108]

---

[105] Subpara. 6(1)(a)(iv).

[106] Subs. 5(1)

[107] Para. 8(1)(b).

[108] Para. 6(1)(j).

(m) Wrongful Dismissal

A taxpayer can deduct legal expenses associated with establishing a right to a pension benefit or retiring allowance (including payments for wrongful dismissal).[109] Any reimbursement of legal expenses as a result of an action to collect such an amount must be included in income to the extent of the deduction claimed.[110]

(n) Strike Pay

The taxation of strike pay is a sensitive and politically contentious issue. Strike pay has not generally been taxed as income as a matter of administrative policy. Revenue Canada exempts certain types of financial assistance paid by unions to their members during the course of a strike.[111] The exemption does not, however, extend to all forms of financial assistance. For example, funds from the operation of a business by the union are taxable, regardless of whether or not the recipients actively participate in the business activity. Similarly, amounts paid by a union to its members when they act as consultants or as members of temporary committees are taxable.

Although strike pay is not taxable as income, union dues are deductible as expenses from employment income.[112]

Political considerations aside, it is not at all clear why strike pay should not be taxable. "Income" in section 3 is realized accretion to wealth from a source. The concept is clearly not restricted to the specifically named sources (office, employment, business and property) in that section. The named sources of income do not constitute an exhaustive list. Income from *any* source inside or outside Canada is taxable under paragraph 3(*a*) of the *Income Tax Act*.

Hence, apart from the common law exclusions of windfall gains and gifts from income, all other income receipts would usually be taxable as income, whether or not identifiable with an office, employment, business or property.[113]

---

[109] Para. 60(*o*.1).

[110] Para. 56(1)(*l*.1).

[111] IT-334R2, "Miscellaneous Receipts" (February 21, 1992), paras. 3, 12.

[112] Subpara. 8(1)(*i*)(iv).

[113] But see *Fries v. M.N.R.*, [1989] 1 CTC 471, 89 DTC 5240; reversed [1990] 2 CTC 439, 90 DTC 6662 (S.C.C.); see discussion in Chapter IV "What is Income".

(o) Other Inclusions

The above list of inclusions in income is not exhaustive. Note also the following inclusions in income from employment:

Item	Statutory Reference
Directors' fees	para. 6(1)(c)
Employees' profit sharing plans	para. 6(1)(d)
Employee benefit plans	para. 6(1)(g)
Group life insurance premiumy	subs. 6(4)
Accident and disability benefits	para. 6(1)(f)
Allocations from employee trusts	para. 6(1)(h)

5. DEDUCTIONS FROM EMPLOYMENT INCOME

References:

ITA:

S. 8	Deductions from Income
S. 110	Other Deductions
Subs. 78(4)	Unpaid Remuneration
Subs. 146(5)	RRSP Premiums Deductible
Subs. 153(1)	Withholding
Subs. 157(1)	Payment of Tax by Corporations
Subs. 227(4)	Enforcement of Withholding Taxes
Subs. 227(8)	Penalties
Subs. 227.l(1)	Liability of Directors
S. 238	Offences
Para. 249(1)(b)	Taxation Year

BULLETINS, CIRCULARS & RULINGS:

IT-85R2	July 31, 1986	Health and Welfare Trusts for Employees
IT-103R	November 4, 1988	Dues Paid to a Union or to a Parity or Advisory Committee
IT-141	December 31, 1973	Clergymen's Residences
IT-158R2	July 14, 1989	Employees' Professional Membership Dues
IT-160R3	February 19, 1992	Personal Use of Aircraft
IT-167R5	March 14, 1985	Registered Pension Funds or Plans — Employee's Contributions
IT-167SR	February 19, 1990	Registered Pension Funds or Plans — Employee's Contributions

IT-227R	May 26, 1980	Group Term Life Insurance Premiums
IT-339R2	August 8, 1989	Meaning of "Private Health Services Plan"
IT-352R2	August 26, 1994	Employees' Expenses Including Work Space in Home Expenses
IT-357R2	November 6, 1989	Expenses of Training
IT-522	August 25, 1989	Vehicle and Other Travelling Expenses — Employees
IT-525	April 20, 1990	Performing Artists
IC 72-13R8	December 16, 1988	Employees' Pension Plans
IC 73-21R7	March 8, 1991	Away-From-Home Expenses
ATR-2	November 29, 1985	Contribution to Pension Plan for Past Service

(a) General

Deductions from employment income are strictly controlled. Subsection 8(2) prohibits any deduction from employment income unless it is *specifically* authorized by the Act. In contrast, business expenses are usually deductible unless specifically prohibited by the Act. Thus, in most cases, it is to a taxpayer's advantage to have his or her income characterized as business rather than employment income.

The rationale for strictly controlling deductions from employment income is to prevent erosion of the revenue base. With millions of employees filing tax returns every year, even a small deduction can mean a substantial revenue loss.

(b) Salesperson's Expenses

A salesperson may deduct expenses from employment income if she or he is:[114]

- Employed to sell property or negotiate contracts;
- *Required* to pay business expenses;
- *Ordinarily* required to carry out job duties away from the employer's regular place of business;
- Remunerated, at least in part, by commissions related to the volume of sales; and
- Not in receipt of a tax-free allowance for travelling expenses that is excluded from income.[115]

---

[114] Para. 8(1)(f).

[115] Subpara. 6(1)(b)(v). Where the allowance is unreasonably low, the taxpayer may include the allowance in income and deduct his actual expenses; see *Cossette v. M.N.R.* (1955), 13 Tax ABC 170, 55 DTC 365 (T.A.B.).

The employee is required to file a prescribed form wherein it is certified by the employer that the employee has satisfied all of the above conditions.[116]

(i) Limits

A salesperson who meets *all* of the above conditions may, within specified limits, deduct employment-related expenses in calculating employment income. The maximum deduction is limited to the amount of commission income received by him or her in the year. The deduction may be claimed for any expenses incurred to earn employment income.[117]

(ii) Capital Cost Allowance

A salesperson may also deduct capital cost allowance ("CCA")[118] and interest expense in respect of a motor vehicle or aircraft acquired and used in the performance of employment-related duties.[119] The claim for CCA and interest expense on a motor vehicle or aircraft is not limited to the salesperson's commission income and may be used to reduce income from other sources.

Notwithstanding the right to deduct CCA and interest expense (deductions usually associated with the computation of. business and property income), salespeople are employees for tax purposes, *albeit* employees with more generous deduction privileges. Here, as elsewhere in the Act, any expenses claimed must be reasonable in the circumstances.[120]

(c) Travelling Expenses

Employees who are:

- Ordinarily required to carry on their employment duties away from their employer's regular place of business,
- Required to pay their own travelling expenses, and
- Not in receipt of a tax-free allowance

---

[116] Subs. 8(10).

[117] *Laliberté v. M.N.R.* (1953), 9 Tax ABC 145, 53 DTC 370 (T.A.B.)'(travelling salesman allowed to deduct rent for sample rooms); *Sherman v. M.N.R.*, [1970] Tax ABC 618, 70 DTC 1409 (T.A.B.) (advertising expenses by securities salesman allowed as deduction).

[118] See Chapter VIII "Business and Property Income: Deductions" for discussion of CCA.

[119] Para. 8(1)(j); Reg. 1100(1).

[120] S. 67. *Niessen v. M.N.R.* (1960), 60 DTC 489, 25 Tax ABC 62 (T.A.B.) (claim for CCA on Cadillac disallowed as excessive).

are allowed to deduct their travelling expense[121] to the extent that these are not reimbursed by the employer.[122] In this context, "ordinarily" means as a matter of regular occurrence.[123]

The deduction for travelling expenses is available to all employees who qualify and is not restricted to commissioned salespeople. A salesperson who claims a deduction for expenses under paragraph 8(1)(*f*), however, cannot also claim another deduction for travelling expenses under paragraph 8(1)(*h*). But, he or she may claim the deduction under whichever of the two provisions is most advantageous.

(i) Inadequate Compensation

An employee who is not fully reimbursed for his or her employment-related expenses may claim any shortfall as an expense deduction. For example, an employee may spend 30 cents a kilometre to run a motor vehicle and be reimbursed at a rate of 20 cents a kilometre. In these circumstances, the employee can claim an expense deduction equal to 10 cents per kilometre travelled on the employer's business.[124]

(ii) Requirement of Travel

Deductibility of travelling expenses depends upon the employee being required to travel away from his or her employer's place of business. This requirement need not be expressly stated in the employment contract, but may be implied from the surrounding circumstances such as employer expectations, industry practice, etc.[125] The employer must, however, certify that the employee meets all of the statutory requirements.[126]

---

[121] Paras. 8(1)(*h*), (*h*.1).

[122] Subparas. 6(1)(*b*)(v), (vi), (vii).

[123] *The Queen v. Healy*, [1978] CTC 355, 78 DTC 6239; reversed [1979] CTC 44, 79 DTC 5060 (F.C.A.) (jockey club employee not "ordinarily" reporting for work at Fort Erie but spending 1/3 of his time there); *The Queen v. Patterson*, [1982] CTC 371, 82 DTC 6326 (F.C.T.D.) (school principal who made 56 trips to other schools "ordinarily" required to carry out duties in different places; expenses deductible).

[124] *Peters v. M.N.R.*, [1986] 2 CTC 2221, 86 DTC 1662 (T.C.C.).

[125] *Moore v. The Queen*, [1987] 1 CTC 319, 87 DTC 5217 (F.C.T.D.) (principal would have received unfavourable performance reviews had she not attended meetings; expenses allowed); *Rozen v. The Queen*, [1986] 1 CTC 50, 85 DTC 5611 (F.C.T.D.) (requirement to use automobile in course of employment implied term of contract); *The Queen v. Cival*, [1983] CTC 153, 83 DTC 5168 (F.C.A.) (deduction denied where taxpayer not required to use own car under contract of employment).

[126] Subs. 8(10).

(iii) Motor Vehicles, etc.

Motor vehicle and aircraft expenses are deductible by employees.[127] An employee may only deduct aircraft expenses which are reasonable in amount, having regard to the availability of commercial transportation.[128]

Interest paid on money borrowed for the purpose of purchasing a motor vehicle or aircraft used for employment purposes is deductible to the extent that the vehicle or aircraft is used in the course of employment.[129]

Similarly, an employee may deduct a part of the capital cost of a motor vehicle or aircraft, to the extent that the vehicle or aircraft is used in the course of employment.

(iv) Meals

An employee may claim meal expenses as part of travel costs only if the meal is consumed while the employee is away for at least 12 hours from the municipality in which his or her employer is located.[130]

(d) Musicians

An employed musician who is required to furnish his or her own musical instruments may deduct amounts paid on account of the maintenance, insurance or rental of such instruments.[131] Where the musician owns the musical instrument used in employment, he or she is entitled to depreciate it at a rate of 20 per cent on a declining balance basis.[132]

(e) Canadian Residents Employed Overseas

As a general rule, Canadian residents are taxable on their global income, regardless of where it is earned.[133] Canadian residents who are employed outside Canada may, however, be eligible for special tax concessions in respect of their overseas employment income. This concession allows Canadian employers to compete for international contracts by reducing the net payroll cost of sending Canadian residents to work overseas. These tax concessions put Canadian employers on a competitive footing with employers from other countries that offer similar tax subsidies.

---

[127] Para. 8(1)(*h*.1).

[128] Subs. 8(9).

[129] Para. 8(1)(*j*).

[130] Subs. 8(4).

[131] Para. 8(1)(*p*).

[132] Reg. 1100(1)(a)(viii).

[133] Subs. 2(1), s. 3.

A Canadian resident is entitled to the overseas tax credit if:[134]

- He or she is employed by a "specified employer";[135]

- His or her employment related duties are performed outside Canada for a period of *at least* six consecutive months; and

- The employer is in the construction, exploration, engineering, or agricultural business, or in some other *prescribed* activity.

An employee who satisfies these requirements is entitled to a tax credit equal to 80 per cent of his or her net overseas earnings up to a maximum of $80,000 annually. These amounts are prorated over the number of days the employee works abroad in a year. The employee may apply the credit against the taxes otherwise payable in respect of his or her overseas employment income.

(f) Other Deductions

Section 8 also lists other deductions from employment income. Note particularly:

Type of Expense	Statutory Reference
Legal expenses incurred by employee in collecting or establishing right to salary or wages owed by employer	para. 8(1)(*b*)
Value of cleric's residence, or rent paid by cleric or member of a religious order	para. 8(1)(*c*); IT-141
Contribution by a teacher to a fund established for the benefit of Commonwealth teachers present in Canada on an exchange program	para. 8(1)(*d*)
Expenses of certain railway company employees employed away from ordinary place of residence or home terminal	para. 8(1)(*e*); IC 73-21R7
Expenses for meals, lodging and travel incurred by a transport business employee while carrying out duties of employment	para. 8(1)(*g*)

---

[134] Subs. 122.3(1); see also Chapter XIII "Computation of Tax Payable".

[135] Para. 122.3(2)(*a*).

Annual professional membership dues, where required to maintain professional status by law	subpara. $8(1)(i)(i)$[136]
Trade union or public servant association annual dues	subpara. $8(1)(i)(iv)$
Annual dues retained by employer from employee's remuneration and paid to a trade union or association	subpara. $8(1)(i)(v)$
Dues required to be paid to a parity or advisory committee under provincial law	subpara. $8(1)(i)(vi)$
Office rent or salary to an assistant paid by employee as required by contract of employment	subpara. $8(1)(i)(ii)$
Cost of supplies consumed directly in the performance of duties of employment	subpara. $8(1)(i)(iii)$
Interest on borrowed money for the purchase of and capital cost allowance for a motor vehicle or aircraft used in the performance of duties of employment	para. $8(1)(j)(i)$; Reg. $1100(1)(a)(viii)$
Canada Pension Plan contributions and unemployment insurance premiums paid by an employee to an individual employed as an assistant	para. $8(1)(l.1)$
Employee RCA contributions	para. $8(1)(m.2)$
Certain amounts paid by employee as reimbursement for amounts paid to him or her as workers' compensation	para. $8(1)(n)$

---

[136] *Lucas v. M.N.R.*, [1987] 2 CTC 23, 87 DTC 5277 (F.C.T.D.).

| Amounts forfeited under salary deferral arrangement | para. 8(1)(*o*) |
| Certain employment expenses of artists | para. 8(1)(*q*) |

(g) Employee Benefit Plans

References:

BULLETINS, CIRCULARS & RULINGS:

IT-502	March 28, 1985	Employee Benefit Plans and Trusts
IT-502SR	May 31, 1991	Employee Benefit Plans and Trusts
ATR-17	February 9, 1987	Employee Benefit Plan — Purchase of Company Shares

(i) General

As a general rule, an employee is taxable on all benefits *received* or *enjoyed* in respect of, in the course of, or by virtue of employment. Thus, employees are taxable on a current basis for the value of benefits received or enjoyed in the calendar year. There are, however, special rules that apply to payments into and out of deferred compensation plans such as employee benefit plans ("EBPs"), salary deferral arrangements ("SDAs"), employee trusts ("ETs"), and retirement compensation arrangements ("RCAs").

EBPs synchronize the employer's deduction for contributions into the plan with the timing of the inclusion of benefits in the employee's income. An employee is not taxable on any benefit derived by virtue of his or her employer's contributions into an EBP, but is taxable only when he or she actually receives an amount out of the plan. An employer is not entitled to deduct an amount paid into an EBP until such time as the plan pays out benefits and the payments are allocated to the employers. Thus, the rules focus on the timing of employer deductions and employee inclusions. There are no rules in respect of the investment activities of such plans.

(ii) Meaning of "Employee Benefit Plan"

An employee benefit plan is an arrangement under which an employer (or any person with whom the employer does not deal at arm's length) makes contributions to another person who acts as the "custodian" of the plan, and the payments are made for the future benefit of employees (or former employees) of the employer.[137]

Thus, the essential ingredients of an "employee benefit plan" are a payment or contribution by an employer to a third party "custodian" and a future benefit (other than an excluded benefit) for the employee.

---

[137] Subs. 248(1) ("employee benefit plan").

A payment of an amount to another specified type of plan or where the amount is excluded under section 6 of the Act does not give rise to an employee benefit plan contribution. Apart from these requirements, there is no particular formality that is required for an arrangement to constitute an EBP. Payments into and out of the plan may be in cash or kind. An EBP may cover an entire group of employees or be limited to a few persons.

Certain types of payments are specifically excluded from the definition of an employee benefit plan. Payments on account of:[138]

- a registered pension fund or plan,
- a sickness or accident insurance plan,
- a private health services plan,
- a supplementary unemployment benefit plan,
- a deferred profit sharing plan,
- a group term life insurance policy,
- an employee profit-sharing plan,
- a disability insurance plan,
- an income maintenance insurance plan,
- a vacation pay trust,
- an employee trust,
- an arrangement to provide education or training to an employee,
- a salary deferral arrangement,
- a retirement compensation arrangement, and
- certain other prescribed plans,

do *not* create an EBP. Apart from these exceptions, however, the employee benefit plan rules apply to all plans (including non-profit organizations) that fall within its definition in subsection 248(1).

(iii) Benefit Required

An EBP only arises from a payment that would confer a benefit on an employee. Thus, the first question to be determined is whether payments made to a plan on behalf of employees would constitute a "benefit" to the employee under section 6 if the payments were paid to the employee directly instead of through the plan.

"Benefit" from employment is broadly interpreted and includes virtually all perquisites and payments related to employment. In *Savage*,[139] for example, the Supreme Court interpreted the phrase "benefits of any kind whatever" in paragraph

---

[138] *Ibid.*

[139] *Savage v. The Queen*, [1983] CTC 393, 83 DTC 5409 (S.C.C.).

6(1)(*a*) of the Act to mean any material acquisition which confers an economic benefit on an employee and that does not fall within an excluded category of receipt. Similarly, in *Nowegijick*:[140]

> The words "in respect of" are, in my opinion words of the widest possible scope. . . . The phrase "in respect of" is probably the widest of any expression intended to convey some connection between two related subject matters.

(iv) Tax Consequences to Employer

(A) Employer Contributions

An employer is entitled to a deduction for its contributions to an EBP. The employer's contribution may be in either cash or kind.[141] The deduction is synchronized with the employee's inclusion in income of payments received from the plan. More specifically, an employer is entitled to a deduction for contributions to an EBP equal to the amount allocated to him or her by the custodian of the plan.

An employer's deduction for a particular taxation year is limited to the amount allocated by the custodian of the plan. The employer cannot deduct an amount in excess of the amount contributed (net of refunds) for the year and preceding years for which deductions have not previously been made.[142]

An employer is also entitled to a deduction where all of the obligations of the plan to its beneficiaries have been fully satisfied and there is no remaining property in the plan. In these circumstances, the employer's deduction is limited to the amount of net contributions made to the plan, less any deductions previously claimed by her or him in prior years.

(B) Constructive Payments

A beneficiary may be considered to have constructively received an amount where, for example, an amount is credited or applied to an outstanding debt. A beneficiary may also be considered to have indirectly received an amount if she or he directs its payment to a third party. An amount constructively received by an employee is also considered to have been constructively paid at that time and the employer may take the deduction at that time.

There are no limits on the amount of an employer's contribution in respect of an employee. The employer may make contributions as are appropriate and reasonable in

---

[140] *Nowegijick v. The Queen*, [1983] CTC 20 at 25, 83 DTC 5041 at 5045 (S.C.C.).

[141] See, e.g., *M.N.R v. Chrysler Canada Ltd.*, [1991] 2 CTC 156, 91 DTC 5526; additional reasons [1992] 1 CTC 61, 92 DTC 6061 and [1992] 2 CTC 95, 92 DTC 6346 (F.C.T.D.) (employer corporation contributed shares to its EBP).

[142] Subs. 32.1(1).

the circumstances. The general limitation in the Act in respect of the non-deductibility of unreasonable amounts also applies to employee benefit plans.[143]

(C) Allocation by Custodian

The custodian of an EBP is required to allocate annual amounts contributed into the plan.[144] The amount allocated to an employer is the amount by which payments out of the plan to employees (or their estates or beneficiaries) in the year (excluding a return of contributions) exceed the income of the plan for the year. There does not appear to be any specific penalty for failure to make the required allocation.

The "income" of a plan for a year is determined by reference to special rules,[145] as discussed below.

(D) Sequence of Payments

Payments from an EBP are considered to occur in the following sequence:

- A return of the beneficiary's contributions,
- A distribution of the plan's income for the year,
- A distribution of the employer's contributions, and
- A distribution of the plan's prior years' income, if any.

Thus, the employer does not get a deduction until the income of the plan has been distributed.

(v) Tax Consequences to Employees

(A) Taxable Receipts

A member of an EBP is not taxable on the value of any benefit that results from an employee's contribution into the plan. The member is taxable only on amounts paid out of the plan to the extent that the payment exceeds his or her contributions. Regardless of the nature of the income earned by the plan, amounts paid out (other than a return of contributions) of an employee benefit plan are taxable as income from an office or employment.

An amount paid out in a form other than cash is included in income at the fair market value of the property dispersed.

(B) Non-deductible

An employee's contributions to an employee benefit plan are not deductible for tax purposes and the employee is not taxable on a return of his or her own contributions

---

[143] S. 67.

[144] Subs. 32.1(2).

[145] Subs. 32.1(3).

from the plan.[146] The custodian of the plan is responsible for determining the portion of the payment that represents a return of the employee's return of contribution from the plan.

(C) Non-taxable receipts

An EBP payment to an employee is not taxable as ordinary income to the employee if the payment represents:

- a death benefit, or
- a superannuation or pension benefit attributable to services by a person in a period throughout which the person was not resident in Canada.

Benefits from these sources are taxable under other provisions of the Act.

(D) Timing

An employee is taxable only when he or she receives, whether actually or constructively, an amount out of an employee benefit plan. An amount is considered to be received when payment has actually been made or when the employee has an unfettered right to the payment. Restrictions (for example, forfeiture of non-vested amounts) are considered as evidence that the employee does not have an unrestricted right to the plan's funds. There is no restriction on the form in which benefits are paid or on the timing or duration of payments from an EBP.

A member of a plan is considered to receive payment out of the plan on the *earlier* of:

- the date of actual payment to him or her, and
- the date when he or she constructively receives payment.

An amount constructively received by an employee/beneficiary is considered to have been paid to him or her and is, therefore, included in income.[147]

(vi) Nature of Income Received

Amounts paid from an EBP are considered income from an office or employment. Thus, any capital gains and dividend income earned by the plan lose their identity as such and are taxable in the employee's hands as employment source income.

(vii) Employer Contributions

An employee may direct an employer to make future payments, to which the employee will be entitled, into an employee benefit plan. Provided that the direction is given to the employer *before* the employee becomes entitled to receive the payment, the payment is considered an employer contribution and, as such, there are no immediate income tax consequences from the payment to the plan.

---

[146] Para. 6(1)(*g*).

[147] Subs. 104(13).

(viii) *Tax Consequences to the Plan*

An EBP may be structured as a trust or as any other arrangement. In fact, most EBPs are structured as trusts for ease of administration.

(A) EBP Not a Trust

Where an EBP is not a trust, the custodian of the plan is taxable on its income at the applicable tax rate. The applicable rate depends upon the legal nature of the custodian. Contributions into the plan are not included in gross income and payments by the plan out of its contributions are not deductible by the custodian.

(B) EBP as Trust

The income of an EBP structured as a trust is determined according to the general rules applicable to trusts. Contributions into the trust are not included in gross income and payments out of contributions are not deductible by the trust in computing its income for the year. A trust is required to include in its income any investment or other incidental income that it earns in the year.

A trust is entitled to deductions in the following order:

- first, all expenses incurred in earning its investment or other income for the year;
- second, any expenses related to its normal operations to the extent that those expenses are not expressly disallowed under the Act; and
- finally, any amounts paid to its beneficiaries out of income.

Any amount remaining as income in the trust is taxable under the general rates applicable to *inter vivos* trusts.

(C) Payments in Later Years

Where an EBP trust pays an amount out of its after-tax income to a beneficiary in a later year, the beneficiary is taxable on the income in the year in which payment is received. Thus, the beneficiary is taxable on any income (but not return of contributions) received from the trust, regardless that it is paid out of the trust's after-tax income.

(ix) *Withholding Taxes*

(A) Payments Considered Salary

A payment out of an EBP is considered to be income from an office or employment[148] and, as such, comes within the definition of "salary or wages" in subsection 248(1). Hence, an amount paid from the plan is subject to the withholding provision[149] of the Act.

---

[148] Para. 6(1)(*g*).

[149] S. 153.

A custodian who makes a payment out of an EBP to an employee is required to deduct tax from the payment and to remit the tax on the employee's behalf to the Receiver General of Canada. The amount of the tax to be withheld is determined in accordance with the rules prescribed under Part I of the Regulations.

(B) Failure to Withhold

A person who fails to deduct or withhold income tax as required under subsection 153(1) is subject to a penalty of 10 per cent of the amount that should have been deducted or withheld.[150] Where the failure to withhold tax is not the first offence in the year (that is, the taxpayer has been assessed a penalty on a prior occasion in the year), the penalty is 20 per cent of the amount that should have been deducted or withheld.[151]

A taxpayer who fails to withhold or remit tax as required is liable for interest on the tax. Interest is payable on a compounded daily basis[152] at the prescribed rate (set quarterly) on all amounts not deducted or withheld on the 15th day of the month following the month in which the amounts should have been deducted or withheld. Interest continues to accrue until the day that the amount which should have been deducted or withheld is actually remitted to the Receiver General of Canada.[153]

(C) Penalties

Persons who withhold tax but who fail to remit the tax as required are subject to penalties.[154] The penalty is in addition to the withholder's liability to remit the *full amount* of the tax deducted to the Receiver General of Canada.

(x) *Summary*

Employee Benefit Plan ("EBP")

General Scheme	• Employer's deduction is synchronized with inclusion in employee's income.
Structure	• No particular structure required — can apply to any type of arrangement, trust or otherwise.
Application	• Applies to all organizations, including non-profit organizations.

---

[150] Para. 227(8)(*a*).

[151] Para. 227(8)(*b*).

[152] Subs. 248(11).

[153] Subs. 227(8.3).

[154] Subs. 227(9).

Effect on Employer	• Cannot take deduction until amount allocated by custodian.
	• Deduction limited to contributions.
	• Can be considered to have made constructive payment to employees.
Limits on Deduction	• None, though must be reasonable in the circumstances.
	• Annual allocation by custodian required.
	• Cannot get deduction until plan's income is distributed.
Effect on Employee	• Taxable on payments out of the plan, except return of contributions.
	• Contributions into plan are not deductible.

(h) Trusts

(i) General

The statutory scheme for the taxation of trusts is to treat trusts as conduits: A trust is taxable on income that it retains and may deduct amounts paid or payable to its beneficiaries. Thus, trusts are sometimes taxed as if they are taxable entities in their own right and, at other times, as conduits of income for their beneficiaries.[155]

The income of a trust is calculated by deducting amounts paid or payable by it to its beneficiaries in the year.[156] A beneficiary of a trust is required to include in income for a year, any amount payable to him or her in that year by the trust, regardless of whether or not the income is actually received.[157]

An amount is considered to be "payable to a beneficiary" if it is paid to that person or if the beneficiary is legally entitled to enforce payment of the amount at that time.[158]

A beneficiary is considered to be "entitled" to the income of a trust if possessed of the legal right to enforce payment of the amount, regardless of whether or not he or she actually makes an attempt to enforce payment. A beneficiary who is *entitled* to trust

---

[155] Subss. 104(2), (6).

[156] Subs. 104(6).

[157] Subs. 104(13).

[158] Subs. 104(24); see also *Wood v. M.N.R.* (1964), 37 Tax ABC 37, 64 DTC 780.

income is required to include the amount payable (whether or not he or she actually receives it) in income in the year in which it is payable.

To be deductible by the trust and taxable to the beneficiary, both the amount payable and the person to whom it is payable must be clearly identified. Amounts required to be included in computing the income of a beneficiary for a taxation year are considered to have been earned by the beneficiary on the last day of the taxation year of the trust.

(ii) *Health and Welfare Trusts*

References:

BULLETINS, CIRCULARS & RULINGS:

IT-85R2	July 31, 1986	Health and Welfare Trusts for Employees
ATR-8	May 12, 1986	Self-Insured Health and Welfare Trust Fund

The *Income Tax Act* does not contain a definition of "health and welfare trust". The concept of what constitutes a "health and welfare trust" has been developed administratively by Revenue Canada. A health and welfare trust is a trust that provides certain specified benefits relating to the health and welfare of employees.

Revenue Canada's administrative view is that a "health and welfare trust" is a trust arrangement under which the trustees receive contributions from employers and, in some cases, from employees, to provide health and welfare benefits agreed to by the employer and the employees.[159] In order to qualify as a "health and welfare trust", the funds of the trust cannot revert to the employer or be used for any purpose other than providing the health and welfare benefits for which the contributions are made. Furthermore, payments by the employer cannot be made on a voluntary or gratuitous basis. They must be enforceable by the trustees in the event that the employer decides not to make the payments legally required of him or her. Thus, a health and welfare trust is one in which the trustees act independently of the employer.

Revenue Canada also takes the administrative position that a health and welfare trust is a trust that restricts its benefits to group sickness or accident insurance plans, private health services plans, group term life insurance policy plans and plans which provide for a combination of these benefits. Further, in their view, in order to qualify as a health and welfare trust the funds of the trust must not be used for any purposes other than providing the health and welfare benefits for which the contributions are made. Finally, the administrative position is that the employer's contributions to a health and welfare trust must not exceed the amounts required to provide the health and welfare benefits.

---

[159] IT-85R2, "Health and Welfare Trusts for Employees" (July 31, 1986).

(A) Tax Consequences to Employers

Subject to certain limitations, contributions to a health and welfare trust by an employer are deductible in the taxation year in which the employer is legally obliged to make the contributions. To be deductible, however, the contributions must be reasonable in amount[160] and be incurred for the purposes of earning income from business or property.[161]

(B) Tax Consequences to Employees

An employee does not receive a benefit at the time that his or her employer makes a contribution to a health and welfare trust on his or her employee's behalf if the contribution is in respect of *non-taxable* benefits in paragraph 6(1)(*a*) of the Act.[162]

(C) Tax Consequences to the Trust

A health and welfare trust is taxable on its net investment income after deductions on account of:

- Expenses incurred in earning its investment or other income;
- Expenses related to its normal operations; and
- Premiums and benefits payable to beneficiaries.

Any income remaining in the trust after deductions is subject to tax at the usual rate applicable to *inter vivos* trusts.[163] The applicable federal rate is 29 per cent, which is equivalent to the highest marginal rate of tax for individuals. A trust is also subject to provincial tax, provincial and federal surtaxes and supersurtaxes, which can raise the effective tax rate to approximately 53 per cent.

(iii) Employee Trusts

Employee trusts are considered conduits for tax purposes. An employer may deduct contributions to an employee trust on a current basis and the beneficiaries of the trust are also taxable on a current basis, regardless of when the funds are received. Thus, the deduction of employer contributions is synchronized with inclusion of benefits in the employee's income.

An "employee trust" is defined in subsection 248(1) as an arrangement under which an employer makes a payment to a trustee in trust for the sole benefit of that person's employees or former employees. The definition requires that:

- The beneficiary's right to benefits vest in him or her at the time each payment is made;

---

[160] S. 67.

[161] S. 9.

[162] IT-85R2, "Health and Welfare Trusts for Employees" (July 31, 1986).

[163] S. 122.

- The amount of the benefit does not depend upon the employee's position, performance or compensation as an employee;
- The trustees allocate both the trust's non-business income and capital gains (net) annually; and
- The trustee elects in the trust's tax return, within 90 days of its first taxation year, to consider the trust as an employee trust for tax purposes.

(A) Tax Consequences to Employer

An employer is generally allowed to take a deduction on a current basis for any contributions to an employee trust.[164] The deduction is subject to the general rule that it must be reasonable in amount.[165]

The employer is not required to deduct or withhold any amount from any payments that it makes to the trustee of the employee trust in accordance with the terms of the trust.

The trustee is not required to deduct or withhold any amounts paid to employees out of the employee trust. The trustee does not incur any liability for withholding taxes in respect of allocation or payments to the beneficiaries out of or under an employee trust. The trustee must, however, file an information return[166] to report amounts allocated under an employee trust to the beneficiaries of the trust.

(B) Tax Consequences to Employees

Employees who are beneficiaries of an employee trust are taxable annually on amounts allocated to them for the year by the trustee, regardless of whether such amounts are actually distributed or received in that year. Any amount allocated to the employee (beneficiary) is taxable as employment source income, regardless of the nature of the income received by the trust.

The amount to be allocated to an employee during the year is the aggregate of:

- The employer's contributions for the year into the trust;
- The trust's net income for the year from investments; and
- Capital gains realized on the disposition of trust property.

Business income of the employee trust may *not* be allocated to the beneficiary.[167] The trust is entitled to deduct certain losses from the allocable amounts in calculating the net annual amount to be allocated to employees.

---

[164] Subs. 9(1).

[165] S. 67.

[166] Form T4A is used for this purpose.

[167] Subs. 104(6).

(C) Tax Consequences to the Trust

An employee trust is required to make an annual allocation of all of its *non-business* income to its beneficiaries. Amounts allocated to beneficiaries may be deducted from the trust's income in the year in which the allocation is made. Thus, an employee trust is not taxable on its non-business income.

An employee trust may not allocate business income to its beneficiaries. The trust's net business income is taxable to the trust at the rate applicable to *inter vivos* trusts.[168]

Example V.7

Assume:

In 1994, A Ltd. contributed $400 on behalf of each of 300 employees to an employee trust plan. The trust is *non-contributory* on the part of the employees. In 1994, the trust allocated $500 (comprised of $400 received from A Ltd. and $100 in income earned by the trust) to employee B. In 1995, the trust paid out $500 to employee B.

Then:

1994	Employee B includes in employment income	$ 500
1994	Employer A Ltd. may deduct	$ 400
1995	Include in B's employment income	NIL

Example V.8

Assume:

In 1994, M Ltd. contributed $100 on behalf of each of 500 employees to an employee benefit plan (EBP). The plan is *non-contributory* on the part of the employees. In 1995, the EBP allocated $250 to employee N. In 1996, the EBP paid out $250 to employee N.

Then:

1994	Tax effect on employee N	NIL
1994	Tax effect on employer M Ltd.	NIL
1995	Tax effect on employee N	NIL
1995	Tax effect on employer M Ltd.	NIL
1996	Include in N's employment income	$ 250
1996	Employer M Ltd. may deduct contribution	$ 250

---

[168] S. 122.

Example V.9

Assume:

In 1994, C Corp. Ltd. contributed $100 on behalf of each of 300 employees to an employee benefit plan (EBP). The plan is *contributory* to the extent that C Corp. Ltd. (employer) matches each dollar contributed by employees to a maximum limit of $100 per employee. The trust agreement provides that payments out of the plan are first made out of employee contributions and then out of employer contributions. In 1995, the EBP paid out $400 to employee D.

Then:

1994	Tax effect on employee D	NIL
1995	Include in D's employment income	$ 400
	Less: Return of contributions for 1994	(100)
	Net inclusion in income	$ 300

Example V.10

Assume:

In 1994, X Ltd.contributed $30,000 to an employee benefit plan. The plan is organized as a trust. During 1994, the trust does not earn any income and pays out $15,000 to employees. One employee (T) receives a payment of $500.

Then:

(a)	Effect on T:	
	Amount included in income in 1994	$ 500
(b)	Effect on EBP trust:	NIL
(c)	Effect on X Ltd.:	
	Amount of payments to employees	15,000
	Exceeds: income of EBP trust	NIL
	Amount deductible by X Ltd. in 1994	$ 15,000*

*Since the trust did not earn any income in 1994, this amount is, in effect, a return of capital.

(i) Employee Pensions

(i) Tax Incentives

Registered employee pension funds receive substantial tax assistance under the *Income Tax Act*. The assistance takes three forms:

1. A tax exemption for the registered pension fund;
2. Exclusion of employer contributions from the employee's income; and
3. A deduction for permissible employee contributions to a registered plan.

The combined effect of these three forms of tax assistance (exemption of earnings, non-taxation of employer contributions and deductibility of employee contributions) can be quite substantial and, consequently, registered pension plans are strictly controlled by Revenue Canada.[169]

(ii) Registration

In order to derive the benefits described above, a pension plan must be "registered" with Revenue Canada. An employer-funded arrangement that provides benefits to employees in connection with their retirement and that is not registered with Revenue Canada is considered to be a "retirement compensation arrangement" ("RCA"). The principal difference between a registered plan and an RCA is that the latter is subject to a "refundable tax" under section 207.7 of the Act. The refundable taxes equal 50 per cent of all contributions to the RCA plus 50 per cent of the net income of the trust. These taxes, *albeit* refundable, make RCAs far less attractive than registered pension plans. Hence, registration is one of the essential elements of tax-assisted retirement savings.

(iii) Retirement Savings

The cornerstone of the regime in respect of registered pension plans is that an employee is entitled to deduct contributions to such plans but subject to an overall dollar limit. The overall limit is 18 per cent of earnings, subject to an absolute dollar limit that is set for each year. The absolute dollar limit is as follows:

1990 — $11,500
1991 — $12,500
1992 — $12,500
1993 — $13,500
1994 — $14,500
1995 — $15,500

(iv) Employee Contributions

An employee is allowed to deduct amounts contributed to a registered pension plan. The amount deductible depends upon whether the plan is a defined benefit plan or a money purchase plan.

(A) Types of Plans

A money purchase plan is one in which contributions are paid to an account in respect of a particular employee and in which the employee's benefits are paid from the money that is accumulated in that particular plan. Thus, the amount contributed into a particular plan determines, in effect, the benefit that will be derived from the plan. In contrast, a defined benefit plan is one in which the employee's pension benefit is determined by reference to some formula of a defined nature. The formula is generally

---

[169] See ss. 147.1 – 147.3.

stated in terms of the years of service and the employee's average earnings during the last years of service.

(B) Contribution Limits

An employee's current service contribution is limited to the lesser of:

- 9 per cent of his or her compensation for the year; or
- $1,000 plus his or her pension adjustment in respect of the employer for the year.

An employee's "pension adjustment" with respect to a money purchase plan is the sum of that person's own contributions together with the employer's contributions to the plan on his or her behalf. The rules for determining an employee's "pension adjustment" with respect to a defined benefit plan are much more complicated, and the calculation is made by Revenue Canada on behalf of the taxpayer.

(j) Retirement Compensation Arrangements ("RCA")

(i) Nature of RCA

An RCA is an arrangement in which an employer (or former employer) makes contributions to a trust or other third party (the "custodian") to be held in respect of an employee's retirement or other severance from employment. There are three essential ingredients of an RCA:

1. Funding of a plan or trust by an employer, a former employer, or a person with whom the employer is at arm's length;
2. Custodianship of funds by a third party; and
3. A provision for benefits that may be received or enjoyed by an employee on retirement, termination from employment, or substantial change in employment.

An RCA must be a *funded* arrangement. Unfunded arrangements do not qualify as RCAs. An employer who retains funds in trust, however, is considered a "custodian" for the purpose of the RCA rules. Revenue Canada considers an arrangement or plan backed by a letter of credit from the employer to constitute an RCA.

The RCA rules are intended to thwart the improper use of deferred compensation arrangements. For example, a non-taxable employer could set up an "employee benefit plan" for high income employees in order to circumvent the statutory limits on tax assistance permitted to registered pension plans and other retirement plans. The employer's contributions into the employee benefit plan would not be currently deductible, but the employee would not be taxable on the value of the benefit. If the employer was a non-taxable entity, the non-deductibility of contributions into the plan would not be a disadvantage. The high income employee would, however, benefit from the tax-deferred investment in the plan. The RCA rules eliminate such tax benefits that would otherwise be available under "off-side" retirement arrangements.

(ii) Tax Consequences

(A) To the Employer

Employer contributions to a RCA are deductible on a current basis under paragraph 20(1)(r) of the Act.

(B) To the Employee

An employee who receives payments from an RCA is taxable upon receipt of the payment. The refund to the RCA is synchronized with the inclusion in income of amounts paid to the employee. Hence, there is no tax deferral or rate advantage in using an RCA. The 50 per cent tax on contributions to, and any income earned by, the plan is approximately equal to the top corporate and personal tax rates.

Only funded plans qualify as RCAs. Unfunded plans cannot be RCAs. Thus, one way to circumvent the RCA rules is to leave the employee's retirement arrangement unfunded and rely upon the employer being sufficiently solvent to meet the financial obligations of the arrangement as and when they fall due. This may not, however, be the most satisfactory option for the employee.

(C) To the Trust

An RCA is subject to tax under Part XI.3 of the Act. Contributions to an RCA and any income generated by the plan are subject to a "refundable tax" at the rate of 50 per cent. The tax is refundable to the plan at a rate of $1 of refund for every $2 paid out to a beneficiary of the plan.

The effect of the refundable tax structure in respect of RCAs is that it negates any potential for tax deferral on contributions into the plan. In effect, the payment and refund mechanism amounts to a prepayment of the tax that the employee might be expected to pay when the plan's funds are distributed in accordance with the terms of the arrangement.

The "custodian" of an RCA is under an obligation to withhold the refundable tax. The custodian also has the responsibility to file tax returns in respect of the trust and to pay any refundable tax owing within 90 days of the end of its taxation year.

An RCA trust is considered to be an *inter vivos* trust and, as such, is taxable on a calendar year basis.

(iii) Withholding Tax

An employer is required to withhold tax on his or her contributions to an RCA. The "custodian" of the plan is required to pay the trust's taxes within 90 days of its fiscal year-end. The "custodian" of the plan is also required to withhold tax on amounts paid out of an RCA to a beneficiary of the plan. The employer is, however, secondarily liable for taxes that may not have been withheld if the "custodian" does not pay the tax as it becomes due.

(k) Limitations on Deductions

(i) Overall Limitation

Section 67 is an overriding limitation on the deduction of expenses for tax purposes. Expenses that might otherwise be deductible according to accounting principles are not deductible if they are unreasonable in the circumstances. Thus, the deductibility of an expense depends upon two factors: substantive authority and the amount claimed.

Whether an expense is reasonable in the circumstances is a question of fact in each case. In the context of salary and bonuses paid to employees, for example, the following factors may be relevant in determining whether the amount is reasonable:

- Rank or level within organization,

- Special knowledge, skills or connections,

- Comparable compensation paid to persons in similar businesses with similar responsibilities, and

- Past practices with respect to compensation in the particular business community concerned.

(ii) Food and Entertainment

The general rule is that all expenses must be reasonable in amount.[170] There is, however, an additional restriction for expenses incurred for food, beverages, and entertainment. The deduction in respect of these three categories of expenditures is restricted to 50 per cent of the lesser of:

- the amount actually paid, or

- an amount that would be reasonable in the circumstances.[171]

Thus, an expenditure that is unreasonable in amount may be disallowed to the extent that it is unreasonable. If the expenditure is in respect of food, beverages, or entertainment the taxpayer may claim only 50 per cent of the amount that is otherwise reasonable in the particular circumstances under consideration.

---

[170] S. 67.

[171] S. 67.1.

COMPREHENSIVE EXAMPLES

Problem V.11   Computation of Net Employment Income

Assume:

Ms. Reynolds is a part-time employee of AC Ltd. In 1995 she received the following amounts:

Gross salary	$ 21,000
Reimbursement of travelling expenses*	800
Reimbursement of tuition fees upon	
completion of technical training course**	120
Interest on Canada Savings Bonds	2,000

AC Ltd. withheld the following amounts from her salary:

Income tax	3,200
Canada Pension Plan contribution	320
Contribution to company registered pension plan	720
Contribution to RRSP	500
Group medical insurance premiums	240
Unemployment insurance premiums	480

The company's contribution to the pension fund in respect of her current services amounted to $580. Ms. Reynold's T4 slip shows taxable benefits for the year totalling $60.***

   * The travelling expenses include $300 worth of meals, but see inclusion of taxable benefit.

  ** Course taken on the instruction of her employer to upgrade her work skills.

*** 20% of the travelling expenses for meals purchased have been included on Ms. Reynold's T4.

Then:

Ms. Reynold's 1995 Net Employment Income

Gross salary	$ 21,000
Reimbursement of travelling expenses	800
Reimbursement of tuition	120
Taxable benefits	60
	21,980
Deductions:	
Travelling expenses	(800)
Tuition	(120)
Contribution to company RPP	(720)
Contribution to RRSP	(500)
Employment income for the year	$ 19,840

Problem V.12   Aggregation of Income Under Section 3

Assume:

Mr. Turner has provided you with the following information in respect of his income and losses for 1995:

Income from employment (net)	$ 35,000
Income from property (net)	10,000
Taxable capital gains	20,000
Allowable capital losses (including allowable business investment losses of $35,000)	(45,000)
Loss from business A	(30,000)
Income from business B	40,000
Taxable *net* gains on dispositions of listed personal property (LPP)	16,000
Dividends received from foreign corporations (Canadian dollars)	5,000

Mr. Turner paid fees of $15,000 for professional services rendered on the appeal of the reassessment of his 1990 income tax return.

Then, Mr. Turner's income for 1995 is:

Para. 3(a):

Income from employment (net)		$ 35,000
Income from property (net)		10,000
Income from business B		40,000
Dividends from foreign corporations		5,000
		$ 90,000

Para. 3(b):

Taxable capital gains	$ 20,000	
Taxable net gains on LPP	16,000	
	$ 36,000	
Allowable capital losses minus allowable business investment losses: ($45,000-$35,000)	(10,000)	26,000
		116,000

Para. 3(c):

Legal fees		(15,000)
		101,000

Para. 3(d):

Loss from business A	30,000	
Allowable business investment losses	35,000	(65,000)

<u>Recall</u>: Income = 3(a) + 3(b) − 3(c) − 3(d)

INCOME $ 36,000

SELECTED BIBLIOGRAPHY TO CHAPTER V

General

Atiyah, P.S., *Vicarious Liability in the Law of Torts* (London: Butterworths, 1967).

Baston, Paul F., "Tax Planning for Executive Hiring and Firing", [1991] *Corp. Mgmt. Tax Conf.* 10:1.

Chegus, Bruce, "Taxation of Employer-sponsored Plans: Current Practice" (1993), 5 *Tax. of Executive Compensation and Retirement* 792.

"Computing Income from Employment: The August 1993 Technical Amendments" (1993), 5 *Tax. of Executive Compensation and Retirement* 828.

"Controversy Surrounding the Adjustment of Earnings and Profits for Accrued Tax By a Cash Method Taxpayer (The): How Should the Conflict Be Resolved?" (Spring 1989), 42 *The Tax Lawyer* 821.

Dewling, Alan, "U.S. Residents Rendering Temporary Services in Canada may be subject to Canadian Tax on Remuneration Received from U.S. Employer" (1990), 2 *Tax. of Executive Compensation and Remuneration* 355.

Dionne, Andre, "SDAs and RCAs: Escaping Both Nets" (1993), 5 *Tax. of Executive Compensation and Retirement* 799.

Drache, Arthur B.C., "Employee Compensation", [1986] *Special Lectures of the Law Society of Upper Canada* 17.

Drache, Arthur B.C., *Taxation and the Arts: A Practical Guide* (Ottawa: Canadian Conference of the Arts, 1987).

Goodison, Don, "Tax Forum — Office Is Where the 'Head' Is" (October 1990), 24 *CGA Magazine* 24.

Gray, Kerry, "U.S. Citizens Employed in Canada" (1986), 34 *Can. Tax J.* 1463.

Hansen, Krishna and Rendall, eds., "The Taxation of Employees" (Chapter 6), *Canadian Taxation* (Toronto: De Boo, 1981) 187.

Hayes, Lawrence I., "Income Receipts and Deductions in the Computation of Income from Employment, Business and Property", in *Proceedings of 31st Tax Conf.* 381 (Can. Tax Foundation, 1979).

Hoey, D. Graham, "Shareholder-manager Compensation" in *Proceedings of 42 Tax Conf.* 6:1 (Can. Tax Foundation, 1990).

Income Tax and Goods and Services Tax Planning for Executive and Employee Compensation and Retirement (Toronto: Can. Tax Foundation, 1992).

Johnston, William, "Taxation of Non-registered Pension Plans", [1991] *Corp. Mgmt. Tax Conf.* 9:1.

Krishna, Vern, "Converting Salary into Management Fees" (1993), 4 *Can. Current Tax* C-1.

Krishna, Vern, "International Employment Income" (1993), 4 *Can. Current Tax* C-23.

Krishna, Vern, "*Surrogatum* Principle Applies to Employment Source Income" (1994), 5 *Can. Current Tax* 1

Krishna, Vern, "The Scope of Employment Benefits", [1994] *Can. Current Tax* C-55

Lax, Sharon M., "Retiring Allowance" (1994), 4 *Employment Bulletin No. 1* 2.

Lessard, Pierre, "Tax Planning for the Migrant Executive: A Canadian Perspective", [1991] *Corp. Mgmt. Tax Conf.* 11:1.

MacLagan, Billa, "Tax Tips" (1991), 1 *Employment and Labour Law Review* 21.

McCallum, J. Thomas, "Defining 'Employee'" (February 1992), 26 *CGA Magazine* 21.

McKie, A.B., "Artists and Athletes: Tax Acts" (1990), 3 *Can. Current Tax* C-17.

Montgomery, Amme, "Developments in Executive Compensation" (1992), 3 *Can. Current Tax* T-21.

Muto, Alexander D., "Same-sex Benefits and the Income Tax Act" (1994), 5 *Tax. of Executive Compensation and Retirement* 854.

Ramaseder, Brigitte M., "Incentives and Benefits" (1993), 4 *Tax. of Executive Compensation and Retirement* 779.

Ramaseder, Brigitte M., "New Rules Apply to Executive Transfers" (1993), *Tax. of Executive Compensation and Retirement* 825.

Swiderski, Tony, "Some New Wrinkles on an Old Problem: U.S. Retirement Plans Held by Canadians" (1991), 39 *Can. TaxJ.* 231.

Weil, Robert D., "A Revenue Canada Perspective", in *Proceedings of 38th Tax Conf.* 18 (Can. Tax Foundation, 1986).

White, Jerry S. *et al.*, *Wealth Creation for the Salaried Executive: A Canadian Guide to Executive/Managerial Compensation and Tax Planning* (Don Mills, Ont.: CCH Canadian, 1900).

The Characterization of Employment Income

Anderson, Eric W., "Owner-Manager Remuneration", in *Proceedings of 38th Tax Conf.* 11 (Can. Tax Foundation, 1986).

Davidson, D.L.H., "Executive and Employee Compensation: A Perspective from Revenue Canada", *Corporate Management Tax Conf.* 238 (Can. Tax Foundation, 1979).

Degnon, Theodore E., "Escaping the 'Employee Burden'" (March 1986), 64 *Taxes* 172.

Douglas, William O., "Vicarious Liability and the Administration of Risk" (1928-29), 38 *Yale L.J.* 584.

Drache, A.B.C., "Employee Compensation" (1986), *Special Lectures LSUC* 17.

Drache, A.B.C., "Employee Compensation" (1988), 10 *Can. Taxpayer* 66.

Drache, A.B.C. and Goldstein, "The Professional as an Employee" (Chapter 4), *Tax Planning for Professionals* (Toronto: De Boo, 1979), 22.

"Executive and Employee Compensation" (1979), 4-5 *Can. Tax News* 49.

Flannigan, Robert, "Employment Status for Income Tax Purposes" (1988), 36 *Can. Tax J.* 145.

Goodison, Don, "Questionable Income" (December 1989), 23 *CGA Magazine* 17.

Gordon, Hugh A., "Management Companies, Personal Services Businesses, Incorporated Professionals and Specified Investment Businesses", in *Proceedings of 36th Tax Conf.* 165 (Can. Tax Foundation, 1984).

Khan, A.N., "Who is a Servant?" (1979), 53 *Austr. L.J.* 832.

McCallum, J. Thomas, "Defining 'Employee'" (February 1992), 26 *CGA Magazine* 21.

Motz, Robert, "Employee vs. Independent Contractor" (November 1990), 64 *CMA Magazine* 26.

Noel, Marc, "Contract for Services, Contract of Service — A Tax Perspective and Analysis", in *Proceedings of 29th Tax Conf.* 712 (Can. Tax Foundation, 1977).

Perelmuter, Jack, "Taxation of Real Estate Agents" (1978), 3 *CA Magazine* 60.

Richards, G.M.R., "Employee or Independent Contractor?" (1986), 1 *Can. Current Tax* J-158.

Robinson, I. Michael, "Personal Service Corporations: New Opportunities and Old Concerns", *Corporate Management Tax Conf.* 165 (Can. Tax Foundation, 1985).

Scott, William, "The Outlook for Executive Compensation: Accountability and Shareholder Value", *Corporate Management Tax Conf.* 1 (Can. Tax Foundation, 1985).

Wilson, Brian J., "Employment Status Under the Income Tax Act", *Corporate Management Tax Conf.* 2:1 (Can. Tax Foundation, 1991).

Timing of Inclusions

Gordon, Hugh A., "Deferred Compensation", in *Proceedings of 38th Tax Conf.* 34 (Can. Tax Foundation, 1986).

Inclusions in Employment Income

(a) *General*

Beaubier, Beaty F., "Not Easily Dismissed" (October 1990), 24 *CGA Magazine* 56.

Bernstein, Jack, "Fringe Benefits and Equity Participation", *Corporate Management Tax Conf.* 5:1 (Can. Tax Foundation, 1991).

Corn, George, "Expense Reimbursements — Not Taxable as Employee Benefits" (October 1990), 3:10 *Can. Current Tax* J-49.

Crawford, William E., "Executive and Employee Benefits", *Corporate Management Tax Conf.* 8:1 (Can. Tax Foundation, 1990).

Drache, A.B.C., "Tax-Free Goodies" (1991), XIII *Can. Taxpayer* 68.

"Employee or Shareholder Benefit" (1983), 5 *Can. Taxpayer* 202.

Innes, William J., "The Taxation of Indirect Benefits: An Examination of Subsections 56(2), 56(3), 56(4), 245(2) and 245(3) of the Income Tax Act", in *Proceedings of 38th Tax Conf.* 42:1 (Can. Tax Foundation, 1986).

"Is the Sec. 6(1)(a) Confusion Finally at an End?" (1990), 44 DTC 7022.

Krishna, Vern, "Employee Benefits" (1984), 1 *Can. Current Tax* C7.

Krishna, Vern, "Taxation of Employee Benefits" (1986), 1:35 *Can. Current Tax* C-173.

Krishna, Vern, "Taxation of Employee Benefits" (August 1987), 21 *CGA Magazine* 25.

Lee, Julie Y., "Purchase of Annuity in lieu of Periodical Payment may Alter Tax Implications" (1992), 3 *Tax. of Executive Compensation and Retirement* 619.

MacKnight, Robin, "Planning for Year-end Bonuses" (1993), 4 *Can. Current Tax* 25.

Perry, Harvey, "Federal Individual Income Tax: Income Computation", *Tax Paper No. 89* 42 (Can. Tax Foundation, 1990).

"Personal Tax Planning — Employee Benefit Plans Revisited" (1984), 32 *Can. Tax J.* 773.

Philp, Barrie M., "Executive and Employee Compensation After Tax Reform", in *Proceedings of 40th Tax Conf.* 28:1 (Can. Tax Foundation, 1988).

(b) *Allowances*

Beam, Robert E., and Stanley N. Laiken, "Employee Allowances" (1989), *Can. Tax J.* 141.

Drache, A.B.C., "Allowances or Reimbursements" (1993), 15 *Can. Taxpayer* 23.

Drache, A.B.C., "Housing Allowance Again Held To Be Tax Free" (1991), 13 *Can. Taxpayer* 70.

Drache, A.B.C., "Tax Exempt Expenses for Moonlighting Employees" (1991), 13 *Can. Taxpayer* 154.

Goodison, Don, "Tax Forum — Travel 'Tax Tips'" (January 1992), 26 *CGA Magazine* 16.

Weatherby, Brian, "Tax 'On Wheels'" (March 1991), 25 *CGA Magazine* 17.

(c) *Automobiles*

Auster, Rolf, "Minimizing Gross Income From the Personal Use of Employer-Provided Autos: Strategies and Options" (April 1990), 68 *Taxes* 295.

Car Expenses and Benefits: Tax Strategy (Toronto: Price Waterhouse, 1988).

Company Cars and Automobile Expenses (Toronto: Coopers & Lybrand Canada, 1991).

Drache, A.B.C., "Automobile Benefits" (1980), 6 *Can. Taxpayer* 51.

Drache, A.B.C., "Clergy Losses under Reformed Car Allowance System" (1988), 10 *Can. Taxpayer* 142.

Drache, A.B.C.,"Partners Now Hit By Standby Charges" (1988), 10 *Can. Taxpayer* 147.

Drache, A.B.C., "Reimbursing Automobile Expenses" (1988), 10 *Can. Taxpayer* 66.

Glover, George, "Effect of Tax Reform on Auto Expenses" (November-December 1987), 61 *CMA Magazine* 60.

Jason, Robert R., "Personal Use of an Employer-Supplied Automobile" (1983), 116:6 *CA Magazine* 48.

Keller, Cameron, "The Company Car" (1983), 57 *Cost and Management* 47.

"Revenue Canada's Framework for Automobile Deductions" (1993), 5 *Tax. of Executive Compensation and Retirement* 839

Tang & Hyatt, "Business-Use Automobiles: The Complex New Tax Rules" (1988), 36 *Can. Tax J.* 195.

Thompson, R.C., "Automobile Stand-by Charge", *Can. Tax Letter,* June 24, 1983.

Yull, Karen, "New Automobile Rules Call for Review of Remuneration for Strategy" (1994), 5 *Tax. of Executive Compensation and Retirement* 883.

(d) *Imputed Interest on Low Cost Loans*

Drache, A.B.C., "Home Purchase Loans" (1983), 5 *The Can. Taxpayer* 76.

"Revenue Canada Established Policies on Loan-related Benefits" (1991), 2 *Tax. of Executive Compensation and Retirement* 451.

(e) *Stock Option Plans*

Atnikov, D., "Stock Options, Stock Purchase Plans and Death Benefits", *Prairie Provinces Tax Conf.* 1 (Can. Tax Foundation, 1980).

Beam and Laiken, "An Employee Stock Option Update" (1987), 33 *Can. Tax J.* 1275.

Bernstein, Jack, "Fringe Benefits and Equity Participation", [1991] *Corp. Mgmt. Tax Conf.* 5:1.

Bowman, S.W., "Employment Benefits — Stock Options Not Falling under S. 7" (1990), 38 *Can. Tax J.* 82.

Corn, George, "Stock Options" (1986), 1 *Can. Current Tax* J-131.

Crawford, William E., "Tax Treatment of the Executive Minority Shareholder", in *Proceedings of 39th Tax Conf.* 14:1 (Can. Tax Foundation, 1987).

Dionne, Andre, "Stock Purchase Arrangements can be Structured to Allow Deduction for Employers" (1992), 3 *Tax. of Executive Compensation and Retirement* 604.

Drache, A.B.C., "Stock Option Plans" (1979), 11 *The Can. Taxpayer* 86.

Dunbar, Alisa E., "Sale of Stock Plan Shares may Produce Freely Deductible Loss" (1991), 3 *Tax. of Executive Compensation and Retirement* 499.

"Employment Benefits — Stock Options Not Falling Under Section 7" (1990), 38 *Can. Tax J.* 82.

Finkelstein, David N., "Equity Compensation", *Corporate Management Tax Conf.* 22 (Can. Tax Foundation, 1985).

Holmes, William R., "Stock-based Deferred Compensation may be Provided to Employees of Private Corporations" (1990), 2 *Tax. of Executive Compensation and Retirement* 375.

Kellough, Howard J., "Techniques of Transferring Ownership of a Private Corporation to Employees or Other Shareholders — Tax and Financing Implications", in *Proceedings of 29th Tax Conf.* 160 (Can. Tax Foundation 1977).

Knight and Knight, "Have Incentive Stock Options Lost Their Value as a Management Compensation Tool?" (1988), 40 *Tax Executive* 131.

Krishna, Vern, "Stock Options Exercised after Becoming Non-resident" (1993), 4 *Can. Current Tax* C-27.

Le Gallais, "Stock-Oriented Compensation Techniques", in *Proceedings of 29th Tax Conf.* 792 (Can. Tax Foundation, 1977).

Lee, Julie Y., "Stock-Based Compensation: Selected Regulatory and Taxation Issues", *Corporate Management Tax Conf.* 4:1 (Can. Tax Foundation, 1991).

MacKnight, Robin, "Hidden Problems in Selling Employee Ownership" (1994), 5 *Can. Current Tax* 7.

MacKnight, Robin, "Planning for Stock Option Benefits: Traps for the Unwary" (1993), 4 *Can. Current Tax* P-13.

MacKnight, Robin, "Pyrrhic Policy: Fixing the Phantom Loophole in Paragraph 7(3)(b)" (1993), 41 *Can. Tax J.* 429.

Michaelson, Suzanne, "Employee Stock Options Revisited" (1992), 40 *Can. Tax J.* 114.

"Personal Tax Planning — An Employee Stock Option Update" (1987), 35 *Can. Tax J.* 1275.

Ramaseder, Brigitte, "Stock Option Benefit Depends on Fair Market Value Determination" (1991), 2 *Tax. of Executive Compensation and Retirement* 455.

Richards, Gabrielle M.R., "Stock Incentive Plans" (June 1990), 3:6 *Can. Current Tax* J-31.

"Share Split may Upset Share Option Plan" (1990), 1 *Tax. of Executive Compensation and Retirement* 302.

Slutsky, Sam, "Innovations in Employee Compensation: The Employee Stock Option and the Tax Exempt Employer", *Prairie Provinces Tax Conf.* 171 (Can. Tax Foundation, 1983).

Snider, Ken, "Employee Share Purchase Loans and the Predicament of Declining Share Values" (1993), 41 *Can. Tax J.* 1001.

"Stock Options Plan Involving Foreign Corporations may be Disqualified from Stock Benefit Deduction" (1990), 1 *Tax. of Executive Compensation and Retirement* 300.

Thomas, Richard B., "Gain Arising from Exercise of stock Option by Shareholder-Director" (1993), 41 *Can. Tax J.* 505.

Tobias, Norman C., "Employee Stock Options: Taxing Benefits Realized by Former Canadian Residents" (1994), 5 *Tax. of Executive Compensation and Retirement* 889.

Tunney, Wayne L., "Taking Stock: The Pros and Cons of Stock-Based Compensation", *Corporate Management Tax Conf.* 3:1 (Can. Tax Foundation, 1991).

Wentzell, David, "Stock Purchase Plans: Two Views" (1991), 39 *Can. Tax J.* 1556.

(f) *Damages and Wrongful Dismissal*

Brown, Elizabeth and Julie Y. Lee, "Putting Employees on Notice: Tax Treatment of Amounts Paid on Termination of Employment" (1994), 5 *Tax. of Executive Compensation and Retirement* 908.

Bush, Kathryn and Caroline L. Hilbronner, "Some Tax Considerations Regarding Employment Terminations" (1994), 3 *Employment and Labour Law Rev.* 111.

Drache, A.B.C.,"Legal Expenses in Wrongful Dismissal Not Deductible" (1988), 10 *Can. Taxpayer* 120.

Hugo, Sharon J. amd L. Alan Rautenberg, "Damages and Settlements: Taxation of the Recipient" (1993), 41 *Can. Tax J.* 1.

Krishna, Vern, "Characterization of Wrongful Dismissal Awards for Income Tax" (1977), 23 *McGill L.J.* 43.

MacKnight, Robin J., "Termination Payments for Mental Distress and Loss of Reputation", [1993], *Can. Current Tax* P-21.

McDonnell, T. E., "Deductibility of Legal Expenses Incurred to Recover Damages for Wrongful Dismissal" [Case Comment *Lalonde v. M.N.R.*, [1988] 2 CTC 2032 (TCC)] (1988), 36 *Can. Tax J.* 697.

Morgan, M.A., "Compensatory Payments Made in a Litigation Context: Tax Treatment to the Recipient" (1986), *Special Lectures LSUC* 109.

O'Brien, M.L., "Litigation Structured Settlements" (1986), *Special Lectures LSUC* 119.

Olsen, D.C., "Tax Treatment of Damages for Wrongful Dismissal" (1986), *Special Lectures LSUC* 135.

Trotter, Paul D., "Severance and Downsizing: Ongoing Tax and Benefits Issues" (1992), 5 *Can. Petroleum Tax J.* 21.

(g) Reimbursed Legal Expenses

Dunbar, Alisa E., "Legal Services Provided to Employee Results in Tax Benefit" (1991), 2 *Tax. of Executive Compensation and Retirement* 403.

Krasa, Eva M., "The Income Tax Treatment of Legal Expenses" (1986), 34 *Can. Tax J.* 757.

(h) Other

Billinger, Jo-anne, "Flexible Benefits a Practical Approach for Employers and Employees in the Cost-conscious '90s" (1993), 4 *Tax. of Executive Compensation and Retirement* 747.

Boulanger, Claude, "Disability Insurance Plans can be Structured to Avoid Taxable Payout" (1991), 2 *Tax. of Executive Compensation and Retirement* 435.

Bush, Kathryn M., "Executive Compensation: Supplemental Pension Plans" (1991), 8 *Bus. and the Law* 46.

Buyers, D.R., and D.E. Harvey, "The Cost of Terminating Employees: Tax and Unemployment Insurance Consequences" (1987), 4 *Bus. & L.* 9.

Dewling, Alan M., "RCA may be Used to Pre-fund Health and Other Post-Retirement Benefits" (1993), 4 *Tax. of Executive Compensation and Remuneration* 707.

Dionee, Andre, "RCA Cash Flow Problems may be Alleviated by Filing Early Trust Tax Return" (1990), 2 *Tax. of Executive Compensation and Retirement* 371.

Drache, A.B.C., "Clup Memberships as a Taxable Benefit" (1993), 15 *Can. Taxpayer* 163.

Drache, A.B.C., "FCA Upholds Revenue Canada on Employee Reimbursement" (1994), 16 *Can. Taxpayer* 49.

Drache, A.B.C., "Group Life Insurance: New Interpretations" (1980), 17 *Can. Taxpayer* 152.

Fitzgerald, Brian A.P., "Tax-effectiveness may be Enhanced by Maximizing Ancillary Benefits" (1993), 4 *Tax. of Executive Compensation and Retirement* 760.

"Home Purchase Loans to Employee/Shareholder may have Extended Term" (1992), 3 *Tax. of Executive Compensation and Retirement* 552.

Krishna, Vern, "Retiring Allowances" (1994), 4 *Can. Current Tax* C-53.

Krishna, Vern, "How Will They Tax Frequent Flyer Programs?" (1985), 5:21 *Ont. Lawyers Weekly* 7.

Laushway, Keith, "Retiring Allowances and Future Employment by Affiliates" (1993), 4 *Can. Current Tax* P-15.

Maclagan, Bill, "Taxable Benefits on Employer Relocation" (1993), 3 *Employment and Labour Law Rev.* 25.

McKie, A.B., "Benefical Occupation" (1994), 4 *Can. Current Tax* C-49.

Novek, Barbara L., "Employment Benefits may be Tax-free if Provided in Connection with Special Work Site or Remote Location" (1991), 3 *Tax. of Executive Compensation and Retirement* 505.

Novek, Barbara L., "Retiring Allowances are subject to Administrative Guideline" (1991), 3 *Tax. of Executive Compensation and Retirement* 523.

Novek, Barbara L. "RCT Expands Unpublished Guidelines in Salary Leave Plans" (1993), 4 *Tax. of Executive Compensation and Retirement* 715.

"Owner-managers may be Eligible for Tax-free Reimbursement of Medical Expenses" (1990), 1 *Tax. of Executive Compensation and Retirement* 299.

Pound, R.W., "Fringe Benefits: Management 'Perks'", *Corporate Management Tax Conf.* 63 (Can. Tax Foundation, 1979).

"Revenue Canada Clarifies Policy on Relocation Assistance" (1992), 3 *Tax. of Executive Compensation and Retirement* 559.

"Revenue Canada Clarifies Position on Temporary Accommodation" (1992), 3 *Tax. of Executive Compensation and Retirement* 563.

Roux, Clement, "Current Planning for Fringe Benefits", in *Proceedings of 35th Tax Conf.* 478 (Can. Tax Foundation, 1983).

Schwartz, Alan M., "Tax Considerations on Being Hired and Fired: Some Exotica", *Corporate Management Tax Conf.* 212 (Can. Tax Foundation, 1985).

Simon, Karla W., "Fringe Benefits and Tax Reform: Historical Blunders and a Proposal for Structural Change" (1984), 36 *Univ. of Florida Law Rev.* 871.

Solursh, John M., "Pension Arrangements can be Funded to Avoid RCA Tax" (1991), 3 *Tax. of Executive Compensation and Retirement* 469.

Deductions from Employment Income

(a) *General*

Beam, Robert E., and Stanley N. Laiken, "Employee Deductions" (1991), 39 *Can. Tax J.* 338.

Canadian Teachers' Federation, *Lexicon Retirement Savings* (Ottawa: Can. Teachers' Federation, 1990).

Goodison, Don, "Tax Forum — Deduction Dilemma" (July 1990), 24 *CGA Magazine* 14.

Grieve, John F., "Directors Beware: Personal Liability for Employee Deductions Under the Income Tax Act" (1987), 4:2 *Bus. & L.* 14.

Hershfield, J.E., "Recent Trends in the Deduction of Expenses in Computing Income", in *Proceedings of 41st Tax Conf.* 44:1 (Can. Tax Foundation, 1989).

Hugget, Donald R., "Oyez, Oyez , Oyez" (1990), 18 *Can. Tax News* 97.

McGregor, Ian, "Employee's Deductions under the Income Tax Act", *Tax Paper No. 21* (Can. Tax Foundation, 1960).

Morgan, M.A., "Recent Developments in Federal Taxation Income and Deductions", in *Proceedings of 29th Tax Conf.* 59 (Can. Tax Foundation, 1977).

Neville, Ralph T., "Deductibility of Automobiles, Meals and Entertainment and Home Office Expenses After Tax Reform", in *Proceedings of 40th Tax Conf.* 25:1 (Can. Tax Foundation, 1988).

New Rules on Tax Assistance for Retirement Savings (Montreal: Sobeco, 1990).

Perry, Harvey, "Federal Individual Income Tax: Income Computation", *Tax Paper No. 89* 42 (Can. Tax Foundation, 1990).

Teichman, Lyle S., "Deducting Employee Expenses: A Hard Act to Follow" (1994), 5 *Tax. of Executive Compensation and Retirement* 859.

Templeton, Michael D., "Employee Expenses — A Practical Approach" (1990), 38 *Can. Tax J.* 666.

(b) *Contributions to Registered Pension Plans*

Bauslaugh, Randy V., "Past Service Contribution and the Subsection 8503(15) Anti-avoidance Rule" (1994), 5 *Tax. of Executive Compensation and Retirement* 899.

Bissell, Thomas S.G., "Distribution of U.S. Pension Plan into RRSP may be Tax-free via IRA" (1992), 3 *Tax. of Executive Compensation and Retirement* 619.

Boulanger, Claude, "Registered Retirement Saving Plan may Provide Greater Tax-assisted Accumulation under Certain Circumstances" (1990), 2 *Tax. of Executive Compensation and Retirement* 339.

Clare, James, and Paul F. Denna Penna, "Tax Aspects of Employees' Pension Plans", *Tax Planning and Management,* 9:28 of *Canadian Income Tax Revised* (Toronto: Butterworths and Co. (Canada) Ltd., 1977).

Crawford, William E., "Tax Planning for Retirement", in *Proceedings of 38th Tax Conf.* 19:1 (Can. Tax Foundation, 1986).

Cudlipp, Ian and Alan Macnaughton, "Transferring Funds from a Pension Plan to an Eligible RRSP or RRIF: The New Opportunities" (1994), 42 *Can. Tax J.* 222.

Dewtering, June, *Reforming Retirement Saving Tax Incentives* (Ottawa: Library of Parliament, Research Branch, 1992).

Dionne, Andre, "Significant Changes Affecting Executives are Made to Pension Reform Legislation during Study by Parliament" (1990), 2 *Tax. of Executive Compensation and Retirement* 307.

Drache, A.B.C., "Foreign Property and RRSPs" (1994), 16 *Can. Taxpayer* 19.

Drache, A.B.C., "Manufacturing Pension Credits" (1993), 15 *Can. Taxpayer* 47.

Drache, A.B.C., "Pension Plans for Family Companies" (1980), 19 *Can. Taxpayer* 161.

Drache, A.B.C., "RRSP Contributions: Maximizing Cash Flow" (1993), 15 *Can. Taxpayer* 24.

Drache, A.B.C., "RRSP Over-contributions" (1994), 16 *Can. Taxpayer* 191.

Drache, A.B.C., "RRSPs: The Final Moves" (1994), 16 *Can. Taxpayer* 107.

Drache, A.B.C., "Top Hat Pension Plans: A Rethink" (1983), 5 *Can. Taxpayer* 155.

Dutka, Randall J., *Pensions and Retirement Income Planning, 90-91: New Tax Rules and Stragegies* (Don Mills, Ont.: CCH Canadian, 1990).

Dutka, Randall J., *Pensions and Retirement Planning: Impact of the May 1985 Budget* (C.C.H. Canadian, 1985).

Fisher, G.B., "Early Retirement Tax Considerations" (1983), 31 *Can. Tax J.* 828.

Forgie, Jeremy J., "Pension Design: Tax and Regulatory Environment may Favour Conversion of Defined Benefit Plan to Money Purchase Arrangement" (1992), 4 *Tax. of Executive Compensation and Retirement* 627.

Gignac, Lorraine, "New Revenue Canada Rules can Prove Tax-effective for Plan Sponsors" (1993), 4 *Tax. of Executive Compensation and Retirement* 771.

Guerard, Yves, "An Overview of the Main Developments in Pension Reform" in *Proceedings of 38th Tax Conf.* 16:1 (Can. Tax Foundation, 1986).

Harris, Peter H., "Using Insurance Policies to Fund Pension Plans" (1993), 5 *Tax. of Executive Compensation and Retirement* 819.

Horner, Keith, "Policy Foundations of the New Tax Treatment of Retirement Savings", in *Proceedings of 38th Tax Conf.* 17:1 (Can. Tax Foundation, 1986).

Howe, David, "Registered Pension Plans must Undergo Redrafting in order to Ensure Maximum Benefits" (1992), 3 *Tax. of Executive Compensation and Retirement* 563.

Johnston, H.B. William, "Individual Executive Pension Plan may Provide Greater Tax Assisted Retirement Saving" (1990), 1 *Tax. of Executive Compensation and Retirement* 291.

Krelove, Russell and Samuel A. Rea, "Private Pensions and the Tax Systems: Twenty Years after the Carter Commission" in *The Quest for Tax Reform, the Royal Commission on Taxation Twenty Years Later* (Toronto: Carswell, 1988), at 121-135.

Leach, Darryl, "PSPA Requirements Impose Constraints on Pension Plan Negotiations" (1992), 2 *Tax. of Executive Compensation and Retirement* 611.

Lewis, Frederick, "Downsizing Program Rules may Provide Substantial Pension Enhancement" (1991), 3 *Tax. of Executive Compensation and Retirement* 483.

Mills, Michael D. and John M. Christie, "Pension Reform Curtails Tax Assistance for Profit Sharing" (1992), *Tax. of Executive Compensation and Retirement* 659.

Muto, Alexander D., "Revenue Canada Clarified its Position on 'Eligible Service' and Other Matters" (1993), 5 *Tax. of Executive Compensation and Retirement* 815.

Richardson, Kathryn M. and Randy V. Bauslaugh, "Continuation of Pension Plan Contributions in a Severance Period" (1993), 4 *Tax. of Executive Compensation and Retirement* 744.

Roberts, David G., "Registered Retirement Savings Plans" (1989), 37 *Can. Tax J.* 64.

Rotenberg, Charles M., "RRSP Investments: Breaking Rules of Thumb" (1994), 16 *Can. Taxpayer* 26.

Singer, Paul B., "Personal Guarantee by Shareholder may Avoid RCA Tax on Supplemental Pension Funding" (1990), 1 *Tax. of Executive Compensation and Retirement* 293.

Straker, Andy Y., "Tax-assisted Retirement Plans: A Practical Approach" in *Proceedings of 43rd Tax Conf.* (Can. Tax Foundation, 1991), at 33:1.

Summerville, A. Dean, "Retirement Compensation Arrangements", in *Proceedings of 39th Tax Conf.* 27:1 (Can. Tax Foundation, 1987).

Taxation of Registered Retirement Plans — The Final Rules (North York, Ont.: Hewitt Associates, 1990).

Theroux, Marcel, "Foreign Service under Canadian Pension Plans" (1993), 41 *Can. Tax J.* 518.

Theroux, Marcel and Brad Rowse, "The Individual Pension Plan: A Complete Guide", [1991] *Corp. Mgmt. Tax Conf.* 8:1.

Yull, Karen, "Individual Pension Plans may Permit Greater Tax Sheltered Accumulation" (1992), 3 *Tax. of Executive Compensation and Retirement* 595.

(c) *Other*

Austin, Barbara, "RRSP Implications of the New Foreign Pension Plan Rules" (1993), 1 *RRSP Plan.* 53.

Boulanger, Claude, "Employee Profit Sharing Plans may Provide Framework for Incentive Payments" (1991), 2 *Tax. of Executive Compensation and Retirement* 508.

"Can I, as an Employee, Deduct My Home-Office Expenses?" (1990), 44 DTC 7028.

Corn, George, "Expense Reimbursements: Not Taxable as Employee Benefits" (1990), 3 *Can. Current Tax* J-24.

Expenses of Sales Representatives: Tax Treatment (Don Mills, Ont: CCH Canadian, 1990).

Kingissepp, Andrew H., "Canadian Officers and Directors can Treat Indemnity Payment as Tax-free Receipt" (1993), 4 *Tax. of Executive Compensation and Retirement* 763.

Krasa, Eva M., "Recent Developments in Retirement Savings and Deferred Compensation: A Pot Pourri", [1992] *Can. Tax Foundation* 18:1.

Krishna, Vern, "A Striking Decision" (November 1989), 23 *CGA Magazine* 43.

Novek, Barbara L., "Part-time and Interrupted Employment Included in Computing Portion of Retiring Allowance Eligible for Rollover to RRSP" (1992), 4 *Tax. of Executive Compensation and Retirement* 637.

Novek, Barbara L., "Sector Specific Tax Relief for Canadian Residents Working Overseas" (1993), 5 *Tax. of Executive Compensation and Retirement* 808.

Roberts, David G., "Registered Retirement Savings Plans" (1989), 37 *Can. Tax J.* 64.

"Sec. 8(1)(f): Is the Frustration Over?" (1990), 44 *DTC* 7021.

Thomas, Richard B., "No To Nanny Expense Deduction" (1991),39 *Can. Tax J.* 950.

"Why Not Work at Home and Deduct the Home-Office Expense?" (1990), 44 DTC 7014.

CHAPTER VI

BUSINESS AND INVESTMENT INCOME: GENERAL

1. GENERAL

References:

ITA:

S. 9	Income from Business or Property
S. 12	Income Inclusions
S. 18	Limitations on Deductions
S. 20	Deductions in Computing Income from Business or Property
Subs. 11(1)	Proprietor of Business

BULLETINS, CIRCULARS & RULINGS:

IT-206R	October 29, 1979	Separate Businesses
IT-419	July 10, 1978	Meaning of Arm's Length

(a) Segregation by Source

We saw in Chapter IV "What is Income" that income is calculated by determining income from each source separately. Business income and investment income are calculated according to subdivision (b) of Division B of Part I of the Act.

Although income from business and investment income (technically referred to as "income from property") are both covered by subdivision (b), they are two distinct and separate sources of income. Most of the rules dealing with the computation of these sources of income are common to both, but there are important differences in how these sources are taxed. For example:

- The attribution rules in sections 74.1 and 74.2 only apply to investment income and do not apply to income from business;

- The small business deduction is available only in respect of income from business and does not apply to investment income.

Hence, the distinction between the two sources of income can be important and, in the context of private corporations, is crucial.

It follows, then, that the determination of income or loss for tax purposes involves two distinct steps: (1) Characterization of a receipt or loss as flowing from a particular source that is taxable under section 3 of the Act; and (2) Measurement of the amount of income or loss according to the particular rules applicable to that source.

(b) "Business"

The concept of "business", which is central to the income tax system, is not a defined term. The *Income Tax Act* merely says that "business" *includes* a profession, calling, trade, manufacture or undertaking of any kind whatever, and, for most purposes, also includes an adventure or concern in the nature of trade.[1]

Generally speaking, "business" refers to economic, industrial, commercial, or financial *activity* and involves more than mere passive ownership of property.

A "trade" is the business of selling, with a view to profit, goods that the trader has either manufactured or purchased.[2]

The quintessential characteristics of business are activity, enterprise, entrepreneurship and commercial risk. How many or how much of each of these characteristics need be present in order for income to be characterized as business income? At what point does one cross over from passive ownership of property to the active process of earning business income? There are no certain answers to these questions.

One thing is clear: The nature of income does not determine its source for tax purposes. The nature of income is essentially a question of law, regardless of who receives the income. Interest, rent, royalties or dividends, for example, may be passive income or business income. In contrast, the source of income is usually a question of fact determined by its character to the recipient.

"Business" implies economic activity. But economic activity by itself is not enough to establish a "business": The activity must be undertaken for the purpose of realizing a profit.[3] The taxpayer must have profit motive.[4] It is profit motive that differentiates a trade or business from a hobby or pastime.

The profit motive test is crucial to the integrity of the tax system. It draws the line between providing limitless tax subsidies for personal pursuits with minimal economic flavour and economic enterprises conducted on a commercial basis for profit. Taxpayers cannot expect other taxpayers to subsidize their personal hobbies. On the other hand, the legal test should not be so stringent as to discourage valid entrepreneurial activities.

---

[1]   Subs. 248(1) ("business").

[2]   *Grainger & Son v. Gough*, [1896] AC 325 (H.L.).

[3]   See, e.g., *Fleming v. M.N.R.*, [1987] 2 CTC 2113, 87 DTC 425 (T.C.C.) (university professors did not have expectation of profit in publishing research); *Shaker v. M.N.R.*, [1987] 2 CTC 2156, 87 DTC 463 (T.C.C.) (keen desire, talent and determination did not necessitate reasonable expectation of profit in an undertaking); *Kusick v. M.N.R.*, [1988] 1 CTC 2052, 88 DTC 1069 (T.C.C.) (taxpayer changed type of business, obviously realized no chance of profits); *Ianson v. M.N.R.*, [1988] 1 CTC 2088, 88 DTC 1074 (T.C.C.) (horse racing carried on as hobby).

[4]   *Issacharoff v. M.N.R.*, [1988] 1 CTC 2006, 87 DTC 673 (T.C.C.).

Thus, the test is a reasonable *expectation* of profit and not an expectation of reasonable profit.

Whether a taxpayer has a reasonable expectation of profit is a question of fact based on the surrounding circumstances. There are literally hundreds of cases in which the issue has been litigated, but the cases are of little guidance. Each is predicated upon its own factual circumstances. Many of the cases involve farming operations; others are concerned with hobbies such as photography, art, authorship, yacht charters, condominium rentals, minor league hockey, beauty products, etc.

The reasonableness of expectations in particular circumstances depends upon:[5]

- The extent of time devoted to the endeavour;

- Financial capitalization of the venture in the context of the normal requirements of similar businesses;

- The industry norm for profitability in similar enterprises;

- The extent to which the taxpayer acts as others would who are engaged in similar businesses;

- The amount of time devoted to promoting and marketing the taxpayer's works;

- The amount of revenue received as a result of sales or services provided by the taxpayer in the pursuit of the endeavour;

- The historical record of annual profits or losses for the taxpayer's economic endeavour in the context of trade or industry norms;

- The taxpayer's qualifications, education and training to pursue the particular activity; and

- Membership in professional associations and organizations to which other similarly situated taxpayers belong.

No single factor is controlling. The criteria relevant to the particular enterprise need to be evaluated to formulate a composite objective opinion as to whether the taxpayer's

---

[5]   *Moldowan v. The Queen*, [1977] CTC 310, 77 DTC 5213 (S.C.C.) (scrap metal businessman also had farming business for purpose of training, boarding and breeding race horses); see also *Dale v. M.N.R.*, [1981] CTC 2320, 81 DTC 278 (T.R.B.) (lack of promotion of vintage car collection precluded any real expectation of profit from rentals); *Escudero v. M.N.R.*, [1981] CTC 2340, 81 DTC 301 (T.R.B.) (hobby dog breeder best in country but operations had no potential for profit; operations did not constitute "business"); *Warden v. M.N.R.*, [1981] CTC 2379, 81 DTC 322 (T.R.B.) (teacher claimed farming loss on cattle and business loss on antique telephone restorations; claim disallowed); *Cork v. M.N.R.*, [1981] CTC 2367, 81 DTC 346 (T.R.B.) (Minister agreed to allow some expenses, not able to limit amounts if reasonable for drafting business on available facts); *Schip v. M.N.R.*, [1983] CTC 2221, 83 DTC 190 (T.R.B.) (full-time photography teacher showed no profit in 8 years of freelance art photography; Court allowed two more years to turn profit).

activities reveal a sufficient profit motive. If they do not, the activity is a hobby even though it may have economic overtones.

Although the law on what constitutes a reasonable expectation of profit is factually driven, one can make certain generalizations. For example, Revenue Canada is more likely to challenge activities that involve:

- Substantial elements of personal pleasure;

- Non-cash expense write-offs; or

- Haphazard management arrangements.

Activities that involve sports (minor league hockey teams, semi-professional baseball teams, drag racing, scuba diving instruction, etc.), hobbies (photography, collecting, etc.) and recreation (yacht charters, etc.) are closely scrutinized for profit motive. Inherently pleasurable activities that create a loss are also more closely screened than other activities.

Activities that are incidental to a related business require careful evaluation. A pleasurable activity that is claimed as a business must have an independent potential for profit and not rely on the profitability of some other business to which it is incidentally related. For example, a taxpayer may operate a business retailing equestrian clothing and gear and also maintain and breed horses as an adjunct business. In these circumstances, the horse breeding business must be evaluated independently from the retail store. Unless the two operations are so closely integrated as to constitute a single business, each business must stand on its own profit potential.

The profit motive test must be satisfied on a pre-tax basis. It is not enough for a taxpayer to make a gross profit or a net profit *after taxes* if the net profit depends solely on non-cash write-offs, such as accelerated depreciation. Hence, an enterprise that is set up for the sole purpose of obtaining tax refunds cannot be considered a "business" if it does not otherwise satisfy the profit motive test.[6]

Further, the "reasonable expectation of profit" must be satisfied on an annual basis and not on a once-and-for-all evaluation of profitability. Thus, it is entirely possible that a taxpayer who is engaged in business may cease to operate as such if there are significant financial or other structural shifts in the business that preclude continuing profit potential.

Finally, and for greater certainty, paragraph 18(1)(*a*) of the Act restates the necessity of a profit motive: A taxpayer is not entitled to deduct an expense unless he or she incurs the expenditure for the *purpose* of gaining or producing income from a business or property. In other words, the taxpayer must have a reasonable expectation of profit.

---

[6]   *Moloney v. Canada,* [1992] 2 CTC 227, 92 DTC 6570 (F.C.A.).

(c) "Property"

Investment income is the yield on invested capital. For example: shares yield dividends, bonds yield interest, patents, copyrights and resources yield royalties, real property yields rent, and so on.

(i) Definition

"Property" is defined in broad terms to include virtually every type of economic interest:[7]

> "[P]roperty" means property of any kind whatever whether real or personal or corporeal or incorporeal and, without restricting the generality of the foregoing, includes
>
> (a) a right of any kind whatever, a share or a chose in action,
>
> (b) unless a contrary intention is evident, money,
>
> (c) a timber resource property, and
>
> (d) the work in progress of a business that is a profession.

A right of property may exist in and over any subject, including the right to possess, use, lend, alienate, consume or otherwise deal with it. A right of property implies the power to exercise possession to the exclusion of others.[8]

A right of property represents a bundle of distinct rights, some of which may be relinquished while others are retained. For example, the right of ownership is a right distinct from the right of possession. One can own without possessing and possess without owning.

(ii) Capital Gains (Losses) Excluded

There is one important exclusion from property income: "income from a property" does *not* include a capital gain from a disposition of the property. So also, "loss from a property" does not include a capital loss from a disposition of the property.[9]

---

[7] Subs. 248(1) "property"; see also *Fasken Estate v. M.N.R.*, [1948] CTC 265, 4 DTC 491 (Ex. Ct.); *Jones v. Skinner* (1835), 5 LJ Ch. 87 at 90:

> It is well-known, that the word "property" is the most comprehensive of all the terms which can be used, inasmuch as it is indicative and descriptive of every possible interest which the party can have.

[8] *West. Electric Co. v. M.N.R.*, [1969] CTC 274 at 289, 69 DTC 5204 at 5212; affirmed [1971] CTC 96, 71 DTC 5068 (S.C.C.) (amounts paid to appellant claimed not to be rentals, royalties or otherwise for the use of property; court determined that payments equivalent to royalties under treaty); *The Queen v. St. John Shipbldg. & Dry Dock Co.*, [1980] CTC 352, 80 DTC 6272 (F.C.A.); leave to appeal to S.C.C. refused 34 NR 348 (lump sums paid for computerized information not related to use, sales or benefit derived; not within classes of property in treaty).

[9] Subs. 9(3).

2. CHARACTERIZATION OF INCOME

References:

ITA:

S. 3	Income for Taxation Year
S. 12	Income Inclusions
Subss. 39(4)–(6)	Disposition of Canadian Securities
S. 74.2	Deemed Gain or Loss

BULLETINS, CIRCULARS & RULINGS:

IT-92R2	December 29, 1983	Income of Contractors
IT-102R2	July 22, 1985	Conversion of Property, Other than Real Property, From or To Inventory
IT-218R	September 16, 1986	Profit, Capital Gains and Losses from the Sale of Real Estate, Including Farmland and Inherited Land and Conversion of Real Estate from Capital Property to Inventory and Vice Versa
IT-479R	February 29, 1984	Transactions in Securities

The first step in the computation of income is to characterize it according to its source. The four specifically named sources are:[10]

1. Employment income,

2. Business income,

3. Investment (property) income, and

4. Capital gains.

In Chapter V "Income From an Office or Employment" we looked at the characterization of employment income and the distinction between employment and business. In this chapter we look at two other distinctions: (1) Income vs. Capital Gains; and (2) Business Income vs. Investment Income.

(a) Income vs. Capital Gains

The Act does not define either "capital gain" or "income". The so-called definitions in paragraphs 39(1)(a) and (b) of the Act are circular and of limited value. The distinction between "capital gains" and "income" is derived from the case law.

---

[10] S. 3.

The legal test for distinguishing between capital gains and income is deceptively simple: Income is the periodic yield of an investment; capital gains derive from sale or realization of the investment. The distinction is often put in the form of an analogy. Income is the fruit of a tree; capital gains are the profits realized upon sale of the tree:[11]

> The fundamental relation of "capital" to "income" has been much discussed by economists, the former being likened to the tree or the land, the latter to the fruit or the crop; the former depicted as a reservoir supplied from springs, the latter as the outlet stream, to be measured by its flow during a period of time.

The tree is the capital used to produce an annual yield (the fruit) and income is the profit from the sale of the fruit. Any gain from the sale of the tree itself is on account of capital. Some examples: A building is capital, rent derived from the building is income; Shares are capital, dividends on the shares are income; Bonds are capital, interest payments on the bonds are income. And so on. Thus, investment of property represents capital and the flow from the investment represents income.

Capital gains derive from a disposition of investments that constitute "capital property". Income gains derive from a sale of trading assets or inventory or as the yield from investments.

The importance of characterization of a gain as being on account of income or capital is the difference in amount of tax payable. Capital gains are not fully taxed, either because of non-inclusion or partial inclusion of such gains in income, or because of specific exemptions.

In this segment we distinguish between business income from sales of trading assets and capital gains from sales of investments. Later, we will look at the distinction between business income from trading and investment income as the yield from investments.

(i) The Meaning of "Investment"

To say that a capital gain or loss arises from the disposition of an investment is not very helpful in determining what constitutes a capital gain. The important question is: What is an "investment"? How do we distinguish between an investment (the sale of which yields a capital gain) and trading assets (the sale of which yields income)? This problem is much more difficult than appears on the surface, as illustrated in the following judicial statement:[12]

> It is quite a well-settled principle that where the owner of an ordinary investment chooses to realize it, and obtains a greater price for it than he originally acquired it at, the enhanced price is not profit. . . . But it is equally well established that enhanced values obtained from realisation or conversion of securities may be so assessable, where what is done is not merely a realisation or change of investment, but an act done in what is truly the carrying on, or carrying out, of a business. . . .

---

[11] *Eisner v. Macomber*, 252 US 189 (1929); see also Chapter IX "Capital Gains".

[12] *Californian Copper Syndicate Ltd. v. Harris* (1904), 5 Tax Cas. 159 at 165-66 (Scot. Ex. Ct. 2nd Div.).

Thus, the distinction between business income and capital gains rests upon whether the taxpayer is trading or investing. The distinction does not rest upon the taxpayer's desire to make a profit, but on the manner in which the profit is made. Trading implies a profit-making scheme to earn income by buying and selling property. Investment implies acquiring and holding an asset for its potential yield, but with the possibility that the investment may, at some time, be sold for a profit. In *Sissons*, for example:[13]

> Here the clear indication of "trade" is found in the fact that the acquisition of the securities was a part of a profit-making scheme. The purpose of the operation was not to earn income from the securities but to make a profit on prompt realization. The operation has therefore none of the essential characteristics of an investment; it is essentially a speculation.

An expectation of profit or profit motive is the *sine qua non* of business. But, since traders and investors are both in search of profit, profit motive by itself is not sufficient to distinguish between business income and capital gains. The distinction rests upon the taxpayer's operative intention at the time the property is acquired: Did the taxpayer intend to trade and turnover the asset for a profit or hold the asset for its potential yield?

(ii) Taxpayer Intention

An "investment" is an asset acquired with the *intention* of holding or using the asset *to produce* income. Where a taxpayer acquires property with an intention to trade — that is, to purchase and resell the property itself at a profit — any gain or loss from the trade is characterized as business income (loss). Thus, the distinction between an investment and inventory depends not upon the nature of the property acquired, but upon the intention with which it is acquired by the taxpayer.

Taxpayer intention at the time an asset is acquired is the basic issue in most characterization cases. The determination is made on the basis of evidence that provides an insight into the taxpayer's state of mind at the relevant time. The taxpayer's conduct, rather than any *ex post facto* declarations, usually provides the key to his or her intention. A taxpayer's intention may, however, be inferred from another taxpayer's conduct. For example, the intentions of a person may be attributed to his or her spouse where the latter is clearly relying on the knowledge and information of the former.[14]

How do we evaluate a taxpayer's intentions? *No single factor is conclusively determinative.* We look at the circumstances of the transaction and balance multiple, often conflicting, indicia to determine the taxpayer's intention. As one judge put it: "...a common sense appreciation of *all* the guiding features will provide the ultimate

---

[13] *M.N.R. v. Sissons*, [1969] CTC 184 at 188, 69 DTC 5152 at 5154 (S.C.C.).

[14] See, e.g., *Darch v. Canada*, [1992] 2 CTC 128, 92 DTC 6366; affirmed [1994] 2 CTC 1 (F.C.A.).

answer".[15] Not a very helpful statement in the determination of the issue, but one which judges frequently rely upon to make a decision.

In addition to looking at intention for the purpose of characterizing income or gain, we also look to see if the taxpayer had a secondary intention to trade. Where a taxpayer has a *secondary* intention to trade, any gain or loss resulting from the trade is business income (loss).[16]

Therefore, a taxpayer who claims that a gain is a capital gain must show two things: (1) That his or her primary intention at the time of entering into the transaction was to make an investment; and (2) That he or she had no secondary intention at that time to trade in the particular property.

Secondary intention to trade is a question of fact and the trier of fact may draw inferences from the taxpayer's conduct.[17] Both intention and secondary intention are determined on a balance of probabilities.[18] Hence, taxpayer credibility is always in issue. The same rules apply to distinguish between business (non-capital) losses and capital losses.[19]

A taxpayer is considered to have a secondary intention to trade if the possibility of early resale at a profit was a *motivating* consideration at the time that he or she acquired the property. Although motive to trade or invest is a subjective criterion, its

---

[15] *B.P. Australia Ltd. v. Commr. of Taxation of Commonwealth of Australia*, [1966] AC 224 at 264 (P.C.), *per* Lord Pearce, approved by the S.C.C. in *Johns-Manville Can. Inc. v. The Queen*, [1985] 2 CTC 111 at 125, 85 DTC 5373 at 5383 (S.C.C.) (thorough analysis of law; purchase of land to allow expansion of mining pit so that slope could be maintained at safe angle was an operational expense); see also *The Queen v. Canadian General Electric. Co. Ltd.*, [1987] 1 CTC 180, 87 DTC 5070 (F.C.A.) (heavy water production "know how" and licence sold; amount received was income because sales replaced taxpayer's business); *Paco Corp. v. The Queen*, [1980] CTC 409, 80 DTC 6215 (F.C.T.D.) (losses for demonstration plant constituted operating expense; determined by taxpayer's intention).

[16] *Bayridge Estates Ltd. v. M.N.R.*, [1959] CTC 158, 59 DTC 1098 (Ex. Ct.) (profit one of motives in sale of raw land); *Fogel v. M.N.R.*, [1959] CTC 227, 59 DTC 1182 (Ex. Ct.) (by-laws necessitated abandonment of building plans; subsequent sale for profit found to have been alternative intention); *Regal Heights Ltd. v. M.N.R.*, [1960] CTC 384, 60 DTC 1270 (S.C.C.) (plans for shopping centre frustrated and parcels of land sold; profits of highly speculative venture constituted income).

[17] *Reicher v. The Queen*, [1975] CTC 659, 76 DTC 6001 (F.C.A.).

[18] *Factory Carpet Ltd. v. The Queen*, [1985] 2 CTC 267, 85 DTC 5464 (F.C.T.D.).

[19] *M.N.R. v. Freud*, [1969] SCR 75, [1968] CTC 438, 68 DTC 5279.

absence or presence is ascertained by inference from objective evidence — that is, the taxpayer's conduct and the circumstances surrounding the particular transaction.[20]

Secondary intention is determined as of the time the property is purchased. Thus, the critical times are just before, and the moment that, the taxpayer enter into a binding agreement to purchase the property in question.[21]

Mere awareness at the time that the property is acquired that future events might dictate a change of investments does not *necessarily* lead to the inference that the transaction is an adventure in the nature of trade. Nor does sensitivity to the probability of capital appreciation necessarily imply a trading intention. Such sensitivity indicates no more than a prudent investment decision.[22]

A gain or loss that results from a taxpayer's response to a changing investment climate is not an adventure in the nature of trade. That is, an intention at the time of acquiring an asset that one will sell the asset if the purchase proves unprofitable merely indicates a prudent investment decision. It does not imply a secondary intention to engage in business or an adventure in the nature of trade.

There is a difference, however, between a taxpayer who responds to a *changing* investment climate and a taxpayer who actively contemplates the potential of profit on resale at the time of investment. Where the potential of profit is a motivating consideration, it suggests a secondary intention to engage in an adventure in the nature of trade:[23]

> . . . an intention at the time of acquisition of an investment to sell it in the event that it does not prove profitable does not make the subsequent sale of the investment the completion of an "adventure or concern in the nature of trade". Had the alleged assumption been that there was an expectation on the part of the purchaser, at the time of purchase, that, in the event that the investment did not prove to be profitable, it could be sold at a profit, and that such expectation was one of the factors that induced him

---

[20] *Reicher v. The Queen*, [1975] CTC 659 at 664, 76 DTC 6001 at 6004 *per* Le Dain J. A. (F.C.A.):
The issue on this appeal is whether at the time they acquired the property the appellant... had a secondary ention, as an operating motivation for such acquisition, to sell the property at a profit should a suitable opportunity present itself.
See also *Hiwako Invt. Ltd. v. The Queen*, [1978] CTC 378, 78 DTC 6281 (F.C.A.) (whether or not onus on taxpayer to disprove Minister's stated assumption that taxpayer primarily motivated by intention to trade); *Kit-Win Hldgs. (1973) Ltd. v. The Queen*, [1981] CTC 43, 81 DTC 5030 (F.C.T.D.) (Minister did not precisely allege exclusive motivation to develop property for profit).

[21] *Dickson v. The Queen*, [1977] CTC 64, 77 DTC 5061 (F.C.A.) (resolution to sell land dated 1964 but agreement dated 1967; purchaser's financial plight at date of signing agreement relevant to intention); *Racine v. M.N.R.*, [1965] CTC 150, 65 DTC 5098 (Ex. Ct.) (to constitute "secondary intention", purchaser must have possibility of reselling as operating motivation for acquisition at moment of purchase).

[22] *Hiwako Invt. Ltd. v. The Queen, ante; The Queen v. Bassani*, [1985] 1 CTC 314, 85 DTC 5232 (F.C.T.D.) (mere expectation that price of property would rise did not constitute "secondary intention" without operating motivation).

[23] *Hiwako Investments Ltd. v. The Queen, ante*, [1978] CTC at 383, 78 DTC at 6285.

to make the purchase, such assumption, if not disproved, might (I do not say that it would) support the assessments based on "trading" if not disproved.

(iii) Criteria Used to Determine Taxpayer Intention

A taxpayer's intention, whether primary or secondary, is always a question of fact. We look objectively at various criteria as aids in determining intention. No single criterion is conclusive. They merely offer clues from which we draw inferences about taxpayer intention.

(A) Number of Similar Transactions

Evidence that a taxpayer engaged in similar transactions to the one at issue provides equivocal, but potentially prejudicial, proof that the taxpayer is a trader or engaged in a business. All other things being equal (although they rarely are), the greater the number of similar transactions in the past, the greater the likelihood that the gain or loss in issue is business income or loss. The converse, however, does not apply. Merely because a transaction is an isolated event does not mean that it is not business income or loss. As the Exchequer Court stated:[24]

> [w]hile it is recognized that, as a general rule, an isolated transaction of purchase and sale outside the course of the taxpayer's ordinary business does not constitute the carrying on of a trade or business so as to render the profit therefrom liable to the income tax . . . it is also established that the fact that a transaction is an isolated one does not exclude it from the category of trading or business transactions of such a nature as to attract income tax to the profit therefrom.

A gain from an isolated transaction can give rise to business income or loss if the transaction is either closely related to the taxpayer's ordinary business activities or the property disposed of is of a type characterized as a "trading" property.[25] Lord President Clyde put it succinctly:[26]

> . . . A single plunge may be enough provided it is shown to the satisfaction of the Court that the plunge is made in the waters of trade. . . .

(B) Nature of Asset

The nature of the asset can be important in the characterization of any gain or loss from its disposition. Land, for example, *particularly raw land*, is viewed suspiciously as a trading, rather than an investment, asset. This attitude also extends to the sale of shares of corporations incorporated *solely* for the purpose of holding raw land.[27]

---

[24] *Atlantic Sugar Refineries Ltd. v. M.N.R.*, [1948] CTC 326 at 333-34, 4 DTC 507 at 511; affirmed [1949] CTC 196, 4 DTC 602 (S.C.C.).

[25] *M.N.R. v. Taylor*, [1956] CTC 189, 56 DTC 1125 (Ex. Ct.).

[26] *Balgownie Land Trust Ltd. v. I.R.C.* (1929), 14 Tax Cas. 684 (Scot.).

[27] *Fraser v. M.N.R.*, [1964] CTC 372, 64 DTC 5224 (S.C.C.); see also *Mould v. The Queen*, [1986] 1 CTC 271, 86 DTC 6087 (F.C.T.D.) (156 acres of land sole asset of corporation: "...the acquisition of the shares was merely a method of obtaining an interest in the land").

In contrast, transactions involving corporate shares are generally seen as on account of capital. As the Supreme Court observed:[28]

> . . . a person who puts money into a business enterprise by the purchase of the shares of a company on an isolated occasion, and not as a part of his regular business, cannot be said to have engaged in an adventure in the nature of trade merely because the purchase was speculative in that, at that time, he did not intend to hold the shares indefinitely, but intended, if possible, to sell them at a profit as soon as he reasonably could. I think that there must be clearer indications of "trade" than this before it can be said that there has been an adventure in the nature of trade.

Thus, a purchase of shares with an intention to resell at a profit is not, *by itself,* likely to result in the characterization of any gain or loss from their sale as resulting from an adventure in the nature of trade. An isolated transaction in shares, however, can give rise to business income or loss if there are other factors that indicate an intention to trade.[29] For example, a "quick flip" of shares may suggest a trading intention unless it can be explained on other grounds. An isolated transaction in speculative penny mining shares may well give rise to business income or loss if the taxpayer is acting like a mining promoter. *A fortiori,* speculative and highly leveraged trading in high risk, non-yielding shares and options may be seen as trading in securities.[30]

All investors hope, *albeit* sometimes unrealistically, that their investments will increase in value. Thus, the mere expectation of profit is not, by itself, sufficient to characterize a transaction as an adventure in the nature of trade. Certain types of assets, though, and typically those that cannot possibly provide any investment yield, are always under suspicion as "trading assets". Profits resulting from the sale of these types of assets are summarily classified as business income. As Lord Carmont stated:[31]

> [t]his means that, although in certain cases it is important to know whether a venture is isolated or not, that information is really superfluous in many cases where *the commodity itself* stamps the transaction as a trading venture, and the profits and gains are plainly income liable to tax. [Emphasis added.]

In contrast, assets with a *potential, even if somewhat remote,* of yielding income, are generally seen as "investment assets" and profits resulting from transactions in these types of assets are usually, though not inevitably, characterized as capital gains. Corporate shares in particular enjoy this status. Corporate shares tend to be viewed as investment assets because they have the *potential* to yield dividends. Are corporate

---

[28] *Irrigation Industries Ltd. v. M.N.R.*, [1962] CTC 215 at 219, 62 DTC 1131 at 1133 (S.C.C.).

[29] *Osler Hammond & Nanton Ltd. v. M.N.R.*, [1963] SCR 432, [1963] CTC 164, 63 DTC 119 (investment dealer sold shares arranged for during underwriting); *Hill-Clarke-Francis Ltd. v. M.N.R.*, [1963] SCR 452, [1963] CTC 337, 63 DTC 1211 (lumber dealer purchased all outstanding shares of supplier; court looked at intention at time of acquisition and sale of shares).

[30] See, e.g., *Oakside Corporation Ltd.*, [1991] 1 CTC 2132, 91 DTC 328 (T.C.C.).

[31] *I.R.C. v. Reinhold* (1953), 34 Tax Cas. 389 at 392 (Scot.); see also *Rutledge v. I.R.C.* (1929), 14 Tax Cas. 490 (Scot. Ct. of Sess.) (isolated transaction in toilet paper characterized as adventure in nature of trade); *I.R.C. v. Fraser*, 27 Tax Cas. 502 (Scot.) (isolated transaction in whiskey gave rise to funds taxable as business income); *M.N.R. v. Taylor*, [1956] CTC 189, 56 DTC 1125 (Ex. Ct.) (isolated transaction in lead).

shares really any different from other assets? The Supreme Court thought so in *Irrigation Industries Ltd. v. M.N.R.*:[32]

> [t]he nature of the property in question here is shares issued from the treasury of a corporation and we have not been referred to any reported case in which profit from one isolated purchase and sale of shares, by a person not engaged in the business of trading in securities, has been claimed to be taxable. . . . *Corporate shares are in a different position because they constitute something the purchase of which is, in itself, an investment.* They are not, in themselves, articles of commerce, but represent an interest in a corporation which is itself created for the purpose of doing business. Their acquisition is a well recognized method of investing capital in a business enterprise. [Emphasis added.]

The Court adopted a more stringent approach, however, in *Freud* where Pigeon J. said:[33]

> It is clear that while an acquisition of shares may be an investment . . . it may also be a trading operation depending upon circumstances. . . .

The converse is equally true. It is generally difficult, but by no means impossible, for a taxpayer to establish that he or she was engaged in a speculative venture or an adventure in the nature of trade in trading shares.[34] Thus, share losses are seen as capital transactions.

Assets other than "trading assets" and "investment assets" fall into some middle ground in which the nature of the asset does not play as important a role as the taxpayer's conduct in relation to the asset. Real estate, other than vacant land, falls into this middle ground.

To summarize:

- *By itself,* nothing conclusive can be determined from the fact that a transaction is an isolated one in the taxpayer's experience;

- If there are other factors indicative of trade, a profit from an isolated transaction will be taxable as ordinary income resulting from an adventure in the nature of trade;

- Even if there are no other business attributes, a transaction may still give rise to business income if the asset traded is of a trading, and not of an investment nature;

---

[32] *Irrigation Indust. Ltd. v. M.N.R.*, *ante* (gain from speculative mining shares purchased with short-term loan on account of capital).

[33] *M.N.R. v. Freud*, [1969] SCR 75 at 80-81, [1968] CTC 438 at 442, 68 DTC 5279 at 5282.

[34] *Becker v. The Queen*, [1983] CTC 11, 83 DTC 5032 (F.C.A.) (purchase of shares in business with intention of transforming it into profitable enterprise); *Factory Carpet Ltd. v. The Queen*, [1985] 2 CTC 267, 85 DTC 5464 (F.C.T.D.) (purchase of shares with substantial deductible non-capital losses with intention of revamping and reselling business, therefore trading).

- If the asset in question is an investment asset (e.g., corporate shares), and there are no other factors indicative of trading, the transaction will *usually* (not inevitably) be viewed as a capital transaction. This is so even though the investment asset is acquired *for the purpose of resale at a profit.*

(C) Related Activity

A taxpayer's profits and losses from transactions that are closely related to his or her other ordinary business activities is usually characterized as business income or losses.[35] It is very difficult for a taxpayer to maintain successfully that a profit arising out of a transaction connected in any manner with ordinary business activity is a capital gain. As Thorson P. put it:[36]

> . . . they were transactions in the same commodity as that which it had to purchase for its ordinary purposes. In my view, they were of the same character and nature as trading and business operations as those of its business in its ordinary course, even though they involved a departure from such course.

To summarize: There is a strong presumption that a transaction connected in any way with a taxpayer's usual business is intrinsically part of that business. The presumption is rebuttable. It may be rebutted through evidence that the transaction was not part of the taxpayer's ordinary business, but was an unrelated capital investment. *Actual* use of the property as an investment asset over some period of time, or a plausible explanation for selling the investment, may also rebut the presumption.

---

[35] See generally: *Smith v. M.N.R.* (1955), 12 Tax ABC 166, 55 DTC 101 (mortgage discounting closely related to taxpayer's business as realtor; treated as trading since so related); *Darius v. M.N.R.,* [1971] Tax ABC 889, 71 DTC 609 (shareholder in construction company sold land parcels in her own name to achieve better tax result than company able to achieve); *Morrison v. M.N.R.,* [1917-27] CTC 343, 1 DTC 113 (Ex. Ct.) (taxpayer with skill and knowledge in trade acquired through experience who then traded privately in the same commodity was carrying on a business); *McDonough v. M.N.R.,* [1949] CTC 213, 4 DTC 621 (Ex. Ct.) (trading not precluded by mere fact that isolated transaction; prospector became promoter of mines in one trade of over a million shares); *No. 351 v. M.N.R.* (1956), 15 Tax ABC 351, 56 DTC 375 (frequent trading of grain futures); *Boivin v. M.N.R.,* 70 DTC 1364 (a dozen property "flips" by wife on direction of building contractor husband motivated by profit and deemed "trading"); *Kinsella v. M.N.R.* (1963), 34 Tax ABC 196, 64 DTC 56 (frequency of sales and modernization of buildings indicated carefully-planned method of increasing income); *M.N.R. v. Spencer,* [1961] CTC 109, 61 DTC 1079 (Ex. Ct.) (lawyers acted as mortgagees for bonuses; although held to maturity, deemed business and not investments); *Kennedy v. M.N.R.,* [1952] CTC 59, 52 DTC 1070 (Ex. Ct.) (stated intention of taxpayer on purchase only relevant if supported by evidence; see editorial note at CTC 59); *No. 13 v. M.N.R.* (1951), 3 Tax ABC 397, 51 DTC 117 (real estate developer treated one property specially, holding it for 10 years as an investment apart from his ordinary business); *Everlease (Ont.) Ltd. v. M.N.R.,* [1968] Tax ABC 162, 68 DTC 180 (building sold to cover lack of funds was trade due to owner's close association with real estate developers and managers).

[36] *Atlantic Sugar Refineries Ltd. v. M.N.R.,* [1948] CTC 326 at 513, 4 DTC 507 at 513; affirmed [1949] CTC 196, 4 DTC 602 (S.C.C.).

(D) Corporate Objects and Powers

A corporation has the capacity, rights, powers and privileges of a natural person.[37] Thus, unless specifically restricted by its articles of incorporation, a corporation may engage in any business other than those from which it is specifically precluded by statute. A corporation may restrict its scope of business activities by specifying the restrictions in its articles of incorporation or other constating documents.[38]

For tax purposes, characterization of corporate income depends upon the business actually conducted by the corporation and not on any restrictions in its incorporating documents.[39] Thus, corporate income is characterized according to the intention and secondary intention tests and not according to any stipulations in the corporation's constating documents.

(E) Degree of Organization

Where a taxpayer deals with property in much the same way as a dealer would with similar property, any resulting profit is likely to be characterized as business income. Thus, a transaction, *albeit* isolated and unrelated to the taxpayer's ordinary business activity, may have the stamp of business purpose if it is organized and carried on in the manner of a trader. As Lord Clyde said in *I.R.C. v. Livingston:*[40]

> I think the test, which must be used to determine whether a venture such as we are now considering is, or is not, "in the nature of 'trade'"; is whether the operations involved in it are of the same kind, and carried on in the same way, as those which are characteristic of ordinary trading in the line of business in which the venture was made.

For example, a taxpayer who purchases undeveloped land which he or she then subdivides and sells for profit, behaves as a developer would in the normal course of business. In the absence of a convincing explanation, the taxpayer's profits would constitute income from business.[41]

---

[37] See, e.g., *Business Corporations Act*, R.S.O. 1990, c. B.16, s. 15.

[38] See, e.g., *Canada Business Corporations Act*, R.S.C. 1985, c. 44, para. 6(1)(f), and *Ontario Business Corporations Act*, R.S.O. 1990, c. B.16, para. 5(1)(f).

[39] *Sutton Lumber & Trading Co. v. M.N.R.*, [1953] CTC 237, 53 DTC 1158 (S.C.C.).

[40] *I.R.C. v. Livingston* (1927), 11 Tax Cas. 538 at 542 (Scot.).

[41] See, e.g., *Moluch v. M.N.R.*, [1966] CTC 712 at 720, 66 DTC 5463 at 5468 (Ex. Ct.) where the Court observed:
> [m]oreover I am unable to distinguish what the appellant did after his decision to subdivide had been reached from what a person engaged in the business of land development would do once he had acquired a parcel of property.

See also IT-218R, "Profit, Capital Gains and Losses from the Sale of Real Estate, Including Farmland and Inherited Land and Conversion of Real Estate from Capital Property to Inventory and Vice Versa" (September 16, 1986).

It is clear that dealing with an asset as a businessperson would deal with similar assets may, by itself, be sufficient to show an intention to trade. It is also clear that a taxpayer's intention at the time of acquisition can be quite different from his or her intention at the time of sale. For example, in *Moluch*,[42] the taxpayer did not originally acquire the lands with an intent to sell them at a profit. The taxpayer's intention to use the land as a capital asset and his actual use as such for an extended period of time were never in question. Nevertheless, the taxpayer's activities subsequent to the acquisition showed that the investment property had been converted into inventory, presumably, on the basis of a change in the taxpayer's intention. The Court said:[43]

> . . . even if at the time of acquisition, the intention of turning the lands to account by resale was not present, it does not necessarily follow that profits resulting from sales are not assessable to income tax. If at some subsequent point in time, the appellant embarked upon a business, using the lands as inventory in the business of land subdividing for profit, then clearly the resultant profits would not be merely the realization of an enhancement in value, but rather profits from a business and so assessable to income tax. . . .

(b) Electing Capital Gains

To reduce the uncertainty associated with the troublesome question of whether a gain is on account of income or capital, individuals and corporations may elect "guaranteed" capital gains or capital loss treatment on a disposition of certain types of properties.[44] The following rules apply:

- The election is only available upon the disposition of a "Canadian security".

- To qualify as a "Canadian security", the issuer of the security must be a Canadian resident, and the security must be either equity or debt. Warrants and options do not qualify as "Canadian securities".[45]

- Once a taxpayer elects to have a gain deemed a capital gain, all subsequent dispositions of "Canadian securities" by the taxpayer are similarly characterized. Hence, all losses would also be considered capital losses.[46]

- The election is available to both individuals and corporations, but it is not available to a trader or dealer in securities.[47]

---

[42] *Moluch v. M.N.R., ante.*

[43] *Moluch v. M.N.R., ante,* [1966] CTC at 718, 66 DTC at 5466; see also *Hughes v. The Queen,* [1984] CTC 101, 84 DTC 6110 (F.C.T.D.) (apartment building acquired as investment asset; converted into inventory upon application to turn it into condominium).

[44] Subs. 39(4).

[45] Subs. 39(6); Reg. 6200.

[46] Subs. 39(4).

[47] Subs. 39(5).

- The election must be made on a prescribed form and filed together with the tax return for the year.

Traders and dealers in securities may not use the election. Whether a person is a trader or dealer is in itself a question of fact to be determined by the taxpayer's intentions and conduct. A person who participates in the promotion or underwriting of securities is considered a trader or dealer.[48] The Department also considers corporate "insiders" who trade for a quick profit to be "traders".

(c) Conversion of Property

Reference:

BULLETINS, CIRCULARS & RULINGS:

IT-102R2   July 22, 1985   Conversion of Property, Other than Real Property, From or To Inventory

Capital property may be converted into inventory and vice versa. The timing of a conversion is a question of fact requiring a clear and unequivocal act implementing such a change of intention as to clearly indicate a change in the character of the property.[49]

(d) Business Income vs. Investment Income

Having drawn a line between "income" and "capital gains", we now refine the process and distinguish between business income from trading and investment income. The characterization of income as resulting from business or investments (more technically, income from property) is a question of fact.[50]

Since most businesses use property to generate income, it is not particularly helpful to ask whether the income is derived from the *use* of property. The critical question is: Does the income flow *from* property or *from* business?[51] It is the subtlety of this distinction which can give rise to difficulties in characterizing the source of income. There is no bright line test that clearly answers the question.

---

[48] IT-479R, "Transactions in Securities" (February 29, 1984).

[49] *Magilb Dev. Corp. v. The Queen*, [1987] 1 CTC 66, 87 DTC 5012 (F.C.T.D.) (father made plans for development of family farm corporation; actions did not convert farm from a capital to a trading asset); *Cantor v. M.N.R.*, [1985] 1 CTC 2059, 85 DTC 79 (T.C.C.) (townhouses purchased by law partners proved unprofitable and sold as condominiums; no change in character of investment where diversification occurred to dispose of property most profitably).

[50] *Cdn. Marconi Co. v. The Queen*, [1986] 2 SCR 522 at 530-31, [1986] 2 CTC 465 at 470, 86 DTC 6526 at 6529 *per* Wilson J.: "It is trite law that the characterization of income as income from a business or income from property must be made from an examination of the taxpayer's whole course of conduct viewed in the light of surrounding circumstances."

[51] Para. 3(*a*); subs. 9(1); see also IT-258R2, "Transfer of Property to a Spouse" (May 11, 1982).

In many, perhaps most, cases the distinction between business income and property income does not affect the end result. A taxpayer's income for a taxation year from a source that is business *or* property is his or her profit therefrom for the year.[52] Income from both of these sources is generally calculated according to the same commercial and statutory rules.

There are, however, circumstances in which the distinction between the two is important. For example:

- The attribution rules apply only to income from property and do not apply to business income;[53]

- Active business income earned by a Canadian controlled private corporation is eligible for special tax credits which substantially reduce the effective tax rate on such income;[54]

- Income from property is subject to a different scheme of taxation and at different rates for different sources of such income.

Generally speaking, income from property is the investment yield on an asset. Rent, dividends, interest, and royalties are typical examples. The yield on the investment is earned by a relatively passive process. For example, where an individual invests in land, stocks, bonds, or intangible property[55] and collects investment income therefrom without doing much more than holding the property, the income is investment income or income *from* property.

In contrast, business income implies activity in the earning process: it is generally generated from the *use* of property as part of a process that combines labour and capital. To take a simple example: a taxpayer may *invest* in bonds and clip the coupons to earn the interest income therefrom; alternatively, she or he may actively *trade* in bonds to earn a profit from trading activities. In the first case, the earnings are derived from a passive process and are investment income; in the second case, the income is from business.[56]

Although the distinction between income from business and investment income is easy to state in general terms, the borderline between the two is often blurred. What is the level of activity beyond which a passive holding becomes an active process of

---

[52] Subs. 9(1).

[53] S. 74.1.

[54] Subs. 125(1); see Chapter XVII "Private Corporations: Business Income".

[55] Such as, copyrights, trademarks, etc.

[56] It is important to note that profits from an isolated trade may be business income. The phrase "adventure in the nature of trade" implies an isolated transaction: see subs. 248(1) ("business").

earning income?[57] The issue has been complicated by statements from the Supreme Court that there is a rebuttable presumption that income earned by a corporate taxpayer in the exercise of its duly authorized objects is income from a business.[58]

Traditionally, a corporation carrying on activities described in the objects clause (if any) of its constating documents is presumed to earn income from business. The presumption appears as early as 1880 in *Smith v. Anderson*:[59]

> You cannot acquire gain by means of a company except by carrying on some business or other, and I have no doubt if any one formed a company or association for the purpose of acquiring gain, he must form it for the purpose of carrying on a business by which gain is to be obtained.

But these judicial statements were born of a foreign tax system with a different structure.

It is less clear whether corporations created in jurisdictions which do not require objects clauses should also be subject to this presumption.[60] One answer is that the rebuttable presumption applies to all corporations, but that it is more readily rebuttable in the case of private corporations subject to the Part IV tax on investment income.[61] But why should the choice of form of business organization determine the characterization of the source of income?

(i) Real Estate

The issue to be determined in characterizing rental income from real estate is whether the income is generated as a result of activity and services associated with a

---

[57] *Cdn. Marconi Co. v. The Queen*, [1986] 2 SCR 522, [1986] 2 CTC 465, 86 DTC 6526 ($18 million invested yielded interest that was included in manufacturing and processing profits); *Wertman v. M.N.R.*, [1964] CTC 252, 64 DTC 5158 (Ex. Ct.) (concerning rent from apartment units: "the concepts of income from property and income from business are not mutually exclusive but blend completely"); *Walsh v. M.N.R.*, [1965] CTC 478, 65 DTC 5293 (Ex. Ct.) (ordinary janitorial services did not convert property to business, as would maid, linen, laundry and breakfast services); *Burri v. The Queen*, [1985] 2 CTC 42, 85 DTC 5287 (F.C.T.D.) (services provided by owners incidental to the making of revenue from property through the earning of rent).

[58] *Cdn. Marconi Co. v. The Queen, ante,* [1986] 2 SCR at 529, [1986] 2 CTC at 468-470, 86 DTC at 6528-6529; see also *Supreme Theatres Ltd. v. The Queen*, [1981] CTC 190 at 193, 81 DTC 5136 at 5138 *per* Gibson J. (F.C.T.D.); *Queen & Metcalfe Carpark Ltd v. M.N.R.*, [1973] CTC 810 at 817-18, 74 DTC 6007 at 6011 *per* Sweet D.J. (F.C.T.D.); *Calvin Bullock Ltd. v. M.N.R.*, [1985] 1 CTC 2309 at 2312, 85 DTC 287 at 289 *per* St-Onge T.C.J. (T.C.C.); *No. 585 v. M.N.R.* (1958), 21 Tax ABC 56 at 66, 58 DTC 754 at 759 *per* Mr. Boisvert; *Tenir Ltée v. M.N.R.*, [1968] Tax ABC 772, 68 DTC 589 at 595 *per* Mr. Davis; *SBI Properties Ltd. v. M.N.R.*, [1981] CTC 2288 at 2297, 81 DTC 263 at 270-271 *per* Mr. St-Onge (T.R.B.); *King George Hotels Ltd. et al. v. The Queen*, [1981] CTC 78 at 80, *per* Smith D.J.; affirmed [1981] CTC 87, 81 DTC 5082 (F.C.A.).

[59] *Smith v. Anderson*, [1880] 15 Ch. D. 247 at 260 (C.A.).

[60] *Smith v. Anderson, ante,* at 530-31.

[61] See Chapter XVI "Private Corporations: Investment Income" for a discussion of the Part IV tax and the statutory scheme in connection therewith.

commercial enterprise or from passive ownership of the property with only minimal ancillary activity. Income derived from passive ownership of real estate is investment income; income derived from the use of real estate as an asset in a commercial endeavour is business income.[62]

The critical test in distinguishing an investment in real estate from a real estate business is the level of services provided as a supplement to the rental of the real property.[63] The greater the level of services provided as an adjunct to the rental of real estate, the greater the likelihood that the income therefrom is business income.[64]

The distinction does not rest on any single criterion but upon an assessment of the aggregate level of activity associated with the generation of the income. To be sure, one factor may outweigh several others, but the test is always one that is resolved on the facts of each particular case.

Here, as elsewhere in the law, it is easy to characterize at either extreme of the spectrum. It is clear, for example, that a traditional hotel rents its guests more than a room, whereas a tenant in an apartment usually rents only space with minimal services. The distinction is less clear, however, between an apartment that provides extensive ancillary services and a hotel that makes minimal provision beyond accommodation.

The provision of maid, linen, laundry and food services suggest business. In contrast, routine and necessary ancillary services such as heating, cleaning and snow removal, are seen as mere adjuncts to the ownership of property. In either case, time spent on managing the property is not the determining factor.[65]

---

[62] *Martin v. M.N.R.*, [1948] CTC 189 at 193, 3 DTC 1199 at 1201 (Ex. Ct.).

[63] The phrase "meer [sic] investment" has sometimes been used to describe a passive investment which gives rise to income from property. See, e.g., *Marks v. M.N.R.* (1962), 30 Tax ABC 155, 62 DTC 536.

[64] *Fry v. Salisbury House Estate Ltd.*, [1930] AC 432 at 470 (H.L.) (management company operated elevators, provided porters, security guards, heating and cleaning at extra charge; property ownership, not trade); see also *Crofts v. Sywell Aerodrome Ltd.*, [1942] 1 KB 317 (C.A.) (activities, though varied and extensive, consisted of exercise and exploitation of property rights of aerodrome); *Malenfant v. M.N.R.*, [1992] 2 CTC 2431, 92 DTC 2065 (T.C.C.) (income from hotel and motel rooms was income from rental property as services provided were only those required to maintain rooms).

[65] See, e.g., the comments of Thurlow J., in *Wertman v. M.N.R.*, [1964] CTC 252 at 267, 64 DTC 5158 at 5167 (Ex. Ct.):

> The nature of the services provided, in my opinion, also has a bearing on the question; some, such as maid service and linen and laundry service, being more indicative of a business operation than the heating of the building which, in my view, is so closely concerned with the property itself as to offer no definite indication one way or the other. Nor do I think that the fact that the management of the property occupies the appellant's time or the fact that he uses his car to go to and from the property indicate that the operation is a business, for, at most, these facts indicate that he renders a service to himself and to the other owners of the building which, so far as charged for, represents a proper outgoing against revenue for the purpose of ascertaining the net profit divisible among the owners regardless of whether the rentals are mere income from property or income from a business.

(ii) Short-term Investments

The characterization of income from short-term investments raises more subtle distinctions. The issue is particularly important for Canadian corporations because of the special rules in respect of the small business deduction, the manufacturing and processing credit, and the refundable dividend tax on investment income.

The small business deduction and the manufacturing and processing credit may only be claimed on Canadian "active business" income. Income must first qualify as business income before it can be characterized as "active" business income. The refundable tax on income from property may only be claimed on "investment income" earned by a Canadian-controlled private corporation.[66]

(A) Integration Test

An "active business" is ". . . *any* business carried on by the taxpayer *other than* a specified investment business or a personal services business . . ."[67] and for some purposes ". . . includes an adventure or concern in the nature of trade".[68]

"Investment income" is ". . . income for the year from a source . . . that is property . . .".

The characterization of a taxpayer's income from short-term investments involves a two-step process:

- Determine whether the taxpayer's investments are an integral part of his or her business activities; if they are, income from the investments is business income; and

- If they are not, determine whether the taxpayer's investment activities constitute a separate business; if they do, the income from those activities is business income. If the investment activity does not constitute a separate business, the income from those activities is income from property.

---

[66] See Chapter XVI "Private Corporations: Investment Income".

[67] Subs. 248(1) ("active business").

[68] Subs. 125(7) ("active business").

(B) "Employed and Risked" Test

A taxpayer's investments are considered to be an integral part of a business if his or her funds are "employed and risked" in the business.[69] One asks: Is the making of investments a part of the mode of conducting the business? If the answer is yes, then the income from the investments is part of the income of the business.

Business income from investments represents the fruit derived from a fund "employed and risked" in the taxpayer's business. Thus, the temporary investment of working capital constitutes an intrinsic part of the business.

---

[69] See *Ensite Ltd. v. The Queen*, [1986] 2 CTC 459, 86 DTC 6521 (S.C.C.) (property yielding interest must be linked to some "definite obligation or liability of the business"); *Bank Line Ltd. v. I.R.C.* (1974), 49 Tax Cas. 307 (Scot. Ct. of Sess.) (no actual risk or employment of reserve funds in the company's business of owning, operating and replacing ships). In *The Queen v. Marsh & McLennan Ltd.*, [1983] CTC 231, 83 DTC 5180 (F.C.A.), for example, the taxpayer, an insurance broker, temporarily invested its insurance premiums in short-term paper. The taxpayer could do so because of the lag between the time that it received a premium from its customer and the time that it remitted the premium to the customer's insurer. The taxpayer's business involved two dimensions: brokerage and investment. The two activities were so interdependent that its investments were an integral part of its business; hence, its investment income was income from a business and *not* income from property. See also the speech of Lord Mersey in *Liverpool & London & Globe Ins. Co. v. Bennett* (1913), 6 Tax Cas. 327 (H.L.) at 379-80:

> It is said that the dividends in question are derived from investments made...and that such investments form no part of the "business" of the Company. In my opinion there is no foundation either in fact or in law for this contention. It is well known that in the course of carrying on an insurance business, large sums of money derived from premiums collected and from other sources accumulate in the hands of the insurers, and that one of the most important parts of the profits of the business is derived from the temporary investment of these moneys. These temporary investments are also required for the formation of the reserve fund, a fund created to attract customers and to serve as a standby in the event of sudden claims being made upon the insurers in respect of losses. It is, according to my view, impossible to say that such investments do not form part of this Company's insurance business, or that the returns flowing from them do not form part of its profits. In a commercial sense the directors of the Company owe a duty to their shareholders and to their customers to make such investments, and to receive and distribute in the ordinary course of business, whether in the form of dividends, or in payment of losses, or in the formation of reserves, the moneys collected from them.

(C) Separate Business Test

Where a taxpayer's investments are not an integral part of his or her business operations, the question arises whether the investment activities constitute a separate business.[70] The answer to this question depends upon several factors:

- The number and value of transactions;

- The time devoted to investment activities;

- The relationship between the taxpayer's investment income and his or her total income; and

- The relationship between the value of the taxpayer's investment and the total value of his or her assets.

Is the taxpayer merely managing personal investments or carrying on an investment business? The greater the amount of time devoted to, and the greater the value of, investment activities as compared to business activities, the more likely it is that the investment segment constitutes a separate business.

3. MEASUREMENT OF INCOME

References:

ITA:

S. 3   Income for Taxation Year

S. 9   Income/Loss from Business or Property

S. 69   Inadequate Consideration, Deemed Proceeds

S. 75   Trust Income

S. 81   Amounts not Included in Income

BULLETINS, CIRCULARS & RULINGS:

IT-179R   May 28, 1993   Change of Fiscal Period

IT-433R   June 4, 1993   Farming or Fishing — Use of Cash Method

IT-526   May 28, 1993   Farming — Cash Method of Inventory Adjustments

---

[70] *Cdn. Marconi Co. v. The Queen*, [1986] 2 SCR 522, [1986] 2 CTC 465, 86 DTC 6526. The taxpayer, a manufacturer of electronic equipment, divested itself of its broadcasting division and found itself with surplus funds of approximately $20 million. While awaiting a suitable opportunity to invest in another business, the taxpayer invested these surplus funds in short-term interest bearing securities. During the period under assessment, the taxpayer earned substantial interest income (approximately $5 million) on which it claimed the manufacturing and processing credit on the basis that its income from its short-term investments represented "business income" and, therefore, "active business income". The Supreme Court of Canada applied the presumption that income earned by a corporate taxpayer is business income. The facts were not sufficient to rebut the presumption in favour of the taxpayer. See also *Colonial Realty Services Ltd. v. M.N.R.*, [1987] 1 CTC 2343, 87 DTC 259 (T.C.C.) (excess funds placed in investment certificates; no corporate activity or circumstances converted the yield to active business income).

(a) The Concept of "Profit"

Having characterized income as flowing from a particular source, the next step is to determine the amount to be included for tax purposes.

A taxpayer's income for a taxation year from a business or property is his or her *profit* therefrom for the year.[71] The term "profit" means *net* profit: The amount of revenue remaining after the deduction of expenses incurred for the purpose of earning the revenue.[72] But how do we determine which expenses are deductible from revenues?

(i) Accounting Principles

The first step in the calculation of net profit is to look to accounting and commercial principles. In *Daley v. M.N.R.*, for example:[73]

> . . . the first inquiry whether a particular disbursement or expense is deductible should not be whether it is excluded from deduction by [paragraph 18(1)(*a*) or (*b*)] but rather whether its deduction is permissible by the ordinary principles of commercial trading or accepted business and accounting practice. . . .

See also, *Dom. Taxi Cab Assn. v. M.N.R.*:[74]

> The expression "profit" is not defined in the Act. It has not a technical meaning and whether or not the sum in question constitutes profit must be determined on ordinary commercial principles unless the provisions of the *Income Tax Act* require a departure from such principles.

---

[71] Subs. 9(1).

[72] *Montreal Light, Heat & Power Consolidated v. M.N.R.*; *Montreal Coke & Mfg. Co. v. M.N.R.*, [1940-41] CTC 217, 2 DTC 506; affirmed [1942] CTC 1, 2 DTC 535; affirmed [1944] CTC 94, 2 DTC 654 (P.C.).

[73] *Daley v. M.N.R.*, [1950] CTC 254 at 260, 4 DTC 877 at 880 (Ex. Ct.) (fee for call to Bar not deductible expense as preceding commencement of the practice of law). See also, *The Queen v. Metro. Prop. Co.*, [1985] 1 CTC 169, 85 DTC 5128 (F.C.T.D.) (in absence of specific statutory provisions, generally accepted accounting principles applied); *Imperial Oil Ltd. v. M.N.R.*, [1947] CTC 353, 3 DTC 1090 (Ex. Ct.) (damages paid on negligence settlement incurred as consequence of operations by which business income earned; damages deemed deductible expenses); *Royal Trust Co. v. M.N.R.*, [1957] CTC 32, 57 DTC 1055 (Ex. Ct.) (club fees allowed executives to meet new clients; expenses need not be directly related to income); *M.N.R. v. Frankel Corp. Ltd.*, [1958] CTC 314, 58 DTC 1173 (Ex. Ct.) (sale of capital assets of one of four of taxpayer's businesses not taxable as inventory sales but, oddly, taxable as deemed receipt because of diversion tactics); *C.G.E. Co. v. M.N.R.*, [1961] CTC 512, 61 DTC 1300 (S.C.C.) (debts decreased due to change in foreign exchange rate; profit apportioned amongst tax years rather than upon actual payment of note); *M.N.R. v. Irwin*, [1964] CTC 362, 64 DTC 5227 (S.C.C.) (concept of profit for tax purposes clarified); *Quemont Mining Corp. v. M.N.R.*, [1966] CTC 570, 66 DTC 5376 (Ex. Ct.) (disagreement in formula used to calculate mining taxes paid to province); *M.N.R. v. Atlantic Engine Rebuilders Ltd.*, [1967] CTC 230, 67 DTC 5155 (S.C.C.) (valuation of inventory consistent and coincidentally correct though original basis of evaluation flawed); *Sherritt Gordon Mines Ltd. v. M.N.R.*, [1968] CTC 262, 68 DTC 5180 (Ex. Ct.) (generally accepted business and commercial principles used in respect of capitalization of interest expenses during construction period).

[74] *Dom. Taxi Cab Assn. v. M.N.R.*, [1954] CTC 34 at 37, 54 DTC 1020 at 1021 (S.C.C.).

(ii) Departure from Accounting Principles

Having determined the appropriate treatment of a receipt or expenditure according to commercial and accounting practice, the next step is to determine whether the Act or case law prescribes a different treatment for the particular item. Although accounting principles are a guide to interpretation of the Act, they cannot be used where the Act prescribes otherwise.[75]

Where the deduction of an expenditure is specifically prohibited by the Act, the statute obviously prevails over commercial and accounting principles and the expenditure is not deductible in computing profit. For example, under generally accepted accounting principles, a taxpayer is entitled to deduct depreciation as an expense in calculating income. Since the Act, however, specifically prohibits the deduction of depreciation, any depreciation calculated for financial statement purposes is not deductible as an expense for tax purposes.[76]

Similarly, case law may also prohibit the use of a particular method of calculating income that is otherwise acceptable in commercial practice. For example, although the last-in, first-out (LIFO) method of valuing inventory is generally acceptable for financial statement purposes, it cannot be used to calculate income for tax purposes.[77]

But a general prohibition against the deduction of a type of an expenditure[78] may be overridden by *specific* authority. For example, interest payable on indebtedness would be a non-deductible payment on account of capital[79] were it not for paragraph 20(1)(c), that specifically allows for its deduction in computing income from a business or property. This is simply a reflection of the rule of statutory construction that a specific rule prevails over a general rule.

(b) Measurement and Timing

Measurement and timing of income are different concepts. They are, however, as a practical matter, inextricably related. For example, suppose a business started up in

---

[75] *The Queen v. Consumers' Gas Co. Ltd.*, [1987] 1 CTC 79, 87 DTC 5008 (F.C.A.).

[76] Para. 18(1)(*b*).

[77] *M.N.R. v. Anaconda Amer. Brass Ltd.*, [1955] CTC 311, 55 DTC 1220 (P.C.).

[78] See, e.g., the general prohibitions in paras. 18(1)(*a*) (expenditure must be incurred for the purpose of earning income), 18(1)(*b*) (expenditure cannot be on account of capital), 18(1)(*h*) (expenditure cannot be on account of personal or living expenses).

[79] *Can. Safeway Ltd. v. M.N.R.*, [1957] CTC 335, 57 DTC 1239 (S.C.C.) (use of borrowed money important in characterization of interest expense as business or property; acquisition of shares of subsidiary complicated issue); *Interprovincial Pipeline Co. v. M.N.R.*, [1967] CTC 180, 67 DTC 5125, affirmed [1968] CTC 156, 68 DTC 5093 (S.C.C.) (tax loophole in treaty cured; incidental interest earned deducted from interest expense to determine loss); *Sherritt Gordon Mines Ltd. v. M.N.R., ante.* See Chapter VII "Business and Property Income: Inclusions" for discussion of interest deductions.

1928 and closed down in 1995. There are a number of difficulties involved in measuring the aggregate income over the 67 years. If all we needed to know was the income figure for the 67 year period, questions of timing would not arise. As soon as we decide that we require the income figure for the year 1995, however, or for the month of June 1995, serious problems of timing intrude in the measurement exercise.

These problems are best illustrated by the concepts of "realization", "recognition", and "matching".

(i) Realization

A simple definition of "realization" would refer to the point of sale, the time at which X parts with Black Acre and receives a real gain in the form of cash. The inadequacy of this simple definition is seen in the following examples. If X sells Black Acre and takes back a mortgage, she or he realizes a gain which should be recognized for tax purposes. Similarly, an exchange of Black Acre for White Acre, a property of equal value, or for stock in Black Acre Developments Ltd., will normally be treated as a realization. Even if X gives Black Acre away, she or he will realize a gain. In all these cases the rationale is the same: X has parted with her or his investment in Black Acre, and for tax purposes, X is treated as though the property was sold for cash.

There is a fundamental question, however, as to *when* a gain or loss is "realized". Suppose, for example that X buys Black Acre for $50,000. By the end of the year the property is worth $60,000. Has X experienced a $10,000 gain? Certainly he or she has a potential gain, a "paper gain", an accrued gain in the Haig-Simons sense. Traditional accounting practice, however, ignores the gain as unrealized.

In the following year, X's property might decline in value to $45,000 or might rise to $70,000. Suppose, in either case, that X then sells the property. According to traditional practice, X is treated as "realizing" a $5,000 loss or a $20,000 gain in the year that the property is sold. In the first case, the $5,000 loss represents a $10,000 paper gain in Year 1 combined with a paper loss of $15,000 in Year 2. In the second case, X had a paper gain of $10,000 in each of the years 1 and 2.

(ii) Recognition

"Recognition", for our purposes, is the taking into account of an amount in computing income under the Act. Some accounting systems would recognize all the "paper" gains and losses in a year even though they are "unrealized". For the most part, however, the Act does not recognize "unrealized" amounts.

There are good reasons for not recognizing paper gains. Accountants, true to the axiom of their conservatism in estimating income, normally disregard such gains because they may prove illusory if values decline in a subsequent period. From the perspective of a taxpayer, the recognition of unrealized gains could prove a hardship. If X were required to recognize a $10,000 paper gain on Black Acre, and to pay tax on it, X would have to find the money to pay the tax at the end of Year 1. Attempts in the past to tax unrealized gains on certain corporate shares met with considerable taxpayer resistance and only limited success.[80]

On the other hand, the failure to recognize paper gains, and recognition of the entire gain at the point of realization, gives rise to problems of irregularity and "lumping" of income.

There are some cases in which the Act recognizes an unrealized gain. For example, when a taxpayer ceases to be a Canadian resident, he or she is *deemed* to have disposed of any capital property and realized any accrued gain or loss for tax purposes. In other situations the Act does not recognize a gain even though it has been realized through an actual disposition. For example, a realized gain may not be recognized when appreciated capital property is conveyed from one spouse to the other. These exceptions are based upon overriding policy considerations in the tax system.

Accountants are not as reluctant to recognize unrealized losses as they are to recognize unrealized gains. Consistent with accounting conservatism in estimating income, and depending upon the nature of the asset concerned, it is sometimes considered good accounting practice to recognize a "paper" loss. Understandably, the revenue authorities usually do not agree that this conservatism should be applied to calculations of income for tax purposes. To forestall the possibility of complete accounting doom and gloom in such matters, the Act denies recognition of most paper losses for tax purposes.

We have explored, in a very simple way, the concept of realization of gain. There remain a number of slightly more sophisticated problems concerning the time when gains should be recognized.

Suppose that X starts a business of manufacturing and selling widgets. The business cycle can be broken down into the following steps:

(1)   acquisition of inventory of raw metal;

(2)   fabrication of metal into an inventory of widgets;

(3)   sales activity which results in orders for widgets;

(4)   delivery of widgets to customers;

(5)   invoicing of customers; and

(6)   payment of invoices.

An argument could be made for choosing any one of the last five steps as the point at which X's gain should be recognized for the purposes of calculating income. Our earlier discussion would probably suggest that the gain should not be recognized at any point before step (4). Standard accounting would lead to a choice of step (5) as the

---

[80]   *Proposals for Tax Reform* (Ottawa: Finance Canada, 1969), ss. 1.30 and 3.36.

point at which X should recognize a gain. In any event, as a matter of usual business practice, steps (4) and (5) are merged. Commonly, the invoice accompanies the delivery of widgets. As we shall note below, if X's business adopts a cash basis of accounting, the gain will not be recognized until step (6), when payment is actually received.

(iii) Matching

So far we have been talking about the appropriate time to recognize gains and "losses". In an accounting sense gains and losses are measured by reflecting expenditures and receipts. "Gain" or "loss" in themselves are net concepts, as is the "income" of a business since it reflects all the expenditures and all the receipts.

Accountants are concerned that an accurate estimate of income is possible only if receipts and the expenditures which are intended to produce revenues, are properly "matched" in the same time period. This leads accountants into a number of practices designed to ensure that the appropriate expenses are offset against the receipts for a particular period. The following example illustrates the resolution of the problem of matching.

Assume that City Dairy Ltd. delivers milk door to door and for this purpose requires 100 trucks costing $6,000 each. The trucks will have a useful life of about five years and will be disposed of for $1,000 each at the end of that time. Thus, over the course of five years, each truck represents a $5,000 expense of City Dairy's business. If, however, City Dairy bought and expensed 100 trucks in its first business year it would dramatically distort its income for the year by recognizing the entire cost of $600,000 as an expenditure for that year. This particular problem is resolved by applying the notion of "depreciation" in order to spread the cost which arises from exhaustion of such assets over an appropriate number of years.

(c) Accounting Statements

The two most common accounting statements used in taxation are the balance sheet and the income statement (sometimes called a statement of profit and loss).

A balance sheet is designed to reflect, *as at a particular date,* the condition of the business as it may be judged by a statement of what the business owns (assets) and a statement of its obligations (liabilities).

The liabilities side of the balance sheet is divided into two parts: a statement of indebtedness to outsiders and a statement of the owner's equity. All business financing must come from these two sources: capital and debt. The owner may make an initial contribution of capital to the business and the business may borrow money from a bank or purchase goods on credit. The traditional balance sheet equation:

$$A = L + E$$
(assets = liabilities + owner's equity)

is true because owner's equity is a constantly shifting amount that represents the difference between assets and liabilities. Whatever the owner of the business may in fact have contributed, that owner's equity at any time is simply this difference:

$$E = A - L$$

A business is a distinct entity for accounting purposes. This is so regardless of its legal status. City Dairy Ltd., for example, is both an accounting entity and a legal entity separate from its incorporators. Assuming that X Widgets is a sole proprietorship carried on by X, it is not a distinct entity in law. It is, however, a business activity requiring separate accounting treatment.

An income statement is a summary of the receipts and expenditures of a business *for a stated period of time.*

The two statements, the balance sheet and the income statement, are closely interrelated and must be read together in order to present a complete and meaningful picture of the profitability and solvency of a business.

As an illustration, assume that A and B open a retail business on January 1, 1995 with each person contributing $2,500, and a bank loan of $10,000. The opening balance sheet *as at* January 1, 1996, would appear as follows:

BALANCE SHEET			
As at January 1, 1996			
ASSETS		LIABILITIES and EQUITY	
Cash	$ 15,000	Bank loan	$ 10,000
		Owner's equity:	
		Capital A	2,500
		Capital B	2,500
	$ 15,000		$ 15,000

The first point to observe is that the balance sheet balances: The left side of the statement that lists all the property owned by the business is *exactly equal* to the right side of the statement that lists its sources of financing. In other words, the left side of the statement informs the reader as to *what* the business owns (assets), and the right side discloses *how* the assets were financed (liabilities and equity). Hence, the above balance sheet informs any reader without further explanation of the statement that the business entity (the retail business) owned $15,000 of property (assets) as at January 1, 1996, and that it held it in the form of cash. Further, it informs the reader that the firm was financed from two sources, one external (bank loan $10,000) and the other internal (owner's equity $5,000).

The following transactions illustrate the operation of the fundamental accounting equation, A = L + E:

On January 2, 1996, the business leases office space at an annual rent of $6,000 and pays two months' rent on that date.

BALANCE SHEET
As at January 2, 1996

ASSETS		LIABILITIES and EQUITY	
Cash	$ 14,000	Bank loan	$ 10,000
Prepaid rent	1,000	Owner's equity:	
		Capital A	2,500
		Capital B	2,500
	$ 15,000		$ 15,000

On January 4, 1996, the business acquires office furniture at a cost of $3,000, paying $1,500 in cash with a promise to pay the balance in 90 days.

BALANCE SHEET
As at January 4, 1996

ASSETS		LIABILITIES and EQUITY	
Cash	$ 12,500	Accounts payable	$ 1,500
Prepaid rent	1,000	Bank loan	10,000
Office furniture	3,000	Owner's equity:	
		Capital A	2,500
		Capital B	2,500
	$ 16,500		$ 16,500

On January 15, 1996, the business hires two employees at a monthly salary of $1,000 each, and pays their salaries on January 31, 1996.

BALANCE SHEET
As at January 31, 1996

ASSETS		LIABILITIES and EQUITY	
Cash	$ 11,500	Accounts payable	$ 1,500
Prepaid rent	500	Bank loan	10,000
Office furniture	3,000	Owner's equity:	
		Capital A	1,750
		·Capital B	1,750
	$ 15,000		$ 15,000

During the month of February 1996, the business sells merchandise and collects $6,000 in cash, again paying its staff $2,000 in salary.

BALANCE SHEET
As at February 28, 1996

ASSETS		LIABILITIES and EQUITY	
Cash	$ 15,500	Accounts payable	$ 1,500
Office furniture	3,000	Bank loan	10,000
		Owner's equity:	
		Capital A	3,500
		Capital B	3,500
	$ 18,500		$ 18,500

Each of the transactions described has been recorded using the fundamental equation: $A = L + E$. The reader sees that the business owns property (assets) which cost $18,500, now held in two forms, cash and office furniture and that the firm is financed as at February 28, 1996, by outsiders to the extent of $11,500 with insiders (owner's equity) providing the balance of $7,000. The balance sheet does not, however, disclose any information as to *how* and *why* the owners' interest in the business increased from $5,000 to $7,000 during the two months of operations. Based on the balance sheet alone it would be difficult, if not impossible, for any user to decide on the profitability of the business.

Should the owners, A and B, be required to pay income tax on the increase in their equity of $2,000, or on some other amount? The answer can only be found in the income statement. The purpose of the income statement is to disclose *how* a business has performed between two successive points in time. In this sense, it is a connecting link between successive balance sheets. Whereas a balance sheet informs a reader *where* a business stands as at a given time, an income statement reveals *how* the business moved from the opening balance sheet to the closing balance sheet.

Continuing with the previous illustration, the income statement reveals the following information:

INCOME STATEMENT
For the *Two Months* ending February 28, 1996

SALES REVENUE		$ 6,000
EXPENSES		
Wages	$ 3,000	
Rent	1,000	
		4,000
NET INCOME:		$ 2,000

ALLOCATION OF NET INCOME
  To A at 50% of $2,000 = $1,000
  To B at 50% of $2,000 = $1,000.

This statement now informs the reader *how* owner's equity increased by $2,000. Specifically, the business generated revenues of $6,000 and expended $4,000 in the process of generating those revenues, leaving an excess of revenues over expenses (net income) of $2,000. Thus, the purpose of the income statement is to match revenues earned with expenses incurred to generate the revenue. The statement can usually explain the change in owners' equity between successive points in time. Accounting principles and conventions deal with the methodology behind the task of matching revenues and expenses.

The net income figure derived from the matching process provides a starting point in calculating a taxpayer's income tax liability. One observes this starting point in subsection 9(1) of the *Income Tax Act*: ". . . a taxpayer's income for a taxation year from a business or property is his *profit* therefrom for the year". The terms "income" and "profit" are often used interchangeably, and it is now well established that in the absence of specific statutory provisions, "profit" is to be computed in accordance with commercial principles.

(d) Accounting Methods

To this point, the term "income" has been used to denote the excess of revenues earned over expenses incurred to generate those revenues. Hence, in one sense income is the increase in net wealth; conversely, a loss is the decrease in net wealth. This definition is terse and obvious but mathematically demonstrable. The essence of the concept is thereby reduced to "gain during an interval of time". Thus, "gain" is the *sine qua non* of income. While this definition satisfies the purpose of conceptual explanation, it is necessary to adapt it for use in the preparation of financial statements.

(i) Time Intervals

As a preliminary matter, it is essential to select the appropriate "interval of time" between successive financial statements. For no other reason than that of administrative convenience, it has been conventionally established that financial statements should be prepared on an annual basis. Thus, annual financial statements for external reporting and tax purposes are now, with limited exceptions, the general statutory rule. It is this statutory requirement of annual reporting that gives rise to several income measurement problems.

(ii) Cash vs. Accrual Accounting

The first of these measurement problems is to determine whether financial statements should be prepared on a "cash basis" or on an "accrual basis". In cash basis accounting, business transactions are recorded at the time, and in the accounting period, when cash is received or disbursed. Assuming an accounting period of January 1 to December 31 and the sale of merchandise on December 15, 1996 for $3,000 with payment received on January 15, 1997, a cash basis business would record and report the $3,000 revenue earned in 1997. Further assume that the cost of the merchandise to the business was $1,000, paid in cash at time of purchase on December 1, 1996. A cash basis business would record and report the cost of merchandise sold in the year 1996. The effect of the purchase and sale of merchandise would be reflected in the Income Statements of the business as follows:

(Cash Basis)

	Year		COMBINED
	1996	1997	
Sales Revenue	$ 0	$ 3,000	$ 3,000
Cost of Merchandise Sold	(1,000)	0	(1,000)
Net Income (Loss)	$ (1,000)	$ 3,000	$ 2,000

It is worthy of emphasis that, regardless of the accounting method, the *combined* net income of the business in the circumstances described would always amount to $2,000. The disadvantage of the cash basis method lies, however, in the mismatching in a particular accounting (fiscal) period of revenues earned and expenses incurred to earn those revenues. Thus, year 1996 shows a net loss of $1,000 due to the combined effect of early expense recognition coupled with delayed revenue recognition. A year later the statement shows net income of $3,000 by ignoring the earlier expense write-off. Each of the years 1996 and 1997 viewed in isolation would present a distorted result of the underlying business transaction: an economic increase of $2,000 in net wealth.

We saw earlier that net income can only be determined with absolute accuracy when the reporting period for financial statements covers the entire life of a business. The selection of a shorter period of time than the life of the business, changes the task from income determination to estimation of net income. The sacrifice in mathematical accuracy, however, is well justified by the enhanced administrative and business convenience that results from timely financial statements.

The fact that cash basis accounting, in most situations, distorts the financial statements of an entity and more readily conceals the true impact of business transactions has, with very limited exceptions, led to its rejection as an appropriate method of financial reporting. A notable exception is found in the reporting of employment income, which must be repeated on a cash basis. This requirement results from a balancing of the enhanced administrative convenience to the employee, employer, and Revenue Canada and the minimal distortion that occurs in measuring employment income on a cash basis.

In contrast with the cash basis of accounting, accrual accounting recognizes revenue when it is realized and expenses are reported in the same time period as the revenues for which they were incurred. The accrual basis is premised on the rationale that reporting revenues earned and expenses incurred in the same accounting period provides a better "matching" and that such "matching" more accurately depicts the underlying business transaction. Using the same figures as in the previous example, an income statement prepared on an accrual basis would disclose the following:

(Accrual Basis)

	Year		COMBINED
	1996	1997	
Sales Revenue	$ 3,000	$ 0	$ 3,000
Cost of Merchandise Sold	(1,000)	0	(1,000)
Net Income (Loss)	$ 2,000	$ 0	$ 2,000

Although the combined net incomes of the two years is the same in both the cash basis and accrual basis methods of reporting, the latter method reveals more accurately the increase in net wealth in each period. (The outstanding accounts receivable of $3,000 as at December 31, 1996, represents a debt that has increased net wealth.)

Regardless of when cash is actually received, accrual accounting requires the reporting of revenue in the fiscal period in which it is realized. The rationale that debt, as much as cash, represents an increase in wealth is one which is particularly appropriate to any modern economy. At the same time, the accrual method requires that expenses incurred to earn revenue be matched with corresponding revenues earned in the same fiscal period. The important task remains to determine the criteria for selection of a given time when revenue may be considered to be realized, and thus recognized as earned, in a particular fiscal period.

(iii) Tests for Revenue Recognition

Two tests determine the selection of the appropriate time period for revenue recognition. First, the major economic activity concerned with the earning process must have been substantially completed. Second, there should be some objective measurement available. Thus, revenue should only be recognized when major uncertainties in respect of its measurement have been substantially resolved.

When one examines these criteria it is easy to see the rationale for selection of point of sale as the most usual time of revenue recognition. In most merchandising and service businesses, the point of sale represents completion of the major portion of economic activity. In these situations the point of sale is assumed to be the primary economic event and it provides an objective measurement yardstick, namely, sale price.

At the same time a sale generates a flow of assets that converts inventory into accounts receivable. Concurrently with the objective measurement of revenue, related expenses are determinable with reasonable certainty, and any remaining uncertainty is reduced, for pragmatic purposes, to an acceptable level. Finally, the point of sale is clear and determinable. For all these reasons, time of sale is considered to be the point of revenue recognition in most business transactions.

(e) Accounting Adjustments

Let us assume that X Widgets is preparing its accounting statements for its fiscal year ending October 31, 1996. Some special accounting entries are required to implement the system of accruing expenses incurred and revenue earned in order to comply with the matching principle. In the preceding section we saw that entries are made when an invoice is received or rendered even though no cash changes hands. At the year end, some special entries are required to reflect expense or income that has accrued but as to which no transaction is currently taking place. These entries are designed to adjust the "timing" and recognition of expenses and revenue. A further group of entries may also be made to adjust the "measurement" of revenues or expenses.

(i) The "Timing" Adjustments

Some transactions that give rise to normal accounting entries represent expense or revenue for a period that straddles the year-end. Assume the following about X Widgets:

(1) On July 1, 1996 it paid a $900 premium for insurance for one year to June 30, 1997;

(2) Its employees are paid monthly on the 15th of the month and the monthly salary expense is $8,000;

(3) It holds a Canada Savings Bond that pays $1,200 interest each November 30;

(4) It rents an unused part of the land adjacent to its building to a company that parks its trucks there. The annual rent is $1,200, paid each January 31 and July 31 in advance.

To avoid a misstatement of the expenses and revenues for the year ending October 31, 1996, four adjustments are necessary:

(1) A reduction in insurance expense to reflect the fact that 2/3 of the insurance benefit paid for in July still remains;

(2) An increase in salary expense to reflect the one-half month's labour already enjoyed by the business, but which will not be paid for until November 15;

(3) An increase in investment income to reflect the 11/12 of the bond interest accrued to October 31; and

(4) A decrease in rental income to reflect the receipt of three months' rent not yet earned.

The following four adjusting entries will be made:

(1) Insurance expense will be reduced by $600 and a balance sheet asset, "prepaid expense", will be set up;

(2) Salary expense will be increased by $4,000 and a balance sheet liability, "salary expense payable", will be set up;

(3) Investment income will be increased by $1,100 and a balance sheet asset, "accrued bond interest", will be set up; and

(4) Rental income will be reduced by $300 and a balance sheet liability, "rent received in advance", will be set up.

(ii) The "Measurement" Adjustments

It is consistent with accounting conservatism to reflect, at the year-end, that the value of some of the business assets may be overstated and therefore, that business profitability may be exaggerated.

One of the most obvious adjustments to correct for this danger is an allowance for doubtful debts. If X Widgets shows $20,000 in accounts receivable at the year end, it may well be realistic to predict that some of the debts will never be collected. On that assumption, the balance sheet asset, "Accounts Receivable", would be reduced by an amount (referred to as an allowance for doubtful accounts) that would also reduce the current year's income.

A business may face many contingencies and hazards which a careful accountant and a prudent business manager would like to recognize by making similar "allowances" to provide for these potential developments. All of them will have the effect of reducing the statement of current profitability. It may be obvious that the revenue authorities are not prepared to be as gloomy in their forecasting of business hazards, and that the Act will not permit, for the purpose of reporting income for taxation, all of the allowances that the accountant and the business manager might wish.

One adjustment that must be mentioned is the allowance for depreciation. In our earlier hypothetical situation, City Dairy will experience, over five years, a cost of $500,000 in respect of its fleet of trucks. To allocate this cost appropriately in order to match expense and revenue, it may reflect a depreciation expense of $100,000 at the end of each year. This is essentially a "timing" adjustment designed to spread a large cost over the appropriate accounting periods. There is, however, an element of measurement involved: both the assumed useful life of the trucks and their assumed salvage value are based on estimates.

(f) Other Accounting Methods

Some businesses involve such unusual features that the standard accrual basis of accounting fails to achieve an appropriate matching of expenses and revenues. For example, some businesses involve a high volume of sales on terms that call for instalment payments over an extended period of time. Such a business may have significant costs associated with the selling activity but, notionally, a large "profit margin" as judged by the difference between selling price and cost of sales. The incidence of uncollectible accounts in such a business, however, is usually higher than for most businesses. At best, the accounts are not "receivable" on a current basis, but are going to be received over a much longer period than is usual for businesses generally. This kind of business might adopt the instalment method of accounting which does not recognize the accounts receivable in revenue. In effect, the business uses a hybrid accounting system which recognizes all expenses except the cost of goods sold on an accrual basis but recognizes revenue on a cash basis by ignoring its accounts receivable.

Other businesses carry on long-term projects that may involve several years' work to complete. Payment for work completed may be by way of advances or there may be significant delay in receiving payment; and there may be a holdback to satisfy liens or to give the payer a guaranteed opportunity to judge whether the work is satisfactory. Again, because of the difficulty of appropriately matching expenses and revenues, such a business may use a "completed contract" method of accounting.

4. BASIC INCOME TAX ACCOUNTING

References:

ITA:

S. 76	Security for Income Debts
Subs. 125(1)	Small Business Deduction
Subs. 249(1)	Definitions: Taxation Year

BULLETINS, CIRCULARS & RULINGS:

IT-109R2   April 23, 1981   Unpaid Amounts

(a) Accounting Period

The division of a business lifetime into arbitrary segments gives rise to problems of accurate income calculation. A taxpayer's lifetime is similarly segmented into annual periods and this segmentation also gives rise to some special problems.

The Act prescribes for individuals a tax year coincident with the calendar year. Corporations are allowed to choose their own fiscal periods for tax purposes.[81]

---

[81] Subs. 249(1).

Businesses carried on in partnership or as a sole proprietorship, although distinct accounting entities, do not have a separate legal personality and are not taxpayers as such. The income from such businesses must be reported by the partners or the proprietor in their personal capacity. The business may, however, use a fiscal period that is different from the calendar year. For example, X Widgets will calculate its income for its fiscal year ending October 31, 1996; that income will be included in X's income for the taxation year 1996.[82] This means that any income earned in 1996 by X Widgets, after November 1, 1996, need not be reported until X files a 1997 tax return in the spring of 1998.

(b) Accounting Methods

(i) General

While employees must report their income according to the cash basis of accounting, businesses are generally required to use the accrual method. The accrual method is considered particularly appropriate for a trading business.[83] There are, however, other methods of accounting that may be more appropriate for some businesses, particularly businesses with peculiar or unique cash flow patterns.

(ii) Instalment Sales

As noted above, for tax accounting, a variation of the accrual method may be adopted by certain sales businesses. The instalment method of accounting, for example, is considered appropriate for a taxpayer whose business involves instalment sales requiring a small downpayment with the balance due over an extended period.[84]

(iii) Completed Contract

In other circumstances, the completed contract method of accounting has been rejected for tax purposes although it might be an appropriate accounting method. Under this method, the taxpayer defers recognition of all expenses and all revenues in respect of long-term contracts until the contract is complete.[85]

(iv) Cash

Income from office or employment is usually reported on a cash basis. This is confirmed by the use of the words "received" and "enjoyed" in sections 5 and 6 of the Act.

The decision to allow certain taxpayers to use the cash method of accounting is based primarily on a concern for administrative convenience. It would be quite difficult,

---

[82] S. 11.

[83] *Ken Steeves Sales Ltd. v. M.N.R.*, [1955] CTC 47, 55 DTC 1044 (Ex. Ct.).

[84] *M.N.R. v. Publishers Guild of Can. Ltd.*, [1957] CTC 1, 57 DTC 1017 (Ex. Ct.).

[85] *Wilson & Wilson Ltd. v. M.N.R*, [1960] CTC 1, 60 DTC 1018 (Ex. Ct.).

if not impossible, for millions of employees to prepare their annual income tax returns on an accrual basis of accounting. The accrual basis requires at least some rudimentary knowledge of accounting principles (realization, timing, etc.) that is beyond the inclination of most non-accountants.

It is also important to remember that accrual basis statements require more careful auditing by the tax authorities. Since employee income tax returns represent approximately 80 per cent of all tax returns filed, mandatory accrual basis returns from all taxpayers would place an intolerable burden on Revenue Canada's resources. The incremental auditing and accounting fees incurred by both taxpayers and Revenue Canada as a result of accrual accounting cannot be justified by the marginal improvement in the accuracy of annual net income calculations.

Having said that, however, it is important to note that the requirement of cash accounting for employees does allow for some modest amount of tax planning. Employees can, within limits, reduce their immediate tax liabilities by accelerating payment of their expenses and delaying receipt of their income.

(v) Accrual

In contrast with the requirement of cash basis accounting for employment income, business and property income is usually required to be reported on an accrual basis. The Act does not specifically stipulate a particular method for calculating business or property income. Section 9 says only that a taxpayer's income from a business or property is his or her *profit* therefrom. The term "profit", however, has been judicially interpreted to mean profit calculated in accordance with commercial practice, and commercial practice favours accrual accounting for most businesses. Hence, the accrual method is mandated indirectly through the requirement to adhere to generally accepted accounting principles.

(vi) Modified Accrual

There are certain specific departures from the usual rule that business and property income is calculated in accordance with the rules of accrual accounting. First, an important exception is made in the case of farmers and fishers; these two categories of taxpayers are specifically authorized to use the cash basis method of accounting.[86] The theoretical justification for this particular variation is that, in most circumstances, the distortion of net income when using the cash basis method is minimal and, hence, justifiable in that it is easier for taxpayers to maintain cash basis books of account.

More pragmatically, one recognizes that it would be politically inconvenient to withdraw a tax concession that has been made available to farmers for so long. If anything, the pull is in the opposite direction: Until 1980 only farmers could use the cash basis of accounting; in that year the cash basis of accounting was extended to

---

[86] S. 28.

fishers, a practice that had been administratively tolerated by Revenue Canada for many years.

A second exception from the accrual basis of accounting is found in the "modified accrual method" applicable to professionals. Professionals, like their business counterparts, are required to calculate income on an accrual basis. Professionals can, however, elect to exclude their work-in-progress in calculating net income for tax purposes.[87]

(vii) Holdbacks

Reference:

BULLETINS, CIRCULARS & RULINGS:

IT-92R2   December 29, 1983   Income of Contractors

We have already stated that, in applying the accrual basis of accounting, the time of sale of goods and services is usually the most convenient time to recognize revenue. The time of sale is not, however, the only time for revenue recognition. Certain businesses may deviate from the norm and recognize revenue at some other time. For example, contractors (persons engaged in the construction of buildings, roads, dams, bridges and similar structures) can, by administrative grace, defer recognition of their income until such time as "holdback payments" become *legally* receivable. This rule varies from the usual accrual accounting test which does not use legal entitlement as the determining criterion for recognizing revenue. Contractors may, however, also accelerate the recognition of profit by bringing into income amounts that may not be legally receivable by virtue of a mechanics' lien or similar statute.

(viii) Net Worth

To this point, we have discussed the more conventional methods of income determination: cash basis, accrual accounting and modified accrual. There remains one other technique for calculating income which can be particularly painful to a taxpayer and particularly useful to Revenue Canada. This technique is the "net worth" method of calculating income.

A net worth assessment is usually issued by Revenue Canada when a taxpayer does not file a return or, in some cases, when Revenue does not accept the taxpayer's figures.[88] The theoretical principle underlying the calculation of income using the net worth basis is simple: Income is equal to the difference between a taxpayer's wealth at the beginning and at the end of a year, plus any amount consumed by the taxpayer during the year. We saw in Chapter IV "What is Income" that this principle derives from the Haig-Simons definition of income.

---

[87] Para. 34(*a*).

[88] Subs. 152(7).

Algebraically, the principle is stated as follows:

$$\text{Income} = (\text{WE} - \text{WB}) + \text{C}$$

where,

WE = Wealth at end of year,
WB = Wealth at beginning of year, and
C = Consumption

Note, however, that, unlike the Haig-Simons formulation of income, the formula does not take into account any accrued but unrealized gains in the value of property. For example, assume that a taxpayer started out a year owning $100,000 in property, such as a house, car, clothing, furniture, cash, etc. At the end of the year it is estimated that the taxpayer owns $105,000 in property. It is also estimated that the taxpayer spent $45,000 during the year on food, clothing, mortgage payments, vacations, children's education, etc. If the taxpayer has not engaged in any borrowing or repayment of loans, his or her net income for the year is $50,000, i.e., ($105,000 – $100,000) + $45,000. If in fact, the taxpayer borrowed $8,000 during the year, his or her wealth at the end of the year is only $97,000 and his or her income for the year would be only $42,000.

Notice the resemblance between the net worth basis of determining income and the Haig-Simons concept of income.[89] When a taxpayer does not, or cannot, use conventional accounting records to calculate her or his income and Revenue Canada does not have any other way of assessing the delinquent taxpayer's income, the system must rely on fundamental concepts: Income is the money value of the net accretion of economic power between two points of time.

5. GENERALLY ACCEPTED ACCOUNTING PRINCIPLES

References:

ITA:

S. 20   Deductions in Computing Business or Property Income

BULLETINS, CIRCULARS & RULINGS:

IT-405   January 23, 1978   Inadequate Considerations — Acquisitions and Dispositions

(a) General

Income from business or property is determined by reference to subsection 9(1):

Subject to this Part, a taxpayer's income from a taxation year from a business or property is his profit therefrom for the year.

---

[89] See Chapter IV "What is Income?".

At one time there was a tentative proposal to incorporate into the Act a general statement to the effect that business profits should be calculated according to generally accepted accounting principles ("GAAP"). The proposal was never implemented because of the difficulty in establishing just what GAAP means in all cases. The absence of a statutory provision requiring the computation of profits according to GAAP did not, however, inhibit the development of a similar doctrine in case law. Indeed, if anything, we have arrived at virtually the same result through judicial decisions.

(b) Section 9

Although there may be disagreement among accountants concerning the best practice in respect of certain matters, it is now well established that section 9 imports into the Act, *as a starting point,* the standard accounting methods used in the business world. Thorson P. dealt with this matter in *Imp. Oil v. M.N.R.,*[90] in *Daley v. M.N.R.*[91] and in *Royal Trust Co. v. M.N.R.*[92] In this last case, dealing with the deductibility of a claimed expenditure, he said:[93]

> . . . it may be stated categorically that . . . the first matter to be determined . . . is whether it was made or incurred by the taxpayer in accordance with the ordinary principles of commercial trading or well accepted principles of business practice.

The determination of what constitutes "net profit" is a question of law and not a matter of generally accepted accounting principles.[94] Although a court may look at the treatment of particular items by reference to GAAP, they are at best only representative of the principles used for preparing financial statements. To be sure, GAAP may well be influential in determining what is deductible, but they are not the operative *legal* criteria. The legal test rests upon well accepted principles of business practice and commercial trading.

---

[90] *Imperial Oil v. M.N.R.*, [1947] CTC 353, 3 DTC 1090 (Ex. Ct.).

[91] *Daley v. M.N.R.*, [1950] CTC 254, 4 DTC 877 (Ex. Ct.).

[92] *Royal Trust Co. v. M.N.R.*, [1957] CTC 32, 57 DTC 1055 (Ex. Ct.); see also *The Queen v. Metropolitan Properties Ltd.*, [1985] 1 CTC 169, 85 DTC 5128 (F.C.T.D.) (GAAP normal rule for measuring income).

[93] *Royal Trust Co. v. M.N.R.*, *ante*, [1957] CTC at 42, 57 D.T.C. 1060 (Ex. Ct.).

[94] *Symes v. Canada*, [1994] 2 CTC 40, 94 DTC 6001 (S.C.C.); *Neonex International Ltd. v. The Queen*, [1978] CTC 485, 78 DTC 6339 (F.C.A.).

Subsection 9(1) only represents a starting point, however, and normal accounting practices for tax purposes may be overborne by specific statutory provisions, judicial precedent, or commercial practice.[95]

(c) Tax Profits

What is the relationship between accounting profit and profit as determined for income tax purposes? For tax purposes, the starting point requires an examination of generally accepted commercial practice: Is a particular expenditure deductible in computing income according to the rules of general commercial and accounting practice? Or is a particular receipt included in computing income according to commercial rules? Once these preliminary questions are answered, other factors may come into play in determining the appropriate tax treatment.

Take depreciation as an example.[96] The general commercial and accounting rule is that, in calculating net income, a reasonable amount of depreciation can be deducted from revenues. Indeed, commercial practice recognizes many different methods of calculating depreciation (for example, straight-line, declining balance, sum of the years, etc.). Provided that the method is acceptable and the amount is reasonable, depreciation expense is a deductible expense in determining net income for financial statement purposes.

The Act, however, *specifically* prohibits a deduction for depreciation[97] and, therefore, such an expense cannot be taken into account in calculating net income for tax purposes. In lieu of depreciation, the Act allows a deduction for capital cost allowance ("CCA") in an amount which may or may not be related to accounting depreciation. Thus, tax profits and accounting income may be substantially different.

---

[95] See generally: *Associated Investors of Canada Ltd. v. M.N.R.*, [1967] CTC 138, 67 DTC 5096 (Ex Ct.); *Neonex International Ltd. v. The Queen*, [1978] CTC 485, 78 DTC 6339 (F.C.A.); *The Queen v. Metropolitan Properties Co. Ltd.*, [1985] 1 CTC 169, 85 DTC 5128 (F.C.T.D.); *MHL Holdings Ltd. v. The Queen*, [1988] 2 CTC 42, 88 DTC 6292 (F.C.T.D.); *Coppley Noyes & Randall Ltd. v. The Queen*, [1991] 1 CTC 541, 91 DTC 5291 (F.C.T.D.); and *West Kootenay Power & Light Co. v. The Queen*, [1992] 1 CTC 15, 92 DTC 6023 (F.C.A.).

[96] Numerous other examples may be found in subdivision b of Division B, Part I of the Act.

[97] Para. 18(1)(*b*).

Example VI.1

A business, with only one fixed Class 8 asset (an antique desk and chair) has a net income of $10,000 in the year 1996. This income is net of depreciation expense in the amount of $200. The oak Louis XIV desk and chair were purchased in 1996 at a cost of $20,000 and it is estimated that the two pieces will functionally endure for another 100 years. It is also anticipated that the market value of the desk and chair will increase at a rate of approximately 15 per cent per year. Ignoring all other factors, for income tax purposes the business will have a net income of $8,200 calculated as follows:

Net income per financial statements	$ 10,000
Add: non-deductible depreciation expense	
(para. 18(1)(*b*))	200
	$ 10,200
Less: Capital cost allowance allowed*	(2,000)
Net income for tax purposes	$ 8,200

*$20,000 x 20% x ½; See Chapter VIII "Business and Property Income: Deductions" for calculation of CCA and first year, half rate rule.

Thus, in this example, net income for tax purposes is $1,800 lower than net income reported for other financial purposes because the CCA allowed for tax is more generous than the equivalent depreciation for financial statements.

Example VI.1 involves at least four steps in working logically through the Act.

Step 1: By subsection 9(1) business income is the "profit" from the business; thus, depreciation should be taken into account according to normal commercial practice;

Step 2: Paragraph 18(1)(*b*), however, denies a deduction for "an allowance in respect of depreciation...except as expressly permitted...";

Step 3: Para. 20(1)(*a*) authorizes deduction of a capital cost allowance "as is allowed by regulation"; and

Step 4: Reg. 1100(1)(*a*)(viii), read together with Schedule II to the Regulations, authorizes a capital cost allowance of 20 per cent, with only one-half permitted in the year the asset is acquired.

(d) Statutory Deviations

The Act deviates from accounting principles in many areas. Three important statutory deviations from standard accounting practice are discussed below.

(i) Reserves and Allowances

Accountants sometimes prefer to anticipate certain contingencies by setting up an allowance that has the effect of reducing income in the current period. The Act seriously inhibits this conservative and quite normal accounting practice by denying, as a deduction, "an amount transferred or credited to a reserve, contingent account or sinking fund except as expressly permitted by this Part".[98] Instead, the Act sets out a specific and rigid regime in respect of accounting for reserves.[99] Thus, there can be a significant difference between accounting reserves and tax reserves.

(ii) Depreciation

At one time, depreciation expense was recognized as a legitimate deduction for tax purposes, subject to showing a sound accounting basis for the deduction. As we have noted, it is indisputable that many capital assets depreciate with use, but the amount of loss in value and the rate at which it occurs are frequently quite speculative. To control the speculations, and to minimize disputes, the Act details a Capital Cost Allowance (CCA) system which imposes limits on the amount of depreciation deductible in calculating income for tax purposes.

Although, in general, CCA rates are designed to be reasonably realistic, there is no attempt to guarantee that the rates for tax purposes conform to depreciation recognized for accounting purposes. The rates are the same for all taxpayers although their depreciation experience may differ greatly. Further, the CCA system is also used to achieve other socio-economic objectives. It may, for example, be used to stimulate economic activity in depressed regions of the country. Thus, income for tax purposes can differ quite significantly from income reported to shareholders or creditors, and there is nothing unusual or improper in this.

(iii) Inventory

A major component of the expenses of some businesses, and thus a major factor in determining income, is the cost of goods sold. To calculate the cost of goods sold, a business must establish its inventory of goods on hand at the year-end, and determine its value. There are a number of accounting approaches to inventory valuation. One method that is commonly used by accountants for financial statement purposes, LIFO, has been judicially rejected for tax purposes as being inappropriate.[100] Here once again, the use of one method for accounting and another for tax purposes can cause a significant difference in the final net income figure.

---

[98] Para. 18(1)(e).

[99] See Chapter VIII "Business and Property Income: Deductions".

[100] M.N.R. v. Anaconda Amer. Brass Ltd., [1955] CTC 311, 55 DTC 1220 (P.C.).

6. REALIZATION AND RECOGNITION OF INCOME

References:

REGULATIONS:

1100(1)   Capital Cost Allowance — Deductions Allowed

BULLETINS, CIRCULARS & RULINGS:

IT-128R   May 21, 1985   Capital Cost Allowance — Depreciable Property

IT-182   October 28, 1974   Compensation for Loss of Business Income, or of Property Used in a Business

There are many problems relating to realization and the appropriate time to recognize income for tax purposes. Some of these problems are simply difficulties inherent in the nature of the transaction, but others arise from attempts by taxpayers to apply the realization concept to their best advantage.

Stock options are an example of the inherent difficulty in correctly applying the concepts of realization and revenue recognition in tax law. Suppose that ABC Ltd. gives employee E an option to buy 1,000 shares of its stock at a price of $10/share, exercisable at any time within three years. The option is given in year 1 at a time when the stock is trading publicly at $12/share. E exercises the option in year 2 when the stock is trading at $15/share. In year 3, E sells the stock for $16/share.

Assuming that the transaction gives rise to income in E's hands, two questions arise: (1) How much income? (2) In what year? It is arguable that E should be treated as having received $2,000 in year 1; the company conferred on E, in that year, a benefit in the form of an opportunity to buy for $10,000 what a stranger would pay $12,000 to acquire. It is also arguable, however, that E's benefit is purely potential; if the stock drops below $10 and stays down for three years the option will be worthless.

It could be said that the benefit was received in year 2 when E actually bought the stock at $5,000 below its market value. Our discussion of the conventional approach to paper gains might suggest, however, as a third alternative, that E should not recognize any income until the shares are sold or otherwise parted with. If the shares rise or fall in value before E parts with them, the actual benefit to E will be greater or less, accordingly. Using this reasoning, we would tax E in year 3 on income of $6,000.

The Act provides an arbitrary, but reasonable, solution to the two problems of timing and quantification. Subsection 7(1) stipulates that E's income will be recognized in the year in which she or he exercises the option or disposes of it. The amount of income is either the difference between the option price and the current value of the shares or the amount received on disposition of the option.[101] Thus, in our hypothetical situation, E would recognize $5,000 of income in year 2. This solution really involves identifying the option as the source of E's gain. It is consistent with our basic discussion of realization to say that E's gain is only a paper gain so long as E holds the option, but becomes a real gain when she or he parts with the option by exercising it or disposing of it to someone else.

7. CONFORMITY OF ACCOUNTING METHODS

A taxpayer's income for a taxation year from a business or property is the profit therefrom for the year.[102]

(a) Use of GAAP

The term "profit" means *net* profit. In the absence of any specific proscription, profit is determined according to commercial and generally accepted accounting principles. Hence, absent an express or implicit statutory or judicial proscription against the use of a particular accounting method, a taxpayer is entitled to determine income for tax purposes according to any appropriate accounting method. Thorson P. explained the rule in *Publishers Guild of Canada Ltd.*:[103]

> If the law does not prohibit the use of a particular system of accounting then the opinion of accountancy experts that it is an accepted system and is appropriate to the taxpayer's business and most nearly accurately reflects his income position should prevail with the Court if the reasons for the opinion commend themselves to it.

---

[101] Actually, subs. 7(1) is somewhat more complex to provide against artificial dealings through non-arm's length transactions. Further, subs. 7(1.1) provides for different treatment in the case of Canadian-controlled private corporations. See Chapter V "Income From an Office or Employment" under the heading "(g) Stock Option Plans".

[102] Subs. 9(1).

[103] *Publishers Guild of Canada v. M.N.R.*, 54 DTC 1017 at 1026 (Ex. Ct.); see also *The Queen v. Nomad Sand and Gravel Limited*, [1991] 1 CTC 60, 91 DTC 5032 at 5034-5035 (F.C.A.); *Assoc. Investors of Can. Ltd. v. M.N.R.*, [1967] CTC 138, 67 DTC 5096 at 5098-99 (Ex. Ct.); *Maritime Telegraph & Telephone Co. v. The Queen*, [1991] 1 CTC 28, 91 DTC 5038 at 5039 (F.C.T.D.), affirmed [1992] 1 CTC 264, 92 DTC 6191 (F.C.A.).

Similarly, in *Silverman:*[104]

> ... the statute does not define what is to be taken as the profit from a business, nor does it describe how or by what method such profit is to be computed, though it does contain provisions to which, for income tax purposes, any method is subject . . . the method must be one which accurately reflects the result of the year's operation, and where two different methods, either of which may be acceptable for business purposes, differ in their results, for income tax purposes the appropriate method is that which most accurately shows the profit from the year's operations.

(b) Conformity of Methods

A taxpayer can use one generally accepted accounting method for financial statement purposes and another for income tax purposes. In the absence of any statutory requirement that a taxpayer use the same method of accounting to calculate income both for tax and financial statement purposes, a taxpayer can select the most appropriate method of accounting for tax purposes.

The purpose for which income is calculated determines the appropriate method of accounting. An accounting method which is suitable for a particular purpose is not necessarily the appropriate measure of income for tax purposes.[105]

What is appropriate for tax purposes? The general rule is to apply that principle or method which provides the proper picture of net income. In MacGuigan J.'s words:[106]

> ... it would be undesirable to establish an absolute requirement that there must always be conformity between financial statements and tax returns and I am satisfied that the cases do not do so. *The approved principle* is that whichever method presents the "truer picture" of a taxpayer's revenue, which more fairly and accurately portrays income, and which "matches" revenue and expenditure, if one method does, is the one that must be followed. [Emphasis added.]

---

[104] *Silverman v. M.N.R.*, [1960] CTC 262 at 266, 60 DTC 1212 at 1214; see also, *Bank of Nova Scotia v. The Queen*, [1980] CTC 57 at 62, 80 DTC 6009 at 6013:

> . . . generally recognized accounting and commercial principles and practices are to be applied to all matters of commercial and taxation accounting unless there is something in the taxing statute which precludes them from coming into play. The legislator, when dealing with financial and commercial matters in any enactment, including of course a taxing statute, is to be presumed at law to be aware of the general financial and commercial principles which are relevant to the subject-matter covered by the legislation. The Act pertains to business and financial matters and is addressed to the general public. It follows that where no particular mention is made as to any variation from common ordinary practice or where the attainment of the objects of the legislation does not necessarily require such variation, then common practice and generally recognized accounting and commercial principles and terminology must be deemed to apply.

[105] *Friedberg v. M.N.R.*, [1993] 2 CTC 306, 93 DTC 5507 (S.C.C.).

[106] *West Kootenay Power & Light Co. v. The Queen*, [1992] 1 CTC 15 at 22, 92 DTC 6023 at 6028 (F.C.A.). See also: *Maritime Telegraph and Telephone Company v. The Queen*, [1992] 1 CTC 264, 92 DTC 6191 (F.C.A.) ("earned method" of reporting income for accounting and tax purposes produced "truer picture" of taxpayer's income).

(c) A "Truer Picture" of Income?

It is not always easy to apply the rule that a taxpayer may adopt whichever accounting method presents the "truer picture" of revenues and expenses. There are cases where a particular accounting principle presents a "truer picture" for income statement purposes at the expense of some accuracy or relevance in the balance sheet. In other cases, the adoption of a particular accounting method more accurately summarizes a taxpayer's closing balances while sacrificing accuracy on the income statement. *West Kootenay*[107] rightly emphasized a proper matching of revenues and expenses and accuracy of the net income figure for tax purposes.

A classic example of the conflict between income statement and balance sheet values is seen in accounting for inventory values.

Under the last-in, first-out ("LIFO") method of inventory accounting, the cost of goods most recently purchased or acquired is the cost that is assigned to the cost of goods sold. Hence, the inventory on hand at the end of an accounting period is valued at the cost that was attributed to the inventory at the beginning of the period (first-in, still here). Any increases in quantity during a period are valued at the cost prevailing during the time the accumulations are deemed to have occurred. Any decreases in quantities are considered to have first reduced the most recent accumulations.[108]

Under the first-in, first-out ("FIFO") method, the process is reversed: The cost of goods first acquired is assigned to the first goods sold. The closing inventory comprises the cost of the most recent purchases (last-in, still here).

The use of the FIFO method of accounting for the flow of inventory costs tends to overstate net income during inflationary periods and more accurately reflect the current value of closing inventory on the balance sheet. In contrast, the LIFO method more realistically measures "real" net income, while sacrificing some accuracy in year-end balance sheet values.

Most accountants and business people argue that the use of LIFO for inventory accounting during inflationary periods results in a more meaningful and "truer picture" of business income during inflationary periods. The Privy Council in *Anaconda Brass*,[109] however, rejected the use of the LIFO method of inventory valuation for tax purposes on the basis that it was proscribed by the Act. Their Lordships were concerned that the method would permit the creation of hidden reserves:[110]

> . . . the evidence of expert witnesses, that the LIFO method is generally acceptable, and in this case the most appropriate, method of accountancy, is not conclusive of the question that the Court has to decide.

---

[107] *West Kootenay Power & Light Co. v. The Queen, ante.*

[108] See *CICA Handbook* §3030.07.

[109] *M.N.R. v. Anaconda Amer. Brass Ltd.*, [1955] CTC 311, 55 D.T.C. 1220 (P.C.).

[110] *M.N.R. v. Anaconda Amer. Brass Ltd.*, [1955] CTC at 321, 55 DTC at 1225.

> That may be found as a fact by the Exchequer Court and affirmed by the Supreme Court. The question remains whether it conforms to the prescription of the Income Tax Act. As already indicated, in their Lordships' opinion it does not.

The accounting principle for selecting the proper method of inventory valuation is clear: The most suitable method for determining cost is that which results in charging against operations those costs that most fairly match the sales revenue for the period. The *CICA Handbook* states the principle as follows:[111]

> The method selected for determining cost should be one which results in the fairest matching of costs against revenues regardless of whether or not the method corresponds to the physical flow of goods.

Anaconda Brass was an unfortunate decision based upon a misunderstanding of accounting methods. The decision rests on two notions: (1) The physical flow of inventory determines values; and (2) The potential for creation of "hidden" reserves. Both premises are fundamentally flawed. The determination of cost does not depend upon the physical flow of goods but on the fairest matching of revenues and expenses. The "fairest" matching of costs against revenues is, presumably, also the method which presents the "truer picture" of income for tax purposes. Thus, the question is: Which method of accounting produces the best and fairest picture of annual profits? Equally, the hidden reserve argument ignores the primary purpose served by the method, namely, the determination of a fair measure of an enterprise's annual income.

8. NON-ARM'S LENGTH TRANSACTIONS

References:

ITA:

S. 74.1   Transfers and Loans to Spouses and Minors

S. 251   Arm's Length

The Act contains stringent anti-avoidance rules to govern transfers of property between persons who do not deal with each other at arm's length. The purpose of these rules is to discourage taxpayers who have close social, family, or economic relationships with each other from artificially avoiding tax through the manipulation of transaction values.

Related persons are deemed not to deal with each other at arm's length.[112]

---

[111] See *CICA Handbook* §3030 and the virtually identical language of *AICPA*, ARB 43, Ch. 4.

[112] S. 251.

It is a question of fact whether unrelated persons deal with each other at arm's length. Parties are not considered to be dealing with each other at arm's length if one person dictates the terms of the bargain on both sides of a transaction.[113]

The anti-avoidance rules are as follows:[114]

- Where, in a non-arm's length transaction, a purchaser acquires anything for a price in *excess* of its fair market value, he is deemed to have acquired the property at its fair market value. Consequently, notwithstanding that he actually paid a price higher than fair market value, the purchaser is *deemed* to acquire the property at a cost equal to fair market value.

Example VI.2

A taxpayer buys land from his mother at a cost of $70,000 when, in fact, the land has a fair market value of $50,000 (this may happen if the mother deliberately wants to trigger a higher capital gain to offset unused capital losses). The son is deemed to have acquired the land at a cost of $50,000. The mother calculates her gain on the basis of her *actual* proceeds of $70,000.

- Where, in a non-arm's length transaction, a vendor has disposed of anything at *less* than its fair market value, the vendor is deemed to have received proceeds equal to fair market value. Thus, notwithstanding that she actually received a lower price, the vendor is taxed on the basis of her deemed proceeds.

Example VI.3

A taxpayer sells land that has a fair market value of $50,000 to his daughter for $40,000. Paragraph 69(1)(*b*) *deems* the father to have received $50,000. His daughter, however, acquires the property for her *actual* cost of $40,000, leaving her with the potential of a larger gain when she sells the property.

The overall effect of these rules is that taxpayers can be liable to double taxation in non-arm's length transactions. Section 69 can have a punitive effect: It is structured

---

[113] *Swiss Bank Corp. v. M.N.R.*, [1971] CTC 427, 71 DTC 5235, affirmed [1972] CTC 614, 72 DTC 6470 (parties acted in concert, exerting considerable influence together; money transactions merely moved funds from one pocket to another); *Millward v. The Queen*, [1986] 2 CTC 423, 86 DTC 6538 (F.C.T.D.) (members of law firm who dealt with each other at less than commercial rates of interest not at arm's length); *Noranda Mines Ltd. v. M.N.R.*, [1987] 2 CTC 2089, 87 DTC 379 (T.C.C.) (existence of arm's length relationship excluded where one party has *de facto* control over both parties).

[114] S. 69.

to discourage non-arm's length parties from dealing with each other at prices other than fair market value.

Example VI.4

Assume:
  An individual owns a property to which the following applies:

Cost	$ 1,000
FMV	$ 5,000

She sells the property to her son for $4,000.

Then:
  Tax consequences to mother:

Deemed proceeds of sale	$ 5,000
Cost	(1,000)
Gain	$ 4,000

If the son sells the property at its fair market value of $5,000, he also realizes a gain of $1,000:

Actual proceeds of sale	$ 5,000
Actual cost of property	(4,000)
Gain	$ 1,000
Total gain:	
Realized by mother	$ 4,000
Realized by son	$ 1,000
	$ 5,000

Thus, an asset with an accrued gain of $4,000 triggers an actual gain of $5,000. The $1,000 that is exposed to double taxation represents the shortfall between the fair market value of the property ($5,000) and the price at which it is sold ($4,000).

---

9. TIMING OF INCOME

References:

ITA:

S. 28	Farming or Fishing
S. 34	Professional Business
S. 78	Unpaid Amounts

BULLETINS, CIRCULARS & RULINGS:

IT-129R	November 7, 1986	Lawyers' Trust Accounts and Disbursements
IT-433R	June 4, 1993	Farming or Fishing — Use of Cash Method

IT-457R   July 15, 1988   Election by Professionals to Exclude Work-In-
                                    Progress from Income

(a) General

We saw earlier that employment income is generally taxed on a cash basis. In contrast, with a few important exceptions, business and property income are normally calculated on an accrual basis. Thus, generally speaking, income from business and property are recognized for tax purposes when services are performed or goods are sold, rather than when payment for the goods or services is actually received. In other words, although a taxpayer may have to wait for some time to receive payment for goods sold or services rendered, he or she will be taxed on income in the year in which it is earned.

The accrual method of accounting is generally considered to be the appropriate method of determining profit in most circumstances. It warrants emphasis, however, that this is *not* the only acceptable method for tax purposes. Since subsection 9(1) is silent on the method of accounting to be used to calculate "profit", a taxpayer is free to use generally accepted accounting principles appropriate to his or her circumstances, provided that use of the method is not prohibited by the Act or by judicial precedent.[115]

(b) Payments in Advance

The accrual method is modified by the Act for certain payments. For example, payments received in advance of rendering a service or sale of goods are included in income even though the payments represent unearned amounts which would usually be excluded from income for accounting purposes. Under accounting principles, unearned revenue is considered a liability. For tax purposes, unearned revenue is included in income in the year the payment is received, rather than when the revenue is earned. A taxpayer may, however, claim a reserve for goods and services to be delivered in the future.[116]

(c) Receivables

A taxpayer is to include in income all amounts *receivable* by him or her in respect of property sold or services rendered in the course of business carried out during the year.[117]

---

[115] *Oxford Shopping Centres Ltd. v. The Queen*, [1980] CTC 7, 79 DTC 5458; affirmed [1981] CTC 128, 81 DTC 5065 (F.C.A.).

[116] Paras. 12(1)(*a*) and 20(1)(*m*).

[117] Para. 12(1)(*b*).

"Receivable" means that the taxpayer has a clearly established *legal right* to enforce payment at the particular time under consideration:[118]

> In the absence of a statutory definition to the contrary, I think it is not enough that the so-called recipient have a precarious right to receive the amount in question, but he must have a clearly legal, though not necessarily immediate, right to receive it.

For example, in the construction industry, it is usual practice, when work is performed under a contract extending over a lengthy period of time, for interim payments to be made to the contractor. These payments, which are based on progress reports, are usually subject to a percentage holdback to ensure satisfactory completion of the project. In these circumstances, holdbacks need not be brought into income as "receivables" until such time as the architect or engineer has issued a final certificate approving the completion of the project.[119]

An amount is deemed to be receivable on the earlier of the day the account is actually rendered and the day on which it *would have been* rendered had there been "no undue delay" in rendering the account.

(d) Professionals

(i) Modified Accrual

The rules in respect of the computation of income of certain professionals (accountants, dentists, lawyers, medical doctors, veterinarians and chiropractors) vary somewhat from the normal accrual basis of accounting. These professional businesses may report income on a so-called modified accrual basis. These professionals may elect to exclude work in progress in the computation of income.[120] On the sale of the professional business, any work in progress previously excluded is brought into the income of the vendor.[121]

(ii) Work in Progress

Generally speaking, if a professional elects to exclude work in progress in the computation of income, his or her income is computed on the basis of fees billed, subject to any adjustment for undue delay in billing. The election is binding on the taxpayer for subsequent years unless it is revoked with the consent of the Minister.[122]

---

[118] *M.N.R. v. Colford (J.) Contr. Co.*, [1960] CTC 178 at 187, 60 DTC 1131 at 1135; affirmed without written reasons [1962] CTC 546, 62 DTC 133 (S.C.C.).

[119] *M.N.R. v. Colford (J.) Contr. Co.*, [1962] CTC 546, 62 DTC 1338 (S.C.C.).

[120] Para. 34(*a*).

[121] Para. 10(5)(*a*) and s. 23.

[122] Para. 34(*b*); see IT-457R, "Election by Professionals to Exclude Work-In-Progress from Income" (July 15, 1988).

(iii) Advance Payments

Amounts received in advance of performance of services are included in income unless the funds are deposited in a segregated trust account.[123] For example, a lawyer who obtains a retainer which must be returned to the client in the event of non-performance of services may exclude the retainer from income if the funds are deposited in a trust account.[124] The taxpayer may, however, claim a deduction in respect of services that will have to be rendered after the end of the year.[125]

(e) Farmers and Fishers

Income from a farming or fishing *business* may be calculated on a cash basis. Thus, the income of a taxpayer from a farming or fishing business is computed by aggregating amounts *received* in the year and deducting therefrom amounts *paid* in the year.

Accounts receivable are included in income only when they are disposed of by the taxpayer.[126]

10. DAMAGES

Reference:

BULLETINS, CIRCULARS & RULINGS:

IT-365R2   May 8, 1987   Damages, Settlements and Similar Receipts

The taxation of damages depends upon the nature of the legal right which gives rise to the payment. The test is: On what account are the damages paid? Damages paid in lieu of taxable receipts are taxable; payments in lieu of non-taxable receipts are not taxable. The difficulty is in determining which receipts are taxable and which are not. As the Court said in *London & Thames Haven Oil Wharves Ltd. v. Attwooll:*[127]

> Judges have from time to time been careful to say that no clear and comprehensive rule can be formulated, and no clear line of demarcation can be drawn, by reference to which it can be determined in every case whether the sum received should be regarded as a capital receipt or as a revenue receipt to be taken into account in arriving at the profit or gains of the recipient's trade. Each case must be considered on its own facts.

---

[123] Para. 12(1)(*a*).

[124] IT-129R, "Lawyers' Trust Accounts and Disbursements" (November 7, 1986).

[125] Para. 20(1)(*m*).

[126] S. 28.

[127] *London & Thames Haven Oil Wharves Ltd. v. Attwooll*, [1966] 3 All ER 145 at 149; reversed [1967] 2 All ER 124 (C.A.).

(a) Breach of Contract

(i) Nature of Claim

Damages for breach of contract are generally arrived at on the principle of compensation with a view to restoring the plaintiff to the financial position she or he would have enjoyed had the defendant performed the contract.[128] The plaintiff is entitled to the economic value of the bargain or "expectation" interest. Exemplary or punitive damages are rarely awarded in contract cases.[129]

(ii) The Surrogatum Principle

Damages paid in lieu of receipts which would otherwise have been taxable to the taxpayer are taxable as income. Diplock L.J. stated the general principle as follows:[130]

> Where, pursuant to a legal right, a trader receives from another person, compensation for the trader's failure to receive a sum of money which, if it had been received, would have been credited to the amount of profits (if any) arising in any year from the trade carried on by him at the time when the compensation is so received, the compensation is to be treated for income tax purposes in the same way as that sum of money would have been treated if it had been received instead of the compensation. The rule is applicable whatever the source of the legal right of the trader to recover the compensation. It may arise [1] from a primary obligation under a contract, such as a contract of insurance; [2] from a secondary obligation arising out of non-performance of a contract, such as a right to damages, either liquidated, as under the demurrage clause in a charter party, or unliquidated; [3] from an obligation to pay damages for tort . . .; [4] from a statutory obligation; [5] or in any other way in which legal obligations arise.

---

[128] *Livingstone v. Rawyards Coal Co.* (1880), 5 App. Cas. 25 at 39, *per* Lord Blackburn (H.L.) (damages represent "that sum of money which will put the party who has been injured, or who has suffered, in the same position as he would have been in if he had not sustained the wrong for which he is now getting his compensation or reparation"); see Street, *Principles of the Law of Damages* (London: Sweet & Maxwell, 1962), at 3; *Yetton v. Eastwoods Froy Ltd.*, [1967] 1 WLR 104 at 115, *per* Blain J.; Ogus, *The Law of Damages* (London: Butterworths, 1973), at 17-21, 283-8; *Admiralty Commrs. v. S.S. Susquehanna*, [1926] AC 655 at 661 (H.L.) (loss to damaged ship owners not constituting lost profits from mercantile charter where ship would not have been chartered); *Victoria Laundry (Windsor) Ltd. v. Newman Indust. Ltd.*, [1949] 2 KB 528 at 539, *per* Asquith L.J. (C.A.) (damages for late delivery of boiler deemed foreseeable business losses); *Robinson v. Harman* (1848), 1 Ex. 850 at 855, 154 ER 363 at 365, *per* Parke B. (Ex. Ct.) (tenant knew lessee did not have title to property leased; damages assessed at entire amount of loss notwithstanding); *Koufos v. C. Czarnikow Ltd.*, [1969] 1 AC 350 at 400, *per* Lord Morris (H.L.) (sugar cargo depreciated as market price dropped while ship·dallying *en route*; shipowner expected to have contemplated such result); *British Westinghouse Electric Mfg. Co. v. Underground Electric Rys. Co. of London*, [1912] AC 673 at 689, *per* Viscount Haldane L.C. (H.L.) (measure of damages where defective turbines replaced and replacement turbines achieved greater efficiency than the ones in question).

[129] *Addis v. Gramophone Co.*, [1909] AC 488 (H.L.) (although discredited by wrongful dismissal, employee not able to claim compensation for injured feelings or lack of notice); *Dobson v. Winton & Robbins Ltd.* (1959), 20 DLR (2d) 164 (S.C.C.) (vendor suing on contract of sale of land entitled to specific performance or damages equal to decrease in price eventually received plus interest). See, however: *Jarvis v. Swan Tours Ltd.*, [1973] 1 QB 233 (C.A.) (damages awarded against travel agent when plaintiff's holiday failing to meet advertised description).

[130] *London & Thames Haven Oil Wharves Ltd. v. Attwooll*, [1967] 2 All ER 124 at 134 (C.A.). See also: *Schwartz v. Canada*, [1994] 2 CTC 99, 94 DTC 6249 (F.C.A.) on appeal to S.C.C. (*surrogatum* principle also applies to employment contracts, whether anticipatory or otherwise).

The characterization of damages as taxable income or non-taxable capital receipts depends upon the nature of the legal right adjudicated or settled. It does not depend upon the method by which the damages are calculated.

(iii) Nature of Interest Settled

Since damages represent compensation equal to the economic value of the underlying bargain, they are usually computed by reference to the profit lost through non-performance of the contract. The mere fact that lost profits are used as the reference point in the calculation of damages does not, however, conclusively determine whether the damages are taxable or non-taxable. *Taxability is determined by the nature of the interest settled.* Take a simple example. A taxpayer is a party to a contract which will render him or her a profit of $10,000 per year for the next 15 years. Upon non-performance of the contract, the taxpayer's lost profits amount to $150,000. Ignoring problems of mitigation, etc., he or she would usually be entitled to the present value of that amount, say $100,000. Whether the $100,000 is taxable as income depends upon the nature of the contract breached and not upon the fact that the damages were determined by reference to annual profits which would have been taxable if received during the tenure of the contract.

(iv) Global Payments

A global payment covering several different heads of damages, for example, loss of earnings and payment on account of capital, should be broken down and distributed into its taxable and non-taxable segments. The allocation is fairly easy where damages are awarded as a result of litigation and the judgment sets out the various heads of damages. An amount paid in settlement of a cause of action is more difficult to allocate and the allocation should be made during negotiation of the settlement.

(v) Capital Receipts

Payments on account of capital receipts are not taxable. This is so whether the payment is on account of judicially assessed damages or pursuant to a settlement. For example, a payment to compensate the plaintiff for the destruction of the entire structure of his or her income earning apparatus is a capital receipt.

The distinction between income and capital receipts is easy to state in principle. The difficulty lies in the application of the principle to the particular facts. Are damages for the cancellation of a lucrative service contract, for example, taxable in lieu of the profit that would have been earned on the contract? What if the contract is the entire substratum of the business and its cancellation renders the enterprise a hollow shell? The difference between the two cases is one of degree.[131]

---

[131] See, e.g., *Schofield Oil Ltd. v. Canada*, [1992] 1 CTC 8, 92 DTC 6022 (F.C.A.) ($1.37 million payment to release party from remaining 20 months of contractual obligations considered compensation for future profits and taxable as lost income).

(vi) Non-performance

Damages for non-performance of a service contract are usually taxable as income unless non-performance materially dislocates the taxpayer's business structure. Lord Russell explained the principle as follows:[132]

> The sum received by a commercial firm as compensation for the loss sustained by the cancellation of a trading contract or the premature termination of an agency agreement may, in the recipient's hands, be regarded either as a capital receipt or as a trading receipt forming part of the trading profit. It may be difficult to formulate a general principle by reference to which in all cases the correct decision will be arrived at since in each case the question comes to be one of circumstance and degree. When the rights and advantages surrendered on cancellation are such as to destroy or materially to cripple the whole structure of the recipient's profit-making apparatus, involving the serious dislocation of the normal commercial organisation and resulting perhaps in the cutting down of the staff previously required, the recipient of the compensation may properly affirm that the compensation represents the price paid for the loss of sterilisation of a capital asset and is therefore a capital and not a revenue receipt.

In *Van Den Berghs Ltd. v. Clark*,[133] for example, the taxpayer entered into an agreement with its competitor which provided for, among other things, profit-sharing, joint arrangements, control of supply, and restrictions on entering into other pooling arrangements. The contract was terminated following a dispute between the parties and the taxpayer was compensated for cancellation of its future rights under the contract. The compensation payment was considered to be on account of a non-taxable capital receipt. In Lord MacMillan's words:[134]

> [T]he cancelled agreements related to the whole structure of the appellants' profit-making apparatus. They regulated the appellants' activities, defined what they might and what they might not do, and affected the whole conduct of their business. I have difficulty in seeing how money laid-out to secure, or money received for the cancellation of, so fundamental an organization of a trader's activities can be regarded as an income disbursement or an income receipt.

(b) Breach of Warranty of Authority

(i) Nature of Claim

An agent is liable for breach of warranty of authority for misrepresenting his or her authority to a person who suffers damage by acting on the strength of the misrepresentation. The obligation is imposed because ". . . a person, professing to contract as an agent for another, impliedly, if not expressly, undertakes to or promises

---

[132] *I.R.C. v. Fleming & Co. (Machinery) Ltd.* (1951), 33 Tax Cas. 57 at 63 (Scot.).

[133] *Van Den Berghs Ltd. v. Clark*, [1935] AC 431 (H.L.).

[134] *Van Den Berghs Ltd. v. Clark, ante,* at 442; see also *Barr, Crombie & Co. v. J.R.C.* (1945), 26 Tax Cas. 406 at 411 (Scot.) where Lord Normand L.P. said:
> In the present case, virtually the whole assets of the appellant company consisted in this agreement. When the agreement was surrendered or abandoned practically nothing remained of the company's business. It was forced to reduce its staff and to transfer into other premises, and it really started a new trading life. Its trading existence as practised up to that time had ceased with the liquidation of the shipping company.

the person who enters into such contract, upon the faith of the professed agent being duly authorized, that the authority which he professes to have does in point of fact exist".[135]

(ii) Damage Principles

Damages for breach of warranty of authority are determined according to the usual contract rule: Compensate the injured party and restore the person to the position he or she would have enjoyed had the authority claimed by the professed agent truly vested in him or her.[136]

The taxation of damages for breach of warranty of authority also follows the usual *surrogatum* rule: Damages that substitute for amounts that would have been taxable are taxable. Thus, here too, characterization for tax purposes depends upon the anterior determination as to the nature of the receipts that the damage award is intended to replace and not upon the method of calculating the amount.

In *Manley*,[137] for example, the taxpayer was awarded damages of $587,400 in lieu of a finder's fee that he would have received had the professed agent with whom he was dealing had the authority the agent claimed. Having determined that the finder's fee would have constituted "profit" from an adventure in the nature of trade, the damages in lieu thereof were also taxable as income from a business:[138]

> In the present case, the [taxpayer] was a trader; he had engaged in an adventure in the nature of trade. The damages for breach of warranty of authority, which he received . . . pursuant to a legal right, were compensation for his failure to receive the finder's fee. . . . Had the [taxpayer] received that finder's fee it would have been profit from a business required by the *Income Tax Act*, to be included in his income in the year of its receipt. The damages for breach of warranty of authority are to be treated the same way for income tax purposes.

Thus, at least in contract and agency, damages are always taxed on the *surrogatum* principle.

(c) Tort Damages

(i) General Principle

Tort damages are generally taxable on the basis of the same principles applied to other damages: Compensation for income receipts is included in income, compensation for capital receipts is not. There are, however, important differences in the manner in

---

[135] *Collen v. Wright* (1857), 8 E & B 647 at 657 (Ex. Ch.).

[136] See, for example, *Manley v. Levy* (1974), 47 DLR (3d) 67 (S.C.C.) (action for commission payment turned on credibility of witnesses); *Re National Coffee Palace Co.* (1883), 24 Ch. D. 367 (C.A.) (broker purchased shares from wrong company; purchaser repudiated; outstanding purchase price exacted from broker by liquidator).

[137] *Manley v. The Queen*, [1985] 1 CTC 186, 85 DTC 5150 (F.C.A.).

[138] *Manley v. The Queen, ante,* [1985] 1 CTC at 191, 85 DTC at 5155.

which the courts apply this principle to torts involving damage to business or investments and torts involving personal injuries or fatal accidents.

(ii) Business or Investments

Compensation for tortious injury to business or property is taxable if the payment is intended to compensate for lost profits and is not taxable if made on account of capital receipts.[139] Thus, the taxation of damages depends upon the nature of the hole that is filled by the damage award or settlement payment. Lord Clyde illustrated the principle as follows:[140]

> Suppose someone who chartered one of the Appellant's vessels breached the charter and exposed himself to a claim of damages . . . there could, I imagine, be no doubt that the damages recovered would properly enter the Appellant's profit and loss account for the year. The reason would be that the breach of the charter was an injury inflicted on the Appellant's trading, making (so to speak) a hole in the Appellant's profits, and damages recovered could not be reasonably or appropriately put . . . to any other purpose than to fill that hole. Suppose on the other hand, that one of the taxpayer's vessels was negligently run down and sunk by a vessel belonging to some other shipowner, and the Appellant recovered as damage the value of the sunken vessel, I imagine that there could be no doubt that the damages so recovered could not enter the Appellant's profit and loss account because the destruction of the vessel would be an injury inflicted, not on the Appellant's trading, but on the capital assets of the Appellant's trade, making (so to speak) a hole in *them,* and the damages could therefore...only be used to fill that hole.

Thus, damages for injury to a business resulting in a loss of profits are taxable as income; compensation for destruction of an entire business is a non-taxable capital receipt. This rule applies regardless of the method used to estimate the loss of profits. As Lord Buckmaster said:[141]

> It appears to me to make no difference whether it be regarded as the sale of the asset out and out, or whether it be treated merely as a means of preventing the acquisition of profit which would otherwise be gained. In either case the capital asset of the company to that extent has been sterilized and destroyed, and it is in respect of that action that the sum . . . was paid. . . . It is now well settled that the compensation payable in such circumstances is the full value of the minerals that are left unworked, less the cost of working, and that is of course the profit that would have been obtained were they in fact worked. But there is no relation between the measure that is used for the purpose of calculating a particular result and the quality of the figure that is arrived at by means of the application of that test.

Here too, there is no bright-line test to determine when compensation for lost earnings constitutes income or the capitalized value of earnings. It is a question of fact in each case.

---

[139] *London & Thames Haven Oil Wharves Ltd. v. Attwooll,* [1967] 2 All ER 124 (C.A.).

[140] *Burmah S.S. Co. v. I.R.C.* (1930), 16 Tax Cas. 67 at 71-72 (Scot.) (contract damages for late delivery of ship included in income as being on account of lost profits).

[141] *Glenboig Union Fireclay Co. v. I.R.C.* (1922), 12 Tax Cas. 427 at 464 (H.L.).

(iii) Depreciable Property

Compensation for damages to depreciable property is included in the taxpayer's income to the extent that money is expended to repair the damage.[142] In effect, inclusion of the compensation in and deduction of the repair costs from income constitute a "wash transaction", which means that the net tax effect is neutral.

(iv) Capital Property

Damages for total loss or destruction of capital property are considered "proceeds of disposition" and go towards determining the capital gain or loss on the disposition of the property.[143] Thus, total loss or destruction of property is considered equivalent to a sale of the property.

(v) Eligible Capital Property

Compensation for damage to eligible capital property (for example, goodwill) is usually considered an eligible capital amount. If the damage is so severe as to destroy the substrata of the taxpayer's business, compensation for such damage is a capital receipt.[144]

(vi) Personal Injuries

Income tax considerations are also relevant to damages for torts involving personal injuries. There are two instances when the issue of taxability can be considered: (1) At trial when liability is determined and damages are assessed and, (2) When the plaintiff receives payment of the award.

(A) Determination of Settlement

Tax factors are not taken into account in determining the amount that a defendant pays to the plaintiff in a personal injury case.[145] The plaintiff is compensated for the loss of earning *capacity* and not for lost earnings. It does not matter that the value of the plaintiff's capacity is determined by direct mathematical reference to his or her lost earnings. Dickson J. explained the rule as follows:[146]

> . . . an award for prospective income should be calculated with no deduction for tax which might have been attracted had it been earned over the working life of the plaintiff. This results from the fact that it is earning capacity and not lost earnings which is the subject of compensation. For the same reason,

---

[142] Para. 12(1)(f).

[143] S. 54 ("disposition") and ("proceeds of disposition").

[144] See IT-182, "Compensation for Loss of Business Income, or of Property Used in a Business" (October 28, 1974).

[145] *Andrews v. Grand & Toy Alta. Ltd.*, [1978] 2 SCR 229, 83 DLR (3d) 452 (plaintiff awarded $69,981 for prospective loss of earnings determined by discounting at 7 per cent the sum of $564 (monthly earnings) over a period of 30.81 years (estimated working life)).

[146] *Andrews v. Grand & Toy Alta. Ltd., ante,* [1978] 2 SCR at 259, 83 DLR (3d) at 474.

no consideration should be taken of the amount by which the income from the award will be reduced by payment of taxes on the interest, dividends, or capital gain. A capital sum is appropriate to replace the lost capital asset of earning capacity. Tax on income is irrelevant either to decrease the sum for taxes the victim would have paid on income from his job, or to increase it for taxes he will now have to pay on income from the award.

Thus, damage awards for personal injuries can be substantial where a person who is rendered incapable of working has a normal life expectancy. The plaintiff's pretax earnings must be capitalized to determine the value of his or her lost earning capacity.

(B) Taxation of Settlement

Damages for personal injuries are not taxable to the plaintiff when he or she receives the judgment amount. This is so, regardless of whether the amount paid is on account of special damages for loss of earnings up to trial, or general damages for loss of prospective earnings.[147] Here too, the courts say that damages compensate for capacity even though they are measured by reference to earnings.[148] Thus, the *surrogatum* principle does not apply in respect of damages for personal injuries. The theory is quite different, however, with respect to fatal accidents.

(vii) Fatal Accidents

Damages under fatal accident statutes are typically determined on a net of tax basis by capitalizing the deceased's *net* take-home pay and not his or her gross earnings. De Grandpré J. explained this rule as follows:[149]

> It seems to me that what the widow and the child have lost in this case is the support payments made by the deceased, support payments which could only come out of funds left after deducting the cost of maintaining the husband, including the amount of tax payable on his income. I cannot see how this pecuniary loss could be evaluated on any other basis than the take-home pay, that is the net pay after deductions on many items, including income tax.

---

[147] *Cirella v. The Queen*, [1978] CTC 1, 77 DTC 5442 (F.C.T.D.).

[148] See *Graham v. Baker* (1861), 106 CLR 340; see also *Groves v. United Pacific Transport Pty. Ltd.*, [1965] Qd. R. 62 where Gibbs J. observed at p. 65:

> Although it is usual and convenient in an action for damages for personal injuries to say that an amount is awarded for loss of wages or other earnings, the damages are really awarded for the impairment of the plaintiff's earning capacity that has resulted from his injuries. This is so even if an amount is separately quantified and described as special damages for loss of earnings up to the time of trial. Damages for personal injuries are not rightly described as damages for loss of income.

[149] *Keizer v. Hanna*, [1978] 2 SCR 342 at 371, 82 DLR (3d) 449 at 467; see also *Andrews v. Grand & Toy Alta. Ltd.* (1978), 83 DLR (3d) 452 at 474, *per* Dickson J. (S.C.C.):

> In contrast with the situation in personal injury cases, awards under the Fatal Accident Act, R.S.A. 1970, c. 138, should reflect tax considerations, since they are to compensate dependants for the loss of support payments made by the deceased. These support payments could only come out of take-home pay, and the payments from the award will only be received net of taxes....

As difficult as it may be to reconcile with the theory in non-fatal personal injury settlement, the capacity theory does not apply in the context of fatal accident cases.[150] The beneficiary is placed in the same financial position that she or he would have enjoyed had the deceased lived and continued to earn income.

(viii) Investment Income

(A) General

Interest and dividends earned on investments acquired with a damage award are generally taxable as income from property.[151] Similarly, taxable capital gains realized on property acquired with the proceeds of a damage award are included in income.

(B) Personal Injury Awards for Minors

An exception is made in respect of personal injury awards paid to, or on behalf of, persons under the age of 21. Interest and property income received from, or accrued on, the investment of a personal injury award is exempt from tax until the end of the taxation year in which the injured person attains the age of 21. Taxable capital gains from dispositions of property acquired with the proceeds of damage awards or settlements are also exempt from tax if the injured person was less than 21 years of age at any time in the year.[152] Amounts earned from the reinvestment of exempt income are also exempt.[153]

The purpose of this exception is to provide relief for young persons who have suffered personal injuries. It is unclear why the plight of young persons who have been injured warrants preferential treatment over older persons in similar circumstances.

(C) Interest on Special Damages

Tort damages are crystallized as at the time of the tortious act. In determining the amount of damages it is usual to breakdown the award into two components: (1) Special damages up to the date of trial; and (2) General damages for future losses. Interest on special damages is excluded from income.[154]

---

[150] *Keizer v. Hanna*, [1978] 2 SCR 342 at 372, 82 DLR (3d) 449 at 467, *per* Grandpré J.: "I cannot consider that the deceased here was a capital asset".

[151] Paras. 12(1)(*c*) and (*k*).

[152] Para. 81(1)(*g*.1). In his or her 21st year, the injured person can elect to recognize any accrued capital gains; see subs. 81(5).

[153] Para. 81(1)(*g*.2).

[154] See IT-365R2, "Damages, Settlements and Similar Receipts" (May 8, 1987).

11. RESERVES AND ALLOWANCES

References:

BULLETINS, CIRCULARS & RULINGS:

IT-152R3	June 18, 1985	Special Reserves — Sale of Land
IT-154R	February 19, 1988	Special Reserves
IT-215R	January 2, 1981	Reserves, Contingent Accounts and Sinking Funds
IT-397R	February 23, 1990	Amounts Excluded From Income — Statutory Exemptions and Certain Service or RCMP Pensions, Allowances and Compensation
IT-442R	September 6, 1991	Bad Debts and Reserve for Doubtful Debts

(a) Prohibition Against Reserves

The term "reserve" is now in disfavour among accountants because it has been applied so widely as to lose any specific meaning. Nevertheless, the term continues to be employed in commercial jargon. The Act specifically sets its face against "reserves".[155]

The general prohibition in paragraph 18(1)(*e*) of a deduction for any reserve, "contingent account" or "sinking fund", except as specifically permitted by the Act, not only causes accounting for tax purposes to deviate significantly from accounting for other purposes, it also produces inconsistencies within the system of income tax accounting.

Whether we refer to "reserve", "allowance", "contingency fund" or some other expression, the fact is that accountants recognize that a simplistic presentation of accrual basis financial statements fails to estimate profitability accurately. The failure results from overlooking *future* risks or obligations which affect *present* profitability. An obvious example is depreciation of capital assets. It would be foolish, and poor accounting, to fail to recognize an asset's ultimate obsolescence or exhaustion over a period of time. As already noted, the *Income Tax Act* concedes the wisdom of depreciating capital assets and provides for this by way of the capital cost allowance or tax depreciation system.

A clear line must, however, be drawn between depreciation and a decline in the market value of an asset. Although an accountant might think it is prudent for financial statement purposes to recognize a paper loss on investments, the tax system does not allow such an accounting practice for the purpose of determining net income. In *M.N.R. v. Consolidated Glass Ltd.*,[156] for example, the taxpayer attempted to deduct as a capital loss, an amount which reflected the decline in value of the shares of its

---

[155] Para. 18(1)(*e*).

[156] *M.N.R. v. Consolidated Glass Ltd.*, [1957] CTC 78, 57 DTC 1041 (S.C.C.).

subsidiary company. A majority of the Supreme Court of Canada held that the taxpayer could not claim a loss in respect of assets of a fluctuating value until such time as the assets were sold or became worthless so that the loss was irrevocable.

(b) Doubtful and Bad Debts

Reference:

BULLETINS, CIRCULARS & RULINGS:

IT-442R   September 6, 1991   Bad Debts and Reserves for Doubtful Debts

Accounts receivable is a major balance sheet asset for many businesses. Receivables are normally recorded on the books at face value, i.e., at the value stated on the invoice. As with depreciation, it would be foolish to ignore the obvious risk that all of the accounts of a business are not collected. Every business that sells on credit suffers some credit risk. Although this is the sort of contingent risk which the Act is careful to prevent taxpayers from exploiting, it specifically authorizes a deduction for a reserve for doubtful debts[157] and bad debts.[158]

A taxpayer's doubtful debt reserve may be based on an analysis of the likelihood of collection of individual accounts. Alternatively, it may be stated as a percentage of total accounts receivable. In either case, the deduction must be reasonable. The mere fact that a debt has remained unpaid for a considerable time is not determinative that it is bad.[159]

The deduction for bad debts is in respect of debts "that are established [by the taxpayer] to have become bad debts in the year".[160]

(c) Prepaid Income

Earlier in this chapter we saw an example of an adjusting entry to reduce current income by setting up a balance sheet liability reflecting the fact that some income received was unearned. In the example, X Widgets set up a liability, "rent received in advance", for the purpose of moving $300, received in its fiscal period ending October 31, into the following accounting period. If the prepayment were a deposit and subject

---

[157] Para. 20(1)(*l*).

[158] Para. 20(1)(*p*).

[159] See *No. 81 v. M.N.R.* (1953), 8 Tax ABC 82, 53 DTC 98 (factors to consider are time element, history of account, finances of client, taxpayer's past experiences with bad debts, business conditions in locality and in country, and relative sales volume); *No. 409 v. M.N.R.* (1957), 16 Tax ABC 409, 57 DTC 136 (delay in payment not sufficient to justify reserve after two months, in circumstances); *Atlas Steels Ltd. v. M.N.R.* (1961), 27 Tax ABC 331, 61 DTC 547 (reserve of 3 per cent of accounts receivable allowed in circumstances despite unfavourable comparison with company's history of collections).

[160] Para. 20(1)(*p*).

to refund on demand, it could be said that X Widgets had not "realized" the amount and should not recognize it in income at that time.

Assuming, however, that X Widgets can retain the $300 even if the payer discontinues use of the rented property, it is incorrect, from an accrual accounting point of view, to recognize the $300 in the period ending October 31.

There are two ways of expressing the accountant's concern that current income is being overstated. One is to say that revenue is overstated because the $300, though received, has not yet been earned. The other is to say that income is overstated as a result of failure to recognize a business liability in the next accounting period, i.e., the obligation to make the rented property available for three months. Although these two ways of expressing the matching concept boil down to the same thing in accounting terms, they are not at all alike for income tax purposes.

(i) Inclusion in Income

Paragraph 12(1)(a) reads as follows:

> There shall be included in computing the income of a taxpayer for a taxation year as income from a business or property such of the following amounts as are applicable:
>
> (a) any amount received by the taxpayer in the year in the course of a business
>
> (i) that is on account of services not rendered or goods not delivered before the end of the year or that, for any other reason, may be regarded as not having been earned in the year or a previous year, or
>
> (ii) under an arrangement or understanding that it is repayable in whole or in part on the return or resale to the taxpayer of articles in or by means of which goods were delivered to a customer. . . .

Obviously, this requires X Widgets to bring the $300 into income, whether or not it has been earned. The question which then arises is whether X Widgets can make an entry to reflect the overstatement of income. The reference in paragraph 12(1)(a) to amounts "regarded as not having been earned" confirms that the adjustment cannot be made directly to the statement of revenues. In any event, normal accrual accounting practice would recognize the receipt and make the adjustment by setting up the liability (unearned income) to reflect the future obligation to provide the rental property.

(ii) Deduction from Income

This brings us back to paragraph 18(1)(e) which prohibits all reserves except those expressly permitted. Fortunately for X Widgets, subparagraph 20(1)(m)(iii) expressly allows "a reasonable amount as a reserve in respect of...periods for which rent or other amounts for the possession or use of land or chattels have been paid in advance".

X Widgets is a simple example of future obligations which affect current income and that can easily be accommodated because the future obligation can be precisely quantified and its occurrence can be precisely predicted. Thus, there are no problems of measurement or timing. Other examples may be found in the publishing business, that receive prepaid subscriptions for which the publisher must provide magazines for a determined future period, and the entertainment business, that sells tickets for future performances with each ticket referable to a specified seat on a specified date.

(iii) Uncertainty

In other circumstances, however, businesses may legitimately claim future obligations, but the amount of the obligation may be uncertain both in respect of quantum and timing. Contrast the sale of season tickets to hockey games with the sale by a movie theatre chain of gift books of tickets for cinema performances. In the first case, the hockey club knows the date of each performance for which ticket revenue has been received. Whether or not the seats are occupied, the revenue is earned, and the club's obligation is satisfied on a game-by-game basis as each game is played. In the second case, the theatre company knows neither when the gift tickets will be used, nor how many will go forever unused.

There may be an intermediate situation in which a business cannot accurately predict the amount of its future obligation, but it can at least predict the timing within reasonable limits. An example would be the dinner-of-the-month arrangement under which a group of restaurants participate in a promotional scheme of selling books of tickets for free dinners at participating restaurants. Each book contains 12 tickets; each ticket is usable at a specified restaurant during a specified month. As each ticket entitles the user to a free meal equal in value to another purchased at the same time by the user's dinner partner, Restaurant A cannot be certain of its maximum obligation. Perhaps it can make a reliable estimate based on past experience. In any event, each month, the obligation for that month is determined, and at the end of 12 months the entire obligation has been quantified and satisfied.

A common business situation, rather like the one just described, is that of the insurance agent or broker who receives commissions in respect of insurance contracts extending into a future period. The broker knows that clients will have to be serviced over the period remaining under each contract, but the extent of the potential obligation in each case is highly speculative. Subsection 32(1) resolves the difficulty arbitrarily by allowing the agent or broker to set up a *pro rata* reserve in respect of unearned commissions.

(iv) Reserve for Future Goods and Services

Paragraph 20(1)(*m*) authorizes a reserve for a "reasonable amount" for goods or services "that it is reasonably anticipated will have to be delivered [or rendered] after the end of the year".[161] The same provision allows a reasonable reserve for anticipated refunds of deposits made on containers or other "articles in or by means of which goods were delivered to a customer".[162] The uncertainty involved in determining the amount

---

[161] Subparas. 20(1)(*m*)(i) and (ii).

[162] Subparas. 20(1)(*m*)(iv) and 12(1)(*a*)(ii).

of these future obligations is apparent from the requirement of the provision that the reserve be a "*reasonable* amount" and that the obligation be "*reasonably* anticipated".

A special problem of future obligations arises from a certain promotional technique used by some retailing businesses. A customer making a purchase at a Canadian Tire Store, for example, receives some "funny money", a form of scrip that can be applied to future purchases at Canadian Tire. Other businesses have used trading stamps that, after a sufficient quantity were accumulated, could be redeemed for merchandise. For a time, some of the major oil companies issued a card in which a hole was punched on the occasion of a purchase from one of the company stations. When the prescribed number of holes had been punched, the card could be redeemed for a set of dishes or cutlery. In all of these cases, the business is being carried on in such a way that current profitability will be overstated unless the future obligation to redeem the scrip, the trading stamps, or the cards is recognized. The problems inherent in any attempt to determine the amount and the timing of future obligations generated by such promotional schemes are, however, very difficult: the proportion of the trading stamps thrown away or lost is probably high, just as it is very likely that the "funny money" will be carried around in the wallets of Canadian Tire customers for years.

In *Dominion Stores Ltd. v. M.N.R.*,[163] the Minister argued that the taxpayer was not entitled to a deduction under paragraph 20(1)(*m*), which is conditional upon showing that the reserve is in respect of amounts that have been included in the taxpayer's income pursuant to paragraph 12(1)(*a*). The Minister argued that the "green stamps" given to customers were free, as they were advertised to be, and that the entire payment by the customer was referable to the food and other items being purchased at the time. Accordingly, Dominion Stores had no income in respect of the green stamps and was not entitled to any reserve to recognize the future obligation to redeem them. Cattanach J. held that the price paid at the check-out desk was a combined price for both the goods being purchased and the green stamps which accompanied them. The taxpayer was, therefore, entitled to take a reserve. It is interesting to note that only this narrow legal issue was submitted to the Court. The parties had, by agreement, fixed the appropriate amount of the reserve if the taxpayer was permitted to take it. Obviously, the determination of a "reasonable reserve" would require careful analysis of past experience with green stamp redemptions, and some speculative estimate as to the proportion which would never be redeemed.

12. ACCOUNTING FOR INVENTORY

References:

ITA:

S. 10   Valuation of Inventory

S. 23   Sale of Inventory

---

[163] *Dominion Stores Ltd. v. M.N.R.*, [1966] CTC 97, 66 DTC 5111 (Ex. Ct.).

BULLETINS, CIRCULARS & RULINGS:

IT-51R2	May 11, 1982	Supplies on Hand at the End of a Fiscal Period
IT-287R	July 15, 1988	Sale of Inventory
IT-473	March 17, 1981	Inventory Valuation
IT-473SR	April 30, 1993	Inventory Valuation

(a) Cost of Goods Sold

The largest single item of expense in a trading or manufacturing business is likely to be the cost of the goods sold. In most businesses which handle a large volume of items which cannot be individually identified, it is neither possible nor desirable to keep a running total of the cost of the goods being sold on a daily basis. The only feasible way to determine the cost of all the goods sold in an accounting period is to add the value of the inventory on hand at the beginning of the period to the cost of inventory purchased during the period and then subtract the value of the inventory on hand at the end of the period. The formula becomes:

Cost of Goods Sold = Opening Inventory + Acquisitions − Closing Inventory

If prices are stable, this formula may give rise to little difficulty. An important problem of valuing opening and closing inventory arises, however, if prices are rising or falling. For example, assume 10,000 units of inventory on hand at the opening of the period, and a current price of $1 per unit;[164] assume 10,000 units on hand at the end of the period and a current price of $4 per unit. Assume also that 100,000 units are traded during the period, the price having risen steadily as the business bought units each month. In many businesses, it will be impossible to say whether the 10,000 units in closing inventory are the same ones as those in the opening inventory, or whether some or none remain from the opening of the period.

If both opening and closing inventory are valued at $10,000, the cost of goods sold will be shown as $30,000 more, and profits will be $30,000 less, than if closing inventory is valued at $40,000.

(b) Alternative Methods

The Act permits two general methods of valuing inventory:[165]

- valuation at the *lower* of cost or fair market value for *each* item of inventory; or

- valuation of the entire inventory at fair market value.

---

[164] Note that we are here assuming a price of $1 to the taxpayer and are ignoring the "value" to the taxpayer in the sense of its current resale price. This would obviously add further complexities to the problem of appropriate valuation of inventory.

[165] Subs. 10(1); Reg. 1801. Artists and writers may elect a nil value for their inventory under subs. 10(6).

A taxpayer's inventory at the beginning of the year must be valued at the same amount at which it was valued at the end of the immediately preceding year.[166]

(c) Change of Method

A taxpayer is required to use the same method of valuation from year to year in the absence of permission from the Minister.[167]

Interpretation Bulletin IT-473R provides:[168]

A change in method of valuing inventory will be accepted if it can be shown that the new method:

- is a more appropriate way of calculating the taxpayer's income,

- will be used for financial statement purposes by the taxpayer, and

- will be used consistently in subsequent years.

13. THE ANNUAL ACCOUNTING REQUIREMENT

The arbitrary division of a business lifetime into annual segments produces numerous accounting problems. These problems are greatly exacerbated because of the annual accounting for income tax purposes. Under a progressive rate structure, a taxpayer whose income fluctuates widely over a number of years will pay more tax than another taxpayer with the same aggregate income over the period but with little annual fluctuation.

A serious problem occurs when income falls below zero in some years. Without a system of negative income tax and refunds, there is no automatic solution for a taxpayer with a net loss tax year. Some relief is available in section 111 for the carryover of losses from one tax year to another. Loss carryovers and related issues are discussed in Chapter XII "Computation of Taxable Income".

---

[166] Subs. 10(2).

[167] Subs. 10(2.1).

[168] IT-473R, "Inventory Valuation" (March 17, 1981), para. 4 (as revised).

SELECTED BIBLIOGRAPHY TO CHAPTER VI

General

Anderson, William D., "A Potpourri of Elements in Computing Business Income: Part 2", *Corporate Management Tax Conf.* 6:1 (Can. Tax Foundation, 1987).

Carr, Brian R., "A Potpourri of Elements in Computing Business Income: Part 1", *Corporate Management Tax Conf.* 5:1 (Can. Tax Foundation, 1987).

Drache, A.B.C., "A Dog is Not a Horse or a Fish" (1991), XIII *Can. Taxpayer* 135.

Durnford, John, "The Distinction Between Income From Business and Income From Property and the Concept of Carrying on Business" (1991), 39 *Can. Tax J.* 1131.

Harris, Edwin C., "Measuring Business Income", in *Proceedings of 19th Tax Conf.* 78 (Can. Tax Foundation, 1967).

Khan, D. and B. Sakich, "Business Income" (1985), 13 *Can. Tax News* 90.

McGregor, Ian, "Another Look at First Principles" (1962), 10 *Can. Tax J.* 65.

Roberts, J.R. and William Leiss, "Technology and Accounting Innovation: Can They Mesh?", in *Proceedings of 38th Tax Conf.* 25 (Can. Tax Foundation, 1986).

Characterization of Income

Brayley, C.A.M., "Income or Capital — The Spin of a Coin" (1986), 8 *Sup. Ct. L.R.* 405.

Boyle, J. Ladson, "What is a Trade or Business?" (1986), 39 *The Tax Lawyer* 737.

Corn, George, "Interest Income: Business Income or Investment Income", [1992] *Can. Current Tax* J141.

Corn, George, "Reasonable Expectation of Profit", [1994] *Can. Current Tax* J61.

Corn, George, "Taxation of Gain on Appreciation of Shares — Capital Gain or Income from an Adventure in the Nature of Trade", [1994] *Can. Current Tax* J39.

Craig, J.D., "Other than in the Ordinary Course of Business" (1980), 54 *Cost and Management* 45.

Drache, A.B.C., "Opting to Be a Market Trader" (1991), XIII *Can. Taxpayer* 175.

Durnford, John W., "Profits on the Sale of Shares: Capital Gains or Business Income — A Fresh Look at Irrigation Industries" (1987), 35 *Can. Tax J.* 837.

Durnford, John W., "The Distinction Between Income from Business and Income from Property, and the Concept of Carrying on Business" (1991) 39 *Can. Tax J.* 1131.

Hodgson, John, "What is Income? What is Capital?" (1988), 7 *The Philanthropist* 24.

Karp, "Rental Income: Property or Business?" (1968), 16 *Can. Tax J.* 191.

Krishna, Vern, "Characterization of 'Income from Business' and 'Income from Property'" (1984), 1 *Can. Current Tax* C-37.

Krishna, Vern, "Sale of Franchises: Receipts on Account of Eligible Capital Property or Income from Business?" (1986), 1 *Can. Current Tax* J-157.

Ladson, Boyle F., "What Is a Trade or Business?" (1986), 39 *Tax Lawyer* 737.

McDonnell, T.E., "Interest Income: Whether Income from Active Business or Income from Property" (1986) 34 *Can. Tax J.* 1431.

McGregor, Ian, "Capital Gainsay" (1964), 12 *Can. Tax J.* 116.

McGregor, Ian, "Secondary Intention" (1961), 9 *Can. Tax J.* 33.

McKie, A.B., "Properly Taxing Property" (1988), 2 *Can. Current Tax* C-91.

McLean, Bruce M., "Sourcing of Business Income", *Corporate Management Tax Conf.* 9:1 (Can. Tax Foundation, 1987).

Morris, D. Bernard, "Capital versus Income: Loans and Real Estate" (1992), *Can. Tax Foundation* 26:1.

Motz, Robert, "Employee vs. Independent Contractor", (November 1990), 64 *CMA Magazine* 26.

Richards, Gabrielle M.R., "Quick Flips as Adventure in Nature of Trade", [1993] *Can. Current Tax* J9.

Richardson, Elinore J., "Holding Real Estate for the Production of Income", *Corporate Management Tax Conf.* 1 (Can. Tax Foundation, 1983).

Strother, Robert C., "Income Tax Implications of Personal-Use Real Estate", *Corporate Management Tax Conf.* 59 (Can. Tax Foundation, 1983).

Thomas, Richard B., "Reasonable Expectation of Profit: Are Revenue Canada's and the Court's Expectations Unreasonable?" (1993) 41 *Can. Tax J.* 1128.

Warnock, Bruce A., "Income or Capital Gains on Dispositions of Property", in *Proceedings of 42nd Tax Conf.* 48:1 (Can. Tax Foundation, 1990).

Measurement of Income

Arnold, Brian J., "Timing and Income Taxation: The Principles of Income Management for Tax Purposes", in *Proceedings of 35th Tax Conf.* 133 (Can. Tax Foundation, 1983).

Harris, Edwin C., "Measuring Business Income", in *Proceedings of 19th Tax Conf.* 78 (Can. Tax Foundation, 1967).

Drobny, Sheldon, "Inventory and Accounting Methods: Controversy and Paradoxes" (October 1990), 68 *Taxes* 764.

Kaplow, L. and A.C. Warren, "The Bankruptcy of Conventional Tax Timing Wisdom is Deeper Than Semantics: A Rejoinder to Professors Kaplow and Warren, [Discussion of An Income Tax By Any Other Name — A Reply to Professor Strand]" (1986), 38 *Stan. L. Rev.* 399.

Robertson, D.A., "Timing is Everything" (1988), 121:3 *CA Magazine* 32.

Strand, J., "Tax Timing and the Haig-Simons Ideal: A Rejoinder to Professor Popkin [Discussion of Tax Ideals in the Real World: A Comment on Professor Strand's Approach to Tax Fairness]" (1986), 62 *Ind. L.J.* 73.

White, Robert, "Profits and Prophets — An Accountant's Afterword" (1987), 8 *Br. Tax Rev.* 292.

Basic Income Tax Accounting

Cooper, Graeme S., "Some Observations of Tax Accounting" (1986), 15 *Aust. Tax Rev.* 221.

Knight & Knight, "Recent Developments Concerning the Completed Contract Method of Accounting" (1988), 41 *Tax Exec.* 73.

Roberts, J.R. and William Leiss, "Technological and Accounting Innovation: Can They Mesh?" (1986), 36 *Can. Tax Foundation Conf., Report of Proceedings* 25:1.

Strand, J., "Tax Timing and the Haig-Simons Ideal: A Rejoinder to Professor Popkin [Discussion of Tax Ideals in the Real World: A Comment on Professor Strand's Approach to Tax Fairness]" (1986), 62 *Ind. L.J.* 73.

Generally Accepted Accounting Principles

Drobny, Sheldon, "Inventory and Accounting Methods: Controversy and Paradoxes" (October 1990), 68 *Taxes* 764.

McDonnell, T.E., "Falling Between the GAAP's?" (1991), 39 *Can. Tax J.* 1313.

Murray, K.J. and Nicole Mondou, "The Relevance of GAAP in Cyprus Anvil Mining Corporation v. The Queen" (1990), 3 *Can. Current Tax* P5.

Padwe, Gerald W., "The Death of G.A.A.P. Reporting — A Tale from the Folks Who Brought You U.S. Tax Reform", *Corporate Management Tax Conf.* 11:1 (Can. Tax Foundation, 1987).

Strain, William J., "Now You See It, Now You Don't: The Elusive Relevance of G.A.A.P. in Tax Accounting", in *Proceedings of 37th Tax Conf.* 38 (Can. Tax Foundation, 1985).

Realization and Recognition of Income

Callard, Rosalind M., "When to Recognize Revenue" (1986), 119 *CA Magazine* 67.

Durnford, John W., "If it Is Payable, Is it Due?", *Can. Tax Letter,* June 3, 1983 (De Boo).

Freedman, Judith, "Profit and Prophets — Law and Accountancy Practice on the Timing of Receipts — Recognition Under the Earnings Basis (Schedule D, Cases 1 and 11)" (1987), *Brit. Tax Rev.* 61 and 104.

Non-Arm's Length Transactions

Eng, Susan, "The Arm's Length Rules", in *Proceedings of 40th Tax Conf.* 13:1 (Can. Tax Foundation, 1988).

McCallum, J. Thomas, "Choosing the Right End" (February 1991), 25 *CGA Magazine* 20.

Moskowitz, Evelyn P., "Dealing at Arm's Length: A Question of Fact", in *Proceedings of 39th Tax Conf.* 33:1 (Can. Tax Foundation, 1987).

Realization of Income: Timing

Arnold, Brian J., "Timing and Income Taxation: The Principles of Income Management for Tax Purposes", in *Proceedings of 35th Tax Conf.* 133 (Can. Tax Foundation, 1983).

Grower, Kenneth W., "Tax Reform and Farmers", in *Proceedings of 40th Tax Conf.* 24:1 (Can. Tax Foundation, 1988).

McNair, D.K., "The Taxation of Farmers and Farming", [1986] *Special Lectures LSUC* 77.

McNair, D.K., *Taxation of Farmers and Fishermen* (Toronto: Richard De Boo, 1986).

O'Brien, M.L., "Taxation of Profits Derived From Criminal or Illegal Activities" (1988), 2 *Can. Current Tax* J-85.

Robertson, D.A., "Timing is Everything" (1988), 121:3 *CA Magazine* 32.

Tiley, John, "More on Receivability and Receipt" (1986), *Br. Tax Rev.* 152.

Turner, Paul E., "The Reform 'Down On The Farm'" (July 1990), 24 *CGA Magazine* 25.

Turner, Paul E., "Restricted Farm Losses" (December 1990), 24 *CGA Magazine* 47.

Damages

Bowman, D.G.H., "Tax Treatment of Payments Made in the Context of Litigation", [1986] *Special Lectures LSUC* 96.

Corn, George, "Award of Damages — Non-Taxable Capital Receipt or Taxable Reimbursement" (July 1990), 3 *Can. Current Tax* J-85.

Corn, George, "Incorrect Assessment Liability for Damages" (1986), 1 *Can. Current Tax* A-29.

Drache, A. B.C., "Tort Damages and Retiring Allowances", (1991), XIII *Can. Taxpayer* 79.

Harris, Peter H., "Tax Treatment of Civil Litigation and Damage Awards, Alimony and Maintenance Payments" (1985), 6 *Advocates' Q.* 346.

Income Tax: *Maintenance, Alimony and Employment Termination Benefits* (Audio Archives of Canada, 1984).

Krishna, Vern, "The Taxation of Damages" (1985), 1 *Can. Current Tax* C-107.

Weir, J.P., "Taxation of Prejudgment Interest: Historical and Current Developments" (1985), 33 *CCLT* 149.

Reserves and Allowances

Cadesky, Michael, "Corporate Losses", in *Proceedings of 42nd Tax Conf.* 19:1 (Can. Tax Foundation, 1990).

Frankovic, Joseph V., "Taxing Times: Foreclosures, Default Sales, Debt Forgiveness, Doubtful and Bad Debts" (1991), 39 *Can. Tax J.* 889.

Krishna, Vern, "Meaning of 'Allowance'" (1986), 1 *Can. Current Tax* J-144.

Land, Stephen B., "Contingent Payments are the Time Value of Money" (1987), 40 *Tax Lawyer* 237.

Lokken, Lawrence, "The Time Value of Money Rules" (1986), 42 *Tax Rev.* 1.

Accounting for Inventory

Arnold, Brian J., "Conversions of Property To and From Inventory: Tax Consequences" (1976), 24 *Can. Tax J.* 231.

Arnold, Brian J., "Recent Developments in the Tax Treatment of Inventory", in *Proceedings of 31st Tax Conf.* 865 (Can. Tax Foundation, 1979).

Cadesky, Michael, "Corporate Losses", in *Proceedings of 42nd Tax Conf.* 19:1 (Can. Tax Foundation, 1990).

Innes, William I., "The Tax Treatment of Accrued Gains on Inventory at Death" (1992), 12 *Estates and Trust J.* 122.

Looney, Steve R., "Using L.I.F.O. to Value Costs Under the Completed Contract Method: A Tale of Two Accounting Methods" (1986), 39 *Tax Lawyer* 235.

McDonnell, Thomas E., "An Inventory Adventure" (1993), 41 *Can. Tax J.* 965.

McQuillan, Peter E., "Real Estate Inventory Valuation" (1992), *Canada Tax Foundation* 5:35.

Other

Beninger, Michael, J., "The Scope and Application of Section 79 of the Income Tax Act" (1985), 33 *Can. Tax J.* 929.

Bernstein, Jack, "Hotels and Motels as Tax Shelters" (1983), 116:10 *CA Magazine* 1972.

Burke, Harold A., "Real Estate Breakups: Tax, Valuation, and Division Issues", in *Proceedings of 38th Tax Conf.* 43 (Can. Tax Foundation, 1986).

Crawford, R.W., "Sales of Real Estate: Tax Planning for the Seller", *Corporate Management Tax Conf.* 138 (Can. Tax Foundation, 1983).

Curtis, "Isolation, Intention and Income", in *Legal Essays in Honour of Arthur Moxon* 239 (University of Toronto Press, 1953).

"Deferred Compensation: Diabolus Ex Machina", *Can. Tax Letter*, November 25, 1983 (De Boo).

Drache, A.B.C., "Renewed Attack on Management Companies" (1983), 5 *Can. Taxpayer* 157.

Dwyer, Blair P., "Deductibility of Tenant Inducement Payments", [1987-89] *Can. Current Tax* C53.

Krishna, Vern, "Does Supreme Court Expand Deductibility of Business Expenses in *Symes*?", [1994] *Can. Current Tax* J35.

MacInnis, Ian V., "Deduction of Rental Losses Require Reasonable Expectation of Profit" (1990), 7 *Business and the Law* 39.

O'Brien, Martin L., "Commodity Trading — Convertible Hedges", [1994] *Can. Current Tax* J31.

Popkin, W.D., "Tax Ideals in the Real World: A Comment on Professor Strand's Approach to Tax Fairness, [Discussion of Taxation of Income from Capital — A Theoretical Reappraisal]" (1986-87), *Ind. L.J.* 63

Valliere, Charles E., "Both Deduction and Capitalization Treatment Denied with respect to Real Estate that Produces No Income" (1991), 39 *Can. Tax J.* 1033.

CHAPTER VII

BUSINESS AND PROPERTY INCOME: INCLUSIONS

1. GENERAL

References:

ITA:

S. 12   Income From Business or Property

S. 12.2   Amounts to be Included

BULLETINS, CIRCULARS & RULINGS:

IT-154R	February 19, 1988	Special Reserves
IT-165R	February 16, 1984	Returnable Containers
IT-365R2	May 8, 1987	Damages, Settlements and Similar Receipts
IT-457R	July 15, 1988	Election by Professionals to Exclude Work in Progress from Income

We saw in Chapter VI "Business and Investment Income: General" that income from business or property is the "profit" therefrom. We also saw that profit is generally determined according to accounting principles and commercial practice. The Act does, however, also specify inclusion of certain receipts in income. These specific inclusions are of three types:

1. Timing adjustments,

2. Modifications of the common law concept of income, and

3. Rules which clarify uncertain issues.

(a) Accrual Basis of Accounting

Reference:

BULLETINS' CIRCULARS & RULINGS:

IT-170R	August 25, 1980	Sale of Property — When Included in Income Computation

"Profit" from business or property is generally calculated on an accrual basis of accounting.

Paragraph 12(1)(*b*) reinforces this concept and requires a taxpayer to include in income in a year any receivables on account of goods sold or services rendered in the year, regardless of when the amounts are due or actually collected. An amount is considered "receivable" when the taxpayer completes the sale or service so that his or her right to receive the amount is perfected.

(b) Unearned Income

Generally accepted concepts of accrual accounting require inclusion in income only of amounts that have been earned. Unearned revenue is a liability and not income. For tax purposes, however, paragraph 12(1)(a) modifies the general accounting rule: All receipts, whether earned or unearned, are included in income for the year. Thus, an amount received on account of services to be rendered in the future is included in income in the year of receipt and not in the year in which the income is earned. The taxpayer may, however, claim a reserve against unearned income.

2. INTEREST INCOME

References:

ITA:

Para. 12(1)(c)	Interest
S. 16	Combined Income and Capital
Para. 20(1)(f)	Discount on Certain Obligations
S. 80.4	Loans
Para. 81(1)(m)	Interest on Certain Obligations
Subss. 258(3)–(5)	Deemed Interest

BULLETINS, CIRCULARS & RULINGS:

IT-396R   May 29, 1984   Interest Income

(a) The Meaning of "Interest"

"Interest" is defined as the return or material consideration given for the use of money belonging to another person. Interest must be referable to a principal sum of money or an obligation to pay money.[1] Thus:[2]

---

[1]   *Ref. re s. 6 of Farm Security Act 1944 of Sask.,* [1947] SCR 394 at 411; affirmed [1949] AC 110 (*sub nom. A. G. Sask. v. A.G. Can.*) (P.C.); *The Queen v. Melford Dev. Inc.,* [1982] CTC 330, 82 DTC 6281 (S.C.C.); see also, *Halsbury's Laws of England* 4th ed., vol. 32 (London: Butterworths, 1980), at 53, where "interest" is defined as "...the return or compensation for the use or retention by one person of a sum of money belonging to or owed to another. Interest accrues from day to day even if payable only at intervals...."; *Miller v. M.N.R.,* [1985] 2 CTC 139, 85 DTC 5354 (F.C.T.D.) (interest on arbitration award is "interest" income and not income from employment even if payable by reference to salary).

[2]   *Re Euro Hotel (Belgravia),* [1975] 3 All ER 1075 at 1084 *per* Megarry J.

... there must be a sum of money by reference to which the payment which is said to be interest is to be ascertained. A payment cannot be "interest of money" unless there is the requisite "money" for the payment to be said to be "interest of".

The quintessential characteristic of interest is the relationship between the obligation that is outstanding and payment on account of the obligation. The relationship encompasses payments labelled under other names. For example, a bonus or premium payable on maturity, or a lump sum payable on prepayment of a loan, may constitute interest:[3]

... The word "interest" is not, then, a technical term and it is not restricted in any sense to compensation determinable by the application of a rate per centum to the principal amount of a loan. It may be for a fixed sum of money whether denominated a bonus, discount or premium, provided that it is referable to a principal money or to an obligation to pay money.

Not all courts, however, interpret "interest" in this broad sense. Some, including the Supreme Court of Canada,[4] have said that daily accrual is the essential characteristic of interest. This view rests upon the interpretation (or misinterpretation) of *Halsbury's Laws of England:*[5]

... [i]nterest accrues from day to day even if payable only at intervals, and is, therefore, apportionable in respect of time between persons entitled in succession to the principal.

But *Halsbury* merely says that where an amount is considered to be "interest", it is *deemed* to accrue from day to day.[6] Unfortunately, the statement was read to mean that a payment *cannot* be interest *unless* it accrues from day to day even if payable only at intervals. This interpretation of *Halsbury* has caused a good deal of misunderstanding as to the meaning of "interest".

Interest may vary with the gross revenues or profits of the borrower.[7] Payments payable as a percentage of profit are less likely to constitute interest.[8] Profit percentage arrangements are more usually associated with a partnership relationship between the parties.[9]

---

[3] *Re Unconscionable Transactions Relief Act*, [1962] OR 1103 at 1108; reversed (*sub nom. A.G. Ont v. Barfried Ent. Ltd.*) [1963] SCR 570.

[4] *A. G. Ont. v. Barfried Ent. Ltd.*, *ante*; *Tomell Invt. Ltd. v. East Markstock Lands Ltd.*, [1978] 1 SCR 974, *per* Pigeon J.

[5] *Halsbury's Laws of England*, 4th ed., vol. 32 (London: Butterworths, 1980), at 53.

[6] See generally *Metro. Trust Co. v. Morenish Land Dev. Ltd.*, [1981] 1 SCR 171; *A.G. Ont. v. Barfield Ent. Ltd.*, *ante*; *Immeubles Fournier Inc. v. Const. St-Hilaire Ltée*, [1975] 2 SCR 2; *Tomell Invts. Ltd. v. East Markstock Lands Ltd.*, *ante*; *Riches v. Westminster Bank Ltd.*, [1947] 1 All ER 469 at 478 (H.L.).

[7] *Pooley v. Driver* (1876), 5 Ch. D. 459 (C.A.); *Cox v. Hickman* (1860), 11 All ER 431 (H.L.); see *Partnerships Act*, R.S.O. 1990, c. P.5, para. 3(*d*).

[8] See, e.g., *Balaji Apts. Ltd. v. Mfrs. Life Ins. Co.* (1980), 25 OR (2d) 275.

[9] See, e.g., *Sedgwick v. M.N.R.*, [1962] CTC 400, 62 DTC 1253 (Ex. Ct.).

A payment in advance (for example, withholding an amount from the principal advanced under a loan) may nevertheless, constitute interest.[10]

(b) Methods of Reporting

There are several ways to account for interest income for tax purposes: the cash basis, modified cash basis, receivable basis, accrual basis and modified accrual basis. Different rules apply to individuals, corporations, and partnerships.

(i) Meaning of "Receivable"

For tax purposes, "receivable" means *legally* receivable and not "receivable" in the sense that it is used in accounting.[11] Thus, the word has a narrower meaning for tax purposes than it has in general accounting.

An amount is "receivable" for tax purposes only when the taxpayer has a clear legal right to it. The right must be enforceable, even though it is not enforced — for example, by the taxpayer not clipping a bond coupon.[12] For example, assume a taxpayer buys a bond for $1,000 on December 1, and the bond pays interest at a rate of 12 per cent per year payable in May and November of each year. By December 31, the taxpayer will have earned 1/12 of his or her annual interest income. In accrual accounting, the taxpayer is considered to have *earned* $10 in the month of December even though he or she may not have received payment. The $10 would be accrued as a receivable for general accounting purposes. For tax purposes, however, the $10 is not a "receivable" because there is no legal obligation on the issuer of the bond to pay the interest as at December 31. The legal obligation to pay the interest will arise on the date stipulated in the bond contract. This date is fixed at intervals that do not necessarily coincide with the fiscal year.

(ii) Consistency

A taxpayer who selects a particular method of reporting interest income for a particular property must conform to that method from year to year. Although a taxpayer is required to account for interest income on a consistent basis from year to year, there is no requirement that the taxpayer follow the same basis for reporting interest income from all sources. For example, a taxpayer may report interest income from Canada Savings Bonds on a cash basis and, in the same year, report interest income from a mortgage on a receivable basis.[13] Paragraph 12(1)(*c*) merely requires that interest from

---

[10] See, e.g., *Asconi Bldg. Corp. v. Vocisano*, [1947] SCR 358 at 368 [Que.].

[11] *M.N.R. v. J. Colford Contr. Co.*, [1962] CTC 546, 62 DTC 1338 (S.C.C.).

[12] *Hall v. M.N.R.*, [1971] CTC 401, 71 DTC 5217 (S.C.C.).

[13] *Indust. Mtge. & Trust Co. v. M.N.R.*, [1958] CTC 106, 58 DTC 1060 (Ex. Ct.); see also IT-396R, "Interest Income" (May 29, 1984).

the *same source* be reported on a consistent basis — that is, interest from the same debtor on the same type of obligation.

(iii) Annual Reporting

As a general rule, an individual may report interest income on a cash or accrual basis.[14] Thus, an individual can use cash basis reporting to defer the recognition of income.

There are, however, special restrictions in respect of "investment contracts". Income from "investment contracts" must be reported on an annual basis, regardless of whether or not the income has been paid out in the year.[15] The rule is intended to prevent prolonged deferral of investment income.

An "investment contract" is a debt such as a note, bond, debenture, or guaranteed investment contract. An "investment contract" does not include the following:[16]

- salary deferral arrangements,
- income bonds and debentures,
- retirement compensation arrangements,
- employee benefit plans,
- small business development bonds,
- small business bonds, or
- debt obligations in respect of which investment income is otherwise included in income at least annually.

(c) Blended Payments

Reference:

BULLETINS, CIRCULARS & RULINGS:

IT-265R3   October 7, 1991   Payments of Income and Capital Combined

A taxpayer is *not legally* obliged to charge interest on money loaned to another.[17] A taxpayer who receives a blended payment (that is, a single payment in which interest and principal are blended into one amount) on repayment of a loan must, however,

---

[14] Para. 12(1)(c).

[15] Subs. 12(4).

[16] Para. 12(11) ("investment contract").

[17] *M.N.R. v. Groulx*, [1966] CTC 115, 66 DTC 5126; affirmed [1967] CTC 422, 67 DTC 5284 (S.C.C.). Note, however, that the recipient of an interest-free loan may be taxable on the benefit imputed on the loan; see s. 80.4 and Chapter V "Income From an Office or Employment".

segregate the interest component (if any) of the payment from the principal amount and include the former portion in income.[18]

(i) Meaning

The first question to be determined is whether an amount represents a blend of interest and principal. Where the constituent elements (i.e., interest and principal) of an amount are *definitely* known, the payment is not a blended payment. For example, where an individual deposits $1,000 in a trust company in return for repayment of $1,610 in five years from the date of the deposit, it is quite clear that $1,000 is principal and $610 is interest calculated at a rate of 10 per cent compounded annually. The $1,610 is *not* a blended payment for the purposes of subsection 16(1). The $1610 is a repayment of the principal sum with interest thereon. Each component of the payment is clearly identifiable. In other words, the mere fact that the interest rate is not specifically spelled out in the contract does not mean that the contract does not contain an interest component.

Interest and principal may be blended by issuing a debt instrument at a discount and redeeming it at its face value upon maturity. Government Treasury Bills, for example, do not stipulate any interest rate or amount on their face, but are issued at a discount from their face value. The discount rate is a direct function of the prevailing interest rate, and the substance of the transaction is that the redemption value is, in effect, made up of principal and interest. Thus, the payment on maturity must be broken down into interest and principal.[19]

Whether an amount represents a blended payment of interest and principal is a question of fact to be determined by the terms of the agreement, the course of the negotiation between the parties and, of particular importance, the price at which the property is sold.

Property sold in an arm's length transaction at a price in excess of its fair market value suggests that the total price represents a blended payment of interest and principal. As we have seen, capital gains are either tax exempt[20] or taxed at lower than the normal rate applicable to ordinary income.[21] Interest income is taxable at the full rate. Sales in excess of market value always raise the question: Why would a taxpayer in an arm's length transaction buy property at a price that is higher than its fair market value? In *Vestey v. I.R.C.*,[22] for example:

---

[18] Subs. 16(1).

[19] *O'Neil v. M.N.R.* (1991), 91 DTC 692 (T.C.C.); see also *Beck v. Lord Howard de Walden*, [1940] T.R. 143; *Lomax v. Peter Dixon & Sons Ltd.*, [1943] 1 K.B. 671.

[20] See Chapter XII "Computation of Taxable Income".

[21] See Chapter IX "Capital Gains".

[22] *Vestey v. I.R.C.*, [1962] Ch. 861.

[i]t is necessary to decide whether or not we are bound to confine our attention to the words of the agreement and the related transfer of shares, and not to have regard for any surrounding circumstances. It appears clear to us on the authorities that we are not only entitled but are bound to consider such of the surrounding circumstances as are proved and admitted in evidence; not in order to vary the legal effect of the agreement and transfer, nor to decide the matter by the doctrine (now exploded) of the "substance" of the matter, but in order to ascertain the true nature of the transaction comprised in the agreement. We have to look first at the legal effect of the agreement and then at the surrounding circumstances.

(ii) Amounts Previously Included

The interest component of a blended payment that has been previously included in income is excluded from the ambit of subsection 16(1). For example, accrued interest income on a debt obligation that is included in income under the accrual rule does not have to be included in income under subsection 16(1) when the interest is actually paid.

(iii) Accrual Basis

The interest component of a blended payment is considered interest on a debt obligation rather than simply income from property. Hence, corporations, partnerships and trusts must account for the interest portion of blended payments on an accrual basis.

(d) Discounts

(i) Rate Adjustments

A debt instrument issued at a discount effectively raises the rate of interest on the debt. The real rate is raised above the nominal rate of interest specified on the face of the instrument. For example, if a $1,000 bond with a nominal rate of interest of 10 per cent is issued at $960, the real rate of interest is some number higher than 10 per cent. Thus, discounting the issue price of a bond is simply another way of changing the "real" rate of interest paid on the bond.

Example VII.1

Assume that S Ltd. issued bonds on April 28, 1992 at a price of $88 3/8. The bonds have a coupon rate of 6.75 per cent and will mature on June 4, 2006.

Then:

Nominal yield	= 6.75%	($67.50 per $1,000 bond)
Effective yield	= 8.15%	
Discount on bond	= $11 5/8	

At common law, the discount on a bond was not considered interest. Instead, the difference between the issue price and the face value of a bond was considered a capital gain.[23] Hence, the common law rules were an invitation to convert interest income into

---

[23] *Wood v. M.N.R.*, [1969] CTC 57, 69 DTC 5073 (S.C.C.).

capital gains. The Minister of Finance described the difficulties of this interpretation in the budget speech of December 20, 1960:

> Unfortunately, increasing use is deliberately being made of a device to pay bondholders the equivalent of interest in a form that is tax-free. If a borrower issues a one-year $100 bond for, say, $96 and the bond bears a coupon rate of 1 per cent, the bondholder will receive $4 more than he paid for it when the bond matures at the end of the year. This excess over purchase price, plus the $1 in interest, will give the lender a 5.2 per cent return on his investment but it has been found difficult to collect tax on more than the $1 designated as interest.

The statutory rules in respect of bond discounts vary depending upon the tax status of the issuer of the bond.

(ii) Tax Exempt Organizations

Where a tax exempt organization, a non-resident person not carrying on business in Canada, or a governmental body issues a bond at a "deep discount", the *entire* discount is income in the hands of the first taxable Canadian resident to hold the bond.[24] A bond is considered to have a "deep discount" if the effective rate of interest on the bond exceeds the nominal rate by more than one-third.

(iii) Taxable Entities

Where a taxable entity issues a bond at a discount, a purchaser of the bond can treat the difference between the issue price and its par value as a capital gain. If the discount is a "deep discount", the taxable entity issuing the bond can deduct only three-quarters of the discount as interest expense. If the discount is "shallow" (i.e., the effective rate of interest does *not* exceed the nominal rate by more than one-third), the taxable entity can deduct the entire discount.[25]

Example VII.2

Assume:

A municipality issues bonds with a face value of $1,000 (coupon rate of 4.5 per cent, maturity five years) at a price of $930.

Then:

Nominal rate of interest	4.50%
Effective rate of interest	(6.14)
Difference	1.64%

Since 6.14 per cent is more than 4/3 × 4.50 per cent, the *entire* discount of $70 per bond is income in the hands of the first Canadian resident, taxable owner of the bond.

---

[24] Subs. 16(3).

[25] Para. 20(1)(f).

Example VII.3		
	Shallow Discount	Deep Discount
Issue price of bond	$ 990	$ 960
Nominal rate of interest	8%	8%
Effective rate of interest	10%	12%
Discount on bond	10	40
Amount deductible by issuer	$ 10	$ 30

3. PAYMENTS BASED ON PRODUCTION OR USE OF PROPERTY

References:

BULLETINS, CIRCULARS & RULINGS:

IT-462   October 27, 1980   Payments Based on Production or Use

The selling price of a property may be determined in several ways. The price may be fixed at the time the parties enter into the agreement of purchase and sale. Alternatively, the price may be determined by reference to a formula based upon production from, or use of, the property. For example, a taxpayer may sell land containing sand for a fixed amount of $15,000 or on the basis that the purchaser shall pay 5 cents for every ton of sand extracted from the land. In the latter case, the sales price is dependent upon the quantity of sand taken from the land, and the total price is not determined until all of the sand is extracted.

A taxpayer must include in income all amounts that he or she receives and that are dependent upon the use of, or production from, property.[26] This rule prevents

---

[26] Para. 12(1)(*g*); IT-462, "Payments Based on Production or Use" (October 27, 1980). The rationale of the provision is captured in the following analysis by Rowlatt J. in *Jones v. I.R.C.*, [1920] 1 KB 711:

There is no law of nature or any invariable principle that because it can be said that a certain payment is consideration for the transfer of property it must be looked upon as price in the character of principal. In each case, regard must be had to what the sum is. A man may sell his property for a sum which is to be paid in instalments, and when that is the case the payments to him are not income: *Foley v. Fletcher* (1858), 3 H. & N. 769. Or a man may sell his property for an annuity. In that case the Income Tax Act applies. Again, a man may sell his property for what looks like an annuity, but which can be seen to be, not a transmutation of a principal sum into an annuity, but in fact, a principal sum payment which is being spread over a period and is being paid with interest calculated in a way familiar to actuaries — in such a case, income tax is not payable on what is really capital: *Secretary of State [in Council of] India v. Scoble*, [1903] A.C. 299 (H.L.). On the other hand, a man may sell his property nakedly for a share of the profits of the business. In that case the share of the profits of the business would be the price, but it would bear the character of income in the vendor's hands. *Chadwick v. Pearl Life Assurance Co.*, [1905] 2 K.B. 507, 514, was a case of that kind. In

taxpayers from converting what would otherwise be fully taxable rent or royalty income into capital.

For example:

- A sells land containing 300,000 tons of sand for $15,000. The purchase price is payable at a rate of $5,000 per year for three years.

  Paragraph 12(1)(g) does *not* apply to the transaction. The payments are not related to the "use of" or "production from" property.

- B sells land containing sand to X. The sales price is determined at 5 cents per ton of sand extracted over the next three years. X extracts 300,000 tons and pays the vendor $15,000.

  Paragraph 12(1)(g) applies; the $15,000 is income to B.

- C sells land containing sand to Y. The sales price is determined at 5 cents per ton of sand extracted in the next three years, provided that the total price cannot exceed $10,000. Y extracts 300,000 tons and pays C $10,000.

  Paragraph 12(1)(g) applies; the $10,000 is income to C. The payment is based upon production from property.

- D sells land containing sand to Z. The sales price is determined at 5 cents per ton of sand extracted in the next three years but *not to be less than* $10,000. In fact, Y extracts 300,000 tons and pays $15,000.

  Paragraph 12(1)(g) does *not* apply to the $10,000 since this amount is not dependent upon production; $5,000 is included in D's income by paragraph 12(1)(g).

4. STOCK DIVIDENDS

References:

ITA:

Subs. 52(3)	Cost of Stock Dividend
S. 82	Dividends Received
Subs. 248(1)	"Dividend"

BULLETINS, CIRCULARS & RULINGS:

IT-88R2	May 31, 1991	Stock Dividends

---

such a case the man bargains to have, not a capital sum but an income secured to him, namely, an income corresponding to the rent which he had before. I think, therefore, that what I have to do is to see what the sum payable in this case really is.

The ascertainment of an antecedent debt is not the only thing that governs, although in many cases it is a very valuable guide.

Dividends on shares represent the investment yield of equity capital. As a general rule, a taxpayer is taxable on dividend income on a cash basis.[27] A "dividend" includes stock dividends.[28]

5. INDUCEMENT PAYMENTS

An "inducement payment" is an economic incentive to lead or persuade a person to perform a particular action or decision. Examples include government subsidies to business(es) to locate in a particular place, landlord inducements to tenants to sign a lease in a shopping plaza, etc.

An inducement receipt, whether from a governmental or private organization, is taxable as income.[29] This is so whether the payment is a grant, subsidy, forgivable loan, deduction from tax, or allowance. A taxpayer may, however, elect to treat an inducement payment as a reduction in the cost or capital cost of any property that he or she acquires with the payment.[30] The effect of the election is that it allows the taxpayer to defer recognition of the income until such time as he or she disposes of the property.

6. AUTO STANDBY CHARGE TO PARTNERS

A member of a partnership (or an employee of a member of a partnership) who is entitled to make personal use of an automobile provided by his or her partnership is subject to a standby charge.[31] The standby charge is calculated according to the rules generally applicable to employees (see Chapter V "Income From an Office or Employment").

7. OTHER INCLUSIONS IN INCOME

References:

ITA:

S. 12.1	Cash Bonus on CSBs
S. 12.3	Net Reserve Inclusion
S. 12.4	Bad Debt Inclusion

---

[27] Paras. 12(1)(*j*), 82(1)(*a*)

[28] Subs. 248(1) ("dividend").

[29] Para. 12(1)(*x*).

[30] Subs. 53(2.1).

[31] Para. 12(1)(*y*).

Item	Statutory Reference	Comments
Amounts received for goods and services to be rendered in the future	subpara. 12(1)(*a*)(i)	
Amounts received for deposits on returnable items	subpara. 12(1)(*a*)(ii)	IT-165R
Amounts received for property sold or services rendered, due in a future tax year	para. 12(1)(*b*)	IT-129R, IT-170R
Amounts received as interest (or in lieu of interest) if not previously included	para. 12(1)(*c*)	IT-396R
Amount deducted in preceding year as a reserve for doubtful debts	paras. 12(1)(*d*)	IT-442R; authorization for deduction in preceding year: 20(1)(*l*)
Amounts deducted in preceding year as reserve for guarantee	paras. 12(1)(*d.1*); 20(1)(*l.1*)	authorization for deduction: 20(1)(*l.1*)
Amount deducted in preceding year as a reserve for:	subpara. 12(1)(*e*)(i)	IT-145R; authorization for deduction in preceding year
• deposits on returnable containers	subpara. 20(1)(*m*)(iv)	
• goods delivered and services performed after end of year	subparas. 20(1)(*m*)(i), (ii); subs. 20(6)	
• a manufacturer's warranty	para. 20(1)(*m*.1)	
• prepaid rent	subpara. 20(1)(*m*)(iii)	
• policies of an insurer	para. 20(7)(*c*)	
Amount deducted in preceding year as unrealizable receivable	subpara. 12(1)(*e*)(ii)	IT-154R; authorization for deduction in preceding year: para. 20(1)(*n*)
Insurance proceeds used to repair depreciable property	para. 12(1)(*f*)	costs of repairs deductible from income
Amounts received based on production or use of property disposed	para. 12(1)(*g*)	IT-423, IT-426, IT-462; exception: sale of agricultural land

Item	Statutory Reference	Comments
Amount deducted in preceding year for quadrennial survey	para. 12(1)(*h*)	autorization for deduction in preceding year: para. 20(1)(*o*)
Recovered bad debts, previously deducted	para. 12(1)(*i*)	IT-442R authorization for deduction in previous years: paras. 20(1)(*l*), (*p*), subs. 20(4)
Dividends from corporations resident in Canada and other corporations	paras. 12(1)(*j*), (*k*)	IT-67R3, IT-269R3
Income from partnership	para. 12(1)(*l*)	IT-138R
Income from trusts	para. 12(1)(*m*)	
Benefits from profit sharing plan and employee trust to employer	paras. 12(1)(*n*)	IT-502
Net amounts received from employee benefit plan	para. 12(1)(*n*.1)	
Royalties paid or payable to government authority	para. 12(1)(*o*)	IT-438R
Amount received under *Western Grain Stabilization Act*	para. 12(1)(*p*)	deduction of amount: para. 20(1)(*ff*)
Amount deducted employment tax	para. 12(1)(*q*)	eligibility for credit under federal Employment Tax Credit
Cost of inventory at year end representing an allowance for depreciation	para. 12(1)(*r*)	
Reinsurer must include maximum amount which insurer may claim as reserve	para. 12(1)(*s*)	insurer's reserve: para. 20(7)(*c*)
Amount deducted as investment tax credit if not previously included	para. 12(1)(*t*)	IC 78-4R3
Government of Canada grant for home insulation or energy income conversion	para. 12(1)(*u*)	for property used principally for earning income from business or property

Item	Statutory Reference	Comments
Forfeited salary deferral amounts	para. 12(1)(*n*.2)	
Amounts received from retirement compensation arrangement	para. 12(1)(*n*.3)	
Amount of negative balance arrived at in scientific research deduction	para. 12(1)(*v*)	calculation for research made under subs. 37(1)
Benefit received from non-interest bearing or low interest loan by virtue of services performed by corporation carrying on a personal services business	para. 12(1)(*w*)	deemed taxable benefit by subs. 80(4.1)
Inducement or assistance payments	para. 12(1)(*x*); *French Shoes Ltd. v. The Queen*, [1986] 2 CTC 132, 86 DTC 6359 (F.C.T.D.)	all amounts received not already included in income
Cash bonus on Canada Savings Bonds	s. 12.1	IT-396R
Certain amount in respect of fuel tax rebates under *Excise Tax Act*	para. 12(1)(*x*)	
Automobile provided to partner	para. 12(1)(*y*)	
Amateur athlete trust payments	para. 12(1)(*z*)	required by s. 143.1 to be included in income

SELECTED BIBLIOGRAPHY TO CHAPTER VII

General

Anderson, William D., "A Potpourri of Elements in Computing Business Income: Part 2", *Corporate Management Tax Conf.* 6:1 (Can. Tax Foundation, 1987).

Carr, Brian R., "A Potpourri of Elements in Computing Business Income: Part 1", *Corporate Management Tax Conf.* 5:1 (Can.

Drache, A.B.C., "Timing of a Receipt: Part II", 13 *Can. Taxpayer* 148.Tax Foundation, 1987).

Drache, A.B.C., "Timing of an Income Receipt (The)", 13 *Can. Taxpayer* 122.

Freedman, Judith, "Profit and Prophets — Law and Accountancy Practice on the Timing of Receipts — Recognition under the Earnings Basis (Schedule D, Cases I and II)" (1987), *Brit. Tax Rev.* 61.

Freedman, Judith, "Profit and Prophets — Law and Accountancy Practice on the Timing of Receipts — Recognition Under the Earnings Basis (Schedule D, Cases I and II), Continued" (1987), *Brit. Tax Rev.* 104.

Harris, Edwin C., "Timing of Income and Expense Items", *Corporate Management Tax Conf.* 84 (Can. Tax Foundation, 1975).

Knechtel, Ronald C., "Role of Generally Accepted Accounting Principles in Determining Income for Tax Purposes", in *Proceedings of 31st Tax Conf.* 845 (Can. Tax Foundation, 1979).

Krishna, Vern, "Conformity of Accounting Methods for Tax and Financial Statement Purposes: A Search for the 'Truer Picture' of Income", [1992] *Can. Current Tax* C95.

Perry, Harvey, "Federal Individual Income Tax: Taxable Income and Tax", *Tax Paper No. 89* 58 (Can. Tax Foundation, 1990).

Pickford, Barry W., "Tax Accounting for Contract Earnings", in *Proceedings of 31st Tax Conf.* 885 (Can. Tax Foundation, 1979).

Reed, "The Dilemma of Conformity: Tax and Financial Reporting", *Corporate Management Tax Conf.* 20 (Can. Tax Foundation, 1981).

Smith, David W., "New Income Attribution Rules 'Muddified' Income Tax Act" (1986), 13 *Nat. (C.B.A.),* No. 1, 12.

"Ss. 15(2) and 80.4(1) and (2) — Are These Subsections Really all that Difficult?" (1990), 44 DTC 7036.

"Timing of Receivables and Expenses for Tax Purposes", *Cana. Tax Letter,* January 3, 1977 (De Boo).

Tremblay, Richard G., "The Meaning of Earned Income in Sub-Paragraph 12(1)(*a*)(i)" [Case Comment: *Versatile Pacific Shipyards Inc. v. R.,* [1988] 2 C.T.C. 90 (F.C.A.)].

Interest Income

Couzin, Robert, James R. Daman, Michael Hiltz and William R. Lawlor, "Tax Treatment of Interest: Bronfman Trust and the June 2, 1987 Release", *Corporate Management Tax Conf.* 10:1 (Can. Tax Foundation, 1987).

"Discounts, Premiums and Bonuses and the Repeal of IT-114: What Happens Now?" (1994), No. 1181 *Tax Topics* 1.

"Income Tax Treatment of Interest — What's Happening" (1995), No. 1181 *Tax Topics* 2.

Kraayeveld, Serena H., "Accrual Basis of Reporting Interest Income", *Prairie Provinces Tax Conf.* 245 (Can. Tax Foundation, 1983).

"Personal Tax Planning — Recognition of Interest Income by Individuals — the New Complexity" (1984), 33 *Can. Tax J.* 134.

Razienne, Robert, "Accrual of Interest Income", in *Proceedings of 40th Tax Conf.* 23:1 (Can. Tax Foundation, 1988).

Ulmer, John M., "Taxation of Interest Income", in *Proceedings of 42nd Tax Conf.* 8:1 (Can. Tax Foundation, 1990).

Stock Dividends

Le Rossignol, Dan G., "Stock Dividends and Stock Options" (1979), 112 *CA Magazine* 67.

Ware, J.G., "Public Corporations — Stock Dividends", *Corporate Management Tax Conf.* 74 (Can. Tax Foundation, 1978).

Inducement Payments

Dwyer, Blair P., "Deductibility of Tenant Inducement Payments (Income Tax)" (1987-89), 2 *Can. Current Tax* C-53.

Harris, Neil H., "Tax Aspects of Condominium Conversions and Lease Inducement Payments to Recipients" (1986), in *Proceedings of 38th Tax Conf.* 45 (Can. Tax Foundation, 1986).

Ward, David A., and Neil Armstrong, "Corporate Taxation: Lease Inducement Payments" (1986), 5 *Legal Alert* 98.

Other Inclusions in Income

Drache, A.B.C., "Reviewing Life Insurance Needs" (1988), 5 *Bus. & L.* 6.

MacNaughton, Alan, "New Income Tax Rules for Holders of Life Insurance Policies and Annuities" (1983), 31 *Can. Tax J.* 921.

Sanger, John H., "Certain Aspects of the Taxation of Life Insurance Policies in Canada After 1982", *Prairie Provinces Tax Conf.* 453 (Can. Tax Foundation, 1983).

Other

Burger, George, "International Aspects of the Taxation of Discounted Securities" (1987), 35 *Can. Tax J.* 1131.

Haney, M.A., "Payments Dependent on Use or Production: Paragraph 12(1)(*g*)" (1987), 35 *Can. Tax J.* 427.

"Having Your Cake" (1979), 7 *Can. Tax News* 41.

Lawlor, "Income Debentures and Term-Preferred Shares" (1978), 26 *Can. Tax J.* 200.

Sohmer, David H., "Purchase and Sale of a Closely-Held Business (2)" (1979), 112 *CA Magazine* 70.

Stewart, Edward C., "Non-Arm's Length Transactions" (1974), 48 *Cost & Management* 40.

Strain, W.J., "All in Good Time . . .", in *Proceedings of 29th Tax Conf.* 74 (Can. Tax Foundation, 1977).

CHAPTER VIII

BUSINESS AND PROPERTY INCOME: DEDUCTIONS

References:

ITA:

S. 9	Income or Loss — Basic Rules
S. 18	Deductions — General Limitations
Paras. 54(*a*)–(*d*)	Definitions
Subs. 69(1)	Inadequate Consideration

BULLETINS, CIRCULARS & RULINGS:

IT-233R	February 11, 1983	Lease-Option Agreements; Sale-Leaseback Agreements
IT-265R3	October 7, 1991	Payments of Income and Capital Combined
IT-323	May 20, 1976	Sale of Mortgage Included in Proceeds of Disposition of Depreciable Property
IT-405	January 23, 1978	Inadequate Considerations — Acquisitions and Dispositions
IT-521	August 25, 1989	Motor Vehicle Expenses Claimed by Self-Employed Individuals

1. GENERAL

In Chapter VI "Business and Investment Income: General", we saw that the computation of business and investment income begins with the determination of profit from each of those sources. We also examined basic principles and methods with respect to the determination of income. In this chapter, we will look at additional rules for the computation of income from these sources.

We saw in Chapter V "Income From an Office or Employment" that the rules in respect of deductions from business income are considerably more generous than those governing deductions from employment income. The differences in the rules between the deduction of expenses in the computation of business and employment incomes has significant financial consequences for taxpayers. The disparity of treatment between differently placed taxpayers does not, however, contravene the equality provisions of section 15 of the Charter.[1]

---

[1] *O.P.S.E.U. v. National Citizens Coalition Inc.* (1987), 60 OR (2d) 26 (Ont. H.C.) (statement of claim on Charter argument not disclosing cause of action); *Symes v. Canada*, [1991] 2 CTC 1; affirmed 94 DTC 6001 (S.C.C.). See discussion, *obiter*, of protection of the right to work and of economic rights in general under s. 15 of the Charter.

(a) Meaning of "Profit"

The term "profit" in subsection 9(1) means *net* profit: Revenues earned minus expenses incurred for the purpose of earning revenue. The right to deduct expenses in determining profit rests not on any express statutory provision, but on the authority of commercial principles and the absence of any express prohibition. Net profit is

determined according to accounting principles insofar as they do not conflict with specific statutory provisions or judicial decisions.

(b) Rules of Deductibility

To be deductible from revenue, an expense must satisfy the following general criteria:

[handwritten: our purpose is to measure income]

- It must be of an income nature as opposed to a capital expenditure;
- It must be reasonable in amount; *[handwritten: - no acctg rule says this]*
  [handwritten: our one of tax objectives is amt of revenue collected]
- It must be incurred for the purpose of earning income;

[handwritten left margin: 2 rules / s 67- all exp. / reas. / s 67(1)-50% / (meals/ent)]

- It must not be a personal expenditure;
- It must not be expressly prohibited by the Act; and
- It must not be "abusive" tax avoidance.

These criteria serve different purposes from those which are served by generally accepted accounting and commercial principles. For example, the requirement that an expenditure should be reasonable in amount is not an accounting rule, but a constraint to protect the taxable base.

The prohibition against the deductibility of expenses that are specifically proscribed by the Act allows the statute to be used to implement or foster socio-economic policies. For example, the general prohibition in section 19 against the deduction of expenses incurred through advertising in non-Canadian periodicals promotes political and economic policy. The rule has no connection with accounting or commercial principles.

2. CURRENT EXPENSE OR CAPITAL EXPENDITURE?

References:

BULLETINS, CIRCULARS & RULINGS:

IT-296	March 1, 1976	Landscaping of Grounds
IT-350R	June 6, 1977	Investigation of Site
IT-485	April 19, 1982	Cost of Clearing or Levelling Land

(a) General Principles

Expenditures on account of capital or in respect of depreciation or depletion are not deductible for tax purposes.[2] At its simplest, this prohibition does no more than

---

[2] Para. 18(1)(*b*).

reinforce the accounting concept that income is the excess of *revenues* over *expenses* incurred during the relevant period.

Thus, to be deductible, an expenditure must satisfy at least two tests: (1) It must be incurred for the purpose of gaining or producing income from a business or property, and (2) It must be a current expense. There is an interrelationship between these two requirements:[3]

> . . . Since the main purpose of every business undertaking is presumably to make a profit, any expenditure made "for the purpose of gaining or producing income" comes within the terms of [paragraph 18(1)(*a*)], whether it be classified as an income expense or a capital outlay.
>
> Once it is determined that a particular expenditure is one made for the purpose of gaining or producing income, in order to compute income tax liability it must next be determined whether such disbursement is an income expense or a capital outlay.

(b) Accounting Principles

Expenditures which benefit more than one accounting period are generally considered capital outlays for accounting purposes. For example, expenditures on fixed assets, goodwill, incorporation fees, patents and trademarks are typically expenses of a capital nature. This distinction between current expenses and capital expenditures is at the very core of the measurement of income.

Since income is measured for a finite period of time, usually annually, income accounting requires a matching of revenues and expenses during the period in question. Thus, expenditures intended to benefit subsequent fiscal periods are not current expenses, but capital outlays. This seems straightforward enough, but how do we in law distinguish an expenditure that benefits the current period from one that benefits the future?

(c) Legal Meaning

The characterization of expenditures as current expenses or capital outlays is a mixed question of law and fact.[4] The determination of the question depends, not upon the nature of property acquired,[5] but upon the nature of the expenditure: What was the payment expended for?

---

[3] *B.C. Electric Ry. v. M.N.R.*, [1958] CTC 21, 58 DTC 1022 (S.C.C.).

[4] *Johns-Manville Can. Inc. v. The Queen* (1985), 85 DTC 5373 (S.C.C.).

[5] *Golden Horse Shoe (New) Ltd. v. Thurgood*, [1934] 1 KS 548 at 563 (C.A.).

There are several legal principles to distinguish between capital and revenue expenditures, but they are applied flexibly to particular factual situations.[6] A test that may be useful in one set of circumstances may not be relevant in another.[7] There is no single definitive or conclusive test for determining whether an expenditure is of a capital or revenue nature.[8]

The classic description of what constitutes a capital expenditure is in *Br. Insulated & Helsby Cables v. Atherton:*[9]

> . . . where an expenditure is made, not only once and for all, but with a view to bringing into existence an asset or an advantage for the enduring benefit of a trade, I think that there is very good reason (in the absence of special circumstances leading to an opposite conclusion) for treating such an expenditure as properly attributable not to revenue but to capital.

Two features of this definition warrant emphasis: (1) It is the *purpose,* rather than the result, of an expenditure that determines whether it is characterized as a capital outlay or a current expense; and (2) The focus of the test is on whether or not the expenditure brings into existence an asset of enduring value, rather than on the determination of the frequency or recurrence of the expenditure.[10]

---

[6] *Johns-Manville Can. Inc. v. The Queen, ante*; *B.P. Australia Ltd. v. Commr. of Taxation of the Commonwealth of Australia*, [1966] AC 224 (P.C.) (deductibility of amount paid to gas stations to secure monopoly of station, i.e., that it sell only B.P. gas in furtherance of marketing reorganization plan), approved by the Supreme Court of Canada in *M.N.R. v. Algoma Central Railway*, [1968] CTC 161, 68 DTC 5096 (S.C.C.) (Court agreed with test enunciated in *B.P. Australia Ltd.*, then decided without reasons); see also *Bowater Power Co. v. M.N.R.*, [1971] CTC 818, 71 DTC 5469 (F.C.T.D.):

> The solution, therefore, depends on what the expenditure is calculated to effect from a practical and business point of view, rather than upon the juristic classification of the legal rights, if any, secured, employed or exhausted in the process. The question of deductibility of expenses, must also, therefore, be considered from the standpoint of the company or its operations, as a practical matter.

[7] *Comm. of Taxes v. Nchanga Consol. Copper Mines Ltd.*, [1964] AC 948 at 959, per Lord Radcliffe (P.C.).

[8] *B.P. Australia Ltd. v. Commr. of Taxation of the Commonwealth of Australia, ante.*

[9] *Br. Insulated & Helsby Cables v. Atherton*, [1926] AC 205 at 213-14 (H.L.).

[10] *Hinton v. Maden & Ireland Ltd.* (1959), 38 Tax Cas. 391 (H.L.) (replacement cost of knives and lasts in shoe manufacturing machinery characterized as capital; equipment essential to functioning of plant); *MacMillan Bloedel (Alberni) Ltd. v. M.N.R.*, [1973] CTC 295, 73 DTC 5264 (F.C.T.D.) (although fan belts and oil were operating costs deductible in maintaining fleet of trucks, tires lasting a year were not; tires comprising 10 — 15 per cent of value of truck; truck purchased intact not in individual parts); *Oxford Shopping Centres Ltd. v. The Queen*, [1980] CTC 7, 79 DTC 5458; affirmed [1981] CTC 128, 81 DTC 5065 (*sub nom. The Queen v. Oxford Shopping Centres Ltd.*) (F.C.A.) ("once and for all" payment by taxpayer to municipality to assist with road changes deductible); see also *The Queen v. Johns-Manville Can. Inc.*, [1982] CTC 56, 82 DTC 6054 (F.C.A.) in which the Court stated:

> I recognize that the regular recurrence of the acquisitions is relevant in determining whether the outlays for the lots are income or capital in nature. But it is in no way decisive. As Dixon J. (as he then was) put it in *Sun Newspapers Limited v. The Federal Commissioner of Taxation* (1938), 61 C.L.R. 337 at page 362 [(Aust. HC)], "recurrence is not a test, it is no more than a consideration, the weight of which depends upon the nature of the expenditure".

Thus, annual expenditures can be on account of capital if they bring into existence assets of enduring value. Conversely, a one-time expenditure may be a current expense if the entire benefit derived from the expenditure is consumed or exhausted in one fiscal period.

(i) Enduring Benefit

What constitutes an "enduring benefit"? The test refers to benefits that endure in the sense that some assets have a life longer than one year. Benefits that accrue from saving payments over a number of years are not indicative of a capital asset. Rowlatt J. explained the distinction in *Anglo-Persian Oil Ltd. v. Dale*:[11]

> ... a benefit which endures, in the way that fixed capital endures; not a benefit that endures in the sense that for a good number of years it relieves you of a revenue payment. It means a thing which endures in the way that fixed capital endures. It is not always an actual asset, but it endures in the way that getting rid of a lease or getting rid of onerous capital assets . . . endures.

An enduring benefit can derive just as well from discharging a liability as from the acquisition of an asset.[12]

> ... the disposition of a source of liability may be equivalent to the acquisition of a source of profit — an extension perhaps, but not an exception, to the principle that in some sense or other an asset of a capital nature, tangible or intangible, positive or negative, must be shown to be acquired.

The "enduring benefit" test is easier to state than it is to apply. To be sure, it provides an answer in self-evident cases. Common sense and accounting principles tell us that a taxpayer who purchases a building for rental purposes should not be entitled to write-off its entire cost in the year of acquisition, and that the purchase price should be considered a capital expenditure. It is equally clear that the costs of heating the building are annual costs and should be charged off as current expenses against revenues in each year.

But what of the in-between cases? Consider the following:

- The taxpayer expends $20,000 on advertising the building for rent;[13]
- The taxpayer spends $40,000 on lobbying against rent control legislation;[14]

---

[11] *Anglo-Persian Oil Ltd. v. Dale* (1931), 16 Tax Cas. 253 at 262 (C.A.), approved by Lord Wilberforce in *Tucker v. Granada Motorway Services Ltd.*, [1979] STC 393 at 396 (H.L.).

[12] *I.R.C. v. Carron Co.* (1968), 45 Tax Cas. 18 at 75 (H.L.).

[13] *M.N.R. v. Tower Invt. Inc.*, [1972] CTC 182 (T.A.B.) (Court allowed deferral of deduction, in effect, matching expense to period when most of the resulting revenue would accrue).

[14] *Morgan v. Tate & Lyle Ltd.*, [1955] AC 21, 35 Tax Cas. 367 (H.L.) (expenditure on propaganda campaign to prevent nationalization of sugar refining industry was current expense); *Boarland v. Kramat Pulai Ltd.* (1953), 35 Tax Cas. 1 (cost of pamphlet circulated to shareholders, critical of government policy not wholly on account of trade).

• The taxpayer installs a concrete lining in the basement of the building to protect it against an oil nuisance created by a nearby refinery.[15]

These subtle distinctions are not as easy to resolve, and some judges are quite candid about the difficulty of characterizing such expenditures. As Sir Wilfred Greene M.R. said:[16]

> . . . there have been . . . many cases where this matter of capital or income has been debated. There have been many cases which fall upon the borderline: indeed, in many cases it is almost true to say that the spin of a coin would decide the matter almost as satisfactorily as an attempt to find reasons. . . .

(ii) Direct vs. Indirect Consequences

Does the expenditure "bring into existence an asset of enduring value"? This test is also difficult. Does one look to the direct and immediate consequence of an expenditure, or to its ultimate effect on the taxpayer's business? The term "enduring" should not be interpreted literally, but in its commercial and accounting context. Many current expenses have enduring benefits in the sense that advantages accruing from the expenditure continue for a long time. For example, a payment to be rid of an incompetent employee is a current expense even though the payment will, hopefully, have enduring beneficial consequences.[17] An oil change is of enduring benefit to the life of an automobile, but would be considered a current expense.

Expenditures on account of the development or acquisition of goodwill illustrate some of the subtle difficulties inherent in the process of expenditure characterization.

(A) Purchased Goodwill

In *M.N.R. v. Algoma Central Ry.*,[18] the taxpayer expended funds to obtain a geological survey of the mineral potential of the area through which the railway operated. The expenditure was a once-and-for-all cost intended to stimulate its railway traffic by attracting developers to engage in mining the area. There were two issues: (1) Did the expenditures bring into existence an asset of enduring value? and (2) Was enduring value to be tested by looking to the immediate or ultimate consequences of the expenditures? The Exchequer Court held that the *direct* consequences of the expenditures did not bring into existence an asset of an enduring nature; the expenses were deductible as a current expense.

Clearly, *purchased* goodwill is an asset of enduring value and the purchase price is a capital outlay. In contrast, funds expended on account of routine institutional advertising, which generates goodwill, are usually current deductible expenses. In both these situations, the direct use of the funds can easily be traced and identified.

---

[15] *Midland Empire Packing Co. v. Commr.* (1950), 14 TC 635 (U.S.) (concrete lining essentially a repair; deductible as expense).

[16] *I.R.C. v. Br. Salmson Aero Engines Ltd.* (1938), 22 Tax Cas. 29 at 43 (C.A.).

[17] *Mitchell v. B.W. Noble Ltd.*, [1927] 1 KB 719 (C.A.) (payment to get rid of a director was a revenue expense).

[18] *M.N.R. v. Algoma Central Ry.*, ante.

(B) Protecting Goodwill

It is the intermediate case, funds expended to protect existing goodwill, that presents the most difficulties. In *Canada Starch Co. v. M.N.R.*,[19] for example, the taxpayer spent $80,000 to develop a new brand name, "Viva". When faced with opposition to its registration as a trade mark on the grounds that "Viva" was confusing with another registered trade mark, the taxpayer paid $15,000 in return for withdrawal of the opposition to registration. Jackett P. described the difference between acquired assets and developed assets as follows:

- an expenditure for the acquisition or creation of a business entity, structure or organization, for the earning of profit, or for an addition to such entity, structure or organization, is an expenditure on account of capital, and

- an expenditure in the process of operation of a profit making entity, structure or organization is an expenditure on revenue account.

Since the expenditures made *in the course of the taxpayer's operations* which gave rise to the trade mark were current expenses, the $15,000 payment was part of the process of the registration of an asset which was already in existence and, therefore, was deductible as an expense.

On the general question of expenditures on account of promotion, advertising, and goodwill, Jackett P. said:

> [I]n my view, the advertising expenses for launching the new product in this case were expenses on revenue account. I expressed a similar view in *Algoma Central Railway v. M.N.R.* . . . a decision that was upheld on appeal. As I indicated there, "According to my understanding of commercial principles . . . advertising expenses paid out while a business is operating, and directed to attract customers to a business, are current expenses". Similarly, in my view, expenses of other measures taken by a businessman with a view to introducing particular products to the market — such as market surveys and industrial design studies — are also current expenses. They also are expenses laid out while the business is operating as part of the process of inducing the buying public to buy the goods being sold.

> It remains to consider expenses incurred by a businessman, during the course of introducing new products to the market, to obtain the additional protection for his trade mark that is made available by trade mark legislation. A new mark adopted and used in the course of marketing a product gradually acquires the protection of the laws against passing off (assuming that it is, in fact, distinctive). This is something that is an incidental result of ordinary trading operations. Additional expenditure to acquire the additional protection made available by statute law seems to me to be equally incidental to ordinary trading operations. It follows that, in my view, the fees paid to the trade mark lawyers and to the trade mark office are deductible. In this case, no submission was presented to me as to any principle whereby I should distinguish between the ordinary cost of acquiring trade mark registration and the $15,000 payment that, in this case, was necessary in the judgment of the appellant to obtain registration of the trade mark . . . and I have been able to conceive of no such principle.

---

[19]   *Can. Starch Co. v. M.N.R.*, [1968] CTC 466, 68 DTC 5320 (Ex. Ct.); *Border Chem. Co. v. The Queen* (1987), 87 DTC 5391 (F.C.T.D.) (legal fees to defend a taxpayer's senior officials against criminal prosecution not deductible as expenses if cost incurred to prevent damage to taxpayer's goodwill).

In contrast, legal fees to defend a taxpayer's senior officials against criminal prosecution are not deductible as expenses if the cost is incurred to prevent damage to the taxpayer's goodwill.[20]

(iii) Preservation of Capital Assets

The distinction between a current expense and capital expenditure becomes even more blurred when the question arises in the context of expenditures to maintain or preserve capital assets already in existence. Is an expenditure incurred for the protection or maintenance of a capital asset a capital expenditure? The answer depends more upon the *type* of property on which the expenditure is incurred than on any clear-cut, black-letter rule.

(A) Legal Expenses

The deductibility of legal expenses incurred in the course of protecting a capital asset is unclear. The weight of the cases would appear to be against deductibility. In an early case, *Dom. Natural Gas Co. v. M.N.R.*,[21] the Supreme Court of Canada held that legal expenses incurred in successfully protecting the taxpayer's gas franchise were capital outlays and not deductible from income. In reaching his decision, Duff C.J.C. enlarged Lord Cave's test (bringing into existence an asset of enduring benefit to the business) as follows:

> The expenditure was incurred *both* "once and for all" and it was incurred for the purpose and with the effect of procuring for the company "the advantage of an enduring benefit".

In contrast to a decision of the English court in the same year,[22] the court did not accept that the expenses were incidental to the ordinary course of the taxpayer's business. Thus, it required that a two-step hurdle be overcome in order to establish that an expenditure is current and deductible.

---

[20]   *Border Chemical Co. v. The Queen, ante.*

[21]   [1940-41] CTC 155, 1 DTC 499-133 (S.C.C.).

[22]   See *Southern v. Borax Consol. Ltd.*, [1940] 4 All E.R. 412 at 416 and 419, per Lawrence J.:

> . . . In my opinion, the principle which is to be deducted from the cases is that where a sum of money is laid out for the acquisition or the improvement of a fixed capital asset it is attributable to capital, but *if no alteration is made* in the fixed capital asset by the payment, then it is properly attributable to revenue, being in substance a matter of maintenance, the maintenance of the capital structure or the capital assets of the company. . . .

> It appears to me that the legal expenses which were incurred . . . did not create any new asset at all but were expenses which were incurred in the ordinary course of maintaining the assets of the company, and the fact that it was maintaining the title and not the value of the company's business does not, in my opinion, make it any different. [Emphasis added.]

See also *Mitchell v. B. W. Noble Ltd.* (1927), 11 Tax Cas. 372 at 421:

> The object (of the expenditure) . . . was that of preserving the status and reputation of the company which the directors felt might be imperilled . . . to avoid that and to preserve the status and divided-earning power of the company seems to me a purpose which is well within the ordinary purpose of the trade.

The stature of *Dom. Natural Gas Co. v. M.N.R.* has, however, been eroded by subsequent decisions, and its sphere of influence considerably reduced. In *M.N.R. v. Kellog Co. of Can.*,[23] for example, the taxpayer successfully deducted substantial legal fees incurred in defending an allegation of trade mark infringement. The Supreme Court distinguished its earlier decision in *Dom. Natural Gas Co. v. M.N.R.* on the basis that the trademark action in *M.N.R. v. Kellogg Co. of Can.* was neither a right of property nor an exclusive right. The court held the expenses to be ordinary legal expenses and deductible in the ordinary course of business.[24]

In *Evans v. M.N.R.*,[25] the taxpayer, who was entitled to one-third of an estate left to her by her husband and by her father, incurred legal fees when her right to the income of the estate was challenged. Once again, the Supreme Court held that the legal fees were a current expense and were not paid on account of capital. Cartwright J., speaking for the majority of the court, distinguished *Dom. Natural Gas Co. v. M.N.R.* on the basis that the legal fees in that case were "expenses to preserve a capital asset in a capital aspect", whereas, in the court's opinion, Mrs. Evans's right to the income of the estate was not a capital asset.

Thus, the distinction between a capital expenditure and an expense comes down to whether the expenditure has been incurred to preserve a capital asset in a capital aspect or in a revenue aspect. But what is the distinction between "a capital aspect" and "a revenue aspect"?[26] Does this test add anything to the other tests? Probably not: Eventually, the resolution of the entire question depends upon a facts and circumstances approach. As the Privy Council said in *B.P. Australia Ltd. v. Commr. of Taxation of Commonwealth of Australia*:[27]

> [T]he solution to the problem is not to be found by any rigid test or description. It has to be derived from many aspects of the whole set of circumstances, some of which may point in one direction, some in the other. One consideration may point so clearly that it dominates other and vaguer indications in the contrary direction. It is a commonsense appreciation of all the guiding features which must provide the ultimate answer.

---

[23] *M.N.R. v. Kellogg Co. of Can.*, [1942] CTC 51, 2 DTC 548; affirmed [1943] CTC 1, 3 DTC 601 (S.C.C.).

[24] *M.N.R. v. Kellogg Co. of Can.*, *ante*, in which the learned Chief Justice said:

> The right upon which the (taxpayer) relied was not a right of property, or an exclusive right of any description, but the right (in common with all other members of the public) to describe their goods in the manner in which they were described.

[25] *Evans v. M.N.R.*, [1960] CTC 69, 60 DTC 1047 (S.C.C.); see also *Farmer's Mutual Petroleums Ltd. v. M.N.R.*, [1966] CTC 283, 66 DTC 5225; affirmed [1967] CTC 396, 67 DTC 5277 (S.C.C.) (legal expenses incurred in defending title to mineral rights were capital outlays); *B.C. Power Corp. v. M.N.R.*, [1966] 454, 66 DTC 5310; affirmed [1967] CTC 406, 67 DTC 5258 (S.C.C.) (legal expenses incurred in preserving right to shares that had purportedly been expropriated by a provincial government were non-deductible capital expenditures).

[26] See, e.g., *The Queen v. Jager Homes Ltd.*, 88 DTC 6119 (F.C.A.) (legal fees to defend action to wind-up company on capital account and not deductible as current expense).

[27] *B.P. Australia Ltd. v. Commr. of Taxation of Commonwealth of Australia*, [1966] AC 224 at 264 (P.C.), cited with approval by the S.C.C. in *Johns-Manville Can. Inc. v. The Queen* (1985), 85 DTC 5373 at 5383.

(B) Repairs, Maintenance and Alterations

The dividing line between capital expenditures and current expenses due to routine maintenance and repairs is also blurred. Here too, the underlying principle is easy to state, but difficult to apply. An expenditure in one fiscal period that enhances, substantially improves, enlarges, or prolongs the life of an asset beyond that period, is a capital outlay. In contrast, an expenditure that merely maintains an asset or restores it to its original condition is a deductible current expense.

Here, as elsewhere in tax law, it is easy to identify the correct answer in polar cases; it is the grey areas in between that cause the problems and litigation. For example, it is clear that the extension of an existing building by adding new floor space is a capital expenditure; it brings into existence an asset of enduring value. It is equally clear that routine maintenance of an existing building, for example, performance of minor repairs, replacement of light bulbs, cleaning, and maintenance of heating and ventilation systems, are current expenditures.

Between these extremes, however, there are cases which cause considerable difficulty. Each expenditure should be characterized *in the context of the taxpayer's activities* and not in the abstract. For example, a taxpayer who expends money to restore a decrepit and rundown building incurs capital expenditures even though routine maintenance by the previous owner, that would have involved current expenditures, would have prevented the building from deteriorating to a decrepit state. Similarly, a business that regularly expends funds to change the oil in its fleet of automobiles incurs current expenses. Neglecting to change the oil in its automobiles may, at a later date, involve substantial costs by way of engine replacements that would result in capital outlays.[28]

(C) "Repair" vs. "Renewal"

"Repair" and "renew" do not necessarily imply different meanings. "Repair" means, "restoration by renewal or replacement of subsidiary parts of a whole". "Renewal" means, "reconstruction of the entirety, meaning by the entirety, not necessarily of the whole".[29] The relationship between repairs and renewals was considered by the Privy Council in *Rhodesia Rys. Ltd. v. Bechuanaland Collector of IT:*[30]

> The periodical renewal by sections, of the rails and sleepers of a railway line as they wear out through use, is in no sense a reconstruction of the whole railway and is an ordinary incident of railway administration. The fact that the wear, although continuous, is not and cannot be made good annually, does not render the work of renewal when it comes to being effected, necessarily a capital charge. The expenditure here in question was incurred in consequence of the rails having been worn out in earning the income of the previous years on which tax had been paid without deduction in respect of such wear, and represented the cost of restoring them to a state in which they could continue to earn income. It did

---

[28] *Better Plumbing Co. v. M.N.R.* (1952), 6 Tax ABC 177 (T.A.B.); see also *Glenco Invt. Corp. v. M.N.R.*, [1967] CTC 243, 67 DTC 5169 (Ex. Ct.) (cost of plumbing and electrical installations in a warehouse acquired and converted into a commercial building suitable for rental was capital outlay).

[29] *Lurcott v. Wakely*, [1911] 1 KB 905 (C.A.).

[30] *Rhodesia Rys. Ltd. v. Bechuanaland Collector of IT*, [1933] AC 368 at 374 (P.C.).

not result in the creation of any new asset; it was incurred to maintain the appellant's existing line in a state to earn revenue.

(D) Replacements

Renewal costs which go beyond financing the replacement of worn-out parts, and transforms one asset into another, are capital expenditures. In *Highland Ry. Co. v. Balderston*,[31] the taxpayer was not allowed to deduct the costs of replacing iron rails with steel rails. As the Lord President of the Scottish Court of Exchequer put it:

> [T]hen when we come to the question of the alteration of the main line itself, it must be kept in view that this is not a mere relaying of the line after the old fashion; it is not taking away rails that are worn out o[r] partially worn out, and renewing them in whole or in part along with the whole line. That would not alter the character of the line; it would not affect the nature of the heritable property possessed by the Company. But what has been done is to substitute one kind of rail for another, steel rails for iron rails.

In other words, steel rails are a different asset from iron rails, although either may be used for the same purpose — transporting trains.

Whether replacement costs are deductible as a current expense depends upon the magnitude of the replacement in the context of the complete unit of which it forms a part. The replacement of spark plugs in an automobile is routine maintenance; replacement of the entire engine is a capital outlay. The test in each case is: Are the expenditures on account of repair of the larger property by replacement of a component, or on account of replacement of an entire unit, complete in itself?[32] The question is often pragmatically resolved by comparing the cost of replacement with the cost of ordinary repairs in the context of the total unit of which the replacement is a part. The higher the cost of replacement compared to the costs of the total unit, the greater the likelihood that the costs are on account of capital.

(iv) Discharge of Obligations

A payment to get rid of an enduring disadvantage or an onerous obligation may have enduring benefits and constitute a capital expenditure. Here too, the polar cases are clear. A *surrogatum* payment to discharge a revenue expense is deductible, for example, a payment to dismiss an unsatisfactory employee.[33] Similarly, a payment to discharge a capital liability is a capital expenditure.[34] The intermediate cases are not

---

[31] *Highland Rwy. Co. v. Balderston* (1889), 2 Tax Cas. 485 at 488; see also *Tank Truck Transport Ltd. v. M.N.R.* (1965), 38 Tax ABC 332 (T.A.B.) (replacement of 12 cast iron tanks with stainless steel tanks held to be capital outlay).

[32] *M.N.R. v. Vancouver Tugboat Co.*, [1957] CTC 178, 57 DTC 1126 (Ex. Ct.) ($42,000 replacement of tugboat engine held to be replacement of substantial part of the whole, hence capital outlay); *Can. S.S. Lines Ltd. v. M.N.R.*, 66 DTC 5205 (Ex. Ct.) (cost of replacing boiler in ship held to be capital expenditure).

[33] *Mitchell v. B.W. Noble Ltd.*, [1927] 1 K.B. 719 (C.A.) (payment to secure retirement of director whose conduct likely to damage taxpayer's business was revenue payment).

[34] *Countess Warwick S.S. Co. v. Ogg*, [1924] 2 K.B. 292 (payment to secure cancellation of contract to acquire capital asset was capital expense).

as clear cut. The emphasis is on the permanency of the advantage secured by discharging the liability.[35]

(v) Factual Ambiguity

As the above discussion illustrates, the characterization of expenditures is a factual determination in the context of broadly defined legal principles. At the very least, the process is shrouded in uncertainty and factual ambiguity. In whose favour is factual ambiguity to be resolved? Factual ambiguity in respect of expenditure characterizations is to be resolved in the taxpayer's favour.[36] As Mr. Justice Estey, speaking for a unanimous Supreme Court, put it:[37]

> . . . Such a determination is, furthermore, consistent with another basic concept in tax law, that where the taxing statute is *not explicit, reasonable uncertainty or factual ambiguity resulting from lack of explicitness in the statute should be resolved in favour of the taxpayer.* This residual principle must be the more readily applicable in this appeal where otherwise, annually recurring expenditures completely connected to the daily business operation of the taxpayer, afford the taxpayer no credit against tax either by way of capital cost or depletion allowance with reference to a capital expenditure, or an expense deduction against revenue. [Emphasis added.]

(vi) Summary

There is no single test that can be applied to all circumstances. There are, however, three broad criteria that offer a useful starting point in determining whether an expenditure is on account of capital or revenue:

1. The character of the advantage or enduring benefit sought and how permanent the benefit (the more enduring the benefit the more likely that the expenditure is on account of capital);

2. Recurrence and frequency of the expenditure (the more frequent the expenditure the less enduring the benefit); and

3. Identification of the payment as a *surrogatum* for expenditures that would be on account of capital or revenue (a substitute for a capital expenditure is more likely a capital expenditure).

---

[35] *Whitehead (Inspector of Taxes) v. Tubbs (Elastics) Ltd.*, [1984] STC 1 at 3 (C.A.) (payment to secure release from onerous term in loan agreement which significantly limited taxpayer's power to borrow constituting capital payment), per Oliver L.J.:

> Here the advantage sought to be achieved was one which was permanent in the sense that the company was relieved, for the balance of the loan period, of the disadvantages arising from the restrictions and relieved of restrictions attributable to a non-recurring transaction. One cannot separate the payment made from the origins of the restrictions in respect of which it was made. In effect these restrictions -and whether they were contained in the agreement or the debenture is really immaterial, for they clearly went and were intended to go hand-in-hand - were the price or premium paid by the company for the loan, and the loan, it is not in dispute, was clearly a transaction of a capital nature.

[36] *The Queen v. Johns-Manville Can. Inc.* (1985), 85 DTC 5373 (S.C.C.).

[37] *The Queen v. Johns-Manville Can. Inc., ante,* at 5384.

Lord Pearce suggested a solution to the problem:[38]

> ... It is a commonsense appreciation of all the guiding features which must provide the ultimate answer. . . . That answer "depends on what the expenditure is calculated to effect from a practical and business point of view rather than upon the juristic classification of the legal rights, if any, secured, employed or exhausted in the process": per Dixon J., in *Hallstroms Pty. Ltd. v. Federal Commr. of Taxation.*

3. UNREASONABLE EXPENSES

References:

ITA:

S. 67   Expenses — General Limitation

BULLETINS, CIRCULARS & RULINGS:

IT-487   April 26, 1982   General Limitation on Deduction of Outlays or Expenses

For the purpose of calculating income, a taxpayer may not deduct an expense, except to the extent that the expense is reasonable in amount.[39] This general rule relates to the *quantum,* and not to the type, of the expense. The purpose of the rule is to prevent taxpayers from artificially reducing income by deducting inordinately high expenses.

What is a "reasonable" expense is a question of fact to be determined by comparing the expense in question with amounts paid in similar circumstances in comparable businesses. Although Revenue Canada does not invoke this rule often, its presence is an important factor to consider when arranging business transactions.[40] In *Doug Burns Excavation,*[41] for example, the Tax Court denied the corporate taxpayer a deduction for a bonus of $100,000 paid to its president's wife for general clerical functions in the office.

---

[38] *B.P. Australia Ltd. v. Commr. of Taxation*, [1966] AC 224 at 264 (P.C.).

[39] S. 67.

[40] *Doug Burns Excavation Contr. Ltd. v. M.N.R.*, [1983] CTC 2566, 83 DTC 528 (T.C.C.); *W.J. Kent and Co. v. M.N.R.*, [1971] Tax ABC 1158 (T.A.B.) (taxpayer not allowed to claim a part of the capital cost allowance in respect of a Rolls Royce automobile); *Mulder Bros. Sand & Gravel Ltd. v. M.N.R.*, [1967] Tax ABC 761 (T.A.B.) (salary of $13,000 paid by corporation to wife of shareholder for performing office work reduced to $8,500); *Cohen v. M.N.R.* (1963), 31 Tax ABC 216 (T.A.B.) (annual office rent of $12,000 paid by doctor to wife reduced to $5,000).

[41] *Doug Burns Excavation Contr. Ltd. v. M.N.R, ante.*

4. PURPOSE OF EXPENDITURE

Reference:

BULLETINS, CIRCULARS & RULINGS:

IT-487   April 26, 1982   General Limitation on Deduction of Outlays
                                        or Expenses

(a) Purpose, Not Result

An expenditure is deductible as an expense in computing income only if it is incurred for the *purpose* of earning income.[42] It is the *purpose,* and not the result, of the expenditure which determines deductibility. Thus, an expense for the purpose of earning income from a business is deductible, regardless of whether or not it actually produces income. For example, if a taxpayer incurs advertising expenses for the purpose of promoting sales of a product, failure of the advertising program to stimulate sales does *not* disqualify the expenditure as a deductible expense.

The Exchequer Court explained the scheme for the deductibility of expenses as follows:[43]

> Thus, it may be stated categorically that in a case under the Income Tax Act the first matter to be determined in deciding whether an outlay or expense is outside the prohibition of paragraph 18(1)(a) of the Act is whether it was made or incurred by the taxpayer in accordance with the ordinary principles of commercial trading or well accepted principles of business practice. If it was not, that is the end of the matter. But if it was, then the outlay or expense is properly deductible unless it falls outside the expressed exception of paragraph 18(1)(a) and, therefore, within its prohibition. . . .

The essential limitation in paragraph 18(1)(a) is that the outlay or expense should have been made by the taxpayer "for the purpose" of gaining or producing income "from the business". The purpose must be that of gaining or producing income from the business in which the taxpayer is engaged. *A fortiori,* the business must be in existence at the time the expenditure is incurred.

---

[42] Para. 18(1)(a). This rule does little more than reinforce subs. 9(1) which states that the income from a business or property is the profit therefrom. To constitute an "expense", the taxpayer must be under an obligation to pay money to someone. An obligation to do something which may entail an expenditure in the future is *not* an expense; see *The Queen v. Burnco Industries Ltd.,* [1984] CTC 337, 84 DTC 6348 (F.C.A.).

[43] *Royal Trust Co. v. M.N.R.,* [1957] CTC 32 at 42, 44, 57 DTC 1055 at 1060, 1062 (Ex. Ct.); see also *B.C. Electric Ry. v. M.N.R.,* [1958] CTC 21, 58 DTC 1022 (S.C.C.) (payments made by taxpayer to enable it to become more profitable not deductible even though made for purpose of producing income on account of capital; case departing from previous law; see editorial note at [1958] CTC 21).

(b) Primary Purpose

Expenditures may be broken down into deductible and non-deductible portions.[44] An expenditure does not have to be wholly and exclusively expended for business purposes in order to be deductible.[45]

What constitutes a business purpose is a question of fact. The focus is on the *primary* purpose of the expenditure. For example, a lawyer who travels from Toronto to Paris for a business meeting may deduct her travel expenses for the trip even though she stays on for the weekend for personal reasons. She may also deduct any *incremental* expenditures (such as, additional hotel and meal charges) associated with the personal portion of her visit, if the expenses are part of the cost of waiting for meetings to resume on Monday. The personal pleasure is secondary to the primary business purpose of the visit.

5. PERSONAL AND LIVING EXPENSES

(a) General

A taxpayer cannot deduct personal or living expenses in computing income from a business or property.[46] This rule does not add anything substantive to the general rule that a deductible expense must be incurred for the purpose of earning income.[47] It does, however, reinforce to the general rule.

(b) Not "But For" Test

The purpose test should not be confused with the "but for" test. The test for deductibility is *not*: "But for this expense, could the taxpayer have earned his or her income?" Such a broad test would completely obliterate the distinction between business

---

[44] *Consumer's Gas Co. of Toronto v. M.N.R.* (1955), 13 Tax ABC 429 (T.A.B.) (taxpayer obtained gas export permit to improve business; permit and fees for securing permit capital in nature; remainder of fees referable to particular business difficulties, not assets); *KVP Co. v. M.N.R.*, [1957] CTC 275, 57 DTC 1208 (Ex. Ct.) (extensive aerial surveys required by province to preserve timber cutting rights; current expense to the extent of previous average survey expense).

[45] Considerable care should be taken in reading English cases on the deductibility of expenses incurred for business and personal purposes. Under the English statute, an expenditure must be *wholly and exclusively* for business purposes if it is to be deductible; see *Mallalieu v. Drummond*, [1983] 2 AC 861 (H.L.).

[46] Para. 18(1)(*h*) and subs. 248(1) ("personal or living expenses"). The prohibition does not cover travelling expenses (including the full cost of meals and lodging) incurred on a business trip.

[47] Para. 18(1)(*h*) was originally implemented as para. 2(2)(*e*) of c. 55, S.C. 1919 which amended s. 3 of the *Income War Tax Act*, 1917. In response to a question in the House regarding the purpose of this section, asked by a questioner who noted that it was already "quite evident that no one has the right to deduct his personal and living expenses from income before he declares it for the purposes of this Act", the Minister of Finance stated that the section was "just to make it clear that deduction must not be made" and to "make it perfectly clear that the full net income must be assessed" (Commons Debates, June 24, 1919).

expenses and personal expenses and negate the value of the purpose test. For example:[48]

> . . . The fee to the doctor, but for whose healing service, the earner of the family income could not leave his sickbed; the cost of the laborer's raiment, for how can the world proceed about its business unclothed; the very home which gives us shelter and rest and the food which provides energy, might all by an extension of the same proposition be construed as necessary to the operation of business and to the creation of income. Yet these are the very essence of those "personal" expenses the deductibility of which is expressly denied.

The proper test is more subtle and involves three questions: (1) What is the need that the expense meets? (2) Would the need exist apart from the business? and (3) Is the need intrinsic to the business? The answer to these questions are essentially a question of fact.[49]

> If a need exists even in the absence of business activity, and irrespective of whether the need was or might have been satisfied by an expenditure to a third party or by the opportunity cost of personal labour, then an expense to meet the need would traditionally be viewed as a personal expense. Expenses which can be identified in this way are expenses which are incurred by a taxpayer in order to relieve the taxpayer from personal duties and to make the taxpayer available to the business. Traditionally, expenses that simply make the taxpayer *available* to the business are not considered business expenses since the taxpayer is expected to be available to the business as a *quid pro quo* for business income received.

The needs test alone does not provide an unequivocal answer. The expense must also be intrinsic to the business. In *Symes*, for example, the taxpayer's child care expenses met the needs test because her business could not function without her presence. But, the expenses were merely to make her *available* to practice her profession, rather than for any purpose intrinsic to the operation of the business itself. The expenses got her to her business, but they were not an integral part of the business.

(c) Type of Expenditure

Given the subjective nature of the purpose test, many courts look to the nature of an expenditure to determine its purpose. Is the expenditure of a type that is ordinarily and usually considered a direct expenditure in the pursuit of business or one that is primarily personal and only tenuously related to business? Consider the distinction between a businessperson who entertains an out-of-town client at home and one who takes a client out for dinner to an expensive restaurant. It is likely that the expenses of entertaining at home are personal, even though the entire discussion may be devoted to business matters. This is because home entertainment is ordinarily and usually considered to be a personal affair. In contrast, 50 per cent of the cost of the dinner in a restaurant would be deductible as a business expense, even though the cost may be

---

[48] *Smith v. Commr.*, 113 F 2d 114 (US 2nd Cir., 1940).

[49] *Symes*, [1993] 4 SCR 695, [1994] 1 CTC 40, 94 DTC 6001
". . . In another case, the arguments might be differently balanced, since the existence of a business purpose within the meaning of s. 18(1)(a) *is a question of fact*, and that the relative weight to be given to the factors analyzed will vary from case to case. . . . It can be difficult to weigh the personal and business elements at play. [Emphasis added.]

substantially higher than the cost of an equivalent meal at home. Entertaining in restaurants is ordinarily and usually associated with business, and expenses in respect thereof are considered "business expenses".[50]

Some courts have said that the distinction between business and personal expenses depends upon the taxpayer's discretionary power to incur the expense. For example, Thorson P. denied a deduction for commuting expenses on the basis that:[51]

> . . . The personal and living expenses referred to . . . are those over which the taxpayer has a large amount of personal control, depending upon the scale of living which he may choose. Such expenses would probably not be deductible even if there were no provision in the statute relating to the matter, for if personal and living expenses were deductible from income and only the balance left for taxation purposes, the amount of net or taxable income would depend upon the taxpayer's own choice as to the scale of living that he might adopt and in many cases there would be no taxable income at all. It is obvious that the determination of what the taxable income of a taxpayer shall be cannot depend upon or be left to the taxpayer's own choice as to whether his personal and living expenses shall be up to the extent of his income or not.

The rationale that personal expenses should not be deducted because they are within the discretion of the taxpayer is not persuasive. Most expenses, including business expenses, are ultimately within the taxpayer's discretion. The simpler explanation is sufficient: Personal expenses are not deductible against business income because they are not incurred for business purposes and, as such, they are not relevant in determining income from business.

"Personal or living expenses" include expenses incurred to maintain a property where the property is not maintained in connection with a business that is being carried

---

[50] *Vuicic v. M.N.R.* (1960), 24 Tax ABC 253 (T.A.B.) (tavern keeper not allowed to deduct capital cost allowance in respect of $7,000 boat); *Brown v. M.N.R.* (1950), 1 Tax ABC 373 (T.A.B.) (special clothing required by radio technician posted in north not deductible); *No. 431 v. M.N.R.* (1957), 17 Tax ABC 300 (T.A.B.) (salary paid to physician's housekeeper entirely personal or living expense notwithstanding housekeeper's answering physician's telephone); *Macquistan v. M.N.R.* (1965), 38 Tax ABC 23 (T.A.B.) (babysitter employed by physician in order to permit her to carry on practice was personal expense); *Nadon v. M.N.R.* (1965), 40 Tax ABC 33 (T.A.B.) (housekeeper engaged during illness of taxpayer's wife not deductible); *Lawlor v. M.N.R.*, [1970] Tax ABC 369 (T.A.B.) (lawyer not entitled to deduct cost of babysitters employed to permit business entertaining); *Cree v. M.N.R.*, [1978] CTC 2472 (T.R.B.) (auto racing not carried on with reasonable expectation of profit; losses not deductible); *Hume v. M.N.R.*, [1980] CTC 2645, 80 DTC 1542 (T.R.B.) ("hobby" investor denied deduction for cost of investment periodicals); *Warden v. M.N.R.*, [1981] CTC 2379, 81 DTC 322 (T.R.B.) (high school principal denied deduction of losses from farming and other operations since no expectation of profit); *Peters v. M.N.R.*, [1981] CTC 2451, 81 DTC 454 (T.R.B.) (bank employee denied deduction of losses from bee keeping and sheep raising); *White v. M.N.R.*, [1981] CTC 2456, 81 DTC 457 (T.R.B.) (taxpayer's losses from breeding and racing quarter horses disallowed for lack of reasonable expectation of profit); *Beyer v. M.N.R.*, [1978] CTC 2026 (T.R.B.) (car racing losses not deductible); *Payette v. M.N.R.*, [1978] CTC 223, 78 DTC 1181 (T.R.B.) (writing and publication of books without reasonable expectation of profit; outlays not deductible); *Fluet v. M.N.R.*, [1978] CTC 2902 (T.R.B.) (bank manager's cost and maintenance of guard dog for family protection not deductible); *Merchant v. M.N.R.*, [1980] CTC 2336 (T.R.B.) (expenses incurred in attempt to secure leadership of Saskatchewan Liberal Party not deductible); *Symes v. Can.*, [1991] 2 CTC 1; affirmed 94 D.T.C. 6001 (S.C.C.) (lawyer's nanny expenses not deductible).

[51] *Samson v. M.N.R.*, [1943] CTC 47 at 64 (Ex. Ct.).

on for profit or with a reasonable expectation of profit. They also include expenses incurred for purchasing a life insurance policy, the proceeds of which are payable to the taxpayer, or to a person related to the taxpayer.[52]

(d) Reasonable Expectation of Profit

How do we distinguish between business and personal expenditures? What is the difference, for example, between an expenditure incurred by a serious amateur photographer and a professional photographer? The distinction depends upon whether the taxpayer has a reasonable expectation of profit in the conduct of his or her activities. It is not enough that the expense was incurred in order to earn gross income.[53] To be deductible, an expense must have been incurred in order to make a *profit*.

What constitutes a "reasonable expectation of profit" can be a difficult question of fact. Two aspects of this question warrant emphasis: (1) The focus is on the reasonable *expectation* of profit, not on the realization of actual profits; and "reasonable expectation of profit" is not synonymous with "expectation of reasonable profit".[54] The word "reasonable" modifies "expectation", and not the word "profit". Thus, the expectation need not be of a reasonable amount of profit.

(i) Criteria for Evaluation

Whether a taxpayer has a reasonable expectation of profit from an activity or operation is to be determined by examining all of the factors surrounding the operation. The determination is objective and based on all of the facts.[55] Equally important, the "expectation" is determined as of the time when the expenses are claimed, not in the retrospective light of actual results determined later.

The following criteria are relevant:[56]

- the profit and loss experience of *prior* years;
- the taxpayer's training and qualifications for the undertaking;
- the financial viability of the undertaking; and
- the stage of development of the undertaking.

The mere fact of a taxpayer's incidentally deriving personal pleasure from an activity in which he or she is involved does not disqualify the activity as "business".[57] Nor

---

[52] Subs. 248(1) ("personal or living expenses").

[53] *Dep. Min. of Revenue (Que.) v. Lipson*, [1979] 1 SCR 833.

[54] *The Queen v. Matthews*, [1974] CTC 230 at 236 (F.C.T.D.), per Mahoney J.

[55] *Moldowan v. The Queen*, [1977] CTC 310, 77 DTC 5213 (S.C.C.).

[56] *Moldowan v. The Queen, ante* at 314.

[57] *The Queen v. Matthews, ante* at 235.

does the absence of profit over an extended period of time necessarily determine the issue. *Nat. Trust Co. (McLaughlin Executors) v. M.N.R. is an extreme example:*[58] An independently wealthy individual devoted 30 years to farming on a scientific, unprofitable, basis but was considered to be operating his farm "with a reasonable expectation of profit".

The expectation of profit must be "reasonable" in the circumstances. Whether an expectation is "reasonable" is determined by applying intuitive probabilistic factors to the success of the undertaking. The "reasonable expectation" test is certainly much more stringent than the "objective of making a profit" test. The Joint Committee of the U.S. Congress stated the difference between these two tests as follows:[59]

> . . . In making the determination of whether an activity is not engaged in for profit, it is intended that an objective rather than a subjective approach be employed. Thus, although a reasonable expectation of profit is not required, the facts and circumstances (without regard to the taxpayer's subjective intent) have to indicate that the taxpayer entered the activity, or continued the activity, with the objective of making a profit. A taxpayer who engaged in an activity in which there was a small chance of a large profit, e.g., a person who invested in a wildcat oil well or an inventor, could qualify under this test even though the expectation of profit might be considered unreasonable.

(ii) Department's Views

Revenue Canada's views on the relevant criteria are as follows:[60]

1) *Profit and loss experience in past years.* Although it may be an indication, the fact that a taxpayer may have incurred continuous losses for several years is not sufficient in and by itself to establish no reasonable expectation of profit. The nature of the activity may require a lengthy start-up period — for example a tree farm, an artist, a writer.

2) *Significance and growth of gross revenue.* The most usual indication that an activity does not constitute a business is that it reports no, or a very small amount of gross income for several years. Conversely, where a gross revenue of some significance has been reported or the gross revenue has been increasing year by year, it is an indicator that there is a reasonable expectation of profit.

3) *Development of the operation to date.* Factors include the amount of capital invested in the operation, the extent to which markets have been developed, or the efforts expended to promote sales.

4) *Planned or intended course of action.* The taxpayer's planned or intended course of action for developing a profitable operation is considered along with the progress made to date.

---

[58] *Nat. Trust Co. v. M.N.R.*, [1952] CTC 264, 52 DTC 1159 (Ex. Ct.); but see s. 31 (deductibility of farming losses restricted in certain circumstances).

[59] *General Explanation of the Tax Reform Act of 1969*, at 94 (Staff of Joint Committee on Internal Revenue Taxation, Dec. 3, 1970).

[60] "Revenue Canada Round Table", in *Proceedings of 36th Tax Conf.* 834 (Can. Tax Foundation, 1984).

5) *Time spent on the activity in question.* The time spent on the activity in comparison to that spent in employment or other income-earning activities is considered. If very little time is spent on the activity in question, there is a presumption that the taxpayer is not carrying on a business unless a substantial amount of the work is contracted out or done by employees.

6) *Education, background, and experience.* The taxpayer's education, background, and experience are considered when evaluating the feasibility of the operation to date and the plans for the future.

7) *Extent of activity in relation to that of business of a comparable size.* One of the tests for determining whether or not a particular operation is economically viable is its size. If it is too small to give any hope of profit, the presumption is that it is being carried on without a reasonable expectation of profit.

(e) Statutory Exceptions

Some expenses which are obviously personal expenses are, nevertheless, deductible under specific statutory provisions. For example, moving expenses,[61] child care expenses,[62] and tuition fees[63] are all personal expenditures that are deductible from income or creditable against taxes in narrowly defined circumstances. The deduction of these types of personal expenses is permitted only after a careful and fully balanced consideration of the social and economic policies underlying the deduction. The deductibility of personal expenses for tax purposes is usually premised on social or economic policy considerations, for example, mobility of labour, access to labour markets, and investment in human capital and resources.

6. GENERAL ANTI-AVOIDANCE RULE

Reference:

ITA:

S. 245   GAAR

The general anti-avoidance rule ("GAAR") applies to "abusive" income tax avoidance transactions and arrangements. The thrust of the rule is that Revenue Canada can ignore an offensive "avoidance transaction" and redetermine its income tax consequences.[64]

---

[61] S. 62; see Chapter XI "Other Deductions".

[62] S. 63; see Chapter XI "Other Deductions".

[63] S. 118.5; see Chapter XIII "Computation of Tax Payable".

[64] S. 245.

An "avoidance transaction" is any transaction or series of transactions that gives rise to a tax benefit, unless the transaction is one that is undertaken for *bona fide* purposes other than that of obtaining a tax benefit.

But even a tax motivated transaction is not an "avoidance transaction" if it does not misuse the Act.[65] See Chapter XXVI "Administration" for a detailed discussion of GAAR.

7. EXEMPT INCOME

Expenses incurred to earn exempt income are not deductible for tax purposes.[66] Generally speaking, "exempt income" is any income that is not included in computing income under Part I of the Act.[67] The purpose of this rule is to ensure that expenditures incurred to earn exempt income are not offset against other taxable income.

8. SPECIFIC DEDUCTIONS

We saw in Chapter VI "Business and Investment Income: General" that the starting point in computing income from business or property is to determine the *net* profit therefrom according to generally accepted accounting principles. In this chapter, we have looked at additional statutory provisions affecting the determination of net profit. We have seen that in determining "net profit", a deduction for expenses that may otherwise be permitted by accounting principles may be prohibited by the Act.

In addition to the deductions allowed according to commercial and accounting principles, the Act also specifically authorizes the deduction of certain expenses. The rationale for this specific list of deductions varies: some of the rules regulate deductions that might otherwise be governed by unclear or flexible accounting principles (e.g., reserves); others (capital cost allowances, for example) replace accounting rules with more specific and detailed tax rules; some (such as restrictions on financing passenger motor vehicles) reflect a concern that the tax system should not subsidize personal expenditures; and some are concerned with political and cultural value judgments (for example, restrictions on advertising in non-Canadian periodicals). There is no single thread connecting the deductions discussed hereunder; each deduction is supported by its own rationale.

9. RESERVES AND CONTINGENT LIABILITIES

References:

BULLETINS, CIRCULARS & RULINGS:

IT-152R3   June 18, 1985   Special Reserves — Sale of Land

---

[65] Subs. 245(4).

[66] Para. 18(1)(c).

[67] Subs. 248(1) ("exempt income").

IT-154R	February 19, 1988	Special Reserves
IT-215R	January 12, 1981	Reserves, Contingent Accounts and Sinking Funds
IT-345R	October 4, 1982	Special Reserve — Loans Secured by Mortgages
IT-436R	November 24, 1983	Reserves — Where Promissory Notes are Included in Disposal Proceeds
IT-442R	September 6, 1991	Bad Debts and Reserves for Doubtful Debts

(a) General Scheme

In the absence of specific authority, a taxpayer may not claim a reserve or deduct a contingent liability in computing income.[68] Reserves are an appropriation of income, rather than expenses incurred for the purpose of earning it. There are, however, many exceptions to this general prohibition against reserves.

The term "reserve" has a much broader meaning in tax law than it does in accounting. For accounting purposes, a "reserve" denotes an appropriation of income from retained earnings. Such appropriation may be pursuant to a contractual stipulation (for example, pursuant to a trust indenture) or at the discretion of the taxpayer.[69] For tax purposes, however, a "reserve" generally refers to an amount set aside that is available for future use.

It is important to distinguish between reserves and unpaid liabilities. A "reserve" represents an amount set aside as a provision against a future uncertain event. A liability is a known and existing obligation.[70] Thus, an obligation is only considered a liability for tax purposes if all of the conditions precedent to create the liability have been satisfied.[71]

A contingent liability is a potential liability that may become actual if, and only if, certain events occur. Thus, contingent liabilities are not real liabilities, but have the potential of becoming real if some uncertain event takes place.

Generally speaking, a taxpayer may claim a reserve in a year only if the Act specifically authorizes the deduction. A reserve claimed in a particular year is added back into the taxpayer's income in the following year. A new reserve may then be claimed according to the terms and conditions of the authorizing provisions. Thus, there is an annual renewal of the reserve on an annual justification for its deduction.

---

[68] Para. 18(1)(e); IT-215R, "Reserves, Contingent Accounts and Sinking Funds" (January 12, 1981) as amended by Special Release dated November 30, 1989.

[69] *CICA Handbook*, s. 3260.01.

[70] *No. 297 v. M.N.R.* (1955), 14 Tax ABC 100 (T.A.B.) (amount set aside by taxpayer for employee bonuses not a reserve since liability to pay definite).

[71] *Kerr Farms Ltd. v. M.N.R.*, [1971] Tax ABC 804 (T.A.B.) (conditions precedent outstanding; accrued employee bonuses not liabilities).

(b) Deductible Reserves

Deduction allowed for:	ITA Reference	To be included in income in following year
Reserve for doubtful debts	20(1)(*l*)	12(1)(*d*)
Reserve for goods delivered and services performed after end of year	20(1)(*m*)(i), (ii)	12(1)(*e*)
Reserve for deposits on returnable containers	20(1)(*m*)(iv)	12(1)(*e*)
Manufacturer's warranty reserve	20(1)(*m*.1)	12(1)(*e*)
Reserves for amounts not due on instalment sales contracts	20(1)(*n*)	12(1)(*e*)
Reserve for quadrennial survey	20(1)(*o*)	12(1)(*h*)

(i) Doubtful Debts

A taxpayer may deduct a reasonable amount for doubtful trade accounts if the amounts receivable in respect of the accounts were included in income, either in the year in which the reserve is sought or in a previous year.

A reserve may also be claimed for doubtful debts arising on loans or lending made in the ordinary course of business where the taxpayer is an insurer or involved in the business of lending money.[72]

A reserve calculated for financial statement purposes is not necessarily the amount deductible for tax purposes. Whether the collectibility of a debt is sufficiently "doubtful" to justify a reserve is a question of fact that must be answered in light of all of the particular circumstances of the relationship between the debtor and creditor. This requires specific analysis of each account. As a matter of practice, however, Revenue Canada does accept reserves calculated as a percentage of doubtful accounts, provided

---

[72] Para. 20(1)(*l*); IT-442, "Bad Debts and Reserve for Doubtful Debts" (February 11, 1980).

that the taxpayer can support the percentage by reference to his or her actual loss experience. A reserve computed as a simple percentage of the taxpayer's total accounts receivable is not acceptable for tax purposes.

The factors usually taken into account in determining the collectibility of an account receivable are as follows:[73]

- History and age of the overdue account,
- The debtor's financial position,
- Past experience in respect of the debtor's bad debts,
- General business conditions,
- Specific business conditions in the debtor's industry,
- Specific business conditions in the debtor's locality, and
- Changes in sales and accounts receivable as compared with previous years.

A taxpayer who claims a reserve for doubtful accounts in one year must include the amount in income in the following year.[74] The taxpayer can then make a fresh evaluation of the collectibility of accounts receivable and deduct a new reserve in the current year. Thus, unlike accounting practice that permits incremental additions to and subtractions from the previous year's reserve, the *entire* amount of the reserve is deducted in the year in which it is claimed. This amount is then added to income in the following year, a new amount is deducted, and so on.

This scheme allows Revenue Canada to challenge the entire reserve in the year it is claimed, without any risk that a portion of the reserve is statute barred. Under accounting practices, it is arguable that only the incremental portion is current. The base of the reserve could be statute barred.[75]

A taxpayer may also deduct actual losses from accounts receivable.[76] Thus, the initial claim for a reserve is a tentative one that is added back to income in the following year. The taxpayer may either collect the amount in a subsequent year or claim a write-off for actual bad debts. An amount written off that is subsequently collected by the taxpayer is brought back into income in the year of collection.[77]

---

[73] *No. 81 v. M.N.R.* (1953), 8 Tax ABC 82 at 98 (T.A.B.).

[74] Para. 12(1)(*d*).

[75] Subs. 152(4).

[76] Para. 20(1)(*p*).

[77] Para. 12(1)(*i*).

Example VIII.1

Assume:

Year	Accounts Receivable (year end)	Reserve for doubtful debts	Bad Debts Deducted	Bad Debts Recovered
1994	$100,000	$10,000	—	—
1995	$120,000	$12,000	$6,000	—
1996	$150,000	$15,000	$4,000	$5,000

Then, the *net* deduction from income in each year is determined as follows:

1994

Reserve for doubtful debts	$10,000
Net deduction (1994)	$10,000

1995

Reserve for doubtful debts	$12,000
Bad debts deducted	6,000
	$18,000
Less: reserve deducted (1994)	(10,000)
Net deduction (1995)	$ 8,000

1996

Reserve for doubtful debts	$15,000
Bad debts deducted	4,000
	$19,000
Less: reserve deducted (1995)	(12,000)
bad debts recovered	(5,000)
Net deduction (1996)	$ 2,000

(ii) Goods and Services

Payments on account of goods to be delivered or services to be rendered in the future are included in income in the year received.[78] This rule overrides the generally accepted accounting principle that income is recognized when it is realized and not when it is received.[79]

---

[78]   Paras. 12(1)(*a*) and (*b*). This is a variation from accounting principles which do not recognize income until it is earned. See Chapter VII "Business and Property Income: Inclusions".

[79]   See Chapter VI "Business and Investment Income: General" under the heading 3(b) "Measurement and Timing".

A taxpayer is, however, entitled to deduct a reasonable amount in respect of goods that will be delivered, or services that will be rendered, in a subsequent year.[80] The reserve is available only in computing income from a business and *not* in computing income from property.

A taxpayer is also allowed to deduct a reserve for deposits that may be refundable (excluding deposits on bottles), prepaid rent for the use of land or chattels, and for amounts which are receivable but not yet due.[81]

Both paragraphs 20(1)(*m*) and 20(1)(*n*) refer to the deduction of a reasonable amount as a reserve. What is "reasonable" is a question of fact depending upon the circumstances. A reasonable reserve is not necessarily equal to the amount included in income under paragraph 12(1)(*a*). For example, a taxpayer who sells tokens that are redeemable for products, would include the proceeds from the tokens in income. If all the tokens have not been redeemed at the end of the taxation year, the taxpayer may claim a reserve equal to the value of the tokens that it is expected will be redeemed by customers. Where, however, the history of the taxpayer's business indicates that some of the tokens sold will never be redeemed, the reserve must be reduced by the amount of the tokens that are not expected to be redeemed.

(iii) Amounts Not Due

In calculating income from a *business*, a taxpayer may deduct a reserve for the purchase price of property sold that is not due until some time after the end of the year.[82]

(A) Property Other Than Land

Where the subject matter of the sale is property other than land, a reserve may be claimed only if the proceeds of the sale are not due until a time more than two years after the date of sale. In effect, the taxpayer may allocate profit over an extended period in much the same way as under instalment sales accounting.

The reserve, which must be reasonable in amount, is normally calculated by comparing the amount due as at the end of the taxation year to the gross sales proceeds. This ratio is applied against the gross profit realized on the sale and the resulting amount is the reserve for that sale for the year.

---

[80] Para. 20(1)(*m*).

[81] Paras. 20(1)(*m*), (*n*).

[82] Para. 20(1)(*n*); *Home Provisioners (Man.) Ltd. v. M.N.R.*, [1958] CTC 334, 58 DTC 1183 (Ex. Ct.) (absolute assignment of right to receive instalment payments precluded right to claim reserve).

Example VIII.2

Assume:

Sale price		$200,000
Cost		100,000
Gross profit		$100,000

Cash received:

Year 1	$125,000	
Year 2	50,000	
Year 3	25,000	

Then:

Year 1:

Profit on sale		$100,000
Less reserve:	$\dfrac{75,000}{200,000} \times \$100,000$	(37,500)
Income (A)		$ 62,500

Year 2:

Previous year's reserve		$ 37,500
Less reserve:	$\dfrac{25,000}{200,000} \times \$100,000$	(12,500)
Income (B)		$ 25,000

Year 3:

Previous year's reserve		$ 12,500
Less reserve:	$\dfrac{0}{200,000} \times \$100,000$	0
Income (C)		$ 12,500

Total gain included in income	
(A + B + C)	$100,000

(B) Land

A taxpayer may claim a reserve when he or she sells land if part of the proceeds of sale are payable after the end of the taxation year in which the land is sold.[83]

---

[83] Subpara. 20(1)(n)(ii); IT-152R3 "Special Reserves — Sale of Land" (June 18, 1985).

(c) Limitations on Reserves

(i) Food, Drink and Transportation

Where a taxpayer claims a reserve in respect of food, drink or transportation to be delivered or provided after the end of the year, the reserve cannot exceed the revenue from these sources included in income for the year.[84]

Example VIII.3

Assume:

Transportation tickets used in year	$ 60,000
Tickets unused at the end of the year	$ 10,000

Then:

The reserve under paragraph 20(1)(*m*) and subsection 20(6) is $10,000 unless experience indicates that a portion of the tickets will never be redeemed. If experience indicates, for example, that 5 per cent of all tickets issued are never redeemed, a reasonable reserve would be computed as follows:

Tickets unused at the end of the year	$ 10,000
Tickets which will not be redeemed	
[5% x $60,000]	(3,000)
Reasonable reserve	$ 7,000

(ii) Non-residents

A taxpayer who ceases to be a Canadian resident and who does not carry on business in Canada may not deduct a reserve in respect of unrealized receivables. Since a reserve claimed in one year is added to income in the following year, this rule ensures that a resident taxpayer cannot avoid tax simply by giving up Canadian residence.[85]

(iii) Guarantees, Indemnities and Warranties

When a taxpayer sells property or services and provides a guarantee, indemnity or warranty for those goods or services, the cost of the guarantee is usually included in the sale price. The taxpayer may not claim a reserve in respect of the expected liabilities under the guarantees, indemnities or warranties.[86]

---

[84] Subs. 20(6).

[85] Subs. 20(8); paras. 20(1)(*n*) and 12(1)(*e*).

[86] Subs. 20(7). For obvious reasons, taxpayers computing income on a cash basis are not entitled to claim a reserve under para. 20(1)(*m*).

10. INTEREST

References:

ITA:

Para. 20(1)(*c*)	Interest Expense
Para. 20(1)(*d*)	Compound Interest
Para. 20(1)(*e*)	Financing Expenses
Para. 20(1)(*e*.1)	Annual Expenses
Para. 20(1)(*f*)	Discounts
S. 21	Borrowed Money
S. 67.2	Interest for Passenger Vehicle Loan

BULLETINS, CIRCULARS & RULINGS:

IT-59R3	September 26, 1984	Interest on Debts Owing to Specified Non-Residents (Thin Capitalization)
IT-80	November 27, 1972	Interest on Money Borrowed to Redeem Shares, or to Pay Dividends
IT-121R3	May 6, 1988	Election to Capitalize Cost of Borrowed Money
IT-153R3	October 7, 1991	Land Developers — Subdivision and Development Costs and Carrying Charges on Land
IT-360R2	December 8, 1989	Interest Payable in a Foreign Currency
IT-410R	September 4, 1984	Debt Obligations — Accrued Interest on Transfer
IT-445	February 23, 1981	The Deduction of Interest on Funds Borrowed Either to be Loaned at Less Than a Reasonable Rate of Interest or to Honour a Guarantee Given for Inadequate Consideration in Non-Arm's Length Circumstances
IT-498	October 6, 1983	The Deductibility of Interest on Money Borrowed to Reloan to Employees or Shareholders

(a) General

The deduction of interest expense is one of the more important deductions for businesses and investors. One starts with the simple accounting premise that interest represents the cost of the use of money over a period of time and, therefore, should be deductible as an expense if incurred for the purpose of earning income.

Unfortunately, the Supreme Court of Canada decreed early on that interest on borrowed money is an expenditure on account of capital because a deduction on account of borrowed money would necessitate a similar deduction on account of invested capital:[87]

> It is important to remember that, in the absence of an express statutory allowance, interest payable on capital indebtedness is not deductible as an income expense. If a company has not the money capital to commence business, why should it be allowed to deduct the interest on borrowed money? The company setting up with its own contributed capital would, on such a principle, be entitled to interest on its capital before taxable income was reached, but the income statutes give no countenance to such a deduction.

Thus, in the absence of specific authority, expenditures on account of interest would not be deductible as an expense.[88]

The Act does, however, specifically authorize the deduction of interest in the following circumstances:[89]

- it is paid or payable in the year,
- it arises from a legal obligation, and
- it is payable on money borrowed used for the purpose of earning income (other than exempt income) from a business or property.

These seemingly simple requirements are mired in technical detail accumulated as a result of judicial interpretation and reinterpretation over the years.[90]

(b) Definition

"Interest" is the return or consideration for the use or retention by one person, of a sum of money belonging or owed to another.[91] It represents a legal obligation calculated by reference to a principal sum of money that is owing. The obligation to pay interest may arise from an express agreement, by legal implication, or, in some cases, by statute.

---

[87] *Can. Safeway Ltd. v. M.N.R.*, [1957] CTC 335 at 344, 57 DTC 1239 at 1244 (S.C.C.).

[88] Para. 18(1)(*b*).

[89] Para. 20(1)(*c*).

[90] *Interprov. Pipeline Co. v. M.N.R.*, [1967] CTC 180, 67 DTC 5125; affirmed [1968] CTC 156, 68 DTC 5093 (S.C.C.) (total interest payments deductible in proportion to various sources of income generated by borrowed money); *Sherritt Gordon Mines Ltd. v. M.N.R.*, [1968] CTC 262, 68 DTC 5180 (Ex. Ct.) (commitment fee deductible as part of cost of borrowing capital for exploration and development of mine, plant and refinery); *Montreal Light, Heat and Power Consol. v. M.N.R.; Montreal Coke & Mfg. Co. v. M.N.R.*, [1944] CTC 94, 2 DTC 654 (P.C.) (company claiming premium, foreign exchange and discount on new bonds as deductions; financial arrangements held to be distinct from expenditures strictly applied toward earning income).

[91] *Ref re s. 6 of Farm Security Act. 1944 of Sask.*, [1947] SCR 394 at 411; affirmed [1949] AC 110 (*sub nom. A.G. Sask. v. A.G. Can.*) (P.C.).

Whether a payment is actually called interest is totally irrelevant to its characterization.

(c) Legal Obligation

To be deductible as an expense by the borrower, the lender must have *legal* rights to enforce payment of the amounts due. There is no such thing in law as gratuitous interest. The obligation to pay interest must be actual rather than contingent. There is no general requirement in law that indebtedness must be documented to constitute a legal debt. It is, however, prudent to reduce to paper any obligations to pay interest.

(d) Use of Money

Paragraph 20(1)(c) of the *Income Tax Act* allows a taxpayer to deduct from income ". . . an amount paid in the year or payable in respect of the year . . . pursuant to a legal obligation to pay interest on borrowed money *used for the purpose of* earning income from a business or property . . . or a reasonable amount in respect thereof, whichever is the lesser". The phrase ". . . used for the purpose of . . ." incorporates two interrelated tests in determining the deductibility of interest expense: use and purpose. Both tests must be satisfied.

The use test is concerned with the physical flow of funds in determining the application of borrowed money. It is the use to which borrowed funds are *actually* put that determines the deductibility of interest payable on the funds.[92]

(i) Direct vs. Indirect Use

There are two ways in which one can look at the use of borrowed funds. Direct use can be traced by following the funds from the lender to the investment in which the funds are applied. Indirect use implies the use of money in a way that facilitates the investment of *other* funds in an income producing process.

The use test is concerned with the physical flow of funds. It is the use to which borrowed funds are *actually* put that generally determines the deductibility of interest payable on the funds.[93] In other words, in most cases, deductibility of interest expense is determined by the *direct* use test. In *Sinha v. M.N.R.,*[94] for example, a student borrowed from the Canada Student Loan Plan at a low rate of interest and reinvested the borrowed funds at a higher rate. The Board rejected the Minister's argument that the purpose of the borrowing was personal and allowed the taxpayer to deduct his interest expense since he *actually* utilized the borrowed money for investment purposes.

---

[92] *Bronfman Trust v. The Queen,* [1987] 1 CTC 117, 87 DTC 5059 (S.C.C.).

[93] *Bronfman Trust v. The Queen,* [1987] 1 CTC 117, 87 DTC 5059 (S.C.C.).

[94] *Sinha v. M.N.R.,* [1981] CTC 2599, 81 DTC 465 (T.R.B.).

(ii) *Purpose of Borrowing*

The second aspect of the test to determine the deductibility of interest is that the funds must be borrowed for the *purpose* of earning income from business or property. Thus, the taxpayer must have a *bona fide* intention to use the borrowed money for income earning purposes. Actual realization of income is irrelevant. The purpose test is concerned with the taxpayer's intention. *Bronfman Trust* considered the inter-relationship between the use and purpose tests:[95]

> Eligibility for the deduction is contingent on the use of borrowed money for the purpose of earning income. It is well established in the jurisprudence, however, that it is not the purpose of the borrowing itself which is relevant. What is relevant, rather, is the taxpayer's purpose in using the borrowed money in a particular manner. . . . Consequently, the focus of the inquiry must be centred on *the use to which the taxpayer put the borrowed funds.* [Emphasis added.]

For example, a taxpayer who borrows money at a given rate of interest and lends out the funds at less than his borrowing cost cannot be said to be borrowing for the *purpose of* earning income. Thus, the absence of an intention to earn income might cause interest to be non-deductible, even when the actual use to which borrowed funds are put would otherwise qualify the payment as a deductible expense.

The deduction for interest expense is restricted to amounts expended for the purpose of earning income from business or property. Interest incurred to earn capital gains is not deductible against income.[96]

(iii) *The "Real" Purpose*

The purpose of borrowing is generally determined by tracing the direct use of the borrowed money. In multi-step arrangements, however, the deductibility of interest may depend upon the *real* purpose of the series of transactions.

In *Mark Resources Inc.*,[97] for example, the Tax Court of Canada looked to the ultimate purpose of borrowing for an investment in the taxpayer's subsidiary. The facts were as follows:

- The taxpayer, a Canadian corporation ("Canco") borrowed funds from a bank for a predetermined period at a specified interest rate;
- Canco contributed the borrowed funds to its U.S. subsidiary ("Subco") as contributed capital;

[95] *Bronfman Trust v. The Queen, ante,* [1987] 1 CTC at 125, 87 DTC at 5064.

[96] See., e.g., *Ludmer,* [1992] 1 CTC 2494, 93 DTC 1353 (T.C.C.) (interest on money used to purchase shares not deductible if *income* from shares cannot yield profit). *Hastings v. M.N.R.,* [1988] 2 CTC 2001, 88 DTC 1391 (T.C.C.) (interest expense on commodities trades not deductible); *Sterling v. The Queen,* [1985] CTC 275, 85 DTC 5199 (F.C.A.) (interest and safekeeping charges for purchase of gold bullion not deductible in determining capital gain); *The Queen v. Can. Pacific Ltd.,* [1977] CTC 606, 77 DTC 5383 (F.C.A.) (deduction of interest under old subs. 8(3) only allowable where corporation subject to Part I tax); *Birmingham Corp. v. Barnes,* [1935] AC 292 (clarification of capital costs for laying tramway lines where expenditure contributed to by another party).

[97] *Mark Resources Inc. v. The Queen,* [1993] 2 CTC 2259, 93 DTC 1004 (T.C.C.).

- Subco had ceased to carry on business and was, in essence, a shell corporation whose only real value lay in its accumulated U.S. losses;

- Subco invested the funds in a term deposit equal to the term of the loan, but at a rate of interest lower than that payable by Canco on its loan payable to the bank;

- Subco posted the term deposit with the bank as security for Canco's loan;

- The amount of the loan, its term and the purchase of the term deposit was calculated to raise income equal to Subco's accumulated losses;

- Subco's interest income from its term deposit was offset against its accumulated U.S. losses;

- Subco did not pay U.S. taxes on its interest income;

- Subco used its interest from the term deposit to pay a tax-free (net of 10 per cent withholding tax) dividend to Canco;

- Canco used its dividend income to pay the interest on its bank borrowing;

- When Subco's accumulated U.S. losses were exhausted, the term deposit matured and the funds received were loaned back to Canco;

- Canco used the funds to repay its own loan to the bank;

- Subco was then liquidated and the inter-corporate loan and contributed capital were offset against each other;

- Canco deducted its interest expense on its bank borrowing from its income for Canadian tax purposes.

Each step in the series of transactions was properly executed: (1) Canco's transactions with the bank were at arm's length and the rate of interest charged was quite reasonable in the circumstances; (2) The income from the term deposits arose out of a normal commercial transaction and there was nothing improper about the payment of the dividends; (3) The documentation that was necessary to implement each of the steps in the arrangement was properly prepared and executed. Thus, the transactions were legitimate and properly executed. They were real transactions and the rights and obligations created by each step of the arrangement were those which they purported to be. In short, the arrangement was not a sham.

The purpose of the arrangement was to utilize Subco's accumulated U.S. losses (which would otherwise expire) and to do so on a tax efficient basis by making Canco's interest deductible for Canadian tax purposes. The essence of the scheme required four elements:

1. No cost to Subco on the funds that it invested in the term deposits;

2. Deducible interest to Canco on its borrowing from the bank;

3. Tax-free interest income to Subco on the term deposit in the U.S. because of its offsetting losses; and

4. Tax-free dividends from Subco to its parent (Canco) by virtue of the deduction for dividends (section 113) from foreign affiliates.

Were the borrowed funds *used for the purpose* of earning income from a business or property under paragraph 20(1)(c) of the Act?

The Tax Court looked to the "real purpose" of the use of the borrowed funds in the entire series of transactions and not at the purpose of their immediate use:[98]

> Here the immediate step of investing in a subsidiary that in accordance with the scheme must necessarily pay dividends was not the real purpose of the use of the funds. The earning of interest income . . . and the payment . . . of dividends . . . were integral but subservient and incidental steps to the real objective that lay behind the implementation of the plan. . . . It is true that the overall economic result, if all the elements of the plan work, is a net gain to the appellant, but this type of gain is not from the production of income but from a reduction of taxes otherwise payable in Canada.

The Tax Court concluded that Canco was not entitled to the deduction for its interest expense because it did not satisfy the test in paragraph 20(1)(c) of the Act.

The decision implies that, in multi-step arrangements, the deductibility of interest expense depends upon the real purpose of the "series of transactions" and not only on the immediate purpose and direct use of the funds. *Mark Resources* clearly involved blatant tax avoidance: Subco's accumulated losses were about to expire, the funds were directly traceable in a series of transactions from the bank to the investment, the terms deposits, and back again to the bank; Subco was liquidated immediately after its losses were utilized. The loan from the bank, the issuance of the term deposit and its deposit with the bank as security were all done through a foreign branch of the Canadian bank. No money was ever transferred either to Canada or the U.S. or used in the operations of either Canco or Subco. Thus, the series of transactions used to implement the scheme constituted "tax avoidance" intended to utilize Subco's losses on a tax efficient basis.

Today, such a scheme would need to be analyzed under the general anti-avoidance rule ("GAAR") in section 245. The rule did not apply to the assessment years under review. Prior to the enactment of GAAR, tax avoidance was not, *per se*, offensive, and business transactions did not require a business purpose to be valid.[99] Tax reduction was a sufficient justification.

What are the implications of *Mark Resources* under GAAR and other circumstances where the purpose of transactions may not be as clearly obvious? For example, assume that a taxpayer liquidates some shares to purchase personal-use property and then, some time later, borrows funds at a commercial rate of interest to repurchase either substitute or identical income-earning investments. It is clear that the immediate use of the funds would be traceable to a borrowing for investment in business or property. But the *real* purpose of the borrowing may need to be tested by looking at the series of transactions: Was the sequence preordained to produce a given result without any purpose other than

---

[98] *Mark Resources Inc. v. The Queen, ante,* [1993] 2 CTC at 2270, 93 DTC at 1012.

[99] *Stubart Invt. Ltd. v. The Queen,* [1984] CTC 294, 84 DTC 6305 (S.C.C.).

tax mitigation and no likelihood that the pre-planned events would take place in any other order than the one ordained?[100]

What if the taxpayer first purchased the personal-use property on the basis of a loan, sold his investments to pay off his personal loan, then borrowed funds to invest in shares? In either case, the "real purpose" of the arrangement would, under the doctrine in *Mark Resources*, disqualify the borrowing costs from deductibility if the entire series of transactions was viewed as a composite arrangement.

(e) Indirect Use

What happens if borrowed moneys are only indirectly used to earn or preserve income? *Bronfman Trust*[101] dealt with this point. Samuel Bronfman created a trust in favour of his daughter, under the terms of which the beneficiary was to receive annually, 50 per cent of the income from the trust property and such additional allocations as the trustees in their discretion might have decided. The capital of the trust was invested in income-earning securities, some in family enterprises and others in marketable securities. The trustees, having decided to make capital allocations of $2 million to the beneficiary, chose to borrow the funds rather than liquidate trust capital to make the payment. They chose to borrow the funds because they considered it to be financially inexpedient to liquidate any portion of the trust's investments at that time. Was the borrowed money used for the purpose of earning income from property?

By borrowing money and using the money to pay the capital allocations, the trustees had preserved intact the income yielding capacity of the trust's investments. That was not sufficient, however, to characterize the borrowed money as having been *used for the purpose* of earning income from property. In Chief Justice Dickson's words:[102]

> . . . In my view, the text of the Act requires tracing the use of borrowed funds to a specific eligible use, its obviously restricted purpose being the encouragement of taxpayers to augment their income-producing potential. This, in my view, precludes the allowance of a deduction for interest paid on borrowed funds which indirectly preserve income-earning property but which are not directly "used for the purpose of earning income from . . . property".

This principle applies to all taxpayers including corporations, trusts and individuals.[103]

Deductibility depends upon the intention of the borrower at the time the funds are invested rather than upon the actual materialization of income at some later date. Provided that the funds are employed in a venture that has the *potential* for earning net income, the actual results of the income earning process are irrelevant to the

---

[100] *Craven v. White*, [1988] 3 WLR 423.

[101] *Bronfman Trust v. The Queen, ante.*

[102] *Bronfman Trust v. The Queen, ante*, [1987] 1 CTC at 129, 87 DTC at 5067.

[103] *Bronfman Trust v. The Queen, ante.*

determination of deductibility of the interest expense.[104] For example, interest on borrowed funds invested in a business venture that loses money is deductible. The intention must be to earn income from business or property and *not* from capital gains. Income from capital gains is not income from property.[105] Thus, interest expenses incurred *solely* to earn capital gains or avoid capital losses are not deductible in computing income from business or property.[106]

(f) Current Use

It is quite clear that it is the *current* use to which borrowed funds are put that determines the deductibility of interest as an expense. As Jackett P. said in *Trans-prairie*:[107]

> . . . interest should be deductible for the years in which the borrowed capital is employed in the business rather than that it should be deductible for the life of a loan as long as its first use was in the business. . . .

Similarly, in *Bronfman Trust*:[108]

> . . . a taxpayer who uses or intends to use borrowed money for an ineligible purpose, but later uses the funds to earn non-exempt income from a business or property, ought not to be deprived of the deduction for the current, eligible use.

Hence, if a taxpayer initially borrows money to invest in income earning property and then diverts those funds to a non-income earning purpose (for example, personal use), any interest incurred on the borrowed funds will cease to qualify for deductibility as of the date of change of use of the funds.[109]

Conversely, interest on funds initially borrowed for personal purposes and later used for business purposes qualifies for deduction as of the date of change of use. For example, a taxpayer who borrows money to purchase a residential cottage and then sells the cottage to use the proceeds for investment purposes is entitled to deduct the interest payable on the funds as of the date of the investment.

---

[104] See: *Lessard v. M.N.R.*, [1993] 1 CTC 2176, 93 DTC 680 (T.C.C.) (interest on funds used to acquire shares deductible even though taxpayer was sole shareholder because shares constituted a potential source of income).

[105] Subs. 9(3). See: *Ludmer v. M.N.R.*, [1993] 2 CTC 2494, 93 DTC 1351 (T.C.C.).

[106] *Bronfman Trust v. The Queen, ante* (". . . The fact that the loan may have prevented capital losses cannot assist the taxpayer in obtaining a deduction from income which is limited to use of borrowed money for the purpose of earning income"). See also, *The Queen v. Mandryk*, [1992] 1 CTC 317, 92 DTC 6329 (F.C.A.) (taxpayer not entitled to deduct interest expense to honour personal guarantees of corporate indebtedness).

[107] *Trans-Prairie Pipelines Ltd. v. M.N.R.*, [1970] CTC 537, 70 DTC 6351 (Ex. Ct.), approved by S.C.C. in *Bronfman Trust v. The Queen, ante*.

[108] *Bronfman Trust v. The Queen, ante*, [1987] 1 CTC at 125, 87 DTC at 5065.

[109] Subpara. 20(1)(c)(i).

(g) Reloaned Funds

Where an individual borrows money and then relends that money to his or her corporation, deductibility of any interest depends upon the *purpose* in lending the money to the corporation. It is quite clear that funds borrowed by a taxpayer at a commercial rate of interest and reloaned at a lower rate cannot be considered to be funds used by the taxpayer for the *purpose* of earning income from a business or property. Hence, any interest payable on the funds is not deductible. Revenue Canada does, however, allow a deduction to the extent of the income actually earned.

Revenue Canada generally takes the view that interest on borrowed money is not deductible *in whole or in part* if the money is reloaned at a lesser rate of interest than that at which it is borrowed. It does, however, permit exceptions where a shareholder borrows and relends to his or her corporation. Revenue Canada's position is outlined in the following paragraphs:[110]

> . . . the Department will generally permit a deduction for the full interest expense incurred when a taxpayer borrows money at interest to be loaned to a Canadian corporation of which he is a shareholder, or to its Canadian subsidiary, at less than a reasonable rate of interest, (or at no interest), if the following conditions are met:
>
> (a) the proceeds of the loan are used by that corporation in its own operations to produce income from business or property which will be subject to Part I tax in Canada, or are used by that corporation to loan to its Canadian subsidiary, at less than a reasonable rate of interest (or at no interest), to be used in its operation to produce income from business or property which will be subject to Part I tax in Canada,
>
> (b) the corporation has made every effort to borrow the necessary funds through the usual commercial money markets but cannot obtain financing, without the guarantee of the shareholder, at interest rates at which the shareholder could borrow, and
>
> (c) the loan from the shareholder to the corporation at less than a reasonable rate of interest (or at no interest) does not result in any undue tax advantage being conferred on either the shareholder or the corporation. The Department does not consider that any undue tax advantage is conferred on either the shareholder or the corporation where the use of loans with interest at less than market rates between associated corporations is for the purpose of offsetting non-capital losses within the group of associated corporations.

Examples of situations where the Department considers that an undue tax advantage has been conferred on either the shareholder or the corporation are as follows:

> (a) the capital cost allowance restrictions of subsection 1100(11) or (15) of the Regulations are circumvented by the corporation being able to claim capital cost allowance in excess of the maximum that would have been allowed had the corporation borrowed the money from the shareholder at a reasonable rate of interest, or

---

[110] IT-445, "The Deduction of Interest on Funds Borrowed Either to be Loaned at Less Than a Reasonable Rate of Interest or to Honour a Guarantee Given for Inadequate Consideration in Non-arm's Length Circumstances" (February 23, 1981), paras. 7, 8.

(b)   provincial income tax is reduced through loans made to a corporation reporting its income in a province with a lower tax rate than that in which the shareholder who made the loan reports and it is evident that there was no other substantial business purpose for the loan. . . .

(h) Exempt Income

The interest expense incurred on money borrowed to acquire property, the income from which is exempt, or to acquire a life insurance policy is not deductible.[111]

(i) Compound Interest

A taxpayer is entitled to deduct interest on interest, otherwise known as compound interest, if all of the other conditions of deductibility are satisfied.[112] Compound interest is deductible only when it is paid and not when it is merely payable.

Where a taxpayer makes a blended payment of capital and interest, an amount equal to the interest component may be deducted.[113]

(j) Discounts

A discount is the amount by which the face value of a debt obligation exceeds its issue or selling price. The discount can arise on issuance of the obligation or later, in accordance with market fluctuations in interest rates.

Discounts on obligations may be deductible in whole or in part in the year paid.[114]

Where an obligation is issued at a price of at least 97 per cent of its principal amount and does not yield an amount in excess of 4/3 of the nominal interest rate, the entire amount of the discount is deductible in computing income. Where a bond is issued for an amount less than 97 per cent of its face amount, or its yield exceeds 4/3 of its nominal interest rate, only 3/4 of the discount is deductible in computing income.

A discount on a debt obligation that does not normally stipulate an interest rate (strip coupon bonds, for example) is considered to be interest if the discount is reasonable in the circumstances.

---

[111] "Exempt income" is defined as money or property received or acquired by a person in such circumstances that it is, by reason of any provision in Part I, not included in computing income, but does not include a dividend on a share. See subs. 248(1) ("exempt income").

[112] Para. 20(1)(d).

[113] Subs. 16(1).

[114] Para. 20(1)(f).

(k) Refinancing

Where money is borrowed to repay money previously borrowed, the second borrowing is deemed to be made for the same purposes as the original borrowing.[115] In *Bronfman*, however, the Supreme Court indicated in *dicta* that refinancing transactions may be scrutinized to determine whether they constitute a formality or a sham.[116] In determining whether a refinancing constitutes a sham, a court may look at the interval of time between the original and refinanced loan.

(l) Existence of Source

An essential requirement for the deduction of interest used to be the continued existence of the source of income to which the interest expense related.[117]   Interest on borrowed money must be traceable to an eligible use in order for the expense to be deductible. For example, a taxpayer who finances the purchase of investment securities may claim any directly related interest expense as a deduction.

What happens if the income-producing source ceases to exist? For example, what if a taxpayer borrows $40,000 to purchase shares for $50,000. A year later, the taxpayer sells the shares for $20,000, which he or she then invests in the shares of another company. There remains, however, an outstanding bank loan of $30,000.

Subsection 20.1(1) allows the taxpayer to claim a proportional amount of the interest in the outstanding loan as deductible interest. In the above example, the deductible portion would be calculated as follows:

Unpaid balance of the loan	$ 30,000
Less	
Portion of the original loan	
attributable to the consideration	$ 16,000
Balance	$ 14,000

The $14,000 is deemed to be used to earn income and, hence, any interest paid on this amount to the loan continues to be deductible under the general rules. The interest on the other $16,000 is also deductible because the taxpayer used the proceeds of

---

[115] Subs. 20(3); see also ATR-4, "Exchange of Interest Rates" (November 29, 1984).

[116] *Bronfman Trust v. The Queen*, [1987] 1 CTC 117, 87 DTC 5059 (S.C.C.).

[117] *Emerson v. The Queen*, [1986] 1 CTC 422, 86 DTC 6184 (F.C.A.); leave to appeal to S.C.C. refused (1986), 70 NR 160 (S.C.C.) (taxpayer not allowed to deduct interest on money used to purchase shares after selling shares at loss); see also *Deschenes v. M.N.R.*, [1979] CTC 2690, 79 DTC 461 (T.R.B.); *Alexander v. M.N.R.*, [1983] CTC 2516, 83 DTC 459 (T.R.B.); *Lyons v. M.N.R.*, [1984] CTC 2690, 84 DTC 1633 (T.C.C.); *McKay v. M.N.R.*, [1984] CTC 2804, 84 DTC 1699 (T.C.C.); *Botkin v. M.N.R.*, [1989] 2 CTC 2110, 89 DTC 398 (T.C.C.); *The Queen v. Malik*, [1989] 1 CTC 316, 89 DTC 5141 (F.C.T.D.); *Dockman v. M.N.R.*, [1990] 2 CTC 2229, 90 DTC 1804 (T.C.C.); *Kornelow v. M.N.R.*, [1991] 1 CTC 2403, 91 DTC 431 (T.C.C.).

$50,000 from investments to purchase other investments. Hence, in these circumstances, the entire $30,000 loan is eligible for deductible interest.

(m) Accrued Interest

A purchaser of a debt obligation (other than an income bond, income debenture, small business development bond, or small business bond) is allowed to deduct interest accrued but unpaid to the date of the purchase, to the extent that the amount is included as interest in computing income for the year. The accrued interest paid to the vendor of the debt obligation is included in computing the vendor's income.[118]

(n) Financing Costs

A taxpayer may deduct financing expenses incurred in issuing shares or in borrowing money for the purpose of earning income from a business or property.[119] Financing expenses, which typically include legal and accounting fees, printing costs, commissions, etc., would otherwise be caught by the prohibition against deducting expenses not directly related to the income-earning process.[120] These expenses are deductible on a rateable basis over a five-year period.

(o) Capitalizing Interest

(i) General

In certain circumstances, a taxpayer may prefer not to write off interest expense against current operations. For example, there may be little advantage in taking a deduction for interest expense on money borrowed to construct an asset if the asset is not currently producing income. Where the deduction of interest would merely create a loss that cannot be used within the time limits allowed for carryover of losses,[121] the taxpayer may prefer to treat interest charges as part of the cost of the asset and then write off the total cost of the asset when it begins to produce income. In other words, she or he may prefer to treat interest costs as a capital expenditure rather than as a current expense.

---

[118] Subs. 20(14); IT-410R, "Debt Obligations — Accrued Interest on Transfer" (September 4, 1984). This rule only operates where there has been an assignment or transfer of title. Evidence of registration of title would likely be necessary; *Hill v. M.N.R.*, [1981] CTC 2120, 81 DTC 167 (T.R.B.) ("bond flip" case; interest payment for carrying cost of bonds not deductible); *Smye v. M.N.R.*, [1980] CTC 2372, 80 DTC 1236 (T.R.B.) (purchase of bonds plus accrued interest; upon sale, taxpayer deducted price for accrued interest from investment yield of bond).

[119] Para. 20(1)(*e*).

[120] *Montreal Light, Heat & Power Consol. v. M.N.R.*, [1944] CTC 94, 2 DTC 654 (P.C.); *The Queen v. Royal Trust Corp. of Can.*, [1983] CTC 159, 83 DTC 5172 (F.C.A.) (whether or not payment constitutes "commission" is a question of fact).

[121] See para. 111(1)(*a*) (limitation period in respect of non-capital losses).

(ii) Depreciable Property

A taxpayer who acquires depreciable property with borrowed money may elect to capitalize the interest charges.[122] Only those costs which would *otherwise have been deductible* as interest expense or as an expense of borrowing money may be capitalized. Interest expense to earn exempt income is not deductible and may not be capitalized. The election is available not only in respect of costs incurred in the year in which the asset is acquired, but also in respect of costs incurred in the three immediately preceding taxation years. The extension of the election to the three preceding years recognizes that large undertakings extend over many years and that money may be borrowed, and expenses incurred, prior to the period in which the money is actually used for its intended purpose of constructing a capital asset.

(iii) Election

The election must be made for the taxation year in which:

- the depreciable property is *acquired,* or
- the money borrowed has been used for exploration, development, or the acquisition of property.

A taxpayer may not elect to capitalize interest in anticipation of the acquisition of depreciable property or the use of borrowed money for exploration or development; she or he can only elect *after* acquiring the property or expending the funds. When the election is made, however, it is effective for borrowing costs and interest incurred in the current year and in the three preceding years.

A taxpayer may elect under subsection 21(1) only for the taxation year in which he or she acquires the depreciable property. Where a building or other structure is being erected by a taxpayer, it is considered to have been "acquired" at any time to the extent of the construction costs at that time. Hence, a taxpayer must file a separate election for each taxation year in respect of the interest expense related to that year.

The election does not have to be in respect of the full amount of the costs of borrowing; a taxpayer may elect to capitalize only part of the interest charges and deduct the remainder as a current expense.

The portion of the interest that is capitalized is added to the capital cost of the depreciable property acquired. Thus, the capitalized cost will eventually be written off through capital cost allowance. The adjusted cost base of the property is increased for the purpose of determining capital gains upon disposition of the property.[123]

---

[122] S. 21. Special restrictions on "soft costs" are discussed below; see subs. 18(3.1).

[123] S. 54 ("adjusted cost base").

(iv) Reassessment

Where the taxpayer has elected to capitalize interest charges, the Minister is required to reassess the taxpayer for those taxation years. Having made the election, the taxpayer may continue to capitalize interest in succeeding years if, in each of those years, the *entire* amount of the interest on the property is capitalized.

(v) Compound Interest

A taxpayer is also permitted to capitalize, compound interest and the expense of raising money. For example, a taxpayer may be required to pay a commitment fee to a financier during the time when the necessary funds have not yet been advanced to the taxpayer. The commitment fee, or standby interest, may be capitalized as part of the cost of borrowed money.[124]

(vi) "Soft Costs"

"Soft costs" (such as interest expense, mortgage fees, property taxes, commitment fees, etc.) incurred in respect of the construction, renovation or alteration of a building, may not be deducted as current expenses during construction and must be added to the cost of the building.[125] Similarly, "soft costs" in respect of land subjacent to a building under construction must be capitalized. The restriction on deducting these expenses applies only in respect of outlays incurred before completion of construction, renovation or alteration of the building.

The scope of the prohibition against writing off soft costs as current expenses is very broad. Included in interest expenses are expenses incurred on borrowed money used to finance working capital if it *"can reasonably be considered"* that the borrowed money freed up other funds for the construction of the building. In other words, "indirect financing" is caught by the prohibition.[126]

(p) Limitations on Deduction

(i) Real Estate

(A) General Limitation

A taxpayer cannot deduct carrying charges (interest and property taxes) in respect of vacant land to the extent that the expenses exceed income from the land[126A]. Thus, carrying charges on land are deductible only to the extent of the taxpayer's net revenues from the land. The purpose of this rule is to discourage speculation in real estate.

---

[124] *Sherritt Gordon Mines Ltd. v. M.N.R.*, [1968] CTC 262, 68 DTC 5180 (Ex. Ct.).

[125] Subs. 18(3.1). This rule does not apply to capital cost allowance, landscaping costs or scientific research expenditures.

[126] Subs. 18(3.2).

[126A] Subs. 18(2).

(B) Exceptions

Land that is used in the course of a business is exempt from the limitation in respect of carrying charges for land. The exemption from the rule does not apply, however, to property developers whose business is the sale or development of land, or to land that is held, but not used, in a business.

(C) Corporations

A special rule applies to corporations whose principal business is the leasing, rental, sale or development of real property. Corporations in these businesses may deduct their carrying charges on vacant land. The maximum deduction is equal to the *lesser* of:

• the income, net of all deductions, from the land, and

• the corporation's "base level deduction" for the year.

A corporation's base level deduction for a taxation year is the amount of interest for the year in respect of $1 million of debt outstanding for the year, computed at the prescribed rate of interest.[126B] Thus, the base level deduction is, in effect, the absolute maximum a corporation can deduct in a year. For example, at a prescribed rate of 10 per cent, the absolute maximum deduction for carrying charges would be $100,000.

The base level deduction of a corporation that is a member of an associated group of corporations is determined by reference to a prescribed agreement that each corporation must file. The $1 million to which the prescribed rate is applied must be allocated amongst the associated members of the group. The Minister has the power to allocate the deduction if the corporations do not file their agreements.

(ii) *Thin Capitalization*

The "thin capitalization"[127] rules limit the deduction a corporation may claim for interest on debts owing to non-residents and persons who are related to such persons. The rules apply to limit the deductibility of interest where the corporation's debt to equity ratio in relation to the specified non-residents exceeds 3:1.

(iii) *Automobiles*

Certain expenditures (for example, automobile expenses) incurred in the course of earning income can involve elements of both business and personal use. The Act attempts to regulate the deduction of the personal component of some of these expenditures in various ways. The rule for automobile financing is arbitrary and simple: Deductible interest expense in respect of financing a passenger vehicle cannot exceed

---

[126B] Subs. 18(2).

[127] Subss. 18(4)–(8); IT-59R3, "Interest on Debts Owing to Specified Non-Residents (Thin Capitalization)" (September 26, 1984).

$300 times the number of months in respect of which the expense is payable. Hence, the maximum deductible interest expense in respect of an automobile is $3,600 per year.[128]

11. CAPITAL COST ALLOWANCE

References:

ITA:

S. 13	Recapture, Exchanges, Deemed Cost
S. 16	Income and Capital Combined
Subs. 39(1)	Capital Gain and Loss — General
Sub. 39(2)	Capital Gain and Loss — Foreign Currency

REGULATIONS:

1100	Deductions Allowed
1102	Property Rules
1103	Inclusions In and Transfers Between Classes

BULLETINS, CIRCULARS & RULINGS:

IT-147R3	September 14, 1992	CCA — Accelerated Write-Off of Manufacturing and Processing Machinery and Equipment
IT-285R2	March 31, 1994	CCA — General Comments

See also:

IT-267R	IT-327	IT-476
IT-274R	IT-336R	IT-477
IT-283R2	IT-367R3	IT-478R
IT-304R	IT-441	IT-482
IT-306R	IT-464R	IT-492
IT-317R	IT-469R	IT-501
IT-324	IT-472	

IC 84-1	July 9, 1984	Revision of Capital Cost Allowance Claims and Other Permissive Deductions
IC 87-5	December 11, 1987	Capital Cost of Property Where Trade-In is Involved

---

[128] S. 67.2 and Reg. 7307(2).

(a) General

A taxpayer may not deduct expenditures on account of capital outlays, depreciation, obsolescence, or depletion.[129] The Act does, however, allow for the deduction of capital cost allowance (CCA) in lieu of such expenses in prescribed circumstances. In computing income from a business or property, a taxpayer may deduct[130] ". . . such part of the capital cost to the taxpayer of property, or such amount in respect of the capital cost to the taxpayer of property, if any, as is allowed by regulation." Thus, a taxpayer may not deduct depreciation calculated for financial statement purposes but may claim a deduction for capital cost allowance calculated according to prescribed rules.

The basic concept underlying the capital cost allowance system is fairly straightforward: CCA is a deduction from income which is intended to allocate the approximate cost of capital assets over their useful lives. Thus, in a sense, the CCA system is nothing more than statutory depreciation at predetermined rates.

The technical application of the capital cost allowance system is, however, quite detailed and extremely complex. This is because the CCA system is also used as an instrument of social, economic, and political policy. The system is sometimes used to stimulate investment by providing for accelerated capital cost allowance; in other circumstances, the CCA system is used to discourage particular types of investment by denying or restricting the allowance on those investments. For example, prior to 1988, the system allowed for a fast write-off of the cost of Canadian films. A taxpayer could claim 100 per cent of the cost of film ownership in one year. This was intended to encourage the development of Canadian culture. In 1988, the CCA rate was reduced to a 30 per cent write-off so as to discourage the use of films as tax shelters by high income taxpayers. In either case, the decision to set the rate was made without reference to the life of films.

(b) Structure of System

(i) Classification

There are three basic questions to be answered in respect of the capital cost allowance system:

1. Is the capital property depreciable capital property?
2. To which class of assets does the property belong?
3. What is the rate of depreciation applicable to the particular class in question?

---

[129] Para. 18(1)(*b*).

[130] Para. 20(1)(*a*); Regulations Pt. XI (Regs. 100–1106). The phrase "capital cost allowance" refers to an allowance in respect of the capital cost of depreciable property.

The system is designed to permit a taxpayer to deduct the actual cost of depreciable assets over a period of time.[131] The rate at which CCA on an asset may be claimed is prescribed in the Regulations and is the same for all taxpayers with similar assets performing similar activities. Generally speaking, the rates are structured so that the deduction for tax purposes in the early years of an asset's life will exceed the comparable depreciation allowed on the asset for accounting and financial statement purposes. Thus, in part at least, the capital cost allowance system compensates taxpayers for the effects of inflation on asset replacement costs. It also gives rise to deferred tax accounting problems because of the difference between tax and accounting depreciation.

(ii) Permissive

The deduction of capital cost allowance is permissive: A taxpayer may, but does not have to, claim capital cost allowance in a particular taxation year. The amount of capital cost allowance that may be deducted in any year is, however, subject to prescribed upper limits. Thus, taxpayers have some flexibility in determining the amount of income they will recognize for tax purposes in any year.

To be eligible for capital cost allowance, an asset must be described in one of the classes listed in the Regulations. These classes list most tangible assets that are expected to depreciate over time. The list also includes intangible assets with limited lives (such as patents and limited life franchises).[132]

(iii) General Structure

The general structure of the CCA system is as follows:

- A taxpayer is entitled to deduct CCA within the terms of the Regulations.
- A taxpayer may deduct a portion or all of the maximum allowance prescribed or forego the claim and postpone amortization of the class of assets.
- Eligible assets are grouped into prescribed classes with approximately similar lives.
- The balance of each class is increased by acquisitions in that class.
- The balance is reduced by dispositions and by the deduction of amounts of capital cost allowance allowed.
- Each class is allowed a *maximum* percentage rate of capital cost allowance.
- CCA may only be claimed when assets are available for use.
- The diminishing balance, rather than the straight line,[133] method is used in computing the annual allowance for most classes of assets. Each year, the rate

---

[131] IT-285R2, "Capital Cost Allowance — General Comments" (March 31, 1994).

[132] Regs., Part XI (1100–1106); Sched. II.

[133] The straight line method may be used in a few situations, e.g., depreciation of Class 13 leasehold interests.

is applied to the balance remaining in the class after deduction of amounts previously allowed, so that the balance remaining to be depreciated diminishes until new assets of the class are acquired.

- Proceeds from the disposition of assets reduce (up to a maximum equal to the cost of the asset) the balance of the class.
- On disposal of assets, capital cost allowance previously taken is "recaptured" to the extent that the proceeds of disposition exceed the "undepreciated capital cost" of the group of assets in the particular class.
- The undepreciated capital cost of a class can never be a negative amount.
- To the extent that the proceeds of disposition of an asset exceed its original capital cost, they are considered a capital gain.
- Upon disposal of *all* the assets in a particular class, any remaining balance of "undepreciated capital cost" for the class is deductible in the year as a "terminal loss".

These relationships are illustrated in the following examples.

Example VIII.4

Assume:

In 1995 a taxpayer acquires one tangible asset to which the following data applies:

Capital cost	$10,000
Capital cost allowance claimed	$ 2,000

In 1997 the taxpayer disposes of the asset, which is the only asset in its class. Assume, alternatively, that the taxpayer receives the following amounts:

Example (A)	$11,000
Example (B)	$ 9,000
Example (C)	$ 6,000

Then:

	(A)	(B)	(C)
Capital cost	$10,000	$10,000	$10,000
CCA claimed	(2,000)	(2,000)	(2,000)
Undepreciated capital cost	$ 8,000	$ 8,000	$ 8,000
CCA recaptured	$ 2,000	$ 1,000	—
Capital gain	$ 1,000	—	—
Terminal loss	—	—	(2,000)

(c) Eligibility

Capital cost allowance is claimable only on depreciable property of a prescribed class.[134] The expression "depreciable property" is defined as "property acquired by the taxpayer in respect of which he or she has been allowed, or is entitled to, "capital cost allowance".[135] This is not a very helpful definition.

The Act is much more precise in its listing of exclusions of property from the prescribed classes. For example, the following properties are definitely *not* eligible for capital cost allowance:

- Property, the cost of which is *deductible as an* ordinary expense.[136]
- Property that is "described in" or is part of, the taxpayer's inventory.[137]
- Property not acquired for the purpose of gaining or producing income.[138]
- Property for which the taxpayer is entitled to a deduction for scientific research.[139]
- Property that is a yacht, camp, lodge, golf course, or membership in any club whose main purpose is to provide recreational, dining or sporting facilities for members.[140]
- Certain works of art created by non-residents.[141]
- Land.[142]
- Animals, trees and plants, radium, intangible assets, rights of way.[143]
- Property situated outside of Canada which belongs to a non-resident.[144]

---

[134] Reg. 1100(1)(*a*).

[135] Subs. 248(1) ("depreciable property") and para. 13(21) ("depreciable property").

[136] Reg. 1102(1)(*a*).

[137] Reg. 1102(1)(*b*). See Chapter VI "Business and Investment Income: General" for distinction between income from business on sale of inventory and capital gains on sale of capital assets. See also IT-128R, "CCA — Depreciable Property" (May 21, 1985) and IT-102R2, "Conversion of Property, Other than Real Property, From or to Inventory" (July 22, 1985).

[138] Reg. 1102(1)(*c*).

[139] Reg. 1102(1)(*d*).

[140] Reg. 1102(1)(*f*).

[141] Reg. 1102(1)(*e*).

[142] Reg. 1102(2).

[143] Reg., Sched. II, Class 8, subpara. (i).

[144] Reg. 1102(3).

(d) Classes of Property

References:

BULLETINS, CIRCULARS & RULINGS:

IT-79R3	May 24, 1991	CCA — Buildings or Other Structures
IT-102R2	July 22, 1985	Conversion of Property From or To Inventory
IT-128R	May 21, 1985	CCA — Depreciable Property
IT-190R2	December 29, 1989	CCA — Transferred and Misclassified Property

Capital cost allowance is claimed on depreciable property of a prescribed class.

The general rule is that similar properties are placed in the same class and, therefore, are subject to the same rate of allowance. For example, all of a taxpayer's automobiles costing $24,000 or less would be placed in Class 10, and capital cost allowance claimed at the rate applicable to that class. Similarly, all passenger vehicles costing more than $24,000 each[145] are grouped in Class 10.1.

There are, however, some exceptions to the general rule: some similar properties are segregated into separate classes. The effect of segregating similar properties into separate classes is that the provisions relating to "recapture" and "terminal loss" are then applied separately to each property rather than to a collective whole. The principal reason for maintaining separate classes is to accelerate the timing of recapture of capital cost allowance or the deduction of terminal loss that might otherwise be wholly or partially deferred by subsequent acquisitions of similar properties. For example, each rental property having a cost of $50,000 or more constitutes a separate class of property.[146] Hence, it is not possible to defer recapture of capital cost allowance upon a disposition of one property by replacing it with a similar property in the same class and of the same type.[147]

In certain circumstances, a depreciable property may satisfy the requirements of two or more classes. Revenue Canada takes the position that where the description of two or more possible classes includes the words ". . . property not included in any other class . . .", and the property in question fits both classes, the taxpayer is entitled to choose the applicable class.[148] For example, a frame building acquired before 1979 could be included in Class 6; it is also a building for the purposes of Class 3. Since

---

[145] Para. 13(7)(*g*) (vehicles purchased after December 31, 1990 included in Class 10.1 if purchase price, excluding GST and provincial sales tax, exceeds $24,000).

[146] Regs. 1101(5*b*), 1101(1*ac*).

[147] See "Recapture", *infra*.

[148] IT-285R2 "Capital Cost Allowance — General Comments" (March 31, 1994).

Classes 3 and 6 are both described to include "property not included in any other class", a taxpayer can choose to place the building in either Class 3 or Class 6. Note, however, that a brick building *must* be included in Class 3 since it is not described in Class 6.

The principal classes of property are described in Schedule II of the Regulations.

(e) Determination of Capital Cost

References:

BULLETINS, CIRCULARS & RULINGS:

IT-285R2	March 31, 1994	CCA — General Comments
IT-95R	December 16, 1980	Foreign Exchange Gains and Losses
IT-217	May 26, 1975	Capital Property Owned on December 31, 1971 — Depreciable Property
IT-218R	September 16, 1986	Profit, Capital Gains and Losses from the Sale of Real Estate, Including Farmland and Inherited Land and Conversion of Real Estate from Capital Property to Inventory and Vice-Versa

(i) General

The allowance is based upon the "capital cost" of an asset. In the simplest situation, the capital cost of a property is determined by calculating the taxpayer's laid-down acquisition cost of the property;[149] it includes legal, accounting, engineering, or other fees incurred to acquire the property and land where it is to be used.

The cost of a depreciable property is the amount paid by the taxpayer. In Lord Atkins' words:[150]

> What a man pays for construction or for the purchase of a work seems to me to be the cost to him; and that whether someone has given him the money to construct or purchase for himself; or, whether before the event, has promised to give him the money after he has paid for the work; or, after the event, has promised or given the money which recoups him what he has spent.

The term "cost" refers to the actual cost of the property to the taxpayer, whether paid in money or some other property. Where the value of the consideration paid is not

---

[149] Para. 20(1)(*a*); IT-285R2, "Capital Cost Allowance — General Comments" (March 31, 1994), paras. 8–12; see also R. M. Skinner, *Accounting Principles: A Canadian Viewpoint*, CICA (1972), at 5: "The recorded cost of a tangible capital asset should include all costs necessary to put the asset in a position to render service".

[150] *Birmingham Corp. v. Barnes*, [1935] AC 292 at 298.

readily apparent (such as when payment is made by the issuance of shares), it is usual to obtain an appraisal to determine the capital cost of the property acquired.[151]

"Cost" includes the *entire laid-down cost* of equipment even though certain expensive parts of the equipment might require frequent replacement.[152] The cost of property paid for in foreign currency is its Canadian dollar equivalent as at the date of acquisition.[153]

Where a taxpayer manufactures an asset for personal use, all outlays attributable to the construction of the asset are included in its cost.[154] The governing criterion is the treatment accorded costs by generally accepted accounting principles.[155] Testing and start-up costs may be considered part of the capital cost of assets in some situations.[156]

In certain circumstances, a taxpayer may capitalize interest costs as part of the capital cost of depreciable property instead of deducting these costs as current expenses.[157]

---

[151] *Tuxedo Hldg. Co. v. M.N.R.*, [1959] CTC 172, 59 DTC 1102 (Ex. Ct.); *Craddock v. Zevo Finance Co.*, [1944] 1 All ER 566; affirmed [1946] 1 All ER 523n (H.L.) (price paid by company *prima facie* nominal value of shares but contrary may be established in appropriate cases).

[152] *MacMillan Bloedel (Alberni) Ltd. v. M.N.R.*, [1973] CTC 295, 73 DTC 5264 (F.C.T.D.) (taxpayer claimed cost of tires for logging equipment as current expense; practice held contrary to generally accepted accounting principles); see also *Cockshutt Farm Equip. of Can. Ltd. v. M.N.R.* (1966), 41 Tax ABC 386, 66 DTC 544 ("capital cost to the taxpayer" means actual, factual, or historical cost of depreciable property at time of acquisition).

[153] IT-285R2, "Capital Cost Allowance — General Comments" (March 31, 1994).

[154] See IT-285R2, "Capital Cost Allowance — General Comments" (March 31, 1994).

[155] *B.P. Refinery (Kwinana) Ltd. v. Fed. Commr. of Taxation*, [1961] ALR 52, 12 ATD 204 (H.C.).

[156] *Weinberger v. M.N.R.*, [1964] CTC 103, 64 DTC 5060 (Ex. Ct.).

[157] Para. 21(1)(*b*); *Sherritt Gordon Mines Ltd. v. M.N.R.*, [1968] CTC 262 at 283, 68 DTC 5180 at 5193 (Ex. Ct.) it was stated that:

> . . . at least where the amount is significant in relation to the business of a company, it is in accordance with generally accepted business and commercial principles to charge, as a cost of construction, payments of interest in respect of the construction period on borrowed money expended by the company for such construction and to write such payments off over a period of years.

See also *Lions Equipment Ltd. v. M.N.R.* (1963), 34 Tax ABC 221, 63 DTC 35 (limitation of deduction to actual source of farming income; hoped-for source excluded); *Ben-Odeco Ltd. v. Powlson* (1978), 52 Tax Cas. 459 (H.L.) (commitment fees and interest charges on loan used to acquire capital asset not included in capital cost despite accord with accounting principles); *S.I.R. v. Eaton Hall (Pty.) Ltd.* (1975), (4) SA 953, 37 SATC 343 (A.D.).

Where a taxpayer acquires property by way of a gift, he or she is deemed to have acquired it at a cost equal to its fair market value at that time.[158] Inherited assets are deemed to be acquired at a cost equal to their fair market value at the date of the taxpayer's death.[159] This rule is modified when the recipient of the gift or inheritance is the spouse of the donor.[160]

(ii) Foreign Currency Transactions

It is a fundamental principle of tax law that income is measured in local currency. Hence, foreign currency transactions must be translated into Canadian dollars. Generally speaking, the translation of foreign currency into Canadian dollars must be at the exchange rate prevailing on the date of the particular transaction. For example, where a taxpayer acquires a capital asset in the United States, the capital cost of the asset will be its purchase price translated into Canadian dollars, plus any custom duties, sales taxes, shipping charges, insurance fees, and handling costs.

Assets which are purchased and sold in foreign currencies may trigger a gain or loss in Canadian dollars. It is important to distinguish between the portion of a gain or loss that is attributable to the intrinsic market value of the asset itself and the portion that is attributable to foreign exchange fluctuations between the time of purchase of the asset and the time of its disposition. The foreign exchange gain or loss from holding the asset is to be accounted for separately from the purchase and sale of the asset. The foreign exchange gain or loss is not an adjustment to the cost of the property acquired or sold.

Gains and losses on account of foreign exchange transactions are characterized as capital gains (losses) or revenue gains (losses) and treated according to the rules applicable to each category. Generally speaking, the characterization of foreign exchange gains and losses depends upon the nature of the property giving rise to the gain or loss. Hence, gains and losses on account of inventory transactions give rise to business income (losses); gains and losses on account of capital transactions give rise to capital gains (losses).

Foreign exchange gains and losses on account of income transactions are included in the taxpayer's income according to the general rules.[161] In contrast, foreign exchange gains and losses on account of capital transactions are governed by the capital gains rules.[162]

---

[158] Para. 69(1)(c).

[159] Subs. 70(5).

[160] Para. 70(6)(c).

[161] S. 9.

[162] Subs. 39(2).

(iii) *Change of Use of Property*

Where a taxpayer changes the use of depreciable property acquired for the purpose of earning income to some other use (for example, from business use to personal use), he or she is deemed to have disposed of it at the time the use is changed for proceeds equal to its fair market value. The taxpayer is also deemed to reacquire the property immediately thereafter at a cost equal to its fair market value.[163] Thus, a change of use can trigger a capital gain, a recapture of capital cost allowance, or a terminal loss.

A change in use of property from personal to business purposes also triggers a deemed disposition of the property. Here, however, the rules are more complicated. The taxpayer's cost of acquisition is determined as follows: Where the fair market value at the time of change in use of the property is[164] less than its capital cost, the acquisition is equal to fair market value; where fair market value is more than its capital cost, the acquisition cost is limited to the aggregate of the cost of the property and three-quarters of the excess of fair market value over its cost, to the extent that the taxpayer did not claim a capital gains exemption for that excess.

(iv) *Non-arm's Length Transactions*

There are special rules for determining the cost of depreciable property acquired in non-arm's length transfers. The following outlines some of the more frequently encountered non-arm's length property acquisitions:

Description	Reference
Depreciable property acquired from partnership	para. 13(7)(*e*)
Bequest of farm property to child	subss. 70(9), (9.1)
Gift of farm property to child	subs. 73(3)
Transfer to corporation from shareholder	subs. 85(1)
Transfer to corporation from partnership	subs. 85(2)
Winding up of partnership	subs. 85(3)
Amalgamation	subs. 87(2)
Winding up of 90 per cent owned Canadian subsidiary	subss. 88(1)–(1.6)
Contribution of property to partnership	subs. 97(2)
Rules applicable where partnership ceases to exist	subss. 98(3), (5)
Distribution by trust	subs. 107(2)

---

[163] Para. 13(7)(*a*).

[164] Para. 13(7)(*b*).

(v) Luxury Automobiles

The depreciable capital cost of passenger vehicles is limited to $24,000, exclusive of provincial sales tax and GST. The capital cost of a passenger vehicle that has an actual cost in excess of $24,000 is deemed to be $24,000. It is expected that this amount will be adjusted in the future to take into account inflation and changed circumstances.

Paragraph 13(7)(*h*) prevents the $24,000 limit on the depreciable capital cost of a passenger vehicle from being circumvented by a transfer of the vehicle between parties not dealing with each other at arm's length. Where a passenger vehicle is acquired by a taxpayer from a person with whom the taxpayer was not dealing at arm's length, the capital cost to the taxpayer of the vehicle shall be deemed to be the least of:

- $24,000 (or such other prescribed amount),
- the fair market value of the vehicle, and
- its undepreciated capital cost to the transferor immediately before the transfer.

(vi) Reduction for Government Assistance

A taxpayer is required to reduce the capital cost of depreciable property to the extent that he or she has deducted a federal investment tax credit or received other governmental assistance in respect of that property.[164A] This rule does not apply to governmental assistance received under an Appropriation Act in respect of scientific research and experimental developments ("R&D") expenditures. These items are not deducted from the capital cost of depreciable property because they reduce the taxpayer's pool of R&D expenditures under subsection 37(1) of the Act.

(f) Exchanges of Property

References:

ITA:

Subs. 44(1)	Exchanges of Property
Subs. 44(4)	Deemed Election

BULLETINS, CIRCULARS & RULINGS:

IT-259R2	September 30, 1985	Exchanges of Property
IT-259R2 SR	November 7, 1986	Exchanges of Property
IT-490	July 5, 1982	Barter Transactions

The capital cost of an asset acquired in a barter transaction is generally considered to be equal to the value of the property traded or exchanged. Thus, it is the value of the

---

[164A] See subs. 13(7.1).

asset used to purchase that determines the cost of the asset purchased. As Jackett P., put it:[165]

> . . . if A conveys Blackacre to B in exchange for a conveyance by B to A of Whiteacre, the cost of Whiteacre to A is the value of Blackacre (being what he gave up to get Whiteacre) and the cost of Blackacre to B is the value of Whiteacre (being what he gave up in order to get Blackacre). Assuming both parties were equally skilful in their bargaining, there is a probability that the values of the two properties are about the same but this does not mean that A's "cost" is the "value" of what he acquired or that B's "cost" is the "value" of what he acquired.

Of course, in most arm's length transactions the value of the property given up is equal to the value of property acquired. Where, however, it is impossible to value the asset given up and the value of the asset acquired is known, it is permissible to use the latter.[166] Ultimately, the question is one of credibility and proof of cost.

(g) Undepreciated Capital Cost

(i) General

The starting point in calculating capital cost allowance (CCA) is determining the capital cost of depreciable property. When CCA is deducted from the capital cost of property, the residue is described as the "undepreciated capital cost" (UCC) of the property.[167] Thus, "undepreciated capital cost" represents the as yet undepreciated cost of the class of assets or in accounting terms, the net book value of the asset.

(ii) Technical Meaning

The "undepreciated capital cost" of any class of depreciable property is determined, first, by aggregating the following:[168]

- the capital cost of all depreciable property of that class acquired by the taxpayer since 1948;

- government assistance repaid by the taxpayer subsequent to the disposition of property in respect of the acquisition of which the assistance was received;

- any amount recaptured in respect of the class; and

- repayment of contributions and allowances received by the taxpayer which were previously deducted from the capital cost of that class.

---

[165] *D'Auteuil Lumber Co. v. M.N.R.*, [1970] CTC 122 at 128, 70 DTC 6096 at 6099 (Ex. Ct.) (timber cutting rights received from province in exchange for transfer of remaining timber limit; value of former in issue); see also *The Queen v. Can. Pac. Ltd. (No. 1)*, [1977] CTC 606, 77 DTC 5383 (F.C.A.) (interest from subsidiary deemed to be dividends and not deductible by railway company).

[166] See IT-490, "Barter Transactions" (July 5, 1982).

[167] Para. 13(21) ("undepreciated capital cost"); Reg. 1100(1)(a).

[168] Para. 13(21) ("undepreciated capital cost"); Reg. 1100(1)(a).

The second step is to make the following deductions from the aggregate:

- the total capital cost allowance to the taxpayer since 1948 for property of that class;
- the proceeds of disposition of any property of that class disposed of (such proceeds are not to exceed the original capital cost of the property); and
- government assistance received as well as investment tax credits claimed subsequent to the disposition by the taxpayer of the property to which such assistance or tax credit related.

For the purpose of calculating CCA in a year an asset is acquired, only one-half of the net additions to the class is generally added to the UCC balance.[169] The remaining one-half is added to the UCC after CCA for the year of acquisition is calculated. The effect of this rule is that CCA on a newly acquired asset may be claimed at only one-half of the normal rate in the year of acquisition.

(iii) Method of Determining

Instead of recomputing totals for all preceding years, the undepreciated capital cost calculation can be updated annually by using the following formula:

Undepreciated capital cost of		
the class at the beginning of the year		$ xxx
Add: purchases during the year		xxx
		$ xxx
Deduct: dispositions during the		
year at the *lesser* of:		
• capital cost	$ xxx	
• proceeds of disposition	$ xxx	(xxx)
Undepreciated capital cost before adjustment		$ xxx
Deduct: 1/2 net additions to class		(xxx)
Undepreciated capital cost before CCA		$ xxx
Deduct: capital cost allowance in		
the class for the year		(xxx)
Add: 1/2 net additions to class		xxx
Undepreciated capital cost of the		
class at the end of the year		$ xxx

The UCC of a class can never be a negative amount. In the event that the amount of the inclusions in a class is less than the amount of the deductions in the class, the

---

[169] Reg. 1100(2). There are limited exceptions to this rule.

negative balance is included in income[170] and added back into the calculation of UCC of that class.[171]

Example VIII.5

Assume:

Alpha Ltd. acquires one Class 8 asset (depreciable at 20 per cent) for $40,000 in 1995, its first year of operation. In 1996 *Alpha* disposes of the asset for $34,000 and acquires another Class 8 asset for $50,000. Assuming that the maximum CCA is claimed in each year, the UCC of the class at the end of 1996 is determined as follows:

		Class 8
Opening UCC	$ NIL	
Add:		
50% of net additions	20,000	
Balance before CCA	$ 20,000	
CCA claimed (1995)		
($20,000 × 20%)		(4,000)
Balance before adjustment		$ 16,000
Add:		
Remaining 50% of net additions		20,000
UCC at the end of 1995		$ 36,000
Add:		
Additions in 1996	$ 50,000	
Dispositions in 1996	(34,000)	
Net additions	$ 16,000	
50% × $16,000		8,000
Balance before CCA		$ 44,000
CCA claimed (1996) (20% × $44,000)		(8,800)
Balance before adjustment		$ 35,200
Add:		
Remaining 50% of net additions		8,000
UCC at the end of 1996		$ 43,200

---

[170] Subs. 13(1).

[171] Subpara. 13(21) ("undepreciated capital cost", B).

(h) Terminal Loss

References:

BULLETINS, CIRCULARS & RULINGS:

IT-418	June 26, 1978	CCA — Partial Dispositions of Property
IT-478R	February 26, 1992	CCA — Recapture and Terminal Loss

(i) General

The theory underlying the capital cost allowance system is that the cost of depreciable property can be written off over its useful life by applying predetermined rates of depreciation. Subsequent events may show, however, that a taxpayer claimed insufficient capital cost allowance over a period of time. This may occur where the taxpayer voluntarily claims less than the maximum CCA allowable, or where the maximum rate applicable to a class of assets is too restrictive. Thus, the UCC of depreciable property may be higher than its fair market value.

Where a taxpayer disposes of the property of a class for less than its UCC, he or she will suffer a shortfall in the depreciation claimed on the particular class. In these circumstances the taxpayer is entitled to recoup the amount of the shortfall in depreciation previously claimed. This shortfall is called a "terminal loss".

(ii) Dispose of All Assets

A taxpayer who disposes of *all* of the property of a class and who owns no property of the class at the end of a taxation year, is required to deduct from income any remaining balance of the undepreciated capital cost of that class.[172] This balance is referred to as a "terminal loss".

A terminal loss created in a year *must* either be claimed in that year or lost forever. Thus, unlike a claim for CCA, the claim for a terminal loss is not permissive. An amount *deductible* as a terminal loss is *deemed* to have been deducted as capital cost allowance in the year and so is not available for deduction in a subsequent year.

---

[172] Subs. 20(16).

Example VIII.6

Assume:

Beta Ltd. has an undepreciated capital cost (UCC) Class 8 balance of $45,000 at
the beginning of 1996. During the year it acquires another Class 8 asset at a cost
of $10,000. In 1997, *Beta Ltd.* disposes of all of its Class 8 assets for $38,000.
Assuming that it claims the maximum capital cost allowance in each year, *Beta's*
terminal loss is determined as follows:

Opening UCC (1996)	$ 45,000
Add:	
50% of net additions	5,000
Balance before CCA	$ 50,000
CCA claimed (1996) (20% × $50,000)	(10,000)
Balance before adjustment	$ 40,000
Add:	
Remaining 50% of net additions	5,000
UCC at the end of 1996	$ 45,000
Subtract:	
Proceeds of disposition (1997)	(38,000)
Balance in class (1997)	$ 7,000
Terminal loss claimed (1997)	(7,000)
UCC at the end of 1997	NIL

(iii) Automobiles

Special rules apply to terminal losses on motor vehicles. A taxpayer may not claim
a terminal loss in respect of a motor vehicle costing more than $24,000.[173]

(i) Recapture

References:

BULLETINS, CIRCULARS & RULINGS:

IT-220R2	May 25, 1990	CCA — Proceeds of Disposition of Depreciable Property
IT-478R	February 26, 1992	CCA — Recapture and Terminal Loss

Just as a taxpayer may claim too little capital cost allowance on a class of assets,
it is also possible that subsequent events show that the taxpayer was allowed too much

---

[173] Subs. 20(16.1). The $24,000 is exclusive of GST and provincial sales tax.

capital cost allowance. Thus, a sale of the assets of a class at fair market value may show that the assets were "over-depreciated" in the past. The amount by which the assets were "over-depreciated" is subject to "recapture" into income.[174]

(i) Effect of Negative Balance

As noted earlier, the undepreciated capital cost of a class of assets is calculated by adding certain amounts and deducting others. Where the class has a negative balance *at the end of the year*, the amount of the balance is recaptured into income for that year.[175] Any amount recaptured into income is then added back to the UCC of the class, which brings the asset balance of that particular class back to nil.[176]

In theory, recapture of capital cost allowance represents an adjustment for excessive claims of depreciation in earlier fiscal periods. In most cases, however, the amount of CCA subject to recapture in any taxation year can be reduced to the extent that additional property of the same class is acquired during the taxation year. Thus, in practice, it is possible to manipulate the amount of recapture recognized in a particular year by timing new acquisitions of depreciable capital assets.[177]

(ii) Limited to Capital Cost

Recapture of CCA on a class is limited to the capital cost of depreciable property in the class. Proceeds of disposition in excess of the capital cost of an asset do *not* give rise to recapture of CCA. Rather, the excess of proceeds of disposition over the capital cost of an asset is a capital gain.[178] This difference is important because recapture of CCA is fully taxable as income, whereas capital gains are, in effect, taxed at lower rates.

---

[174] Para. 13(21) ("undepreciated capital cost"); see also para. 13(21.1)(*a*); *Malloney's Studio Ltd. v. M.N.R.*, [1979] CTC 206, 79 DTC 5124 (S.C.C.) (house demolished prior to sale of land; no part of proceeds from sale of land apportionable to demolished building).

[175] Subs. 13(1).

[176] Subpara. 13(21)(*f*)(ii); IT-220R2, "Capital Cost Allowance — Proceeds of Disposition of Depreciable Property" (May 25, 1990).

[177] Subpara. 13(21) ("undepreciated capital cost", A).

[178] Subpara. 13(21) ("undepreciated capital cost", E). Note: this rule does not apply to timber resource properties.

Example VIII.7

Assume:

Capital cost of asset	$10,000
CCA claimed	(5,000)
UCC of class	$ 5,000
Proceeds of disposition (net)	$ 8,000

Then:

UCC before disposition		$ 5,000
Deduct *lesser* of:[179]		
(i) Net proceeds	$ 8,000	
(ii) Capital cost	$10,000	
Lesser amount		(8,000)
Recapture of CCA		$ (3,000)

Example VIII.8

Assume only one asset in class:

Capital cost	$10,000
CCA claimed	(4,000)
UCC	$ 6,000

CASE:	A	B	C	D
Proceeds of disposition:	$4,000	$6,000	$9,000	$11,000
UCC	6,000	6,000	6,000	6,000
Terminal loss	$2,000	NIL	—	—
Recapture	—	—	$3,000	$ 4,000
Capital gain	—	—	—	$ 1,000

(iii) Deferral

In certain circumstances, a taxpayer may defer the recapture of capital cost allowance to a later period. A taxpayer who receives proceeds of disposition by way of insurance compensation for stolen or lost property (or by way of compensation for expropriated property) may elect to defer recognition of any recapture provided that the

---

[179] Subpara. 13(21) ("undepreciated capital cost", E).

property is replaced with more expensive property.[180] This election is also available upon disposition of a "former business property".[181]

A "replacement property" is a property acquired for the same or similar use as the property being replaced. A replacement property need only be a substitute for the original property; it need only be capable of being put to a similar use. It does *not* have to be an identical property.[182]

To obtain the benefit of the deferral, the taxpayer must make an election when filing a return for the year in which the replacement property is acquired. Upon election, part of the proceeds of disposition of the former property are, in effect, transferred from the year in which the disposition occurs, to the year in which the replacement property is acquired.

An election to defer recapture of CCA is also an automatic election to defer any capital gain triggered on the disposition.[183]

(iv) Automobiles

There is no recapture in respect of passenger vehicles costing in excess of $24,000 (or such other prescribed amount). ·

(j) First Year Half-rate Rule

As a general rule, the capital cost allowance on assets acquired during a year is restricted in the first year to one-half the allowance that is otherwise deductible.[184] The purpose of this rule is to blunt the incentive to acquire depreciable property at the end of a year in order to claim the full year's allowance. For example, a taxpayer might buy an asset on December 31 and claim CCA for the full year.

This problem is solved by excluding from the undepreciated capital cost (UCC) of a class, one-half of the net additions of property of that class in the year. The one-half that is excluded is then added back to the UCC of the class, after the capital cost allowance (CCA) claim is determined.

---

[180] Subs. 13(4).

[181] Subss. 13(4); 248(1) ("former business property").

[182] Subs. 13(4.1).

[183] Subs. 44(4); IT-259R2, "Exchanges of Property" (September 30, 1985), as amended by Special Release (November 7, 1986); *Korenowsky v. M.N.R.* (1964), 35 Tax ABC 86 (T.A.B.) (delay beyond specified periods precluding deferral).

[184] Reg. 1100(2). This rule applies only to acquisitions made subsequent to November 12, 1981. For acquisitions made prior to that date, the taxpayer was able to claim the full allowance in the year of acquisition. As to when a taxpayer acquires property, see *M.N.R. v. Wardean Drilling Ltd.*, [1969] CTC 265, 69 DTC 5194 (Ex. Ct.).

Example VIII.9		
Assume:		Class 8 (20%)
UCC beginning of year		$ 10,000
Acquisitions during the year		$ 7,000
Proceeds from dispositions during		
the year		$ 2,000
Then:		
Opening UCC		$ 10,000
Additions during year	$ 7,000	
Dispositions during year	(2,000)	
Net additions	$ 5,000	
One-half of net additions		2,500
UCC before allowance		$ 12,500
CCA (20% × $12,500)		(2,500)
		$ 10,000
Add:		
Remaining one-half of net additions		2,500
UCC at end of year		$ 12,500

Thus, where a taxpayer acquires depreciable property in a year, the capital cost allowance that may be deducted equals one-half of the *net* additions to the class during the year, plus the full allowance on the UCC of the class at the beginning of that year. The remaining one-half of the net additions on which CCA is not claimed in the year of acquisition, is added back to the UCC of the class; in effect, the capital cost allowance on this half is deferred to future years.

The first year half-rate rule does not apply to certain types of properties.[185] Nor does the rule apply to certain business reorganizations in which there is a change in legal title without any effective change in economic ownership.[186]

(k) Available for Use

A taxpayer is not considered to have acquired a property until the taxation year in which the property becomes available for use, or until 24 months after the actual acquisition of the property.[187] The purpose of the first test is to match income and

---

[185] Most Class 12 (small items for which a 100 per cent deduction is available in the year); Class 13 (leasehold interests, which are subject to special rules — see Reg. 1100(1)(b)); Class 14 (patents and limited period franchises, etc.); Class 15 (timber rights); Classes 24, 27 and 34 (pollution control equipment), and Class 29 properties, are excluded.

[186] Reg. 1100(2.2).

[187] See subss. 13(26)–(32).

expenses more accurately; the purpose of the second test is to accommodate long-term construction projects.

The first year half-rate rule applies to the tax year in which the property is considered to have been acquired according to calculations for CCA purposes.

(l) Taxation Year of Less Than 365 Days

Reference:

BULLETINS, CIRCULARS & RULINGS:

IT-172R   August 25, 1980   CCA — Taxation Year of Individuals

The usual rule is that capital cost allowance is calculated on the undepreciated capital cost of assets of a class at the *end* of the taxation year. This rule is subject to the proviso noted above that only one-half of the full CCA may be claimed on an asset in the year that in which it is acquired.

Where the taxpayer's taxation year is less than 12 months, CCA is limited, in certain cases, to a proportional amount. This amount is calculated as follows:

$$\frac{\text{No. of days in the taxation year}}{365} \times \text{Maximum CCA allowable}$$

This rule applies to all depreciable assets except Classes 14 (limited life intangibles) and 15 (wood assets) and industrial mineral mines.[188]

(m) Separate Classes for Similar Properties

Reference:

BULLETINS, CIRCULARS & RULINGS:

IT-206R   October 29, 1979   Separate Businesses

(i) Separate Business, Separate Class

Where a taxpayer operates more than one business, capital cost allowance for *each* business must be calculated separately.

Similarly, a taxpayer who has income from a business as well as income from property must use separate classes for the assets used to derive income from the business and the property.[189] For example, a taxpayer may own a building that he or she uses in business while also owning a rental property. Although the two buildings

---

[188] Reg. 1100(3).

[189] Reg. 1101(1); IT-206R, "Separate Businesses" (October 29, 1979); see also *Vincent v. M.N.R.*, [1966] CTC 147, 66 DTC 5123 (S.C.C.) (requirement that taxpayer calculate income from each source separately also applies to calculation of capital cost allowance); *Midwest Hotel Co. v. M.N.R.*, [1972] CTC 534, 72 DTC 6440 (S.C.C.) (taxpayer who sold business then purchased another later in year subject to recapture).

may be similar in all respects, each of the buildings must be placed into a separate class. Thus, it is quite possible that a taxpayer may trigger a recapture of capital cost allowance on the disposition of one asset when he or she owns a similar property which would, but for this rule, have been included in the same class.

Whether two or more business operations carried out simultaneously can be part of the same business depends upon the degree of interconnection or interdependence between the operations of the various units. Revenue Canada's views on "interconnection and interdependence" are set out in IT-206R:[190]

> When determining the degree of interconnection or interdependence between simultaneous business operations, factors to be considered could include, among others, the following:
>
> • The extent to which the two operations have common factors. For example, do the two operations have the same processes, products, customers, services offered to customers, types of inventories, employees, machinery or equipment?
>
> • Whether the operations are carried on in the same premises. For example, if a hardware store and a sporting goods store are operated in two distinct locations, it is possible that they should be looked upon as separate businesses, but if they are in one store, it is almost certain that they are one business.
>
> • One operation may exist primarily to supply the other. An example of this might be the carrying on of market-garden operations chiefly for the purpose of supplying a hotel with fresh produce. In these circumstances, the two operations likely should be regarded as one business, even if a small amount of the market-garden produce is sold elsewhere.
>
> • Whether the operations have differing fiscal year-ends.
>
> • Whether the taxpayer's accounting system records the transactions of both operations as if they were those of one business, or whether separate complete sets of records are maintained throughout the year; if the latter, too much weight should not be given to the possible merging of the results into one statement at the year-end for tax and other reporting purposes.

(n) Rental Buildings Over $50,000

Each rental building that costs $50,000 or more must be placed in a separate class.[191] The purpose of this rule is to prevent taxpayers from artificially avoiding recapture of CCA upon the disposition of a rental property by acquiring another similar property of the same class.

These rules also apply to rental properties acquired for less than $50,000, but to which additions have been made to increase the total capital cost above $50,000. In these circumstances, the properties must be transferred into a separate class. Where a taxpayer acquires a rental property consisting of numerous units, the cost of all of the units within the same building must be aggregated to determine whether the total cost is in excess of $50,000.

---

[190] IT-206R, "Separate Businesses" (October 29, 1979), para. 3.

[191] Reg. 1101(1ac); IT-304R, "Capital Cost Allowance — Condominiums" (May 13, 1991). Rental and non-rental properties must be placed in separate classes: Reg. 1101(1ae).

The capital cost allowance claimable on "rental properties" in excess of $50,000 is restricted to the *net* of rental incomes and losses for the year from all such properties owned by the taxpayer. In other words, CCA on this class of assets cannot be used to create a loss from property.

(o) Transfers of Property Between Classes

References:

BULLETINS, CIRCULARS & RULINGS:

IT-190R2	December 29, 1989	CCA — Transferred and Misclassified Property
IT-491	September 3, 1982	Former Business Property

A taxpayer is allowed to transfer all assets in Classes 2–12 that are used to produce income from the *same* business into Class 1.[192] To do so, the taxpayer must elect the transfer on or before the day on which he or she is required to file an income tax return for the year.[193]

Class 1 provides for a lower capital cost allowance rate than any of Classes 2 to 12. In normal circumstances then, it will not be to a taxpayer's advantage to transfer assets into Class 1. A taxpayer may, however, use the rules to his or her advantage to establish a terminal loss or to defer a recapture of capital cost allowance. For example, a taxpayer may have a large UCC in one class but very few assets remaining in the class, and the remaining assets may have a very low capital cost. If these items were transferred out of the class into another class, the taxpayer may recognize a terminal loss in the class from which the property has been transferred.

Conversely, the UCC of a class may be low when the market value of the property in the class is high. If the taxpayer sold the property he or she would have to recognize a recapture of CCA. The taxpayer could, however, transfer the property into another class with a lower rate of capital cost allowance. It would then be possible to defer the recognition of recapture by reducing the UCC of the class into which the property is transferred.[194]

---

[192] Reg. 1103(1).

[193] Reg. 1103(3).

[194] See also Regs. 1103(2)–(2c).

Example VIII.10

Assume the following profile:

Class	UCC	Additions	Disposals	CCA
1	$100,000			$ 4,000
3	35,000		$75,000	(40,000)
8	12,000	$3,000		2,700
10	30,000			9,000
				$(24,300)

The taxpayer faces a potential recapture of $24,300. He may either purchase a new Class 3 asset or elect to transfer all assets in Classes 3, 8 and 10 to Class 1. If he transfers the assets into Class 1, his CCA profile would appear as:

Class	UCC	Additions	Disposal	Adjustments	CCA	UCC
1	$ 100,000	$ 3,000	$ 75,000	$ 77,000	$ 4,200	$ 100,800

The taxpayer may claim CCA of $4,200.

(p) Employees

The general rule is that capital cost allowance is a deduction in computing income from a business or property. Capital cost allowance is not generally deductible in computing income from an office or employment. There are limited circumstances, however, in which an employee is allowed to deduct capital cost allowance.[195]

(q) Leasehold Improvements

Capital cost allowance may be deducted from the cost of certain leasehold improvements (Class 13) in accordance with Schedule III.[196] Thus, a taxpayer may deduct the *lesser* of:

- 1/5 of the capital cost of any leasehold improvements, or
- the amount obtained by dividing the capital cost of leasehold improvements by the term of the lease in years, plus the term of the first option to renew, if any (not exceeding 40 years in total).

For example, the cost of a leasehold improvement made under a three-year lease with no option to renew will be deducted at the rate of 1/5 of the capital cost per year. If, at the end of the three years, the lease is surrendered and no other leasehold interests are owned or acquired, a terminal loss may be deducted. If the lease is for a term of

---

[195] See paras. 8(1)(f), (j); see also Chapter V "Income From an Office or Employment".

[196] Reg. 1100(1)(b).

ten years with an option to renew for five years, then the capital cost will be deducted in computing income at the rate of 1/15 per year.

The capital cost allowance that may be deducted in the year of acquisition of a Class 13 property is limited to one-half of the full year amount.[197]

(r) Patents, Franchises, Concessions, or Licences

Reference:

BULLETINS, CIRCULARS & RULINGS:

IT-477   April 30, 1981   Capital Cost Allowance — Patents, Franchises, Concessions and Licences

CCA may be deducted on a patent, franchise, concession, or licence provided that the asset has a limited life.[198] CCA is determined by prorating the cost of the asset over the life of the asset. Alternatively, where the asset is a patent, the taxpayer may claim a deduction dependent on the use of the patent.[199]

(s) Foreign Works of Art

A taxpayer is entitled to claim CCA on certain types of works of art created by Canadian artists. These include:[200]

- prints, etchings, drawings and paintings costing in excess of $200; and
- hand-woven tapestries and carpets costing more than $215 per square metre.

A taxpayer may *not* claim CCA on other types of works of art such as:

- antique furniture more than 100 years old costing more than $1,000;
- prints, etchings, drawings, paintings and carpets which are not the work of Canadian artists; and
- engravings, lithographs, etchings, woodcuts or charts made before 1990.

(t) Capital Cost of Automobiles

As a general rule, the full, laid-down cost of an asset is considered to be the capital cost of the asset for CCA purposes. A special rule applies to automobiles. For tax purposes, the maximum cost on which CCA may be claimed is $24,000. Any amount in excess of $24,000 (excluding provincial sales tax and GST) is not eligible for capital

---

[197] Reg. 1100(1)(*b*).

[198] Reg. 1100(1)(*c*); Sched. II, Class 14.

[199] Reg. 1100(9).

[200] Reg. 1102(1)(*e*).

cost allowance. Each passenger vehicle that costs more than $24,000 is segregated in a separate class, within Class 10.1, and is subject to special rules. For example, there is no recapture or terminal loss on Class 10.1 passenger vehicles.

12. ELIGIBLE CAPITAL PROPERTY

References:

ITA:

S. 14   Eligible Capital Property

BULLETINS, CIRCULAR & RULINGS:

IT-123R5	October 30, 1992	Transactions Involving Eligible Capital Property
IT-187	November 12, 1974	Customer Lists and Ledger Accounts
IT-344R	May 8, 1987	Eligible Capital Property — Deceased Persons
IT-345R	October 4, 1982	Special Reserve — Loans Secured by Mortgages
IT-386R	October 30, 1992	Eligible Capital Amounts

(a) General

An eligible capital property is a capital expenditure on account of intangible property. Typical examples include goodwill, franchises, customer lists and incorporation fees.

Expenditures on account of eligible capital property are deductible in computing business income, but deductibility is subject to stringent statutory limits and rules. Three-quarters of such expenditures are deductible at a maximum rate of 7 per cent per year on a declining balance basis.

Similarly, 75 per cent of the proceeds from the disposition of an eligible property is included in income, but only for amounts in excess of the taxpayer's "cumulative eligible capital account".[201] The "cumulative eligible capital amount" is the balance remaining in a notional account, or pool, to which amounts are credited and debited.

The general structure in respect of the tax treatment of eligible capital expenditures centres around the operation of a notional account containing the "cumulative eligible capital amount". It functions as follows:

---

[201] Para. 20(1)(*b*), s. 14.

- 75 per cent of outlays on account of eligible capital expenditures are included in the taxpayer's "cumulative eligible capital" account;[202]

- 75 per cent of the proceeds of disposition from eligible capital properties are credited to the "cumulative eligible capital" account;[203]

- The balance in the "cumulative eligible capital" account at the end of the year may be amortized against business income at a maximum rate of 7 per cent per year on a declining balance basis;[204]

- Any negative balance in the account as at the end of the year is recaptured and included in the taxpayer's income for the year.[205]

Thus, the tax structure for eligible capital property is a hybrid between the capital cost allowance rules (declining balance, fixed rate, recapture, etc.) and the capital gains rules (three-quarters inclusion and deduction).

(b) Cumulative Eligible Capital

"Cumulative eligible capital" (CEC) is the amount by which the aggregate of 75 per cent of the eligible capital expenditures made in respect of the business, and amounts previously included in income under subsection 14(1), exceed:

- amounts previously deducted in computing income from the business under paragraph 20(1)(*b*); and

- 75 per cent of the proceeds of sale less selling expenses from a disposition of eligible capital property.[206]

---

[202] Para. 14(5) ("cumulative eligible capital").

[203] Para. 14(5) ("cumulative eligible capital").

[204] Para. 20(1)(*b*).

[205] Subs. 14(1).

[206] Para. 14(5)(*a*).

Example VIII. 11

Assume:

A taxpayer enters into the following transactions in respect of eligible capital properties.

Year	Transaction	Amount
1995	Purchase	$53,334
1996	—	—
1997	Sale	$40,000
1998	Sale	$13,334

The taxpayer claims the maximum 7 per cent amortization each year.

Then:

	Cumulative Eligible Capital Account			
	1995	1996	1997	1998
Opening balance	NIL	$37,200	$34,596	$4,274
75% × purchases	$40,000	—	—	—
75% × sales	—	—	30,000	10,000
Balance before deduction from account	$40,000	$37,200	$ 4,596	$(5,726)
Amortization [7%] (Deducible from business income)	2,800	2,604	322	—
Included in income	—	—	—	$5,726
Ending Balance	$37,200	$34,596	$4,274	NIL

(c) Eligible Capital Expenditures

Reference:

BULLETINS, CIRCULARS & RULINGS:

IT-143R2   August 10, 1983   Meaning of Eligible Capital Expenditure

(i) Meaning

An eligible capital expenditure is a *capital* expenditure incurred to earn income from a business, but which is not deductible under any other provision of the Act. More specifically, "eligible capital expenditures" are capital expenditures of an intangible nature incurred to gain or produce *business* income.

The following expenditures are specifically excluded from "eligible capital expenditures":[207]

- an outlay otherwise deductible in computing income or deductible under some provision of the Act, other than paragraph 20(1)(*b*);
- outlays made specifically non-deductible by some provision of the Act, other than paragraph 18(1)(*b*);
- an outlay made to earn exempt income;
- the cost of tangible property or an interest therein, or the right to acquire same;[208]
- the cost of intangible property that is depreciable property, or an interest therein, for example, leasehold interests, patents and franchises with a limited life, all of which costs would be deductible under the capital cost allowance provisions;
- the cost of property which would otherwise be deductible in computing a taxpayer's business income, or an interest therein, or the right to acquire same;
- an amount paid to a creditor in settlement of a debt;
- an amount paid to a person in his or her capacity as a shareholder of the corporation;
- the cost, or part of the cost, of an interest in a trust, or a right to acquire the same;
- the cost, or part of the cost, of an interest in a partnership, or a right to acquire the same; and
- the cost or part of the cost of a share, bond, etc., or a right to acquire the same.

(ii) "Eligible Capital Amount"

"Eligible capital amount" is defined as three-quarters of the proceeds of the disposition of property which would represent an eligible capital expenditure to the purchaser. That is, if the purchaser has made an eligible capital expenditure, the vendor is in receipt of an eligible capital amount equal to three-quarters of that expenditure, less any outlays and expenses incurred on disposition.[209]

---

[207] Para. 14(5) ("eligible capital expenditures").

[208] In most cases, a deduction in respect of tangible property would be available under the capital cost allowance provisions.

[209] Subpara. 14(5) ("cumulative eligible capital, E); subs. 14(1).

(iii) "Eligible Capital Property"

"Eligible capital property" is any property that, if sold, would require the inclusion, in computing the taxpayer's income, of three-quarters of the proceeds under subsection 14(1).[210]

(iv) Characterization of Expenditures and Receipts

Amounts incurred or received on the purchase and sale of property are not necessarily characterized as mirror images of each other. In *Samoth*,[211] for example, the taxpayer acquired the exclusive right to sell Century 21 franchises in Canada to licensed real estate brokers. The taxpayer paid $100,000 for this right. The taxpayer acted as a trader in selling the Century 21 franchises, but maintained that the receipts from those sales were on account of eligible capital property. The Federal Court of Appeal held the receipts from the sale of the franchises to be on account of business income and not on account of capital. Hence, not being on account of capital, the receipts could not constitute amounts received on account of eligible capital property. In other words, although the purchase of the franchises might have been on account of eligible capital property, the sale of the franchises did not necessarily require a mirror image characterization of the proceeds of sale. In Justice Mahoney's words:[212]

> In applying the so-called "mirror image rule" . . . the face to be seen in the mirror by the [taxpayer] is not that of the actual purchaser of one of its franchises acquiring a capital asset but its own face, that of a trader in franchises.

Example VIII.12

Assume:

In 1996, A sold her entire business operations to B. B acquired the following assets:

Inventory	$ 10,000
Accounts receivable	15,000
Investments	5,000
Land	20,000
Buildings	25,000
Equipment	6,000
Goodwill	28,000
	$109,000

---

[210] Subs. 14(1); para. 54 ("eligible capital property").

[211] *Samoth Financial Corp. v. The Queen*, [1986] 2 CTC 107, 86 DTC 6335 (F.C.A.).

[212] *Samoth Financial Corp. v. The Queen, ante*,[1986] 2 CTC 107 at 108, 86 DTC at 6335.

Example VIII.12 (continued)

All of the assets listed above, except inventory and accounts receivable, are capital assets. Of the capital assets, only goodwill is an eligible capital expenditure. In computing income for the first year of operations, B can deduct a maximum of $1,470.

The cumulative eligible capital account is as follows:

Opening balance (3/4 of $28,000)	$ 21,000
Amortization - Year 1 [7% × $21,000]	(1,470)
Balance end of Year 1	$ 19,530

If A originally started the business, she would include, as an eligible capital amount, three-quarters of the proceeds of $28,000 in income.

Example VIII.13

Assume:

In 1997, B sells his business assets to C and receives $35,000 for goodwill. B would include $6,720 in income.

Eligible capital amount	
(3/4 of $35,000)	$ 26,250
Balance of cumulative eligible capital	(19,530)
Income	$ 6,720

Note, 75% of the proceeds from goodwill is considered an eligible capital amount, regardless of its purchase cost. A disposition of eligible capital property cannot give rise to a capital gain.[213]

(d) Exchanges of Property

Where a taxpayer disposes of an eligible capital property and acquires a replacement property[214] before the end of the first taxation year following the year of disposition, he or she may elect to defer recognition of any amount that might otherwise be recaptured.[215]

---

[213] Subpara. 39(1)(a)(i).

[214] Subs. 14(7).

[215] Subss. 14(1) and (6).

(e) Goodwill

"Goodwill" has been described as ". . . the probability that the old customers will resort to the old place".[216] In other words, it is the advantage that accrues to a person as a result of a reputation, which may be built up by honest dealing, hard work or advertising.[217] In financial terms, goodwill translates into a premium sales price on the disposition of a business.

The premium compensates for the "excess" earning power of the business because of its goodwill. Accountants define goodwill as:[218]

> . . . [a]n intangible asset of a business when the business has value in excess of the sum of its net identifiable assets. . . . It has been said to fall into the three classes of commercial, industrial, and financial goodwill, which are the consequences of favourable attitudes on the part of customers, employees, and creditors, respectively. As to its value, the most common explanations emphasize the present value of expected future earnings in excess of the return required to induce investment.

"Goodwill" is also defined in terms of excess earning power over the "normal" rate of return of a business. For example, in *Dominion Dairies v. M.N.R.*:[219]

> . . . [g]oodwill can be viewed as the purchase of earning power in excess of a normal return on the investment. . . . This advantage evidences itself in the form of earnings in an amount greater than that expected in a typical firm in the industry with a similar capital investment.

---

[216] *Cruttwell v. Lye* (1810), 34 ER 129 at 134.

[217] *Trego v. Hunt*, [1896] AC 7 (H.L.).

[218] CICA, *Terminology for Accountants*.

[219] *Dominion Dairies Ltd. v. M.N.R.*, [1966] CTC 1 at 12-13, 66 DTC 5028 at 5033-34 (Ex. Ct.).

The determination of the existence of and the amount attributable to goodwill is a question of fact; it may result from location,[220] reputation,[221] brand loyalty,[222] competent management, good labour relations and trade marks.[223]

The tax system treats purchased goodwill differently from expenditures incurred in building up goodwill. A taxpayer who expends money on advertising, customer relations, employee relations, etc., may write off the expenditures on a current basis even though the expenditures cultivate an asset. Where, however, a taxpayer purchases goodwill built up through such expenditures, the cost is an "eligible capital expenditure" which can only be amortized in the manner described.

(f) Recapture of Negative Balances

(i) General Rule

Generally speaking, where, at the end of a taxation year the amounts required to be deducted from a taxpayer's pool of expenditures in respect of eligible capital property exceed the amounts required to be added to the pool, the excess ("negative balance") must be included in the taxpayer's income for the year.

(ii) Individuals

Where an individual's cumulative eligible capital has a negative balance at the end of a taxation year, the amount that must be included in income is limited to that portion of the negative balance that represents the recapture of previous deductions claimed in respect of eligible capital property. The remainder of the negative balance is deemed to be the taxpayer's taxable capital gain from the disposition of capital property and is eligible for the capital gains exemption (see Chapter IX "Capital Gains").

---

[220] *The Queen v. Shok*, [1975] CTC 162, 75 DTC 5109 (*sub nom. The Queen. v. Waldorf Hotel (1958) Ltd.*) (F.C.T.D.) (contract specifying value of goodwill not upheld by court as appraisal differing and vendor was never consulted about allocation); *Saskatoon Drug & Stationery Co. v. M.N.R.*, [1975] CTC 2108, 75 DTC 103 (T.R.B.) (court outlined types of goodwill as well as premium payable to succeed lease of choice location).

[221] *Can. Propane, Gas & Oil Ltd. v. M.N.R.*, [1972] CTC 566, 73 DTC 5019 (F.C.T.D.) (proper assessment of value of goodwill that amount assigned by opposing parties after hard bargaining); *Pepsi Cola Can. Ltd. v. The Queen*, [1979] CTC 454, 79 DTC 5387 (F.C.A.) (characterization of payment as on account of goodwill not termination of franchise).

[222] *Herb Payne Tpt. Ltd. v. M.N.R.*, [1963] CTC 116, 63 DTC 1075 (Ex. Ct.) (trucking business name part of good will; review of law on "goodwill"); *Schacter v. M.N.R.*, [1962] CTC 437, 62 DTC 1271 (Ex. Ct.) (court upheld agreement between taxpayer and vendor of accounting firm, absent contrary evidence of value of goodwill).

[223] *Morin v. M.N.R.*, [1978] CTC 2976, 78 DTC 1693 (T.R.B.) (partnership held to have goodwill, and elements comprising goodwill); *Saskatoon Drug & Stationery Co. v. M.N.R.*, ante; *Herb Payne Tpt. Ltd. v. M.N.R.*, ante.

(iii) Bad Debts

Where a taxpayer has a negative balance in his or her cumulative eligible capital at the end of a taxation year, the negative balance is included in income for the year. This is so, regardless of whether or not the taxpayer has been paid for the disposition of the property that triggered the negative balance. If the amount proves uncollectible, the taxpayer may deduct three-quarters of the amount receivable upon the disposition of an eligible capital property that did not generate a taxable capital gain.[224]

13. HOME OFFICE EXPENSES

Reference:

BULLETINS, CIRCULARS & RULINGS:

IT-514   February 3, 1989   Work Space in Home Expenses

There are special restrictions on the deductibility of home office expenses incurred on account of "workspace" in a domestic establishment. An individual may not deduct from business income, an amount in respect of an office in his or her home unless it is:

- The principal place of business, or

- Used by that person exclusively on a regular and continuous basis for meeting clients, customers or patients.

Home office expenses may only be deducted to the extent of the taxpayer's income from the business for the year. Thus, an individual may not create a loss on account of such expenses. To the extent that there is a loss, however, it may be carried forward and used in the year immediately following the one in which the loss was incurred. This restriction does not apply to the computation of income from property[225].

14. SUPERFICIAL LOSSES

A taxpayer in the business of lending money in Canada (for example, a financial institution) may not claim a "superficial loss" when it disposes of debt or equity securities used or held by it in its business. This rule is similar to the superficial loss rules applicable to capital properties (see Chapter IX "Capital Gains").

A superficial loss arises where a taxpayer disposes of debt or equity securities and reacquires the same or identical property ("substituted property") during the period commencing 30 days before and ending 30 days after the disposition, and where he or she owns the substituted property at the end of that period. The superficial loss may be added to the cost of the substituted property acquired by the taxpayer.[226]

---

[224] Subs. 20(4.2).

[225] Subs. 18(12).

[226] Subs. 18(13)

15. CONVENTION EXPENSES

Reference:

BULLETINS, CIRCULARS & RULINGS:

IT-131R2   November 24, 1989   Convention Expenses

(a) General

Taxpayers who are in business or practice a profession may deduct their expenses for attending up to two conventions per year, provided the conventions are in connection with their business or profession. This deduction is subject to several limitations.

(b) Territorial Scope

The convention must be at a location that can reasonably be regarded as falling within the territorial scope of the convening organization.[227] The taxpayer does not have to be a member of the sponsoring organization. An organization that is national in character may convene at any location in Canada; an organization that is international in character may convene abroad. A convention held during an ocean cruise is considered to be held outside Canada.

It is the character of the sponsoring organization, and not the nature of the taxpayer's business, that determines what is acceptable in terms of territorial scope.[228] The taxpayer's actual business may, however, reflect on the purpose of the trip.

(c) Primary Purpose

The *primary* purpose of the taxpayer's visit to the convention must be connected to business. Is the taxpayer entitled to enjoy being at the convention? To be sure, provided that such personal enjoyment is incidental to, and not the "raison d'être" of, the trip.

The question of the purpose of attendance at a convention should be determined by the relationship between the taxpayer's business and the subject matter covered at the convention.[229] The closer the relationship between the two, the easier it is to justify the business purpose of the trip. That is not to suggest, however, that a taxpayer who is expanding a business from one field into another is not entitled to attend a convention that discusses the subject matter of the new field.

---

[227] Subs. 20(10).

[228] *Michayluk v. M.N.R.*, [1988] 2 CTC 2236, 88 DTC 1564 (T.C.C.).

[229] *Rovan v. M.N.R.*, [1986] 2 CTC 2337, 86 DTC 1791 (T.C.C.).

(d) Blended Purposes

If a taxpayer combines a vacation with attendance at a convention, the personal portion of the trip is not deductible from income. The taxpayer should allocate, on some reasonable basis, the portion of the trip that is considered personal. A reasonable basis could be, for example, the number of days spent at the convention versus the total time spent away from home. The taxpayer is, however, entitled to deduct the entire cost of travel to and from the convention as a business expense. Thus, it is only the portion of the total expenditure that is directly attributable to the vacation portion (apart from travel expenses) that is considered non-deductible for tax purposes.

Costs incurred for taking the taxpayer's spouse and family to the convention are not usually deductible for tax purposes. Of course, if it can be shown that the presence of the taxpayer's spouse at the convention is *necessary* for business or professional purposes, that portion is also deductible as a business expense. The burden of proving the necessity of the presence of the taxpayer's spouse rests squarely, and heavily, on the taxpayer.

(e) U.S. Conventions

A special rule applies to Canadian businesses and professional organizations that are national in character and that hold conventions in the United States. In these circumstances, the *Canada-U.S. Tax Treaty* provides that expenses incurred for attending the organization's convention in the U.S. are deductible on the same basis as if the convention had been held in Canada. This special provision only applies to organizations that are "national" in character and does not apply to regional or local organizations.

(f) Intra-Company Meetings

(i) Corporations

The limit of two conventions per year also applies to corporate taxpayers. Thus, where a corporation "attends" a convention through its officers or agents, it is subject to the maximum of two per year. Revenue Canada does accept, however, that where a corporation has diversified business interests (as in the case of an integrated oil company), the limit applies separately to each of its business interests. For example, the corporation may send representatives to attend conventions held on the subjects of administration, accounting, chemistry, geology, etc., and deduct expenses for up to two conventions per subject grouping per year for each of its personnel.

COMPREHENSIVE EXAMPLE

Computation of Net Income for Tax Purposes

Assume:

A taxable Canadian corporation with June 30 as its year-end provides the following statement of income for its 1996 taxation year:

Income Statement — 1996

Revenue		$ 2,000,000
Costs of goods sold:		
Inventory — opening	$ 300,000	
Purchases	800,000	
Cost of goods available	1,100,000	
Inventory — closing	(200,000)	(900,000)
Gross profit		$ 1,100,000
General, administrative and selling expenses:		
Depreciation and amortization	$ 120,000	
Accounting & legal	15,000	
Commission	80,000	
Donations	30,000	
Bad debts	25,000	
Rental	120,000	
Salary, wages and fringe	250,000	
Interest	35,000	
Insurance	5,000	
Travel (airline)	20,000	
Utilities	45,000	
General	100,000	(845,000)
Income before under-noted items		$ 255,000
Other income:		
Dividends	$ 20,000	
Interest	15,000	
Receipt on disposal of investment	50,000	85,000
Income before income tax expense		$ 340,000
Current	$ 30,000	
Deferred	140,000	(170,000)
Net income		$ 170,000

Comprehensive Example (continued)

Additional information on the above income statement is as follows:

(a) The $50,000 receipt on disposal of investment was the result of the sale of some securities that were acquired in 1974 at a cost of $10,000, resulting in a capital gain of $40,000.

(b) The interest income was derived from the accounts receivable for late payments.

(c) The $20,000 dividends were received from shares that are held for investment purposes.

(d) Included in the general expenses of $100,000 is $5,000 paid as an entrance fee to a social club. In addition, $50,000 was accrued as bonus to be paid to the two senior executives of the company. As of August 10, 1996, the bonus accruals of 1994 and 1995 taxation years of $30,000 and $35,000, respectively, remained unpaid.

(e) The $8,500 interest paid for a late instalment payment of corporate tax was charged to interest expense.

(f) The $25,000 bad debts expense was determined for accounting purposes. For income tax purposes, a reserve for bad debts of $35,000 was made at the end of the preceding year; $10,000 was determined to be bad in 1996 and was written off: $4,000 has been collected in 1996 from the accounts written off in previous years; and a reserve for bad debts at the end of the 1996 taxation year was determined to be $50,000.

(g) The maximum capital cost allowance that could be claimed for the year is $100,000. The balance of the cumulative eligible capital account is $64,285 before amortization.

(h) Donations are made up of the following payments:

i) Canadian Red Cross	$10,000
ii) Federal political parties	15,000
iii) United Nations	5,000

Comprehensive Example (continued)

Then:

DETERMINATION OF 1996 NET INCOME FOR TAX PURPOSES

Net income per financial statements		$ 170,000
ADD:		
Income tax expense	$ 170,000	
Taxable capital gain	30,000	
Entrance fee	5,000	
Accrued bonus (1995)	35,000	
Interest on late instalment	8,500	
Bad debts	25,000	
Reserve (1995)	35,000	
Bad debts recovered	4,000	
Depreciation & amortization	120,000	
Donations	30,000	$ 462,500
		$ 632,500
LESS:		
Gain on investment	$ 50,000	
Bad debts	10,000	
Reserve (1996)	50,000	
CCA	100,000	
CEC deduction at 7%	4,500	(214,500)
Net income for tax purposes		$ 418,000

SELECTED BIBLIOGRAPHY TO CHAPTER VIII

General Deductions

Brooks, Neil, "The Principles Underlying the Deduction of Business Expenses", *Canadian Taxation,* Hansen, Krishna, Rendall, eds. (Toronto: Richard De Boo, 1981), chapter 5.

Cruikshank, Allan B., "Business Expenses Under the White Paper on Tax Reform", in *Proceedings of 39th Tax Conf.* 24:1 (Can. Tax Foundation, 1987).

Goodison, Don, "Allowable Business Expenditures" (May 1989), 23 *CGA Magazine* 14.

Hershfield, J.E., "Recent Trends in the Deduction of Expenses in Computing Income", in *Proceedings of 41st Tax Conf.* 44:1 (Can. Tax Foundation, 1989).

Lawrence J., "Income Receipts and Deductions in the Computations of Income from Employment, Business and Property", in *Proceedings of 31st Tax Conf.* 381 (Can. Tax Foundation, 1979).

Krishna, Vern, "Does Supreme Court Expand Deductibility of Business Expense in Symes?", [1994] *Can. Current Tax J.* 35.

McCart, Janice, "Deductibility of Business Expenses: Recent Developments", in *Proceedings of 37th Tax Conf.* 41 (Can. Tax Foundation, 1985).

Neville, Ralph T., "Deductibility of Automobiles, Meals and Entertainment and Home Office Expenses After Tax Reform", in *Proceedings of 40th Tax Conf.* 25:1 (Can. Tax Foundation, 1988).

Perry, Harvey, "Federal Individual Income Tax: Taxable Income and Tax", *Tax Paper No. 89* 58 (Can. Tax Foundation, 1990).

Verchere, Bruce, "Deductible Expenses", *Corporate Management Tax Conf.* 55 (Can. Tax Foundation, 1975).

Unreasonable Expenses

McGregor, G., "The 'Reasonable' Test for Business Expenses" (1959), 7 *Can. Tax J.* 318.

McIntyre, J.M., "The Deduction of Illegal Expenses" (1965), 2 *U.B.C.L. Rev.* 283.

Personal and Living Expenses

Hershfield, J.E., "Recent Trends in the Deduction of Expenses in Computing Income", in *Proceedings of 41st Tax Conf.* 44:1 (Can. Tax Foundation, 1989).

Perry, Harvey, "Federal Individual Income Tax: Taxable Income and Tax", *Tax Paper No. 89* 58 (Can. Tax Foundation, 1990).

Ramaseder, Brigitte, "Department Continues to Hold Restrictive View on Deductibility of Costs Related to Acquisition of New "Residence" (1993), 5 *Tax of Executive Compensation and Retirement* 844.

Current Expense or Capital Expenditure

Cunningham, Noel B., and Deborah H. Schend, "How to Tax The House That Jack Built" (Spring 1988), 43 *Tax Law Review* 447.

"Distinguishing Between Capital Expenditures and Ordinary Business Expenses: A Proposal for a Universal Standard" (Spring 1986), 19 *U. Mich. J.L. Ref.* 711.

Spiro, D.E., "'Genuine Repair Crisis': A Gloss is Added to the Capital 'Improvement' Test for Repair Expenses" (1987), 35 *Can. Tax J.* 419.

Tremblay, Richard G. and Helen Aston, "The Deductibility of Environmental Clean-Up Costs" (September 1991) 3 *Can. Current Tax* C77.

Reserves

Champagne, Donald C., "Bad and Doubtful Debts, Mortgage Foreclosures and Conditional Sales Repossessions", in *Proceedings of 27th Tax Conf.* 682 (Can. Tax Foundation, 1975).

Dzau, Vivien, "Reserves: A Tool for Deferring Taxes" (1980), 113 *CA Magazine* 57.

Krishna, Vern, "Reserves" (1984), 1 *Can. Current Tax* J-41.

McCullogh, J.D., "Deferred Income Reserves — Improving Cash Flow" (1975), 106 *CA Magazine* 51.

Merrell, David L., "Bill C-139: New Reserve Provisions and the Forward Averaging Refundable Tax Rules", *Prairie Provinces Tax Conf.* 195 (Can. Tax Foundation, 1983).

Mida, Israel H., "Deductibility of Reserves: Contractors, Maintenance Contracts, Captive Insurance Arrangements", *Corporate Management Tax Conf.* 4:1 (Can. Tax Foundation, 1987).

Nitikman, Bert W., "Reserves", in *Proceedings of 25th Tax Conf.* (Can. Tax Foundation, 1973).

Smyth, "Accounting for Reserves — Tax Relationship and Gross Earnings" (1959), 75 *Can. Chartered Accountant* 549.

Interest

Arnold, Brian J., and Gordon D. Dixon, "Rubbing Salt into the Wound: The Denial of the Interest Deduction After the Loss of a Source of Income" (1991), 39 *Can. Tax. J.* 1473.

Atsidis, Elisabeth, "Technical Amendments to the Interest Deductibility Rules in the Income Tax Act as Proposed on 20 December 1991" (1993), 2 *Dal. J. Leg. Studies* 265.

Bale, Gordon, "The Interest Deduction Dilemma" (1973), *Can. Tax J.* 317.

Bankman, Joseph, and William A. Klein, "Accurate Taxation of Long-Term Debt: Taking Into Account the Term Structure of Interest" (Winter 1989), 44 *Tax Law Review* 335.

Berger, Sydney H., and Mark Potechin, "When is Interest Expense Deductible?" (1986), 119:5 *CA Magazine* 54.

Birnie, David A.G., "Consolidation of Corporate Structures", in *Proceedings of 31st Tax Conf.* 177 (Can. Tax Foundation, 1979).

Block, Cheryl D., "The Trouble with Interest: Reflections on Interest Deductions After the Tax Reform Act of 1986" (Fall 1988), 40 *University of Florida Law Review* 689.

Bouman, Donald G.H., "Debt Financing-II", *Corporate Management Tax Conf.* 88 (Can. Tax Foundation, 1974).

"Bronfman Panacea or Pandora's Box" (1990), 44 *DTC* 7009.

Couzin, Robert, James R. Daman, Michael Hiltz and William R. Lawlor, "Tax Treatment of Interest: Bronfman Trust and the June 2, 1987 Release", *Corporate Management Tax Conf.* 10:1 (Can. Tax Foundation, 1987).

Crawford, William E., "The Deductibility of Interest", in *Proceedings of 42nd Tax Conf.* 4:10 (Can. Tax Foundation, 1990).

Crowe, Ian, "Tax — I'm Tired of Yoghurt" (June 1991), 124 *CA Magazine* 29.

Damji, Nazee, "Interest and Penalty Charges" (April 1990), 64 *CMA Magazine* 15.

Discounts, Premiums and Bonuses and the Repeal of IT-114: What Happens Now" (1994), No. 1181 *Tax Topics* 1.

Drache, Arthur B.C., "Draft Interest Expense Legislation" (1992), 14 *Can. Taxpayer* 11.

Drache, Arthur B.C., "Interest Deductibility: Loans to Shareholders and Employees" (1983), 5 *Can. Taxpayer* 179.

Drache, Arthur B.C., "Interest Deductibility : Planning Still Worthwhile" (1991), 13 *Can. Taxpayer* 102.

Drache, Arthur B.C., "Interest Deductibility Reviewed" (1991), 13 *Can. Taxpayer* 189.

Drache, Arthur B.C.,"Mortgage Interest Deductible...For Now" (1987), 9:4 *Can. Taxpayer* 29.

Edgar, Tim, and Brian J. Arnold, "Reflections on the Submission of the CBA-CICA Joint Committee on Taxation Concerning the Deductibility of Interest" (1992), 38 *Can. Tax J.* 847.

Edwards, Stanley E., "Debt Financing-I", *Corporate Management Tax Conf.* 70 (Can. Tax Foundation, 1974).

Ewens, Douglas S., "The Thin Capitalization Restrictions" (1994), *Can. Tax J.* 954.

Fox-Revett, Melissa G., "Interest Deductibility", [1993] *Can. Current Tax* P19.

Gagnon, Guy A., "Deducting Shareholder Interest the Hard Way" (1992), 40 *Can. Tax J.* 1343.

Glover, Paul, "Interest is Deductible — Isn't It?" (July-August 1987), 61 *CMA Magazine* 28.

Henly, K.S.M., "Late Payment Charges: Interest for the Purpose of Thin Capitalization Rules?" (1987), 35 *Can. Tax J.* 143.

Hickey, Paul B., "The Proposed New Interest Deductibility Regime: Strategies and Pitfalls" in *Processing of 46th Tax Conference* (Can. Tax Foundation, 1992).

Huggett, Donald R., "A Matter of Interest" (1987), 14 *Can. Tax News* 105.

Huggett, Donald R. (ed.), "Speculators Beware" (1980), 7 *Can. Tax News* 114.

"Income Tax Treatment of Interest — What's Happening" (1995), No. 1196 *Tax Topics* 2.

"Interest Deductibility Revisited" (1990), 44 DTC 7026.

"Interest Expense Detailed" (1992), 4:11 *Tax Notes Inter.* 513.

Krever, Richard, " 'Capital or Current': The Tax Treatment of Expenditures to Preserve a Taxpayer's Title or Interest in Assets" (1986), 12 *Monash Univ. L.R.* 49.

Krishna, Vern, "Deducting Interest Expenses" (1983), 17:11 *CGA Magazine* 21.

Krishna, Vern, "Interest Deductibility: More Form Over Substance", [1993] *Can. Current Tax* C17.

Krishna, Vern, "Interest Expenses" (1983), 17:7 *CGA Magazine* 39.

Krishna, Vern, "Is There a Choice of Methods in Accounting for Interest Expenses?" (1984), 1 *Can. Current Tax* C-21.

Krishna, Vern, "More Uncertainty on Deduction of Interest Expenses" [Case Comment: *Attaie v. Canada (M.N.R.)* (1987) T-1319-85 (T.C.)] (1987-89), 2 *Can. Current Tax* J-59.

Latimer, W.R., "Capitalization of Interest" (1969), 17 *Can. Tax J.* 331.

Lavelle, P.M., "Deductibility of Interest Costs" (1981), 29 *Can. Tax J.* 536.

Lawlor, William B., "Interest Deductibility: Where to After Bronfman Trust?", in *Proceedings of 39th Tax Conf.* 19:1 (Can. Tax Foundation, 1987).

Lindsay, Robert F., "Tax Aspects of Real Estate Financing", *Corporate Management Tax Conf.* 258 (Can. Tax Foundation, 1983).

Loveland, Norman C., "Income Tax Aspects of Borrowing and Lending", [1986] *Special Lectures LSUC* 289.

McDonnell, T.E., "Without a Trace" (1993), 41 *Can. Tax J.* 134.

McNair, D. Keith, "Restricted Interest Expense" (1987), 35 *Can. Tax J.* 616.

Mitchell, George, "Current Assessing Trends" (1979), 27 *Can. Tax J.* 256.

Neville, Ralph T., "Tax Considerations in Real Estate Development and Construction", *Corporate Management Tax Conf.* 7:1 (Can. Tax Foundation, 1989).

Riehl, Gordon W., "Debt Instruments", in *Proceedings of 27th Tax Conf.* 764 (Can. Tax Foundation, 1975).

Shoup, Carl S., "Deduction of Homeowners' Mortgage Interest, Interest on Other Consumer Debt, and Property Taxes Under the Individual Income Tax: The Horizontal Equity Issue" (1979), 27 *Can. Tax J.* 529.

Smith, David W., "Supreme Court Shakes Up Interest-Deduction Rules" (April 1987), 14:4 *Nat.* 17.

Smith, Ronald, J., "Sales of Real Estate: Tax Planning for the Buyer", *Corporate Management Tax Conf.* 159 (Can. Tax Foundation, 1983).

Steiss, "Deductibility of Financing Charges", in *Proceedings of 24th Tax Conf.* 126 (Can. Tax Foundation, 1972).

Stikeman, H.H. (ed.), "Interest Deductibility — The Purpose Test", *Canada Tax Letter*, April 21, 1980 (De Boo).

Stikeman, H.H. (ed.),"The Deduction of Interest and the 'Use' of Money", *Canada Tax Letter*, July 10, 1974 (De Boo).

Thomas, Douglas, "As a Matter of Interest" (1978), 3 *CA Magazine* 84.

Ward, David A., "Arm's Length Acquisition Relating to Shares in a Public Corporation", *Corporate Management Tax Conf.* 108 (Can. Tax Foundation, 1978).

Wraggett, Cathy, "Minimizing Your Personal Tax Burden" (March 1990), 64 *CMA Magazine* 21.

Capital Cost Allowance

Arnold, Brian J., "Conversions of Property to and from Inventory: Tax Consequences" (1976), 24 *Can. Tax J.* 231.

Arnold, Brian J., "Recent Developments in the Tax Treatment of Inventory", in *Proceedings of 31st Tax Conf.* 865 (Can. Tax Foundation, 1979).

Bird, R.W., and J.R. Williamson, "Capital Cost Allowance" (1981), *Can. Taxation* 251.

Carter, Ronald W., "CCA and Eligible Capital Property: Tax Reform Implications", in *Proceedings of 40th Tax Conf.* 27:1 (Can. Tax Foundation, 1988).

Colley, Geoffrey M., "More on Capital Cost Allowance" (1976), 109 *CA Magazine* 62.

Daniels, C. Paul, "Real Estate Investment as a Tax Shelter", in *Proceedings of 28th Tax Conf.* 179 (Can. Tax Foundation, 1976).

"Distinguishing Between Capital Expenditures and Ordinary Business Expenses: A Proposal for a Universal Standard" (Spring 1986), 19 *U. Mich. J.L. Ref.* 711.

Harris, N.H., "Capital Cost Allowance" (1984), 1 *Computer L.* 26.

Harris, N.H., "Tax Aspects of Condominium Conversions and Lease Inducement Payments to Recipients", in *Proceedings of 38th Tax Conf.* 45 (Can. Tax Foundation, 1986).

Harris, N.H., "Capital Cost Allowances", in *Proceedings of 21st Tax Conf.* 200 at 231 (Can. Tax Foundation, 1968).

Harris, N.H., "Replacement Property", in *Proceedings of 29th Tax Conf.* 395 (Can. Tax Foundation, 1977).

Huggett, Donald R. (ed.), "Capital Cost Allowances" (1974), 11 *Canadian Tax News* 71.

Louis, David, *Canada's Best Real Estate Tax Shelters* (Toronto: Hume Pub. Co., 1985).

MacDonald, R.C., "Capital Cost Allowances" (1973), 47 *Cost and Management* 43.

Matheson, David I., "Acquisition and Disposition of Depreciable Assets" (1969), 17 *Can. Tax J.* 277.

Milrad, L.H., "Computers and the Law: The Taxation of Computer Systems — An Overview" (1984), 1 *Bus. & L.* 65.

Revenue Canada Round Table, *Corporate Management Tax Conf.* 601 (Can. Tax Foundation, 1979).

Revenue Canada Round Table, in *Proceedings of 36th Tax Conf.* 834-35 (Can. Tax Foundation, 1984).

Silver, Sheldon "Tax Implications of Different Forms of Holding Real Estate", in *Proceedings of 25th Tax Conf.* 425 (Can. Tax Foundation, 1973).

Sterritt, Deborah, "Partnerships and the Rental Property CCA Restriction: News to Some, Relief to Others", [1987-89] *Can. Current Tax* P35.

Stikeman, H.H. (ed.), "A Brave New World of Recapture", *Canada Tax Letter*, September 10, 1976 (De Boo).

Strain, W.J., "Capital Cost Allowances", *Corporate Management Tax Conf.* 26 (Can. Tax Foundation, 1975).

Weyman, C. David, "Manufacturing and Processing, Valuations and Business Deductions Including Capital Cost Allowances", in *Proceedings of 31st Tax Conf.* 254 (Can. Tax Foundation, 1980).

Witterick, Robert G., "Syndicated Acquisitions and Financing of Businesses", *Corporate Management Tax Conf.* 3:1 (Can. Tax Foundation, 1990).

Eligible Capital Property

Carter, Ronald W., "CCA and Eligible Capital Property: Tax Reform Implications", in *Proceedings of 40th Tax Conf.* 27:1 (Can. Tax Foundation, 1988).

Dwyer, Blair P., "Deductibility of Tenant Inducement Payments (Income Tax)" (1987-89), 2 *Can. Current Tax* C-53.

Grant, Carl T., "The Valuation and Tax Treatment of Goodwill", in *Proceedings of 24th Tax Conf.* 467 (Can. Tax Foundation, 1972).

Huggett, Donald R. (ed.), "Eligible Capital Expenditures" (1974), 11 *Can. Tax News* 46.

Johnston, Albert N., "All About Nothings" (1977), 110 *CA Magazine* 47.

Krishna, Vern, "Indirect Payments and Transfers of Income" (1986), 1:28 *Can. Current Tax* J-137.

Krishna, Vern, "Sale of Franchises: Receipts on Account of Eligible Capital Property or Income from Business?" (1986), 1 *Can. Current Tax* J-157.

McCallum, J.Thomas, "The Right Rollovers" (October 1991), 25 *CGA Magazine* 17.

McKay, Russell E., "Income Taxation of a Professional Partnership", in *Proceedings of 24th Tax Conf.* 421 (Can. Tax Foundation, 1972).

Mogan, Murray A., "Recent Developments in Federal Taxation of Income and Deductions", in *Proceedings of 29th Tax Conf.* 59 (Can. Tax Foundation, 1977).

Stikeman, H.H.,"Goodwill or Illwill: When is a Nothing Something?", *Canada Tax Letter*, Feb. 19, 1975 (De Boo).

Stikeman, H.H. (ed.),"Payments for Know-How or Research", *Canada Tax Letter*, March 31, 1975 (De Boo).

Ward, David A., "Tax Considerations Relating to the Purchase of Assets of a Business", *Corporate Management Tax Conf.* 22 (Can. Tax Foundation, 1972).

Ward, David A. and Neil Armstrong, "Corporate Taxation: Lease Inducement Payments" (1986), 5 *Legal Alert* 98.

Home Office Expenses

Neville, Ralph T., "Deductibility of Automobiles, Meals and Entertainment and Home Office Expenses After Tax Reform", in *Proceedings of 40th Tax Conf.* 25:1 (Can. Tax Foundation, 1988).

Convention Expenses

Drache, Arthur B.C., "Deductible Convention Expenses" (1992), 13 *Can. Taxpayer* 7.

Drache, Arthur B.C., "Medical Convention Expenses" (1983), 5 *The Can. Taxpayer* 124.

Selected Other Deductions

"Automobile Expense Deduction Limits for 1995" (1994), No. 1185 *Tax Topics* 2.

Bacal, Norman, and Richard Lewin, "Once Bitten, Twice Shy? The Canadian Film Industry Revisited", in *Proceedings of 38th Tax Conf.* 46 (Can. Tax Foundation, 1986).

Colley, Geoffrey M., "Tax Relief for Overseas Employment Income" (1983), 116:11 *CA Magazine* 71.

Colley, Geoffrey M., "The 3% Inventory Allowance" (1978), 4 *CA Magazine* 106.

"Company Cars and Automobile Expense" (Toronto: Coopers & Lybrand Canada, 1991).

Corn, G., "Deductibility of Landscaping Costs" (1984), 1 *Can. Current Tax* J-27.

"Deductible Advertising Expenses" (1995), No. 1195 *Tax Topics* 3.

Drache, Arthur B.C., "Top Hat Pension Plans: A Rethink" (1983), 5 *Can. Taxpayer* 155.

Farwell, Peter M., "Scientific Research and Experimental Development", *Corporate Management Tax Conf.* 7:1 (Can. Tax Foundation, 1986).

Gillespie, Thomas S., "Lease Financing: An Update", in *Proceedings of 41st Tax Conf.* 24:1 (Can. Tax Foundation, 1989).

Goldstein, D.L., "Whether a Charitable Donation is Deductible as a Business Expense" [Case Comment: *Impenco Ltd. v. M.N.R.*, [1988] 1 C.T.C. 2339 (T.C.C.)] (1988), 36 *Can. Tax J.* 695.

Huggett, Donald R. (ed.), "Inventory Allowance" (1980), 7 *Can. Tax News* 98.

Huggett, Donald R., "Training Costs for Professionals and Other Independent Businessmen" (1980), 8 *Canadian Tax News* 26.

Krasa, Eva M., "The Income Tax Treatment of Legal Expenses" (1986), 34 *Can. Tax J.* 757.

Krasa, Eva M., "The Deductibility of Fines, Penalties, Damages and Contract Termination Payments" (1992), 38 *Can. Tax Journal* 1399.

Krishna, Vern, "Deductibility of Legal and Accounting Fees in Defending Tax Evasion Charges (IT-99R3)" (1986), 1 *Can. Current Tax* C-129.

Krishna, Vern, "Deducting Fines and Penalties" (September 1988), 22 *CGA Magazine* 35.

Langlois, Robert, et al., "Mid-Year Amalgamations", *Canada Tax Letter*, Jan. 20, 1978 (De Boo).

McDonnell, T.E., "Issue Costs of Interests in Real Estate Syndicate Deductible" (1992), 40 *Can. Tax Journal* 710.

Murray, Kenneth J., "The Definition of Scientific Research for Income Tax Purposes", in *Proceedings of 36th Tax Conf.* 563 (Can. Tax Foundation, 1984).

Neville, Ralph T., "Tax Considerations in Real Estate Development and Construction", *Corporate Management Tax Conf.* 7:1 (Can. Tax Foundation, 1989).

Novek, Barbara L., "Deductibility of Financing Expenses", *Corporate Management Tax Conf.* 3:1 (Can. Tax Foundation, 1992).

Pitfield, Ian H., "Prepaid Expenses and Other Deductions — Recent Developments" (1980), 14 *CGA Magazine* 41.

"Revenue Canada's Framework for Automobile Deductions" (1993), 5 *Tax. of Executive Compensation and Retirement* 839.

Shafer, Joel, "Income Tax Aspects of Real Estate Financing", *Corporate Management Tax Conf.* 1:1 (Can. Tax Foundation, 1989).

Tremblay, Richard G. and Helen Aston, "The Deductibility of Environmental Clean-up Costs", [1991] *Can. Current Tax* C77,

Valliere, Charles E., "Both Deduction and Capitalization Treatment Denied for Expenses with Respect to Real Estate that Produces No Income" (1991), 39 *Can. Tax J.* 1033.

Other

Anthony, Irene, "Franchising" (1983), 116:10 *CA Magazine* 20.

Beam, R.E., and S.N. Laiken, "Personal Tax Planning — Changes in Use and Non-Arm's Length Transfers of Depreciable Property" (1987), 35 *Can. Tax J.* 453.

Dean, Jacklyn I., "The January 15, 1987 Draft Amendments Relating to the Acquisition of Gains and Losses", *Corporate Management Tax Conf.* 2:1 (Can. Tax Foundation, 1987).

Drache, Arthur B.C., "Indirect Gifting: The Taxman's Approach" (1980), 2 *Can. Taxpayer* 167.

Drache, Arthur B.C., "On the Move?" (1979), 1 *The Canadian Taxpayer* 96.

Fairwell, Peter M., "Debt and Capital Gains Taxation" (1972), 20 *Can. Tax J.* 101.

Goodison, Donald, "Sex Discrimination and the Income Tax Act" (1979), 13 *CGA Magazine* 20.

O'Brien, Martin L., "Sale of Assets: The Vendor's Position", *Corporate Management Tax Conf.* 1 (Can. Tax Foundation, 1972).

Romano, Dianne L., "Reducing Immediate Tax Liabilities on Asset Disposals" (1979), 53 *Cost and Management* 44.

Strother, Robert C., "Transfer of Losses and Deduction Between Unrelated Taxpayers" (1987), 2 *Can. Current Tax* C-19.

Scace, Arthur R.A., and Michael G. Quigley, "Zero Coupon Obligations, Stripped Bonds, and Defeasance — An Update" (1984), 32 *Can. Tax J.* 689.

Williamson, W. Gordon, "Transfers of Assets to and from a Canadian Corporation", in *Proceedings of 38th Tax Conf.* 12 (Can. Tax Foundation, 1986).

CHAPTER IX

CAPITAL GAINS

Reference:

ITA:

S. 3   Basic Rule — Computation of Income

1. GENERAL

(a) Structure

Capital gains are considered a separate and distinct source of income. Thus, capital gains (including losses) are brought into income as a separate category and are calculated by reference to a distinct set of rules in subdivision c of Division B. Generally speaking, a taxpayer is required to include in income three-quarters of capital gains and may deduct therefrom three-quarters of capital losses.[1] Hence, strictly speaking, there is no separate tax on capital gains; capital gains and losses merely expand or contract the taxable base upon which tax is calculated at the normal rates.

(b) Inclusion Rates

The amount of capital gains included in, and capital losses deducted from, income has varied as follows:

Prior to 1972   —   Nil
1972–1987   —   One-half (1/2)
1988–1989   —   Two-thirds (2/3)
1990–   —   Three-quarters (3/4)

It is important to note that certain taxpayers are entitled to a complete exemption from tax in respect of certain capital gains. The capital gains exemption is claimed by way of a deduction from income in computing taxable income.[2] In effect, the capital gains exemption comes into play in two steps: first, capital gains are included in income;[3] then, within specified limits, a taxpayer may deduct exempt gains in computing taxable income. In this chapter we look at the rules in respect of including capital gains in, and deducting capital losses from, income. The capital gains exemption is discussed in detail in Chapter XII "Taxable Income".

---

[1] S. 38.

[2] See s. 110.6.

[3] Para. 3(*b*).

(c) Segregation by Type

Capital gains are brought into income according to the rules outlined in section 3. The specific inclusions provided for in paragraph 3(b) are as follows:

- *net* taxable capital gains from dispositions of property other than listed personal property ("LPP"); and

- taxable *net* gains from dispositions of LPP.

"Net" refers to the excess of gains over losses. As a general rule, capital losses are deductible only against capital gains; any excess of capital losses over capital gains cannot be used to reduce income from other sources.[4] There is one exception to this rule: business investment losses may be applied against "ordinary" income.

The scheme of section 3 in respect of capital gains and losses is as follows:

Taxable capital gains from property other than listed personal property	XXX	
Add: taxable *net* gain from listed personal property	XXX	
		XXX
Exceeds:		
The amount, if any, by which allowable capital losses from property other than listed personal property *exceeds* allowable business investment losses	XXX	(XXX)
Amount included in income		(XXX)

The effect of the statutory provisions is to treat capital gains and losses as income from a separate source. Thus, the term "income" is a generic term which includes "ordinary" income and capital gains.

Example IX.1

Assume:	1995
The following data applies to Alesia Ng:	
Employment income (gross)	$ 64,500
Business income	15,550
Business losses	9,000
Rental income	12,500
Capital gains	3,000
Taxable listed personal property gain	5,000
Taxable listed personal property loss	7,500
Capital losses	13,500
Alimony expenses	5,000
Allowable business investment losses ("ABIL")	2,000

---

[4] See paras. 3(d)–(f).

Example IX.1 (continued)

Then:

paragraph 3(*a*):

Employment income	$ 64,500	
Business income	15,550	
Property income	12,500	
		$ 92,550

paragraph 3(*b*):

Taxable capital gains	$ 2,250	
Net LPP gains	0	
Net gains	$ 2,250	
Allowable capital losses		
exceeds ABIL*	8,125	0
		$ 92,550

Exceeds paragraph 3(*c*):

Alimony expenses		5,000
		$ 87,550

Exceeds paragraph 3(*d*):

Business losses	$ 9,000	
ABIL	2,000	
		11,000
Income		$ 76,550

* Capital losses times inclusion rate equals allowable capital losses ($13,500 × 3/4 = $10,125); minus ABIL ($2,000).

2. CAPITAL PROPERTY

References:

BULLETINS, CIRCULARS & RULINGS:

IT-102R2	July 22, 1985	Conversion of Property, Other than Real Property, From or To Inventory
IT-176R2	April 23, 1993	Taxable Canadian Property — Interests in and Options on Real Property and Shares
IT-285R2	March 31, 1994	Capital Cost Allowance — General Comments
IT-407R3	April 27, 1990	Disposition after 1987 of Canadian Cultural Property
IT-484R	May 5, 1989	Business Investment Losses
IC 70-6R2	September 28, 1990	Advance Income Tax Rulings

(a) Meaning

A capital gain or loss arises when a taxpayer disposes of capital property. "Capital property" is defined as property, the disposition of which will give rise to a capital gain.[5] As such, with the exception of items that are specifically addressed by the Act, the characterization of a gain or loss as being on account of income or capital is determined by reference to common law principles.[6]

(b) Specific Exclusions

The following properties are specifically excluded from property which can give rise to a capital gain:[7]

- property the disposition of which gives rise to income from a business, a property, or an adventure in the nature of trade;
- eligible capital property;
- cultural property disposed of pursuant to the *Cultural Property Export and Import Act*;[8]
- Canadian and foreign resource properties, which include mineral, oil and gas rights;
- insurance policies, including life insurance policies within the meaning of section 138, except for a taxpayer's deemed interest in a related segregated fund trust; and
- timber resource properties.

Dispositions of eligible capital properties, Canadian and foreign resource properties, insurance policies as described above, and depreciable properties cannot give rise to a capital loss. They are, *ipso facto*, not capital properties.[9] Note, however, that the disposition of a cultural property can give rise to a capital loss.[10]

To summarize: a capital gain (or loss) is a gain or loss from the disposition of property *to the extent that* it is not ordinary income or loss and does not arise from the disposition of one of the special types of property listed above. Thus, generally, a capital gain or loss arises from the disposition of an investment acquired for the purpose of producing income rather than as a trading asset.[11]

---

[5]   S. 54 ("capital property", B).

[6]   Revenue Canada does not give advance rulings on the characterization of gains.

[7]   Para. 39(1)(*a*).

[8]   *Cultural Property Export and Import Act*, R.S.C. 1985, c. C-51.

[9]   S. 54 ("capital property", B).

[10]   IT-407R3, "Disposition of Canadian Cultural Property" (April 27, 1990).

[11]   See Chapter VI "Business and Investment Income: General".

(c) Types of Capital Property

The terms "capital gain" and "capital loss" are used in a broad sense to denote a gain or loss from the disposition of a capital property. There are, however, different types of capital properties, which give rise to different types of capital gains and losses. Capital properties are subdivided into the following categories:

- personal-use property;[12]
- listed personal property;[13]
- "business investment" property;[14] and
- other capital properties.

The gain or loss from each of these subcategories of capital property is calculated separately, according to special rules.

(d) Deemed Capital Property

Where a person disposes of *all or substantially all* of the assets used in an active business to a corporation, any shares received in consideration for the assets are considered capital property of that person.[15] Thus, a disposition of the shares will give rise to a capital gain or loss. For example, a parent corporation may transfer a business to its subsidiary and subsequently sell the shares of the subsidiary corporation. Any gain on the sale of the subsidiary's shares is a capital gain. Similarly, an individual might sell his or her business to a newly-formed corporation in exchange for its shares and then dispose of the shares of the corporation. Any gain on the sale of the shares would be considered to be a capital gain.

The rule is intended to provide certainty to taxpayers who engage in business and corporate reorganizations. It is important to note, however, that the rule deems the shares to be capital property only if:

- the taxpayer disposes of "all or substantially all" of the assets of the business; and
- the business is an "active" business.

The rule does not apply to dispositions of non-business assets or in circumstances where some, but not substantially all, of the assets are disposed of to the corporation. Nor does the rule apply to the disposition of assets used in an adventure or concern in the nature of trade. Thus the rule cannot be used to convert an income gain into a capital gain by exchanging the asset for shares and then selling the shares.

---

[12] S. 54 ("personal-use property").

[13] S. 54 ("listed personal property").

[14] Para. 39(1)(*c*); IT-484R, "Business Investment Losses" (May 5, 1989).

[15] S. 54.2.

3. COMPUTATION OF CAPITAL GAIN OR LOSS

References:

ITA:

| Ss. 38-55 | Rules — Taxation of Capital Gains, Allowable Capital Losses |
| S. 110.6 | Capital Gains Deduction |

BULLETINS, CIRCULARS & RULINGS:

IT-236R3	June 28, 1991	Reserves — Disposition of Capital Property
IT-395R	July 31, 1991	Foreign Tax Credit — Foreign-Source Capital Gains and Losses
IC 74-3R2	February 5, 1979	Supplementary Schedules for Calculating Capital Gains and Losses

(a) General

A capital gain from a disposition of property is the difference between the "proceeds of disposition" from the property and the sum of its "adjusted cost base" ("ACB") and the expenses of disposition.[16]

For present purposes, we can assume that "proceeds of disposition" means selling price and "adjusted cost base" means the cost of property. The technical meaning of these terms is discussed later.

Example IX.2

Assume:

A taxpayer sells a capital property for $10,000. The asset was purchased for $6,000. He incurs expenses of $800 in selling the property.

Then:

Selling price		$ 10,000
Less: cost (ACB)	$ 6,000	
Selling expenses	800	(6,800)
Capital gain		$ 3,200

The taxpayer's taxable capital gain is $2,400, that is, the capital gain times the inclusion rate ($3,200 × 3/4).

---

[16] Para. 40(1)(*a*).

A taxpayer's capital loss from a disposition of property is the amount by which the "adjusted cost base" and selling expenses exceed the "proceeds of disposition."[17]

Example IX.3

Assume:

T sells a capital property that cost $16,000 for cash proceeds of $2,000; T also incurs $80 as expenses of sale.

Then:

Proceeds of Sale		$ 2,000
Less: Cost (ACB)	$ 16,000	
Selling expenses	80	(16,080)
Capital loss		$(14,080)

T's allowable capital loss is $10,560, that is, the capital loss times the inclusion rate ($14,080 × 3/4).

(b) Reserves

(i) General Structure

A taxpayer who disposes of property in a year may be entitled to claim a reserve if he or she is not paid in full for the property. The amount of the reserve is determined by reference to the proceeds that are not *payable* to the taxpayer until after the end of the taxation year.

An amount deducted as a reserve in one year is brought into income as a capital gain in the following year. The taxpayer can then claim a further reserve in each of the following years to the extent that part of the proceeds of sale remain outstanding at the end of the year.[18]

A reserve for unpaid proceeds of disposition cannot exceed the amount of the reserve claimed in the immediately preceding year in respect of the property. Thus, if a taxpayer claims less than the maximum allowed in one year, he or she cannot claim a larger reserve in respect of the same property in the next year.[19]

(ii) Limitations

A reserve may not be deducted except as expressly permitted by the Act.[20]

---

[17] Para. 40(1)(*b*).

[18] Subpara. 40(1)(*a*)(iii); see also the various restrictions on claiming reserves in subs. 40(2).

[19] Subpara. 40(1)(*a*)(ii).

[20] Para. 18(1)(*e*).

The maximum reserve that may be claimed in a year is limited to the *lesser* of two amounts:[21]

1. a "reasonable" amount; and
2. an amount determined by reference to formula.

(A) "A Reasonable Reserve"

What constitutes a reasonable reserve is a question of fact in each case. A reserve may be calculated on the basis of the following formula:

$$\frac{\text{Amount not payable until after the end of the year}}{\text{Total proceeds of sale}} \times \text{Capital gain}$$

Such a reserve is considered "reasonable" by Revenue Canada. This formula is only one of many ways of calculating a reserve. A taxpayer is free to choose any other "reasonable" method.[22]

Example IX.4

Assume:

In 1995, T sold a capital property in an arm's length transaction. The property, which cost $63,000, was sold for $100,000, payable $20,000 on completion of the sale and $20,000 per year for the next four years. Expenses of selling the property came to $7,000.

Then

Proceeds of sale		$ 100,000
Less: Cost (ACB)	$ 63,000	
Selling expenses	7,000	(70,000)
Capital gain		$ 30,000
Less: Reasonable reserve (see below)		(24,000)
Capital gain recognized in 1995		$ 6,000

---

[21] Subpara. 40(1)(*a*)(iii).

[22] *The Queen v. Ennisclare Corp.*, [1984] CTC 286, 84 DTC 6262 (F.C.A.).

Example IX.4 (continued)

A "reasonable" reserve may be calculated as follows:

Year	Calculation	Reserve	Capital Gain Recognized
1995	$\frac{80,000}{100,000} \times \$30,000 = \$24,000$		$ 6,000
1996	$\frac{60,000}{100,000} \times \$30,000 = \$18,000$		$ 6,000
1997	$\frac{40,000}{100,000} \times \$30,000 = \$12,000$		$ 6,000
1993	$\frac{20,000}{100,000} \times \$30,000 = \$ 6,000$		$ 6,000
1994		NIL	$ 6,000
Total capital gain recognized			$ 30,000

(B) Maximum Reserve

The second limitation restricts the period during which a taxpayer may claim a reserve to a maximum of five years. This limitation ensures that the cumulative amount of capital gain recognized is *not less* than 20 per cent of the total gain times the number of taxation years that have elapsed since the disposition.

Example IX.5

Assume:

In 1995, T sells a capital property to which the following data applies:

Proceeds of sale	$90,000
Cost of property (ACB)	$35,000
Selling expenses	$ 5,000

The property was sold on the basis that the purchase price was payable in five equal instalments commencing in 1996.

Example IX.5 (continued)

Then in 1990 the maximum reserve allowed is:

Proceeds of sale		$90,000
Less: Cost (ACB)	$35,000	
Selling expenses	5,000	(40,000)
Capital gain		$50,000
Maximum reserve ($50,000 × 4/5)		(40,000)
Capital gain recognized		$10,000*

*$50,000 × 20% = $10,000

Thus at least one-fifth of the gain is included in income in the year of sale even though the taxpayer did not receive any proceeds in that year. In contrast, a "reasonable reserve" under the first test would be $50,000.

(C) Special Reserves

The maximum five-year period applicable to general reserves is extended to ten years if the property transferred is:[23]

- a family farm;
- a share in a family farm corporation;
- an interest in a family partnership; or
- a share in a small business corporation

and the property is transferred to the taxpayer's child.

(iii) Amounts "Not Payable"

A taxpayer may claim a reserve on only the portion of the sale proceeds that are "not payable" to him or her until after the end of the year. Note the distinction between "not payable" and not collected. Fixed-maturity debt instruments are payable on the date indicated on the face of the instrument, whether or not they are actually paid or collected. A demand note is payable at the time when the note is signed, unless the note is otherwise qualified.[24] Thus, to claim a reserve on a demand note, the note should be made payable a number of days (for example, ten days) *after* demand for payment.

---

[23] Subs. 40(1.1).

[24] Subpara. 40(1)(a)(iii); *The Queen v. Derbecker*, [1984] CTC 606, 84 DTC 6549 (F.C.A.). In the words of Parke B. in *Norton v. Ellam* (1837), 2 M & W 461 at 464: ". . . a promissory note, payable on demand, is a present debt, and is payable without any demand". See also *Pineo v. The Queen*, [1986] 2 CTC 71, 86 DTC 6322 (F.C.T.D.) (demand promissory note secured by share escrow agreement remained present debt).

(c) Selling Expenses

A taxpayer is entitled to deduct expenses incurred in disposing of a capital property. Only expenses incurred in connection with the *disposition* of capital property are deductible in calculating a capital gain or loss. Expenses incurred for the purposes of earning income from a capital property are not deductible in calculating the amount of a capital gain or loss.

Expenses incurred in putting capital property into a saleable condition, or those connected directly with the disposition of the property are deductible from the proceeds of disposition. Thus, fixing-up expenses, finder's fees, sales commissions, brokers' fees, surveyor's fees, transfer taxes, title registration fees and legal expenses which relate to the disposition, are deductible.

4. DISPOSITIONS

References:

ITA:

Para. 2(3)(c)	Disposition by Non-Resident
Subss. 13(4), (7)	Exchanges of Property
Subs. 70(5)	Capital Property of Deceased Taxpayer
S. 80	Debt Forgiveness
Subs. 104(4)	Deemed Disposition by Trust
S. 115	Taxable Income — Non-Resident
S. 116	Disposition by Non-Resident

BULLETINS, CIRCULARS & RULINGS:

IT-95R	December 16, 1980	Foreign Exchange Gains and Losses
IT-134R	November 24, 1975	Capital Gains and Losses on Disposition of Business Property by an Individual
IT-170R	August 25, 1980	Sale of Property — When Included in Income Computation
IT-173R2	January 30, 1989	Capitals Gains Derived in Canada by Residents of the United States
IT-209R	May 18, 1983	Inter Vivos Gifts of Capital Property to Individuals Directly or Through Trusts
IT-259R2	September 30, 1985	Exchanges of Property
IT-264R	December 29, 1980	Part Disposition
IT-264SR	October 19, 1984	Part Dispositions
IT-268R3	February 13, 1987	Inter Vivos Transfer of Farm Property to a Child

IT-271R	May 16, 1980	Expropriations — Time and Proceeds of Disposition
IT-285R2	March 31, 1994	Capital Cost Allowance — General Comments
IT-381R2	November 29, 1991	Trusts — Deduction of Amounts Paid or Payable to Beneficiaries and Flow-Through of Taxable Capital Gains to Beneficiaries
IT-405	January 23, 1978	Inadequate Considerations — Acquisitions and Dispositions
IT-444R	March 26, 1993	Corporations — Involuntary Dissolutions
IT-448	June 6, 1980	Dispositions — Changes in Terms of Securities
IT-448SR	June 21, 1982	Dispositions — Changes in Terms of Securities
IT-451R	March 25, 1987	Deemed Disposition and Acquisition on Ceasing to be or Becoming Resident in Canada
IT-460	October 6, 1980	Disposition — Absence of Consideration
IC 72-17R4	April 24, 1992	Procedures Concerning the Disposition of Taxable Canadian Property by Non-Residents of Canada — Section 116
ATR-1	November 29, 1985	Transfer of Legal Title in Land to Bare Trustee Corporation — Mortgagee's Requirements Sole Reason for Transfer

(a) General

A capital gain or capital loss generally arises upon a disposition of capital property.[25] "Dispositions" are of two types: actual and deemed. An actual disposition occurs when a taxpayer legally alienates his or her property rights.[26] A deemed disposition occurs when the Act *deems* a taxpayer to have disposed of his or her property even though he or she may not have physically or legally alienated his or her property rights.[27]

---

[25] Subs. 39(1).

[26] See, generally, s. 54 ("disposition").

[27] See, e.g., s. 45 (deemed disposition on change of use of property); subs. 50(1) (deemed disposition of bad debt); subs. 70(5) (deemed disposition on death).

(b) "Property"

The term "property" is broadly defined.[28] It includes real and personal property (whether corporeal or incorporeal), shares, choses in action and timber resource properties. Indeed, the term comprises virtually every possible interest a person may have.[29]

Corporeal properties are substances which may be seen and handled. In contrast, incorporeal properties are "merely an idea and abstract contemplation, though their effects and profits may frequently be objects of the bodily senses".[30]

Incorporeal property is a right issuing out of a thing corporate (whether real or personal) or concerning, annexed to or exercisable within the same. It is not the thing corporate itself (such as land, houses or jewels), but something collateral thereto, such as a rent issuing out of the land or houses. Incorporeal property includes such intangibles as reversions, remainders and executory interests in property, life interests, rights-of-way and rights to sunlight.

(c) "Disposition"

The concept of "disposition" is one of the key elements of the capital gains system. The term is not defined in the Act, although there is a fairly comprehensive description of the types of transactions included within its meaning.

A disposition involves an alienation of property rights, such as the rights of possession and use of property. But not every alienation of every right is a "disposition" of the property; there must be a substantial alienation of rights.

A "disposition" includes:[31]

Any event entitling a taxpayer to "proceeds of disposition", such as proceeds from:[32]

- the sale price of property;
- compensation for stolen property;
- compensation for property lost or destroyed;

---

[28] Subs. 248(1) ("property").

[29] *Re Lunness* (1919), 46 OLR 320 (C.A.).

[30] *Re Christmas; Martin v. Lacon* (1886), 33 Ch D 332 at 338 (C.A.); *Blackstone's Commentaries on the Laws of England* (1765), vol. 2, at 20.

[31] S. 54 ("disposition").

[32] S. 54 ("proceeds of disposition").

- compensation for expropriated property (including any interest penalty or damages that is part of the expropriation award);[33]
- compensation for damaged property (unless funds have been expended in repairing the damage within a reasonable time);
- mortgage settlements upon foreclosure of mortgaged property (including reductions in the liability of a taxpayer to a mortgagee as a result of the sale of mortgaged property);
- the principal amount of a debtor's claim that has been extinguished as a result of a mortgage foreclosure or conditional sales repossession;[34]
- a winding-up (or redemption) dividend, to the extent that it does not exceed the corporation's pre-1972 capital surplus on hand;
- redemptions or cancellations of shares, bonds and other securities;
- settlements or cancellations of any debt owing to a taxpayer;
- conversion of shares on an amalgamation;
- expiry of options to acquire or dispose of property; and
- transfers of property to or by a trust (including transfers to an RRSP, DPSP, EPSP or RRIF, even if the transfer does not involve a change of beneficial ownership).

A "disposition" does *not* include any of the following types of transactions:[35]

- transfers of property to, or by, a creditor for securing or releasing a debt;
- *issuance* by a corporation of its own bonds or debentures;
- transfer of property without change in beneficial ownership (except transfer by resident trust to non-resident trust or transfer to a trust governed by RRSP, DPSP, EPSP, RRIF);
- *issuance* by a corporation of its own shares;
- amounts which represent a deemed dividend on a winding-up or share redemption; and
- amounts deemed to be dividends paid to a non-resident person in a non-arm's length sale of shares of one Canadian corporation to another Canadian corporation.

---

[33] *E.R. Fisher Ltd. v. The Queen*, [1986] 2 CTC 114, 86 DTC 6364 (F.C.T.D.) (interest paid pursuant to *Expropriation Act*, R.S.C. 1985, c. E-21, as penalty, because Crown's offer inappropriate, constituted "proceeds of disposition"); *Sani Sport Inc. v. The Queen*, [1987] 1 CTC 411, 87 DTC 5253; affirmed [1990] 2 CTC 15, 90 DTC 6230 (F.C.A.) (*sub nom. Sani Sport Inc. v. Can.*) (amount paid as damages for loss of business opportunity included in proceeds of disposition).

[34] See s. 70.

[35] S. 54 ("disposition"), ("proceeds of disposition").

It is important to repeat that these lists are not exhaustive. A "disposition" includes any event which implies a loss of ownership, whether such loss occurs by voluntary action on the owner's part or is involuntarily suffered by the owner. The words "disposed of" embrace every event by which property ceases to be available to the taxpayer for use in producing income, either because the property ceases to be physically accessible to him or her or because it ceases to exist.[36] Note particularly that for tax purposes "disposition" has a much broader meaning than "sale".[37]

A transfer of legal title of property to a "bare trustee" is not a disposition if there is no change in beneficial ownership.[38]

(d) Proceeds of Disposition

In the simplest case, the proceeds from a disposition of property are equal to the consideration received for the property. The value of consideration received for property should be determined from the terms of the contract of sale or deed. For example, the face value of the proceeds of disposition may be adjusted by the assumption or discharge of debt obligations attached to the transaction.[39]

---

[36] See, generally, *Victory Hotels Ltd. v. M.N.R.,* [1962] CTC 614, 62 DTC 1378 (Ex. Ct.) (determination of disposition when documentation conflicting); *M.N.R. v. Wardean Drilling Ltd.*, [1969] CTC 265, 69 DTC 5194 (Ex. Ct.) (asset paid for in 1963, delivered in 1964; deductible in 1964, when all incidents of title passed); *The Queen v. Cie Immobilière BCN Ltée,* [1979] CTC 71, 79 DTC 5068 (S.C.C.) (meaning of "disposed of"); *Lord Elgin Hotel Ltd. v. M.N.R.* (1964), 36 Tax ABC 268 (T.A.B.), appeal quashed [1969] CTC 24, 69 DTC 5059 (winding-up of company and distribution of shares constituted "disposition" of hotel); *The Queen v. Malloney's Studio Ltd.*, [1979] CTC 206, 79 DTC 5124 (S.C.C.) (demolition of building constituted disposition of building even though taxpayer did not receive proceeds of disposition); see also *Rose v. Fed. Commr. of Taxation* (1951), 84 CLR 118 (Aust. H.C.); *Gorton v. Fed. Commr. of Taxation* (1965), 113 CLR 604 (Aust. H.C.); *Henty House Pty. Ltd. v. Fed. Commr. of Taxation* (1953), 88 CLR 141 at 151 (Aust. H.C.), where the Australian High Court commented upon the meaning of the term "disposition" as follows:

> The entire expression "disposed of, lost or destroyed" is apt to embrace every event by which property ceases to be available to the taxpayer for use for the purpose of producing assessable income, either because it ceases to be his, or because it ceases to be physically accessible to him, or because it ceases to exist . . . the words "is disposed of" are wide enough to cover all forms of alienation . . . and they should be understood as meaning no less than 'becomes alienated from the taxpayer', whether it is by him or by another that the act of alienation is done.

[37] *Olympia & York Dev. Ltd. v. The Queen*, [1980] CTC 265, 80 DTC 6184 (F.C.T.D.) (instalment contract; transfer of possession but not title constituted "disposition", although no "sale" until later); *The Queen v. Imp. Gen. Properties Ltd.*, [1985] 1 CTC 40, 85 DTC 5045; leave to appeal to S.C.C. refused 16 DLR (4th) 615n (sale complete when conditions precedent satisfied); Attis v. M.N.R., [1984] CTC 3013, 85 DTC 37 (T.C.C.) (Minister entitled to fix proceeds of disposition by reference to sale price).

[38] See ATR-1, "Transfer of Legal Title in Land to Bare Trustee Corporation — Mortgagee's Requirements Sole Reason for Transfer" (November 29, 1985).

[39] *The Queen v. Demers*, [1986] 2 CTC 321, 86 DTC 6411 (F.C.A.) (proceeds reduced by difference between principal amount of debt and its fair market value).

(e) Changes in Terms of Securities

A change in the terms or attributes of securities may or may not constitute a disposition of the security. The determining factor is whether the amended security is in substance the same property as the security which underwent the change.

Revenue Canada's position is that any one of the following changes usually constitutes a disposition:[40]

Debt securities

- an interest-bearing debt becoming non-interest-bearing, or *vice versa*;
- the repayment terms or maturity date being altered significantly;
- the principal amount of the debt being changed;
- the addition, alteration or elimination of a repayment premium;
- a change in the debtor; or
- the conversion of a fixed interest debt into a variable interest debt, or *vice versa*.

Equity securities

- a change in voting rights which results in a change in the control of the corporation;
- the addition or elimination of, or any change in, a preferential right to share in the assets of the corporation upon winding-up;
- the addition or elimination of a right to dividends beyond a fixed preferential rate or amount; or
- the conversion of a cumulative right to dividends into a non-cumulative right, or *vice versa*.

The following changes in the terms of a share are not considered a disposition of the share:[41]

- the addition of a right to elect a majority of the board of directors, if the class of shares carries sufficient voting power to control the election of the board at that time;
- a change in the number of votes per share, unless the influence of a particular shareholder over the day-to-day operation of the corporation is enhanced or impaired;
- the elimination of contingent voting rights, unless the exercise of such rights would carry control of the corporation;
- a change in transfer restrictions;

---

[40] IT-448, "Dispositions — Changes in Terms of Securities" (June 6, 1980), para. 7.

[41] IT-448, "Dispositions — Changes in Terms of Securities" (June 6, 1980), para. 15.

- the addition of a right to redeem shares at the option of the corporation;
- a stock split or consolidation;
- the conversion of par value shares to non-par value shares, or *vice versa*;
- a change in ranking or preference features; and
- a change in the amount or rate of a fixed dividend, other than the addition or deletion of the right itself.

(f) Foreign Currencies

(i) Characterization

Gains and losses in foreign currency transactions are taxable according to the usual rules, either as income gains (or losses) or as capital gains (or losses). Thus the first step is to determine whether a gain or loss is on account of income or capital. The characterization of the currency gain or loss usually follows the transaction from which it results. Hence, gains and losses from business transactions are treated as income items; gains and losses from transactions in capital assets are considered capital gains and losses. A foreign exchange loss is not *per se* an "outlay or expense" for the purposes of determining a capital gain or loss.[42]

(ii) Method of Accounting

The general rule is that a capital gain or loss can occur for income tax purposes only if there is a disposition of property.[43] This rule also applies to capital gains and losses from foreign currency transactions. Revenue Canada considers that a taxpayer has "made a gain" only if there is a completed transaction.

A capital gain or loss may result from a fluctuation in the value of a foreign currency relative to the Canadian dollar. Such a gain or loss may arise in respect of a cash balance held in a foreign currency or on account of foreign debts. Three-quarters of the *net* amount of such gains and losses is brought into income. To avoid administrative and recordkeeping difficulties, individuals are allowed to exclude the first $200 of any *net* foreign currency capital gain or loss sustained in a year.[44]

---

[42] *Avis Immobilier GMBH v. The Queen*, [1994] 1 CTC 2204, 94 DTC 1029 (T.C.C.).

[43] S. 39.

[44] Subs. 39(2).

Example IX.6

Assume:

In 1995, an individual purchased U.S. shares for $2,000 U.S. at a time when the U.S. dollar was worth $.90 Cdn. The shares cost her $1,800 Cdn. She sold these shares for $3,000 U.S. at a time when the U.S. dollar equalled $1.30 Cdn., and received $3,900 Cdn.

Then her taxable gain is calculated as follows:

Gain on sale of shares	$ 2,100
($3,900 − $1,800)	
Actual foreign exchange gain*	$ 840
Deductible foreign exchange gain**	(200)
Capital gain	$ 2,740
Taxable capital gain (3/4)	$ 2,055

  * $2,100 × ($1.30 − $.90)
** A maximum foreign exchange gain of $200 is exempt under subsection 39(2).

(iii) Determination of Cost

The cost of a capital property is determined in Canadian dollars as at the date when it is acquired, and not as at the date of its disposition.[45] This is so even if the asset is acquired by payment in foreign currency. Thus the capital cost of a property is its actual, factual or historical cost when it is acquired.

(g) Purchase of Bonds by Issuer

We saw earlier that a taxpayer is generally considered to realize a capital gain or loss only when he or she disposes of a capital property. Thus, a taxpayer who issues a bond (or similar debt obligation) does not trigger a gain or loss at the time of issuance. A purchase by the issuer of its own debt obligation may trigger a capital gain or loss if the purchase is on the open market. The gain or loss is calculated as follows:[46]

---

[45] See *Gaynor v. M.N.R.,* [1987] 1 CTC 2359, 87 DTC 279; affirmed [1988] 2 CTC 163, 88 DTC 6394 *(sub nom. Gaynor v. R.)* (F.C.T.D.) (capital cost of portfolio securities imported into Canada determined as at acquisition date).

[46] Subs. 39(3); see also ITAR 26(1.1) (obligations outstanding on January 1, 1972).

Capital gain:

Issue price	$ 900
Less: purchase price	(600)
Capital gain	$300

Capital loss:

Purchase price	$ 700
Less issue price	(500)
Capital loss	$ 200

Thus, a gain results where the issue price is greater than the purchase price paid by the taxpayer. Conversely, a capital loss arises where the purchase price exceeds the issue price of the bond, debenture or similar obligation.[47]

(h) Deemed Dispositions

The Act deems certain transactions and events to be dispositions of property. These deemed dispositions give rise to deemed proceeds of disposition. Some of the more common transactions which are subject to these deemed disposition rules are discussed in the following paragraphs.

(i) *Change in Use of Property*

(A) Personal to Commercial

A taxpayer who has acquired property for personal use is deemed to have disposed of the property for proceeds equal to its fair market value if he or she begins to use the property for commercial purposes.[48] For example, suppose a taxpayer who owns and lives in a house which cost $100,000 begins to rent out the house at a time when its fair market value is $170,000. The act of renting out the house is a change in use of property. Upon the change of use, the taxpayer is *deemed* to have disposed of, and immediately reacquired, the house for $170,000. Thus the taxpayer would realize a capital gain of $70,000.

Where a taxpayer changes the use of property from personal to commercial, he or she may *elect* to have the change in use ignored for income tax purposes. The effect of such an election is that the taxpayer is deemed not to have begun to use the property for commercial purposes.[49] The election may be rescinded at any time. Upon rescission of the election, the taxpayer is deemed to have changed the use of the property on the first day of the year in which the rescission was made.

The election allows the taxpayer to defer recognition of any capital gain arising by virtue of a change in the use of the property. Consequently, the taxpayer can defer

---

[47] Subs. 39(3).

[48] Para. 45(1)(*a*).

[49] Subs. 45(2).

payment of tax until such time as either the property is actually disposed of or the election is rescinded. Note, however, that during the tenure of the election the taxpayer is not allowed to claim capital cost allowance on the property.[50]

(B) Commercial to Personal

A taxpayer who has acquired property for commercial purposes is deemed to have disposed of the property at its fair market value at the time when he or she begins to use it for personal purposes.[51] In the example above, if the taxpayer had changed back the use of the house from commercial to personal use at a time when the fair market value of the house was $200,000, the change of use would have triggered a capital gain of $30,000.

The change of use does not apply where the change in use of property is from commercial use to use as a principal residence, provided that the taxpayer makes the appropriate election in writing.[52] The deadline for the election is the earlier of two dates:

1. 90 days after the Minister demands the election; or

2. April 30 of the year following the year in which the property is actually disposed.

(C) Mixed Use Property

Where a property is used for both commercial and personal purposes, any change in the *proportion* of use for either of these purposes triggers a deemed disposition.[53] Where the change involves a decrease in the proportion of commercial use of the property, the deemed proceeds of disposition are added to the cost base of the property available for personal use.[54] In other words, the taxpayer is deemed to have reacquired that proportion of the property at a cost equal to the same proportion of the cost for the entire property. Similarly, where the change involves an increase in the business use of the property, the deemed proceeds of disposition are added to the cost base of the property available for business use.[55] Note that the adjustment to the capital cost of the property under subsection 13(7) is an adjustment made *solely* for the purpose of

---

[50] Reg. 1102(1)(c) (excludes from depreciable property any property not acquired by taxpayer for purpose of gaining or producing income).

[51] Para. 45(1)(a); *Woods v. M.N.R.,* [1978] CTC 2802, 78 DTC 1576 (T.R.B.) (capital gain on deemed disposition in respect of taxpayer's dwelling when he occupied it after renting it out for nine years); *Leib v. M.N.R.,* [1984] CTC 2324, 84 DTC 1302 (T.C.C.) (change in use of principal residence deemed to be disposition despite taxpayer not receiving funds).

[52] Subss. 45(3), (4).

[53] Para. 45(1)(c).

[54] Subpara. 45(1)(c)(i).

[55] Subpara. 45(1)(c)(ii) (for example, duplex which is partly rented and partly owner-occupied).

capital cost allowance and recapture; it is *not* an adjustment for capital gains purposes under subdivision c of Division B. Revenue Canada may allow a taxpayer to step up the cost base of the property, but the taxpayer does not have statutory authority to insist on the step-up in cost.

Example IX.7

Assume:

An individual owns a building which he uses for both business and personal use.

Cost	$ 50,000
Proportion of business use	60%
Proportion of personal use	40%

He takes over an additional 10 per cent of the building for his personal use and decreases the portion occupied for business purposes to 50 per cent. The fair market value at that time is $70,000.

Then, to calculate the capital gain for the 10 per cent change in use:

Deemed proceeds of disposition	
(10% of $70,000)	$ 7,000
ACB (10% of $50,000)	(5,000)
Capital gain	$ 2,000

Calculation of Revised ACB of Property:

	Business Use	Personal Use	Total
Original ACB	$ 30,000	$ 20,000	$ 50,000
Deemed disposition	(5,000)		(5,000)
Deemed acquisition		7,000	7,000
Revised ACB	$ 25,000	$ 27,000	$ 52,000*

* The revised ACB takes into account the capital gain resulting from the change of use:

Original cost	$ 50,000
Capital gain	2,000
Revised ACB	$ 52,000

Example IX.7 (continued)

If immediately thereafter the building was sold at its fair market value of $70,000, the business and personal portions of the resulting capital gain would be allocated as follows:

	Business Portion (50%)	Personal Portion (50%	Total
Proceeds of disposition	$35,000	$35,000	$70,000
Revised ACB	25,000	27,000	52,000
Capital gain	$10,000	$ 8,000	18,000
Capital gain previously recognized			2,000
Total capital gain			$20,000**

** Thus, the full amount of the capital gain of $20,000 ($70,000-$50,000) is eventually recognized.

(ii) Leaving Canada

(A) "Departure Tax"

A taxpayer who ceases to be resident in Canada is deemed to dispose of his or her property immediately before giving up residence. This deemed disposition may give rise to a capital gain, resulting in a "departure tax" being levied on the taxpayer.[56]

The following properties are not subject to the departure tax:

Description	Reference
Where the taxpayer is an individual, property that would be taxable Canadian property if the taxpayer had not been resident in Canada at any time in the year;	subpara. 128.1(4)(b)(i)
Where the taxpayer is an individual, property that is inventory of a business carried on by the taxpayer in Canada;	subpara. 128.1(4)(b)(ii)

---

[56] Para. 128.1(4)(b); *Davis v. The Queen*, [1978] CTC 536, 78 DTC 6374; affirmed [1980] CTC 88, 80 DTC 6056 (F.C.A.).

Description	Reference
The right to receive payments under certain pension plans, deferred income arrangements, retiring allowances, death benefits and unemployment insurance benefits;	subpara. 128.1(4)(*b*)(iii)
If the taxpayer is an individual other than a trust, any other property in respect of which the taxpayer has made a prescribed election and furnished acceptable security;	subpara. 128.1(4)(*b*)(iv); Reg. 1300
Where the taxpayer is an individual other than a trust and during the preceding ten years was resident in Canada for a total of 60 months or less, property that the taxpayer owned when he or she last became resident in Canada or that was acquired by him or her by inheritance or bequest after he or she last became resident in Canada;	subpara. 128.1(4)(*b*)(v)
A right to acquire shares under a stock option.	subpara. 128.1(4)(*b*)(vi)

Resident taxpayers may, however, elect to defer or trigger accrued gains on their capital property.

(B) Election of Date

A taxpayer may elect under subparagraph 128.1(4)(*b*)(iv) to deem the elected property to be taxable Canadian property of the taxpayer (and therefore not subject to departure tax) from the time immediately after he or she ceased to be resident in Canada until the earlier of the time when he or she:[57]

- disposes of it, or
- next becomes resident in Canada.

This election is useful to a departing resident who does not want to realize capital gains. Concurrently with the deemed disposition, the taxpayer is also deemed to reacquire the property at its fair market value.

---

[57] Para. 128.1(4)(*e*).

(C) Election to Dispose

An individual (other than a trust) may elect to be considered to have disposed of taxable Canadian property at its fair market value.[58] This election is for the benefit of departing residents who want to realize accrued capital gains to take advantage of the capital gains exemption.[59]

Note that the two elections are available only to departing residents of Canada. Non-resident taxpayers are liable for tax on capital gains realized upon disposition of taxable Canadian property.[60]

(iii) Options

(A) Nature

An option is a right that gives its holder the power to buy or sell property at some time in the future at a fixed or otherwise determinable price. Since an option is a right, it is "property" for income tax purposes.[61] An option right can be sold, exercised or allowed to expire.

(B) Characterization on Issuance

The issuance of an option may be considered an income transaction or a capital transaction. The usual tests in characterizing gains as income gains or capital gains also apply to options: the determination depends upon the taxpayer's intention to invest or trade in the property on which the option is granted.[62]

(C) Grant and Exercise

As a general rule, a taxpayer who *grants* an option in respect of a capital property is deemed to have disposed of the property at that time.[63] The adjusted cost base of the option is deemed to be nil. Thus the issuance of an option for valuable consideration will trigger a capital gain in the year in which it is issued. This rule does not apply to options to buy or sell a principal residence, options issued by a corporation to acquire its debt or equity capital, or options granted by a trust to acquire units of the trust.

---

[58]   Para. 128.1(4)(*d*).

[59]   S. 110.6; see Chapter XII "Taxable Income".

[60]   Para. 2(3)(*c*).

[61]   Subs. 248(1) ("property"); *Day v. M.N.R.,* [1971] Tax ABC 1050, 71 DTC 723.

[62]   *Cook v. The Queen,* [1987] 1 CTC 377, 87 DTC 5231 (F.C.T.D.); see also *Day v. M.N.R., ante* (meaning of "option").

[63]   Subs. 49(1).

(1) Call Options

Where a taxpayer grants a call option (that is, an option to acquire property), the granting of the option is considered to be a disposition of property. The adjusted cost base of the property is deemed to be nil, and the taxpayer must report the gain on the option in the year.[64]

If the option is exercised, the granting of the option is retrospectively deemed not to have been a disposition of property.[65] Thus, upon the exercise of the option the earlier transaction is, in effect, retrospectively cancelled for tax purposes. The grantor must include the price of the option in the proceeds of disposition from the property sold pursuant to the option.[66] The purchaser includes the cost of the option in the adjusted cost base of the property acquired.[67] The grantor is entitled to make a retrospective adjustment to its tax return for the year in which the option was issued, to recalculate its earlier option gain.[68]

Example IX.8

Assume:

In 1993, *Alpha Ltd.* grants T a call option to purchase a parcel of land for $400,000. T pays $15,000 for the option, which T exercises in 1997. The adjusted cost base ("ACB") of the land is $50,000.

Then:

1. Effect on *Alpha Ltd.* upon *issuance of* option:

Proceeds of disposition	$ 15,000
ACB (deemed)	NIL
Capital gain	$ 15,000

2. Effect on *Alpha Ltd.* upon exercise of option:

Proceeds from sale of land	$ 400,000
Add: proceeds from option	15,000
Total proceeds of disposition	$ 415,000
ACB of land	(50,000)
Capital gain	$ 365,000

---

[64]   Subs. 49(1).

[65]   Subs. 49(3).

[66]   Para. 49(3)(*a*).

[67]   Para. 49(3)(*b*).

[68]   Subs. 49(4).

Example IX.8 (continued)

Subsequently, *Alpha Ltd.* may file an amended return in 1997 to retroactively reduce its capital gain in 1993 to nil.

3. Adjusted cost base of land to purchaser (T):

Exercise price	$ 400,000
Option price	15,000
ACB	$ 415,000

(II) Put Options

Where a taxpayer issues a put option (an option to sell property), any consideration received for the option is considered as proceeds of disposition in the year of issuance.[69] Where the option is subsequently exercised by the grantee, the granting and exercise of the option are deemed not to have taken place. Instead, the grantor's and grantee's proceeds of disposition and the cost of the property are adjusted for the price of the option.[70]

(iv) Bad Debts

(A) General

Where a taxpayer establishes that an amount owing to him or her on account of a disposition of capital property has become uncollectable, he or she can elect to be deemed to have disposed of the debt.[71] Similarly, a taxpayer who establishes that a corporation in which he or she holds shares has become bankrupt or is subject to a winding-up order can elect to be deemed to have disposed of any shares.[72] The taxpayer is entitled to claim a capital loss even though the shares may not have been disposed. Where the election is made, the taxpayer is deemed to have disposed of the bad debt or the shares for nil proceeds at the end of the year, and to have then acquired it for a cost of nil.

(B) Subsequent Recovery

A taxpayer can take a deduction for bad debts arising from the sale of capital property only when the debt is *actually* established to have become bad. The Act does not permit the deduction of a reserve for doubtful accounts in respect of debts created

---

[69] Subs. 49(1).

[70] Subs. 49(3.1).

[71] Subs. 50(1).

[72] Para. 50(1)(*b*).

from dispositions of capital property. Since a taxpayer who disposes of a bad debt can elect to do so for nil proceeds and to reacquire it for the same amount, any recovery on account of a debt previously written off will give rise to a capital gain.[73]

(C) Insolvent Corporations

Shareholders of a corporation that has ceased to carry on business and is insolvent can elect to be deemed to have disposed of their shares, and therefore may be entitled to claim a capital loss. A shareholder is deemed to have disposed of his or her shares in an insolvent corporation only if:[74]

- the fair market value of the shares is nil;
- it is reasonable to expect that the corporation will be wound up;
- neither the corporation nor a corporation controlled by it carries on business; and
- the shareholder elects to have the provision apply.

(v) Death

A taxpayer who dies is deemed to have disposed of all capital properties *immediately before* death.[75] The deemed disposition gives rise to deemed proceeds of disposition. The amount of the proceeds depends upon the type of capital property and the date of death.

(A) Depreciable Capital Property

Prior to 1993, depreciable property was deemed to be disposed of for proceeds midway between the undepreciated capital cost ("UCC") of the property and its fair market value at that time. Hence the deceased could defer tax on a portion of any gain accrued on depreciable property. For dispositions after 1992, however, depreciable property is deemed to be disposed of at its fair market value.[76] Thus the full amount of any gain accrued on depreciable property is included in the proceeds of disposition.

A beneficiary who inherits property as a consequence of the death of a taxpayer is deemed to acquire the property at an amount equal to the deceased's (deemed) proceeds of disposition (fair market value).[77] A special rule applies, however, if the deceased's capital cost exceeds the beneficiary's deemed acquisition cost. In this circumstance, *for purposes of capital cost allowance and recapture only,* the beneficiary assumes the deceased's original cost, and any difference between this cost and the

---

[73] See also subpara. 40(2)(*g*)(ii).

[74] Subpara. 50(1)(*b*)(iii).

[75] Para. 70(5)(*a*).

[76] Para. 70(5)(a).

[77] Para. 70(5)(*b*).

beneficiary's acquisition cost is deemed to have been claimed as capital cost allowance by the beneficiary.[78] The effect of this special rule is to bump up the beneficiary capital cost, so that the deeming provision does not obscure the true nature of the proceeds of a future disposition by the beneficiary. The bump up in the cost could result in the characterization of proceeds as recapture rather than capital.

Example IX.9

Assume:

D dies owning a depreciable property which cost $200,000. At the time of his death, the property had a UCC of $120,000 and a fair market value ("FMV") of $320,000.

Then, D's capital gain is $120,000, calculated as follows:

Deemed proceeds	$ 320,000*
Original cost	(200,000)
Capital gain	$ 120,000

D is also subject to recapture of capital cost allowance of $80,000.

(B) Other Capital Property

Capital properties other than depreciable properties are deemed to be disposed of immediately before death for proceeds equal to the fair market value of the property.[79]

Example IX.10

Assume: D dies owning a depreciable property to which the following data applies:

Original cost	$ 200,000
UCC at death	$ 120,000
FMV at death	$ 180,000

Then:
Effect on D's Terminal Tax Return:

Deemed proceeds of disposition	$ 180,000
UCC at death	(120,000)
Recapture of CCA	$ 60,000

---

[78] Para. 70(5)(*c*).

[79] Para. 70(5)(*a*).

Example IX.10 (continued)

Effect on B:

Capital cost for CCA purposes	$ 200,000
CCA deemed allowed to B	(20,000)
UCC to B	$ 180,000

Upon Sale by B:

Deemed capital cost	$ 200,000
UCC on sale	(180,000)
Recapture of CCA	$ 20,000
Proceeds of disposition	$ 240,000
Cost (ACB)	(200,000)
Capital gain	$ 40,000

(vi) Trusts

To discourage indefinite accumulations of property in trusts, the Act provides for periodic deemed dispositions of all property held in trust. A trust is deemed to dispose of all of its capital property on the 21st anniversary of the day on which the trust was created. For trusts created before 1972, the first deemed disposition will occur on January 1, 1993; thereafter, the trust will be deemed to dispose of all of its capital property every 21 years.[80]

(i) Involuntary Dispositions

In certain circumstances, a taxpayer may be considered to have involuntarily disposed of property, for example, when the property is stolen or expropriated. It can cause hardship, in these circumstances, to tax a taxpayer on the full value of any proceeds received. To relieve against such hardship, the Act allows a taxpayer who has involuntarily disposed of property to elect to defer any capital gain from the disposition,[81] provided that he or she replaces the property with a substitute property before the end of the second taxation year following its disposition.[82]

---

[80] Subs. 104(4).

[81] Subs. 44(1).

[82] IT-259R2, "Exchanges of Property" (September 30, 1985).

(i) Election to Defer Gain

The deferral is available in respect of the following types of receipts:[83]

- compensation for property[84] that has been lost or destroyed;
- compensation for property that is stolen;
- compensation for property that is expropriated under statutory authority; or
- sale proceeds from property sold under the duress of an intention to expropriate under statutory authority.

The deferral is available only where the taxpayer acquires a replacement for the property before the end of the second taxation year following the year in which the proceeds became receivable.[85] The taxpayer must acquire a capital property to replace the former property; a business asset must be replaced with a business asset.

(ii) Proceeds of Disposition

Proceeds of an involuntary disposition are deemed to become receivable on the *earliest* of the following days:[86]

- the day when the taxpayer agrees to an amount as full compensation for property lost, stolen or destroyed;
- where an appeal or other proceeding has been taken before a court or tribunal, the day on which the taxpayer's compensation for the property is finally determined by the court or tribunal;
- where no such appeal or other proceeding has been taken before a court or tribunal within two years of the loss, destruction or expropriation of property, the second anniversary day of the loss, destruction or expropriation;
- the day on which the taxpayer ceases to be resident in Canada;
- the day on which the taxpayer dies; or,
- where the taxpayer is a corporation (other than a taxable Canadian corporation that is 90 per cent owned by another taxable Canadian corporation), immediately before the corporation is wound up.

---

[83] Subs. 44(1).

[84] *Sani Sport Inc. v. Can.*, [1990] 2 CTC 15, 90 DTC 6230 (F.C.A.) (compensation for property includes damages suffered by business loss).

[85] Para. 44(1)(*c*).

[86] Subs. 44(2).

Example IX.11

Assume:

Jones owns a parcel of land to which the following data applies:

ACB of land	$ 80,000
Proceeds upon expropriation	$ 140,000
Expenses of disposition	$ 2,000
Cost of replacement land (FMV)	$ 160,000

Then, Jones's capital gain is determined as follows:

Without Election:

Proceeds of disposition		$ 140,000
Less: ACB of land	$ 80,000	
Expenses of disposition	2,000	(82,000)
Capital gain		$ 58,000

With Election under Section 44:

Capital gain otherwise determined		$ 58,000*
Proceeds from former property		$ 140,000
Cost of replacement land	$ 160,000	
Expenses of disposition	2,000	162,000
Excess of proceeds over replacement cost		NIL**
Deemed capital gain, lesser of * and **		NIL

ACB of Replacement Land After Election:

Cost of replacement land		$ 160,000
Less excess of:		
Capital gain otherwise determined	$ 58,000	
Excess of proceeds over replacement cost	NIL	(58,000)
ACB of replacement land		$ 102,000

Note: if Jones immediately sold the replacement land at its FMV of $160,000, she would realize a capital gain of $58,000 ($160,000 less $102,000), which is, in effect, the amount of the capital gain that she deferred.

Thus, in general terms, a taxpayer can defer the entire capital gain that would otherwise be recognized provided that he or she replaces the disposed of property with more expensive property. The deferred gain reduces the cost base of the new property.[87] In Example IX.11, the deferred capital gain of $58,000 reduces the cost of the new property from $160,000 to $102,000. Thus the gain on the sale of the new property will be $58,000 greater than it would otherwise have been.

5. ADJUSTED COST BASE

References:

ITA:

S. 7	Inclusions — Employees Stock Options
Subs. 69(1)	Inadequate Consideration

BULLETINS, CIRCULARS & RULINGS:

IT-88R2	May 31, 1991	Stock Dividends
IT-96R5	May 13, 1991	Options Granted by Corporations to Acquire Shares, Bonds or Debentures
IT-338R	May 28, 1979	Partnership Interests — Effects on Adjusted Cost Base Resulting from the Admission or Retirement of a Partner
IT-353R2	September 14, 1982	Partnership Interests — Some Adjustments to Cost Base
IT-384R	January 14, 1987	Reassessment Where Option Exercised in Subsequent Year
IT-384SR	November 6, 1989	Reassessment Where Option Exercised in Subsequent Year
IT-387R2	July 14, 1989	Meaning of "Identical Properties"
IT-403R	May 29, 1984	Options on Real Estate
IT-456R	July 9, 1990	Capital Property — Some Adjustments to Cost Base
IC 87-5	December 11, 1987	Capital Cost of Property Where Trade-In is Involved

(a) General

As a general rule, the capital cost of a property is the amount expended for the acquisition of the property, including the amount of any liabilities assumed by the taxpayer. The "adjusted cost base" of a property means:[88]

---

[87] Para. 44(1)(*e*).

[88] S. 54 ("adjusted cost base").

- where the property is depreciable property, its capital cost; and

- where the property is any other property, the cost of the property as adjusted by section 53.

The terms "capital cost" and "cost" are not defined, and should be interpreted according to their commercial usage.

"Cost" refers to the price that the taxpayer gives up in order to acquire the property.[89] It includes incidental acquisition costs such as brokerage, legal, accounting, engineering and valuation fees. Carrying costs (such as interest expense) for the unpaid price of property are not part of the "cost" of the asset for purposes of the capital gains rules.[90]

There are special rules for determining the adjusted cost base of properties owned by a taxpayer at the start of the "new system" on January 1, 1972. These rules are set out in the Income Tax Application Rules (ITARs).

(b) Deemed Adjusted Cost Base

Numerous provisions of the Act *deem* the cost of a property to be a certain amount. Note that whenever the Act deems a disposition of property for deemed proceeds, it also deems a reacquisition of the property at a deemed cost base. Thus every capital property always has an adjusted cost base.

(i) Change of Use

Where a taxpayer changes the use of a capital property from business to personal use, or *vice versa,* he or she is deemed to have acquired the property for the new purpose at a cost equal to its fair market value at the time of the change in use.[91] Similarly, where a taxpayer changes the proportions of business and personal use of a capital property, he or she may be deemed to have acquired the portion of the property subject to the new use at a cost proportional to its fair market value at that time.[92]

---

[89] *The Queen v. Stirling*, [1985] 1 FC 342 (F.C.A.) (interest expense on unpaid portion of price of gold bullion, and safe-keeping charges, not part of cost of bullion).

[90] *The Queen v. Stirling, ante,* at 343; see also *The Queen v. C.P. Ltd.*, [1977] CTC 606, 77 DTC 5383 (F.C.A.) (taxpayer not entitled to CCA on perishable product or expenditures in respect of property not owned); *The Queen v. Consumer's Gas Co.*, [1984] CTC 83, 84 DTC 6058 (F.C.A.) (taxpayer to add cost of pipelines to UCC without reduction for reimbursement); *Birmingham Corp. v. Barnes*, [1935] AC 292 (H.L.) (deductibility of grant received and renewal costs in determination of "actual cost" to build tramway).

[91] S. 45.

[92] Para. 45(1)(c).

(ii) Identical Properties

The cost of identical properties is their weighted average cost at any time.[93] A new average is to be determined each time another identical property is acquired and added to the pool. The cost of identical capital properties (other than depreciable property or an interest in a partnership) owned by a taxpayer on December 31, 1971, is also the weighted average cost of the properties.[94] Note, however, that this calculation is made separately from the one for identical properties acquired after December 31, 1971. In effect, a taxpayer is required to maintain two separate pools of identical properties: one for pre-1972 properties and the other for post-1971 properties.

Where a taxpayer issues debt (bonds, debentures, notes, etc.) and equity securities at different times, the securities are considered to be identical to each other if they have the same rights in all respects and differ only in the face value or principal amount of the security. [95]

(iii) Becoming a Canadian Resident

When a taxpayer becomes resident in Canada, he or she is deemed to have acquired each property already owned by him or her at that time, at a cost equal to its fair market value.[96] This rule does not apply to property which would be "taxable Canadian property" if the taxpayer were not resident in Canada, in which case the cost of the property for Canadian tax purposes is its actual cost to the taxpayer.[97]

(iv) Options

When a taxpayer exercises an option to acquire property, the adjusted cost base of the property to the purchaser includes the cost of the option.[98]

(v) Conversions

Where a taxpayer acquires shares of a corporation in exchange for convertible shares, bonds, debentures or notes issued by the corporation, and the acquisition is made without any cash consideration, the taxpayer's cost of the shares is deemed to be his or her adjusted cost base of the convertible property immediately before the exchange.[99]

---

[93] S. 47.

[94] ITAR 26(8).

[95] Subs. 248(12).

[96] Para. 128.1(4)(c).

[97] Subpara. 128.1(4)(b)(i).

[98] Subs. 49(3); see Example IX.8.

[99] S. 51.

(vi) Non-arm's Length Transactions

Where a taxpayer acquires property in a non-arm's length transaction at an amount greater than its fair market value, he or she is deemed to have acquired the property at its fair market value at the time of acquisition.[100] If the property is acquired at less than its fair market value, the adjusted cost base of the property is the taxpayer's actual cost.

(vii) Prizes

A taxpayer who wins a prize in a lottery is deemed to acquire the property at a cost equal to its fair market value at the time of winning the prize.[101] Although a lottery prize is exempt from tax, a life annuity in lieu of the prize is *fully* taxable on both the capital and interest components.

(viii) Dividends in Kind

A taxpayer who receives a dividend in kind (other than a stock dividend) is deemed to have acquired the property at its fair market value.[102]

(ix) Stock Dividends

A stock dividend includes any dividend paid by the issuance of shares of any class of a corporation.[103]

The value of a stock dividend is the amount by which the paid-up capital of the corporation paying the dividend is increased by virtue of the payment of the dividend. In the case of a stock dividend which does not qualify as a "dividend", the cost is nil.[104] Note that the cost of stock dividends received by a taxpayer will affect the adjusted cost base of all other identical shares owned by the taxpayer.[105]

A corporation which pays a stock dividend with a low paid-up capital and high fair market value and then repurchases the stock may be liable to a special corporate distributions tax.[106]

---

[100] Para. 69(1)(a).

[101] Subs. 52(4); see *Rumack v. M.N.R.*, [1984] CTC 2382, 84 DTC 1339 (T.C.C.).

[102] Subs. 52(2).

[103] See subs. 248(1) ("dividend").

[104] Para. 52(3)(a.1).

[105] S. 47.

[106] Pt. II.1, (ss. 183.1, 183.2).

(c) Adjustments to Cost Base

(i) General

The cost base of a property is determined by reference to commercial principles and the aforementioned deeming provisions. The cost base may also be adjusted for various events and transactions from time to time. The adjusted cost base of a property is always determined *as of a particular time,* and any adjustments are made up to that time.

There are two types of adjustments to the cost base of property: additions to the cost base[107] and deductions from the cost base.[108]

Generally, additions to the cost base of property are made when a taxpayer receives an amount which either has previously borne tax or was exempt from tax. Thus additions to the adjusted cost base of property prevent double taxation of the same amount. For example, where an employee is taxed on a stock option benefit that is included in employment income,[109] the value of the benefit is added to the cost base of the shares.[110] Without this addition, the taxpayer would be taxed again on the same gain when he or she disposed of the shares.

Conversely, deductions from the cost base of property are made when a taxpayer has previously received an amount free of tax. The following is illustrative of some of the adjustments made to the cost base of the more common types of property.

(ii) Acquisition of Land

A deduction for interest expense on debt relating to the acquisition of vacant land is precluded to the extent that the expense exceeds any income from the land.[111] The taxpayer is allowed to add the disallowed carrying charges to the cost base of the land.[112]

The phrase "interest on debt relating to the acquisition of land" includes certain interest expenses incurred by a taxpayer in respect of money that is borrowed to finance the acquisition of land by another person with whom the taxpayer does not deal at arm's length.[113] For example, it also includes interest on borrowed money used to finance the acquisition of land by a corporation of which the taxpayer is a specified

---

[107] Subs. 53(1).

[108] Subs. 53(2).

[109] S. 7; see Chapter V "Income From an Office or Employment" section (g) "Stock Option Plans".

[110] Para. 53(1)(*j*).

[111] Subs. 18(2).

[112] Subpara. 53(1)(*h*)(i).

[113] Subs. 18(3) ("interest on debt relating to the acquisition of land").

shareholder or by a partnership in which the taxpayer has a 10 per cent or greater interest. All of the amounts denied under subsections 18(2) and (3) may be added to the cost base of the land.[114]

(iii) Stock Dividends or Options

Stock dividends have an adjusted cost base equal to the aggregate of the value of the dividend and any amount included in the taxpayer's income as a shareholder benefit.[115]

Where an employee has acquired shares of a corporation and, as a consequence of the acquisition, is deemed to have received a "stock option" benefit under section 7, the amount of the benefit is added to the adjusted cost base of the shares acquired.[116]

(iv) Forgiveness of a Debt

Where a debtor settles a debt for less than the principal amount of the debt, an amount (not exceeding the amount of the gain on settlement of the debt) may be deducted in calculating the cost base of any non-depreciable property (other than restricted property) owned by the debtor.[117]

(d) Negative Adjusted Cost Base

As a general rule, the adjusted cost base of a property at the time of its disposition cannot be less than nil.[118] If at any time the deductions from the cost of property exceed the sum of the cost of the property and subsequent additions to cost, so that, in effect, the adjusted cost base of the property becomes a negative amount, the negative amount is immediately deemed to be a capital gain from the disposition of the property. The amount of the deemed gain is then immediately added to the cost of the property, thereby raising the adjusted cost base to nil.[119] Where the adjusted cost base of the capital property falls below nil in a particular year, the negative amount is generally considered to be a capital gain for the year. The capital gain is eligible for the capital gains exemption under section 110.6.

---

[114] Para. 53(1)(h).

[115] Subs. 52(3); subs. 15(1.1); subs. 248(1) ("stock dividend"); see Chapter XIX "Shareholder Benefits".

[116] Para. 53(1)(j).

[117] Para. 53(2)(g); see s. 80.

[118] S. 54 ("adjusted cost base")(d).

[119] Subs. 40(3).

Example IX.12

Assume:

A taxpayer owns a capital property with an adjusted cost base of $2,000. During the year, the cost base is adjusted by subsection 53(1) additions of $300 and subsection 53(2) deductions of $2,700.

Then the taxpayer's adjusted cost base is calculated as follows:

Cost of property	$ 2,000
Subsection 53(1) additions	300
	$ 2,300
Subsection 53(2) deductions	(2,700)
Deemed capital gain	$ (400)
Paragraph 53(1)(*a*) addition	400
ACB of property	$ NIL

---

6. PART DISPOSITIONS

Reference:

BULLETINS, CIRCULARS & RULINGS:

IT-264R   December 29, 1980   Part Disposition

Where a taxpayer disposes of only a part of a capital property, the adjusted cost base of that part is calculated by taking a "reasonable" proportion of the cost base of the part to the whole. The adjusted cost base of the part of the property that was disposed of is then deducted from the adjusted cost base of the whole property. The balance becomes the cost base of the remaining part.[120]

---

[120] S. 43; there are special rules governing partial dispositions of personal-use property.

Example IX.13

Assume:

A taxpayer disposes of a part of a capital property for its fair market value of $3,000, at a time when the fair market value of the entire property is $14,000. The adjusted cost base of the entire property is $7,000.

Then, (i) the ACB of the disposed of property, (ii) the taxpayer's capital gain, and (iii) the ACB of the remaining property, are calculated as follows:

(i) ACB of portion of property disposed of:

$$\frac{\$\,3,000}{14,000} \times \$7,000 = \$1,500$$

(ii)	Proceeds of disposition	$ 3,000
	ACB of disposed of portion	(1,500)
	Capital gain	$ 1,500
(iii)	ACB of entire property	$ 7,000
	ACB of disposed of portion	(1,500)
	ACB of remaining portion	$ 5,500

---

7. PERSONAL-USE PROPERTY

References:

BULLETINS, CIRCULARS & RULINGS:

IT-159R3	May 1, 1989	Capital Debts Established to be Bad Debts
IT-264R	December 29, 1980	Part Dispositions
IT-332R	November 28, 1984	Personal-Use Property

(a) General

There are special rules for determining capital gains and losses from dispositions of "personal-use property". These special rules serve two purposes: first, they eliminate the need for any recordkeeping in connection with the purchase and sale of low-value capital assets used primarily for the taxpayer's personal use or enjoyment; second, they prohibit a deduction for capital losses on the disposition of this particular category of capital property.

(b) Meaning

Personal-use property includes:[121]

- Property owned by a taxpayer that is used *primarily* for the personal use or enjoyment of the taxpayer or:
  - — a relative of the taxpayer; or
  - — if the taxpayer is a trust, a beneficiary under the trust or any relative of the beneficiary;
- A debt owing to a taxpayer in respect of the disposition of personal-use property; and
- An option to acquire property that would, if it were acquired, be personal-use property of a taxpayer.

Cars, boats, furniture, clothing and residences are common examples of personal-use property.

A partnership may also own personal-use property. For example, any partnership property that is used primarily for the personal use or enjoyment of any member of the partnership, or for the personal use or enjoyment of one or more of a group of individuals consisting of a member of the partnership and persons related to him or her, would be personal-use property. Similarly, property owned by a corporation may be personal-use property if the property is primarily for the personal use of a shareholder of the corporation.

(c) Listed Personal Property

There is also a special category of personal-use property, described as "listed personal property" ("LPP"). This special category is a list of capital assets that consists of the following:[122]

- prints, etchings, drawings, paintings, sculptures or other similar works of art;
- jewellery;
- rare folios, rare manuscripts or rare books;
- stamps; and
- coins.

An interest in or right to any of these items is also considered listed personal property.

Listed personal property items are typically assets which are acquired for dual reasons: personal consumption and investment value. Gains from listed personal property are taxable; losses are not deductible from income.

---

[121] S. 54 ("personal-use property").

[122] S. 54 ("listed personal property").

(d) Computational Rules

To minimize recordkeeping for low-value items of personal-use property, the *minimum* adjusted cost base and proceeds of disposition of personal-use property are deemed to be $1,000.[123] Consequently, if both the *actual* cost and the *actual* proceeds on disposition of an item of personal-use property are less than $1,000, the transaction does not give rise to any capital gain or capital loss. Thus taxpayers do not need to keep a detailed record of low-value transactions for income tax purposes.

Example IX. 14

A taxpayer purchases and then sells personal-use property for the amounts indicated. The gain or loss in each case is calculated as follows:

	A	B	C
Proceeds of disposition	$ 900*	$1,200	$2,000
Cost	(600)*	(600)*	(1,500)
Capital gain	$ NIL	$ 200	$ 500

	D	E	F
Proceeds of disposition	$ 400*	$ 800*	$1,200
Cost	(60)*	(1,500)	(1,500)
Capital loss**	$ NIL	$ (500)	$ (300)

* Deemed to be $1,000
** Capital loss is deemed to be nil unless the personal-use property qualifies as listed personal property.

(e) Bad Debts

Where a debt owing to a taxpayer from a sale of personal-use property is established to have become a bad debt, the taxpayer may offset any prior capital gain recognized on the sale of the property by recognizing a capital loss when the debt becomes bad.[124]

---

[123] Subs. 46(1).

[124] Subs. 50(2).

Example IX.15

Assume:

A taxpayer sells personal-use property with an ACB of $9,000 for proceeds of $10,000 in 1995. The taxpayer receives $6,000 cash and accepts a note for $4,000. In 1997, the debtor defaults on the note and the debt is established to have become bad.

Then:

1995 Proceeds of disposition	$ 10,000
ACB of property	(9,000)
Capital gain	$ 1,000
1997 Deemed proceeds of debt*	$ 3,000
ACB of debt	(4,000)
Capital loss	$ (1,000)

* Calculated as the amount which will give rise to a capital loss equal to the prior capital gain.

Since a debt arising from a sale of personal-use property is itself personal-use property, a strict interpretation of this rule would preclude the taxpayer from deducting the capital loss of $1,000. Revenue Canada does, however, by administrative discretion, permit a deduction for the capital loss of $1,000 in these circumstances.

(f) Part Dispositions

To prevent taxpayers from taking unfair advantage of the minimum $1,000 adjusted cost base and proceeds of disposition rule by selling sets of property in bits and pieces, a special rule requires that the $1,000 be allocated whenever the various parts of a personal-use property are sold individually or when a set of personal-use property is sold piecemeal. The $1,000 amount is allocated in the following proportion:

$$\$1,000 \times \frac{\text{Adjusted cost base of part disposed}}{\text{Adjusted cost base of the whole property}}$$

The deemed cost and deemed proceeds of disposition rules are then applied in relation to the part of the personal-use property that has been disposed of on the basis of this reduced amount.[125]

---

[125] Subs. 46(2). Note that these allocation rules apply only when a taxpayer disposes of a part of a personal-use property and retains another part. Accordingly, upon the disposition of the final remaining part, no allocation is required, since the taxpayer would not be retaining another part.

The second aspect of this rule applies to dispositions of a set of personal-use properties which have an *aggregate* fair market value in excess of $1,000 and which would *ordinarily* be disposed of together. If a set of personal-use properties is sold in more than one transaction to the same person, or to a group of persons who do not deal with each other at arm's length, the set is deemed to be a single property and the $1,000 amount is proportionally reduced.[126]

(g) Capital Losses

Capital losses arising from a disposition of personal-use property (other than listed personal property) are deemed to be nil.[127] An additional rule provides that, where a capital gain is reduced, or a capital loss is increased, on the disposition of a share of a corporation (or an interest in a partnership or trust), and it may reasonably be regarded that the reduction in value of the share results from a decrease in the value of any personal-use property of the corporation (or partnership or trust), then the capital gain or capital loss is adjusted to the amount that it would have been if the particular personal-use property had not decreased in value.[128] This rule applies even if the particular personal-use property is listed personal property.

Finally, there are special rules for calculating losses on listed personal property ("LPP"). The general thrust of these rules is that capital losses on LPP can be offset only against capital gains on LPP. Any remaining balance can be carried back three years and carried forward seven years; in each of those years, the LPP loss can be offset only against LPP gains.[129]

8. IDENTICAL PROPERTIES

References:

BULLETINS, CIRCULARS & RULINGS:

IT-78	November 27, 1972	Capital Property Owned on December 31, 1971 — Identical Properties
IT-199	February 17, 1975	Identical Properties Acquired in Non-Arm's Length Transactions
IT-387R2	July 14, 1989	Meaning of "Identical Properties"

Where a taxpayer acquires a capital property identical to other properties which he or she owns, the cost of each of the properties is calculated by taking the weighted average of their adjusted cost bases. The weighted average cost of properties must be

---

[126] Subs. 46(3).

[127] Subpara. 40(2)(g)(iii).

[128] Subs. 46(4).

[129] Subs. 41(2).

recalculated each time the taxpayer acquires another property identical to property already owned by him or her.[130] The weighted average cost of identical properties is determined by dividing the aggregate of their adjusted cost bases by the number of properties owned.

Whether property acquired by a taxpayer is "identical" to property already owned by him or her is a question of fact. Corporate shares of the same class and with the same rights are identical properties, notwithstanding that they may be physically identifiable as separate properties by virtue of their serial numbers.

Bonds and debt obligations issued by a corporation are considered similar to other debts issued by the debtor if they are identical in respect of their legal and equitable rights. This is so even if the principal amounts are different.[131]

Land can never be an identical property for tax purposes; this is so even if the lots are adjoining lots and of the same size and quality. Each plot of land is unique.

Example IX.16

A taxpayer owns 100 common shares of *XYZ Co.*, which she acquired at a cost of $20 per share. The taxpayer acquires a further 200 shares of the same class and kind of the same corporation at $30 per share.

The weighted average cost of the shares is calculated as follows:

100 shares × $20/share	$ 2,000
200 shares × $30/share	6,000
300	$ 8,000

Weighted Average Cost per Share $ 26.67
($8000/300)

Properties owned by a taxpayer as at December 31, 1971, are segregated in a separate pool from identical properties acquired by the taxpayer after that date. In other words, a weighted average cost is calculated for identical properties owned on December 31, 1971, and a separate average cost is calculated for properties acquired subsequently. Note that a disposition of identical properties is always deemed to be made first out of the pre-1972 pool.[132]

---

[130] S. 47.

[131] Subs. 248(12).

[132] ITAR 26(8)–(8.3).

To summarize: identical properties are divided into two pools, one pool consisting of the properties on hand at December 31, 1971, and the other group comprising post-1971 acquisitions. The pre-1972 group is deemed to be disposed of first.

Example IX.17

Assume:

Jane Henry, a Canadian resident, has bought and sold shares of *Gamma Ltd.*, a CCPC, as an investment since 1993. In 2001 she liquidated part of her holdings. The following is a history of her transactions:

	Bought		Sold	
	(#)	($)	(#)	($)
1993	6,000	18,000		
1994	5,000	32,000		
1995	7,500	42,000		
1996	6,500	35,000		
1997			6,500	40,000
1998	5,500	28,000		
1999	8,000	36,000		
2000	6,000	25,000		
2001			7,500	45,000

Question: Determine Jane's capital gain for the year 2001.

Then:

  Acquisitions:

1993	$ 18,000.00
1994	32,000.00
1995	42,000.00
1996	35,000.00

Total cost of shares to date: $ 127,000.00

  Average cost/shares: $5.08

Example IX.17 (continued)

Number of shares sold:

1997	6,500
Cost of shares sold:	$ 33,020.00
ACB of remaining shares:	$ 93,980.00

Acquisitions:

1998	$ 28,000.00
1999	36,000.00
2000	25,000.00
	$ 89,000.00

| Total cost of shares to date: | $ 182,980.00 |
| Average cost/share: | $4.82 |

Number of shares sold:

2001	7,500	
Cost of shares sold:		$ 36,114.47
ACB of remaining shares:		$ 146,865.53
Proceeds of disposition		$ 45,000.00
ACB of shares sold		36,114.47
Capital gain realized		$ 8,885.53

9. LOSSES DEEMED TO BE NIL

References:

ITA:

Subs. 85(4)   Disposition to Controlled Corporation

BULLETINS, CIRCULARS & RULINGS:

IT-302R3   February 28, 1994   Losses of a Corporation — The Effect that Acquisitions of Control, Amalgamations and Windings-Up have on Their Deductibility — After January 15, 1987

(a) General

The Act may deem a capital loss to be nil, with the result that the capital loss is not recognized in computing income. The circumstances when the Act deems a capital loss to be nil are varied. The general thrust of these deeming provisions is to prevent a taxpayer from creating or accelerating an "artificial" capital loss by structuring transactions within a group of related economic entities. Sometimes the non-recognition of the capital loss is permanent; at other times the amount of the capital loss that is deemed to be nil is added to the cost base of some other property owned by the taxpayer, so that there will be a corresponding reduction in the capital gain (or increase in the capital loss) on the disposition of the other property.

(b) Disposition of "Controlled" Corporation

(i) Denial of Loss

Where a taxpayer disposes of a capital property to a "controlled" corporation or to a corporation controlled by his or her spouse, any capital loss resulting from the disposition is deemed to be nil.[133]   "Control" refers to the taxpayer's control of the corporation *before* the disposition.[134]

The taxpayer may, however, step up the adjusted cost base of his or her shares of the transferee corporation.[135] If the taxpayer owns several classes of shares in the transferee corporation, the addition to the cost base of the shares is proportional to their respective fair market values.

(ii) Rule of General Application

The rule that a taxpayer cannot recognize a loss upon a transfer of property to a controlled corporation is a rule of general application. Thus, although the rule is contained in subsection 85(4), it is not confined only to transfers under section 85.

Example IX.18

Assume that Mr. X transfers his shares (capital property) in *Opco* to *Holdco*, a corporation that he controls. The following data applies to the transfer:

ACB of *Opco* shares	$300,000
FMV of *Opco* shares	$200,000

Mr. X receives *Holdco* shares valued at $200,000 in exchange for his *Opco* shares. He cannot recognize the loss of $100,000 at the time of the transfer, but the unrecognized loss is added to the adjusted cost base of his *Holdco* shares.

ACB of *Holdco* shares	$200,000
Add: unrecognized loss	100,000
ACB of *Holdco* shares	$300,000

Thus the loss is carried over into the new shares.

---

[133]   Subs. 85(4).

[134]   *Plant Nat. Ltd. v. M.N.R.*, [1989] 2 CTC 2145, 89 DTC 401 (T.C.C.).

[135]   Para. 85(4)(*b*).

(c) Lotteries

A taxpayer who fails to win a lottery is not entitled to claim a capital loss in respect of the cost of the ticket.[136]

(d) Superficial Losses

A taxpayer may not claim a "superficial loss".[137]

A superficial loss arises when a taxpayer, or certain related parties, disposes of property and replaces it with "substituted property" within a period of 61 days.[138] For the purpose of this rule, the 61-day period commences 30 days before and ends 30 days after the day of disposition of the property. Note that this rule applies to property acquired by the taxpayer, his or her spouse, or a corporation controlled by him or her. In this context, a corporation is controlled by a taxpayer if he or she controls it directly, indirectly *or in any manner whatever.*

The cost base of the "substituted property" is increased by the amount of the taxpayer's superficial loss.[139] Consequently, when the "substituted property" is disposed of, any gain on the property is reduced; alternatively, any loss is increased by the amount of the taxpayer's superficial loss.

The superficial loss rules do not apply in a number of situations where the Act deems property to have been disposed of and reacquired by the taxpayer. Thus losses arising from the following deemed dispositions do not give rise to superficial losses:[140]

- emigration;
- a debt becoming a bad debt;
- death;
- change in use of property;
- realization by a trust under subsection 104(4); and
- an employee's profit-sharing plan as a result of an election made in accordance with subsection 144(4.1) or (4.2).

Also, the superficial loss rules do not apply if the loss results from the expiry of an option, from the disposition of a property to a controlled corporation, where the loss is deemed to be nil under subsection 85(4).

---

[136] Para. 40(2)(*f*).

[137] Subpara. 40(2)(*g*)(i).

[138] S. 54 ("superficial loss").

[139] Para. 53(1)(*f*).

[140] S. 54 ("superficial loss"). Deemed dispositions under subss. 33.1(11), 138(11.3), 149(10) also do not give rise to superficial losses.

(e) Disposition of a Debt

A capital loss from a disposition, whether actual or deemed, of a debt is deemed to be nil unless the debt was acquired for the purpose of gaining or producing income from a business or property (other than exempt income), or as consideration for the disposition of capital property in an arm's length transaction.[141]

(f) Disposition of Personal-use Property

A taxpayer's loss from a disposition of personal-use property is deemed to be nil unless the property qualifies as listed personal property.[142] The non-recognition of the loss is permanent.

10. PRINCIPAL RESIDENCE

References:

BULLETINS, CIRCULARS & RULINGS:

IT-120R4	March 26, 1993	Principal Residence
IT-218R	September 16, 1986	Profit, Capital Gains and Losses From the Sale of Real Estate, Including Farmland and Inherited Land and Conversion of Real Estate from Capital Property to Inventory and Vice Versa
IT-366R	May 4, 1984	Principal Residence — Transfer to Spouse, Spouse Trust or Certain Other Individuals
IT-437R	February 21, 1994	Ownership of Property (Principal Residence)
News Release	April 9, 1987	

(a) Exemption from Tax

As a general rule, a Canadian resident is not taxable on a capital gain from his or her principal residence.[143] The entire amount of the gain is tax exempt, regardless of the value of the property sold. This makes the principal residence exemption the most generous exemption in the Act and one which should be taken into account in every individual's financial planning. Note that the residence does not have to be in Canada to be eligible for the exemption.

---

[141] Subpara. 40(2)(*g*)(ii).

[142] Subpara. 40(2)(*g*)(iii).

[143] Para. 40(2)(*b*).

(b) Meaning of "Principal Residence"

(i) Minimum Requirements

There are several requirements to qualify a property as a "principal residence". Generally speaking, these requirements address four separate criteria:[144]

1. The type of property:
   - the property may consist of a housing unit, a leasehold interest in a housing unit or a share in a co-operative housing corporation;[145]

2. Owner occupation:
   - the property must be owned by the taxpayer; and
   - the property must be "occupied" by the taxpayer during the year;[146]

3. The period of ownership:
   - the property must be ordinarily inhabited at some time during the year by the taxpayer or his or her spouse, former spouse or child; or
   - if the property was acquired for the purpose of gaining or producing income and the use changes to that of a principal residence, an election can be made under subsection 45(3) to prevent the deemed disposal and reacquisition in subsection 45(1) from operating;

4. Designation on tax return:
   - the property must be designated by the taxpayer as his or her sole principal residence for the year.

(ii) Included Land

A principal residence includes the land under and adjacent to the housing unit. Any adjacent land must contribute to the taxpayer's use and enjoyment of the housing unit as a residence. It is statutorily presumed that land up to 0.5 ha qualifies as part of the principal residence. Where the total area of land exceeds 0.5 ha (one acre), the excess land is presumed not to qualify as a principal residence unless the taxpayer can establish that the excess land is *necessary* to the use and enjoyment of the housing unit as a residence.[147] Minimum lot size restrictions may be taken into account in

---

[144] S. 54 ("principal residence").

[145] *Flanagan v. M.N.R.*, [1989] 2 CTC 2395, 89 DTC 615 (T.C.C.) (van, trailer or mobile home can qualify as housing unit eligible for exemption).

[146] *Ennist v. M.N.R.*, [1985] 2 CTC 2398, 85 DTC 669 (T.C.C.) (24-hour occupancy of condominium not sufficient to satisfy requirement that residence be "ordinarily inhabited").

[147] *Fourt v. M.N.R.*, [1988] 2 CTC 2060, 88 DTC 1420 (T.C.C.) (additional land must be "necessary", not merely convenient, to taxpayer's use and enjoyment of housing unit); *The Queen v. Yates*, [1986] 2 CTC 46, 86 DTC 6296 (F.C.A.) (minimum lot size can be used to determine amount of land necessary for use and enjoyment).

determining the amount of land that is exempt as part of a principal residence.[148] The severability of land is also a relevant factor in determining the value assigned to any portion in excess of the exempt amount.

Given that the exemption is restricted by the physical dimensions of the residence and land and not by its value, it is obviously advantageous to own as much land as possible as part of the residence. For example, a residence located on 0.5 ha of land in, say, Rosedale (Toronto) is entitled to the same exemption as 0.5 ha in Moose Jaw (Saskatchewan), even though one may be worth 100 times the other.

(iii) Designation

Strictly speaking, a property does not qualify as a principal residence for a particular year unless the taxpayer designates it as such in his or her income tax return for the year in which he or she disposes of it. Revenue Canada does not, however, call for the designation unless the taxpayer makes a *taxable* capital gain on the disposition of his or her principal residence after deducting the exempt portion of the gain.

(c) Exempt Gains

The exempt portion of a capital gain realized on the disposition of a principal residence is determined by the following formula:[149]

$$\frac{1 + \text{number of taxation years ending after the acquisition date for which the property was the taxpayer's principal residence and during which he or she was resident in Canada}}{\text{Number of taxation years ending after the acquisition date during which the taxpayer owned the property}} \times \text{Capital gain realized}$$

A taxpayer is eligible for this exemption in respect of a capital gain on the disposition of a property if it was his or her principal residence *at any time* in the year. The effect of the "1 +" in the numerator of the fraction for determining the exempt

---

[148] *Baird v. M.N.R.*, [1983] CTC 2651, 83 DTC 582 (T.C.C.) (taxpayer cannot make a partial disposition of principal residence); *The Queen v. Mitosinka*, [1978] CTC 664, 78 DTC 6432 (F.C.T.D.) (each half of duplex separate housing unit); *The Queen v. Yates*, [1983] 2 FC 730; affirmed [1986] 2 CTC 46, 86 DTC 6296 (F.C.A.) (where taxpayer legally unable to occupy housing unit as residence on less than ten acres, excess portion necessary for taxpayer's use and enjoyment). The *Yates* decision has been accepted by Revenue Canada: see News Release (April 9, 1987).

[149] Para. 40(2)(*b*).

portion of the capital gain is that a taxpayer may obtain the exemption in respect of the disposition of two principal residences in the same year.

Example IX.19: <u>Where the taxpayer owns one principal residence</u>

Assume:

A taxpayer purchased a house in 1993 at a cost of $50,000 and sold it in 1999 for $200,000 (net of $10,000 selling expenses). He made no capital expenditures on the house while he owned it. He was resident in Canada during the relevant period, and he designated the house as a principal residence for the years 1993 to 1998 inclusive.

Then:

Proceeds of disposition	$ 210,000	
Less:		
Adjusted cost base	$ 50,000	
Expenses of disposition	10,000	(60,000)
Capital gain otherwise determined		$ 150,000
Less:		
Exempt portion of capital gain		
$\dfrac{1+6}{7} \times \$150{,}000$		(150,000)
Capital gain		$ NIL

Where a taxpayer lives in a residence for only a portion of the period of ownership, the exemption is allocated according to the formula set out above.

Example IX.20: Where there is a change in use of residence

Assume the same facts as in Example IX.19 (above), except that the taxpayer lived in the residence only during the period 1993-95. The rest of the time the building was rented out to a tenant.

Then (ignoring any elections under section 45):

Proceeds of disposition	$ 210,000	
Less:		
ACB of property	$ 50,000	
Selling expenses	10,000	(60,000)
Capital gain otherwise determined		$ 150,000
Less:		
Exempt portion of capital gain		
$\dfrac{1 + 3}{7} \times \$150{,}000$		(85,714)
Capital gain		$ 64,286

(d) Limits on Exemptions

The general rule is that a family unit living together can together designate only one principal residence per year. For the purpose of this rule, a "family unit" comprises: the taxpayer, his or her spouse and unmarried children under the age of 18.[150]

(i) Two Exempt Residences

The "1+" in the numerator of the fraction, used to determine the exempt portion of the gain, allows a taxpayer to claim an exemption in respect of two principal residences in the same year. Such a situation typically arises when a taxpayer sells his or her principal residence during the course of the year and purchases another residence in the same year. In these circumstances the taxpayer would own and occupy two residences in the same year, both of which could be eligible for the principal residence exemption.

---

[150] Subpara. 54(*g*)(iii).

Example IX.21: Where the taxpayer owns more than one residence

A taxpayer purchased a house in 1993 and lived in it until he sold it on February 28, 1996. He purchased a second house on February 1, 1996, and moved into it on March 1, 1996, living there until he sold it on October 1, 1996. He purchased a third house on September 30, 1996, and moved into it on November 1, 1996.

First House

Designated as principal residence for 1993-95
Exempt portion of capital gain on its sale

$$\frac{1 + 3}{4}$$

Therefore, any capital gain is exempt.

Second House

Designated as principal residence for 1996
Exempt portion of capital gain on its sale

$$\frac{1 + 0}{1}$$

Hence, any capital gain is also exempt.

If the third house was also sold in 1996, the taxpayer could not take advantage of the principal residence exemption on both the second and third houses. This is because only one of these houses could be designated as a principal residence for 1996. In these circumstances, however, the taxpayer may choose which house to designate for exemption. Alternatively, the taxpayer could arrange to have the closing on the third house delayed until January 1997.

(ii) Extended Family Unit

Where the taxpayer claiming the principal residence exemption is an unmarried person or an individual under 18 years of age, the concept of the family unit is extended to include the taxpayer's mother, father and unmarried brothers and sisters under 18 years of age.[151] Note, however, that the concept of the family unit does not extend to include common law spouses. Hence individuals cohabiting with, but not married to, each other may be able to claim the benefit of the exemption in respect of two principal residences.

(iii) "Ordinarily Inhabited"

The principal residence exemption is available only if the residence was ordinarily occupied by the taxpayer, his or her spouse or former spouse, or his or her child.

---

[151] S. 54 ("principal residence")(c).

The question of whether a residence was "ordinarily inhabited" during the taxation year by the taxpayer (or by a related person) is one of fact, and depends upon the circumstances of each case. Generally speaking, Revenue Canada is quite generous in its interpretation of what constitutes habitation of a residence. Thus the Department will accept seasonal occupation of a taxpayer's vacation house (such as a cottage or ski chalet) as sufficient to qualify the premises for the principal residence exemption. The Department goes even further: it will accept a seasonal residence as eligible for the exemption even where the taxpayer rents out the premises for incidental rental income. That is, provided that the rental is not a commercial or business enterprise, the taxpayer may occupy the premises for a limited portion of the season, rent it out for the remainder of the year and still claim the exemption.

(e) Farm Houses

Special rules apply to taxpayers engaged in a farming business. An individual who disposes of land and a principal residence used by him or her in a farming business is allowed to calculate the exempt portion of the capital gain attributable to the residence in one of two ways.

(i) Alternative 1

The taxpayer can treat the property as comprising two portions, the first portion being the principal residence and the second the balance of the farmland. Any capital gain realized from the disposition is allocated between these two portions on a reasonable basis.[152] The excmpt portion of the capital gain on the principal residence is then determined in accordance with the general rules described above.

Example IX.22

Anne Jones acquired a farm in 1983 at a cost of $145,000. The purchase price was allocated $25,000 to the farmhouse and $120,000 to the farmland. She sold the property in 1997 for $250,000 (net of selling expenses), of which $30,000 was allocated to the farmhouse and $220,000 to the farmland. The farmhouse was the taxpayer's principal residence throughout the period. The first method applies automatically.

Gain on farmland ($220,00 − 120,000)	$ 100,000
Gain on farmhouse ($30,000 − 25,000)	$ 5,000
Less: Exempt portion	(5,000)
Capital gain	$ 100,000

---

[152] Subpara. 40(2)(c)(i).

(ii) Alternative 2

Under the second method, the individual may elect not to allocate his or her proceeds between the residence and the farmland. Instead, the rule is that the exempt portion of the total capital gain realized by the taxpayer is set at $1,000, plus an additional $1,000 for each taxation year ending after the acquisition date for which the property was the taxpayer's principal residence and during which the taxpayer was resident in Canada.[153] This method applies only if the taxpayer elects to use it.

Example IX.23

Assume the same facts as in Example IX.22.

Gain on property ($250,00 − 145,000)		$ 105,000
Less: Exempt portion		
• standard	$ 1,000	
• ($1,000 × 15 years)	$ 15,000	$ (16,000)
Capital gain		$ 89,000

(f) Change in Use Elections

(i) Personal to Income-earning Use

We saw earlier in this chapter that a taxpayer who changes the use of capital property from personal to income-earning use may elect under subsection 45(2) to have the change in use ignored for income tax purposes. The effect of the election is that the taxpayer is deemed not to have changed the use of the property from personal to business and not to have disposed of the property at its fair market value at that time.

(A) Application to Principal Residence

The "change in use" election is particularly useful in respect of a principal residence. The election has two effects:

1. it allows the property to retain its status as a principal residence for four years after the year in which the taxpayer moved out of the property; and

2. the election deems the taxpayer not to have changed his or her use of the property.

Hence, if the taxpayer changes use of the property again, and resumes habitation of the premises, the second change will not give rise to a deemed disposition; the taxpayer will be considered never to have changed the use of the property in the first place. Thus there will be no income tax consequences when the taxpayer moves back into the

---

[153] Subpara. 40(2)(c)(ii).

property. This is because during the tenure of the election the taxpayer is *deemed* to be using the property for his or her own personal use (whether or not the property still qualifies as a principal residence); when the taxpayer moves back into the property, he or she will actually be using it for his or her own personal use.

(B) Timing of Election

An election under subsection 45(2) can be made only in respect of a change of use which occurs when the taxpayer moves out of the property, that is, when he or she changes his or her use from personal to business. A taxpayer who does not make an election on moving out of the residence cannot avoid the resultant deemed disposition, and related tax consequences, on moving back into the property at a later date.

(C) Duration

The election continues in effect until it is rescinded by the taxpayer, at which time the property is deemed to have been disposed of by the taxpayer.

(ii) Income-earning Use to Principal Residence

A taxpayer who converts income property into a principal residence may elect to ignore the change in use if he or she has not claimed capital cost allowance on the property after 1984. This election allows the taxpayer to defer the recognition of any accrued capital gain on the property, but does not allow him or her to defer recapture of capital cost allowance claimed on the property after 1984.[154]

11. CAPITAL LOSSES

References:

ITA:

Para. 111(1)(*b*) Net Capital Losses

Subs. 111(1.1) Deductibility of Net Capital Losses
Subs. 111(2) Year of Death
Subs. 111(3) Limitation on Deductibility
Subs. 111(4) Acquisition of Control
Para. 111(8)(*a*) Meaning of Net Capital Losses

---

[154] Subss. 45(3), (4).

BULLETINS, CIRCULARS & RULINGS:

IT-232R2	December 30, 1987	Non-Capital Losses, Net Capital Losses, Restricted Farm Losses, Farm Losses and Limited Partnership Losses — Their Composition and Deductibility in Computing Taxable Income
IT-239R2	February 9, 1981	Deductibility of Capital Losses from Guaranteeing Loans for Inadequate Consideration and from Loaning Funds at Less than a Reasonable Rate of Interest in Non-Arm's Length Circumstances
IT-262R	August 30, 1985	Losses of Non-Residents and Part-Year Residents
IT-484R	May 5, 1989	Business Investment Losses

(a) General

A taxpayer's income for a taxation year is determined by aggregating income from each source on a separate basis. As a general rule, capital losses can be used only to offset capital gains.[155] Unused capital losses may, however, be carried forward indefinitely and applied against capital gains in future years; they may also be carried back three years and applied against capital gains reported in those years.[156]

(b) Current Year Losses

(i) Listed Personal Property Losses

Capital gains and losses from listed personal property ("LPP") are calculated separately from capital gains and losses on all other types of capital properties. Thus a taxpayer is required to include his or her "taxable *net* gain" for the year from dispositions of LPP with his or her capital gains.[157] Losses from dispositions of LPP are deductible only to the extent of gains for the same year from dispositions of LPP. In other words, if LPP losses exceed LPP gains, the excess cannot be deducted in computing the taxpayer's income for that year, even if he or she has other net taxable capital gains from dispositions of other types of capital property. LPP losses may not be deducted from capital gains on non-LPP.

---

[155] Para. 3(*b*).

[156] Para. 111(1)(*b*).

[157] Para. 3(*b*); s. 41.

(ii) Allowable Capital Losses

A taxpayer may also deduct his or her allowable capital losses (net of allowable business investment losses) from dispositions of property for the year to the extent of his or her taxable capital gains from dispositions of property and his or her taxable *net* gain from dispositions of listed personal property.

The effect of these rules is that a taxpayer may deduct his or her allowable capital losses realized on property (other than LPP) from his or her taxable net gains on listed personal property.

(iii) Allowable Business Investment Losses ("ABIL")

(A) General

A business investment loss is a special type of capital loss which receives preferential treatment for income tax purposes. A business investment loss arises on the disposition of shares or debt of a "small business corporation".[158] An allowable business investment loss is three-quarters of a business investment loss.[159]

Unlike ordinary capital losses, which may be deducted only against capital gains, an allowable business investment loss may be deducted against income from any source. Thus an allowable business investment loss may be deducted from business income.

A taxpayer's deduction for business investment losses is restricted if he or she has previously claimed the capital gains exemption.[160]

A business investment loss arises upon the disposition of the shares or debt of a corporation that qualified as a small business corporation *at any time* within the preceding 12 months.[161] The disposition of the shares or debt may be triggered either by an actual disposition (for example, sale or transfer) or through a deemed disposition.[162]

(B) "Small Business Corporation"

A "small business corporation" is a Canadian-controlled private corporation that uses all or substantially all (as measured by fair market value) of its assets in an active business in Canada.[163] A corporation may also qualify as a small business corporation

---

[158] Para. 39(1)(c).

[159] Para. 38(c).

[160] Subs. 39(9).

[161] Subs. 248(1) ("small business corporation").

[162] See, for example, subs. 50(1).

[163] Subs. 248(1) ("small business corporation").

if all, or substantially all, of its assets are invested in shares of another small business corporation with which it is connected.

(C) Deemed Disposition

A taxpayer is deemed to have disposed of his or her shares of a small business corporation if:

- the corporation is insolvent, bankrupt or wound up *and* has ceased to carry on its business;
- the fair market value of the shares is nil;
- it is reasonable to expect that the corporation will be dissolved, and the corporation does not commence any business in the year in which the deduction is claimed or within 24 months following the end of that year.

The term "insolvent" is not defined, but is reasonable to expect that it has the usual meaning of insolvency, namely, the inability to pay liabilities as they come due.

(c) Unused Losses

Capital losses which are not deductible in the year in which they are sustained may be "carried over" and deducted in other years. In dealing with capital loss carryovers, it is important to distinguish between losses from dispositions of listed personal property and losses from dispositions of property other than listed personal property.

(i) LPP Losses

Where a taxpayer's losses for a year from LPP exceed his or her gains for the year from dispositions of LPP, the excess is his or her "listed personal property loss" for that year.[164] A listed personal property loss for a particular year can be deducted, in computing the "net gain", only from dispositions of listed personal property for the three preceding and the seven succeeding years.[165]

(ii) Net Capital Losses

Allowable capital losses from dispositions of property other than listed personal property which are not deductible in computing a taxpayer's income in the year in which they are sustained, become part of the taxpayer's "net capital loss".[166] A taxpayer's net capital loss for a year may be carried back and deducted in computing his or her *taxable income* for the three preceding years. Also, subject to certain limitations, the loss may be carried forward indefinitely.[167] In either case, net capital

---

[164]   Subs. 41(3).

[165]   Para. 41(2)(*b*).

[166]   Subs. 111(8)("net capital loss").

[167]   Para. 111(1)(*b*).

losses may be deducted against only the excess of taxable gains over allowable capital losses of other years.

(A) Change of Corporate Control

A net capital loss from an earlier year cannot be deducted by a corporation if, before the end of the year, control of the corporation changes hands and the corporation is acquired by a person who did not control it at the time when the net capital loss was sustained. This rule does not generally affect the deductibility of capital losses sustained *in the year* in which control is acquired by the new person or persons.[168]

(B) Death

Where a taxpayer dies with unclaimed net capital losses, the losses may be applied as follows:[169]

- against his or her net taxable capital gains for the year of death, and
- against his or her other sources of income in the immediately preceding year, to the extent that the losses exceed his or her lifetime capital gains exemption.[170]

Thus exemptions claimed in respect of capital gains during a taxpayer's lifetime reduce his or her unused net capital losses on death.

---

[168] Subs. 111(4).

[169] Subs. 111(2).

[170] The capital gains exemption is discussed in Chapter XII "Taxable Income".

Example IX.24

Assume:

Net capital losses carried forward	$ 25,000
Taxable capital gains in year of death	10,000
Allowable capital losses in year of death	4,000
Capital gains exemption claimed during lifetime	15,000

Then, maximum claim in respect of net capital losses in year of death:

Taxable capital gains		$ 10,000
Less: allowable capital losses		(4,000)
Net taxable capital gains		$ 6,000
Net capital losses	$ 25,000	
Prior year gains exemption	(15,000)	
Terminal year gains exemption	(6,000)	
Excess claimable		4,000
Maximum claim		$ 10,000

---

12. TRANSITIONAL RULES

References:

BULLETINS, CIRCULARS & RULINGS:

IT-107	June 14, 1973	Costs of Disposition of Capital Property Affected by the Median Rule
IT-370	April 25, 1977	Trusts — Capital Property Owned on December 31, 1971

(a) General

With the introduction of the tax on capital gains as of January 1, 1972, it became necessary to ensure that capital gains and capital losses which had accrued prior to 1972 would not be retroactively taxed. Thus there are transitional rules to ensure smooth passage from the old system to the new. Although the rationale of the transitional rules is simple, the rules are technically complex. The essential purpose of the transitional rules is to provide a taxpayer with either a deemed cost or deemed proceeds of disposition for the capital property which he or she owned on December 31, 1971, so that, on selling the property, he or she can calculate any gain or loss from that date.

Generally, the transitional rules apply to capital property *actually* owned by a taxpayer on December 31, 1971. In some cases, however, the person to whom the property is disposed of may be *deemed* to have owned it on December 31, 1971, so that the transitional rules will apply to him or her when disposing of the property. The rules can therefore apply to dispositions of property acquired after 1971. Note, however, that the transitional rules do not apply to the property of a taxpayer who becomes resident in Canada after 1971.[171]

(b) Valuation Day

The concept of Valuation Day value is fundamental to the structure of the transitional rules. The Valuation Day value of a capital property is its value at the beginning of the new system, when capital gains were first subjected to tax. The "V-Day value" of a property is its fair market value on Valuation Day, which was December 22, 1971, for publicly-traded shares or securities and December 31, 1971, for all other capital property.[172]

The fair market value of publicly-traded securities on Valuation Day is deemed to be the greater of the amount prescribed[173] in respect of the security and the fair market value of the security on December 22, 1971, "as otherwise determined". Any "other determination" of the fair market value of a publicly-traded share or security as at that date must be made by the taxpayer. If this value is greater than the prescribed amount, the taxpayer may use it for the purpose of determining the capital gain or loss realized on the disposition of the security in question.

The Valuation Day value of all other capital properties (i.e., properties other than publicly-traded securities) is their fair market value on December 31, 1971. It is the taxpayer's responsibility to determine this value for the purpose of reporting a capital gain or loss on the disposition of capital property.

(c) Depreciable Property

For depreciable property acquired by a taxpayer before 1972 and owned by him or her continuously since that time, the transitional rules eliminate any capital gain accrued as at December 31, 1971, from the total capital gain realized upon disposition of the property. There is no corresponding rule in respect of a capital loss accrued as at December 31, 1971, because a taxpayer cannot realize a capital loss on depreciable property.[174] Where depreciable property is disposed of in a non-arm's length transaction, the transitional rules preserve the tax-free character of any accrued capital gains.[175]

---

[171] ITAR 26(10).

[172] ITAR 24.

[173] Reg., Sched. VII.

[174] Subpara. 39(1)(*b*)(*i*).

[175] ITAR 20(1).

The transitional rules in respect of depreciable property owned on December 31, 1971, operate by deeming the proceeds of disposition of the property to be the amount determined by the following formula:

$$\begin{matrix} \text{Deemed proceeds} \\ \text{of disposition} \end{matrix} = \begin{matrix} \text{capital} \\ \text{cost} \end{matrix} + \begin{matrix} \text{excess, if any, of actual} \\ \text{proceeds of disposition} \\ \text{over fair market value on} \\ \text{Valuation Day} \end{matrix}$$

The transitional rules do not apply if the actual proceeds of disposition of depreciable property do not exceed the capital cost of that property, since, in this instance, a capital gain could not possibly result.

Example IX.25

Capital cost to taxpayer T of a depreciable property acquired by him in 1970:	$ 10,000
Fair market value of this property on Valuation Day (December 31, 1971):	12,600
Selling price of the property in 1986:	17,200
T's deemed proceeds of disposition: $10,000 + ($17,200 – $12,600)	14,600
T's capital gain is therefore: $14,600 – $10,000	4,600

Arithmetically, the capital gain equals the excess of the actual selling price of the depreciable property over its Valuation Day value, although the gain is not actually computed in this way. The capital gain of $2,600 accrued on the property as at December 31, 1971, is not subject to tax at all. Where depreciable property is disposed of after 1971 at a price greater than its original cost but less than its Valuation Day value (e.g., $12,000, in the above illustration), the transitional rules apply in the following manner:

T's deemed proceeds of disposition are: $10,000 + ($12,000 – $12,600)*	$ 10,000
T's capital gain is $10,000 – $10,000	NIL

*The amount in the brackets cannot be less than zero.

Since the depreciable property has been disposed of for less than its Valuation Day value, this is the result one would expect.

(d) Interest in a Partnership

Transitional rules are also provided for taxpayers who were members of a partnership on December 31, 1971, and have remained so continuously since that date. These rules are provided for the purpose of computing the adjusted cost base of the partnership interest at any time after 1971. These rules affect the amount of the taxable capital gain or allowable capital loss realized by the partner when disposing of his or her partnership interest.

These transitional rules operate by deeming the partner's cost of the partnership interest to be an amount that is the median[176] of the following three amounts:

1. its "actual cost" to the partner;
2. his or her share of the partnership's "tax equity", subject to certain adjustments; and
3. the fair market value of the partnership interest, again subject to certain adjustments.

The "actual cost" of a partnership interest and the partnership's "tax equity" are both defined amounts, and all three amounts in this formula are determined as of the particular time when the deemed cost is relevant.[177] If two or more of these amounts are the same, that amount is the median.

(e) Other Capital Property

There are also transitional rules for the purpose of computing the capital gain or loss of capital property other than the two previous examples. The effect of these rules is to deem a cost to be the taxpayer's adjusted cost base of capital property owned. The capital gain or loss of the property is then computed on the basis of this deemed cost.

There are two distinct methods of determining the deemed cost. The first of these methods is the "median rule" or "tax-free zone" method. This method applies automatically to capital property that was owned on December 31, 1971, by *any taxpayer*. The second method, known as the "Valuation Day value election," is available only to *individuals* (including trusts), and applies only to capital property *actually* owned on December 31, 1971.[178]

---

[176] If two or more of these amounts are the same, that amount is the median.

[177] ITAR 26(9)–(9.3).

[178] The tax-free zone method cannot then be used in respect of any of these properties, although it must still be used in respect of any "other capital property" which the individual taxpayer making the Valuation Day value election did not actually own on December 31, 1971, but which he or she is deemed by the Act to have owned on that date.

For individuals, the two methods for determining the deemed cost of capital property owned on December 31, 1971, are mutually exclusive alternatives. Thus an individual *either* uses the tax-free zone method to determine the deemed cost of *each and every* item of capital property which he or she owned on December 31, 1971, or makes the Valuation Day value election, in which case he or she must use this method to determine the deemed cost of *each and every* item of capital property which he or she actually owned on December 31, 1971.

(i) Median Rule or Tax-free Zone Method

The median rule (tax-free zone) method operates by deeming a taxpayer's initial cost of capital property which he or she owned on December 31, 1971, to be the amount that is the median of the following three amounts:[179]

1. its actual cost (or, if the property is an "obligation", its "amortized cost") to him or her on January 1, 1972;

2. its fair market value on Valuation Day; and

3. the proceeds of disposition of the property, subject to certain adjustments, which are described below.

If two or more of these amounts are the same, that amount is the median.

If a particular item of capital property has been owned continuously since December 31, 1971, and it is necessary to compute its adjusted cost base at a point in time *before* it is disposed of (in which case there would be no actual proceeds of disposition), the median rule is applied by deeming the proceeds of disposition of the particular property to be its fair market value at that time.[180]

The adjustments to the proceeds of disposition of the property can be summarized as follows:

- *Add* amounts that will be deducted from the deemed cost in computing the adjusted cost base of the particular property.

- *Deduct* amounts that will be added to the deemed cost in computing the adjusted cost base of the particular property.

These adjustments are necessary for the purpose of applying the median rule to avoid double-counting of the additions and deductions which are made in computing the adjusted cost base of the property under section 53.

"Proceeds of disposition" in this context means gross proceeds before the deduction of any outlays or expenses incurred for the purpose of making the disposition.

---

[179] ITAR 26(3).

[180] ITAR 26(4).

Therefore a capital loss equal to the amount of these outlays and expenses may be realized if the deemed cost of a particular property equals the proceeds of disposition.

Example IX.26

Assume:

The actual cost of a capital property that was owned on December 31, 1971 is $4,000. Its Valuation Day value is $8,000. The proceeds of disposition of the property before deducting the sales commission of $800 are $8,000.

Then:

  Applying the median rule, the deemed cost of the property is $8,000.

Proceeds of disposition		$ 8,000
Deduct:		
Deemed cost	$ 8,000	
Sales commission	800	(8,800)
Capital loss		$ (800)

(ii) Valuation Day Value Election

As its name implies, the "Valuation Day value" election allows a taxpayer to determine the cost of each capital property (other than depreciable property and partnership interests) *actually* owned by him or her on December 31, 1971, as its value on Valuation Day. This alternative method is administratively convenient; it provides individuals with a deemed cost for every capital property which they actually owned at the start of the new system, and accommodates taxpayers who have not maintained a record of the actual cost of their properties.[181]

13. ANTI-AVOIDANCE PROVISIONS

There are several anti-avoidance provisions which are intended to prevent or discourage taxpayers from artificially converting fully taxable income into income that is either non-taxable or taxable at a lower rate. Some of these provisions are quite specific and narrow in scope. For example, the rules in respect of "superficial losses" are directed squarely at preventing the creation of capital losses by transferring and reacquiring properties.[182] The following additional provisions should be noted:

---

[181] ITAR 26(7); *Knight v. M.N.R.*, [1984] CTC 2643, 84 DTC 1586 (T.C.C.) (failure to elect V-Day value "in prescribed manner" results in automatic application of median rule).

[182] Subpara. 40(2)(*g*)(i), s. 54 ("superficial loss"), as discussed in section 9(d) of this chapter.

Subs. 55(2)	specific provision to prevent "capital gains strips";
Subs. 110.6(7)	intended to prevent conversion of taxable capital gains of corporations into exempt capital gains of individuals;
Subss. 110.6(8), (9)	intended to prevent the conversion of dividend income into exempt capital gains of individuals;
S. 245	general anti-avoidance provision ("GAAR").

COMPREHENSIVE EXAMPLES

1. Capital Gain or Loss of Listed Personal Properties

Assume:

A taxpayer sells the following listed personal properties in the years (all of which are subsequent to 1971) indicated:

Year	Property	ACB	Proceeds
1	A print	$ 600	$ 4,000
	A coin	1,500	600
2	A rare book	8,000	4,000
	A painting	2,000	2,500
3	Jewellery	500	2,500

Then net gain from the above is as follows:

	Actual	Deemed Subs. 46(1)	
Year 1			
PRINT:			
Proceeds	$ 4,000	$ 4,000	
ACB	(600)	(1,000)	
Gain			$ 3,000
COIN:			
Proceeds	$ 600	$ 1,000	
ACB	(1,500)	(1,500)	
Loss			(500)
Gain			$ 2,500
Loss carryback from year 2			$ (2,500)*
NET GAIN			NIL

Comprehensive Examples (continued)

	Actual	Deemed Subs. 46(1)	
Year 2			
BOOK:			
Proceeds	$ 4,000	$ 4,000	
ACB	(8,000)	(8,000)	
Loss			$ (4,000)
PAINTING:			
Proceeds	$ 2,500		
ACB	(2,000)		
Gain			500
Loss			$ (3,500)
Loss carryback to year 1			2,500*
NET GAIN			NIL
Year 3			
JEWELLERY:			
Proceeds	$ 2,500	$ 2,500	
ACB	(500)	(1,000)	
Gain			$ 1,500
Loss carryforward from year 2			(1,000)*
NET GAIN			$ 500

2. Capital Gain or Loss Where Replacement of Property

Assume:

X Ltd. owns a building to which the following data applies:

Cost	$ 200,000
UCC	$ 50,000

The building is expropriated under statutory authority, and *X Ltd.* is paid $250,000. In the same taxation year, *X Ltd.* acquires a substitute building in the same vicinity. The cost of the replacement property is $400,000. *X Ltd.* makes an election under subsection 13(4).

Comprenhensive Examples (continued)

Then:

(a) Election under subsection 13(4):

Proceeds otherwise determined	$ 200,000
Minus, lesser of:	
(i) $200,000 − 50,000 = $150,000	
(ii) $400,000	(150,000)
Elected proceeds of disposition	$ 50,000
UCC	(50,000)
Recapture of CCA	NIL
Deemed capital cost of replacement of property	$ 350,000*
Less: Amount of CCA deferred	(150,000)
Deemed UCC of replacement of property	$ 200,000

(b) Election under subsection 44(1):

Proceeds of disposition	$ 250,000
Less: ACB	(200,000)
(A) Capital gain otherwise determined	$ 50,000
Proceeds of disposition	$ 250,000
Exceeds:	
Capital cost of replacement	400,000
(B) Amount determined	NIL
Capital gain (lesser of (A) and (B))	NIL

(c) Capital cost of replacement property:*

Actual capital cost of replacement property	$ 400,000
Less: capital gain deferred	(50,000)
Deemed capital cost of replacement property	$ 350,000

*Paragraph 44(1)(f).

SELECTED BIBLIOGRAPHY TO CHAPTER IX

General

Allan, J.R., et al., "The Effects of Tax Reform and Post Reform Changes in the Federal Personal Income Tax, 1972-75" (1978), 26 *Can. Tax J.* 1.

Barbacki, Richard, "Use It or Lose It?" (July 1989), 122 *CA Magazine* 43.

Bernstein, Jack, "Tax Planning for Holding Canadian Real Estate" (1984), 3:8 *Ont. Lawyers Wkly.* 8.

Binavince, E., "The Taxation of Capital Gains and Losses: General Principles", in Hansen, Krishna and Rendall (eds.), *Canadian Taxation* (Toronto: De Boo, 1981), p. 297.

Bird, Richard M., "Capital Gains Taxation in Canada: A Review of a Review", in *Proceedings of 3lst Tax Conf.* 525 (Can. Tax Foundation, 1980).

Birnie, David A.G., "Shareholders' Buy-Sell Agreements: Some New Opportunities", in *Proceedings of 38th Tax Conf.* 13 (Can. Tax Foundation, 1986).

Boehmer, G.C., "Personal Tax Planning — Small Business Corporations — Capital Gains Planning Opportunities and Pitfalls" (1987), 35 *Can. Tax J.* 987.

Boehmer, G.C., "Small Business Corporations: Capital Gains Planning Opportunities and Pitfalls" (1987), 35 *Can. Tax J.* 987.

Bossons, John, "Economic Effects of the Capital Gains Tax" (1981), 29 *Can. Tax J.* 809.

Bossons, John, "Implementing Capital Gains Reforms" (1979), 27 *Can. Tax J.* 145.

Broadway, Robin W., and Harry M. Kitchen, "Canadian Tax Policy", *Tax Paper No. 63* (Canadian Tax Foundation, 1980) 71-77.

Bucovetsky, Meyer W., "Inflation and the Personal Tax Base: The Capital Gains Issue" (1977), 25 *Can. Tax J.* 77.

Colley, G.M., "Capital Gains Tax — A Perspective" (1981), 14 *CA Magazine* 63.

Corn, George, "Taxation of Gain on Appreciation of Shares: Capital Gain or Income from an Adventure in the Nature of Trade" (1994), 4 *Can. Current Tax* J39.

Crawford, R.W., "Sales of Real Estate: Tax Planning for the Seller", *Corporate Management Tax Conf.* 138 (Can. Tax Foundation, 1983).

Cullity, Maurice C., "The Capital Gains Exemption: Implications for Estate Planning", in *Proceedings of 37th Tax Conf.* 18 (Can. Tax Foundation, 1985).

Daly, Michael J., et al., "Toward a Neutral Capital Income Tax System" (1986), 34 *Can. Tax J.* 1331.

Daly, Michael J., et al., "The Taxation of Income from Capital in Canada: An International Comparison" (1987), 35 *Can. Tax J.* 88.

Davies, James B., and France St-Hilaire, *Reforming Capital Income Taxation in Canada: Efficiency and Distributional Effects of Alternative Options* (Economic Council of Canada, 1987).

Dean, Jacklyn I., "The January 15, 1987 Draft Amendments Relating to the Acquisition of Gains and Losses", *Corporate Management Tax Conf.* 2:1 (Can. Tax Foundation, 1987).

Drache, A.B.C., "Real Estate Capital Gains Change Raises Strategic Questions" (1992), 14 *Can. Taxpayer* 21.

Durnford, John W., "Profits on the Sale of Shares: Capital Gains or Business Income? A Fresh Look at Irrigation Industries" (1987), 35 *Can. Tax J.* 837.

Ewens, Douglas S., "The Capital Gains Exemption and the Butterfly" (1986), 34 *Can. Tax J.* 914.

James, Larry W., "Capital Gains Exemption, Planning Techniques", in *Proceedings of 38th Tax Conf.* 33 (Can. Tax Foundation, 1986).

James, Larry W., "Disposing of Real Estate", *Corporate Management Tax Conf.* 5:1 (Can. Tax Foundation, 1989).

Jordan, Barbara Ann, "An Economic Evaluation of the Tax Treatment of Capital Gains in Canada" (microform) (Ottawa: National Library of Canada, 1987).;

Kellough, Howard J., and K. Travers Pullen, "Planning for the Lifetime Capital Gains Exemption" (1986), 3 *Bus. & L.* 3.

Kirby, F.P., "The Capital Gains Exemption: Other Than Qualified Small Business Shares", in *Proceedings of 40th Tax Conf.* 30:1 (Can. Tax Foundation, 1988).

Krishna, V., *The Taxation of Capital Gains* (Toronto: Butterworths, 1983).

Kroft, Edwin G., and Bruce W. Aunger, "Some Issues Relating to the Taxation of Insider Trading Transactions — Comments on Interpretation Bulletin IT-479" (1983), 31 *Can. Tax J.* 763.

Lawlor, William R.G., "Surplus Stripping and Other Planning Opportunities With the New $500,000 Capital Gains Exemption", in *Proceedings of 37th Tax Conf.* 8 (Can. Tax Foundation, 1985).

Maloney, Maureen A., "Capital Gains Taxation: Marching (Oh So Slowly) into the Future" (1988), 17 *Man. L. J.* 299.

Mayhall, "Capital Gains Taxation — The First One Hundred Years" (1980), 41 *L.A. L. Rev.* 81.

Messere, Kenneth C., "Capital Gains and Related Taxation in OECD Member Countries", in *Proceedings of 31st Tax Conf.* 505 (Can. Tax Foundation, 1980).

Mida, Israel H., *Capital Gains and the May 1985 Federal Budget* (C.C.H. Can., 1986).

Perry, David B., "Importance of Capital Gains and Losses in the Personal Income Tax System (The)" (1984), 32 *Can. Tax J.* 178.

Perry, David B., "Selected Statistics on the Evolution of the Personal Income Tax System Since 1970" (1987), 35 *Can. Tax J.* 207.

Quinton, Cathy, "The Additional Capital Gains Exemption" (December-January 1989), 62 *CMA Magazine* 47.

Richards, Gabrielle M.R., "Proceeds of Disposition of Property" (1986), 1 *Can. Current Tax* J-164.

Richards, Gabrielle M.R., "Quick Flips: Capital Gains or Income Treatment?" (1991), 3 *Can. Current Tax* C57.

Richards, Gabrielle M.R., "The Timing of Dispositions of Property" (1986), 1 *Can. Current Tax* C-131.

Richardson, Elinore J., "Holding Real Estate for the Production of Income", *Corporate Management Tax Conf.* 1 (Can. Tax Foundation, 1983).

Rotenberg, Charles M., "Making the Deal Work" (1991), 13 *Can. Taxpayer* 60.

Ruby, Stephen S., "A Glimpse at the Lifetime Capital Gains Exemption (Part I)" (1986), 3:12 *Bus. & L.* 93.

Ruby, Stephen S., "A Glimpse at the Lifetime Capital Gains Exemption (Part III)" (1987), 4:1 *Bus. & L.* 6.

Sauve, Marc, *L'imposition des gains en capital et l'égalité fiscale* (Université de Montréal, Faculté de droit, 1987).

Sheppard, Anthony F., "Capital Gains: Twenty Years Later a Buck is Still Not a Buck" in *The Quest for Tax Reform: The Royal Ciommission on Taxation Twenty Years Later* (Toronto: Carswell, 1988).

Silver, Sheldon, "Capital Gains", in *Proceedings of 23rd Tax Conf.* 68 (Can. Tax Foundation, 1971).

Stack, Thomas J., "Capital Gains and Losses on Shares of Private Corporations", in *Proceedings of 39th Tax Conf.* 17:1 (Can. Tax Foundation, 1987).

Tam, Anthony, "Capital Gains Exemption: Small Business Corporations" (1987-89), 2 *Can. Current Tax* P-5.

Tax Treatment of Real Estate Gains: Working Group Report (Toronto: Fair Tax Commission, 1992).

Thompson, A.E.J., and B.R. Sinclair, "Capital Gains" (1985), 13 *Can. Tax News* 81.

Walker, Michael A., "Perspectives on Capital Gains Taxation", in *Proceedings of 31st Tax Conf.* 535 (Can. Tax Foundation, 1980).

Ward, David A., and John M. Ulmer, "Corporate Taxation: Shares Eligible for the Capital Gains Exemption" (1986), 5 *Legal Alert* 81.

Warnock, Bruce A., "Income or Capital Gains on Dispositions of Property" in *Proceedings of 42nd Tax Conf.* 48:1 (Can. Tax Found., 1990).

Watchuk, Jeanne, "Are Gains on SRTC Debt Flips Capital or Income? Two Opposing Opinions" (1990), 38 *Can. Tax J.* 380.

Zinn, J.A., "The Taxation of Capital Gains: Selected Topics" (1981), *Can. Taxation* 363.

Capital Property

Drache, A.B.C., "Real Estate Capital Gains Change Raises Strategic Questions" (1992), 14 *Can. Taxpayer* 21.

Goodman, Wolfe D., "Charitable Gifts of Appreciated Capital Property" (1986), 8 *Estates and Trusts J.* 189.

Williamson, W. Gordon, "Transfers of Assets to and from a Canadian Corporation", in *Proceedings of 38th Conf.* 12 (Can. Tax Foundation, 1986).

Computation of Capital Gain or Loss

Corn, G., "Capital Gains — Calculation of Proceeds of Disposition" (1984), 1 *Can. Current Tax* J-24.

Dzau, Vivien, "Reserves: A Tool for Deferring Taxes" (1980), 113 *CA Magazine* 57.

Krishna, Vern, "Reserves" (1984), 1 *Can. Current Tax* J-41.

Nitikman, Bert W.,"Reserves", in *Proceedings of 25th Tax Conf.* 355 (Can. Tax Foundation, 1973).

Rotenberg, Charles M., "Making the Deal Work" (1991), 13 *Can. Taxpayer* 60.

Stack, Thomas J., "Capital Gains and Losses on Shares of Private Corporations" in *Proceedings of 39th Tax Conf.* 17:1 (Can. Tax Found., 1987).

Webb, K., "Escalator Clauses, Earn-Outs and Reserves", in *Proceedings of 26th Tax Conf.* 55 (Can. Tax Foundation, 1974).

Dispositions

Alliston, Paul F., "Rental of Real Estate" (1976), 109 *CA Magazine* 57.

Arnold, Brian J., "An Analysis of the Amendments to the FAPI and Foreign Affiliate Rules" (1983), 31 *Can. Tax J.* 183.

Arnold, Brian J., "Conversions of Property to and from Inventory: Tax Consequences" (1976), 24 *Can. Tax J.* 231.

Arnold, Brian J., and David A. Ward, "Dispositions — A Critique of Revenue Canada's Interpretation" (1980), 28 *Can. Tax J.* 559.

Beam, Robert E., and Stanley N. Laiken, "Personal Tax Planning — Changes in Use and Non-Arm's-Length Transfers of Depreciable Property" (1987), 35 *Can. Tax J.* 453.

Bittker, "Capital Gains and Losses — The 'Sale' or 'Exchange' Requirements" (1981), 32 *Hastings L.J.* 743.

Brown, R.D., "Can You Take It With You?" (1972), 20 *Can. Tax J.* 470.

Chapman, "The Time of Sale Under the Internal Revenue Code" (1964), 22 *N.Y.U. Tax Inst.* 139.

Corn, George, "Capital Gains — Calculation of Proceeds of Disposition" (1984), *Can. Current Tax* J-24.

Denega, M.A., "The Migrating Executive: Leaving Canada and Working Abroad", *Corp. Management Tax Conf.* 189 (Can. Tax Foundation, 1979).

Drache, A.B.C., "Foreign Exchange" (1979), 1 *Can. Taxpayer* 52.

Drache, A.B.C., "Real Estate Capital Gains Change Raises Strategic Questions" (1992), 14 *Can. Taxpayer* 21.

Ewens, Douglas S., "When Is a 'Disposition'?" in *Proceedings of 26th Tax Conf.* 515 (Can. Tax Foundation, 1974).

Goodison, Don, "Tax Forum — Not a Threat" (1990), 24 *CGA Magazine* 19.

Kroft, Edwin G., and Bruce W. Aunger, "Disposition of Canadian Securities" (1983), 31 *Can. Tax J.* 763.

Masson, Guy, et al., "The Expatriate's Departure", *Can. Tax Letter,* August 18, 1980 (De Boo).

Matheson, David I., "Taxation of Investments in Commodities Futures, Precious Metals, Options, Objects of Art, Foreign Exchange and Other Exotica", in *Proceedings of 27th Tax Conf.* 918 (Can. Tax Foundation, 1975).

Middleton, David W., "Tax Implications of Departure From Canada" (1983), 116 *CA Magazine* 44.

Richards, Gabrielle M.R., "Proceeds of Disposition of Property" (1986), 1 *Can. Current Tax* J-164.

Richards, Gabrielle M.R., "The Timing of Dispositions of Property" (1986), 1 *Can. Current Tax* C-131.

Richardson, Elinore, "Currency Swaps — A Canadian Perspective" (1984), 32 *Can. Tax J.* 345.

Tkachenko, Lorissa V., "Expropriations: The Income Tax Aspects" (1985), 33 *Can. Tax J.* 1.

White, Michael J., "Isolated Foreign Currency Transactions and Foreign Exchange Contracts", in *Proceedings of 30th Tax Conf.* 490 (Can. Tax Foundation, 1978).

Adjusted Cost Base

Champagne, Donald C., "Bad and Doubtful Debts, Mortgage Foreclosures and Conditional Sales Repossessions", in *Proceedings of 27th Tax Conf.* 682 (Can. Tax Foundation, 1975).

Corn, George, "Computation of Adjusted Cost Base of Shares" (December 1990), 3:12 *Can. Current Tax* J-59.

Couzin, Robert, "Of Arm's Length and Not Dealing Threat" (1978), 26 *Can. Tax J.* 271.

Crawford, William E., "Taxation of Land Developers", *Corporate Management Tax Conf.* 75 (Can. Tax Foundation, 1977).

Farwell, Peter M., "Debts and Capital Gains Taxation" (1972), 20 *Can. Tax J.* 101.

Goldspink, Tom, and David Allgood, "Tax Treatment of Personal Guarantees" (1983), 31 *Can. Tax J.* 1042.

Hogg, R.D., "Stock Option Benefits in Canadian-Controlled Private Corporations" (1978), 26 *Can. Tax J.* 85.

Riehl, Gordon W., et al., "Intercompany Non-Arm's Length Transactions — Income Tax Consequences", in *Proceedings of 26th Tax Conf.* 102 (Can. Tax Foundation, 1974).

Smith, David W., "Transferring the Family Business" (1979), 27 *Can. Tax J.* 1.

Stikeman, H.H. (ed.), "Stock Dividends", *Can. Tax Letter,* October 30, 1975 (De Boo).

Zinn, John A., "The Taxation of Capital Gains: Selected Topics", in Hansen, Krishna & Rendall (eds.), *Canadian Taxation* (Toronto: De Boo, 1981).

Personal-use Property

Arbuckle, J.E., "Investment in Art — For Pleasure and Profit" (1980), 54 *Cost & Mgmt.* 46.

Bernstein, J., "Investing in Art and Other Collectibles", in *Proceedings of 35th Tax Conf.* 124 (Can. Tax Foundation, 1983).

Dewling, A.M., "Intergenerational Transfers of Personal-use Property" (1989), 37 *Can. Tax J.* 1292.

Drache, A.B.C., "Real Estate Capital Gains Change Raises Strategic Questions" (1992), 14 *Can. Taxpayer* 21.

Edwards, S.E., "Personal Investments", [1986] *Special Lectures LSUC* 221.

Feingold, Fred, and Marlene F. Schwartz, "Source of Income from Sales of Personal Property" (1987), 35 *Can. Tax J.* 473.

Rotenberg, Charles M., "Inflation and Personal Property" (1980), 2 *Can. Taxpayer* 37.

Strother, Robert C., "Income Tax Implications of Personal-Use Real Estate", *Corporate Management Tax Conf.* 59 (Can. Tax Foundation, 1983).

Identical Properties

Lynch, John H., "Income Splitting Among Family Members", in *Proceedings of 32nd Tax Conf.* 752 (Can. Tax Foundation, 1980).

McDonnell, T.E.J., "Capital Gains: Tax Planning for the Individual" (1972), 20 *Can. Tax J.* 382.

Losses Deemed to be Nil

Brown, Robert D., and Thomas E. McDonnell, "Capital Gains Strips", in *Proceedings of 32nd Tax Conf.* 51 (Can. Tax Foundation, 1980).

Burpee, Thomas R., "Utilization of Tax Losses: A Reasonable Expectation of Profit", in *Proceedings of 37th Tax Conf.* 32:1 (Canadian Tax Foundation, 1985).

Drache, A.B.C., "Superficial Gains" (1980), 2 *Can. Taxpayer* 17.

Grover, Warren, "Superficial Losses" (1974), 22 *Can. Tax J.* 253.

Huggett, Donald R. (ed.), "Restrictions on Loss Transfers" (1987), 14:8 *Can. Tax News* 87.

Income Tax, Capital Gains Strips (Audio Archives of Canada, 1984).

Kirkpatrick, Paul K., "Tax Consequences of a Corporation Dealing in its Own Stock" (1964), 13 *Tulane Tax Ins.* 85.

Riehl, Gordon W., "Debt Instruments", in *Proceedings of 27th Tax Conf.* 764 (Can. Tax Foundation, 1975).

Stewart, E.C., "Capital Gains Considerations" (1974), 48 *Cost & Mgmt.* 45.

Sweet, David G., "Capital Losses", in *Proceedings of 24th Tax Conf.* 348 (Can. Tax Foundation, 1972).

Watts, David E., "Recognition of Gain or Loss to a Corporation on a Distribution of Property in Exchange for its own Stock" (1968), 22 *Tax Lawyer* 161.

Zimmer, Henry B., "Using Your Losses" (1974), 104 *CA Magazine* 58.

Principal Residence

Bergen, Rodney C., "The Tax Treatment of Principal Residences: An Update" in *Proceedings of 44th Tax Conf.* 12:1 (Can. Tax Found., 1992).

Boivin, Marc, "La 'résidence principale' lors d'un déménagement", *Recueil de fiscalité*, AQPFS, vol. 83-2, 151.

Drache, A.B.C., "The Best Investment" (1991), 13 *Can. Taxpayer* 134.

Drache, A.B.C., "Buying Your Student a Home" (1991), 13 *Can. Taxpayer* 115.

Freedman, Martin H., "The Home Owner", in *Proceedings of 25th Tax Conf.* 224 (Can. Tax Foundation, 1973); reprinted and revised in *Butterworth's Canadian Income Tax Revised* 9:5.

Fulton, Patricia, "Tax Preferences for Housing: Is There a Case for Reform?", in Thirsk and Whalley (eds.), "Tax Policy Options in the 1980's", *Tax Paper No. 66* (Can. Tax Foundation, 1982), 73.

Goldstein, D.L., "Capital Gain — Whether the Principle Residence Exemption may be taken on a Gain brought in from a Reserve" (1987), 37 *Can. Tax J.* 1522.

Goodison, Don, "Tax Forum — Necessary Excess" (1991), 25 *CGA Magazine* 14.

Gray, W.D., "When Does Land in Excess of One-half Hectare From Part of a Principal Residence?" (1989), 37 *Can. Tax J.* 113.

Harris, Edwin C., "A Case Study in Tax Reform: The Principal Residence" (1983), 7 *Dal. L.J.* 169.

Kehler, J.A., "Capitalizing on a Change of Residence or in its Use" (1985), 118 *CA Magazine* 12:52.

McGregor, G., "Principal Residence: Some Problems" (1973), 21 *Can. Tax J.* 116.

Moore, D.H., "Does a 'Principal Residence' Include Separate Buildings" (1987), 35 *Can. Tax J.* 702.

"Personal Tax Planning — The Principal Residence Designation Decision: The New Complexity" (1984), 32 *Can. Tax J.* 572.

Rotenberg, Charles M., "My Second Home" (1983), 5 *Can. Taxpayer* 199.

Shead, Richard G., "The Current Status of Real Estate as a Tax Shelter", in *Proceedings of 38th Tax Conf.* 48 (Can. Tax Foundation, 1986).

Simmons, Howard S., *The Family Home and Income Tax* (Toronto: Carswell, 1986).

Strother, Robert C., "Income Tax Implications of Personal-Use Real Estate", *Corporate Management Tax Conf.* 59 (Can. Tax Foundation, 1983).

Thomas, R.B., "Associated Corporations; Principal Residence", in *Proceedings of 35th Tax Conf.* 689 (Can. Tax Foundation, 1983).

William, "Private Residence: Tax Incidence and Exemptions" (1977), 41 *Convey. & Prop. Lawyer* 389.

Capital Losses

Arnold, Brian J., and D. Keith McNair, "The Stop-Loss Rule in Subsection 97(3): An Analysis" (1980), 28 *Can. Tax J.* 131.

Burpee, Thomas R., "Utilization of Tax Losses: A Reasonable Expectation of Profit", in *Proceedings of 37th Tax Conf.* 32:1 (Canadian Tax Foundation, 1985).

Cadesky, Michael, "Corporate Losses", in *Proceedings of 42nd Tax Conf.* 19:1 (Can. Tax Foundation, 1990).

Conkwright, Glen E., "The Utilization of Losses in Corporate Groups and Further Relief that Might be Taken", in *Proceedings of 31st Tax Conf.* 316 (Can. Tax Foundation, 1979).

Drache, A.B.C., "Corporate Loss Strategies" (1991), 13 *Can. Taxpayer* 70.

Drache, A.B.C., "New Treatment for Losses" (1983), 5 *Can. Taxpayer* 183.

Eaton, K.E., "The Death of the 'Profit Earning Process Test' " (1957), 5 *Can. Tax J.* 271.

Farwell and Mathew, "The Costs of Corporate Complexity" (1979), 112 *CA Magazine* 28.

Hirsch, Morley P., "The Corporate Loss Transfer System", in *Proceedings of 37th Tax Conf.* 31:1 (Canadian Tax Foundation, 1985).

Kleinman, Robert A. and Jeffrey Gerstein, "Planning to Maximize the Eligibility and Utilization of Capital Losses for Individuals" (1993), 41 *Can. Tax J.* 324.

Nowoselski, Barry, "Should You Buy or Sell a Company for Its Tax-Loss Carryovers?" (1983), 116 *CA Magazine* 64.

Reid, Robert J., "Capital and Non-Capital Losses", in *Proceedings of 42nd Tax Conf.* 20:2 (Can. Tax Foundation, 1990).

Silver, Sheldon, "Utilization of Real Estate Losses", *Corporate Management Tax Conf.* 91 (Can. Tax Foundation, 1983).

Stacey, John A., "The Treatment of Losses", in *Proceedings of 35th Tax Conf* 29 (Can. Tax Foundation, 1983).

Sweet, David G., "Capital Losses", in *Proceedings of 24th Tax Conf.* 348 (Can. Tax Foundation, 1972).

Wraggett, Cathy, "Accelerated Deduction of Business Losses" (1990), 64 *CMA Magazine* 33.

Zimmer, Henry B., "Using Your Losses" (1974), 104 *CA Magazine* 58.

Transitional Rules

Cadesky, Michael, "Corporate Losses", in *Proceedings of 42nd Tax Conf.* 19:1 (Can. Tax Foundation, 1990).

Reid, Robert J., "Capital and Non-Capital Losses", in *Proceedings of 42nd Tax Conf.* 20:2 (Can. Tax Foundation, 1990).

Wise, Richard M., "The V-Day Value of Publicly Traded Shares" (1980), 28 *Can. Tax J.* 253.

Anti-avoidance Provisions

Goodison, Don, "Tax Forum — Not a Threat" (1990), 24 *CGA Magazine* 19.

Lahmer, Craig, "New Measures Against Tax Avoidance Transactions" in *Proceedings of 40th Tax Conf.* 19:1 (Can. Tax Found., 1988).

Templeton, Wendy, "Anti-Avoidance and the Capital Gains Exemption" (1986), 34 *Can. Tax J.* 203.

Other

Attridge, Ian, "Create Conservation Gains, Not Capital Gains" (1994), 19 *Intervenor No.* 6 8.

Ballon, Naomi L., "Section 68: Judicial Deference?" (1989), 2 *Can. Current Tax* P67.

Campbell, Ian R., "Valuation-related Issues: Tax Planning and Post-transaction Follow-up" in *Proceedings of 45th Tax Conf.* 40:1 (Can. Tax Found., 1993).

Drache, A.B.C., "Stock Dividends: Beneficial to the Few" (1981), 3 *Can. Taxpayer* 99.

Hanson, Suzanee I.R., "Planning for a Share Sale" in *Proceedings of 44th Tax Conf.* 27:1 (Can. Tax Found., 1992).

Hayos, Gabriel J., "The Capital Gains Exemption: Planning Strategies to Meet the Criterial of a 'Qualified Small Business Corporation'" in *Proceedings of 40th Tax Conf.* 15:1 (Can. Tax Found., 1988).

Krishna, Vern, "Using the Capital Gains Exemption for Matrimonial Settlement" (1993), 4 *Can. Current Tax* C5.

Peters, Steven, "Enhancing the Exemption" (1992), 125 *CA Mag. No. 5* 33.

Potvin, Jean, "The Capital Gains Deduction for Qualified Small Business Corporation Shares Revisited" in *Proceedings of 44th Tax Conf.* 5:50 (Can. Tax Found., 1992).

Sapona, Ingrid, "Canada's Tax Treaties: A Comparison of the Treatment of Capital Gains" (1992), 40 *Can. Tax J.* 720.

Silver, Sheldon, "Estate Freezing With Discretion" (1978), 26 *Can. Tax J.* 705.

Stewart, Donald A.C., "Stock Option Plans: Bright Past, Dim Future" (1972), 20 *Can. Tax J.* 299.

Tam, Anthony, "Capital Gains Exemption: Small Business Corporations" (1987-89), *Can. Current Tax* P5.

Wise, Richard M., "Fair Market Determinations — A Few More Requirements" (1983), 31 *Can. Tax J.* 337.

CHAPTER X

OTHER SOURCES OF INCOME

References:

ITA:

S. 3   Income for Taxation Year

1. GENERAL

To this point, we have examined the rules governing the computation of income from the following specifically identified sources: office, employment, business, property and capital gains. We have seen that income from these sources enters into the computation of total income according to the sequence and manner set out in section 3. There are, however, certain types of income that cannot conveniently be identified as originating from, or relating to, these named sources. These are loosely categorized as "other sources of income" in subdivision d of Division B.

The rationale for the "other sources of income" is as varied as the types of income in this category. Pension benefits and retirement allowances are closely related to the earning of employment income, but may be received after the taxpayer's employment has terminated. Other items (such as indirect payments, family allowances, etc.) just do not conveniently relate to any particular source of income. Thus, in a sense, "other sources of income" is nothing more than a residual category for receipts that have the characteristics of income but that cannot be conveniently linked with an office or employment, business or property, and that do not result from a disposition of capital property.

2. SUPERANNUATION OR PENSION BENEFITS

References:

ITA:

S. 57   Pension or Superannuation Benefits

S. 147.1   Registered Pension Plans

BULLETINS, CIRCULARS & RULINGS:

IT-499R   January 17, 1992   Superannuation or Pension Benefits

Pension income is taxable upon receipt and not upon payment of contributions into the pension plan.

Employer contributions to employee registered pension plans are not taxable as employment source income.[1] Within specified limits, employees are also entitled to deduct contributions to a registered pension fund or plan.[2]

Pension benefits from a pension plan (not including benefits from an employee benefit plan) are taxable upon their withdrawal from the plan, and are included in income in the year payment is received.[3]

An employee is required to include all pension benefits in income as they are received. This is so whether the payments are made under a formal plan, received lump sum, or meted out periodically. Pensions and supplementary pensions received under the *Old Age Security Act* and the *Canada Pension Plan* are also taxable as income.[4]

It is important to observe that all payments made out of a superannuation or pension plan, whether registered or not, are included in income. Registration is of importance only in determining the deductibility of contributions to a plan; it has no bearing on the taxability of receipts out of a plan.

The source of a pension is also irrelevant to its inclusion in income calculations; all pension income is taxable when received by a taxpayer resident in Canada. Hence, in the absence of a tax treaty, a foreign taxpayer who takes up residence in Canada becomes liable to tax on a pension income, even though he or she may not have been entitled to a deduction at the time the contributions were made into the pension plan.[5]

3. DEATH BENEFITS

References:

ITA:

S. 148   Life Insurance Policies

BULLETINS, CIRCULARS & RULINGS:

IT-301	April 6, 1976	Death Benefits — Qualifying Payments
IT-508	June 30, 1987	Death Benefits — Calculation

A payment on account of a death benefit is included in income in the year of receipt. A "death benefit" is defined as a payment made upon the death of an employee

---

[1] Subpara. 6(1)(*a*)(i); subs. 248(1) ("superannuation or pension benefit").

[2] Para. 8(1)(*m*).

[3] Subpara. 56(1)(*a*)(i); *Muller v. M.N.R.* (1960), 26 Tax ABC 295, 61 DTC 246 (pension does not have to be related to an office or employment to be taxed).

[4] Equivalent payments under Quebec plans are also included in the taxpayer's income.

[5] *The Queen v. Herman*, [1978] CTC 442, 78 DTC 6311 (F.C.T.D.).

in recognition of his or her service in an office or employment. A death benefit paid to an employee's spouse is tax-free to a maximum of $10,000.[6]

4. ALIMONY AND MAINTENANCE

References:

ITA:

S. 56.1   Maintenance and Prior Payments

BULLETINS, CIRCULARS & RULINGS:

IT-118R3   December 21, 1990   Alimony and Maintenance

The statutory provisions in respect of alimony and maintenance are divided into two segments: receipts are included in income under subdivision d; deductions are permitted under subdivision e. The inclusion and deduction provisions are mirror images of each other.[7] A payment that is deductible by the payer is required to be included in income by the payee. A payment that is taxable to the recipient may be deducted by the payer. These provisions are discussed further in Chapter XI "Other Deductions".

5. INDIRECT PAYMENTS

References:

BULLETINS, CIRCULARS & RULINGS:

IT-335R   September 11, 1989   Indirect Payments

IT-440R   November 30, 1989   Transfer of Rights to Income

The Act seeks to prevent high income taxpayers from diverting income to taxpayers in lower tax brackets. In certain circumstances, a taxpayer who diverts income to another may be deemed to be in "constructive" receipt of the income.[8] The doctrine of constructive receipt is used to control income splitting and income shifting. The purpose of the doctrine has been described as follows:[9]

> It is to cover cases where the taxpayer seeks to avoid the receipt of what in his hands would be income, by arranging to transfer that amount to some other person he wishes to benefit, or for his own benefit in doing so. Apart from any moral satisfaction, the practical benefit to the taxpayer is the reduction in his income tax.

---

[6]   Subpara. 56(1)(*a*)(iii), subs. 248(1) ("death benefit").

[7]   Paras. 56(1)(*b*), (*c*), s. 56.1; paras. 60(*b*), (*c*), s. 60.1. See: *Thibaudeau v. Canada*, [1995] 1 CTC 382 (S.C.C.) (para. 56(1)(b)) does not impose a burden on recipient so as to attract section 15 of the Charter.

[8]   Subs. 56(2).

[9]   *Murphy v. The Queen*, [1980] CTC 386 at 390, 80 DTC 6314 at 6318 (F.C.T.D.).

A taxpayer is considered to be in constructive receipt of income if:[10]

- He or she makes a payment or transfers property to some other person;
- The transfer or payment is made at the taxpayer's direction, or with his or her concurrence; and
- The transfer is for the benefit of the taxpayer or some other person whom the taxpayer wishes to benefit.

In these circumstances, the taxpayer is taxable on the amount transferred to the extent that he or she would have been taxable had the payment or property been received directly.

The term "transfer" is broadly interpreted. Justice Thorson said in *Fasken Estate*:[11]

> The word "transfer" is not a term of art and has not a technical meaning. It is not necessary to a transfer of property from a husband to his wife that it should be made in any particular form or that it should be made directly. All that is required is that the husband should so deal with the property as to divest himself of it and vest it in his wife, that is to say, pass the property from himself to her. The means by which he accomplishes this result, whether direct or circuitous, may properly be called a transfer.

Whether a taxpayer acquiesces in a payment or transfer of property to another is a question of fact. The taxpayer's concurrence in a transfer may be either implicit or explicit and apparent indifference or failure to protest may be construed as approval of the transfer.[12]

There are three categories of circumstances in which the Department frequently invokes the doctrine of constructive receipt. These circumstances involve:

1. Delegated payments;
2. Interposed corporations; and
3. Income splitting.

(a) Delegated Payments

The first category involves payments delegated or diverted by one taxpayer to another. For example:

- A taxpayer may divert employment income to another taxpayer;[13]

---

[10] Subs. 56(2).

[11] *Fasken Estate v. M.N.R.*, [1948] CTC 265 at 279, 4 DTC 491 at 497 (Ex. Ct.); see *Dunkelman v. M.N.R.*, [1959] CTC 375, 59 DTC 1242 (Ex. Ct.) (loan of money by father to trustees for purchase of building for benefit of children did not constitute a transfer of property from father to children); *Oelbaum v. M.N.R.*, [1968] CTC 244, 68 DTC 5176 (Ex. Ct.) (loan from husband to wife not same as transfer of property, investment income derived from borrowed funds not taxable in hands of lender).

[12] Unlike the attribution rules in subss. 74.1(1) and (2), subs. 56(2) does not state clearly whether the transferee of the property is also taxable under this subsection.

[13] *Watts v. M.N.R.* (1961), 27 Tax ABC 432, 61 DTC 592.

- A corporation may make a gift to the relatives of its principal shareholders or directors;[14]

- A corporation may lease property at less than its fair rental value to a relative of its principal shareholder;[15] or

- A corporation may discharge its shareholder's legal obligations to a third party.[16]

All of these examples involve fairly blatant diversions of receipts which would otherwise have been income in the hands of the taxpayer who has caused, or acquiesced in, the diversion.

(b) Interposed Corporations

An individual who interposes a personal service corporation between himself or herself and an employer in order to render services to that employer may be considered in constructive receipt of payments made to the corporation. Whether or not the individual is in constructive receipt of payments made to the corporation depends upon two principal factors: (1) documentation of the arrangement; and (2) legality of the scheme.

The corporation must be created pursuant to *bona fide* and lawful arrangements and the transactions must be implemented by proper documentation. Thus, corporations have been successfully used to render coaching services to a football club,[17] and deliver medical[18] and sales services.[19] But the veil of a corporation that has been created improperly may be pierced.[20]

In addition to the general rules controlling indirect payments, there are also special rules that govern the use of corporations to earn "personal service business" income. These rules are discussed in Chapter XV "Corporate Finance".

---

[14] *Copp v. M.N.R.* (1954), 11 Tax ABC 147, 54 DTC 376; *M.N.R. v. Bronfman*, [1965] CTC 378, 65 DTC 5235 at 5239-40 (Ex. Ct.).

[15] *New v. M.N.R.*, [1971] Tax ABC 400, 70 DTC 1415.

[16] *M.N.R. v. Bisson*, [1972] CTC 446, 72 DTC 6374 (F.C.T.D.).

[17] *Sazio v. M.N.R.*, [1968] CTC 579, 69 DTC 5001 (Ex. Ct.).

[18] *Campbell v. M.N.R.*, [1979] CTC 279, 79 DTC 5202 (F.C.A.); affirmed [1980] CTC 319, 80 DTC 6239 (*sub nom. The Queen v. Campbell*) (S.C.C.).

[19] *M.N.R. v. Cameron*, [1972] CTC 380, 72 DTC 6325 (S.C.C.). See, however, the "incorporated employee" rules in s. 125 which deny the small business deduction to "personal service businesses": subs. 125(7) ("personal services business").

[20] *The Queen v. Daly*, [1981] CTC 270, 81 DTC 5197; leave to appeal to S.C.C. refused 40 NR 134 (S.C.C.).

Similarly, unlawful corporate arrangements may be pierced. In *Kindree v. M.N.R.*,[21] for example, a medical doctor was personally taxed on income diverted to his corporation on the basis that a medical practice could be conducted only by a licensed medical practitioner in his personal capacity and that it is unlawful to conduct such a practice through a corporation.

(c) Income Splitting

The third category of circumstances in which the doctrine of constructive receipt is sometimes applied involves situations in which corporate share structures are designed to facilitate income splitting. This category of cases has created the greatest number of problems and the most uncertainty in tax planning.

(i) Corporate Law

From the viewpoint of corporate law, it is arguable that the tax doctrine of constructive receipt should not apply to corporate dividends since the decision to declare dividends is made by the directors *in their capacity as directors.*[22] Shareholders cannot usually compel directors to declare a dividend and, in most circumstances, they must acquiesce in, or concur with, decisions of the board of directors if the directors are acting in good faith.[23]

Absent *mala fides* or a breach of fiduciary duty, there is no jurisdiction to interfere in the internal management of a corporation. In *Burland v. Earle*,[24] for example, Lord Davey said:

> It is an elementary principle of law relating to joint-stock companies that the Court will not interfere with the internal management of companies acting within their power, and in fact has no jurisdiction to do so. [Emphasis added.]

The notion that a shareholder, *qua* shareholder, can direct a corporation to divert a payment is an idea that is conceptually foreign to corporate law. The directors' decision to pay a dividend is usually made in their capacity as directors and not in their capacity

---

[21] *Kindree v. M.N.R.*, [1964] CTC 386, 64 DTC 5248 (Ex. Ct.).

[22] See Howard J. Kellough, "Selecting an Appropriate Share Capital Structure for Private Corporations", in *Proceedings of 33rd Tax Conf.* 49 at 73 (Can. Tax Foundation, 1981): "...[i]n summary, it is suggested that the payment of a dividend does not fit within the meaning of subs. 56(2)".

[23] *Bond v. Barrow Haematite Steel Co.*, [1902] 1 Ch. 353 (Court cannot easily override director's discretion not to pay dividends); *Lambert v. Neuchatel Asphalt Co.* (1882), 51 L.J. Ch. 882 (question of whether or not to set aside reserve fund in sole discretion of directors); *Burland v. Earle*, [1902] AC 83 (P.C.); *Kehoe v. Waterford & Limerick Ry.* (1888), 32 LR Ir. 221; *Leslie v. Can. Birkbeck Co.* (1913), 24 OWR 407; affirmed 25 OWR 513 (Ont. C.A.) (shareholder wanted usual dividend either paid out or credited on company books from time to time); *Denault v. Stewart, Denault & Co.* (1918), 54 Que. SC 209 (Que. S.C.) (directors alone had right and authority to declare dividend).

[24] *Burland v. Earle, ante*, at 93.

as shareholders.[25] In this sense, the payment of corporate dividends is quite different from the gifting of corporate property to persons who are not shareholders of the corporation. Indeed, gifting away corporate property may give rise to an action for breach of fiduciary duty.[26]

(ii) Business Purpose

The absence of a business purpose in designing a share capital structure is not, *per se*, sufficient to invalidate the structure.[27] A properly designed share structure may be valid for tax purposes, even if it is used for income splitting between taxpayers, provided that the arrangement can withstand the general anti-avoidance rule in section 245.

(iii) Discretionary Dividends

Where a corporation's share structure is intended to facilitate income splitting, its articles of incorporation will generally provide that the directors may pay dividends on the various classes of shares on a discretionary basis. For example, a clause such as:

> Each class of shares has the right to receive dividends exclusive of other classes of shares in the corporation and the corporation is authorized to issue an unlimited number of shares in each class.

permits the directors of the corporation to sprinkle dividends on the class or classes of shares to maximize income splitting possibilities for the shareholders.

A corporate dividend paid to an arm's length person is not considered a benefit diverted to a third party. Hence, subsection 56(2) does not generally apply to tax corporate dividends as an indirect benefit.[28] This is so whether or not the dividend is paid pursuant to a discretionary dividend clause. Thus, the use of discretionary dividend clauses is a valid means whereby directors of a corporation can distribute dividends to facilitate income splitting.

(iv) Non-arm's Length Relationships

The scope of subsection 56(2) is less certain where the relationship between the parties constitutes a non-arm's length business relationship. There is a suggestion in *McClurg*, for example, that subsection 56(2) may apply where a discretionary power to distribute dividends is used to benefit a shareholder who is not at arm's length with the corporation and who has made no legitimate contribution to the corporation:[29]

---

[25] Shareholders may declare a dividend if authorized to do so by virtue of a shareholders agreement: see, e.g., *Canada Business Corporations Act*, R.S.C. 1985, c. 44, s. 107.

[26] See, e.g., *Cook v. Deeks*, [1916] 1 AC 554 (P.C.).

[27] *Stubart Invt. v. The Queen*, [1984] CTC 294, 84 DTC 6305 (S.C.C.).

[28] *McClurg v. M.N.R.*, [1991] 1 CTC 169 at 185, 91 DTC 5001 at 5012 (S.C.C.).

[29] *McClurg v. M.N.R., ante*, [1991] 1 CTC at 185, 91 DTC at 5012.

[I]f a distinction is to be drawn in the application of s. 56(2) between arm's length and non-arm's length transactions, it should be made between the exercise of a discretionary power to distribute dividends when the non-arm's length shareholder has made no contribution to the company (in which case s. 56(1) [*sic*] may be applicable), and those cases in which a legitimate contribution has been made.

What constitutes a "legitimate contribution" is a question of fact in each case. A contribution may be financial (whether by way of equity or back-up guarantees), or it may be through active management involvement, business connections, or know-how, to name a few possibilities.

A court may look through a corporation to the "economic and commercial reality of the taxpayer's actions".[30] A discretionary dividend may be considered an indirect benefit if the "economic and commercial reality" of the circumstance indicates that the corporation's capital structure is nothing more than a scheme for tax avoidance.

The Supreme Court's vague *obiter* in *McClurg* adds to Revenue Canada's arsenal of anti-avoidance measures. How much weight will Revenue Canada and the courts give to such dicta? Bowen L. J. said of dicta:[31]

I believe that *obiter dicta*, like the proverbial chickens of destiny, come home to roost sooner or later in a very uncomfortable way to the judges who have uttered them and are a great source of embarrassment in future cases.

McClurg should not be read as creating an independent anti-avoidance test that is intended to be applied differently from the now defunct business purpose rule[32] or the general anti-avoidance rule in section 245.[33]

6. RETIRING ALLOWANCES

Reference:

BULLETINS, CIRCULARS & RULINGS:

IT-337R2   May 22, 1984   Retiring Allowances

In the absence of a specific statutory provision, a retiring allowance for the loss of employment would be compensation *for the loss of* a source of income, rather than compensation *from* a source of income. The Act, however, specifically brings retiring allowances into income.[34]

A "retiring allowance" is defined as a payment in recognition of long service. It also includes certain payments in situations where the worker has not *retired*, such as

---

[30] *McClurg v. M.N.R.*, ante, [1991] 1 CTC at 183, 91 DTC at 5011.

[31] *Cooke v. New River Co.* (1888), 38 Ch. D. 56 at 71.

[32] *Stubart Invt. Ltd v. The Queen*, [1984] CTC 294, 84 DTC 6305 (S.C.C.).

[33] See, for example, *The Queen v. Neuman*, [1994] 1 CTC 354, 94 DTC 6094 (F.C.T.D.).

[34] Subpara. 56(1)(*a*)(ii).

compensation for loss of an office or employment, or damages for wrongful dismissal.[35]

A payment pursuant to the terms of an employment contract is generally not a retiring allowance; it is remuneration.[36] In exceptional circumstances, a contractual payment to an employee upon termination of employment may be considered to be a "retiring allowance" if the payment is in recognition of the length of the employee's service to the company. There is generally an element of gratuitousness in the making of the payment, even though it may result from a threat of litigation.

7. SCHOLARSHIPS, BURSARIES, FELLOWSHIPS, RESEARCH GRANTS AND PRIZES

References:

BULLETINS, CIRCULARS & RULINGS:

IT-75R3	October 4, 1993	Scholarships, Fellowships, Bursaries, Prizes, and Research Grants
IT-257R	March 31, 1995	Canada Council Grants
IT-340R	September 26, 1984	Scholarships, Fellowships, Bursaries and Research Grants — Forgivable Loans, Repayable Awards and Repayable Employment Income

(a) General

Scholarships, fellowships, bursaries and prizes for achievement are included in income to the extent that the amount received in the year exceeds $500.[37] Work-related and business-related awards, prizes and similar payments do not qualify for the $500 exemption.

The terms "scholarship", "fellowship" and "bursary" are often used interchangeably to mean financial assistance to selected students pursuing further education. A "prize for achievement" is an award for accomplishment. The phrase does not necessarily imply an award for victory in a competition or contest.[38] An award is only considered a "prize" if the winner of the prize is aware of the existence of and enters the contest.[39]

---

[35] Subs. 248(1) ("retiring allowance").

[36] Para. 6(3)(*b*).

[37] Para. 56(1)(*n*).

[38] *The Queen v. Savage*, [1983] CTC 393 at 400, 83 DTC 5409 at 5415 *per* Dickson J. (S.C.C.).

[39] *The Queen v. McLaughlin*, [1978] CTC 602, 78 DTC 6406 (F.C.T.D.).

(b) Research Grants

A fellowship, scholarship or bursary should be distinguished from a research grant. A research grant is a sum of money given to a person to defray expenses in connection with a research project. Research grants sometimes include remuneration for the researcher.

The term "research" is undefined; it generally involves a critical or scientific inquiry aimed at discovering new facts and exploring the potential for their practical application. Usually, the terms of the grant will establish that the primary purpose of the grant is the carrying out of research.

A research grant is taxable only if it is received directly by an individual. In other words, a payment of funds to the taxpayer's educational or research institution to finance research by the taxpayer is not taxable to the researcher.[40]

Research-related expenses are deductible from a research grant to the extent of the total value of the grant.

A taxpayer who has to travel to conduct his or her research may deduct travelling expenses (including the full amount expended for meals and lodging) incurred in the carrying out of the research. Revenue Canada takes the view, however, that a researcher who resides temporarily in a place while engaged in research is "sojourning" rather than travelling. Amounts paid for meals and lodging while the researcher is sojourning in a place are considered personal and living expenses and are not deductible from the research grant. It is not clear how long a taxpayer must stay in a place in order to be considered to be sojourning rather than travelling.[41]

(c) Prizes

Prizes for achievement are included in income in the year received.[42] The word "prize" is broadly interpreted to include any award for accomplishment. To be included in income, however, the prize must be for achievement in a field of endeavour ordinarily carried on by the taxpayer. Thus, prizes won in games of chance or for athletic achievement are not taxable.[43] Prescribed prizes of recognition by the general public for particularly meritorious endeavours are also excluded from income.[44]

---

[40] Para. 56(1)(*o*).

[41] Subpara. 56(1)(*o*)(i).

[42] Para. 56(1)(*n*).

[43] *The Queen v. Savage, ante*, [1983] CTC at 401, 83 DTC at 5415.

[44] Reg. 7700.

8. NON-ARM'S-LENGTH LOANS

(a) General

The attribution rules are intended to prevent a taxpayer from splitting income with family members so as to reduce the total amount of tax which would otherwise be payable on his or her income. The general rule in section 74.1 deals with transfers or loans to the taxpayer's spouse or to a person who is under 18 years of age and with whom the taxpayer does not deal at arm's length.

Subsection 56(4.1) extends the attribution rules even further for loans between persons who are not at arm's length with each other. The general effect of these rules is that income from property that is diverted by one individual to another, non-arm's length individual through a low-interest or an interest-free loan is taxable in the first individual's hands. This rule supplements and extends the attribution rules in section 74.1 insofar as loans are concerned.

(b) Application

Subsection 56(4.1) does not apply to outright transfers of property. It applies only where an individual loans property to another with whom he or she does not deal at arm's length *and* one of the main reasons for the loan is to reduce or avoid tax on income from the property.[45] The result is that the income is considered to be income of the individual who made the loan and not of the individual who actually received the income from the property.[46] This rule does not apply where the attribution rules in section 74.1 apply.

There is no attribution of income on loans that bear a commercial rate of interest. To be exempt, however, interest on the loan must be charged at a rate that is not less than either the prescribed rate of interest or the rate that would prevail between persons dealing with each other at arm's length in comparable commercial circumstances. To obtain the benefit of the exemption, however, the interest on the loan must have been paid in the year or, at the very latest, no later than 30 days after the end of the year.[47]

9. SOCIAL ASSISTANCE PAYMENTS

Most social assistance payments are not taxable. A taxpayer in receipt of social assistance payments must, however, include the amount received in income[48] in determining taxable income. The taxpayer may then claim a deduction for the amount

---

[45] Or from substituted property.

[46] Subs. 56(4.1).

[47] Subs. 56(4.2).

[48] Para. 56(1)(*u*).

included in income.[49] Although the net effect is that such payments are not taxable, the inclusion of social assistance payments in a taxpayer's income may have other consequences. For example, it may reduce the amount of other tax incentives, such as refundable tax credits, to which the taxpayer might otherwise be entitled.

The trend in recent Canadian tax legislation is to shift the tax burden of social welfare payments to the payer of the highest rate of tax in a family. Social assistance payments are taxed to the spouse with the higher marginal tax rate. This ensures that a family's access to any other income-tested tax incentives is determined by reference to the income of the spouse with the higher tax rate.

10. OTHER INCLUSIONS

Other Inclusions in Income	Statutory Reference	Comment
amounts paid for benefit of taxpayer and/or children in taxpayer's custody	56.1	
unemployment insurance benefits	56(1)(*a*)(iv)	
transitional assistance benefit	56(1)(*a*)(v)	received by employees of automotive industry covered by the 1965 Canada-U.S. pact on automotive products
prescribed benefit under government assistance program to extent not already included in income	56(1)(*a*)(vi)	
annuity payments	56(1)(*d*), (*d*.2)	
amount received from the disposition of an income-averaging annuity contract	56(1)(*e*), (*f*); 61(4) ("income-averaging) annuity contract")	
benefits under a supplementary unemployment benefit plan	56(1)(*g*); 145	

---

[49] Para. 110(1)(*f*).

Other Inclusions in Income	Statutory Reference	Comment
benefits received under an RRSP or a RRIF	56(1)(*h*); 146	
home buyers' plan	56(1)(*h*.1); 146.01	
benefits from a deferred profit sharing plan	56(1)(*i*); 147	
amount received from the disposition of an interest in a life insurance policy	56(1)(*j*); 148(1), (1.1)	
legal costs awarded by a court on an appeal for tax assessment, interest or penalties, and costs reimbursed from a decision of Canada Employment and Immigration Commission or under *Unemployment Insurance Act, Canada Pension Plan*	56(1)(*l*)	provided costs of the appeal or decision are deductible under para. 60(*o*)
reimbursement of legal expenses paid to collect or establish right to a retiring allowance or pension benefit	56(1)(*l*.1)	
training allowance paid under *National Training Act*	56(1)(*m*)	except to extent paid on account of an allowance for away-from-home living expenses
amount received from an RESP	56(1)(*q*); 146.1	
home insulation or conversion grants	56(1)(*s*); Regs. 5500, 5501	
benefits from an RRIF	56(1)(*t*); 146.3	
worker's compensation	56(1)(*v*)	

Other Inclusions in Income	Statutory Reference	Comment
amounts received from some other person's salary deferral arrangement	56(1)(*w*)	amount included in income to the extent that it was not included in the other person's income
proceeds from disposition of an interest in a RCA	56(1)(*y*)	
value of benefits received or enjoyed in respect of workshops, seminars, training programs, etc.	56(1)(*aa*)	received by reason of membership in a registered national arts service organization

SELECTED BIBLIOGRAPHY TO CHAPTER X

Superannuation or Pension Benefits

Baston, Paul F., "Individual Pension Plans Revisited: Are they Really Worthwhile" (1994), 6 *Tax. of Exec. Compensation and Retirement* 19.

Bauslaugh, Randy V., "Past Service Enhancement and the Subsection 8503(15) Anti-avoidance Rule" (1994), 5 *Tax. of Exec. Compensation and Retirement* 899.

Broley, John A., "Overcoming Benefit Limitations for Executives Through Design and Use of Pension and Nonstatutory Arrangements", in *Proceedings of 33rd Tax Conf.* 869 (Can. Tax Foundation, 1981).

Bush, Kathryn M., "Executive Compensation: Supplemental Pension Plans" (1991), 8 *Bus. L.* 46.

Dutka, Randall J., *et al.*, *Pensions and Retirement Income Planning 1993: Tax Rules and Strategies* (Toronto: CCH Canadian, 1993).

Johnston, William, "Taxation of Non-registered Pension Plans", *Corp. Mgmt. Tax Conf.* 9:1 (Can. Tax Foundation, 1991).

Krasa, Ewa M., "Recent Developments in Retirement Savings and Deferred Compensation: A Potpourri", in *Proceedings of 44th Tax Conf.* 18:1 (Can. Tax Foundation, 1992).

Muto, Alexander D., "Recent Changes to the Income Tax Regulations on Retirement Savings" (1994), 5 *Tax. of Exec. Compensation and Retirement* 942.

Pensions: Significant Issues and Developments (Toronto: Law Society of Upper Canada, Dpt. of Education, 1990).

Solursh, John M. and Jeremy J. Forgie, "Tax-assisted Retirement Savings: An Overview of the New System and its Application to Registered Pension Plans", *Corp. Mgmt Tax Conf.* 7:1 (Can. Tax Foundation, 1991).

Theroux, Marcel and Brad Rowse, "The Individual Pension Plan: A Complete Guide", *Corp. Mgmt. Tax Conf.* 8:1 (Can. Tax Foundation, 1991).

Wolpert, Michael, "Pension Plans and the Income Tax Act: The Other Side of the Equation" (1992), 2 *Can Corp. Counsel* 10.

Death Benefits

Atnikov, D., "Stock Options, Stock Purchase Plans, and Death Benefits", *Prairie Provinces Tax Conf.* 1 (Can. Tax Foundation, 1980).

Alimony and Maintenance

"Alimony and Maintenance Trusts" (1993), 8 *Money and Family Law* 81.

"Alimony Insurance could be Tax Deductible" (1992), 7 *Money and Family Law* 36.

Arnold, Brian J., "Income Tax Consequences of Separation and Divorce", in *Proceedings of 29th Tax Conf.* 193 (Can. Tax Foundation, 1977).

Barnett, Jim, "Alimony and Maintenance Payments" (1979), 112 *CA Magazine* 65.

Bowman, Stephen W., *et al.*, "The Taxability of Child Support Payments and the Charter of Rights and Freedoms" (1994), *Can. Tax J.* 907.

Corn, George, "Child Care Expenses — Deductibility as Business Expenses or Personal Living Expenses" (1991), 3 *Can. Current Tax* J-91.

Douglas, Kristen, "Child Support: Quantum, Enforcement and Taxation" (Ottawa: Library of Parliament, Research Branch, 1994).

Drache, A.B.C., "Reducing Expenses is Not Gaining Income" (1991), 13 *Can. Taxpayer* 156.

Drache, A.B.C., "Support Payments: All Tax Aspects Should Be Considered" (1991), 13 *Can. Taxpayer* 160.

Drache, A.B.C., "Tax Act Creates Problems in Joint Custody" (1992), 14 *Can. Taxpayer* 31.

Drache, A.B.C., "Written Separation Agreements" (1991), 13 *Can. Taxpayer* 61.

Durnford, John W. and Stephen J. Troope, "Spousal Support in Family Law and Alimony in the Law of Taxation" (1994), 42 *Can. Tax J.* 1.

Freedman, Andrew J., "Arrears Payments: To Tax or Not to Tax?" (1993), 8 *Money and Family Law* 61.

Goodison, Don, "Tax Forum — Not a Business Expense" (1991), 25 *CGA Magazine* 17.

Harris, J., "Alimony and Maintenance Payments: Unexpected Results" (1988), 2 *Can. Current Tax* P-25.

Harris, Peter H., "Tax Treatment of Civil Litigation and Damage Awards, Alimony and Maintenance Payments" (1985), 6 *Advocate's Q.* 346.

Income Tax and Costs: Setting Aside Separation Agreements: Appeals, Choosing the Right Forum (Audio Archives of Canada, 1984).

Income Tax: Maintenance, Alimony and Employment Termination Benefits (Audio Archives of Canada, 1984).

Klein, William A., "Tax Effects of Nonpayment of Child Support" (1990), 45 *Tax Lawyer* 259.

Krishna, Vern, "To Love, Honor or Pay" (1990), 24 *CGA Magazine* 28.

McCallum, J. Thomas, "Deferring the Inevitable" (1990), 24 *CGA Magazine* 23.

"Post-Marital Trusts" (1984), 6 *Can. Taxpayer* 15.

Raich, Robert, "Characterization of Income and Third Party Alimony Receipts", in *Proceedings of 32nd Tax Conf.* 238 (Can. Tax Foundation, 1980).

Richards, Gabrielle M.R., "Support Payments: An Update" (1992), 3 *Can. Current Tax* J-115.

Shillington, Richard and Ellen Zweibel, "Child Support Policy: Income Tax Treatment and Child Support Guidelines" (Toronto: Policy Research Centre on Children, Youth and Families, 1993).

Shultz, Clayton G., "Income Tax Law and Policy Applicable to Periodic Maintenance and Division of Matrimonial Assets" (1987), 1 *Can. Fam. L. Q.* 293.

"Taxation of Support Payments Received from Non-residents" (1994), 9 *Money and Family Law* 78.

"Taxation of Support Payments Simplified?" (1992), 7 *Money and Family Law* 75.

Indirect Payments

Davidson, A. Barrie, "Personal Service and Professional Corporations Incorporating Employment and Professional Income", in *Proceedings of 32nd Tax Conf.* 212 (Can. Tax Foundation, 1980).

Desaulniers, Claude P., "Choix d'une structure du capital", *J. d'études fiscales* 79 (Can. Tax Foundation, 1981).

Drache, A.B.C., "Controlling a Company Without Shares" (1992), 14 *Can. Taxpayer* 56.

Drache, A.B.C., "Gifting Without a Transfer" (1991), 13 *Can. Taxpayer* 164.

Drache, A.B.C., "Income Splitting 'Loophole' Closed" (1992), 14 *Can. Taxpayer* 21.

Drache, A.B.C., "McClurg Obiter Creates Problems" (1992), 14 *Can. Taxpayer* 47.

Drache, A.B.C., "Technical Hitches Ruin Income Split" (1991), 13 *Can. Taxpayer* 62.

"Estate Planning Time Bomb" (1983), 5 *Can. Taxpayer* 42.

Grafton, S., "Income-Splitting" (1985), 13 *Can. Tax News* 88.

Graschuk, Harry S., "The Professional Corporation in Alberta" (1977), 25 *Can. Tax J.* 109.

Harris, Neil H., "Tax Aspects of Condominium Conversions and Lease Inducement Payments to Recipients", in *Proceedings of 38th Tax Conf.* 45 (Can. Tax Foundation, 1986).

Innes, William I., "The Taxation of Indirect Benefits: An Examination of Subsections 56(2), 56(3), 56(4), 245(2) and 245(3) of the Income Tax Act", in *Proceedings of 38th Tax Conf.* 42 (Can. Tax Foundation, 1986).

Krishna, Vern, "Corporate Share Capital Structures and Income Splitting" (1991), 3 *Can. Current Tax* C-71.

Krishna, Vern, "Corporate Share Structures and Estate Planning" (1983), 6 *E. & T.Q.* 168.

Krishna, Vern, "Designing Share Capital Structures for Income Splitting" (1984), 1 *Can. Current Tax* C-51.

Krishna, Vern, "Indirect Payments and Transfer of Income" (1986), 1 *Can. Current Tax* J-137.

Kroft, E.G., "Income Splitting" (1983), 17 *CGA Magazine* 28.

Kwan, Stanley P.W., and Kenneth J. Murray, "Remuneration Planning for the Owner-Manager" (1982), 29 *Can. Tax J.* 603.

Levine, Risa, "Incorporation and the Taxation of a Private Corporation", *British Columbia Tax Conf.* 1 (Can. Tax Foundation, 1980).

Zaytsoff, J.J., "Accountant's Comment: Innovative Share Capital Structures to Split Income Effectively" (1984), 42 *Advocate (Van.)* 177.

Retiring Allowances

Colley, Geofferey, M., "Retirement and Termination" (1980), 113 *CA Magazine* 57.

Fisher, G.B., "Early Retirement Tax Considerations" (1983), 31 *Can. Tax J.* 828.

Income Tax: Maintenance, Alimony and Employment Termination Benefits (Audio Archives of Canada, 1984).

Levine, Risa, "Retiring Allowances Part 1: How Do You Know if You Have One?" (1994), 2 RRSP Plan. 125.

Matheson, D.I., "Termination of Employment", *Corporate Management Tax Conf.* 219 (Can. Tax Foundation, 1979).

Murill, Raymond F., "Easing the Pain of Severance Pay" (1984), 117 *CA Magazine* 38.

Novek, Barbara L., "Retiring Allowances are subject to Administrative Guidelines" (1991), 3 *Tax. of Exec. Compensation and Retirement* 523.

Rayside J.W., "Retirement Planning for Owner-Managers" (1982), 30 *Can. Tax J.* 83.

"Retiring Allowance Reasonableness" (1980), 2 *Can. Taxpayer* 205.

Non-arm's Length Loans

Brahmst, Oliver C., "Beware of the Breadth of Subsection 56(4.1)" (1991), 3 *Can. Current Tax* P-43.

Brahmst, Oliver C., "Subsection 56(4.1) — An Update" (1992), 3 *Can. Current Tax* P-47.

Drache, A.B.C., "Income Splitting Needs Advance Planning" (1991), 13 *Can. Taxpayer* 181.

Drache, A.B.C., "Income Splitting Through Lending" (1991), 13 *Can. Taxpayer* 174.

Other

Duncan, Garry R., "Passing the Hat (The Orderly Succession of a Business to a Worthy Heir)" (Jan/Feb 1989), 122 *CA Magazine* 39.

Finkelstein, David N., "Tax Problems in Estate Planning for the Corporate Executive", in *Proceedings of 33rd Tax Conf.* 952 (Can. Tax Foundation, 1981).

Harris, Peter H., "Tax Treatment of Civil Litigation and Damage Awards, Alimony and Maintenance Payments" (1985), 6 *Advocate's Q.* 346.

Wakeling, Audrey A., "Tax Planning with Trusts", in *Proceedings of 42nd Tax Conf.* 35:1 (Can. Tax Foundation, 1990).

CHAPTER XI

OTHER DEDUCTIONS

References:

ITA:

S. 60   Deductions in Computing Income

1. GENERAL

Just as the *Income Tax Act* includes in income various miscellaneous receipts that are not directly attributable to a particular source,[1] it also allows for the deduction of certain expenses that are not directly related to a particular source of income. These deductions (described here as "other deductions") constitute an open category of expenses, each with its own rationale. A common theme, however, that runs through many, though not all, of these "other deductions" is that they are on account of personal expenditures that would not be deductible under the general rules for determining income.

2. ALIMONY AND MAINTENANCE PAYMENTS

References:

ITA:

S. 60.1   Maintenance Payments

BULLETINS, CIRCULARS & RULINGS:

IT-118R3   December 21, 1990 Alimony and Maintenance

(a) General Structure

As a general rule, a taxpayer may not deduct his or her personal and living expenses in computing income for tax purposes. Alimony and maintenance payments are an exception to this rule. Within narrow and strictly-circumscribed circumstances, taxpayers may deduct alimony and maintenance payments in computing income.

The rationale for this exception is to provide financial relief to taxpayers who are required to maintain more than one household or support more than one family. Thus, the deduction for alimony and maintenance payments reflects the principle of tax equity that the burden of tax should be determined by the taxpayer's ability to pay. In recent

---

[1] See Chapter X "Other Sources of Income".

years, however, the deduction has also been justified on the basis that it encourages the payment of support entitlements.

The alimony and maintenance provisions have a significant effect on federal and provincial treasuries. Since alimony or maintenance is usually paid by the spouse with the higher marginal tax rate to the spouse with the lower tax rate, deduction of payments by the payor and inclusion in income by the payee involves a rate shift that has revenue consequences. For example, a man with a marginal tax rate of 50 per cent who pays $12,000 alimony to his spouse receives a deduction that is worth $6,000 in tax savings. In other words, the *net* cost of his alimony payments is only $6,000. If his spouse has a marginal rate of 20 per cent, her tax cost is only $2,400. The net loss of revenue caused by the difference in marginal rates is $3,600. Recent estimates (1995) suggest that the loss to the federal treasury is approximately $300 million per year.

There are three principal provisions that deal with the deduction of alimony and maintenance payments, and three reciprocal provisions that require inclusion of such payments in income.[2] The rules that require the inclusion of alimony and maintenance payments in income and the rules that allow a deduction for these types of payments are mirror images of each other.

Payments that qualify for a deduction of a payment from income under paragraph 60(*b*) or (*c*) require inclusion of the receipt in the recipient's income under paragraph 56(1)(*b*) or (*c*). The constitutional validity of paragraph 56(1)(*b*) was upheld by the Supreme Court in *Thibaudeau.*[3]

(i) Alimony

A payment by a taxpayer in respect of alimony is deductible if, and only if:[4]

- It is paid pursuant to a decree, order or judgment of a competent tribunal or pursuant to a written agreement;
- It is in the nature of alimony or other allowance *payable* on a periodic basis;
- It is paid to the taxpayer's spouse or former spouse;
- It is for the *maintenance* of the recipient and/or children of the recipient; and
- The taxpayer is living separate and apart from the recipient at the time of the payment because of the breakdown of the taxpayer's marriage and *throughout* the remainder of the year.

---

[2]   Paras. 56(1)(*b*), (*c*), s. 56.1 and paras. 60(*b*), (*c*), s. 60.1.

[3]   *Thibaudeau v. The Queen*, [1995] SCJ No. 42, File No. 24154, May 25, 1995.

[4]   Para. 60(*b*).

For tax purposes, "spouse" includes a person of the opposite sex with whom the individual cohabits for at least 12 months in a conjugal relationship. "Spouse" also includes the natural or adoptive unmarried parents of a child of the "spouses".[5]

(ii) Maintenance

A payment by a taxpayer in respect of maintenance is deductible if, and only if:[6]

- It is paid *pursuant to* an order of a competent tribunal, in accordance with provincial law;

- It is in the nature of an allowance *payable* on a periodic basis;

- It is for the *maintenance* of the recipient and/or children of the recipient;

- The taxpayer is the natural parent of a child of the recipient; and

- The taxpayer is living apart from the recipient at the time of the payment and *throughout* the remainder of the year.

Alimony and maintenance are deductible and taxable on a cash basis: Deductions may be claimed only for amounts actually paid in the year; the recipient is required to include in his or her income only those payments that he or she receives in the year.

(b) Order or Written Agreement

(i) Payments Prior to Agreement

A payment is deductible only if it is made pursuant to an order of a competent tribunal or, in certain cases, a written agreement. Amounts paid by a taxpayer *before* he or she is required to do so by a court order, or *before* he or she enters into a written agreement, are deductible,[7] but only if the order or agreement incorporates the payments and is made or entered into before the end of the year following the payments.[8]

---

[5] Subs. 252(4).

[6] Para. 60(*c*).

[7] See IT-118R3, "Alimony and Maintenance" (December 21, 1990); *Hardtman v. M.N.R.*, [1977] CTC 358, 77 DTC 5219 (F.C.T.D.) (although Court able to distinguish between sham and equitable maintenance, even prior to any agreement, Court without such equitable jurisdiction); *Pezet v. M.N.R.*, [1974] CTC 2315, 77 DTC 5219 (F.C.T.D.) (no retroactivity of deductibility where payments made prior to agreement, unless legislation provides otherwise); *Gagné v. M.N.R.*, [1976] CTC 2315, 74 DTC 1246 (T.R.B.) (husband's letter listing expenses which he would pay did not constitute "agreement", since no evidence of consent); *Brooks v. M.N.R.*, [1977] CTC 2048, 77 DTC 38 (T.R.B.) (amounts paid prior to agreement and order not deductible; even amount of arrears paid pursuant to order not deductible).

[8] Subs. 60.1(3).

(ii) Written Agreement

A "written agreement" is a legal document signed by both parties to the agreement. It is not enough that the parties exchange correspondence with each other or that their lawyers or accountants exchange correspondence and discuss draft agreements.[9] Anything less than a clear-cut "written agreement" signed by both parties precludes deductibility of the payments. An exchange of correspondence may, however, crystallize into a "written agreement" in the same way that contracts are sometimes formed through an exchange of letters.[10]

(iii) Pursuant to Agreement

A payment is *pursuant to* an order or agreement if it complies with the legal obligation created in the agreement.[11] Thus, only those amounts that are actually set out in the court order or written agreement are deductible by the payor and taxable to the payee. Voluntary payments in excess of the agreed-upon amounts are not "pursuant to" the order or agreement. Conversely, payments that are pursuant to a court order or agreement are taxable as income to the recipient even though the order or agreement might stipulate that the amounts are to be paid on a "tax-free" basis.[12]

(c) "Allowance"

An "allowance" is a sum of money that is:[13]

- Limited and predetermined in amount;
- Paid on account of maintenance; and
- At the complete disposition of the person to whom it is paid.

---

[9] *Feinstein v. The Queen*, [1979] CTC 329, 79 DTC 5236 (F.C.T.D.) (agreement destroyed by fire in attorney's office; payments not deductible in these exceptional circumstances); *Chamberland v. M.N.R.*, [1981] CTC 2302, 81 DTC 288 (T.R.B.) (agreement in principle, signed by one spouse is insufficient even if payments actually made); *Ardley v. M.N.R.*, [1980] CTC 2126, 80 DTC 1106 (T.R.B.) (legal fees for separation agreement paid, but no proof of execution of agreement); *Hardy v. M.N.R.*, [1978] CTC 3120, 78 DTC 1802 (T.R.B.) (and cases cited therein) (payments made pursuant to a written agreement which the payor refused to sign not deductible); *Andrychuck v. M.N.R.*, [1986] 2 CTC 2214, 86 DTC 1667 (T.C.C.) (informal correspondence between spouses does not constitute "written agreement"; wife's letter requesting $300 support per month insufficient); *Jacoby v. M.N.R.*, [1981] CTC 2935, 81 DTC 824 (T.R.B.) (unsigned written agreement insufficient); *Jaskot v. M.N.R.*, [1992] 1 CTC 2145, 92 DTC 1102 (T.C.C.) (increase in support payments not deductible as only written evidence in correspondence of recipient's solicitor).

[10] *Burgess v. M.N.R.*, [1991] 1 CTC 163, 92 DTC 5076 (*sub nom. Burgess v. The Queen*) (F.C.T.D.).

[11] *The Queen v. Sills*, [1985] 1 CTC 49, 85 DTC 5096 (F.C.A.).

[12] *The Queen v. Sigglekow*, [1985] 2 CTC 251, 85 DTC 5471; additional reasons at 85 DTC 5594 (F.C.T.D.).

[13] *Gagnon v. The Queen*, [1986] 1 SCR 264, [1986] 1 CTC 410, 86 DTC 6179 ($360 paid to spouse pursuant to divorce decree, for purpose of paying two mortgages and interest was "allowance"); *The Queen v. Pascoe*, [1975] CTC 656, 75 DTC 5427 (F.C.A.).

The amount paid must be at the complete disposition of the recipient: The recipient must be able to dispose of the amount received for his or her own benefit. An amount paid constitutes an allowance if the recipient is *entitled* to use the money for his or her own benefit, even though there may be restrictions on the types of expenditures for which the money may be used.[14] The amount paid on account of a mortgage, for example, is income to the recipient, because he or she benefits from the payment despite the restriction on the purpose for which the money may be used.

How do we test whether a person is able to dispose of an amount for his or her benefit? Does "able to dispose" mean the power or the legal right to dispose? In *Gagnon*,[15] the Supreme Court held that a payment which was allocated to a mortgage was a deductible allowance, on the basis of cases dealing with the nature of income.

In *Helvering*,[16] for example, the United States Supreme Court had to consider whether insurance commissions, which were potentially subject to partial reimbursement if reinsurance policies were cancelled, constituted income for the agent in the year in which they were received. The commissions were considered income because "when received, the general agent's right to it was absolute. It was under no restriction, *contractual or otherwise*, as to its disposition, use or enjoyment".[17] Thus, the focal point of the decision characterizing the commissions as income was the absence of legal restrictions, contractual or otherwise, on the recipient's right to use the amounts received for his or her own benefit.

Gagnon[18] restates the broad concept of "income" used in *Rutkin:*[19]

[A] . . . gain . . . constitutes taxable income when its recipient has such control over it that, as a practical matter, he derives readily realizable economic value from it.

Thus, a mortgage allowance is income even though the funds are restricted to a single use.

---

[14] *Gagnon v. The Queen, ante,* at 273-74, Beetz J. said:
   . . . the recipient must be able to dispose of the amount completely, and that, provided she benefits from it, it is not relevant that she has to account for it and that she cannot apply it to certain types of expense at her complete discretion. . . . What matters is not the way in which a taxpayer may dispose of, or be required to dispose of, the amounts he receives, but rather the fact of whether he can dispose of them or not.

[15] *Gagnon v. The Queen, ante.*

[16] *Brown v. Helvering,* 91 US 193 (1934).

[17] *Brown v. Helvering, ante,* at 199 [Emphasis added].

[18] *Gagnon v. The Queen, ante.*

[19] *Rutkin v. U.S.* (1952), 343 US 130 at 137, 96 L. ed. 833 at 836.

As a general rule, reimbursement by one spouse of specific expenses paid by the other does not qualify for deduction.[20] There are, however, a few reimbursed payments on account of medical, education and accommodation expenses which are deductible to the payor and taxable to the recipient.[21]

(d) Payable on a Periodic Basis

Alimony and maintenance payments are deductible by the payor, and taxable to the payee, but only if they are payable on a periodic, rather than a lump sum, basis. Thus, the deduction is confined to expenses and does not extend to capital settlements. Lump sum capital payments are not deductible in the determination of income.[22] For example, a lump sum payment in satisfaction of all future monthly payments payable under a decree is not considered a periodic payment.[23]

The term "periodic" means recurring at fixed or regular intervals. To be deductible, the payment must be *payable* on a periodic basis and the requirement of periodic payment must be set out in the court order or in the written agreement. It is not enough that the payments have actually been made on a periodic basis, if the payments have not been made pursuant to a legal obligation that requires the payments be made on a periodic basis.[24]

---

[20] See, e.g., *The Queen v. Fisch*, [1978] CTC 438, 78 DTC 6332 (F.C.T.D.) (since wife feared being financially irresponsible amounts for education paid directly; payments not deductible); *The Queen v. Guay*, [1977] CTC 266, 77 DTC 5420 (F.C.A.) (payments for repairs, heating, electricity, insurance, medical expenses and mortgage not deductible); *A.G. Can. v. Weaver*, [1975] CTC 646, 75 DTC 5462 (F.C.A.) (strict definition of "maintenance", dissenting judge would have allowed deduction for monthly mortgage payments); *Roper v. M.N.R.*, [1977] CTC 602, 77 DTC 5408 (F.C.T.D.) (payments made to creditors directly rather than included in monthly sum paid to wife, not deductible); *Cotton v. The Queen*, [1976] CTC 406, 76 DTC 6232 (F.C.T.D.) (*A.G. Can. v. Weaver, ante,* applied; exemption from taxation to be strictly construed); *Goldenburg v. M.N.R.*, [1979] CTC 3082, 79 DTC 851 (T.R.B.) (benefit of mortgage payments made by spouse and deductibility dependent upon percentage of ownership held by spouse); *Guay v. M.N.R.*, [1979] CTC 2981, 79 DTC 589 (T.R.B.) (transfer of equity in matrimonial home not "maintenance"); *Hellyer v. M.N.R.*, [1979] CTC 3037, 79 DTC 831 (T.R.B.) (expenses paid to separated wife's creditors not "allowance"; see test at 3040); *Barron v. M.N.R.*, [1978] CTC 3162, 78 DTC 1856 (T.R.B.) (mortgage payments deductible pursuant to amended legislation authorizing third-party payments, but not for period prior to application); *Riddoch v. M.N.R.*, [1978] CTC 2190, 78 DTC 1163 (T.R.B.) (mortgage payments not "allowances"); *Brooks v. M.N.R.*, [1977] CTC 2048, 77 DTC 38 (T.R.B.) ("alimony" defined as payments providing *current* support and assurance of future support).

[21] Subss. 56.1(2), 60.1(2).

[22] There are other provisions which allow for tax-free capital settlements: see, e.g., subs. 73(1).

[23] *M.N.R. v. Armstrong*, [1956] CTC 93, 56 DTC 1044 (S.C.C.).

[24] Paras. 60(*b*), (*c*).

(i) Periodic vs. Lump Sum Payments

It is important to distinguish between an allowance payable on a periodic basis and an obligation to pay a specified lump sum amount by way of regular instalments. The determination of whether a payment is an allowance payable on a periodic basis is sometimes quite difficult, and requires careful study of the document which creates the obligation to make the payments.

An allowance is a limited, predetermined sum of money that is paid to enable the recipient to provide for certain kinds of expenses. Its amount is determined in advance and, once paid, it is at the complete disposition of the recipient, who is not required to account for it. A lump sum payment also represents a limited, predetermined sum of money. Thus, the distinction between an allowance and a lump sum payment is blurred if the lump sum payment is payable in equal instalments on a periodic basis.

The problem is essentially one of legal characterization rather than economic substance. For example, what is the economic difference between a settlement of $100,000 payable in ten equal instalments and an agreement to pay $10,000 annually for the support of a child aged 11 until such time as the child attains the age of 21? In purely financial terms, allowing for the appropriate discount factor, the two alternatives can be structured to yield identical financial results.

To be "periodic", the obligation to pay should recur at fixed intervals and not at variable times. The requirement of periodicity refers to the regularity of time over which payments are payable. The obligation to pay at predetermined times should not be left to the discretion of the payor, but should arise from an antecedent legal obligation.[25]

Some of the earlier jurisprudence dealing with the meaning of the word "periodic" required that payments be on at least a monthly basis to qualify as being on a periodic basis. In recent years, however, the courts and Revenue Canada have become more flexible. Now, even annual payments sometimes qualify as periodic.[26] It would, however, be quite unusual for payments that recur less frequently than annually to qualify as periodic payments. Note: The statutory requirement is that the payment be *payable* on a periodic basis, not that it actually be paid periodically.[27]

---

[25] *Jones v. Ogle* (1872), 8 Ch. App. 192 at 198 (in construction of will, partnership profits did not come within meaning of "periodical payment in the nature of income"); *No. 427 v. M.N.R.* (1957), 57 DTC 291 (T.A.B.) (single $5,000 payment which was one of several of increasing value to be paid over 12 years was periodic in nature).

[26] *Hanlin v. The Queen*, [1985] 1 CTC 62, 85 DTC 5052 (F.C.T.D.) (three annual payments held to be part of series of payments payable on periodic basis).

[27] *The Queen v. Sills*, [1985] 1 CTC 49, 85 DTC 5096 (F.C.A.) (lump sum payments for arrears of periodic alimony characterized as periodic notwithstanding tardiness and manner of payment); *James v. The Queen*, [1985] 1 CTC 239, 85 DTC 5173 (F.C.T.D.) (recipient taxable on payments made pursuant to order even though payments were late and amounts less than specified in order).

A lump sum payable in instalments is not deductible and not taxable. The *Income Tax Act* taxes only income, not capital receipts. Similarly, it allows deductions only for expenses, not for capital payments. Thus, the distinction between lump sum amounts and periodic allowances reflects the basic distinction between income and capital. A lump sum settlement is a capital payment that is not deductible as an expense and not taxable as income.

Generally speaking, an obligation to pay a lump sum represents a finite debt as between the parties. The property right represented by the debt is assignable by the person to whom it is owed, and survives his or her life. Hence, the debt can pass to his or her estate in the event of death. In contrast, alimony and maintenance payments are usually linked to the duration of the life of the payor and the payee. They are also usually linked to the period of time during which the payments are necessary for the maintenance of the recipient.

The following are considered important and indicative of trends in this area. The list is not categorical or exhaustive.[28]

INDICIA	PERIODIC	LUMP SUM
Frequency of payments	Weekly Monthly Annually (?)	More than annually
Ratio of payment in relation to income and living standards	Low Small percentage of annual income of payor	High In excess of annual income of payor
Interest payments prior to due date	None	Yes
Acceleration by payee as penalty on default	No	Yes
Prepayment at option of payor	No	Yes
Amount allows for significant capital accumulation by recipient	No	Yes
Liability to pay is for definite and fixed time	No	Yes

---

[28] See, generally, *McKimmon v. Can.*, [1990] 1 CTC 109, 90 DTC 6088 (F.C.A.).

INDICIA	PERIODIC	LUMP SUM
Payments for indefinite period or until some identifiable family event (e.g., age of child)	Yes	No
Assignability of payments	No	Yes
Survival of obligation to pay after death of payor	No	Yes
Release from future obligations to pay	No	Yes

None of the above criteria is absolute or unequivocal. They do, however, provide some measure against which the obligation to pay and the right to receive payments can be tested.

(A) Frequency of Payments

"Periodic" payments imply an obligation to pay at fixed intervals and not at variable times. Moreover, the payments should be payable on a reasonably regular basis, whether, weekly, monthly or quarterly. Payments made at intervals of greater than one year are rarely considered to be allowances on account of maintenance.

(B) Amount Paid in Relation to Living Standards

To be deductible for tax purposes, the payment must be on account of maintenance and not on account of capital. A payment that represents a very substantial portion of a taxpayer's income is unlikely to be considered an allowance for maintenance. On the other hand, a payment that is clearly intended to maintain the recipient's standard of living qualifies as an allowance for maintenance. There is no hard-and-fast rule as to what constitutes maintenance. The answer depends upon the lifestyle of the parties and their standard of living and income levels.

(C) Interest

Payments that bear interest are generally lump sum payments payable by instalments, rather than a true allowance for maintenance. Maintenance payments do not typically bear interest.

(D) Acceleration Clauses

Prepayment and acceleration clauses are generally associated with obligations to pay lump sum capital obligations, not with maintenance allowances. The presence of an acceleration clause in a settlement contract suggests that the debt is a non-deductible capital obligation rather than an amount paid on account of periodic maintenance.

(E) Accumulation of Capital

The quantum of payments is important: Maintenance payments are for the recipient's living costs. They are not intended to allow for an accumulation of capital over a short period of time. It is accepted, however, that modest payments on account of capital accumulation may qualify as maintenance. For example, blended monthly mortgage principal and interest payments allow for a modest accumulation of capital over time, but are considered to be a normal living expense and may be part of a maintenance allowance.

(F) Term of Payments

Alimony and maintenance support payments are either payable for an indefinite or unspecified period of time or, where time is specified, the payments generally relate to a significant event in the life of the parties. For example, alimony payments may depend upon the coming of age of a child, because such an event is anticipated to cause a material change in the recipient's needs. In contrast, a lump sum generally represents a finite debt between the parties and payments on account thereof are expected to continue for a fixed and specified term.

(G) Assignment of Obligation

Maintenance allowances are personal to the recipient and are not assignable to third parties. A maintenance obligation usually terminates upon the death of the recipient and does not pass on to his or her estate. Thus, the obligation is both personal and non-assignable. In contrast, lump sum capital payments are assignable debts and form part of the recipient's estate.

(H) Release From Future Obligations

An agreement that releases the payor from all future obligations to pay maintenance is generally a lump sum settlement and not a payment on account of maintenance. The consideration for the release from future maintenance is the capitalized present value of the payments that would have been made on account of maintenance. The capital payment may be made in cash or by assumption of a liability (such as a mortgage) on the recipient's behalf. For example, a husband may assume a mortgage on his wife's property in exchange for his release from further liability.

(ii) Rollovers

Capital settlements between spouses and ex-spouses are subject to a different set of rules than are periodic payments. Section 73 allows an individual two choices when transferring capital property to his or her spouse or ex-spouse. He or she may:

1. Roll over the property on a tax-free basis, or

2. Elect to realize any capital gain accrued up to the date of the transfer.

In either case, the recipient takes the property at a cost equal to the transferor's proceeds of disposition. If the transferor elects a rollover, the recipient assumes the property at the transferor's cost; if the transferor realizes a capital gain, the recipient acquires the property at its fair market value.

(iii) Arrears

What happens when payments fall into arrears and the payor eventually makes one or several lump sum payments in satisfaction of all, or some part of, the amount due? In *Sills*,[29] the taxpayer received three lump sum payments on account of alimony arrears. The Federal Court of Appeal held that the taxpayer was taxable on the amounts received, since the amounts paid were identifiable under the terms of the agreement. Payments payable on a periodic basis do not change in character merely because they are not made on time. As stated earlier, the test is whether the payments are *payable* on a periodic basis and not whether they are actually paid on a periodic schedule.[30]

(e) Maintenance

The term "maintenance" is generally understood to mean a payment made for the support of an individual. Whether a payment constitutes "maintenance" depends upon the lifestyle of the parties involved, their standard of living and their legitimate expectations. The courts are fairly strict, and have denied taxpayers deductions for educational expenses, medical expenses, camping expenses, hospital insurance premiums and life insurance premiums.[31]

(f) Children

The term "children" as used in the alimony provisions has the same meaning that the term "child" has in other provisions of the Act.[32] Alimony payments are deductible if they are made in respect of children of the recipient of the payments.[33]

For the purposes of paragraphs 56(1)(c) and 60(c), the payer must be the natural parent of a child of the recipient.

---

[29] *The Queen v. Sills, ante.*

[30] *The Queen v. Pascoe,* [1975] CTC 656, 75 DTC 5427 (F.C.A.).

[31] *Urichuk v. The Queen,* [1993] 1 CTC 226, 93 DTC 5120 (F.C.A.) (characterization in separation agreement of instalment payments as additional maintenance does not prevent a contrary finding); *Golightly v. M.N.R.,* [1970] Tax ABC 161, 70 DTC 1120 (various payments, including insurance, university room and board, tuition and medical insurance paid directly to institution pursuant to separation agreement were not "maintenance"); *Ivey v. M.N.R.,* [1969] Tax ABC 903, 69 DTC 630 (payments of school fees, summer camp fees and medical expenses for child with cystic fibrosis outside meaning of "maintenance"); *Shaw v. M.N.R.,* [1978] CTC 3230, 79 DTC 26 (T.R.B.) (payment by taxpayer of spouse's income tax on maintenance payments and spouse's moving expenses not "alimony" or "maintenance"); *Evans v. M.N.R.,* [1960] CTC 69, 60 DTC 1047 (S.C.C.) (car payments made for spouse not "maintenance" although car highly useful).

[32] Subs. 252(1).

[33] Paras. 56(1)(b) and 60(b).

(g) "Living Apart From"

The payor and the payee must be living apart from each other at the time when the payment is made, and must also be living apart *throughout the remainder of the year in which the payments are made*. Whether individuals are living apart from each other is a question of fact in each situation. Persons living under a common roof may be considered to be living apart from each other.[34]

Where a payor taxpayer and the payee resume cohabitation during a taxation year, the payor is not entitled to deduct any payments made prior to the resumption of cohabitation.

(h) Third-party Payments

Alimony and maintenance payments are generally structured so that they are tax-deductible by the payor and taxable to the recipient. Payments are deductible if they are paid by a person to his or her spouse and the payments are pursuant to a judicial order or a written agreement and in the nature of an allowance payable on a periodic basis.

There are certain circumstances, however, when it is more convenient, and sometimes financially prudent, to pay some or all of the support payments (for example, mortgage payments) directly to a third party (for example, a financial institution) instead of making the payment to the spouse. Unfortunately, the tax rules in respect of support payments, which are complex enough when payments are made directly to the spouse, increase exponentially in complexity when payments are made directly to a third party. The governing provision, subsection 60.1(2), is the quintessence of Canadian tax legislation: Long-winded (392 words in one sentence), replete with double negatives, layered with qualifying clauses designed to block every possible avenue of fiscal escape, and crafted so that a minimum number of people can understand it in either official language.

---

[34] *Rushton v. Rushton* (1968), 66 WWR 764 (B.C.S.C.) ("separate" means having withdrawn from marriage with intent to destroy bond; "apart" means physically separate); *Rousell v. Rousell* (1969), 69 WWR 568 (Sask. Q.B.) (essence of evidence of separation being cessation of marital relationship); *Galbraith v. Galbraith* (1969), 69 WWR 390 (Man. C.A.) (examination of law on cruelty as grounds for separation though couple living in same dwelling); *M.N.R. v. Longchamps*, [1986] 2 CTC 2231 at 2233, 86 DTC 1694 at 1695 (T.C.C.) ("the termination of all rapport between a husband and his wife of the kind evidenced in this appeal is certainly in my opinion within the meaning that must be attributed to the expression, 'living apart'"; "there was no communication between them, no socializing whatsoever, each attending to his or her own affairs without consultation between them"); *Boos v. M.N.R.* (1961), 27 Tax ABC 283, 61 DTC 520 (on facts, husband so withdrawn and separated from wife and children as to be in desertion, though still occupying same home).

(i) Conditions for Deduction

Third-party alimony payments are deductible where the payments are:[35]

- Paid pursuant to either a judicial order of a competent tribunal or a written agreement, which stipulates that subsections 56.1(2) and 60.1(2) apply;
- For the maintenance of the payor's spouse, former spouse, an individual of the opposite sex who is the natural parent of a child of the taxpayer, and/or children;
- Payable on a periodic basis;
- Incurred at a time when the payor and the recipient were living separate and apart; and
- In respect of support expenses incurred either in the year or in the preceding taxation year.

There are additional requirements if the payment to a third party is in respect of mortgage payments on the family home. In these circumstances a payment is deductible only if:[36]

- The payor does not reside in the family home;
- The payment is not in respect of the purchase of tangible property; and
- The payment for principal and interest is not in excess of 20 per cent of the original amount of the loan incurred to finance the home.

In order for a third-party payment to be deductible, the judicial order or written agreement must *specifically* provide that subsections 60.1(2) and 56.1(2) of the Act apply to the payments. Failure to enumerate the subsections in the terms of settlement disqualifies the payments for deduction! Some courts[37] have blunted the severity of this harsh approach and accepted an oblique reference in the minutes of settlement as sufficient to satisfy the statutory requirement. But it is better to specify in the minutes of settlement that the subsections apply.

(ii) Deemed Allowance

Spousal support payments paid to a third party are *deemed* to have been paid as an allowance. Such payments are deductible by the payor and taxable in the hands of the person for whose benefit the payments are made.

---

[35] Subs. 60.1(2).

[36] Subs. 60.1(2).

[37] See, e.g., *Cottrell v. M.N.R.*, [1990] 2 CTC 2031, 90 DTC 1581 (T.C.C.) (payments deductible where minutes of settlement referred to payments in issue); *Bishop v. M.N.R.*, 93 DTC 333 (T.C.C.) (payment of support arrears to welfare authorities neither taxable nor deductible; payment constituted discharge of indebtedness).

Typically, third-party payments are made on account of, for example, medical and dental bills, mortgage payments, tuition fees, household utilities, camp fees and condominium maintenance fees. Of these expenses, mortgage fees, utilities and tangible property associated with medical, dental or educational requirements can easily be made tax-deductible.

It is less clear, however, whether condominium maintenance expenses (common area charges) paid directly to the condominium corporation are deductible for tax purposes. Expenditures incurred on account of the family home are deductible in respect of the *acquisition* or *improvement* of the home to the extent that they do not exceed 20 per cent of the original cost of financing the home. Condominium fees cannot be considered to qualify as either an acquisition or an improvement cost. Hence, it is generally better to include condominium fees as part of the negotiated allowance that is paid directly to the spouse.

(iii) Prior Payments

Support payments made prior to obtaining a judicial order or entering into a written agreement are also tax-deductible, provided that the order or agreement *specifically* so provides.[38] In effect, the order or agreement can retroactively render the payments deductible even though they were not paid *pursuant to* the order or agreement.

(iv) Payments to Non-residents

Alimony payments to non-residents are subject to withholding tax unless the non-resident elects to pay Part I tax on the amounts received.[39]

3. MATRIMONIAL SETTLEMENTS

An individual is entitled to a general capital gains exemption of $500,000 in respect of shares of a Qualified Small Business Corporation ("QSBC").[40] For a high rate taxpayer, the $500,000 exemption means a tax saving of approximately $187,000. The exemption can be used to minimize tax upon matrimonial breakdown.

(a) Capital Gains Exemption

The three basic requirements to qualify for the super exemption are as follows:[41]

1. The gain must be from a disposition of shares of a "small business corporation" ("SBC");

2. The shareholder must satisfy a holding period test; and

3. The corporation's assets must satisfy a holding period test.

---

[38] Subs. 60.1(3).

[39] Para. 212(1)(f), s. 217.

[40] Subss. 110.6(2.1) and (4). See Chapter IX "Capital Gains".

[41] Subs. 110.6(1) ("qualified small business corporation share").

Generally speaking, a SBC is a Canadian-controlled private corporation that uses all or substantially all of its assets (as measured by fair market value) in an active business carried on primarily in Canada.[42] Shares and debt of another SBC that is connected with the corporation also qualify as SBC shares. The phrases "all or substantially all" and "primarily" basically mean 90 per cent and 50 per cent, respectively. Thus, the first test is that at the time that its shares are disposed of the corporation uses at least 90 per cent of its assets (measured by fair market value) in an active business carried on at least 50 per cent in Canada.

The second requirement is that *throughout* the 24 months immediately before the disposition, the shares must not have been owned by anyone other than the individual or a person or partnership related to the individual. The individual does not have to own the shares for the continuous period of 24 months. The test is stated in the negative: They cannot have been owned in that period by a person who is *not* related to the individual.

(b) Share Settlements

Share transfers as part of a property settlement upon matrimonial breakdown require particular attention. There are two decisions that need to be made: (1) Who will claim the exemption?; and (2) When to claim the exemption.

An individual who transfers capital property to his or her spouse, former spouse or common-law spouse in settlement of matrimonial rights has a choice as to the amount of proceeds that he will recognize for tax purposes: He or she can elect to transfer the property either at its fair market value or at its adjusted cost base.[43] If the individual elects QSBC share proceeds equal to fair market value, he or she can shelter up to a maximum of $500,000 capital gain from the shares from tax. The transferee spouse takes the shares at the elected proceeds (fair market value) and any subsequent gain or loss on the shares is calculated from that point on.

Where the gain accrued on the QSBC shares exceeds $500,000, the transferor can split the share transfer into two separate transactions to minimize his or her tax on the transfer: (1) Transfer sufficient shares to trigger the maximum amount of the available capital gains exemption; (2) Transfer the remainder at the adjusted cost base of the shares.

For example, assume that a family corporation has issued and outstanding 100 common shares to H who is married to W. The shares have an adjusted cost base of $100 and a fair market value of $2 million. The property settlement between H and W provides that one-half of the shares are to be transferred from H to W. Thus, each share can trigger a capital gain of $20,000. If H transfers 25 shares at their fair market value

---

[42] Subs. 248(1) ("small business corporation").

[43] Subs. 73(1).

of $500,000 for a capital gain of $500,000 and then, separately transfers another 25 shares at their adjusted cost base of $25, he can claim the capital gains exemption in respect of $500,000 and, in effect, shelter the entire disposition of 50 shares from immediate tax.

W will acquire the 50 shares at a total cost base of approximately $500,000 or $10,000 per share. The shares will have a fair market value of $1 million and an accrued capital gain of $500,000. Any capital gain from the disposition of the transferred shares will be attributed to H and taxable as if he had in fact realized the gain himself. Thus, W's tax liability can come back to haunt H and should be taken into account in the property settlement. Otherwise, the transferor may subsequently be liable for tax that was not reflected in the division of the family assets.

A transferor can avoid liability for capital gains arising from a subsequent disposition of the transferred shares if he or she elects *jointly* with the transferee not to have the capital gain attributed to him. Clearly, it is best to have this joint election signed at the time of the property settlement so that both parties are fully aware of the income tax consequences of the settlement.

Thus, the ultimate decision as to the quantum of a settlement depends upon the availability of the capital gains exemption and the decision as to who will ultimately bear the tax liability for any capital gains that result. It is generally preferable for the transferor to trigger the maximum gain in his or her hands so as to utilize the full extent of his or her capital gains exemption. If the recipient spouse takes the shares at their fair market value, she or he will be more likely to consent to a joint election not to have any subsequent capital gains attributed to the transferor. Any subsequent capital gain would reflect her or his economic gain for which she or he should bear the burden of tax.

In the event that the transferor cannot claim the capital gains exemption because he or she has previously utilized the exemption in respect of other properties, he or she will be better off by deferring his or her tax liability. He or she can do this by rolling over the shares to his spouse at their adjusted cost base. In these circumstances, however, it is important that the parties make some adjustment for the subsequent tax liability that will be attributed to the transferor. In the above example, there is a potential capital gain of $1 million from the 50 transferred shares rolled over to W. The potential tax liability from the accrued gain is (approximately) $375,000. This liability will attach to H unless *both* parties jointly elect not to have the gain attributed to the transferor. In these circumstances, it is generally preferable for each party to keep their own one-half of the potential income tax liability that attaches to their respective shares.

(c) Timing

Timing is also an important element in a matrimonial settlement and can result in the claim for the exemption being granted or denied. In the above example, W can claim the capital gains exemption if she sells her 50 QSBC shares while she is separated from H provided that she and H owned the shares for 24 months between them. If, however, W acquires title to the shares *after* her divorce, she will not be able to claim the capital gains exemption if she disposes of the shares before owning them for at least 24 months. She will be restricted in her ability to access the exemption.

4. CHILD CARE EXPENSES

References:

ITA:

S. 63   Child Care Expenses

BULLETINS, CIRCULARS & RULINGS:

IT-495R   March 6, 1989   Child Care Expenses

(a) Policy

Expenditures on account of "child care" are personal expenses. Indeed, it is difficult to conceive of a more personal decision than to have a family.

The argument is made, however, that child care expenses are a necessary expenditure to allow parents (particularly women) to earn income in the marketplace. Proponents of this view adopt the "but for" test: But for the child care expenditure, the parent could not earn income. *Ergo*, the expenditure should be fully deductible for tax purposes. If carried to the extreme, the "but for" line of reasoning could extend to virtually any type of personal expenditure being justified as a business expense. As Professor McIntyre put it:[44]

> No one would suggest that the costs of caring for a pet elephant are deductible, simply because it is impossible to go to work and leave the baby elephant alone. What made child care expenses different was that a parent, after making the quintessential personal choice to have a child, could not undo that decision by giving the child to the local zoo. This difference, however, is not sufficient to convert child care into a business deduction.

The Act allows a measure of tax relief to parents who incur such expenses so that they may pursue financial gain outside of the home.[45] But the deduction is subject to strict limits. Child care expenses are not deductible as business expenses.[46] As we shall see in Chapter XII "Computation of Taxable Income", most "personal" expenses are eligible only for tax credits. Child care expenses, however, are *deductible* from

---

[44] M.J. McIntyre, "Evaluating the New Tax Credit for Child Care and Maid Services" (1977), *Tax Notes* 7 at 8.

[45] S. 63.

[46] *Symes v. The Queen*, [1994] 2 CTC 40, 94 DTC 6001 (S.C.C.).

income. Mr. David Dodge, Assistant Deputy Minister, Tax Policy and Legislation Branch, Finance Department explained the variance of policy as follows:[47]

> Turning to the first question, on why some deductions were converted to credits and not others, there are a large number of reasons, I think, that went behind the choices that were made, but for the particular ones that are not being converted to credits I can give the committee the main reasons why these were not converted to credit. The first one, the child care expense deduction, which has been left as a deduction, has been done pending government decisions on day care and what is to be done in day care policy. The decision was made not to make conversion at this time, pending the review of all the issues surrounding day care.
>
> I should note that there is no theoretical reason why it should be a deduction or why it should be a credit. You can argue on both sides. But the key reason it was not dealt with now is it was felt it should be dealt with and whatever decision is taken should be taken in the context of decisions related to the government's day care policy.

In most cases, the deduction for child care expenses is available only to working mothers. Only in extremely rare situations may a father claim a deduction for expenses in respect of child care.

(b) Definition of "Child Care Expense"

The phrase "child care expense" is restrictively defined. The following requirements qualify an expenditure as "child care expense":[48]

- The child care services must be provided in Canada;
- The child must be either under 14 years of age or, if older, physically or mentally infirm;
- The child care services must be provided to allow the taxpayer either to earn income from employment or business, to conduct funded research or to undertake an occupational training course;
- The services must be provided by a Canadian resident (other than the child's parents) for whom the taxpayer or his or her spouse does not claim a dependency credit; and
- The person providing the service must not be under 18 years of age if he or she is related to either the taxpayer or his or her spouse.

The Department also accepts certain incidental expenses as being on account of child care expenses. For example, the Department considers advertising expenses, agency placement fees and transportation expenses to locate, interview or bring to Canada a care-giver as "child care expenses".

---

[47] Testimony before the Commons Committee on Finance and Economic Affairs, August 24, 1987.

[48] Subs. 63(3) ("child care expense").

(c) Deductible Limits

(i) *Claim by Lower-Income Parent*

The general rule is that in two-parent families child care expenses are deductible only by the spouse with the lower income. It is only in exceptional circumstances that the higher-income spouse is entitled to the child care deduction.[49]

The parent with the lower income may claim a deduction equal to the least of:[50]

- the aggregate of
  - $5,000 multiplied by the number of eligible children (under 7 years of age or with severe and prolonged physical or mental impairment) for whom child care expenses have been paid; and
  - $3,000 per other eligible child under 15 years of age or with physical or mental impairment for whom child care expenses have been paid; or
- two-thirds of the taxpayer's "earned income" for the year.

(ii) *Claim by Higher-Income Parent*

The higher income parent may make a claim for child care expenses, but only if the other parent is:[51]

- In full time attendance at a designated educational institution;
- Certified by a medical doctor to be either mentally or physically ill and incapable of looking after children;
- Certified by a doctor to be mentally or physically ill to the extent that the person is confined to a bed or wheelchair or is a patient in a hospital for a period of at least two weeks in the year;
- Imprisoned for at least two weeks in the year; or
- Living apart from the taxpayer for at least 90 days in the year by reason of marriage breakdown.

In these circumstances the amount deductible by the higher income parent is restricted to the *least* of the following amounts:

- the aggregate of
  - $5,000 per eligible child under 7 years of age or with severe and prolonged physical or mental impairment; and
  - $3,000 per other eligible child for whom child care expenses were incurred;

---

[49] Subs. 63(2).

[50] Subs. 63(1).

[51] Para. 63(2)(*b*).

- two-thirds of the taxpayer's "earned income" for the year;
- the number of weeks the taxpayer was eligible to make the claim multiplied by the sum of the following:
  - $150 for each child under 7 years of age (or with severe impairment); and
  - $90 per other eligible child (under 15 years).

(iii) Nil Income

Where one of the parents has no income whatsoever ("nil income"), the other parent may claim the deduction for child care expenses even though he or she has the higher income. In other words, the question as to who has the higher income arises only if both parents have income. Subsection 63(2) does not apply where the supporting person has no income at all.[52]

5. MOVING EXPENSES

References:

ITA:

S. 62   Moving Expenses

BULLETINS, CIRCULARS & RULINGS:

IT-178R3   May 28, 1993   Moving Expenses

(a) General

Moving expenses are essentially personal expenses and are not incurred to earn income. Hence, in the absence of a provision to the contrary, a taxpayer would not be entitled to deduct moving expenses. To promote the mobility of labour in Canada, however, the Act allows taxpayers to deduct moving expenses in certain circumstances.

Moving expenses are deductible where the taxpayer:[53]

- Commences employment in Canada;
- Commences business in Canada; or
- Commences full time studies at a post-secondary educational institution.

Moving expenses are not deductible against investment income.[54]

---

[52] *McLaren v. M.N.R.*, [1990] 2 CTC 429, 90 DTC 6566 (*sub nom. The Queen v. McLaren*) (F.C.T.D.) ("income" implies existence of positive amount; concept does not apply where no income or zero income).

[53] Para. 62(1)(*a*); see also IT-178R3, "Moving Expenses" (May 28, 1993).

[54] *Schultz v. The Queen*, [1988] 2 CTC 293, 88 DTC 6468 (*sub nom. Schultz v. M.N.R.*) (F.C.T.D.).

(b) Eligibility for Deduction

An individual who moves to a place in Canada for the purpose of employment or to carry on a business may deduct moving expenses if he or she satisfies three conditions:[55]

1. Both the old residence and the new residence are in Canada;

2. The new residence is at least 40 km closer to the new employment or business location than was the old residence;[56] and

3. The move must be *related to* the commencement of the business, employment or studies.[57]

Students may deduct expenses of moving into or out of Canada.

The change in the taxpayer's residence must be by *reason* of the commencement of his or her business, employment or studies.

(c) Definition of "Moving Expenses"

The phrase "moving expenses" is not defined in the Act. Thus, any expenses which fall within the common understanding of "moving expenses" are deductible. One looks at the economic substance of the expenditure to determine whether it constitutes a "moving expense". The following expenditures are specifically included as deductible "moving expenses":[58]

- Travelling costs, including reasonable expenses for meals and lodging, incurred in the course of the move;

- Movers' costs, including storage charges;

- The cost of meals and lodging either near the old residence or near the new residence, for a period not exceeding 15 days;

- The cost of cancelling a lease;

- Selling costs[59] to dispose of the old residence; and

- Legal expenses, registration and land transfer taxes in respect of the acquisition of a new residence in the new location, if the taxpayer sells the old residence.

---

[55] Subs. 62(1).

[56] *Cameron v. M.N.R.*, [1993] 1 CTC 2745, 93 DTC 437 (T.C.C.) (40 kms is measured "as the crow flies"); *Haines v. M.N.R*, [1984] CTC 2422, 84 DTC 1375 (T.C.C.) (distance to be measured in straight line).

[57] *Kubryk v. M.N.R.*, [1987] 1 CTC 2125, 87 DTC 75 (T.C.C.).

[58] Subs. 62(3).

[59] *Collin v. M.N.R.*, [1990] 2 CTC 92, 90 DTC 6369 (*sub nom. The Queen v. Collin*) (F.C.T.D.) (lump sum paid by vendor to reduce purchaser's effective mortgage rate constituted "cost of selling property").

Expenditures not listed above are also deductible as "moving expenses" if they qualify under the general understanding of that phrase.

The following expenditures are not deductible:[60]

- Expenses reimbursed to the taxpayer by his or her employer;
- Expenses paid directly by the individual's employer;
- Expenses that are deductible under any other section of the Act;
- Expenses in excess of the individual's income in the year of the move from his or her employment or business at the new location; and
- Where the taxpayer is a student, any expenses in excess of the taxable portion of scholarships, fellowships, bursaries and research grants.

Moving expenses are generally deductible only in the year in which the move occurs. Expenses in excess of the deductible limit for a year may, however, be carried over and deducted against income in the following year. To be deductible in the year following the move, the expenses must not have been *deductible* in the year in which they were incurred. Thus, deductible moving expenses that are not claimed by the taxpayer in the year of the move are forever lost.[61]

Example XI.1

Horace Rumpole graduated from the University of Ottawa in 1995 and found a job as an accountant in Vancouver. He commenced his job on November 1, 1995, at a starting salary of $30,000 per year.

As part of his contract of employment, his new employers reimbursed Horace $2,000 to defray the cost of his move to Vancouver.

On October 1, 1995, Horace moved out of his Ottawa apartment and into a hotel, where he stayed for seven days. As a consequence of his move to Vancouver, Horace incurred the following expenditures:

• Lease cancellation costs on his apartment in Ottawa	$ 400
• Hotel and meal expenses in Ottawa and Vancouver (21 days)	2,100
• Airfare and ground transportation	600
• Movers' charges	3,500
• Storage charges	600
• Legal fees re acquisition of house in Vancouver	1,400
• Airfare for house-hunting trip in September 1995 and associated living costs	850

---

[60] Subs. 62(1).

[61] Para. 62(1)(*d*).

Example XI.1 (continued)

Unfortunately for Horace, there was a fire in his mover's premises in Vancouver, where his furniture and belongings were being stored. The storage company did not carry sufficient insurance, and Horace's goods, worth $7,000, were destroyed.

The maximum deduction available to Horace for 1995 is calculated as follows:

Eligible moving expenses under subsection 62(3):

Lease cancellation costs		$ 400
15 days hotel and meal expenses		
15/21 × $2,100		1,500
Airfare and ground transportation		600
Movers' charges		3,500
Storage charges		600
		$ 6,600
Reimbursed amount		$ (2,000)
Net moving expenses		$ 4,600
Income at new job		
2/12 × $30,000		$ 5,000
Maximum deduction		$ 4,600

Note:

1. The legal fees ($1,400) for the acquisition of the new house in Vancouver are not deductible as moving expenses, because the taxpayer did not dispose of a residence at his old location: paragraph 62(3)(f).

2. The "income at new job" limits deductibility of expenses: subparagraph 62(1)(f)(i). Horace worked for November and December, 1995, for 2/12 of his annual salary.

6. OTHER DEDUCTIONS

References:

ITA:

S. 61   Income-averaging Annuity Contracts

BULLETINS, CIRCULARS & RULINGS:

IT-99R4	August 2, 1991	Legal and Accounting Fees
IT-111R	February 27, 1984	Annuities Purchased from Charitable Organizations
IT-118R3	December 21, 1990	Alimony and Maintenance

IT-124R6	January 31, 1995	Contributions to Registered Retirement Savings Plans
IT-167R5	March 14, 1985	Registered Pension Funds or Plans — Employees' Contributions
IT-203	February 24, 1975	Interest on Death Duties
IT-301	April 6, 1976	Death Benefits — Qualifying Payments
IT-340R	September 26, 1984	Scholarships, Fellowships, Bursaries and Research Grants - Forgivable Loans, Repayable Awards, and Repayable Employment Income
IT-363R2	May 28, 1993	Deferred Profit Sharing Plans — Deductibility of Employer Contributions and Taxation of Amounts Received by a Beneficiary
IT-513	February 3, 1989	Personal Tax Credits
IT-517	March 28, 1989	Pension Tax Credit
IC 79-8R3	January 29, 1993	Forms to Use to Directly Transfer Funds to or Between Plans, or to Purchase an Annuity

Other deductions to be found in various sections of the Act or in Income Tax Rulings include the following:

Type of Deduction	Statutory References
Capital element of each annuity payment, if paid under a contract, will or trust	para. 60(*a*); IT-111R
Alimony payments	para. 60(*b*); IT-118R3
Maintenance payments	para. 60(*c*); IT-118R3
Repayment of support payments	para. 60(*c*.2)
Annual interest accruing on succession duties, inheritance taxes or estate taxes	para. 60(*d*); IT-203
Premium or payment under registered retirement savings plan	para. 60(*i*); IT-124R6

Type of Deduction	Statutory References
Transfer of superannuation benefits	para. 60(*j*); IT-167R5
Transfer of surplus under a defined benefit provision of a registered pension plan	para. 60(*j*.01)
Certain payments to registered pension plan	para. 60(*j*.02)
Repayment under prescribed statutory provision of pension benefits included in income	para. 60(*j*.03), 60(*j*.04);
Transfer of retiring allowances	para. 60(*j*.1); IT-337R2
Transfer to a spousal RRSP	para. 60(*j*.2)
Transfer of refund of a premium under a registered retirement savings plan	para. 60(*l*)
Estate tax applicable to property to which the taxpayer is the successor	para. 60(*m*)
Succession duties payable on property to which the taxpayer is the successor	para. 60(*m*.1)
Amount of overpayment of pension or benefits received by the taxpayer to the extent repaid by him or her	para. 60(*n*)
Amount in respect of fees or expenses in the preparation, institution or prosecution of an objection or an appeal regarding certain decisions	para. 60(*o*); IT-99R4
Amount in respect of legal fees to collect or establish a right to pension benefits	para. 60(*o*.1); IT-99R4
Overpayment of an allowance, to the extent repaid or recovered	para. 60(*p*)

Type of Deduction	Statutory References
Refund of income payments in an arm's length transaction	para. 60(*q*); IT-340R
Repayment in respect of a policy loan under a life insurance policy, to the extent the amount was included in income and not otherwise deductible	para. 60(*s*)
Certain amount included in income in respect of a retirement compensation arrangement	para. 60(*t*)
Amount included in income as proceeds from a disposition of an interest in a retirement compensation arrangement	para. 60(*u*)
Contribution to a provincial pension plan	para. 60(*v*)
Repayment of unemployment insurance benefit to the extent not otherwise deductible	para. 60(*v*.1)
Tax on old age security benefits	para. 60(*w*)
Refund of undeducted additional voluntary contributions to a registered pension plan in respect of services rendered	para. 60.2
Payments made as consideration for an income-averaging annuity contract	subs. 61(1)
Moving expenses	s. 62
Child care expenses	s. 63
Attendant care expenses incurred by taxpayer with mental or physical impairment	s. 64

SELECTED BIBLIOGRAPHY TO CHAPTER XI

General

Drache, A.B.C., "Charter Offers No Tax Breaks" (1991), 13 *Can. Taxpayer* 188.

Ross, David W., "Income Tax Consequences of Property Transfers and Payments Made as a Result of Marriage Breakdown and Divorce", in *Proceedings of 41st Tax Conf.* 12:1 (Can. Tax Foundation, 1989).

Alimony and Maintenance Payments

"Alimony and Maintenance Trusts" (1993), 8 *Money and Family Law* 81.

Arnold, Brian J., "Income Tax Consequences of Separation and Divorce", in *Proceedings of 29th Tax Conf.* 193 (Can. Tax Foundation, 1977).

Arnold, Brian J., "Tax Aspects of Alimony and Maintenance", 9:7 *Tax Planning and Management of Canadian Income Tax, Revised* (Toronto: Butterworth and Co. (Canada) Ltd., 1975).

Benotto, Mary Lou, "An Income Tax Checklist", [1993] *Special Lectures L.S.U.C.*, 297.

Barnett, Jim, "Alimony and Maintenance Payments" (1979), 112 *CA Magazine* 65.

Bowman, Stephen W. *et al.*, "The Taxability of Child Support Payments and the Charter of Rights and Freedoms" (1994), 42 *Can. Tax J.* 907.

Brahmst, Oliver C., "A Definition for the Term 'Spouse': Far-reaching Changes on the Horizons" (1993), 4 *Can. Current Tax* P1.

Cole, Stephen R. and Andrew J. Freeman, *Property Valuation and Income Tax Implications of Marital Dissolution* (Toronto: Thomson Professional Publishing Canada, 1991).

Coleman, Gene C. and Gary S. Opolsky, "Alimony Insurance Could Be Tax Deductible" (1992), 7 *Money and Family Law* 36.

Drache, A.B.C., "Post-Marital Trusts" (1984), 6 *Can. Taxpayer* 15.

Drache, A.B.C., "Reducing Expenses is Not Gaining Income" (1991), 13 *Can. Taxpayer* 156.

Drache, A.B.C., "Support Payments: All Tax Aspects Should Be Considered" (1991), 13 *Can. Taxpayer* 160.

Drache, A.B.C., "Tax Act Creates Problems in Joint Custody" (1992), 14 *Can. Taxpayer* 31.

Durnford, John W. and Stephen J. Trope, "Spousal Support in Family Law and Alimony in the Law of Taxation" (1994), 42 *Can. Tax J.* 1.

Financial Implications of Child Support Guidelines: Research Report (Ottawa: Department of Justice, Federal/Provincial Territorial Family Law Committee)

Goldstein, D. Lisa, "Until Death Do Us Part" (1991), 39 *Can. Tax J.* 513.

Goodison, Don, "Taxation of Maintenance Income" (1988), 22 *CGA Magazine* 18.

Goodison, Don, "Tax Forum — Deduction Denied" (1991), 25 *CGA Magazine* 17.

Harris, P.H., "Tax Treatment of Civil Litigation and Damage Awards, Alimony and Maintenance Payments" (1985), 6 *Advocates' Q.* 346.

Income Tax: Maintenance, Alimony and Employment Termination Benefits, Audio Archives of Canada, 1984.

Income Tax and Costs: Setting Aside Separation Agreements: Appeals, Choosing the Right Forum, Audio Archives of Canada, 1984.

Klein, William A., "Tax Effects of Nonpayment of Child Support" (1990), 45 *Tax Lawyer* 259.

Krishna, V., "Alimony and Maintenance, 'Payable on a Periodic Basis?'; Paragraphs 56(b), (c), (c.1) and 60(b), (c) and (c.1)" (1985), 1 *Can. Current Tax* J-83.

Krishna, V., "Spousal Payments" (1989), 23 *CGA Magazine* 44.

Krishna, V., "Structuring Matrimonial Settlements" (1990), 3:3 *Can. Current Tax* J-19.

Krishna, V., "To Love, Honor or Pay" (1990), 24 *CGA Magazine* 28.

Krishna, Vern, "Using the Capital Gains Exemption for Matrimonial Settlement" (1993), 4 *Can. Current Tax* C5.

Kroft, E.G., "Some Income Tax Considerations Relating to Support Payments Made After 1983" (1985), 4 *Can. J. Fam. L.* 499.

Maisel, Neil and Steve Z. Ranot, "Who Pays the Tax on Tax?" (1992), 7 *Money and Family Law* 93.

McCue, David J., "Maintenance and Alimony Payments" (1979), 13 *CGA Magazine* 27.

McGivney, Evelyn L., "Just the Tax Ma'am, Just the Tax!" (1991), 13 *Advocates Quarterly* 129.

McGregor, Gwyneth, "Alimony and Maintenance Payments" (1983), 5 *Can. Taxpayer* 169.

Penner, Michael S. and Neil Maisel, "Understanding Capital Gains and the Capital Gains Exemption" (1992), 7 *Money and Family Law* 9.

Penner, Michael S. and Steve Z. Ranot, "When is Alimony Paid?" (1992), 7 *Money and Family Law* 65.

Richards, Gabrielle M.R., "Support Payments: An Update" (1992), 3 *Can. Current Tax* J-115.

Roher, Bruce, "Transferring Shares to a Separated Spouse: Who Pays the Tax?" (1994), 9 *Money & Family Law* 75.

Sandler, Daniel, "Family Law and the Family Jewels" (1991), 39 *Can. Tax J.* 513.

Sands, H., and A. Zylberlicht, "The Tax Consequences of Support Payments" (1985), 118:6 *CA Magazine* 56.

"Second Time Around (The): How Much Does It Cost?", *Can. Tax Letter,* May 10, 1976.

"Sections 60(b) and (c) — A Trap for the Unwary" (1990), 44 DTC 7035.

Sherman, David M., "Till Tax Do Us Part: The New Definition of 'Spouse'" in *Report of Proceedings of 44th Tax Conf.* 20:1 (Canada Tax Foundation, 1992).

Shillington, Robert and Ellen Zweibel, *Child Support Policy: Income Tax Treatment and Child Support Guidelines* (Toronto: Policy Research Centre on Children, Youth and Families, 1993).

Shultz, Clayton G., "Income Tax Law and Policy Applicable to Periodic Maintenance and Division of Matrimonial Assets" (1987), 1 *Can. Fam. L.Q.* 293.

"Spousal Trust Rollovers" (1990), 44 DTC 7040.

"Taxation of Support Payments Simplified?" (1992), 7 *Money and Family Law* 75.

"The Written Separation Agreement: Not Quite Dead Yet!" (1993), 18 *Money and Family Law* 89.

Child Care Expenses

Arnold, B.J., "Section 63: The Deduction for Child Care Expenses" (1973), 21 *Can. Tax J.* 176.

Bittker, "A Comprehensive Tax Base As A Goal of Income Tax Reform" (1967), 80 *Harvard L.R.* 925.

Buckley, Melina, "Symes v. The Queen" (1993), 2 *National* No. 437.

Drache, Arthur B.C., "Child Care Expenses: Planning Leeway" (1983), 5 *Can. Taxpayer* 3.

Drache, Arthur B.C., "Sexism, Human Rights and Tax" (1979), 1 *Can. Taxpayer* 114.

Goodison, Don, "Child Care Expenses Deduction" (1988), 22 *CGA Magazine* 5.

Goodison, Don, "Nanny Means Business" (1989), 23 *CGA Magazine* 15.

Goodison, Don, "Tax Forum — Not a Business Expense" (1991), 25 *CGA Magazine* 20.

MacGowan, J.M., "The Tax Consequences of Marriage", in *Proceedings of 26th Tax Conf.* 275 (Can. Tax Foundation, 1974).

McAllister, Debra M., "The Supreme Court in Symes: Two Solitudes" (1994), 4 *N.J.C.L.* 248.

Young, Claire F.L., "Child Care: A Taxing Issue?" (1994), 39 *McGill Law J.* 539.

Young, Claire F.L., "Child Care and the Charter: Privileging the Privileged" (1994), 2 *Rev. Constit. Studies* 20.

Moving Expenses

Finlay, Joe, "Staggered Relocations May Disqualify Moving Expenses" (1991), 49 *Advocate* 358.

Goodison, Donald, "It's Your Move" (1979), 13 *CGA Magazine* 16.

Goodison, Donald, "Moving On" (1981), 15 *CGA Magazine* 37.

Hugget, Donald R., "Moving Employees" (1991), 19 *Can. Tax News* 44.

"Interest-Free Loans to Employees and Shareholders", *Can. Tax Letter,* November 10, 1977.

Lemon, K.W., "Tax Considerations Arising from Household Relocation" (1981), 46 *Bus. Q.* 86.

"On the Move?" (1979), 1 *Can. Taxpayer* 96.

"Reimbursement of Moving Expenses for Same City Move Could Be Tax Free" (1992), 4 *Tax. of Exec. Comp. and Retirement* 667.

Schnek, M., "Employee Relocation" (1981), 29 *Can. Tax J.* 71.

"Student Moving Expenses" (1983), 5 *Can. Taxpayer* 151.

Thomas, Richard B., "A Hole That You Could Drive a Moving Van Through" (1990), 38 *Can. Tax J.* 937.

Other Deductions

Beach, Wayne G., "Tax Aspects of Registered Retirement Savings Plans", 9:30 *Tax Planning and Management* of *Canadian Income Tax, Revised* (Toronto: Butterworth and Co. (Canada) Ltd., 1978).

Boyle, "The Treatment of RRSP Proceeds on Maturity" (1979), 27 *Can. Tax J.* 68.

Budd, John S., "Two Unlikely Havens from Capital Gains Tax" (1979), 112 *CA Magazine* 70.

Clare, James L., and Paul F. Della Penna, "Tax Aspects of Employee's Pension Plans", 9:28 *Tax Planning and Management of Canadian Income Tax, Revised* (Toronto: Butterworths and Co. (Canada) Ltd., 1977).

Colley, Geoffrey M., "What's New in Personal Investment" (1977), 110 *CA Magazine* 63.

Connors, Raymond J., "DPSPs — The Ideal Tax Shelter for Employers and Employees" (1982), 115:2 *CA Magazine* 50.

Dancey, Kevin J., "Specific Expenditures: Timing and Deductibility", *Corp. Mgmt. Tax Conf.* 116 (Can. Tax Foundation, 1981).

Drache, Arthur B.C., "Estate Planning: Depreciable Property" (1980), 2 *Can. Taxpayer* 22.

Drache, Arthur B.C., "Religious School Decision" (1981), 3 *Can. Taxpayer* 33.

Drache, Arthur B.C., "Single Premium Deferred Annuities" (1981), 3 *Can. Taxpayer* 27.

Drache, Arthur B.C., "Tax Planning for Higher Education" (1981), 3 *Can. Taxpayer* 44.

Drache, Arthur B.C., "Tuition Fee Deductibility" (1980), 2 *Can. Taxpayer* 208.

Eng, Susan, and Goodman, "Education Trusts and Other Provisions for Education Expenses" (1979-81), 5 *E. & T.Q.* 246.

Farres, Alan E., "RRSPs: The Tax Shelter That Wasn't Meant To Be" (1982), 115:4 *CA Magazine* 48.

Finkelstein, David N., "Tax Problems in Estate Planning for the Corporate Executive", in *Proceedings of 33rd Tax Conf.* 952 (Can. Tax Foundation, 1981).

Fisher, G.B., "Early Retirement Tax Considerations" (1983), 31 *Can. Tax J.* 828.

Griffith, Thomas D., "Theories of Personal Deductions in Income Tax" (January 1989), 40 *Hastings L. J.* 343.

Jarman, Robert E., "Administrative and Tax Problems with Self-Administered RRSP's" (1975), 2 *E. & T.Q.* 105.

Knechtel, Ronald C., "Federal Income Taxation of Life Insurance Policyholders under the Present Law and under the Current Proposals", in *Proceedings of 29th Tax Conf.* 612 (Can. Tax Foundation, 1977).

Krishna, V., "Registered Retirement Savings Plans (RRSP's) — Availability of Funds for Judgment Creditors" (1984), 1 *Can. Current Tax* J-43.

Lengvari, George F., "Deferred Annuities as Tax Shelters" (1978), 111 *CA Magazine* 90.

Le Rossignol, Dan G., "Stock Dividends and Stock Options" (1979), 112 *CA Magazine* 67.

MacNaughton, Alan, "New Income Tax Rules for Holders of Life Insurance Policies and Annuities" (1983), 31 *Can. Tax J.* 921.

McGregor, Gwyneth, "Forward Averaging" (1983), 5 *Can. Taxpayer* 7.

McReynolds, D. Shawn, "Sheltering RRSP Assets from Creditors on Death" (1982-84), 6 *E. & T.Q.* 106.

Murray, L.C., "Statutory Deferred Income Plans", *Corp. Mgmt. Tax Conf.* Management Tax Conf. 121 (Can. Tax Foundation, 1979).

"1979 Year-End Planning for Individuals", Can. Tax Letter, November 30, 1979.

Rea, Samuel A., "Registered Retirement Savings Plans as a Tax Expenditure" (1980), 28 *Can. Tax J.* 459.

Schmidt, Rosemary, "Students and Taxation" (1991), 39 *Can. Tax J.* 673.

Young, Clair F.L., "Deductibility of Entertainment and Home Office Expenses: New Restrictions To Deal with Old Problems?" (1989), 37 *Can. Tax J.* 227.

CHAPTER XII

TAXABLE INCOME

1. GENERAL

To this point, we have examined the rules determining liability for tax and the rules for calculating net income. Now, we look at the rules that determine "taxable income"[1] earned by a resident of Canada. In Chapter XIII "Computation of Tax Payable", we will review the computation of tax payable.

Taxable income is the base on which tax is calculated. Canadian residents are subject to tax on their *taxable income* for the year.[2] Subject to treaty provisions, non-residents are taxable on taxable income earned in Canada during a taxation year.[3]

There are two particularly controversial issues in designing an appropriate structure to determine the taxable base.

1. What relief, if any, should be provided for individual and personal circumstances?

2. Should the relief take the form of a deduction from income or a credit against taxes payable?

(a) "Taxable Income"

As used in the *Income Tax Act*, "taxable income" is simply a mathematical measure of the taxable base. A resident's "taxable income" is his or her net income plus or minus the adjustments and deductions in Division C. Thus, "taxable income" is the mathematical residue of net income adjusted by various items contained in Division C.

The rationale for the Division C deductions is varied and, in some cases, quite controversial. It would certainly be easier to calculate tax on net income. An income tax calculated by reference only to net income might, however, create serious inequities between taxpayers of differing financial ability.

It is easy to see that taxpayers who have the same amount of *net* income do not necessarily have equal amounts of disposable income with which to pay their tax. For example, consider two individuals, each of whom earns $50,000: An unmarried person with no dependants and a married person with a family of six, one of whom is seriously

---

[1] Subs. 2(2); Div. C (ss. 110-114.2).

[2] Subs. 2(1); see also Chapter III "Who is Taxable".

[3] Subs. 2(3). A non-resident's taxable income is determined by reference to the rules in Div. D (ss. 115–116).

ill and requires expensive medication. It is clear that these two individuals have different abilities to pay tax. Should the individual with substantial financial responsibilities be allowed a measure of tax relief to ease the burden of his or her responsibilities?

The adjustments in Division C are of three types: (1) those available only to individuals; (2) those available only to corporations; and (3) those which are available to both individuals and corporations.

(b) Deduction or Credit?

References:

ITA:

Sub. 2(2)   Definition of "Taxable Income"

Subs. 110(1)   Deductions Permitted

Should relief for persons in different financial circumstances be provided through tax deductions or tax credits? A tax deduction is a deduction from income in computing taxable income. The saving which results from a deduction is measured by multiplying the deduction by the taxpayer's marginal tax rate. For example, a deduction of $1,000 reduces tax by $450 if the taxpayer's marginal rate is 45 per cent, and by $300 if the tax rate is 30 per cent. Thus, the higher the marginal tax rate, the more valuable the deduction to the taxpayer and the more expensive it is to the government's treasury.

A tax credit is a reduction of the tax that would otherwise be payable. The savings resulting from a tax credit are constant, regardless of the taxpayer's marginal tax rate. For example, a tax credit of $500 reduces tax by that amount, regardless of whether the taxpayer's marginal tax rate is 45 per cent or 30 per cent. Hence, tax credits distribute tax savings equally.

A tax credit is subtracted directly from the amount of tax payable rather than from income. Thus, each individual achieves the same saving regardless of his or her income level or marginal tax rate. For example, the basic tax credit applies to all individuals regardless of their income level. Hence, a person earning $100,000 per year receives the same basic credit as a person earning $8,000 per year.

2. CHARITABLE DONATIONS

References:

ITA:

S. 110.1   Deduction for Gifts

BULLETINS, CIRCULARS & RULINGS:

IT-297R2   March 21, 1990   Gifts in Kind to Charity and Others

IT-407R3   April 27, 1990   Disposition after 1987 of Canadian Cultural Property

(a) General

The tax system provides financial incentives for taxpayers to contribute to charitable, philanthropic, and other public service organizations.

The rationale for providing tax relief for charitable donations is to encourage private financial support of philanthropic activities that are beneficial to the community at large and might otherwise require direct financial support from public funds. The incentives are justified on the basis of social policy, but they have a cost to the federal and provincial treasuries.

The nature and extent of the incentives depend upon two criteria: (1) The type of taxpayer, and (2) The dollar amount contributed.

(b) Individuals

changed 50% now

An individual may claim a tax credit for donations of up to 20 per cent of his or her net income. The rate at which the credit may be claimed depends upon the amount donated. The credits are linked to the lowest and highest marginal tax brackets: 17 per cent on the first $200 of the amount of gifts; 29 per cent on any excess.[4]

(c) Corporations

A corporation is entitled to a *deduction* for its charitable donations.

Gifts to charitable and certain other organizations are deductible by a corporation up to an annual maximum of 20 per cent of its income for the year.[5] The 20 per cent limitation does not apply to gifts to the Crown.[6]

Donations in excess of 20 per cent of net income may be carried forward for five years and, in any of those years, deducted to the extent that they were not deducted in a previous year.

(i) Criteria for Deduction

There are two substantive criteria for determining the deductibility of a donation:

1. Does the contribution constitute a gift? and

---

[4]   Subs. 118.1(3).

[5]   Para. 110.1(1)(*a*).

[6]   Para. 110.1(1)(*b*).

2. Was the gift to a registered charity or other public service organization?

(ii) *What Constitutes a Gift?*

The word "gift" is not defined in the Act. A gift is a voluntary transfer of property for no consideration. The word "gift" is given its ordinary meaning. As Deane J. said:[7]

> The word "gift" . . . is intended to bear the meaning which it bears as a matter of ordinary language. . . . [I]t is not to be assumed that its ambit can properly be defined, with a lawyer's or logician's precision, by reference to a number of unqualified propositions or tests. . . .

(A) Voluntary Transfer

Generally speaking, a "gift" is a voluntary and gratuitous transfer of property from one person to another; it may be conditional but, once the condition is satisfied, it is not revocable.[8] A transfer of property is a gift where it is made:[9]

- by way of benefaction,[10]
- without exchange for material reward or advantage, and
- without contractual obligation.

---

[7] *Leary v. Fed. Commr. of Taxation* (1980), 32 ALR 221 at 241 (F.C.A.).

[8] "Gift" is defined in *Halsbury's Laws of England*, 4th ed., Vol. 20, §1 as follows:
> A gift *inter vivos* may be defined shortly as the transfer of any property from one person to another gratuitously while the donor is alive and not in expectation of death. . . .
In *Black's Law Dictionary*, 4th ed., (1968), "gift" is defined as:
> [a] voluntary transfer of personal property without consideration.
and:
> [b] parting by owner with property without pecuniary consideration . . .
The *Shorter Oxford Dictionary* defines "giving" as
> . . . [a] transfer of property in a thing, voluntarily and without any valuable consideration . . .
See also *Commr. of Taxation (Cth.) v. McPhail* (1968), 41 ALR 346 at 348 (Aust. H.C.), where Owen J. said,
> [b]ut it is, I think, clear that to constitute a "gift," it must appear that the property transferred was transferred voluntarily and not as the result of a contractual obligation to transfer it and that no advantage of a material character was received by the transferor by way of return....
This definition was approved by the Federal Court in *The Queen v. Zandstra*, [1974] CTC 503, 74 DTC 6416 (F.C.T.D.).

[9] *Leary v. Fed. Commr. of Taxation, ante*, at 243 (quoted with approval by the Federal Court of Appeal in *The Queen v. McBurney*, [1985] CTC 214, 85 DTC 5433 (F.C.A.)).

[10] *Collector of Imposts (Vic.) v. Cuming Campbell Invt. Pty. Ltd.* (1940), 63 CLR 619 (Aust. H.C.) (transfer by way of benefaction being "essential idea" of gift, *per* Dixon, J. at 642). Some courts speak of a "detached and disinterested generosity"; see, e.g., *Commr. v. Lo Bue*, 351 US 243 at 246 (1956) (gift of affection, respect, admiration, charity or like impulses); *Robertson v. U.S.*, 343 US 711 at 714 (U.S., Utah, 1952); *C.I.R. v. Duberstein*, 363 US 278 at 285 (1960); see also, *Savoy Overseers v. Art Union of London*, [1896] AC 296 at 308 and 312 (H.L.) (charitable donation made where donor not looking "for any return in the shape of direct personal advantage", *per* Lord McNaghten); *Collector of Imposts (Vic.) v. Cuming Campbell Investments Pty. Ltd., ante*, at 641.

The essence of a gift is that it is a transfer without *quid pro quo,* a contribution motivated by detached and disinterested generosity.[11]

(B) No Consideration

A person cannot be considered to have made a gift where he or she receives valuable consideration equal to his or her "donation".[12] For example, payment for a dinner organized by a charity may involve both charitable and non-charitable elements.[13] Regardless of the form and documentation of the arrangements, it is the substance of the contribution that determines whether it is a gift or a disguised payment for services. But there is no litmus paper test: One looks to the substance of the contribution.[14]

Although a payment made pursuant to a contractual obligation to the donee is not a gift, the absence of a contractual obligation does not necessarily imply that the payment is a gift. Note also, a contractual obligation between the donor and a third party does not necessarily deprive a payment of its character as a gift. For example, a contract between A and B that each will contribute an amount to a registered charity does not *per se* disqualify their contributions as gifts.

(iii) Blended Payments

Blended contributions should be broken down into its component parts. For example, the admission price to a charity event may cover the costs of goods and services rendered to the patron (such as food and entertainment) and a premium intended as a gift.[15]

Similarly, a global payment to a charity that offers both religious and secular education might comprise a payment for tuition fees and a gift for charitable purposes. The tuition component is a personal expenditure; the gift for charitable purposes is deductible as a donation. The allocation between the deductible and the non-deductible

---

[11] *Tite v. M.N.R.,* [1986] 2 CTC 2343, 86 DTC 1788 (T.C.C.).

[12] *Tite v. M.N.R., ante* (taxpayer's claim for charitable donation denied where evidence demonstrated that payment to acquire print equal to value of work).

[13] *Burns v. M.N.R.,* [1988] 1 CTC 201, 88 DTC 6101 (F.C.T.D.) (taxpayer's payments to amateur athletic association not "gifts" because taxpayer expected and received benefit in return for payments).

[14] See, e.g., *C.I.R. v. Duberstein, ante,* at 289, *per* Justice Brennan:
    Decision of the issue presented in these cases must be based ultimately on the application of the fact-finding tribunal's experience with the mainsprings of human conduct to the totality of the facts of each case. The nontechnical nature of the statutory standard, the close relationship of it to the data of practical human experience, and the multiplicity of relevant factual elements, with their various combinations, creating the necessity of ascribing the proper force to each, confirm us in our conclusion that primary weight in this area must be given to the conclusions of the trier of fact.

[15] *Aspinall v. M.N.R.,* [1970] Tax ABC 1073, 70 DTC 1669.

portions is a question of fact that requires an analysis of the services rendered in exchange for the payment.[16]

(iv) Eligible Organizations

Donations to the following organizations are deductible to the extent of the annual maximum limit:[17]

- Registered charities,
- Registered Canadian amateur athletic associations,
- Resident housing corporations that provide low-cost housing accommodations for the aged,
- Canadian municipalities,
- The United Nations and its agencies,
- Prescribed foreign universities that admit Canadian students,[18] and
- Certain foreign charitable organizations to which the federal government has contributed in the year or in the preceding year.

The deduction for charitable donations must be supported by receipts that disclose prescribed information.[19]

(v) Charities

References:

ITA:

Subs. 149.1(1)   Definitions: Charities

BULLETINS, CIRCULARS & RULINGS:

IC 87-1   February 25, 1987   Registered Charities — Ancillary and
                                        Incidental Political Activities

A "charity" can be either a charitable organization or charitable foundation.[20]

---

[16] *The Queen v. McBurney*, [1985] CTC 214, 85 DTC 5433 (F.C.A.).

[17] Para. 110.1(1)(a).

[18] Reg. 3503.

[19] Reg. 3501.

[20] Subs. 149.1(1) ("charity").

A "charitable organization" is an organization that devotes itself to charitable activities[21] and a "charitable foundation" is, more specifically, a trust or corporation that operates exclusively for charitable purposes.[22]

(A) Charitable Purposes

It is now well accepted that "charity" in its legal sense comprises the four divisions set out by Lord McNaghten in *Commrs. for Special Purposes of the Income Tax v. Pemsel*:[23]

1. Trusts for the relief of poverty,
2. Trusts for the advancement of education,
3. Trusts for the advancement of religion, and
4. Trusts for other purposes beneficial to the community.

In addition, however, the organization must also have a charitable purpose that is within "the spirit and intendment" of the Preamble to the *Charitable Uses Act*.[24]

At first blush, the fourth division appears to be a broad, inclusive category for all sorts of beneficent activities. In fact, this category is fairly narrowly construed because of the additional requirement that the charitable purpose must meet the spirit and intendment of the *Charitable Uses Act*, a statute enacted in 1601. Stated in modern English, but reflecting social perceptions of a bygone era, the statute's list of charitable purposes read as follows:[25]

> The relief of aged, impotent, and poor people; the maintenance of sick and maimed soldiers and mariners, schools of learning, free schools, and scholars in universities; the repair of bridges, ports, havens, causeways, churches, seabanks, and highways; the education and preferment of orphans; the relief stock, or maintenance of houses of correction; marriage of poor maids; supportation, aid, and help of young tradesmen, handicraftsmen, and persons decayed; the relief or redemption of prisoners or captives; and the aid or ease of any poor inhabitants concerning payment of fifteens, setting out of soldiers, and other taxes.

Thus, only activities that are beneficial to the community *and* that come within the spirit and intendment of the above Preamble are recognized as "charitable."[26]

---

[21] Subs. 149.1(1) ("charitable organization").

[22] Subs. 149.1(1) ("charitable foundation").

[23] *Commrs. for Special Purposes of Income Tax v. Pemsel*, [1891] AC 531 at 583 (H.L.). These categories are well accepted in Canadian law; see *Guar. Trust Co. v. M.N.R.*, [1967] SCR 133 at 141, [1966] CTC 755 at 759, 67 DTC 5003 at 5005.

[24] 1601 (43 Eliz. I, c. 4).

[25] *Per* Slade J. in *McGovern v. A.G.*, [1982] Ch. 321 at 332.

[26] See, e.g., *National Anti-Vivisection Soc. v. I.R.C.*, [1948] AC 31 (H.L.) (main object political; unclear whether public benefit advanced if such scientific research curtailed); *Re Strakosch*, [1949] Ch. 529 (C.A.) (gift must be beneficial to community in way which law regards as charitable).

The double-headed aspect of the qualification causes difficulty for organizations that seek registration as a charity. Revenue Canada typically applies the tests in a rigid and dogmatic manner, without accommodation or adaptation to the nuances of modern Canadian society. But, as Lord Wilberforce said, "the law of charity is a moving subject".[27] What must be taken into account is not the literal wording of the Preamble, but its scope as determined by decisions. These decisions have kept the law of charities moving as new social needs arise or old ones become obsolete. As Lord Upjohn put it:[28]

> This so-called fourth class is incapable of further definition and can to-day hardly be regarded as more than a portmanteau to receive those objects which enlightened opinion would regard as qualifying for consideration under the second heading.

Thus, the Preamble of 1601 should not be applied *verbatim* as only for the benefit of the aged, impotent, and poor maids, but should be read in the context of the contemporary needs of Canadian society.[29]

It is clear, however, that despite some relaxation of the rules for registration, the basic focus remains: Are the activities of a public character or are they "member-oriented"?[30]

(B) Tax-exempt Status

A registered charity is a tax-exempt organization. Thus, the tax subsidy in respect of registered charities is double-barrelled: The charity is tax exempt and its benefactors obtain a tax deduction or credit.

The tax exemption is justifiable on the basis that it encourages private organizations to engage in philanthropic activities that would otherwise fall to the public sector. To control the subsidy, the tax system imposes stringent requirements on charitable registration and annual accounting.

(C) Political Activities

An organization is not a charity if its main or principal object is political.[31] For example, tenants and ratepayer groups formed with the purpose of lobbying governments to act in support of societal change do not qualify as charitable

---

[27] *Scottish Burial Reform & Cremation Soc. v. Glasgow Corp.*, [1968] AC 138 at 154 (H.L.).

[28] *Scottish Burial Reform & Cremation Soc. v. Glasgow Corp.*, *ante*, at 150.

[29] See, for example, *Native Communications Soc. of B.C. v. M.N.R.*, [1986] 4 CNLR 79 (F.C.A.).

[30] *Nat. Model Rairoad Assn. v. M.N.R.*, [1989] 1 CTC 300, 89 DTC 5133 (*sub nom. Seventh Div., Pac. N.W. Region, Nat. Model Railroad Assn. v. M.N.R.*) (F.C.A.).

[31] *Re Patriotic Acre Fund* (1951), 1 WWR (NS) 417 at 427 (Sask. C.A.):
> . . . the Court has no means of judging whether a proposed change in the law will or will not be for the public benefit and therefore cannot say that a gift to secure the change is a charitable gift.

organizations if their primary focus is political activity.[32] Similarly, anti-pornography groups that are, in effect, "political" organizations lobbying for legislative change under the guise of education are denied registration as charitable organizations.[33]

Charities that engage in non-partisan political activities that are "ancillary and incidental" to their charitable purposes or activities can maintain registration as tax-exempt organizations.[34] For example, a charity may use mass mailings or media campaigns to influence public opinion or government policy. More active involvement in partisan political activities, however, endanger a charity's registration.[35]

It is not always easy to draw the line between political activity and public education. Generally speaking, there is a reluctance to recognize organizations that engage in lobbying for legislative change. The following, however, would amount to "political purposes" and disqualify an organization's charitable status:[36]

- The furthering of the interests of a particular political party;
- The procuring of changes to the laws of the country;
- The procuring of changes to the laws of a foreign country;
- The procuring of a reversal of government policy or of particular decisions of governmental authorities in the country; or
- The procuring of a reversal of government policy or of particular decisions of governmental authorities in a foreign country.

(vi) Donations of Capital Property
Reference:
BULLETINS, CIRCULARS & RULINGS:

IT-288R2   January 16, 1995   Gift of Capital Properties to a Charity and
                                            Others

Where a person donates capital property to a registered charity, it may designate the value of the gift at any amount between its fair market value and adjusted cost base. The designated value then becomes the taxpayer's proceeds of disposition. Thus, a

---

[32] *N.D.G. Neighbourhood Assn. v. Revenue Can. Taxation Dept.*, [1988] 2 CTC 14, 88 DTC 6279 (F.C.A.) (tenants' association denied registration as charity).

[33] *Positive Action Against Pornography v. M.N.R.*, [1988] 1 CTC 232, 88 DTC 6186 (F.C.A.).

[34] Subs. 149.1(6.1).

[35] Para. 149.1(6.1)(c).

[36] *McGovern v. A.G.*, [1982] Ch. 321, [1982] 2 WLR 222 (Ch. D.).

taxpayer has some flexibility in determining the amount of its capital gain on the disposition of the property.[37]

(d) Valuation

(i) Fair Market Value

Having determined that a contribution to an eligible organization qualifies as a gift, the next task is to attach a value to the gift. Gifts are generally valued at their fair market value at the time that the property is transferred to the donee.

The fair market value of an asset is its exchange value.[38] Where there is a regular and efficient market for the asset (for example, widely-held shares on a stock exchange), its trading price is probably the best, though not necessarily the only, measure of fair market value.[39] Where there is no efficient market for the asset, it is necessary to determine fair market value through other criteria, such as, earnings value, liquidation value, replacement value, etc.

The "fair market value" of an asset for tax purposes is the highest price that it "might reasonably be expected to bring if sold by the owner in the normal method applicable to the asset in question, in the ordinary course of business in a market not exposed to any undue stresses, and composed of willing buyers and sellers dealing at arm's length and under no compulsion to buy or sell".[40] Thus, the focus of the determination of fair market value is on an efficient, normal and knowledgeable market.

(ii) Expert Evidence

Valuation is a sophisticated art that calls for the expertise and judgement of people trained in its discipline. It is also an art that is vulnerable to manipulation and the expert testimony of professional valuators should be carefully considered. Expert evidence should, in Lord Wilberforce's words, ". . . be, and should be seen to be, the independent product of the expert, uninfluenced as to form or content by the exigencies of litigation".[41] Unfortunately, some experts have a propensity for moulding their opinions to identify with, and accommodate, their client's positions. As Adrian Keane says in the *Modern Law of Evidence*:[42]

---

[37] Subs. 110.1(3). A non-resident can also make the designation in respect of certain types of real property situated in Canada.

[38] See generally, *Re Mann*, [1972] 5 WWR 23; affd [1973] 4 WWR 223; affd [1974] 2 WWR 574 (S.C.C.) [B.C.].

[39] *Re Mann*, ante, at 27.

[40] *Henderson v. M.N.R.*, [1973] CTC 636, 73 DTC 5471; affirmed [1975] CTC 485, 75 DTC 5332 (F.C.A.).

[41] *Whitehouse v. Jordan*, [1981] 1 WLR 246 at 256 (H.L.).

[42] Keane, *Modern Law of Evidence* (London: Butterworths, 1985), at 377.

... the danger is particularly acute in the case of opinions expressed by expert witnesses, of whom it has been said, not without some sarcasm, "it is quite often surprising to see with what facility and to what extent, their views can be made to correspond with the wishes or the interests of the parties who call them".

Valuation experts find it equally difficult to distance themselves from the purse-strings determining their livelihood. As Professor Bonbright said:[43]

... few, if any, appraisers can take an unbiased position when they take the witness stand under an engagement from one of the contesting parties ... a court must choose between the tremendous errors implicit in a capitalization of audited reported earnings, and the tremendous errors implicit in a capitalization of prejudiced prophecies.

(e) Registration as Charity

To receive the benefits of tax-exempt status, a charity must be registered with the Minister of National Revenue. To secure or maintain its registration, a registered charity must be operated exclusively for charitable purposes and must not carry on any business that does not qualify as a "related business".

The Minister may revoke the registration of a charitable organization if it carries on any business other than a business related to that charity.[44] A "related business" includes "a business that is unrelated to the objects of the charity if substantially all of the people employed by the charity in the carrying on of that business are not remunerated for such employment".[45]

Where a charity carries on a business, there are, in effect, two separate tests that must be satisfied in order to acquire or maintain its registration. (1) The taxpayer must operate exclusively for charitable purposes; and (2) The business must be a "related business".

(i) Related Business

How do we determine whether a business is related or unrelated to the charitable organization? Do we look at the nature of the business activities to determine whether or not they are of a type which flow naturally from the charity's purposes and activities, or do we look to the use to which the profits of the business are put? It appears that the latter test may determine whether or not a business is "related" to a charity. It remains, unclear, however, how far the destination of funds test can be applied.[46]

---

[43] Bonbright, *Valuation of Property* (New York: McGraw-Hill, 1937), vol. 1, at 251.

[44] Para. 149.1(2)(*a*).

[45] Subs. 149.1(1) ("related business").

[46] *Alta. Inst. on Mental Retardation v. The Queen*, [1987] 3 FC 286, [1987] 2 CTC 70, 87 DTC 5306 (F.C.A.); leave to appeal to S.C.C. refused 87 NR 397. See *Br. Launderer's Research Assn. v. Hendon Borough Rating Authority*, [1949] 1 KB 462; followed by Supreme Court of Canada in *Guar. Trust Co. v. M.N.R.*, [1967] SCR 133, [1966] CTC 755, 67 DTC 5003.

In *AIMR*, Heald J., speaking for the majority, said:[47]

> [W]here *all* of the monies received are dedicated to the charitable purposes for which the appellant was incorporated and where the business aspect of the operation is merely incidental to the attainment of its charitable objects, the appellant can, indeed, be said to be operating exclusively for charitable purposes.

The majority also favoured the destination of funds test as ". . . the clear intention of Parliament to recognize the contemporary reality insofar as the fundraising activities of modern charitable organizations are concerned".[48] The concept of charity must be kept moving with changing social needs.[49] In Justice Heald's words:[50]

> If the operation of a cafeteria on the premises of an art gallery or the operation of a parking lot adjacent to and on premises owned by a hospital, for example, can be said to be related businesses even though the cafeteria and the parking lot may be operated by concessionaires for profit, then surely an activity such as that of this [taxpayer] must be in the same category.

Thus, charities may carry on any type of business so long as the profits of the business are ultimately diverted to charitable purposes.

3. RESIDENTS OF REMOTE REGIONS

References:

ITA:

S. 110.7   Residing in Prescribed Zone

REGULATIONS:

7303.1   "Prescribed Northern Zone" and "Prescribed Intermediate Zone"

Individuals who reside in prescribed isolated posts in the near and far north are entitled to special deductions when computing taxable income.[51] These special deductions are intended as relief from the high cost of living in remote regions.

The deduction is the lesser of:

- 20 per cent of the taxpayer's net income for the year; and

---

[47] *Alta. Inst. on Mental Retardation v. The Queen, ante,* [1987] 2 CTC at 75, 87 DTC at 5310.

[48] *Alta. Inst. on Mental Retardation v. The Queen, ante,* [1987] 2 CTC at 77, 87 DTC at 5306.

[49] *Native Communications Soc. of B.C. v. M.N.R.,* [1986] 4 CNLR 79 (F.C.A.).

[50] *Alta. Inst. on Mental Retardation v. The Queen, ante,* [1987] 2 CTC at 77.

[51] S. 110.7. In certain circumstances, the deduction may apply to residents of any isolated or sparsely populated area of the country.

- $7.50 multiplied by the number of days in the year that the individual resided in the area plus an additional $7.50 for each day that the taxpayer maintained a dwelling in the area.

Individuals employed in a prescribed area are also entitled to special deductions in respect of travel expenses. These deductions are of two types: (1) Travel for medical purposes and (2) General travel. Travel for trips to obtain medical services is deductible where such services are not available locally. Employees may claim a deduction for up to two trips per calendar year for other purposes.[52]

The full amounts of the maximum deductions described above are available only to residents of the "prescribed northern zone". The deductions are reduced by 50 per cent for residents of the "prescribed intermediate zone".

4. LOSSES

References:

ITA:

S. 3	Income for Taxation Year
S. 4	Income from a Source
S. 111	Losses

(a) General

The use of the fiscal year as the unit of time to measure income can create problems for taxpayers whose incomes fluctuate between years. For example, a taxpayer who earns income in one year which is followed by an equal loss in the next would, in the absence of relieving provisions, face financial hardship as a result of paying tax in the first year without relief in the second. Consider the following scenario:

Taxpayer	Year 1	Year 2	Year 3	Total
A	$ 120,000	$ (40,000)	$ (80,000)	NIL
B	$ (80,000)	$ 120,000	$ (40,000)	NIL
C	$ (40,000)	$ (80,000)	$ 120,000	NIL

It is obvious that the economic well-being of all three taxpayers is identical over the three-year period. There are, however, important differences if the three taxpayers are taxed on an annual basis. Taxpayer A must pay tax on income of $120,000 in year 1, Taxpayer B in year 2, and Taxpayer C in year 3. In the absence of special provisions which allow losses from one period to be used in another period, taxpayers could end up paying tax on illusory income.

---

[52] Para. 110.7(1)(*a*); subs. 110.7(3).

A taxpayer may offset losses from one source against income from other sources in the same year.[53] There are, however, several restrictions. For example, capital losses may be offset only against capital gains; listed personal property losses may be used only against listed personal property gains.[54]

Losses that are not used in the year in which they occur may, within certain limits, be used to offset income in other years.

(b) Types of Losses

References:

ITA:

S. 111	Deductibility of Various Losses
Subs. 39(1)	Meaning of Capital Gain and Loss

BULLETINS, CIRCULARS & RULINGS:

IT-232R2	December 30, 1987	Non-Capital Losses, Net Capital Losses, Restricted Farm Losses, Farm Losses and Limited Partnership Losses — Their Composition and Deductibility in Computing Taxable Income

Given the compartmentalized structure of the Act, the characterization of losses is as important as the characterization of income. There are different rules for each type of loss. Some losses (such as non-capital losses) are more valuable to a taxpayer than others (such as capital losses) because the entire loss may be written off against all sources of income.

But capital losses have a longer shelf life than non-capital losses. Thus, the first step in determining the tax treatment of a loss is to determine the nature and character of the loss. There are five major categories of losses:

1. Non-capital losses; — *business losses.*
2. Net capital losses;
3. Restricted farm losses;
4. Farm losses; and
5. Limited partnership losses.

---

[53] S. 3.

[54] Para. 3(*b*); subs. 41(2).

Capital losses are further subdivided into three categories:

1. personal-use property losses,
2. listed personal property losses, and
3. business investment losses.

A taxpayer's loss from a source first offsets other sources of income for the purpose of calculating *income* for the current year. Losses that cannot be used in the current year to reduce income from other sources may be carried back or forward to other years and deducted in computing the taxpayer's *taxable income* for those years. Thus, current year losses are deductible in the computation of net income. Losses carried over to other years (whether prior or subsequent) are deductible only in the computation of taxable income.

(i) Non-Capital Losses

A non-capital loss (loosely referred to as a "business loss") is deductible from income in any of the three taxation years preceding, and the seven taxation years following, the year in which the loss is incurred.[55] Thus, non-capital losses may be used to offset income over a period of 11 years: the year of the loss, three years prior to the loss, and seven years subsequent to the loss.

Farmers and fishers may use losses over a period of 14 years: the year of the loss, three years prior to the loss and ten years subsequent to the loss.[56]

(A) Meaning

A taxpayer's non-capital loss includes the following amounts:[57]

- A loss from any business (including losses from a farming or fishing business);
- A loss from the ownership of any property;
- A loss from any office or employment;
- An allowable business investment loss for the year;
- Any used portion of the deduction for Part VI.1 special taxes on dividends;
- An amount deductible by a life insurer in computing taxable income in respect of taxable dividends received from taxable Canadian corporations;[58]
- One-quarter of the amount included in the taxpayer's income as an employee benefit in respect of the exercise or disposition of prescribed shares;[59]

---

[55] Para. 111(1)(a).

[56] Para. 111(1)(d).

[57] Subs. 111(8) ("non-capital loss").

[58] Subs. 138(6).

[59] Para. 110(l)(d).

- One-quarter of the amount included in the taxpayer's income as an employee benefit in respect of a stock option plan issued by a Canadian-controlled private corporation;[60]
- One-quarter of the amount included in the taxpayer's income as prospectors' shares;[61]
- An amount deductible by a corporation in computing its taxable income in respect of dividends received from other corporations;[62]
- One-quarter of the amount included in the taxpayer's income in respect of certain deferred profit-sharing benefits;[63]
- An amount deducted from taxable income in respect of a home relocation loan;[64]
- A net capital loss carryover deduction made by the taxpayer for the taxation year;[65]
- An amount claimed as a capital gains exemption;[66]
- Certain amounts deducted under paragraph 110(1)(f), such as amounts exempt under a tax convention, social assistance payments, and workers' compensation; and
- Amounts added to a corporation's taxable income for foreign tax deductions.[67]

The following amounts are then deducted from the aggregate of the above:

- the amount determined under paragraph 3(c);
- any accumulated averaging amount which the taxpayer elects to include in income;
- the taxpayer's farm loss;
- an amount deducted under subsection 111(10) (fuel tax rebate); and
- the amount by which non-capital loss must be reduced under section 80 (debt forgiveness).

---

[60] Para. 110(1)(d.1).

[61] Para. 110(1)(d.2).

[62] S. 112; subs. 113(1).

[63] Para. 110(1)(d.3).

[64] Para. 110(1)(j).

[65] Para. 110(1)(b). This provision allows non-capital losses to be reinstated where they have reduced taxable capital gains in a year and net capital losses from other years are carried over to that year.

[66] S. 110.6.

[67] S. 110.5.

Thus, a taxpayer's losses from non-capital sources are initially applied against income in the *current* year. The residue less any portion that is a farm loss becomes the taxpayer's non-capital loss. There are special rules for farm losses.[68]

A non-capital loss cannot be increased by the deductions permitted under subdivision e of Division B (sections 60–66.8). These deductions may, however, reduce other income in the year. For example, an individual who suffers a business loss in a particular year cannot increase his or her loss carryforward by including in the non-capital loss amounts paid as alimony. If, however, the individual was also employed in the same year, he or she could use any alimony payments to reduce or eliminate his or her employment income and carry forward his or her business loss.

(B) Non-residents

Reference:

BULLETINS, CIRCULARS & RULINGS:

IT-262R   August 30, 1985   Losses of Non-Residents and Part-Year
                                          Residents

A non-resident taxpayer may not include as a non-capital loss any losses from businesses that are not carried on in Canada.[69]

A resident taxpayer may not deduct non-capital losses incurred while he or she was a non-resident and had no Canadian source of income.[70] Thus, a corporation which becomes resident in Canada cannot import its non-capital losses accumulated while it was a non-resident corporation without any Canadian income source.

(C) Order of Deductions

Non-capital losses must be deducted in the order in which they are incurred.[71]

(D) Transfer of Losses

A loss is generally deductible only by the taxpayer who incurs it. For example, where an individual incurs a non-capital loss, the loss cannot be claimed by another taxpayer to whom the business is sold. Similarly, a sole proprietor cannot transfer the losses of the proprietorship on selling his or her business to a corporation. This is so even if the individual owns all the shares of the corporation that acquires the business.

Since a corporation is a legal entity in its own right, any losses incurred by the corporation belong to it, and it is only in very rare circumstances that its losses can be

---

[68] Para. 111(1)(*d*).

[69] Subs. 111(9).

[70] *Oceanspan Carriers Ltd. v. The Queen*, [1987] 1 CTC 210, 87 DTC 5102 (F.C.A.).

[71] Subpara. 111(3)(*b*)(i).

used by another corporation. Note, however, that even though a corporation owns its losses, a change of control of the corporation may extinguish its non-capital losses.[72]

(ii) Net Capital Losses

References:

BULLETINS, CIRCULARS & RULINGS:

IT-134R	November 24, 1975	Capital Gains and Losses on Disposition of Business Property by an Individual
IT-328R3	February 21, 1994	Losses on Shares on Which Dividends Have Been Received

Allowable capital losses may only offset taxable capital gains. Listed personal property losses may be used only to offset gains on listed personal property and not against other capital property.[73]

(A) Meaning

A taxpayer's "net capital loss" is made up of:[74]

• The excess of its allowable capital losses over taxable capital gains, and

• Any unutilized allowable business investment losses previously included in its non-capital losses in respect of which the carryover period expired in the year.

Net capital losses may be carried back three years and carried forward indefinitely. Hence, they may have an unlimited life. They may, however, be applied only against capital gains in other years.[75]

(B) Technical Adjustments

Net capital losses are adjusted to account for the difference between the inclusion rate for capital gains for the year in which the loss was incurred and the particular year in which the loss is actually deducted. The purpose of this adjustment is to ensure that a capital loss offsets an equivalent amount of capital gain, regardless of the year in which it is ultimately deducted. The adjustment compensates for the difference in inclusion rates prior to 1988 (one-half of capital gains), those in 1988 and 1989 (two-

---

[72] Subs. 111(5).

[73] Para. 3(b).

[74] Subs. 111(8)("net capital loss"). The taxpayer's net capital loss is also reduced as required by s. 80 (debt forgiveness). Capital losses which also qualify as "allowable business investment losses" are initially treated as non-capital losses and may be written off against income from any source. If they cannot be used as non-capital losses within the seven year carryforward period, they are added to net capital losses and may be carried forward indefinitely.

[75] Para. 111(1)(b).

thirds of capital gains), and inclusion in income after 1990 (three-quarters of capital gains).

The adjustments are implemented by applying a ratio to the net capital loss claimed. The net capital loss that a taxpayer may claim in a particular year is increased when the loss is carried forward from a loss year in which the inclusion rate was lower than the inclusion rate prevailing at the time of the deduction. Similarly, the net capital loss claimed is reduced for the purposes of the deduction if the loss is carried back from a loss year in which the inclusion rate is greater than the rate prevailing in the year for which the loss is claimed.

(iii) Farm Losses

References:

ITA:

S. 31   Farming Losses

BULLETINS, CIRCULARS & RULINGS:

IT-322R   October 25, 1978   Farm Losses

There are three types of farm losses:

1. Business "farm losses";
2. Restricted farm losses; and
3. Hobby farm losses.

Where a taxpayer in the *business* of farming incurs a "farm loss", the loss is subject to the rules generally applicable to business losses.[76] A taxpayer's "farm loss" is the excess of his or her losses from farming and fishing over any income from these sources.[77]

Farm losses may be carried back three years and forward ten years and applied against income from any source.[78]

---

[76] Para. 111(1)(*d*) and subs. 111(8) ("farm loss"); *Brown v. The Queen*, [1975] CTC 611, 75 DTC 5433 (F.C.T.D.).

[77] Subs. 111(8) ("farm loss"). For the meaning of "farm loss", see *Moldowan v. The Queen*, [1977] CTC 310, 77 DTC 5213 (S.C.C.) (three classes of farmers; tests for "chief source of income"); *Graham v. The Queen*, [1983] CTC 370, 83 DTC 370; affirmed [1985] 1 CTC 380 (*sub nom. The Queen v. Graham*), 85 DTC 5256 (F.C.A.) (although Hydro employee, taxpayer's main preoccupation farming); *Hadley v. The Queen*, [1985] 1 CTC 62, 85 DTC 5058 (F.C.T.D.) (sizeable investment in farming made employment more a source of investment finance; losses allowed); *Bender v. M.N.R.*, [1986] 1 CTC 2437, 86 DTC 1291 (T.C.C.) (four-pronged test for deductibility of farm losses); *Crouch v. The Queen*, [1986] 2 CTC 246, 86 DTC 6453 (F.C.T.D.) (no reasonable expectation of profit from horse breeding operation).

[78] Para. 111(1)(*d*).

(iv) Restricted Farm Losses

A taxpayer whose chief source of income is neither farming nor a combination of farming and some other source of income is limited to $8,750 in any year in respect of "farming losses".[79] Any loss in excess of the limit becomes the taxpayer's "restricted farm loss" for the year and can be carried over to future years.[80]

A "restricted farm loss" is a farming loss suffered by a taxpayer who carries on business with an expectation of profit, but whose *chief* source of income is *neither* farming nor a combination of farming and some other source of income.[81]

A restricted farm loss may be carried back three years and forward ten years.[82] The amount of a restricted farm loss that is deductible in any year is limited to the amount of the taxpayer's income from farming for the year.[83]

Where a farmer disposes of farmland and has unclaimed restricted farm losses which were not deductible in prior years, he or she may add the unclaimed losses to the adjusted cost base of the land. Thus, any capital gain on the eventual disposition of the land will be reduced by the amount of the unclaimed losses.[84]

A hobby farm loss is a loss from a farming operation that is conducted without a profit motive or a reasonable expectation of profit.[85]

(v) Allowable Business Investment Losses
Reference:
BULLETINS, CIRCULARS & RULINGS:

IT-484R   May 5, 1989   Business Investment Losses

A "business investment loss" is a hybrid loss:[86] A capital loss that is deductible from income from *any* source.

(A) Capital Loss

A business investment loss is a particular type of capital loss. Thus, characterization of a loss as a capital loss is a necessary precondition to its

---

[79] Subs. 31(1).

[80] Subs. 31(1.1).

[81] *Moldowan v. The Queen*, [1977] CTC 310, 77 DTC 5213 (S.C.C.).

[82] Para. 111(1)(c).

[83] Para. 111(1)(c).

[84] Para. 53(1)(i).

[85] See, generally, Chapter VI "Business and Investment Income: General".

[86] Para. 39(1)(c); subs. 111(8) ("non-capital loss")(i).

characterization as a business investment loss. A capital loss that is deemed to be nil (for example, a superficial loss) cannot give rise to a business investment loss.[87]

A "business investment loss" is a loss incurred on a disposition of capital property under the following conditions:[88]

- The capital property is a share of a "small business corporation" or a debt owed to the taxpayer by such a corporation;
- Where the taxpayer is a corporation and the capital property is a debt, the debtor corporation is at arm's length from the taxpayer; and
- The shares or debt are, unless subsection 50(1) applies, disposed of to a person dealing with the taxpayer at arm's length.

(B) Hybrid Nature of Loss

An allowable business investment loss is a hybrid form of loss that has features of both business and capital losses: It results from a disposition of capital property, but it may be used to offset income from *any* source.[89]

An unused portion of an allowable business investment loss is considered to be a non-capital loss, and may be applied against income from any source.

Since an unused allowable business loss is treated as a non-capital loss, it has a limited life. It may be carried back three years and carried forward only for seven years.[90] As previously noted, net capital losses may be carried back three years and carried forward indefinitely.

An allowable business loss that is not used within the seven year carryforward period applicable to non-capital losses reverts to a net capital loss.[91] Thereafter, it may be carried forward indefinitely but applied only against taxable capital gains.

(C) Transfer to Controlled Corporation

Where a taxpayer transfers capital property or eligible capital property to a corporation which, immediately after the transfer, is controlled by the taxpayer, or controlled by a related person, any capital loss resulting from the transfer is added to the adjusted cost base of the shares owned by the taxpayer after the transfer.[92] In these circumstances, the capital loss is deferred until such time as the taxpayer disposes of his or her shares.

---

[87] Para. 40(2)(*g*).

[88] Para. 39(1)(*c*); see also subs. 248(1) ("small business corporation").

[89] S. 3.

[90] Para. 111(1)(*a*), subs. 111(8) ("non-capital loss").

[91] Subs. 111(8) ("net capital loss").

[92] Subs. 85(4).

Where the loss is a business investment loss, it is reduced by any increase in the adjusted cost base of the shares as a result of the application of the above rule.[93] The purpose of this rule is to prevent double deduction of the loss by the taxpayer.

(vi) Net Capital Losses in Year of Death

A taxpayer's net capital losses may be deducted against net taxable capital gains in the year of his or her death and in the immediately preceding year. Unused capital losses can be carried back and written off against income in the year before the taxpayer's death, but only to the extent that such losses exceed any capital gains exemption claimed by that person in his or her lifetime.[94]

Capital losses in excess of capital gains realized by a deceased's estate within its first taxation year may also be written off *as if* they had been realized by the deceased in the year of his or her death. Thus, the deceased's estate is given credit for the amount of income tax that the deceased would have saved in the year of his or her death if the excess capital losses had been sustained by him or her rather than by his or her estate.

This relief is available only where the legal representative of the deceased makes an election and designates the amount of the excess capital losses to be carried back. The amount designated is deemed not to have been a capital loss of the estate.[95] The representative must file an amended return for the deceased taxpayer for the year in which he died.

(vii) Limited Partnership Losses

A taxpayer may carry forward limited partnership losses indefinitely and apply them against income from any source. The deduction for limited partnership losses is restricted to the amount that the taxpayer is "at risk" in the partnership in the year.[96]

(c) Change of Corporate Control

References:

ITA:

Subs. 85(4)	Disposition to Controlled Corporation
Subs. 249(4)	Year-End on Change of Control
Subs. 256(7)	Control Deemed Not to be Acquired

---

[93] Subpara. 39(1)(c)(v).

[94] Subs. 111(2).

[95] Subs. 164(6).

[96] Para. 111(1)(e).

BULLETINS, CIRCULARS & RULINGS:

IT-302R23   February 28, 1994   Losses of a Corporation — The Effect that Acquisitions of Control, Amalgamations and Windings-up have on their Deductibility — After January 15, 1987

(i) General

The Act discourages taxpayers from trading in "loss companies", that is, corporations with accumulated losses purchased and sold primarily for the sake of tax, rather than business, advantages. It does this by streaming the carryforward of losses when control of a corporation changes hands.[97] In the absence of these rules, a taxpayer could purchase a "loss company", inject a new profitable business into it and shelter the profits of the new business from tax.[98]

(ii) Meaning of "Control"

(A) *De Jure* Control

"Control" implies ownership of sufficient shares to carry with them the ability to cast a majority of the votes on election of a board of directors. Thus, at common law, control means *de jure* and not *de facto* control. As Jackett P. said in *Buckerfield's*:[99]

> [M]any approaches might conceivably be adopted in applying the word "control" in a statute such as the *Income Tax Act* . . .
>
> It might, for example, refer to control by "management", where management and the Board of Directors are separate, or it might refer to control by the Board of Directors. The kind of control exercised by management officials of the Board of Directors is, however, clearly not intended by [s. 256] which contemplates control of one corporation by another as well as control of a corporation by individuals. . . . The word "control" might conceivably refer to *de facto* control by one or more shareholders whether or not they hold a majority of the shares. I am of the view, however, that in [s. 256 of] the *Income Tax Act*, the word "control" contemplates the right or control that rests in ownership of such a number of shares as carries with it the right to a majority of the votes in the election of the Board of Directors.

The lack of power to elect a majority of the board of directors, however, does not necessarily imply a lack of control; control can also be determined by some other tests like, for example, the power to wind up the corporation.[100]

(B) Statutory Exceptions

There are circumstances, however, in which the Act deems control of a corporation not to have changed. For example, a person who acquires shares of a corporation is

---

[97] Subss. 111(4), 111(5).

[98] See also, Chapter XXV "Purchase and Sale of a Business".

[99] *Buckerfield's Ltd. v. M.N.R.*, [1964] CTC 504 at 507, 64 DTC 5301 at 5303 (Ex. Ct.).

[100] *The Queen v. Imp. Gen. Properties Ltd.*, [1985] 2 CTC 299, 85 DTC 5500 (S.C.C.).

deemed *not* to have acquired control by virtue of the acquisition, redemption or cancellation of shares, if immediately before such transaction he or she was related to the acquired corporation.[101]

(C) Restrictions on Losses

There are stringent restrictions on the use of accumulated losses following a change of corporate control. The general thrust of these rules is to limit transfers of losses between unrelated corporate taxpayers and to discourage business arrangements which are nothing more than "loss-trading" or "loss-offset" transactions. For example, in the typical "loss-trading" transaction, a taxpayer would sell property with an accrued gain (profit) and use an intermediary corporation with accumulated losses as a conduit. Any gain from the transaction could then be offset against the intermediary's losses to reduce taxable income.

(D) Non-capital Losses

A corporation may carry forward its non-capital and farm losses following a change of control, but only if it satisfies two conditions: Prior year's losses are deductible against income from the *same* business if the corporation which sustained the loss continues to carry on business for profit or with a reasonable expectation of profit. The acquired business must be maintained with a reasonable expectation of profit *throughout the year* following the time of its acquisition.[102]

The acquired business by which the losses were originally sustained must be continuously maintained for profit or with a reasonable expectation of profit. The substitution of a new or similar, but more profitable, business does not satisfy this requirement.

Following a change of control, a corporation may only deduct its non-capital and farm losses from prior years to the extent of the aggregate of:[103]

- Its income for the year from the acquired business; and,
- Any other business income substantially derived from the sale, lease, rental, or development of properties, or the rendering of services, which are similar to those properties sold, leased, rented, or developed or the services rendered, as the case may be, in the course of carrying on the *particular* business in question, prior to the change in control.

---

[101] Para. 256(7)(*a*).

[102] Subpara. 111(5)(*a*)(i).

[103] Subpara. 111(5)(*a*)(ii); *Yarmouth Indust. Leasing Ltd. v. The Queen*, [1985] 2 CTC 67, 85 DTC 5401 (F.C.T.D.) ("control" includes both direct and indirect control).

(E) Deemed Year-end

A corporation is deemed to have a year-end immediately before its control changes hands.[104] Any losses incurred in the year in which control changes are subject to the restrictions on loss carryovers. Thus, a change of corporate control can speed up the timetable for the use of losses.

(F) Capital Losses

The restrictions on capital losses are even more stringent than for non-capital losses.

Net capital losses for preceding years may not be deducted in computing its income for the year of change of control or in any subsequent year. Further, losses incurred in years subsequent to the change of control cannot be carried back to offset income earned in the years prior to the change of control.[105]

Following a change of corporate control, the corporation is deemed to have realized any losses accrued on its *non-depreciable* capital properties.[106] Its deemed capital losses then become subject to the restrictions on the carryover of capital losses. The adjusted cost base of the non-depreciable capital properties is reduced by the amount of the capital loss.[107] The purpose of these rules is to make it less attractive to trade in corporations that are pregnant with capital losses.

5. CAPITAL GAINS EXEMPTION

References:

ITA:

S. 110.6   Capital Gains Exemption

BULLETINS, CIRCULARS & RULINGS:

IT-451R   March 25, 1987   Deemed Disposition and Acquisition on Ceasing to Be or Becoming Resident in Canada

(a) Purpose

The capital gains exemption was introduced in 1985. The exemption is intended to encourage risk-taking and stimulate investment in small businesses while assisting farmers and broadening the participation of individuals in the equity markets. In short,

---

[104] Subs. 249(4).

[105] Subs. 111(4), see also Chapter XXV "Purchase and Sale of a Business".

[106] Para. 111(4)(*d*).

[107] Para. 53(2)(*b*.2).

the exemption was intended to ". . . unleash the full entrepreneurial dynamism of individual Canadians".[108]

Capital gains from dispositions of shares of farm properties and qualified small business corporations are exempt from tax to a maximum of $500,000. Thus, at a tax rate of 50 per cent, the full exemption for taxable capital gains of $375,000 is worth $187,500 in tax savings.

(b) Structure

The capital gains exemption is available in respect of two categories of capital properties:

1. "Qualified farm property";[109] and
2. Shares of qualified small business corporations.[110]

An individual's exemption depends upon three principal factors:

1. his or her residence;
2. the type of capital property that gives rise to the gain; and
3. the net cumulative amount of his or her investment income and financing expenses in the year in which the gain is realized.

These three factors determine who is eligible for the exemption and how much of the gain may be sheltered from tax in a particular year.

(c) Eligible Taxpayers

(i) Residents

Only individuals resident in Canada may claim the exemption. An individual may claim the exemption if:

- He or she is resident in Canada *throughout* the year; or
- He or she is resident in Canada for part of the year, if he or she was resident in Canada throughout the year preceding or the year following the year in which the gain is realized.[111]

A trust is not entitled to the exemption. A trust may, however, flow through its capital gain to its beneficiaries by making a special designation.[112]

---

[108] Budget speech, May 23, 1985.

[109] Subs. 110.6(2).

[110] Subs. 110.6(2.1).

[111] Subs. 110.6(5).

[112] Subs. 104(2.1).

A spouse trust may claim a deduction in respect of its eligible taxable capital gains in the year in which the spouse dies.[113]

(ii) Deemed Residents

For the purposes of the exemption, an individual who was resident in Canada at any time in a taxation year is deemed to have been resident in Canada throughout the year if he or she was resident in Canada throughout either the year immediately preceding, or the year immediately following the taxation year.[114] Thus, a person who becomes a non-resident in a particular year is entitled to the exemption if he or she was resident in Canada throughout the year immediately preceding it.

An immigrant may claim the exemption on becoming resident in Canada if he or she remains a resident throughout the following year.

(d) Eligible Properties

The exemption is available in respect of $500,000 of capital gains from the disposition of shares of a "qualified small business corporation" or "qualified farm property".

(e) Restrictions

Generally speaking, an individual (other than a trust) resident in Canada may claim an exemption equal to the least of the following three amounts:

1. His or her unused capital gains exemption of $500,000;
2. His or her annual gains limit for the year; and
3. His or her cumulative gains limit at the end of the year.

(f) Farm Property

The general purpose of the farm property rules is to limit the exemption to taxpayers who are engaged in the business of farming for a minimum stipulated period of time and to circumstances in which farming constitutes the taxpayer's main source of income.

(i) "Qualified Farm Property"

A taxpayer is entitled to the exemption in respect of "qualified farm property". The phrase "qualified farm property" refers to farm property held personally or through a partnership or family farm corporation.

---

[113] Subs. 110.6(12), paras. 104(4)(a), (a.1).

[114] Subs. 110.6(5).

More specificàlly, an individual's "qualified farm property" includes any real property which has been used by:[115]

- The individual;
- His or her spouse;
- His or her child or parent;
- The individual's family farm corporation; or
- A family farm partnership in which he or she has an interest.

The property must have been used to carry on the business of farming in Canada. The business may be or may have been carried on by the individual who owns the farm property, that person's spouse or children, a family farm corporation, or, family farm partnership in which the individual, or his or her spouse, children, or parents have an interest. For the purposes of these rules, grandchildren qualify as children.

(ii) The Business of Farming

To qualify as farm property eligible for the exemption, the property must be used or must have been used in the course of carrying on the business of farming in Canada. What constitutes "the business of farming" is a question of fact.

(iii) Additional Tests

The following two tests must also be met:[116] (1) The property must have been owned by the individual, his or her spouse, children or parents, a family farm partnership, or a personal trust *throughout* the 24 months immediately preceding its disposition, (2) During a period of at least two years while the property was so owned, the individual's gross revenue from the property used in farming must have exceeded his or her income from all other sources for the year.

(g) Small Business Corporation Shares

The exemption is also available in respect of capital gains realized from the disposition of qualified small business corporation ("QSBC") shares.

A QSBC share is a share of a "small business corporation", which is defined as follows:[117]

- a Canadian-controlled private corporation all or most of the fair market value of the assets of which is attributable to assets used principally in an active business carried on primarily in Canada; and

---

[115] Subs. 110.6(1) ("qualified farm property").

[116] Subs. 110.6(1) ("qualified farm property")(*a*).

[117] Subs. 248(1); see also, subs. 110.6(1) ("qualified small business corporation share").

- a Canadian-controlled private corporation the assets of which, throughout a period of 24 months immediately preceding the corporation's disposition, have not been owned by any person other than the individual claiming the exemption, or by a person or partnership related to him or her.

Shareholders of newly incorporated small business corporations are, however, entitled to claim the exemption, even where the corporation has existed for less than 24 months. Thus, a sole proprietor can dispose of his or her active business by transferring all of the business to a corporation and then selling the shares of the corporation rather than the assets of the business.

(h) Reporting Requirements

A taxpayer who claims a capital gains exemption is required to disclose the amount claimed on his or her tax return for the year. In other words, a taxpayer may not simply omit net taxable capital gains from income on the basis that they are not, in effect, subject to tax. Failure to file an income tax return within one year of its due date or failure to report the capital gain in income may nullify the exemption.[118] The taxpayer can only be denied an exemption, however, if the Minister of National Revenue can establish that failure to file the return or to disclose the amount of the capital gain was attributable to the taxpayer's gross negligence or that the taxpayer "knowingly" failed to conform to the reporting requirements.

(i) Anti-avoidance Rules

Given that the capital gains exemption is a generous tax preference, taxpayers have an incentive to convert income that is taxable into non-taxable capital gains. There are several anti-avoidance provisions in place in anticipation of such manoeuvres. Some of the provisions are very specific. Others are broad provisions that cast a wide net. Indeed, in some cases, the net has been cast so widely that it is impossible to determine the types of transactions it might catch.

The primary focus of the anti-avoidance provisions, however, is the prevention of three types of tax avoidance:

1. Conversion of capital gains earned by corporations into capital gains earned by individuals ("Type A");

2. Conversion of dividend income into capital gains ("Type B"); and

3. Disproportionate allocations of gains between taxpayers.

---

[118] Subs. 110.6(6).

(i) Type A Conversions

As already noted, only individuals may claim the exemption in respect of capital gains. Consequently, there is every incentive to convert potential corporate capital gains into gains attributable to individual shareholders.

The exemption may not be claimed by an individual in respect of a gain realized as a consequence of a corporation or partnership's acquisition of property at a price that is significantly less than its fair market value.[119] For example, where a corporation disposes of a property by transferring it to another corporation for less than its fair market value, any capital gain from a sale of the shares of either corporation is not eligible for the exemption if the dispositions of property are part of a series of transactions. This rule applies where the transformed gain *results* from a "series of transactions or events".[120] It is not necessary to establish any intention or purpose on the part of the taxpayer to transform the gain. The sequence of events must, however, be sufficiently connected to constitute a "series of transactions".

(ii) Type B Conversions

The second category of anti-avoidance provisions is concerned with the conversion of dividend income into capital gains. In the simplest case, the value of shares may be enhanced by restricting the dividend payout on the shares. In these circumstances, the taxpayer's claim for an exemption in respect of the gain from a disposition of the shares may be denied.[121]

More specifically, an individual may not claim the capital gains exemption in respect of gains realized on shares where:[122]

- It is reasonable to conclude that a significant part of the gain is attributable to non-payment of dividends on the shares; or

- The dividends paid in the year *or in any preceding taxation year* were less than 90 per cent of the average annual rate of return on the shares for that year.

The individual need not have an intention to convert dividend income into capital gains. It is sufficient that there is a causal connection between significant enhancement in the value of the shares and inadequacy of the payment of dividends. The onus is then on the individual to provide an alternative explanation for the enhanced value of the shares.

---

[119] Para. 110.6(7)(*b*).

[120] See subs. 248(10) (defining "series of transactions").

[121] Subs. 110.6(8).

[122] Subs. 110.6(8).

This rule does not apply to prescribed shares.[123] A "prescribed share" is one that is commonly referred to as a "common share", that is, a share not restricted to a maximum dividend, or to a maximum amount upon winding up of the corporation. Shares issued as part of an estate freeze[124] and shares issued by mutual fund corporations are also prescribed for the purposes of this rule.[125]

The average annual rate of return on a share is the rate of return that a "knowledgeable and prudent investor" would expect to receive on such a share.[126] In determining the rate, any delay, postponement, or failure to pay dividends in respect of the shares is to be ignored. Similarly, variations in the amount of dividends payable from year to year are to be ignored.

Finally, the return is to be determined on the assumption that the shares may only be disposed of for proceeds equal to their issue price. These assumptions are intended to provide a nearly mechanical formula for determining a rate of return without regard to all the factual financial nuances that might otherwise influence the return on shares.

6. ADJUSTED TAXABLE INCOME

High income taxpayers may be subject to an "alternative minimum tax" ("AMT") even though they do not have any taxable income.[127] The federal alternative minimum tax is payable at a flat rate of 17 per cent on "adjusted taxable income". Combined with a provincial tax rate of approximately 50 per cent, the AMT is 26 per cent.

The alternative minimum tax was introduced in 1986 for the purpose of improving tax equity and making the tax system "fairer". There was a perception that the tax was necessary because many high income taxpayers were not paying their fair share of taxes.

The alternative minimum tax applies only to individuals and trusts (other than mutual fund trusts); it does not apply to corporations. AMT is an alternative tax. Thus, it only applies if the amount computed under it exceeds the individual's regular tax calculated on regular taxable income. The AMT is a substitute for the regular tax.

Generally speaking, a taxpayer's "adjusted taxable income" for the alternative minimum tax is his or her regular taxable income plus certain add-backs in respect of tax preference items.[128] These tax preference items are deductions which might be

---

[123] Reg. 6205.

[124] Reg. 6205(2)(a).

[125] Reg. 6205(2)(b).

[126] Subs. 110.6(9).

[127] Subss. 127.5-127.55.

[128] S. 127.52.

used to shelter income. For example, the exempt portion of capital gains, contributions to registered retirement savings plans, deferred savings plans, registered pension plans, write-offs for resource expenses, Canadian films, multiple-unit residential buildings, and stock option deductions are added back into taxable income.

In computing "adjusted taxable income" for AMT purposes, a taxpayer is entitled to a basic exemption of $40,000.[129]

---

[129] S. 127.53.

SELECTED BIBLIOGRAPHY TO CHAPTER XII

General

McQuillan, Peter E., "Computation of Income for Tax Purposes", in *Proceedings of 44th Tax Conf.* 5:27 (Canada Tax Foundation, 1992).

Swanson, Julie Anne, "The Alternative Minimum Tax" (Don Mills, Ont.: CCH Canadian, 1991).

Personal Exemptions

"A Green Wedding" (1981), 3 *Can. Taxpayer* 77.

Arnold, Brian J., "Income Tax Consequences of Separation and Divorce", in *Proceedings of 29th Tax Conf.* 193 (Can. Tax Foundation, 1977).

Brown, C., and F. Woodman, "Taxation of the Family" (1981), *Can. Taxation* 987.

Dulude, Louise, "Taxation of Spouses: A Comparison of Canadian, American, British, French and Swedish Law" (1985), 23 *Osgoode Hall L. J.* 129.

"Non-Resident Dependants" (1980), 2 *Can. Taxpayer* 149.

Novek, Barbara L., "Sector Specific Tax Relief for Canadian Residents Working Overseas" (1993), 5 *Tax of Executive Compensation and Retirement* 808.

Charitable Donations, Medical Expenses, etc.

Anderson, Alec R., "The Statutory Non-charitable Purpose Trust: Estate Planning in the Tax Havens" in *Equity, Fiduciaries and Trusts* (Ont.: Carswell, 1993).

Arbuckle, J.E., "Investment in Art — For Pleasure and Profit" (1980), 54 *Cost & Mgt.* 46.

Bale, G., "Construing a Taxing Statute or Tilting at Windmills: Charitable Donation Deduction and the Charter of Rights and Freedoms" (1985), 19 *E.T.R.* 55.

Bromley, E. Blake, "A Response to 'A Better Tax Administration in Support of Charities'" (1991), 10 *Philanthrop. No. 3* 3.

Bromley, E. Blake, "Parallel Foundations and Crown Foundations" (1993), 11 *Philanthrop. No. 4* 37.

"Charity Lotteries" (1983), 5 *Can. Taxpayer* 112.

"Corporate Donations" A Double Winner" (1980), 2 *Can. Taxpayer* 200.

Dickson, M.L., and Lawrence C. Murray, "Recent Tax Developments" (1985), 5 *Philanthrop.* 50, 52.

Dickson, M.L., and Laurence C. Murray, "Recent Tax Developments" (1986), 6 *Philanthrop.* 40, 59.

Dickson, M.L., and Lawrence C. Murray, "Recent Tax Developments (Charitable Organizations)" (1985), 5 *Philanthrop.* 56.

Dickson, M.L., and Lawrence C. Murray, "Recent Tax Developments" (1991), 10 *Philanthrop.* 42.

Drache, A.B.C., "Abortion Clinic Recognized as Charitable" (1992), 14 *Can. Taxpayer* 18.

Drache, A.B.C., *Canadian Tax Treatment of Charities and Charitable Donations* (Toronto: De Boo, 1978).

Drache, A.B.C., *Canadian Taxation of Charities and Donations* (Scarborough, Ont.: Carswell, 1994).

Drache, A.B.C., "Complaints Against 'Charitable Business'" (1992), 14 *Can. Taxpayer* 20.

Drache, A.B.C., "Residual Gift to Charity Recognized" (1992), 14 *Can. Taxpayer* 15.

Drache, A.B.C., "Tax Exempt Organizations" (1991), 13 *Can. Taxpayer* 165.

Erlichman, Harry, "Profitable Donations: What Price Culture?" (1992), *Philanthrop. No. 2* 3.

Farrow, Trevor C.W., "The Limits of Charity: Redefining the Boundaries of Charitable Trust Law" (1994), 13 *Estates and Trusts J.* 306.

Finkelstein, David N., "Tax Problems in Estate Planning for the Corporate Executive", in *Proceedings of 33rd Tax Conf.* 952 (Can. Tax Foundation, 1981).

Forster, George V., "Tax-effective Compensation for the Employees of Charitable Organizations" (1986), 6 *Philanthrop.* 24.

Goldstein, Lisa D., "Non-profit Organization Can Be Profitable" (1993), 41 *Can. Tax J.* 720.

Goodison, Don, "Tax Deductible Donations" (1988), 22 *CGA Magazine* 11.

Goodman, Wolfe D., "Charitable Gifts of Appreciated Capital Property" (1986), 8 *Estates & Trusts Q.* 189.

Goodman, Wolfe D., "The Impact of Taxation on Charitable Giving: Some Very Personal Views" (1984), 4 *Philanthrop.* 5.

Gotlieb, Maxwell, *Charities and the Tax Man and More* (Toronto: Canadian Bar Association — Ontario, Continuing Legal Education, 1990).

Gotlieb, Maxwell, "Taxation of, and Tax Planning for, Charitable Donations" (1993), 11 *Philanthrop. No. 4* 3.

Haney, Mary-Anne, "Abortion Too Controversial for Revenue Canada" (1992), 40 *Can. Tax J.* 171.

Innes, William I., "Gifts of Cultural Property by Artists" (1993), 12 *Estates and Trusts J.* 219.

Juneau, Carl D., "Some Major Issues Affecting Evaluation of the Charities Tax Incentive" (1990), 9 *Philanthrop. No. 4* 3.

Krishna, Vern, "Advantages des dons de charité au Canada (Les)" (soc. canadienne du cancer, 1984).

Krishna, Vern, "Charitable Donations: What Constitutes a 'Gift'?" (1985), 1 *Can. Current Tax* J107.

Krishna, Vern, "Charitable Donations: What is a Charitable Purpose?" (1986), 1 *Can. Current Tax* C159.

Law, Tax, and Charities: The Legislative and Regulatory Environment for Charitable and Non-profit Organizations (Toronto: The Canadian Centre for Philanthropy, 1990).

Midland, Christina H., "Limitations on Charities Under the Income Tax Act" (1992), 44 *E.T.R.* 111.

Monaco, Joseph C., *Charitable Donations: 'Gifts in Kind'* (Hamilton, Ont.: Thorne Ernst and Whinney, 1989).

"Personal Tax Planning: Charitable Giving" (1987), 35 *Can. Tax J.* 182.

Pintea, Hans O., "Taxation of Ongoing Partnership Operations", in *Proceedings of 33rd Tax Conf.* 195 (Can. Tax Foundation, 1981).

"Private Religious Schools in Jeopardy" (1980), 2 *Can. Taxpayer* 203.

"Religious School Problem: Final Resolution" (1982), 4 *Can. Taxpayer* 83.

Schusheim, Pearl E., "Charities and the Federal Income Tax Provisions: Getting and Staying Registered" (1986), 6 *Philanthrop.* 11.

Senecal, David, "The Tax Sleepers: Charitable and Nonprofit Organizations" (1975), 107 *CA Magazine* 52.

"Special Fund-Raising Events" (1983), 5 *Can. Taxpayer* 196.

Stephen, Peter R., "Charitable Giving" (1987), 35 *Can. Tax J.* 182.

Tamagno, Edward, "The Medical Expenses Deduction" (1979), 1 *Can. Taxation* 58.

Watson, Rod, "Charity and the Canadian Income Tax: An Erratic History" (1985), 5 *Philanthrop.* 3.

Zweibel, Ellen B., "A Truly Canadian Definition of Charity and a Lesson in Drafting Charitable Purposes: A Comment on *Native Communications Society of B.C. v. M.N.R.*" (1987), 26 E.T.R. 41.

Zweibel, Ellen B., "Looking the Gift Horse in the Mouth: An Examination of Charitable Gifts Which Benefit the Donor" (1986), *31 McGill L.J.* 417.

Zweibel, Ellen B., "Registration as Charity — Political Activities (case comment on *Scarborough Community Legal Services v. R.*)" (1985), 1 *Can. Current Tax* A20.

Interest and Dividend Income

Alter, Dr. A., "Different Techniques for Adjusting Taxable Income Under Inflationary Conditions" (1986), *Br. Tax Rev.* 347.

Birnie, David A.G., "Shareholders' Buy-Sell Agreements: Some New Opportunities" in *Proceedings of the 38th Tax Conf.* 13 (Can. Tax Foundation, 1986).

Boultbee, Jack, "Tax Gimmicks", in *Proceedings of 33rd Tax Conf.* 300 (Can. Tax Foundation, 1981).

Colley, Geoffrey M., "Is Indexing a Necessary Evil?" (1986), 119 *CA Magazine* 52.

Colley, Geoffrey M., "Personal Tax Planning and You" (1976), 109 *CA Magazine* 45.

Colley, Geoffrey M., "Planning Ahead for Your Tax Exemption" (1981), 14 *CA Magazine* 59.

Colley, Geoffrey M., "What's New in Personal Investment?" (1977), 110 *CA Magazine* 63.

Communications Directorate, Revenue Canada Taxation, "Application for Registration: A Revenue Canada Taxation Perspective" (1986), 6 *Philanthrop.* 4.

Gould, Lawrence I., and Stanley N. Laiken, "Dividends vs. Capital Gains under Share Redemptions" (1979), 27 *Can. Tax J.* 161.

Gould, Lawrence I., and Stanley N. Laiken, "Effects of the Investment Income Deduction on Investment Returns" (1982), 30 *Can. Tax J.* 228.

Guilbault, P., "Individuals" (1985), 13 *Can. Tax News* 97.

"Interest Deductibility" (1979), 1 *Can. Taxpayer* 20.

"Juggling Dividends" (1980), 2 *Can. Taxpayer* 27.

Kennedy, James F., "The Use of Trust in Tax and Estate Planning", in *Proceedings of 33rd Tax Conf.* 577 (Can. Tax Foundation, 1981).

McNair, D. Keith, *Taxation of Farmers and Fishermen* (Toronto: De Boo, 1986).

Pintea, Hans O., "Taxation of Ongoing Partnership Operations", in *Proceedings of 33rd Tax Conf.* 195 (Can. Tax Foundation, 1981).

Pipes, Sally, and Michael Walker, with Douglas Wills, *Tax Facts 5: The Canadian Consumer Tax Index and You* (Vancouver: Fraser Institute, 1986).

Thomas, Douglas, "As A Matter of Interest" (1978), 111 *CA Magazine* 84.

Forward Averaging

McGregor, Gwyneth, "Forward Averaging" (1983), 5 *Can. Taxpayer* 7.

Merrell, David L., "Bill C-139: New Reserve Provisions and the Forward Averaging Refundable Tax Rules", *Prairie Provinces Tax Conf.* 195 (Can. Tax Foundation, 1983).

Miscellaneous Deductible Losses

Amighetti, Leopole, "Income Tax Events Triggered by Death, an Examination of Selected Problems", in *Proceedings of 31st Tax Conf.* 652 (Can. Tax Foundation, 1979).

Blom, J., "Deductions for Personal Expenditures (Subdivision e and Divison C)" (1981), *Can. Taxation* 473.

Cadesky, Michael, "Corporate Losses", in *Proceedings of 42nd Tax Conf.* (Can. Tax Foundation, 1990).

Burpee, Thomas R., "Utilization of Tax Losses: 'A Reasonable Expectation of Profit'", in *Proceedings of 37th Tax Conf.* 32:1 (Can. Tax Foundation, 1985).

Clarkson Gordon Foundation, *Policy Options for the Treatment of Tax Losses in Canada* (Scarborough, Ont.: Clarkson Gordon Foundation, 1991).

Dean, Jacklyn I., "The January 15, 1987 Draft Amendments Relating to the Acquisition of Gains and Losses" (1987), *Corporate Management Tax Conf.* 2:1.

Dunbar, Alisa E., "Sale of Stock Plan Shares May Produce Freely Deductible Loss" (1991), 3 *Tax. of Exec. Compensation and Retirement* 499.

Farden, Eric N., "Income Tax for Farmers" (Sask.: E.N. Farden, 1985).

Flynn, Gordon W., "Tax Planning for Corporations with Net Capital and Noncapital Losses", *Corporate Management Tax Conf.* 208 (Can. Tax Foundation, 1981).

Foster, David R., "Restoration of Non-capital Losses" (1992), 3 *Can. Current Tax* A7.

Hirsch, Morley P., "The Corporate Loss Transfer System", in *Proceedings of 37th Tax Conf.* 31 (Can. Tax Foundation, 1985).

Krishna, Vern, "Farm Losses; Subsection 31(1); 'Chief Source of Income'" (1985), 1 *Can. Current Tax* J-91.

LePan, Nicholas, "Federal and Provincial Issues in the Corporate Loss Transfer Proposal", in *Proceedings of 37th Tax Conf.* 13 (Can. Tax Foundation, 1985).

Neville, Ralph J., "Acquisition of Control and Corporate Losses" in *Proceedings of 44th Tax Conf.* 25:25 (Can. Tax Foundation, 1992).

"New Treatment for Losses" (1983), 5 *Can. Taxpayer* 183.

Nowoselski, Barty, "Should You Buy or Sell a Company for Its Tax-Loss Carryovers?" (1983), 116 *CA Magazine* 64.

Pearson, Hugh, "Farming and the Income Tax Act" (1993), 41 *Can. Tax J.* 1135.

Reid, Robert J., "Capital and Non-capital Losses", in *Proceedings of 42nd Tax Conf.* 20:1 (Can. Tax Foundation, 1990).

Richardson, Stephen R., "A Corporate Loss Transfer System for Canada: Analysis of Proposals", in *Proceedings of 37th Tax Conf.* 12 (Can. Tax Foundation, 1985).

Silver, Sheldon, "Utilization of Real Estate Losses", *Corporate Management Tax Conf.* 91 (Can. Tax Foundation, 1983).

Slutsky, Sam, "Insolvency: A Refresher from a Taxation Perspective" (1982), 30 *Can. Tax J.* 528.

Swirsky, Benjamin, "Utilization of Losses", *Corporate Management Tax Conf.* 213 (Can. Tax Foundation, 1978).

Thomas, Richard B., "A Farm Loss with a Difference: The Farmer is Successful" (1993), *Can. Tax J.* 513.

Ward, David A., "Arm's Length Acquisitions Relating to Shares in a Public Corporation", *Corporate Management Tax Conf.* 108 (Can. Tax Foundation, 1978).

Wilson, Michael H., *A Corporate Loss Transfer System for Canada*, Dept. of Finance, Canada, 1985.

Wise, Richard M., "Fair Market Determinations — A Few More Requirements" (1983), 31 *Can. Tax J.* 337.

Wraggett, Cathy, "Accelerated Deduction of Business Losses" (1990), 64 *CMA Magazine* 33.

Capital Gains Exemption

Attridge, Ian, "Create Conservation Gains, Not Capital Gains" (1994), 19 *Intervenor No. 6* 8.

Barbacki, Richard, "Use It or Lose It?" (1989), 122 *CA Magazine* 43.

Colley, G.M., "What Price the Capital Gains Exemption?" (1985), 118 *CA Magazine* 10:75.

Cullity, Maurice C., "The Capital Gains Exemption: Implications for Estate Planning", in *Proceedings of 37th Tax Conf.* 18 (Can. Tax Foundation, 1985).

Goodison, Don, "Business Losses" (1987), 21 *CGA Magazine* 6.

Goodman, S.H., and N.C. Tobias, "The Proposed $500,000 Capital Gains Exemption" (1985), 33 *Can. Tax J.* 721.

Hayos, Gabriel J., "The Capital Gains Exemption: Planning Strategies to Meet the Criteria of a Qualified Small Business Corporation", in *Proceedings of 40th Tax Conf.* 15:1 (Can. Tax Foundation, 1988).

James, Larry W., "Capital Gains Exemption: Planning Techniques", in *Proceedings of 38th Tax Conf.* 33 (Can. Tax Foundation, 1986).

Kellough, Howard J., and K. Travers Pullen, "Planning for the Lifetime Capital Gains Exemption" (1986), 3 *Bus. & L.* 3.

Kirby, F.P., "The Capital Gains Exemption: Other Than Qualified Small Business Shares", in *Proceedings of 40th Tax Conf.* 30:1 (Can. Tax Foundation, 1988).

Lawlor, W.R., "Surplus Stripping and Other Planning Opportunities with the New $500,000 Capital Gains Exemption" (1986), 34 *Can. Tax J.* 49.

Peters, Steven, "Enhancing the Exemption" (1992), 125 *CA Mag. No. 5* 33.

Potvin, Jean, "The Capital Gains Deduction for Qualified Small Business Corporation Shares Revisited", in *Proceedings of 44th Tax Conf.* (Can. Tax Foundation, 1992).

Quinton, Cathy, "The Additional Capital Gains Exemption" (1989), 62 *CMA Magazine* 34.

Rotenberg, Charles M., "Making the Deal Work" (1991), 13 *Can. Taxpayer* 60.

Ruby, Stephen S., "A Glimpse at the Lifetime Capital Gains Exemption (Part I)" (1986), 3 *Bus. & L.* 93.

Ruby, Stephen S., "A Glimpse at the Lifetime Capital Gains Exemption (Part III)" (1987), 4 *Bus. & L.* 6.

Stack, Thomas J., "Capital Gains and Losses on Shares of Private Corporations", in *Proceedings of 39th Tax Conf.* 17:1 (Can. Tax Foundation, 1987).

Tam, Anthony, "Capital Gains Exemption: Small Business Corporations" (1987-89), 2 *Can. Current Tax* P-5.

"Taxation of Corporate Reorganizations (The): New Measures to Restrict Netting of Gains and Shelter" (1987), 35 *Can. Tax J.* 198.

Templeton, Wendy, "Anti-Avoidance and the Capital Gains Exemption" (1986), 34 *Can. Tax J.* 203.

Templeton, Wendy, "The Taxation of Corporate Reorganizations: Anti-Avoidance and the Capital Gains Exemption" (1986), 34 *Can. Tax J.* 203.

Templeton, Wendy, "The Taxation of Corporate Reorganizations: Anti-Avoidance and the Capital Gains Exemptions: Part 2" (1986), 34 *Can. Tax J.* 446.

Tax Credits

Kraayeveld, S.H., "Tax Credits" (1985), 13 *Can. Tax News* 93.

Sayyed, A., "Choosing Between Tax Credits and Exemptions for Dependent Children" (1985), 33 *Can. Tax J.* 975.

CHAPTER XIII

COMPUTATION OF TAX PAYABLE

1. GENERAL

The focus of the preceding chapters has been on the computation of income and taxable income, i.e., determination of the base upon which tax is calculated. We now turn to the second variable in determining a taxpayer's liability for income tax: Application of a rate to the taxable base. As we shall see, the computation of tax is not just a simple process of applying a rate, or schedule of rates, to taxable income. The computation involves multiple calculations and adjustments. The basic tax determined by applying a tax rate to taxable income is adjusted by various credits, surtaxes and reductions. Having determined the tax payable under Part I of the *Income Tax Act*, some taxpayers may also have to make another calculation to see if they are liable for the "alternative minimum tax".

It is important to recognize the difference between a deduction and a tax credit. A deduction reduces taxable income, and therefore *indirectly* reduces the amount of tax payable; a tax credit is a *direct* reduction of the amount of tax that would otherwise be payable by the taxpayer. The difference between the two can be quite substantial, as taxpayers discovered after the 1987 tax reform, when many deductions were replaced with lower-value tax credits.

The provisions relating to the computation of tax, set out in Division E of Part I of the Act, are subdivided into three parts:

1. Rules applicable to individuals;
2. Rules applicable to corporations; and
3. Rules applicable to all taxpayers.

2. INDIVIDUALS

Reference:

ITA:

S. 117 Computation of Tax — Individuals

(a) Basic Tax Rate

(i) General Rates

Section 117 sets out the federal tax rates applicable to individuals. The general basic tax rates in subsection 117(2) are as follows:

Taxable Income		Rate
$1	– 27,500	17%
$27,501	– 55,000	26%
$55,001+		29%

(ii) Indexation

The individual tax rates are indexed by a formula that is linked to the Consumer Price Index ("CPI").[1]

The indexed rate schedule for 1995 is as follows:

First	$ 29,590		17%
Next	$ 29,590	$ 5,030	plus 26% on remainder
Over	$ 59,180	$12,724	plus 29% on remainder

(iii) Provincial Taxes

The rates of tax set out in section 117 are only the federal rates of tax. In addition to the federal tax, an individual resident in Canada is also liable to pay provincial income tax. In most cases, the provincial income tax is calculated by applying the provincial rate of tax to the federal tax payable. In nine of the provinces, the provincial income tax on individuals is calculated as a percentage of the taxpayer's federal tax payable (referred to in the income tax return as "Basic Federal Tax"). Quebec is the exception.

Thus, for most resident individuals the provincial income tax payable is determined by reference to their federal tax payable and not by reference to their taxable income. For example, Ontario imposes a basic provincial income tax of 58 per cent (1995) of the basic federal tax payable. Hence, a taxpayer with a federal marginal rate of 29 per cent has a *combined* basic marginal rate of approximately 46 per cent (1995).

Apart from the indexing of tax brackets, the rate schedule remains fairly stable; the rates are not usually altered from year to year. Instead, governments can and do increase or lower taxes by imposing a surtax or by allowing for a special tax credit.

---

[1] S. 117.1. From 1974 to 1985 the indexing formula was, with two exceptions, directly linked to changes in the CPI. The two exceptions were in respect of the years 1983 and 1984, when the federal government introduced a restraint program known as "6 and 5". In 1983, notwithstanding a much higher inflation rate, the Minister of Finance capped the indexing of marginal tax brackets and personal exemptions at 6 per cent; for 1984, indexing was capped at 5 per cent in accordance with the federal government's "6 and 5 program". Although full indexing was resumed in 1985, there was no provision to make up for the reductions in 1983 and 1984. In 1986, the federal government, faced with an ever-increasing deficit, cut back on indexation of tax rates to reflect only that portion of the increase in CPI over 3 per cent. Thus individuals may be bumped up into higher tax brackets on the basis of inflationary income gains up to 3 per cent.

(b) Surtaxes

Adjustments to tax rates are usually implemented through surtaxes (often labelled as "temporary") or tax credits. A surtax is a tax calculated by reference to another tax, usually the basic federal tax.

(i) Basic Surtax

The surtax rate has been adjusted frequently in the past few years. The "temporary" surtax was set at 3 per cent in 1987 and 1988, increased to 4 per cent in 1989 and 5 per cent in 1990 and 1991, reduced to 4.5 per cent in 1992, and 3 per cent in 1993 and subsequent years.

(ii) Super Surtax

In April 1989 the Minister of Finance announced a super surtax (also "temporary") that now affects individuals with income in excess of approximately $58,300. The super surtax rate was set at 1.5 per cent in 1989, 3 per cent in 1990 and 5 per cent in 1991 and subsequent years. Thus, the combined surtax rate on high income taxpayers is 8 per cent in 1995.

(c) Tax Credits

An individual taxpayer may be entitled to certain credits towards his or her tax. A tax credit reduces the tax that would otherwise be payable. For example, a taxpayer may claim a credit on account of:

- Personal tax credits;
- Pension income;
- Dividends from taxable Canadian corporations;
- Tuition and education;
- Medical expenses;
- Charitable donations;
- Eligible children;
- Overseas employment; or
- Foreign taxes.

The credits are calculated according to a formula that applies a percentage to the aggregate of the claimable amounts. The credits are indexed and, as such, are partially adjusted each year to reflect inflationary increases as measured by the Consumer Price Index.

Some tax credits are refundable, that is, the taxpayer receives a cash refund if the credits exceed his or her income for the year. Others are non-refundable credits: The credit is lost if it cannot be deducted from tax otherwise payable for the year.

(i) Personal Tax Credits

References:

ITA:

S. 118   Personal Tax Credits

BULLETINS, CIRCULARS & RULINGS:

IT-513   February 3, 1989   Personal Tax Credits

Personal tax credits may be claimed on account of:

- Single status;
- Spousal status;
- Equivalent-to-spouse status;
- Dependants; and
- Age.

The personal tax credits are not refundable.

(A) Method of Calculation

A taxpayer is first required to determine the aggregate dollar value of all of the amounts to which he or she is entitled, and then to multiply this value by the "appropriate percentage" for the year.[2] The "appropriate percentage" for a taxation year is the *lowest* marginal tax rate applicable in the particular year. The lowest "appropriate percentage" is 17 per cent.[3] (See Form A below.)

FORM A

CALCULATION OF NON-REFUNDABLE TAX CREDITS (1995)

Basic personal amount	$ 6,456.00
Age amount (65 or older, maximum)	$ 3,482.00
Spousal amount (maximum)	$ 5,380.00
Equivalent-to-spouse amount (maximum)	$ 5,380.00
Amounts for infirm dependants age 18 or older (various)	$ 1,583.00

---

[2] Subs. 118(1).

[3] Subs. 248(1) ("appropriate percentage"); subs. 117(2).

Form A (continued)

Canada or Quebec Pension Plan contributions:

Contributions through employment (maximum)	$ 806.00
Contribution payable on self-employment earnings (various)	
Unemployment Insurance premiums (maximum)	$ 1,293.03
Eligible pension income amount (maximum)	$ 1,000.00
Disability amount	$ 4,233.00
Disability amount transferred from dependant other than spouse	
Tuition fees (for self)	
Education amount (for self (maximum))	$ 960.00
Tuition fees and education amount transferred from child (maximum)	$ 4,000.00
Amounts transferred from spouse (various)	
Medical expenses:	
Subtract 3% of "Net Income" = allowable portion of medical expenses (maximum)	$ 1,614.00
SUBTOTAL	$_____
Creditable portion of subtotal (17%)	
Add:	
Charitable donations	
Gifts to Canada or a province or gifts of cultural property	
Total donations	$_____
Credit of 17% on the first $200 or less	
Credit of 29% on the balance	
TOTAL NON-REFUNDABLE TAX CREDITS	$_____

(B) Single Status

An individual may claim an amount of $6,456 (1995), which is the minimum claim, to which every individual is entitled.[4] This amount is multiplied by the "appropriate percentage". For example, in 1995 the credit for a single person was $1,098, that is, 17 per cent of $6,456.

---

[4]   Para. 118(1)(c).

(C) Spousal Status

An individual who supports his or her spouse is allowed to claim an additional amount as a tax credit. In 1995 the additional amount is $5,380. Thus, in the simplest case, an individual is entitled to claim a total of $11,836 in 1995, comprised of the basic personal amount plus the spousal amount. This translates into a personal tax credit of $2,012, that is, 17 per cent of $11,836.

The status claim is reduced dollar for dollar by the amount that the income of the taxpayer's spouse exceeds $538 (1995). For example, in 1995 the additional spousal status claim is reduced to zero when the spouse's income exceeds $5,918.

A person is considered to be "married" if he or she undergoes a form of marriage recognized by the laws of Canada and is not a widow or widower, or divorced.[5] Subsection 252(4) expands the meaning of "spouse" to include individuals of the opposite sex who have cohabited in a conjugal relationship for a 12-month period or who are the parents of a child. Thus a "common law" spouse is eligible for the spousal credit, is permitted spousal RRSPs, but is unable to claim the equivalent-to-spouse credit.

"Income" means *net* income determined under the Act. The spouse's income for the entire year is taken into account in determining whether the supporting taxpayer is entitled to the claim for spousal status.[6] Thus, a taxpayer who marries, or qualifies as a common law spouse, late in the year may claim a deduction for supporting his or her spouse only if the spouse's income for the entire year is less than $5,918. Both spouses may not claim a deduction for each other in the same taxation year.

An individual who is *entitled* to claim a deduction for alimony or maintenance payments may not also claim the married status tax credit in respect of his or her spouse. Where the individual was living apart from his or her spouse at the end of the year by reason of marriage breakdown, the spouse's income for the period during the year in which the parties were not separated is taken into account in determining the claim.[7]

(D) Wholly-dependent Persons

The credit for a wholly-dependent person (also referred to as the "equivalent-to-spouse credit") is available to a person who is not entitled to the spousal status credit

[5] *The Queen v. Scheller*, [1975] CTC 601, 75 DTC 5406 (F.C.T.D.); *McPhee v. M.N.R.*, [1980] CTC 2042, 80 DTC 1034 (T.R.B.); *The Queen v. Taylor*, [1984] CTC 244, 84 DTC 6234 (F.C.T.D.).

[6] *Johnston v. M.N.R.*, [1948] CTC 195, 3 DTC 1182 (S.C.C.) (husband considered to support his wife if contributing to her support, even though she may supply some money towards meeting expenses of household).

[7] Para. 118(1)(*a*).

but who supports a person dependent upon him or her.[8] The amount claimable in 1993 was $5,380, reduced by any income over $538 earned by the wholly-dependent person in the year. Thus, the amount claimable under this provision is equivalent to the amount claimable by a married person whose spouse does not earn more than the total threshold amount.

The equivalent-to-spouse credit is available only to an individual who maintains (either alone or jointly with another person), and lives in, a self-contained domestic establishment and actually supports therein the dependent person. For example, a single parent supporting a child would qualify for the credit under this provision.

There are two additional qualifications for the claim on account of wholly-dependent persons. First, except where the claim is in respect of the taxpayer's child, the credit is available only in respect of dependants who are resident in Canada.[9] A taxpayer is not entitled to claim the credit in respect of foreign resident dependants.

Second, except in the case of a claim for a parent or grandparent, a taxpayer cannot claim an amount in respect of a dependant who is 18 years of age or older unless the person is dependent because of a mental or physical infirmity.[10]

(E) Dependants

A taxpayer may claim an amount in respect of individuals who are dependent upon him or her for support. The claim depends upon five criteria:[11]

1. Dependency;
2. Relationship between the taxpayer and the individual claimed as a dependant;
3. Residence;
4. Age; and
5. Mental or physical infirmity of dependant.

(1) Dependency

Whether an individual is dependent upon a taxpayer is a question of fact in each case. In the event that a person is partially dependent upon two or more taxpayers, their aggregate claim in respect of that dependant cannot exceed the maximum amount that would be deductible in respect of a claim by one taxpayer. Where the supporting individuals cannot agree on the portion of the total that each is to deduct, the Minister may allocate the amount between them.

---

[8] Para. 118(1)(*b*).

[9] Cl. 118(1)(*b*)(ii)(A).

[10] Cl. 118(1)(*b*)(ii)(D).

[11] Para. 118(1)(*d*).

(II) Relationship

The term "dependant" in respect of a taxpayer or his or her spouse means:[12]

- their children or grandchildren;
- their nieces or nephews, if resident in Canada;
- their brothers or sisters, if resident in Canada; and
- their parents, grandparents, aunts or uncles, if resident in Canada.

(III) Residence

Except in respect of a claim for the taxpayer's, or his or her spouse's, children or grandchildren, the dependency deduction is available only for the support of dependants who are resident in Canada. This distinction between the various categories of dependants reflects the administrative concerns of the tax authorities who monitor dependency claims.

(IV) Age

The dependency deduction is available only in respect of qualified dependants over the age of 18. The amount claimable in 1995 was $1,583 less the excess of the dependant's income over $2,690. The maximum credit in 1993 was $269, that is, 17 per cent of $1,583.

(V) Mental or Physical Infirmity

The dependency deduction is only available for individuals dependent on the taxpayer by reason of mental or physical infirmity.[13]

(F) Age

An individual who becomes 65 years of age or older in the year may claim an additional amount.[14] In 1995 the maximum amount claimable was $3,482, which amounted to a credit of $592, that is, 17 per cent of $3,482.

For individuals whose income exceeds $25,291, the maximum amount claimable is reduced by 15 per cent of the amount by which his or her income exceeds $25,291.

(ii) Pension Income

Reference:

BULLETINS, CIRCULARS & RULINGS:

IT-517   March 28, 1989   Pension Tax Credit

---

[12] Subs. 118(6).

[13] Subpara. 118(1)(d)(ii).

[14] Subs. 118(2).

The pension income credits are intended to provide some relief from inflation, particularly for individuals who have to live on fixed incomes. The credit depends upon two factors: (1) The source of the pension, and (2) The recipient's age.

An individual who is 65 years of age or over may claim a credit in respect of pension income. The claim is determined by applying the appropriate percentage (17 per cent in 1995) to the lesser of $1,000 and the pension income in the year.[15] Hence in 1995 the maximum credit in respect of pension income is $170, that is, 17 per cent of $1,000.

The claim of an individual who has not attained the age of 65 is restricted to the lesser of $1,000 and his or her "qualified pension income" for the year.[16] The credit is determined by applying the appropriate percentage for the year to this amount. For example, in 1995 the maximum credit was $170, that is, 17 per cent of $1,000.

"Pension income" includes:[17]

- Life annuity payments out of a superannuation or pension fund;
- Annuity payments out of registered retirement savings plans;
- Payments out of registered retirement income funds;
- Payments out of deferred profit-sharing plans; and
- Accrued income on an annuity or life insurance policy included in income.

But lump sum payments out of pension plans and deferred income plans are not eligible for the pension income credit. The credit is determined by reference to *annuity* payments out of these plans.

Pensions paid under the *Old Age Security Act*, the Canada Pension Plan or the Quebec Pension Plan, retirement allowances, death benefits, exempt income, and payments out of an employee benefit plan, an employee trust, a salary deferral arrangement or a retirement compensation arrangement do not qualify for the credit.

The concept of "qualified pension income" is much narrower than "pension income". "Qualified pension income" includes:[18]

- Life annuities paid out under a superannuation or pension fund plan; and
- Amounts paid as a consequence of the death of a taxpayer's spouse on account of registered retirement savings plans, registered retirement income funds, deferred profit-sharing plans or certain annuity payments.

---

[15] Subs. 118(3).

[16] Subs. 118(3).

[17] Subs. 118(7) ("pension income").

[18] Subs. 118(7) ("qualified pension income").

For example, where an individual takes out a guaranteed term annuity under a registered retirement savings plan and designates his or her spouse as a beneficiary under the plan, any payments made under the guaranteed term of the plan to the beneficiary are eligible for the pension income credit.

(iii) Tuition Fees

References:

ITA:

S. 118.5	Tuition Credit

BULLETINS, CIRCULARS & RULINGS:

IT-516R	March 25, 1994	Tuition Tax Credit

Tuition fees on account of education are personal and capital expenditures. Thus, an individual may not, without specific authorization, claim a deduction or a credit for tuition fees. For social policy reasons, however, the tax system allows individuals a credit against taxes for tuition fees paid to certain educational institutions.

There are two different sets of conditions which regulate the credit for tuition fees: the first deals with students attending educational institutions in Canada, the second with those attending educational institutions outside Canada. The rules in respect of the former category are considerably less stringent than those in respect of the latter.

(A) Institutions in Canada

A student may claim a credit for fees paid to attend:[19]

- A post-secondary educational institution; or
- An institution certified by the Minister of Employment and Immigration to provide courses that furnish or improve occupational skills.

The credit is determined by applying the "appropriate percentage" to the eligible tuition fees paid in the year. For a student to qualify for the credit, the total fees paid to the particular educational institution must exceed $100.

(B) Deemed residence

Where a student is deemed to be a resident of Canada,[20] the credit is available even if he or she attends an educational institution outside Canada. The credit is available on the same terms and conditions as if the student were attending an institution in Canada.[21]

---

[19] Para. 118.5(1)(*a*).

[20] S. 250.

[21] Subs. 118.5(2).

(C) Transfer of Unused Credits

A portion of the tuition tax credit may be transferred to the student's spouse.[22] The amount transferrable (maximum $680) is the excess of the amounts which the student may claim for the year as his or her tuition and education tax credit.

Where a student is unmarried, or a married student's spouse does not claim a personal tax credit for him or her, the education and tuition tax credit may be transferred to the student's parents or grandparents.[23]

(D) Fees Paid by Employer

Tuition fees paid by a student's employer are also creditable by the student, but only to the extent that the student includes the fees in income. The employer may deduct the fees as a business expense if the fees are paid for business purposes.[24]

(E) "Tuition Fees"

Tuition fees include:

- Admission fees;
- Charges for the use of a library, or laboratory fees;
- Exemption fees;
- Examination fees;
- Application fees;
- Confirmation fees;
- Charges for a certificate, diploma or degree;
- Membership or seminar fees specifically related to an academic program and its administration;
- Mandatory computer service fees; and
- Academic fees.

Fees for student activities (whether social or athletic), medical care fees, transportation and parking charges, board and lodging, equipment costs of a capital nature and initiation or entrance fees to professional organizations are not creditable for tax purposes.

(F) Books

Although the cost of books does not usually qualify as a tuition fee, a student may claim a credit for such costs if he or she is enrolled in a correspondence course and the cost of the books is an integral part of the fee paid for the course.

---

[22] S. 118.8.

[23] S. 118.9.

[24] S. 9.

(G) Period Covered by Fees

Only tuition fees paid *in respect of a particular year*[25] are creditable in that year. Fees paid to cover tuition for an academic session which straddles the calendar year are eligible for the tax credit only for the year to which they relate. For example, where the academic year is from September in one year to May of the next year, the tuition tax credit must be allocated so that the portion from September to December is claimable in one year and the portion from January to May is claimable in the subsequent year.

(H) Educational Institutions Outside Canada

A full-time student enrolled at a university outside Canada is entitled to claim a credit by applying the "appropriate percentage" to the amount of eligible tuition fees paid in respect of the year to the university.[26] The qualifications to claim the tuition fee credit for attending a university outside Canada are considerably more stringent than those for institutions in Canada.

The credit is available only if the student satisfies the following conditions:

- He or she attends a course that is of not less than 13 consecutive weeks' duration;
- The program of study leads to a *degree* (not a diploma) from the institution;
- The institution attended by the student is a *university*, not a college or other educational institution; and
- The student attends on a full-time basis.

Students are considered to be in "full-time attendance" at a university if the institution regards them to be full-time students for academic purposes. A certificate from a university stating that a student was in full-time attendance in a particular academic year or semester is acceptable for tax purposes. Hence, a student who holds a full-time job and takes a full course load at a university is considered to be in full-time attendance at the educational institution for tax purposes.

Revenue Canada interprets the 13 consecutive weeks' attendance requirement quite liberally. For example, the requirement is satisfied if the student drops out of the course before completing the program of studies, the particular academic term falls a little short of 13 weeks, or the term is broken by official holidays.

(I) Post-graduate Studies

A student enrolled in a post-graduate program of studies on a regular basis is considered to be in "full-time attendance" if he or she is registered for the regular academic year. This is so even if the requirements for attendance in class are minimal. For example, a registered post-graduate student who spends most of his or her time in

---

[25] Subs. 118.5(1).

[26] Para. 118.5(1)(*b*).

a laboratory or a library engaged in research, whether on or off campus, is usually considered to be in full-time attendance. Similarly, a post-graduate student who holds a full-time job is not necessarily precluded from claiming the tuition tax credit.

(J) Commuting to United States

The tuition tax credit is also available in respect of fees paid by a Canadian resident who commutes to a post-secondary level educational institution in the United States.[27] This credit is available only to students who reside throughout the year near the Canada-U.S. border.

(iv) Education Credit

Reference:

BULLETINS, CIRCULARS & RULINGS:

IT-515R   March 25, 1994   Education Tax Credit

In addition to the tuition fee credit, a student is also entitled to claim an "education credit" for full-time attendance at a designated educational institution, provided that he or she is enrolled in a qualifying educational program at that institution.[28] As with the other tax credits, the education tax credit is determined by applying the "appropriate percentage" for the year to the number of months of full-time attendance at the institution, multiplied by $80. For example, the credit for a student who attended a university for eight months in 1995 was $109, that is, $80 x 8 months x 17 per cent.

(v) Medical Expenses

Reference:

BULLETINS, CIRCULARS & RULINGS:

IT-519R   February 20, 1995   Medical Expense and Disability Tax Credits and Attendant Care Expense Deduction

Medical expenditures are personal and, therefore, would be non-deductible expenses for tax purposes. There is, however, some relief for "extraordinary" medical expenses over a minimum threshold limit.

(A) Computation of Credit

The medical expense credit is determined by applying the "appropriate percentage" (17 per cent in 1995) to the sum of the taxpayer's medical expenses in excess of a threshold amount.[29] The threshold amount is the lesser of $1,614 (1995) and 3 per cent of the individual's income from the year.

---

[27] Para. 118.5(1)(*c*).

[28] S. 118.6.

[29] Subs. 118.2(1).

Thus, the first step is to determine the taxpayer's total medical expenses for the year. The second step is to deduct from the total medical expenses the *lesser* of $1,614 (1995) and 3 per cent of the taxpayer's income for the year. The final step is to determine the medical expense credit by applying the appropriate percentage to the amount by which the medical expenses exceed the threshold.

(B) Meaning of "Medical Expenses"

A taxpayer may deduct medical expenses incurred on behalf of:[30]

- himself or herself;
- his or her spouse;
- his or her children, or spouse's children, who were dependent on the taxpayer for support; or
- the taxpayer's, or his or her spouse's parent, grandparent, brother, sister, uncle, aunt, niece, or nephew who was resident in Canada and dependent on the taxpayer for support.

The claim for the credit must be supported by receipts filed with the taxpayer's return for the year.

To constitute "medical expenses", the amount must be paid to a medical practitioner, dentist, nurse, public or licensed private hospital. At first glance, the phrase "medical expenses" appears to include any expenditures that an individual may incur as a consequence of disability or illness. In fact, the phrase is circumscribed by several restrictive conditions that are fairly rigidly interpreted.

Payments for full-time nursing care in a nursing home and payments for a full-time attendant to look after an individual also qualify as medical expenses if the individual who requires the care is suffering from severe and prolonged mental or physical impairment.[31] A person is considered to be suffering from severe and prolonged impairment if his or her disability markedly restricts his or her daily activities and can be expected to last for a continuous period of at least 12 months.[32]

Payments for a part-time attendant to look after an individual qualify as medical expenses to the extent that the total paid does not exceed $5,000 (or $10,000, where the individual died in the year).

The restrictions in respect of eligible medical expenses are long and detailed. It is important to note that an individual is required to satisfy all of the requirements before he or she can claim the credit. The courts have traditionally been very strict in permitting a claim for medical expenses. They have applied a rigid and literal

---

[30] Subss. 118.2(2), 118(6).

[31] See paras. 118.2(2)(*b*), (*b*.1).

[32] Subs. 118.4(1).

interpretation to the statutory rules.[33] It remains to be seen whether the courts will become more liberal in their interpretation of the provisions following the Supreme Court of Canada's guidelines that the *Income Tax Act* should be read in context and that ambiguous provisions should be interpreted according to the "object and spirit" of the rule.[34]

(vi) Mental or Physical Impairment

Reference:

ITA:

S. 118.3   Credit for Mental or Physical Impairment

An individual with a severe and prolonged mental or physical impairment may claim a tax credit.[35] In 1995, the credit was $720. The claim must be supported by a doctor's certificate in prescribed form certifying the impairment.

A person is considered to have a "severe and prolonged impairment" only if he or she is markedly restricted in the ability to perform a basic activity of daily living and the impairment lasts, or can reasonably be expected to last, for a continuous period of at least 12 months.[36]

A "basic activity of daily living" includes:[37]

- Perceiving, thinking and remembering;
- Feeding and dressing oneself;
- Speaking so as to be understood by a familiar person;
- Hearing so as to understand a familiar person;
- Eliminating (bowel or bladder functions); or
- Walking.

Other activities, such as housekeeping, working or social activities, do not qualify.

---

[33] See, e.g., *Witthuhn v. M.N.R.* (1959), 17 Tax ABC 33, 57 DTC 174 (T.A.B.) (board denied claim for medical expenses for amounts paid to attendant to look after infirm spouse; taxpayer claimed expenses on basis that spouse was confined to bed or wheelchair; spouse in fact did not own wheelchair, instead sat in a special rocking chair; claim denied as rocking chair not a "wheelchair").

[34] *Stubart Invt. Ltd. v. The Queen*, [1984] 1 SCR 536, [1984] CTC 294, 84 DTC 6305; See Chapter II "Interpretation of Tax Law".

[35] S. 118.3.

[36] S. 118.4.

[37] Paras. 118.4(1)(*c*), (*d*).

An individual may claim the credit in respect of his or her dependants with mental or physical impairments who were resident in Canada at any time in the taxation year.[38] The claim may be made in respect of the following dependants of the taxpayer:

- Persons for whom the equivalent-to-spouse credit may be claimed; or
- Children or grandchildren of the taxpayer, or his or her spouse; or
- The taxpayer's, or his or her spouse's, parents or grandparents who reside with the taxpayer.

(d) Dividend Tax Credit

References:

ITA:

Para. 82(1)(*b*)   Taxable Dividends

S. 121   Deduction for Taxable Dividends

(i) Tax Integration

An individual who receives a taxable dividend from a taxable Canadian corporation is required to include 125 per cent of the dollar amount of the dividend in his or her income.[39] In other words, the cash value of the dividend is "grossed up" by 25 per cent. Thus, the tax payable on the dividend is initially calculated by reference to a figure that is higher than the actual income. The gross-up is intended to reflect the underlying corporate tax (at an assumed rate of 20 per cent) paid by the corporation. The individual may, however, apply a dividend tax credit against the amount of federal tax.[40]

This two-step process of "grossing up" taxable dividends followed by a tax credit is a structural device designed to prevent double taxation of corporate income. The tax credit integrates the tax paid by Canadian corporations with the tax paid by shareholders on dividends. This process, referred to as "tax integration", is discussed in greater detail in Chapter XVII "Private Corporations: Business Income". For present purposes, it is sufficient to state that an individual in receipt of a dividend from a Canadian corporation is entitled to a credit against tax payable.

(ii) Federal Credit

The dividend tax credit is equal to two-thirds of the value of the gross-up applied to the dividend. For example, an individual who receives a dividend of $800 is taxable on $1,000, and may claim a federal dividend tax credit of $133. Since provincial tax

---

[38] Subs. 118.3(2).

[39] Para. 82(1)(*b*).

[40] S. 121.

is calculated on the basis of the basic federal tax,[41] the provincial tax is, in effect, also reduced by the federal dividend tax credit. For example, at a provincial tax rate of 50 per cent, the combined federal/provincial dividend tax credit is equal to 150 per cent of $133, that is, $200.

Example XIII.1

Assume that in 1995 Harry Smith receives $40,000 in dividends from taxable Canadian corporations. The tax payable (ignoring personal credits and surtaxes) on the dividend income would be as follows:

Cash dividends		$ 40,000
Gross-up by 25%		10,000
Taxable amount		$ 50,000
Tax thereon (1995 rates)		
On first $29,590	$ 5,030	
On next $20,410	$ 5,307	
Federal income tax		$ 10,337
Federal dividend tax credit		(6,667)
Basic federal tax		$ 3,670
Provincial tax @ 50%		1,835
Tax payable on dividend		$ 5,505

(iii) Provincial Credit

Since the provincial tax payable is calculated by reference to the basic federal tax payable, which is net of the federal dividend tax credit, the provinces, in effect, indirectly also allow a dividend tax credit. Stated another way, since the provincial tax payable is calculated by reference to the federal tax payable, a reduction in the basic federal tax payable by virtue of the dividend tax credit *automatically* reduces the provincial tax payable. In the above example, the provincial tax is $1,835, which is 50 per cent of the federal tax of $3,670. The provincial dividend tax credit is equal to 50 per cent of the federal dividend tax credit, or 50 per cent of $6,667. Thus, in Example XIII.1 the provincial dividend tax credit is $3,333 and the *combined* dividend tax credit is equal to $10,000. The $10,000 is a credit for the underlying corporate tax of an equivalent amount ($50,000 x 20%) paid by the corporation.

---

[41] Except in Quebec.

(e) Overseas Employment Tax Credit

References:

ITA:

S. 122.3   Employment out of Canada

BULLETINS, CIRCULARS & RULINGS:

IT-497R2   June 29, 1990   Overseas Employment Tax Credit

(i) General

As a general rule, Canadian residents are subject to full tax liability on their world-wide income.[42] Non-residents are not generally subject to Canadian tax.

An individual employed on an overseas contract may be entitled to a tax credit. The credit is available only in limited circumstances, but it is extremely generous. The generosity of the credit is justified on the basis that it allows Canadian businesses employing Canadian workers to compete in international markets with other countries that offer similar tax relief to their residents.

(ii) Application

The credit is available only to an individual who is employed by a *specified* employer, and then only if the employee works overseas for a period of at least six consecutive months in certain *approved* activities. Thus the credit is limited in four ways:[43]

- The taxpayer must work for a "specified employer";
- The employer must be engaged in an approved activity;
- The employee must work abroad for more than six consecutive months; and
- The amount of the credit is subject to a ceiling.

A "specified employer" is generally an employer resident in Canada.[44] The employer must be engaged in an approved activity such as construction, exploration for and exploitation of natural resources, or an agricultural project.

The amount of the credit is subject to a ceiling:[45] The credit is equal to that portion of the tax otherwise payable that the *lesser* of $80,000 and 80 per cent of the employee's net overseas employment income is of his or her total income.

---

[42] Subs. 2(1); see also Chapter III "Who is Taxable?".

[43] Subs. 122.3(1); IT-497R2, "Overseas Employment Tax Credit" (June 29, 1990).

[44] Subs. 122.3(2) ("specified employer").

[45] Paras. 122.3(1)(c), (d).

(f) Alternative Minimum Tax ("AMT")

High income taxpayers may be liable for tax even though they do not have any taxable income. This is because taxpayers may be liable for an alternative minimum tax ("AMT"), payable at a flat rate on taxable income computed for AMT purposes.[46] The AMT is an adjunct to the regular tax system. It is targeted at a limited group of high income taxpayers who derive their income from certain sources.

The AMT, which applies to individuals and trusts (other than mutual fund trusts), is an alternative tax. It applies only if the amount computed under it exceeds the individual's regular tax. The AMT is not added on to, but is a substitute for, the regular tax.[47]

Most Canadians will not pay the minimum tax. This is because the basic exemption for the AMT is $40,000 and the federal AMT rate of 17 per cent is about one-half of the top rate for regular tax purposes.

AMT is determined by multiplying "AMT taxable income" by the applicable AMT rate. Then, the AMT is reduced by some, but not all, of the tax credits allowed for regular tax purposes.

The AMT taxable income calculation begins with net income for regular income tax purposes.[48] This figure is then adjusted by adding back certain amounts which are deductible or non-taxable for regular tax purposes. There is a basic exemption of $40,000.[49]

For federal tax purposes, the AMT rate is 17 per cent (1995). Assuming that the provinces also impose a similar tax, the combined federal/provincial AMT rates range between approximately 24 per cent and 28 per cent, depending upon the individual's province of residence.

An individual's federal tax liability is the greater of his or her liability as determined under the AMT and the "regular" income tax. The greater of these two numbers becomes the taxpayer's basic federal tax payable, which is then used to calculate the federal surtax, the provincial tax and the various tax credits.

3. RULES: CORPORATIONS

References:

ITA:

S. 123   Corporations — Rates, Surtax, Deduction

---

[46] S. 127.51.

[47] S. 127.5.

[48] Subs. 127.52(1).

[49] Subs. 127.53(1).

S. 124	Deduction — Provincial Abatement
S. 125	Deduction — Small Business
S. 125.1	Deduction — Manufacturing and Processing

BULLETINS, CIRCULARS & RULINGS:

IT-67R3	May 15, 1992	Taxable Dividends from Corporations Resident in Canada
IT-73R4	February 13, 1989	The Small Business Deduction — Income from an Active Business, a Specified Investment Business and a Personal Services Business
IT-145R	June 19, 1981	Canadian Manufacturing and Processing Profits-Reduced Rate of Corporate Tax
IT-177R2	May 4, 1984	Permanent Establishment of a Corporation in a Province and of a Foreign Enterprise in Canada
IT-295R4	April 27, 1990	Taxable Dividends Received after 1987 by a Spouse
IT-411	March 23, 1978	Meaning of "Construction"
IT-458R	May 31, 1990	Canadian-Controlled Private Corporation

The rules that deal with the computation of tax payable by corporations are more detailed and complex than the rules applicable to individuals. This is because corporate taxation depends upon numerous variables: (i) Type and size of the corporation, (2) Ownership structure, (3) Type and source of income; and (4) Amount of income earned in a year. In this Chapter we look at the general rules applicable to all corporations. In following chapters[50] we will examine the rules in respect of special types of corporations and specific types of income.

(a) General Tax Rate

The general basic rate of federal tax payable by a corporation is 38 per cent.[51]

(b) Surtax

In addition to the general tax, corporations are also liable to pay a surtax of 4 per cent of their basic federal tax. The surtax is calculated on the basis of the federal

---

[50] See Chapters XVI "Private Corporations: Investment Income" and XVII "Private Corporations: Business Income" for the taxation of private corporations.

[51] Para. 123(1)(a).

corporate tax payable before deductions for the small business deduction and the manufacturing and processing deduction.[52]

(c) Tax Adjustments

Few, if any, corporations actually pay tax at the basic rate. The following are some of the adjustments to the basic corporate tax:

- Provincial tax credit;
- Foreign tax credit;
- Small business deduction;
- Manufacturing and processing profits deduction;
- Logging tax deduction;
- Investment tax credit; and
- Political contributions credit.

Also, certain types of corporations are taxed at special rates because of their special status.[53]

(d) Provincial Tax Credit

A corporation may claim a tax credit of 10 per cent of its taxable income earned in a province.[54]

The provincial tax credit vacates part of the tax field to the provinces so that they may levy a corporate tax of their own. Where a province imposes a corporate tax of 10 per cent, the total burden of corporate tax (ignoring special tax adjustments) is 38 per cent. Where, however, a province imposes a provincial corporate tax in excess of 10 per cent, the effective corporate tax burden (ignoring special tax adjustments) exceeds 38 per cent.

The provincial tax credit is applicable only to a corporation's "taxable income earned in a province". This amount is determined by allocating the corporation's total taxable income to its "permanent establishments" in the provinces.[55] Thus, the calculation of a corporation's provincial tax credit involves four steps:

1. Determine whether the corporation has a "permanent establishment" in one or more provinces;

---

[52] S. 123.2.

[53] For example, investment corporations are subject to the special rules in s. 130 and non-resident-owned investment corporations are taxed at a special rate under subs. 133(3).

[54] S. 124.

[55] Regs. 401, 402.

2. Allocate the taxable income of the corporation to the various provinces in accordance with the prescribed formulae;

3. Calculate the provincial tax abatement as 10 per cent of the amount of "taxable income earned" in the provinces; and

4. Deduct the provincial tax abatement from the corporation's "tax otherwise payable".

The phrase "tax otherwise payable" is not defined and should be read as the tax that is payable after the deduction of *all* permissible deductions.

(i) "Permanent Establishment"

A "permanent establishment" is a fixed place of business of a corporation. A fixed place of business includes:[56]

- an office;
- a branch;
- a mine;
- an oil well;
- a farm;
- timberland;
- a factory;
- a workshop; or
- a warehouse.

Where a corporation does not have a fixed place of business, the term "permanent establishment" means the principal place in which the corporation's business is conducted.[57]

A corporation may be *deemed to* have a permanent establishment in a particular place. For example:

- Where a corporation carries on business through an employee (or agent), established in a particular place, who has general authority to contract or who has a stock of merchandise owned by his or her employer or principal, from which he or she regularly fills orders, that place is deemed to be a permanent establishment.[58]

---

[56] Reg. 400(2).

[57] Reg. 400(2)(*a*).

[58] Reg. 400(2)(*b*).

- Where a corporation which *otherwise* has a permanent establishment in Canada also owns land in a province, the land is deemed to be a permanent establishment.[59]

- Where a corporation uses substantial machinery or equipment in a particular place *at any time in a taxation year*, it is deemed to have a permanent establishment in that place.[60]

- An insurance corporation registered or licensed to do business in a province is deemed to have a permanent establishment in that province.[61]

The mere fact, however, that a corporation's subsidiary does business in a particular place does not necessarily mean that the parent corporation has a permanent establishment in that same place.[62] Similarly, the maintenance of an office solely for the purchase of merchandise does not *necessarily* imply the presence of a permanent establishment in that location.[63]

(ii) Allocation of Taxable Income

Having determined that a corporation has one or more permanent establishments, the next step is to allocate its taxable income to the provinces in which it maintains the establishments. The allocation is as follows:[64]

- Where a corporation has only one permanent establishment, its entire taxable income is allocated to the province in which it has that permanent establishment; and

- Where the corporation has a permanent establishment in more than one province, its taxable income is allocated on the basis of the following formula:

$$\frac{1}{2} \left(\frac{\text{Provincial Gross Revenue}}{\text{Total Gross Revenue}} + \frac{\text{Provincial Salary \& Wages}}{\text{Total Salary \& Wages}} \right) \times \text{Taxable Income}$$

A Canadian resident corporation which has only one permanent establishment in Canada and no other permanent establishment outside Canada is *deemed* to have earned its entire taxable income in that province.[65]

---

[59] Reg. 400(2)(*d*).

[60] Reg. 400(2)(*e*).

[61] Reg. 400(2)(*c*).

[62] Reg. 400(2)(*g*).

[63] Reg. 400(2)(*f*).

[64] Reg. 402. The phrase "gross revenue" is defined in subs. 248(1), and detailed rules are prescribed for determining the gross revenue attributable to a permanent establishment.

[65] Reg. 402(1).

(iii) Computation of Provincial Tax Credit

The final step in the determination of the provincial tax credit is to calculate 10 per cent of its total taxable income allocated to the provinces in which the corporation has permanent establishments. This amount is deducted from the federal tax otherwise payable.

The provincial tax credit applies only to taxable income earned in a province. It does not apply to taxable income earned in a foreign jurisdiction.

Example XIII.2

Assume that a corporation has permanent establishments in Nova Scotia, Ontario, British Columbia and the U.S., and that its gross revenues and wages are allocated as follows:

	Gross Revenue	Salaries & Wages
Nova Scotia	$ 500,000	$ 150,000
Ontario	1,300,000	400,000
B.C.	700,000	250,000
U.S.	500,000	200,000
Total	$3,000,000	$1,000,000

Total Taxable Income (assumed): $ 500,000

Then the corporation's taxable income is allocated to the *three* provinces in which it has a permanent establishment, in the following manner:

Nova Scotia

$$\frac{1}{2} \left(\frac{500,000}{3,000,000} + \frac{150,000}{1,000,000} \right) \times \$500,000 \qquad \$\ \ 79,167$$

Ontario

$$\frac{1}{2} \left(\frac{1,300,000}{3,000,000} + \frac{400,000}{1,000,000} \right) \times \$500,000 \qquad \$\ 208,333$$

B.C.

$$\frac{1}{2} \left(\frac{700,000}{3,000,000} + \frac{250,000}{1,000,000} \right) \times \$500,000 \qquad \$\ 120,833$$

Total Taxable Income Allocated to Provinces $ 408,333

Provincial Tax Credit (10% × $408,333) $ 40,833

(e) Small Business Deduction

A Canadian-controlled private corporation ("CCPC") that earns active business income in Canada is entitled to an annual tax credit (the "small business deduction") equal to 16 per cent of the first $200,000 of its active business income.[66] Thus, in effect, a CCPC pays federal tax at a rate of 13.12 per cent on the first $200,000 of its business income. This rate is determined as follows:

	%
Basic federal rate	38.00
Less provincial abatement	(10.00)
Federal rate before surtax	28.00
Surtax at 4%	1.12
	29.12
Small business deduction	16.00
Total federal tax	13.12

(f) Manufacturing and Processing Credit

The manufacturing and processing credit is intended to encourage manufacturing and processing in Canada. It is available to corporations that carry on an active business in Canada and derive gross revenue from the sale of goods manufactured or processed in Canada.

Corporations engaged in manufacturing and processing are entitled to a tax credit in respect of their profits from such activities. The tax credit for manufacturing and processing profits is 7 per cent of manufacturing and processing profits that do not qualify for the small business deduction.[67] The credit is not available in respect of income eligible for the small business deduction.

---

[66] S. 125.

[67] Subs. 125.1(1). As to the meaning of "manufacturing and processing", see *Can. Marconi Co. v. The Queen*, [1986] 2 CTC 465, 86 DTC 6526 (S.C.C.) (investments of funds necessary or ancillary to manufacturing and processing business); *Modern Miss Sportswear Ltd. v. The Queen*, [1980] CTC 521, 80 DTC 6390 (F.C.T.D.) (independent contractors sewing for garment manufacturer; not creditable); *Levi Strauss of Can. Inc. v. The Queen*, [1980] CTC 480, 80 DTC 6345; affirmed [1982] CTC 65, 82 DTC 6070 (F.C.A.) (payments made to independent contractor for the making of shirts not part of taxpayer's "cost of labour"; payments ineligible for manufacturing and processing credit); *Louben Sportswear Inc. v. M.N.R.*, [1979] CTC 2526, 79 DTC 531 (T.R.B.) (payments made to independent contractor for labour performed on supplied material not eligible for manufacturing and processing credit).

(i) Manufacturing and Processing Profits

(A) Formula

The formula for determining the portion of a corporation's profits that is derived from its manufacturing and processing activities is set out in the Regulations.[68] The formula does not directly determine the amount of manufacturing and processing profits earned by a corporation. Rather, it requires the identification of those activities that are considered to be manufacturing and processing activities and the identification of the cost of labour and the cost of capital employed in those activities. The formula is then used to allocate the total income of the corporation between "manufacturing and processing" and "other income". If, however, a corporation can qualify as a "small manufacturer", its entire "adjusted business income" is deemed to be Canadian manufacturing and processing profits. In these circumstances no formula is required.

The following is the prescribed formula to allocate manufacturing and processing income:[69]

$$MP = ABI \times \frac{(MC + ML)}{C + L}$$

where:

MP = Canadian manufacturing and processing profits
ABI = Adjusted business income
MC = Cost of manufacturing and processing capital
C   = Cost of capital
ML = Cost of manufacturing and processing labour
L   = Cost of labour

To qualify for the manufacturing and processing tax credit, the taxpayer must:

- be a corporation liable to tax under Part I of the Act;
- carry on an active business in which it processes or manufactures in Canada goods for sale or lease; and
- derive at least 10 per cent of its gross revenue in the year from manufacturing or processing in Canada goods for sale or lease by it or others.

(B) "Manufacturing or Processing"

The first step is to determine whether the activity carried on by a corporation constitutes "manufacturing or processing". The terms "manufacturing" and "processing" are not defined. The Act does, however, specifically exclude the following activities:[70]

---

[68] Regs. 5200–5204.

[69] Reg. 5200.

[70] Subs. 125.1(3) ("manufacturing or processing").

- farming or fishing;
- logging;
- construction;
- operating an oil or gas well or processing heavy crude oil produced in Canada to a stage not beyond the crude oil stage or its equivalent;
- extracting minerals from a mineral resource;
- producing industrial minerals;
- producing or processing electrical energy or steam for sale;
- processing ore (other than iron ore or tar sands) from a mineral resource not beyond the prime metal stage;
- processing iron ore from a mineral resource to the pellet stage.
- processing tar sands from a mineral resource not beyond the crude oil stage;
- producing industrial minerals other than sulphur by processing natural gas; or
- processing gas for sale or distribution by a public utility.

Since the terms "manufacturing" and "processing" are not defined, the starting point in interpreting these words is to look at their everyday meaning. The "manufacture" of goods normally involves the creation of an object or the shaping, stamping or forming of an object out of something. The "processing" of goods usually refers to a technique of preparation, handling or other activity designed to effect a physical or chemical change in an article or substance, other than by the process of natural growth.

It is important to note, however, that, even if an activity falls within the general understanding of "manufacture" or "process", the Act specifically excludes from the meaning of the terms any activities the revenue from which constitutes less than 10 per cent of the corporation's gross revenue.

(ii) Small Manufacturers

The Canadian manufacturing and processing profit of a small manufacturer is equal to its "adjusted business income".[71] To qualify as a "small manufacturer", a corporation must satisfy the following requirements:

- its activities during the year must be *primarily* the manufacturing or processing, in Canada, of goods for sale or lease;
- its active business income less its active business losses plus the net active business income of its associated corporations must not exceed $200,000;
- it must not carry on any active business outside Canada in the year; and
- the corporation must not carry on any of the activities specifically excluded from "manufacturing and processing";

---

[71] Reg. 5201.

- the corporation must not engage in processing of ore (other than iron ore or tar sands) from a mineral resource outside Canada to any stage that is not beyond the prime metal stage;
- the corporation must not engage in the processing of iron ore from a mineral resource outside Canada to any stage that is not beyond the pellet stage; and
- the corporation must not engage in the processing of tar sands located outside Canada to any stage that is not beyond crude oil.

(g) Large Corporations Capital Tax

Large corporations are subject to a special tax on their taxable capital employed in Canada.[72] The tax is set at an annual rate of 0.2 per cent of a corporation's taxable capital employed in Canada in excess of its capital deduction for the year and is payable in monthly instalments. The tax applies to all corporations, but the threshold of $10,000,000 effectively exempts small businesses.[73] The 4 per cent corporate surtax[74] may be deducted from the amount payable.[75]

4. RULES: ALL TAXPAYERS

(a) Foreign Tax Credit

References:

ITA:

Subs. 20(11)	Foreign Tax on Income from Property
Subs. 20(12)	Foreign Non-Business Income Tax
S. 126	Foreign Tax Credit

BULLETINS, CIRCULARS & RULINGS:

IT-183	October 28, 1974	Foreign Tax Credit — Member of a Partnership
IT-194	January 16, 1975	Foreign Tax Credit — Part-Time Residents
IT-270R2	February 11, 1991	Foreign Tax Credit
IT-395R	July 31, 1991	Foreign Tax Credit — Foreign-Source Capital Gains and Losses

---

[72] Part. I.3 (ss. 181–181.7).

[73] S. 181.5

[74] S. 123.2.

[75] Subs. 181.1(4).

| IT-506 | January 5, 1987 | Foreign Income Taxes as a Deduction From Income |
| IT-520 | May 1, 1989 | Unused Foreign Tax Credits — Carryforward and Carryback |

(i) General

Canadian residents are subject to full tax liability on their world-wide income. Hence, a taxpayer may be subject to double taxation: To a foreign government for income taxed at source and for Canadian tax on the basis of residence. There is, however, some relief.

A resident taxpayer may claim a credit against Canadian tax for taxes paid to a foreign government.[76] The foreign tax credit is calculated separately in respect of *each* country.[77]

The tax credit is available only in respect of obligatory taxes paid to a foreign government. Discretionary foreign taxes levied by a foreign government which would not have been imposed if the taxpayer were not entitled to a Canadian foreign tax credit are not eligible for credit in Canada.[78] The rationale for this rule is that the Canadian government does not want to finance foreign governments by encouraging them to levy taxes upon Canadians resident in their country in the expectation that the taxpayers will receive a rebate for the tax under Canadian tax law.

The foreign tax credit rules deal with three different circumstances:

1. Foreign taxes paid by a resident on non-business income;
2. Foreign taxes paid by a resident on business income; and
3. Taxes paid by non-residents in respect of certain capital gains.

(ii) Non-business-income Tax

A resident taxpayer may deduct from "tax otherwise payable" under Part I an amount equal to the non-business-income taxes[79] paid to a foreign jurisdiction. The tax credit cannot exceed the amount of Canadian tax that would have been payable on the foreign income had that income been earned in Canada.[80]

---

[76] S. 126.

[77] Subs. 126(6).

[78] Subs. 126(4).

[79] Subs. 126(7) ("non-business income tax").

[80] This is the effect of the formula in subs. 126(1).

(A) Definition

"Non-business-income tax" generally means taxes paid to a foreign jurisdiction, whether a foreign country or a subdivision of a foreign country. It does not include:[81]

- Amounts included in calculating the taxpayer's "business income tax" (the credit for business income taxes is calculated separately);

- Taxes in respect of which the taxpayer has already taken a *deduction* in computing income;[82]

- Taxes attributable to income eligible for the overseas employment tax credit;[83]

- Taxes payable to a foreign country based solely on the taxpayer being a citizen of that country if the taxes are attributable to income earned in Canada;[84]

- Taxes relating to an amount that is refunded to any person or partnership;[85]

- Taxes reasonably attributable to a taxable capital gain for which the taxpayer or his or her spouse has claimed a deduction;[86]

- Taxes reasonably attributable to a loan received by the taxpayer;[87] and

- Taxes relating to an amount that was exempt by treaty.[88]

The credit is available only for foreign taxes *actually paid* by the taxpayer *for the year*. Hence, tax refunded by a foreign government in a subsequent year because of a loss carryback necessitates a recalculation of the foreign tax credit for the year to which the refund applies.[89]

---

[81] Subs. 126(7) ("non-business income tax").

[82] Subs. 20(11) (deduction for tax in excess of 15 per cent paid to foreign government on income from property, other than real property); subs. 20(12) (deduction for tax paid to foreign government in respect of income from business or property, other than from shares of a foreign affiliate, to the extent of the "non-business-income" tax paid by taxpayer); subs. 104(22.3) (recalculation of trust's foreign tax).

[83] See subs. 122.3(1).

[84] Subs. 126(7) ("non-business income tax")(d); for example, a United States citizen who pays U.S. tax on employment income earned in Canada is not entitled to the foreign tax credit for the U.S. taxes.

[85] Subs. 126(7) ("non-business income tax")(e); some countries, such as Brazil, refund taxes withheld from payments to foreigners to the local payor; the purpose of these refunds is to subsidize domestic operations and borrowings.

[86] Subs. 126(7) ("non-business income tax")(g); s. 106.

[87] Subs. 126(7) ("non-business income tax")(h); subs. 33.1(1).

[88] Subs. 126(7) ("non-business income tax")(i); subpara. 110(1)(*f*)(i).

[89] *Icanda Ltd. v. M.N.R.*, [1972] CTC 163, 72 DTC 6148 (F.C.T.D.).

The credit is available only in respect of "income or profits" taxes paid to a foreign government. A corporate taxpayer cannot claim a credit for foreign taxes on income from a share in a foreign affiliate.[90]

(B) Limits

The foreign tax credit is subject to a limit calculated according to the following formula:

$$\frac{\text{Amount of foreign non-business income}}{\text{Income from all sources}} \times \text{Canadian tax otherwise payable}$$

The effect of this formula is that the credit for Canadian income tax purposes cannot exceed a rate that is higher than the rate that would have been payable by the taxpayer had the income been earned in Canada rather than in the foreign jurisdiction.[91]

(C) No Carryover

There is no carryover for non-business-income tax. Thus in Example XIII.3 foreign tax of $869 cannot be applied to reduce the Canadian tax payable in other fiscal periods; it may, however, be deducted as an expense in calculating income from business or property.[92]

Example XIII.3

Assume:

Mr. X, a Canadian resident, earned the following amounts in the U.S.:

Employment income (net of deductions)	$ 15,000
Tax thereon: federal	(3,600)
state	(250)
	$ 11,150
Interest income	$ 500
Tax thereon	(75)
	$ 425

He also earned $20,000 of business income in Canada and paid Canadian tax of $7,000.

---

[90] Para. 126(1)(a).

[91] Para. 126(1)(b).

[92] Subs. 20(12).

Example XIII.3 (continued)

Mr. X's non-business foreign tax credit (U.S.) is calculated as follows:

Non-business-income tax paid	$ 3,925 (A)
Non-business income	$ 15,500
Income for the year	$ 35,500
Canadian income tax	$ 7,000

Foreign tax credit limit = $\dfrac{\text{U.S. income}}{\text{Total income}} \times$ TOP*

$\dfrac{15,500}{35,500} \times \$7,000$ $ 3,056 (B)

Foreign tax credit for non-business
   income [Lesser of (A) and (B)] $ 3,056

*Tax otherwise payable determined according to subs. 126(7) ("tax for the year otherwise payable under this Part").

(iii) Business-income Tax

The credit for foreign business income tax is for the benefit of Canadian resident taxpayers who have branch operations in foreign countries.

(A) Definition

"Business-income tax" means tax paid by the taxpayer which may reasonably be regarded as a tax in respect of the income of the taxpayer from any business carried on by him or her in a foreign country.[93]

(B) Separate Calculation

As with the tax credit for non-business-income tax, the tax credit for business income taxes must be calculated separately for each country in which the taxpayer carries on business.

(C) Carryover

Business-income taxes paid to a foreign jurisdiction may exceed the amount that the taxpayer can claim as a credit against Canadian taxes. Any excess may be carried forward as an "unused foreign tax credit" for seven years and carried back for three years.[94] The foreign tax credit in respect of the current year must be claimed before any unused credits from other years.[95]

---

[93] Subs. 126(7) ("business-income tax).

[94] Para. 126(2)(a), subs. (7) ("unused foreign tax credit").

[95] Subs. 126(2.3).

(D) Limits

The credit in respect of business-income tax is limited to the amount of tax that would have been payable on a comparable amount of income earned in Canada.[96] Note: Non-business income tax credits are to be deducted before business income tax credits.[97]

(iv) Non-residents

References:

ITA:

Subs. 128.1(4)   Changes in Residence

BULLETINS, CIRCULARS & RULINGS:

IT-451R   March 25, 1987   Deemed Disposition and Acquisition on
                                          Ceasing to be or Becoming Resident in
                                          Canada

A Canadian resident who gives up residency in Canada is deemed to have disposed of his or her property immediately before the time of relinquishing residence.[98] This deemed disposition can trigger a "departure tax". In certain circumstances, the departing resident may elect to defer the tax resulting from the deemed disposition until such time as he or she actually disposes of the property.[99]

A non-resident taxpayer who defers his or her departure tax may claim a credit against Canadian tax for any non-business-income tax paid to a foreign jurisdiction when he or she actually disposes of the property.[100] There are, however, two important restrictions in respect of this credit: (1) It is available only in respect of taxes paid on account of the disposition of the *property* that was the subject of the election; and (2) The foreign tax credit must reasonably be regarded as having been paid for the year in respect of any gain on the disposition of *that* property.

(v) Employees of International Organizations

Employees of international organizations are usually exempt from income tax levied by the country in which they are stationed. Some of these organizations (for example, the United Nations) impose a levy upon their employees for the purpose of defraying the expenses of the organization. The levy is calculated in the same manner as an income tax.

---

[96] Para. 126(2)(*b*), subs. 126(2.1).

[97] Para. 126(2)(*c*).

[98] Para. 128.1(4)(*b*).

[99] Subpara. 128.1(4)(*b*)(iv).

[100] Subs. 126(2.2).

Since a Canadian resident working abroad is subject to Canadian income tax on his or her world-wide income, the imposition of this additional levy constitutes double taxation of the income. To prevent double taxation, Canadian residents employed by international agencies are allowed either a deduction or a credit for foreign income.

An employee of a *prescribed* international organization may deduct his or her employment income in calculating taxable income.[101]

Employees of other international organizations may claim a tax credit for foreign taxes paid to the organization.[102]

(b) Political Contributions Credit

Reference:

BULLETINS, CIRCULARS & RULINGS:

IC 75-2R4	January 17, 1992	Contributions to a Registered Political Party or to a Candidate at a Federal Election

Contributions to political parties and to candidates for political office are not deductible from income for tax purposes.[103] The Act does, however, allow a credit for political contributions *against tax payable*.[104] The purpose of the credit is to encourage taxpayers to support the democratic process.

The credit is available in respect of contributions to a "registered party" or to an "officially nominated candidate" in a federal election. Some of the provinces also allow for a credit against provincial taxes for contributions to provincial political parties and officially nominated candidates in provincial elections.

The amount of the credit is restricted: The percentage claimable declines as the amount of the contribution increases:

	Contribution	Tax Credit
on the first	$ 100	75%
on the next	$ 450	50%
on the next	$ 600	33 1/3%
on any excess over	$ 1,150	nil

Thus, the maximum credit is $500.

---

[101] Subpara. 110(1)(*f*)(iii).

[102] Subs. 126(3).

[103] Para. 18(1)(*n*); *Stasiuk v. The Queen*, [1986] 2 CTC 346 (F.C.T.D.) (taxpayer denied deduction for amounts expended on publicizing her political views).

[104] Subs. 127(3).

A claim for the credit must be supported by filing an official receipt signed by a registered agent of the party or candidate. The receipt must disclose certain prescribed information.[105]

(c) Other Tax Credits

There are other special tax credits available to taxpayers who derive income from particular types of activities.

(i) Logging Tax Credit

Reference:

ITA:

Subs. 127(1)   Logging Tax Credit

Subsection 127(1) allows a credit for "logging taxes" paid by a taxpayer to a province in respect of logging operations. (British Columbia and Quebec impose logging taxes.)

(ii) Investment Tax Credit

An investment tax credit is available for most current and capital expenditures on account of research and development carried on in Canada.[106]

The investment tax credit is intended to stimulate investment in certain types of activities and in certain regions of the country.

Generally speaking, the credit is available to a taxpayer in respect of acquisitions of depreciable property used by the taxpayer in Canada primarily for the purpose of:[107]

- Manufacturing or processing of goods for sale or lease;
- Operating an oil or gas well;
- Processing heavy crude oil recovered from a natural reservoir in Canada to a stage that is not beyond the crude oil stage or its equivalent;
- Extracting minerals from a resource;
- Processing ore (other than iron or tar sands) to the prime metal stage or its equivalent;
- Exploring or drilling for oil or gas;
- Prospecting or exploring for or developing a mineral resource;
- Logging;

---

[105] Reg. 2000.

[106] Subs. 127(5).

[107] Subs. 127(9) ("qualified property").

- Farming or fishing;
- Storing grain;
- Producing industrial minerals;
- Harvesting peat;
- Processing iron ore to the pellet stage; or
- Processing tar sands to the crude oil stage.

The amount of the credit depends upon the type of investment made by the taxpayer, the region in which the investment is made, whether the property is "available for use" and, in certain cases, the taxpayer's status.

The investment tax credit is deductible against taxes otherwise payable. Unused credits may be carried back three years and carried forward for ten years.[108]

---

[108] Subs. 127(9) ("investment tax credit") (*c*)(ii).

SELECTED BIBLIOGRAPHY TO CHAPTER XXIII

General

Account of the Cost of Selective Tax Measures (Dept. of Finance, Canada, 1985).

Bale, Gordon, "The Tax Reform Bill and the Problem of Income Fluctuation" (1971), 19 *Can. Tax J.* 487.

Carlyle, William M., and Howard J. Kellough, "Tick-Tock, or Timing Problems under the Income Tax Act" (1973), 21 *Can. Tax J.* 85.

Drache, A.B.C., "General Averaging" (1981), 3 *Can. Taxpayer* 11.

Individuals

As True As Taxes: Disability and the Income Tax System: Report of the Standing Committee on Human Rights and the Status of Disabled Persons (Ottawa: The Committee, 1993).

Ballantyne, Janet L., "The Alternative Minimum Tax and Dividends" (1986), 34 *Can. Tax J.* 242.

Beam, Robert E., and Karen Wensley, "Personal Tax Planning: Alternative Minimum Tax — The Political Tax" (1986), 34 *Can. Tax J.* 174.

Bernstein, Jack, "Family Succession", in *Proceedings of 38th Tax Conf.* 15 (Can. Tax Foundation, 1986).

Bernstein, Jack, "Shelter Benefits Gone With Minimum Personal Law" (1986), 5:37 *Ont. Lawyers Wkly.* 6.

Berry, David B., "1988 Provincial Tax Comparisons (Part I)" (1988), 36 *Can. Tax J.* 1054.

Bromley, Blake E., "A Response to 'A Better Tax Administration in Support of Charities'" (1991), 10 *Philanthrop.* 3.

Colley, G.M., "Do We Need a Minimum Tax?" (1986), 119:11 *CA Magazine* 56.

Colley, G.M., "Proposed Minimum Tax Poses Maximum Problems" (1986), 119:2 *CA Magazine* 49.

Dart, Robert J., "A Critique of an Advance Corporate Tax System for Canada" (1990), 38 *Can. Tax J.* 1245.

Drache, A.B.C., "Child Tax Credit (The)" (1979), 1 *Can. Taxpayer* 23.

Drache, A.B.C., "Delaying Credit Claims" (1995), 17 *Can. Taxpayer* 59.

Drache, A.B.C., "A Gift by Any Other Name" (1995), 17 *Can. Taxpayer* 7.

Drache, A.B.C., "Income Splitting with Charitable Tax Credits" (1995), 17 *Can. Taxpayer* 54.

Drache, A.B.C., "Making Gold from Straw" (1995), 17 *Can. Taxpayer* 80.

Drache, A.B.C., "Medical Tax Credits: Too Often Wasted" (1995), 17 *Can. Taxpayer* 51.

Drache, A.B.C., "Personal Tax Credits Frozen" (1995), 17 *Can. Taxpayer* 11.

Drache, A.B.C., "Revenue Hard on Disability Claims" (1995), 17 *Can. Taxpayer* 15.

Drache, A.B.C., "Spousal Dividend Swaps" (1995), 17 *Can. Taxpayer* 53.

Drache, A.B.C., "Spousal Tax Return" (1981), 3 *Can. Taxpayer* 38.

Drache, A.B.C., "Tax-Free Dividend Level: (1983)" (1983), 5 *Can. Taxpayer* 41.

Erlichman, Harry, "Profitable Donations: What Price Culture?" (1992), 11 *Philanthrop.* 3.

Goodman, Sheldon H., "The Alternative Minimum Tax", in *Proceedings of 38th Tax Conf.* 32 (Can. Tax Foundation, 1986).

Gotlieb, Maxwell, "Taxation of, and Tax Planning for, Charitable Donations" (1993), 11 *Philanthrop.* 37.

Huggett, Donald R., "Alternative Minimum Tax (A Fiscal Albatross)" (1986), 13 *Can. Tax News* 109.

Huggett, Donald R., "Minimum Income Tax (A)", in *Proceedings of 37th Tax Conf.* 10:1 (Can. Tax Foundation, 1985).

Huggett, Donald R., "Minimum Tax (The)" (1985), 13 *Can. Tax News* 75.

Huggett, Donald R., "Personal Income Tax Rates — 1986" (1986), 13 *Can. Tax News* 111.

Huggett, Donald R., "Temporary Surtax" (1985), 13 *Can. Tax News* 97.

Innes, William I., "Gifts of Cultural Property by Artists" (1993), 11 *Philanthrop.* 3.

Jenkins, Glenn P., "The Role and Economic Implications of the Canadian Dividend Tax Credit", *Discussion Paper No. 307* (Ottawa: Economic Council of Canada, June 1986).

Kitchen, Brigitte, "The Refundable Child Tax Credit" (1979), 1 *Can. Taxation* 44.

Larin, Gilles N. and Marie N. Jacques, "Is the Alternative Minimum Tax a Paper Tiger?" (1994), 42 *Can. Tax J.* 804.

Low Income Tax Relief Working Group of Fair Tax Commission, *Working Group Report* (Toronto: Fair Tax Commission, 1992).

Lynch, John, "Alternative Minimum Tax" (1986), 14:6 *Can. Tax News* 66.

Marsel, Neil, "Taking into account Tax Credits where Tax Credits are Due" (1991), 6 *Money and Family Law* 65.

McKie, A.B., "Minimum Tax" (1985), 92:1 *Can. Bank* 40.

McDonnell, T.E., "In Tax Law, Form Matters" (1992), 40 *Can. Tax J.* 384.

Medland, Christina H., "Limitations on Charities Under the Income Tax Act" (1992), 44 *E.T.R.* 111.

Newman, Eric J., "Tax Indexing — What Does It Mean to You?" (1974), 105:5 *CA Magazine* 54.

Novek, Barbara L., "Sector Specific Tax Relief for Canadian Residents Working Overseas" (1993), 5 *Tax. of Exec. Compensation and Retirement* 808.

Petrie, Deborah A., and Pierre M. Turgeon, *The Alternative Minimum Tax: Impact on Canadian Taxpayers* (CCH Canadian, 1986).

Pintea, Hans O., "Accounting Methods, Deductions and Averaging Provisions", in *Proceedings of 26th Tax Conf.* 590 (Can. Tax Foundation, 1974).

Sayeed, Adil, "Choosing Between Tax Credits and Exemptions for Dependent Children" (1985), 33 *Can. Tax J.* 975.

Sherbeniuk, Douglas J., "Future Trends in Tax Policy: Focus on the Alternative Minimum Tax and the Corporate Income Tax Discussion Papers," [1986] *Special Lectures L.S.U.C.* 425.

Shinerock, Stanley, "Dividends and All That" (1979), 13:9 *CGA Magazine* 14.

Smith, David W., "Alternative Minimum Tax Provisions Set for 1986 Taxation Year: No Rule of Thumb to Determine When Payable" (1986), 13:9 *Nat. (C.B.A.)* 22.

Smith, David W., "Wilson's Minimum-Tax Proposals Treat Dividends Unfairly" (1986), 13:2 *Nat. (C.B.A.)* 22.

Smith, Roger S., "Rates of Personal Income Tax: The Carter Commission Revisited" (1987), 35 *Can. Tax J.* 1226, and in *The Quest for Tax Reform,* W. Neil Brooks, (ed.) (Toronto: Carswell, 1988), p. 173.

Sunley, Emil M., "Minimum Income Taxation", in *Proceedings of 37th Tax Conf.* 11:1 (Can. Tax Foundation, 1985).

Swanson, Julie Anne, *The Alternative Minimum Tax* (Don Mills: CCH Canadian Ltd., 1991).

Wilson, Michael H., *A Minimum Tax for Canada*, Dept. of Finance, Canada, 1985.

Wilson, Michael H., *A Minimum Tax for Canada: Executive Summary*, Dept. of Finance, Canada, 1985.

Rules: Corporations

Allgood, David R., "Tax Planning for Private Corporations and Their Shareholders: Implications of Recent Changes on the Use of Holding Companies", in *Proceedings of the 38th Tax Conf.* 10 (Can. Tax Foundation, 1986).

Blais, A., and F. Vaillancourt, "The Federal Corporate Income Tax: Tax Expenditures and Tax Discrimination in the Canadian Manufacturing Industry, 1972-1981" (1986), 34 *Can. Tax J.* 1122.

Corn, George, "Manufacturing or Processing of Goods for Sale" (1994), 5 *Can. Current Tax* 11.

Dale, Michael, "A Comparison of Effective Marginal Tax Rates on Income Capital in Canadian Manufacturing" (1985), 33 *Can. Tax J.* 1154.

Drache, A.B.C., "Corporate Donations - Personal Tax Savings" (1995), *Can. Taxpayer* 30.

Drache, A.B.C., "Pre-Mortem Planning" (1991), 13 *Can. Taxpayer* 86.

Horne, Barry D. and Tim S. Wach, "Canadian Taxation of Foreign Sourced Income: The Foreign Tax Credit" (1991), 3 *Imm. & Cit.* 4.

Huggett, Donald R., "Temporary Surtax" (1985), 13 *Can. Tax News* 97.

Lahmer, Craig, "Recent Developments in Manufacturing and Processing" in *Proceedings of 44th Tax Conf.* (Can. Tax Found., 1992) 52:1.

McDonnell, T.E., "Manufacturing and Processing Profits: Some Interpretive Questions" (1994), 40 *Can. Tax J.* 929.

Nolke, David, "All in the (Corporate) Family" (1991), 25 *CGA Magazine* 17.

Sennema, James R., "Temporary Business Operations as 'Permanent Establishments'" (1992), 5 *C.U.B.L.R.* 171.

Vytas, Nalaitas, "Large Corporation's Tax" (1990), 64 *CMA Magazine* 34.

Rules: All Taxpayers

Attridge, Ian, "Create Conservation Gains, Not Capital Gains" (1994), 19 *Intervenor* 8.

Baillie, William J., "Expanded Investment Tax Credits a Boon to Canadian Business" (1984), 117:5 *CA Magazine* 42.

Baillie, William J., "Investment Tax Credits" (1984), 18 *CGA Magazine* 30.

Brown, Robert D., "The Investment Tax Credit: Mysteries Unravelled, or Up the Down Escalator?", in *Proceedings of 35th Tax Conf.* 77 (Can. Tax Foundation, 1983).

Clark, W. Steven, "Canada's R & D Tax Incentives: Recent Developments" in *Proceedings of 44th Tax Conf.* (Can. Tax Foundation, 1992) 32:1.

Colley, Geoffrey M., "The Latest on Investment Tax Credits" (1983), 116:9 *CA Magazine* 53.

Drache, A.B.C., "Canadian Taxation of Charities and Donations" (Scarborough, Ont.: Carswell, 1994).

Farrow, Trevor C.W., "The Limits of Charity: Redefining the Boundaries of Charitable Trust Law" (1994), 13 *Estates and Trusts J.* 306.

Farwell, Peter M., "Scientific Research and Experimental Development", *Corporate Management Tax Conf.* 7:1 (Can. Tax Foundation, 1987).

Goodman, Wolfe D. and Barry Naiberg, "Holding Companies: Why They're Still Attractive" (1983), 116:3 *CA Magazine* 44.

Gotlieb, Maxwell, *Charities and the Tax Man and More* (Toronto: Canadian Bar Association — Ontario, Continuing Legal Education, 1990).

Juneau, Carl D., "Some Major Issues Affecting Evaluation of the Charities Tax Incentive" (1990), 9 *Philanthrop.* 3.

Kamin, Shelley J., "Scientific Research and Experimental Development Tax Incentives" (1993), 10 *C.I.P. Rev.* 487.

Kraayeveld, S.H., "Tax Credits" (1985), 13 *Can. Tax News* 93.

Law, Tax, and Charities: The Legislative and Regulatory Environment for Charitable and Non-profit Organizations (Toronto: The Canadian Centre for Philanthropy, 1990).

"Mandatory Social Security Contributions Abroad Produce Tax Relief at Home" (1994), 5 *Tax. of Exec. Compensation and Retirement* 907.

McKie, A.B., "Foreign Tax Credit — Some Thoughts" (1984), 1 *Can. Current Tax* C-11.

Monaco, Joseph C., *Charitable Donations: 'Gifts in Kind', Cultural Proprty Export and Import Act Gifts: Tax Considerations* (Hamilton, Ont.: Thorne, Ernst & Whinney, 1989).

Murray, Kenneth J., "Complying With the R & D Rules", *Corporate Management Tax Conf.* 3:1 (Can. Tax Foundation, 1988).

Ntiamoa, K.T., "Investment Tax Credits" (1983), 17 *CGA Magazine* 58.

Rotfleisch, David J., "Unquestionable Incentives" (1993), 126 *CA Mag.* 27.

Shultis, Roy, "Revenue Canada's Administration of R & D Tax Incentives: Overview of Current Administrative Practices" in *Proceedings of 44th Tax Conf.* (Can. Tax Foundation, 1992) 33:1.

Sweeney, Terrance A., and Larissa V. Tkachenko, "Cape Breton Investment Tax Credit", in *Proceedings of 38th Tax Conf.* 47 (Can. Tax Foundation, 1986).

Tremblay, Richard G., "Foreign Tax Credit Planning" (1993), *Corp. Mgmt. Tax Conf.* 3:1.

Wensley, Karen, "Scientific Research and Experimental Development: An Update on the Status of the Canadian Tax Incentives" in *Proceedings of 44th Tax Conf.* (Can. Tax Foundation, 1992) 31:1.

Other

Bernstein, Jack, and Suzanne I.R. Hanson, "The Taxation of Accumulating Income of Personal Trusts" (1980), 28 *Can. Tax J.* 715.

Birnie, David A.G., "Shareholders' Buy-Sell Agreements: Some New Opportunities", in *Proceedings of the 38th Tax Conf.* 13 (Can. Tax Foundation, 1986).

Clemen, Phillipe, *Environmentally Perverse Government Incentives* (Ottawa: National Round Table on the Environment and the Economy: IRPP Institute for Research on Public Policy, 1992).

Johnston, Albert N., "Farm Taxation" (1982), 115:5 *CA Magazine* 67.

Routley, Tom C., "Research and Development Tax Incentive Policy: A Call to Action", in *Proceedings of 38th Tax Conf.* 24 (Can. Tax Foundation, 1986).

Strain, H. Larry, "Integration Revisited", in *Proceedings of the 38th Tax Conf.* 9 (Can. Tax Foundation, 1986).

CHAPTER XIV

CORPORATIONS AND SHAREHOLDERS: GENERAL

To this point, we have been looking at the general rules in respect of the computation of taxable income and tax payable. Most of these rules apply to all taxpayers, including individuals, corporations, and trusts. In this and subsequent chapters, we focus on the rules that apply specifically to corporations and their shareholders.

1. THE CORPORATE ENTITY

Reference:

ITA:

S. 112   Deduction of Taxable Dividends

(a) Separate Legal Entity

A corporation is a "person", and therefore a "taxpayer" in its own right.[1] A corporation is a legal entity that is brought into existence by its constating documents and is an entity distinct from its shareholders. A corporation has been described as:[2]

> . . . [an] artificial person established for preserving in perpetual succession certain rights, which being conferred on natural persons only, would fail in process of time. . . . The royal charter gives it a legal immortality, and a name by which it acts and becomes known. It has power to make by-laws for its own government, and transacts its business under the authority of a common seal — its hand and mouthpiece; it has neither soul nor tangible form, so it can neither be outlawed nor arrested; it only enjoys a legal entity, sues, and is sued by its corporate name, and holds and enjoys property by such name. The several members of a corporation and their successors constitute but one person in law. . . . The distinction between corporations and trading partnerships is, that in the first the law sees only the body corporate and knows not the individuals, who are not liable for the contracts of the corporation in their private capacity, their share in the capital only being at stake : but in the latter the law looks not to the partnership, but to the individual members of it, who are therefore answerable for the debts of the firm to the full extent of their assets.

Unlike a partnership, which is a *relationship* between persons carrying on business in common with a view to profit,[3] a corporation is an entity that has a legal existence separate and apart from its shareholders.

The concept that a corporation is a legal entity separate and distinct from its shareholders gives rise to difficult problems in taxation. Since a corporation is a

---

[1] Subs. 248(1) ("person"), ("taxpayer").

[2] *Wharton's Law Lexicon*, 8th. ed. (London: Stevens, 1889): "corporation or body politic".

[3] See, e.g., *Partnerships Act*, R.S.O. 1990, c. P.5, s. 2.

separate entity, its property, assets and liabilities belong to, or flow from, the corporation. This is so even if there is only one shareholder of the corporation who owns all of its issued and outstanding shares. The "one person company" is no less of a corporation and a separate legal identity than a publicly-held corporation.

(b) The *Salomon* Doctrine

Salomon[4] is the *locus classicus* upholding the principle that a corporation has a separate legal identity that is distinct from its shareholders. Mr. Salomon incorporated a company to which he sold his unincorporated shoe manufacturing business in return for all but six of the issued shares of the company and £10,000 of secured debentures. When the company fell upon hard times and was wound up a year later, the unsecured creditors, alleging that the company was a mere alias or agent of its principal shareholder, claimed that Mr. Salomon was personally liable to indemnify their claims. The House of Lords held that all of the requirements of the corporate statute authorizing the creation of the company had been complied with, that the corporation was not a sham, and that Salomon had not acted fraudulently. As a secured creditor of the corporation, Mr. Salomon ranked ahead of its unsecured creditors. As Lord Macnaghten said:[5]

> The company attains maturity on its birth. There is no period of minority — no interval of incapacity. . . . The company is, at law, a different person altogether from the subscribers to the memorandum; and, though it may be that after incorporation the business is precisely the same as it was before, the same persons are managers, and the same hands receive the profits, the company is not in law the agent of the subscribers or trustee for them. Nor are the subscribers, as members liable, in any shape or form, except to the extent and in the manner provided by the Act.

---

[4] *Salomon v. Salomon & Co.*, [1897] AC 22 (H.L.).

[5] *Salomon v. Salomon & Co.*, *ante*, at 51. Although Mr. Salomon had not committed any fraud on his creditors, it was found that he had sold his business to his company at an extravagant price. As Lord Macnaghten put it, the price "represented the sanguine expectations of a fond owner rather than anything that can be called a businesslike or reasonable estimate of value". (p. 49)

Hence, where a corporation is created according to the terms of the relevant corporate statute, it becomes an entity legally distinct from its shareholders.[6]

(c) Parent and Subsidiary

The principle that a corporation is a legal entity separate from its shareholders carries through to the relationship between a parent company and its subsidiary. Thus, in the absence of a specific statutory provision to the contrary, a parent corporation and its subsidiary are separate and distinct legal entities. This is so even where the parent owns all the shares of its subsidiary and the two are, in effect, one economic entity.[7]

Since a parent corporation and its subsidiaries are separate entities, one cannot automatically be considered to be an agent of the other. Nor, as a general rule, can a parent corporation be held liable for its subsidiary's debts, or *vice versa.*[8]

(d) Multiple Relationships

An important consequence of the doctrine of separate corporate personality is that a shareholder can have multiple legal relationships with a corporation.[9] An individual may be employed by a corporation, be its director or have a debtor/creditor relationship

---

[6] *Army & Navy Department Store v. M.N.R.*, [1953] CTC 293 at 308, 53 DTC 1185 at 1193 (S.C.C.), *per* Cartwright J.: "With the greatest of respect for those who hold the contrary view, I do not think that shareholders, either individually or collectively, have any ownership direct or indirect in the property of the company in which they hold shares"; see, generally, *Rielle v. Reid* (1899), 26 OAR 54 (C.A.); *Kodak Ltd. v. Clark*, [1902] 2 KB 450, affirmed [1903] 1 KB 505 (C.A.); *Janson v. Driefontein Consol. Mines Ltd.*, [1902] AC 484 at 497, 498, 501 (H.L.); *Rainham Chem. Works Ltd. v. Belvedere Fish Guano Co.*,[1921] 2 AC 465 at 475, 476, 501 (H.L.); *Meadow Farm Ltd. v. Imp. Bank of Can.*(1922), 18 Alta. LR 335 (C.A.); *British Thomson-Houston Co. v. Sterling Accessories Ltd.*, [1924] 2 Ch. 33; *Assoc. Growers of B.C. Ltd. v. Edmunds*, [1926] 1 WWR 535 (B.C.C.A.); *Export Brewing & Malting Co. v. Dom. Bank*, [1937] 2 WWR 568 (P.C.); *The Queen v. Meilicke*, [1938] 2 WWR 97; leave to appeal to P.C. granted [1938] 2 WWR 424; *Hydro-Elec. Power Comm. of Ont. v. Thorold Township* (1924), 55 OLR 431 at 435 (Ont. C.A.); *Beckow v. Panich* (1940), 69 Que. KB 398 (C.A.); *White v. Bank of Toronto*, [1953] OR 479 (C.A.); *Bank Voor Handel en Scheepvaart N.V. v. Slatford*, [1953] 1 QB 248 at 269; *Lee v. Lee's Air Farming Ltd.*, [1961] AC 12 (P.C.). See also: *Kosmopoulos v. Constitution Ins. Co. of Can.*, [1987] 1 SCR 2 at 10, 36 BLR 233 at 240, *per* Wilson, J.: "As a general rule, a corporation is a legal entity distinct from its shareholders".

[7] *Aluminum Co. of Can. v. Toronto*, [1944] SCR 267 (S.C.C.); *Barnes v. Sask. Co-op. Wheat Producers Ltd.*, [1946] 1 WWR 97 at 113; affirmed [1947] SCR 241 (S.C.C.) [Sask.]; *Ebbw Vale Urban Dist. Council v. South Wales Traffic Licensing Authority*, [1951] 2 KB 366 (C.A.), *per* Cohen L.J. (under ordinary rules of law, parent and wholly-owned subsidiary are distinct legal entities; in absence of agency contract between companies, one cannot be said to be agent of other).

[8] *Hartford Accident & Indemnity Co. v. Millsons Const. Ltd.* (1939), 44 Que. PR 170 (S.C.); see *Discount & Loan Corp. v. Supt. of Ins.*, [1938] Ex. CR 194; affirmed [1939] SCR 285 (S.C.C.) (corporate veil may, of course, be pierced); *Ebbw Vale Urban Dist. Council v. South Wales Traffic Licensing Authority, ante* (statute may deem acts of subsidiary corporation to be acts of its parent corporation).

[9] *Lee v. Lee's Air Farming Ltd., ante.*

with the corporation. Each of these relationships gives rise to different types of income subject to different rules of computation:

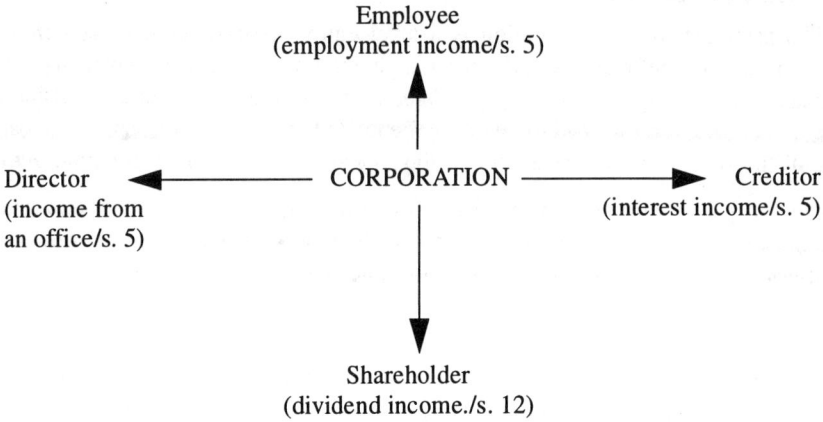

Employee
(employment income/s. 5)

Director   CORPORATION   Creditor
(income from   (interest income/s. 5)
an office/s. 5)

Shareholder
(dividend income./s. 12)

(e) Piercing the Corporate Veil

A corporation's separate legal existence may be disregarded and its veil lifted to reach through the corporate entity to its individual members. Legal ownership may be ignored for certain purposes in favour of economic ownership.

(i) Common Law Piercing

Having said that the corporate veil may be pierced, it is not at all easy to identify the circumstances in which a court will do so.[10] The courts will usually only ignore a corporation's separate legal personality where it is used to defeat public convenience, justify wrong, protect fraud or defend crime.[11] As Lord Denning said in *Littlewoods*:[12]

---

[10] *Kosmopoulos v. Constitution Ins. Co. of Can., ante*, [1987] 2 SCR at 10, 36 BLR at 240 *per* Wilson J.:
As a general rule a corporation is a legal entity distinct from its shareholders. The law on when a court may disregard this principle "lifting the corporate veil" and regard the company as a mere "agent" or "puppet" of its controlling shareholder or parent corporation follows no consistent principle. The best that can be said is that the "separate entities" principle is not enforced when it would yield a result "too flagrantly opposed to justice, convenience or the interests of the Revenue".

[11] See Durnford, "The Corporate Veil in Tax Law" (1979), 27 *Can. Tax. J.* 282; Feltham, "Lifting the Corporate Veil", [1968] *LSUC Lectures* 305; see also Wormser, *The Disregard of the Corporate Fiction & Allied Corporate Problems* (1927); Latty, "The Corporate Entity as a Solvent of Legal Problems" (1936), 34 *Mich. L. Rev.* 597; Horowitz, "Disregarding the Entity of Private Corporations" (1939), 14 *Wash L. Rev.* 285; *Ballantine on Corporations* (Chicago: Callaghan and Company, 1946), at 292. *Gower's Principles of Modern Company Law*, 4th ed. (London: Stevens, 1979), at 112-38 (English parallel).

[12] *Littlewoods Mail Order Stores v. McGregor*, [1969] 3 All ER 855 at 860 (C.A.).

The doctrine laid down in *Salomon* has to be watched very carefully. It has often been supposed to cast a veil over the personality of a limited company through which the courts cannot see. But that is not true. The courts can and often do draw aside the veil. They can, and often do pull off the mask. They look to see what really lies behind. The legislature has shown the way with group accounts and the rest. And the courts should follow suit.

Two points warrant emphasis. First, the principle that the veil can be pierced for the protection of public convenience, prevention of wrong, avoidance of fraud or prevention of crime applies equally in corporate and tax law. There is no separate legal doctrine for piercing the corporate veil in tax cases. Judges are, however, more willing to pierce the corporate veil in tax cases.[13]

Second, merely because a court lifts a corporation's veil for a particular purpose does not imply that its separate legal personality is to be ignored for all other purposes. Where the veil is lifted, it is lifted only for the specific purpose of the litigated issue and not for other purposes.[14]

Thus, merely because a corporation's veil is lifted for tax purposes does not imply that its shareholders also automatically become personally liable for its debts. The corporation's separate personality remains intact for all other purposes, including that of limiting the liability of its shareholders for corporate debts.[15]

(ii) Statutory Piercing

The legislature can also, to use Lord Devlin's phrase, forge a sledgehammer capable of cracking open the corporate shell.[16] Thus, a statute can reach through a corporation and tax its shareholders in their personal capacity, or regard an affiliated group of corporations *as if* they comprised one legal entity.

---

[13] *Consol.-Bathurst Ltd. v. The Queen*, [1985] 1 CTC 142, 85 DTC 5120 at 5124; additional reasons at [1985] 1 CTC 351, 85 DTC 5244; reversed in part [1987] 1 CTC 55, 87 DTC 5001 (F.C.A.).

[14] *Nedco Ltd. v. Clark*, [1973] 6 WWR 425 at 433 (Sask. C.A.) *per* Culliton C.J.S.:
    While the principle laid down in *Salomon* is, and continues to be, a fundamental feature of Canadian law, there are instances in which the court can and should lift the corporate veil, but whether it does so depends upon the facts in each particular case. Moreover, the fact that the court does lift the corporate veil for a specific purpose in no way destroys the recognition of the corporation as an independent and autonomous entity for all other purposes.

[15] See, e.g., *Canada Business Corporations Act*, R.S.C. 1985, c. C-44, subs. 45(1); *Business Corporations Act*, R.S.O. 1990, c. B.16, subs. 92(1).

[16] *Bank Voor Handel en Scheepvaart N.V. v. Slatford*, [1953] 1 QB 248 at 278.

Examples of Statutory Piercing		
Statutory Reference	**Item**	**Comment**
Subs. 256(2.1) discretionary	Associated corporations	The Minister has discretionary power to deem two or more corporations to be associated with each other. Associated corporations are, in effect, treated as one corporation for the purpose of certain tax deductions and credits, such as the small business deduction.
S. 227.1	Liability of directors for failure of corporation to remit taxes	Directors may be *personally* liable for certain taxes which the corporation failed to deduct, withhold, remit or pay.
Para. 18(1)(*p*); subs. 125(7) ("personal services business")	Personal services income	In determining whether a business is a "personal service business", the relationship between the "incorporated employee" and the person to whom services are rendered is examined *as if* the corporation did not exist.

(iii) Related Corporations

A corporation may incorporate another corporation by signing articles of incorporation and complying with the relevant statutes.[17] The legal rule that govern corporations owned by individuals also apply to corporations owned by other corporations.

Corporations may be related through a vertical relationship (for example, parent-subsidiary) or a horizontal relationship (for example, affiliated corporations). In either case, related corporations are generally treated as separate and distinct legal persons. This is so even if a corporation owns all of the shares of its related corporation. But just as a court can pierce the veil of a single corporation, it can also pierce the veils of a group of related corporations and regard the group as one economic entity.

---

[17] See, for example, *Canada Business Corporations Act,* R.S.C. 1985, c. C-44, subs. 5(2); *Business Corporations Act*, R.S.O. 1990, c. B.16, subs. 4(1).

There are various theories used to ignore the separate legal personality of a group of related corporations. Some courts refer to one corporation being under the control or dominance of another; others say that one of the corporations is an instrumentality of the other; still others describe one corporation as being the agent of the other. Berle's thesis is as follows:[18]

> Another illustration of judicial erection of a new entity occurs in situations where the corporate personality (as embodied in its charter, books and so forth) does not correspond to the actual enterprise, but merely to a fragment of it. The result is to construct a new aggregate of assets and liabilities. Typical cases appear where a partnership or a central corporation owns the controlling interest in one or more other corporations, but has so handled them that they had ceased to represent a separate enterprise and have become, as a business matter, more or less indistinguishable parts of a larger enterprise. The decisions disregard the paper corporate personalities and base liability on the assets of the enterprise. The reasoning by which courts reach this result varies: it is sometimes said that one corporation has become a mere "agency" of another; or that its operations may have been so intermingled that it has lost its identity; or that the business arrangements indicate that it has become a "mere instrumentality".

But words such as "agency", "control" and "instrumentality" offer little by way of guidance. As Latty has said: "What the formula comes down to, once shorn of verbiage about control, instrumentality, agency and corporate entity, is that liability is imposed to reach an equitable result".[19] The difficulty, as Professor Gower has stated, "is that the attitude of the courts is unpredictable. Each case where they have regarded the subsidiary as agent of the parent can be matched with another in which they have refused to do so".[20]

All that can be said is that a court is more likely to pierce the corporate veil of a group of related corporations where the corporate, economic and managerial relationships are so closely intertwined that the corporations can be considered as one enterprise. Berle puts it as follows:[21]

> If it be shown that the enterprise is not reflected and comprehended by the corporate papers, books and operations, the court may reconstruct the actual enterprise, giving entity to it, based on the economic facts. Thus one corporation may be shown to be in fact only an "instrumentality" of a large enterprise, or to be so intermingled with the operations of such larger enterprise as to have lost its own identity.

(f) Personal Liability for Shareholders

Limited liability companies were created to attract capital investment without exposing shareholders to the unlimited liability usually associated with proprietorships and partnerships. The corporate veil may be pierced to attach personal liability to shareholders but, generally, only in clearly convincing cases of fraud, shams, outrageously offensive conduct, and overriding considerations of public policy.

---

[18] Berle, *Theory of Enterprise Entity* (London: Stevens, 1979).

[19] Latty, *Basic Business Associations* (Boston: Little, Brown, 1963).

[20] *Gower's Principles of Modern Company Law*, 4th ed. (London, Stevens, 1979), at 129.

[21] Berle, *Theory of Enterprise Entity* (London: Stevens, 1979).

Shareholders can, however, be personally liable for corporate tax even though they act in good faith. *Algoa Trust*[22] illustrates the potential risks: The corporation paid cash dividends to its shareholders at a time when it had satisfied all of its assessments and was current in respect of its tax liabilities. Some time later, however, Revenue Canada issued reassessments in respect of the corporation's earlier (but not statute barred) taxation years. When the corporation failed to pay its reassessed tax, the Minister pursued the shareholders personally for the unpaid tax on the basis that a corporation and its shareholders are jointly and severally liable for tax under section 160 of the *Income Tax Act.*

Section 160 is intended to prevent a taxpayer from rendering himself or herself judgment-proof by transferring his or her property to, *inter alia*, persons with whom he or she does not deal at arm's length. Paragraph 160(1)(*c*) is triggered when a corporation pays dividends to a person with whom it does not deal at arm's length (such as an owner/manager or relative) and the corporation is at that time liable for tax. Section 160 is a strict liability provision. It does not require any intent to avoid taxes on the part of the transferor or any knowledge by the transferee that the dividend was paid when the corporation's past tax years were open to potential reassessment.

What is less obvious, however, is that the section can be triggered *retroactively* through a subsequent reassessment. This is because the legal obligation to pay tax arises when income is *earned*, not when it is assessed for tax. Since the Minister may reassess a corporation three or four years after its assessment, a shareholder's liability for the corporation's tax can be retroactively regenerated when the corporation is subsequently reassessed. Thus, shareholders in receipt of dividends are never free of the potential burden to pay corporate taxes until such time as the corporation's particular taxation year is statute barred.

2. STRUCTURE OF CORPORATE TAXATION

(a) Basic Structure

The first and most obvious question in corporate taxation is: Should we have a corporate tax at all? It is arguable that all corporate income should be attributed to, and taxed in the hands of, individual shareholders as it is earned, regardless of whether or not the income is actually distributed through dividends. Only individuals ultimately bear the burden of tax. Artificial entities do not really "pay" tax — they act merely as conduits for individuals who are the real taxpayers.

The concept of *notionally* flowing through corporate income to individual shareholders has conceptual appeal. The concept is, however, fraught with several practical problems. Notional flow-through of corporate income that would be taxed in the hands of individuals would create severe liquidity problems for taxpayers if the flow-through was not accompanied by cash dividends. There would be substantial

---

[22] *Algoa Trust et al. v. The Queen,* [1993] 1 CTC 2294, 93 DTC 405 (T.C.C.).

pressure on corporations to make dividend payments to cover tax liabilities resulting from the notional flow-through of income. This could have a significant effect on capital markets.

There could also be significant corporate control shifts if individual shareholders were compelled to sell a portion of their shareholdings in order to raise the cash necessary to pay tax liabilities that would result from the notional flow-through of corporate income. Corporate control could change from the liquidation of shares and family-owned businesses in particular would be vulnerable. Private corporations might encounter difficulties in finding a suitable market for their shares, which would need to be valued annually. These concerns strongly influenced the *Carter Commission Report*:[23]

> Equity and neutrality would best be achieved under a tax system in which there were no taxes on organizations as such, and all individuals and families holding interests in organizations were taxed on the accrued net gains from such interests on the same basis as all other net gains. . . .
>
> Although we can see no grounds in principle for taxing corporations and other organizations, we have reluctantly reached the conclusion that there are good and sufficient reasons for continuing to collect a tax from them. The main reason is the practical difficulty of taxing accrued share gains as required under the ideal approach we have just described. Another reason is the loss in economic benefit to Canada that would result if non-residents holding shares in Canadian corporations were not taxed by Canada on their share of corporate income at approximately the rates that now prevail.

The rationale for the structure of our corporate tax model becomes clearer if we accept the proposition that corporate income should not flow through and be taxed in the hands of individual shareholders on an annual basis. In the absence of a flow-through of income to shareholders, corporate income must bear its own tax annually if we are to prevent deferral of tax. If corporate income is not taxed at its full rate, there would be incentive to accumulate income in the corporation in order to defer any tax that would otherwise be payable if it were paid out to shareholders. Thus, the prevention of tax deferral is an important reason for levying an annual tax on corporate income.

If there is to be a separate corporate tax, what is the ideal tax rate? The problem now assumes additional dimensions.

The corporate tax rate determines the extent of tax deferral or penalty that is payable through the use of corporations. A corporate tax rate lower than individual rates invites deferral; a higher rate invokes a penalty and biases the system. The corporate tax rate is determined by several factors, but the desirability of competitive international tax rates plays a pre-eminent role. Canadian corporations must compete in an international environment, and the tax rates of our principal trading partners have a significant influence on the structure of Canadian corporate taxation.

---

[23] *Report of the Royal Commission on Taxation* (Ottawa: Queen's Printer, 1966) (Chair: K.M. Carter), vol. 4, at 4.

A more difficult question is whether the corporate tax rate for private corporations should equal the highest marginal rate for individuals. If it did, the tax system would be substantially neutral at the top end, and businesses could make their decisions on the basis of non-tax criteria. There would be no tax deferral advantage to earning income through a corporation.

A corporate rate equal to the top individual tax rate (approximately 53 per cent) would also remove business and economic incentives from those who are entitled to special low rates of taxation, for example small businesses. Thus, any gain in tax neutrality between different types of taxpayers would carry with it the cost of lost tax incentives for certain sectors of the economy.

There are also other questions: Should there be special incentives for domestic investment over foreign investment? Should the corporate tax system favour Canadian corporations that earn income within Canada over Canadian corporations that earn income in foreign countries? Should there be special tax incentives for foreign corporations that come into Canada to do business in Canada?

(b) Double Taxation

One can argue that in an ideal world the corporate tax should be nothing more than a withholding tax for individuals who ultimately bear the real economic burden of taxation. In fact, one of the most acute problems of the corporate tax system is the potential for "double taxation" of corporate income. Corporate income is typically taxed at the corporate level, when it is earned, and is taxed again at the shareholder level, when it is distributed as a dividend.

Where a corporation earns income and distributes it to shareholders who are individuals, both the corporation and the individuals pay tax on the distributed income. The problem of "double taxation" is compounded, however, where there is a chain of corporations, and income passes through the chain to the ultimate shareholder. In these circumstances, the double tax problem becomes a multiple taxation problem.

The Canadian tax system unilaterally provides some relief against both of these forms of double/multiple taxation of corporate and shareholder income. The nature of the relief varies depending upon whether the corporate/shareholder relationship is between:

- Corporation and individual;
- Domestic corporation and domestic corporation;
- Domestic corporation and foreign corporation; or
- Individual and foreign corporation.

In addition, Canada has numerous bilateral tax treaties that also provide relief from double taxation.

(c) Integration

Should corporate and individual taxes be fully integrated to prevent double taxation and, if so, how?

There are two basic methods used to integrate corporate and shareholder taxes:

- The imputation model; and
- The advanced corporate tax model.

(i) The Imputation Model

Under the imputation model (which is the system used in Canada), corporate tax is imputed to the corporation's shareholders who are individuals. The imputation is made when dividends are paid. An individual who receives a dividend from a corporation is required to "gross up" the cash value of the dividend to a value that is notionally equivalent to the corporation's pre-tax income. The amount of the gross-up is simply a mathematical function of the underlying corporate tax rate. For example, where a corporation earns $100 of income and pays tax of 20 per cent on the income, it has $80 to distribute to its shareholders. Assuming that the corporation pays a dividend of $80 to an individual shareholder, the shareholder would gross up the dividend by 25 per cent and include $100 in his or her income. Thus, assuming that the corporation had previously paid 20 per cent tax on the income, the shareholder would calculate his or her tax liability on the equivalent of the corporation's pre-tax income.

The individual then pays tax on the equivalent of the corporation's pre-tax income (in this case, $100) and is given a credit for taxes that are *assumed* to have been previously paid by the corporation (in this case, $20). Thus, the essence of the imputation model is that the corporation's income and taxes are imputed to the individual to whom the corporation distributes its after-tax income as dividends.

The imputation model is not without its problems. One of the more significant problems is that the individual receives a notional credit for taxes supposedly paid by the corporation even though the corporation may not actually have paid any tax on the income. For example, a corporation may earn $100 income but pay no tax because it can reduce its taxable income to zero by applying $100 of losses carried forward from previous years. The imputation model would, however, allow the individual a notional tax credit for the tax supposedly paid by the corporation. The disadvantage of the imputation model is its reliance on an assumption that is precariously perched.

(ii) The Advance Corporate Tax Model

The advance corporate tax ("ACT") model operates on a different theoretical premise: It involves an actual tracking of taxes and dividends paid by a corporation. Under the ACT model, where a corporation pays taxes, it establishes a "taxes payable" account. When it pays a dividend to its shareholder, it withholds tax on behalf of the shareholder and claims the tax withheld from the shareholder to reduce its corporate tax payable account. The essence of the ACT system is that it relies on a direct dividend tax credit, rather than a notional credit as under the imputation model. The tax withheld on distribution to shareholders is equal to the correct amount of tax paid by the corporation. The limitation of the system is that there is double taxation of corporate income if the corporation does not pay enough dividends to cover the full corporate tax liability.

(d) Taxable Income

The corporate tax structure is influenced by two doctrines, one legal, the other economic. A corporation is *legally* a separate person in its own right. Thus a corporation is liable for its own taxes and must file its own tax returns.[24] The tax structure also recognizes the close *economic* link between a corporation and its shareholders. For example, the structure takes into account that corporate income bears tax before distribution to shareholders and, therefore, should be taxed more leniently than income that has not been previously taxed.[25]

Thus, the corporate tax system is pulled in opposite directions by two doctrines. The doctrine that a corporation is a separate *legal* entity calls for taxation of the corporation as a person in its own right. The doctrine that there is an economic link between a corporation and its shareholders requires the system to reduce the potential for multiple taxation of the same income. One sees the conflict between these doctrines in the loss transfer rules: a sole proprietor who sells his or her business to a corporation is not allowed to transfer his or her non-capital losses to the corporation, even if the seller owns all of the corporation's shares. Similarly, a parent corporation and its wholly-owned subsidiaries may not use each other's losses to offset income generated by the economic group.[26]

(e) Revenues

Although corporate income taxes are the second largest source of federal revenues (12 per cent in 1990-91), they represent a comparatively small contribution to the national accounts when compared with the tax revenue collected from individuals (45 per cent in 1990-91). Thus, from a revenue perspective, the corporate tax system is not nearly as important as the individual tax.

---

[24] Para. 150(1)(*a*); subs. 248(1) ("person").

[25] See, e.g., s. 121 (dividend tax credit); subs. 112(1) (tax-free intercorporate dividends).

[26] Para. 111(1)(*a*) (taxpayer may only deduct *his or her* non-capital losses from preceding years); see also paras. 111(1)(*b*), (*c*), (*d*), (*e*).

(f) Tax Rates

(i) General Rates

The taxation of corporate income depends upon four principal factors:

- The type of corporation;
- The source of its income;
- The timing of its distribution to shareholders; and
- The relationship between the corporation and its shareholders.

The theoretical federal tax rate for all corporations is 38 per cent of taxable income.[27] This rate is reduced by an amount equal to 10 per cent of the corporation's taxable income earned in the year in a province.[28] In effect, then, the basic federal rate of tax on corporate taxable income earned in Canada is 28 per cent.

The purpose of the 10 per cent reduction in the federal corporate tax rate is to vacate an area of the income tax field to the provinces to allow them to levy their own corporate income taxes. In fact, all of the provinces have entered the tax field, and levy corporate taxes at varying rates. Thus the total tax on corporate taxable income is calculated by adding the applicable provincial rate to the federal rate. For example, where a province levies corporate tax of 16 per cent, the combined federal-provincial corporate tax is 44 per cent.

The actual rate of federal tax on corporate income depends upon various factors which can increase or decrease the theoretical rate. For example, some corporations receive tax credits for certain types of income, while surtaxes can raise the effective corporate tax rate above the nominal rate.

(ii) Flat Rate

The basic federal corporate tax is levied at a flat rate, that is, it is applied at a uniform rate to the corporation's taxable income. Because the tax is applied at a flat rate, the average rate of tax paid by a corporation is usually the same as its marginal rate. Thus, with some exceptions, that are discussed below, the rate of tax paid by a corporation on its "top dollar" is the same as the rate paid on its first dollar of taxable income. This characteristic of the corporate tax structure is extremely important when considering the interplay between the tax paid by a corporation and the tax paid by its individual shareholders. It might, for example, influence the decision as to how much an-owner-manager should extract from a corporation by way of salary (that is deductible to the corporation) or dividends (that are not deductible) and taxable to the individual at progressive marginal rates.

---

[27] Subs. 123(1).

[28] Subs. 124(1). The basic rate of federal tax is subject to various adjustments in the form of tax credits and surtaxes.

(iii) Special Rates

Having said that corporate tax is levied at a flat rate, it is important to note that there are, in fact, several different flat rates. The rate applicable to a particular corporation depends upon the type of corporation, the amount that it earns in the year, the source and type of its income, and its shareholdings. Each of these factors plays a role in determining the rate at which a corporation is taxable.[29] For example, the federal tax on active business income earned by a Canadian-controlled private corporation is approximately 13.12 per cent (1995):

	%
Basic federal rate	38.00
Federal abatement	(10.00)
	28.00
Federal surtax (4% of 28%)	01.12
	29.12
	(16.00)
Small business deduction	13.12

(g) Taxation of Shareholders

When a corporation pays dividends, its shareholders may also be liable for tax on their dividend income. The taxation of shareholders depends upon the following:

- Type of shareholders (corporate or individual);
- Status (Canadian or foreign) of the payor corporation;
- Size of shareholdings (controlling shareholder or portfolio investor);
- Type of dividend (taxable or capital); and
- Source of income from which the dividend is paid (active or passive).

One of the complicating features of the corporate tax system is the potential for double taxation of income in the corporation and again in the hands of its shareholders. The Act does, however, provide some relief from double taxation. For example, dividends between taxable Canadian corporations flow through on a tax-free basis.[30] Individuals who receive dividends from taxable Canadian corporations are entitled to a dividend tax credit,[31] which reduces the net tax rate on such income.

Whether the relief from double taxation of corporate income is complete or partial depends upon the status of the payer corporation and the source and amount of its income. Generally, the tax system is most generous to shareholders of "small" Canadian

---

[29] See, e.g., ss. 125, 125.1.

[30] Subs. 112(1).

[31] S. 121.

corporations engaged in active business. Shareholders of "large" or non-Canadian corporations are subject to some double taxation.

(h) Factors Affecting Corporate Taxation

The factors that determine the tax payable by a corporation are set out below:

Type of Corporation:

- Canadian vs. non-Canadian
- Taxable corporation vs. non-taxable corporation
- Public
- Private
  - Canadian-controlled
  - Foreign-controlled
- Other (non-public/non-private)
- Special status
- Exempt

Type of Income:

- Business:
  - Active
  - Manufacturing and processing
  - Personal services
  - Other
- Property:
  - Dividends
  - Interest
  - Specified investment business
  - Other
- Capital gains

Geographic Source of Income:

- Domestic
- Foreign

Nature of Income:

- Active business income
- Passive income

Time of Distribution by Corporation:

- Immediate
- Deferred

Size of Shareholdings:

- Insignificant (under 10 per cent)
- Significant (over 10 per cent)
- Control holding
- Foreign affiliate
  - — Controlled foreign affiliate

Size of Capital Base:

- Various levels are significant

It should be apparent that the permutations and combinations of these factors introduce a significant degree of complexity into the corporate tax system.

3. TYPES OF CORPORATIONS

(a) Canadian Corporation

Reference:

ITA:

Subs. 89(1)   "Canadian Corporation"

A Canadian corporation is a corporation that is resident in *or* incorporated in Canada.[32] There is no requirement that the corporation be owned by Canadian citizens or nationals.

A corporation incorporated in Canada after April 26, 1965, is *deemed* to be resident in Canada.[33]

A corporation incorporated in Canada before April 27, 1965, that has either become a resident of Canada or carried on business in Canada after that date is also *deemed* to be a resident of Canada.[34]

---

[32] Subs. 89(1) ("Canadian corporation").

[33] Para. 250(4)(*a*).

[34] Subs. 250(4).

(b) Taxable Canadian Corporation

A taxable Canadian corporation is a Canadian corporation that is not exempt from Part I tax.[35]

(c) Public Corporations

References:

ITA:

Subs. 89(1)   "Public Corporation"

REGULATIONS:

3200   Prescribed Stock Exchanges

4800   Prescribed Conditions for Corporation Going Public

4803   Definitions

Generally, public corporations are listed corporations with widely-dispersed shareholdings.

More specifically, a "public corporation" is a corporation that is resident in Canada that has:[36]

- its shares listed on a prescribed stock exchange in Canada;[37]

- elected to become a public corporation and has complied with certain prescribed conditions; or

- been designated by the Minister to be a public corporation and has complied with certain prescribed conditions.

(i) Electing Public Corporation Status

Listed corporations are public corporations.

A corporation that is not listed on a prescribed[38] stock exchange may elect to be treated as a public corporation for income tax purposes if it meets certain conditions relating to:[39]

- the number of its shareholders;

---

[35] Subs. 89(1) ("taxable Canadian corporation").

[36] Subs. 89(1) ("public corporation").

[37] Over-the-counter trading of shares does not qualify a corporation as a public corporation.

[38] Reg. 3200.

[39] Reg. 4800.

- the dispersal of ownership of its shares;
- the public trading of its shares; and
- the size of the corporation.

The conditions are similar to the requirements imposed on corporations listed on stock exchanges. Thus, an unlisted corporation may, by satisfying requirements similar to those imposed on listed corporations, qualify as a public corporation.[40]

A corporation that elects to become a "public corporation" must have:[41]

- at least 150 shareholders (excluding "insiders") holding "equity shares", with each shareholder owning at least one "block of shares" of the class having a total fair market value of not less than $500; or
- at least 300 shareholders (excluding "insiders"), with each shareholder holding at least one "block of shares"[42] of the class having a total fair market value of not less than $500.

An "equity share" is a share with an unrestricted right to share in dividends and the right to participate in the capital of the corporation in the event that the corporation reduces its capital or is wound up; this generally means the common shares of the corporations, but the category can include shares with special rights.[43]

To determine the number of shareholders[44] of a particular class of shares, shareholders owning less than one block of shares with a market value under $500 are arranged so as to form the greatest possible number of groups such that each group owns at least one block of shares with a fair market value of $500 or more; no shareholder is included in more than one group, and each group is considered to be one shareholder for the purpose of meeting the 150 or 300 shareholders requirements.[45]

---

[40] Note that co-operative corporations and credit unions cannot *elect* public corporation status, and can qualify as public corporations only by having their shares listed on a prescribed stock exchange.

[41] Reg. 4800(1).

[42] Reg. 4803(1). A "block of shares" is 100 shares if the fair market value of each share is less than $25, 25 shares if the fair market value of each share is $25 or more but less than $100, and 10 shares if the fair market value of each share is $100 or more.

[43] S. 204 ("equity share").

[44] Reg. 4800(1). For the purpose of calculating the number of shareholders of a class of shares to determine whether the 150 or 300 minimum numbers are satisfied: each shareholder must hold not less than one "block of shares" of the class; the shares held by each shareholder must have an aggregate fair market value of $500 or more; and insiders must not hold more than 80 per cent of the shares of the class.

[45] Regs. 4803(3), (4).

The class of shares that forms the basis for the election must qualify for distribution to the public. Thus, the corporation must file a prospectus, registration statement or similar document with a public authority, pursuant to the laws of the jurisdiction to which the corporation is subject (such document must have been accepted for filing by the public authority) and there must have been a distribution to the public of that class of shares in accordance with the filed document.[46]

(ii) Ministerial Designation

The Minister may designate a corporation as a public corporation if it complies with all of the conditions that would entitle it to elect public corporation status at the time of the designation.[47] He or she does so by giving 30 days' written notice.

(iii) Electing Out Of Public Corporation Status

A listed corporation may not elect out of its public corporation status.

An unlisted public corporation may elect *not* to be a public corporation if it complies with certain conditions. These conditions concern:[48]

- the number of its shareholders;
- the dispersal of ownership of its shares; and
- the public trading of its shares.

The election must be supported by an authorization for the election and a statutory declaration by the directors as to compliance with prescribed conditions.

A corporation that elects not to be a public corporation must either have fewer than 50 equity shareholders (excluding insiders) or fewer than 100 shareholders (excluding insiders) if the shares are not equity shares.[49] In addition, insiders must own more than 90 per cent of the shares of the class.

A corporation that elects not to be a public corporation must also establish that at the time of the election it does not have any other class of shares that could form the basis of an election to be a public corporation.

---

[46] Reg. 4800(1).

[47] Subs. 89(1) ("public corporation"(b)(ii)).

[48] Subs. 89(1) ("public corporation"(c)(i)).

[49] Reg. 4800(2). Each shareholder of the class of shares forming the basis of the election must hold not less than one "block of shares" of the class, and the shares must have an aggregate fair market value of $500 or more.

(d) Private Corporations

Reference:

ITA:

Subs. 89(1)   "Private Corporation"

Private corporation status is determined by applying a negative test. A private corporation is a corporation that is:[50]

- resident in Canada;
- *not* a public corporation; and,
- *not* controlled by one or more public corporations.

Whether a corporation is controlled by a public corporation is determined on the basis of the *de jure* test.

A corporation may be *neither* a private corporation nor a public corporation. Thus, the mere fact that a corporation does not qualify as a public corporation does not automatically make it a "private corporation". For example, a resident unlisted subsidiary of a public corporation is neither a public nor a private corporation. In contrast, a resident subsidiary of a non-resident corporation whose shares are widely held may qualify as a private corporation.

A corporation that was a private corporation at the commencement of its 1972 taxation year and has continued since then to be a private corporation is deemed to have become a private corporation at the end of its 1971 taxation year.[51]

A corporation incorporated after 1971 that was a private corporation at the time of its incorporation and that has continued without interruption to be a private corporation is deemed to have become a private corporation immediately before its incorporation.[52]

(e) Canadian-controlled Private Corporations

References:

ITA:

Subs. 125(7)   Canadian-Controlled Private Corporation

BULLETINS, CIRCULARS & RULINGS:

IT-458R   May 31, 1990   Canadian-Controlled Private Corporation

---

[50] Subs. 89(1) ("private corporation").

[51] Subs. 89(1) ("private corporation"(a)).

[52] Subs. 89(1) ("private corporation"(b)).

A Canadian-controlled private corporation ("CCPC") is a private "Canadian corporation" that is *not* controlled by non-residents or by a public corporation.[53]

(f) Special Status Corporations

References:

ITA:

S. 130	Investment Corporations
S. 131	Mutual Fund Corporations
S. 132	Mutual Fund Trusts
Ss. 133, 134	Non-Resident-Owned Investment Corporations
S. 136	Co-operative Corporations
S. 137	Savings and Credit Unions
Ss. 138, 140, 141, 142	Insurance Corporations
S. 143	Communal Organizations

Certain types of corporations carrying on business in Canada are subject to special rules under the Act. There are various reasons for granting corporations special status. Certain investment-type corporations are treated as financial intermediaries for their shareholders, and the Act provides a mechanism to integrate the tax imposed at the corporate and individual level. In other cases, corporations such as credit unions and co-operative organizations are accommodated by special provisions which take into account the special needs of the businesses that these entities conduct.

(g) Exempt Corporations

Certain corporations are completely exempt from tax. Exempt corporations are of two types:

* Those exempt from tax by virtue of their status (for example, a municipality in Canada or a municipal or public body performing a function of government in Canada);[54] and

* Those exempt from tax by virtue of a particular status *and* additional tests (e.g., a registered charity is exempt from tax on its income if it complies with certain rules in respect of its activities).[55]

---

[53] Subs. 125(7) ("Canadian-controlled private corporation").

[54] Paras. 149(1)(*d*), (*e*).

[55] Para. 149(1)(*f*); see, generally, s. 149.1.

4. ADVANTAGES OF OPERATING THROUGH A CORPORATION

A business may be incorporated for tax or business benefits.

(a) Personal Liability

The most significant legal result of incorporating a business is that, as a rule, the corporation becomes responsible for all its financial debts, commercial actions and negligence in the operation of the business. The owners, managers and employees are generally sheltered from personal liability in their work-related activities. Shareholders may, however, be liable for the non-payment of corporate taxes.[56]

(b) Capital Gains Exemption

Individuals who dispose of shares of a "qualified small business corporation" ("QSBC") are entitled to a special capital gains exemption of $500,000.[57] This special exemption is available only in respect of the shares of a QSBC. The shares must be held for a prescribed minimum holding period, and the corporation must satisfy an active business asset test.

Generally, a small business corporation ("SBC") is defined as a Canadian-controlled private corporation that uses all or substantially all of its assets in an active business carried on primarily in Canada.[58] An SBC can also be a Canadian-controlled private corporation that is a holding company for other corporations which qualify as small business corporations.

The holding period requirement is that, throughout the period of *24 months immediately preceding* the date of disposition, the shares must not have been owned by any person or partnership other than the individual.[59]

In addition, the corporation must satisfy an active business asset test. This test requires that, throughout that part of the immediately preceding 24 months during which the shares were held, more than 50 per cent of the fair market value of the corporation's assets must have been used in active business.[60]

(c) Deferral of Tax

A corporation allows for greater flexibility in retaining funds in the business. Canada does not tax accumulated earnings.

---

[56] See, e.g., *Davis v. Canada*, [1994] 2 CTC 2033, 94 DTC 1934 (T.C.C.).

[57] Subs. 110.6(2.1); see also Chapter XII "Computation of Taxable Income".

[58] Subs. 248(1) ("small business corporation").

[59] Subs. 110.6(1) ("qualified small business corporation share"(b)).

[60] Subs. 110.6(1) ("qualified small business corporation share"(c)).

Canadian source business income is taxable at a comparatively low rate of tax, approximately, 23 per cent. Business income retained in the business and not distributed as dividends to shareholders is not subject to any additional tax burden. Thus, shareholders can *defer* tax on funds retained in the corporation.

In contrast, profits earned by a sole proprietorship or partnership are fully taxable in the owner's or partners' hands, regardless whether they are retained in the business. The top marginal rate of tax is approximately 54 per cent (1994).

(d) Choice Between Salary and Dividends

A corporation allows for greater flexibility in determining whether business profits should be extracted in the form of salary or dividends.

Salary paid by a corporation is deductible to the corporation and taxable to the employee to whom it is paid. Dividends are paid out of after-tax dollars. An individual who receives a dividend is taxable on it, but is entitled to a dividend tax credit. The ideal salary/dividend mix is a function of several factors: marginal rates, other sources of income, pension plans, and so on.

The use of a corporation allows one to select the optimum balance between salary and dividend income, and the decision can be made annually in light of the business and tax circumstances that prevail at the particular time.

(e) Bonuses, Retiring Allowances and Employment Benefits

An individual cannot be an employee of his or her own unincorporated business or partnership. An individual shareholder may, however, be an employee of his or her corporation, even if he or she owns all of the shares of the corporation. Hence, it is possible to use bonuses and retiring allowances to reduce the corporation's active business income to the $200,000 threshold level, in order to take maximum advantage of the low rate of tax available to Canadian-controlled private corporations.[61]

It is also possible for an employee/shareholder to obtain employment benefits such as club memberships, insurance and interest-free loans on a tax-preferred basis. These advantages are not available through an unincorporated business.

(f) Income Splitting

The share capital of a family corporation can be structured to allow family members to participate in the corporation's shareholdings. The income of the corporation can be paid out through discretionary dividends[62] and sprinkled among several shareholders to attract lower marginal tax rates. This will reduce the total tax burden.

---

[61] Subss. 125(1), (2); see also Chapter XVII "Private Corporations: Business Income".

[62] See, e.g., *McClurg v. M.N.R.*, [1991] 1 CTC 169, 91 DTC 5001 (S.C.C.).

(g) Recapture of Depreciation

Where a corporation owns real estate, it can dispose of its "ownership" of the property (that is, the shares) without triggering any recapture of depreciation. This can amount to a substantial saving if the corporation has previously claimed capital cost allowance (depreciation) on its depreciable property.

Further, a sale of corporate shares is considered to be a transaction in personal property and not a transaction in real property. Hence, a disposition of corporate shares does not trigger any land transfer taxes.

(h) Flexibility in Corporate Financing

Incorporation generally allows considerably greater flexibility in financing than is possible through a sole proprietorship. For example, it is easy to create a variety of share and debt capital structures that accommodate different business and estate planning interests. Combined with the use of stock options, corporations also permit more flexible financing and compensation vehicles.

(i) Provincial Advantages

Provincial governments allow corporations tax holidays from time to time. These tax holidays can provide for significant (10 to 14 per cent) reductions in the effective tax rate applicable to corporations.

SELECTED BIBLIOGRAPHY TO CHAPTER XIV

General

Byrd, Clarence and Ida Chen, *Taxation and Business Decisions* (Chelsea, Quebec: Clarence Byrd Inc., 1991).

Cadesky, Michael, "Owner-Manager Remuneration", in *Proceedings of 39th Tax Conf.* 13:1 (Can. Tax Foundation, 1987).

Cadesky, Michael, "Planning Considerations in Owner-Manager Remuneration" in *Proceedings of 40th Tax Conf.* (Can. Tax Foundation, 1988), 9:1.

"Workshop: Tax Planning for Private Corporations and Their Shareholders", in *Proceedings of 41st Tax Conf.* 54:1 (Can. Tax Foundation, 1989).

The Corporate Entity

Krishna, Vern, "Blowing Hot and Cold at the Same Time" (1994), 5 *Can. Current Tax* 7.

Ross, David W., "Incorporation and Capitalization of a Private Corporation", in *Proceedings of 39th Tax Conf.* 11:1 (Can. Tax Foundation, 1987).

Structure of Corporate Taxation

Blais, André and Francois Vallaincourt, *The Political Economy of Tax: The Corporate Income Tax and the Canadian Manufacturing Industry* (Montreal: Dep de science econmique, Université de Montreal, 1986).

Cumming, Peter, *The Taxation of Business Enterprises* (Toronto: York University, Osgoode Hall Law School, 1992-1993).

Ewens, Douglas S., "New Considerations in Structuring Share-for-Share Exchange Offers" (1988), 36 *Can. Tax J.* 449.

Holland, David and Alain Castonguay, "The Corporate Income Tax: Preliminary Results in the Impact of Tax Reform" in *Proceedings of the 43rd Tax Conference* (Can. Tax Foundation, 1991), 20:1-20:18.

Mintz, Jack M., "Alternative Views of the Corporate Tax: A Reassessment of the Carter Report" in *The Quest for Tax Reform: The Royal Commission on Taxation Twenty Years Later* (Toronto: Carswell, 1988).

Mintz, Jack M., "Competitiveness and Tax Policy: How does Canada Play the Game?" in *Proceedings of 43rd Tax Conf.* (Can. Tax Foundation, 1991), 5:1-5:14.

Mintz, Jack M., *An Empirical Estimate of Corporate Tax Refundability and Effective Tax Rates* (Ottawa, Department of Economics, Carleton University, 1987).

Scace, Arthur, and M. Quigley, "New Developments in Debt Financing", in *Proceedings of 34th Tax Conf.* 579 (Can. Tax Foundation, 1982).

Sullivan, Daniel, "New Developments in Corporate Financing", in *Proceedings of 34th Tax Conf.* 532 (Can. Tax Foundation, 1982).

Thornton, Daniel, *Management Tax Planning: A Canadian Perspective* (Toronto: J. Wiley & Sons, 1993).

Types of Corporations

Beach, Wayne G. and Mark F. Wheeler, "Associated Corporations" in *Proceedings of 40th Tax Conf.* (Can. Tax Foundation, 1988), 10:1.

Cherniak, Janice L.E., "Going Private: Tax Planning Aspects" in *Corporate Structure, Finance and Operations* (Toronto: Carswell, 1990), at 83.

Couzin, Robert, and Robert J. Dart, "The New Preferred Share Rules", in *Proceedings of 39th Tax Conf.* 18:1 (Can. Tax Foundation, 1987).

Drache, A.B.C., "Tax Exempt Organizations" (1991), 13 *Can. Taxpayer* 165.

Dukac, Jules, "An Analysis of the Proposals for the Taxation of Life Insurance Companies", in *Proceedings of 39th Tax Conf.* 35:1 (Can. Tax Foundation, 1987).

Flynn, Gordon, "Creative Equity Financing", in *Proceedings of 34th Tax Conf.* 615 (Can. Tax Foundation, 1982).

Loveland, Norman C., "Securities Lending and Repurchase Agreements: Canadian Tax Issues" (1989), 4 *SCRR* 205.

MacKight, Robin J., "What's in a Name?: Classifying Partnerships, Associations and Limited Liability Companies for Income Tax Purposes", [1993] *Corp. Mgmt. Tax Conf.* 21:1.

Ort, Harry W., "Recent Issues in the Taxation of Lending Institutions: A New Playing Field for Lenders", in *Proceedings of 39th Tax Conf.* 38:1 (Can. Tax Foundation, 1987).

Raich, Robert, "Flow-Through Financing: Present and Future", in *Proceedings of 39th Tax Conf.* 43:1 (Can. Tax Foundation, 1987).

Skingle, Leslie E., "Carve-Outs and Flow-Through Shares", in *Proceedings of 38th Tax Conf.* 50:1 (Can. Tax Foundation, 1986).

Thompson, A.E. John, "Taxation of the Life Insurance Industry and Cooperatives: The Post-Carter Evolution" in *The Quest for Tax Reform: The Royal Commission on Taxation Twenty Years Later* (Toronto: Carswell, 1988), at 239-248.

Advantages of Operating Through a Corporation

Anderson, Eric W., "Owner-Manager Remuneration", in *Proceedings of 38th Tax Conf.* 11:1 (Can. Tax Foundation, 1986).

Cadesky, Michael, "Planning Considerations in Owner-Manager Remuneration", in *Proceedings of 41st Tax Conf.* 9:1 (Can. Tax Foundation, 1989).

Drache, A.B.C., "Retirement Compensation Arrangements" (1992), 14 *Can. Taxpayer* 15.

Krishna, Vern and J. Anthony VanDuzer, "Corporate Share Capital Structures and Income Splitting: McClurg v. Canada" (1993), 21 *Canadian Business Law J.* 335.

Krishna, Vern, "Income Splitting Corporate Structures" (1994), 4 *Can. Current Tax* C-45).

Larter, Ron W., "Tax Aspects of Earning Various Sources of Income through a Canadian Corporation", in *Proceedings of 44th Tax Conf.* 36:1 (Can. Tax Foundation, 1992).

Menulz, Karen, and Paul Glover, "Reducing Tax with Scientific Research" (1992), 65 *CMA Magazine* 8.

Sklar, Murray, "Does It Pay to Incorporate?" (1989), 122 *CA Magazine* 42.

Sommerfeldt, Don R., "Tax Advantages to Incorporation: Tax Planning" (1993), 17 *Law Now No. 6* 10.

"Tax Planning for Private Corporations and Their Shareholders: Implications of Recent Changes on the Use of Holding Companies", in *Proceedings of 38th Tax Conf.* 10:1 (Can. Tax Foundation, 1986).

"Workshop: Tax Issues Concerning the Owner-Manager", in *Proceedings of 39th Tax Conf.* 48:1 (Can. Tax Foundation, 1987).

CHAPTER XV

CORPORATE FINANCE

1. GENERAL

Reference:

ITA:

Subs. 20(1)   Deductions in Computing Income from Business or Property

A corporation can be funded in several ways. The conventional sources of corporate funding are:

- Share or equity capital,
- Debt capital,
- Retained cash earnings,
- Off-balance-sheet financial instruments (warrants, options, leases, etc.), and
- Government grants and subsidies.

The method used to finance a corporation depends upon the type of corporation, its size, access to capital markets, and the residence of its shareholders.

Small businesses have access only to the first three sources of financing: debt, share capital, and retained earnings. Contractual options (for example, rights and warrants) are usually issued only by large, publicly listed corporations with access to sophisticated capital markets.

The financial structure of a corporation is determined by two principal factors:

1. Access to funds, and
2. The cost of available funds.

The cost of funds is influenced by market and tax considerations. Thus, where a corporation has a choice between alternative sources of funding, the decision to opt for one source over another, or to balance between different sources of funds, may be significantly influenced by income tax considerations. For example, the ratio of debt to equity capital raised may be determined by tax considerations such as the residence of shareholders (which determines the withholding tax rate), or the thin capitalization rules,[1] which determine the deductibility of interest.

---

[1]   Subs. 18(4).

2. GENERAL CHARACTERISTICS OF DEBT AND SHARE CAPITAL

Reference:

BULLETINS, CIRCULARS & RULINGS:

IT-67R3   May 15, 1992   Taxable Dividends from Corporations Resident in
                                 Canada

The capital structure of most small businesses and private corporations is essentially comprised of two elements: equity and debt.

Equity comprises two categories: Share capital and retained earnings.

(a) Share Capital

Equity or share capital represents an ownership interest in the corporation. The nature of the interest is determined by the rights, restrictions, terms and conditions attached to the shares. In the absence of any special provisions, all shares of a corporation are presumed to be equal.

The single most significant income tax characteristic of shares is that dividends paid on shares are not deductible from income. Dividends represent a distribution of earnings and not an expense incurred for the purpose of earning income. Hence, dividends are paid out of a corporation's after-tax dollars.

(b) Debt Capital

Debt is a sum of money due by agreement, whether express or implied, that includes not only the obligation of the debtor to pay, but also the right of the creditor to receive and enforce payment. Debt generally arises from a contractual obligation whereby one person lends money to another on terms and conditions negotiated between the parties.

The quintessential characteristics of corporate debt are as follows:

- Debt does not represent ownership in a corporation but merely creates a relationship of debtor and creditor between the lender and the corporation;

- Corporate creditors generally rank ahead of shareholders in any claims to the corporation's assets;

- Debt may be secured by corporate assets; and

- Interest on debt is generally deductible for tax purposes.

(c) Hybrid Capital

Hybrid financial instruments have characteristics of both debt and share capital. Due to the significant tax differences in the treatment of debt and equity capital, corporations have an incentive to devise hybrid financial instruments that afford them the best of both worlds. From a corporation's perspective, it is attractive to issue a hybrid instrument that has all the characteristics of share capital, but which can be classified as debt for tax purposes. The tax authorities are understandably concerned about such instruments and have devised complex rules to minimize their use. These rules circumscribe the use of hybrids such as "taxable preferred shares", "term preferred shares", and "income bonds".

3. CORPORATE LAW OF EQUITY FINANCING

A corporation's share capital for tax purposes (referred to as "paid-up capital" in the *Income Tax Act*) is initially determined from its "stated capital" for the purposes of corporate law. Thus, we start with a general discussion of the corporate law applicable to corporate financing through the issuance of shares, and then proceed to a discussion of the income tax consequences of the various forms of corporate financing.

(a) General

The concept of "stated capital" in corporate law serves two distinct interests:

1. Protection of creditors, and
2. Protection of shareholders.

A corporation's creditors have a right to look to its stated capital as a measure of the pool from which the corporation will draw to pay its debts. Hence, creditors have an interest in the capital structure of the corporation to which they have loaned, money and are concerned that the corporation does not dissipate its capital through unauthorized corporate distributions.[2]

The concept of stated capital also serves as a measure of limiting shareholder liability for corporate debts. A shareholder's exposure for corporate liabilities is generally limited to his or her contributions to the corporation's stated capital.

"Capital" is not defined in the *Canada Business Corporations Act*[3] ("CBCA") or in the *Business Corporations Act* of Ontario[4] ("OBCA"). Generally speaking, "capital" refers to proceeds from the sale of capital stock and represents money paid by a purchaser for an undivided interest in the assets of a corporation.[5]

The term "capital" can also have other meanings depending upon the context in which it is used and the adjective by which it is modified. For example, "working capital" is used in accounting to denote the excess of current assets over current

---

[2] *Re Inrig Shoe Co.* (1924), 27 OWN 110 (S.C.); see *J.M.P.M. Ent. Ltd. v. Danforth Fabrics (Humbertown) Ltd.*, [1969] 1 OR 785 (H.C.) (issuance of additional shares to affect a change in control being "sale or other disposition" of control).

[3] *Canada Business Corporations Act*, R.S.C. 1985, c. C-44.

[4] *Business Corporations Act*, R.S.O. 1990, c. B.16.

[5] *Toronto v. Consumers' Gas Co.*, [1927] 4 DLR 102 (P.C.) [Ont.].

liabilities, "liquid capital" sometimes denotes cash and marketable securities, etc. In corporate law, however, the term "capital" is used to describe only the share capital of a corporation.

(b) Share Capital

(i) Nature of Shares

A share represents the proportional financial interest of a shareholder in a corporation. It measures the liability of the shareholder to outside interests and the size of his or her financial interest in the corporate undertaking.

A share is not a sum of money: it is an interest measured by a sum of money. A share represents a bundle of rights contained in the share contract.[6] Thus, a share is that fraction of the capital of a corporation which confers on its owner a proportional proprietary interest in the corporation.

Shareholders are not part owners of the assets of the undertaking.[7] Instead, they share certain rights, such as the right to participate in profits and capital.

A share is a chose in action that forms a separate right of personal property.[8] It represents a fractional interest in the capital of the corporation.

(ii) Rights of Shares

There are three rights usually associated with shares:

1. The right to vote,

2. The right to participate in profits by way of dividends, and

3. The right to share in the property of the corporation upon its dissolution.

Under the CBCA, where there is only one class of shares, these three rights attach to each share. Under the OBCA, however, only the right to vote and the right to receive property upon dissolution automatically attach to a single class of shares.[9]

A corporation may issue more than one class of shares. The rights, privileges, restrictions and conditions that attach to each class of shares must be set out in its

---

[6] *Borlands Trustee v. Steel Bros. & Co.*, [1901] 1 Ch. 279 at 288 *per* Farwell J.; see also *Re Paulin*, [1935] 1 KB 26 (C.A.); *I.R.C. v. Crossman*, [1937] AC 26 (H.L.).

[7] *Short v. Treasury Commrs.*, [1948] 1 KB 116. The term "shareholder" merely describes a person who is a holder of shares; it does not mean that that person shares property in common with another.

[8] OBCA, s. 41; *Bradbury v. English Sewing Cotton Co.*, [1923] AC 744. The term "chose in action" only means that a share does not confer a right to possession of a physical thing; instead, it gives a personal right of property claimable by legal action.

[9] CBCA, subs. 24(3); OBCA, subs. 22(3). Although there is no statutory right to dividends under the OBCA, all shareholders must be treated equally where there is only one class of shares.

articles of incorporation.[10] If a corporation issues more than one class of shares, it must ensure that each of the rights (the right to vote, the right to receive dividends and the right to share in property) are attached to at least one of the classes of shares.[11]

Under the OBCA, however, the only rights required to be attached to at least one class of shares are the right to vote and the right to participate in property upon dissolution.[12] Unlike the CBCA, the OBCA does not address the right of a shareholder to receive dividends.

(c) Issuance of Shares

(i) No Par Value

Shares must be issued in registered form without nominal or par value.[13] Shares are considered to be issued when all the formalities in respect of their issuance are satisfied.[14] Shares with nominal or par value issued *prior to the enactment of* the CBCA and the OBCA *are deemed to be shares without nominal or par value.*[15]

A share is issued in registered form if it satisfies one of two conditions: it names a person who is entitled to the share such that its transfer may be recorded on a securities register, or it bears a statement that it is in registered form.[16]

(ii) Unlimited Number

In the absence of a specific restriction in its articles of incorporation, a corporation is allowed an unlimited number of shares of each class provided for in the articles. A corporation can set an upper limit, however, on the number of shares it will issue, even if the articles specify no such limit.[17]

A corporation that restricts the number of shares it may issue may, at any time, by special resolution, amend its articles of incorporation to remove and or amend the

---

[10] CBCA, subs. 24(4); OBCA, subs. 22(4).

[11] CBCA, para. 24(4)(*b*).

[12] OBCA, cl. 22(4)(*b*).

[13] CBCA, subs. 24(1); OBCA, subs. 22(1).

[14] See: *Dale v. The Queen*, 94 DTC 1100 (T.C.C.); *National Westminster Bank v. I.R.C.*, [1994] STC 184 (C.A.).

[15] CBCA, subs. 24(2); OBCA, subs. 22(2).

[16] CBCA, subs. 48(4); OBCA, subs. 53(1) ("registered form").

[17] CBCA, para. 6(1)(*c*); OBCA, cl. 5(1)(*c*).

restriction.[18] An amendment to a corporation's authorized capital entitles a shareholder of the corporation to dissent from the change and, if the appropriate procedural steps are followed, the shareholder is entitled to be paid the fair value of his or her shares.[19]

(iii) Limited Liability

Shares issued by a corporation are non-assessable against its shareholders who cannot be called upon to pay additional amounts either to the corporation or to its creditors.[20] Shareholders are not, *qua shareholders*, liable for the acts or default of the corporation.[21]

(iv) Full Consideration

A corporation may not issue any shares until such time as it receives full consideration in the form of money, property or past services, in return for the shares. If past services constitute the consideration for issued shares, the fair value of those services must not be less than the money the corporation would have received had the shares been issued for cash.[22]

A corporation may issue shares for non-cash property provided that the property is no less than equivalent in value to the fair cash consideration the corporation would have received had its shares been issued for money.[23]

The directors of a corporation determine the value of consideration received by the corporation in exchange for its shares (whether in the form of property or past services). They must ensure that this amount is not less than the cash equivalent that it would have otherwise received.[24] In determining what constitutes a fair equivalent value for property or past services, directors may take into account reasonable charges and any expenses of organization that are expected to benefit the corporation.[25]

---

[18] CBCA, para. 173(1)(d); OBCA, clause 168(1)(d). "Special resolution" is a defined term and, in effect, means a two-thirds majority; *Trans-Prairie Pipelines Ltd. v. M.N.R.*, [1970] CTC 537, 70 DTC 6351 (Ex. Ct.) (interest on money borrowed used to redeem preferred shares deductible).

[19] CBCA, s. 190; OBCA, s. 185.

[20] CBCA, subs. 25(2); OBCA, subs. 23(2).

[21] CBCA, subs. 45(1); OBCA, subs. 92(1).

[22] CBCA, subs. 25(3); OBCA, subs. 23(3).

[23] CBCA, subs. 25(3); OBCA subs. 23(3).

[24] CBCA, subs. 25(3); OBCA, subs. 23(4). The CBCA does not specifically require directors to act on the determination of equivalent fair value. The power of determining share consideration is, however, an incident of the power and duty to manage the affairs of the corporation.

[25] CBCA, subs. 25(4); OBCA, subss. 23(4) and 23(5).

(d) Stated Capital Account

The concept of "stated capital" is particularly important in corporate law. As we shall see, it is also the springboard for determining the "paid-up capital" of a corporation for tax purposes.

Stated capital is the amount of money "committed" by a shareholder to the corporation and, in most cases, represents the shareholder's maximum liability to corporate creditors. Thus, in a sense, it is the financial measure of the limited liability of shareholders and represents to creditors the amount of funds or assets initially invested by shareholders.

(i) Separate Accounts for Each Class

A corporation must maintain a separate stated capital account for each class and series of shares that it issues.[26] Generally, the stated capital account is credited with the *full* amount of any consideration received in respect of the particular shares issued by the corporation.[27] There are some exceptions (discussed below) to this rule in respect of non-arm's length transactions.

Shares must be without nominal or par value and, as noted above, the full consideration received must be credited to the stated capital account.

(ii) Shares Issued for Property

A corporation may not issue shares in exchange for any property (or past service) which is valued at less than the amount the corporation would have received had the shares been issued for money.[28] It can, however, issue shares for consideration of greater value than the cash equivalent of property or past services.

(A) Credit Full Consideration

Generally speaking, the *full* amount of the consideration received must be credited to the stated capital account.

A corporation may not credit to a stated capital account an amount that is greater than the amount of the consideration that it receives for its shares.[29] This restriction plays an important role in tax law because a corporation can generally pay back its stated capital without any income tax cost to shareholders.

---

[26] CBCA, subs. 26(1); OBCA, subs. 24(1).

[27] CBCA, subs. 26(2); OBCA, subss. 24(2), (8) (stated capital account may be maintained in foreign currency).

[28] CBCA, subs. 25(3); OBCA, subs. 23(3).

[29] CBCA, subs. 26(4); OBCA, subs. 24(4).

(B) Non-arm's Length Transactions

There are several exceptions to the general rule that a corporation must credit the full amount of consideration that it receives to its stated capital account. A corporation may add to its stated capital account an amount that is less than the consideration that it receives for its shares if the shares are issued:[30]

- in exchange for property of a person who, immediately before the exchange, does not deal with the corporation at arm's length;

- in exchange for shares of a body corporate that immediately before the exchange, or because of the exchange, does not deal with the issuing corporation at arm's length;

- pursuant to an amalgamation with another corporation; or

- pursuant to an "arrangement" that is, in effect, an amalgamation of the issuing corporation with another corporation.

In each of the above circumstances, the corporation may add either all or *some lesser part of* the consideration that it receives for its shares to the appropriate stated capital account. As already noted, it cannot add an amount that is greater than the amount it receives.[31] These exceptions are intended to facilitate corporate reorganizations under the *Income Tax Act*.[32]

(iii) Stock Dividends

Where a corporation pays a stock dividend, it must add to the stated capital account of the class of shares on which the dividend is paid, the full financial equivalent of the declared amount of the dividend.[33] In other words, the amount that it capitalizes from retained earnings to share capital for accounting purposes is also the amount that must be credited to the share capital account for corporate law purposes.

(iv) Continuances

A corporation continued under either the CBCA or the OBCA may add to its stated capital accounts any consideration received for shares issued prior to its continuance.

---

[30] CBCA, subs. 26(3); OBCA, subs. 24(3). These exceptions all cater to income tax transactions and are intended to facilitate various rollovers under the *Income Tax Act*.

[31] CBCA, subs. 26(4); OBCA, subs. 24(4). Since March 31, 1977 the general rule is that "paid-up capital" for income tax purposes is calculated by reference to the rules of corporate law. In the absence of technical adjustments, the paid-up capital of a class of shares of a corporation is determined by dividing the stated capital account for that class of shares by the number of issued shares of that class.

[32] See Chapter XX "Reorganizations: Transfer of Property to a Corporation".

[33] A stock dividend is a dividend paid by issuing additional fully paid shares of the corporation to existing shareholders; see CBCA, subs. 43(2); OBCA, subs. 38(2).

It may also, at any time, add to its stated capital account any amount credited to its retained earnings or other surplus accounts.[34]

(v) Resolutions

Where a corporation has more than one class of shares outstanding, any addition to the stated capital account of a class or series of shares must be approved by a special resolution if the amount that is to be added was not received as consideration for the issue of shares.[35] An Ontario corporation does not need to pass a special resolution if the amount credited to the stated capital account arises by virtue of the payment of a stock dividend.

The OBCA also requires a corporation to conduct a special class vote if an addition to its stated capital account affects the shareholders of one of its classes or series of shares in a manner different from the way in which it affects holders of another of its classes or series of shares. The right to vote separately as a class attaches to the shares whether or not the particular shares would otherwise entitle the holder to vote under normal circumstances.[36]

(e) Reduction of Stated Capital

A corporation's stated capital account serves two important corporate purposes: (1) It serves as a measure of the maximum liability of its shareholders to outsiders; (2) The amount shown in the account represents the initial investment of its shareholders, which serves as a measure of security for creditors who loan money to the corporation. Thus, corporate statutes stringently control adjustments, particularly downward adjustments, in these accounts.

The general rule is that a corporation may not reduce its stated capital.[37] There are exceptions to this rule but the exceptions apply only in narrowly circumscribed circumstances.

Generally speaking, a corporation may reduce its stated capital only if it satisfies two financial requirements: the reduction must not impair the solvency or the liquidity of the corporation. Thus, a corporation may reduce its stated capital if it is able to pay its obligations as they fall due and it is able to discharge its obligations to its shareholders and creditors.

The stringency of the financial tests depends upon the reason for the reduction of capital and the potential for harm to investors. The less the risk of harm and the lower

---

[34] CBCA, subs. 26(6); OBCA, subs. 24(5).

[35] CBCA, subs. 26(5); OBCA, subs. 24(6). Under the CBCA, a special resolution is not required if there are only two classes of shares and all of the issued shares are convertible from one class into the other.

[36] OBCA, subs. 24(7).

[37] CBCA, subs. 26(10); OBCA, subs. 24(9). This prohibition does not apply to mutual funds.

the potential for abuse, the less stringent the test that must be satisfied to reduce stated capital.

(i) Acquisition of Corporation's Own Shares

At common law, a corporation was not allowed to reduce its capital except with judicial approval. Thus, a corporation was also prohibited from purchasing its own shares, since the purchase of its own shares would be tantamount to a reduction of capital.[38]

The common law rule has been incorporated into both the CBCA and the OBCA, but with substantial exceptions.[39] A corporation may reduce its capital if the financial interests of its investors and creditors are protected.

(A) Financial Tests

Subject to restrictions in its articles, a corporation may purchase its own shares if it does not have reasonable grounds for believing that the purchase will:[40]

- render the corporation unable to pay its liabilities as they come due, or

- cause the realizable value of its assets to be less than the aggregate of its liabilities and the stated capital of all of its classes of shares.

Thus, the corporation must satisfy two financial tests: it must be both liquid *and* solvent after it purchases its shares. The determination of corporate liquidity is fairly clear cut in most cases and can be ascertained from professionally prepared financial statements expressed in terms of current market values. Long term solvency is more difficult to measure.

Directors of a corporation who authorize the purchase of its shares in contravention of the solvency and liquidity tests are jointly and severally liable to the corporation for the amount of the unauthorized disbursement of funds.[41] A director who dissents from the resolution authorizing the purchase of shares is absolved from liability if his or her dissent is recorded at the meeting. If the director is not present at the meeting, he or she must notify the secretary of the corporation and cause his or her dissent to be placed in the minutes of the meeting.[42]

---

[38]   *Trevor v. Whitworth* (1887), 12 App. Cas. 409 (H.L.).

[39]   CBCA, s. 30; OBCA, s. 28.

[40]   CBCA, s. 34; OBCA, s. 30. Note that an Ontario corporation may also purchase its warrants. The financial tests are somewhat less stringent if the purchase of shares is to settle a claim against the corporation, eliminate fractional shares, or fulfil the terms of a non-assignable agreement under which the corporation is obliged to purchase the shares.

[41]   CBCA, subs. 118(2); OBCA, subs. 130(2).

[42]   CBCA, s. 123; OBCA, s. 135.

A director is entitled to rely upon reports presented by professionals who are qualified to comment on matters requiring technical expertise. As such, a director who relies upon the report of an accountant, appraiser, or other professional qualified to make valuation judgments is not liable if the purchase of shares subsequently proves to be in contravention of the statutory financial tests.[43]

(B) Dissenting Shareholders

A corporation that purchases its own shares to satisfy a dissenting shareholder's claim pursuant to the appraisal remedy faces a less stringent financial test.[44] For example, under a buy-out pursuant to the appraisal remedy, a corporation is only prohibited from purchasing its own shares from a dissenting shareholder if the purchase would render the corporation unable to pay its obligations as they fall due (the liquidity test), or if the realizable value of its assets is reduced by the purchase to less than the value of its outstanding liabilities.[45] In these circumstances, the corporation's stated capital is not taken into account in the second prong of the two tests. In other words, a corporation may reduce its stated capital to purchase its own shares provided it does not impair its liquidity and solvency insofar as its creditors are concerned.

(C) Court Order

A corporation may also purchase its own shares to comply with a court order to do so.[46] In complying with the court order, the corporation does not have to satisfy the liquidity and solvency tests applicable to other purchases.[47] The corporation need only satisfy two tests: (1) That it will be able to pay its liabilities as they become due (the liquidity test); (2) That the realizable value of its assets after the purchase does not fall below the aggregate of its liabilities.[48]

(ii) Alternative Acquisition of Corporation's Own Shares

There are three additional circumstances in which a corporation may acquire its own shares by satisfying a somewhat less stringent financial test than those generally applicable. Subject to its articles, a corporation may purchase its own shares to:[49]

1. Settle or compromise debts asserted by or against the corporation;
2. Eliminate fractional shares; or

---

[43] CBCA, subs. 123(4); OBCA, subs. 135(4).

[44] CBCA, para. 35(2)(*a*); OBCA, cl. 31(2)(*a*).

[45] CBCA, subs. 190(26); OBCA, subs. 185(30).

[46] CBCA, s. 241; OBCA, s. 248.

[47] CBCA, para. 35(2)(*b*); OBCA, cl. 31(2)(*b*).

[48] CBCA, subs. 241(6); OBCA, s. 248(6).

[49] CBCA, subs. 35(1); OBCA, subs. 31(1).

3. Fulfil the terms of a non-assignable agreement under which the corporation has an option or is obligated to purchase shares owned by a director, officer or employee of the corporation.

In any of these situations, the corporation may purchase its shares *unless:*[50]

- there are reasonable grounds for believing that the purchase will render the corporation unable to pay its obligations as they fall due; or

- the realizable value of the corporation's assets after the purchase will be less than the aggregate of its liabilities and the amount required to redeem all of its shares the holders of which have the right to be paid *prior to* the holders of the shares to be purchased.

The second prong of the financial tests ensures that a corporation that purchases its own shares does not prejudice the rights of senior shareholders who have a higher ranking claim to the assets of the corporation than the holders of the shares purchased. Thus, the rights of preferred shareholders cannot be prejudiced by the corporation purchasing shares that rank lower in corporate rights.

(iii) Redemption of Shares

A corporation is entitled to redeem its redeemable shares, but it cannot pay an amount in excess of the redemption price stipulated in its articles of incorporation.[51] A "redeemable share" is defined as a share that is redeemable at the option of either the corporation or the shareholder.[52]

A corporation may not redeem its shares unless it satisfies two financial tests. First, a corporation may redeem its shares only if there are reasonable grounds for believing that the redemption would not render the corporation unable to pay its obligations as they fall due.[53] Thus, the corporation must be liquid enough to pay its debts as they mature.

Second, the realizable value of the corporation's assets after the redemption must not be less than the aggregate of its liabilities and the amount required to pay other shareholders who rate equally with or have a higher claim than the holders of the redeemed shares.[54] The concern here is to protect only those who have a claim equal to or higher than the shares redeemed. The financial tests are less stringent because the

---

[50] CBCA, subs. 35(3); OBCA, subs. 31(3).

[51] CBCA, subs. 36(1); OBCA, subs. 32(1).

[52] CBCA, subs. 2(1) ("redeemable share"); OBCA, subs. 1(1) ("redeemable share"). In financial jargon, a share that is redeemable at the option of the shareholder is referred to as a "retractable share".

[53] CBCA, para. 36(2)(*a*); OBCA, cl. 32(2)(*a*).

[54] CBCA, para. 36(2)(*b*); OBCA, cl. 32(2)(*b*).

shares would have been issued on the basis that they were redeemable and this information is available to the public.

(iv) Other Reductions of Stated Capital

A corporation may by special resolution reduce its stated capital account at any time and for *any* purpose provided that it satisfies certain financial tests.[55] Under this general, broad-based power the corporation can proceed only by way of a special resolution of its shareholders. The resolution must identify the particular stated capital accounts that are to be reduced.[56]

(A) Financial Tests

In addition to the special resolution, the corporation must satisfy two financial tests: liquidity and solvency. These tests are similar, though not identical, to the tests applicable to a purchase or redemption of corporate shares. Thus, a corporation may not reduce its stated capital if there are reasonable grounds for believing that the reduction will render the corporation unable to pay its obligations as they fall due.[57]

Second, the stated capital account may not be reduced if there are reasonable grounds for believing that the reduction will cause the realizable value of the corporation's assets to be less than the aggregate of its liabilities.[58] Since the liabilities of a corporation include its contingent liabilities, it may be quite difficult to determine whether the solvency test is satisfied in borderline cases.

Where an Ontario corporation plans to reduce its capital in circumstances in which the reduction will have a different effect on different classes of shares, it must allow a separate class vote for the purposes of obtaining the special resolution from each of the affected classes. The right to a separate class vote does not depend upon whether or not the shares affected would otherwise be entitled to vote.[59]

---

[55] CBCA, subs. 38(1); OBCA, subs. 34(1).

[56] CBCA, subs. 38(2); OBCA, subs. 34(3). A "special resolution" is a resolution passed by a majority of two-thirds of votes cast, or one signed by all of the shareholders entitled to vote on the resolution; see, CBCA, subs. 2(1) ("special resolution"), OBCA, subs. 1(1)("special resolution").

[57] CBCA, para. 38(3)(a); OBCA, cl. 34(4)(*a*). A corporation reducing its stated capital must *always* satisfy the liquidity test so that the rights of creditors are not prejudiced. It is only the solvency test which is more or less stringent depending upon the circumstances surrounding the reduction.

[58] CBCA, para. 38(3)(b); OBCA, cl. 34(4)(*b*).

[59] OBCA, subs. 34(2).

(B) Creditor's Rights

A creditor of a corporation that reduces its stated capital in contravention of either the CBCA or the OBCA is entitled to apply to a court for relief. The court may order the shareholder *or other recipient* who has benefited from the reduction:[60]

- To pay to the corporation an amount equal to any liability of the shareholder that was either extinguished or reduced contrary to the statutory provisions; or

- To deliver to the corporation any money or property paid or distributed to the shareholder or other recipient as a consequence of the improper reduction of capital.

This remedy is in addition to any other remedies that the creditor may have against the directors of the corporation who have authorized an unlawful reduction of capital.[61] There is, however, a limitation period: The creditor must commence action within two years of the alleged unlawful reduction of capital.[62]

Shareholders of Ontario corporations are entitled to apply to bring the suit as a class action.[63]

A shareholder who holds shares as a trustee (or other fiduciary) is not personally liable on an improper reduction of stated capital. Rather, it is the beneficial owner of the shares who assumes all the liabilities flowing from an infringement of the statutory provisions.[64]

(f) Adjustments of Stated Capital Accounts

A corporation is required to maintain a separate stated capital account for each class and series of shares that it issues.[65] Generally, the full amount of any consideration received upon issuing shares is credited to the appropriate stated capital account.[66]

---

[60] CBCA, subs. 38(4); OBCA, subs. 34(5).

[61] CBCA, subs. 38(6); OBCA, subs. 34(9).

[62] CBCA, subs. 35(5); OBCA, subs. 34(6).

[63] OBCA, subs. 34(7).

[64] OBCA, subs. 34(8), subs. 1(1) ("personal representative").

[65] CBCA, subs. 26(1); OBCA, subs. 24(1).

[66] CBCA, subs. 26(2); OBCA, subs. 24(2). A lesser amount may be credited to the stated capital account where the shares are issued in exchange for property in a non-arm's length transaction: CBCA, subs. 26(3); OBCA, subs. 24(3). The rationale of this exception is to accommodate income tax planning, particularly under s. 84.1 of the *Income Tax Act*.

(i) Reduction

When a corporation reduces its share capital, it is required to adjust the amount shown in its stated capital account. The amount of the adjustment depends upon the manner in which the corporation acquires its own shares.

Where the reduction in the share capital of a corporation is pursuant to:

- an acquisition of the corporation's own shares;[67]
- a settlement or compromise of a claim asserted against the corporation;[68]
- a plan to eliminate fractional shares;[69]
- the terms of a non-assignable agreement under which the corporation was obliged to purchase shares owned by its directors, officers or employees;[70]
- a redemption of its shares;[71]
- the enforcement of a lien against its shares;[72]
- a transaction whereby a dissenting shareholder of the corporation exercised appraisal rights;[73] or
- a court order relieving a shareholder from oppression by the corporation,[74]

the amount to be deducted from the stated capital account is calculated according to a formula that reduces the stated capital account by the *average* issue price of all of the shares of the particular class or series.[75]

The formula reduces the stated capital account of the shares in proportion to the amount that was credited to the account when the shares were issued. The premium paid to a shareholder on the redemption of shares in any of the above listed circumstances is not deducted from the stated capital account.[76]

---

[67] CBCA, s. 34; OBCA, s. 30.

[68] CBCA, para. 35(1)(*a*); OBCA, cl. 31(1)(*a*).

[69] CBCA, para. 35(1)(*b*); OBCA, cl. 31(1)(*b*).

[70] CBCA, para. 35(1)(*c*); OBCA, cl. 31(1)(*c*).

[71] CBCA, s. 36; OBCA, s. 32.

[72] CBCA, subs. 45(3); OBCA, subs. 40(3).

[73] CBCA, s. 190; OBCA, s. 185.

[74] CBCA, s. 241; OBCA, s. 248.

[75] CBCA, subs. 39(1); OBCA, subs. 35(1).

[76] Ibid.

In contrast, if a corporation is required to compensate a shareholder for the purchase price of his or her shares because of its oppressive conduct, the reduction in the stated capital account is the full amount paid to the shareholder.[77] This amount will not necessarily coincide with the amount credited to the corporation's stated capital account when the shares were initially issued as the shareholder may have purchased the shares from another shareholder at a later date.

Where a corporation reduces its stated capital account pursuant to a special resolution, the amount specified in the resolution as the amount of the reduction is the amount deducted from the appropriate stated capital account.[78] The determination of this amount depends entirely upon the particular circumstances calling for the reduction.

(ii) Conversion or Change of Shares

When shares are converted from one class into another, the stated capital accounts of both of the classes must be adjusted to reflect the conversion. Similarly, when shares are changed from one class or series into shares of another class or series, the stated capital account of both classes or series must be adjusted.[79] In either of these situations, conversion or change, the stated capital account of the class from which the shares are converted is reduced by the amount derived from a formula.

The stated capital account of the shares into which the shares are converted or changed is increased by an equivalent amount *plus* any additional consideration payable on the conversion or change of shares.[80]

Where a corporation has two classes of shares with rights of conversion from one class into the other (that is, interconvertible shares), the adjustment to the stated capital account upon the conversion of a share from one class to the other is equal to the weighted average of the stated capital accounts of both classes of shares.[81]

When shares of one class or series are converted or changed into shares of another class or series, the old shares (that is, the converted or changed shares) are considered to be issued shares of the class or series into which the shares have been converted or changed.[82] Thus, to the extent of the number of shares converted, the issued capital of the old class or series *automatically* becomes issued shares of the new class or series.

---

[77] CBCA, subs. 39(2); OBCA, subs. 35(2).

[78] CBCA, subs. 39(3); OBCA, subs. 35(3).

[79] CBCA, subs. 39(4); OBCA, subs. 35(4). A "conversion" of shares from one class into another occurs pursuant to the terms and conditions of the shares as described in the articles of incorporation. A "change" of shares from one class into another is usually pursuant to a subsequent amendment to the terms and conditions attached to the shares.

[80] CBCA, para. 39(4)(*b*); OBCA, cl. 35(4)(*b*).

[81] CBCA, subs. 39(5); OBCA, subs. 35(5).

[82] CBCA, subs. 39(9); OBCA, subs. 35(8).

The automatic conversion of shares from one class into another applies only to the *issued* shares and does not apply to any *unissued* shares. The articles must be amended to convert the unissued shares of the old class into unissued shares of the new class.

(g) Effect of Change of Shares on Authorized Capital

There are circumstances where a corporation may wish to restrict the amount of share capital that it issues.[83] Where a corporation limits the number of shares that it may issue by stipulating a maximum authorized capital, a conversion of shares from one class into another will have the effect of increasing the unissued but authorized shares of the old class by the number of shares converted or changed into shares of the new class. In other words, the authorized share capital of the old class is restored by the number of shares converted or changed into the new class.[84]

(h) Cancellation of Shares

If its articles of incorporation do not limit the number of shares that a corporation may issue, any shares (or fractions of shares) issued and later acquired by the corporation are automatically cancelled. Where, however, the authorized share capital of a corporation is limited, any of its shares acquired by the corporation are restored to the status of authorized but unissued shares of the particular class.[85] The rationale of these provisions is to prevent the corporation and its senior officials from manipulating the market in the corporation's shares or using corporate assets to acquire, or enhance, voting power.

(i) Corporation Holding Its Own Shares

The common law rule against corporations "trafficking" in their own shares also prohibited a corporation from holding its shares: The retention of cancelled shares would be tantamount to a reduction of capital.[86]

The common law rule is entrenched in both the CBCA and the OBCA.[87] The general rule is that a corporation may not hold shares in itself; nor may it hold shares

---

[83]   CBCA, para. 6(1)(c); OBCA, cl. 5(1)(c).

[84]   CBCA, subs. 39(10); OBCA, subs. 35(8).

[85]   CBCA, subs. 39(6); OBCA, subs. 35(6).

[86]   *Trevor v. Whitworth* (1887), 12 App. Cas. 409 at 423 (H.L.):

   Paid-up capital may be diminished or lost in the company's trading; that is a result which no legislation can prevent; but persons who deal with, and give credit to a limited company, naturally rely upon the fact that the company is trading with a certain amount of capital already paid, as well as upon the responsibility of its members for the capital remaining at call; and they are entitled to assume that no part of the capital which has been paid into the coffers of the company has been subsequently paid out, except in the legitimate course of its business.

[87]   CBCA, subs. 30(1); OBCA, subs. 28(1).

in its parent corporation. A parent corporation is specifically prohibited from issuing its shares to any of its subsidiaries.[88] Although there are exceptions to these rules, each exception is circumscribed by financial tests which are intended to protect the interests of investors and creditors.

4. TAX ASPECTS OF EQUITY FINANCING

References:

BULLETINS, CIRCULARS & RULINGS:

IT-67R3	May 15, 1992	Taxable Dividends from Corporations Resident in Canada
IT-143R2	August 10, 1983	Meaning of Eligible Capital Expenditure
IT-386R	October 30, 1992	Eligible Capital Amounts

(a) General

A corporation's share capital represents its permanent capital base. A corporation is generally under no legal obligation to re-purchase its shares and return capital to shareholders.

Since, in most cases, the payment of dividends is within the sole discretion of the board of directors, a corporation need not pay dividends when it is not financially secure. Indeed, as already noted, a corporation is prohibited from paying dividends if the payment would impair its financial ability to repay its debts.

A shareholder's ownership of a corporation is measured by the number of shares that he or she owns. Each share is represented by its "paid-up capital" in the corporation.

There are two fundamental tax aspects of corporate share capital:

1. Dividends are paid from after-tax dollars and are not deductible from income; and

2. The paid-up capital of shares can be returned to shareholders on a tax-free basis.

These two characteristics of the corporate tax system have an enormous influence on the structure of the system and their effect is seen in many anti-avoidance rules.

(b) Types of Shares

Unless otherwise stated or provided for in the articles of incorporation, all shares are presumed to be equal in respect of their fundamental rights. These rights include:

---

[88] CBCA, subs. 30(2); OBCA, subs. 28(2) (a corporation acquiring a subsidiary that holds its shares must cause the subsidiary to dispose of those shares within five years of its becoming a subsidiary).

the right to vote; the right to participate in dividends; and the right to share in any proceeds on liquidation of the corporation.

The fundamental rights can, however, be modified to suit the needs of the corporation and its investors. Thus, shares can be made voting or non-voting, and voting shares can be differently weighted. Similarly, shares can be granted priority in respect of the timing and amount of dividends payable on them. Shares can be redeemable at the option of the corporation and retractable at the option of the shareholder. Shares can be given priority in respect of the return of capital upon liquidation, and so on. These variable attributes permit a very large number of combinations and permutations of share characteristics. Thus, share conditions can be crafted to suit the particular purposes for which they are to be used.

The particular terms, conditions, rights and restrictions attached to shares can have a significant effect upon their fair market value and this can be important for the purposes of determining capital gains and losses. For example, the types of conditions attached to shares used in an estate freeze are quite different from share conditions in a public offering. In the former case, the objective is to freeze the fair market value of shares so that they do not increase in value; in the latter case, the objective is to facilitate growth in the value of the shares in the public market.

(c) Paid-up Capital

References:

ITA:

S. 84	Deemed Dividends
Subs. 89(1)	"Paid-up Capital"

BULLETINS, CIRCULARS & RULINGS:

IT-463R	July 12, 1991	Paid-up Capital

In corporate law, the concept of stated capital serves two distinct purposes: (1) It is a measure of the cushion upon which creditors may rely for the repayment of their debts, and (2) it is a measure of the limit of shareholder liability.

"Paid-up capital" for tax purposes is analogous to the concept of "stated capital": It measures the amount of capital that may be returned to shareholders on a tax-free basis. Payments to shareholders in excess of the paid-up capital of their shares are deemed to be income.[89]

---

[89] See, e.g., *Income Tax Act*, s. 84.

The "paid-up capital" of a class of shares is initially determined under the applicable corporate statute.[90] Hence, the concept of paid-up capital can vary between different corporate jurisdictions in Canada.

The paid-up capital of a share is specific and particular to *the share* — it does not attach to the shareholder. Thus, it does not necessarily change when the share is sold.

The paid-up capital of shares is determined as at a point in time: it is equal to the stated capital of the shares plus or minus any adjustments prior to that time.

Example XV.1

Assume:

Holdco is a corporation incorporated under the *Canada Business Corporations Act* which has not issued any shares prior to the transactions described below. Assume also that the shares are issued to, and held by, individual shareholders. *Holdco* is authorized to issue the following classes of shares:

Class	Rights
Class A	Voting, unlimited participation in dividends and on liquidation ("common shares").
Class B	Voting, no dividend entitlement, preferential participation on liquidation to the extent of $100 per share, redeemable and retractable for $100 per share, convertible into Class D on a 1:1 basis.
Class C	Non-voting, no dividend entitlement, preferential participation on liquidation to the extent of $100 per share, retractable for $100 per share.
Class D	Non-voting, unlimited participation in dividends and on liquidation.

Holdco issues one Class A share for $100.

Then:
  Stated capital (Class A shares):

Before issuance	$ 0
Increase	100
After issuance	$ 100

  Paid-up capital (Class A shares):

Stated capital	$ 100
Adjustment	0
Paid-up capital	$ 100

Hence, paid-up capital equals stated capital of shares.

---

[90] Subs. 89(1) ("paid-up capital").

(i) Classes of Shares

All shares are presumed equal and to confer the same rights unless it is expressly stated otherwise. In order for shares to be considered to belong to different classes, they must, *in substance*, have different rights, conditions, privileges or restrictions. As Dickson C.J., said in *McClurg*:[91]

> ... In my view, a precondition to the derogation from the presumption of equality, both with respect to entitlement to dividends and other shareholder entitlements, is the division of shares into different "classes". The rationale for this rule can be traced to the principle that shareholder rights attach to the shares themselves and not to shareholders. The division of shares into separate classes, then, is the means by which shares (as opposed to shareholders) are distinguished, and in turn allows for the derogation from the presumption of equality. ...

(ii) Interconvertible Shares

The stated capital and paid-up capital of shares of interconvertible classes are determined as if they were combined in one class.[92]

(iii) Capitalizing Retained Earnings

The amount of retained earnings capitalized will affect the stated capital and the paid-up capital of the shares and may also trigger a deemed dividend.[93]

Example XV.2	
Assume:	
Holdco capitalizes $50 of its retained earnings to its Class A shares.	
Then:	
Stated capital (Class A shares):	
Before capitalization	$ 100
Capitalization	50
After capitalization	$ 150
Paid-up capital (Class A shares):	
Stated capital	$ 150
Adjustment	0
Paid-up capital	$ 150

---

[91] *McClurg v. The Queen*, [1991] 1 CTC 169, 91 DTC 5001 at 5007 (S.C.C.); see also *Int. Power Co. v. McMaster Univ.*, [1946] SCR 178 [Que.].

[92] CBCA, subs. 39(5); OBCA, subs. 35(5).

[93] *Income Tax Act*, subs. 84(1).

The shareholder of the Class A shares is also deemed to have received a dividend to the extent that the paid-up capital of the shares is increased without a corresponding increase in Holdco's net assets — in the above example, $50.

(iv) Stock Dividends

A stock dividend is the payment of a dividend in shares. Shares are issued to existing shareholders without consideration. Typically, stock dividends are prompted by a desire to ostensibly allocate retained earnings to shareholders, but without distribution of cash.

Subsection 43(2) of the CBCA requires the "declared amount" of a stock dividend to be added to the stated capital of the class of shares on which the dividend is paid.[94] The "declared amount" of a dividend is the amount *declared* by the directors in the corporation's resolutions.

Example XV.3

Assume:

Holdco declares and pays a dividend in the amount of $10 on its Class A share payable by the issue of one Class B share that has a fair market value of $100.

Then:

Stated capital (Class B shares):

Before stock dividend	$ 0
Stock dividend	10
After stock dividend	$ 10

Paid-up capital (Class B shares):

Stated capital	$ 10
Adjustment	0
Paid-up capital	$ 10

It is arguable that, pursuant to subsection 26(2) of the CBCA, the "full amount" of the consideration for the stock dividend is the fair value of the dividend — here, $100 per Class B share — and that this is the amount to be added to the stated and paid-up capital of the shares. This view better accords with the policy of the corporate and tax statutes. It is also in keeping with commercial and accounting practice. For example, the American Institute of Certified Public Accountants states:[95]

> . . . a stock dividend does not, in fact, give rise to any change whatsoever in either the corporation's assets or its respective shareholders' proportionate interests therein. However, it cannot fail to be

---

[94] See also OBCA, subs. 38(2).

[95] ARB 43, c. 7 (1953).

recognized that, merely as a consequence of the expressed purpose of the transaction and its characterization as a *dividend* in related notices to shareholders and the public at large, many recipients of stock dividends look upon them as distributions of corporate earnings and usually in an amount equivalent to the fair value of the additional shares received. Furthermore, it is to be presumed that such views of recipients are materially strengthened in those instances, which are by far the most numerous, where the issuances are so small in comparison with the shares previously outstanding that they do not have any apparent effect upon the share market price and, consequently, the market value of the shares previously held remains substantially unchanged. The committee, therefore, believes that where these circumstances exist the corporation should, in the public interest, account for the transaction by transferring from earned surplus to the category of permanent capitalization (represented by the capital stock and capital surplus accounts) an amount equal to the fair value of the additional shares issued. . . .

(v) Conversion of Shares

Subsection 39(4) of the CBCA requires stated capital adjustments to be made on a conversion of shares from one class into another class.[96] The stated capital of the class from which shares are converted is reduced by the appropriate percentage. The stated capital of the class into which the shares are converted is increased by a corresponding amount.

Example XV.4	
Holdco's shareholder elects to convert its Class B share into a Class D share.	
Stated capital (Class B shares):	
Before conversion	$ 10
Deduction on conversion	(10)
After conversion	$ 0
Paid-up capital (Class B shares):	
Stated capital	$ 0
Adjustment	0
Paid-up capital	$ 0
Stated capital (Class D shares):	
Before conversion	$ 0
Increase on conversion	10
After conversion	$ 10
Paid-up capital (Class D shares):	
Stated capital	$ 10
Adjustment	0
Paid-up capital	$ 10

---

[96] See also OBCA, subs. 35(4).

(d) Adjustments to Paid-up Capital

The paid-up capital of a share starts off equal to its stated capital for corporate purposes. The two measures of capital can, however, diverge because of adjustments that may have to be made for tax purposes. For example, the paid-up capital of a class of shares may be adjusted for transactions under any of the following provisions of the *Income Tax Act*:

- subsections 66.3(2) and (4) (flow-through shares);
- sections 84.1 and 84.2 (non-arm's length sales);
- section 85 (transfer of property to a corporation);[97]
- subsections 87(3) and (9) (amalgamation);
- subsection 192(4.1) (designation by corporation); and
- section 212.1 (non-arm's length purchase of shares from non-resident).

Thus, a corporation's paid-up capital for tax purposes may be quite different from its stated capital for financial accounting purposes. The difference between paid-up capital and stated capital can be a trap for anyone who relies solely on the corporation's financial statements to determine the paid-up capital of shares. For example, where a corporation redeems its shares, any amount paid over the paid-up capital of the shares is deemed to be a dividend to the shareholder.[98] Since paid-up capital may be lower than stated capital for accounting purposes, what appears to be a tax-free return of stated capital for tax purposes may, in fact, be a taxable dividend in the hands of the shareholder.

To avoid the risk of unexpected deemed dividends, it is desirable to reduce a corporation's stated capital for corporate purposes to accord with its paid-up capital for income tax purposes. This reduces the risk of inadvertently triggering income tax consequences on the basis of corporate share transactions.

(e) Cost of Issuing Shares

(i) General

The cost of issuing equity capital is not a deductible expense under the general rules: The cost is on account of capital and is caught by the prohibitions in paragraphs 18(1)(a) and (b). The Act, however, permits the deduction of financing charges, but only according to a specific amortization formula.[99]

---

[97] See Chapter XX "Transfer of Property to a Corporation".

[98] *Income Tax Act*, subs. 84(3).

[99] Para. 20(1)(e).

(ii) Commissions to Agents

A corporation may deduct expenses associated with the issuance of its shares. Deductible expenses include any commissions, fees, or other amounts payable to salespersons, agents, or securities dealers in the course of issuing shares. The deduction is available only to the taxpayer who issues the shares and not to any other person. A parent corporation, for example, may not deduct expenses incurred in respect of shares issued by its subsidiary. The subsidiary may, however, be able to deduct fees paid to its parent corporation in respect of the shares issued.

(iii) Commissions to Purchaser

A commission, fee or bonus paid to the person to whom the shares are sold is not deductible as part of the cost of issuing equity. Such expenses are considered to be a discount of the share price rather than an expense of issuing the shares.

(iv) Deductible Expenses

The following expenses are deductible by a corporation when it issues shares:

- Legal fees in connection with the preparation and approval of a prospectus related to the issuance of shares;
- Accounting or auditing fees in connection with the preparation of financial statements, and related data, for inclusion with the prospectus;
- Printing costs for the prospectus, share certificates, etc.;
- Registrars' and transfer agents' fees; and
- Filing fees payable to any regulatory authorities with whom the prospectus must be filed.

Incorporation expenses, which include legal and accounting fees, are not considered to be part of the cost of issuing shares and are not deductible expenses for tax purposes. Incorporation expenses qualify as eligible capital expenditures.[100]

(v) Amortization of Issuance Expenses

Expenses of issuing securities are only deductible in equal portions over a period of five years.[101] Corporations with short taxation years must pro rate the deduction for the short year. Where a corporation with an undeducted balance of financing expenses is wound up into, or amalgamated with, another corporation, the parent or new corporation may continue to deduct the expenses over the remainder of the five-year period.

---

[100] Subs. 14(5) ("eligible capital expenditure").

[101] Subpara. 20(1)(e)(iii).

(f) Share Redemptions

Where a corporation redeems its shares for an amount in excess of the paid-up capital of the shares, the excess is considered to be a dividend.[102]

(g) Taxable Preferred Shares

Reference:

ITA:

S. 191   Dividends on Taxable Preferred Shares

(i) Background

We saw in Chapter XIV "Corporations and Shareholders: General" that one of the fundamental structural characteristics of the corporate tax system is that dividends are paid out of after-tax earnings. In contrast, interest expense is generally deductible to a corporate debtor. On the other side of the coin, dividends generally flow on a tax-free basis between taxable Canadian corporations;[103] interest income is taxable to a corporate creditor. Thus, there is a built-in structural bias in the system. A taxable corporation usually prefers dividend income as opposed to interest income.

On the other hand, a corporate debtor usually prefers to pay interest on debt because interest is deductible for tax purposes.

Hence, in most cases, the opposing economic interests of creditor and debtor corporations in arm's length relationships will cause the parties to arrive at the most appropriate and market-efficient solution for corporate financing needs. Typically, there is a rate differential between interest charged on debt obligations and dividends on shares. The differential takes into account their disparate income tax treatment. The market model breaks down, however, if one of the parties to the financing transaction is not taxable.

The tax-free flows of intercorporate dividends is justified on two bases: (1) The dividends are paid out of previously taxed profits to an entity that has an economic interest in the payor; (2) The dividends will eventually be taxed again when paid out to individual shareholders. Thus, the disparity between dividend and interest income is premised on the prevention of double taxation of the same income within an economic unit of corporations.

The disparate tax treatment of dividend and interest income creates other problems, however, because of hybrid equities with the features and characteristics of both — instruments that look like shares, but that have all the important characteristics of debt, such as a fixed and predetermined life. One of the prominent features of these "shares"

---

[102] Subs. 84(3); see also Chapter XVIII "Corporate Distributions".

[103] See subs. 112(1).

is that they are underwritten by guarantees and have a specific term. Hence, they are known as "term preferred shares".

Term preferred shares are, in substance, equity instruments with preferences usually associated with preferred shares, but with a limited term, and usually supported by guarantees for repayment. This type of financial instrument is most attractive when the borrower (for example, a taxable corporation) does not need, and cannot use, an interest deduction because it does not have sufficient taxable income to absorb the deduction. (The taxable corporation may not be able to utilize the interest deduction because it has, for example, accumulated losses, low profit margins, or accelerated write-offs.) In these circumstances, the corporation can usually negotiate more favourable borrowing terms on a hybrid, rather than a conventional debt, instrument if the lending institution is paid in the form of tax-free dividends.

Similarly, even if both the lender and the borrower are taxable entities, there can be a tax advantage if the borrower's tax rate is lower than that of the lending institution. The net result of this ingenious, tax-driven financial arrangement is that otherwise profitable enterprises (but without taxable income because of available tax write-offs) can transform what are, in effect, payments on debt-type instruments into tax-free dividends in exchange for a lower borrowing cost.

The financial institutions were the principal beneficiaries of these arrangements and were able to increase their income through the receipt of tax-free dividends. In 1978, the annual cost of this form of after-tax financing to federal and provincial governments was approximately $500,000,000.[104]

In 1978, the government introduced new rules to curb the use of after-tax financing. These rules (known as the "term preferred share" rules) are among the most complex provisions in the statute. They are intended to disallow the manipulation of the inter-corporate dividend deduction by financial institutions. They were also intended to ensure that dividends on preferred shares are paid out of a corporation's taxed earnings with after-tax dollars. The rules were substantially amended in 1988 and a new concept, the "taxable preferred share", was introduced into the Act.

(ii) "Taxable Preferred Shares"

(A) General Scheme

Part VI.1 of the Act levies a special tax to be paid by a corporation that has paid taxable dividends on taxable preferred shares. This tax was introduced in 1988 in a renewed effort to control the use of after-tax financing, which continued to be popular despite the term preferred share rules introduced a decade earlier.

---

[104] See Budget Papers, *Notice of Ways and Means Motions and Supplementary Information*, November 16, 1978.

The tax under Part VI.1 is, in effect, a refundable tax on large corporations that use after-tax financing. The tax is imposed at three different rates as follows:[105]

Rate	Application
66 2/3%	Taxable dividends (other than excluded dividends) on "short-term" preferred shares in excess of dividend allowance;
40%	Where issuing corporation makes an election at the time of issue and where the terms of the shares so provide; and
25%	In all other cases where taxable dividends are paid on taxable preferred shares.

The rate of 66 2/3 per cent is intended to approximate the amount of tax that would be paid on an equivalent amount of interest if we assume a 40 per cent rate of corporate tax. Assuming a combined federal and provincial corporate tax rate of 40 per cent and an individual dividend tax credit of 25 per cent, the underlying rationale of these rates is to ensure that sufficient income tax is paid at the corporate level to recover the tax benefit given to the recipient corporation for the inter-corporate dividend deduction or to individuals for the dividend tax credit.

(B) Meaning of "Taxable Preferred Shares"

The Part VI.1 tax is built around the concept of "taxable preferred shares". Generally speaking, a "taxable preferred share" is a share with a special liquidation or dividend entitlement, or that is subject to a guarantee in respect of its proceeds of sale or return of income. In effect, the definition probably encompasses all preferred and special shares issued after June 18, 1987.

Thus, a share is a taxable preferred share if:

- the shareholder is entitled to a fixed annual dividend, as and when declared by the directors of the issuing corporation,

- the shareholder is entitled to a fixed entitlement on a winding-up or a redemption of the share,

- it has any preference to dividends in relation to any other share, or

- it is convertible into a share that would be a taxable preferred share.

More specifically, a "taxable preferred share" includes a share that can be described in any of the following ways:[106]

- it is a "short-term preferred share" issued after December 15, 1987;

---

[105] Subs. 191.1(1).

[106] Subs. 248(1) ("taxable preferred share").

- it may reasonably be considered that the amount of any dividends payable on the share is fixed, limited to a maximum, or established to be not less than a minimum;

- it may reasonably be considered that the amount that a shareholder is entitled to receive for the share upon the dissolution, liquidation, or winding-up of the issuing corporation is fixed, limited to a maximum, or established to be not less than a minimum amount;

- it may reasonably be considered that the amount that a shareholder is entitled to receive upon a redemption, acquisition or cancellation of the share or on a reduction of the paid-up capital of the share is fixed, limited to a maximum, or established not to be less than a minimum amount;

- the share is convertible or exchangeable, unless the share is convertible or exchangeable into something that would not be a taxable preferred share; or

- the share is one the shareholder's investment in which any person (other than the issuing corporation) has undertaken to guarantee.

A "taxable preferred share" does not include prescribed shares or shares issued by a corporation in financial difficulty. (The concept of "financial difficulty" is itself defined in paragraph (e) of the definition of "term preferred share" definition in subsection 248(1).)

The definition of taxable preferred shares is comprehensive enough to include shares that are considered to be "common shares" in most other circumstances. Given the broad definition of "taxable preferred share", the term encompasses ordinary "common shares" that have rights, conditions, privileges or restrictions attached to them that fall within the definition. For example, it is not unusual to see so-called "common shares" that may be redeemable at a pre-determined ("fixed") amount. Such a share is caught within the definition of "taxable preferred share" for the purposes of the special taxes.

(iii) Tax on Preferred Shares

The Part VI.1 tax on dividends on taxable preferred shares is, in effect, a refundable tax. The tax is structured to prevent taxable corporations that do not have taxable income from using after-tax financial instruments to pay tax-free dividends to taxable lending institutions.

A corporation pays the tax on its taxable dividends on taxable preferred shares, but is entitled to claim a refund of the tax in certain circumstances. The refund is in the form of a deduction from income in an amount equal to 9/4 of the tax paid.[107] The tax is fully refundable only if the corporation that pays the dividend has sufficient income against which it can use the deduction. Thus, the payor corporation cannot use its Part VI.1 tax to reduce income if it does not have any income that is subject to tax.

---

[107] Para. 110(1)(k).

(iv) Exemptions

There are several exemptions from the special tax on taxable preferred shares.

(A) "Substantial Interest"

There are exemptions in respect of substantial interest shareholdings that are, essentially, dividends received by a related party or those received by a shareholder who owns at least 25 per cent of the votes and of the value of the capital stock of the paying corporation.[108] A dividend paid to a shareholder with a substantial interest in the corporation is an "excluded dividend" for the purposes of the tax.[109]

(B) "Dividend Allowance"

The Part VI.1 tax applies only to dividends paid in excess of the corporation's dividend allowance. The dividend allowance is set at $500,000, which must be shared among associated corporations. The allowance is reduced on a dollar-for-dollar basis by preferred share dividends paid in the preceding year in excess of $1,000,000.[110] Thus, small corporations may issue taxable preferred shares without getting caught by the tax.

(C) Financial Intermediaries

There are also special exemptions in respect of dividends paid and received by financial intermediary corporations and certain deemed dividends that arise on corporate reorganizations.[111]

(v) Short-term Preferred Shares

The tax rate on short-term preferred shares is 66 2/3 per cent. This rate reflects the basic 40 per cent tax rate plus the effect of the denial of the inter-corporate dividend deduction to the recipient. Thus, in effect, this rate combines the two taxes into one rate and levies it on the issuer of the share, subject to a full refund if the issuer is a taxable corporation. In a sense, then, the tax on taxable preferred shares is the equivalent of an advance corporation tax.

Generally speaking, a short-term preferred share is a share issued after December 15, 1987 that is retractable within five years of its issue, or that is potentially subject to a guarantee of proceeds of disposition which may be effective within five years of the issuance of the shares.[112]

---

[108] Subss. 191(1) and (2).

[109] Subss. 191(1) and 191.1(1).

[110] Subs. 191.1(2).

[111] Subs. 191(1).

[112] Subs. 248(1) ("short-term preferred share").

5. TAX ASPECTS OF DEBT FINANCING

References:

BULLETINS, CIRCULARS & RULINGS:

IT-265R3   October 7, 1991   Payments of Income and Capital Combined

IT-410R   September 4, 1984   Debt Obligations — Accrued Interest on Transfer

There are several factors to be taken into account in selecting an appropriate method of debt financing. It is important to consider, for example, the cost of capital, its availability, and the risk exposure of the enterprise. There is no formula that can be applied to every corporation. Each corporation must take into account the terms and conditions attached to its debt financing in the context of the economic climate at the particular time.

Debt is often the primary source of capitalization of a small business corporation in the early stages of its life. There are advantages to using debt capital to capitalize a small business corporation. If the loan is properly structured, interest paid on the debt is deductible for tax purposes. The owner of the business can secure the debt and rank ahead of other creditors to the extent of the security.

Thus, an individual can start an enterprise with a small amount of share capital and contribute the balance of the capital by way of a secured shareholder loan. External lenders (for example, banks) will, however, usually require the owner/ shareholder to provide a personal guarantee for borrowed funds.

Debt financing falls into one of two broad categories: long-term or short-term debt. Long-term debt, typically with a maturity of 15 to 20 years, is used to finance the purchase of assets that have a long life. Shorter term debt financing is appropriate only for short-term needs.

(a) Discounts and Premiums

References:

ITA:

S. 16   Income and Capital Combined

Debt obligations may be issued at face value, at a discount, or at a premium from their face value. A discount or premium generally reflects economic adjustments to the nominal rate of interest to bring it into line with the effective market rate applicable at the time that the obligation is issued.

An amount paid as a premium or bonus or on account of a discount may be characterized as being on account of interest or capital. What is the "true nature" of the discount or premium? Does the debt obligation have a commercial rate of interest? Does the bonus or discount vary with the length of time that the loan funds are outstanding, the extent of capital at risk, and the nature of the financial operation? For example, discounts on financial market instruments, such as treasury bills, bankers' acceptances, and call loans, are generally considered to be on account of interest. In these cases, the discount is the economic reward for simply holding the instrument for a period of time, determined by reference to the principal amount payable on maturity of the debt.

Where the yield on a debt obligation exceeds four-thirds of the stipulated interest rate, the discount is considered to be income to the first Canadian-resident, taxable owner of the debt obligation.[113]

The issuer of a debt obligation is entitled to deduct a discount on a debt obligation. The amount of the deduction depends upon whether the discount is "deep" or "shallow".

(b) Interest

(i) Nature of Expenditure

Interest on borrowed money is an expenditure on account of capital.[114] Hence, in the absence of specific statutory authority, expenditures on account of interest would not be deductible as an expense of earning income.[115] The Act does, however, specifically authorize the deduction of interest expense and other financing costs.

Interest expense is deductible where:[116]

• it is paid or payable in the year;

• arises from a legal obligation; and

• is payable on money borrowed to earn income (other than exempt income) from a business or property or in respect of the unpaid purchase price of property acquired to earn such income ("borrowed money").

(ii) Meaning

The Act does not define the term "interest". "Interest" is the return or consideration for the use or retention by one person of a sum of money belonging to or owed to

---

[113] Subss. 16(2) and (3).

[114] *Can. Safeway Ltd. v. M.N.R.*, [1957] CTC 335 at 344, 57 DTC 1239 at 1248 (S.C.C.); *The Queen v. Bronfman Trust*, [1987] 1 CTC 117, 87 DTC 5059 (S.C.C.); *Interprov. Pipeline Co. v. M.N.R.*, [1968] CTC 156, 68 DTC 5093 (S.C.C.); *Sherritt Gordon Mines Ltd. v. M.N.R.*, [1968] CTC 262, 68 DTC 5180 (Ex. Ct.); *Montreal Light, Heat & Power Consol. v. M.N.R.*, [1944] CTC 94, 2 DTC 654 (P.C.).

[115] Para. 18(1)(*b*).

[116] Para. 20(1)(*c*).

another.[117] It is a payment for the use of property (money) and is determined, *inter alia*, by the length of time that the property is used.

Interest is a legal obligation calculated by reference to a principal sum of money that is owing. The obligation to pay interest may arise from an express agreement, by legal implication, or, in some cases, by statute.

Thus, there are two essential requirements for a payment to be considered interest: (1) There must be a sum of money by reference to which the payment is ascertained; (2) The sum of money must be an amount that is *due* to the person entitled to the payment.[118] The label attached to a payment is totally irrelevant to its characterization; it is the substance of the arrangement that determines whether or not a payment or receipt is on account of interest.

(iii) Legal Obligation

Interest is deductible as an expense by the borrower if the lender has a *legal* right to enforce payment of the amounts due. There is no such thing in law as gratuitous interest. There must be a legal obligation to pay the interest. There is, however, no requirement in law that the indebtedness must be documented to constitute a legal debt.

(iv) Use of Money

The borrowed money must be used for the purpose of earning income from business or property, that is, for an "eligible or qualifying use". The phrase "used for the purpose of" incorporates two separate tests: use and purpose.

(A) Direct Use

The use test is concerned with tracking the physical flow of funds to determine the application of borrowed moneys. There are two ways in which one can examine the use of borrowed funds: direct use and indirect use.

The direct use of funds is traced by following the funds from the lender to the investment to which the funds are applied.[119] It is the actual and direct use of borrowed funds that generally determines the deductibility of interest payable on the funds.[120] In *Sinha*,[121] for example, a student borrowed from the Canada Student Loan Plan at a low rate of interest and reinvested the borrowed funds at a higher rate. The Board rejected the Minister's argument that the purpose of the borrowing was

[117] *Ref. re s. 6 of Farm Security Act, 1944 of Sask.*, [1947] SCR 394 at 411; affirmed [1949] AC 110 (*sub nom. A.G. Sask. v. A.G. Can.*) (P.C.); *Riches v. Westminster Bank Ltd.*, [1947] AC 390; see also Chapter VII "Business and Property Income: Inclusions".

[118] See, e.g., *Re Euro Hotel (Belgravia) Ltd.*(1975), 51 TC 293 at 301-302.

[119] *R. v. Attaie*, [1990] 2 CTC 157, 90 DTC 6413 (F.C.A.).

[120] *The Queen v. Bronfman Trust*, [1987] 1 CTC 117, 87 DTC 5059 (S.C.C.).

[121] *Sinha v. M.N.R.*, [1981] CTC 2599, 81 DTC 465 (T.R.B.).

personal and allowed the taxpayer to deduct his interest expense, since he *actually* used the borrowed money for investment purposes.

Thus, a taxpayer should "stream" the use of borrowed money in order to maximize tax deductions: Borrow for business and use savings for pleasure.

(B) Indirect Use

The indirect use of funds is determined by asking: Did the use of the borrowed funds facilitate the investment of *other* funds in an income-producing process?

What happens if borrowed moneys are used indirectly used to earn or preserve income? The law is not clear. *Bronfman*[122] suggests that indirect use does not qualify for deduction. However, the comments of the Supreme Court in *Bronfman* cannot be reconciled with earlier decisions. In Chief Justice Dickson's words:[123]

> . . . the text of the Act requires tracing the use of borrowed funds to a specific eligible use, its obviously restricted purpose being the encouragement of taxpayers to augment their income-producing potential. This, in my view, precludes the allowance of a deduction for interest paid on borrowed funds which indirectly preserve income-earning property but which are not directly "used for the purpose of earning income from . . . property".

It is unclear whether these comments effectively overrule *Trans-Prairie Pipelines*,[124] which permitted a deduction in certain circumstances on the basis of the indirect use of borrowed funds.

(C) Purpose of Borrowing

The second test is that the funds must be borrowed for the *purpose* of earning income from business or property. The taxpayer must have a *bona fide* intention to use the borrowed money for income-earning purposes. Actual realization of income is irrelevant. The purpose test is concerned with the taxpayer's intention. In *Bronfman Trust, for example*:[125]

> Eligibility for the deduction is contingent on the use of borrowed money for the purpose of earning income. It is well established in the jurisprudence, however, that it is not the purpose of the borrowing itself which is relevant. What is relevant, rather, is the taxpayer's purpose in using the borrowed money in a particular manner. . . . Consequently, the focus of the inquiry must be centred on the use to which the taxpayer put the borrowed funds.

The use of funds, however, may reveal the purpose of borrowing. For example, a taxpayer who borrows money at a rate of 10 per cent interest and then lends out the funds for 6 per cent cannot be said to be borrowing for the *purpose* of earning net

---

[122] *The Queen v. Bronfman Trust, ante.*

[123] *The Queen v. Bronfman Trust, ante,* [1987] 1 CTC at 129, 87 DTC at 5067; see also *Trans-Prairie Pipelines Ltd. v. M.N.R.,* [1970] CTC 537, 70 DTC 6351 (Ex. Ct.).

[124] *Trans-Prairie Pipelines Ltd. v. M.N.R., ante.*

[125] *The Queen v. Bronfman Trust, ante,* [1987] 1 CTC at 125, 87 DTC at 5064.

income. Thus, the absence of an intention to earn net income might preclude a deduction for interest (or a portion thereof), even when the actual use to which borrowed funds are put would otherwise qualify the payment as a deductible expense.

(D) Capital Gains

The deduction for interest expense is restricted to amounts expended to earn business or property income. Interest incurred to earn capital gains is not deductible against income.[126] Hence, interest on funds invested in bullion, commodities, paintings, etc. is not usually deductible for tax purposes because these assets do not yield income. But a trader may deduct interest expense from business income as a cost of carrying inventory.

(E) Realization of Income

Deductibility of interest expense depends upon the borrower's intention at the time the funds are invested, rather than upon the actual materialization of income at some later date. Provided that the funds are employed in a venture that has the *potential* for earning net income, the actual results of the income-earning process are irrelevant. For example, interest on borrowed funds invested in a business venture that loses money is deductible.

The borrower's intention, however, must be to earn income from business or property and *not* from capital gains. Income from capital gains is not income from property.[127] Thus, interest expenses incurred *solely* to earn capital gains or avoid capital losses are not deductible in computing income from business or property.[128]

What of investments in non-dividend-paying common stocks? Interest expense on account of common stock investments is deductible even if the stocks do not pay dividends, provided that there is a reasonable prospect that they will pay dividends sometime in the future.

---

[126] See, e.g., *Hastings v. M.N.R.*, [1988] 2 CTC 2001, 88 DTC 1391 (T.C.C.) (interest expense on commodities trades not allowed as deduction); *The Queen v. Stirling*, [1985] 1 CTC 275, 85 DTC 5199 (F.C.A.) (interest and safe keeping charges for purchase of gold bullion not deductible in determining capital gain); *The Queen v. C.P. Ltd.*, [1977] CTC 606, 77 DTC 5383 (F.C.A.); *Birmingham Corp. v. Barnes*, [1935] AC 292 (H.L.).

[127] Subs. 9(3).

[128] *The Queen v. Bronfman Trust, ante* (fact that loan may have prevented capital losses did not assist taxpayer in obtaining a deduction from income; deduction limited to borrowed money used for the purpose of earning *income*).

(F) Current Use

It is the *current* use to which borrowed funds are put which determines the deductibility of interest as an expense. As Jackett P. said in *Trans-Prairie:*[129]

> ... interest should be deductible for the years in which the borrowed capital is employed in the business rather than that it should be deductible for the life of a loan as long as its first use was in the business.

Similarly, in *Bronfman Trust:*[130]

> ... a taxpayer who uses or intends to use borrowed money for an ineligible purpose, but later uses the funds to earn non-exempt income from a business or property, ought not to be deprived of the deduction for the current, eligible use.

Hence, if a taxpayer initially borrows money to invest in income-earning property and then diverts those funds to a non-income-earning purpose (e.g., personal use), any interest incurred on the borrowed funds will cease to qualify for deductibility as of the date of change of use of the funds.[131]

Conversely, interest on funds initially borrowed for personal purposes and later used for business purposes also qualifies for deduction as of the date of change of use. For example, a taxpayer who borrows money to purchase a residential cottage and then sells the cottage to use the proceeds for investment purposes is entitled to deduct the interest payable on the funds as of the date of the investment.

(G) Reloaned Funds at Lower Rate

Generally, if a taxpayer borrows funds at a commercial rate of interest and reloans the funds at a lower rate, he or she cannot be considered to have used the funds for the *purpose* of earning net income from a business or property. The taxpayer may, however, be entitled to deduct a portion of the interest for tax purposes. Revenue Canada will usually allow a deduction to the extent of the income actually earned.

Where an individual borrows money and then relends the money to a corporation, the individual may be entitled to an interest deduction in certain circumstances. Revenue Canada generally takes the view that interest on borrowed money is not deductible *in whole or in part* if borrowed money is reloaned at a lesser rate of interest than that at which it is borrowed.

---

[129] *Trans-Prairie Pipelines Ltd. v. M.N.R.,* [1970] CTC 537, 70 DTC 6351 at 6354 (Ex. Ct.), approved by S.C.C. in *The Queen v. Bronfman Trust, ante.*

[130] *Bronfman Trust v. The Queen, ante,* [1987] 1 CTC at 125, 87 DTC at 5065.

[131] Subpara. 20(1)(*c*)(i).

The Department does, however, allow for some exceptions where a shareholder borrows and relends to his or her corporation. The Department states its position in IT-445:[132]

> ... the Department will generally permit a deduction for the full interest expense incurred when a taxpayer borrows money at interest to be loaned to a Canadian corporation of which he is a shareholder, or to its Canadian subsidiary, at less than a reasonable rate of interest (or at no interest), if the following conditions are met:
>
> (a) the proceeds of the loan are used by that corporation in its own operations to produce income from business or property which will be subject to Part I tax in Canada, or are used by that corporation to loan to its Canadian subsidiary, at less than a reasonable rate of interest (or at no interest), to be used in its operation to produce income from business or property which will be subject to Part I tax in Canada,
>
> (b) the corporation has made every effort to borrow the necessary funds through the usual commercial money markets but cannot obtain financing, without the guarantee of the shareholder, at interest rates at which the shareholder could borrow, and
>
> (c) the loan from the shareholder to the corporation at less than a reasonable rate of interest (or at no interest) does not result in any undue tax advantage being conferred on either the shareholder or the corporation. The Department does not consider that any undue tax advantage is conferred on either the shareholder or the corporation where the use of loans with interest at less than market rates between associated corporations is for the purpose of offsetting non-capital losses within the group of associated corporations.

Despite Revenue Canada's declared policy in IT-445, it has been known to disallow the deduction of interest on reloaned funds even when the above conditions are satisfied. In *Scott*,[133] for example, the Department successfully challenged the taxpayer's deduction of interest expense on a $25,000 loan incurred to finance a restaurant business through a corporation. The taxpayer borrowed the money and reloaned it to the corporation as a non-interest-bearing shareholder's loan. The Tax Court sustained the Minister's disallowance of the deduction on the basis that the words in paragraph 20(1)(c) were quite clear and, as such, could not be amended by an administrative bulletin. Taylor T.C.J. said:[134]

> It is not for this Court to enlarge on the operative words of the Act in paragraph 20(1)(c), when their meaning as fundamental legislation is quite clear. The deductions sought in this matter do not qualify as interest expense. . . .

---

[132] IT-445, "The Deduction of Interest on Funds Borrowed either to be Loaned at Less than a Reasonable Rate of Interest or to Honour a Guarantee Given for Inadequate Consideration in Non-arm's Length Circumstances" (February 23, 1981), para. 8 (deduction of interest on funds borrowed either to be loaned at a less than reasonable rate of interest or to honour a guarantee given for inadequate consideration in non-arm's length circumstances).

[133] *Scott v. M.N.R.*, [1989] 1 CTC 2305, 89 DTC 218 (T.C.C.).

[134] *Scott v. M.N.R., ante*, [1989] 1 CTC at 2307, 89 DTC at 220.

(v) Exempt Income

Interest on money borrowed to acquire property the income from which would be exempt or to acquire a life insurance policy is not deductible.[135]

(vi) Compound Interest

Interest on interest, that is, compound interest, is deductible.[136] Compound interest is deductible only when it is paid. It is not deductible on a "payable" basis.[137]

Where a taxpayer makes a blended payment of capital and interest, he or she may deduct an amount equal to the interest component.[138]

(vii) Discounts

Discounts on debt obligations are deductible from income.[139] Where an obligation is issued at a price that is equal to at least 97 per cent of its principal amount and it does not yield an amount in excess of four thirds of the nominal interest rate, the entire amount of the discount is deductible in computing income.

Where, however, a bond is issued for an amount that is less than 97 per cent of its face amount, for a yield in excess of four thirds of its nominal interest rate, only three quarters of the discount is deductible in computing income for tax purposes.

(viii) Refinancing

Where money is borrowed to repay money previously borrowed, the second borrowing is deemed to have been undertaken for the same purpose as the original borrowing.[140] Refinancing transactions are looked at closely to determine whether they constitute a formality or a sham.[141] The interval of time between the original and refinanced loans is an important consideration. The shorter the interval, the more suspect the transaction.

---

[135] Subs. 248(1) ("exempt income") (exempt income is money or property received or acquired by person in circumstances such that it is, by reason of any provision in Part I, not included in computing income; dividends on shares not included in exempt income).

[136] Para. 20(1)(d).

[137] Para. 20(1)(d).

[138] Para. 16(1)(a).

[139] Para. 20(1)(f).

[140] Subs. 20(3); see also, ATR-4, "Exchange of Interest Rates" (November 29, 1985).

[141] *The Queen v. Bronfman Trust, ante.*

(ix) Source of Income

One of the requirements for the deduction of interest is the existence of the source of income to which the interest expense relates.[142] For example, a taxpayer who finances the purchase of investment securities may claim any directly related interest expense as a deduction. The deduction is available so long as the taxpayer continues to hold the original investment or substituted securities. This is so even if the security declines in value or becomes worthless.

The deduction may also be claimed, however, in certain circumstances if the investment is sold and the funds are used for another eligible purpose.

Interest on money that was used to acquire income earning property may be deductible even if the property is disposed of. The conditions for continued deductibility are as follows:[143]

- The borrowed money must have been used for the purpose of earning income from capital property (other than real property or depreciable property); and

- The property must have been disposed of at its fair market value.

(x) Accrued Interest

A taxpayer who purchased a debt obligation (other than an income bond, income debenture, small business development bond, or small business bond) is allowed to deduct interest accrued on the debt to the date of the purchase. The deduction is restricted to the extent that the amount is included as interest in computing income for the year. The accrued interest paid to the vendor of the debt obligation is included in computing the vendor's income.[144]

(xi) Expenses of Issuing Debt

Reference:

BULLETINS, CIRCULARS & RULINGS:

IT-341R2   October 31, 1990   Expenses of Issuing or Selling Shares, Units in a Trust, Interests in a Partnership or Syndicate, and Expenses of Borrowing Money

---

[142] *Emerson v. The Queen*, [1986] 1 CTC 422, 86 DTC 6184; leave to appeal to S.C.C. refused, 70 NR 160 (taxpayer not allowed to deduct interest on money used to purchase shares after shares sold at loss); *The Queen v. Bronfman Trust, ante* (interest not deductible where principal borrowed to make capital distribution to trust beneficiary).

[143] Subs. 20.1(1).

[144] Subs. 20(14); IT-410R, "Debt Obligations — Accrued Interest on Transfer" (September 4, 1984). This rule only operates where there has been an assignment or transfer of title. Evidence of registration of title would likely be necessary; see *Hill v. M.N.R.*, [1981] CTC 2120, 81 DTC 167 (T.R.B.); *Smye v. M.N.R.*, [1980] CTC 2372, 80 DTC 1326 (T.R.B.); *Antosko v. Canada*, [1994] 2 CTC 2073, 94 DTC 6314 (S.C.C.).

A taxpayer is allowed to deduct expenses incurred in borrowing money for the purpose of earning income from a business or property.[145] In the absence of specific authorization, financing expenses (which typically include legal and accounting fees, printing costs, commissions, etc.) would be caught by the prohibition against deducting expenses not directly related to the income-earning process.[146] Financing expenses are deductible on a rateable basis over a five-year period.

(xii) Lump-sum Payments

Interest may be paid lump-sum at the end of the term of a loan.[147]

(c) Capitalizing Interest

References:

ITA:

S. 21   Cost of Borrowed Money

BULLETINS, CIRCULARS & RULINGS:

IT-121R3   May 6, 1988   Election to Capitalize Cost of Borrowed Money

(i) General

A taxpayer may prefer not to write-off his or her interest expense against current operations. For example, there may be little advantage in taking a deduction for interest expense on money borrowed to construct an asset if the asset is not currently producing income. The deduction of interest would merely create a loss that may not be utilized within the time limits allowed for carryover of losses.[148] In such circumstances, the taxpayer may prefer to treat his or her interest expense as part of the capital cost of the asset and write-off the total cost of the asset at a later time when it begins to produce income. In other words, a taxpayer may treat interest costs as a capital expenditure rather than as a current expense.

(ii) Depreciable Property

A taxpayer who acquires depreciable property with borrowed money can elect to capitalize related interest charges.[149] Only those costs which would *otherwise have been deductible* as interest expense or as an expense of borrowing money may be

---

[145] Para. 20(1)(e).

[146] *Montreal Light, Heat & Power Consol. v. M.N.R.*, [1944] CTC 94, 2 DTC 654 (P.C.); see *The Queen v. Royal Trust Corp. of Can.*, [1983] CTC 159, 83 DTC 5172 (F.C.A.) (payment was commission for services rendered therefore qualified as an eligible capital expenditure).

[147] *Lomax v. Dixon*, [1943] 1 KB 671 (C.A.).

[148] See para. 111(1)(a) (limitation period in respect of non-capital losses).

[149] S. 21. Special restrictions on "soft costs" are discussed below; see subs. 18(3.1).

capitalized. Interest expense to earn exempt income is not deductible and may not be capitalized.

The election is available not only in respect of costs incurred in the year in which the asset is acquired, but also in respect of costs incurred in the three immediately preceding taxation years. The extension of the election to the three preceding years recognizes that large undertakings extend over many years and that interest may be incurred on money borrowed prior to the period in which the money is actually used for its intended purpose.

(iii) Election

(A) Timing

The election must be made for the taxation year in which:

- the depreciable property is *acquired*,[150] or
- the money borrowed has been used for exploration, development, or the acquisition of property.[151]

A taxpayer may not elect to capitalize interest in anticipation of the acquisition of depreciable property or the use of borrowed money for exploration or development. The taxpayer may elect only *after* the property has been acquired or the funds have been expended. When the election is made, however, it is effective for borrowing costs and interest incurred in the year and in the three preceding years.

A taxpayer may elect only under subsection 21(1) for the taxation year in which she or he acquires the depreciable property. Where a building or other structure is being erected by a taxpayer, it is considered to have been "acquired" at any time to the extent of the construction costs to that time. Hence, a taxpayer must file a separate election for each taxation year in respect of the interest expense related to that year.

(B) Amout Capitalized

The election to capitalize interest does not have to be in respect of the full amount of the costs of borrowing. A taxpayer may elect to capitalize only a part of the interest charges and deduct the remainder as a current expense.

The portion of any capitalized interest is added to the capital cost of the depreciable property acquired. Thus, any capitalized interest can be written off through capital cost allowance charges in the future. The adjusted cost base of the property is also increased for the purpose of determining capital gains upon disposition of the property.[152]

---

[150] Subs. 21(1).

[151] Subs. 21(2).

[152] Para. 54(*a*).

(iv) Reassessment

Where a taxpayer elects to capitalize interest charges in respect of prior years, the Minister is required to reassess the taxpayer's preceding taxation years if the interest would have been otherwise deductible in those years. Having made the election, the taxpayer may continue to capitalize interest in succeeding years if, in each of those succeeding years, the *entire* amount of the interest on the property is capitalized.

(v) Compound Interest

A taxpayer may also capitalize compound interest and the expense of raising money. For example, a taxpayer may be required to pay a commitment fee to a financier before funds are advanced. The commitment fee, or standby interest, may be capitalized as part of the cost of borrowed money.[153]

6. HYBRID DEBT

Reference:

ITA:

S. 51   Convertible Property

Just as a corporation can issue hybrid share capital (that is, share capital with substantial debt characteristics), so also can it issue hybrid debt — debt capital with all of the characteristics of equity. There are two advantages of hybrid debt: (1) In the absence of special rules, payments on debt are generally deductible for tax purposes; (2) Payments can be discretionary and, in this sense, resemble dividends paid on share capital. To prevent inappropriate exploitation of these advantages, there are special rules controlling the deductibility of interest on hybrid debt capital.

(a) Income Bonds and Debentures

(i) General Rule

An income bond or debenture is a debt instrument that pays interest or dividends only when and to the extent that the issuing corporation makes a profit.[154] An income bond or debenture allows its issuer the flexibility of making interest or dividend payments only if it is in a profitable position and able to do so. Thus, an income bond or debenture is similar to share capital.

More technically, an "income bond" or "income debenture" is a bond or debenture in respect of which interest or dividends are payable only to the extent that the issuing

---

[153] *Sherritt Gordon Mines Ltd. v. M.N.R.*, [1968] CTC 262, 68 DTC 5180 (Ex. Ct.).

[154] Subs. 248(1) ("income bond").

corporation makes a profit, the bond or debenture, does not, in any circumstances, exceed a term of five years, and is issued:[155]

- as part of a proposal or arrangement with creditors that is approved under the *Bankruptcy Act* and *Insolvency Act*;
- at a time when all or substantially all of its assets were under the control of a receiver, or similar person; or
- at a time when the issuing corporation or a resident non-arm's length corporation was in default, or reasonably expected to be in default, on a debt obligation,

The proceeds of the issue must be used in a business that is carried on immediately before its issue by the issuing corporation, or by a corporation with which it does not deal at arm's length.

Interest or dividends paid by a resident corporation on an income bond or debenture are deemed to be dividends[156] and are not deductible from income for tax purposes.

(ii) Financial Difficulty

Interest on income bonds issued by a resident corporation in financial difficulty is not deemed to be a dividend if the bond is issued for a term that does not exceed five years.

(iii) Taxable as Dividends

Payments on income bonds or debentures that are deemed to be dividends are taxable as such in the recipient's hands. Thus, in the case of individuals, the dividend is treated as a taxable dividend subject to the usual gross-up and dividend tax credit rules.[157]

Where the recipient is a corporation, the dividend may be deductible as an inter-corporate dividend under section 112 of the Act. The dividend may also be subject to the refundable tax under Part IV if the recipient is a private corporation.

(b) Convertible Debt

Convertible debt is debt that is convertible into equity. Convertible debt allows the lender the best of two worlds: The security of debt capital and the growth potential of share capital. The corporation that issues convertible debt also benefits in that it can deduct interest payments on the debt. Interest on convertible debt is usually lower than that on conventional debt as a trade-off for the convertibility feature.

---

[155] Ibid.

[156] Subs. 15(3).

[157] Para. 82(1)(*b*), s. 121.

(i) Roll Over Into Shares

A holder of convertible debt can roll over the debt into share capital of the issuing corporation without triggering a disposition.[158] Thus, the lender can defer recognition of any accrued capital gain on the conversion of the debt instrument into share capital.

The rollover is available in the following circumstances:[159]

- The convertible debt constitutes capital property to the taxpayer;
- The capital property is exchanged for shares in the same corporation; and
- The taxpayer receives no additional consideration for the conversion other than the shares of the corporation.

In these circumstances, the taxpayer is deemed not to have disposed of the convertible debt and the cost of the debt is rolled over into the cost of the newly acquired shares. Hence, there are no immediate income tax consequences of the conversion.

The rollover under section 51 is not elective: it applies automatically if all of the conditions of the provision are satisfied.

The rollover is available only in respect of certain types of convertible properties: bonds, debentures, notes, and shares. It does not extend to other debt instruments such as mortgages. The rollover is available only in respect of "capital property" and does not extend to any property, a gain or loss from the disposition of which would constitute a capital gain or loss.

(ii) Indirect Gifts

The rollover is not available where the fair market value of the convertible debt before the exchange exceeds the fair market value of the shares immediately after the exchange *and* it is reasonable to regard the excess of the value of the debt over the value of the shares as a benefit that the taxpayer desires to confer on a related person.[160] Thus, a taxpayer cannot dispose of high valued debt in exchange for lower value shares and have the difference accrue to the benefit of a person related to him or her. In the absence of such a rule, a taxpayer could divest himself or herself of capital property without triggering a capital gain or loss.

It is not always clear what constitutes a "gift" or benefit in these circumstances. It is not enough that a related taxpayer benefits from the conversion: subsection 51(2) applies only if the taxpayer who converts a debt actually desires to have the benefit conferred on a person related to him or her. The test is objective. The taxpayer must have at least some minimum threshold level of intention to benefit a person related to him or her.

---

[158] Para. 51(1)(c).

[159] Subs. 51(1).

[160] Subs. 51(2).

Where subsection 51(2) applies, the taxpayer is deemed to receive proceeds of disposition for the convertible property equal to the lesser of its fair market value immediately prior to the exchange and the aggregate of its adjusted cost base and the "gift" portion. Thus, the capital gain or loss is deferred on the conversion, except to the extent that the gain is decreased (or loss increased) as a result of the indirect gift. The taxpayer's capital loss from the disposition is deemed to be nil.

7. ATTRIBUTION RULES

(a) Deemed Interest

An individual may be deemed to receive interest income in respect of property that she or he transfers or loans to a corporation, if her or his spouse (or any of certain minors) owns 10 per cent or more of the issued share of any class of its capital stock.[161] These "attribution rules" are intended to prevent taxpayers from diverting investment income to their families in order to reduce the overall tax burden through income splitting.

(b) Intention

The corporate attribution rules apply only if one of the main purposes of the transfer or loan is to reduce the transferor's income and to benefit, either directly or indirectly, his or her spouse, or relatives who are minors.

(c) Convertible Debt

The corporate attribution rules also apply where a taxpayer rolls over convertible debt into shares of the corporation under section 51. For example, if an individual who owns high-yield debt converts it into low-yield shares, she or he could, in effect, transfer high-yield interest payments to persons whom she or he desires to benefit. Where the taxpayer's spouse owns 10 per cent or more of the shares of the issuing corporation, it is likely that the attribution rules apply.

8. LEASES

Reference:

BULLETINS, CIRCULARS & RULINGS:

IT-233R   February 11, 1983   Lease-Option   Agreements;   Sale-Leaseback
                                  Agreements

A lease is a contractual arrangement whereby one of the parties (the "lessor") grants to another party ("the lessee") the use, possession and enjoyment of an asset for a period of time in consideration of rental payments. Since a lease is a contract, its terms and conditions can be as varied as contract law permits.

---

[161] S. 74.4, subs. 74.5(5).

The terms and conditions of a lease can be tailored to meet the financial needs of the lessor and the lessee. Almost any asset that can be purchased can be leased. The most common forms of leases in business, however, deal with automobiles, furniture, equipment and real property.

Leasing is a form of "off-balance sheet" financing that has grown in popularity in recent years. Part of the popularity of leasing assets is attributable to the financial advantage of keeping debt off the balance sheet, which allows for a more favourable debt to equity ratio. Another advantage of leasing is that it does not drain the cash flow of an enterprise in the same way as a purchase of assets.

(a) Advantages

The principal advantages of leasing are as follows:

- Since leasing is an "off-balance sheet" form of financing, it does not enter into the computation of debt/equity ratios. These ratios may be governed by covenants in debt instruments issued by the enterprise.

- Since leases are not reported as liabilities on the balance sheet, they do not reflect adversely on the enterprise's access to the credit markets.

- Small businesses do not usually have easy access to the capital markets in order to purchase substantial amounts of tangible assets. A lease is an alternative to long-term financing to purchase equipment.

- Leasing terms and conditions are flexible and, therefore, can be readily adapted to the particular needs of the business. Lease payments can be linked to the enterprise's profits.

(b) Disadvantages

There are also certain disadvantages associated with leases:

- Since the leased asset belongs to the lessor, any appreciation in the value of the asset belongs to the lessor and not to the lessee. This can be a significant financial consideration in leases involving real property.

- Leases tend to be fixed term contracts (*albeit* often with options to renew) and during the term of the contract the lessee is committed to the contract. It is not usually easy to exit from the contract without paying a penalty or premium. Thus, unlike the owner of an asset who may be able to dispose of it if circumstances change, a lessee may be contractually locked in even when economic circumstances change or become unattractive.

(c) Tax Treatment

The income tax considerations of leasing depend upon three principal factors:

1. The nature of the agreement;
2. The tax status of the lessee and the lessor; and
3. The type of property leased.

(i) Nature of Lease

What constitutes a "lease" for tax purposes? The answer to this question is crucial in the context of property acquisitions. The leasing rules apply to property financed through a lease. The capital cost allowance rules apply to purchases of property.

In the absence of specific tax rules, the characterization of a contractual arrangement depends upon the law of the jurisdiction in which the contract is regulated. The nature of an acquisition is determined by reference to the normal incidents of ownership of property: title (actual or constructive), possession, use and risk. This can be a complicated matter.

At common law, the nature of the relationship that exists between a vendor and a purchaser of real property is governed by legal and equitable principles of ownership. In the Province of Quebec, the matter is determined by reference to the Civil Code.

(ii) Rentals or Instalments

Payments for the use of leased property may represent rental payments or instalments on account of its purchase price. Payments on account of rent are deductible as a current expense in the computation of income.[162] Payments on account of the purchase of depreciable property are subject to capital cost allowance on the property.[163] The distinction between these two types of payments is blurred, however, where the contract provides for a lease with an option to purchase the property. In such cases, one must determine the true nature of the contract: Is it, in substance, a lease or an instalment purchase?

There are two different types of lease option agreements:

1. Leases that are financing arrangements for the purchase of an asset to be acquired at a later date pursuant to a predetermined or determinable option price; and

2. Leases that are genuine agreements for the rental of an asset, but which give the lessee an option to purchase the asset at a later date.

A lease option agreement that is, in effect, a financing arrangement, represents a transaction involving the purchase of an asset: The lease is merely the vehicle to finance the purchase. In contrast, a "genuine" lease-option agreement is, in both substance and form, a rental agreement, but one which allows the lessee the privilege of changing his or her mind and purchasing the asset at a later date.

The distinction between these two types of lease options is subtle and there is no bright line test to distinguish between them. Obviously, they both involve the same arrangements, namely, periodic payments with an option to purchase the asset at a later

---

[162] S. 9.

[163] Para. 20(1)(a).

date. The two arrangements, however, differ substantially in both their legal effects and tax results.

Revenue Canada's administrative position is that the following factors point toward a sale rather than a lease:[164]

- The lessee *automatically* acquires title to the property after payment of a specified amount in the form of rental payments;
- The lessee is *required* to buy the property from the lessor during or at the termination of the lease;
- The lessee has the right, during or at the expiration of the lease, to acquire the property at a price which, *at the inception* of the lease, is substantially less than the probable fair market value of the property at the time that the lessee is allowed to acquire the property; or
- The lessee has the right, during or at the expiration of the lease, to acquire the property at a price, or under terms and conditions which, *at the inception* of the lease, are such that no reasonable person would fail to exercise the option.

The above criteria indicate that the determination of whether a contract is a lease or a purchase of property is almost always a question of fact to be made in the light of all of the circumstances of the transaction. The determination is made by examining the conduct of the parties, the nature of the legal obligations created and, where relevant, past dealings between the parties in similar transactions.

The examination requires more than a superficial enumeration of the relevant criteria. For example, in a "financial lease", it is quite usual for the lessee to assume the responsibility for paying the expenses of the leased property, such as taxes, insurance, maintenance, etc. The obligation to pay these expenses, which are normally associated with the ownership rather than the rental of property, does not, in and by itself, necessarily imply that the transaction is, in substance, a purchase. Such an obligation is only one factor to be evaluated in determining the characterization of a particular contract. The fact that the expenses are assumed by the lessee does not necessarily render the contract something other than a true lease.

(A) Option to Purchase at Fair Market Value

An option agreement that is in substance a purchase agreement is not considered to be a genuine "lease". The so-called "lessee" is not entitled to deduct lease payments. Where, however, the lease-option agreement is a genuine lease, the taxpayer is entitled to deduct lease payments during the tenure of the lease.

(B) Option to Purchase at Less Than Fair Market Value

A special rule applies to options to purchase property at less than its fair market value. Where a taxpayer purchases an asset at less than its fair market value pursuant

---

[164] IT-233R, "Lease-option Agreements; Sale-leaseback Agreements" (February 11, 1983), para. 3.

to an option, any amounts previously paid for the use of the property (for example, rent) are considered as amounts previously claimed as capital cost allowance in respect of the property.[165] The effect of this rule is that a subsequent disposition of the property may trigger recapture of capital cost allowance.

More specifically, this rule applies where a taxpayer acquires a depreciable capital property or real property in respect of which:

- the taxpayer (or a person with whom he or she was not dealing at arm's length) was entitled to a deduction from income for use (for example, rent) of the property; and

- the capital cost of acquisition is less than the fair market value of the property, determined without reference to the option price.

The purpose of the rule is to prevent the taxpayer from receiving the best of both worlds: Current deductions of lease payments and capital gains treatment on any gains realized when the asset is eventually sold. This rule applies only in circumstances in which, *even though the lease-option agreement is a genuine lease,* the option allows the taxpayer to acquire the property at less than its fair market value. The rule does not apply to instalment purchases whereby the purchaser is not, in any event, entitled to a rental deduction.

Subsection 13(5.2) deems a taxpayer who exercises an option to acquire property at less than its fair market value to have acquired the property at the *lesser* of:

- its fair market value at the time the option is exercised; and,

- its actual cost at that time *plus* all payments previously paid on account of rent for the use of the property.

If the actual cost of the property to the taxpayer is less than its deemed cost, the difference is deemed to have been previously claimed by the taxpayer as capital cost allowance on the property. Thus, the taxpayer may be subject to recapture of capital cost allowance at a later date if the property is disposed of at a profit.

Example XV.5
Assume:
In 1992, X Ltd. leased some land from T Ltd. at an annual rental of $20,000. The lease allows X Ltd. to purchase the land at the end of five years at an agreed upon price of $80,000, which is a reasonable estimate of its fair market value at that time. In 1997 X Ltd. exercises its option to purchase the land and it is determined at that time that the fair market value of the land is $120,000. X Ltd. sells the land in 1999 for $200,000.

---

[165] Subs. 13(5.2)

Example XV.5 (continued)

Then:

Upon exercise of the option in 1997

Exercise price of option		$ 80,000(A)
Lesser of:		
(i) FMV of land	$ 120,000	
(ii) Cost of land $ 80,000		
Rental payments $100,000	$ 180,000	
Deemed cost of land		$120,000(B)
Depreciation deemed		
claimed ((B) minus (A))		$ 40,000

Upon sale of the land in 1999

Proceeds of disposition	$ 200,000
Deemed cost	$ 120,000
Capital gain	$ 80,000
Recapture of depreciation	$ 40,000

Subsection 13(5.2) applies to all capital properties, including land. Thus, in the above example, the land is deemed to be depreciable property of a separate prescribed class and, therefore, the rental payments (or a portion thereof) on the land are subject to "recapture", and are taxable as income.

To prevent a taxpayer from circumventing this rule by disposing of, instead of exercising, the option to acquire the property, subsection 13(5.3) deems that any difference between the proceeds of disposition of the option itself and its cost, is taxable as "recaptured" income.

(d) Restrictions on After-tax Financing

We have seen that leasing can be used as an alternative to the more usual methods of financing. The tax advantages of leasing arise because capital cost allowance ("CCA") for leased property often exceeds its actual depreciation, particularly in the early years of a lease. This allows non-taxable lessees to trade off accelerated CCA against reduced rental payments.

The use of leases as a form of after-tax financing for tax-exempt entities and taxpayers who are not currently taxable is restricted through the capital cost allowance rules.

(i) The Lessor's Position

A taxpayer ("the lessor") who leases specified leasing property (other than exempt property) with a fair market value of more than $25,000 to another person for more than one year is restricted in the amount that he or she may claim for capital cost allowance on the property. The CCA claimable is limited to the amount that would have been a repayment of principal if the lease had been a loan and the rental payments were considered blended payments that represented principal and interest.[166] Thus, the entire regime depends upon the concept of notional loans and repayments.

The lessor is regarded as having made a loan to the lessee in an amount equal to the fair market value of the leased property, and the rental payments on the lease are considered to be a blend of principal and interest. Generally speaking, the capital cost allowance that may be claimed by the lessor on each property is restricted to the difference between rental income and a notional value for interest.

The capital cost allowance that is deductible by the lessor in respect of such property is restricted by Regulation 1100(1.1) to the *lesser* of:

- the amount that would be received by the lessor in the year as a return of principal had the lessor made a loan to the lessee at a prescribed rate of interest in an amount equal to the fair market value of the leased property; and

- the amount by which the total capital cost allowance that the lessor could have claimed in respect of the property in the absence of any special leasing rules, over the amount of any capital cost allowance previously claimed by the lessor in respect of the property.

A rate of interest is prescribed for each month.

"Specified leasing property" is depreciable property (other than exempt property) that is used principally to earn leasing revenue from a lease that has a term of more than one year.[167]

"Exempt property" includes automobiles, light trucks and trailers, buildings, home furnishings, appliances, office furniture, office equipment and computers. The exemption in respect of office furniture, office equipment and electronic data processing equipment does not apply to individual assets that have a capital cost in excess of $1,000,000.[168]

(ii) The Lessee's Position

Lessees are generally entitled to claim the full amount of lease payments that relate to the use of the property in the year in the normal manner.

A lessee may, however, jointly elect with the lessor to have the lease considered as money borrowed to purchase the asset leased.[169] The lessee is entitled to claim

---

[166] Reg. 1100(1.1).

[167] Reg. 1100(1.11).

[168] Reg. 1100(1.13).

[169] Subs. 16.1(1).

capital cost allowance and deduct the interest portion of the deemed blended payments of principal and interest. Thus, *both* the lessee and the lessor may be able to claim capital cost allowance in certain circumstances.

Where the lessor and lessee *jointly* elect in prescribed form and agree upon the fair market value of the leased property, the lessee is considered to have borrowed an amount equal to the fair market value of the property and to have acquired the property. In these circumstances, rental payments under the lease are not considered to be rent, but are treated as blended payments of principal and interest on the loan.

To the extent that the property is used to earn income, the lessee is able to claim capital cost allowance in respect of the property, and to deduct the interest portion of each rental payment. This rule applies only in computing the income of a lessee who leases property (other than prescribed property) for a term of more than one year from an arm's-length person who is resident in Canada, or who carries on business in Canada through a permanent establishment.

Example XV.6

Assume:

A taxpayer leases an asset with a fair market value of $10,000 in an arm's length transaction. The lease is for a period of five years at an annual rental of $1,314. The capital cost allowance rate applicable in respect of the property is 25 per cent (diminishing balance basis) subject to the half-year rule. Both the lessor and the lessee jointly elect to treat the lease as a loan and purchase for the term of the lease. The prescribed rate in effect at the time of the lease is 10 per cent.

Then:

The lessee may deduct interest expense and capital cost allowance as follows:

Year	Lease Payments	Principal	Interest	CCA	UCC
					$10,000
1	$1,314	$ 314	$1,000	$1,250	8,750
2	1,314	345	969	2,188	6,562
3	1,314	380	934	1,641	4,921
4	1,314	418	896	1,230	3,691
5	1,314	460	854	923	2,768
TOTAL	$6,570	$1,917	$4,653	$7,232	

At the end of the five-year lease period, the lessee is deemed to have disposed of the property for the remaining principal amount of the deemed loan, that is, $8,083. Assuming that the property was the only property in that class of assets, the lessee is subject to recapture of capital cost allowance of $5,315:

Example XV.6 (continued)

Principal amount of loan	$10,000
Loan (principal) payments	(1,917)
Principal balance outstanding	$ 8,083
Undepreciated capital cost (UCC)	(2,768)
Recapture of CCA	$ 5,315

Thus, the total deductions allowed to the lessee with respect to the property over the term of the lease is $6,570, that is, interest expense of $4,653 and capital cost allowance of $7,232 less the recapture of capital cost allowance of $5,315.

(iii) Anti-avoidance Rule

Leases which are entered into for less than one year, but which are then extended are subject to an anti-avoidance rule. Property is deemed to be the subject of a lease that is longer than one year if it is reasonable to conclude that the lessor knew, or ought to have known, that the lessee would lease the property for more than one year. The burden is on the lessor to establish that she or he could not have known that the lessee would extend the term of the lease beyond one year.

Where a taxpayer acquires a lease that has a remaining term of more than one year, with certain exceptions, the taxpayer is treated as having entered into a new lease of the property at that time for a term of more than one year.[170] There is an exception for acquisitions from a non-arm's length person or in the course of certain rollover transactions, for example, an amalgamation of corporations.[171] Apart from these exceptions, however, the acquiring taxpayer steps into the shoes of the vendor in respect of the property covered by the lease.

---

[170] Reg. 1100(1.15).

[171] Reg. 1100(1.16).

SELECTED BIBLIOGRAPHY TO CHAPTER XV

General

Andison, Douglas, "Categories of Corporations", in *Proceedings of 24th Tax Conf.* 73 (Can. Tax Foundation, 1972).

Ashton, R.K., "Does the Tax System Favour Incorporation?" (1987), *Br. Tax Rev.* 256.

Bonham, D.H., "Corporations", [1986] *Special Lectures LSUC* 259.

Darling, C. Brian, "Revenue Canada Perspectives" in *Corp. Management Tax Conf.* (Can. Tax Foundation, 1992).

Edgar, Tim, "The Classification of Corporate Securities for Income Tax Purposes" (1990), 38 *Can. Tax J.* 1141.

Ewens, Douglas S., "Proposed Amendments Affecting Debt and Equity Reorganizations" (1993), 6 *Can. Petro. Tax J.* 49.

Novek, Barbara L., "Deductibility of Financing Expenses" in *Corp. Management Tax Conf.* (Canada Tax Foundation, 1992).

Richardson, Stephen R., "New Financial Instruments: A Canadian Tax Perspective" in *Corp. Management Tax Conf.* (Canada Tax Foundation, 1992).

Ruby, Stephen S., "Recent Financing Techniques", in *Proceedings of 41st Tax Conf.* 27:1 (Can. Tax Foundation, 1989).

Shafer, Joel, "Income Tax Aspects of Real Estate Financing", [1989] *Can. Tax Foundation, Corp. Management Tax Conf.* 1:1.

Spindler, Robert J., "New Investment Products", in *Proceedings of 44th Tax Conference* 19:1 (Can. Tax Foundation, 1992).

Sullivan, Daniel F., and James P. O'Sullivan, "Recent Developments in Corporate Financing" in *Corp. Management Tax Conf.*(Can. Tax Foundation, 1992).

Teltscher, Lawrence, "Small Business Financing" in *Corp. Management Tax Conference* (Can. Tax Foundation, 1992).

General Characteristics of Debt and Share Capital

Andison, Douglas, "Categories of Corporations", in *Proceedings of 24th Tax Conf.* 73 (Can. Tax Foundation, 1972).

Ashton, R.K., "Does the Tax System Favour Incorporation?" (1987), *Br. Tax Rev.* 256.

Barry, David B., "The Relative Importance of Personal and Corporation Income Tax" (1986), 34 *Can. Tax J.* 460.

Bonham, D.H., "Corporations", [1986] *Special Lectures LSUC* 259.

Dart, Robert J., "An Analysis of the Tax Position of Public, Private and Canadian-Controlled Private Corporations" (1972), 20 *Can. Tax J.* 523.

Dart, Robert J., "Specific Uses of Companies in Tax Planning", in *Proceedings of 31st Tax Conf.* 117 (Can. Tax Foundation, 1979).

Hariton, David P., "The Taxation of Complex Financial Instruments" (1988), 43 *Tax Lawyer* 731.

Corporate Law Aspects of Equity Financing

Baillie, William J., "To Incorporate or Not to Incorporate — From an Income Tax Perspective" (1983), 41 *Advocate* 615.

Barry, David B., "The Relative Importance of Personal and Corporation Income Tax" (1986), 34 *Can. Tax J.* 460.

Bonham, D.H., "Corporations", [1986] *Special Lectures LSUC* 259.

Brean, Donald J.S., "The Redemption of Convertible Preferred Shares: The Implications of Terms and Conditions" (1985), 33 *Can. Tax J.* 957.

Broadway, Robin W., "Reforming the Corporate Tax System", in *Proceedings of 37th Tax Conf.* 5 (Can. Tax Foundation, 1985).

Brown, Robert D., "Corporate Tax Reform: Necessary but not Sufficient", in *Proceedings of 37th Tax Conf.* 5 (Can. Tax Foundation, 1985).

Chanin, Faralee, "Paid-up Capital Pitfalls" (1990), 3 *Can. Petroleum Tax J.* 117.

Colley, Geoffrey M., "Are Corporate Tax Changes Imminent?" (1986), 119 *CA Magazine* 60.

Daly, M.J. and P. Mercier, "The Impact of Tax Reform on the Taxation of Income from Investment in the Corporate Sector" (1988), 36 *Can. Tax J.* 345.

Dart, Robert J., "An Analysis of the Tax Position of Public, Private and Canadian-Controlled Private Corporations" (1972), 20 *Can. Tax J.* 523.

Dart, Robert J., "Specific Uses of Companies in Tax Planning", in *Proceedings of 31st Tax Conf.* 117 (Can. Tax Foundation, 1979).

Durnford, John W., "Tax Essay — The Corporate Veil in the Tax Law" (1979), 27 *Can. Tax J.* 282.

"Equity Investment As An Alternative to Stock Incentive Arrangement" (1990), 2 *Tax Profile* 256.

Hariton, David P., "The Taxation of Complex Financial Instruments" (1988), 43 *Tax Lawyer* 731.

Hiseler, Gregory R., "Judicial Decisions Relating to the Taxation of Corporations and Their Shareholders", in *Proceedings of 35th Tax Conf.* 429 (Can. Tax Foundation, 1983).

Impact of Income and Other Taxes (The), Audio Archives of Canada, 1984.

Jones, David Phillip, "Corporations, Double Taxation and the Theory of Integration" (1979), 27 *Can. Tax J.* 405.

Krishna, Vern, "Common Law Piercing of the Corporate Veil to Reach Individual Shareholders" (1985), 1 *Can. Current Tax* J-101.

Krishna, Vern, "Corporate Share Capital Structures and Income Splitting", [1991] *Can. Current Tax* C71.

Krishna, Vern, "Income Splitting Corporate Structures", [1994] *Can. Current Tax* C45.

Krishna, Vern and Anthony VanDuzer, "Corporate Share Capital Structures and Income Splitting: McClurg v. Canada" (1993), 21 *Can. Business Law J.* 335.

Marble, Del, and Mark Walsh, "The Emphasis is Misplaced (Exposure Draft on Corporate Income Taxes)" (1989), 122:1 *CA Magazine* 253.

McIvor, R. Craig, "Canadian Cooperatives and Credit Unions: The Tax Scene Revisited" (1972), 20 *Can. Tax J.* 32.

McKie, A.B., "Corporations and Shareholders: Tax Reform or Reforming" (1986), 93 *Can. Banker* 46.

McLure, Charles E., "Rationalizing the Corporate Income Tax: The Recent U.S. Proposals", in *Proceedings of 37th Tax Conf.* 6 (Can. Tax Foundation, 1985).

Morin, Robert et Marc Papillon, *Impôt sur le revenu des particuliers et des corporations* (Éditions Merlin, 1985).

Reid, Robert J., *Tax Aspects of Incorporations* (Toronto: Butterworths, 1983).

Richards, Gabrielle M.R., "When are Shares Issued?", [1994] *Can. Current Tax* J43.

Rixon, F.G., "Lifting the Veil Between Holding and Subsidiary Companies" (1986), 102 *L.Q.R.* 415.

Roberts, David G., "Some Issues in the Determination of Paid-up Capital" (1992), 40 *Can. Tax J.* 338.

Schwartz, Alan M., "Income Tax Aspects of Shareholders' Agreements", [1986] *Special Lectures LSUC* 327.

Thomas, R.B., "Associated Corporations; Principal Residence", in *Proceedings of 35th Tax Conf.* 689 (Can. Tax Foundation, 1983).

Tremblay, Richard, "Contributions to Capital: Cost Basis", [1987-89] *Can. Current Tax* P1.

Weyman, C. David, "Restructuring the Corporate Income Tax", in *Proceedings of 37th Tax Conf.* (Can. Tax Foundation, 1985).

Wilson, James R., and Stuart F. Bollefer, *Taxation of Corporations and their Shareholders* (Toronto: Carswell, 1986).

Tax Aspects of Equity Financing

Brean, Donald J.S., "The Redemption of Convertible Preferred Shares: The Implications of Terms and Conditions" (1985), 33 *Can. Tax J.* 957.

Brussa, John A., "Flow-through Share Financing for Oil and Gas Companies: An Update" (1993), 6 *Can. Petro. Tax J.* 1.

Colley, Geoffrey M., "Tax Affairs Aren't Just an April Filing" (1989), 122 *CA Magazine* 46.

Couzin, Robert, and Robert J. Dart, "The New Preferred Share Rules", in *Proceedings of 39th Tax Conf.* 18:1 (Can. Tax Foundation, 1987).

Dixon, G.D., and B.J. Arnold, "Rubbing Salt into the Wound: The Denial of the Interest Deduction after the Loss of a Source of Income" (1991), 39 *Can. Tax J.* 1473.

Dunn, A.W., "The Draft Associated Corporation Rules: New Ways to Skin a Cat" (1988), 2 *Can. Current Tax* P17.

"Equity Investment As An Alternative to Stock Incentive Arrangement" (1990), 2 *Tax Profile* 256.

Ewens, Douglas S., "Forced Share Conversions" (1992), 40 *Can. Tax J.* 1407.

Fiscal Figures — Selected Statistics on the Evolution of the Corporate Income Tax System Since 1965" (1987), 35 *Can. Tax J.* 502.

Fitchett, Gary A., "Creative Structuring of Equity" (1990), 64 *CMA Magazine* 22.

Fooladi, Iraj, Patricia A. McGraw, and Gordon S. Roberts, "Preferred Share Rules Freeze Out the Individual Investors" (1988), 121 *CA Magazine* 38.

Hariton, David P., "The Taxation of Complex Financial Instruments" (1988), 43 *Tax Lawyer* 731.

Jans, Gord, "Stripping 'Safe Income'" (1991), 65 *CMA Magazine* 9.

Gradey, Patrick, "The Recent Corporate Income Tax Reform Proposals in Canada and the United States" (1986), 34 *Can. Tax J.* 111.

Kennedy, Henry A., *Introduction to Business Taxation* (Edmonton: Univ. of Alberta, Dept. of Accounting, 1984).

Malach, David, and Barbara Worndl, "Waltzing Though the Preferred Share Maze" (1988), 121 *CA Magazine* 47.

Raich, Robert, "Flow-Through Financing — Present and Future", in *Proceedings of 41st Tax Conf.* 43:1 (Can. Tax Foundation, 1989).

Roberts, David G., "Some Issues in the Determination of Paid-up Capital" (1992), 40 *Can. Tax J.i 338*.

Ruby, Stephen S., "Recent Financing Techniques", in *Proceedings of 41st Tax Conf.* 27:1 (Can. Tax Foundation, 1989).

Sinclair, B.R., "Paid-up Capital" (1986), 34 *Can. Tax J.* 1483.

Tax Aspects of Debt Financing

Arnold, Brian J., "Canada's Draft Legislation on Deductibility of Interest Expense Detailed" (1992), 4:11 *Tax Notes Int.* 513.

Arnold, Brian J., "Is Interest a Capital Expense?" (1992), 40 *Can. Tax J.* 533.

Arnold, Brian J. and Tim Edgar, "The Draft Legislation on Interest Deductibility: A Technical and Policy Analysis" (1992), 40 *Can. Tax J.* 267.

Bankman, Joseph, and William A. Klein, "Accurate Taxation of Long-Term Debt: Taking Into Account the Term Structure of Interest" (1989), 44 *Tax Lawyer* 335.

CBA and CICA, Joint Committee on Taxation, "Submission to the Minister of Finance on the Issue of Deductibility of Interest", in *Can. Tax Reports, Special Report No. 964* (Don Mills, Ont.: CCH Canadian, August, 1990).

Crowe, Ian, "I'm Tired of Yoghurt" (1991), 124 *CA Magazine* 29.

Drache, A.B.C., "Draft Interest Expense Legislation" (1992), 14 *Can. Taxpayer* 11.

Drache, A.B.C., "Interest Deductibility: Planning Still Worthwhile" (1991), 13 *Can. Taxpayer* 102.

Dunn, A.W., "The Draft Associated Corporation Rules: New Ways to Skin a Cat" (1988), 2 *Can. Current Tax* P17.

Edgar, Tim, and Brian J. Arnold, "Reflections on the Submission of the CBA-CICA Joint Committee on Taxation Concerning the Deductibility of Interest" (1990), 38 *Can. Tax J.* 847.

Edgar, Tim, "The Thin Capitalization Rules: Role and Reform" (1992), 40 *Can. Tax J.* 1.

Ewens, Douglas S., "The Thin Capitalization Restrictions" (1994), 42 *Can. Tax J.* 954.

Farden, Eric N., *Income Tax for a Small Business* (E.N. Farden, 1985).

Felesky, Brian A. and Sandra E. Jack, "Is there Substance to 'Substance over Form' in Canada?", [1992] *Can. Tax Foundation* 50:1

"Fiscal Figures — Selected Statistics on the Evolution of the Corporate Income Tax System Since 1965" (1987), 35 *Can. Tax J.* 502.

Flatters, Michael J., "Assumption of Debt Obligations" (1992), 40 *Can. Tax J.* 509.

Fox-Revett, Melissa G., "Interest Deductibility", [1993] *Can. Current Tax* P19.

Gradey, Patrick, "The Recent Corporate Income Tax Reform Proposals in Canada and the United States" (1986), 34 *Can. Tax J.* 111.

Hariton, David P., "The Taxation of Complex Financial Instruments" (1988), 43 *Tax Lawyer* 731.

Hickey, Paul B., "The Proposed New Interest Deductibility Regime: Strategies and Pitfalls", [1992] *Can. Tax Foundation* 23:1.

Hugget, Donald R., "It Certainly Does Make A Difference!" (1990), 17 *Can. Tax News* 69.

Kennedy, Henry A., *Introduction to Business Taxation* (Edmonton: University of Alberta, Dept. of Accounting, 1984).

Krishna, Vern, "Interest Deductibility: More Form Over Substance", [1993] *Can. Current Tax* C17.

Loveland, Norman C., "Income Tax Aspects of Borrowing and Lending", [1986] *Special Lectures of the LSUC* 289.

McDonnell, T.E., "Without a Trace" (1993), 41 *Can. Tax J.* 134.

McKie, A.B., "Interest: A Taxing Problem" (1987), 35 *Can. Banker* 20.

McNair, D. Keith, "Restricted Interest Expense" (1987), 35 *Can. Tax J.* 616.

Richardson, Stephen R., "Current Developments in Debt Financing: A Canadian Perspective", in *Proceedings of 40th Tax Conf.* 22:1 (Can. Tax Foundation, 1988).

Ruby, Stephen S., "Recent Financing Techniques", in *Proceedings of 41st Tax Conf.* 27:1 (Can. Tax Foundation, 1989).

Small Business Taxation (Audio Archives of Canada, 1984).

Ulmer, John M., "Index-linked Debt and Other Derivatives: Canadian Income Tax Implications" (1992), 11 *National Banking Law Rev.* 65.

Wraggett, Cathy, "Minimizing Your Personal Tax Burden" (1990), 64 *CMA Magazine* 21.

Hybrid Debt

Burgoyne, Terrence R. and David J. Tetrault, "Distress Preferred Shares: Re-structuring with After-tax Financing (Part 1)" (1992), 9 *Nat. Insolvency Rev.* 91.

Burgoyne, Terrence R. and David J. Tetrault, "Distress Preferred Shares: Re-structuring with After-tax Financing (Part 2)" (1993), 10 *Nat. Insolvency Rev.* 1.

Dunn, A.W., "The Draft Associated Corporation Rules: New Ways to Skin a Cat" (1988), 2 *Can. Current Tax* P17.

Edgar, Tim, "Distress Preferred Shares and Small Business Development Bonds: A Tax Expenditure Analysis" (1994), 42 *Can. Tax J.* 659.

Ewens, Douglas S., "Amending Grandfathered Preferred Share Conditions" (1994), 42 *Can. Tax J.* 548.

Ewens, Douglas S., "Convertible Property: Section 51 — Part 1" (1994), 42 *Can. Tax J.* 1413.

Ewens, Douglas S., "Forced Share Conversions" (1992), 40 *Can. Tax J.* 1407.

Ewens, Douglas S., "The New Preferred Share Dividend Tax Regime" in *Report of Proceedings of 40th Tax Conference* (Can. Tax Foundation, 1988.

"Fiscal Figures — Selected Statistics on the Evolution of the Corporate Income Tax System Since 1965" (1987), 35 *Can. Tax J.* 502.

Gradey, Patrick, "The Recent Corporate Income Tax Reform Proposals in Canada and the United States" (1986), 34 *Can. Tax J.* 111.

Hariton, David P., "The Taxation of Complex Financial Instruments" (1988), 43 *Tax Lawyer* 731.

Kennedy, Henry A., *Introduction to Business Taxation* (Edmonton: University of Alberta, Dept. of Accounting, 1984).

Loveland, Norman C., "Securities Lending and Repurchase Agreements: Canadian Tax Issues" (1989), 4 *Securities and Corp. Regulation Rev.* 205.

Meredith, P. Mark, "Securities Lending: Evolving Tax Problems and Issues" (1992), 11 *National Banking Law Rev.* 18.

Robinson, Chris and Alan White, "Guaranteed Preferred Shares: Debt or Equity" (1986/87), 1 *Banking & Finance Law Rev.* 211.

Ross, David W., "Equity Preferred Shares" (1992), 40 *Can. Tax J.*

Sugg, Donald M., "Preferred Share Review: Anomalies and Traps for the Unwary", [1992] *Can. Tax Foundation* 22:1.

Leases

Athanassakos, George and Margaret Klatt, "Lease or Buy?: How Recent Tax Changes have Affected the Decision" (1993), 41 *Can. Tax J.* 444.

Atlas, Michael I., "Income Tax Issues in Real Estate Leasing", *Corp. Mgmt. Tax Conf.* 3:1 (Can. Tax Foundation, 1989).

Bowman, Stephen W., "Equipment Leasing Revisited" (1994), 42 *Can. Tax J.* 206.

Bowman, Steve, "Lease or Buy? Tax Considerations" (1990), 64 *CMA Magazine* 22.

Bowman, Steve, "Leasing Rules — Tax Simplification?" (1989), 63 *CMA Magazine* 18.

Birnie, David A.G., "Shareholders' Buy-sell Agreements: Some New Opportunities", in *Proceedings of 38th Tax Conf.* 13 (Can. Tax Foundation, 1986).

Gillespie, Thomas S., "Lease Financing" in *Corp. Management Tax Conf.* (Canada Tax Foundation, 1992).

Haney, M.A., "Leasing Property — Use in the Year" (1987), 35 *Can. Tax J.* 970.

Hugget, Donald R., "Leasing Property Rules" (1990), 17 *Can. Tax News* 70.

McDonnell, Thomas E., "Questions About Leasing" (1993), 41 *Can. Tax J.* 509.

McKie, A.B., "Corporations and Shareholders: Tax Reform or Reforming" (1986), 93 *Can. Banker* 46.

Ross, David W., "Corporate Taxation and Tax Avoidance", in *Proceedings of 31st Tax Conf.* 400 (Can. Tax Foundation, 1979).

Templeton, Michael D., "Not a Lease But Not a Sale" (1991), 39 *Can Tax J.* 288.

Ward, David A., and John M. Ulmer, "Corporate Taxation: 1986 Federal Budget" (1986), 5 *Legal Alert* 81.

Weyman, C. David, "Restructuring the Corporate Income Tax", in *Proceedings of 37th Tax Conf.* (Can. Tax Foundation, 1985).

Wilson, Michael H., *The Corporate Income Tax System: A Direction for Change*, Dept. of Finance Canada, 1985.

Zinn, John A., "Advancements in Off-balance Sheet Financing (Part 1)" (1994), 13 *Nat. Banking L. Review* 24.

CHAPTER XVI

PRIVATE CORPORATIONS: INVESTMENT INCOME

Reference:

ITA:

S. 129   Rules Applicable to Private Corporations

1. GENERAL

The taxation of income earned by a private corporation depends upon the source of the income. In general terms, corporate income is classified into two broad categories: "investment" and "business". In this chapter we examine the taxation of investment income earned by a private corporation. In Chapter XVII "Private Corporations: Business Income" we will look at the taxation of business income earned by a private corporation.

2. TAX OBJECTIVES

The rules in respect of the taxation of investment income earned by a private corporation serve two objectives: (1) To "integrate" the amount of tax paid by a corporation on its investment income with the tax paid by its individual shareholders; and (2) To discourage individuals from deferring tax by placing their investments in private holding companies.

"Integration" means that an individual should pay the same amount of tax on investment income, regardless of whether the income is earned personally or indirectly through a corporation. Integration is achieved by synchronizing the corporate tax rate with the effective rate of tax paid by an individual on investment income earned through a corporation.

The second objective is implemented by initially taxing corporate investment income at a high rate to prevent tax deferral. Thus, investment income (other than taxable dividends) earned by a Canadian-controlled private corporation is initially taxed at the full corporate rate (approximately 40 per cent). A portion of this tax is refunded to the corporation when it pays taxable dividends. The initial tax of approximately 40 per cent has the effect of blunting any advantage derived from tax deferral. The tax refund reduces the effective rate of tax to a level that is approximately equivalent to the rate that would be paid on such income received directly by an individual.

3. TYPES OF INVESTMENT INCOME

Investment income is income from property and income from capital gains.

Income from property is of two types: "dividends" and "other" investment income (such as rent, interest, royalties, etc.). The following chart sets out some of the more common sources of investment income:

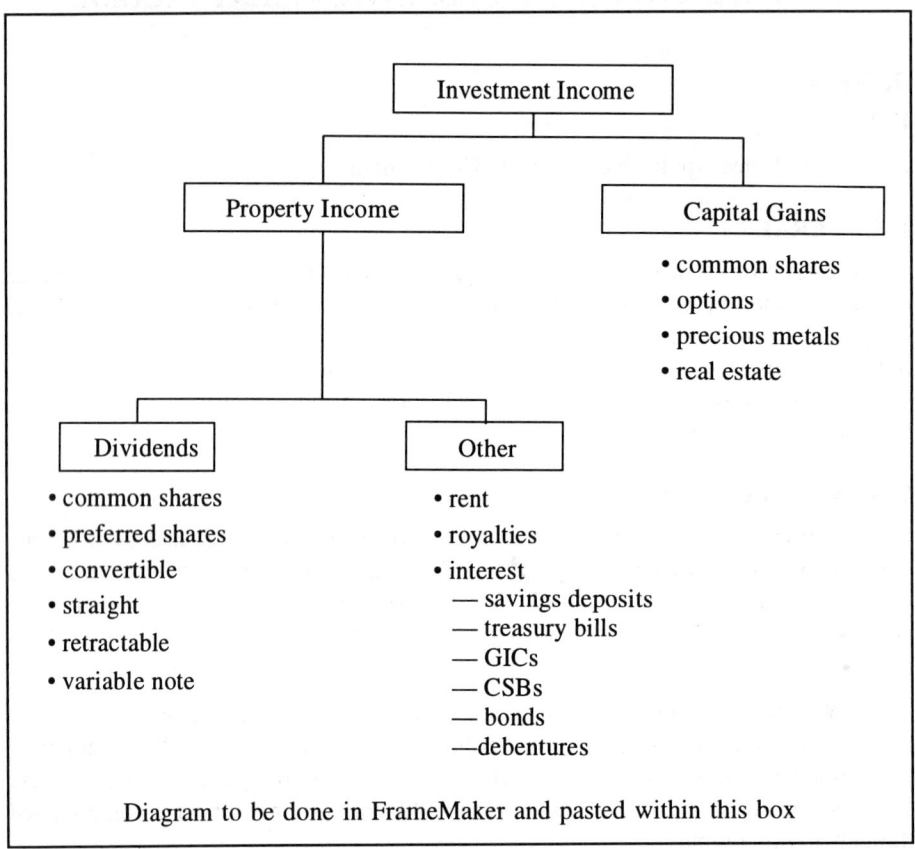

Diagram to be done in FrameMaker and pasted within this box

4. DIVIDEND INCOME

References:

ITA:

Para. 12(1)(*j*)	Dividends from Resident Corporations
Para. 12(1)(*k*)	Dividends from Other Corporations
Subs. 112(1)	Deduction for Taxable Dividends in Computing Taxable Income
S. 121	Deduction for Taxable Dividends in Computing Tax
S. 186	Part IV Tax on Taxable Dividends Received by Private Corporations

BULLETINS, CIRCULARS & RULINGS:

IT-67R3	May 15, 1992	Taxable Dividends from Corporations Resident in Canada
IT-88R2	May 31, 1991	Stock Dividends
IT-243R3	May 21, 1985	Dividend Refund to Private Corporation
IT-269R3	Nov. 29, 1991	Part IV Tax on Taxable Dividends Received by a Private Corporation or a Subject Corporation

Generally speaking, a corporation must include in its income all taxable dividends that it receives from other corporations.[1] In computing its taxable income, however, a corporation may deduct taxable dividends that it has received from:[2]

- a "taxable Canadian corporation"; or
- a resident corporation (other than a non-resident-owned corporation) that it controls.

The basic structure for the taxation of inter-corporate dividends prevents multiple taxation of income passing through several different corporations. Including taxable dividends in income and then deducting these dividends in the computation of taxable income effectively exempts inter-corporate dividends from Part I tax. (It should be noted, however, that increasingly in recent years the mechanism for the tax-free flow-through of inter-corporate dividends has been curtailed. There are now numerous exceptions to the general rule.[3])

Thus, an individual who places his or her portfolio investments in a holding company can defer tax on dividends received by the corporation. To prevent this deferral, a special tax is levied on private corporations that receive "portfolio dividends".[4] This tax is fully refundable to the corporation when it pays out taxable dividends to its shareholders.[5]

---

[1] Paras. 12(1)(j), (k).

[2] Subs. 112(1); dividends from non-resident investment corporations may *not* be deducted.

[3] See Chapter XV "Corporate Finance", for a discussion on "Taxable Preferred Shares".

[4] Subs. 186(1). The phrase "portfolio dividends" is used to describe taxable dividends from corporations *other than* payor corporations "connected" with the receiving corporation, in respect of which a deduction may be claimed under subss. 112(1), 113(1) and (2).

[5] Subs. 129(1).

(a) Theoretical Model

The underlying purpose of the scheme in respect of the Part IV tax is:

1. To prevent tax deferral through the use of holding companies; and

2. To "integrate" the personal and corporate tax on investment income.

These objectives are achieved through a three-part mechanism: (1) A Part IV tax on portfolio dividend income; (2) A dividend refund to the corporation; and (3) A dividend gross-up and tax imputation credit for individuals.

Since inter-corporate dividends flow tax-free, an individual could defer personal taxes by placing his or her investments in a holding company. The Part IV tax, which is fully refundable, prevents tax deferral.

An individual who receives a dividend from a taxable Canadian corporation is taxable on 125 per cent of the cash value of the dividend. The 25 per cent "gross-up" is on account of corporate taxes previously paid by the corporation. The individual may claim a tax credit equal to two-thirds of the "gross-up" of 25 per cent included in his or her income.[6] The effect of including a grossed-up value of the dividend in income followed by a dividend tax credit is to "integrate" the total tax paid by the individual with the tax paid by the corporation. Thus, the dividend tax credit imputes taxes paid by the corporation to the shareholder.

The combined effect of the Part IV tax and the dividend tax credit is to prevent tax deferral and integrate corporate and shareholder taxes. Example XVI.1 illustrates the theoretical model for integrating dividend income.

Example XVI.1

Portfolio Dividends: Theoretical Model

Assume a combined (federal and provincial) tax rate of 40 per cent for both personal and corporate tax.

Corporate Tax:

Portfolio dividends	$ 10,000
Part IV tax payable	$ 3,333
Net income after tax	$ 6,667
Refund of tax on payment of dividend	$ 3,333
Amount available for dividend	$ 10,000

---

[6] S. 121.

Example XVI.1 (contiued)

Shareholder Tax:

Dividend income	$ 10,000
Gross-up	$ 2,500
Taxable amount	$ 12,500
Federal/provincial tax @ 40% (Assumed)	$ 5,000
Dividend tax credit (Assumed)	$ 2,500
Net tax payable	$ 2,500
Income retained	$ 7,500

Effective Tax Rate on Dividend **25%**

Hence, an individual with a combined federal-provincial tax rate of 40 per cent would end up paying $2,500 tax on a dividend of $10,000, regardless of whether he or she receives the dividend directly or through a holding corporation. Thus, in theory at least, the tax on portfolio dividends earned by a private corporation is integrated with the personal tax system.

(b) Actual Rates

The theoretical model begins to break down as we move away from its underlying assumptions. To the extent that the combined federal/provincial tax rate varies from 40 per cent, the integration of the corporate and personal tax systems is less than perfect.

Example XVI.2

Portfolio Dividends: Theory vs. Actual

Corporate Tax:	Integration Model	Actual Taxes (Ontario-1995)
Portfolio dividends	$ 10,000	$ 10,000
Part IV tax payable	$ 3,333	$ 3,333
Net income after tax	$ 6,667	$ 6,667
Refund of tax on payment of dividend	$ 3,333	$ 3,333
Amount available for dividend	$ 10,000	$ 10,000

Example XVI.2 (continued)

Shareholder Tax:

Dividend income	$ 10,000	$ 10,000
Gross-up of dividend	$ 2,500	$ 2,500
Taxable amount	$ 12,500	$ 12,500
Federal/provincial tax @ 40%	$ 5,000	
Dividend tax credit	$ 2,500	
Federal tax (at top marginal rates)		$ 2,115
Ontario tax (at top marginal rates)		$ 1,477
Net tax payable	$ 2,500	$ 3,592
Income retained	$ 7,500	$ 6,408
Tax deferral		$ 259
Effective Tax Rate on Dividend	**25%**	**36%**

As federal and provincial taxes have increased, the effective tax rate on dividends has risen to approximately 36 per cent (Ontario, 1995).

(c) Part IV Tax

(i) Rationale

The Part IV tax is an anti-deferral mechanism. It places an individual who holds portfolio investments through a holding company in the same position as a person who holds portfolio investments directly. Thus, the income tax effects of owning portfolio investments are neutral regardless of the vehicle selected to hold the investments.

(ii) Application

The Part IV tax is a fully refundable tax. It applies to two types of corporations:[7]

1. Private corporations; and
2. "Subject corporations".

A "subject corporation" is a corporation (*other than* a private corporation) resident in Canada that is controlled directly or indirectly in any manner by, or for the benefit of, an individual or a related group of individuals.[8]

---

[7] Subs. 186(1).

[8] Subs. 186(1).

An individual or a related group of individuals is considered to be in control of a corporation if its shares are indirectly controlled by another corporation, partnership or trust.[9]

(iii) Taxable Dividends

A private corporation is subject to Part IV tax on:

- Taxable dividends from *non-connected*[10] Canadian corporations resident in Canada, if the dividends are deductible in computing the recipient's taxable income;[11]

- Certain taxable dividends from foreign affiliates;[12] and

- Taxable dividends from connected private corporations in proportion to the dividend refund obtained by the payor corporation.[13]

In determining its liability for Part IV tax, a corporation may deduct its non-capital losses and farm losses for the current year[14] and its non-capital and farm loss carryover.[15] A corporation has the option of deducting its loss carryovers to reduce its Part IV tax or in calculating its taxable income.

(iv) Connected Corporations

The critical factor in determining the liability of a corporation for Part IV tax is its relationship with the corporation from which it receives a dividend (the "payor" corporation). If the payor and recipient corporations are *not* connected with each other, the recipient corporation is liable to Part IV tax on its taxable dividends from the payor. If the corporations are connected, the recipient corporation is liable for Part IV tax, *but only if* the payor corporation obtains a dividend refund by paying the dividend.

A payor and a recipient corporation are "connected" with each other if:[16]

- The recipient corporation controls the payor; or

---

[9] See subs. 251(5); but see, generally, s. 256.

[10] Subs. 186(4).

[11] Subpara. 186(1)(*a*)(i).

[12] Subpara. 186(1)(*a*)(ii).

[13] Para. 186(1)(*b*). This provision ensures that, until such time as dividends are paid out to individuals or non-connected corporations, the payor corporation's tax refund is matched with the payee corporation's liability to Part IV tax.

[14] Para. 186(1)(*c*).

[15] Para. 186(1)(*d*).

[16] Subs. 186(4).

- The recipient corporation owns more than 10 per cent of the issued fully-voting shares of the payor and the fair market value of *all* the shares owned by the recipient exceeds 10 per cent of the fair market value of *all* issued shares of the payor.

Thus, a private corporation that receives a taxable dividend is not subject to Part IV tax if it owns more than 10 per cent of the payor corporation, *unless* the payor obtains a dividend refund in respect of the dividend.

Example XVI.3

Assume:

A Ltd., a private corporation, owns 60 per cent of the issued and outstanding shares of *S Ltd.* which pays a dividend of $150,000. *S Ltd.* receives a dividend refund of $30,000.

Total dividend paid by *S Ltd.*	$150,000
Dividend received by *A Ltd.* (60% of $150,000)	$ 90,000

Then *A Ltd.* is liable for $18,000 Part IV tax calculated as follows:

$$1/3 \, \frac{\text{Taxable dividend}}{\text{Total taxable dividend}} \times 3 \, (\text{Dividend refund})$$

$$= 1/3 \, \frac{\$ \, 90,000}{150,000} \times 3 \, (\$30,000)$$

$$= \$18,000$$

For the purpose of determining whether one corporation controls another corporation, "control" means the ownership of more than 50 per cent of the issued fully-voting shares of a corporation.[17] Note that, for the purposes of the Part IV tax, one corporation can control another with a direct holding of less than 50 per cent in that corporation. This can occur where one corporation that controls another corporation has an interest in a third corporation. For example:

---

[17] Subs. 186(2). This definition of control does not apply for the purpose of determining whether a corporation is a "subject corporation".

Example XVI.4

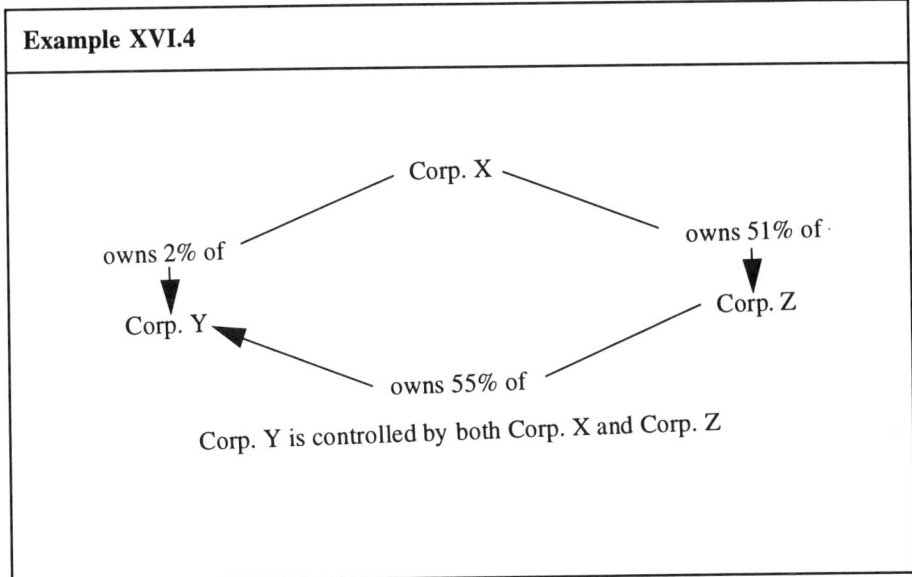

Corp. X

owns 2% of

owns 51% of

Corp. Y

Corp. Z

owns 55% of

Corp. Y is controlled by both Corp. X and Corp. Z

In Example XVI.4, Corp. X and Corp. Z are not at arm's length with each other. Since Corp. Z owns more than 50 per cent of Corp. Y, Corp. X is considered to "control" Corp. Y for the purposes of the Part IV tax.

(v) Excluded Dividends

Inter-corporate dividends generally flow tax-free between corporations. There are certain dividends, however, which do not flow on a tax-free basis between corporations. For example, subsections 112(2.2) and (2.4) deny the inter-corporate dividend deduction on certain "guaranteed" shares and "collateralized preferred shares" that have security guarantees to protect any loss on the shares. In these circumstances, Part IV tax does not apply, since the corporation is fully taxable under Part I on the dividends. Paragraph 186(1)(*b*) excludes from Part IV tax any taxable dividends received from a *connected* corporation.

The following example illustrates the operation of the Part IV tax in theory and in practice.

Example XVI.5 (Theoretical model)

Assume:

A private corporation receives $1,000 interest income. The corporation pays Part I tax at a rate of 40 per cent and pays a dividend to its sole shareholder, an individual with a marginal tax rate of 40 per cent.

Then:

	CORP.	PERSONAL
Tax effect on corporation:		
Interest income	$ 1,000	
Corporate Part I tax 40%	400	
Net income after tax	$ 600	
Refund of tax on payment of dividend	200	
Available for dividend	800	
Effective corporate tax rate	20%	
Tax effect on individual:		
Interest income earned directly by individual		$ 1,000
Dividend received	$ 800	
Gross-up @ (equal to corporate tax)	200	
Taxable amount	$ 1,000	$ 1,000
Tax thereon:		
Personal tax before dividend tax credit 40%	$ 400	$ 400
Dividend tax credit (equal to corporate tax)	200	
Tax payable	$ 200	$ 400
Net income retained by individual	$ 600	$ 600
Effective individual tax rate	20%	40%
Combined corporate/personal tax rate	40%	40%

5. OTHER INVESTMENT INCOME

References:

ITA:

Subs. 125(7)   "Specified Investment Business"

BULLETINS, CIRCULARS & RULINGS:

IT-524   March 16, 1990   Trust — Flow-Through of Taxable Dividends
                                        to a Beneficiary — After 1987

"Other investment income" describes investment income other than portfolio dividends; it includes taxable capital gains, income from property and income from a "specified investment business".[18]

(a) Tax Integration

The rules in respect of the taxation of "other investment income" also neutralize the use of holding companies to earn investment income. Thus, an individual who places investments in a holding company does not enjoy any tax advantage over an individual who holds his or her investments directly.

The rules apply to investment income earned by a *Canadian-controlled* private corporation and not just any private corporation. The general structure for the taxation of investment income involves four steps:

1. A Canadian-controlled private corporation is initially taxed on its investment income at full corporate tax rates;[19]

2. When the corporation pays a dividend, it receives a refund for a portion of the taxes that it previously paid on that income;[20]

3. When the dividend is paid to an individual, the "grossed-up" value of the dividend is included in his or her income;[21]

4. The individual may then claim a dividend tax credit to adjust for the net amount of corporate tax that was notionally paid on his or her behalf by the corporation.[22]

---

[18] Subs. 125(7) ("specified investment business").

[19] That is, starting at a basic federal rate of 38 per cent (1995).

[20] The refund is processed through an account described as the "refundable dividend tax on hand account" ("RDTOH").

[21] Para. 82(1)(*b*).

[22] S. 121.

(b) "Investment Income"

There are two types of investment income: "Canadian investment income" and "foreign investment income".

(i) Canadian Investment Income

"Canadian investment income" comprises:[23]

- The excess of taxable capital gains over allowable capital losses to the extent that such gains and losses are from sources in Canada; and
- Net property income *(including* income from a "specified investment business") from Canadian sources.[24]

(A) Presumptions

Investment income does not include income from a business.[25] The distinction between investment income and business income is essentially a question of fact.[26] In the case of corporate taxpayers, however, there is a rebuttable presumption that income earned in the pursuit of the corporation's objects (as stated in its constating documents) is income from a business.[27] Although the question is open,[28] there does not appear to be any compelling reason why the presumption would not also apply to corporations that do not require objects clauses in their constating documents.

Thus, depending upon the rigidity with which the presumption is applied, corporations have some flexibility in characterizing the source of their income as flowing from business or investments. The presumption should not, however, be applied in such a manner as to destroy the legislative scheme distinguishing between active business income and investment income.[29]

(B) Specified Investment Business

A "specified investment business" is a business the principal purpose of which is to derive income from property.[30] A "specified investment business" does *not* include the business of leasing personal property, but it does include the business of leasing real property.

---

[23] Subs. 129(4) ("Canadian investment income").

[24] Subs. 129(4.1) *deems* income from a "specified investment business" to be income from property.

[25] Subs. 129(4.1) *deems* income from a "specified investment business" to be income from property; see also Chapter XVII "Private Corporations: Business Income".

[26] *Can. Marconi Co. v. The Queen*, [1986] 2 CTC 465 at 470, 86 DTC 6526 at 6529 (S.C.C.).

[27] *Can. Marconi Co. v. The Queen, ante,* [1986] 2 CTC at 468, 86 DTC at 6528.

[28] *Can. Marconi Co. v. The Queen, ante,* [1986] 2 CTC at 470, 86 DTC at 6529.

[29] *Ensite Ltd. v. The Queen,* [1986] 2 CTC 459 at 464, 86 DTC 6521 at 6524 (S.C.C.).

[30] Subs. 125(7) ("specified investment business").

A business that employs more than five full-time employees throughout the year is not a "specified investment business". Thus, a "specified investment business" includes any business with less than six full time employees that has as its principal purpose the earning of income from property or the leasing of real property.

(ii) Foreign Investment Income

"Foreign investment income" is calculated in the same way as "Canadian investment income", except that it takes into account only income earned from non-Canadian sources.[31] "Foreign investment income" does not include any income or loss from property that is used incidentally in, or pertains to, an active business.[32]

(c) Refund of Tax

Where a Canadian-controlled private corporation earns investment income (other than portfolio dividends), it is eligible for a *partial refund* of taxes when it pays out dividends.[33] The effective rate of tax (net of refunds) on investment income (other than portfolio dividends) is 20 per cent. Hence, individual and corporate taxes payable by Canadian-controlled private corporations on investment income are approximately integrated where the individual's combined federal-provincial marginal rate of tax is 40 per cent.

(i) Theoretical Model

The theoretical scheme of the refundable tax is as follows: we assume that a Canadian-controlled private corporation pays tax on its investment income at 40 per cent; when it pays out dividends, it receives a refund of 20 per cent on its Canadian investment income. (This is the "refundable portion" of its Part I tax[34].) The grossed-up value (125 per cent) of the cash dividend is included in the individual shareholder's income and the individual is allowed a dividend tax credit equal to the value of the dividend gross-up. The corporate tax is imputed to its shareholders to avoid double taxation.

Thus, where an individual has a marginal tax rate of 40 per cent, corporate and personal taxes are "integrated": The tax burden is neutral, regardless of whether the shareholder receives the investment income directly or through a holding company.

---

[31] Subs. 129(4) ("foreign investment income").

[32] Subs. 129(4.2); see also *Aqua-Gem Invt. Ltd. v. M.N.R.*, [1986] 1 CTC 2528, 86 DTC 1392 (T.C.C.) (interest from short-term investments was income "incident to" taxpayer's business).

[33] Subs. 129(1); para. 129(3)(*a*). Note that the corporation must be a Canadian-controlled private corporation *throughout the taxation year*.

[34] Subs. 129(1); subpara. 129(3)(*a*)(ii).

(ii) Actual Rates

Since federal/provincial tax rates in Canada generally exceed 40 per cent, there is less than perfect integration of corporate and personal taxes in most provinces. In Ontario, for example, the combined federal provincial corporate tax rate on investment income is 51.29 per cent.

Example XVI.6 (Actual rates)

Assume:

A private corporation receives $1,000 interest income. The corporation pays Part I tax at a rate of 51.29 per cent and pays a dividend to its sole shareholder, an Ontario resident in the top marginal tax bracket and subject to Ontario surtaxes. The corporation receives a refund of $1 for every $3 paid out in dividends.

Then:

	CORP.	PERSONAL
Tax effect on corporation:		
Interest income	$ 1,000	
Corporate Part I tax (Ontario)	512	
Net income after tax	$ 487	
Refund of tax on payment of dividend	243*	
Available for dividend	$ 730	
Effective corporate tax rate	26%	
Tax effect on individual:		
Interest income earned directly by individual	$ 1,000	
Dividend received	$ 730	—
Gross-up @ 1/4	182	—
Taxable amount	$ 913	$ 1,000

Example XVI.6 (continued)

Tax thereon:

Federal tax before dividend tax credit (29%)	$ 264	$ 290
Dividend tax credit	121	
Basic federal tax (BFT)	$ 143	$ 290
Surtax on federal tax (3% BFT)	4	8
Additional federal surtax (5% BFT)	7	14
Federal tax payable	$ 154	$ 313
Ontario tax (58% of BFT)	83	168
Ontario surtax (20% Ontario tax)	16	33
Additional Ontario surtax (10% Ontario tax)	8	16
Combined federal/provincial tax payable	$ 262	$ 531
Net income retained by individual	$ 468	$ 468
Effective personal tax rate	35%	53%
Combined corporate/personal tax rate	53%	53%

* The refund is equal to the *lesser* of the balance in the RDTOH account and one-third of the dividend paid.

(iii) Capital Gains

"Canadian investment income" also includes the excess of Canadian source taxable capital gains over Canadian source allowable capital losses. The theory in respect of the taxation of capital gains is to integrate the tax payable on corporate capital gains with the tax that would be payable by an individual who receives such income directly.

As with other sources of investment income, interest, rent, etc.), the theory is that a corporation pays Part I tax on its capital gains at 40 per cent, but is entitled to a refund of 20 per cent on dividends that it pays out. Since only three-quarters of capital gains are taxable, this results in an effective corporate tax rate of 15 per cent on capital gains.

There is one significant difference between the tax structure in respect of corporate capital gains and other sources of investment income: Capital gains are only partially taxable. Only 75 per cent of capital gains are included in income as taxable capital gains, and only 75 per cent of capital losses are allowed as a deduction from taxable capital gains. The non-taxable portion (that is, 25 per cent of the capital gain) goes into a special account called the "Capital Dividend Account", which may be paid out on a tax-free basis to shareholders. Thus, capital gains earned through a corporation are treated in a similar manner to gains earned directly by an individual.

The following examples illustrate the flow-through of capital gains through a corporation. (The theoretical model assumes a combined corporate/personal tax of 30 per cent on capital gains.)

Example XVI.7 (Theoretical model)

Assume:

A private corporation earns $1,000 capital gains. The corporation pays a dividend to its sole shareholder, an individual with a marginal tax rate of 40 per cent. The corporation pays Part I tax at a rate of 40 per cent.

Then:

	CORP.	PERSONAL
Tax effect on corporation:		
Capital gains	$ 1,000	
Tax-free portion of gain (25%)	250	
Taxable capital gain	$ 750	
Corporate Part I tax (40%)	300	
Net income after tax	$ 450	
Refund of tax on payment of dividend	150	
Available for dividend	$ 600	
Effective corporate tax rate on gain	15%	
Tax effect on individual:		
Capital gains realized directly by individual		$ 1,000
Taxable dividend received	$ 600	—
Gross-up @ 1/4 (equal to corporate tax)	150	—
Taxable amount	$ 750	$ 750
Tax thereon:		
Personal tax before dividend tax credit (40%)	$ 300	$ 300
Dividend tax credit (equal to corporate tax)	150	—
Tax payable	$ 150	$ 300
Capital dividend (tax free)	$ 250	
Net income retained by individual	$ 700	$ 700
Effective personal tax rate	15%	30%
Combined corporate/personal tax rate	30%	30%

Example XVI.8 (Actual rates)

Assume:

A private corporation earns $1,000 in capital gains, which it pays out in dividends to its sole shareholder, an Ontario resident in the top marginal tax bracket and subject to Ontario surtax. The corporation pays Part I tax on its income at a rate of 51.29% and receives a refund of $1 for every $3 of dividends paid.

Then:

	CORP.	PERSONAL
Tax effect on corporation:		
Capital gains	$ 1,000	
Tax-free portion of gain (1/4 of gain)	250	
Taxable capital gain	$ 750	
Corporate Part I tax @ 51.29%	385	
	$ 365	
Refund of tax on payment of dividend	182	
Available for dividend	$ 547	
Effective corporate tax rate on gain	20%	
Tax effect on individual:		
Capital gains realized directly by individual		$ 1,000
Dividend received	$ 547	—
Gross-up @ 1/4	137	—
Taxable amount	$ 684	$ 750
Tax thereon:		
Federal tax before dividend tax credit (29%)	$ 198	$ 218
Dividend tax credit	91	
Basic federal tax (BFT)	$ 107	$ 218
Surtax on federal tax (3% BFT)	3	7
Additional federal surtax (5%* BFT)	5	11
Federal tax payable	$ 115	$ 236
Ontario tax (58% BFT)	62	126
Ontario surtax (20% Ontario tax)	12	25
Additional Ontario surtax (10% Ontario tax)	6	13
Combined federal/provincial tax payable	$ 195	$ 400
Capital dividend	$ 250	—
Net income retained by individual	$ 602	$ 600
Effective personal tax rate	24%	36%
Combined corporate/personal tax rate on gain	40%	40%

(d) Capital Dividends

The non-taxable portion of capital gains is credited to an account called the "Capital Dividend Account".[35] A dividend paid out of the "Capital Dividend Account" is tax-free to the shareholder and does not affect the adjusted cost base of his or her shares.[36]

(e) Integration

As the preceding examples illustrate, the tax payable on investment income by an individual is approximately the same whether such income is earned directly or through a corporation. The structure integrates the personal and corporate tax through the refund and dividend tax credit mechanism. In each case the amount taxable in the individual's hands is approximately equal to the corporation's pre-tax income. In addition, the combined federal-provincial dividend tax credit approximately equals the tax paid by the corporation.

Two factors can distort the tax integration model as it applies to investment income: (1) The combined federal-provincial corporate tax rate can shift because of surtaxes and variations in provincial rates; (2) The amount of the dividend tax credit varies because of provincial tax rates. Thus, perfect integration of taxes on investment income occurs only when federal corporate tax rates are exactly synchronized with provincial tax rates.

(f) Refundable Dividend Tax on Hand ("RDTOH")

The "refundable dividend tax on hand" ("RDTOH") account is a notional account used to calculate a corporation's entitlement to a tax refund.

The refundable tax in respect of portfolio dividend income is available to all private corporations. For non-portfolio dividend income, however, the refund is available only in respect of the investment income of a corporation that was a *Canadian-controlled private corporation throughout* the taxation year.[37]

The tax refund is equal to one third of taxable dividends paid by the corporation, subject to a maximum equal to the corporation's RDTOH.[38] The refund is usually credited against other corporate taxes that are payable by the corporation or will become so in the future.

---

[35] Subs. 89(1) ("capital dividend account").

[36] Subs. 83(2).

[37] Para. 129(3)(a).

[38] Subs. 129(1).

The balance in the refundable dividend tax on hand account at the end of a particular year is reduced in the following year by the amount of dividend refunds to which the corporation has become entitled as a result of the payment of taxable dividends to its shareholders.[39]

Where a corporation loses its private corporation status, its RDTOH account is erased. The only income credited to the RDTOH of a corporation is its investment income earned after it *last became a private corporation.* Hence, once its RDTOH is erased, the amount is never again available for future refunds of tax.

Where a private corporation has a balance in its refundable dividend tax on hand account, the Minister may, at the time of mailing of the notice of assessment, refund to the corporation an amount equal to the *lesser* of:[40]

- one third of all taxable dividends paid by the corporation in the year; and

- the balance in its RDTOH account at the end of that year.

The Minister is required to make the refund if the corporation applies for it after the notice of assessment has been mailed and within three years from the end of the year.[41] The Minister may, however, apply the refund to offset the corporation's existing or prospective income tax liability.

---

[39] Para. 129(3)(c).

[40] Subs. 129(1).

[41] The limitation period is extended to six years in certain circumstances, when the refund arises from a reassessment involving losses carried over and tax credits; para. 129(1)(b).

SELECTED BIBLIOGRAPHY TO CHAPTER XVI

General

Allgood, David R., "Tax Planning for Private Corporations and Their Shareholders: Implications of Recent Changes in the Use of Holding Companies", in *Proceedings of 38th Tax Conf.* 10 (Can. Tax Foundation, 1986).

Colley, Geoffrey M., "Are Corporate Tax Changes Imminent?" (1986), 119 *CA Magazine* 60.

Deloitte, Haskins & Sells Canada, Taxation of a Private Corporation (1981).

Fenwick, "Incorporation of Investment Income", in *Proceedings of 29th Tax Conf.* 141 (Can. Tax Foundation, 1977).

Goodman, Wolfe D., and Barr Naiberg, "Holding Companies: Why They're Still Attractive" (1983), 116:3 *CA Magazine* 44.

Hiseler, "Judicial Decisions Relating to the Taxation of Corporations and Their Shareholders", in *Proceedings of 34th Tax Conf.* 429 (Can. Tax Foundation, 1982).

Institute for Fiscal Studies, *Equity for Companies: A Corporation Tax for the 1990's* — A Corporation Tax for the 1990's — A Report of the IFS Capital Taxes Group (London, 1991).

Jones, D.P., "Corporations, Double Taxation and the Theory of Integration" (1979), 27 *Can. Tax J.* 405.

Jones, D.P., "Sources of Income", in *Proceedings of 34th Tax Conf.* 911 (Can. Tax Foundation, 1982).

McDonnell, Thomas E., "The Taxation of Investment Income of Private Corporations and Personal Services Business Income", in *Proceedings of 34th Tax Conf.* 103 (Can. Tax Foundation, 1982).

Provenzano, Louis J., "The Impact of Escalating Provincial Tax Rates on an Owner-manager's Decision to Earn Investment and Active Business Income Directly or through a Corporation", in *Proceedings of 45th Tax Conf.* 33:1 (Can. Tax Foundation, 1993).

Strain, H. Larry, "Integration Revisited", in *Proceedings of 38th Tax Conf.* 9:1 (Can. Tax Foundation, 1986).

Dividends

Boultbee, I.A., "Minimizing the Taxation Effects of Dividends", in *Proceedings of 37th Tax Conf.* 7 (Can. Tax Foundation, 1985).

Drache, A.B.C., "Ontario Budget Produces Highest Corporate Tax Rate" (1991), 13 *Can. Taxpayer* 86.

Drache, A.B.C., "These Days, Dividends Look Better Than Interest" (1991), 13 *Can. Taxpayer* 172.

Institute for Fiscal Studies, *Equity for Companies: A Corporation Tax for the 1990's* — A Report of the IFS Capital Taxes Group (London, 1991).

Kennedy, Henry, "Tax Integration" (1990), 123 *CA Magazine* 43.

Lanthier, "A Critical Analysis of the Part IV Tax Provisions" (1978), 26 *Can. Tax J.* 625.

McCallum, J. Thomas, "Taxation of Portfolio Dividends" (1995), 5 *Can. Current Tax* 67.

McQuillan, Peter, "Investment Income and Active Business Income Earned By an Individual and Through a Corporation; A Comparative Analysis, 1987-1988", in *Proceedings of 39th Tax Conf.* 12:1 (Can. Tax Foundation, 1987).

Strain, William J., "Integration Revisited", in *Proceedings of 38th Tax Conf.* 9:1 (Can. Tax Foundation, 1986).

Other Investment Income

Broadhurst, David G., "Income Tax Treatment of Investment Corporations and Nonresident-Owned Investment Corporations", in *Proceedings of 37th Tax Conf.* 44 (Can. Tax Foundation, 1985).

Drache, A.B.C., "Ontario Budget Produces Highest Corporate Tax Rate" (1991), 13 *Can. Taxpayer* 86.

Drache, A.B.C., "These Days, Dividends Look Better Than Interest" (1991), 13 *Can. Taxpayer* 172.

Lanthier, "A Critical Analysis of the Part IV Tax Provisions" (1978), 26 *Can. Tax J.* 625.

McLean, D.S., "Canadian Investment Income — Property Used or Held by a Corporation in the Course of Carrying on a Business" (Comment on *R. v. Ensite Ltd.*, [1983] CTC 296 (F.C.A.); *R. v. Brown Boveri Howden Inc.*, [1983] CTC 301 (F.C.A.)) (1983), 31 *Can. Tax J.* 1006.

Nathanson, David D., "Active Versus Passive Once Again: Active Business Income and Investment Income of Canadian-Controlled Private Corporations", in *Proceedings of 33rd Tax Conf.* 908 (Can. Tax Foundation, 1981).

Novis, Derrick, "Tax Incentives: More Good Reasons to Invest" (1987), 120 *CA Magazine* No. 5, 68.

Other

Birnie, David A.G., "Shareholder's Buy-Sell Agreements: Some New Opportunities", in *Proceedings of 38th Tax Conf.* 13 (Can. Tax Foundation, 1986).

Drache, A.B.C., "A Handy-Dandy Formula" (1983), 5 *Can. Taxpayer* 109.

Durnford, John W., "Profits on the Sale of Shares: Capital Gains or Business Income? A Fresh Look at Irrigation Industries" (1987), 35 *Can. Tax J. 837.*

Farden, Eric N., *Income Tax for a Small Business* (E.N. Farden, 1985).

Potter, Christopher J., "Part IV Tax Implications in Butterfly Transactions" (1992), 40 *Can. Tax J.* 992.

Small Business Taxation, Audio Archives of Canada, 1984.

Williamson, Gordon, "Transfer of Assets To and From a Canadian Corporation", in *Proceedings of 38th Tax Conf.* 12:1 (Can. Tax Foundation, 1986).

CHAPTER XVII

PRIVATE CORPORATIONS: BUSINESS INCOME

References:
ITA:

S. 123   Corporate Tax Rate

S. 124   Deduction from Corporation Tax

BULLETINS, CIRCULARS & RULINGS:

IT-364   March 14, 1977   Commencement of Business Operations

We saw in Chapter XIV "Corporations and Shareholders: General" that there are various types of corporations: private, public, exempt, investment, etc. The scheme of taxation in respect of each of these types of corporations is different and takes into account their special needs and circumstances.

In Chapter XVI "Private Corporations: Investment Income" we looked at the rules for the taxation of investment income earned by private corporations. In this chapter we look at the taxation of the business income of private corporations.

1. THE STATUTORY SCHEME

The statutory scheme for private corporations reflects three distinct objectives:

1. High income taxpayers should not be able to defer tax on investment income by holding investments in personal holding corporations;

2. Corporate income should not be subject to double taxation; and

3. The income tax system should be used to support "small businesses" through tax incentives.

We saw in Chapter XVI that a special refundable tax on investment income prevents tax deferral on such income. In this chapter we look at the mechanism for controlling double taxation of business income and the tax incentives for small and family owned businesses.

There are three principal criteria that determine the amount of corporate tax on business income:

1. Type of corporation;

2. Type of income earned; and

3. Source of income.

The tax system encourages small and family owned businesses through rate incentives for Canadian-controlled private corporations, that are taxed at special low rates on certain forms of business income.

The taxation of private corporations also depends upon the type and source of income earned. Corporate income may derive from:

- Active business;
- Personal service business;
- Specified investment business; or
- Investment.

Each of these types of income may be earned in or outside of Canada and different rules apply in each case.

2. TAX INTEGRATION

One of the important objectives of the tax system is to control double taxation of corporate and shareholder income. Thus, the system seeks to "integrate" the tax payable by a corporation with the tax payable by its shareholders. "Integration" means that the amount of tax paid by a corporation and its shareholders on income should be the same, regardless whether the income is earned through a proprietorship, partnership or a corporation.

Corporate and shareholder taxes are integrated through a notional credit or imputation of corporate taxes against shareholder taxes. The shareholder receives a credit at the personal level for taxes previously paid at the corporate level. Thus, the two systems theoretically "integrate" the total amount of tax payable by corporations and their shareholders.

The model for tax integration is premised on certain assumptions:

- The combined federal and provincial corporate tax is 20 per cent on business income;
- Dividends to individual shareholders are included in their income at a grossed-up value to take into account the corporate tax previously paid; and
- Individual shareholders pay tax at 40 per cent and receive a tax credit equal to the amount of the tax previously paid by the corporation.

If all of these assumptions apply, the tax payable by a corporation on its business income will be exactly equal to the amount of tax that would have been paid by the individual shareholder if he or she had earned the income directly instead of through the corporation. In other words, the corporate tax would be fully "integrated" with the individual's tax. Example XVII.1 illustrates the theoretical framework of tax integration.

Example XVII.1

THEORETICAL MODEL OF INTEGRATION

Assume:

Federal corporate tax rate	12%
Provincial corporate tax rate	8%
Combined federal/provincial tax rate	20%
Shareholder federal/provincial marginal rate	40%
Dividend gross-up	25%
Active business income	$ 100

Then:

Corporate Tax:

Business income	$ 100
Corporate tax	20
Net income paid as dividend	$ 80
Shareholder Tax: *(only if shareholder is "individual")*	
Dividend received	$ 80
Gross-up for corporate tax *(1/4)*	20
82(1)(b) Amount taxable	$ 100
Tax thereon:	
Federal/provincial tax	$ 40
Credit for corporate taxes	20
Net tax payable	$ 20
Net cash	$ 60
Amount retained if dividend earned personally	$ 60
Tax differential *neutral system*	0

The model works perfectly if, and only if, *all* of the underlying assumptions apply.

(a) Over- and Under-integration

As previously noted, an underlying premise of the tax integration model is that the corporation pays corporate tax at a rate of 20 per cent (12 per cent federal plus 8 per cent provincial). Another premise is that the shareholder is taxed at a rate of 40 per cent. Both of these assumptions are essential to the model. Any variation from the assumed rates causes distortion and causes over- or under-integration.

In fact, the theoretical model does not operate in any of the provinces. There is always some over- or under-integration of corporate/shareholder taxes because:

- The combined rate of the federal/provincial corporate tax is not equal to 20 per cent in any province. The provinces levy tax independently of the federal government and set their own corporate tax rates regardless of the federal government's theoretical assumptions.

- Federal and provincial governments sometimes impose surtaxes, which effectively increase the basic tax rates. For example, there is a federal corporate surtax of 4 per cent (1995) payable on top of the basic federal tax. This immediately distorts the underlying assumption, namely, that the federal rate is 12 per cent. In addition, there can also be provincial surtaxes.

- The corporation may have a fiscal year that does not coincide with the calendar year. Thus, assumptions made about corporate tax rates on a fiscal year basis do not necessarily coincide with actual tax rates applicable to individuals who are taxable on a calendar year basis.

- A corporation is entitled to the 20 per cent rate of tax on a maximum of $200,000 of its active business income. Income in excess of $200,000 is taxable at the full federal tax rate of 28 per cent. The average provincial rate on income in excess of $200,000 is 16 per cent on top of the federal tax. This raises the "normal" tax rate to approximately 44 per cent plus surtaxes.

- The marginal tax rate of individuals in the top bracket is well in excess of 40 per cent. In 1994, for example, the top marginal rate varied from a low of 44 per cent (NWT) to a high of 54 per cent (Nova Scotia).

Thus, any combination of these factors distorts tax integration and results in double taxation of corporate income. The distortion is small for income levels below $200,000 and increases above that level.

Example XVII.2

INTEGRATION OF CORPORATE AND SHAREHOLDER TAXES

	Integration Model	Actual Taxes (Ontario)	Income Earned by Individual
Corporate income	$200,000	$ 200,000	
Taxable income	$200,000	$ 200,000	
Corporate tax	40,000	45,240	
Net income after tax	$160,000	$ 154,760	
Dividends paid	$160,000	$ 154,760	

Example XVII.2 (continued)

	Integration Model	Actual Taxes (Ontario)	Income Earned by Individual
Personal tax:			
Dividend income	$160,000	$ 154,760	
Gross-up	$ 40,000	$ 38,690	
Income earned directly			$200,000
Taxable Income	$200,000	$ 193,450	$200,000
Tax thereon:			
Federal tax	$ 27,313	$ 57,221	
Ontario tax		17,605	38,485
Federal/provincial tax	$ 40,000	$ 44,918	$ 95,707
Net income after tax	$120,000	$ 109,842	$104,293
Total tax paid:			
Corporate tax	$ 40,000	$ 45,240	$ 0
Personal	40,000	44,918	95,707
Total tax	$ 80,000	$ 901,158	$ 95,707
Net cash to individual:			
Income earned	$160,000	$ 154,760	$200,000
Personal tax paid	40,000	44,918	95,707
Net cash retained	$120,000	$ 109,842	$104,293

As the above example illustrates, notwithstanding the distortion of underlying assumptions, there is substantial integration of corporate and shareholder taxes for income less than $200,000. Indeed, there is a small advantage to earning $200,000 of income through a corporation because of the value of the dividend tax credit.

(b) Limits on Integration

The tax incentives for "small business" are an important part of the Canadian tax system. The incentives take two forms: Low rates of tax on business income and partial integration of corporate and shareholder taxes. But there is a cost to the incentives. They are, in effect, "tax expenditures". Hence, the system restricts the incentives. The low tax rate is available only to Canadian-controlled private corporations ("CCPCs") on active business income ("ABI") earned in Canada.

The basic rate of federal tax on a CCPC's active business income is 12 per cent on the first $200,000 of income, as compared with 28 per cent for other corporations. Assuming a provincial tax rate of approximately 11 per cent, the total rate of tax is 23 per cent. This rate of tax is available only to CCPCs that earn active business income in Canada.

Active business income in excess of $200,000 is taxable at the full corporate tax rate. Since the dividend tax credit is premised on the assumption that the corporation paid tax at a rate of 20 per cent, even in theory, there is a penalty for doing business through the corporate form on income in excess of $200000. As Example XVII.3 illustrates, double taxation of corporate income over $200,000 is systemic.

Example XVII.3

CORPORATE ABI IN EXCESS OF $200,000		
	Case A	**Case B**
Assume:		
Federal corporate tax rate	12%	
Provincial corporate tax rate	8%	
Federal/provincial corporate tax rate on ABI	20%	
Federal/provincial corporate tax (other income)	40%	
Shareholder federal/provincial marginal rate	40%	
Dividend gross-up	25%	
Active business income (ABI)	$ 200,000	$400,000
Business limit	$ 200,000	$200,000
Then:		
Corporate tax:		
Active business income	$ 200,000	$400,000
Corporate tax	40,000	120,000
Net income paid as dividend	$ 160,000	$280,000
Shareholder tax:		
Dividend received	$ 160,000	$280,000
Gross-up for corporate tax	40,000	70,000
Amount taxable	$ 200,000	$350,000
Tax thereon:		
Federal/provincial tax	$ 80,000	$140,000
Credit for corporate tax	40,000	70,000
Net tax payable	$ 40,000	$ 70,000
Total tax paid:		
Corporate	$ 40,000	$120,000
Personal	40,000	70,000
	$ 80,000	$190,000
Tax paid if income earned directly by individual	$ 80,000	$160,000
Penalty of earning income through corporation	$ 0	$ 30,000

Example XVII.4

DOUBLE TAXATION OF CORPORATE AND SHAREHOLDER INCOME

	Integration Model	Actual Taxes (Ontario)	Income Earned by Individual
Corporate income	$400,000	$ 400,000	
Taxable income	$400,000	$ 400,000	
Corporate tax	120,000	134,480	
Net income after tax	$280,000	$ 265,520	
Dividends paid	$280,000	$ 265,520	
Personal Tax:			
Dividend income	$280,000	$ 265,520	
Gross-up	$ 70,000	$ 66,380	
Income earned directly			$400,000
Taxable Income	$350,000	$ 331,900	$400,000
Tax thereon:			
Federal tax		$ 50,739	$119,861
Ontario tax		33,960	82,217
Federal/provincial tax	$ 70,000	$ 84,699	$202,079
Net income after tax	$210,000	$ 180,821	$197,921
Total tax paid:			
Corporate tax	$120,000	$ 134,480	$ 0
Personal	70,000	84,699	202,079
Total tax	$190,000	$ 219,179	$202,079
Net cash to individual:			
Income earned	$280,000	$ 265,520	$400,000
Personal tax paid	70,000	84,699	202,079
Net cash retained	$210,000	$ 180,821	$197,921
Double Tax Penalty		$ 17,100	9%

The double tax penalty increases substantially as income exceeds $200,000. This is because any income in excess of $200,000 is taxed at full corporate rates of approximately 45 per cent. In Example XVII.4 the penalty on $400000 income is approximately 9 percentage points for doing business through a corporation.

3. CANADIAN-CONTROLLED PRIVATE CORPORATIONS
Reference:
BULLETINS, CIRCULARS & RULINGS:

IT-458R	May 31, 1990	Canadian-Controlled Private Corporation
IT-484R	May 5, 1989	Business Investment Losses

A Canadian-controlled private corporation ("CCPC") is a private corporation that is resident in Canada and that is not controlled, directly or indirectly, in any manner whatsoever, by one or more non-resident persons, by one or more public corporations or by any combination of non-residents and public corporations.[1] The definition of CCPC does not require control by Canadian residents. Rather, a CCPC is defined as a private corporation that is *not controlled* by non-residents. Hence, a private corporation that is owned 50 per cent by non-residents and 50 per cent by residents qualifies as a CCPC.

4. ACTIVE BUSINESS INCOME
The basic federal corporate rate of tax is 38 per cent. This is reduced by the provincial tax credit of 10 per cent, which leaves the basic federal tax at 28 per cent. Thus, all corporations are initially taxable at 28 per cent.

A corporation that is a Canadian-controlled private corporation *throughout its taxation year* is entitled to a special tax credit. The credit (that is inaccurately referred to as the "small business *deduction*") is equal to 16 per cent of its first $200,000 of net Canadian "active business income" earned in the year.[2] Thus, the tax credit reduces the corporate tax payable by a CCPC on the first $200,000 of its active business income from 38 per cent to approximately 23 per cent.

Basic rate:	38.00%
Provincial abatement	(10.00)
	28.00%
Federal surtax (4%)	1.12
	29.12%
Small business deduction	(16.00)
Total federal	13.12
Provincial tax (Ontario)	9.50
Combined federal/provincial	22.62%

---

[1] Subs. 125(7) ("Canadian-controlled private corporation); IT-458R, "Canadian-Controlled Private Corporation" (May 31, 1990).

[2] Subs. 125(1).

The phrase "active business" is broadly defined to include *any business other than* a "specified investment business" or a "personal service business". Active business income includes income from an adventure or concern in the nature of trade.[3]

"Business" is defined to include "a profession, calling, trade, manufacture or undertaking of any kind whatever".[4]

The adjective "active" is also expansively interpreted. For example, in *Cadboro Bay:*[5]

> [A]ny quantum of business activity that gives rise to income in a taxation year for a private corporation in Canada is sufficient to make mandatory the characterization of such income as income from an "active business carried on in Canada".

Revenue Canada also accepts the broad interpretation of an "active" business:[6]

> Where a corporation was incorporated to earn income by doing business, there is a general presumption that profits arising from its activities are derived from a business. . . . Thus, from the time that the activities contemplated commence until they permanently cease, most corporations will be carrying on one or more businesses. . . .

(a) Presumptions

There is a *rebuttable* presumption that corporate income derives from business. In *Can. Marconi,*[7] for example, Madam Justice Wilson said:

> It is frequently stated in both the English and Canadian case law that there is in the case of a corporate taxpayer a rebuttable presumption that income received from or generated by an activity done in pursuit of an object set out in the corporation's constating documents is income from a business. . . .

> The question whether particular income is income from business or property remains a question of fact in every case. However, the fact that a particular taxpayer is a corporation is a very relevant matter to be considered because of the existence of the presumption and its implications in terms of the evidentiary burden resting on the appellant.

The presumption, coupled with the generous judicial interpretation of "active", gives an expansive meaning to the phrase "active business".

The presumption is not ironclad, however, and should be read in the context of the statutory structure for the taxation of corporate income. Business income is taxed quite differently from investment income. The judicial presumption should not be applied to negate the structure of the Act.

---

[3]   Subs. 125(7) ("active business").

[4]   Subs. 248(1) ("business").

[5]   *The Queen v. Cadboro Bay Hldg., ante,* [1977] CTC at 199, 77 DTC at 5123.

[6]   IT-73R4, "The Small Business Deduction — Income from an Active Business, a Specified Investment Business and a Personal Services Business" (February 13, 1989), para. 5.

[7]   *Can. Marconi Co. v. The Queen,* [1986] 2 CTC 465 at 468, 470, 86 DTC 6526 at 6528, 6529 (S.C.C.).

(b) Business vs. Investment Income

The distinction between investment income and business income is essentially a question of fact that depends upon:[8]

- Activity associated with the generation of the income;
- Number and value of transactions;
- Relationship between the income in question and total income; and
- Relationship between the value of the assets producing the income in question and total assets.

The greater the volume of activity and the value of transactions, the closer the relationship between the income earned and the total income and assets of the taxpayer, the greater the likelihood that the income is "business income".

Once it is determined that a corporation's activities constitute a business, its income therefrom is almost invariably characterized as flowing from an "active business", *unless* the income is from a "specified investment business" or a "personal service business".[9]

(c) Incidental Business Income

Cash and short-term liquid investments that are an integral part of a business are considered business assets. Hence, they generate business income.[10] The critical element is whether there is a substantive dependence and reliance upon the investments for the operation of the business.[11]

A business engaged in the lending of money under security of mortgages, investing in securities and the renting of property can qualify as an active business.[12]

---

[8] *Can. Marconi Co. v. The Queen, ante.*

[9] Subs. 125(7) ("active business"), ("personal service business"), ("specified investment business").

[10] *Irving Garber Sales Canada Ltd. v. Canada*, [1992] 2 CTC 260, 92 DTC 6498 (F.C.T.D.).

[11] *Majestic Tool & Mold Ltd. v. The Queen*, [1993] 2 CTC 2813, 94 DTC 1220 (T.C.C.) (interest from term deposits was active business income).

[12] *The Queen v. Rockmore Invt. Ltd., ante.*

Income that is incidental to an active business, such as investment of surplus cash, rental of excess space, interest on accounts receivable and certain investment income from associated corporations is also active business income.[13]

5. THE SMALL BUSINESS DEDUCTION

References:

ITA:

S. 125   Small Business Deduction

BULLETINS, CIRCULARS & RULINGS:

IT-73R4	February 13, 1989	The Small Business Deduction — Income From an Active Business, a Specified Investment Business and a Personal Services Business
IT-206R	October 29, 1979	Separate Businesses

The small business deduction is a tax incentive for small and family owned Canadian businesses. Hence, the deduction is limited by three parameters:

1. The corporation's active business income;
2. The corporation's Canadian source taxable income; and
3. An overall limit of $200,000.

These restrictions ensure that the deduction is claimed only by small corporate businesses with Canadian-source active business income. The small business deduction is not available to proprietorships and partnerships, no matter that they are small or family owned.

More specifically, a corporation's small business deduction in any year is limited to 16 per cent of the *least* of its:[14]

- *Net* Canadian active business income for the taxation year;

---

[13] Subs. 125(7) ("income of the corporation"); see subs. 129(4.1) ("specified investment business" income specifically excluded from active business income and included in income from property); *The Queen v. Marsh & McLennan Ltd.,* [1983] CTC 231, 83 DTC 5180; leave to appeal to S.C.C. refused 52 NR 231 (meaning of what is ancillary, incidental or subsidiary to active business); *The Queen v. Ensite Ltd.,* [1983] CTC 296, 83 DTC 5315; affirmed [1986] CTC 459, 86 DTC 6521 (S.C.C.) (test is whether property employed and risked in business; property used to fulfil a mandatory condition precedent to trade was property used or held in the business); *Alamar Farms Ltd. v. The Queen,* [1993] 1 CTC 2682, 93 DTC 121 (T.C.C.) (rental payments from surface leases and royalty income was incidental to taxpayer's principal activity of farming and, therefore, active business income). See also subs. 129(6) (investment income from associated corporation deemed to be active business income).

[14] Subs. 125(1). Prior to 1985 there was a fourth restriction: the small business deduction was not available to a CCPC with a cumulative deduction account in excess of $1,000,000.

- Taxable income for the taxation year less 10/3 of its foreign non-business income tax credit and 10/4 of its foreign business income tax credit; and

- Business limit, which is $200,000 unless the corporation is associated with another corporation.

The effect of these three limiting factors is to restrict the availability of the small business deduction to the active business income of "small" Canadian corporations.

Each of the three limits to the small business deduction plays a different role. The first limitation ensures that the deduction is confined to "active business income" and excludes investment income and income from a personal service business.[15]

The second limitation ensures that the small business deduction is confined to domestic source income and is not claimed on foreign income that has not been taxed in Canada and on account of which the corporation claims a foreign tax credit.[16]

The corporation's taxable income is reduced by 10/3 of its foreign non-business income tax credit. The factor (10/3) is based on the assumption that the corporation paid a tax of 30 per cent on its foreign non-business income. For example, assume that a corporation earns $100 foreign non-business income on which it pays $30 tax. Then, 10/3 × $30 = $100, which is the amount deducted from the corporation's taxable income. Similarly, the multiplication factor of 10/4 assumes that the corporation has paid foreign tax at a rate of 40 per cent on its foreign business income.

The third restriction limits the *annual* deduction to a maximum of $200,000[17] so as to restrict the deduction to "small" businesses. The overall limit also restricts the revenue loss from the tax expenditure.

6. CORPORATE PARTNERSHIPS

Partnership income is generally calculated at the partnership level and allocated to the partners according to their respective shares. Each partner then includes in income his or her own share of the partnership's income or loss for the fiscal period.

For the purposes of the small business deduction, a corporation is required to include in its income its share of the active business income or loss of any partnership of which it is a member. A corporation does this by including in its income its "specified partnership income" and deducting therefrom its "specified partnership losses".[18]

---

[15] Para. 125(1)(a), subs. 125(7) ("active business").

[16] Para. 125(1)(b).

[17] Para. 125(1)(c); subss. 125(2), (3) (business limit of $200,000 to be allocated among group of associated corporations).

[18] Paras. 125(1)(a), (7)(f), (g).

Since the maximum amount of active business income on which a corporation may claim the small business deduction is limited to $200,000, it is necessary to ensure that corporations cannot multiply the limit by carrying on business in partnerships. Otherwise, corporations carrying on business in partnership might be able to claim a much larger deduction.

There are two anti-avoidance rules to ensure that the $200,000 maximum limit is not abused: (1) a specific formula; and (2) a general rule.

A corporation's "specified partnership income" is the lesser of its share of the partnership's income from active businesses in Canada and the proportion of the $200,000 limit that is its share of the total partnership income.[19] For example, where a partnership comprised of five equal corporate partners earns active business income of $1,000,000, each corporate partner has "specified partnership income" of $200,000 (that is, 1/5 × $1,000,000) for the purpose of calculating its small business deduction.

There is also an additional anti-avoidance rule that can be used against corporate partnerships. Where a corporation becomes a member of multiple partnerships in order to claim an increased small business deduction, the Minister is entitled to disregard the multiple partnerships and reduce the amount of the partnership income that can qualify for the deduction in the hands of the corporate partner.[20]

The Minister may also "look through" several tiers of partnerships. For example, where a corporation is a member of a partnership which in turn is a member of another partnership, the corporation can be deemed to be a member of the second tier partnership. Its share of income can be deemed to be the amount to which it is directly or indirectly entitled through the first and second partnerships.[21] Thus, the corporation's share of the small business deduction may be determined by looking through multiple tiers of partnership to ensure that it does not obtain a larger claim than that to which it would otherwise be entitled.

The small business deduction is intended to benefit Canadian-controlled private corporations. To ensure that corporate partnership income is treated in the same manner as if the business were carried on directly by the corporation, income of a partnership that is controlled, *directly or indirectly, in any matter whatever,* by non-resident persons or public corporations does not qualify for the small business deduction.[22] Hence, an otherwise non-qualifying corporation cannot claim the small business deduction by structuring its affairs through a partnership.

---

[19] Subs. 125(7) ("specified partnership income").

[20] Subs. 125(6).

[21] Subs. 125(6.1).

[22] Subs. 125(6.2).

7. ASSOCIATED CORPORATIONS

References:

ITA:

Subs. 251(5)   Control by Related Groups, Options, etc.

S. 256   Associated Corporations

BULLETINS, CIRCULARS & RULINGS:

IT-64R3   March 9, 1992   Corporations: Association and Control — After 1988

The attractiveness of the small business deduction is an obvious incentive for taxpayers to set up multiple corporations that are created solely for the purpose of multiplying the deduction. A special set of rules controls artificial multiplication of the deduction by restricting the maximum amount that may be claimed by a group of associated corporations.[23]

Where two or more Canadian-controlled private corporations are "associated" with each other, the aggregate claim of the associated group is restricted to $200,000. The group is required to file an agreement allocating the annual business limit among the associated corporations. The agreement must be filed annually with the Minister.[24] The allocation may be in any amount agreed upon by the group.[25]

Where a corporation in an associated group fails to sign and file the prescribed form allocating its annual business limit, the Minister is required, after 30 days and proper notice, to assess the corporation on the basis of the Minister's own allocation.[26]

Corporations can be associated with each other because of interrelated shareholdings[27] or through Ministerial discretion.[28]

(a) Interrelated Shareholdings

Corporations are associated with each other if they are subject to common control and common ownership of shares by a person or a related group of persons.

---

[23] Subs. 125(2).

[24] Subs. 125(3).

[25] Subs. 125(3).

[26] Subs. 125(4).

[27] Subs. 256(1).

[28] Subs. 256(2.1).

The central element underlying "association" is control, whether *de jure* or *de facto*. There are five basic rules to determine association between corporations. There are also several anti-avoidance rules to prevent taxpayers from circumventing the basic rules.

(i) Control of One Corporation by Another

A corporation is associated with another corporation in a taxation year if at any time in the year one of the corporations controls (directly, indirectly *or in any manner whatever*) the other.[29]

Example XVII.5

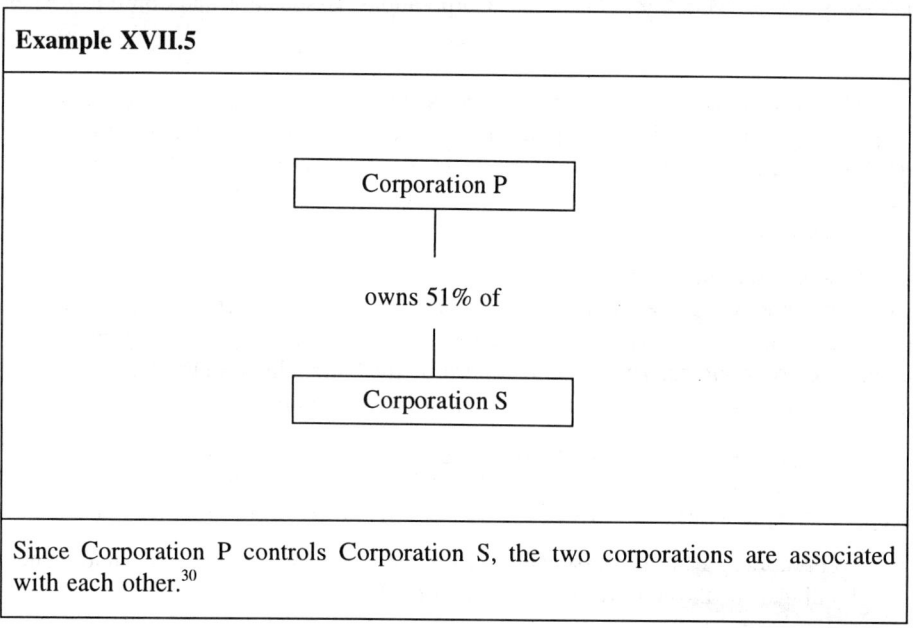

Since Corporation P controls Corporation S, the two corporations are associated with each other.[30]

"Control" is generally manifested through voting rights. Thus, 51 per cent of voting power is usually sufficient to secure control for most corporate purposes. Control may,

---

[29] Para. 256(1)(*a*).

[30] Subs. 251(5) expands the meaning of "control" set out in, e.g., *Buckerfield's Ltd. v. M.N.R.*, [1964] CTC 504, 64 DTC 5301 (Ex. Ct.)(corporations associated due to common ownership of shares by third party); see also *Dworkin Furs (Pembroke) Ltd. v. M.N.R.*, [1967] CTC 50, 67 DTC 5035 (S.C.C.) (absence of majority votes in election of board of directors indicated that one corporation was not controlled by the other); *Br. Amer. Tobacco Co. v. I.R.C.*, [1943] 1 All ER 13 (H.L.) (owners of majority of voting power in a company are persons who are in effective control of its affairs and fortunes, *per* Viscount Simon LC at 15).

however, also exist by virtue of other factors. For example, the power to wind up a corporation and appropriate the majority of its assets may constitute effective control.[31]

(ii) Control of Corporations by Same Person

A corporation is associated with another corporation in a taxation year if at any time in the year both corporations are controlled (directly, indirectly *or in any manner whatever*) by the same person or group of persons.[32]

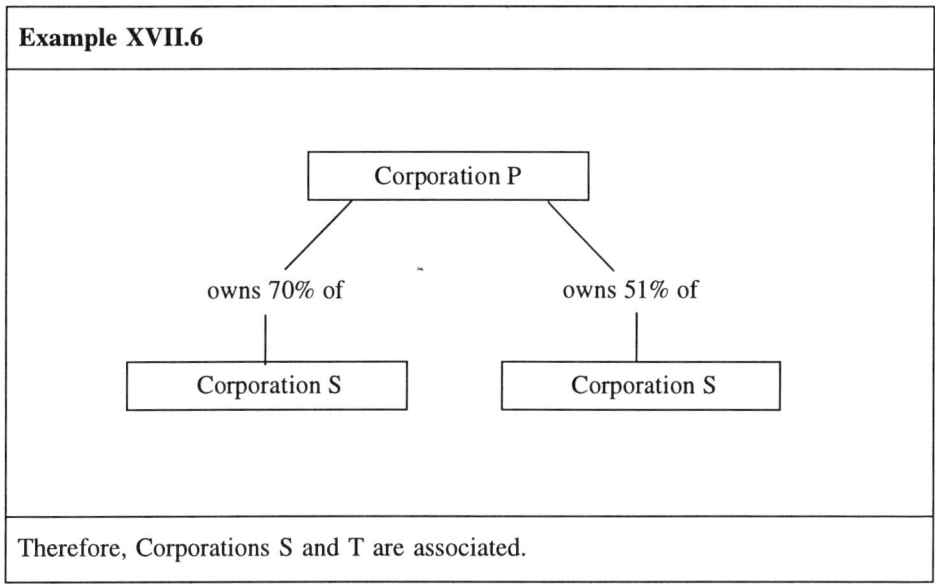

Example XVII.6

owns 70% of   owns 51% of

Corporation P

Corporation S   Corporation S

Therefore, Corporations S and T are associated.

---

[31] *The Queen v. Imp. Gen. Properties Ltd.*, [1985] 2 CTC 299 at 302, 85 DTC 5500 at 5503 (S.C.C.) (in interpreting subs. 256(1), "the court is not limited to a highly technical and narrow interpretation of the legal rights attached to the shares of a corporation").

[32] Para. 256(1)(*b*).

Example XVII. 7

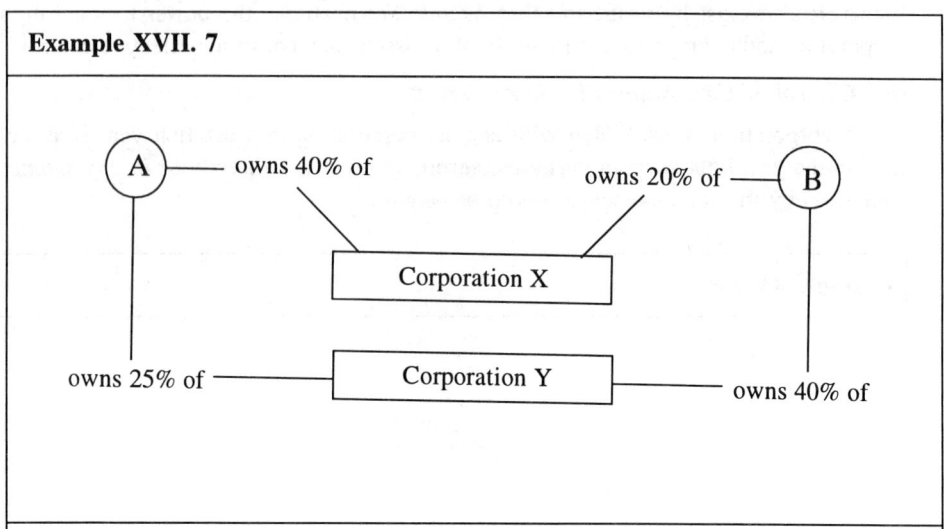

Therefore, Corporations X and Y are controlled by the same group of persons, A and B. Note that two persons can constitute a "group" despite the absence of any familial relationship between them.[33]

(iii) Cross-ownership of Shares

A corporation is associated with another corporation in a taxation year if at any time in the year each of the corporations is controlled (directly, indirectly, or *in any manner whatever*) by one person, and the person who controls one of the corporations is related to the person who controls the other, and *either one* of those persons owns, in respect of each corporation, not less than 25 per cent of the issued shares of any class (other than a specified class) of the capital stock thereof.[34]

---

[33] See also para. 251(5)(*b*).

[34] Para. 256(1)(*c*).

Example XVII. 8

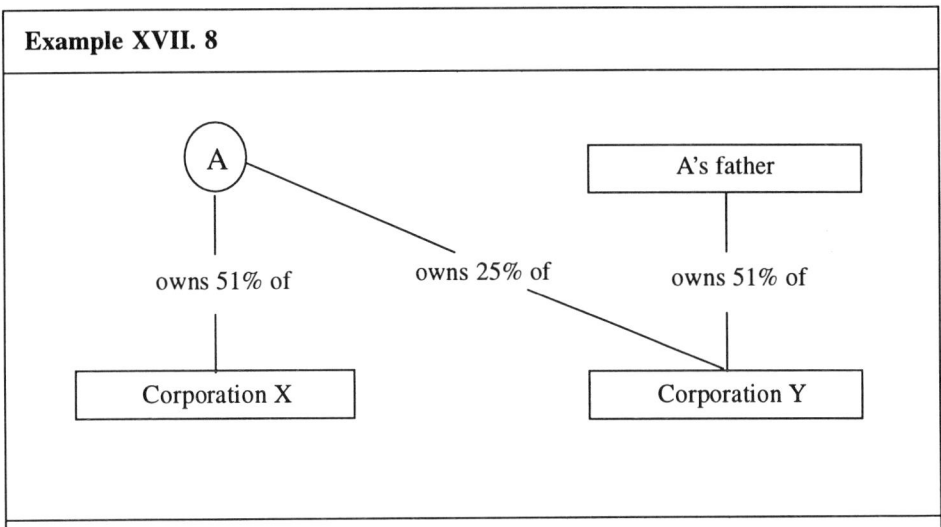

owns 51% of   owns 25% of   owns 51% of

Corporations X and Y are associated; each is controlled by one person, those persons are related, and there is a 25 per cent cross-ownership in the shares of Corporation Y.

(iv) Group Control and Cross-ownership

A corporation is associated with another corporation in a taxation year if at any time in the year one of the corporations is controlled (directly, indirectly, or *in any manner whatever*) by one person and that person is related to each member of a group of persons that controls the other corporation, and that person owns not less than 25 per cent of the issued shares of any class (other than a specified class) of the capital stock of the other corporation.[35]

---

[35] Para. 256(1)(*d*).

Example XVII. 9

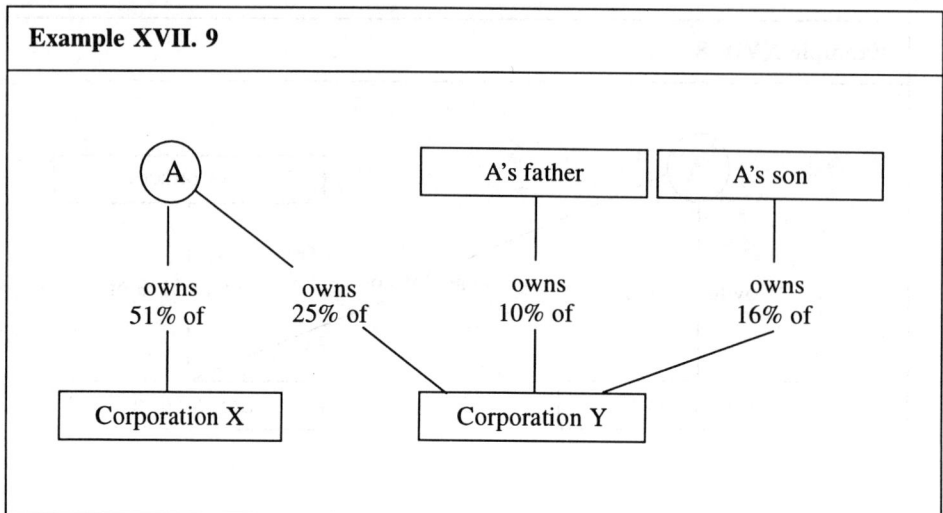

Corporations X and Y are associated; Corporation X is controlled by A, who is related to each member of a group of persons (himself, his father and his son) who together control Corporation Y. In addition, A has cross-ownership of 25 per cent of the shares of Corporation Y.

(v) Control by Related Group and Cross-ownership

A corporation is associated with another corporation in a taxation year if at any time in the year each of the corporations is controlled (directly, indirectly, *or in any manner whatever*) by a related group and each of the members of one of the related groups is related to *all* of the members of the other related group, and one or more persons who are members of both related groups owns not less than 25 per cent of the issued shares of any class (other than a specified class) of the capital stock of each corporation.[36]

---

[36]   Para. 256(1)(*e*).

Example XVII. 10

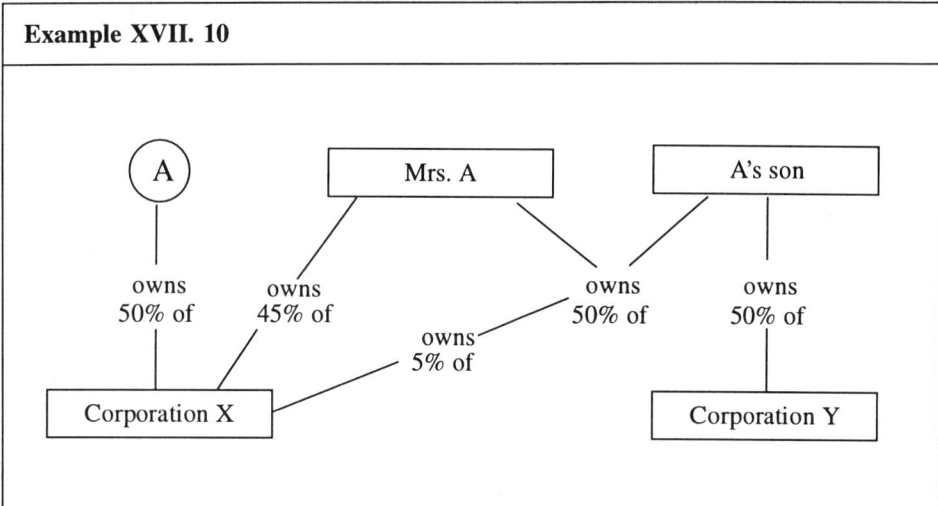

A and Mrs. A are a related group in control of Corporation X. Mrs. A and her son are a related group in control of Corporation Y. Each member of the group in control of Corporation X is related to each member of the group in control of Corporation Y. The related group in control of Corporation Y (Mrs. A and her son) own 25 per cent or more of Corporation X. Therefore, Corporations X and Y are associated.

(b) Specified Class of Shares

The 25 per cent cross-ownership rules do not apply to shares of a "specified class". "Specified shares" are generally non-voting preferred shares that confer minimal shareholder power.

More specifically, a class of shares is a "specified class" if:[37]

- the shares are neither convertible nor exchangeable;
- the shares are non-voting;
- dividends payable on the shares are fixed in amount or rate;
- the annual dividend rate on the shares, as a percentage of the fair market value of the consideration for which the shares were issued, does not exceed the prescribed rate of interest at the time when the shares were issued; and
- the amount that a holder of the shares is entitled to receive on their redemption, cancellation or acquisition by the corporation (or a person with whom the corporation does not deal at arm's length) does not exceed the fair market value of the consideration for which the shares were issued plus any unpaid dividends.

---

[37] Subs. 256(1.1).

Thus, a person can invest funds in a corporation that is controlled by a related person without subjecting his or her own corporation to a reduced small business deduction if the investment is in fixed-rate, non-voting, preferred shares.

(c) Association with Third Corporation

Two otherwise unassociated corporations are associated with each other if they are both associated with the same third corporation.[38] For example, if Alpha Limited is associated with Beta Limited and Gamma Limited, then Beta Limited and Gamma Limited are also associated with each other.

This rule does not apply for the purposes of the small business deduction if the third corporation does not claim the deduction. The third corporation may not claim the deduction either because it explicitly elects not to do so or because it does not qualify for the deduction because it is not a "Canadian-controlled private corporation".

8. CORPORATE CONTROL

Reference:

BULLETINS, CIRCULARS & RULINGS:

IT-419   July 10, 1978   Meaning of Arm's Length

There are two forms of corporate control: *De jure* and *De facto*. The word "control" without any qualifier means *de jure* control. The phrase "controlled, directly or indirectly in any manner whatever" is used to describe *de facto* control. Either form can result in corporations being associated with each other.

(a) *De Jure* Control

(i) *Voting Power*

Generally speaking, *de jure* corporate control means the ownership of a sufficient number of shares to be able to elect a majority of the board of directors of a corporation.[39] Thus, *de jure* control is the legal power to manage a corporation's affairs and the power to exercise corporate control in the long run.[40]

This test does not always provide a clear answer. For example, where a corporation's shareholdings are divided equally between two shareholders, neither has the power to elect a majority of the directors, and the corporation may not be legally controlled by either person.

---

[38] Subs. 256(2).

[39] *Buckerfields' Ltd. v. M.N.R., ante.*

[40] *Donald Applicators Ltd. v. M.N.R.*, [1969] CTC 98, 69 DTC 5122; affirmed [1971] CTC 402, 71 DTC 5202 (S.C.C.).

(ii) Appropriation of Assets

The lack of power to elect a majority of the board of directors is not always determinative of *de jure* corporate control. Control may be inferred from some other form of corporate power, for example, the power to wind up a corporation and appropriate its assets.[41]

(iii) "Group of Persons"

For the purposes of determining whether a corporation is controlled by a group of persons, "group" means *any* two or more persons each of whom owns the corporation's shares.[42]

The existence of a group of persons does not depend upon common links between the persons, the size of the collectivity, or a common intention to obtain a tax benefit. Ownership of shares in the corporation by two or more persons is sufficient to constitute a group.

(iv) Control by Two Groups

A corporation may be controlled by a person or a particular group of persons notwithstanding that it is also controlled by another person or group of persons.[43] Hence, it is possible for a corporation to be controlled by several persons or groups of persons.

Where a group of persons owns shares of the capital stock of a corporation, the fact that an individual member of the group owns, by himself or herself, enough shares to control the corporation does not alter the fact that the group also controls the corporation. Hence, a corporation may be controlled by different persons or groups of persons at the same time. This can cause it to be associated with several corporations each of which may otherwise be unconnected with each other.

(v) Market Value Control

A corporation may be controlled by virtue of a person owning more than 50 per cent of the fair market value of its shares, even though the shares do not represent majority voting power in the corporation.

A corporation is deemed to be controlled by another corporation, person or a group of persons where the "controller" owns:[44]

- Shares that represent more than 50 per cent of the fair market value of *all* of the corporation's issued and outstanding shares; or

- Common shares that represent more than 50 per cent of the fair market value of all of the corporation's issued and outstanding common shares.

---

[41] *The Queen v. Imp. Gen. Properties Ltd.*, [1985] 2 CTC 299, 85 DTC 5500 (S.C.C.).

[42] Para. 256(1.2)(*a*).

[43] Subpara. 256(1.2)(*b*)(ii).

[44] Para. 256(1.2)(*c*).

This test is based on the premise that the fair market value of an individual's shareholdings in a corporation may be as relevant an indication of real power as a test based on the legal ability of shareholders to elect a majority of the corporation's board of directors.

The market value test does, however, raise very difficult valuation issues, particularly in the context of corporations that have complex share capital structures. Hence, in certain circumstances access to the small business deduction may be uncertain and subject to challenge on the basis of a share valuation conducted after the claim for the deduction has been made.

The fair market value of shares must be determined without regard to the voting attributes of the shares of the capital stock of the corporation.[45] Hence, it is quite possible that the control of a corporation may shift between different groups as the value attributable to the shares of the corporation changes over time. Since the value of a corporation is usually attributable to the capitalized value of its earnings, common shares valued without voting rights may not have any value where the corporation does not have a history of established earnings. This rule is particularly difficult to apply in the context of common shares of a newly-created corporation.

Since the common shares of a new enterprise may not have any substantial market value if they are valued on the basis that they are non-voting shares with no evidence of established earning power, it is possible that such a corporation may be associated with another corporation on the basis of its issued preferred shares. Similarly, the control of a corporation may shift when the corporation is in financial difficulty, because the common shares will presumably reflect those difficulties and diminish in value. Hence, it is entirely possible for a corporation to be denied access to the full small business deduction and low tax rate at the very time when it is most likely in need of financial assistance.

(vi) Holding Corporations

A shareholder of a holding corporation that has a subsidiary is considered to have an equity ownership in the subsidiary corporation.[46] The Act "looks through" the holding corporation and attributes ownership of the subsidiary's shares directly to the shareholder of the holding corporation. The attributed ownership of the shares is in the proportion that the fair market value of the holding corporation's shares owned by the shareholder is to the fair market value of all of the issued and outstanding shares of the holding corporation at that time. The fair market value of the shares is determined on the assumption that all of the outstanding shares are non-voting.[47]

---

[45] Para. 256(1.2)(g).

[46] Para. 256(1.2)(d).

[47] Para. 256(1.2)(g).

(vii) Partnerships

A similar "look through" rule also applies to shares owned by a partnership. A member of a partnership that owns shares of a corporation is considered to directly own his or her proportionate interest in those shares.[48] Where the income and loss of the partnership for its fiscal period is nil, the proportion is calculated on the assumption that the partnership's income is $1,000,000 in that period.

(viii) Trusts

Under trust law, a trustee is the legal owner of shares held in trust by him or her. For tax purposes, corporate shares owned by a trust are considered to be owned by the beneficiaries of the trust and, in some cases, by the person from whom the trust property was received.[49]

(A) Testamentary Trusts

Where, in a testamentary trust, some of the beneficiaries are entitled to all of the income of the trust prior to the death of one of them or all of them, and no other person is entitled to any capital of the trust before that time, the shares are deemed to be owned by the beneficiaries before that time.[50] If the trust is a discretionary trust, all of the discretionary beneficiaries are deemed to own the shares.[51]

(B) Other Trusts

Where the trust is not a testamentary trust, each beneficiary is deemed to own a proportion of the shares based upon the fair market value of his or her interest in the trust.[52] If the trust is a discretionary trust, all of the discretionary beneficiaries are deemed to own the shares.[53]

(C) Reversionary Trusts

Where a trust is a "reversionary" trust, the person from whom the property of the trust was received is also deemed to own the shares.[54] The result of these rules is that it is entirely possible that more than one person can be deemed to own the same shares at the same time.

---

[48] Para. 256(1.2)(*e*).

[49] Para. 256(1.2)(*f*).

[50] Cl. 256(1.2)(*f*)(i)(B).

[51] Cl. 256(1.2)(*f*)(i)(A).

[52] Subpara. 256(1.2)(*f*)(iii).

[53] Subpara. 256(1.2)(*f*)(ii).

[54] Subpara. 256(1.2)(*f*)(iv).

(ix) Attribution Rules

Where the shares of a corporation are owned (or deemed to be owned) by a child who is under 18 years of age, the shares are considered to be owned by the child's parents.[55] This rule does not apply if the child manages the business and affairs of the corporation without significant influence by the parents. The shares may be attributed to either parent, depending upon the purpose of the determination.

(x) Options and Rights

A person who has an option or a right to acquire or to control the voting rights of shares is treated as if he or she owned those shares.[56] This rule does not apply where the option or right is not exercisable until the death, bankruptcy or permanent disability of a designated individual. Thus, an option or right that is triggered under a shareholders' agreement may be exempt from the deeming provision, provided that the option or right is exercisable only upon the death, bankruptcy or permanent disability of the individual designated in the agreement.

Similarly, where a person has a right to cause a corporation to redeem, acquire or cancel its shares owned by *other shareholders,* he or she is deemed to be in the same position in relation to the control of the incorporation and ownership of its shares *as if* the shares had already been redeemed, acquired or cancelled by the corporation.[57]

(xi) Tax Avoidance

The Act also contains a special anti-avoidance rule to catch any cases that may escape through the net of the specific rules described above.

Two or more corporations may be associated with each other where *one* of the main reasons for the separate existence of the corporations in a taxation year is to reduce the amount of tax that would otherwise have to be paid.[58] For example, where two parts of what could reasonably be considered to be one business (for example, manufacturing and sales of a single product line) are carried out by two corporations each of which is controlled by different persons, the two separate corporations may be deemed to be associated with other for the purposes of the small business deduction. If they are associated, the two corporations may claim only one small business deduction in respect of the income generated by both businesses.

To avoid association under this rule, it is necessary for the taxpayer to establish, in effect, that *none* of the main reasons for the existence of multiple corporations is to

---

[55] Subs. 256(1.3).

[56] Para. 256(1.4)(*a*).

[57] Para. 256(1.4)(*b*).

[58] Subs. 256(2.1).

reduce the amount of tax that would otherwise be payable.[59] The intention of the corporations is to be inferred from those by whom it is managed and controlled. The taxpayer must establish that the separate existence of the corporations was dictated *solely* by business expediency and not by tax considerations.[60]

(b) *De Facto* Control

The *de facto* test focuses on the influence, as opposed to the power, that a person or group of persons may have on a corporation. It is premised on the theory that there is more to control than mere legal power as expressed in voting rights.

Although the purpose of the *de facto* test is to prevent artificial manipulation of the associated corporation rules, it does not provide any greater certainty than the more traditional common law doctrines. Thus, the *de facto* test merely substitutes statutory uncertainty for judicial uncertainty.

(i) *"Directly or Indirectly in Any Manner Whatever"*

A corporation is associated with another corporation if the two corporations are controlled "directly or indirectly in any manner whatever" by the same person or by persons with common and related interests.[61] A corporation is considered to be "controlled, directly or indirectly in any manner whatever" by a person where the person has any *"direct or indirect influence"* that, *if exercised*, would result in control in fact of the corporation.[62]

The critical test in each case is to determine whether a person or group of persons ("the controller") has the requisite direct or indirect influence over the affairs of a corporation. The controlling person may be another corporation, an individual or a group of persons. For example, a corporation may be controlled by a person who owns less than 50 per cent of the voting shares of the corporation if the remaining shares are widely distributed among other persons (such as employees) who could reasonably be considered to be amenable to the wishes of the person with "influence".

(A) Influence

The test does not require the "controller" to have any legally-enforceable right or power over the corporation. It is sufficient that the controller have *influence*, whether direct or indirect, over the affairs of the corporation.

---

[59] See *Maritime Forwarding Ltd. v. The Queen*, [1988] 1 CTC 186, 88 DTC 6114 (F.C.T.D.)(incorporating to reduce leasing costs not sustainable as main reason for creation of multiple corporations); *Kencar Ent. Ltd. v. M.N.R.*, [1987] 2 CTC 246, 87 DTC 5450 (*sub nom. Kencar Ent. Ltd. v. The Queen*) (F.C.T.D.) ("Minister's direction could only be challenged by establishing that none of the main reasons for the separate existence of the corporations was to reduce the amount of tax payable").

[60] *Doris Trucking Co. v. M.N.R.*, [1968] CTC 303, 68 DTC 5204 (Ex. Ct.).

[61] Subs. 256(5.1).

[62] Subs. 256(5.1).

(B) Potential Influence

The test is predicated upon the presence of potential influence, and not upon the actual exercise of influence in a particular case. In other words, the "controller" does not have to actually exercise influence over the affairs of the corporation; he or she merely has to have sufficient influence that, *if exercised*, could result in control in fact of the corporation. The taxpayer faces a difficult task to discharge his or her burden of proof. He or she must prove a negative proposition, namely, that he or she does not have influence over the corporation.

(C) Exceptions

A person may have influence over another by virtue of a legal arrangement between them that governs the manner in which a business is carried on by a corporation. Provided that the corporation and the "controller" are dealing with each other at arm's length, the *de facto* control test does not apply where the controller's influence derives only from an agreement or arrangement the main purpose of which is to govern the business relationship between the corporation and the controller. For example, where a franchise agreement or lease gives the franchisor or lessor some power to regulate the products sold by the corporation or the hours during which it conducts its business, the power does not, *in and of itself,* result in the franchisor or lessor having *de facto* control over the corporation.

9. PERSONAL SERVICES BUSINESS INCOME

Reference:

BULLETINS, CIRCULARS & RULINGS:

IT-525   April 20, 1990   Performing Artists

Employment income is taxed at progressive marginal rates.[63] Corporate income is taxed at a flat rate.[64] Since the corporate tax rate applied to active business income earned by a Canadian-controlled private corporation is approximately 23 per cent, there is a considerable advantage in converting employment income (which can be taxed at a rate as high as 54 per cent) into business income.

The most common technique of converting employment income into business income was to use a corporation to render personal services. Thus X, an employee of *Opco Ltd.*, might incorporate *Newco* to render services to *Opco*. In *Sazio,*[65] for example, the taxpayer, a football coach, persuaded his football club to hire his personal corporation to provide the club with coaching services, which he had previously

---

[63] S. 117; see also Chapters V "Income From an Office or Employment", XIII "Computation of Tax Payable".

[64] S. 123.

[65] *Sazio v. M.N.R.,* [1968] CTC 579, 69 DTC 5001 (Ex. Ct.).

provided directly to the club. The fees paid to the corporation were then taxed as business, instead of employment, income.

To discourage the conversion of personal services into business income, "personal services business income" ("PSBI") is taxed on a gross income basis, with only minimal deductions. Thus, PSBI is taxed on the same basis as employment income, and is not eligible for the small business deduction.

A personal services business is a business in which a major shareholder of a corporation provides services through the corporation in circumstances where he or she would normally provide the services as an employee. Thus, in effect, the shareholder is an "incorporated employee".

More specifically, a "personal services business" is a business carried on by a corporation where the services are performed on behalf of the corporation by an individual (or any person related to the individual) who is a specified shareholder of the corporation, and the individual can, ignoring the interposition of the corporation between him- or herself and the person to whom the services are rendered, "reasonably be regarded" as an officer or employee of the entity *to which* the services are provided.[66]

The test comes down to this: if one notionally ignores the existence of the "incorporated employee's" corporation, can the relationship between the individual and the person to whom he or she renders services be regarded as an employment relationship?[67] If so, the income is PSBI, and is taxed accordingly.

There is no clear cut and obvious answer in every case to determine whether corporate income is active business income or PSBI. For example, Revenue Canada accepts that self-employed real estate agents who incorporate to provide real estate services are considered independent contractors and not "incorporated employees". Thus, their income is eligible for the small business deduction. In contrast, the Department is hesitant to extend independent contractor status to corporate directors who provide management services on an exclusive contract basis. An individual who provides management services to, and is a director of, several corporations may, however, be in a better position.

(a) Specified Shareholder

A "specified shareholder" of a corporation is a person who owns directly or indirectly 10 per cent or more of the issued shares of *any* class of the capital stock of the corporation or a related corporation.[68]

---

[66] Subs. 125(7) ("personal services business").

[67] See, generally, *Wiebe Door Services Ltd. v. M.N.R.*, [1986] 2 CTC 200, 87 DTC 5025 (F.C.A.).

[68] Subs. 248(1) ("specified shareholder"); s. 251.

A taxpayer is deemed to own each share of the capital stock of a corporation that is owned by a person with whom he or she does not deal at arm's length. Hence, for example, where a taxpayer's spouse owns 10 per cent or more of the issued shares of a corporation, the taxpayer is also a "specified shareholder" of the corporation.

Each beneficiary of a trust is deemed to own his or her proportion of all the shares owned by the trust. The proportion is determined by reference to the total fair market value of the beneficial interests at the particular time. Similarly, each member of a partnership is deemed to own his or her proportionate share of all the shares owned by the partnership.

There are two exceptions to PSBI:[69]

1. The income of a corporation that throughout the year employs more than five full time employees is not considered PSBI; and

2. Amounts paid to a corporation by an associated corporation are not PSBI.

(b) Deductions

In computing PSBI, a corporation generally may deduct only expenses in respect of salaries and benefits paid to the "incorporated employee".[70] In effect, PSBI is taxed on a gross income basis, which puts it on the same footing as employment income.

PSBI is taxable at the full federal corporate rate of 38 per cent. It is not eligible for the small business deduction or the refund of tax on dividends.

10. SMALL BUSINESS CORPORATIONS

Reference:

ITA:

Subs. 110.6(2.1)   Capital Gains Deduction — Qualified Small Business Corporation Shares

Generally speaking, an individual may claim a capital gains exemption of $500,000 for gains on the sale of shares of a small business corporation ("SBC").[71]

The exemption is available on a disposition of SBC shares, but only if the shares "qualify". The additional qualifications deal with minimum share ownership periods and asset use during the qualifying period. Thus an individual who disposes of qualified small business corporation ("QSBC") shares may claim a capital gains exemption in respect of the disposition up to a maximum amount of $500,000 — that is, $375,000 of *taxable* capital gains.

---

[69] Subs. 125(7) ("personal services business")(c), (d).

[70] Para. 18(1)(*p*).

[71] Subs. 110.6(2.1).

(a) Meaning of "Small Business Corporation"

A "small business corporation" is a Canadian-controlled private corporation where all or substantially all of the fair market value of its assets are attributable to assets that are:[72]

- used in an active business carried on primarily in Canada;
- shares or debt of one or more small business corporations connected with it; or
- used in a combination of the above.

Thus, a holding company or an operating company can qualify as a "small business corporation".

The phrase "all or substantially all" is not defined in the Act. Revenue Canada's view is that "substantially all" means that at least 90 per cent of a corporation's assets are used in a qualifying activity.

There are two additional tests that must be satisfied to claim the exemption in respect of small business corporation shares:[73]

- The individual who claims the exemption (or a person or partnership related to him or her) must have owned the shares throughout the period of 24 months immediately prior to their disposition; and
- Throughout the minimum holding period of 24 months preceding the disposition of the shares, more than 50 per cent of the fair market value of the corporation's assets must be attributable to assets used directly or indirectly in an active business.

The general rule is that a corporation must use more than 50 per cent of the fair market value of its assets directly in an active business carried on primarily in Canada throughout the required holding period.

Where a corporation holds shares or debt of connected corporations, the shares or debt also qualify as active business assets of the corporation if they satisfy two conditions: a holding period test and an active business test. These conditions are similar to those which apply to shares of the corporation held directly by an individual.

(b) New Corporations

Shares issued from a corporation's treasury must also be held for the full 24-month holding period if the shareholder intends to claim the capital gains exemption. The 24-

---

[72] Subs. 248(1) ("small business corporation").

[73] Subs. 110.6(1) ("qualified small business corporation share").

month holding period restriction does not apply, however, to new issues of treasury shares if the shares are issued:[74]

- As consideration for other shares;
- On a transfer of all or substantially all of the assets used in active business; or
- On a transfer of certain active partnership interests.

Thus, shareholders of newly-incorporated small business corporations may claim the superexemption for QSBC shares even though the corporation has been in existence for less than 24 months. For example, a sole proprietor can transfer an active business carried on in Canada to a corporation in exchange for its shares and then dispose of the shares to claim the capital gains exemption.

(c) Purifying a Small Business Corporation

The superexemption in respect of QSBC shares is generous, and it is important that Canadian-controlled private corporations not go offside by holding non-qualifying assets. There are various ways to purify a corporation that might not otherwise qualify as a "small business corporation". For example, an offside corporation can:

- Distribute its non-qualifying assets to its shareholders as a taxable dividend prior to the disposition of its shares;
- Distribute non-qualifying assets as a dividend on a tax-free basis to the extent of its capital dividend account (a dividend out of the capital dividend account is tax-free without any adjustment to the adjusted cost base of the shares);
- Dispose of its non-qualifying assets to another corporation through a "butterfly" reorganization; or
- Transfer its shares to a holding company, with an election under section 85 to realize sufficient gains to fully absorb the $500,000 exemption. The exemption is then locked into the cost base of the holding company's shares.

---

[74] Para. 110.6(14)(*f*).

COMPREHENSIVE EXAMPLE

Assume:

Theta Ltd. is a Canadian-controlled private corporation. The following data applies to *Theta:*

	1996
Active business income	$100,000
Capital gains	30,000
Canadian interest income	10,000
Dividends from non-connected Canadian corporations	9,000
Federal corporate tax rate	38.00%
Provincial abatement	10.00%
Small business deduction	16.00%
Federal corporate surtax	4.00%
Provincial tax rate (Ontario)	9.50%

Then:

1. Calculation of taxable income:

Active business income	$100,000
Taxable capital gains	22,500
Interest income	10,000
Dividend income	9,000
Net income	$141,500
Less: intercorporate dividends	9,000
Taxable income	$132,500

2. Calculation of Part I tax payable:

Federal tax (38%)	$ 50,350
Provincial tax abatement (10%)	13,250
	$ 37,100
Federal surtax (4%)	1,484
	$ 38,584
Small business deduction	16,000
Federal tax payable	$ 22,584
Provincial tax payable (9.5%)	12,588
Total tax payable	$ 35,172

Comprehensive Example (continued)

3. Small business deduction:

Least of	
(i) ABI	$100,000
(ii) Taxable income	$132,500
(iii) Annual business limit	$200,000
Least amount	$100,000
Small business deduction	$ 16,000

4. Refundable taxes:

Dividends	$ 3,000
Capital Gains	2,000
Interest Income	890
	$ 5,890

5. RDTOH:

Refundable portion of Part I tax	$ 8,668
Part IV tax	3,000
	$ 11,668

SELECTED BIBLIOGRAPHY TO CHAPTER XVII

General

Andersson, Krista, "Implications of Integrating Corporate and Shareholder Taxes" (1991), 50 *Tax Notes* 1523.

Birnie, David A.G., "Capping the Small Business Deduction", in *Proceedings of 35th Tax Conf.* 13 (Can. Tax Foundation, 1983).

Brookes, Geoff, and Vinneau, "Taxation: Downside Protection" (1992), 125 *CA Magazine* 53.

Couzin, Robert, "Business and Property Income", *Corp. Mgmt. Tax Conf.* 41 (Can. Tax Foundation, 1981).

Cranston, Ann M., "Bill C-17 and the Small Business Deduction" (1980), 54 *Cost and Mgmt.* 46.

Dent, Douglas Edward, *The Small Business Deduction and a Canadian Tax on Unreasonable Accumulations* (Vancouver: University of British Columbia, 1985).

Doane, H. Lawrence, "Income Tax Treatment of Specified Investment Business Income, Capital Gains Rollovers for Small Businesses and Business Investment Losses Under Bill C-17", in *Proceedings of 31st Tax Conf.* 106 (Can. Tax Foundation, 1979).

Farden, Eric N., *Income Tax for a Small Business* (E.N. Farden, 1985).

"Getting the Needle" (1981), 3 *Can. Taxpayer* 23.

Gillix, Marlene, "The New Small Business Tax Rules" (1984), 117:6 *CA Magazine* 72.

Graham, Douglas D., "Taxation of a Private Corporation", *B.C. Tax Conf.* 66 (Can. Tax Foundation, 1980).

Institute for Fiscal Studies, *Equity for Companies: A Corporation Tax for the 1990's — A Report of the IFS Capital Taxes Group* (London: Institute for Fiscal Studies, 1991).

Jones, David Phillip, "Further Reflections on Integration: The Modified Small Business Deduction, Non-qualifying Businesses, Specified Investment Income, Corporate Partnerships, and Personal Service Corporations" (1982), 30 *Can. Tax J.* 1.

Kennedy, Henry, "Tax Integration" (May 1990), 123 *CA Magazine* 43.

Larter, Ronald W., "The Small Business Deduction, Corporate Partnerships, Personal and Facility Corporations and Other Related Matters", *B.C. Tax Conf.* 101 (Can. Tax Foundation, 1981).

Louis, David, *How to Make More Money Out of Your Company With Less Tax* (Toronto: Hume, 1984).

McQuillan, Peter, "Investment Income and Active Business Income Earned by an Individual and Through a Corporation: A Comparative Analysis, 1987-1988", in *Proceedings of 39th Tax Conf.* 12:1 (Can. Tax Foundation, 1987).

O'Brien, Martin L., "Carrying on Business in Canada" (1985), 1 *Can. Current Tax* J-111.

"Round Table Discussion — Tax Problems of Small Business", in *Proceedings of 33rd Tax Conf.* 342 (Can. Tax Foundation, 1981).

Shead, Richard G., "The 1978 Tax Changes Affecting Family Farms and Small Businesses", in *Proceedings of 30th Tax Conf.* 275 (Can. Tax Foundation, 1978).

Shinder, Bernard, "The Taxation of Small Business: An Historical and Technical Overview" (1984), 32 *Can. Tax J.* 1.

"Simplifying Tax for Small Business", Budget Papers (1984), Department of Finance, Canada.

Small Business Taxation, Audio Archives of Canada, 1984.

Strain, William J., "Integration Revisited", in *Proceedings of 38th Tax Conf.* 9:1 (Can. Tax Foundation, 1986).

Taxation of a Private Corporation (Deloitte, Haskins & Sells, 1981).

Tax Minimization Strategies for Small Business (Toronto: Insight Educational Services, 1983).

Yin, George K., "A Different Approach to the Taxation of Corporate Distributions: Theory and Implementation of a Uniform Corporate — Level Distributions Tax" (1990), 78 *Georgetown L.J.* 1837.

Canadian-Controlled Private Corporations

"Active Business Income: A Retroactive Break!" (1980), 2 *Can. Taxpayer* 83.

Andersson, Krista, "Implications of Integrating Corporate and Shareholder Taxes" (1991), 50 *Tax Notes* 1523.

Beach, Wayne G., and Mark F. Wheeler, "Associated Corporations", in *Proceedings of 40th Tax Conf.* 10:1 (Can. Tax Foundation, 1988).

Berand, Daniel, "Corporations associées — Les nouvelles règles de jeu" (1989), 37 *Can. Tax J.* 37.

Bowden, Gregory T.W., "Associated Corporations — A New Test?" (1986), 44 *Advocate (Van.)* 391.

Bowden, Gregory T.W., "Associated Corporations: Recent Developments", in *Proceedings of 38th Tax Conf.* 40:1 (Can. Tax Foundation, 1986).

Brookes, Geoff, and Vinneau, "Taxation: Downside Protection" (1992), 125 *CA Magazine* 53.

Colley, Geoffrey, "Small Business Deduction Rules Revisited" (1981), 114:12 *CA Magazine* 46.

Drache, A.B.C., "Pre-Mortem Planning" (1991), 13 *Can. Taxpayer* 86.

Glover, Paul, "CCPC's May Lose Low Tax Rate" (April 1988), 62 *CMA Magazine* 46.

Hierlihy, Thomas G., "Planning to Maximize the Tax Saving from the Small Business Deduction", in *Proceedings of 32nd Tax Conf.* 174 (Can. Tax Foundation, 1980).

Hogg, R.D., "Stock Option Benefits in Canadian-Controlled Private Corporations" (1978), 26 *Can. Tax J.* 85.

Hugget, Donald R., "The $500,000 Exemption — Fact or Fiction" (1990), 17 *Can. Tax News* 79.

Lemon, K.W., "Small Business Deduction" (1979), 44 *Bus. Q.* 18, 85.

Lewin, Richard, "Income Tax Planning and the Rules of Association", in *Proceedings of 39th Tax Conf.* 32:1 (Can. Tax Foundation, 1987).

Mandel, Jeffrey, "New Life for the Small Business Deduction — The Dividend Straddle" (1981), 3 *Can. Taxpayer* 129.

McCallum, J. Thomas, "Choosing the Right End" (1991), 25 *CGA Magazine* 20.

Nathason, David C., "Active Versus Passive Once Again: Active Business Income and Investment Income of Canadian-Controlled Private Corporations", in *Proceedings of 33rd Tax Conf.* 908 (Can. Tax Foundation, 1981).

Nolke, David G., "All in the (Corporate) Family" (1991), 25 *CGA Magazine* 16.

Nolke, David G., *Income Taxes and the CCPC* (Vancouver: CGA Canada, 1993).

Quinton, Cathy, "The Additional Capital Gains Exemption" (December — January 1989), 62 *CMA Magazine* 47.

Stack, Thomas J., "Capital Gains and Losses on Shares of Private Corporations", in *Proceedings of 39th Tax Conf.* 17:1 (Can. Tax Foundation, 1987).

Strain, W.J., "The Small Business Rules: 'O What a Tangled Web...!' ", in *Proceedings of 34th Tax Conf.* 53 (Can. Tax Foundation, 1982).

Tremblay, Richard G., "Active Business Income" (1992), 3 *Can. Current Tax* 47.

Ulmer, John M., "Family Members as Shareholders of a Small Business Corporation", in *Proceedings of 38th Tax Conf.* 14:1 (Can. Tax Foundation, 1986).

Yin, George K., "A Different Approach to the Taxation of Corporate Distributions: Theory and Implementation of a Uniform Corporate-Level Distributions Tax" (1990), 78 *Georgetown L.J.* 1837.

Corporate Control

Chyfetz, Bill and Don Jakubowicz, *Associated Corporations in Canada* (Don   Mills, Ont.: CCH Canadian, 1992).

Corn, George, "Control — De Jure or De Facto?" (August 1990), 3:8 *Can. Current Tax* J-43.

"Corporate Control: A Judicially Enacted De Facto Test?" (1990), 44 *DTC* 7023.

Drache, A.B.C., "Controlling a Company Without Shares" (1992), 14 *Can. Taxpayer* 56.

Eng, Susan, "The Arm's Length Rules", in *Proceedings of 40th Tax Conf.* 13:1 (Can. Tax Foundation, 1988).

Glover, Paul, "Changes in Control — Corporate Taxpayers Beware" (1988), 62 *CMA Magazine* 42.

Halpern, Jack V., "Determination of Control for the Purposes of Being a 'CCPC' " (1990), 38 *Can. Tax J.* 942.

Hiseler, Gregory R., "Corporate Control", in *Proceedings of 40th Tax Conf.* 12:1 (Can. Tax Foundation, 1988).

Hugget, Donald R., "$500,000 Exemption (The) — Fact or Fiction" (1990), 17 *Can. Tax News* 79.

Hugget, Donald R., "Guilt By Association" (1990), 14 *Can. Tax News* 103.

Jerrold, J., "How to Assess the Value of Deferral" (1989), 67 *Taxes* 384.

Krishna, Vern, "The Power of Influence" (February 1990), 24 *CGA Magazine* 48.

Moskowitz, Evelyn P., "Dealing at Arm's Length: A Question of Fact", in *Proceedings of 39th Tax Conf.* 33:1 (Can. Tax Foundation, 1987).

Sheffield, Jeffrey T., "Holding Company Formations" (1986), 64 *Taxes* 846.

Wikenfeld, David, "Taxation: Tenuous Connections" (1991), 124 *CA Magazine* 32.

Personal Services Business Income

Batten, L.J. Dick, "Personal Services Business", *Prairie Provinces Tax Conf.* 101 (Can. Tax Foundation, 1983).

Krishna, Vern, "Personal Services Business Income" (1983), 17:10 *CGA Magazine* 31.

Small Business Corporations

Boehmer, G.C., "Small Business Corporations: Capital Gains Planning Opportunities and Pitfalls" (1987), 35 *Can. Tax J.* 987.

Durnford, John W., "Profits on the Sale of Shares: Capital Gains or Business Income — A Fresh Look at Irrigation Industries" (1987), 35 *Can. Tax J.* 837.

Hayos, Gabriel J., "The Capital Gains Exemption: Planning Strategies to Meet the Criterion of a 'Qualified Small Business Corporation'", in *Proceedings of 40th Tax Conf.* 15:1 (Can. Tax Foundation, 1988).

Howick, Wallace M., "Assets Versus Shares: An Approach to the Alternatives", *Corp. Mgmt. Tax Conf.* 1:1 (Can. Tax Foundation, 1990).

Hugget, Donald R., "The $500,000 Exemption — Fact or Fiction" (1990), 17 *Can. Tax News* 79.

"Personal Tax Planning — Small Business Corporations — Capital Gains Planning Opportunities and Pitfalls" (1987), 35 *Can. Tax J.* 987.

Quinton, Cathy, "The Additional Capital Gains Exemption" (December — January 1989), 62 *CMA Magazine* 47.

Sider, Vance A., "Corporate Restructuring Issues: Public Corporations", *Corp. Mgmt. Tax Conf.* 6:1 (Can. Tax Foundation, 1990).

Stack, Thomas J., "Capital Gains and Losses on Shares of Private Corporations", in *Proceedings of 39th Tax Conf.* 17:1 (Can. Tax Foundation, 1987).

Tam, Anthony, "Capital Gains Exemption: Small Business Corporations" (1987-89), 2 *Can. Current Tax* P-5.

Truster, Perry, "The Capital Gains Exemption", in *Proceedings of 41st Tax Conf.* 12:1 (Can. Tax Foundation, 1989).

Ward, David A., and John M. Ulmer, "Corporate Taxation: Shares Eligible for the Capital Gains Exemption" (1986), 5 *Legal Alert* 81.

"Workshop: Capital Gains Exemption and Small Business Corporation Shares", in *Proceedings of 41st Tax Conf.* 46:1 (Can. Tax Foundation, 1989).

Other

Anderson, Eric W., "Owner-Manager Remuneration", in *Proceedings of the 38th Tax Conf.* 11 (Can. Tax Foundation, 1986).

Barbacki, Richard, "Estate Freezing in the Light of Recent Income Tax Changes", in *Proceedings of 38th Tax Conf.* 36 (Can. Tax Foundation, 1986).

Beith, Robert M., Scott Brown, Claude McDonald and George Venner, "Revenue Canada Round Table/Table ronde de Revenu Canada", in *Proceedings of 38th Tax Conf.* 51 (Can. Tax Foundation, 1986).

Bernstein, Jack, "Family Succession", in *Proceedings of the 38th Tax Conf.* (Can. Tax Foundation, 1986).

Birnie, David A.G., "Consolidation of Corporate Structures", in *Proceedings of 31st Tax Conf.* 177 (Can. Tax Foundation, 1979).

Boultbee, J.A., "Minimizing the Taxation Effects of Dividends", in *Proceedings of 37th Tax Conf.* 7 (Can. Tax Foundation, 1985).

Brender, Mark, "The De Minimis Dividend Test under Subsection 110.6(8) — Part 1" (1993), 41 *Can. Tax J.* 808.

Brender, Mark, "The De Minimis Dividend Test under Subsection 110.6(8) — Part 2" (1993), 41 *Can. Tax J.* 1034.

Brown, Catharine A., "Spouse Trusts", in *Proceedings of 38th Tax Conf.* 37 (Can. Tax Foundation, 1986).

Corn, George, "Interest Income — Foreign Accrual Property Income or Income from an Active Business", [1990-2] *Can. Current Tax* J141.

Cullity, Maurice C., "The Capital Gains Exemption: Implications for Estate Planning", in *Proceedings of 37th Tax Conf.* 18 (Can. Tax Foundation, 1985).

Dulude, Louise, "Taxation of the Spouses: A Comparison of Canadian, American, British, French, and Swedish Law" (1985), 23 *Osgoode Hall L.J.* 67.

Halpern, Jeffrey N., "The Last Word on Management Companies... Or Is It?" (1984), 6 *Can. Taxpayer* 25.

Minzberg, Samuel, "Income Splitting Still Alive?", in *Proceedings of 38th Tax Conf.* 35 (Can. Tax Foundation, 1986).

Peters, Steven, "Enhancing the Exemption" (1992), 125 *CA Mag.* 33.

Potvin, Jean, "The Capital Gains Deduction for Qualified Small Business Corporation Shares Revisited", in *Proceedings of 44th Tax Conference* 5:50 (Can. Tax Foundation, 1992).

Provenzano, Louis J., "The Impact of Escalating Provincial Individual Income Tax Rates on an Owner-manager's Decision to Earn Income Directly or through a Corporation", in *Proceedings of 45th Tax Conference* 33:1 (Can. Tax Foundation, 1993).

Reid, R.J., "Tax Implications of a Change in Control" (1984), *Income Tax Aspects* 84.

Ross, David W., "Incorporation and Capitalization of a Private Corporation", in *Proceedings of 39th Tax Conf.* 11:1 (Can. Tax Foundation, 1987).

Ruby, Stephen S., "A Glimpse at the Lifetime Capital Gains Exemption (Part I)" (1986), 3:12 *Bus. & L.* 93.

Ruby; Stephen S., "A Glimpse at the Lifetime Capital Gains Exemption (Part III)" (1987), 4:1 *Bus. & L.* 6.

Stack, T.J., "Corporate Partnerships: Non-Qualifying Business and Related Topics", *Prairie Provinces Tax Conf.* 189 (Can. Tax Foundation, 1981).

Tremblay, Richard, "Active Business Income", [1990-2] *Can. Current Tax* P45.

"The Taxation of Corporate Reorganizations — The New Part II.1 Tax" (1987), 35 *Can. Tax J.* 1292.

Weyman, C. David, "Manufacturing and Processing, Valuations and Business Deductions Including Capital Cost Allowances", in *Proceedings of 32nd Tax Conf.* 254 (Can. Tax Foundation, 1980).

Wilson, Brian, "Buy-Sell Agreements", in *Proceedings of 39th Tax Conf.* 16:1 (Can. Tax Foundation, 1987).

CHAPTER XVIII

DIVIDENDS AND CAPITAL DISTRIBUTIONS

1. TYPES OF DISTRIBUTIONS

There are several ways in which a corporation can distribute its property. In the context of owner-managed businesses, a corporation can distribute its profits through:

- Wages and salary;
- Employee loans;
- Shareholder benefits;
- Shareholder loans;
- Dividends; or
- Capital distributions.

Wages, salary and employee loans are taxable as employment source income (see Chapter V "Income From an Office or Employment"). Shareholder benefits and loans are taxable under special rules discussed in Chapter XIX "Shareholder Benefits". In this chapter we look at the other two methods of distributing corporate profits: dividends and capital distributions.

2. DIVIDENDS

References:

ITA:

Subs. 12(1)	Amounts to be Included from Business or Property
S. 52	Cost of Certain Property Value of Which Included in Income
Subs. 82(1)	Taxable Dividends Received
S. 126	Foreign Tax Deduction

BULLETINS, CIRCULARS & RULINGS:

IT-66R6	May 31, 1991	Capital Dividends
IT-67R3	May 15, 1992	Taxable Dividends From Corporations Resident in Canada
IT-149R4	June 28, 1991	Winding-Up Dividend
IT-269R3	November 29, 1991	Part IV Tax on Taxable Dividends Received by a Private Corporation or a Subject Corporation
IT-270R2	February 11, 1991	Foreign Tax Credit

IT-297R2	March 21, 1990	Gifts in Kind to Charity and Others
IT-458R	May 31, 1990	Canadian-Controlled Private Corporation
IT-506	January 5, 1987	Foreign Income Taxes as a Deduction From Income
IT-520	May 1, 1989	Unused Foreign Tax Credits — Carryforward and Carryback

The general policy underlying the taxation of dividends is that corporate distributions from income should be taxable in the shareholder's hands. This policy, however, conflicts with a competing policy consideration: Income should not be subject to double taxation.

The resolution of these two competing policy objectives poses a particularly vexing problem in the context of corporate and shareholder taxation. Since a corporation is a legal entity for tax purposes, it is taxable in its own right separate and apart from any tax payable by its shareholders on distributed income. In economic terms, however, the taxation of shareholders without consideration of their ownership interests in a corporation does not promote the principle of tax neutrality, that is, the tax burden should not depend upon the form of economic interests but rather on their substance.

Take a simple case: *Opco*, a wholly-owned subsidiary of *Holdco*, earns $100 on which it pays tax at 50 per cent; it then pays a dividend of $50 to *Holdco*. Should *Holdco* pay tax at 50 per cent on its dividend income of $50? Suppose that *Holdco* distributes its income to its sole shareholder, an individual. Should the shareholder pay tax again on his or her dividend? How many times should the income be taxed as it passes through a chain of corporations all owned by the same ultimate owners?

How do we reconcile the principle that a corporation is taxed as an independent entity with the principle that we want to avoid double taxation of the same income? There are different approaches to this problem.

At one extreme, a corporation may be considered a completely separate entity without any regard to its shareholdings. Thus, the corporation and its shareholders are each taxed on their respective income without any consideration for their interlinked economic interests. Under this model (the "classical system"), the principle of full taxation of income overcomes the principle of avoiding double taxation.

But even in those countries which use the classical system,[1] there is usually some accommodation for closely-held corporations. The rationale of these exceptions is to encourage commercial enterprises by permitting them to enjoy the benefits of incorporation without suffering double taxation of profits. For example, the United States, which follows the classical system, allows for a flow-through of income for its

---

[1] For example, the United States.

Subchapter S corporations. Subchapter S corporations are fiscally transparent and treated, in effect, on the same basis as partnerships.

At the other extreme, we have the full imputation system: A corporation is treated as a fiscal transparency and all income taxes paid by the corporation are creditable to its shareholders when its profits are distributed as dividends. Thus, under this theory, a corporation is a conduit for its shareholders in so far as the tax system is concerned. Of course, the corporation remains a separate legal entity for business and commercial purposes.

There is also a third alternative that lies between the two extremes of the classical and full imputation systems. Canada, for example, uses a notional imputation system that allow shareholders a credit for corporate taxes, but in fixed amounts so that the shareholder may receive more or less credit for corporate taxes than actually paid.

The following example illustrates the differences between the classical system, full imputation of corporate profits at the shareholder level, and a partial imputation of corporate taxes to shareholders.

Example XVIII.1			
Assume:			
Corporate tax rate:	45%		
Shareholder's marginal tax rate:	40%		
Corporate net income for tax purposes:	1000		
Shareholder credit for corporate tax:	0%	100%	50%
Then:	CLASSICAL SYSTEM	FULL IMPUTATION	PARTIAL IMPUTATION
TAXATION OF CORPORATIONS:	$	$	$
Net income	1000	1000	1000
Corporate tax	450	450	450
Net income after tax	550	550	550
TAXATION OF SHAREHOLDER:			
Dividend received (Gross)	550	550	550
Credit for corporate tax paid	0	450	225
Taxable amount	550	1000	775
Shareholder tax	220	400	310
NET AMOUNT TO SHAREHOLDER	330	600	465
TOTAL CORPORATE/ SHAREHOLDER TAX	670	400	535

The above example illustrates how punitive the classical system can be and why countries which adopt such a system provide for some form of relief for closely-held corporations. The above comparison assumes that the corporate tax rate is the same in all three systems. In fact, it is quite unlikely that a full imputation system will levy corporate tax at the same rate as under a classical system. Countries that use a classical system of taxation typically have a lower rate of corporate tax to accommodate the burden of double taxation for shareholders.

Canada has a partial imputation system of corporate taxation. Four factors affect the taxation of dividends:

- Type of shareholder;
- Status of the payor corporation;
- Source of the underlying income from which the dividend is paid; and
- Type of share on which the dividend is paid.

OVERVIEW OF TAXATION OF DIVIDEND INCOME RECIPIENT			
PAYING CORPORATION	RESIDENT INDIVIDUAL	RESIDENT CORPORATION	NON-RESIDENT TAXPAYER
TAXABLE CANADIAN CORPORATION	Grossed-up value of dividend included in income. Individual entitled to dividend tax credit. Para. 82(1)(b); s. 121.	Dividend included in income [para. 12(1)(j)] and then deducted in computing taxable income [subs. 112(1)].	25% withholding tax on taxable dividends and capital gains. Rate may be reduced by treaty. Subs. 212(2).
NON-RESIDENT CORPORATION THAT IS NOT A FOREIGN AFFILIATE	Dividend received included in income: s. 90. Credit for foreign taxes paid: subs. 126(1).	Dividend received included in income: s. 90. See also subs. 15(4) and 93(1).	N/A
FOREIGN AFFILIATE	Dividend received included in income: s. 90; deduction for portion of dividend paid out of taxable surplus — subs. 91(5). Foreign tax credit.	Divided received included in income: s. 90; deduction for dividends paid out of taxable surplus: subs. 91(5) and exempt surplus: s. 113(1).	N/A

The source of income (business versus investment) from which a dividend is paid can also be an important determinant, particularly in the case of dividends from foreign affiliate. The focus of this chapter is on dividends paid by resident corporations to resident shareholders.

(a) Meaning of "Dividend"

The term "dividend" is not defined in the Act.[2] At common law, a dividend is a share of profits allocated to the shareholders of a corporation.[3] Dividends may be paid in cash, shares or other kinds of property.[4]

(b) Types of Dividends

A dividend is an appropriation of corporate assets pursuant to a resolution of the corporation's board of directors or a shareholders' agreement. The declaration and payment of a dividend creates legal rights and obligations, both under corporate law and tax law.

Whether a payment constitutes a dividend is a question of fact and law. Payments cannot be recharacterized. For example, where a corporation has paid salary to a shareholder, it cannot retroactively "convert" the salary into a dividend through bookkeeping journal entries.[5]

(i) Cash

A cash dividend is usually paid by a cheque drawn upon the corporation. The face amount of the dividend is the amount used to compute the shareholder's income.

(ii) Stock

A stock dividend is a *pro rata* distribution of additional shares by a corporation to its shareholders without any additional subscription of cash or other property for the shares.[6] Stock dividends are usually paid to shareholders in lieu of cash dividends when the corporation has its cash invested in or earmarked for business operations.

---

[2] Subs. 248(1) ("dividend") (definition merely restricts meaning of word in certain circumstances).

[3] The legality of a dividend is a mixed question of fact and law; see, e.g., *Canada Business Corporations Act*, R.S.C. 1985, c. C-44, s. 42.

[4] See, e.g., *Canada Business Corporations Act* ("CBCA"), subs. 43(1).

[5] *Adam v. M.N.R.*, [1985] 2 CTC 2383, 85 DTC 667 (T.C.C.).

[6] See *Income Tax Act*, subs. 248(1) ("dividend").

(iii) In Kind

Dividends may also be paid in kind.[7] A dividend paid in property (other than cash) is valued at the fair market value of the property.[8]

3. RESIDENT INDIVIDUALS

References:

ITA:

Subs. 12(1)	Amounts to be Included from Business or Property
Subs. 82(1)	Taxable Dividends Received
S. 89	Definitions
S. 121	Deduction for Taxable Dividends
S. 126	Foreign Tax Deduction

The taxation of dividends paid to resident individuals depends upon two factors: (1) Status of the payor corporation; (2) Source of the underlying income from which the dividend is paid. Depending upon these factors, dividends may be taxable or non-taxable to shareholders. Dividends paid out of a corporation's income are taxable to individual shareholders. Dividends paid out of the "capital dividend account" are generally not taxable to shareholders.

(a) From Taxable Canadian Corporations

A "taxable dividend" is any dividend other than a tax-exempt or tax-deferred dividend.[9]

(i) Imputation of Corporate Taxes

An individual who receives a taxable dividend from a taxable Canadian corporation must include 125 per cent of the amount received in his or her income.[10] For example, an individual who receives $80 as a dividend must include $100 in his or her income. The extra 25 per cent included in income is referred to as the dividend "gross-up".

The gross-up is a *notional* amount that represents the tax (or part thereof) previously paid by the payor corporation. The gross-up is included in the individual's income, so that he or she is taxable on some *pre-tax* equivalent of the corporation's income. Then, the individual claims a credit for taxes paid by the corporation.[11]

---

[7] See, e.g., CBCA, subs. 43(1); see also *Income Tax Act*, subs. 248(1) ("property").

[8] *Income Tax Act*, subs. 52(2).

[9] Subs. 89(1) ("taxable dividend").

[10] Paras. 12(1)(*j*), 82(1)(*b*).

[11] S. 121.

Thus, the gross-up and the dividend tax credit alleviate double taxation of corporate income and provide for integration of corporate and shareholder taxes. Example XVIII.2 illustrates the theoretical model of tax integration through the imputation of corporate taxes to shareholders.

Example XVIII.2

Assume:

Federal corporate tax rate	12.00%
Provincial corporate tax rate	8.00%
Combined federal/provincial tax rate	20.00%
Shareholder federal/provincial marginal rate	40.00%
Dividend gross-up	25.00%
Active business income	$ 100

Then:

Corporate Tax

Active business income	$ 100
Corporate tax (federal/provincial)	20
Net income after tax (paid as dividend)	$ 80

Shareholder tax

Dividend received	$ 80
Gross-up @ 25%	20
Taxable grossed-up amount	$ 100

Tax thereon:

Combined federal/provincial tax	$ 40
Dividend tax credit (combined)	20
Net tax payable	$ 20
Net cash retained	$ 60
Amount retained if dividend earned personally	$ 60
Tax saving	0

Under the full imputation model, an individual pays the same amount of tax, regardless of whether he or she receives the income directly or indirectly through a corporation.

Since the federal dividend tax credit is a constant percentage (2/3) of the gross-up, the value of the dividend tax credit increases as the marginal rate of tax decreases. In Example XVIII.3, the federal dividend tax credit is a constant $167 in each case, regardless whether the federal tax rate is 29 per cent, 26 per cent or 17 per cent. Hence, the *effective* rate of tax on dividends drops at a faster rate than the marginal rate of tax.

Example XVIII.3

Assume:

An individual receives a dividend of $1,000 from a taxable Canadian corporation. Assume also that the individual is taxable at a federal marginal rate in

Case A @	29%
Case B @	26%
Case C @	17%

The provincial tax rate is 58 per cent and federal surtaxes apply only at the top marginal rate (Case A).

Then (ignoring provincial surtaxes) the tax payable on the dividend in each case is as follows:

	Case A	Case B	Case C
Dividend received	$ 1,000	$ 1,000	$ 1,000
Gross-up @ 1/4	250	250	250
Taxable amount	$ 1,250	$ 1,250	$ 1,250
Tax thereon:			
Federal tax before dividend tax credit	$ 363	$ 325	$ 213
Dividend tax credit	167	167	167
Basic federal tax (BFT)	$ 196	$ 158	$ 46
Surtax on federal tax (3% BFT)	6	0	0
Additional federal surtax (5% BFT)	6	0	0
	$ 212	$ 158	$ 46
Provincial tax (58%)	114	92	27
Tax payable	$ 325	$ 250	$ 73
Effective tax rate on dividend income	33%	25%	7%

Since the provincial tax in all of the provinces (except Quebec) piggybacks the federal tax, the federal dividend tax credit has the effect of reducing the provincial tax payable. The federal dividend tax credit, in effect, also acts as a provincial dividend tax credit. In Example XVIII.3 (Case A), the provincial tax of $114 is equal to 58 per cent of the basic federal tax of $196, which has been reduced by the dividend tax credit of $167.

(b) From Non-resident Corporations

The structure of taxation of dividends from non-resident corporations is quite different from that which applies to dividends from taxable Canadian corporations. Dividends from non-resident corporations are included in income.[12]

There is a less compelling case, however, to integrate the tax paid by a non-resident corporation with the tax payable by its resident shareholders: After all, the tax paid by the corporation is paid to a foreign government. The principal purpose of the structure in respect of foreign source dividends is to prevent double taxation rather than to integrate corporate and shareholder taxes. Thus, the resident shareholder is allowed a credit for foreign taxes withheld at source from the dividend.[13]

The foreign tax credit cannot exceed the rate of Canadian tax that would have been payable on the foreign income had the income been earned in Canada by a resident taxpayer. Thus, Canada does not subsidize foreign governments by allowing Canadian residents to claim a credit for foreign taxes levied at a rate higher than that prevailing in Canada at the relevant time.

The taxation of dividends from non-resident corporations that qualify as foreign affiliates is more complicated. For present purposes, it is sufficient to note that an individual who receives a dividend from a foreign affiliate must include the dividend in income, but may claim a deduction to the extent that the dividend is paid out of the affiliate's "taxable surplus". The individual may also claim a credit for foreign taxes withheld at source from the dividend.[14]

4. INTERCORPORATE DIVIDENDS

References:

ITA:

Subs. 12(1)	Amounts to be Included from Business or Property
S. 83	Qualifying Dividends
S. 89	Definitions
Subs. 112(1)	Deduction of Taxable Dividends Received by Corporation Resident in Canada

(a) General

The taxation of intercorporate dividends depends upon three factors:

1. Status of the payor corporation;

---

[12] Para. 12(1)(*k*), s. 90.

[13] S. 126.

[14] See Chapter XIII.

2. Type of share on which the dividend is paid; and

3. Source of income from which the dividend is paid.

Intercorporate dividends on common shares paid by a taxable Canadian corporation to a resident corporation are tax-free.[15] The rationale for this rule is to prevent multiple taxation of income. In the absence of this rule, intercorporate dividends that pass through a chain of corporations would be taxed in each corporation. Thus, the exemption from tax is restricted to taxable dividends.

(b) "Taxable Dividend"

"Taxable dividends" includes dividends *other than:*[16]

- Exempt dividends in respect of which the paying corporation has made an election;[17] or

- "Qualifying dividends[18] paid by public corporations to certain shareholders.

(c) Deduction for Taxable Dividends

Dividends on common shares are not taxable under Part I. The exemption from tax is implemented in two steps: (1) Taxable dividends are initially included in calculating *net* income; (2) The corporation may then deduct the amount of the dividend in calculating its *taxable income.*

---

[15] Paras. 12(1)(*j*), 112(1)(*a*).

[16] Subs. 89(1) ("taxable dividend").

[17] Subs. 83(2).

[18] Subs. 83(1).

Example XVIII.4

Assume:

A resident corporation receives taxable dividends of $40,000 from taxable Canadian corporations. The corporation has net business income of $100,000 from other sources, and makes a charitable donation of $28,000.

Ignoring other deductions, the corporation's taxable income is calculated as follows:

Income from business	$ 100,000
Add: Taxable dividends	40,000
Net income	$ 140,000
Deduct:	
Charitable donations	
(20% × $140,000)	(28,000)
Intercorporate dividends	(40,000)
Taxable income	$ 72,000

This two-step process can have important implications. Although intercorporate taxable dividends are, in effect, exempt from Part I tax, the inclusion of such dividends in net income can affect the computation of other deductions, e.g., charitable donations. In the above example, the ceiling for deductible charitable donations is raised from $20,000 to $28,000 as a result of the inclusion of $40,000 of taxable dividends in income.[19]

The deduction for intercorporate taxable dividends applies only in respect of dividends from a "taxable Canadian corporation" or resident corporations that it controls.[20]

A "taxable Canadian corporation" is a corporation that:[21]

- is resident in Canada;
- was incorporated in Canada[22] and
- is not exempt from Part I tax.

---

[19] Para. 110.1(1)(a) (annual ceiling of 20 per cent of income for charitable donations).

[20] Other than dividends from NROs (non-resident owned investment corporations).

[21] Subs. 89(1) ("Canadian corporation"), ("taxable Canadian corporation").

[22] If incorporated abroad, has been resident in Canada continuously since June 18, 1971.

(d) Restrictions on Deduction for Dividends

(i) Policy Background

The policy underlying the rule that dividends between Canadian corporations should be allowed to flow through on a tax-free basis is to avoid multiple taxation of income as it passes through a chain of corporations. Thus, the payor corporation pays the dividend with after-tax dollars and the payee corporation is exempted from tax on dividends received from taxable Canadian corporations.

In contrast, interest expense on debt obligations is deductible for tax purposes and must be included in the income of the recipient. This rule applies whether the taxpayer is an individual or a corporation.

Dividends between Canadian corporations flow through on a tax-free basis to avoid multiple taxation of the same income as it flows through a chain of corporations. The exemption of intercorporate dividends from taxation can, however, be used to convert what might otherwise be interest income into dividend income.

The exemption of intercorporate dividends from taxation can, however, also be used to reduce corporate tax. For example, for many years Canadian corporations found it attractive to invest in treasury shares of corporations with accumulated tax losses and unused deductions. The shares were usually preferred shares and came with a "guarantee" to pay a specified investment yield. Typically, the "loss corporation" would invest the money that it received on the issuance of its shares in Canadian treasury bills or similar interest-bearing securities. The accumulated losses and deductions would shelter the corporation's investment income from tax, and the *gross* income would be paid out as an intercorporate dividend on a tax-free basis. In effect, the loss corporation's tax deductions were transferred indirectly to the profitable corporation through the use of secured preferred shares. These shares (which came to be known as "collateralized preferred shares") were, in effect, more like debt securities with a guaranteed return than equity investments.

(ii) Dividends on Collateralized Preferred Shares

Subsection 112(2.4) prohibits the intercorporate dividend deduction for dividends on collateralized preferred shares. Generally speaking, subsection 112(2.4) applies to deny the intercorporate dividend deduction when:

- The issuance of the shares is part of a series of transactions that reduces the tax payable by a corporation on its investment income;
- The proceeds obtained from the issuance of the shares are used to earn passive property income; and
- The financing transaction and the issuance of shares are structured in such a way that the profitable (investor) corporation's equity interest in the loss corporation is secured.

Subsection 112(2.4) is an anti-avoidance rule: It applies only where preferred shares are structured so that they resemble secured debt with a guaranteed return and where the purpose of the transaction is to reduce the tax that would otherwise be payable on passive investment income such as interest income.

(iii) Term Preferred Shares

We saw in Chapter XV "Corporate Finance" that preferred shares are sometimes used as a form of after-tax financing by certain issuers. The attraction of term preferred shares also stems from the different treatment of dividends and interest under the Canadian income tax system.

Generally speaking, a corporate debtor can deduct its interest expense and the creditor pays tax on its interest income.

In contrast, dividends are paid out of after-tax dollars. The tax system, however, provides special relief for dividends paid by taxable Canadian corporations. The relief takes two forms: (1) Individuals are entitled to a dividend tax credit; and (2) Resident corporations are allowed to deduct taxable dividends received in computing their taxable income.

This system works well as long as the assumptions upon which the system is based are valid. Thus, the system functions efficiently if the corporation that pays the dividend has, in fact, paid corporate tax on the income from which it pays the dividend. In these circumstances, the dividend tax credit for individuals reflects previously paid corporate taxes.

There are, however, significant advantages at the expense of the tax system if the payor corporation has not paid tax on its income. Many taxable corporations which are in fact quite profitable do not pay tax because they take advantage of tax incentives and deductions. These corporations can use preferred shares as a form of after-tax financing.

The following example illustrates the advantage of after-tax financing through preferred shares. Assume that a corporation with a tax rate of 40 per cent borrows $1,000 from another corporation and pays interest at the rate of 10 per cent per year, that is, $100. The interest expense is deductible for income tax purposes, and the borrower's after-tax cost of the interest payment is only $60. The lending corporation earns $100 of interest income, on which it pays tax of $40. Thus the lending corporation's net after-tax income is $60. The income tax system is neutral under this regime, since the $100 interest income exactly matches the $100 interest expense deduction.

If, however, the $1,000 financing is restructured as equity financing instead of debt financing, the borrower might be able to reduce its cost of funds to, say, $80 of dividends, and forgo the greater tax deduction associated with an interest payment. This option would be particularly attractive if the borrower was not a tax paying corporation. Since intercorporate dividends are deductible in computing taxable income, the recipient's after-tax return would be $80. Thus, both parties benefit from the arrangement: The borrower's net cost of funds is reduced by $20 and the recipient's after-tax return is increased by $20. Only the public treasury suffers.

This is all done through the substitution of so-called "equity financing" for debt financing. The system is even more attractive to the lending corporation if the equity that it receives for its funds contains guarantees which, in effect, give the share capital all of the security of debt capital. The corporation will then benefit, from both the security of debt financing and the tax advantages of equity capital.

The Act contains several different provisions that are intended to prevent after-tax financing through the use of preferred shares. The provisions ensure that dividends are paid, at least indirectly, from tax-paid earnings by levying a special tax on the issuer of dividends paid on taxable preferred shares and a special tax on certain shareholders who receive dividends on such shares.

In addition to the special taxes paid on taxable preferred share dividends, the Act also denies the deduction for intercorporate dividends to "specified financial institutions" that receive dividends on "term preferred shares". The effect of this rule is that dividends on a term preferred share that are received by a specified financial institution must be included in income, and are subject to tax at normal corporate rates.

Generally speaking, a share is considered to be a "term preferred share" if the holder of the share has the right to require *anyone* to redeem, acquire, cancel or reduce the paid-up capital of the share, or if anyone provides a guarantee, security or covenant with respect to the share.[23] The effect of this rule is to make dividends subject to tax in the same way as interest payments. The important difference, however, is that the amount paid to the "specified financial institution" is not considered to be "interest" and, as such, the amount is not deductible to the payor corporation.

A "specified financial institution" includes the following:[24]

- Banks;
- Corporations licensed to carry on business as trustees (trust corporations);
- Credit unions;
- Corporations whose principal business is the lending of money or the purchasing of debt obligations, and insurance corporations;
  Corporations controlled by, or related to, any of the above.

---

[23] Subs. 248(1) ("term preferred share").

[24] Subs. 248(1) ("specified financial institution").

5. STOCK DIVIDENDS AND STOCK SPLITS

References:

ITA:

S. 52	Cost of Certain Property Value of Which Included in Income
Subs. 82(1)	Taxable Dividends Received

BULLETINS, CIRCULARS & RULINGS:

IT-88R2	May 31, 1991	Stock Dividends
IT-387R2	July 14, 1989	Meaning of "Identical Properties"

A stock dividend involves a capitalization of corporate retained earnings into share capital.[25] Stock dividends may be paid by issuing shares of the same class as the shares on which the dividend is paid, or by issuing shares of another class. For example, a stock dividend on Class A shares may be paid by issuing more Class A shares on a *pro rata* basis to existing shareholders of that class or by issuing Class B shares.

A stock split involves a reduction in the *nominal* value of outstanding shares, accompanied by a *pro rata* increase in the number of shares issued. A stock split does not involve any capitalization of retained earnings.

For example, a corporation with 100,000 outstanding shares trading at $200 per share may split each share into four, so that there will be 400,000 shares (worth approximately $50 per share) outstanding after the split. A stock split neither involves any substantive financial change in the corporation's position, nor does it generate any income tax consequences for the corporation or its shareholders.

(a) Accounting

A stock dividend does not alter the *total* equity of the corporation; it involves a transformation of one form of equity capital (retained earnings) into another (paid-up capital).[26] Although the CICA has not made any recommendation on the value to be assigned to a stock dividend, the preferred accounting treatment is to capitalize the market value of the dividend from retained earnings into stated capital. The Accounting Research Board in the U.S. supports this treatment.[27]

> The Committee therefore believes that where these circumstances exist the corporation should in the public interest account for the transaction by transferring from earned surplus to the category of

---

[25] Subs. 248(1) ("dividend"), ("stock dividend").

[26] Subs. 248(1) ("amount").

[27] ARB No. 43, c. 7.

permanent capitalization (represented by the capital stock and capital surplus accounts) an amount equal to the fair value of the additional shares issued.

Thus, in accounting terms, a corporation with 1,000,000 issued Class A shares (current market value of $50 per share) that declares a stock dividend of 20 per cent on its shares, should transfer $10,000,000 (that is, 20% x 1,000,000 x $50) from its retained earnings to the paid-up capital account of Class A.

(b) Taxable as Dividends

Stock dividends are taxable in the same manner as cash dividends.[28] Thus, individuals must include the grossed-up value of the dividend in income, and may claim a tax credit.

(c) Cost Base of Shares

The cost of a stock dividend is equal to:[29]

- its share of the amount capitalized from retained earnings into paid-up capital;[30] and
- any amount included in the taxpayer's income as a benefit.[31]

Stock dividends are taxed in the same way as cash dividends. The cost of the stock dividend is taken into account in calculating the average cost of identical shares held by the shareholder.[32]

6. PART II.1 TAX OF CORPORATE DISTRIBUTIONS

(a) Anti-avoidance Tax

A special anti-avoidance tax applies only to publicly traded corporations.[33] The tax is intended to prevent individuals from converting dividend income into tax-free capital gains.

Generally speaking, where a corporation purchases its own shares from its shareholders, the shareholder is considered to have received a dividend to the extent that the purchase price paid for the shares exceeds their paid-up capital. If, however, a shareholder sells shares to someone other than the corporation, he or she can realize

---

[28] Subs. 82(1); subs. 248(1) ("dividend").

[29] Subs. 52(3).

[30] Subs. 248(1) ("amount").

[31] Subs. 15(1.1).

[32] S. 47.

[33] See Part II.1 of the *Income Tax Act*.

a capital gain to the extent of the difference between the proceeds of disposition and the adjusted cost of the shares.

To take advantage of these rules and convert dividends into capital gains, some public corporations issued stock dividends in redeemable preference shares instead of paying a cash dividend. The shares would have a nominal paid-up capital and a high redemption value. Thus, individuals were required to recognize only a very small taxable dividend. Since the shares had a substantial redemption price in excess of their paid-up capital, however, they could be disposed of in the open market for a substantial capital gain. Thus individuals were able, in effect, to convert taxable dividends into tax-free capital gains.

The Part II.1 tax applies where it may reasonably be considered that proceeds of disposition have been paid by a corporation (or a person with whom it does not deal at arm's length) as a substitute for dividends that would otherwise have been paid in the normal course of the corporation's activities. In these circumstances, the corporation is required to pay a special tax of 45 per cent of the amount that can reasonably be considered to be a substitute for the dividends it would normally have paid[34] The 45 per cent rate approximates the 29 per cent maximum federal rate of tax payable by individuals on dividend income.

The factors used to determine whether the corporation would have paid a dividend in the "normal course" of its operations are:

- The corporation's past dividend policy;
- The amount of dividends paid for the current year; and
- Evidence of the corporation's intention to pay out other amounts instead of dividends.

(b) Stock Dividends

Subsection 183.1(3) provides a special rule for stock dividends issued at less than fair market value. Where, as part of a transaction or series of transactions or events, a corporation purchases such shares, directly or indirectly, for an amount in excess of their paid-up capital, the excess is considered a "substitute for dividends" which would otherwise have been paid in the normal course of events by the corporation. Thus, any excess redemption value is taxed at an equivalent rate to that which would have been paid on a cash dividend.

---

[34] S. 183.1.

7. DIVIDENDS FROM NON-RESIDENT CORPORATIONS

Reference:

ITA:

Subs. 112(2)   Dividends Received from Non-Resident Corporation

Dividends from non-resident corporations are generally taxable as income from property.[35] A resident corporation may, however, deduct a portion of dividends received from a non-resident corporation (other than a foreign affiliate), if:[36]

- The non-resident corporation has been carrying on a business in Canada continuously from June 18, 1971, to the date that the dividend is received; and

- The non-resident's business is conducted through a permanent establishment in Canada.

This provision exempts from tax the portion of dividends paid to a resident corporation out of a non-resident's Canadian-source income which has borne Canadian tax.

The proportion of the dividend deductible by the resident corporate taxpayer in computing its taxable income is determined as follows:

$$\text{Total dividends received} \times \frac{\text{Payor's taxable income in Canada in preceding year}}{\begin{array}{c}\text{Payor's world-wide taxable income in preceding year}\\ \text{if payor had been resident in Canada}\end{array}}$$

Example XVIII.5

In 1996, *ABC Ltd.*, a resident corporation, received a dividend of $10,000 from *NR Ltd.*, a non-resident corporation with a permanent establishment in Canada. In 1995, *NR Ltd.* derived $50,000 of its taxable income from carrying on business in Canada and earned world-wide taxable income of $200,000. The deductible portion of the dividend to *ABC Ltd.* is $2,500, determined as follows:

$$\$\,10,000 \times \frac{50,000}{200,000} = \$\,2500$$

The definition of "permanent establishment" for the purpose of this subsection differs from the definition of "permanent establishment" used in some of Canada's tax treaties. Therefore, it is possible that a non-resident corporation which has not paid

---

[35] Para. 12(1)(*k*).

[36] Subs. 112(2).

Canadian income tax by virtue of not having a permanent establishment in Canada can pay a dividend which is eligible for the intercorporate dividend deduction.

8. RETURN OF CAPITAL

References:

ITA:

S. 52	Cost of Certain Property Value of Which Included in Income
Subs. 53(1)	Adjustments to Cost Base
Subs. 53(2)	Amounts to be Deducted
S. 54	"Proceeds of Disposition"
Subs. 82(1)	Taxable Dividends Received
S. 84	Deemed Dividend
S. 89	Definitions

BULLETINS, CIRCULARS & RULINGS:

IT-291R2	September 16, 1994	Transfer of Property to a Corporation Under Subsection 85(1)
IT-432R2	February 10, 1995	Benefits Conferred on Shareholders
IT-463R	July 12, 1991	Paid-Up Capital
IT-489R	February 28, 1994	Non-Arm's Length Sale of Shares to a Corporation

(a) Paid-up Capital

The paid-up capital ("PUC") of shares can be returned to a shareholder on a tax-free basis. Thus, PUC is a shareholder's friend: It represents the maximum amount that can be returned on a tax-free basis as a return of capital.

A return of capital in excess of the paid-up capital of shares triggers a deemed dividend and affects the adjusted cost base of the shares.[37]

The Act contains several rules which are intended to ensure that the rule allowing for a tax-free return of capital is not abused. The rationale for these rules is to prevent a corporation from converting what would otherwise be taxable dividend income into a tax-free return of PUC.

---

[37] See, e.g., paras. 53(1)(*b*), (2)(*a*).

A resident corporation is *deemed* to have paid a dividend if it:[38]

- Increases the paid-up capital of a class of its shares without a corresponding decrease in the paid-up capital of another class of its shares, an increase in its net assets or a decrease in its liabilities;

- Distributes property on its winding up, its discontinuance or the reorganization of its business in excess of the paid-up capital of its shares;

- Redeems, acquires or cancels any of its shares and pays an amount in excess of the paid-up capital of its shares; or

- Reduces the paid-up capital of its shares by means other than the redemption or cancellation of its shares.

(i) Corporate Law

The paid-up capital of a class of shares is generally determined according to the corporate law concept of stated capital.[39] In corporate law, stated capital is the amount of money "committed" by a shareholder to the corporation which, in most cases, represents the shareholder's maximum financial exposure to creditors. Thus, in a sense, it is the financial measure of the limited liability of shareholders. Stated capital represents to creditors the amount of funds or assets invested by shareholders.

For tax purposes, paid-up capital is used to measure the maximum share capital which may be returned tax-free to shareholders.[40]

Paid-up capital, except where specific statutory adjustments apply,[41] is determined according to the relevant corporate law. The Department's position is as follows:[42]

> [T]he calculation [of paid-up capital computed without reference to the provisions of the *Income Tax Act*] involves corporate rather than tax law. The result . . . in most cases will be the amount indicated by a corporation's financial statements as the component of its capital stock represented by that class of shares.

(ii) Separate Accounts

A corporation must maintain a separate stated capital account for each class and series of shares it issues.[43] This account is to be credited with the *full* amount of any

---

[38] S. 84.

[39] Subs. 89(1) ("paid-up capital").

[40] See, generally, s. 84.

[41] Subs. 89(1) ("paid-up capital") (b)(iii) (setting out statutory adjustments).

[42] IT-463R, "Paid-up Capital" (July 12, 1991), para. 2.

[43] See, e.g., CBCA, subs. 26(1); *Business Corporations Act*, R.S.O. 1990, c. B.16, subs. 24(1).

consideration received in respect of the particular shares issued by the corporation.[44] Shares must be without nominal or par value.[45]

(iii) Exchange of Property

A corporation may not issue shares in exchange for property (or past services) valued at less than the cash equivalent the corporation would have received had the shares been issued for money. The corporation may, however, issue shares for consideration in excess of the cash equivalent of property or past services.

(iv) Consideration

Generally speaking, the *full* amount of any consideration received for shares must be credited to its stated capital account.[46] There are a few exceptions to this rule. A corporation may add to its stated capital account an amount that is *less* than the consideration received for its shares, if the shares are issued:[47]

- In exchange for the property of a person who, immediately before the exchange, does not deal with the corporation at arm's length;
- In exchange for shares of a body corporate that, immediately prior to the exchange, or because of the exchange, does not deal with the issuing corporation at arm's length;
- Pursuant to an amalgamation with another corporation; or
- Pursuant to an "arrangement" that is, in effect, an amalgamation of the issuing corporation with another corporation.

In each of these cases, the corporation may add either all or a part of the consideration that it receives for its shares to the appropriate stated capital account. It may not, however, add to its stated capital account an amount that is greater than the amount received.[48]

(v) Adjusted Cost Base

It is important to distinguish between the "paid-up capital" and the "adjusted cost base" of a share. The paid-up capital of a share refers to the amount contributed by the shareholder *to the corporation* in return for his or her share. The paid-up capital is a characteristic of the share.

---

[44] CBCA, subs. 26(2); Ontario *Business Corporations Act* ("OBCA"), subs. 24(2); see subs. 24(8) (stated capital account may be maintained in foreign currency).

[45] CBCA, subss. 24(1), (2); OBCA, subss. 22(1), (2). Par value shares tended to be misleading, and the determination of par value in any case was quite arbitrary. Par value also gave rise to difficult accounting and disclosure problems.

[46] CBCA, subs. 26(2); OBCA, subs. 24(2).

[47] CBCA, subs. 26(3); OBCA, subs. 24(3).

[48] CBCA, subs. 26(4); OBCA, subs. 24(4).

The adjusted cost base of a share refers to the shareholder's cost of acquiring the share. Thus, the adjusted cost base of a share is unique to its shareholder. The adjusted cost base of a share will usually equal its paid-up capital only when it is *initially* issued by the corporation. Subsequent transactions and corporate events will cause the adjusted cost base of the share to vary from its paid-up capital.

Suppose, for example, that a new corporation, *A Ltd.*, is formed and that it issues its shares for $10 per share. Suppose further, that B acquires 100 shares. Then, the paid-up capital and adjusted cost base of the shares to B is then $10 per share. If, five years later, B sells shares to C for $200 per share, the paid-up capital of the shares (assuming no adjustments of the type discussed below) remains $10 per share. The adjusted cost base of the shares *to C*, however, is now $200 per share.

(b) Increases in Paid-up Capital

(i) Deemed Dividend

A resident corporation that increases the paid-up capital of its shares is deemed to have paid a dividend, *unless* the increase results from:[49]

- The payment of a stock dividend;
- An issuance of shares for net assets of equal value;
- An issuance of shares to reduce a liability of equal value; or
- A transaction which correspondingly reduces the paid-up capital of some other class of shares of the corporation by an equivalent amount.

In other words, a resident corporation is deemed to have paid a dividend to the extent that it increases its paid-up capital without increasing its *net* assets, reducing its liabilities, or making an equivalent adjustment in the paid-up capital of other classes of its shares. The purpose of this rule is to prevent a corporation from capitalizing its retained earnings and then distributing its PUC on a tax-free basis to its shareholders.

(ii) Inadequate Consideration

Where a corporation issues shares with a paid-up capital in excess of the consideration it received for the shares, *all* of the shareholders of that particular class are deemed to have received a proportional dividend.[50]

(iii) Cost Base

Where an adjustment to PUC triggers a deemed dividend, the dividend is added to the cost base of the shareholder's shares.[51] Thus, the amount taxed as a dividend is

---

[49] *Income Tax Act*, subs. 84(1).

[50] Subs. 84(1).

[51] Para. 53(1)(*b*).

not included again in income in the calculation of the capital gain or loss upon disposition of the shares.

(iv) Stock Dividends

An increase in the paid-up capital of a corporation as a consequence of the declaration of a stock dividend does not give rise to a deemed dividend.[52] The shareholder must include his or her *pro rata* share of the dividend in income. Concurrently, the shareholder increases the adjusted cost base of the shares on which the dividend is paid by the amount included in his or her income.[53]

Example XVIII.6		
Assume: A corporation increases its paid-up capital by capitalizing $50,000 of its retained earnings.		
	Equity Structure	
	Before	After
1,000 Class A shares	$ 50,000	$ 100,000
1,000 Class B shares	10,000	10,000
Retained earnings	100,000	50,000
	$ 160,000	$ 160,000

The Class A shareholders are deemed to receive a dividend of $50 for each share held. The adjusted cost base of *each* Class A share is increased by $50.

(v) Pro Rata *Dividend*

A dividend that is deemed to have been paid on shares as a result of a PUC adjustment is also deemed to have been received by each shareholder of the class on a *pro rata* basis. This is so regardless of the shareholder's actual involvement in the particular transaction.

---

[52] Para. 84(1)(*a*).

[53] Subs. 52(3).

Example XVIII.7

Assume:

A corporation has the following balance sheet:

ASSETS	$ 100,000
Liabilities	$ 20,000
1,000 Class A shares	50,000
Retained earnings	30,000
LIABILITIES AND EQUITY	$ 100,000

In exchange for land valued at $25,000, the corporation issues an additional 500 shares to X, its principal shareholder, and increases its stated capital by $40,000. Another shareholder, T, owns 80 Class A shares, purchased for $50 per share at the inception of the corporation.

Balance Sheet After Share Issue

ASSETS	$ 125,000
Liabilities	$ 20,000
1,500 Class A shares	90,000
Retained earnings	15,000
LIABILITIES AND EQUITY	$ 125,000

In effect, the corporation has "watered" its stock by $15,000.

Then:

Increase in PUC of class	$ 40,000
Increase in net assets	(25,000)
Deemed dividend (subs. 84(1))	$ 15,000
Number of shares outstanding	1,500
Dividend/share	$ 10
Total dividend to T ($10 x 80)	$ 800
ACB of T's share before transaction (per share basis)	$ 50
Add: deemed dividend	10
ACB of T's share after transaction	$ 60

(vi) Conversion of Shares

Where corporate shares are converted from one class into another, the amount paid on the conversion is equal to the increase in the paid-up capital of the new share issue.

Example XVIII.8

Assume:

A corporation's equity structure at the end of its fiscal year is as follows:

1,000 Convertible Class A shares	$ 5,000
1,000 Class B shares	20,000
	$ 25,000

The Class A shares are convertible into Class B shares on a one-for-one basis. If one-half of the Class A shares are converted into Class B shares, the revised equity structure would appear as follows:

500 Convertible Class A shares	$ 2,500
1,500 Class B shares	22,500
	$ 25,000

Since the amount paid on conversion ($2,500) is equal to the paid-up capital of the Class A shares that were converted, the transaction does not give a rise to a deemed dividend.

(c) Liquidating Distributions

At common law, payments to shareholders upon the liquidation of a corporation are considered to be on account of capital. Thus, in the absence of a special rule for tax purposes, liquidation payments paid out of a corporation's *pre-liquidation* earnings transform income into capital.

(i) Deemed Dividends

The Act modifies the common law rule. A resident corporation that distributes its property to its shareholders on its winding-up or discontinuance or on the reorganization of its business is deemed to have paid a dividend.

The dividend is equal to the amount by which the value of the property distributed exceeds the amount by which the paid-up capital of the corporation is reduced through the distribution.[54] Shareholders of the class affected by the distribution are deemed to receive a dividend equal to their *pro rata* shareholding.

(ii) Reduction in Proceeds

The amount of the deemed dividend is excluded from the proceeds of disposition of the shares cancelled upon winding-up.[55]

The effect of these rules is that an amount distributed by a corporation to its shareholders on its winding-up or discontinuance or the reorganization of its business may be divided into two portions: (1) The amount paid in excess of the reduction in paid-up capital is deemed to be a dividend, and is taxed as income; and (2) The remaining portion (the amount that represents the reduction in paid-up capital) is returned to the shareholder as a payment on account of capital, which reduces the adjusted cost base of the shares.[56]

Example XVIII.9

A resident corporation has a paid-up capital of $5,000 divided into 5,000 Class A shares with a paid-up capital of $1 per share. The corporation discontinues its business, makes a cash distribution of $3 per share, and reduces its paid-up capital to nil. The tax consequences to an individual shareholder who owns 500 of the issued Class A shares purchased at $1 per share are as follows:

1. Dividend deemed paid by corporation:

Cash distribution	$ 15,000
Less: reduction in paid-up capital	(5,000)
Dividend deemed by subs. 84(2)	$ 10,000

2. Dividend deemed received by individual:

$$\frac{500}{5,000} \times \$10,000$$

$ 1,000

3. Adjustment to cost base of shares:

ACB of shares before payment (assumed)	$ 500
Less: *pro rata* (10%) reduction in paid-up capital	(500)
ACB of shares after payment	$ NIL

---

[54] Subs. 84(2).

[55] S. 54 ("proceeds of disposition") (j).

[56] Subpara. 53(2)(*a*)(iv).

Example XVIII.9 (continued)

4. Summary:
   Deemed dividend
   $2/share × 500 shares $ 1,000
   Return of capital
   $1/share × 500 shares   500
   $3/share x 500 shares

   Total $ 1,500

(d) Redemption, Acquisition or Cancellation of Shares

(i) Deemed Dividend

A resident corporation that redeems, acquires or cancels any of its shares (except on its winding-up or discontinuance or a reorganization of its business, or on the open market) is deemed to have paid a dividend on the redeemed, acquired or cancelled shares.

The dividend is equal to the excess of the amount paid by the corporation to its shareholders over the paid-up capital of the shares cancelled. The shareholder is deemed to have received a dividend which is directly proportionate to the number of shares cancelled over the total number of shares cancelled.[57]

(ii) Reduction in Proceeds

The deemed dividend is *not* included in the shareholder's proceeds from the disposition of the shares.[58] The purpose of this provision is to ensure that all amounts paid by a resident corporation to acquire its own shares are taxable to the shareholder, except to the extent that the amount paid represents a return of paid-up capital. Thus, the shareholder does not have the payment taxed as a deemed dividend and a capital gain when he or she disposes of the shares.

(iii) Capital Gain

In addition to any amount deemed to be a dividend, a shareholder may also realize a capital gain or loss from the acquisition of shares. Payments to a shareholder on account of a redemption of shares do *not* give rise to a shareholder benefit.[59]

---

[57] Subs. 84(3). A corporation that redeems or otherwise acquires its own shares is deemed to have cancelled them as a matter of corporate law: see, e.g., CBCA, subs. 30(1); OBCA, subs. 28(1).

[58] *Income Tax Act*, s. 54 ("proceeds of disposition") (j).

[59] Para. 15(1)(*a*).

Subsection 84(3) does not apply where a corporation purchases its own shares on the open market in a normal stock market transaction.[60]

Example XVIII.10

Assume:

An individual owns 100 redeemable shares. Consider the following alternatives:

	Case A	Case B
PUC	$ 100	$ 100
ACB	$ 100	$ 300
FMV	$ 500	$ 500

The shares are redeemed at their fair market value in a private (non-market) transaction.

Then:

	Case A	Case B
(i) Redemption price	$ 500	$ 500
PUC	(100)	(100)
Deemed dividend	$ 400	$ 400
(ii) Cash received	$ 500	$ 500
Less: deemed dividend	(400)	(400)
Proceeds of disposition	$ 100	$ 100
ACB	(100)	(300)
Capital gain (loss)	NIL	$ (200)

(e) Reduction of Paid-up Capital

(i) Deemed Dividend

A corporation may return its share capital to its shareholders on a tax-free basis. It cannot, however, convert taxable earnings into a tax-free return of capital. A resident corporation that reduces its paid-up capital[61] and makes a payment to its shareholders in excess of the reduction, is deemed to have paid a dividend equal to the amount by which the payment exceeds the reduction in the paid-up capital of its shares.[62]

---

[60] Para. 84(6)(b).

[61] Other than by a transaction covered by subs. 84(2).

[62] Subs. 84(4).

(ii) Pro Rata *Distribution*

A shareholder who holds shares of the class that has had its paid-up capital reduced is deemed to receive a *pro rata* share of the dividend that is deemed to have been paid by the corporation.[63] At the same time, the adjusted cost base of the shares is reduced by deducting the *pro rata* portion of the reduction in paid-up capital.[64]

(iii) **Public Corporations**

An amount paid by a public corporation on a reduction of its paid-up capital is deemed to be a dividend *unless* the reduction takes place on a redemption, acquisition or cancellation of its shares, on a winding-up or as part of a reorganization of capital.[65]

(f) **Eliminating Double Taxation**

There are special rules to eliminate the possibility of double taxation. Subsection 84(4) does not apply in respect of a reduction in the paid-up capital of a corporation if the transaction leading to the reduction can fit under either subsection 84(2) or 84(4.1).

Similarly, a deemed dividend described in subsections 84(2) and (3) does not arise to the extent that the transaction falls within subsection 84(1); nor is there a subsection 84(3) deemed dividend if the transaction can fit under subsection 84(2). These rules prevent overlapping or double taxation of the same transaction.[66]

Where a portion of a dividend deemed to be paid under any of subsections 84(2), (3) or (4) consists of shares of the corporation paying the dividend, for the purposes of determining the amount of the dividend, the shares are valued at their paid-up capital.[67] As a result of this rule, there is no deemed dividend to the extent of the paid-up capital of the shares.

9. CAPITAL DIVIDENDS

References:

ITA:

S. 83	Qualifying Dividends
S. 89	Definitions
S. 121	Deduction for Taxable Dividends

---

[63] Para. 84(4)(*b*).

[64] Subpara. 53(2)(*a*)(ii).

[65] Subs. 84(4.1).

[66] Para. 84(6)(*a*).

[67] Subs. 84(5).

S. 123   Rate for Corporations

S. 129   Dividend Refund to Private Corporation

S. 184   Additional Tax on Excessive Election

(a) Policy Objectives

A key policy objective in the taxation of investment income earned by private corporations is to "integrate" the tax payable by the corporation with the tax payable by its shareholders. In other words, the tax system tries to ensure that individuals (particularly those in the top bracket) pay the same amount of tax on investment income, regardless whether it is earned personally or indirectly through a corporation. In respect of capital gains, this objective is implemented through the combined structure of the refundable dividend tax on hand ("RDTOH") and the capital dividend account ("CDA").

The capital dividend account represents the non-taxable portion of capital gains and certain other non-taxable receipts. A dividend paid out of the corporation's capital dividend account is not subject to tax in the hands of shareholders.

(b) Integration of Capital Gains

The integration of capital gains earned by a private corporation works as follows:

- Initially, a private corporation is taxed at full corporate rates[68] on three-quarters of its capital gains;

- The remaining one-quarter of its capital gains is credited to a special account called the "capital dividend account";[69]

- 26 2/3 per cent of its net taxable gains goes into the corporation's RDTOH account;[70]

- Upon payment of a taxable dividend, the corporation receives a refund of one-third of the amount of the dividend, up to a maximum of the balance in its RDTOH account;[71]

- An amount paid by the corporation as a taxable dividend to an individual is grossed up by one-quarter, and the individual can claim a dividend tax credit;[72] and

---

[68] S. 123.

[69] Subs. 89(1) ("capital dividend account").

[70] Subpara. 129(3)(a)(i), subs. (4) ("Canadian investment income").

[71] Subs. 129(1).

[72] Para. 82(1)(b); s. 121.

- An amount paid to an individual out of the corporation's capital dividend account is not included in the individual's income and does not reduce the adjusted cost base of the shares on which the dividend is paid.[73]

(c) The Capital Dividend Account

A "capital dividend" is one that is paid out of a private corporation's capital dividend account and for which the corporation has made the necessary election.[74]

A private corporation's capital dividend account is composed of:

- The untaxed one-quarter of its capital gains,
- Proceeds of goodwill, and
- Capital dividends from other private corporations.[75]

Capital gains and losses on property which *accrued* during any period when the property was held by a corporation that was not a private corporation are excluded from the capital dividend account.[76]

(d) The Election

A dividend qualifies as a "capital dividend" only if the corporation that pays the dividend elects in prescribed form and manner.[77] The election must be for the *full* amount of the dividend paid.

The election must be filed no later than the date on which the dividend becomes payable or is paid, whichever is earlier.[78]

The election must be accompanied by certified copies of the board of directors' resolution authorizing the election.

Duplicate copies of schedules showing the calculation must also be filed with the election.

(i) Private Corporation Status

An election to pay a capital dividend is available only to a corporation that is a private corporation *at the time* when the dividend is payable. A capital dividend cannot be paid by a public corporation, even though the corporation may at an earlier time

---

[73] Para. 83(2)(*b*); subpara. 53(2)(*a*)(i).

[74] Subs. 83(2).

[75] Subs. 89(1) ("capital dividend account").

[76] Subs. 89(1) ("capital dividend account") (a)(i)(A).

[77] Reg. 2101.

[78] Reg. 2101.

have been a private corporation with a capital dividend account balance. Thus, the tax-free status of a private corporation's capital dividend account is preserved only during the time when it remains a private corporation.[79]

(ii) *Late-filed Election*

Subject to certain penalties, a corporation may file a capital dividend election after the dividend has been paid. An election filed after a dividend has been paid will retroactively qualify the payment as a capital dividend if the following requirements are satisfied:[80]

- The election is made in prescribed manner and form;
- The election is supported by an authorization from the board of directors; and
- The estimated penalty tax is paid at the time when the election is made.

(iii) *Penalty for Late Filing*

The penalty for a late-filed election is the lesser of 1 per cent per year for the amount of the dividend or $41.67 per month (annual maximum of $500).[81] Upon receipt of the late-filed election, the Minister will assess the corporation on the exact amount of the penalty payable, and the corporation is then required to pay any balance outstanding.[82]

(iv) *Excessive Elections*

A corporation that elects an amount in excess of its capital dividend account balance is liable to pay a penalty tax on the excess portion of the election. The penalty is levied at a rate of 75 per cent of the excess portion of the dividend.[83] Further, since the penalty tax is due at the time when the election is made, any outstanding balance carries interest at the prescribed rate.

A corporation may avoid the penalty tax by electing to treat the excess portion (i.e., the amount in excess of the balance of its capital dividend account) as a separate taxable dividend.[84] This election, which must be made in prescribed manner within 90 days of the mailing of the notice of assessment, is available only if it is made with the concurrence of *all* the shareholders of the corporation whose addresses are known to the corporation.

---

[79] Subs. 83(2).

[80] Subs. 83(3).

[81] Subs. 83(4).

[82] Subs. 83(5).

[83] Subs. 184(2).

[84] Subs. 184(3).

(e) Capital Dividend Transfers

The capital dividend account of a private corporation is a very valuable asset from which non-taxable income may be withdrawn by resident shareholders. The attractiveness of the capital dividend account is also an incentive to transfer such accounts between corporations in order to reduce the tax that might otherwise be payable on taxable distributions to domestic shareholders.

For example, a private corporation controlled by non-residents (who are taxable on capital dividends) may be prepared to sell its shares to a domestic corporation and transfer its capital dividend account in order to permit the domestic corporation to reduce the tax payable on distributions to its domestic shareholders.

There are several anti-avoidance rules to prevent this type of trafficking in capital dividends accounts. Where a capital dividend is paid on a share that was acquired by the holder in a transaction or as part of a series of transactions, and *one* of the main purposes of the transaction or series of transactions is to receive a capital dividend, the capital dividend is treated as a taxable dividend.[85] In these circumstances, the dividend must be included in computing the shareholder's income, and is taxable according to the normal rules in respect of such dividends.

Note, however, that the capital dividend account retains its character as a capital dividend for purposes of determining the corporation's tax in respect of excessive elections, and for purposes of calculating its capital dividend account.

10. DIRECTORS' LIABILITY

(a) Legality of Dividends

The legality of dividends paid by a corporation is determined by the corporate law of the jurisdiction in which the corporation is incorporated. Generally,[86] the legality of a dividend is determined by a two-pronged test: The dividend must not impair either the liquidity or the solvency of the corporation.

A corporation may not declare or pay a dividend if there are reasonable grounds for believing that:[87]

- The corporation is, or, after the payment, would be, unable to pay its liabilities as they become due; *or*
- The realizable value of the corporation's assets would thereby be less than the aggregate of its liabilities and stated capital of all classes of shares.

---

[85] Subs. 83(2.1).

[86] See, e.g., *Canada Business Corporations Act*, R.S.C. 1985, c. C-44 ("CBCA"); *Business Corporations Act*, R.S.O. 1990, c. B-16 ("OBCA").

[87] CBCA, s. 42; OBCA, subs. 38(3).

Similarly, a corporation may redeem its shares only if it satisfies two financial tests: (1) The corporation must be sufficiently liquid to pay its debts as they mature; and (2) The realizable value of its assets after the redemption cannot be less than the aggregate of its liabilities and the amount required to pay other shareholders who rate equally with or have a higher claim than the holders of the shares being redeemed.[88]

The rationale for these rules is to protect corporate creditors and shareholders. Hence, the two-pronged test: The liquidity test protects corporate creditors and the solvency test protects both creditors and shareholders.

(b) Personal Liability of Directors

Directors of a corporation who authorize the payment of a dividend or the redemption of shares in contravention of these two tests may be jointly and severally liable to the corporation for the amount of the unauthorized disbursement of funds.[89]

A director who dissents from the resolution authorizing the improper payment of a dividend or improper redemption of shares is not liable provided that he or she records his or her dissent at the directors' meeting or, if not present at the meeting, he or she notifies the secretary of the corporation and causes a dissent to be recorded in the minutes of the meeting.[90]

A director of a corporation is entitled to rely upon a professional opinion on matters requiring technical expertise.[91] For example, a director may rely upon the opinion of an accountant, appraiser or valuation specialist to value assets to declare a dividend. In these circumstances, he or she is not liable if it is subsequently determined that the valuation was incorrect.

(c) Power of Court

In addition to rendering corporate directors personally liable for improper corporate distributions, most corporate statutes also give the courts wide discretionary powers to remedy improperly declared dividends. For example, where a court is satisfied that the payment of a dividend is "unfairly prejudicial" to the shareholders or creditors of the corporation, it may, upon application by a complainant, make *any order it thinks fit* to rectify the conduct which was the subject of complaint.[92]

---

[88] CBCA, subs. 34(2); OBCA, subs. 32(2).

[89] CBCA, subs. 118(2); OBCA, subs. 130(2).

[90] CBCA, s. 123; OBCA, s. 135.

[91] CBCA, subs. 123(4); OBCA, subs. 135(4).

[92] CBCA, subs. 241(2); OBCA, subs. 248(2).

(d) Complainant

(i) Proper Complainant

"Complainant" is defined broadly to include shareholders, directors, officers, and *any other person* who, in the discretion of the court, is a proper person to seek relief against improper corporate conduct.[93]

The Minister of National Revenue can be a "complainant" to seek an order against any corporate distribution that might be considered prejudicial to his or her interest.[94] To obtain redress, the Minister must show that the impugned dividend was paid in contravention of the appropriate corporate statute.

(ii) Time of Complaint

A taxpayer's obligation for income taxes arises as soon as he or she earns income, not when he or she is assessed by the Department. In *Simard-Beaudry*,[95] Noel A.C.J.F.C. said:

> The general scheme of the *Income Tax Act* indicates that the taxpayer's debt is created by his taxable income, not by an assessment or re-assessment. . . . In principle, the debt comes into existence the moment the income is earned, and even if the assessment is made one or more years after the taxable income is earned, the debt is supposed to originate at that point. . . . Indeed, in my opinion, the assessment does not create the debt but is at most a confirmation of its existence.

Thus, the Minister has the status of a "complainant" where a corporation earns income on which tax is payable and outstanding. Since a corporation may be reassessed several years after it has earned income, the Minister's status as a "complainant" may be resurrected many years after a taxable event.[96]

---

[93] CBCA, s. 238; OBCA, s. 245.

[94] *The Queen v. Sands Motor Hotel Ltd.*, [1984] CTC 612, 84 DTC 6464 (Sask. Q.B.).

[95] *The Queen v. Simard-Beaudry Inc.* (1971), 71 DTC 5511 at 5515 (F.C.T.D.).

[96] *The Queen v. Sands Motor Hotel Ltd.*, *ante.*

SELECTED BIBLIOGRAPHY TO CHAPTER XVIII

General

Colley, Geoffrey M., "Are Corporate Tax Changes Imminent?" (1986), 119 *CA Magazine* 60.

Hiltz, Michael, " Subsection 247(1) and the 1985 Amendments to the Income Tax Act", in *Proceedings of 38th Tax Conf.* 7:1 (Can. Tax Foundation, 1986).

Kellough, Howard J., "Some Current Issues in Corporate Tax" in *Proceedings of 44th Tax Conf.* 21:1 (Can. Tax Found. 1992).

Dividends

Allgood, David R., "Tax Planning for Private Corporations and Their Shareholders: Implications of Recent Changes on the Use of Holding Companies", in *Proceedings of the 38th Tax Conf.* 10 (Can. Tax Foundation, 1986).

Ballantyne, Janet L., "The Alternative Minimum Tax and Dividends" (1986), 34 *Can. Tax J.* 242.

Boultbee, J.A., "Minimizing the Taxation Effects of Dividends", in *Proceedings of 37th Tax Conf.* 7:1 (Can. Tax Foundation, 1985).

Brean, Donald J.S., "The Redemption of Convertible Preferred Shares: The Implications of Terms and Conditions" (1985), 33 *Can. Tax J.* 957.

Couzin, Robert, "Intercorporate Distributions", in *Proceedings of 34th Tax Conf.* 311 (Can. Tax Foundation, 1982).

Drache, Arthur B.C., "A Primer on Dividend Gross-ups" (1986), 3 *Bus. and L.* 78.

Ewens, Dpuglas S., "Amending Grandfathered Preferred Share Conditions" (1994), 42 *Can. Tax J.* 548.

Meredith, P. Mark, "Securities Lending: Evolving Tax Problems and Issues" (1992), 11 *Nat. Banking L. Rev.* 18.

Patterson, David, "Flow-Through Shares: Tax Shelter Financing and Investing" (1986), 1 *SCRR* 4.

Pullen, K.T., and Howard J. Kellough, "Tax Treatment of Intercorporate Dividends, Grandfather Provisions and the Use of Press Releases" (1987), *Current Dev. in Measuring Bus. Income for Tax Purposes* 3.

Skingle, Ken S., "A Guide Through the Preferred Share Maze" (1994), 7 *Can. Petro. Tax J.* 79.

Strain, William J., "Integration Revisited" in *Proceedings of 38th Tax Conf.* 9:1 (Can. Tax Foundation, 1986).

Sugg, Donald M., "Preferred Share Review: Anomalies and Traps for the Unwary" in *Proceedings of 44th Tax Conf.* 22:1 (Can. Tax Found., 1992).

"Taxation of Corporate Reorganizations (The) — Collateralized Preferred Shares" (1987), 35 *Can. Tax J.* 467.

"Taxation of Corporate Reorganizations (The) — Impact of Tax Reform on Preferred Share Financing" (1987), 35 *Can. Tax J.* 1004.

Part II.1 Tax

Boultbee, J.A., "Minimizing the Taxation Effects of Dividends", in *Proceedings of 37th Tax Conf.* 7:1 (Can. Tax Foundation, 1985).

Cronkwright, Dart and Lindsay, "Corporate Distributions and the 1977 Tax Changes", in *Proceedings of 29th Tax Conf.* 279 (Can. Tax Foundation, 1977).

Hogg, Roy D., "Corporate Distributions: The Proposed Part II.1 Tax", in *Proceedings of 39th Tax Conf.* 31:1 (Can. Tax Foundation, 1987).

Return of Capital

Ashton, Raymond, "Cost of Capital and Raising Venture Capital in a Tax Efficient Manner" (1986), *Brit. Tax Rev.* 176.

Ballantyne, Janet L., "The Alternative Minimum Tax and Dividends" (1986), 34 *Can. Tax J.* 242.

Boultbee, J.A., "Minimizing the Taxation Effects of Dividends", in *Proceedings of 37th Tax Conf.* 7:1 (Can. Tax Foundation, 1985).

Cronkwright, Dart and Lindsay, "Corporate Distributions and the 1977 Tax Changes", in *Proceedings of 29th Tax Conf.* 279 (Can. Tax Foundation, 1977).

Ewens, Douglas S., "The New Preferred Share Dividend Tax Regime", in *Proceedings of 40th Tax Conf.* 21:1 (Can. Tax Foundation, 1988).

Hirsch, Morley P., "The Corporate Loss Transfer System", in *Proceedings of 37th Tax Conf.* 31 (Can. Tax Foundation, 1985).

Jackson, Brian, "Thin Capitalisation" (1990), 30 *European Taxation* 319.

Richardson, Stephen R., "A Corporate Loss Transfer System for Canada: Analysis of Proposals", in *Proceedings of 37th Tax Conf.* 12 (Can. Tax Foundation, 1985).

Ross, David W., "Reducing Paid-Up Capital" (1985), 33 *Can. Tax J.* 591.

Simpson, Muriel A., "Planning Around the New Paid-Up Capital Restrictions" (1986), 34 *Can. Tax J.* 631.

Skingle, Leslie E., "Carve-Outs and Flow-Through Shares", in *Proceedings of 38th Tax Conf.* 50 (Can. Tax Foundation, 1986).

Sinclair, B.R., "Paid-Up Capital", (1984), 34 *Can. Tax J.* 1483.

Strain, H. Larry, "Integration Revisited" in *Proceedings of 38th Tax Conf.* 9 (Can. Tax Foundation, 1986).

Tremblay, Richard, "Contributions to Capital: Cost Basis (Practice Note)" (1987-89), 2 *Can. Current Tax* 1.

Turner, Graham, and Mary Turner, "Making Sense of Corporate Share Capital: Part 1" (1985), 118 *CA Magazine* 52.

"Use of Low Paid-up Capital Shares in Estate Freezes (The)" (1985), 33 *Can. Tax J.* 1028.

Capital Dividends

Ballantyne, Janet L., "The Alternative Minimum Tax and Dividends" (1986), 34 *Can. Tax J.* 242.

Boultbee, J.A., "Minimizing the Taxation Effects of Dividends", in *Proceedings of 37th Tax Conf.* 7:1 (Can. Tax Foundation, 1985).

Cronkwright, Dart and Lindsay, "Corporate Distributions and the 1977 Tax Changes", in *Proceedings of 29th Tax Conf.* 279 (Can. Tax Foundation, 1977).

Ewens, Douglas S., "Meaning of Corporate 'Capital' and Distribution of Post-1971 Surplus as Capital Gains", in *Corporate Management Tax Conf.* 1978, 49 (Canadian Tax Foundation, 1978).

Smith, David W., "Wilson's Minimum-Tax Proposals Treat Dividends Unfairly" (1986), 13 *Nat (CBA)*, 22.

Ward, David A., and Neal Armstrong, "Corporate Taxation: Erroneous Capital Dividend Elections" (1986), 5 *Legal Alert* 97.

Directors' Liability

Campbell, R. Lynn, "The Fiduciary Duties of Corporate Directors: Exploring New Avenues" (1988), 36 *Can. Tax J.* 912.

Krishna, Vern, "Improper Corporate Distribution: Liability for Income Tax" (1984), 1 *Can. Current Tax* J61.

Kroft, Edwin G., "The Liability of Directors for Unpaid Canadian Taxes", in *Proceedings of 37th Tax Conf.* 30:1 (Can. Tax Foundation, 1985).

CHAPTER XIX

TAXATION OF SHAREHOLDERS

References:

ITA:

Subs. 9(1)	Income from Business or Property — Rules
S. 15	Benefit Conferred on Shareholder

BULLETINS, CIRCULARS & RULINGS:

IT-63R4	March 31, 1994	Benefits, Including Standby Charge for an Automobile, From the Personal Use of a Motor Vehicle Supplied by an Employer
IT-119R3	October 12, 1984	Debts of Shareholders, Certain Persons Connected With Shareholders, etc.
IT-421R2	September 9, 1992	Benefits to Individuals, Corporations and Shareholders From Loans or Debt
IT-432R	February 10, 1995	Benefits Conferred on Shareholders

Corporate income is taxed at two distinct levels: (1) In the corporation, when it is earned; and (2) At the shareholder level, when it is paid out as a dividend.[1]

But corporate income can be distributed to shareholders in other ways. For example, a corporation can confer indirect benefits upon, or make loans to, its shareholders. In this chapter we examine the taxation of indirect payments and benefits.

1. BENEFITS

A "shareholder" of a corporation is the person registered on its books, whether or not he or she is the beneficial owner of the shares.[2]

A shareholder is generally taxable on the value of any benefits conferred upon him or her by the corporation in his or her capacity as shareholder. This is so whether or not the corporation that confers the benefit is resident, or carries on business, in Canada. The purpose of this rule is to prevent corporate shareholders from indirectly appropriating the corporation's property on a tax-free basis.

---

[1] See Chapter XVIII "Corporate Distributions".

[2] *Reininger v. M.N.R.* (1958), 20 Tax ABC 242, 58 DTC 608.

The scope of the rule is broad. As Cattanach J. said in *Pillsbury Holdings*:[3]

> [The rule] is aimed at payments, distributions, benefits and advantages flowing from a corporation to a shareholder. . . . While the subsection does not say so explicitly, it is fair to infer that Parliament intended . . . to sweep in payments, distributions, and advantages that flow from a corporation to a shareholder by some route other than the dividend route and that might be expected to reach the shareholder by the more orthodox dividend route if the corporation and the shareholder were dealing at arm's length.

Thus, where a corporation appropriates its property for, or confers a benefit upon, a shareholder, the shareholder is required to include the value of the benefit or the amount appropriated in his or her income for the year.

The rule raises three questions:

1. Does the particular appropriation of property or payment constitute a "benefit"?
2. Was the payment or appropriation of property made to the shareholder in his or her capacity as a shareholder? and
3. What is the amount to be included in the shareholder's income for the year?

Whether something constitutes a shareholder benefit is a mixed question of fact and law and each case must be answered on its own merits.

(a) Purpose

Whether a payment or an appropriation of property to a shareholder constitutes a benefit depends upon the purpose for which the payment is made. For whose benefit was the payment made? Was the payment to benefit the corporation in its operations or for the benefit of the recipient? Thus, the corporation's intention in making the payment or appropriating the property is a key determinant in the characterization of benefits. In *Pillsbury Holdings*, for example, the Exchequer Court said:[4]

> Even where a corporation has resolved formally to give a special privilege or status to shareholders, it is a question of fact whether the corporation's purpose was to confer a benefit or advantage on the shareholders or some other purpose having to do with the corporation's business such as in inducing the shareholders to patronize the corporation.

Payments to shareholders are taxable as shareholder benefits only if they are made outside of the ordinary course of business. Thus, a payment to a shareholder in the ordinary course of, and pursuant to, a *bona fide* business transaction does not trigger a benefit under this rule. Such payments are taken into account in the normal accounting for profit.[5] For example, a person who rents a building to a corporation of which he or she is a shareholder does not necessarily receive a shareholder benefit in respect of the rental. If the shareholder rents in his or her capacity as a landlord and

---

[3]   *M.N.R. v. Pillsbury Hldg. Ltd.*, [1964] CTC 294 at 299, 64 DTC 5184 at 5186 (Ex. Ct.).

[4]   *M.N.R. v. Pillsbury Hldg. Ltd.*, *ante*, [1964] CTC at 298, 64 DTC at 5187.

[5]   See, e.g., subs. 9(1).

charges a fair rental value for the building, the shareholder is taxable on the rental income. The payment to the shareholder is made to him or her not *qua* shareholder, but *qua* landlord.

(b) Income

Shareholder benefits and appropriations are taxable as ordinary income and not as dividends.[6] Hence, amounts included in income as shareholder benefits are not eligible for the dividend tax credit.

(c) Prospective Shareholders

A benefit conferred on a person in contemplation of his or her becoming a shareholder is also taxable as income.

(d) Capacity in Which Benefit is Conferred

Section 15 is directed towards benefits conferred on a shareholder in his or her capacity as shareholder. It is not concerned with benefits conferred on a taxpayer in his or her capacity as an employee,[7] which are covered by paragraph 6(1)(*a*). Although it makes little difference to the recipient of the benefit whether an amount is included in his or her income as an employment benefit or as a shareholder benefit, the issue is important to the corporation that pays the benefit. Employee benefits are generally deductible to the payor corporation as a cost of doing business. Shareholder benefits are not deductible to the corporation, even though they are taxable to the shareholder.[8]

2. EXEMPT BENEFITS

The following transactions do not give rise to shareholder benefits:[9]

- Reduction of paid-up capital;
- Redemption, cancellation or acquisition by a corporation of its own shares;
- Winding-up or discontinuance of a corporation or reorganization of its business;
- Payment of a dividend or stock dividend;
- Common shareholder's rights offering;
- Conversion of an insurance corporation's or bank's contributed surplus into paid-up capital; or

---

[6]   Except to the extent that the amount is taxable as a deemed dividend on a corporate distribution.

[7]   *Singing Skies Farms Ltd. v. M.N.R.*, [1986] 2 CTC 2146, 86 DTC 1586 (T.C.C.) (home supplied by corporation to principal shareholder deductible by corporation as expense; conferred as employee benefit).

[8]   *Broitman v. M.N.R.*, [1986] 2 CTC 2283, 86 DTC 1711 (T.C.C.) (payment by corporation to sole shareholder's spouse as part of divorce settlement not deductible as business expense).

[9]   Subs. 15(1). Also excluded are certain shareholder loans under subs. 15(2).

- A transaction that results in a deemed dividend.[10]

The above transactions are covered by specific provisions of the *Income Tax Act*.

The exemption for stock dividends is not available where one of the purposes of the payment is to significantly alter the value of a specified[11] shareholder's interest in the corporation.[12] The purpose of this rule is to prevent the use of stock dividends to affect a change in shareholder interests so as to shift capital gains from one person to another. In these circumstances, the fair market value of the stock dividend is included in the recipient shareholder's income except to the extent that it has otherwise been included in income as a taxable dividend.

3. TAXABLE BENEFITS

Shareholder benefits can be conferred in a multitude of ways. For example:

- A transfer of property by a shareholder to the corporation at a price in excess of its fair market value;[13]

- A sale of property by a corporation to its shareholder at a price less than fair market value;[14]

- Funds embezzled by a shareholder;

- Excessive expense claims reimbursed to a shareholder;[15]

- Supply of services to a shareholder without fair payment;[16] or

---

[10] S. 84.

[11] Subs. 248(1) ("specified shareholder").

[12] Subs. 15(1.1).

[13] See, e.g., *Losey v. M.N.R.*, [1957] CTC 146, 57 DTC 1098 (Ex. Ct.) (distinction between accounting and tax law definitions of "goodwill"); *Neuls v. M.N.R.*, [1975] CTC 2215, 75 DTC 170 (T.R.B.) (valuation of goodwill/salary/other in sale of business).

[14] See, e.g., *No. 403 v. M.N.R.* (1957), 16 Tax ABC 387, 57 DTC 120 (residence sold to president-general manager *cum* shareholder below fair market value); *No. 513 v. M.N.R.* (1958), 19 Tax ABC 243, 58 DTC 301 (valuation of shares of private corporation); *Seeley v. M.N.R.* (1959), 22 Tax ABC 97, 59 DTC 283 (automobile bought by private company, then sold at loss to shareholder); *Carlile v. M.N.R.*(1959), 22 Tax ABC 407, 59 DTC 479 (purchase of underwritten shares by brokers in-house); *Guilder News Co. (1963) v. M.N.R.*, [1973] CTC 1, 73 DTC 5048 (F.C.A.) (benefit conferred; value of benefit not a dividend eligible for dividend tax credit).

[15] See, e.g., *Zakoor v. M.N.R.* (1971), 71 DTC 745 (T.A.B.) (travelling expenses to Florida for shareholder and family in conjunction with citrus fruit business); *Byke Estate v. The Queen*, [1974] CTC 763, 74 DTC 6585 (F.C.T.D.) (company subsidized interest and principal on shareholder's loans).

[16] See, e.g., *Cakebread v. M.N.R.* (1968), 68 DTC 424 (T.A.B.) (expenses of maintaining horses sold to company for promotional advantages); *Gibson Bros. Indust. Ltd. v. M.N.R.*, [1972] CTC 221, 72 DTC 6190 (F.C.T.D.) (ship sold through wholly-owned subsidiary in sham transaction for personal benefit of customer).

• Forgiveness of a debt owed by a shareholder to the corporation.[17]

4. VALUATION OF BENEFITS

One of the more troublesome issues that arises in the context of shareholder benefits is the value to be placed on the benefit. The valuation of shareholder benefits raises subtle issues and is a fertile source of tax litigation.[18]

The amount to be included in the shareholder's income as a benefit is the "value" of the benefit to the shareholder, not its cost to the corporation. "Value" generally means "fair market value". However, it is not always clear how fair market value is determined.

(a) Inadequate Consideration

Where a corporation transfers property to its shareholders for inadequate consideration, it is deemed to have sold the property at its fair market value.[19] Thus, the shareholder may be taxed on the full value of the benefit conferred, while the corporation is taxed on the basis of a deemed sale of its property.

For example, suppose a corporation purchases a painting for $10,000, then gives it to its shareholder when the work is worth $25,000. The shareholder is taxable on the value received — $25,000; the corporation realizes a gain of $15,000.

(b) Excessive Consideration

A corporation may confer a benefit on its shareholder by paying an excessive price for services or goods. In these circumstances, the corporation is not entitled to an expense deduction for the excess portion of the payment.[20] The excessive portion of the payment comes out of after-tax dollars, but the shareholder is required to include the *entire* amount received in his or her income.

---

[17] See, e.g., *Perrault v. The Queen*, [1978] CTC 395, 78 DTC 6272 (F.C.A.) (shareholder not able to overcome effect of agreement to extinguish debt to corporation); *No. 523 v. M.N.R.* (1958), 58 DTC 379 (T.A.B.) (benefit taxable, no matter how minuscule).

[18] See, e.g., *The Queen v. Houle*, [1983] CTC 406, 83 DTC 5430 (F.C.T.D.); *Woods v. M.N.R.*, [1985] 2 CTC 2118, 85 DTC 479 (T.C.C.); *Check v. M.N.R.*, [1987] 1 CTC 2114, 87 DTC 73 (T.C.C.); *Mid-West Feed Ltd. v. M.N.R.*, [1987] 2 CTC 2101, 87 DTC 394 (T.C.C.); *Soper v. M.N.R.*, [1987] 2 CTC 2199, 87 DTC 522 (T.C.C.); *Dudelzak v. M.N.R.*, [1987] 2 CTC 2195, 87 DTC 525 (T.C.C.); *Gendro v. M.N.R.*, [1989] 2 CTC 2378, 89 DTC 575 (T.C.C.).

[19] Subs. 69(4).

[20] S. 67.

(c) Non-arm's Length Transactions

A corporation that disposes of property for less than its fair value in a non-arm's length transaction is *deemed* to have disposed of the property at its fair market value.[21] Where the property is acquired by a shareholder of the corporation, the shareholder is deemed to receive a benefit.

Where the property is capital property, the shareholder may add the amount of any benefit included in his or her income to the cost base of the property.[22] Note, however, that, notwithstanding the step-up on the cost base of the capital property, a portion of the payment is subject to double taxation.

Example XIX.1

Assume:

A corporation owns a capital property with an adjusted cost base of $20,000. The corporation sells the property (which has a fair market value of $80,000) to its controlling shareholder for $60,000.

Then:

1. Tax consequences to corporation

Deemed proceeds of disposition	$ 80,000
Adjusted cost base of property	(20,000)
Capital gain	$ 60,000
Taxable capital gain	$ 45,000

2. Tax consequences to shareholder

Fair market value	$ 80,000
Purchase price of property	60,000
Shareholder benefit	$ 20,000

3. Cost of property to shareholder

Purchase price of property	$ 60,000
Add: shareholder benefit	20,000
Cost of property	$ 80,000

---

[21] Para. 69(1)(*b*).

[22] Subs. 52(1).

In Example XIX.1, the disposition of a capital property with an accrued taxable capital gain of $45,000 results in $65,000 being included in income, namely, the taxable capital gain plus the shareholder benefit of $20,000. Thus, the amount taxable is more than the economic value of the gain. In contrast, had the shareholder personally acquired and disposed of the property, only $45,000 would have been subject to tax as a taxable capital gain.

(d) Repayment of Benefits

Where a shareholder repays a benefit previously included in his or her income, he or she is not entitled to deduct the repayment. Hence, where a corporation confers a benefit on a shareholder in one year and the benefit is repaid in a subsequent year, the shareholder is required to include the benefit in income in the year when he or she receives it, but is not allowed to deduct the amount repaid.[23] In contrast, a shareholder loan that is taxable in one year is deductible in the year that it is repaid.

(e) Fair Market Value

(i) Opportunity Costs

Having said that "value" generally means "fair market value", it is important to note that market prices do not invariably represent fair market value. Opportunity costs and savings are sometimes used to measure the value of benefits.[24]

(ii) Rental Value

The benefit from a property may be measured by reference to its rental value. But rental value may depend upon the purpose for which the property was acquired. In *Soper*,[25] for example, the taxpayer was the controlling shareholder of a corporation that operated a nursing home. The corporation owned several properties in Florida, which were not used for rental or business purposes. The taxpayer and her family used one of the houses for several weeks each year and allowed certain staff members to use it for their holidays. The taxpayer was taxable on the benefit of her personal use of the property, determined by reference to the *annual* fair market rental value of the properties. The court rejected the taxpayer's assertion that the benefit should be measured by reference to the time that she actually used the property. Since the properties were not acquired for business purposes and were available for the taxpayer's personal use throughout the year, she was taxable on the *annual* rental value of the property rather than on a lesser percentage based upon actual use.

---

[23] *Crosbie v. M.N.R.* (1960), 23 Tax ABC 432, 60 DTC 147.

[24] *Youngman v. The Queen*, [1986] 2 CTC 475, 86 DTC 6584 (F.C.T.D.) (benefit measured by reference to investment value of corporate equity in shareholder's residence).

[25] *Soper v. M.N.R.*, [1987] 2 CTC 2199, 87 DTC 522 (T.C.C.).

(iii) Imputed Value

The value of a shareholder benefit may depend upon the corporation's purpose in acquiring the asset. In *Hinkson*,[26] for example, a corporation acquired and maintained a cottage, which its major shareholder used personally for approximately 60 days per year. Since the corporation did not acquire the cottage for business purposes, the benefit was calculated on the imputed value of the savings to the taxpayer. The value of the benefit was the taxpayer's saving of the capital cost that he would otherwise have had to incur to purchase the property.[27]

5. DEEMED DIVIDENDS

Reference:

ITA:

Subs. 84(1)   Deemed Dividends

Where a shareholder transfers property to a corporation, a shortfall in the consideration received may give rise to a dividend and a shareholder benefit. The portion taxable as a dividend is excluded from the portion taxable as the shareholder's benefit.[28]

Example XIX.2	
Assume:	
An individual transfers land worth $20,000 to a corporation in return for shares with a paid-up capital of $40,000 and cash in the amount of $30,000. Then:	
(1) Increase in paid-up capital of corporation	$ 40,000
Increase in net assets of corporation ($20,000 − $30,000)	NIL
Deemed dividend (subs. 84(1))	$ 40,000
(2) Fair market value of asset transferred	$ 20,000
Total consideration received	70,000
Excess consideration	$ 50,000
Deemed dividend (subs. 84(1))	(40,000)
Shareholder benefit (subs. 15(1))	$ 10,000
Total inclusion in income	$ 50,000

---

[26] *Hinkson v. M.N.R.*, [1988] 1 CTC 2263, 88 DTC 1119 (T.C.C.).

[27] See also: *Youngman v. The Queen, ante.*

[28] Subs. 15(1).

6. APPROPRIATIONS

References:

ITA:

Subs. 69(4)   Inadequate Consideration — Shareholder Benefit

BULLETINS, CIRCULARS & RULINGS:

IT-405	January 23, 1978	Inadequate Considerations — Acquisitions and Dispositions
IT-432R2	February 10, 1995	Benefits Conferred on Shareholders

Corporate property that is appropriated to, or for the benefit of, a shareholder can give rise to a taxable benefit unless the appropriation occurs as a result of reduction of capital, redemption of shares, or the winding-up, discontinuance or reorganization of business of the corporation.[29]

The term "appropriation" includes payment for a *quid pro quo*, a gift, a voluntary or gratuitous division of capital, or any act by which a corporation confers a benefit on a shareholder in respect of any of its property. Indeed, in certain circumstances, corporate property may be appropriated to a shareholder even though its ownership does not change. All that is required is that the corporation's property be appropriated for the shareholder's benefit.[30]

(a) Inadequate Consideration

Where a shareholder purchases property from a corporation at less than its fair market value, the excess of the property value over the amount paid is a shareholder benefit. Where a shareholder sells property to a resident corporation and receives excessive share consideration, the amount of the shareholder benefit is calculated in two steps:

1. The amount by which the paid-up capital of the newly-issued shares exceeds the value of the property sold is deemed to be a dividend to the shareholder;[31] and

2. The amount of the shareholder benefit is the difference between the value of the property sold and the amount paid by the corporation less the amount deemed to be a dividend.[32]

---

[29] Subs. 15(1).

[30] *Reid v. M.N.R.* (1961), 26 Tax ABC 321, 61 DTC 263 (shareholders sold contents of hotel to private company at inflated price; amount of price increase included in income); *Olan v. M.N.R.* (1952), 6 Tax ABC 126, 52 DTC 127 (payment of personal and living expenses of shareholder was income to shareholder).

[31] Subs. 84(1).

[32] Subs. 15(1).

Example XIX.3

Assume:

An individual sells a capital property worth $50,000 to a corporation in exchange for redeemable shares that have a paid-up capital ("PUC") of $60,000 and a fair market value of $100,000.

Then:

PUC of shares	$ 60,000
Net increase in assets	50,000
(1) Deemed dividend	$ 10,000
Payment to shareholder	$ 100,000
Value of asset sold	(50,000)
Excess consideration	$ 50,000
Less: deemed dividend	(10,000)
(2) Shareholder benefit	$ 40,000

In Example XIX.3, the individual includes (ignoring gross-up of the dividend) $50,000 in income, which is equal to the excess of the fair market value of the consideration received over the value of the property conveyed. The corporation can redeem the shares for $60,000 without any tax consequences to the shareholder. If the corporation redeems the shares at an amount in excess of their paid-up capital, the shareholder will be deemed to receive the excess amount as a dividend.[33]

Where corporate assets are transferred to shareholders for inadequate consideration, the assets are deemed to have been sold at their fair market value.[34] Thus, a corporation cannot artificially reduce its income by disposing of property to its shareholders for less than fair market value. This rule applies to all transactions between corporations and their shareholders, whether at arm's length or otherwise.[35] In addition, the shareholder is also taxed on the amount of his or her benefit.[36]

(b) Cost of Property

The Act does not provide a generic formula for determining the cost of property acquired by a shareholder. The cost of a property is simply the amount paid for it.

---

[33] Subs. 84(3).

[34] Subs. 69(4).

[35] Subs. 69(4) is considerably broader in scope than subs. 69(1).

[36] Subs. 15(1).

Thus, a shareholder who acquires any property at less than its market value cannot step up its cost amount. A shareholder is, however, entitled to step up the cost base of property by the amount included in income as a shareholder benefit.[37]

(c) Winding-up

Corporate property appropriated to, or for the benefit of, a shareholder upon the winding-up of a corporation is deemed to have been sold at its fair market value immediately before the winding-up.[38] The corporation is required to calculate its income, gains and losses in much the same way as if it had disposed of the property in an ordinary commercial transaction. The shareholder is deemed to acquire the property at a cost equal to its fair market value at that time.[39]

An appropriation of corporate property on the winding-up of a corporation does not give rise to a shareholder benefit.[40] A shareholder who receives property on the winding-up of a corporation may, however, be deemed to receive a taxable dividend to the extent that the value of property appropriated to him or her exceeds the reduction in the paid-up capital of the shares in respect of which the appropriation is made.[41]

7. SHAREHOLDER LOANS

References:

BULLETINS, CIRCULARS & RULINGS:

IT-119R3	October 12, 1984	Debts of Shareholders, Certain Persons Connected with Shareholders, etc.
IT-498	October 6, 1983	The Deductibility of Interest on Money Borrowed to Reloan to Employees or Shareholders

The shareholder loan rules are stringent[42] and intended to discourage corporations from using loans as an indirect means of conferring untaxed economic advantages on shareholders. We have seen that corporate income paid out as dividends is taxable as

---

[37] Subss. 52(1), (1.1).

[38] Subs. 69(5).

[39] Para. 69(5)(*b*); see also Chapter XXVII "General Principles of International Tax".

[40] Subs. 15(1).

[41] Subs. 84(2).

[42] Subs. 15(2); *Kwong v. The Queen*, [1993] 2 CTC 2056, 93 DTC 588 (T.C.C.); IT-119R3, "Debt of Shareholders, Certain Persons Connected with Shareholders, etc." (October 12, 1984); see, generally, John W. Durnford, "Loans to Shareholders" (1988), 36 *Can. Tax J.* 1411.

income.[43] Long term loans are an indirect way of withdrawing corporate funds and, therefore, are subject to tax.

The rules apply to loans and any other form of indebtedness from any source. The lending corporation does not have to be a resident of Canada or be carrying on business in Canada. Thus, a Canadian resident shareholder who borrows from a non-resident corporation may be taxable on the loan. The rules do not, however, apply in respect of indebtedness between non-resident persons.[44]

An individual who is indebted, *qua* shareholder, to a corporation is generally taxable on the amount of the indebtedness. A "connected shareholder" is also taxable on the same basis.[45] A corresponding deduction is available upon repayment of the loan or indebtedness.[46] Thus, in the simplest case, the *principal sum* of a loan by a corporation to its shareholder is included in his or her income in the year in which the loan is made.[47]

(a) Application

The shareholder loan rules apply to:

- Shareholders (other than resident corporations) of the lending corporation;
- Shareholders who are connected[48] to shareholders of the lending corporation; and
- Members of partnerships and beneficiaries of trusts that are shareholders of the lending corporation.

The shareholder loan rules apply whether the loan is made by the corporation in which the borrower holds shares, by any other corporation related to it, or by a partnership in which the corporation or a corporation related to it is a member.

---

[43] *Silver v. M.N.R.*, [1976] CTC 2043 at 2046, 76 DTC 1039 (T.R.B.), *per* Cardin (corporation "received", as compared to "derived", income from dividends); *Olson v. M.N.R.*, [1984] CTC 3029 at 3031, 84 DTC 1826 at 1828 (T.C.C.), *per* Taylor J. (amounts of shareholder loans not reported as income in year or repaid within one year, etc.); *Cerny v. M.N.R.* (1952), 6 Tax ABC 385 at 388, 52 DTC 259 at 261, *per* Monet (burden of proof as to income on hand where loan not incidental to company's business); *Ramsay v. M.N.R.* (1961), 26 Tax ABC 193 at 194, 61 DTC 191 at 192, *per* Panneton (funds used to pay back corporate debts; no proof of deceit or fraud); *Zatzman v. M.N.R* (1959), 23 Tax ABC 193 at 195-96, 59 DTC 635 at 637 *per* Boisvert (purpose of section is to prevent distribution of profits under guise of loan).

[44] Subs. 15(8).

[45] Subs. 15(2.1); IT-119R3, "Debts of Shareholders, Certain Persons Connected with Shareholders, etc." (October 12, 1984).

[46] Para. 20(1)(j).

[47] See *Tick v. M.N.R.*, [1972] CTC 137, 72 DTC 6135 (F.C.T.D.) (meaning of "loan").

[48] See subs. 15(2.1) (meaning of "connected").

(b) Intercorporate Loans

Intercorporate loans to resident corporations are not subject to taxation. Intercorporate dividends are tax-free and, therefore, intercorporate loans do not require special regulation.

(c) Criteria for Taxability

There are three factors which determine whether a loan (or other indebtedness) is included in income:

1. The relationship between the borrower and the lender;

2. The purpose of the indebtedness; and

3. Repayment arrangements.

A shareholder loan (or other indebtedness) is not included in income where the loan is made:[49]

- By a lending institution in the ordinary course of its business;
- To an employee of the lender or to the employee's spouse to enable him or her to acquire residential accommodation;
- To assist an employee of the lender to purchase its shares or the shares of a related corporation; or
- To an employee of the lender to assist him or her in purchasing an automobile that is to be used in the performance of employment duties.

These exclusions are, however, all contingent upon the third requirement: *Bona fide* arrangements for repayment of the debt within a reasonable time.

Thus, there are three distinct tests:

1. The loan must be *bona fide*,

2. The arrangements for repayment must be *bona fide*, and

3. Repayment must be required within a reasonable period of time.

(i) Repayment

A shareholder loan (or other indebtedness) that is repaid within one year after the end of the lender's taxation year is not taxable as income, provided that the repayment is not part of a series of loans and repayments.[50] Where the loan is not repaid within one year, the principal sum of the loan is taxable in the year in which the loan was made.[51]

---

[49] Para. 15(2)(*a*).

[50] Para. 15(2)(*b*).

[51] *Olson v. M.N.R.*, *ante.*

In contrast, however, with the rules in respect of shareholder benefits, an amount repaid on a loan previously included in the shareholder's income is deductible from income in the year in which the loan is repaid.[52]

Paragraph 15(2)(a) requires only that *bona fide* arrangements be made for repayment of the loan within a reasonable time. There is no requirement that actual repayment be made within a reasonable time. Failure to repay a loan within a reasonable time may call into question the *bona fides* of the arrangement, particularly where no effort is made to collect the loan.[53] A demand loan may not constitute a *bona fide* arrangement for repayment.[54]

(d) Excluded Loans

Shareholder loans and indebtedness are not taxable as income if they are made in, or arise from, the ordinary course of business and the lending of money is part of the corporation's ordinary business.[55] Thus, there are two requirements:

1. The loan must be made in the *ordinary* course of business; and

2. The lending of money must be part of the *ordinary* business of the lending corporation.

Corporate loans to employees or to spouses of employees are excluded from income if the loan is to assist the employee or spouse to acquire a dwelling.[56]

The term "dwelling" includes normal residential accommodation, a summer cottage or a self-contained suite in an apartment building. The exemption applies only to loans used to acquire a dwelling for habitation by the employee. A change in circumstances after the loan is made, however, which prevents the employee from inhabiting the dwelling does not disqualify a loan that would otherwise be exempt.

Corporate loans to assist employees to purchase fully-paid shares of the employer corporation (or shares of a related corporation) are not taxable provided that the shares are held for the employee's own benefit.[57] The important point to observe here is that the loan is exempt from inclusion in income only if the shares are purchased *directly* from the corporation. Open market purchases from other shareholders do not qualify for exemption.

---

[52] Para. 20(1)(j).

[53] *The Queen v. Silden*, [1993] 2 CTC 123, 93 DTC 5362 (F.C.A.).

[54] *Perlingieri v. M.N.R.*, [1993] 1 CTC 2137, 93 DTC 158 (T.C.C.).

[55] Subpara. 15(2)(a)(i); *Duquette v. M.N.R.*, [1984] CTC 3008, 84 DTC 1820 (T.C.C.).

[56] Subpara. 15(2)(a)(ii).

[57] Subpara. 15(2)(a)(iii).

These rules apply to all loans that are required to be included in income as a shareholder benefit. Thus, apart from the exceptions noted, the *principal sum* of a loan to a shareholder is included in his or her income even if it is borrowed at the prevailing market rate of interest.

8. IMPUTED INTEREST ON LOANS

Reference:

BULLETINS, CIRCULARS & RULINGS:

IT-421R2   September 9, 1992   Benefits to Individuals, Corporations and Shareholders From Loans or Debt

A shareholder[58] may be taxable on the interest imputed on a loan.[59] The taxability of imputed interest depends upon three factors:

1. The relationship between the borrower and the lending corporation;
2. The rate of interest payable on the loan; and
3. The prescribed rate of interest at the time when the loan was taken out or the indebtedness was incurred.

In the simplest case, a shareholder[60] of a corporation who, *qua* shareholder, obtains a low-interest loan from the corporation is taxable on the benefit from the loan. The value of the benefit is the difference between the shareholder's actual interest cost and the prescribed rate of interest at that time.[61]

The prescribed rate of interest is determined quarterly, based on the average interest rate for 90-day treasury bills during the first month of the preceding quarter.[62]

(a) Relationship Between Parties

The taxability of imputed interest on corporate loans depends upon the relationship between the borrower and the corporation. Where a shareholder of a corporation, a person who does not deal at arm's length[63] with the shareholder, or a person who is a member of a partnership or a beneficiary of a trust that is a shareholder of the corporation is indebted to the corporation, a related corporation, or a partnership to

---

[58] And certain persons related to the shareholder.

[59] S. 80.4; subs. 15(9).

[60] Other than a resident corporate shareholder.

[61] Subs. 80.4(2).

[62] Reg. 4301.

[63] Para. 80.4(2)(*b*); subs. 80.4(8); s. 251.

which that corporation is related, the shareholder is deemed to have received a benefit in the year in which the loan or indebtedness is incurred.[64] The imputed interest provisions do not apply to intercorporate loans to corporate shareholders resident in Canada.

(b) Value of Benefit

The imputed benefit from indebtedness is the difference between the amount that would have been payable in the year on the indebtedness if interest were calculated at the prescribed rate and the interest actually paid on the debt during the year, or within 30 days after the end of the taxation year, by the debtor.

Example XIX.4

Assume:

A Ltd. lends $100,000 at 5% to its shareholder at a time when the prescribed rate of interest is 11%. The loan is outstanding all year.

Then:

Imputed interest (11% × $100,000)	$ 11,000
Less:	
Interest paid (5% × $100,000)	(5,000)
Shareholder benefit included in income	$ 6,000

(c) Exclusions

(i) Commercial Loans

The imputed interest rules do not apply in certain circumstances where the rate of interest payable on the debt is equal to or greater than the rate of interest that would have been payable in an arm's length transaction *at the time when the loan was taken out or the obligation was incurred.*[65]

Interest is not imputed on indebtedness where:

- The shareholder is not indebted by virtue of the shareholding;
- The creditor is in the business of lending money; and
- The debt is repaid by the shareholder and not by any other person on his or her behalf.

---

[64] Subs. 80.4(2).

[65] Subs. 80.4(3).

(ii) Principal Sum Taxed

A shareholder is not taxable on imputed interest on indebtedness if the principal sum of the debt is included in his or her income.[66]

9. AUTOMOBILE STANDBY CHARGE

Reference:

BULLETINS, CIRCULARS & RULINGS:

| IT-63R4 | March 31, 1994 | Benefits, Including Standby Charge for an Automobile, From the Personal Use of a Motor Vehicle Supplied by an Employer |

Where a corporation provides its shareholder (or a person related to the shareholder) with an automobile, the shareholder may be taxable on the benefit derived from the automobile. The shareholder may also be taxable for any operating costs paid by the corporation. The shareholder is taxable on a "standby charge" if he or she (or a person related to him or her) is supplied with an automobile by the corporation or by any person related to the corporation.[67]

10. NON-RESIDENT SHAREHOLDERS AND CORPORATIONS

For the purpose of calculating a resident shareholder's income, the shareholder benefit provisions apply whether or not the corporation or creditor is resident in Canada or carries on business in Canada.[68] Thus, a Canadian resident who borrows from a non-resident corporation may be liable for tax if the loan does not qualify as an "exempt loan".[69]

A loan by a resident corporation to a non-resident shareholder is not subject to the shareholder benefit provisions. The amount of the benefit that *would have* been included in income if the borrower were a resident is deemed to be a dividend to the non-resident shareholder and is subject to withholding tax.[70]

---

[66] Para. 80.4(3)(*b*).

[67] Subs. 15(5); see Chapter IV "What is Income?".

[68] Subs. 15(7).

[69] See the exceptions in subs. 15(2).

[70] Para. 214(3)(*a*).

11. SHAREHOLDER AGREEMENTS

References:

BULLETINS, CIRCULARS & RULINGS:

IT-96R5	May 13, 1991	Options Granted by Corporations to Acquire Shares, Bonds or Debentures
IT-116R3	February 28, 1995	Rights to Buy Additional Shares
IT-405	January 23, 1978	Inadequate Considerations — Acquisitions and Dispositions

(a) General

A shareholders' agreement is a contract among shareholders setting out the terms, conditions and obligations agreed upon between the shareholders. The main purpose of a shareholders' agreement is to govern relations between shareholders and to provide a mechanism for the transfer of shares between shareholders.

Why are shareholders' agreements necessary? The best way to answer this question is to look at what would happen in the absence of such an agreement.

The general rule of corporate law is that the business and affairs of a corporation are to be governed by its board of directors. Thus, in the absence of an agreement, most business policies, acquisitions, mergers, dividend payouts, share issues and repurchases are in the discretion of the board of directors. Obviously, the person who controls the board of directors controls the corporation. Minority shareholders generally do not have enough votes to have representation on the board of directors, and so are vulnerable to corporate actions taken by the majority shareholders.

Where two shareholders have an equal holding of 50 per cent each, the danger lies, not in dominance of one over the other, but in corporate deadlock. The provision of a casting vote to one of the shareholders does not resolve the problem. Such a provision would effectively transform an equal shareholding into absolute control for the person who carries the third vote.

A shareholders' agreement is typically used between shareholders of a closely-held corporation to deal with matters such as:

- Control and management of the corporation;
- Protection of minority shareholders;
- Purchase and sale of its shares;
- Options to acquire additional shares issued by the corporation;
- Expenses that exceed predetermined limits;
- Valuation of the corporation's shares;
- Sale of a substantial part of the corporation's assets; and
- Amalgamation and liquidation.

A shareholders' agreement is particularly valuable in situations where a corporation is closely held and operates, in effect, as a partnership. For example, a shareholders' agreement can be useful in the following types of situations:

- Where there are two shareholders and each of them has a 50 per cent shareholding in the corporation. This situation is analogous to a two-person partnership, and the shareholders' agreement between the shareholders will usually cover many of the same topics found in a typical partnership agreement. The focus of the agreement may be to prevent deadlock.

- Where there are two or more shareholders and one of the shareholders has a controlling interest. In this type of situation the agreement is generally drafted to protect the minority shareholders, who might otherwise be vulnerable to the controlling shareholder's domination.

- Where there are more than two shareholders and none of them has a majority position, so that no single person can control the corporation. In these circumstances the agreement can provide for the smooth and efficient operation of the corporation despite the absence of control in one person.

(b) *Inter Vivos* Agreements

Shareholders' agreements fall into two broad categories: (1) *Inter vivos* agreements, and (2) Agreements that are operative only upon the death of one or more of the shareholders.

A shareholders' agreement is a contract. There are no hard and fast rules as to what should be included in contracts. Typically, such agreements address areas that are of major concern to the parties to the agreement. For example:

- The right to elect members of the board of directors;
- The right to appoint officers of the corporation;
- The right to restrict the powers normally conferred upon directors, particularly powers dealing with corporate borrowing, guarantee of obligations to third parties, and the power to enter into long-term obligations and contracts over a specified value;
- The right of shareholders to enter into competing businesses;
- Dividend policies;
- Preemptive rights of shareholders to acquire new issues of shares;
- Restrictions or prohibitions on the right to transfer shares and the obligation to take up shares offered for sale;
- The right or obligation of other shareholders to purchase shares under certain conditions, such as the death or permanent disability of the shareholder;
- The method of share valuation in the event of compulsory acquisition of the shares or where there is a right of first refusal;

- The provision of adequate funding to ensure that there are sufficient funds to finance any compulsory acquisitions under the agreement;
- Dispute resolution mechanisms; and
- Provisions for the alteration and/or termination of the shareholders' agreement to accommodate new and changed circumstances.

A shareholders' agreement should be comprehensive if it is to adequately address each of the issues listed above.

Some of the provisions that address these concerns can have important income tax consequences which should be taken into account at the time when the agreement is drafted. Others have no income tax consequences and are simply a matter of corporate or contract law.

(i) Control

One of the matters frequently addressed in a shareholders' agreement is the allocation of corporate control. For example, provisions that deal with voting power, options to acquire shares, rights of first refusal, etc., may affect control of the corporation, which in turn can cause the corporation to become associated with other corporations.[71]

The concept of "control" is also important in the following situations:

- Determination of "private corporation" and "Canadian-controlled private corporation" status;
- Availability of the small business deduction;
- Qualification as a "small business corporation" for purposes of the capital gains exemption;
- Limitations on the carryover of capital and non-capital losses;
- Liability for Part IV tax; and
- Allocation of the small business deduction between corporate partnerships and associated corporations.

(ii) Associated Corporations

The Act contains various provisions dealing with "associated corporations". Generally speaking, associated corporations are required to allocate the small business deduction (maximum $200,000 per year) among themselves. Thus, a group of associated corporations is limited in the amount that it may claim in any year on account of the small business deduction.

Section 256 sets out the rules for determining whether two or more corporations are associated with each other. Two or more corporations are considered to be

---

[71] See, for example, subss. 256(6) and (7).

associated with each other if one of the corporations controls the other or the corporations are controlled by a common person. Thus, in the simplest case, if Corporation A controls Corporation B, then corporations A and B are associated with each other. Similarly, if *Redco* controls *Blackco* and *Whiteco*, then *Blackco* and *Whiteco* are associated with each other.[72]

(A) Option to Acquire Shares

A person who has a right to acquire shares in a corporation or who can control the voting rights of shares is considered to be in the same position as if he or she actually owned the shares.

Hence, the use of a buy-sell option (usually inserted for the purpose of ensuring a market for the shares) can inadvertently result in two or more corporations becoming associated with each other for tax purposes.

Options granted to non-residents and public corporations to acquire shares in a private Canadian corporation can cause a shift of control and disqualify the corporation from having status as a Canadian-controlled private corporation.

Similarly, a person who has a right to cause a corporation to redeem, acquire or cancel its shares is considered to be in the same position in relation to the control of the corporation as if the shares had been redeemed, cancelled or acquired by the corporation. Hence, the mere right to acquire shares or the right to redeem or cancel shares can cause a person to be considered in control of a corporation.

The above rules apply, however, only when the right to acquire shares or control the voting rights of shares is exercisable during the lifetime of the shareholders. They do not apply when the right is triggered by the death of a designated shareholder or by the bankruptcy or permanent disability of an individual designated in the shareholders' agreement.

(B) Right of Refusal

Is a right of first refusal also a buy-sell option for the purposes of the above rule? The better view is that a right of first refusal is not a right to acquire shares, but only a right to have the first bid on the shares in the event that the shares are, if ever, offered for sale to a third party. Revenue Canada's position is that paragraph 251(5)(*b*) of the Act does not normally apply to a right of first refusal:[73]

> Shareholder agreements commonly referred to as "the right of first refusal" are considered not to confer a right to acquire a share but rather an option to acquire, in certain future circumstances, a right to acquire a share. It follows from this that paragraph 251(5)(*b*) does not apply in the case of "the right of first refusal". The Department also is of the view that [the paragraph] would not normally apply to what is commonly called "a shotgun arrangement" where a shareholder offers to purchase the shares

---

[72] See Chapter XVII "Private Corporation: Business Income".

[73] IT-64R3, "Corporations: Association and Control — After 1988" (March 9, 1992), para. 37.

of another shareholder and the other shareholder must actually accept the offer to purchase the shares owned by the offering party.

The scope of subparagraph 251(5)(*b*)(ii) is also uncertain. The provision reads as follows:

(*b*) a person [who] has a right under a contract, in equity or otherwise, either immediately or in the future and either absolutely or contingently

(ii)   to cause a corporation to redeem, acquire or cancel any shares of its capital stock owned by other shareholders of the corporation shall...be deemed to have the same position in relation to the control of the corporation as if the shares were so redeemed, acquired or cancelled by the corporation. . . .

Under corporate law, the directors of a corporation have the power to exercise their discretion to redeem, acquire or cancel any shares of capital stock that are issued and outstanding in the hands of shareholders. It would be absurd to interpret this provision to mean that the control of the corporation should be determined *as if* the shares that were issued and outstanding had already been redeemed, acquired or cancelled by the corporation. The better interpretation is that this provision applies only to shareholders who, in their capacity as shareholders, have such a right by virtue of a contract, such as a shareholders' agreement.

(iii) Market for Shares

One of the important reasons for a shareholders' agreement is to ensure a market for the shares of a closely-held corporation. A shareholders' agreement sets out the events that allow for a transfer of shares between shareholders and the manner in which the transfer is to be executed.

The following mechanisms are frequently used to ensure that there is a market for the shares.

(A) Right of First Refusal

A right of first refusal obliges a shareholder who wishes to dispose of shares to offer the shares to the other shareholders before they are offered to outside parties. The offer to the current shareholders must be on the same terms and conditions as any offer to the non-shareholders.

(B) Shotgun Clause

A shotgun clause provides that a shareholder can give notice to the other shareholders of his or her intention to acquire all of the shares belonging to the other shareholders. The notice specifies the purchase price of the shares as well as the other terms and conditions of the offer. The recipient of the notice is required to either sell his or her shares to the offeror, or acquire all of the offeror's shares under the same terms and conditions. A shotgun clause can be particularly useful when shareholders reach an impasse, but it can have unpredictable consequences and should be used only when shareholders have equal bargaining power and financial resources.

(C) Private Auction

A private auction operates in a similar manner to a shotgun clause: All of the shareholders are required to offer their shares for sale to the highest bidder at a private auction that is attended only by the shareholders. A private auction offers a little more flexibility than a shotgun clause, because it allows the offeror to increase the offer during the course of the proceedings.

(D) Compulsory Offer

A compulsory offer clause obliges a shareholder to offer his or her shares to the other shareholders or to buy the shares of the other shareholders. The clause will set out the circumstances in which the obligation arises. Typically, a compulsory offer clause is triggered in the following circumstances:

- Death of a shareholder;
- Retirement of a shareholder;
- Disability of a shareholder;
- Bankruptcy or insolvency of a shareholder;
- Theft, fraud or embezzlement by a shareholder against the company;
- Termination of a shareholder's employment;
- Competition by a shareholder with the company; or
- Non-observance of the shareholders' agreement.

The clause should set out the price for the shares or a method for establishing the price of the shares. The clause should also specify the manner in which the shares are to be paid for by the purchaser.

(E) Piggyback Clause

A piggyback clause obliges the minority shareholders to sell their shares when the shares of the majority shareholder are sold to a third party. A piggyback clause allows minority shareholders to avail themselves of terms and conditions that they might not otherwise be able to negotiate for themselves.

Each of these methods of purchase and sale raises two questions: (1) How will the funds be generated to provide for the purchase and sale of the shares? and (2) What are the tax consequences to the purchaser and vendor of the shares?

(iv) Funding the Agreement

There are several ways to fund a shareholders' buy-sell agreement. The best method depends upon the particular structure of the agreement, the financial capabilities of the parties concerned and, where applicable, the insurability of the parties to the agreement.

(A) Corporation Party to Agreement

Where the corporation itself is a party to the agreement (for example, an "unanimous shareholders' agreement" under the *Canada Business Corporations Act*)[74] and is required to purchase any shares that are offered for sale, the easiest method of financing the purchase is to provide for a reserve or contingency fund to satisfy the terms of the agreement. In most cases, however, closely-held corporations do not segregate their funds for such purposes, and the presence of an accounting reserve on the books does not ensure that liquid funds will be available at the appropriate time to finance the purchase of shares that come onto the market.

A corporation can use a sinking fund to finance the purchase, but this route is rarely followed. A sinking fund is an actual reserve of cash or near-cash assets.

If the corporation is required to borrow money to finance the repurchase of shares, interest paid may be deductible as an expense in computing income.

(B) Corporation Not Party to Agreement

The problem of financing the agreement becomes more complicated if the corporation is not a party to the agreement and the other shareholders are required to take up any shares offered for sale. The purchaser may borrow the necessary funds to purchase the shares. In these circumstances, any interest paid on the borrowed money will generally be deductible in computing income for tax purposes. The use of disability insurance is convenient to finance the purchase of shares that are offered for sale as the result of a shareholder's long term disability.

(v) Capital Gains

A shareholder may realize a capital gain or capital loss upon the disposition of shares to other shareholders. If the shares sold are the shares of a "qualified small business corporation", the vendor may shelter up to $500,000 of capital gains from tax.[75]

The capital gains exemption is subject to several special anti-avoidance rules. One of these rules prevents an individual from claiming the capital gains exemption in circumstances where the gain is, in effect, generated by converting dividend income into a capital gain.[76] In other words, this rule applies where the value of corporate shares is enhanced by the non-payment or restrictive payment of dividends. This rule can have important consequences for a shareholder who is a party to a shareholders' agreement, because such agreements quite typically provide for restricted dividend payments. Thus, although a clause restricting dividends may be financially desirable, it may also prove to be expensive from an income tax perspective.

---

[74] *Canada Business Corporations Act*, R.S.C. 1985, c. C-44.

[75] See Chapter XVII "Private Corporations: Business Income".

[76] See subs. 110.6(8).

(c) Death

Reference:

BULLETINS, CIRCULARS & RULINGS:

IT-140R3   April 14, 1989   Buy-Sell Agreements

(i) Market for Shares

One of the principal attractions of a shareholders' agreement is that it provides a market for the shares of a private corporation. Private corporations typically restrict the transfer of their shares. Such restrictions are usually desirable from a business point of view, but they can seriously inhibit the market for minority shareholders. A shareholders' agreement can overcome this disadvantage by providing for an alternative share transfer mechanism and for the orderly settlement of an estate.

Typically, a private corporation's articles of incorporation will state that the corporation's shares may not be transferred without:

- The approval of the directors of the corporation; or

- The approval of the holders of at least a majority of the common shares of the corporation.

These restrictions do not pose a problem for majority shareholders, but can be difficult for the minority.

A shareholders' agreement is a mechanism for arranging shareholder approval in advance of an event. For example, the agreement can provide that, in the event of a shareholder's death, the surviving shareholders shall purchase, or have the *option* to purchase, the deceased's shares. In the first case, the agreement must provide a mechanism to determine the price at which the shares will be purchased and the appropriate procedural mechanism for an orderly transfer. In the second case, the mechanism for price determination may be left open until the time when the option is put to the purchaser. In either case, the formula for determination of the price may have important tax consequences.

(ii) Deemed Disposition

Subsection 70(5) of the Act provides that a shareholder is "deemed to have disposed, immediately before his death, of each property owned by him at that time". The deemed disposition does not, by itself, create a market for the shares; it simply triggers income tax consequences *as if* the taxpayer had actually disposed of the shares.

The actual transfer of the shares occurs pursuant to principles of succession law, provisions in the corporation's articles of incorporation, and the terms of the shareholders' agreement. Thus, it is important to ensure that the deemed proceeds of disposition for tax purposes are at least equal to the price received for the shares. Otherwise, tax will be payable on an amount that is higher than the cash actually received for the shares.

(iii) Funding

In addition to ensuring the marketability of shares and the determination of the price of shares, it is also important that the parties provide for a method of funding the purchase and sale of the corporation's shares. After all, it serves little purpose to have a contractual obligation that provides for a mandatory purchase of shares without providing for some method to ensure that the purchaser has the necessary funds to fulfil his or her contractual obligations.

Thus, a shareholders' agreement may incorporate funding provisions to ensure the availability of funds at the appropriate time to finance the share purchase and sale transaction. This is particularly important in the case of mandatory share purchase agreements. The method of funding also has income tax consequences.

(iv) Mandatory Purchases

An agreement may provide that the deceased shareholder's estate is entitled to "put" his or her shares to the surviving shareholders and that they are *obliged* to purchase the shares according to the method and formula provided in the agreement. In these circumstances, the surviving shareholders do not have any choice in their decision to purchase the shares, nor is there very much choice as to the price of the shares transferred. The price is determined according to the formula prescribed in the agreement.

Such a clause is generally advantageous to the deceased's estate: It assures a market for the shares at the earliest possible opportunity and with the greatest certainty in respect of the transaction price. A "put" option may, however, place an onerous financial burden on the purchasers by requiring them to purchase the shares at an inopportune time.

(v) Valuation

Paragraph 70(5)(a) of the Act provides that a deceased taxpayer is deemed to have disposed of each non-depreciable capital property owned by him or her immediately before death, for proceeds equal to its fair market value. The person who acquires the property is also deemed to do so at an amount equal to the fair market value of the property. Where there is a shareholders' agreement, the deemed proceeds of disposition may depend upon the relationship of the parties to the agreement.

(A) Arm's Length Relationships

One of the more troublesome questions in respect of shareholder buy-sell agreements is the value to be attached to shares that are the subject of a "put" clause. Where the deceased and the surviving shareholders deal with each other at arm's length, the contract price provided for in the shareholders' agreement will usually be close to the fair market value of the property at the relevant time. It would be unusual for parties who are at arm's length with each other to arrange for a purchase and sale of property at any price other than its fair market value.

It is, however, possible that the stipulated contract price is out of date and does not fully reflect share values at the time of death. It is also possible that the parties may have drafted the transfer price incorrectly or without much thought.[77] In either case, Revenue Canada is not bound by an improper valuation, even if the parties were at arm's length. Fair market value is to be determined objectively.

(B) Non-arm's Length Relationships

Where the parties were not at arm's length with each other, it is quite possible for the fair market value of the transferred property to be different from the transfer price resulting from the agreement. Revenue Canada takes the view that, where the deceased and the surviving shareholders did not deal with each other at arm's length, the fair market value of the shares must be determined *without reference* to the shareholders' agreement.[78]

(C) Insurance

The effect of corporate-owned life insurance may also affect the value of the deceased's shares. Subsection 70(5.3) requires that the cash surrender value of any corporate-owned insurance on the life of the deceased be taken into account in determining the value of the deceased's shares immediately before death. The face value of the policy is irrelevant for this purpose.

Since term life insurance does not generate a cash surrender value, this rule really applies only to whole life policies. The specific rule in subsection 70(5.3) precludes, in effect, the application of any general valuation principle that the discounted expectancy of a term policy should be taken into account in valuing shares immediately before death.[79]

The deceased's estate is deemed to acquire the shares that are deemed to have been disposed of *immediately before death* at an amount equal to the deemed proceeds of disposition. Thus, the cost of the shares to the estate is determined by reference to the value of the shares, which includes the *pro rata* share of the cash surrender value of any whole life policy on the life of the deceased.

It is, however, arguable that the value of the shares to the estate increases *after the death* of the deceased, because the corporation is now actually entitled to the full face value of the whole life policy. In other words, where there is a substantial disparity between the cash surrender value and the face value of a policy, the value of the shares may be enhanced by the corporation's *pro rata* share of the difference between the two values. In these circumstances, the estate may have a gain on the transfer of the shares to the surviving shareholders' pursuant to the shareholders' agreement.

---

[77] See, e.g., *Carrol v. McArthur* (1983), 25 BLR 132 (Ont. Co. Ct.).

[78] IT-140R3, "Buy-Sell Agreements" (April 14, 1989).

[79] See, e.g., *The Queen v. Mastronardi*, [1977] CTC 355, 77 DTC 5217 (F.C.A.).

(vi) Right of First Refusal

A right of first refusal clause usually provides that the deceased's estate is obliged to offer the shares to the surviving shareholders but that they are not obliged to purchase the shares offered. A right of first refusal operates to the advantage of the surviving shareholders, but does not provide the deceased's estate with an assured market for the shares. Thus, a right of first refusal may not be the most appropriate transfer mechanism to use if marketability and liquidity of the estate are the primary concerns.

A right of first refusal does simplify many other aspects of share transfers. It is generally considerably easier to provide for a valuation mechanism as part of a right of first refusal than in the case of a mandatory buy-sell agreement. For example, it is not unusual to provide that the surviving shareholders have a right of first refusal to be exercised within a period of time (say, 30 days), after which the deceased's estate is entitled to offer the shares to any other interested party.

From an income tax perspective, however, the problem of valuation may become more complicated. Where the shareholders' buy-sell agreement does not provide for a formula to value the shares, their fair market value must be determined according to general principles of share valuation. This can be difficult even in the most routine circumstances, and can be a substantial burden, in both financial and administrative terms, for the estate.

12. SOLE PURPOSE CORPORATIONS

Canadians who own vacation properties in the United States may be subject to U.S. estate taxes and the U.S. *Foreign Investment in Real Property Tax Act.* To avoid exposure to these taxes, Canadians can own personal-use real property (for example, vacation homes, condominiums, time-shares, etc.) through a Canadian corporation created for the sole purpose of owning the property. Ownership of such assets through a corporation will avoid United States estate taxes, provided that the corporation is not considered a sham or an agent of the individual.

The use of a sole-purpose corporation may subject the taxpayer to the shareholder benefit rules in subsection 15(1). The Department has indicated that it will not assess a personal shareholder benefit in the following circumstances:

- The corporation's only objective is to hold the property for the personal use or enjoyment of the shareholder;
- The corporation's shares are held by an individual or by an individual related to the shareholder;
- The corporate transactions only relate to the corporation's objectives, namely, the personal use or enjoyment of the property by the shareholder; and

- The shareholder is charged with all of the operating expenses of the property, and as a consequence the corporation does not show a profit or loss with respect to the property.

The Department interprets these conditions quite stringently. The "no-benefit" rule applies only if the corporation does nothing more than hold the property for the personal use and enjoyment of the shareholder. Earning income (e.g., rent) of any kind whatever is inconsistent with the above conditions and can trigger subsection 15(1) benefits.

SELECTED BIBLIOGRAPHY TO CHAPTER XIX

Benefits

Allgood, David R., "Tax Planning for Private Corporations and Their Shareholders: Implications of Recent Changes on the Use of Holding Companies", in *Proceedings of 38th Tax Conf.* 10:1 (Can. Tax Foundation, 1986).

Beam, Robert E. and Stanley N. Laiken, "Benefits under Subsection 15(1)" (1994), 42 *Can. Tax J.* 477.

Bernstein, Jack, "Family Tax Planning", in *Proceedings of 37th Tax Conf.* 46 (Can. Tax Foundation, 1985).

Bernstein, Jack, "Fringe Benefits and Equity Participation", *Corp. Mgmt. Tax Conf.* 5:1 (Can. Tax Foundation, 1991).

Birnie, David A.G., "Shareholders' Buy-Sell Agreements: Some New Opportunities", in *Proceedings of 38th Tax Conf.* 13:1 (Can. Tax Foundation, 1986).

Campbell, Ian R., "Valuation-related Issues: Tax Planning and Post-transaction Followup", in *Proceedings of 45th Tax Conf.* 25:1 (Can. Tax Foundation, 1993).

Corn, George, "Indirect Payments and Shareholder Loans as Income Inclusions" (1993), 4 *Can. Current Tax* J23.

Dan, Robert J., and David W. Smith, "Estate Planning: A New Era" (1986), 34 *Can. Tax J.* 1.

Drache, A.B.C., "Employee or Shareholder Benefit" (1983), 5 *Can. Taxpayer* 202.

Dunbar, Alisa, "Use of Holding Corporation may Elude Shareholder Benefit Provisions" (1992), 3 *Tax. of Exec. Compensation and Retirement* 606.

Durnford, John W., "Benefits and Advantages Conferred on Shareholders" (1984), 32 *Can. Tax J.* 455.

Goldstein, D.L., "Court Places No 'Ceiling' on Shareholder Benefit Valuation" (1990), 38 *Can. Tax J.* 669.

Hickey, Pat, "The New Rules for Intergenerational Transfers of Family Assets" (1985), 33 *Can. Tax J.* 360.

Hoey, D. Graham, "Shareholder-manager Compensation" in *Proceedings of 42nd Tax Conf.* 6:1 (Can. Tax Foundation, 1990).

Hogg, Roy D., "A Canadian Tax Overview of Transfer Pricing" (1983), 116 *CA Magazine* 54.

"Home Purchase Loans to Employee/Shareholders may have Extended Term" (1992), 3 *Tax. of Exec. Compensation and Retirement* 552.

Innes, William I., "The Taxation of Indirect Benefits: An Examination of Subsections 56(2), 56(3), 56(4), 245(2) and 245(3) of the Income Tax Act", in *Proceedings of 38th Tax Conf.* 42:1 (Can. Tax Foundation, 1986).

Jaskolka, Norman, "Employee and Shareholder Loans — Are They a Benefit?" (1983), 116 *CA Magazine* 51.

Jones, D. Alan, "Business Equity Valuations and Real Estate Appraisals in Revenue Canada", in *Proceedings of 45th Tax Conf.* 26:1 (Can. Tax Foundation, 1993).

Krishna, Vern, "Shareholder Benefits" (1990), 3 *Can. Current Tax* C33.

Krishna, Vern, "Who Benefits?" (1991), 5 *CGA Magazine* 45.

Lee, Julie Y., "Stock-Based Compensation: Selected Regulatory and Taxation Issues", *Corp. Mgmt. Tax Conf.* 4:1 (Can. Tax Foundation, 1991).

McCrodan, Andrew, "Tackling Tax-related Troubles" (1993), 126 *CA Magazine No. 4* 45.

Montgomery, Anne, "Developments in Executive Compensation" (1992), 3 *Can. Current Tax* T-21.

"Redemption or Repurchase of Shares (The)", *Can. Tax Letter,* February 22, 1982 (De Boo).

"Revenue Canada Round Table", in *Proceedings of 33rd Tax Conf.* 726 (Can. Tax Foundation, 1981).

Richards, Gabrielle M.R., "A Trap for the Unwary: Subsection 15(2) of the Income Tax Act" (1993), 4 *Can. Current Tax* J27.

"Shareholders Benefits — Vacation Properties" (1988), 15 *Can. Tax News* 121.

Sklar, Murray, "Don't Get Trapped by the New Income Attribution Rules" (1987), 120 *CA Magazine* 42.

Smith, David W., "New Income Attribution Rules 'Muddified' Income Tax Act" (1986), 13 *Nat. (CBA)* 12.

Smith, David W., "Wilson's Minimum-Tax Proposals Treat Dividends Unfairly" (1986), 13 *Nat. (CBA)*2.

Strain, William J., "Life-insured Share Redemption Provides Advantages Over Outright Buyback" (1993), 5 *Tax. of Exec. Compensation and Retirement* 811.

Stubbs, Larry, and Don Goodison, "Planning Ahead" (1990), 4 *CGA Magazine* 42.

Templeton, Michael D., "Loan Made to Shareholder-Employee *qua* Employee Liable to Tax under Subsection 15(2)" (1994), 42 *Can. Tax J.* 201.

Tunney, Wayne L., "Taking Stock: The Pros and Cons of Stock-Based Compensation", *Corp. Mgmt. Tax Conf.* 3:1 (Can. Tax Foundation, 1991).

Ulmer, John M., "Family Members as Shareholders of a Small Business Corporation", in *Proceedings of 38th Tax Conf.* 14:1 (Can. Tax Foundation, 1986).

Ward, David A., and John M. Ulmer, "Corporate Taxation: Shares Eligible for the Capital Gains Exemption" (1986), 5 *Legal Alert* 81.

Zien, Randolph B., "Remuneration of Shareholders and Executives: Selected Problems", *British Columbia Tax Conf.* 149 (Can. Tax Foundation, 1980).

Indirect Benefits

Desaulniers, Claude P., "Choix d'une structure du capital", *J. d'études fiscales* 79 (Can. Tax Foundation, 1982).

Drache, A.B.C., "Estate Planning Time Bomb" (1983), 5 *Can. Taxpayer* 42.

Graschuk, Harry S., "The Professional Corporation in Alberta" (1977), 5 *Can. Tax J.* 109.

Katz, Robert L., "Income Splitting: The Labyrinth of Attribution", *B.C. Tax Conf.* 93 (Can. Tax Foundation, 1980).

Kellough, Howard J., "Selecting an Appropriate Share Capital Structure for Private Corporations", in *Proceedings of 33rd Tax Conf.* 49 (Can. Tax Foundation, 1981).

Krishna, V., "Corporate Share Structures and Estate Planning" (1983), 6 *E. & T.Q.* 168.

Kroft, E.G., "Income Splitting" (1983), 17 *CGA Magazine* 28.

Kwan, Stanley P.W., and Kenneth J. Murray, "Remuneration Planning for the Owner-Manager" (1981), 9 *Can. Tax J.* 603.

Leuser, John, "Income Splitting Within the Family" (1981), 55 *Cost & Mgmt.* 47.

McKenzie, H.G., "Recent Developments in Income Splitting", *Prairie Provinces Tax Conf.* 413 (Can. Tax Foundation, 1981).

Morris, J.S.D., "Freezing Family Business Interests — Inflation and Other Concerns" (1981), 9 *Can. Tax J.*11.

Promislow, Norm, "Estate Planning and Income Splitting: Recent Developments", *Prairie Prov. Tax Conf.* 371 (Can. Tax Foundation, 1983).

Shinerock, Stanley, "Tax Planning for the Canadian-Controlled Private Corporation" (1980), 14 *CGA Magazine* 32.

Zaystoll, J.J., "Accountant's Comment: Innovative Share Capital Structures to Split Income Effectively" (1984), 42 *Advocate (Van.)* 177.

Deemed Dividends

Boultbee, J.A., "Minimizing the Taxation Effects of Dividends", in *Proceedings of 37th Tax Conf.* 7 (Can. Tax Foundation, 1985).

Carten, Michael A., "Income Tax Considerations in the Capitalization of a Corporation", *Corp. Mgmt. Tax Conf.* 50 (Can. Tax Foundation, 1980).

Gould, Lawrence I., and Stanley N. Laiken, "Dividends vs. Capital Gains under Share Redemptions" (1979), 7 *Can. Tax J. 161.*

Hart, Stephen D., "Estate Freezes, Part: Income Splitting" (1982), 115 *CA Magazine* 60.

Hogg, R.D., "Stock Option Benefits in Canadian Controlled Private Corporations" (1978), 6 *Can. Tax J.* 85.

Kellough, Howard J., "Formation, Operation, and Disposition of Closely Held Corporations", in *Proceedings of 30th Tax Conf.* 703 (Can. Tax Foundation, 1978).

"Revenue Canada Round Table", in *Proceedings of 33rd Tax Conf.* 726 (Can. Tax Foundation, 1981).

Sohmer, David H., "Purchase and Sale of a Closely-Held Business (2)" (1979), 112 *CA Magazine* 70.

Spindler, Herbert O., "Article X: Dividends", in *Proceedings of 32nd Tax Conf.* 405 (Can. Tax Foundation, 1980).

Imputed Interest on Loans

Drache, A.B.C., "Reduction of Tax at Source" (1983), 5 *Can. Taxpayer* 130.

Hamill, James R., "Tax Consequences of Corporation-Shareholder Loans" (1989), 67 *Taxes* 608.

Hugget, Donald R., "Obfusclarity" (1992), 9 *Can. Tax News* 57.

Jaskolka, Norman, "Employee and Shareholder Loans — Are They a Benefit?" (1983), 116 *CA Magazine* 51.

Kar, William J., "The Onus of Shareholder Loans" (1993), 126 *CA Magazine* 34.

Novek, Barbara L., "Taxable Benefit from Interest Free Loan may Reduce Capital Gains Exemption" (1992), 3 *Tax. of Exec. Compensation and Retirement* 572.

Shareholder Agreements

Hugget, Donald R., "Shareholder Agreements" (1991), 19 *Can. Tax News* 24.

Krishna, Vern, "Buy-Sell Shareholders' Agreements" (1988), 2 *CGA Magazine* 39.

Krishna, Vern, "Shareholder Agreements" (1988),2 *CGA Magazine* 21.

Magee, J.E., "Shareholder Buy-sell Agreements to Operate on the Winding-up of a Trust" (1991), 39 *Can. Tax J.* 983.

CHAPTER XX

REORGANIZATIONS: TRANSFER OF PROPERTY TO A CORPORATION

References:

ITA:

S. 85	Transfer of Property to Corporation by Shareholders
Subs. 93(1)	Election: Disposition of Share in Foreign Affiliate
Subs. 97(2)	Election: Transfer of Property to Partnership
Subs. 98(3)	Disposition of Partnership Property where Partnership Ceases to Exist

BULLETINS, CIRCULARS & RULINGS:

IT-169	August 6, 1974	Price Adjustment Clauses
IT-170R	August 25, 1980	Sale of Property — When Included in Income Computation
IT-218R	September 16, 1986	Profit, Capital Gains and Losses from the Sale of Real Estate Including Farmland and Inherited Land and Conversion of Real Estate from Capital Property to Inventory and Vice Versa
IT-291R2	September 16, 1994	Transfer of Property to a Corporation Under Subsection 85(1)
IC 76-19R2	June 15, 1990	Transfer of Property to a Corporation Under Section 85
ATR-25	October 9, 1987	Estate Freeze
ATR-26	October 9, 1987	Share Exchange
ATR-27	January 8, 1988	Exchange and Acquisition of Interests in Capital Properties Through Rollovers and Winding-Up ("Butterfly")
ATR-32	July 8, 1988	Rollover of Fixed Assets from Opco into Holdco
ATR-36	November 4, 1988	Estate Freeze

FORMS:

T2057	Election on Disposition of Property by a Taxpayer to a Taxable Canadian Corporation

T2058   Election on Disposition of Property by a Partnership to a Taxable Canadian Corporation

T2059   Election on Disposition of Property by a Taxpayer to a Canadian Partnership

T2060   Election in respect of Disposition of Property upon Cessation of Partnerships

T2107   Election in respect of a Disposition of Shares in a Foreign Affiliate

1. GENERAL PRINCIPLES

As a general rule, a taxpayer who disposes of property will either receive or be *deemed* to have received proceeds of disposition from the property. Where a taxpayer disposes of property to a person with whom he or she does not deal at arm's length, he or she is deemed to receive proceeds of disposition equal to the fair market value of the property.[1] This recognizes the principle of taxation upon realization. Hence, in the absence of special rules, the reorganization of business affairs (e.g., transfer of proprietorship assets into a corporation) would be deemed to occur at fair market value and could result in taxable gains.

The deemed disposition rule could have punitive consequences if it was applied every time a taxpayer reorganized his or her business. For example, a sole proprietor who transfers his or her business assets to a corporation could face a substantial tax on any gains accrued on capital assets, eligible capital property, inventory and for recapture from depreciable property. Since the change in the business would be merely in its legal form rather than its economic substance, a deemed disposition with substantial tax consequences would be inappropriate in the circumstances. The general rule does not promote tax neutrality as between different forms of business organizations.

Section 85 provides a special rule to accommodate business reorganizations. The essence of section 85 is that it overrides the general rule in section 69 and allows a taxpayer to transfer property to a corporation on a tax-deferred basis: Tax that would ordinarily be triggered from a disposition of assets is deferred to a later date when the assets are disposed of by the corporation without cover of a rollover.

Section 85 is an elective provision. It allows taxpayers to recognize transfers of assets at amounts other than their fair market value and to rollover the cost of their assets into other property. To prevent inappropriate use of the provision to avoid tax, however, it is severely circumscribed by various rules, limits, and time constraints.

(a) Meaning of "Rollover"

The term "rollover" is used in tax law to describe transactions in which the tax cost of property disposed of is transferred or "rolled over" into the tax cost of property acquired in exchange for the disposition. Thus, any gain accrued at the time of the

---

[1]   Para. 69(1)(*b*).

rollover is deferred until such time as the newly acquired property is subsequently sold in an "unprotected" transaction.

The general thrust of rollovers is that, in stringently controlled circumstances, a taxpayer can dispose of property without recognizing any immediate gain or loss from the disposition. The property is rolled over at its cost amount to the transferee. The transferor's tax basis in the transferred property becomes the tax basis in the property taken back by the transferor as consideration. The rationale for permitting a taxpayer to rollover assets is that it is undesirable, and perhaps unfair, to impose a tax on transactions that do not involve a fundamental economic change in ownership, even though there may be a change in form or legal structure.

(b) Types of Rollovers

The general thrust of section 69 is to prevent manipulation of asset transfer prices between parties who are not dealing with each other on an economic arm's length basis. The "rollover" provisions of the Act are exceptions to section 69 and allow taxpayers to defer recognition of gains, and sometimes losses, until a subsequent date or event. Thus, the first question to consider in rearranging business or family affairs is whether it is desirable in the particular circumstances to realize any gain or loss accrued on the property.

If it is considered to be undesirable to trigger an accrued gain or loss at the particular time, the proposed disposition of assets should be evaluated in the light of one or more of the "rollover" provisions of the Act. For example, each of the following provisions of the Act permit rollovers in varied circumstances:

- s. 85 — transfers of property to a corporation;
- s. 85.1 — share for share exchanges;
- s. 86 — reorganization of share capital of a corporation;
- s. 87 — amalgamations;
- s. 88 — winding-up of a corporation.

Each provision needs to be considered on its own merits and applicability to the circumstances under review. This chapter begins with an examination of the section 85 rollover; the other corporate rollovers are described in subsequent chapters.

2. SECTION 85

(a) Uses

Section 85 applies:

- Where a taxpayer disposes of an eligible property,
- To a taxable Canadian corporation,
- In exchange for consideration that includes shares of the corporation, and
- Where the parties elect to have the provision apply to the disposition.

Under section 85, a taxpayer who transfers property to a taxable Canadian corporation may *elect* as proceeds of disposition an amount that is less than the fair market value of the property. In other words, section 85 specifically overrides the general rule in section 69 that dispositions of property are deemed to occur at fair market value. Hence, for example, a taxpayer can transfer property with an accrued gain to a taxable Canadian corporation, elect a transfer price equal to the *cost* of the transferred property, and avoid immediate recognition of the accrued gain for tax purposes.[2]

Section 85 may be used to advantage in any of the following circumstances:

- Incorporation of a business carried on by a sole proprietor or by a partnership;
- Transfer of portfolio securities to a holding corporation;
- Transfer of business assets within related corporate groups;
- Transfer of a controlling interest in an operating company to a newly-created holding corporation as part of an estate freeze or an income splitting reorganization;
- Pooling of assets to form a joint venture corporation;
- Split-off of assets held by a joint venture corporation;
- Division of assets of a corporation among its shareholders (a "butterfly" reorganization);[3] and
- Share exchange in a take-over bid.[4]

As the above list suggests, section 85 is a versatile provision that can be used in a variety of familial and business reorganizations, estate planning, and commercial transactions that involve a disposition of assets between taxpayers. But the section is strictly controlled and may be used only in narrowly circumscribed circumstances.[5] The slightest deviation from the technical rules of the section can invalidate the rollover and trigger a deemed disposition at fair market value.

(i) Incorporation of Business

An individual who starts a business may initially structure the enterprise as a sole proprietorship so that he or she can offset business losses against his or her income from other sources. Where a business is financially successful, however, it is generally

---

[2] Para. 85(1)(*a*); see also IT-291R2, "Transfer of Property to a Corporation under Subsection 85(1)" (September 16, 1994).

[3] Para. 55(3)(*b*).

[4] A share-for-share exchange may also be implemented on a rollover basis under s. 85.1; see Chapter XXII "Share-for-Share Exchanges".

[5] Some of these rules deal with the manner of electing and designating values; others deal with the time of filing returns.

advantageous to operate it as a corporation. A Canadian-owned private corporation, for example, can take advantage of the small business deduction and the low rate of tax levied on active business income. Section 85 can be used to transfer the assets of the proprietorship to the incorporated business without triggering any immediate tax liability.

(ii) Capital Gains Exemption

A taxpayer who disposes of shares of a qualified small business corporation may claim an exemption in respect of $500,000 of capital gains realized from the disposition.[6] This exemption is only available on a sale of shares; it is not available to sole proprietors. A sole proprietor may, however, incorporate his or her business and use section 85 in order to take advantage of this generous exemption.

(iii) Tax Deferral

A Canadian-owned private corporation can defer taxes by leaving its income in the corporation. Generally speaking, the tax paid (approximately 23 per cent) by a Canadian-owned small business corporation is substantially lower than the tax payable by an individual in the top tax bracket. Hence, provided that the owner of a business is prepared to leave his or her income in the business, there is a substantial deferral of the tax that would otherwise be payable if the income flowed through to the owner either as salary or dividends. As noted above, section 85 can be used to incorporate a business on a tax deferred basis to take advantage of the low tax rate on active business income.

(iv) Incorporation of Portfolio

In certain circumstances, particularly for taxpayers in the top marginal tax brackets, there may be some tax deferral available in respect of an investment portfolio held in a corporation. The magnitude of the deferral depends upon the difference in tax paid by individuals and corporations on dividend income. For example, a taxpayer in the top tax bracket pays tax at a rate of approximately 35 per cent to 37 per cent on dividend income. If the portfolio is transferred into a taxable Canadian corporation, the effective tax rate on dividend income drops to 33 3/4 per cent. Section 85 allows a taxpayer to incorporate his or her portfolio investments without triggering any immediate income tax liability.

(v) Removing Excess Cash From Corporation

Where an operating company ("Opco") generates cash in excess of its immediate needs, it may wish to utilize the excess cash for investment purposes. It is usually prudent for Opco to segregate its excess cash in a holding company ("Holdco"), which can then invest the funds in a portfolio of investments. In this way, the corporation's investments are not exposed to business risks and Opco can more easily retain its status as a corporation engaged primarily in active business. Section 85 can be used to

---

[6]   Subs. 110.6(2.1).

restructure Opco by transferring its shares to Holdco. Opco then becomes a subsidiary of Holdco. Any excess cash can usually be paid to Holdco as a tax-free dividend.

(vi) Estate Planning and Income Splitting

A taxpayer who owns an operating company ("Opco") may wish to reorganize it so as to minimize the potential for death taxes and to reduce the burden of current income taxes. A reorganization to reduce the impact of death taxes can be implemented through an "estate freeze".

One technique of estate freezing is to transfer the shares of Opco to a holding company ("Holdco") in exchange for "preferred" or "special" shares that will not appreciate in value from the date of the freeze. The effect of such an exchange is that future growth in value is diverted to Holdco's "common" shares, which can be taken up by the taxpayer's children. Such a transaction (referred to as a "holding company freeze") may be implemented on a tax deferred basis under section 85.

Similarly, a taxpayer may wish to reorganize an operating business in order to minimize the amount of current taxes payable. One method is to reorganize the capital structure of the corporation so that its shares are held by the taxpayer and the members of his or her family. This allows the taxpayer to split the corporation's income into several parts and sprinkle it, through dividends, into the hands of the family. Section 85 permits such a reorganization on a tax deferred basis.

(vii) Transfer of Assets Within a Corporate Group

In certain circumstances it may be advantageous to transfer assets within a related corporate group. For example, where one of the corporations in a related group has business losses which it cannot utilize, a profitable corporation in the same group can transfer a profitable asset into the loss corporation. The asset can generate income in the loss corporation that can be sheltered by the losses. Thus, the group as a whole pays less tax. Section 85 can be used to transfer the profitable assets on a tax-free basis without any immediate income tax consequences to the transferor.

(viii) Butterfly Reorganizations

A "butterfly reorganization" is a method of splitting a corporation into two or more separate corporations. This may be necessary if the shareholders of a corporation wish to go their separate ways and to split up an existing corporation. For example, a family-owned business enterprise may require reorganization if the principal shareholders (husband and wife) separate or divorce. In these circumstances, family law legislation may require a sharing of the net value of business assets. A butterfly reorganization allows for the division of the corporation into two or more components on a tax deferred basis under section 85.

(b) Example

The following illustrates a rollover involving the transfer of capital property to a corporation under section 85.

Example XX.1

Assume:

An individual owns a building (capital property) to which the following data applies:

	Land	Building
Adjusted cost base	$150,000	—
Capital cost	—	$120,000
UCC	—	$ 75,000
Fair market value	$225,000	$105,000
Potential capital gain/recapture of CCA witihout rollover	$ 75,000	$ 30,000

The individual transfers the property to a taxable Canadian corporation and the parties elect proceeds of disposition as follows:

Land	$150,000
Building	$ 75,000

Then:

	Land	Building
Deemed proceeds of disposition	$150,000	$ 75,000
Adjusted cost base	(150,000)	—
UCC	—	(75,000)
Capital gain/recapture of transfers	NIL	NIL
Deferred capital gain/recapture of CCA	$ 75,000	$ 30,000

(c) Partnerships

Subsection 85(1) deals with transfers by a taxpayer to a taxable Canadian corporation. There are other provisions that deal with comparable transfers of property by a partnership to a corporation.[7]

(d) Election of Values

Section 85 allows a taxpayer who transfers property to a taxable Canadian corporation to *elect* as proceeds of disposition of the property an amount other than its

---

[7] Subss. 85(2), (3).

fair market value or the value of the consideration received. Thus, section 85 overrides section 69, which would otherwise deem the proceeds of disposition to be equal to the fair market value of the property.

The election is, however, subject to certain limits. The lower limit is generally the cost amount of the property. The upper limit is usually the fair market value of the property transferred. Thus, a taxpayer who elects to use section 85 to transfer property to a taxable Canadian corporation has some latitude in determining the amount, if any, of the gain which he or she will recognize at the time of the transfer. Note, that section 85 does not allow a taxpayer to claim a capital loss from a disposition of capital property or a loss from a disposition of eligible capital property.[8]

3. WHO CAN USE SUBSECTION 85(1)?

(a) Transferors

The rollover is available to any taxpayer (whether resident or non-resident in Canada) who disposes of property to a taxable Canadian corporation. "Taxpayer" includes any person regardless of whether he or she is liable to pay tax.[9] Thus, the rollover can be used by individuals, trusts and corporations. The rollover is also available to partnerships.[10]

(b) Transferees

The transferee must be a *taxable* Canadian corporation. A "taxable Canadian corporation" is a Canadian corporation that is not exempt from tax under Part I of the Act.[11]

A "Canadian corporation" is a resident corporation that was either incorporated in Canada or resident in Canada *throughout* the period from June 18, 1971 to the relevant date, that is, the date of the transfer.[12] It is not generally possible to rollover property to a non-resident corporation.[13]

(c) Exclusion of Subsection 86(1)

Subsection 86(1) applies when a taxpayer exchanges *all* of his or her shares of one class for shares of another class of the same corporation as part of a reorganization of

---

[8] Subs. 85(4).

[9] Subs. 248(1) ("taxpayer").

[10] Subs. 85(2).

[11] Subs. 89(1) ("taxable Canadian corporation").

[12] Subs. 89(1) ("Canadian corporation").

[13] See, however, the foreign affiliate rollover in subsection 85.1(3).

the corporation's capital. Subsection 86(1) does not apply to an exchange of shares if subsection 85(1) or (2) are applicable.[14]

Where a taxpayer transfers *all* of his or her shares in a taxable Canadian corporation in exchange for shares of another class in the *same* corporation, Revenue Canada is of the view that subsection 85(1) applies; hence, subsection 86(1) cannot apply to such an exchange of shares.

4. PROPERTY ELIGIBLE FOR ROLLOVER

(a) Types of Property

Section 85 restricts the rollover to dispositions of the following types of property:[15]

- capital property (except for real property, or an interest therein, or an option in respect thereof, owned by a non-resident);
- eligible capital property;
- inventory,[16] except real property inventory, an interest in real property or an option in respect thereof;
- accounts receivable in respect of which no election has been made;[17]
- Canadian resource properties;
- foreign resource properties;
- certain property used in an insurance business;
- real property that is capital property and is used by a non-resident in the course of carrying on a business in Canada; and
- a NISA Fund No. 2.

Eligible property includes personal property that qualifies as capital property. It also includes debt owing to a corporation by another taxable Canadian corporation.

A Canadian resident may transfer any capital property (depreciable or otherwise) under section 85, regardless whether it is situated in Canada or in a foreign country.

---

[14] Subs. 86(3).

[15] Subs. 85(1.1).

[16] Including a professional's work in progress; see definition of "inventory" in subsection 248(1).

[17] S. 22; see Chapter XXV "Purchase and Sale of a Business".

(b) Real Estate

(i) Inventory

The exclusion of real property inventory is intended to prevent a real estate trader from converting business income into a capital gain by selling inventory to a corporation and then selling the shares of the corporation for a capital gain. Such a transformation of business income into a capital gain would in any event probably fail.[18] Subsection 85(1), however, adds certainty through its outright prohibition of the use of the rollover for real property inventory.

The distinction between capital property and business inventory depends on the intention of the taxpayer who disposes of the property.[19] Therefore, it may be difficult to determine with certainty whether real estate does or does not qualify for the rollover under subsection 85(1). Since the characterization of real estate gains and losses depends on the factual circumstances surrounding its ownership, it is usually not possible to obtain an advance ruling on its status from Revenue Canada.[20] In cases of doubt, it may be prudent not to transfer real property that may later be determined to constitute inventory.

(ii) Non-residents

As a general rule, a non-resident cannot rollover real property even if it constitutes capital property. The purpose of this prohibition is to prevent non-residents from avoiding tax by transferring real estate that is capital property into a corporation, selling the shares of the corporation and then claiming the benefits of a bilateral treaty.

Canada's bilateral tax treaties generally allow Canada to tax capital gains from a non-resident's sale of shares only if the value of the shares is derived principally from Canadian real estate.[21] Since the prohibition does not generally apply to property used by a non-resident in the course of a business carried on in Canada, a non-resident might

---

[18] *Fraser v. M.N.R.*, [1964] CTC 372, 64 DTC 5224 (S.C.C.) (profit realized from sale of shares of corporation is income from business where corporation is an alternative method chosen by the taxpayer to conduct real estate transactions); *Claude Belle-Isle v. M.N.R.*, [1966] CTC 85, 66 DTC 5100 (S.C.C.) (sale of hotel to a corporation followed by the sale of the shares in that corporation generated business income); *Gibson Bros. Industries Ltd. v. M.N.R.*, [1972] CTC 221, 72 DTC 6190 (F.C.T.D.) (rather than selling assets directly to customer, parent sold assets to subsidiary and customer bought shares of subsidiary; sales of assets and shares treated as one transaction); *Burgess v. M.N.R.*, [1973] CTC 58, 73 DTC 5040 (F.C.T.D.) (sale of shares in a corporation with only one asset was an adventure in the nature of trade).

[19] IT-218R, "Profit, Capital Gains and Losses from the Sale of Real Estate, Including Farmland and Inherited Land and Conversion of Real Estate from Capital Property to Inventory and Vice Versa" (September 16, 1994).

[20] See IC 70-6R2, "Advance Income Tax Rulings" (September 28, 1990).

[21] See, generally, Article XIII of Canada's tax treaties.

otherwise avoid the tax if the value of the shares could be substantially attributed to other assets.

(iii) Partnerships

An interest in a partnership is capital property and, as such, is eligible for the rollover under section 85. Thus, although real estate inventory cannot be rolled over under section 85, an interest in a partnerhip that owns real property inventory can be rolled over to a taxable Canadian corporation.[22] Revenue Canada has indicated, however, that it considers such a double rollover to be an abusive form of tax avoidance and contrary to the General Anti-Avoidance Rule ("GAAR").[23]

(c) Receivables

Business accounts receivables are generally considered to be capital property.[24] Hence, they are eligible to be rolled over to a corporation under subsection 85(1). In most circumstances, however, a taxpayer will prefer to transfer accounts receivable to a corporation and use the election available under section 22 rather than the rollover under section 85. The section 22 election is particularly desirable where the transferee corporation is controlled by the person who sells the receivables, since the stop-loss rules in subsection 85(4) would preclude the recognition of any losses on transfers of capital property to a controlled corporation.

An election under section 22 allows the vendor to claim a deduction for the amount by which the consideration received for the receivables is less than their face value. Provided that the election is for the fair market value of the receivables sold, the election is binding upon all parties.[25]

(d) Eligible Capital Property

Eligible capital property generally refers to goodwill, customer lists, patents, trademarks and perpetual franchises.[26] It also includes "know how".[27]

---

[22] Revenue Canada used to accede to this practice; see Question 48 — Revenue Canada Round Table, 36th Tax Conf., pp. 819-820 (Can. Tax Foundation, 1984).

[23] See IC 88-2, "General Anti-avoidance Rule — Section 245 of the *Income Tax Act*" (October 21, 1988), para. 22.

[24] *Doughty v. Commr. of Taxes*, [1927] AC 327 (P.C.); *Crompton v. Reynolds* (1952), 33 Tax Cas. 288 (H.L.).

[25] Subs. 22(2).

[26] Subs. 248(1) ("eligible capital property"); s. 54 ("eligible capital property").

[27] See *Rapistan Canada Ltd. v. M.N.R.*, [1974] CTC 495, 74 DTC 6426 (F.C.A.)

A mere right to receive income without any interest in the property that generates the income does not constitute a capital property. An amount paid to acquire the right is not considered to be an eligible capital expenditure.

5. INDIVIDUAL ASSET TEST

A section 85 rollover is implemented on an asset-by-asset basis. Technically, each property is the subject of a separate election even though several properties may be listed on a single election form. Thus, the transferor must specify a particular transfer price for each asset. Assets that are not listed on the form are subject to section 69.

It is possible to elect different amounts in respect of identical properties such as shares. Thus, a transferor can control the amount of capital gains to be recognized on the transfer.

Where the stop-loss rules apply, a gain on one asset cannot be used to offset a loss on another property transferred at the same time. This is so despite the fact that the form used for the election (T2057) groups assets for the sake of convenience. For example, where a portfolio of securities is transferred to a controlled corporation, gains on one class of securities may not be used to absorb losses on another class. The loss is caught by the stop-loss rules and the rollover is restricted to the accrued gains.

6. THE ELECTION

(a) A Legal Fiction

The rollover is entirely optional: The transferor and the transferee must jointly elect to have subsection 85(1) apply and they must do so in prescribed form and within a certain period of time.[28] Once made, the election is irrevocable[29] and it may be amended only in certain very limited circumstances.[30]

The election is the centrepiece of the rollover under section 85 and requires careful consideration. It determines the amount to be recognized as the transferor's proceeds of disposition and the transferee's cost of acquisition. The transferee's consent to the election causes it to become liable for the tax liability deferred on the transfer of property. The elected amount is, in effect, a legal fiction to the extent that it varies from the contractually determined transaction price. Within certain constraints, however, the elected amount is *deemed* to be the proceeds of disposition and the acquisition cost of the property in respect of which the election is made.

---

[28] Subs. 85(6).

[29] *Walker (A.S.) Holdings Ltd. v. M.N.R.*, [1979] CTC 2112, 79 DTC 132(T.R.B.); *Busch v. M.N.R.*, [1979] CTC 2275, 79 DTC 277 (T.R.B.); *One for Three Ltd. v. M.N.R.*, [1980] CTC 2293, 80 DTC 1244 (T.R.B.); *Deconinck v. The Queen*, [1988] 2 CTC 213, 88 DTC 6410 (F.C.T.D.); affirmed [1990] 2 CTC 464, 90 DTC 6617 (F.C.A.).

[30] Subs. 85(7.1).

(b) Individual Listing of Assets

Technically speaking, a taxpayer is required to separately list *each* property that is transferred and provide a specific transfer amount for *each* asset. For the purpose of these rules, "nil" is not considered to be an amount.

An exception is made in respect of depreciable properties. Where *all* of a class of depreciable property is transferred to a corporation, the election need only show aggregate amounts for each class provided that the taxpayer retains supporting schedules showing the order of disposition of each of the properties in the class.[31] As a matter of practice, it is usually sufficient in a major transaction to list the type and class of asset on the election form.

(c) Late-filed Elections

As a general rule, an election under section 85 is considered to be final and irrevocable as between the parties to the transaction. The Act does, however, permit a late, as opposed to an amended, election to be filed in certain limited circumstances.

(i) Within Three Years

The transferor and the corporation are required to file the election by the date on which the income tax return for the year must be filed.[32] An election filed within three years of that date will, however, be accepted, subject to a late-filing penalty.[33] The taxpayer is liable for an amount equal to one quarter of one per cent per month of the difference between the fair market value of the property transferred and the amount elected in respect of it. The maximum penalty is $8,000.

(ii) Beyond Three Years

A taxpayer may file an election beyond the three year late filing period or may file an amended election where, in the opinion of the Minister, the circumstances are such that it would be "just and equitable" to accept the election.[34] The election must be accompanied by a written submission requesting its acceptance and it must set out the reasons why it is just and equitable that it should be accepted. Revenue Canada is quite stringent in this matter and it will not usually accept an election that is not accompanied by the taxpayer's submission of reasons in support of the election.

The Department generally accepts amended elections if the purpose of the amendment is to revise an agreed upon amount that would otherwise trigger unintended

---

[31] IC 76-19R2, "Transfer of Property to a Corporation under Section 85" (June 15, 1990).

[32] Subs. 85(6).

[33] Subss. 85(7), (8).

[34] Subs. 85(7.1).

tax consequences for the parties involved. It will also usually accept an amended election in order to correct an error, omission or oversight in the original election.

(iii) "Just and Equitable" Reasons

The Department generally accepts amendments that:

- Result from an inaccurate valuation of the property that gives rise to unintended tax consequences;

- Reduce the agreed upon amount of transferred shares to the correct cost amount in circumstances where a transfer at cost was intended or dividends were omitted when calculating the adjusted cost base of the shares;

- Implement a correction where it is quite clear that the amount was entered in error (for example, an entry for depreciable capital property at its net book value instead of at its undepreciated capital cost);

- Correct other situations that give rise to unintended income tax consequences[35] when it is quite clear that the parties really intended to implement the rollover without any immediate income tax consequences but did not in fact do so effectively.

The Department does not accept amended elections where the purpose of the election is:

- To implement retroactive tax planning;

- To take advantage of losses or tax credits that were not originally taken into account at the time the election was filed;

- To take advantage of amendments in the law that were enacted after the election was filed;

- To avoid or evade tax; or

- To increase the agreed amount in a statute-barred taxation year.

7. PRICE ADJUSTMENT CLAUSES

A taxpayer who wants to implement the terms of a price adjustment clause must file an amended election under subsection 85(7.1). The Department's administrative position[36] is that it should be notified in advance of the existence of all agreements with price adjustment clauses.

8. FILING OF ELECTION

The joint election is a prerequisite to the rollover. The assets that are to be rolled over to the corporation must be listed; an estimate of the fair market value of each

---

[35] For example, the application of s. 84.1, subs. 15(1), 84(1) or 84(2.1).

[36] IT-169, "Price Adjustment Clauses" (August 6, 1974).

property must be disclosed. It is particularly important to list eligible capital property (such as goodwill) in the election, even if only at $1. In the event that goodwill is not listed (and it is quite easy to omit listing goodwill since it does not usually appear as an asset on financial statements), it is considered to have been transferred at its fair market value and may trigger an unexpected gain.

9. SALE OF BUSINESS AS GOING CONCERN

Where a business is sold as a going concern, it is prudent to include eligible capital property as an asset in the election. This is so even if the parties believe that there is no eligible capital property to be transferred. A successful business generating income usually has goodwill even if it does not show on the balance sheet. A sale of a business as a going concern includes its goodwill as one of the assets sold. The amount elected is usually set at a nominal $1. "Nil" is not an amount and should not be elected.[37]

10. CONSIDERATION RECEIVED

(a) Share Consideration

The rollover only applies if the transferor receives[38] share consideration of the transferee corporation in exchange for the property transferred. Even one share of the capital stock of the purchasing corporation is sufficient consideration. The purpose of this rule is to ensure that any tax deferred on the transfer of property will eventually be taxable on a subsequent disposition of the share consideration in an unprotected transaction.

The share consideration is allocated to each asset. Although subsection 85(1) speaks of "shares" in the plural, the vendor need take back only a single share in return for all of the property transferred to the corporation.[39] The agreement of purchase and sale can allocate some, even if only a fraction of the shares, to all of the assets that are the subject of the election. A more conservative approach is to allocate at least one share to each asset, or type of property, transferred to the corporation.

(b) Boot

The vendor may also take back non-share consideration (sometimes referred to as "boot") in exchange for the property sold. "Boot" consists of any consideration other than shares of the purchaser corporation. Examples include, cash, assets of the purchaser corporation, a promissory note of the purchaser, or assumption of the vendor's liabilities by the purchasing corporation.

---

[37] IC 76-19R2, "Transfer of Property to a Corporation Under Section 85" (June 15, 1990), para. 5.

[38] *Dale v. The Queen*, [1994] 1 CTC 2303, 94 DTC 1100 (T.C.C.) (on appeal to F.C.A.) (shares do not have to be issued, but there must be a binding obligation to do so at the time of the transfer).

[39] See the *Interpretation Act*, R.S.C. 1985. c. I-21, subs. 33(2).

(c) Allocation

Subject to certain constraints, the amount elected (referred to as the "agreed upon" amount) to be recognized as proceeds of disposition must be allocated between the non-share consideration (if any), preferred shares (if any), and common shares issued to the transferor. The allocation of cost to the share consideration must be made on a class-by-class basis[40] and may affect the cost of other identical properties owned by the transferor.[41]

The allocation of the elected amount, rather than the contractually agreed upon transfer price, allows the transferor to defer recognizing any gain on the property transferred by electing the cost of the property transferred rather than its fair market value. To prevent taxpayers from misusing the rollover, however, the Act imposes four additional restrictions:

1. There are upper and lower limits on the amount that may be elected in respect of different types of property transferred and consideration received;

2. Subsection 84(1) may apply to deem a dividend if the paid-up capital of the shares received as consideration exceeds the fair market value of the property transferred to the corporation;

3. Subsection 85(2.1) may apply to reduce the paid-up capital of the shares received as consideration if the paid-up capital is higher than the tax cost of the asset transferred; and

4. Section 84.1 may deem a dividend in certain circumstances.[42]

The first three of these control devices are discussed hereunder. Section 84.1 is considered in Chapter XXI "Non-arm's Length Share Transfers".

11. ELECTED AMOUNTS

As a general rule, non-arm's length transfers are deemed to occur at fair market value.[43] Subsection 69(11) extends the fair market value rule to certain arm's length transactions.

The general scheme in subsection 85(1) is that both the vendor and the purchasing corporation can agree upon an amount other than fair market value in respect of *each* property transferred to the corporation. Within certain limits, the agreed upon amount

---

[40] Paras. 85(1)(*g*), (*h*).

[41] S. 47.

[42] See Chapter XXI "Non-arm's Length Share Transfers".

[43] Subs. 69(1).

in respect of each property becomes the vendor's deemed proceeds of disposition and the purchaser's cost of that property.[44]

The agreed upon or elected amount is also used to determine the cost base of the consideration paid to the vendor. Thus, within limits, the vendor can control the amount of the capital gain or recapture of capital cost allowance that he or she will recognize in the year of transfer.

(a) General Limits

There are two general upper and lower limits on the amount that may be agreed upon by the vendor and the purchasing corporation.

(i) Elected Amount Cannot Exceed Fair Market Value

First, the amount elected in respect of a property cannot exceed its fair market value; if it does, the fair market value of the property is *deemed* to be the elected amount.[45] This places an upper limit on the election. The purpose of this rule is to prevent the vendor from artificially inflating capital gains on property in order to offset such gains against capital losses. The rule also prevents the purchaser from artificially stepping-up its cost base in the property.

Example XX.2	
Assume:	
ACB	$ 100
FMV	$ 200
Elected amount	$ 250
Then:	
Deemed POD	$ 200
ACB	(100)
Capital gain	$ 100

The fair market value of property transferred must be set out in the prescribed form. The Department accepts a "reasonable estimate" of fair market value where the elected amount is not affected by the fair market value.

---

[44] Para. 85(1)(*a*).

[45] Para. 85(1)(*c*).

(ii) *Elected Amount Cannot be Less than Boot*

Second, the elected amount cannot be less than the value of any *non-share consideration* ("boot") received from the purchaser corporation.[46] This places a lower limit on the election. Where the elected amount is less than the value of boot received, the value of the boot is *deemed* to be the elected amount. The purpose of this limit is to prevent a taxpayer from actually realizing and extracting the economic value of a gain without, at the same time, recognizing the gain for tax purposes.

A corollary of this rule is that a taxpayer can extract boot from the corporation, at least up to the value of the cost in the asset, without triggering a capital gain.

Example XX.3

Assume:

ACB	$ 100
FMV	$ 200
"Boot" (promissory note)	$ 120
Elected amount	$ 100

Then:

Deemed POD	$ 120
ACB	(100)
Capital gain	$ 20

In the absence of this rule the taxpayer could have the promissory note paid off without recognizing the actual gain of $20.

With the exception of the upper limit rule noted above, the value of "boot" sets the floor of the range of amounts that may be elected. Thus, the election can range between the value of "boot" received from the purchaser corporation and the fair market value of the property sold to the corporation. In Example XX.3, the taxpayer can extract up to $100 in boot without triggering a capital gain on the transfer of the asset.

(iii) *Fair Market Value Determines Upper Limit*

A taxpayer cannot elect an amount in excess of the fair market value of the property transferred to the corporation: Fair market value is the upper limit of electable amounts.

Where the value of "boot" exceeds the fair market value of the asset sold to the corporation, the fair market value of the asset determines the upper limit of the election range. Any excess of "boot" over the fair market value of the asset sold is a taxable

---

[46] Para. 85(1)(*b*).

shareholder benefit.[47] The amount of the benefit may be added to the cost base of the "boot" received from the corporation.[48]

Example XX.4

Assume:

	Case A	Case B
ACB	$ 100	$ 100
FMV	$ 200	$ 200
"Boot"(cash)	$ 250	$ 200
Elected amount	$ 225	$ 225
Then:		
Deemed POD	$ 200	$ 200
ACB	(100)	(100)
Capital gain	$ 100	$ 100
Shareholder benefit (subs. 15(1))	$ 50	—

(iv) Liabilities are Boot

Liabilities assumed by the purchaser corporation constitute "boot". Where an asset that has a liability attached to it (e.g., mortgaged land) is sold, the excess of the liability over the cost of the asset may be allocated to other assets involved in the sale in order to avoid triggering a capital gain.[49]

---

[47]   Subs. 15(1).

[48]   Subs. 52(1). It is unclear what would happen if the "boot" takes the form of cash, i.e., if the value of the shareholder benefit is added to the cost of cash so that there is a capital loss on the disposition of the cash.

[49]   IC 76-19R2, "Transfer of Property to a Corporation under Section 85" (June 15, 1990) and TR-41, "Transfer of Property to a Corporation" (October 25, 1976).

Example XX.5	
Assume:	
ACB of land	$ 100
FMV of land	$ 300
Mortgage on land ("boot")	$ 210
Elected amount	$ 100
Cost of other assets sold	$ 200
FMV of other assets	$ 170
Elected amount	$ 170
Then:	
1. Without allocation	
Deemed POD of land ("boot")	$ 210
ACB of land	(100)
Capital gain on land	$ 110
2. With allocation of boot	
To land: $100 of mortgage.	
To other assets: $110 of mortgage.	
Then:	
Deemed POD of land	$ 100
ACB of land	(100)
Capital gain	NIL

(b) Specific Limits

In addition to the general rules dealing with elected amounts, there are a number of special rules designed to prevent taxpayers from artificially avoiding tax.[50]

(i) Inventory and Non-depreciable Capital Property

Where the property transferred to a corporation is inventory or non-depreciable capital property, the elected amount cannot be less than the *lesser* of its fair market value and cost amount to the taxpayer.[51] This rule prevents the taxpayer from creating an artificial loss.

---

[50] Paras. 85(1)(*c*.1), (*d*), (*e*), (*e*.1), (*e*.2).

[51] Para. 85(1)(*c*.1).

Example XX.6

Assume the following applies to inventory or non-depreciable capital property:

ACB/Cost amount	$ 100
FMV	$ 200
"Boot"(cash)	$ 90
Elected amount	$ 90

Then:

Deemed POD	$ 100
ACB	(100)
Capital gain	NIL

Note, the general rule merely disallows an election at less than the value of "boot".[52] This special rule, in effect, raises the election floor to the lower of the fair market value and cost amount of the property.

Example XX.7

Assume the following applies to inventory:

ACB	$ 100
FMV	$ 80
"Boot"(cash)	$ 70
Elected amount	$ 70

Then:

Deemed POD	$ 80
ACB	(100)
Capital loss	(20)

As Example XX.7 illustrates, this rule prevents a taxpayer from creating an *artificial* loss by electing an amount that is less than the fair market value of the property.

The Act also controls tax avoidance, whether artificial or otherwise, through a general loss limitation rule that prohibits a taxpayer from claiming a loss on capital

---

[52] Para. 85(1)(*b*).

property or eligible capital property sold to a controlled corporation.[53] This is a rule of general application and is *not* confined to transactions covered by section 85. The taxpayer may add the amount of the loss that is denied to the adjusted cost base of his or her shares in the corporation.

(ii) Eligible Capital Property

The amount elected in respect of eligible capital property sold to a corporation cannot be less than the *least* of the following amounts:[54]

- 4/3 the vendor's cumulative eligible capital in respect of the business immediately before the transfer;
- the cost of the property to the taxpayer; and
- the fair market value of the property at the time of its disposition.

A taxpayer who elects a lesser amount is deemed to have elected the least of these three amounts.

Example XX.8	
Assume:	
Cost	$ 100
FMV	$ 200
"Boot"(cash)	$ 70
CEC (cumulative eligible capital)	$ 60
Then:	
Deemed POD (4/3 x $60)	$ 80
CEC	$ 60
75% × $80	(60)
Balance CEC	NIL

Here too, the rationale of limiting the vendor to the least of the three amounts is to prevent the creation of an artificial loss on the disposition of eligible capital property.

A terminal loss in respect of eligible capital property may only be claimed where its actual value is less than the balance in the vendor's cumulative eligible account

---

[53] Subs. 85(4).

[54] Para. 85(1)(*d*).

before the transfer of property.[55] Note, again, the general loss limitation rules in respect of transfers of capital property and eligible capital property to a controlled corporation.[56]

(iii) Depreciable Properties

(A) General Rule

There are two rules in respect of dispositions of depreciable properties of a prescribed class. The general rule is that the amount agreed upon by the vendor and the purchaser corporation cannot be less than the *least* of:[57]

- the undepreciated capital cost (UCC) of all property of that class;
- the cost of the property to the taxpayer; and
- the fair market value of the property at the time of disposition.

The purpose of this rule is to prevent the vendor from claiming an artificial terminal loss by electing an unduly low amount. Thus, generally speaking, a taxpayer may only claim a terminal loss where the fair market value of the depreciable property is *actually* less than its undepreciated capital cost.

Example XX.9		
Assume:	Case A	Case B
Cost	$ 100	$ 100
UCC	$ 50	$ 60
FMV	$ 70	$ 40
"Boot"(cash)	$ 40	$ 40
Elected amount	$ 40	$ 40
Deemed POD	$ 50	$ 40
UCC	(50)	(60)
Terminal loss	NIL	$ (20)

The elected amount of $40 in Case A would otherwise produce an artificial terminal loss since the fair market value of the property exceeds its UCC.

---

[55] Subs. 24(1).

[56] Subs. 85(4).

[57] Para. 85(1)(e).

(B) Sale to Controlled Corporation

An additional rule applies in respect of depreciable property transferred to a corporation where, after the transfer, the corporation is either controlled by the vendor, or the corporation and the vendor are both controlled by the same person. A taxpayer cannot claim a terminal loss on a disposition of depreciable property of a prescribed class to a "controlled" corporation.[58] This is so even if there is a real loss in value as in Case B of Example XX.9.

Two aspects of this rule should be noted: (1) "control" means *de facto* and not *de jure* control;[59] (2) "control" is determined *after* the disposition of the depreciable property to the corporation. Thus, share consideration issued by the purchaser corporation in exchange for the depreciable property is taken into account in determining "control".

More specifically, where the fair market value of depreciable property transferred to a controlled corporation is less than its capital cost *and* the undepreciated capital cost (UCC) of the entire class to which it belongs, the proceeds of disposition from the property are deemed to be equal to the *lesser* of the cost and the undepreciated capital cost of the property.[60]

Example XX.10	
Assume the following transfer of depreciable property to a controlled corporation:	
Cost	$ 100
UCC	$ 60
"Boot"(cash)	$ 50
FMV	$ 50
Then:	
Deemed POD	$ 60
UCC	(60)
Terminal loss	NIL

---

[58] Subs. 85(5.1). This rule also applies to partnerships.

[59] This is because of the use of the words "directly or indirectly in any manner whatever" in subs. 85(5.1). See subs. 256(5.1) for meaning of *de facto* control.

[60] Para. 85(5.1)(*e*).

In effect, the terminal loss of $10, which would otherwise have been available to the vendor, is blocked upon the transfer of property to a "controlled" corporation. Note, however, the tax cost of the property to the purchaser corporation is equal to the vendor's proceeds of disposition. Hence, the terminal loss may be retrieved if the asset is subsequently sold in an arm's length transaction.

(C) Company Cars

A taxpayer is restricted in the amount that may be deducted as capital cost allowance on passenger automobiles. Generally speaking, a taxpayer may not claim capital cost allowance on more than $24,000 in respect of the capital cost of a passenger automobile.[61] This $24,000 limit is the prescribed amount effective September 1, 1989 and will be increased from time to time as circumstances warrant.

The $24,000 rule effectively limits the maximum capital cost allowance permitted on passenger automobiles. To prevent taxpayers from circumventing the limit when a passenger automobile is transferred to a corporation under section 85, a special anti-avoidance rule restricts the amount that may be elected in respect of the undepreciated capital cost of the vehicle immediately before its transfer to the corporation.[62] For the purposes of calculating the standby charge,[63] however, the cost of the automobile to the corporation is deemed to be its fair market value immediately before its transfer to the corporation.

(iv) Ordering of Dispositions

Where a taxpayer simultaneously transfers several items of depreciable property of the same class, or several eligible capital properties in respect of a business, the sequence of the dispositions may need to be designated so as to avoid recapture of capital cost allowance previously claimed on the properties.[64] Each of the properties is considered to have been transferred separately in the designated order and the undepreciated capital cost of the class, or the cumulative eligible capital, will be reduced as each asset is transferred. In practice, the order in which properties are transferred is significant only where the vendor receives non-share consideration (e.g., cash) as part of the purchase price. This is because the non-share consideration or "boot" acts as the floor for the taxpayer's election.

---

[61] Para. 13(7)(*g*); Reg. 7307(1).

[62] Para. 85(1)(*e*.4).

[63] See Chapter V "Income From an Office or Employment".

[64] Para. 85(1)(*e*.1).

Example XX.11

Assume that a taxpayer transfers two Class 8 assets:

	Asset #1	Asset #2
Cost	$ 100	$ 500
FMV	80	400
Cash consideration	80	NIL
UCC of Class	$ 300	

The taxpayer stipulates that the properties are to be transferred at their minimum allowable amounts and Asset #1 is transferred first, then:

UCC of class	$ 300
Amount elected (Asset #1)	(80)
UCC remaining	$ 220
Amount elected (Asset #2)	(220)
Recapture	NIL

If the taxpayer had designated in the reverse order, i.e., Asset #2 before Asset #1, then:

UCC of class	$ 300
Amount elected (Asset #2)	(300)
UCC remaining	NIL
Amount elected (Boot for Asset #1)	80
Recapture of CCA	$ 80

As the above example illustrates, the designated order of dispositions is important only if the taxpayer receives boot as part of the consideration for the transfer. The Minister may designate the order of disposition if the taxpayer fails to do so.

12. CONFLICT BETWEEN RULES

Given the numerous rules that limit the upper and lower values of the elected amounts, it is possible that one rule may dictate a result that is in conflict with the result produced by another rule. To resolve such conflicts, an overriding rule deems the order in which the individual rules are to apply.[65] In the event that the application of paragraph 85(1)(c.1), (d), or (e) produces a result which conflict with the result obtained by applying paragraph 85(1)(b), the elected amount is deemed to be the *greater* of the

---

[65] Para. 85(1)(e.3).

two conflicting amounts. Hence, the elected amount cannot be less than the value of the "boot" received and can never be more than the fair maket value of the property transferred.

Example XX.12		
Assume a capital property:		
	Case A	Case B
ACB	$ 60	$ 60
FMV	$ 100	$ 100
"Boot"	$ 40	$ 80
Elected amount	$ 30	$ 30
Then:		
Result under para. 85(1)(b)	$ 40	$ 80
Result under para. 85(1)(c.1)	$ 60	$ 60
Deemed elected amount by para. 85(1)(e.3)	$ 60	$ 80

13. INDIRECT BENEFITS RULE

(a) Purpose

Section 85 contains a specific anti-avoidance rule that is intended to prevent a taxpayer from disposing of property for inadequate consideration in order to benefit a person related to him or her. For example, an individual may dispose of property valued at $1 million to a corporation controlled by his or her child in exchange for consideration valued at $400,000. The shortfall of $600,000 in the value of the consideration received would accrue to the benefit of the controlling shareholder, the transferor's child. Paragraph 85(1)(e.2) adds the value of the benefit conferred to the proceeds of disposition elected by the taxpayer.

Paragraph 85(1)(e.2) only applies where the consideration received by the taxpayer in exchange for property transferred to a corporation is less than the value of the property *and* it is reasonable to regard the difference as a benefit that the taxpayer desires to confer on a person related to him or her. In these circumstances the elected proceeds are increased by the value of the benefit.[66]

---

[66] Para. 85(1)(e.2).

(b) Scope of Rule

More specifically, where the fair market value of property transferred to a corporation exceeds *both*:

- the fair market value of the consideration received from the corporation in exchange for the sale, *and*
- the amount agreed upon (subject to the various deeming provisions discussed above) in respect of the property,

and it is reasonable to infer that any portion of the excess is intended to be a benefit conferred on a person related to the taxpayer, the "excess portion" is added to the elected proceeds of disposition and, as such, may trigger a capital gain on the property transferred.

In the absence of this rule, it would be possible for a taxpayer to dispose of assets to a corporation for less than their fair market value and take back a minimum number of shares in the corporation. This would effectively transfer the assets to the other shareholders of the corporation without triggering any tax on accrued capital gains.

Example XX.13

Assume:

Holdco is a family business owned by:

X	10%
X's spouse	50%
X's child	40%
	100%

X transfers land (capital property) with an ACB of $10,000 and FMV of $60,000 to *Holdco* in exchange for preferred shares with a fair market value of $1,000. The parties elect $10,000.

Then:

FMV of property of land		$ 60,000
Exceeds *greater* of:		
FMV of consideration	$ 1,000	
Elected amount	$ 10,000	
		(10,000)
Inadequate consideration		$ 50,000
Benefit conferred (90% of $50,000)		$ 45,000
Elected amount		10,000
Deemed elected amount		$ 55,000
ACB of property		(10,000)
Capital gain realized		$ 45,000

Example XX.14

Assume:

Ownership of shares prior to transfer:

Father	20
Mother	45
Child	35

Property transferred by father:

ACB	15,000	
FMV	75,000	
Elected amount		15,000
Consideration: shares (PUC and FMV)		15,000

Then:

Inadequate consideration	$ 60,000
Indirect benefit (80% x 60,000)	$ 48,000
Deemed elected amount	$ 63,000
Gain to father	$ 48,000
ACB of property to corporation	$ 63,000
Father's ACB of shares taken back	$ 15,000

(c) Penal Provision

Paragraph 85(1)(*e*.2) operates as a penal provision. The amount of the indirect gift included in the transferor's proceeds of disposition is neither added to the adjusted cost base of the share consideration received in exchange for the property nor to the adjusted cost base of the shares of the shareholder who has benefitted from the transfer.[67] Thus, the tax cost of the "indirect gift" results in a permanent loss that is not recoverable by any person at any time. The value of the indirect gift is, however, added to the cost of the asset transferred to the corporation.

(d) Bump-up

The bump-up to the amount elected by the transferor and the purchaser corporation in their election is made *after* applying all of the other rules in subsection 85(1) and not to the amount actually set out in their joint election.[68] In Example XX.13 above, if X and *Holdco* had initially elected $1,000, the elected amount would have been bumped-

---

[67] Paras. 85(1)(*e*.2) and 53(1)(*c*).

[68] Any other interpretation of para. 85(1)(*e*.2) would undermine its rationale and be contrary to the *Interpretation Act*, R.S.C. 1985, c. I-21, s. 12.

up to $10,000 (paragraph 85(1)(*c*.1)) which would then be bumped up by $45,000 (benefit conferred) to bring it up to $55,000.

(e) Related Persons

The rule only applies to transfers between related persons. Thus, the scope of this rule is similar to its counterpart provisions in other parts of the Act.[69] Of course, it is quite unlikely that a taxpayer would confer a benefit on a complete stranger.

(f) Post-Transfer Benefits

The indirect benefits rule is broad enough to catch a benefit conferred on a person who becomes a shareholder of the transferee corporation *after* the transfer of property to the corporation. Thus, where a taxpayer's children take up shares in the corporation to which he or she has transferred property in circumstances such that it may reasonably be regarded that they have benefitted, the rule will apply to bump-up the taxpayer's proceeds of disposition.[70]

(g) Transfers Between Corporations

The rule also applies to any benefits conferred on the transferee corporation itself unless the corporation is a wholly-owned corporation of the transferor immediately after the disposition.

(h) Value of Transferred Property

The value of the property transferred and the consideration received in exchange is a question of fact in each case. The Department takes the position that the fair market value of the transferred property is not reduced by the amount of the potential deferred tax liability on the asset in the hands of the transferee. For example, where a property with an adjusted cost base of $100 and a fair market value of $700 is transferred to a corporation under section 85, the deferred tax on the $600 potential gain cannot be taken into account in determining the value of the consideration paid to the transferor. In the event that such a deferred gain is taken into account, paragraph 85(1)(*e*.2) will reduce the amount of the consideration paid.

14. COST OF PROPERTY TO CORPORATION

(a) General Rule

The general rule is that a purchaser corporation acquires the property transferred to it at a cost equal to the amount agreed, or deemed to have been agreed, upon by the

---

[69] See, e.g., subss. 86(2), 87(4) and para. 51(2)(*c*).

[70] Any other interpretation would clearly defeat the "object and spirit" of the provision and provide a gaping loophole.

parties in their joint election.[71] Thus, the corporation stands in the shoes of the transferor in respect of properties transferred to it and is liable for any tax payable upon the eventual disposition of the property. Hence the rollover: the transferor's elected amount is, in effect, "rolled over" to the corporation.

(b) Pre-1972 Property

Special rules regulate the transfer of non-depreciable capital property owned by a taxpayer on June 19, 1971. Where a taxpayer who has not elected to use Valuation Day[72] values in respect of pre-1972 capital properties, transfers such property to a corporation with which he or she does not deal at arm's length, the corporation is deemed to have owned the capital property continuously since June 18, 1971. The "actual cost" of the property is deemed to be equal to the cost of the property to the taxpayer.[73] In effect, the corporation steps into the taxpayer's shoes and calculates the cost of its pre-1972 capital property by applying the median rule under ITAR 26(3). Thus, the transferee corporation can take advantage of the tax-free or neutral zone of the property in calculating its gain or loss when it disposes of the property.[74]

(c) Depreciable Properties

Another special rule applies in respect of depreciable property. Where the elected amount in respect of depreciable property is less than the transferor's cost of the property, for the purpose of calculating capital cost allowance and any recapture thereof, the transferee corporation is deemed to:[75]

- acquire the property for an amount equal to the capital cost of the property to the transferor, and
- have claimed capital cost allowance in an amount equal to the difference between the vendor's capital cost and the elected amount.

In effect, the capital cost of the property to the transferor flows through to the purchaser corporation, as does any capital cost allowance previously claimed on the property by him or her. Hence, on a subsequent disposition by the purchaser corporation, the corporation may be liable for recapture of capital cost allowance previously claimed by the transferor in respect of the property.

---

[71] Para. 85(1)(a).

[72] ITAR 26(7). See Part XII.

[73] ITAR 26(5). Note also, a transfer of capital property under s. 85 is deemed not to be an arm's length transfer for the purposes of ITAR 26(5).

[74] ITAR 26(5)(c) provides for various adjustments to the cost of the property.

[75] Subs. 85(5).

This rule only applies in respect of depreciable properties transferred pursuant to subsections 85(1), (2) (transfer from partnership) and (5.1) (transfer to controlled corporation) and does not apply in respect of transfers of property to a corporation where the transfer has not been made under those subsections. If the purchaser corporation disposes of the depreciable property under subsection 85(1), the original capital cost will flow through once again to the new transferee and the potential for recapture will pass through to the new owner of the property.[76]

Example XX.15

Assume one depreciable property:

Capital cost	$ 200
FMV	$ 250
UCC	$ 150

Then:

Deemed elected amount (para. 85(1)(*e*))	$ 150
Purchaser's capital cost (subs. 85(5))	$ 200*
Deemed proceeds	(150)
CCA deemed claimed (potential recapture)	$ 50

*equals vendor's capital cost

---

[76] Unrealized capital gains on depreciable property owned on V-Day that are the subject matter of a section 85 rollover are protected from tax upon their ultimate disposition by the purchaser: ITAR 20(1) and (1.2) (see Example XX.16).

Example XX.16

Assume one depreciable property of a prescribed class:

Capital cost	$ 100
V-Day	$ 200
UCC	$ 70
Sold by purchaser at FMV	$ 250

Then:

(i)	Deemed elected amount on transfer to corporation (para. 85(1)(e))	$ 70
(ii)	Cost of property to purchaser	$ 100
	CCA deemed claimed	(30)
	UCC to purchaser (subs. 85(5))	$ 70
(iii)	On sale by purchaser Recapture of CCA	$ 30
	Capital gain (FMV − V-Day)	$ 50

One aspect of the cost flow-through rules warrants emphasis: Subsection 85(5) only flows through the transferor's capital cost to the purchaser corporation for the purposes of calculating capital cost allowance and recapture thereof. The provision does not flow through such cost to the purchaser corporation for the purposes of calculating the corporation's capital gain or loss on a disposition of the property at a later date. Therefore, it is possible for the same amount (that is, the difference between the vendor's original cost and the agreed upon amount) to be subject to both recapture of capital cost allowance and taxed again as a capital gain. The argument against this view is that there is a general judicial understanding that fiscal statutes are to be interpreted so as to avoid double taxation of the same amount. There is also a statutory presumption against double taxation. As a matter of administrative practice it appears that Revenue Canada will not double tax the same amount.[77]

15. COST OF CONSIDERATION RECEIVED BY THE TRANSFEROR

Subsection 85(1) requires the transferor to take back share consideration from the purchaser corporation. The taxpayer may, of course, also take back non-share consideration. The cost of the consideration received from the corporation is determined by allocating the amount jointly elected (the agreed upon amount) by the transferor and

---

[77] Subs. 4(4). See *Proceedings of the Standing Senate Committee on Banking, Trade and Commerce*, First Session, 30th Parliament, 1974-75-76, issue No. 31, p. 55.

the purchaser corporation to the various classes of consideration.[78] The agreed upon amount is allocated in the following sequence:

- First, to non-share consideration or "boot";
- Next, to preferred shares; and
- Finally, to common shares.

(a) Boot

Non-share consideration ("boot") paid to the transferor is deemed to have a cost equal to the lesser of its fair market value and the fair market value of the property transferred.[79] Where the transferor receives more than one property from the corporation, the cost of *each* property is deemed to be the *lesser* of:[80]

- its fair market value; and
- the proportion of the fair market value of all assets transferred to the corporation that the fair market value of the particular property bears to the fair market value of all "boot" received.

In effect, the cost of boot taken back from the corporation cannot exceed the fair market value of the property transferred to it.

Example XX.17

Assume that property with a fair market value of $100,000 is transferred to a corporation in exchange for:

Cash	$ 5,000
Promissory note (FMV)	$ 65,000
Shares (FMV)	$ 30,000

Then:

Cost of promissory note is lesser of:

  (i) $65,000 and

  (ii) $\dfrac{65 \times 100,000}{70} = \$92,857$

Lesser amount	$ 65,000

---

[78] Paras. 85(1)(f), (g) and (h).

[79] Para. 85(1)(f).

[80] Para. 85(1)(f).

Example XX.18

Assume that an individual transfers a portfolio of shares with a value of $60,000 to a holding company in exchange for four properties valued as follows:

Property #1	$ 10,000
Property #2	15,000
Property #3	20,000
Property #4	55,000
	$ 100,000

Then, the cost of the four properties is determined as follows:

Property #1

$$\frac{10}{100} \times \$60,000 \qquad \$ \quad 6,000$$

Property #2

$$\frac{15}{100} \times \$60,000 \qquad \$ \quad 9,000$$

Property #3

$$\frac{20}{100} \times \$60,000 \qquad \$ \quad 12,000$$

Property #4

$$\frac{55}{100} \times \$60,000 \qquad \$ \quad 33,000$$
$$\$ \quad 60,000$$

Where the transferor receives both shares and "boot" from the purchaser corporation, the cost base of the shares is determined as follows:

- First, calculate the amount to be allocated to the "boot";
- Second, determine the amount to be allocated to any preferred shares received as consideration;[81] and

---

[81] Para. 85(1)(g). A "preferred share" is defined as a share other than a common share (subs. 248(1) ("preferred share")). Although most new corporate statutes have moved away from the terminology of "preferred" and "common" shares, these concepts remain important for income tax purposes.

- Finally, determine the cost to be allocated to any common shares of the purchaser corporation received as consideration in exchange for the transferred property.[82]

(b) Preferred Shares

In the simplest case, where the vendor receives only one class of preferred shares, the cost of each share is the *lesser* of:

- its fair market value, and
- the difference between the agreed upon amount and the fair market value of "boot" received.

Example XX.19

Assume that X transfers securities with a cost of $50,000 and fair market value of $120,000 to *Holdco Ltd.* in exchange for the following:

Consideration	FMV
Land	$ 50,000
Promissory note	40,000
Preferred shares	30,000
	$ 120,000

The agreed upon amount is $100,000.

Then:

Consideration	Cost Base to Transferor
Land	$ 50,000
Promissory note	$ 40,000
Preferred shares	
($100,000 − $90,000)	$ 10,000
	$ 100,000

Where the transferor takes back more than one class of preferred shares, the cost of each class of preferred shares is deemed to be the *lesser* of:[83]

- their fair market value; and

---

[82]   Para. 85(1)(*h*).

[83]   Para. 85(1)(*g*).

- that proportion of the excess of the agreed upon amount over the value of "boot" that the fair market value of the preferred shares of that class is of the fair market value of all preferred shares received as consideration.

In other words, the excess of the deemed proceeds of disposition (agreed upon amount) received by the transferor over the amount of "boot" paid is allocated to the preferred shares in proportion to their fair market value.

Example XX.20

Assume that an individual transfers public securities with a cost of $50,000 and fair market value of $120,000 to *Holdco* in exchange for the following:

Consideration	FMV
Promissory note	$ 50,000
Class A preferred shares	$ 40,000
Class B preferred shares	$ 30,000
	$ 120,000

The parties elect $100,000 as the agreed upon amount.

Then:

Cost of Class A preferred shares
Lesser of:

FMV	$ 40,000	
$(100,000 - 50,000) \times 40/70 =$	$ 28,571	
		$ 28,571

Cost of Class B preferred shares
Lesser of:

FMV	$ 30,000	
$(100,000 - 50,000) \times 30/70 =$	$ 21,429	
		$ 21,429

Consideration	Cost Base to Transferor
Promissory note	$ 50,000
Class A preferred	$ 28,571
Class B preferred	$ 21,429
	$ 100,000

(c) Common Shares

The cost of any common shares received as consideration is simply the residual amount remaining after the deemed cost of boot and any preferred shares is deducted from the elected (or deemed elected) amount. Once again, in the simplest case, if the transferor takes back only one class of common shares from the purchaser corporation, the entire remaining balance, *if any*, is allocated to those shares.

Example XX.21

Assume:

Cost of property transferred	$ 100,000
FMV of property transferred	$ 180,000
Consideration received:	
Boot (FMV)	$ 100,000
Shares	?
Amount elected	$ 100,000

Then:

Amount elected (POD)	$ 100,000
Cost of boot	(100,000)
Cost of shares received	NIL

Example XX.22

Assume Y transfers property with a cost of $100,000 and fair market value of $150,000 to *Opco Ltd.* in exchange for the following:

Consideration	FMV
Cash	$ 20,000
Class A preferred	$ 80,000
Class B preferred	$ 50,000
	$ 150,000

Example XX.22 (continued)

The agreed upon amount is $100,000.

Then:

Proceeds of disposition	$ 100,000
Less: boot	(20,000)
Excess	$ 80,000

Cost of Class A preferred

$$\frac{80,000}{130,000} \times \$80,000$$

$ 49,231

Cost of Class B preferred

$$\frac{50,000}{130,000} \times \$80,000$$

$ 30,769

Consideration	Cost Base to Transferor
Cash	$ 20,000
Class A preferred	$ 49,231
Class B referred	$ 30,769
	$ 100,000

Where the transferor receives more than one class of common shares from the purchaser corporation, the balance is allocated amongst the various classes of common shares in proportion to their fair market value.

Example XX.23

Assume Z transfers property with an adjusted cost base of $100,000 and fair market value of $180,000 to *Newco Ltd.* in exchange for the following:

Consideration	FMV
Cash	$ 20,000
Class A preferred	$ 80,000
Class B preferred	$ 50,000
Class C common	$ 30,000
	$ 180,000

Example XX.23 (continued)

The agreed upon amount is $100,000.

Then:

Proceeds of disposition	$ 100,000
Less: non-share consideration ("boot")	(20,000)
Excess	$ 80,000

Cost of Class A preferred

$$\frac{80,000}{130,000} \times \$80,000 \qquad \qquad \$ \ 49,231$$

Cost of Class B preferred

$$\frac{50,000}{130,000} \times \$80,000 \qquad \qquad \$ \ 30,769$$

Cost of Class C common	$ NIL

Consideration	Cost Base to Transferor
Cash	$ 20,000
Class A Preferred	$ 49,231
Class B Preferred	$ 30,769
Common	NIL
	$ 100,000

16. PAID-UP CAPITAL OF SHARES ISSUED BY PURCHASER CORPORATION

The concept of paid-up capital ("PUC") is fundamental to the corporate income tax system. Generally speaking, a corporation can return paid-up capital to its shareholders on a tax-free basis. Hence, the tax system seeks to prevent artificial increases in the PUC of shares.

(a) In Excess of Fair Market Value of Property Acquired

The paid-up capital ("PUC") of shares issued to the vendor must not exceed the fair market value of the transferred property. To the extent that it does, the vendor is deemed to have received a dividend under subsection 84(1).

Example XX.24	
Assume:	
Cost of property transferred	$ 100,000
FMV of property transferred	$ 200,000
Consideration received:	
Boot	$ 60,000
PUC of preferred shares	$ 40,000
PUC of common shares	$ 120,000
	$ 220,000
FMV of property transferred	(200,000)
Deemed dividend	$ 20,000

Where the paid-up capital of shares issued by the purchaser corporation exceeds the fair market value of the property transferred to it, *each* shareholder of the class of shares is deemed to receive a dividend.[84] Such a transaction may contravene the applicable corporate law. Under the *Canada Business Corporations Act*[85] a corporation may not add to the stated capital account of a class of shares an amount that is greater than the amount of the consideration it receives in exchange for the shares. The purpose of this rule is to prevent taxpayers from converting taxable surpluses into paid-up capital, which can then be returned to shareholders on a tax-free basis.

Example XX.25	
Assume:	
Adjusted cost base of capital property	$ 100
Fair market value of property	$ 400
Mortgage on property	$ 100
Consideration received:	
Paid-up capital/preferred shares	$ 200
Paid-up capital/common shares	130
	$ 330

---

[84] Subs. 84(1).

[85] *Canada Business Corporations Act*, R.S.C. 1985, c. C-44, subs. 26(4). See also, *Business Corporations Act*, R.S.O. 1990, c. B-16, subs. 24(4).

Example XX.25 (continued)	
Then:	
Increase in paid-up capital	$ 330
Net increase in value of assets	(300)
Deemed dividend (subs. 84(1))	$ 30

The *pro rata* value of the dividend is added to the cost base of the shares on which the dividend is deemed to have been paid.[86] Note, that *all* holders of shares of the particular class are affected by an improperly valued transfer of property to a corporation.

The stated capital of shares may be controlled through the use of an appropriate directors' resolution. The following is an example:

BE IT RESOLVED THAT in accordance with Section [ ] of the Canada Business Corporations Act, there be added to the stated capital account maintained for the First Preference shares in the capital of the Corporation, (state number) of which are being issued to the Vendor as consideration for the Property, an amount equal to the fair market value of the Property immediately before the completion of the purchase, which the directors of the Corporation have determined to be (state value); provided, however, that if hereafter the directors of the Corporation become satisfied that such fair market value of the Property was not (state value), then this addition to the said stated capital account shall be changed to such amount as the directors are satisfied is equal to such fair market value.

(b) Reduction of Paid-Up Capital of Shares

A special anti-avoidance rule in subsection 85(2.1) prevents the removal of taxable corporate surpluses as a tax-free capital gain in circumstances when other more particular provisions (such as sections 84.1 and 212.1) might not apply.

Where the paid-up capital of share consideration issued by the purchaser corporation exceeds the cost of property that it acquires less the value of "boot" paid, the paid-up capital of the shares is reduced by the amount of the excess.[87] The rule prevents misuse of the lifetime capital gains exemption. Note that this rule applies to arm's length and non-arm's length transfers, but it does not apply if either section 84.1 or 212.1 applies.

---

[86] *Income Tax Act*, para. 53(1)(*b*). Non-resident shareholders may be subject to withholding tax (subs. 212(2)).

[87] Subs. 85(2.1).

The formula for reducing the paid-up capital of the shares issued by the purchaser corporation (sometimes referred to as a "PUC grind") is as follows:[88]

$$(A - B) \times \frac{C}{A}$$

where:

A = the increase in the corporation's total paid-up capital for corporate purposes as a result of the acquisition;

B = excess of the cost of property to the corporation over "boot" paid;

C = the increase in the paid-up capital of the particular class of shares as a result of the acquisition.

The C/A part of the formula only applies if more than one class of shares is issued as consideration for the property transferred. It has no application if only one class of shares is issued.

Example XX.26

Property transferred to a corporation under subsection 85(1):

Adjusted cost base (ACB)	$ 100
Fair market value (FMV)	$ 300
Consideration received:	
Promissory note	$ 150
Common shares (PUC and FMV)	$ 150
Deemed elected amount	$ 150
ACB of common shares	NIL

Without subsection 85(2.1), the taxpayer could redeem the common shares at their fair market value ($150) for a potentially tax-exempt capital gain of $150. There would be no deemed dividend because the amount paid would be equal to the paid-up capital ($150) of the shares.

Subsection 85(2.1) prevents this from happening:

Stated capital for corporate purposes	$ 150
Less: PUC "grind"	
$(A - B) \times C/A$	
$(150 - 0) \times 150/150$	(150)
PUC for tax purposes	NIL

---

[88] Para. 85(2.1)(a).

Example XX.26 (continued)

Now, on a redemption of the common shares at their FMV, the transferor is
required to recognize a deemed dividend instead of a capital gain.

Redemption price	$ 150
PUC of shares	NIL
Deemed dividend (subs. 84(3))	$ 150
Cash received on redemption	$ 150
Less, deemed dividend	(150)
Proceeds of disposition	
(para. 54 ("proceeds of disposition") (j))	NIL
ACB of shares	NIL
Capital gain	NIL

Thus, subsection 85(2.1) prevents the bump-up in the paid-up capital of the shares
and thereby prevents the transferor from converting the potential deemed dividend
upon redemption of the shares into a tax-free capital gain.

Example XX.27

Assume:

Mr. White transfers land to an operating corporation (*Opco*) in exchange for its
Class A shares. The following data applies to the transaction:

Fair market value (FMV) of land	$ 140,000
Adjusted cost base (ACB) of land	$ 40,000
FMV and PUC of *Opco* shares issued	
in exchange for land	$ 140,000

Assume, alternatively, that the parties elect

Case A	$ 40,000
Case B	$ 140,000

as the transfer price under subsection 85(1) and that the shares are subsequently
redeemed when their fair market value is $140,000.

Example XX.27 (continued)

Then:

Proceeds of disposition	$ 40,000	$ 140,000
ACB of land	(40,000)	(40,000)
Capital gain realized under subs. 85(1)	NIL	$ 100,000
Stated capital of *Opco* shares	$ 140,000	$ 140,000
Less, cost of property to *Opco*	(40,000)	(140,000)
PUC "grind"	$ 100,000	NIL
Stated capital of *Opco* shares	$ 140,000	$ 140,000
Subs. 85(2.1) reduction "grind"	(100,000)	(NIL)
PUC for tax purposes	$ 40,000	$ 140,000
Deemed dividend on redemption of shares (subs. 84(3))	$ 100,000	NIL

17. TAXABLE CANADIAN PROPERTY

Where property transferred to a corporation constitutes "taxable Canadian property", the shares of the purchaser corporation paid to the transferor are also deemed to be taxable Canadian property in his or her hands.[89]

18. IDENTICAL PROPERTIES

A taxpayer who has acquired identical properties before and after Valuation Day is required to segregate the properties into two separate pools.[90] The average cost of each property is calculated separately within each pool. Upon disposition of any of the properties, the taxpayer is deemed to have disposed of properties acquired prior to V-day first; when that pool is exhausted, further dispositions are deemed to come out of the post V-day pool.[91]

---

[89] Para. 85(1)(*i*).

[90] Subs. 47(1) and ITAR 26(8).

[91] ITAR 26(8)(e).

19. LOSSES

(a) Loss Limitation

A taxpayer who transfers capital property or eligible capital property to a "controlled" corporation is not entitled to recognize any loss that results from the disposition.[92] Two points warrant emphasis: first, this rule applies to all dispositions of property by a taxpayer or a partnership to a "controlled corporation", regardless of whether the transaction is governed by section 85; second, the rule applies even where the property is transferred at its fair market value.

The loss limitation rules apply where:[93]

- a taxpayer transfers capital property or eligible capital property to a corporation;
- a corporation is controlled directly or indirectly by,
  — the taxpayer,
  — the taxpayer's spouse, or
  — by a person or group of persons by whom the taxpayer is controlled; and
- the disposition gives rise to a capital loss or a deduction in respect of cumulative eligible capital.[94]

(b) Bump-up

In these circumstances, the amount of the capital loss or the amount deductible as cumulative eligible capital is deemed to be nil. The taxpayer is, however, allowed to "bump up" the cost of his or her share consideration from the purchaser corporation by the amount of the loss or deduction denied. The amount of the "bump-up" is equal to the amount of the disallowed capital loss. The excess of the adjusted cost base of the property over the proceeds of disposition received transferred is added to the cost base of the taxpayer's shares in the purchaser corporation.

In the case of eligible capital property, the "bump-up" is the excess of the cost amount of the property to the taxpayer over the taxpayer's eligible capital amount.[95]

---

[92] Subs. 85(4).

[93] Subs. 85(4).

[94] Para. 24(1)(a).

[95] Para. 85(4)(b).

Example XX.28	
Assume:	
Capital property:	
ACB	$ 1,000
POD (equals FMV)	(700)
Bump-up to cost base of shares taken back	$ 300
Eligible capital property:	
Cost amount	$ 1,000
Eligible capital amount	(700)
Bump-up to cost base of shares	$ 300

(c) Depreciable Property

The loss limitation rule in subsection 85(4) does not apply to dispositions of depreciable capital property since such property cannot give rise to a capital loss.[96] Instead, subsection 85(5.1) applies as described earlier.

20. POTENTIAL FOR DOUBLE TAXATION

As we have seen, subsection 85(1) is a relieving provision. It allows a taxpayer to rollover property to a taxable Canadian corporation, and defer the tax on any gain accrued on the property, in circumstances when the Act would otherwise deem a disposition to occur at fair market value. The section does, however, create problems of double taxation.

(a) The Problem

The rollover comes at a price. It exposes both the taxpayer and the purchaser corporation to the risk of double taxation on the deferred accrued gain: once, when the taxpayer disposes of the consideration which he or she receives from the purchaser corporation; and again when the purchaser corporation disposes of the transferred assets.

The double tax problem is an intrinsic part of every section 85 rollover because the elected amount determines the tax basis of *both* the consideration received from the corporation *and* the property transferred to it. Thus, the deferred accrued gain is a latent tax liability in the hands of both the transferor and the transferee corporation.

---

[96] Subpara. 39(1)(*b*)(i).

Example XX.29

Assume:

F owns land (capital property)

ACB	$200,000
FMV	$700,000

1. If F sold the land to *Holdco Ltd.* at its fair market value of $700,000, he would realize a capital gain of $500,000 and the corporation's ACB in the land would be $700,000.

2. F transfers the land to *Holdco Ltd.* and the parties elect $200,000 as the agreed-upon amount under subs. 85(1) and F receives the following consideration in exchange for the land:

Promissory note (boot)	$200,000
Preferred shares (FMV)	<u>$500,000</u>
	<u>$700,000</u>

Then:

- Consequences to F

POD (elected amount)	$200,000
ACB	<u>(200,000)</u>
Capital gain	<u>$ NIL</u>

- Cost of preferred shares

POD	$200,000
Less: "boot"	<u>(200,000)</u>
Cost of preferred shares	<u>$ NIL</u>
Potential capital gain on preferred shares	<u>$500,000</u>

- Potential consequences to *Holdco*

Cost of land	$200,000
FMV of land	<u>700,000</u>
Potential capital gain on disposition of land	<u>$500,000</u>

Thus, the accrued capital gain of $500,000 has been doubled to potential gains of $1,000,000.

The severity of the double taxation problem will vary with the circumstances. The longer the intended holding period of the shares received from the purchaser corporation, the less severe is the problem. Where the holding period is long, the discounted present value of the tax deferred on the rollover will outweigh the disadvantage of double taxation. Each case must be evaluated on its own facts to determine what, if any, further steps are necessary to solve the problem.

(b) The Cure

In certain circumstances, for example, when the section 85 rollover is used to implement an estate freeze, the double tax problem can be redressed through subsection 164(6) in the year following the taxpayer's death.[97] The problem of double taxation can be avoided if the taxpayer's life is insurable and the corporation takes out a policy to pay for the redemption of the shares.

Subsection 164(6) is an elective provision that allows the legal representative of a deceased taxpayer to amend the deceased's terminal return and offset any net capital losses suffered by the estate in its first taxation year against gains reported in the terminal return.

Thus, the length of the estate's first taxation year has important implications. On the one hand, it is desirable for the taxation year to be as long as possible so as to trigger the maximum number of losses for carryback to the terminal return. On the other hand, a short taxation year allows one to offset the losses as quickly as possible and to trigger the refund of taxes previously paid or to minimize the interest on unpaid taxes.

Example XX.30

Assume:

Mr. Black owns 50 per cent of the shares of *Holdco*, (a Canadian controlled private corporation) which he acquired in exchange for his *Opco* shares rolled over to *Holdco* under section 85. The following data applies to his shares:

ACB	$ 100
PUC	$ 100
FMV	$500,000

---

[97] See, generally, Ronald G. Gravelle, "Estate Freezing Today" in *Special Lectures of the Law Society of Upper Canada* (Toronto: DeBoo, 1980), 249 at 270.

Example XX.30 (continued)

Black has entered into an agreement with *Holdco* that it will redeem his shares on his death. The redemption price is to be the fair market value of the shares at that time. Black's life is insured for $500,000 by *Holdco*. The tax consequences on Black's death will be as follows:

1. Death

Deemed proceeds of disposition (para. 70(5)(*a*))	$500,000
Adjusted cost base	(100)
Capital gain	$499,900

2. Corporate redemption of shares from estate

Redemption price	$500,000
Less: PUC of shares	(100)
Deemed dividend (subs. 84(3))	$499,900
Capital dividend (subs. 83(2))*	$499,900
Taxable amount	NIL

3. Net result to estate

Redemption price	$500,000
Less: deemed dividend	(499,900)
Proceeds of disposition	$ 100
Less: deemed ACB of shares (para. 70(5)(*c*))	$500,000
Capital loss**	$499,900

* elect to treat as capital dividend using the capital dividend account arising from the life insurance proceeds

** may be used to offset taxable capital gain of equal amount per subs. 164(6)

Example XX.31

Assume:

A owns shares of *A Corp.*, (a CCPC).
A dies and *A Corp.* is wound up within one year.

Then:

1. A dies   Tax Cost
   Deemed POD on shares of *A Corp.* (CCPC) $ 150.00
   ACB   100.00
   Gain   50.00
   Tax thereon (45% of 3/4 x $50) $ 16.88

2. *A Corp.* wound-up within one year
   (a) *A Corp.*:
      Deemed proceeds on winding-up
      (subs. 69(5))   150.00
      ACB of property held   100.00
      Capital gain   50.00
      Tax thereon (45% of 3/4 × $50)   16.88
      Less refundable tax (to be triggered)   (7.50)
      Tax payable by *A Corp.* $ 9.38
   (b) Winding-up dividend:
      FMV of property distributed $ 150.00
      Less — taxes payable by *A Corp.*   (9.38)
                                                                       $ 140.62
      Less — PUC of shares   (100.00)
      Deemed dividend   40.62
      Capital dividend (subss. 83(2), 88(2))   (12.50)
      Taxable dividend to estate   28.12
      Gross-up @ 25%   7.03
      Income   35.15
      Tax thereon @ 45%   15.82
      Less dividend tax credit   4.69
      Tax payable by *A Corp.* $ 11.13

3. Capital loss to estate:
   Proceeds — PUC of shares
   (s. 54 ("proceeds of disposition") (j))   100.00
   ACB of shares (equal to FMV at death)   150.00
   Capital loss   50.00
   Refund available on amended terminal return   (16.88)
   NET TAXES PAYABLE $ 20.51

21. TRANSFER OF PROPERTY BY A PARTNERSHIP

A partnership is not a taxpayer under the *Income Tax Act*. For certain purposes, however, a partnership is treated *as if* it were a taxpayer.[98] In the context of transfers of property to a corporation, subsection 85(2) treats a partnership *as if* it were a taxpayer resident in Canada. It is important to note that subsection 85(2) is only available on a transfer of partnership property by the partnership itself; it does not apply to taxpayers who have joint ownership of property but who are not in partnership with each other. Note also, the share consideration paid by the purchaser corporation must be paid directly to the partnership and not to the individual partners.

(a) Real Property

A partnership's assets are to be distinguished from the partnership interests: the assets belong to the partnership; the interests belong to the partners. An interest in a partnership is not considered to be an interest in its underlying assets. Hence, where a partnership owns an inventory of real property, the partnership interest itself is not real property inventory. Thus, a partnership interest of a partnership that owns real property inventory may be rolled over to a corporation under subsection 85(1).

(b) Winding-up

A special rule applies where a partnership has tranferred all of its property to a corporation and the partnership is then wound up within 60 days of the transfer. In these circumstances, the cost of the consideration received by the partnership from the purchaser corporation may be rolled over from the partnership to the partners.[99] Thus, in certain circumstances, share consideration issued by the purchaser corporation in exchange for assets transferred by the partnership may be rolled over to the members of the partnership.

The rollout of property from a partnership to its members is only available where:[100]

- partnership property has been rolled over from the partnership to a taxable Canadian corporation;
- the affairs of the partnership are wound up within 60 days after the disposition of the property; and
- immediately before the winding-up of the partnership, there was no partnership property other than money or property received from the purchaser corporation as consideration for the disposition under subsection 85(2).

---

[98] See, e.g., s. 96.

[99] Subs. 85(3).

[100] Subs. 85(3).

In effect, these requirements prevent a rollout of partnership assets to individual members if property that does not qualify for a rollover is transferred by the partnership to the corporation. Nor is the rollout available unless all of the partnership's property has been transferred to the corporation.

There are several rules to determine the cost of consideration received by the members of the partnership. Thus:

- the cost of "boot" is its fair market value at the time of the winding-up;[101]
- the cost of the preferred shares distributed to a partner is the *lesser* of:[102]
  — the fair market value of the shares immediately after the wind-up, and
  — the adjusted cost base of a partnership interest immediately before the wind-up less the fair market value of any "boot" distributed to the partner;
- the cost to a partner of any common shares is the adjusted cost base of the partnership interest less the fair market value of "boot" and the cost allocated to any preferred shares distributed to him or her.[103]

Each partner is deemed to receive proceeds from the disposition of his or her partnership interest equal to the cost of all of the share and non-share property that is received on the winding-up of the partnership.[104]

---

[101] Para. 85(3)(*d*).

[102] Para. 85(3)(*e*). When no common shares were receivable as consideration, the cost of the preferred shares is the adjusted cost base of a partnership interest immediately before the wind-up less the fair market value of any "boot" distributed to the partner (subpara. 85(3)(*e*)(ii)).

[103] Para. 85(3)(*f*).

[104] Para. 85(3)(*g*).

COMPREHENSIVE EXAMPLE NO.1

(SECTION 85 ROLLOVER)

Assume:

Hilda Rumpole is the sole proprietor of a business to which the following data applies:

	Cost Amount	FMV
Portfolio securities	$ 37,500	$ 28,000
Accounts receivable	56,250	56,250
Inventory	112,500	115,000
Machinery & equipment*	65,625	96,250
Goodwill	—	67,750
Liabilities	(26,250)	(26,250)
	$ 245,625	$ 337,000

*Capital cost of $120,000

She transfers the assets and liabilities of her business to a newly formed Canadian corporation in exchange for the following consideration:

Promissory note	$175,000
Preferred shares (FMV)	87,500
Common shares (FMV)	74,500
	337,000

The corporation also assumes the liabilities of $26,250. Mrs. Rumpole and the corporation elect under subsection 85(1) to minimize taxes. An election is made under section 22 in respect of the accounts receivable.

	Agreed Amount	Gain (Loss)
Then:		
1. Elected amounts		
Portfolio securities	$ 28,000	(9,500)
Accounts receivable (s. 22)	56,250	—
Inventory	112,500	—
Machinery & equipment	65,625	—
Goodwill	1	—
	$262,376	(9,500)**

**Loss deemed to be nil under subsection 85(4).

Comprehensive Example (No. 1) (continued)

2. Cost of consideration received by Mrs. Rumpole

Agreed upon amount		$262,376
Cost of "boot":		
Liabilities assumed	$ 26,250	
Promissory note	175,000	(201,250)
Cost allocated to preferred shares		$ 61,126
Cost allocated to common shares		NIL

3. Allocation of deemed loss on portfolio securities

Cost of preferred shares		$ 61,126
Add: $\dfrac{87,500}{162,000} \times \$9,500$	=	5,131
Adjusted cost base of preferred shares		$ 66,257
Cost of common shares		NIL
Add: $\dfrac{74,500}{162,000} \times \$9,500$	=	$ 4,369
Adjusted cost base of common shares		$ 4,369

COMPREHENSIVE EXAMPLE NO. 2

**(REDUCTION OF PAID-UP CAPITAL
OF SHARES UNDER SUBSECTION 85(2.1))**

Assume:

Mr. Black sells his shares in an operating company (*Opco*) to a company (*Newco*) in an arm's length transaction. The following data applies to the *Opco* shares:

Fair market value (FMV)	$ 500,000
Adjusted cost base (ACB)	$ 1,000
Paid-up capital(PUC)	$ 1,000

Newco pays Mr. Black the following amounts:

Promissory note	$ 200,000
Shares (FMV and PUC)	$ 300,000*
Purchase price	$ 500,000

*Redeemable at $300,000.

Comprehensive Example (No. 2) (continued)

The parties elect $200,000 as the transfer price for the *Opco* shares. The consequences to Mr. Black are as follows:

1. <u>Capital gain on *Opco* shares</u>

Proceeds of disposition (para. 85(1)(*a*))	$ 200,000
ACB of shares	(1,000)
Capital gain	$ 199,000

2. <u>Adjustment to PUC of *Newco*'s shares</u>

Legal PUC of shares		$ 300,000
Less, amount by which		
Cost of *Opco* shares to *Newco*	$200,000	
exceeds		
Non-share consideration	($200,000)	
PUC reduction		NIL
Legal PUC of *Newco* shares		$ 300,000
Less: subs. 85(2.1) reduction		$ 300,000
PUC for tax purposes		(300,000)
		NIL

3. ACB of *Newco's* shares   NIL

4. <u>Upon redemption of shares by *Newco*</u>

Redemption price	$ 300,000
PUC for tax purposes	NIL
Deemed dividend (subs. 84(3))	$ 300,000
Redemption	$ 300,000
Less: deemed dividend	(300,000)
Proceeds of disposition (s. 54 ("proceeds of disposition") (j))	NIL
ACB of shares	NIL
Capital gain	NIL

SELECTED BIBLIOGRAPHY TO CHAPTER XX

General

Battye, George A., "Structuring Corporate Transactions", *British Columbia Tax Conf.* 65 (Can. Tax Foundation, 1981).

Bernstein, Jack, "Corporate Spin-Offs and Creditor Proofing", *Proceedings of 39th Tax Conf.* 30:1 (Can. Tax Foundation, 1987).

Bollefer, Stuart F. and Sheldon M. Rochkin, "The Wingless Butterfly" (January 1986), 119 *CA Magazine* 70.

Boultbee, Jack, "A Survey of the Use of Rollovers in Acquisitions and Mergers" (1980), 28 *Can. Tax J.* 504.

Brown, Robert D. and Thomas E. McDonnell, "Capital Gains Strips: A Critical Review of the New Provisions", in *Proceedings of 32nd Tax Conf.* 51 (Can. Tax Foundation, 1980).

"Butterflies: An Endangered Species?" (1990), 12:17 *The Canadian Taxpayer* 135.

Dart, Robert J., "Specific Uses of Companies in Tax Planning", in *Proceedings of 31st Tax Conf.* 117 (Can. Tax Foundation, 1979).

Dart, Robert J. and Howard J. Kellough, "The Butterfly Reorganization: A Descriptive Analysis", in *Proceedings of 41st Tax Conf.* 20:2 (Can. Tax Foundation, 1989).

Dolan, Claude, "Roulements", *Congres "79"*, Association Quebecoise de Planification Fiscale et Succesorale, 165.

Ewens, Douglas S., "The Butterfly Matures", in *Proceedings of the 36th Tax Conf.* 866 (Can. Tax Foundation, 1984).

Ewens, Douglas S., "The Capital Gains Exemption and the Butterfly" (1986), 34 *Can. Tax J.* 914.

Ewens, Douglas S., "Transfers to a Corporation Under Subsection 85(1)" (1984), 32 *Can. Tax J.* 378.

Ewens, Douglas S. and Sharon J. Hugo, "The Effect of Bill C-139 on Certain Corporate Reorganizations" (1988), 36 *Can. Tax J.* 1021.

Harris, E.C., "Rollovers — Some Practical Questions: Subsection 85(1)" (1981), *Can. Taxation* 1027-1049.

Hausman, James S., "US-Canada Cross-Border Reorganizations" (1990), 38 *Can. Tax J.* 678.

Hiltz, Michael A., "The Butterfly Reorganization: Revenue Canada's Approach", in *Proceedings of 41st Tax Conf.* 20:32 (Can. Tax Foundation, 1989).

Kellough, Howard J., "Splitting Up the Business of a Private Corporation", *Corporate Management Tax Conf.* 12 (Can. Tax Foundation, 1984).

Kellough, Howard J. and Peter E. McQuillan, "Taxation of Private Corporations and Their Shareholders", *Canadian Tax Paper No. 72* 395 (Can. Tax Foundation, 1983).

Middleton, David W., "Common Tax Problems and Pitfalls in Effecting Reorganizations of Private Corporations", in *Proceedings of 41st Tax Conf.* 13:1 (Can. Tax Foundation, 1989).

Muirson, Stephen R., "Transfers of Property Within a Corporate Group" (1986), 34 *Can. Tax J.* 646.

Pitfield, Ian H., "Section 85 Transfers Revisited" (1978), 12 *CGA Magazine* 27.

"Reorganizations — Reorganized" (1991), 13:2 *The Canadian Taxpayer* 13.

Rohde, Richard C., "Section 85 Transfers — Limitations and Pitfalls" (1988), 36 *Can. Tax J.* 1302.

Scwartz, Alan M., "Transferring Shares of Private Corporations Need Not Be So Taxing" (1980), 113 *CA Magazine* No. 5, 49.

Sider, Vance A., *Butterfly Reorganizations* (Don Mills, Ontario: CCH Canadian, 1989).

Singer, Paul, "The Rollover Provisions in Respect of Corporate Reorganizations Provided under the Income Tax Act: Efficiency and Equity as Policy Considerations" (1983), 31 *Can. Tax J.* 569.

Spindler, Robert J., "Butterflies Revisited" (1989), 37 *Can. Tax J.* 808.

Stacey, John A., "Transfer of Assets To and From a Corporation", in *Proceedings of 40th Tax Conf.* 14:1 (Can. Tax Foundation, 1988).

Thomas, James P., "Restructuring the Ownership of Property Within a Closely-Held Group", *Corp. Management Tax Conf.* 6:1 (Can. Tax Foundation, 1989).

Williamson, W.G., "Transfers of Assets To and From a Canadian Corporation", in *Proceedings of 38th Tax Conf.* 12:1 (Can. Tax Foundation, 1986).

Witterick, R.G., "Acquisitions of Shares of Private Corporations in Arms's Length Transactions", *Corporate Management Tax Conf.* 120 (Can. Tax Foundation, 1978).

Property Eligible for Rollover

Murison, Stephen A., "Transfers of Property Within a Corporate Group (Taxation)" (1986), 34 *Can. Tax J.* 646-660.

Spindler, Robert J., "Mutual Fund Reorganizations" (1987), 35 *Can. Tax J.* 736.

Consideration Received

Boultbee, Jack A., "Dividend Stop-Loss Rules" (1985), 33 *Can. Tax J.* 150.

Stein, Boris P., "Part Two: Canadian Case Law Concerning Shares Received on a Rollover", *The Journal of Business Valuation*, Canadian Assoc. of Business Valuators, Vol. 7, 1981, 95.

Elected Amounts

Beam, Robert E. and Stanley N. Laiken, "Changes in Use and Non-Arm's Length Transfers of Depreciable Property" (1987), 35 *Can. Tax J.* 461.

Boultbee, Jack A., "Gifts and Rollovers" (1983), 31 *Can. Tax J.* 84.

Ewens, Douglas S., "Retractable Preferred Shares" (1983), 31 *Can. Tax J.* 713.

Heller, Stephen, "Part One: Valuation of Preferred Shares Received on a Rollover Under the Income Tax Act", *The Journal of Business Valuation*, Canadian Assoc. of Business Valuators, Vol. 7, 1981, 71.

Peters, Steven, "The Effect of Amendments to Paragraph 85(1)(e.2) on Transfers To and Between Wholly-Owned Corporations" (1989), 2:32 *Canadian Current Tax J*-139.

Stainsby, Joseph A., "Recent Developments in Capital Cost Allowance and Eligible Capital Expenditures", *Corporate Management Tax Conf.* 196 (Can. Tax Foundation, 1981).

Wise, Richard M., "Fair Market Value Determinations — A Few More Requirements" (1983), 31 *Can. Tax J.* 337.

Wise, Richard M., "Valuation and the Income Tax Act" (1981), 29 *Can. Tax J.* 626.

Wise, Richard M., "The Valuation of Preferred Shares Issued on a Section 85 Rollover" (1984), 32 *Can. Tax J.* 239.

Paid-Up Capital of Shares Issued by Purchaser Corporation

Roberts, David G.,"Determination of Paid-Up Capital" (1992), 40 *Can. Tax J.* 338.

Simpson, M.A., "Planning Around the New Paid-Up Capital Restrictions" (1986), 34 *Can. Tax J.* 631.

Potential for Double Taxation

Swiderski, Tony, "Transfers of United States Real Property Interests in Canadian Reorganizations: Opportunities, Limitations and Pitfalls" (1989), 37 *Can. Tax J.* 605.

Tremblay, Richard G., "Canada-United States Cross-Border Butterflies", in *Proceedings of 39th Tax Conf.* 22:1 (Can. Tax Foundation, 1987).

Estate Freezing and Subsection 85(1)

Barbacki, Richard, "Estate Freezing in the Light of Recent Income Tax Changes", in *Proceedings of 38th Tax Conf.* 36:1 (Can. Tax Foundation, 1986).

Bowden, Gregory, T.W., "Estate Freezing", *British Columbia Tax Conf.* 266 (Can. Tax Foundation, 1980).

Crawford, William E., "Corporate Freezes — Are You Getting Your Money's Worth?", in *Proceedings of 32nd Tax Conf.* 772 (Can. Tax Foundation, 1980).

Hart, Stephen D., "Estate Freezes, Part 1: Holding Companies" (1982), 115 *CA Magazine* No. 10, 54.

Morris, J.S.D., "Freezing Family Business Interests — Inflation and Other Concerns" (1981), 29 *Can. Tax J.* 211.

Promislow, Norm, "Estate Planning and Income Spliting: Recent Developments", *Prairie Provinces Tax Conf.* 371 (Can. Tax Foundation, 1983).

Rochwerg, Martin J., "Post-Mortem Estate Freezing" (1983), 31 *Can. Tax J.* 69.

Silver, Sheldon, "A Simple Case of Freezing" (1976), 24 *Can. Tax J.* 74.

Silver, Sheldon, "A Simple Case of Freezing — Part 2" (1976), 24 *Can. Tax J.* 171.

Silver, Sheldon, "Has the Dust Settled?" (1977), 25 *Can. Tax J.* 652.

Other

Colley, Geoffrey M., "Tax Planning Implications for New Business" (1980), 113 *CA Magazine* No. 12, 78.

Davidson, Barrie, "Inter Vivos Tax Planning" (1981), 15 *CGA Magazine* 2.

Gordon, Hugh A.,"Discussion by Hugh A. Gordon. C.A.", in *Proceedings of 33rd Tax Conf.* 370 (Can. Tax Foundation, 1981).

Hiltz, Michael A., "Section 55: An Update", *Corp. Management Tax Conf.* 40 (Can. Tax Foundation, 1984).

Hogg, R.D., "Stock Option Benefits in Canadian Controlled Private Corporations" (1978), 26 *Can. Tax J.* 85.

Lindsay, Robert F., "Canadian Holding Corporations for Canadian Subsidiaries of Nonresident Parent Corporations", *Corporate Management Tax Conf.* 347 (Can. Tax Foundation, 1980).

Mida, I.H., "More on Intra Group Transfers" (1986), 34 *Can. Tax J.* 1184.

Playfair, J.L., "Planning for the Successful Tax-Sheltered Investment" (1980), 28 *Can. Tax J.* 647.

Read, Robert J.L., "Section 55: A Review of Current Issues", in *Proceedings of 40th Tax Conf.* 18:1 (Can. Tax Foundation, 1988).

CHAPTER XXI

NON-ARM'S LENGTH SHARE TRANSFERS

References:

ITA:

S. 69	Inadequate Consideration
S. 84	Deemed Dividends
S. 84.1	Non-arm's Length Sale of Shares
Subs. 89(1)	Definition: "Paid-up Capital"

BULLETINS, CIRCULARS & RULINGS:

IT-169	August 6, 1974	Price Adjustment Clauses
IT-419	July 10, 1978	Meaning of "Arm's Length"
IT-463R	July 12, 1991	Paid-up Capital
IT-489R	February 28, 1994	Non-arm's Length Sale of Shares to a Corporation
ATR-27	January 8, 1988	Exchange and Acquisition of Interests in Capital Properties Through Rollovers and Winding-up ("Butterfly")
ATR-32	July 8, 1988	Rollover of Fixed Assets from Opco into Holdco

1. GENERAL

As a general rule, a taxpayer who disposes of capital property is required to recognize the proceeds of disposition in the year of the disposition. There are, however, several important exceptions to this rule. Chapter XX "Reorganizations: Transfer of Property to a Corporation" illustrated how a taxpayer can rollover capital property at its adjusted cost base into a taxable Canadian corporation under subsection 85(1). For example, a taxpayer can transfer shares of an operating company into a holding company without triggering a capital gain on the disposition.

Although the *Income Tax Act* allows taxpayers to rollover capital property to a corporation without triggering capital gains,[1] it also prevents taxpayers from ultimately avoiding tax on the transfer. Two easy methods of avoiding tax would be to convert a corporation's taxable surplus into tax exempt capital gains or to remove the taxable surplus of a corporation as a tax-free return of capital.

---

[1] Subs. 85(1).

2. PURPOSE OF SECTION 84.1

Section 84.1 is essentially an anti-avoidance rule. It prevents the removal of taxable corporate surplus as a tax-free return of capital or as a tax-exempt capital gain when an individual transfers shares to a corporation in a *non-arm's length* transaction.[2] The section only applies to a non-arm's length transfer of shares to a "connected" corporation.

Before looking at the details of section 84.1, it may be useful to consider the type of transactions that the section is intended to safeguard against. Consider the following example: Rodgers is the sole shareholder of an operating small business company ("Opco"). Her shares have a paid-up capital of $1,000, an adjusted cost base of $150,000 and a fair market value of $500,000, all of which is represented in cash. If Opco simply pays a cash dividend to Rodgers, she will be taxed on the dividend. If Opco redeems its shares at their fair market value, Rodgers will be deemed to receive a taxable dividend of $499,000. Thus, Rodgers will be taxed under either option if she extracts the corporation's surplus. But what if Rodgers incorporates a new company, ("Holdco"), and sells her Opco shares to Holdco in exchange for a demand promissory note in the amount of $500,000? Assume that the gain of $350,000 on the sale of Opco's shares qualifies as a tax-exempt capital gain. If Opco and Holdco amalgamate after the sale, the amalgamated corporation could pay off its demand note to Rodgers without any tax cost to her. In effect, Rodgers could extract Opco's taxable surplus without any tax payable either on the proceeds of the disposition of the Opco shares or on the corporation's surplus. Section 84.1 is intended to prevent these types of surplus stripping transactions (see examples XX1.4 and XX1.5 on ways to avoid section 84.1.).

3. NON-ARM'S LENGTH TRANSACTIONS

Section 84.1 is directed solely towards controlling "surplus stripping" in non-arm's length transactions; it does not have any effect whatsoever where a taxpayer sells shares in an arm's length transaction. Similar, though not identical, provisions deal with sales by a non-resident person of shares of a Canadian corporation to another Canadian corporation.[3]

4. SHARE TRANSFERS

Section 84.1 can apply regardless of whether or not the share transfer is the subject of an election under section 85.

---

[2] S. 84.1.

[3] See s. 212.1.

5. APPLICATION OF SECTION 84.1

Section 84.1 applies when an individual or a trust resident in Canada disposes of shares to a corporation in the following circumstances:[4]

- The shares are capital property;

- The shares disposed of are the shares of a corporation resident in Canada;

- The vendor and the purchaser corporation do not deal with each other at arm's length; and

- Immediately after the disposition of the shares the corporation whose shares are disposed of (referred to as the "subject corporation") and the purchaser corporation are "connected" with each other.

Thus, the principal features of section 84.1 are that it applies to non-arm's length transfers of shares where the purchaser corporation and the subject corporation are "connected"[5] to each other.

Three points warrant emphasis: (1) The purchaser corporation does not have to be resident in Canada for the section to apply; (2) The section applies both to pre-1972 and post-1971 shares; (3) The section does not apply to dispositions of shares of non-resident corporations (for example, it does not apply to a disposition of shares in a foreign affiliate).

6. "NON-ARM'S LENGTH" RELATIONSHIPS

Reference:

BULLETINS, CIRCULARS & RULINGS:

IT-419   July 10, 1978   Meaning of "Arm's Length"

Section 84.1 only applies where the vendor and the purchaser corporation do not deal with each other at "arm's length".[6] Although the statutory language is not entirely clear, it appears that the section applies if the parties are not at arm's length at the time of the disposition of the shares even if the parties are at arm's length after the transaction.

---

[4]   Subs. 84.1(1).

[5]   See subs. 186(4).

[6]   S. 251.

(a) Deemed Non-arm's Length Relationships

The vendor and the purchaser corporation are deemed not to be dealing with each other at arm's length if:[7]

- immediately before the disposition, the vendor was one of a group of less than six persons that controlled the "subject corporation";

- immediately after the disposition, the vendor was part of a group of less than six persons who controlled the "purchaser corporation"; and

- each member of the group that controlled the "purchaser corporation" was also a member of the group that controlled the "subject corporation".

The members of the group do not have to be related to each other for these rules to apply. If an individual was part of a group of less than six persons who controlled the subject corporation before, and the purchaser corporation after the disposition of the shares, the individual is deemed not to be at arm's length with the purchaser corporation.

In determining whether a corporation is controlled by a group of persons, a "group" in respect of the corporation means any two or more persons each of whom owns shares of the corporation.[8]

(b) Deemed Ownership of Shares

For the purposes of determining whether or not the vendor and the purchaser corporation are at non-arm's length, the vendor is deemed to own any shares of the corporation that are owned by:[9]

- his or her spouse;

- his or her children under 18 years of age;

- an *inter vivos* trust of which either the vendor or the vendor's spouse or children are beneficiaries;

- an *inter vivos* trust of which a controlled corporation is a beneficiary;

- a corporation that the vendor, the vendor's spouse or children under 18 years of age control; or

- a corporation that is controlled by an *inter vivos* trust of which the vendor or the vendor's spouse or children under 18 years of age are beneficiaries.

---

[7] Para. 84.1(2)(*b*).

[8] Para. 84.1(2)(*e*).

[9] Para. 84.1(2)(*c*).

For the purpose of these rules, "children" includes grandchildren, great-grandchildren and persons under the age of 18 who are wholly dependent on the taxpayer.[10]

7. "CONNECTED" CORPORATIONS

Generally speaking, a purchaser corporation and a subject corporation are connected to each other if the former, either alone or with other non-arm's length parties, controls the latter. They are also connected to each other if the purchaser corporation owns shares of the subject corporation that represent more than 10 per cent of the votes and fair market value of all the shares of the subject corporation.[11]

8. DISPOSITIONS BY TRUSTS

A disposition by a trust to a corporation that is controlled by its beneficiaries (or by persons related to the beneficiaries) of the trust is considered a non-arm's length disposition to the corporation.[12]

9. SCOPE OF SECTION 84.1

Section 84.1 applies to share transfers regardless of whether the transferor has elected to rollover the shares under subsection 85(1). Indeed, the section can apply even if the purchaser corporation has not issued any shares as consideration for the transfer.

The section can have two effects: (1) It can deem a dividend to have been paid to the transferor of the subject shares; and (2) It can reduce the paid-up capital of any new shares issued as consideration for the subject shares. Hence, if the section applies to reduce the paid-up capital of shares, the paid-up capital of the shares can be different from their stated capital for corporate purposes. This can be an important consideration in the purchase and sale of shares.

Generally speaking, the maximum "safe amount" that a person who transfers shares to a corporation can receive from the corporation, either as "hard" consideration or as the paid-up capital of shares, is the *greater* of the paid-up capital and the adjusted cost base of the transferred shares. Any consideration in excess of the greater of these two amounts will trigger a dividend, either immediately or in the future, for the person who transferred the shares.

(a) Reduction in Paid-up Capital of Shares

Where a purchaser corporation issues shares in exchange for other shares and the paid-up capital of the newly issued shares exceeds the excess (if any) of the *greater* of

---

[10] Para. 84.1(2)(*c*); subs. 70(10).

[11] Subs. 186(4).

[12] Para. 84.1(2)(*d*).

the paid-up capital and the adjusted cost base of the shares over the value of "hard" consideration, the excess amount reduces the paid-up capital of the new shares.

The paid-up capital of the newly issued shares is reduced by an amount determined by the following formula:[13]

$$(A - B) \times C/A$$

where, generally:

A = paid-up capital of all new shares issued by purchaser corporation;

B = excess of *greater* of paid-up capital and adjusted cost base of transferred shares over the value of "hard" consideration received; and

C = increase in paid-up capital of particular class of new shares issued.

Hence, where the purchaser corporation issues only one class of shares in exchange for the transferred shares, the formula reduces to:

$$(A - B)$$

Where the amount determined by the formula is negative, the negative amount is deemed to be nil.[14]

---

[13]　Para. 84.1(1)(*a*).

[14]　S. 257.

Example XXI.1

Assume:

	Case		
	1	2	3
PUC of purchaser corporation shares	$ 100	$ 100	$5,000
PUC of transferred shares	100	100	100
ACB of transferred shares	100	1,000	1,000
"Hard" consideration	NIL	1,100	NIL

Then, the reduction in paid-up capital is (A - B), determined as follows:

		1	2	3
A.	PUC of purchaser corporation shares	$ 100	$ 100	$5,000
B.	Greater of:			
	PUC and ACB of transferred shares	$ 100	$1,000	$1,000
	Exceeds:			
	"Hard" consideration	—	$1,100	—
		$ 100	—	$1,000
	PUC reduction (A − B)	NIL	$ 100	4,000
	PUC after reduction	$ 100	NIL	$1,000

Thus, one effect of section 84.1 is that redemption of the new shares for an amount in excess of their revised paid-up capital gives rise to a deemed dividend.

(b) Deemed Dividend

Section 84.1 can also trigger a deemed dividend to the transferor. The purchaser corporation is deemed to have paid a dividend to the transferor where the aggregate of the increase in the paid-up capital of its shares and the value of any "hard" consideration that it issues exceeds the total of:[15]

- the *greater* of the adjusted cost base and the paid-up capital of the transferred shares; and

- the total paid-up capital reduction required in the purchaser corporation's shares.

---

[15] Para. 84.1(1)(*b*).

The amount of the deemed dividend is determined by the formula:

$$(A + D) - (E + F)$$

where, generally:

A = paid-up capital of all new shares issued by purchaser corporation

D = value of "hard" consideration

E = greater of PUC and ACB of transferred shares

F = reduction in paid-up capital of purchaser corporation by application of paragraph 84.1(1)(a)

Example XXI.2

Assume:

PUC of purchaser corporation shares	$2,500
PUC of transferred shares	100
ACB of transferred shares	1,000
"Hard" consideration	$2,500

Then, the paid-up capital reduction is determined as follows:

A. PUC of purchaser corporation shares	$2,500
B. Greater of:	
PUC ($100) and ACB ($1,000) of transferred shares	$1,000
Exceeds: "Hard" consideration	(2,500)
	NIL
PUC reduction (A − B)	$2,500*
PUC after reduction	NIL

The deemed dividend is determined as follows:

A. PUC of purchaser corporation shares	$2,500
D. "Hard" consideration	2,500
A + D	$5,000

Example XXI.2 (continued)

E. Greater of:	
PUC of transferred shares	$ 100
ACB of transferred shares	$ 1,000
Greater amount:	$ 1,000
F. PUC reduction	2,500*
E + F	$ 3,500
Immediate dividend (A + D) − (E + F)	
$5,000 − $3,500	$ 1,500

Example XXI.3

APPLICATION ON SHARE TRANSFER								
	I	II	III	IV	V	VI	VII	VIII
	(dollars)							
A. Paid-up capital of shares of purchaser received for transferred shares (before s. 84.1 reduction)	100	100	100	100	5,000	4,000	2,500	—
B. Paid-up capital of transferred shares	100	100	100	100	100	100	100	100
C. Adjusted cost base of transferred shares	100	1,000	1,000	1,000	1,000	1,000	1,000	1,000
D. Non-share consideration received for transferred shares	—	900	1,000	1,000	—	1,000	2,500	1,500
Paid-Up Capital Reduction: 1. Amount A	100	100	100	100	5,000	4,000	2,500	—
2. Amount by which greater of B and C exceeds D	100	100	—	—	1,000	—	—	—
3. E: Paid-up capital reduction	—	—	100	100	4,000	4,000	2,500	—
4. Paid-up capital after reduction	100	100	—	—	1,000	—	—	—
Immediate Dividend: 1. Aggregate of A and D	100	1,000	1,100	1,100	5,000	5,000	5,000	1,500
2. Aggregate of the greater of B and C plus E	100	1,000	1,100	1,100	5,000	5,000	3,500	1,000
3. Immediate dividend	—	—	—	—	—	—	1,500	500

10. AVOIDING REDUCTION IN PAID-UP CAPITAL

The easiest way to avoid a reduction of paid-up capital under paragraph 84.1(1)(*a*) is to ensure that the fair market value of boot and the paid-up capital of the new shares does not exceed the *greater* of the adjusted cost base and the paid-up capital of the shares transferred to the corporation.

Example XXI.4

Transferred shares:
PUC	$ 1,000
ACB	$150,000
FMV	$500,000

New shares:
PUC	$ 1,000
FMV	$500,000
Boot:	$149,000

There is no reduction in the paid-up capital of the new shares in these circumstances.

---

11. AVOIDING A DEEMED DIVIDEND

It is also possible to have a reduction in the paid-up capital of the purchaser corporation's shares without triggering a deemed dividend.

Example XXI.5

AVOIDING DEEMED DIVIDEND UNDER SECTION 84.1

Assume:

Mr. Black owns the shares of *Blackco* to which the following data applies:

FMV	$ 500,000
ACB	$ 150,000
PUC	$ 1,000

Black transfers the shares to a new corporation ("*Newco*") in exchange for the following consideration:

Promissory note	$ 150,000
Shares (PUC and FMV)	350,000
	$ 500,000

Example XXI.5 (continued)

Section 84.1 applies to the transaction.
Then:

1. PUC Reduction

Legal PUC of *Newco* shares		$ 350,000
S. 84.1 reduction		(350,000)
PUC for tax purposes		NIL
Potential dividend on redemption of shares		$ 350,000

2. Deemed dividend

Increase in PUC of *Newco*		$ 350,000
Non-share consideration		150,000
Total consideration		$ 500,000
Less aggregate of:		
(i) Greater of PUC of *Blackco's* shares and ACB of *Blackco's* shares, and	$ 150,000	
(ii) PUC reduction under s. 84.1	$ 350,000	(500,000)
Deemed dividend		NIL

The safest way, however, to avoid problems under section 84.1 is to take back shares that have a paid-up capital equal to the paid-up capital of the shares transferred. (See Column I in Example XXI.3, above.)

12. PRICE ADJUSTMENT CLAUSES

Reference:

BULLETINS, CIRCULARS & RULINGS:

IT-169   August 6, 1974   Price Adjustment Clauses

(a) Purpose

A price adjustment clause is a term in a contract of purchase and sale that allows the parties to the contract to *retroactively* adjust the price of the subject matter of the sale. A price adjustment clause is usually used in contracts when the parties to the contract intend to transact at fair market value, but where the determination of value is difficult or uncertain in the particular circumstances.[16]

---

[16] See generally, Douglas Ewens, "Use of Adjustment Clauses in Non-arm's Length Reorganizations" (1981), 20 *Can. Tax J.* 718.

To appreciate the purpose served by a price adjustment clause, one should first look at subsection 69(1).

A taxpayer who acquires property in a non-arm's length transaction at a price in excess of its fair market value is deemed to have acquired the property at its fair market value. Thus, for tax purposes, the cost of the property acquired is reduced to its fair market value. For example, a taxpayer who pays $150,000 for an asset that has a fair market value of $100,000 is deemed to have acquired it for $100,000. The reduction in cost increases the purchaser's potential tax liability when he or she disposes of the property in the future. Note, however, that there is no concurrent adjustment to the seller's proceeds of disposition.

A taxpayer who disposes of property at less than its fair market value in a non-arm's length transaction is *deemed* to receive proceeds of disposition equal to its fair market value. For example, a taxpayer who sells an asset worth $100,000 for $75,000 is deemed to have received proceeds of $100,000. Hence, the gain or loss is calculated on the basis of the deemed, rather than actual, proceeds of disposition.[17] The purchaser calculates any subsequent gain on the basis of his or her *actual* cost.

Thus, subsection 69(1) does not provide a mirror image of the same transaction from the purchaser's and the vendor's points of view. Consequently, taxpayers who do not deal at arm's length with each other may be financially penalized if they do not transact at fair market value. Subsection 69(1) is, and is intended to be, a penal provision: It does not allow a taxpayer who has paid less than fair market value for property to "bump-up" the cost base of the property.

The primary purpose of a price adjustment clause is to rectify the mismatch of costs and values. A price adjustment clause allows a taxpayer who purchases property in a non-arm's length transaction for less than its fair market value to *retroactively* "bump-up" the cost base of the property at a later date.

(b) Determination of Fair Market Value

A taxpayer who transfers property to a corporation usually receives consideration equal to the value of the property. If the consideration received is less than the value of the property transferred, there may be an indirect gift.[18] If the assets are transferred in exchange for too much consideration from the corporation, the taxpayer receives a shareholder benefit that is taxable as income.[19] Hence, the determination of the fair market value of property is a critical step in all non-arm's length transfers.

---

[17] Para. 69(1)(*b*).

[18] Para. 85(1)(*e*.2); see Chapter XX "Reorganizations: Transfer of Property to a Corporation".

[19] Subs. 15(1).

The calculation of fair market value, however, is a complex and uncertain process. Subsequent events may show that the values used in an agreement do not in fact reflect market values. The use of a price adjustment clause in an agreement of purchase and sale can alleviate the uncertainty. In the event that the estimate of fair market value set out in the agreement of purchase and sale subsequently proves to be incorrect, the parties to the contract can retroactively adjust the purchase price according to the price adjustment clause in order to reflect the revised figure.[20]

(c) *Bona Fide* Intention

The use of price adjustment clauses is subject to an important qualification. A price adjustment clause is only valid where it reflects the *bona fide* intention of the parties to contract at fair market value.[21] Thus, it is imperative that the parties make a good faith attempt to arrive, by some fair and reasonable valuation method, at the fair market value of the property transferred. A price adjustment clause may be ineffective for tax purposes in the absence of a good faith effort to determine the fair market value of the subject of the purchase and sale.[22]

(d) Administrative Interpretation

Revenue Canada requires taxpayers who use price adjustment clauses in agreements of purchase and sale to notify Revenue Canada of the existence of the clause. There is no legislative authority for this requirement. Notification to Revenue Canada almost certainly "red-flags" the file and is an invitation to a valuation dispute. At the very least, it is a signal to Revenue Canada that the parties to the transaction are uncertain about their valuation.

13. AVERAGING PAID-UP CAPITAL

The paid-up capital of a share of a class of capital stock of a corporation is the average paid-up capital of the entire class. For example, if a corporation issues 1,000 Class A shares at $1 per share and later issues 1,000 Class A shares at $20 per share, the paid-up capital of each Class A share is $10.50, that is, $21,000/2,000.

Paid-up capital adjustments under section 84.1 are similarly averaged. The paid up capital of the issued shares of a particular class of shares is the average of the entire class. Hence, an adjustment under section 84.1 that is triggered by a transaction with one shareholder of a class of shares also affects all other shareholders of the same class.

---

[20] IT-169, "Price Adjustment Clauses" (August 6, 1974).

[21] *Guilder News Co. (1963) Ltd. v. M.N.R.*, [1973] CTC 1, 73 DTC 5048 (F.C.A.).

[22] IT-169, "Price Adjustment Clauses" (August 6, 1974).

14. COMPREHENSIVE EXAMPLE

REDUCTION OF PAID-UP CAPITAL OF SHARES UNDER SECTION 84.1

Assume:

Mr. Green owns the shares of an operating company (*Opco*) to which the following data applies:

Fair market value (FMV)	$ 500,000
Adjusted cost base (ACB)	$ 1,000
Paid-up capital (PUC)	$ 1,000

Green transfers the shares to a holding company (*Holdco*) in exchange for the following consideration:

Promissory note	$ 400,000
Shares (PUC and FMV)	100,000
Total consideration	$ 500,000

Green and *Holdco* are not at arm's length with each other.

Then:

1. The legal paid-up capital of the shares newly issued by *Holdco* (the "purchaser corporation") is reduced for tax purposes as follows:

Legal PUC of shares	$ 100,000
S. 84.1 reduction (Note 1)	(100,000)
PUC for tax purposes	NIL
Potential dividend on redemption of shares	$ 100,000

Note:

PUC reduction = $(A - B) \times \dfrac{C}{A}$

where:

A = Increase in PUC of *all* new shares;

B = Amount by which greater of PUC and ACB of *Opco's* shares exceeds fair market value of non-share consideration; and

C = Increase in PUC of new shares of the *particular* class issued by *Holdco*.

$= (100,000 - 0) \times \dfrac{100,000}{100,000}$

$= \underline{\$100,000}$

Comprehensive Example (continued)

2. *Holdco* is deemed to have paid a dividend of $399,000 to *Opco's* shareholders. The amount of this deemed dividend is determined as follows:

Increase in PUC of *Holdco*		$ 100,000
Non-share consideration		400,000
Total consideration		$ 500,000
Less, aggregate of		
(i) greater of PUC of *Opco's* shares		
($1,000) and ACB of *Opco's* shares		
($1,000), and	$ 1,000	
(ii) PUC reduction under s. 84.1	$ 100,000	(101,000)
Deemed dividend		$ 399,000

3. Hence, a potential capital gain of $499,000 (that is, $500,000 - 1,000) is converted into:

Deemed dividend	$ 399,000
Potential dividend on redemption of shares	$ 100,000
	$ 499,000

SELECTED BIBLIOGRAPHY TO CHAPTER XXI

General

Couzin, Robert, "Of Arm's Length, and Not Dealing Thereat" (1978), 26 *Can. Tax. J.* 271.

Cronkwright, Glen E., Robert J. Dart & Robert F. Lindsay, "Corporate Distributions and the 1977 Tax Changes", in *Proceedings of 29th Tax Conf.* 279 (Can. Tax Foundation, 1977).

Fryer, D.J., "84.1 and Two-Tier Tax Problems" (1980), 28 *Can. Tax J.* 208.

Gordon, Hugh A., "Discussion by Hugh A. Gordon, C.A.", in *Proceedings of 33rd Tax Conf.* 370 (Can. Tax Foundation, 1981).

Hart, Stephen D., "Estate Freezes, Part 1: Holding Companies" (1982), 115 *CA Magazine* No. 10, 54.

Holtz, D.E., "Transfer of a Small Family Business Corporation" (1980), 28 *Can. Tax J.* 357.

Kellough, Howard J., "Acquisition of Shares in a Non-Arm's Length Transaction", *Corporate Management Tax Conf.* 186 (Can. Tax Foundation, 1978).

Kellough, Howard J., "Formation, Operation, and Disposition of Closely Held Corporations", in *Proceedings of 30th Tax Conf.* 703 (Can. Tax Foundation, 1978).

Kellough, Howard J., "Selecting an Appropriate Share Capital Structure for Private Corporations", in *Proceedings of 33rd Tax Conf.* 49 (Can. Tax Foundation, 1981).

Laflamme, Pierre, "Planning an Estate Freeze" (1978), 111 *CA Magazine* No. 7, 57.

Laushway, Keith, "Documentation and Non-arm's Length Transactions" (1992), 3 *Can. Current Tax* P-55.

Lemmon, K.W., "Corporate Distributions" (1978), 43 *Business Quarterly* 90.

Lessard, Pierre, "Nouvelles dispositions des articles 84.1 et 84.2" (1978), 26 *Can. Tax J.* 466.

Little, L.M., "Further Tax Traps for the Unwary" (1978), 12 *CGA Magazine* No. 7, 7.

McQuillan, Peter, "Financing Corporate Acquisitions", *Tax Planning and Management*, Vol. 9, No. 32 of *Canadian Income Tax Revised* (Butterworth and Co. (Canada) Ltd., 1978).

Morris, J.S.D., "Freezing Family Business Interests — Inflation and Other Concerns" (1981), 29 *Can. Tax J.* 211.

Reid, Robert J., "Tax Aspects of Incorporation", *Tax Planning and Management*, Vol. 9, No. 38 of *Canadian Income Tax Revised* (Butterworth and Co. (Canada) Ltd., 1979).

Schwartz, Alan M., "Transferring Shares of Private Corporations Need Not Be So Taxing" (1980), 113 *CA Magazine* No. 5, 49.

Stein, Boris P., "Part Two: Canadian Case Law Concerning Shares Received on a Rollover", *The Journal of Business Valuation*, Canadian Association of Business Valuators, Vol. 7, 1981, 95.

Ward, David A., "Arm's Length Acquisitions Relating to Shares in a Public Corporation", *Corporate Management Tax Conf.* 108 (Can. Tax Foundation, 1978).

Ward, David A. and Neal Armstrong, "Corporate Taxation: Arm's Length Dealings" (1986), 5 *Legal Alert* 49.

Williamson, W. Gordon, "Transfers of Assets To and From a Canadian Corporation", in *Proceedings of 38th Tax Conf.* 12:1 (Can. Tax Foundation, 1986).

Witterick, R.G., "Acquisitions of Shares of Private Corporations in Arm's Length Transactions", *Corporate Management Tax Conf.* 120 (Can. Tax Foundation, 1978).

Application of Section 84.1

Birnie, David A.G., "The New Approach to Dividend Stripping and Its Implications for Share Acquisitions and Capital Reorganizations", in *Proceedings of 29th Tax Conf.* 537 (Can. Tax Foundation, 1977).

Brown, Robert D., "Last Gun-Fight at the Surplus-Stripping Corral", in *Proceedings of 30th Tax Conf.* 590 (Can. Tax Foundation, 1978).

Dixon, Gordon D., "Depreciable Property: Rules Affect Non-Arm's Length Transfers" (January 1988), 22 *CGA Magazine* 24.

Eng, Susan, "The Arm's-Length Rules", in *Proceedings of 40th Tax Conf.* 13:1 (Can. Tax Foundation, 1988).

Ewens, Douglas S., "New Considerations in Structuring Share-for-share Exchange Offers" (1988), 36 *Can. Tax J.* 449.

Moskowitz, Evelyn P., "Dealing at Arm's Length: A Question of Fact", in *Proceedings of 39th Tax Conf.* 33:1 (Can. Tax Foundation, 1987).

Rohde, Richard C., "Section 85 Transfers — Limitations and Pitfalls" (1988), 36 *Can. Tax J.* 1302 at 1315-1318.

Templeton, Wendy, "The Taxation of Corporate Reorganizations — Anti-Avoidance and the Capital Gains Exemption" (1986), 34 *Can. Tax J.* 203.

Price Adjustment Clauses

Ewens, Douglas, "Use of Adjustment Clauses in Non-Arm's Length Reorganizations" (1981), 29 *Can. Tax J.* 718.

Morris, J.S.D., "Freezing Family Business Interests — Inflation and Other Concerns" (1981), 29 *Can. Tax J.* 211.

Wise, Richard M., "Valuation and the Income Tax Act" (1981), 29 *Can. Tax J.* 626.

Averaging Paid-Up Capital

Sinclair, B.R., "Paid-up Capital" (1986), 34 *Can. Tax J.* 1483.

CHAPTER XXII

SHARE-FOR-SHARE EXCHANGES

References:

ITA

S. 85.1   Share-for-Share Exchange

BULLETINS, CIRCULARS & RULINGS:

IT-450R   April 8, 1993   Share for Share Exchange

ATR-26   October 9, 1987   Share Exchange

1. GENERAL

(a) Purpose

The share-for-share exchange rules in section 85.1 are intended to facilitate share exchange transactions on a tax-deferred basis. The rules serve two principal purposes: (1) They allow Canadian corporations to finance takeover bids using share consideration; and (2) They allow for the reorganization of foreign affiliates.[1]

(b) Tax Deferral

Section 85.1 is a flexible provision. It allows shareholders who exchange shares of a taxable Canadian corporation for shares of a Canadian purchaser corporation in an arm's length transaction to obtain a tax-deferred rollover: The tax cost of the shareholder's old shares is rolled over into the tax cost of the new shares. Thus, any capital gain accrued on the old shares is deferred until they are disposed of at a later date.

(c) Not Elective

The share-for-share exchange provisions in section 85.1 do not require an election by the parties. Therefore, they are particularly suitable in arm's length transactions, such as takeover bids. However, the rollover is not mandatory and the vendor may recognize any portion of the capital gain or loss for tax purposes simply by including the amount on his or her tax return for the year. The provision is somewhat unusual in that the acquiring corporation's cost of shares acquired is determined independently of the vendor's tax treatment.

---

[1]   See subs. 95(2).

2. CONDITIONS FOR ROLLOVER

A taxpayer who disposes of shares in a taxable Canadian corporation ("old shares") in exchange for treasury shares of a Canadian corporation ("new shares") may rollover the cost of the old shares into the cost base of the new shares on a tax-free basis in the following circumstances:[2]

- The purchaser of the "old shares" is a Canadian corporation;[3]
- The vendor held the "old shares" as capital property;[4]
- The "old shares" are shares of a taxable Canadian corporation;[5]
- The purchaser corporation issues *its own* (i.e., treasury) shares to the vendor in exchange for the vendor's shares;[6]
- The only consideration the vendor receives for the shares is shares of *one* particular class of the purchaser corporation;[7]
- The vendor and the purchaser are at arm's length with each other immediately before the exchange of shares;[8]
- The vendor and purchaser do not elect for the rollover under subsection 85(1) or (2);[9]
- Immediately after the exchange, the purchaser corporation is not controlled directly, indirectly, or in any manner whatever by the vendor and/or persons with whom the vendor does not deal at arm's length;[10] and
- Immediately after the exchange, the vendor and/or persons with whom the vendor does not deal at arm's length do not beneficially own shares of the purchaser corporation that have a fair market value of more than 50 per cent of the fair market value of all of the purchaser corporation's issued shares.[11]

---

[2] Para. 85.1(1)(*a*); see also IT-450R, "Share for Share Exchange" (April 8, 1993).

[3] Subs. 89(1) ("Canadian corporation").

[4] The rollover is not available to a dealer in securities.

[5] Subs. 85.1(1).

[6] Subs. 85.1(1).

[7] Para. 85.1(2)(*d*). Revenue Canada will allow a vendor to receive up to $200 in cash in lieu of fractional shares without prejudicing rollover; see IT-450R, "Share-for-Share Exchange" (April 8, 1993).

[8] Para. 85.1(2)(a).

[9] Para. 85.1(2)(*c*).

[10] Subpara. 85.1(2)(*b*)(i).

[11] Subpara. 85.1(2)(*b*)(ii).

The rationale of this provision is to facilitate takeovers of corporations by Canadian corporations.

The rollover is not available if the vendor acquires the purchaser's shares from any person other than the corporation; nor is the rollover available if the purchaser corporation gives the vendor shares other than its own shares in return for the shares of the vendor.

Thus, with one exception in respect of *de minimis* payments for fractional shares, the rollover is not available where the purchaser corporation issues non-share consideration for the vendor's shares. By administrative discretion, however, a vendor is allowed to receive up to $200 in cash in lieu of fractional shares without prejudicing the rollover.[12]

An option to acquire additional shares of the purchaser corporation at a later date precludes the rollover. Similarly, a collateral agreement that allows the vendor the right to "put"[13] newly acquired shares from the purchaser corporation to an associated or related corporation is considered to be "other consideration" sufficient to cause the transaction to be outside subsection 85.1(1).[14]

3. PIECEMEAL DISPOSITIONS

A taxpayer may sever his or her shareholdings into two or more distinct parts and dispose of each of the parts separately. For example, a taxpayer may dispose of one part in exchange for one class of shares of the purchaser corporation to obtain the benefit of the rollover and dispose of another part for cash. In these circumstances, each disposition should be separately and clearly identified.[15]

Alternatively, a taxpayer can reorganize share capital into two distinct classes of shares and then dispose of each class separately. It is important to ensure that the different classes of shares are *in fact* different and not merely labelled as such.[16]

4. EFFECT OF EXCHANGE ON VENDOR

The rollover applies automatically unless the vendor opts out of it.[17] Thus, in the absence of an indication on his or her return that the taxpayer is opting out of the

---

[12] IT-450R, "Share for Share Exchange" (April 8, 1993).

[13] A "put" is an option permitting its holder to sell a certain stock or commodity at a fixed price for a stated quantity and within a stated period of time.

[14] Unpublished Revenue Canada technical interpretation (February 11, 1991), Reorganizations and Non-Resident Division.

[15] See paras. 7 and 8 of IT-450R, "Share for Share Exchange" (April 8, 1993).

[16] See, e.g., *Champ v. The Queen*, [1983] CTC 1, 83 DTC 5029 (F.C.T.D.).

[17] Subs. 85.1(1).

rollover, the taxpayer is deemed to have disposed of the shares for proceeds of disposition equal to their adjusted cost base.[18] Concurrently, the taxpayer is deemed to acquire his or her new shares from the purchaser corporation at a cost equal to the adjusted cost base of the old shares.[19]

Where the old shares are taxable Canadian property to the vendor, the new shares are also considered to be taxable Canadian property.[20]

Example XXII.1

Assume:

X owns 100 shares of *Targetco* (a taxable Canadian corporation) that have a total ACB of $1,000. He exchanges his *Targetco* shares for 300 shares of *Hitco* (a Canadian corporation) that have a fair market value of $6,000.

Then:	Under general rules	Under s. 85.1
Proceeds of disposition	$ 6,000	$ 1,000
ACB of old shares	(1,000)	(1,000)
Immediate capital gain	$ 5,000	$ NIL
ACB of new shares	$ 6,000	$ 1,000
FMV of new shares	6,000	6,000
Deferred capital gain	NIL	$ 5,000

---

5. EFFECT OF EXCHANGE ON PURCHASER

The cost of the shares to the purchaser corporation is the lesser of the fair market value of the shares and their paid-up capital immediately before the exchange.[21] Thus, section 85.1 is somewhat unusual in that the purchaser corporation's cost of shares acquired is determined independently of the vendor's tax treatment. In contrast, where the purchaser elects under subsection 85(1) for the share-for-share exchange, the tax cost of the shares to the purchasing corporation is the amount elected in respect of the shares.

---

[18] Subpara. 85.1(1)(*a*)(i).

[19] Subpara. 85.1(1)(*a*)(ii).

[20] Para. 85.1(1)(*a*).

[21] Para. 85.1(1)(*b*).

Example XXII.2

Assume the same facts as in Example XXII.1 and the following additional data:

	PUC	FMV
Per *Targetco* share	$ 10	$ 60

Then, the deemed adjusted cost base of each *Targetco* share to *Hitco* equals the lesser of:

PUC of shares	$ 10
FMV of shares	$ 60
ACB of *Targetco* shares	$ 10/share

6. PAID-UP CAPITAL OF PURCHASER'S SHARES

The paid-up capital of the purchaser corporation's shares issued to the vendor is reduced by the amount by which the total increase in the paid-up capital of the purchaser's shares exceeds the paid-up capital of the exchanged shares.[22] In other words, the paid-up capital of the new shares is reduced by any attempted step-up in their paid-up capital.

Example XXII.3

Assume the same facts as in Example XXII.1 with the following additional data:

	PUC/share	Total PUC
Targetco shares exchanged	$ 10	$ 1,000
Hitco shares exchanged	$ 20	$ 6,000
Then:		
Corporate PUC of *Hitco* shares	$ 20	$ 6,000
Less, PUC of *Targetco* shares	(10)	(1,000)
PUC reduction	$ 10	$ 5,000
Tax PUC of *Hitco* shares	$ 10	$ 1,000

---

[22] Subs. 85.1(2.1).

The purpose of this rule is to prevent vendors in a share-for-share exchange from taking advantage of a step-up in the paid-up capital of the purchaser's shares, which could then be returned to shareholders on a tax-free basis. In Example XXII.3, the vendors of *Targetco* would be entitled to a return of $20 per *Hitco* share if there was no adjustment to the paid-up capital of *Hitco* shares. Following the adjustment to the paid-up capital of *Hitco* shares, only $10 per *Hitco* share may be returned on a tax-free basis. Thus, in effect, the paid-up capital of the exchanged shares is rolled over into the purchaser's shares issued to the vendors.

7. V-DAY VALUE

Reference:

BULLETINS, CIRCULARS & RULINGS:

IT-132R2	December 18, 1978	Capital Property Owned on December 31, 1971 — Non-arm's Length Transactions

The tax-free zone of a taxpayer who exchanges shares owned on December 31, 1971 is preserved[23] provided that he or she has not previously elected under ITAR 26(7) to use V-Day values.

---

[23] ITAR 26(26).

SELECTED BIBLIOGRAPHY TO CHAPTER XXII

General

Singer, Paul, "The Rollover Provisions in Respect of Corporate Reorganizations Provided Under the Income Tax Act: Efficiency and Equity as Policy Considerations" (1983), 31 *Can. Tax J.* 569.

Taxation of Corporate Organization and Reorganization (Montreal: Federated Press, 1993).

Exchange for Shares of Canadian Corporation

Boultbee, Jack, "A Survey of the Use of Rollovers in Acquisitions and Mergers" (1980), 28 *Can. Tax J.* 504.

Boultbee, Jack, "Public Company Split-Ups", *Corporate Management Tax Conf.* 1 (Can. Tax Foundation, 1984).

Cronkwright, Glen E., "Amalgamations and Share-For-Share Exchanges", in *Proceedings of 26th Tax Conf.* 53 (Can. Tax Foundation, 1974).

Ewens, Douglas, "New Considerations in Structuring Share-for-Share Exchange Offers" (1988), 36 *Can. Tax J.* 449.

Ewens, Douglas, "Share-For-Share Exchanges" (1982), 30 *Can. Tax J.* 99.

McNair, D.K., "Share-For-Share Exchange: Section 85.1" (1981), *Can. Taxation* 1051.

Watkins, Donald H., "Income Tax Consequences of Reorganizations and Arrangements", in *Proceedings of 30th Tax Conf.* 452 (Can. Tax Foundation, 1978).

Other

McQuillan, Peter, "Financing Corporate Acquisitions", *Corporate Management Tax Conf.* 145 (Can. Tax Foundation, 1978).

McQuillan, Peter, "Financing Corporate Acquisitions", *Tax Planning and Management*, Vol. 9, No. 32 of *Canadian Income Tax Revised* (Butterworth and Co. (Canada) Ltd., 1978).

Ward, David A., "Arm's Length Acquisitions Relating to Shares in a Public Corporation", *Corporate Management Tax Conf.* 108 (Can. Tax Foundation, 1978).

Witterick, R.G., "Acquisitions of Shares of Private Corporations in Arm's Length Transactions", *Corporate Management Tax Conf.* 120 (Can. Tax Foundation, 1978).

CHAPTER XXIII

EXCHANGE OF SHARES IN A REORGANIZATION OF CAPITAL

References:

ITA:

Subs. 86(1)   Exchange of Shares in a Reorganization of Capital

S. 54   "Disposition"

BULLETINS, CIRCULARS & RULINGS:

IT-65	September 8, 1972	Stock Splits and Consolidations
IT-448	June 6, 1980	Dispositions — Changes in Terms of Securities
TR-36	August 2, 1976	Estate Freeze by Way of a Corporate Reorganization
TR-50	March 7, 1977	Estate Freeze
TR-66	July 11, 1977	Estate Freeze
TR-67	July 11, 1977	Estate Freeze
TR-68	July 11, 1977	Estate Freeze
ATR-22R	April 14, 1989	Estate Freeze Using Share Exchange
ATR-33	October 7, 1988	Exchange of Shares

1. GENERAL

A taxpayer entitled to receive "proceeds of disposition", whether in cash or kind, in respect of a property is considered to have disposed of the property.[1] Hence, a change in the share capital structure of a corporation can trigger a disposition of shares. For example, a shareholder of a corporation that amends its articles, amalgamates with another corporation, continues under the laws of another jurisdiction, or sells all or substantially all of its property is *entitled* to receive the "fair value" of his or her shares.[2] Such an event would be considered a disposition of the shares since the shareholder would be entitled to proceeds. There are, however, special rules in section 86 that allow for a rollover of capital gains when corporate share capital is restructured.

---

[1]   S. 54 ("disposition"), ("proceeds of disposition").

[2]   Under certain corporate statutes (see, e.g., the *Canada Business Corporations Act*, R.S.C. 1985, c. C-44, s. 190; *Business Corporations Act*, R.S.O. 1990, c. B-16, s. 185).

2. USES OF SECTION 86

Section 86 is a versatile provision with many uses. Generally speaking, the section can be used to restructure the share capital of a corporation in circumstances when it is necessary to change the rights, conditions, privileges or restrictions of its existing shares or to create new shares in order to accommodate shareholder needs. The section is particularly useful in estate planning and capital reorganizations to accommodate or restructure family shareholdings. For example, section 86 is often used to:

- Exchange common shares of a corporation for preferred shares with a fixed and pre-determined value (an "estate freeze");

- Reorganize the capital of a corporation to allow for dividend sprinkling among family members or where new shareholders are introduced into the corporation;

- Fight off hostile takeovers by changing the characteristics and rights of existing shares into new weighted voting shares.

3. APPLICATION OF SUBSECTION 86(1)

Section 86 is deceptively straightforward: A taxpayer who exchanges *all* of his or her shares of a class of a corporation for new shares from the corporation may rollover the cost base of his or her old shares into the new shares if the exchange is a reorganization of the share capital of the corporation.

More specifically, the rollover is available where a taxpayer:[3]

- disposes of all of his or her shares ("old shares") of a particular class of a corporation;

- in the course of a reorganization of share capital; and

- the exchange is for consideration from the corporation that includes "new shares" of the corporation.

An important point to note at the outset is that the rollover does not depend upon the nationality or residence of the corporation or upon the residence of the taxpayer who disposes of the shares.

Thus, there are four essential ingredients to the rollover:

1. There must be "a reorganization of the capital of a corporation";

2. The shareholder must "dispose" of the shares "in the course of" the reorganization;

3. The "old shares" must have been the taxpayer's capital property prior to their disposition and exchange for the new shares; and

---

[3]   Subs. 86(1). See Tax Rulings TR-36, "Estate Freeze by Way of a Corporate Reorganization" (August 2, 1976); TR-50, "Estate Freeze" (March 7, 1977); TR-66, "Estate Freeze" (July 11, 1977); and TR-68, "Estate Freeze" (July 11, 1977).

4. The disposition must be in respect of *all* of the shares of a class of the capital stock of the corporation.

The rollover is not available if the taxpayer utilizes the rollover under section 51 or 85.[4]

(a) "Reorganization of Capital"

The phrase "reorganization of capital" is determined according to the corporate law of the jurisdiction in which the reorganization occurs. The following types of transactions generally constitute a reorganization of capital:[5]

- An increase or decrease in authorized capital;
- A subdivision or reclassification of share capital;
- Reclassification or redesignation of shares from one class into shares of another class;
- A variation, deletion or addition to share conditions as described in the articles of incorporation; or
- The creation of a new class of shares.

Typically, a reorganization of capital requires an amendment to the corporation's articles of incorporation and approval of the amendment through a special resolution of shareholders. In effect, any amendment that *substantially* affects the rights, privileges, restrictions or conditions attached to shares qualifies as a reorganization of capital for corporate purposes.[6] The phrase "winding-up, discontinuance or reorganization" is interpreted broadly, and there is no reason to believe that the phrase "reorganization of capital" would not be similarly interpreted.

(b) "In the Course of"

Section 86 only applies if the exchange of shares is pursuant to and "*in the course of*" the reorganization of capital. The exchange of shares must occur concurrently with, or shortly after, the reorganization of the capital of the corporation. Thus, timing is the key: The longer the delay between the reorganization of capital and the exchange of shares, the greater the risk that the exchange may not be seen as being *in the course of* the reorganization. This can cause some uncertainty in complex reorganizations that span an extended period of time.

---

[4] Subss. 51(4), 86(3).

[5] See, e.g., *Canada Business Corporations Act*, R.S.C. 1985, c. C-44, s. 173.

[6] See e.g., *Smythe v. M.N.R.*, [1969] CTC 558, 69 DTC 5361 (S.C.C.).

(c) Disposition of Shares

The taxpayer must *dispose* of the shares. But a transaction that qualifies as a reorganization of capital does not necessarily imply a disposition of shares. For example, although from a corporate perspective, a stock split or consolidation involves a reorganization of the share capital of a corporation, it does not *per se* involve a disposition of shares.[7] Similarly, a reclassification of one class of shares into two separate interconvertible classes which offers shareholders a choice between cash dividends and stock dividends is not considered a disposition of shares.[8]

"Disposition" involves more than a reorganization: It requires cessation, divestiture, alienation or transfer of the incidents of ownership of property. The divestment does not have to be in respect of all of the incidents of ownership, but it should involve an alienation of at least some of the substantive rights of share ownership. The essential question is whether or not the taxpayer alienates a sufficient bundle of rights and privileges in the shares. For example, in the simplest case, a reclassification of shares to alienate voting rights is sufficient to constitute a "disposition" even if all of the other rights (such as the right to dividends and the right to receive residual property) remain intact.[9] But a mere split in the number of shares outstanding does not affect any substantive rights and privileges in the shares.

The term "disposition" is broadly interpreted. For example:[10]

> The entire expression "disposed of, lost or destroyed" is apt to embrace every event by which property ceases to be available to the taxpayer for use for the purpose of producing assessable income, either because it ceases to be his, or because it ceases to be physically accessible to him, or because it ceases to exist . . . the words "is disposed of" are wide enough to cover all forms of alienation . . . and they should be understood as meaning no less than "becomes alienated from the taxpayer", whether it is by him or by another that the act of alienation is done.

The essential test is whether or not it is reasonable to regard the new or amended shares as being in substance the same property as the old shares. If they are, there is no disposition. If they are not, there is a disposition.

---

[7] See IT-65, "Stock Splits and Consolidations" (September 8, 1972).

[8] IT-146R4, "Shares Entitling Shareholders to Choose Taxable or Capital Dividends" (September 6, 1991).

[9] See *Victory Hotels Ltd. v. M.N.R.*, [1962] CTC 614, 62 DTC 1378 (Ex. Ct.); *M.N.R. v. Wardean Drilling Ltd.*, [1969] CTC 265, 69 DTC 5194 (Ex. Ct.); *The Queen v. Cie Immobilière BCN Ltée*, [1979] CTC 71, 79 DTC 5068 (S.C.C.).

[10] *Henty House Pty. Ltd. v. Fed. Commr. of Taxation* (1953), 88 CLR 141 at 151-152 (Aust. HC); see also, *Rose v. Fed. Commr. of Taxation* (1951), 84 CLR 118 (Aust. HC); *Gorton v. Fed. Commr. of Taxation* (1965), 113 CLR 604 (Aust. HC); *Lord Elgin Hotel Ltd. v. M.N.R.* (1964), 36 Tax ABC 268, 64 DTC 637.

The following are some examples of changes in share conditions that Revenue Canada normally considers to be a disposition:[11]

- A change in voting rights attached to shares that effects a change in the voting control of the corporation;

- A change in a defined entitlement (for example, a change in par value) to share in the assets of a corporation upon dissolution;

- The giving up or the addition of a priority right to share in the distribution of assets of the corporation upon dissolution;

- The addition or deletion of a right attaching to a class of share that provides for participation in dividend entitlements beyond a fixed preferential rate or amount; and

- A change from a cumulative to a non-cumulative right to dividends or *vice versa.*

The following are examples of changes in share conditions that the Department does *not* consider as dispositions:

- The addition of the right to elect a majority of the directors of the corporation if, at that time, the shareholders of that class are already in a position to control the election of directors;

- A change in the number of votes per share, if the ability of any one shareholder to influence the day-to-day affairs of the corporation is neither enhanced nor impaired thereby;

- The giving up of contingent voting rights which, in the event they were exercised, would not have been of sufficient number to control the affairs of the corporation;

- Restrictions added or removed concerning transfer of shares;

- Stock splits or consolidations;

- A change of shares with par value to shares without par value or vice versa, provided that there is no change in any pre-set entitlements to dividends and/or distribution of assets upon dissolution;

- A change in ranking concerning preference features (e.g., 1st preference to 2nd preference); and

- An increase or decrease in the amount or rate of a fixed dividend entitlement.

---

[11] IT-448, "Dispositions — Changes in Terms of Securities" (June 6, 1980) as amended by Special Release (June 21, 1982). See also Arnold and Ward, "Dispositions — A Critique of Revenue Canada's Interpretation" (1980), 28 *Can. Tax J.* 559.

It is important to observe, however, that even if each of the above transactions in isolation does not constitute a disposition, a combination of changes taken together may well amount to a disposition.

(d) Capital Property

The rollover is available only in respect of shares that constitute capital property.[12] Generally speaking, "capital property" includes shares, the gain or loss from the disposition of which would be a capital gain or loss. In certain circumstances, however, a taxpayer may elect to have Canadian securities deemed to be capital property.[13] This election is not available to a trader or dealer in securities.[14]

(e) Dispose of All Shares

The final requirement in respect of the rollover is that the taxpayer dispose of *all* of the shares of any particular class owned by him or her. A partial disposition of share holdings of a class does not qualify for the rollover even if all of the other conditions are satisfied.[15]

4. CALCULATION OF GAIN ON "OLD SHARES"

Subsection 86(1) allows a taxpayer to defer the capital gain which he or she might otherwise have been required to recognize on a disposition of shares with accrued gains.

The subsection involves three separate computations:

- The cost of any non-share consideration received from the corporation;
- The cost of the share consideration received from the corporation; and
- The proceeds of disposition of the "old shares".

The cost of non-share consideration received is its fair market value at the time of the disposition.[16]

The cost of share consideration is the difference between the adjusted cost base of the "old shares" and the fair market value of any non-share consideration received.[17]

---

[12] See s. 54 ("capital property"); Chapter VI "Business and Investment Income: General".

[13] Subs. 39(4).

[14] Para. 39(5)(*a*); see also Chapter VIII "Business and Property Income: Deductions".

[15] Subs. 86(1); see generally, TR-50, "Estate Freeze" (March 7, 1977) and TR-66, "Estate Freeze" (July 11, 1977).

[16] Para. 86(1)(*a*).

[17] Para. 86(1)(*b*).

A taxpayer who receives more than one class of new shares is required to allocate the cost between the various classes of shares. The allocation is made on the basis of the relative fair market value of each class of new shares taken back from the corporation.

The proceeds of disposition of the old shares are deemed to be equal to the *cost* of the taxpayer's non-share consideration and the new shares.[18]

Hence, unless the taxpayer receives non-share consideration (for example, cash) in excess of the cost of the "old shares", the proceeds of disposition will always equal the adjusted cost base of the "old shares" and there can be no capital gain. Where the taxpayer receives excessive non-share consideration (that is, an amount in excess of the cost base of the old shares), the proceeds of disposition for the old shares will exceed their ACB and result in a capital gain.

Example XXIII.1

Assume:

Mr. S. exchanges his "old shares" in *S Ltd.* for debt and "new shares" in the corporation. The following data applies to the exchange:

	"Old Shares"	Consideration Received	
		Debt	New Shares
Case A			
ACB	$ 100	$?	$?
FMV	$ 300	$ 80	$ 220
Case B			
ACB	$ 100	$?	$?
FMV	$ 300	$ 110	$ 190

Then:

	Case A	Case B
(1) ACB of "old shares"	$ 100	$ 100
Cost of debt received (FMV)	(80)	(110)
ACB of "new shares"	$ 20	$ NIL
Proceeds of disposition of "old shares"	$ 100	$ 110
ACB of "old shares"	(100)	(100)
Capital gain (immediate)	NIL	$ 10
(2) FMV of "new shares"	$ 220	$ 190
ACB of "new shares"	(20)	(NIL)
Deferred capital gain	$ 200	$ 190

---

[18] Para. 86(1)(*c*).

5. INDIRECT GIFTS

A special rule prevents taxpayers from avoiding tax by indirectly diluting the value of their shares in order to benefit related persons. In the absence of a rule to prevent indirect dilution of shares, a taxpayer could deplete the value of his or her shareholding and eliminate any capital gain that might otherwise be taxable to his or her estate on death.

The special rule is as follows: Where, in a reorganization of capital, a taxpayer exchanges "old shares" in return for inadequate consideration, the amount by which the fair market value of the "old shares" exceeds the value of the consideration that he or she receives from the corporation may be considered a "gift".

The shortfall in consideration is a gift if it can reasonably be considered a benefit which the taxpayer desired to confer on a person related to him or her.[19] In these circumstances, the taxpayer's proceeds of disposition are recalculated to be equal to the *lesser* of:[20]

- the aggregate of any non-share consideration taken back from the corporation *and* the amount of the "gift portion"; and
- the fair market value of the "old shares" immediately before the disposition.

Subsection 86(2) has two effects: (1) The amount of the indirect gift (i.e., the amount by which the share value is diluted) is added to the taxpayer's proceeds of disposition for the purpose of calculating a capital gain from the disposition of the old shares; (2) It affects the adjusted cost base of the new shares.

Example XXIII.2

Mr. T exchanges his "old shares" in *T Ltd.* for "new shares" in the corporation. Assume that the following data and subsection 86(2) apply to the exchange:

	"Old Shares"	"New Shares" Consideration Received	
		Case A	Case B
ACB	$ 100	$?	$?
FMV	$ 300	$ 250	$ 150

---

[19] Subs. 86(2).

[20] Para. 86(2)(c).

Example XXIII.2 (continued)

Then:

	Case A	Case B
(1) POD of old shares is *lesser* of:		
Gift portion, and	$ 50	$ 150
FMV of old shares	$ 300	$ 300
Proceeds of disposition of old		
shares (lesser amount)	$ 50	$ 150
ACB of old shares	(100)	(100)
Capital gain or loss	NIL*	$ 50
*deemed nil by para. 86(2)(*d*)		
(2) ACB of old shares		
Exceeds: "gift portion"	$ 100	$ 100
ACB of new shares	50	(50)
	$ 50	NIL
(3) FMV of new shares	$ 250	$ 150
ACB of new shares	(50)	NIL
Deferred capital gain	$ 200	$ 150

In Example XXIII.2, the gift portion of $150 in Case B causes the proceeds of disposition of the old shares to exceed their ACB and trigger an immediate capital gain of $50. It also drops the ACB of the new shares to nil, thereby increasing the potential capital gain on the shares in the future.

6. COST BASE OF NEW SHARES

The cost base of the taxpayer's "new shares" is the amount by which the adjusted cost base of the "old shares" exceeds the aggregate of:[21]

- any non-share consideration received from the corporation on the exchange of shares, and

- the amount of the indirect gift (the "gift portion") conferred on a related person.

---

[21] Para. 86(2)(*e*).

7. DEEMED DIVIDENDS

A shareholder is deemed to receive a dividend if the paid-up capital of the new shares plus the amount of any non-share consideration received exceeds the paid-up capital of the old shares disposed of in the course of the reorganization of capital.[22]

8. CAPITAL LOSS

The proceeds of disposition of the new shares and any non-share consideration can never be less than the adjusted cost base of the "old shares". Hence, it is not possible to recognize a capital loss on a disposition of shares under section 86.

9. ESTATE FREEZING

Section 86 can be used to freeze the value of an individual's growth shares by exchanging the shares for fixed value preferred shares in the corporation. In a typical estate freeze, a parent exchanges growth common shares for fixed value preferred shares of equal value and the children acquire new common shares with future growth potential. Thus, the value of the parent's shares is frozen at their exchange value and future growth enures to the benefit of the children. The type of business carried on by the corporation is not a material factor and Revenue Canada accepts that the shares of a corporation may be frozen regardless of the nature of its business activity.

Section 86 can also be used to implement a reorganization of capital that is principally motivated by income splitting considerations. In this scenario, the shares of the reorganized corporation are distributed or sprinkled amongst various family members so that they can each participate in dividend distributions. The corporation's share capital is structured so that each class of shares is in substance a different type of property. Dividends may be paid to one class of shareholders to the exclusion of another class.

This type of selective dividend sprinkling through the use of discretionary dividends has been popular for a long time and continues to attract Revenue Canada's ire. Although the Department has had limited success in controlling income splitting through discretionary dividends, they are reluctant to approve of and further encourage such transactions by issuing favourable advance tax rulings. Thus, Revenue Canada will not give an advance ruling on a section 86 reorganization of capital involving an estate freeze in favour of a spouse, because Revenue Canada generally considers such arrangements to constitute income splitting.

The Department's view is that a section 86 reorganization involves a transfer of property, and hence the attribution rules would normally apply to the transaction. The Department will not usually issue a ruling in these circumstances unless the taxpayer can establish to its satisfaction that he or she has *bona fide* business reasons (other than income splitting) for including a spouse in the estate freeze. The rationale is that an

---

[22] See subss. 84(3), (5).

estate freeze in favour of a spouse is not really necessary, since a taxpayer's capital property can be rolled over without any immediate tax consequences to his or her spouse or to a spouse trust.[23] Hence, Revenue Canada may invoke subsection 15(1) (shareholder benefits), 56(2) (indirect payments), or 245(2) (GAAR) to attack such transactions.

Revenue Canada is more disposed, however, towards estate freezing in favour of children and has taken the position that it will not normally invoke GAAR in such circumstances. For example, the Department states[24] that ". . . estate freezes would not ordinarily result in misuse or abuse . . ." of the Act, including those provisions of the statute which deal with income attribution.

Where the freeze is in favour of minor children, however, the Department takes the position that the shares which represent a child's interest must be held in trust and that dividends should not be paid to the trust until such time as the child reaches the age of 18. In other words, given that the Act generally circumscribes income splitting with minors, the Department takes the position that an estate freeze to facilitate such splitting does not accord with the scheme of the Act. It remains unclear whether the Department's reluctance to issue a favourable advance ruling in these circumstances means that they will invoke GAAR to attack the transaction on the theory that such an arrangement constitutes an "abuse of the Act read as a whole".

10. VALUATION OF SHARES

The valuation of the "new shares" received as part of a section 86 rollover can give rise to several difficulties.

(a) Indirect Gifts

The indirect benefit rule in subsection 86(2) can trigger a deemed gift or benefit where the value of consideration received exceeds the value of the "old shares" disposed of by the freezor. The value of the benefit is the difference between the fair market value of the old shares disposed of and the aggregate fair market value of the consideration received in exchange. Subsection 86(2) applies only where the taxpayer confers a benefit on a related person. To be sure, in an arm's length transaction it is quite unlikely that the taxpayer would confer a benefit on a person who was not related to him or her.

---

[23] See subs. 70(6).

[24] IC 88-2, "General Anti-avoidance Rule — Section 245 of the *Income Tax Act*" (October 21, 1988), para. 10.

(b) Redeemable Shares

In order to freeze the value of preferred shares at a given amount, it is necessary to circumscribe their economic attributes so as to prevent any increase or decrease in their value. This may be achieved by setting their redemption value (the price at which the corporation may redeem its shares) and retractable value (the price at which a shareholder may cause the corporation to purchase his or her shares) at a predetermined value. For example, in the simplest case, assume that an individual exchanges shares that have a value of $500,000 for new shares with a value of $100,000 and $400,000 cash. In order to ensure that the new shares remain frozen at a value of $100,000, the shares should be redeemable and retractable for $100,000. Absent any other considerations, this should be sufficient to "freeze" the value of the new shares at that amount.

The proposition that the value of shares can be frozen at their redemption and retraction amounts is both logical and defensible. Why would an arm's length purchaser pay more than $100,000 for the frozen shares if they can be redeemed by the corporation at any time for that amount? Why would the shareholder sell the shares for less than $100,000 if he or she can require the corporation to redeem its shares for the stipulated retraction amount? Thus, absent any special share characteristics or contractual conditions which might cause the value of the shares to deviate from their "frozen" value, the "new shares" should remain frozen at their contractually determined redemption and retraction value.

But what if the corporation is financially incapable of meeting its potential obligation to redeem the preferred shares? Do the preferred shares have to have some inherent minimum investment quality to be considered equal to the value of the common shares for which they are exchanged? Revenue Canada does not have definite answers to these questions. There is a real risk that, in these circumstances, the value of the preferred shares will be considered to be less than the value of the common shares for which they are exchanged. If so, subsection 86(2) may trigger an indirect benefit to the freezor of the common shares.

(c) Reasonable Dividends

The dividend payable on a share can also affect its value. The Department's general position is that preferred shares that are issued as part of an estate freeze should bear a *reasonable* dividend rate. It accepts, however, that the absence of a dividend does not, "in and of itself", reduce the value of the preferred shares.[25] Clearly, an excessive dividend rate can cause the value of the preferred shares to escalate and defeat the estate freeze.

---

[25] See e.g., Revenue Canada Round Table, in *Proceedings of 33rd Tax Conf.* (Can. Tax Foundation, 1981), Question #45 at 759.

COMPREHENSIVE EXAMPLE

Assume:

Ms. Jones owns all of the issued Class A shares of *Opco Ltd.*, a private corporation to which the following data applies:

	Per share	
PUC	$	100
ACB	$	500
FMV	$	1,000

- Pursuant to a reorganization of capital under section 86, Ms. Jones exchanges *each* Class A share for one Class B share plus $300 debt.
- Ms. Jones' children subscribe for new Class C shares which have a PUC, ACB and FMV of $100.
- Each Class B share has paid-up capital (PUC) of $100 and a FMV of $700.
- *Opco Ltd.* cancels the Class A shares previously held by Ms. Jones.

Then:

1. Cost of Class B shares:

ACB of old shares	$	500
Exceeds		
FMV of non-share consideration (debt)		(300)
Cost of Class B shares	$	200

2. Calculation of capital gain:

Cost of Class B shares	$	200
Cost of non-share consideration (debt)		300
POD of old shares	$	500
ACB of old shares		(500)
Capital gain		NIL

3. Deemed dividend on cancellation of old shares

Amount paid by debt	$	300
PUC of Class B shares		100
Total amount paid	$	400
PUC of old shares		(100)
Deemed dividend [subs. 84(3)]	$	300

SELECTED BIBLIOGRAPHY TO CHAPTER XXIII

General

Bennett, Sharon, "Phantom Income, Real Tax: Section 86 Reorganizations" (1990), 3:11 *Canadian Current Tax* P-21.

Boultbee, Jack A., "A Survey of the Use of Rollovers in Acquisitions and Mergers" (1980), 28 *Can. Tax J.* 504.

Boultbee, Jack A. and D.S. Ewens, "The Taxation of Corporate Reorganizations" (1986), 34 *Can. Tax J.* 203.

Deaves, Brian M.P., "Tax and Estate Planning with Section 86" (1982), 115 *CA Magazine* No. 2, 79.

"Estate Planning in Canada" (1975), 23 *Can. Tax J.* 542 at 545.

Ewens, Douglas, "Retractable Preferred Shares" (1983), 31 *Can. Tax. J.* 713.

Kellough, "A Planning Update for Private Corporations — Corporate Reorganizations", *Prairie Provinces Tax Conf.* 131 (Can. Tax Foundation, 1981).

Lindsay, Robert F., "Winding-Up of Corporations: Changes in Capital Structure of Corporations", in *Proceedings of 26th Tax Conf.* 69 (Can. Tax Foundation, 1974).

McNair, D.K., "Exchange of Shares by Shareholder in the Course of a Reorganization of Capital: Section 86" (1981), *Can. Taxation* 1063.

McQuillan, P., et al., "Section 86 — Exchange of Shares Checklist", in *Purchase and Sale of a Business* 5-55 (Toronto: The Canadian Institute of Chartered Accountants, 1982).

Middleton, David W., "Common Tax Problems and Pitfalls in Effecting Reorganizations of Private Corporations", in *Proceedings of 41st Tax Conf.* 13:1 (Can. Tax Foundation, 1989).

Shannon, H., "Part 5: Reorganization of Corporate Share Capital", in *Income Taxation in Canada*, W.A. MacDonald and G.E. Cronkwright (Scarborough: Prentice-Hall Canada Inc., 1977), 63-040.

Stein, Boris P., "Part Two: Canadian Case Law Concerning Shares Received on a Rollover", *The Journal of Business Valuation*, Canadian Assoc. of Business Valuators, Vol. 7, 1981, 95.

Taxation of Corporate Organization and Reorganization (Montreal: Federated Press, 1993).

"The Taxation of Corporate Reorganizations — Section 86 Reorganizations" (1984), 32 *Can. Tax J.* 1165.

Ward, David A. and Brian J. Arnold, "Dispositions — A Critique of Revenue Canada's Interpretation" (1980), 28 *Can. Tax J.* 559.

Wilson, Ronald S., "Cost Adjustments in Corporate Reorganization Transactions: Policy and Practice", in *Proceedings of 38th Tax Conf.* 8:1 (Can. Tax Foundation, 1986).

Wise, Richard M., "Valuation and the Income Tax Act" (1981), 29 *Can. Tax J.* 626.

Witterick, R.G., "Estate Freezing through Corporate Reorganizations of Capital", *Tax Planning and Management*, Vol. 9, No. 24 of *Canadian Income Tax Revised* (Butterworth and Co. (Canada) Ltd., 1977).

Witterick, R.G., "Section 86: a Slumbering Giant" (1975), 23 *Can. Tax J.* 89.

Indirect Gifts

Boultbee, Jack, "Gifts and Rollovers" (1983), 31 *Can. Tax J.* 84.

Estate Freezing and Section 86

Barnett, James J., "Estate Planning and the Life Stages of the Business, Owner and the Business" (1991), 39 *Can. Tax J.* 1576.

Bowden, Gregory T.W., "Estate Freezing", *British Columbia Tax Conf.* 266 (Can. Tax Foundation, 1980).

Cadesky, Michael, "Succession of the Family Business" (1994), *Estates and Trusts J.* 219.

Crawford, William E., "Corporate Freezes — Are you Getting Your Money's Worth?", in *Proceedings of 32nd Tax Conf.* 772 (Can. Tax Foundation, 1980).

Drache, Arthur B.C., "The Flexible Freeze" (1995), *Can. Taxpayer* 21.

Krishna, Vern, "Administrative View on Estate Freezing", [1990-92] *Can. Current Tax* A21.

Louis, David, "Estate Freezing — The Next Generation" (1994), No. 377 *Tax Notes* 1.

Morris, J.S.D., "Freezing Family Business Interests — Inflation and Other Concerns" (1981), 29 *Can. Tax J.* 211.

Morrissette, Andre, "Unfreezing an Estate", in *Proceedings of 44th Tax Conf.* 15:1 (Can. Tax Foundation, 1992).

Rochwerg, Martin J., "Post-Mortem Estate Freezing" (1983), 31 *Can. Tax J.* 69.

Silver, Sheldon, "A Simple Case of Freezing — Part 2" (1976), 24 *Can. Tax J.* 171.

Silver, Sheldon, "Has the Dust Settled?" (1977), 25 *Can. Tax J.* 652.

Silver, Sheldon, "Unplanning an Estate — Part I" (1976), 24 *Can. Tax J.* 652.

Witterick, R.G., "Estate Freezing through a Reorganization of Capital under Section 86", in *Proceedings of 28th Tax Conf.* 732 (Can. Tax Foundation, 1976).

Other

Davidson, Barrie, "Inter Vivos Tax Planning" (1981), 15 *CGA Magazine* No. 1, 2.

Heller, Stephen, "Part One: Valuation of Preferred Shares Received on a Rollover under the Income Tax Act", *The Journal of Business Valuation*, Canadian Assoc. of Business Valuators, Vol. 7, 1981, 71.

Sohmer, David H., "Partnerships and Corporations", [1991] *Meredith Mem. Lect.* 199.

CHAPTER XXIV

MERGERS AND DISSOLUTIONS

1. AMALGAMATIONS

References:

ITA:

S. 87	Amalgamations
S. 111	Deductibility of Losses

BULLETINS, CIRCULARS & RULINGS:

IT-302R3	February 28, 1994	Losses of a Corporation — The Effect that Acquisitions of Control, Amalgamation and Winding-Up have on their Deductibility — After January 15, 1987
IT-315	May 10, 1976	Interest Expense Incurred for the Purpose of Winding-Up or Amalgamation
IT-474R	March 14, 1986	Amalgamations of Canadian Corporations
TR-1	June 24, 1974	Exporting a Corporation — Whether a Disposition — Effect on Incorporation Date
TR-4	July 15, 1974	Designated Surplus
TR-37	August 9, 1976	Amalgamations
TR-49	March 7, 1977	Sale of Assets — Amalgamation
ATR-7	March 31, 1986	Amalgamation Involving Losses and Control

(a) General

A merger or an "amalgamation" is a form of acquisition that involves the fusion of two or more corporations into a new corporate entity. An amalgamation coalesces two or more corporations to create a homogeneous whole. An amalgamation is sometimes described by analogy as "a river formed by the confluence of two streams", or "the creation of a single rope through the intertwining of strands".[1] The amalgamated corporation acquires all of the assets and assumes all of the liabilities of the amalgamating corporations.[2] The shareholders and creditors of the predecessor corporations become the shareholders and creditors of the amalgamated corporation.

---

[1] *The Queen v. Black & Decker Mfg. Co.*, [1975] 1 SCR 411 at 420.

[2] See, e.g., *Canada Business Corporations Act* ("CBCA"), R.S.C. 1985, c. C-44, s. 186.

(i) Distinguished From Other Acquisitions

An amalgamation is to be distinguished from an acquisition of the assets or shares of one corporation by another. Where a corporation purchases all of the assets and liabilities of another corporation, the vendor corporation continues its existence as a separate entity, *albeit* as a "shell" corporation. Where a corporation acquires all of the shares of another corporation, the vendor corporation becomes a subsidiary of the purchaser corporation. In contrast to these two forms of acquisition, an amalgamation involves a fusion of the amalgamated corporations into one corporation.[3] The new corporation is sometimes referred to as the "continuing" or "survivor" corporation.

(ii) Type

There are three different types of amalgamations: "Vertical", "Horizontal" and "Hybrid".

In a vertical amalgamation, a parent corporation is merged with one or more of its subsidiary corporations to form the new amalgamated corporation. Thus, a "vertical" amalgamation is similar in effect to the winding-up of a subsidiary into its parent corporation.

In a "horizontal" amalgamation, two or more corporations which do not own shares of each other are merged to form a new amalgamated corporation.

A "hybrid" amalgamation is a combination of a "vertical" and "horizontal" amalgamation.

"Amalgamation" is both a corporate and a tax concept. For the purposes of corporate law, an amalgamation is implemented according to the law of the relevant jurisdiction.[4] To qualify as an "amalgamation" for tax purposes, however, the merger must satisfy the specific requirements of subsection 87(1) of the Act.

(iii) Form Over Substance

It is important to emphasize at the outset that the income tax consequences of a corporate reorganization (such as an amalgamation) depend entirely on the form in which it is arranged, rather than on the economic consequences which flow from the reorganization. Thus, choice of method and form of implementation, rather than the economic substance of the reorganization, dictate the tax consequences. For example, if Corporation B acquires the assets and liabilities of Corporation A and Corporation A is then wound up, the economic result is identical to that of an amalgamation of Corporations A and B into a new Corporation AB. In both cases, one corporation ends up with all of the assets and liabilities of the other. In both cases, the shareholders of Corporation A end up with shares which may be exchanged for cash, either by way of

---

[3]   *The Queen v. Black & Decker Mfg. Co.*, *ante*, at 417 (amalgamated companies continue as one company; antithesis of notion that amalgamating corporations extinguished or continue in truncated state).

[4]   See, e.g., CBCA, ss. 181-86.

a liquidating dividend on winding-up or by disposition on the open market. The tax consequences of the two alternatives are, however, very different. A purchase and sale of assets triggers a gain or loss at the time of the disposition.[5] An amalgamation can be accomplished on a tax-free basis.

(b) Corporate Law

(i) General

Corporations may amalgamate only with other corporations governed by the same corporate statute. Corporations incorporated under the same corporate statute automatically come within the jurisdiction of that statute. Where one corporation is incorporated under one statute and another corporation is incorporated in some other jurisdiction, the two corporations cannot amalgamate unless one of the corporations is imported into the jurisdiction of the other. For example, assume that Corporation X is incorporated under the *Canada Business Corporations Act* and Corporation Y is incorporated under the Ontario *Business Corporations Act*.[6] For the two corporations to amalgamate, one of them must be imported into the jurisdiction of the other. Either Corporation Y can be continued under the *Canada Business Corporations Act*[7] or Corporation X can be continued under the Ontario *Business Corporations Act*.[8] The corporations may then amalgamate according to the corporate law of the jurisdiction in which they are both incorporated.

Where a corporation is continued from one jurisdiction to another, it is not considered to have disposed of its assets or its shares.[9]

(ii) Amalgamation Agreement

Two or more federal corporations (including holding and subsidiary corporations) may amalgamate and continue as one corporation. The first step in an amalgamation is for the corporations to enter into a proposed agreement to settle, *inter alia*, the following issues:[10]

- Corporate name, registered office, share capital structure, share transfer restrictions;

---

[5] Unless the disposition and purchase of assets is eligible for a rollover under, e.g., s. 85.

[6] *Business Corporations Act*, R.S.O. 1990, c. B.16 ("OBCA").

[7] CBCA, s. 187.

[8] OBCA, s. 180.

[9] TR-1, "Exporting a Corporation — Whether a Disposition — Effect on Incorporation Date" (June 24, 1974); TR-37, "Amalgamations" (August 9, 1976); TR-49, "Sale of Assets — Amalgamations" (March 8, 1977).

[10] CBCA, subs. 182(1); see OBCA, subs. 175(1) (similar requirements set out).

- Number of directors, and restrictions on business activities in respect of the amalgamated corporation;

- Name and address of each proposed director of the amalgamated corporation;

- Description of the method by which the shares of each of the amalgamating corporations is to be converted into the shares of the amalgamated corporation;

- Compensation to be paid to the holders of shares that are not converted into securities of the amalgamated corporation;

- By-laws of the amalgamated corporation, if they are different from those of the amalgamating corporations; and

- Details of arrangements necessary for the subsequent management and operation of the amalgamated corporation.

The proposed amalgamation agreement must be submitted to the shareholders of each of the amalgamating corporations for their approval.[11]

(iii) Voting

Each share of an amalgamating corporation carries the right to vote in respect of the amalgamation regardless of whether the share has voting rights in other circumstances.[12] Where the proposed amalgamation involves a change in the rights of a class of shares, the agreement requires the additional approval of the shareholders of the class voting separately as a class.[13]

An amalgamation agreement is adopted when the shareholders of each amalgamating corporation approve of the amalgamation by special resolutions.[14]

(iv) Effect

The Director of the Corporations Branch will issue a certificate of amalgamation upon receipt of the articles of amalgamation. The effect of the certificate is as follows:[15]

- The amalgamation of the amalgamating corporations and their continuance as one corporation is effective as of the date shown on the certificate;

- The property of each amalgamating corporation continues as the property of the amalgamated corporation;

---

[11] CBCA, subs. 183(1).

[12] CBCA, subs. 183(3).

[13] CBCA, subs. 183(4).

[14] CBCA, subs. 183(5); subs. 2(1) ("special resolution").

[15] CBCA, s. 186.

- The amalgamated corporation continues to be liable for the obligations of each amalgamating corporation;

- Existing causes of action, claims or liabilities remain unaffected;

- Civil, criminal or administrative actions or proceedings pending by or against an amalgamating corporation may be continued to be prosecuted by or against the amalgamated corporation;

- A conviction against, or ruling, order or judgment in favour of or against, an amalgamating corporation may be enforced by or against the amalgamated corporation;

- The articles of amalgamation are deemed to be the articles of incorporation of the amalgamated corporation; and

- The certificate of amalgamation is deemed to be the certificate of incorporation of the amalgamated corporation.

(v) "Short-form" Amalgamation

A "short-form" amalgamation is an amalgamation implemented without shareholder approval. A holding corporation and one or more of its *wholly-owned* subsidiary corporations may amalgamate without shareholder approval if the amalgamation is approved by the directors of each corporation, the shares of each subsidiary corporation are cancelled without repayment of capital, and the amalgamated corporation does not issue new securities as part of the amalgamation.[16]

Similarly, two or more *wholly-owned* subsidiary corporations of the same holding corporation may amalgamate without shareholder approval upon resolution of the directors of each corporation if the shares of the amalgamating corporation are cancelled without repayment of capital.[17]

In both of the above cases, shareholder approval would serve little purpose, since the corporations are wholly owned by the same corporation and the amalgamation does not involve any diminution in the share capital of the amalgamated corporations.

(c) "Amalgamation" for Tax Purposes

For income tax purposes, an amalgamation is a merger of two or more *taxable Canadian corporations* (the "predecessor corporations") into a new corporate entity (the "new corporation"), such that:[18]

- All of the properties of the predecessor corporations become property of the new corporation;

---

[16] CBCA, subs. 184(1) (this type of amalgamation is referred to as "vertical short-form" amalgamation).

[17] CBCA, subs. 184(2) (referred to as "horizontal short-form" amalgamation).

[18] *Income Tax Act*, subs. 87(1).

- All of the liabilities of the predecessor corporations become liabilities of the new corporation; and
- All of the shareholders of the predecessor corporations before the merger receive shares of the capital stock of the new corporation.

Intercorporate accounts receivable, accounts payable and shareholdings are eliminated upon amalgamation.

A "short-form" amalgamation also qualifies as an amalgamation for income tax purposes even though no new shares of the amalgamated corporation are issued as a result of the amalgamation.[19]

The corporate entity created as a result of an amalgamation is considered to be a "new" corporation for certain purposes[20] and a continuation of the predecessor corporations for other purposes.[21] The account balances of the predecessor corporations generally pass through in aggregate to the new corporation. Shareholders of the predecessor corporations can usually exchange their old shares for shares in the new corporation on a tax-free basis.[22]

(d) The New Corporation

(i) Taxation Year

The first taxation year of the new corporation commences at the time of the amalgamation. Thus, the new corporation may adopt any fiscal period commencing from the date of the amalgamation, so long as the period does not exceed 53 weeks.[23]

(ii) Tax Instalments

Although the new corporation is deemed to have come into existence at the time of the amalgamation, the instalment bases of its predecessor corporations are added together and constitute the instalment base of the new corporation for the immediately

---

[19] Subs. 87(1.1).

[20] Para. 87(2)(a).

[21] *The Queen v. Pan Ocean Oil Ltd.*, [1994] 2 CTC 143, 94 DTC 6412 (F.C.A.); *The Queen v. Guaranty Properties Ltd.*, [1990] 2 CTC 94, 90 DTC 6363 (F.C.A.); leave to SCC refused; *The Queen v. Black & Decker Mfg. Co.*, [1975] 1 SCR 411 (S.C.C.) [Ont.]; *Witco Chemical Co. Can. v. Oakville (Town)*, [1975] 1 SCR 273 (S.C.C.) [Ont.] (for corporate law purposes, new corporation considered to be continuation of old). See also subs. 87(1.2) (new corporation continuation of predecessor); para. 87(2)(*l*) (new corporation permitted to utilize unused scientific research expenditures of predecessor corporation by deeming new corporation to be continuation of its predecessors).

[22] Subs. 87(4).

[23] Paras. 87(2)(*a*), 249(1)(*a*), subs. 248(1) ("fiscal period"); see also para. 87(2)(*oo*).

preceding year. Thus, the new corporation is required to make instalment payments *as if* it had been in existence in the preceding taxation year.[24]

(iii) Inventory

As a general rule, inventory is valued at the lower of its cost or market value.[25]

A taxpayer's opening inventory must be valued on the same basis as its closing inventory for the preceding year.[26] Similarly, the closing inventories of the predecessor corporations become the opening inventory of the new corporation. Property that was included in the closing inventory of each predecessor corporation is deemed to have been acquired by the new corporation at the *commencement* of its first taxation year at the same value used by the predecessor corporations in computing their income for their last taxation year.[27] Thus, inventory values are carried over from the predecessor corporations to the new corporation without any loss of inventory basis.

Property which would have been included in the inventory of a predecessor corporation if it had followed the cash method of calculating income is deemed to have been acquired by the new corporation at an amount equal to the value specified in the predecessor's election.[28] This amount will usually be nil where the predecessor corporation accounts for its inventory on a cash basis. It may, however, be equal to fair market value, in the case of livestock inventory.[29]

(iv) Depreciable Property

For the purposes of capital cost allowance and recapture, the new corporation's depreciable property is deemed to have a capital cost equal to the capital cost of the property to its predecessor corporations. The undepreciated capital cost of depreciated property to the new corporation is, in effect, equal to the total of the undepreciated capital cost of property of that class owned by the predecessor corporations. Thus, on a disposition of the property by the new corporation, recapture of capital cost allowance is calculated by reference to the original capital cost of the property to the predecessor corporation.[30]

---

[24] Reg. 5301(4).

[25] See subs. 10(1); Regs. 1801, 1802 (special rules permitting *all* of taxpayer's inventory to be valued at fair market value).

[26] Subs. 10(2).

[27] Para. 87(2)(*b*).

[28] Para. 87(2)(*b*).

[29] Subs. 28(1).

[30] Para. 87(2)(*d*); Reg. 1102(14).

Example XXIV.1

Assume:

	Predecessor A	Corporations B	Total
Depreciable property (Class 8)			
Capital cost	$ 100,000	$ 68,000	$168,000
CCA claimed	(50,000)	(46,000)	(96,000)
UCC	$ 50,000	$ 22,000	$ 72,000

Corporations A and B amalgamate to form *AB Ltd.*

Then:

Capital cost of property to *Corp. A*	$100,000
Capital cost of property to *Corp. B*	68,000
Capital cost to *AB Ltd.*	$168,000

Add:

UCC of property acquired from *Corp. A*	50,000
from *Corp. B*	22,000
	$240,000

Less:

Capital cost to *AB Ltd.*	(168,000)
UCC of class to *AB Ltd.*	$ 72,000*

*This amount is in effect equal to the aggregate UCC of the predecessor corporations.

Example XXIV.2

Assume:

	Predecessor	Corporations	
	C	D	Total
Depreciable property (Class 6)			
Capital cost	$ 150,000	$ 80,000	$ 230,000
CCA claimed	(50,000)	(40,000)	(90,000)
UCC	$ 100,000	$ 40,000	$ 140,000

Corporations C and D amalgamate to form *CD Ltd.*, which disposes of the building previously owned by *C Ltd.* and acquires a new Class 6 building.

Proceeds of disposition of old building	$ 225,000
Cost of new Class 6 building	$ 300,000

Then (ignoring replacement property elections):

Capital cost of property (*C Ltd.*)	$ 150,000
Capital cost of property (*D Ltd.*)	80,000
Capital cost of new property to *CD Ltd.*	300,000
	$ 530,000
Add: UCC of class of predecessors	140,000
Less: Capital cost of class to predecessors	(230,000)
	$ 440,000
Less: Proceeds of disposition	(150,000)*
UCC of class to *CD Ltd.*	$ 290,000

*Being the lesser of the proceeds of disposition of the property ($225,000) and its capital cost ($150,000).

(v) Non-depreciable Capital Property

The new corporation is deemed to acquire non-depreciable capital property (other than an interest in a partnership) from its predecessor corporations at an amount equal to the adjusted cost base of the property to its predecessors immediately before the amalgamation.[31] The tax-free zone of capital property owned by the predecessor corporations is preserved and passed on to the new corporation.[32]

---

[31] Para. 87(2)(*e*).

[32] Subs. 251(3.1); ITAR 26(5).

(vi) Eligible Capital Property

Where the new corporation carries on the business of its predecessor corporation, the predecessor's cumulative eligible capital immediately before the amalgamation is added to the new corporation's cumulative eligible capital account. The new corporation calculates its cumulative eligible capital account by adding 75 per cent of its eligible capital expenditures to, and deducting 75 per cent of its disposition proceeds on account of eligible capital properties from, any amount that it inherits from its predecessor corporations.[33]

Example XXIV.3

Assume:

	Predecessor Corporations		New Corporation
	C. Ltd.	D. Ltd.	CD Ltd.
Cumulative eligible capital	$ 130,000	$ 30,000	—
Eligible capital expenditures	—	—	$ 50,000
Proceeds of disposition of eligible capital property	—	—	$ 26,000

Then:

Eligible capital expenditures (75% of $50,000)	$ 37,500
Inherited from C Ltd. and D Ltd.	160,000
	$ 197,500
Dispositions (75% of $26,000)	(19,500)
	$ 178,000
Less: maximum claim (7%)	(12,460)
Cumulative eligible capital of CD Ltd.	$ 165,540

(vii) Reserves

(A) General

A taxpayer may claim a reserve only if it is *specifically* authorized by the Act.[34] Under the statutory scheme in respect of reserves a taxpayer must include in his or her income the amount of any reserve claimed by him or her in the immediately preceding year, and may deduct an amount as a new reserve in the current year.

---

[33]   Para. 87(2)(*f*).

[34]   Para. 18(1)(*e*).

A reserve claimed by a predecessor corporation in its final year is *deemed* to have been claimed by the new corporation, and is included in the new corporation's income in its first taxation year. Thus, the new corporation inherits the ongoing responsibility for reserves previously claimed by its predecessor corporations.[35] The new corporation may claim a reserve in respect of its first taxation year in the usual manner.

Similarly, the new corporation is deemed to have included in its income in its first taxation year any amounts receivable by it in future years that were included in the predecessor corporation's last taxation year. Here too, the new corporation steps into the shoes of the predecessor corporations and continues to claim the reserve.[36]

(B) Debts

The predecessor corporations' debts, and debts which arose from loans made in the ordinary course of its business which included lending money, are deemed to be debts owing to the new corporation. The new corporation may deduct a reasonable amount as a reserve in respect of doubtful debts.[37]

(C) Capital Gains Reserve

Where an amount owing to a taxpayer in respect of a disposition of capital property is not due at the end of the taxation year, a portion of any gain resulting from the disposition may be claimed as a reserve.[38] A reserve claimed by a predecessor corporation in its last taxation year is included in the income of the new corporation for its first taxation year. The new corporation may claim a reserve in respect of any proceeds of disposition which remain due at the end of its first taxation year.[39]

(viii) Property Lost, Destroyed or Taken

Where a corporation's property is unlawfully taken, lost, destroyed or expropriated prior to its amalgamation, and the new corporation replaces the property within certain time limits, the new corporation can defer any recapture of capital cost allowance or capital gain that results from the disposition of the property. The rollover in respect of replacement properties applies *as if* the new corporation was the same corporation as, and a continuation of, the predecessor corporation.[40]

---

[35] Para. 87(2)(*g*).

[36] Para. 87(2)(*i*).

[37] Para. 87(2)(*h*).

[38] Para. 40(1)(*a*) (note that the critical test is whether the amount is "due", not whether the amount is outstanding).

[39] Para. 87(2)(*m*).

[40] Para. 87(2)(*l*.3).

(ix) Prepaid Expenses

Prepaid expenses for services to be rendered after the end of the taxation year may be claimed as a deduction only in the year to which the expenditure relates.[41] Prepayments of interest, taxes, rent or royalty in respect of a period after the end of the year may be deducted only in the period to which the expense relates.

Following an amalgamation, the new corporation is deemed to be the same corporation as, and a continuation of, each of its predecessor corporations.[42] Thus, the new corporation is subject to the same limitations in respect of its prepaid expense deductions.

(x) Options

Where an option issued by a corporation expires, the corporation is deemed to have disposed of a capital property for proceeds equal to the option price.[43] If the option expires after the corporation has amalgamated with another corporation, it is deemed to have been issued by the new corporation. Thus, option proceeds received by the predecessor are deemed to have been received by the new corporation.[44]

(xi) Attribution Rules

The attribution rules apply where an individual loans or transfers property to a corporation (other than a small business corporation) in which his or her spouse or a person under 18 years of age has an interest.[45] These rules continue to apply if the corporation amalgamates with another corporation. Thus, the new corporation is considered the same as, and a continuation of, its predecessor corporation.[46]

(xii) Partnership Interests

The new corporation's cost of a partnership interest held by its predecessor corporation depends upon the relationship between the corporations. If both the new and predecessor corporations were related[47] to each other, the new corporation's cost of the partnership interest is equal to its cost to the predecessor corporation.[48] The new corporation is treated in the same manner as its predecessor corporation in so far as the partnership interest is concerned. Thus, any adjustments to the adjusted cost base of the

---

[41] Subs. 18(9).

[42] Para. 87(2)(j.2).

[43] Subs. 49(2).

[44] Para. 87(2)(o).

[45] Ss. 74.4; 74.5.

[46] Para. 87(2)(j.7).

[47] Subs. 251(3.1).

[48] Para. 87(2)(e.1).

partnership interest flow through to the new corporation. Any negative adjusted cost base of a partnership interest held by the predecessor corporation is preserved on the amalgamation.[49]

Where the new corporation and its predecessor were not related to each other, the predecessor corporation is deemed to have disposed of its partnership interests to the new corporation for proceeds equal to their adjusted cost base. The new corporation acquires the interests at the same amount. Thus, the predecessor is required to recognize any gain on the disposition of any interests with a negative adjusted cost base.[50]

(xiii) "Stop-loss" Rules

A corporation's loss on the sale of a share may be reduced by the amount of any tax-free dividends that it receives on the share. The loss is reduced if the share was owned for less than 365 days prior to the sale, or if the corporation owned more than 5 per cent of the shares on which the dividend is paid.[51] This rule, known as the "stop-loss" rule, also extends to taxable dividends received by the predecessor corporation. Such dividends are taken into account on a disposition of the share after the amalgamation.[52]

(xiv) Other

The new corporation is also deemed to be the same corporation as each predecessor corporation for the following purposes:

• Employee benefit plans	para. 87(2)($j.3$)
• Lease cancellations	para. 87(2)($j.5$)
• Income accrual rules	para. 87(2)($j.4$)
• Unused investment and employment tax credits	para. 87(2)(qq)
• Repayments of inducements	para. 87(2)($j.6$)
• Salary deferral arrangements	para. 87(2)($j.3$)
• Deferred profit sharing plans	para. 87(2)(q)
• Scientific research and experimental development	para. 87(2)(l)

---

[49] See Chapter IX "Capital Gains".

[50] Subs. 100(2.1); see also subs. 53(2).

[51] Subss. 112(3), (4).

[52] Para. 87(2)(x).

(e) Predecessor Corporations

The taxation year of a corporation that amalgamates with another corporation is deemed to have ended immediately before the amalgamation.[53] The predecessor corporation is required to file an income tax return for the period up to the date of its amalgamation. Capital cost allowance and the inventory allowance in respect of the final taxation year are prorated if the amalgamation does not coincide with the predecessor corporation's taxation year.[54]

In corporate law, a corporation that amalgamates with another corporation does not terminate its existence.

The companies "are amalgamated and are continued as one company" which is the very antithesis of the notion that the amalgamating corporations are extinguished or that they continue in a truncated state.[55]

The status of predecessor corporations for tax purposes is unclear. The general scheme of the Act suggests that the predecessor corporations do not terminate their existence. At the very least, they are not deemed to have disposed of their assets upon amalgamation.

(f) Creditors of Predecessor Corporations

In order for a merger to qualify as an amalgamation for income tax purposes, the new corporation must assume *all* of the liabilities of the amalgamating corporations.[56] Creditors of the predecessor corporation may be entitled to rollover their receivables for new obligations from the new corporation.

Where a creditor of the predecessor corporation receives a debt obligation from the new corporation that has the same amount payable at maturity as was payable on the old obligation, he or she is deemed to dispose of the old debt at its adjusted cost base and to acquire the new debt at a cost equal to the cost base of the old debt. In other words, the creditor can rollover the cost of the old debt into the new debt and defer the recognition of any gain on the instrument. This rollover is available only where the debt obligation is a capital property to the creditor of the predecessor corporation.[57]

Debt obligations of the predecessor corporation assumed by the new corporation are treated as if they were always debts of the new corporation. Thus, there is continuity of treatment in respect of such obligations. For example, the deduction for

---

[53] Para. 87(2)(*a*).

[54] Reg. 1100(3); IT-474R, "Amalgamations of Canadian Corporations" (March 14, 1986).

[55] *The Queen v. Black & Decker Mfg. Co., ante,* at 417.

[56] Other than intercorporate accounts payable to the predecessor corporations.

[57] Subs. 87(6).

discounts on debts issued by the predecessor continues to be available to the new corporation.[58]

(g) Paid-up Capital

A corporation is required to maintain a separate stated capital account for each class and series of shares that it issues.[59] The stated capital account of each class of shares is to be credited with the full amount of any consideration that it receives in respect of the particular shares.[60]

Where shares are issued pursuant to an amalgamation, however, the new corporation may, in certain circumstances, credit the stated capital account with *less* than the consideration that it receives for the shares.[61] The corporation cannot credit its stated capital account with more than it receives.[62]

The computation of the paid-up capital of the new corporation is particularly important for income tax purposes, because, as a general rule, paid-up capital can be returned to shareholders on a tax-free basis.[63] The paid-up capital of shares for income tax purposes is generally determined according to the corporate law concept of stated capital.[64]

For corporate purposes, the paid-up capital of the new corporation usually will not exceed the aggregate of the paid-up capital of its predecessor corporations less the amount eliminated as a result of the cancellation of intercorporate shareholdings. There are circumstances, however, where the paid-up capital of a corporation for tax purposes may be less than its stated capital for corporate purposes.[65]

In the absence of special rules, taxpayers might be inclined to increase the paid-up capital of the new corporation in order to later withdraw it on a tax-free basis. A special rule provides, however, that the paid-up capital of the new corporation is reduced to the extent that it exceeds the aggregate paid-up capital of all classes of shares of its

---

[58] Para. 20(1)(*f*).

[59] CBCA, subs. 26(1); see also Chapter XV "Corporate Finance".

[60] CBCA, subs. 26(2).

[61] CBCA, para. 26(3)(*b*).

[62] CBCA, subs. 26(4).

[63] *Income Tax Act,* subss. 84(2), (3).

[64] Subs. 89(1) ("paid-up capital").

[65] For example, where s. 84.2 or s. 212.1 are applied to reduce the paid-up capital of the predecessor corporation.

predecessor corporations.[66] Any such reduction is allocated among *all* of the classes of shares of the new corporation in proportion to their respective paid-up capital amounts.

Example XXIV.4

Assume:	PUC of Predecessors		Legal (Stated) Capital New Corporation
	A. Ltd.	*B. Ltd.*	*AB Ltd.*
Class A	$ 70,000	$ 40,000	$ 150,000
Class B	$ 25,000	—	$ —
Class C	—	$ 15,000	—
Class D	—	—	$ 50,000
	$ 95,000	$ 55,000	$ 200,000

A Ltd. and *B Ltd.* amalgamate to form *AB Ltd.*

Then:

The increase of $50,000 in the legal stated capital of *AB Ltd.* is allocated to the various classes of shares as follows:

Class A shares of *AB Ltd.*

Stated capital for corporate purposes	$ 150,000
Less:	
$\dfrac{\$150,000}{\$200,000} \times (\$200,000 - 150,000)$	(37,500)
PUC for tax purposes	$ 112,500

Class D shares of *AB Ltd.*

Stated capital for corporate purposes	$ 50,000
Less:	
$\dfrac{\$50,000}{\$200,000} \times (\$200,000 - 150,000)$	(12,500)
PUC for tax purposes	$ 37,500

PUC of *AB Ltd.* for tax purposes

Class A shares	$ 112,500
Class D shares	$ 37,500
Total paid-up capital	$ 150,000

---

[66] Para. 87(3)(*a*).

Note: A reduction in the paid-up capital of one class of shares of a corporation reduces the paid-up capital of *all* other classes of shares if the corporation amalgamates with another corporation. Thus, a reduction in paid-up capital can have a ripple effect on other shareholders of the corporation.

As a general rule, a shareholder who exchanges shares in a predecessor corporation for shares of the new corporation with a paid-up capital in excess of the paid-up capital of the old shares is not considered to have received a dividend.[67] If, however, the shares are redeemed or otherwise cancelled for an amount in excess of their paid-up capital, the shareholder is deemed to receive a dividend.[68] To prevent double taxation of the proceeds, the amount of the dividend that is attributable to the previous reduction of paid-up capital is added back to the paid-up capital of the particular class of shares.[69]

Example XXIV.5

Assume:

	Predecessor Corporations		New Corporation	
	PUC	Legal Capital	PUC	Legal Capital
Whiteco	$ 10,000	$ 10,000		
Blackco	$ 40,000	$ 50,000		
Newco/Class A	—	—	?	$ 20,000
Class B	—	—	?	$ 40,000
Total	$ 50,000	$ 60,000		$ 60,000

Whiteco and *Blackco* amalgamate to form *Newco,* which issues 100 Class A and 400 Class B shares, for a total stated capital of $60,000. *Newco* redeems 60 of its Class A shares for $200 per share.

Then:

1. Reduction in Newco's PUC

Legal capital for corporate purposes	$ 60,000
Less: Paid-up capital of predecessors	(50,000)
Amount by which *Newco*'s PUC is reduced for tax purposes (para. 87(3)(*a*))	$10,000

---

[67] IT-474R, "Amalgamations of Canadian Corporations" (March 14, 1986).

[68] Subss. 84(3), (4), (4.1).

[69] Para. 87(3)(*b*).

2. Allocation of reduction to *Newco*'s shares

Legal capital of Class A shares	$ 20,000
Less: $\frac{20,000}{60,000} \times \$10,000$	(3,333)
PUC of Class A shares	$ 16,667
PUC per Class A share	$ 167
Legal capital of Class B shares	$ 40,000
Less: $\frac{40,000}{60,000} \times \$10,000$	(6,667)
PUC of Class B shares	$ 33,337
PUC per Class B share	$ 83

3. Deemed dividend on redemption
of 60 Class A shares

Redemption price ($200 × 60)	$ 12,000
PUC of shares redeemed ($167 × 60)	$ 10,020
Deemed dividend (subs. 84(3))	$ 1,980
Deemed dividend per Class A share	$ 33

4. Revised computation of PUC of Class A shares

Legal capital of remaining 40 Class A shares (40% × $20,000)	$ 8,000	
Less: para. 87(3)(a) reduction (step 2 above)	(3,333)	
	$ 4,667	
Add *lesser* of (i) and (ii)		
(i) subs. 84(3) deemed dividend	$ 1,980	
exceeds		
deemed dividend *without* reduction in PUC under para. 87(3)(*a*) ($200 − $200)	(NIL)	
	$ 1,980	
(ii) para. 87(3)(*a*) reduction	$ 3,333	
Lesser amount		1,980
Remaining PUC of 40 Class A shares		$ 6,647
Remaining PUC *per* Class A share $\frac{\$6,647}{40}$		$ 166

In effect, the deemed dividend of $1,980 under subs. 84(3) is added back to determine the remaining PUC of the Class A shares to avoid double taxation in the future. For example, if the remaining 40 Class A shares were redeemed for $200 per share, the amount taxable would be:

Redemption price (40 × $200)	$ 8,000
PUC of shares redeemed	(6,646)
Deemed dividend	$ 1,354
Deemed dividend per Class A share	$ 34

Note that shareholders of *Whiteco* who received Class A shares from *Newco* are deemed to receive a dividend even though the PUC of *Whiteco* equals its legal capital prior to the amalgamation.

(h) Amalgamation Involving Issuance of Shares by Parent Corporation

For income tax purposes, an amalgamation is defined as a merger of two or more taxable Canadian corporations in which, *inter alia*, all of the shareholders of the predecessor corporations receive shares of the new corporation as a result of the merger.[70]

An amalgamation may also be arranged by issuing shares of a corporation other than the new corporation (for example, shares of the parent of the new corporation) to the shareholders of the predecessor.[71]

Where two or more taxable Canadian corporations merge to form a new corporation that immediately after the merger is controlled by a taxable Canadian corporation (the "parent" corporation), any shares issued by the parent corporation are deemed to be shares issued by the new corporation.[72] This type of amalgamation (referred to as a "triangular amalgamation") also qualifies for the flow-through provisions even though the shareholders of the predecessor corporation are not shareholders of the new corporation. Similarly, shareholders of the predecessor corporation may rollover their shares on a tax-free basis when they become shareholders of the new corporation's parent.

Here too, the Act controls the paid-up capital of the parent corporation's shares issued to the shareholders of the predecessor corporation. The paid-up capital of the parent corporation's shares is reduced by the amount that the paid-up capital of all the

---

[70] Para. 87(1)(c).

[71] CBCA, subs. 182(1).

[72] *Income Tax Act*, para. 87(9)(a).

shares of the capital stock of the parent, immediately after the amalgamation, exceeds the aggregate of the paid-up capital of the parent corporation and each of its predecessor corporations immediately before the amalgamation. Thus, the parent corporation cannot increase the paid-up capital of its shares by an artificial amount. The increase in the parent's paid-up capital is limited to the amount of the paid-up capital of the shares of its predecessor corporations for which they are issued.[73]

(i) Carryover of Losses

The new corporation may use the non-capital losses, net capital losses, limited partnership losses, restricted farm losses and farm losses of its predecessor corporations.[74] For the purposes of determining the type and amount of losses to be carried forward from the predecessor corporations to the new corporation, the new corporation is deemed to be the same corporation as, and a continuation of, each predecessor corporation. Thus, the character of the predecessor's unused losses is carried through to the new corporation. Subject to certain restrictions, the losses may be used by the new corporation.

The new corporation is deemed to be a continuation of each of its predecessor corporations only for the purpose of calculating the taxable income of, and tax payable by, the *new* corporation. Thus, losses realized in the first taxation year of the new corporation may *not* be carried back to reduce the income, taxable income or tax payable by its predecessor corporations in previous years.

The taxation year of a corporation that amalgamates with another corporation is deemed to have ended immediately before the amalgamation.[75] Hence, unless the amalgamation occurs at the predecessor corporation's year-end, the predecessor corporation will have a short taxation year, which will count towards the number of years available for the carryforward of losses.[76]

There are special rules which govern reorganizations implemented solely for the purpose of utilizing corporate losses. The general thrust of these rules is to restrict the availability of loss carryovers where corporate control changes as a result of an amalgamation.

Where, immediately following an amalgamation, the new corporation is controlled by a person (or group of persons) that did not control its predecessor corporation, control of the predecessor corporation is deemed to have changed. Where control of a predecessor corporation has changed, the corporation's net capital losses for taxation years preceding the change of control may not be carried forward.[77] Similarly, non-

---

[73] Para. 87(9)(*b*).

[74] Subs. 87(2.1).

[75] Para. 87(2)(*a*).

[76] Subs. 111(1).

[77] Subs. 111(4).

capital losses and farm losses may not be carried forward following a change of control unless the business in which the losses were incurred continues to be carried on for profit or with a reasonable expectation of profit, and then only to the extent of income from the particular business or a similar business.[78]

(j) Shareholders of Predecessor Corporations

(i) General

A taxpayer who disposes of shares in a corporation is required to recognize any capital gain or loss realized at that time.[79] A share converted into another share by virtue of an amalgamation or merger is a disposition of property.[80] Thus, in the absence of specific rules, a shareholder of a corporation that amalgamates with another corporation would be required to recognize a capital gain or loss at the time of the amalgamation.

There are, however, special rules which allow the shareholders and creditors of a corporation that has amalgamated with another corporation to exchange their shares or debt obligations for shares or debt obligations of the new corporation. The general thrust of these rules is that the cost of the shareholder's "old shares" becomes the cost of "new shares", and the shareholder is not required to recognize a capital gain or loss at the time of the amalgamation.[81]

This rollover is available only if:[82]

- The "old shares" constitute capital property; and
- The shareholder receives as consideration only the shares of the new corporation.

Where these conditions are satisfied, the shareholder of the predecessor corporation is deemed to have:

- Disposed of his or her "old shares" for proceeds equal to their adjusted cost base immediately before the amalgamation;[83] and
- Acquired the new shares at a cost equal to the adjusted cost base of the old shares.[84]

---

[78] Subs. 111(5); see also subs. 256(7) (special rule in respect of change of control); ATR-7, "Amalgamation Involving Losses and Control" (March 3, 1986); Chapter XII "Taxable Income".

[79] Subs. 40(1) (shares presumed to be capital property of shareholder).

[80] S. 54 ("disposition").

[81] Paras. 87(4)(a), (b).

[82] Para. 87(4)(a), IT-474R, "Amalgamations of Canadian Corporations" (March 14, 1986).

[83] Para. 87(4)(a).

[84] Para. 87(4)(b).

Where a shareholder receives more than one class of shares of the new corporation, the adjusted cost base of his or her old shares is allocated among the various classes of the new shares. The allocation ratio is the fair market value of the new shares of the particular class to the fair market value of all of the shares received by the shareholder.

The shareholder of the predecessor corporation determines the proceeds of disposition from the total adjusted cost base of all of his or her shares of that class. The total adjusted cost base is then allocated among the new shares, but on a class-by-class basis. Where a shareholder of the predecessor corporation holds shares of more than one class, a separate calculation is required for each class of his or her old shares in order to allocate the adjusted cost base of these shares among the various classes of the new shares. The formula for allocation is as follows:

$$\text{Cost of new shares of particular class} = \text{ACB of all old shares} \times \frac{\text{FMV of new shares of the particular class}}{\text{FMV of all new shares of all classes}}$$

Example XXIV.6

Assume:

White owns common shares of *Alpha Ltd.*:

# of shares	ACB/share	Total ACB
10	$10	$100

Alpha amalgamates with *Beta Ltd.* to form *Omega Ltd.*, and White receives the following new shares:

Type	# of shares	FMV/share	Total FMV
Class A	4	$ 25	$ 100
Class B	1	$ 100	100
			$ 200

Then:

Cost of Class A shares to White: $100 \times \dfrac{100}{200} = \$50$

Cost per Class A share: $\dfrac{\$50}{4} = \underline{\$12.50}$

Cost of Class B shares to White: $100 \times \dfrac{100}{200} = \$50$

Cost per Class B share: $\underline{\$50}$

Summary:

Cost of new Class A shares ($12.50 × 4)	$ 50
Cost of new Class B shares ($50.00 × 1)	50
Total cost of all new shares	$ 100

(ii) Indirect Gifts

A special anti-avoidance rule prevents taxpayers from using amalgamations to divert, or reduce the value of, their shareholdings while taking advantage of the rollover. Where a taxpayer exchanges old shares for new shares that have a lesser value, and it is reasonable to regard any portion of the difference between the two values as a gift that the taxpayer has conferred on a related person, the taxpayer is deemed to have disposed of the old shares for an amount that is equal to the *lesser* of:[85]

- The aggregate of the adjusted cost bases of the old shares plus the "gift portion"; and
- The fair market value of the old shares.

The effect of this rule is that the taxpayer is compelled to recognize a capital gain upon the amalgamation. The taxpayer may not, however, recognize a capital loss on the disposition of the old shares.[86]

The capital gain is generally equal to the value of the "gift portion", that is, the value of the benefit conferred on the related person.

The cost base of the new shares is equal to the *lesser* of:[87]

- The aggregate of the adjusted cost bases of the old shares; and
- The aggregate of the fair market value of the new shares *and* any capital loss disallowed to the taxpayer on the disposition of the old shares.

---

[85] Para. 87(4)(c).

[86] Para. 87(4)(d).

[87] Para. 87(4)(e).

Example XXIV.7

Assume:

Black owns all of the shares of *X Ltd.*, to which the following data applies:

Number of shares	100
Total fair market value	$ 200,000
Total adjusted cost base	$ 100,000

X Ltd. amalgamates with *Y Ltd.*, a corporation wholly owned by Black's son, to form *XY Ltd.* In exchange for his shares in *X Ltd.*, Black receives Class A shares of *XY Ltd.* that have a fair market value of $140,000.

Then:

Proceeds of disposition are the *lesser* of:

(i) ACB of shares plus "gift portion"	$ 100,000
	60,000
	$ 160,000
(ii) FMV of shares	$ 200,000
Lesser amount	$ 160,000
ACB of shares	(100,000)
Capital gain to Black	$ 60,000

---

2. WINDING-UP

References:

ITA:

Subs. 69(5)	Shareholder Appropriation — Winding- Up
S. 88	Winding-up
S. 116	Disposition by Non-Resident of Taxable Canadian Property

BULLETINS, CIRCULARS & RULINGS:

IT-126R2	March 20, 1995	Meaning of "Winding-Up"
IT-142R3	January 11, 1988	Settlement of Debts on the Winding-Up of a Corporation
IT-149R4	June 28, 1991	Winding-Up Dividend
IT-259R2	September 30, 1985	Exchanges of Property

IT-302R3	February 28, 1994	Losses of a Corporation — The Effect that Acquisitions of Control, Amalgamation and Winding-Up Have On Their Deductibility - After January 15, 1987
IT-315	May 10, 1976	Interest Expense Incurred for the Purpose of Winding-Up or Amalgamation
IT-451R	March 25, 1987	Deemed Disposition and Acquisition on Ceasing to Be or Becoming Resident in Canada
IT-488R2	June 24, 1994	Winding-Up of 90%-Owned Taxable Canadian Corporations

(a) General

Winding-up or dissolving a corporation refers to the termination or liquidation of corporate existence. The procedure on winding-up is governed by the appropriate corporate law. Consequently, the procedure varies between jurisdictions.

The tax consequences, however, are determined by section 88 of the Act, and are uniform. A corporation is wound up only when all of the corporate steps are completed.

The winding-up of a corporation and distribution of its assets to shareholders results in a deemed disposition of the assets.[88] The amount by which the value of the assets exceeds the paid-up capital of the corporation's shares is deemed to be a dividend to the shareholders.[89]

There are special rules, however, which permit a tax-free rollover of corporate assets when a parent corporation winds up a subsidiary of which it owns at least 90 per cent of the capital stock. In such circumstances, the property distributed by the subsidiary corporation to the parent corporation is deemed to have been disposed of for proceeds of disposition that generally result in a tax-free rollover of the property.[90]

The rollover is not available where the special anti-avoidance rules in respect of partnerships apply.[91] These rules apply where a taxpayer transfers property with an accrued gain to an unrelated corporation or partnership on a tax-free basis so as to shelter the gain from tax upon a subsequent disposition.[92] Where the anti-avoidance rules apply, the property is treated as having been disposed of at its fair market value.

---

[88] Para. 69(5)(a).

[89] Subs. 84(2).

[90] Subs. 88(1).

[91] Subs. 88(1).

[92] Subs. 69(11).

(b) Corporate Law

A corporation can be dissolved only under the authority of the jurisdiction in which it is incorporated.[93] A corporation may be dissolved by action of its shareholders, its directors, the Director of the Corporations Branch, or by court order.

(i) Voluntary Dissolution

Under the *Canada Business Corporations Act*, a corporation may be dissolved voluntarily in several ways: If it has not issued any shares, it may be dissolved at any time by a resolution passed by all of its directors;[94] if it has issued shares but does not have any property or liabilities, it may be dissolved by a special resolution of its shareholders.[95]

Where it has issued more than one class of shares, the special resolution must be passed by the holders of each class of shares, whether or not the shareholders of the class are otherwise entitled to vote.

A corporation with property or liabilities can be dissolved by a special resolution of the shareholders, if it discharges its liabilities prior to dissolution.[96] A parent corporation can, for example, assume its subsidiary's obligations.

Shareholders of a corporation can submit a proposal for dissolution at the annual meeting.[97] If the proposal is approved by a special resolution, a statement of intent to dissolve the corporation must be sent to the Director of the Corporations Branch.[98] The corporation must communicate its intention to dissolve to each known creditor of the corporation.[99]

Following the completion of the appropriate corporate steps, including the completion and filing of all outstanding income tax returns, the Director will issue a

---

[93] See, generally, *Russian Commercial & Indust. Bank v. Comptoir d'Escompte de Mulhouse*, [1925] AC 112 (H.L.); *Banque Int. de Commerce de Petrograd v. Goukassow*, [1925] AC 150 (H.L.); *Employers' Liability Assur. Corp. v. Sedgwick, Collins & Co.*, [1927] AC 95 (H.L.); *Lazard Bros. & Co. v. Midland Bank*, [1933] AC 289 (H.L.); *Russian & Eng. Bank v. Baring Bros.*, [1936] AC 405 (H.L.); *Re Russian & Eng. Bank*, [1932] 1 Ch. 663; *Re Russian Bank for Foreign Trade*, [1933] Ch. 745; *Re Russo-Asiatic Bank*, [1934] Ch. 720. This rule applies whether the winding-up is voluntary or involuntary.

[94] CBCA, subs. 210(1).

[95] CBCA, subs. 210(2).

[96] CBCA, subs. 210(3).

[97] CBCA, subs. 211(1).

[98] CBCA, subs. 211(4).

[99] CBCA, subs. 211(7).

certificate of dissolution. The certificate terminates the existence of the corporation as of its date of issuance.[100]

(ii) Involuntary Dissolution

The Director of the Corporations Branch has the power to dissolve a corporation where the corporation:[101]

- Has not commenced business within three years after the date shown on its certificate of incorporation;
- Has not carried on its business for three consecutive years; or
- Is in default for a period of one year in filing its corporate documents and annual fees.

In these circumstances, the Director can dissolve the corporation by giving 120 days' notice of his or her intention to do so, followed by the issuance of a certificate of dissolution.

(iii) Dissolution by Court Order

Any interested person (including the Director of the Corporations Branch) may apply to a court for an order to dissolve a corporation where the corporation:[102]

- Has failed for two or more consecutive years to comply with the requirements of the *Canada Business Corporations Act* with respect to the holding of annual meetings of shareholders;
- Is carrying on a business that is prohibited by its articles of incorporation;
- Does not make its records available to its shareholders and creditors as required;
- Procured any certificate under the *Canada Business Corporations Act* by misrepresentation;
- Fails to keep proper financial information available for inspection by its shareholders; or
- Fails to distribute its financial statements to its shareholders prior to its annual general meeting.

There are similar provisions under the various provincial statutes.

(c) Winding-up a 90 Per Cent Subsidiary

For corporate purposes, a corporation is considered to have been wound up where it has followed the procedures for winding-up and dissolution in the relevant corporate

---

[100] CBCA, subs. 211(16).

[101] CBCA, s. 212.

[102] CBCA, s. 213.

statute. For income tax purposes, however, a corporation is "wound up" even though it has not completed all of the formalities in respect of winding-up, if there is substantial evidence that the corporation will be dissolved within a short period of time.[103] Thus, the timing of a winding-up may be different for tax purposes and corporate law purposes.

A taxable Canadian corporation that is at least 90 per cent owned by its parent corporation can be wound up into its parent on a tax-free basis. In these circumstances, the subsidiary is considered to have disposed of each of its assets (other than partnership interests) at its "cost amount" immediately before the winding-up, and the parent corporation is deemed to acquire the assets at the same amount. Thus, in general terms, the assets and liabilities of a subsidiary are "rolled over" into its parent corporation without triggering any immediate capital gain or loss.[104] The rollover is not available in respect of assets transferred to minority shareholders.[105]

(i) Eligibility for Rollover

The rollover applies if:[106]

- Both the subsidiary and the parent are taxable Canadian corporations;
- The parent owns at least 90 per cent of the issued shares *of each class* of the subsidiary; *and*
- All of the shares of the subsidiary that are not owned by the parent are owned by persons with whom the parent deals at arm's length.

The rollover is *not* elective: It applies automatically whenever the above conditions are satisfied.

(ii) Property of the Subsidiary Corporation

The general scheme of the rollover is that property of the subsidiary that is distributed to its parent corporation is transferred at its cost amount. Thus, there is no capital gain (or loss) or income recognized at the time of the winding-up. Note: The presumptions in subsection 88(1) do no more than establish the cost of property acquired by a parent on the winding-up of its subsidiary. It does not otherwise flow through the character of the property.[107]

---

[103] IT-126R2, "Meaning of 'Winding-up'" (March 20, 1995)

[104] *Income Tax Act*, subs. 88(1); IT-488R2, "Winding-up of 90%-owned Taxable Canadian Corporations" (June 24, 1994).

[105] Subs. 69(5). The distribution of assets may also give rise to a "winding-up" dividend under subs. 84(2); see also para. 88(2)(*b*).

[106] Subs. 88(1); IT-488R2, "Winding-up of 90%-owned Taxable Canadian Corporations" (June 24, 1994).

[107] *The Queen v. Mara Properties Ltd.*, [1995] ETC 2031, 95 DTC 5168 (F.C.A.) (subsidiary's inventory did not retain character in parent's hands).

The rollover is available only in respect of property distributed by a subsidiary to its parent corporation. Property distributed to minority shareholders is deemed to have been sold at fair market value.[108] Thus, the subsidiary corporation has some flexibility in determining the assets on which it will realize or defer gains and losses.

(A) Eligible Capital Property

The subsidiary is deemed to have disposed of its eligible capital property for proceeds equal to its cost amount.[109] The "cost amount" of eligible capital property is four-thirds of the cumulative eligible capital multiplied by the proportion that the fair market value of the property is of all of the eligible capital property owned. Since the cumulative eligible capital account is reduced by three-quarters of the deemed proceeds, this formula provides for a complete rollover in respect of such property.

Example XXIV.8	
Assume:	
Cumulative eligible capital (CEC) of subsidiary	$ 10,000
Then:	
Proceeds of disposition: "cost amount" 4/3 × CEC	$ 13,333
Eligible capital amount 3/4 × Proceeds of disposition	$(10,000)
Opening balance (CEC)	$ 10,000
Less: Eligible capital amount	$(10,000)
Closing balance (CEC)	NIL

Any eligible capital property acquired by the subsidiary prior to 1972 has a cost amount equal to nil. Thus, the subsidiary is not required to include any amount in its income in respect of its pre-1972 eligible capital property.

(B) Non-depreciable Capital Property

A subsidiary's non-depreciable capital property is deemed to be distributed to its parent corporation for proceeds equal to the adjusted cost base of the property.[110]

---

[108] Subpara. 69(5)(a)(i).

[109] Subpara. 88(1)(a)(iii); subs. 248(1) ("cost amount").

[110] Subpara. 88(1)(a)(iii).

(C) Depreciable Capital Property

Depreciable capital property is deemed to be disposed of at its undepreciated capital cost.[111] Hence, the subsidiary is not liable for recapture of capital cost allowance, and cannot recognize a terminal loss on the distribution of its depreciable property to its parent corporation.

Depreciable capital property acquired by the subsidiary prior to 1972 and owned continuously since December 31, 1971, is deemed to have been owned by the parent corporation prior to 1972. Thus, any capital gain accrued on the property prior to that date is not taxable to the parent corporation when it disposes of the property.[112]

(D) Accounts Receivable and Reserves

A subsidiary's accounts receivable are transferred to its parent corporation at their face amount. In computing its income, however, the subsidiary may claim a reserve for doubtful accounts as if it had not been wound up.[113]

The parent corporation is deemed to have claimed the reserve actually claimed by the subsidiary in the year in which it was wound up. Thus, in the following year the parent is required to add back the reserve to its own income.[114]

(E) Inventory

The subsidiary's inventory is deemed to be distributed to its parent corporation at the lower of its cost and fair market value.[115] It is a question of fact, however, whether the inventory retains its character as such in the hands of the parent corporation.[116]

(F) Partnership Interests

The subsidiary's partnership interests distributed to its parent corporation are not considered to have been disposed of by the subsidiary.[117] Hence the transfer of a partnership interest with a negative cost base will not trigger a capital gain until such time as it is disposed of by the parent corporation.

---

[111] Subpara. 88(1)(*a*)(iii); subs. 248(1) ("cost amount").

[112] ITAR 20(1.2).

[113] Para. 88(1)(*e*.1).

[114] Paras. 88(1)(*e*.2); 87(2)(*g*).

[115] Para. 88(1)(*a*), subs. 248(1) ("cost amount"); s. 10.

[116] *The Queen v. Mara Properties Ltd.*, [1995] ETC 2031, 95 DTC 5168 (F.C.A.).

[117] Para. 88(1)(*a*.2).

(iii) Liabilities of the Subsidiary

(A) Owing to the Parent Corporation

A prerequisite to the legal dissolution of a corporation is that it discharge its obligations to its creditors.[118] A subsidiary may discharge any indebtedness to its parent corporation either by payment in cash or by transferring assets of equivalent value to the parent. Note: The rollover under subsection 88(1) is available only in respect of assets transferred *pursuant* to the liquidation proceedings.

Where a debt payable by the subsidiary to its parent corporation is settled without payment, or by payment of a sum less than the principal amount of the amount payable, the parent can elect to assume the debt at its cost amount.[119] If the parent elects, the subsidiary is deemed to have paid an amount equal to the cost amount of the debt to the parent. The "cost amount" of the debt is its adjusted cost base, if it constitutes capital property, and the lower of its cost and fair market value, if it is inventory.[120]

(B) Owing to Third Parties

Debts owing to third parties must also be settled before a subsidiary is wound up. Here too, the subsidiary may discharge its obligations either in cash or by transferring assets of an equivalent value to its creditors. A disposition of assets in satisfaction of a debt can give rise to capital gains, income or recapture of capital cost allowance.

A subsidiary's obligations to third parties that are assumed by its parent corporation are not considered to be a settlement of a debt if: (1) The indebtedness is assumed by the parent as part of the distribution of the subsidiary's assets on liquidation; and (2) The amount payable by the parent on maturity of the debt is the same as the amount payable by the subsidiary.[121] For example, where a parent corporation acquires mortgaged real estate from its subsidiary, it can assume the mortgage together with the property as part of the liquidation distribution. The parent steps into the shoes of the subsidiary, and is considered to have issued the debt from the outset. Thus, the parent is entitled to any deduction for "deep" or "shallow" discounts to which its subsidiary was entitled.[122]

Third-party creditors can rollover debts owed to them by the subsidiary if the only consideration which they receive in exchange for the debts is new debts issued by the parent corporation and the amount payable on maturity of the new debts is the same as

---

[118] See, e.g., CBCA, para. 211(7)(c).

[119] *Income Tax Act*, subs. 80(3); IT-142R3, "Settlement of Debts on the Winding-up of a Corporation" (January 11, 1988).

[120] Subs. 248(1) ("cost amount"); s. 10.

[121] Para. 88(1)(e.2); subs. 87(7).

[122] Para. 20(1)(f); See Chapter VII "Business and Property Income: Inclusions".

that payable on the old. The rollover is restricted to debts which constitute capital property to the creditor.[123]

(iv) Acquisition of Property by Parent Corporation

(A) General

The rules that govern the acquisition of property by a parent corporation from its subsidiary are the mirror image of the rules in respect of the subsidiary's disposition of the property. Generally, the parent is deemed to receive each asset distributed to it at an amount that is equal to the proceeds of disposition deemed to have been received by the subsidiary.[124] Hence, the tax-free rollover to the parent: In effect, the parent corporation steps into the shoes of its subsidiary corporation by taking over its property at their tax values. These rules are set out below:

COST TO PARENT CORPORATION OF PROPERTIES		
Property	**Cost to Parent Corporation**	**Statutory Reference**
1. Accounts receivable	Face amount of receivables	para. 88(1)(*c*)
	Doubtful accounts deducted by subsidiary deemed deducted by parent in previous year	para. 88(1)(*e*. 2)
2. Inventory (non-farming)	Lower of cost or market	para. 88(1)(*c*); s. 10
Farming inventory (cash basis)	NIL	s. 28
3. Eligible capital property	4/3 of subsidiary's cumulative eligible capital	para. 88(1)(*c*)
4. Depreciable property	UCC (in proportion to capital cost)	para. 88(1)(*c*)
5. Non-depreciable capital property	ACB, with potential step-up in cost base	paras. 88(1)(*c*), (*d*)

---

[123] Para. 88(1)(*e*.2); subs. 87(6).

[124] Para. 88(1)(*c*).

(B) Non-depreciable Capital Property

The parent acquires the subsidiary's non-depreciable capital property at its adjusted cost base. The tax-free zone in respect of any such property owned on June 18, 1971, flows through to the parent corporation.[125]

The cost base of the property can be stepped up by an amount equal to the difference between the cost base of the subsidiary's shares to the parent and the underlying *net* tax cost of the subsidiary's properties.[126] The amount of the step-up allocated to a particular capital property cannot exceed the difference between its fair market value at the time when the parent last acquired control of the subsidiary and the cost amount of the property to the subsidiary immediately before the winding-up. In effect, the amount of any step-up allocated to a property is limited to the *unrealized* gain in respect of the property at the time when the parent last acquired control of the subsidiary.[127]

In the case of partnership interests, the step-up is to the parent's cost of the interest — the cost of the partnership interest to the subsidiary corporation.[128]

The cost base of non-depreciable capital property may be stepped-up only where the property was owned by the subsidiary at the time when the parent last acquired control of it, *and* continuously thereafter until the time when it was distributed to the parent corporation.[129] Note: The election to step-up the cost base of capital property is not available in respect of property transferred in the course of a "butterfly" reorganization.[130]

Specifically, the adjusted cost base of capital properties may be stepped-up by an amount equal to the excess of the adjusted cost base of the parent's shares in its subsidiary over the aggregate of:[131]

- The tax values of the subsidiary's *net* assets (that is, after deducting its liabilities and certain reserves) immediately before the winding-up; and

- Taxable dividends, capital dividends or life insurance capital dividends received by the parent corporation (or any other corporation with which the parent corporation does not deal at arm's length) on the subsidiary's shares.

---

[125] ITAR 26(5).

[126] Paras. 88(1)(*c*), (*d*).

[127] Subpara. 88(1)(*d*)(ii).

[128] Para. 88(1)(*c*).

[129] Subs. 88(4) (for purposes of these rules, amalgamation does not give rise to change of control).

[130] See subs. 55(3).

[131] Para. 88(1)(*d*).

Example XXIV.9

Assume:

On January 1, 1995, *P Ltd.* purchased all of the issued shares of *S Ltd.* for $1,000,000. On December 31, 1996, *S Ltd.* is liquidated and wound up; its assets are distributed to *P Ltd.* The following data applies to S Ltd.:

	January 1, 1995		December 31, 1996	
	Cost Amount	FMV	Cost Amount	FMV
Assets:				
Cash	$ 50,000	$ 50,000	$ 50,000	$ 50,000
Securities	80,000	125,000	80,000	175,000
Inventory	100,000	100,000	100,000	100,000
Land	200,000	350,000	200,000	400,000
Buildings	250,000	400,000	250,000	475,000
	$ 680,000	$ 1,025,000	$ 680,000	$ 1,200,000
Liabilities:				
Payables	$ 100,000	$ 100,000	$ 100,000	$ 100,000
Long-term debt	400,000	400,000	400,000	400,000
	$ 500,000	$ 500,000	$ 500,000	$ 500,000

Then:

1. Maximum designation under para. 88(1)(*d*):

Tax cost of *P Ltd.*'s investment in *S. Ltd.*	$1,000,000
Tax value of *S Ltd.*'s *net* assets	
($680,000 − $500,000)	(180,000)
Maximum overall designation	$ 820,000

2. Cost of *S Ltd.*'s assets to *P. Ltd.*:

Cash		$ 50,000
Inventory		100,000
Buildings		250,000
Land		
FMV at acquisition of control	$ 350,000	
ACB to *S. Ltd.*	(200,000)	
Maximum step-up in cost	$ 150,000	
Revised cost base		$ 350,000
Securities		
FMV at acquisition of control	$ 125,000	
ACB to *S Ltd.*	(80,000)	
Maximum step-up in cost	$ 45,000	
Revised cost base		$ 125,000

(v) Disposition of Property to Minority Shareholders

As a general rule, a shareholder who acquires property from a corporation on its winding-up is deemed to acquire the property at its fair market value immediately before the winding-up.[132] This is also the same value at which the subsidiary corporation is deemed to have sold its property.[133]

(vi) Disposition of Subsidiary's Shares by Parent Corporation

A parent corporation's shares in its subsidiary are cancelled when the subsidiary is wound up. Any payment of an amount in excess of the paid-up capital of the shares is deemed to be a dividend.

A special rule applies, however, where a 90 per cent-owned subsidiary is wound up into its parent corporation. In certain circumstances, the parent is deemed to have disposed of its shares in its subsidiary for proceeds equal to the *greater* of:[134]

- The paid-up capital of the shares *or* the tax value of the subsidiary's net assets after deducting liabilities, *whichever* is the lesser; and
- The adjusted cost base of the shares immediately before the winding-up.

Thus, the parent corporation cannot realize a loss on the disposition of its subsidiary's shares. It may, however, realize a capital gain.

The difference between the fair market value of a subsidiary's *net* assets distributed to its parent and the paid-up capital of the parent's shares in the subsidiary at the time of the distribution is *not* considered a dividend.[135] Instead, the future liability for the dividend is passed on to the shareholders of the parent corporation.

Example XXIV.10		
Assume:	Case A	Case B
PUC of parent's shares in subsidiary	$ 1,000	$ 1,000
Tax value of subsidiary's *net* assets at		
liquidation	$ 10,000	$ 10,000
ACB of subsidiary's shares to parent	$ 15,000	$ 500
Then:		
Deemed POD	$ 15,000	$ 1,000
ACB of shares	(15,000)	(500)
Capital gain (loss)	NIL	$ 500

---

[132] Para. 69(5)(*b*).

[133] Para. 69(5)(*a*).

[134] Para. 88(1)(*b*).

[135] Para. 88(1)(*d*.1).

(vii) Losses

A parent corporation may use the non-capital, net capital, limited partnership, restricted farm, and farm losses accumulated by its subsidiary to reduce its taxable income or Part IV tax if:[136]

- Both the parent and its subsidiary are Canadian corporations;
- Immediately before the winding-up, the parent owns at least 90 per cent of the issued shares *of each class* of its subsidiary; and
- All of the remaining shares (maximum 10 per cent) of the subsidiary are owned by persons with whom the parent is dealing at arm's length.

A corporation is restricted in carrying forward its own accumulated losses when control of the corporation changes. Similarly, the losses of a subsidiary corporation which is wound up into its parent may not be available to the parent corporation where control of the parent or subsidiary changes. The purpose of these restrictions is to discourage artificial tax avoidance through "loss company" trading.

Following a change of control of a parent or a subsidiary corporation, the parent can use its subsidiary's non-capital or farm losses only if the business that incurred the losses has been carried on continuously by either the parent or the subsidiary following the change of control, for profit or with a reasonable expectation of profit.[137] The subsidiary's losses from property and allowable business investment losses before the acquisition of control cannot be carried forward and deducted by the parent after the change of control.

A subsidiary's net capital losses may also be carried over and utilized by its parent corporation, if control of the parent or subsidiary corporation has not been acquired by a person who did not control the parent or subsidiary at the end of the year *in which the net capital loss* was incurred.[138] Thus, a change of control of the parent corporation *after* the winding-up of its subsidiary precludes the parent from claiming the subsidiary's capital loss.

The term "control" is not defined. It usually implies ownership of a sufficient number of shares to elect a majority of the board of directors of the corporation.[139]

---

[136] Subss. 88(1.1), (1.2).

[137] Para. 88(1.1)(*e*).

[138] Subs. 88(1.2).

[139] *Buckerfield's Ltd. v. M.N.R.*, [1964] CTC 504, 64 DTC 5301 (Ex. Ct.); see, generally, *I.R.C. v. B.W. Noble Ltd.* (1926), 12 Tax Cas. 911 at 926; *Br. Amer. Tobacco Co. v. I.R.C.*, [1943] AC 335 (H.L.); *Vancouver Towing Co. v. M.N.R.*, [1947] CTC 18, 2 DTC 706 (Ex. Ct.); *M.N.R. v. Sheldon's Engr. Ltd.*, [1954] CTC 241, 54 DTC 1106; affirmed [1955] CTC 174, 55 DTC 1110 (S.C.C.); *Forand Auto Ltée v. M.N.R.* (1966), 66 DTC 184 (T.A.B.); *Aaron's (Prince Albert) Ltd. v. M.N.R.*, [1966] CTC 330, 66 DTC 5244; affirmed [1967] CTC 50, 67 DTC 5035 (S.C.C.).

The power to wind-up a corporation may, however, confer control despite equality of voting power.[140] Note: The acquisition of shares of a corporation by a person who immediately before the acquisition was related to the corporation does not constitute a change of control.[141]

(d) Winding-up of Other Canadian Corporations

The winding-up of a Canadian corporation *other than* a 90 per cent-owned subsidiary is governed by the usual rules in respect of dispositions of property. The subsidiary is deemed to have sold each of its properties immediately before its liquidation for proceeds of disposition equal to the fair market value of its properties. Capital gains and losses, recapture of capital cost allowance, inventory gains and terminal losses are all taken into account in computing its income in its final year.[142] Note: The subsidiary can use capital losses resulting from a disposition of capital property in the course of its winding-up even if the property is distributed to its controlling shareholder. The loss limitation rules in respect of transfers to controlling shareholders do not apply.[143]

(i) Deemed Dividends

Distribution of a subsidiary's property to its parent corporation can give rise to a deemed dividend where the parent does not own at least 90 per cent of each class of shares of the subsidiary. The dividend is equal to the excess of the value of the property distributed over the reduction in the paid-up capital of the class of shares on which the distribution is made. The dividend is deemed to have been received by each shareholder in proportion to his or her shareholdings.[144]

(ii) Proceeds of Disposition

Each shareholder of a corporation is considered to have disposed of his or her shares for proceeds of disposition equal to the value of the property received by him or her from the corporation. Where the corporation is a Canadian-resident corporation, the proceeds of disposition are reduced by the amount of any dividend deemed to have been paid to the shareholder.[145] Thus, a shareholder may realize a capital gain or loss upon the liquidation of the corporation.

---

[140] *The Queen v. Imp. Gen. Properties* Ltd., [1985] 2 CTC 299 at 302, 85 DTC 5500 (S.C.C.) (in determining control, court not limited to highly technical and narrow interpretation of legal rights attached to shares).

[141] Subs. 256(7).

[142] Para. 69(5)(a).

[143] Subpara. 69(5)(a)(ii).

[144] Subs. 84(2).

[145] S. 54 ("proceeds of disposition")(j).

Example XXIV.11

Assume:

In 1990, Green subscribed for 100 shares of *White Ltd.* at a total cost of $1,000. In 1995, Blue subscribed for 100 shares of *White Ltd.* for $5,000. These were the only share capital transactions. *White Ltd.* was wound up in 1996, and Green received property valued at $4,000 from the corporation in exchange for his shares.

Then:

PUC of all shares ($1,000 + $5,000)	$ 6,000
PUC *per* share ($6,000 ÷ 200)	$ 30
PUC of Green's shares ($30 × 100)	$ 3,000
Value of property distributed on winding-up	(4,000)
Deemed dividend (subs. 84(2))	$ 1,000
Proceeds of disposition ($4,000 − $1,000)	$ 3,000
ACB of shares cancelled	(1,000)
Capital gain	$ 2,000

Summary:

Deemed dividend	$ 1,000	
Capital gain	2,000	
Increase in value of shares ($4,000 − $1,000)		$ 3,000

(e) Non-resident Corporations

The tax-free rollover of assets on the winding-up of a 90 per cent-owned subsidiary into its parent corporation is limited to taxable Canadian corporations.

A non-resident corporation that is wound up is deemed to have sold its property at fair market value.[146] If the non-resident corporation is carrying on business in Canada or owns taxable Canadian property, it is deemed to have disposed of its property, and must take into account any income (loss) or capital gain (loss). The tax treatment of income or capital gains resulting from a deemed disposition may depend upon the relevant international tax treaty.

A winding-up distribution by a non-resident corporation does not give rise to a deemed dividend,[147] nor is any amount distributed to a shareholder by a non-resident

---

[146] Para. 69(5)(*a*).

[147] Subs. 84(2) applies only to a corporation resident in Canada.

corporation considered to be a shareholder benefit.[148] Instead, the entire amount distributed by a non-resident corporation to its resident shareholders is considered to be proceeds of disposition.

(f) Clearance Certificates

An assignee, liquidator or receiver is required to obtain a certificate from the Minister certifying that any taxes, interest or penalties payable out of property under his or her control have been paid or acceptable security has been provided in lieu of payment. A person acting in the capacity of a liquidator of a corporation, whether or not he or she has been formally appointed, is required to comply with this rule and obtain a clearance certificate.[149]

A non-resident who disposes of shares of a corporation that is wound up is obliged to obtain a clearance certificate from the Minister if the shares constitute "taxable Canadian property". The non-resident has two options: (1) To report the details of the *proposed* transaction to the Minister;[150] or (2) To complete the transaction and report the details thereof within ten days.[151]

The information that is reported to the Minister must disclose the actual or estimated selling price of the property and its adjusted cost base. The Minister will issue a clearance certificate upon payment of 33 1/3 per cent of the amount by which the estimated or actual proceeds of disposition exceed the adjusted cost base of the property.[152]

A person who purchases property from a non-resident who has not obtained a clearance certificate is liable to pay tax *on behalf of* the non-resident vendor. The purchaser's liability is for 15 per cent of the *cost* of the property purchased. The purchaser is entitled to withhold that amount from the price paid to the non-resident vendor.[153]

(g) Corporate Emigration

In certain circumstances, a corporation incorporated in one jurisdiction may move out of, or be "exported" from, that jurisdiction and apply for continuance in another jurisdiction. Under the *Canada Business Corporations Act*, for example, a corporation

---

[148] Subs. 15(1) does not apply to the winding-up of a corporation.

[149] Subs. 159(2); IT-368, "Corporate Distributions — Clearance Certificate", para. 2 (March 28, 1977).

[150] Subs. 116(1); See also Chapter XXV "Purchase and Sale of a Business".

[151] Subs. 116(3).

[152] Subss. 116(2), (4).

[153] Subs. 116(5). It is questionable whether the federal government has constitutional power to affect property rights by allowing for the right of set-off through the *Income Tax Act*.

may apply for export to another jurisdiction, and may request that it be continued *as if* it had been incorporated under the laws of that other jurisdiction.[154]

An application to continue a corporation from one jurisdiction to another must be supported by a special resolution of its shareholders.[155] *All* of the shareholders, whether or not they have voting rights, are entitled to vote in respect of the application to move.[156] Upon compliance with the applicable corporate provisions of the continuing jurisdiction, the Director of the Corporations Branch will issue a certificate of discontinuance to the corporation.[157]

The continuance of a corporation from one Canadian jurisdiction to another Canadian jurisdiction is not considered a disposition by the shareholders of their shares in the corporation.[158] Special statutory rules apply, however, where a corporation which is incorporated in Canada is granted Articles of Continuance in a foreign jurisdiction or becomes resident in a foreign jurisdiction and, as a consequence thereof, becomes exempt from Part I tax. In these circumstances the corporation is deemed:[159]

- To have ended its taxation year *immediately before* it is continued under, or takes up residence in, the foreign jurisdiction;
- To have disposed of its property *immediately before* it is "exported", for proceeds equal to the fair market value of the property; and
- To have acquired its property immediately *after* its "export" at the fair market value of the property.

The effect of these rules is that the exported corporation is liable for any recapture of capital cost allowance, capital gains, inventory gains and any other income inclusions resulting from dispositions of property. Note: Since the corporation is deemed to dispose of its property immediately before it is exported, it cannot seek the protection of an international tax treaty to reduce its Canadian taxes payable. Thus, the tax payable by a corporation on its emigration is similar to the liability of an individual who gives up residence in Canada: The corporation is subject to a form of "departure tax".

---

[154] CBCA, subs. 188(1).

[155] CBCA, subs. 188(5).

[156] CBCA, subs. 188(4).

[157] CBCA, subs. 188(7).

[158] TR-1, "Exporting a Corporation — Whether a Disposition — Effect on Incorporation Date" (June 24, 1974); TR-37, "Amalgamations" (August 9, 1976); TR-49, "Sale of Assets — Amalgamation" (March 8, 1977).

[159] *Income Tax Act*, subs. 128.1(4).

Since the corporation's taxation year is deemed to have ended immediately prior to its departure, it is required to file an income tax return within a period of six months after its deemed departure date.

A corporation that "emigrates" from Canada may remain a resident of Canada for tax purposes. This may occur, for example, where the corporation's "central management and control" remain in Canada.[160] In such circumstances, the corporation would continue to be taxable in Canada on its global income even though it had emigrated.

An emigrating corporation is liable to pay 25 per cent on its "net surplus" at the date of emigration.[161] "Net surplus" is the difference between the fair market value of the corporation's assets and the aggregate of its paid-up capital and liabilities. This tax is in lieu of the withholding tax that would be payable had the corporation simply distributed its "net surplus" to non-resident shareholders.[162]

---

[160] Subs. 250(4) (arguably, corporation incorporated in Canada continues to be Canadian resident even if discontinued in Canada).

[161] S. 219.1.

[162] S. 212.

SELECTED BIBLIOGRAPHY TO CHAPTER XXIV

Amalgamations

General

Ahmed, Firoz and Sarah Gagan, "Amalgamations After Pan Ocean" (1994), 4 *Can. Current Tax* J71.

Birnie, David A.G., "Consolidation of Corporate Structures", in *Proceedings of 31st Tax Conf.* 177 (Can. Tax Foundation, 1979).

Boultbee, Jack A., "Public Company Split-Ups", in *Corp. Mgmt. Tax Conf.* 1 (Can. Tax Foundation, 1984).

Boultbee, Jack A., "Survey of the Use of Rollovers in Acquisitions and Mergers (A)" (1980), 28 *Can. Tax J.* 504.

Brown, Robert D., "Corporate Liquidations", in *Proceedings of 25th Tax Conf.* 52 (Can. Tax Foundation, 1973).

Cronkwright, Glen E., "Amalgamations and Share-for-Share Exchanges", in *Proceedings of 26th Tax Conf.* 53 (Can. Tax Foundation, 1974).

Dart, Robert J., "Specific Uses of Companies in Tax Planning", in *Proceedings of 31st Tax Conf.* 117 (Can. Tax Foundation, 1979).

Edwards, Stanley E., "Statutory Amalgamations and Recapitulations", in *Proceedings of 24th Tax Conf.* 401 (Can. Tax Foundation, 1972).

Ewens, Douglas S., "Amalgamations — Part I" (1980), 28 *Can. Tax J.* 661.

Ewens, Douglas S., "Corporate Dissolutions" (1985), 33 *Can. Tax J.* 1246.

Farwell, Peter M., "Statutory Amalgamations", *Corp. Mgmt. Tax Conf.* 82 (Can. Tax Foundation, 1972).

Harris, Edwin C., "New Sections 88.1 and 219.1 and Amendments to Sections 51, 85, 86, 87, 88, and 184", in *Proceedings of 32nd Tax Conf.* 92 (Can. Tax Foundation, 1980).

Hartkorn, D.N., "Income Splitting — The New Rules" (1985), 33 *Can. Tax J.* 1226.

Kellough, H.J., "A Planning Update for Private Corporations — Corporate Reorganizations", *Prairie Prov. Tax Conf.* 131 (Can. Tax Foundation, 1981).

Laflamme, Pierre, "Acquisition Strategies" in *Proceedings of 45th Tax Conf.* (Can. Tax Foundation, 1993) 13:1.

Levin, Jonathon A. *et al., Tax Features of Major Business Agreements: Effectively Structuring the Transactions* (Mississauga, Ont.: Insight, 1991).

Lindsay, Robert F., "Canadian Income Tax Considerations in the Consolidation of Business Operations", in *Proceedings of 27th Tax Conf.* 304 (Can. Tax Foundation, 1975).

Lindsay, Robert F., "Winding-Up of Corporations: Changes in Capital Structure of Corporations", in *Proceedings of 26th Tax Conf.* 69 (Can. Tax Foundation, 1974).

MacDonald, Nancy, "Amalgamations Following Guaranty Properties Limited" (1991), 39 *Can. Tax J.* 1399.

McCallum, J. Thomas, *Amalgamations and Wind-ups* (Vancouver: Certified General Accountants' Association of Canada, 1994).

Mintz, Jack M., *Policy Forum on Takeovers and Tax Policy* (Kingston, Ont.: Queen's University, John Deutsch Institute for the Study of Economic Policy, 1990).

O'Keefe, Michael J., "Liquidation of Corporations under the Income Tax Act" (1973), 102 *CA Magazine* No. 5, 28.

Palmer, J.S., "Amalgamation — Winding-Up", in *Proceedings of 30th Tax Conf.* 469 (Can. Tax Foundation, 1978).

Richler, Ronald, "Triangular Amalgamations" (1985), 33 *Can. Tax J.* 374.

Schwartz, Alan M., "Statutory Amalgamations, Arrangements, and Continuations: Tax and Corporate Law Considerations" in *Proceedings of 43rd Tax Conf.* (Can. Tax Foundation, 1991) 9:1.

Singer, Paul, "The Rollover Provisions in Respect of Corporate Reorganizations Provided Under the Income Tax Act: Efficiency and Equity as Policy Considerations" (1983), 31 *Can. Tax J.* 569.

Skingle, L.E., "Guaranty Properties Ltd. v. R." (1992), 5 *Can. Petro. Tax J.* 171.

Smith, D.W., "Amalgamations: Section 87" (1981), *Can. Taxation* 1079.

Smith, John G., "Winding Up", in *Proceedings of 23rd Tax Conf.* 53 (Can. Tax Foundation, 1972).

Spindler, Herbert O., "Mergers, Acquisitions and Divestitures" (1975), 107 *CA Magazine* No. 3, 65.

Turner, Graham, "Amalgamations and Continuations" (1988), 36 *Can. Tax J.* 1479.

Williamson, David M., "Checklists: Corporate Reorganizations, Amalgamations (Section 87) and Wind-Ups (Subsection 88(1))", in *Proceedings of 39th Tax Conf.* 29:1 (Can. Tax Foundation, 1987).

Wilson, Ronald S., "Cost Adjustments in Corporate Reorganization Transactions: Policy and Practice", in *Proceedings of 38th Tax Conf.* 8:1 (Can. Tax Foundation, 1986).

Williamson, W. Gordon, "Recent Developments Affecting Corporate Reorganizations" in *Proceedings of 42nd Tax Conf.* (Can. Tax Foundation, 1990) 13:1.

Federal Corporate Law

Hansen, Brian G., "Minority Squeeze-Outs", in *Proceedings of 30th Tax Conf.* 408 (Can. Tax Foundation, 1978).

Slutsky, Samuel, "Short-Form Amalgamations — Some Problems" (1984), 32 *Can. Tax J.* 595.

The New Corporation

Boultbee, Jack, "Amalgamations — Part III" (1981), 29 *Can. Tax J.* 83.

"Mid-Year Amalgamations", *Can. Tax Letter*, January 20, 1978 (De Boo).

Thomas, James P., "Restructuring the Ownership of Property Within a Closely Held Group", *Corp. Mgmt. Tax Conf.* 6:1 (Can. Tax Foundation, 1989).

Wilson, Ronald S., "Cost Adjustments in Corporate Reorganization Transactions: Policy and Practice", in *Proceedings of 38th Tax Conf.* 8:1 at 8:37-8:39 (Can. Tax Foundation, 1986).

Predecessor Corporations

Birnie, David A.G., "Consolidation of Corporate Structures", in *Proceedings of 31st Tax Conf.* 177 (Can. Tax Foundation, 1979).
Boultbee, Jack, "Amalgamations — Part III" (1981), 29 *Can. Tax J.* 83.
Richler, Ronald, "Triangular Amalgamations" (1985), 33 *Can. Tax J.* 374.

Paid-Up Capital

Ewens, Douglas, "Amalgamations — Part II" (1980), 28 *Can. Tax J.* 826.
Sinclair, B.R., "Paid-Up Capital" (1986), 34 *Can. Tax J.* 1494.

Carryover of Losses

Arnold, Brian J., and David C. Poynton, "Tax Treatment of Losses on Amalgamation and Winding-up" (1978), 26 *Can. Tax J.* 444.
Cronkwright, Glen E., "The Utilization of Losses in Corporate Groups and Further Relief That Might be Taken", in *Proceedings of 31st Tax Conf.* 316 (Can. Tax Foundation, 1979).
Flynn, Gordon W., "Tax Planning for Corporations with Net Capital and Noncapital Losses", *Corp. Mgmt. Tax Conf.* 208 (Can. Tax Foundation, 1981).
Treharne, R., "Loss Carryforward Rollovers" (1977), 51 *Cost & Mgmt.* 45.

Shareholders of Predecessor Corporations

Cowan, R.I., "Amalgamations — Shareholders and Investors" (1977), 51 *Cost & Mgmt.* 46.
Richler, Ronald, "Triangular Amalgamations" (1985), 33 *Can. Tax J.* 374.

Winding-up

Winding-up of a 90 Per Cent Subsidiary

Alpert, Howard J., "Winding-Up under Section 88" (1974), 22 *Can. Tax J.* 98.
Arnold, Brian J., and David C. Poynton, "Tax Treatment of Losses on Amalgamation and Winding-Up" (1978), 26 *Can. Tax J.* 444.
Cronkwright, Glen E., "The Utilization of Losses in Corporate Groups and Further Relief That Might Be Taken", in *Proceedings of 31st Tax Conf.* 316 (Can. Tax Foundation, 1979).
Flynn, Gordon W., "Tax Planning for Corporations with Net Capital and Noncapital Losses", *Corp. Mgmt. Tax Conf.* 208 (Can. Tax Foundation, 1981).
Nitikman, Bert W., and G. David Eriks, "Macbeth and Subsection 88(1)" (1976), 24 *Can. Tax J.* 1.
Pister, Tom, "Paragraph 88(1)(d) Bump on the Winding Up of a Subsidiary — Part I" (1990), 38 *Can. Tax J.* 148.
Pister, Tom, "Paragraph 88(1)(d) Bump on the Winding Up of a Subsidiary — Part II" (1990), 38 *Can. Tax J.* 426.

Scace, Arthur R.A., "The Purchase and Sale of Shares: Section 88 Winding-Up", *Corp. Mgmt. Tax Conf.* 51 (Can. Tax Foundation, 1972).

Smith, D.W., "Winding-Up: Section 88" (1981), *Can. Taxation* 1141.

Swiderski, Tony, "Transfers of U.S. Real Property Interests in Canadian Reorganizations: Opportunities, Limitations and Pitfalls" (1989), 37 *Can. Tax J.* 605, at pp. 624-25.

Tinker, John B., "Rollovers on Winding Up Wholly-Owned Subsidiaries and Distributing Property of Trusts", in *Proceedings of 23rd Tax Conf.* 407 (Can. Tax Foundation, 1972).

Winding-up of Other Canadian Corporations

Ewens, Douglas S., "The Winding-Up of Corporations Otherwise than Under Section 88" (1973), 21 *Can. Tax J.* 1.

Ewens, Douglas S., "The Winding-Up of Corporations Otherwise than Under Section 88: An Update" (1975), 23 *Can. Tax J.* 352.

Corporate Emigration

Boultbee, J., "Change of Residence and Continuance" (1984), 32 *Can. Tax J.* 792.

Other

Lindsay, Robert F., "Purchase and Sale of a Canadian Business by a Nonresident of Canada", *Corp. Mgmt. Tax Conf.* 305 (Can. Tax Foundation, 1984).

Pooley, Joanne, and Terry Clark, "Comparison Between Canadian and U.S. Reorganizations — Part I" (1982), 30 *Can. Tax J.* 284.

Pooley, Joanne, and Terry Clark, "Comparison Between Canadian and U.S. Reorganizations — Part II" (1982), 30 *Can. Tax J.* 437.

"The Taxation of Corporate Reorganizations — Change of Residence and Continuance" (1984), 32 *Can. Tax J.* 792.

CHAPTER XXV

PURCHASE AND SALE OF A BUSINESS

1. GENERAL

There are three principal decisions to be made in a business acquisition:

1. Do we buy the business?
2. What do we buy? and
3. How do we pay for it?

The first of these decisions is essentially a business decision: Is the business attractive in terms of its potential financial returns? Does it integrate with the purchaser's other businesses? Does the purchaser have the necessary expertise to run the new business? Will it ensure lines of supply or customers that will enhance the purchaser's existing businesses? And so on.

The next two decisions, however, are substantially influenced by tax law. Both the purchaser and the vendor have the same economic interests: They want the best deal. The structure of an acquisition will determine not only its price but also the manner of payment.

The method of financing a business depends upon both financial and tax considerations. Financial considerations concern the state of the debt and equity markets, the availability of funds and, most importantly, the cost of capital at the relevant time. The cost of capital and the available internal rate of return from the invested capital determine whether the acquisition is justifiable on a business basis.

From a tax perspective, the first important consideration is the dichotomy between debt and equity capital. The general rule is that the cost of debt capital is deductible for tax purposes, whereas equity capital is financed with after-tax dollars. The deductibility of interest expenses and the non-deductibility of dividends for tax purposes colours most business acquisitions and explains the enormous amount of debt financing in Canada.

The second structural characteristic of the tax system which influences financing decisions is that intercorporate dividends generally flow on a tax-free basis. This means that equity or near-equity financing can be attractive to the lender if it is paid in the form of dividends. The avenues for after-tax financing are, however, substantially closed with the tightening of the rules in respect of taxable preferred shares.[1]

---

[1] See Parts IV.1 and VI.1 of the Act.

One of the early decisions to be made in the purchase and sale of a business is the manner in which the acquisition will be structured. This decision has an important effect on the ultimate purchase price of the business because it directly affects the net proceeds that the vendor receives from the sale.

Two common methods for the acquisition of a business are through the purchase of its assets or, in the case of a corporation, the purchase of its shares.

There are no absolute rules that indicate invariable preference of one method over the other. Each acquisition is influenced by facts that are unique to the particular business. In general terms, however, the purchaser and vendor should look at the following:

- The tax status of the purchaser, the target business ("Targetco"), and Targetco's shareholders. If Targetco is a Canadian-controlled private corporation ("CCPC"), there will be some integration of corporate and shareholder taxes for its shareholders who are Canadian residents.
- The tax rates of Targetco and its shareholders.
- The tax rate of the purchaser and its marginal cost of capital.
- The type of income that the sale of Targetco will generate. A sale of shares generally triggers capital gains. A sale of assets usually triggers a mixture of ordinary income and capital gains. The relative amount of each of these types of income has a bearing on the net proceeds that Targetco's shareholders receive.
- The basis of Targetco's assets and its shares.
- The amount of "safe income" (generally after-tax retained earnings) on Targetco's books.
- The value of any tax deferrals under each of the alternatives, asset purchase and share purchase.
- The presence of accumulated losses in Targetco and the purchaser's prospects of utilizing the losses.
- The presence of tax free accounts, such as the "capital dividend account", that may be extracted at nil cost prior to the sale of the business.
- The business complexities of completing the transaction as an asset or share acquisition.

2. FINANCIAL STATEMENTS

The decision to acquire a business, whether by purchasing its assets or shares, relies heavily on the accuracy of its financial statements. In an asset acquisition, the financial statements disclose valuable information about the cost and basis of assets, the face value of liabilities and shareholder loans. In a share purchase, the financial statements provide the underpinning of the purchase price, namely, the corporation's earning stream.

But financial statements, despite their aura of exactitude and precision, have limitations. To be sure, an audit of financial statements and the expression of a clean opinion on them provides some level of comfort in their accuracy. It cannot be overstated, however, that an audit opinion is just that: An "opinion". An audit opinion merely expresses the view of the auditors that the financial statements "present fairly the results of operations in accordance with generally accepted accounting principles on a basis consistent with that of the preceding year". It is not a certification of accuracy in respect of every detail of each asset or liability represented on the financial statement.

There are many versions of generally accepted accounting principles, each of which may be suitable in appropriate circumstances, but which produce widely divergent results in the valuation of a business enterprise. Auditors are concerned only that the financial statements do not *materially* misstate the underlying financial picture of a business. Materiality is an elastic concept that will produce varied interpretations in the event of a dispute between the purchaser and the vendor. Hence, it is prudent to carefully consider the content and substance of the financial statements prior to the execution of the agreement of purchase and sale.

There are many aspects of financial statements that should be taken into account in the preparation of an agreement of purchase and sale of a business. For example:

- Financial statements are traditionally prepared on an historical cost assumption and do not reflect, in most cases, the market value of assets unless there is a permanent and substantial decline of market values below cost.

- Financial statements are prepared *as at* a particular date and their usefulness declines exponentially with their age.

- The historical cost of assets shown in the financial statements may not reflect their basis for tax purposes, particularly if they were acquired in non-arm's length transactions at values other than fair market value.

- The market value of accounts receivable depends upon their collectibility. The allowance for doubtful accounts on the balance sheet is only an estimate and reflects management's perception of the collectibility of the outstanding accounts. As will all the other values reflected on the financial statements, the estimate of uncollectible accounts is valid only as of the date at which the estimate was made. Subsequent events (for example, the insolvency of a major customer) may have an important effect on the value of the *net* accounts collectible.

- The valuation of inventory, particularly in a manufacturing enterprise, reflects many accounting assumptions. Inventory may be valued on the basis of any of several equally acceptable accounting principles, each of which produces different results. The value of inventory also reflects management's judgment as to the condition and viability of the inventory.

- Finally, and most importantly, historical cost financial statements do not reflect any value of what may be the enterprise's most valuable asset: Goodwill. A successful business is valued at a premium to the net fair market value of its assets. The premium, which in effect recognizes the enterprise's internally generated goodwill, is an important element in the determination of the ultimate purchase price.

To summarize: The financial statements of a business enterprise are a useful *starting* point in the determination of its value. They are, however, just that: A starting point. The purchaser needs to ensure that the tax values and basis of the business assets are fully and properly disclosed. Thus, the purchaser will want to confirm, and obtain representations on, the amount of tax losses, tax reserves, the capital dividend account balance, the amount of refundable dividend tax on hand, and the status of outstanding tax assessments.

3. MODE OF ACQUISITION

Business acquisitions require an evaluation of:

- Choice of structure;
- Form of acquisition;
- Financing;
- Location of acquiring structure;
- Securitization of assets and contracts;
- Valuation of assets and liabilities;
- Transfer of contracts and statutory relationships and obligations; and
- Tax considerations in respect of all of the above.

Thus, there are two broad categories of tax decisions to be made in the acquisition of a domestic business as a going concern: (1) How is the business to be acquired? and (2) In what form is the business to be held? International acquisitions involve additional considerations such as the location of the acquiring entity and double tax treaties.

Business acquisitions typically occur through:

- A purchase of the assets of a going business;
- An acquisition of shares; or
- An amalgamation of corporations.

The method selected depends upon business and tax factors, the source of financing, and the significance of minority ownership interests.

The term "acquisition" is used in the present context to describe any transaction in which a buyer acquires all or substantially all of the assets and business of a seller or all or a control portion of the share capital of the seller in a voluntary transaction between a willing buyer and a willing seller. The term is not used here to describe a takeover in which the seller's management is an unwilling partner to the acquisition (for example, a hostile takeover).

Traditionally, the most popular methods of acquisitions are the purchase of assets and the purchase of shares. Each of these methods has certain business and tax advantages and disadvantages. Whether a particular method is more suitable than another depends upon the particular circumstances and the reasons for the acquisition.

Business acquisitions involve two different but interrelated decisions: (1) Price; and (2) Form and financing. The latter almost invariably influences the former. The first decision is a business decision, the second is "tax-driven".

(a) Assets vs. Shares

Having decided upon an acquisition, the next decision (if there is a choice) is on the form of the acquisition. Generally speaking, if the business is incorporated, the seller will want to sell his or her shares in the corporation, in order to claim the gain as a capital gain. An asset acquisition generally involves a greater tax liability, because inventory gains and recaptured capital cost allowance are fully taxable as income.[2]

In contrast, the purchaser usually prefers to acquire assets in order to step up the "basis" of the assets acquired so that he or she can claim capital cost allowance on the stepped-up basis. A purchaser of assets also knows exactly what he or she is buying and is not exposed to the risk of assuming any hidden and contingent liabilities.

There are, however, circumstances where the purchaser may prefer to acquire the shares of a corporation rather than its assets. For example, a purchaser may prefer to purchase shares if he or she is interested in acquiring the corporation's losses and intends to continue operating the acquired business.

(b) Amalgamations

The third method of business acquisition is by way of amalgamation. An amalgamation involves a merger of two or more corporations to form a new corporation. In certain circumstances, corporate amalgamation is the preferred method of acquiring a business because of the availability of tax-free rollovers.[3] This method,

---

[2]   Subs. 13(1).

[3]   S. 87.

however, can be used only if all of the corporations to be merged are subject to the same corporate legislation.[4]

4. PURCHASE AND SALE OF ASSETS

(a) General

A business can be acquired by purchasing its assets and liabilities *in toto*. The disposition of an *entire* business constitutes a capital transaction and the proceeds of sale are capital receipts to the vendor. Similarly, the acquisition of a business is usually considered a capital expenditure.[5]

There are, however, a multitude of provisions which vary these general rules, and each category and type of asset must be separately considered to determine the tax consequences that flow from its acquisition or disposition.

(b) Purchaser's Perspective

(i) Advantages

There are several advantages to purchasing a business by acquiring its assets and liabilities *in toto*.

- **Elimination of minority interests:**
  If the business is carried on by a corporation, the purchaser is not encumbered with minority shareholdings from the acquired business. The minority shareholders are, however, entitled to dissent if the corporation sells all of its assets. If they do, they are entitled to be bought out at the fair value of their shares.[6]

- **Limitation of liability:**
  The purchaser acquires only the liabilities stipulated in the agreement of purchase and sale and, subject to "bulk sales" legislation, is not generally liable for the vendor's undisclosed liabilities.

- A purchaser can be more selective in an asset acquisition and exclude any assets that are not required.

---

[4] See Chapter XXIV "Mergers and Dissolutions".

[5] *Frankel Corp. v. M.N.R.*, [1959] CTC 244, 59 DTC 1161 (S.C.C.) (sale of inventory is part of sale of taxpayer's business, proceeds not taxable as business income); *The Queen v. Farquhar Bethune Ins. Ltd.*, [1982] CTC 282, 82 DTC 6239 (F.C.A.) (purchase of customer lists and a covenant of non-competition constituted the acquisition of a capital asset); *Cumberland Invt. Ltd. v. The Queen*, [1975] CTC 439, 75 DTC 5309 (F.C.A.) (payment by insurance agency to competitor for latter's list of sub-agents, insurance policies and card index system was an acquisition of a capital asset).

[6] See, e.g., *Canada Business Corporations Act*, R.S.C. 1985, c. C-44, subss. 189(3), 190(1).

- **Allocation of purchase price:**
  The purchaser can negotiate the allocation of the purchase price among the assets acquired. In an arm's length transaction, the negotiated allocation will usually determine the tax cost or the basis of the acquired assets.[7]

- **Step-up in cost base:**
  The fair market value of business assets will usually exceed their tax basis. By negotiating appropriate purchase price allocations, the purchaser can usually step-up the cost base of the depreciable assets acquired and obtain larger CCA write-offs in future. Similarly, the purchaser can step-up the basis of non-depreciable and other assets and reduce the amount of capital gains that may ultimately be realized on disposition of the assets. This can be particularly important if the purchaser intends to divest any assets with accrued gains in the near future.

(ii) Disadvantages

There are also some disadvantages to asset acquisitions. For example:

- **Complexity:**
  An asset acquisition is a complex transaction, because it involves the transfer of individual assets, registration of title transfers and assignment of leases, contracts and franchises. It can also involve other taxes (e.g., land transfer taxes) on the transfer of certain assets.

- **Consents to transfers:**
  The seller may need consent to transfer non-assignable contracts such as leases, licence agreements and franchises. Obtaining the consent of third parties may be difficult and expensive.

- **Bulk sales laws:**
  To avoid liability to creditors, it is usually necessary to comply with the bulk sales laws of the jurisdiction in which the seller's assets are located.[8] The purpose of bulk sales legislation is to protect the creditors of the seller and to discourage a disposition of assets in bulk, leaving behind unpaid creditors. Non-compliance with the provisions of the relevant bulk sales legislation renders the sale voidable and the purchaser liable to the seller's creditors.

- **Contractual restrictions:**
  The seller's long term debt obligations may contain covenants which restrict the sale of assets that have been pledged as security to creditors.

- Because of the increased tax basis available to the purchaser (and the resulting increased proceeds to the seller), the purchaser will generally have to pay a higher price to acquire assets than for shares. Thus, the purchase price for a

---

[7] See, however, s. 68.

[8] See, e.g., *Bulk Sales Act*, R.S.O. 1990, c. B.14.

business depends upon whether the purchase is structured as an asset or share acquisition.

(c) Seller's Perspective

The shareholders of a corporation generally prefer a share sale over an asset sale.

(i) Advantages

- A share sale usually triggers a capital gain for a shareholder. Since only three-quarters of a capital gain is subject to tax, shareholders usually prefer to dispose of their shares rather than the assets of the corporation. This consideration is that much more important if the shareholder can claim the $500,000 "super-exemption" on the sale of shares of a small business corporation.

- Purchase and sale of shares is generally a less complicated transaction than an asset sale. This is because a share sale does not require individual identification of every asset and allocation of the purchase price to each asset or group of assets. In any event, a sale of assets is simply not possible in the case of a large corporation with a diversified asset base spread over multiple locations in several jurisdictions.

- A sale of appreciated assets results in recaptured capital cost allowance and other income gains to the corporation. A further tax is payable on the distribution of income from the corporation to its shareholders. A share sale bypasses these problems of double taxation by eliminating any direct tax consequences to the corporation.

(ii) Disadvantages

- A share sale may not be advantageous if the corporation has accumulated tax losses. An asset sale may be more beneficial if gains from the sale of assets can be offset against corporate tax losses. In such circumstances, the shareholders may prefer to see the corporation's losses utilized to shelter any gains that result from the disposition of assets. This consideration is relevant if the shareholders do not withdraw funds from the corporation but reinvest their proceeds.

(d) Allocation of Purchase Price

The allocation of the purchase price among the assets purchased is one of the most significant tax issues in an asset acquisition. The allocation affects both the purchaser and the seller and will almost invariably influence the acquisition price of the assets.

The purchase price must be allocated on a reasonable basis among the assets acquired. The allocation should be part of the agreement of purchase and sale. In the absence of a written agreement, the Minister may challenge the allocation of the price between the parties. This can lead to valuation disputes and, in the absence of a satisfactory resolution of such problems, to protracted litigation regarding the fair market value of the assets purchased.

The allocation of the purchase price to the assets determines the proceeds of disposition of each property sold and the cost basis of each property acquired by the purchaser.

(i) Purchaser's Perspective

From the purchaser's perspective, it is generally preferable to allocate the maximum amount possible to assets in the following sequence of priority:

- Inventory;
- Depreciable capital property;
- Eligible capital property; and
- Non-depreciable capital property.

The purchaser should allocate as much of the total purchase price as possible to the first two categories, inventory and depreciable capital property. Costs allocated to inventory will be fully deductible as cost of goods sold. Amounts allocated to depreciable capital property will form the basis of capital cost allowance claims in the future. The larger the cost base, the greater the write-off.

In contrast, only three-quarters of amounts allocated to goodwill and other eligible capital property are deductible on a declining balance basis at a rate of 7 per cent.

Amounts allocated to non-depreciable capital property cannot be deducted at all, but will reduce the amount of any capital gains that may be realized on the disposition of the property in the future.

(ii) Vendor's Perspective

The vendor should negotiate to allocate the global selling price with the opposite priorities. From the vendor's perspective, it is best to assign the highest amounts to assets in the following sequence:

- Non-depreciable capital property;
- Eligible capital property;
- Depreciable capital property; and
- Inventory.

Non-depreciable capital property triggers capital gains; depreciable property triggers recapture and capital gains; and inventory gains are fully taxable as income.

(e) Section 68

The purchaser and the vendor are required to allocate the purchase and sale price to the assets sold. The allocation must be on some reasonable basis, which is generally considered to be the fair market value of the assets at the time of the transaction. Where the seller and the purchaser are at arm's length and bargain with each other with opposing economic interests, Revenue Canada will usually consider the negotiated allocation of the purchase price as fair and reasonable.

But even parties who are at arm's length with each other may not have truly opposing economic interests. For example, a non-taxable entity that sells its assets is unlikely to be concerned about potential recapture of capital cost allowance or inventory gains that may result from the sale. Similarly, a taxable entity with large accumulated losses may be prepared to agree to an allocation of convenience in exchange for a higher overall selling price for its assets.

The allocation of the total price by the seller and the purchaser in the agreement of purchase and sale is usually acceptable for income tax purposes.[9] Where the parties do not make the allocation, it may be necessary to obtain expert testimony supported by a valuation of the various assets.

To prevent manipulations of asset price allocations, section 68 of the Act allows the Minister to set aside an otherwise legal agreement, substitute reasonable amounts in lieu of the amounts allocated by the purchaser and seller, and bind both parties to the revised allocation.[10]

(i) Land and Buildings

Some of the most difficult price allocation problems arise in the context of real property, particularly where land and buildings are sold to a person who is interested in acquiring only the land and not the buildings situated thereon. What happens, for example, if the purchaser demolishes the building immediately after purchasing the property? Can it be said that the seller actually received any proceeds of disposition in respect of the building? Should all of the proceeds be allocated to the land?

---

[9] See, generally, *Herb Payne Tpt. Ltd. v. M.N.R.*, [1963] CTC 116, 63 DTC 1075 (Ex. Ct.) (court arbitrated the values of the assets adopted by each party); *Klondike Helicopters Ltd. v. M.N.R.*, [1965] CTC 427, 65 DTC 5253 (Ex. Ct.); Ward, "Tax Considerations Relating to the Purchase of Assets of a Business", *Corp. Mgmt. Tax Conf. 22* (Can. Tax Foundation, 1972).

[10] *The Queen v. Golden*, [1986] 1 CTC 274, 86 DTC 6138 (S.C.C.) (validity of s. 68 upheld); *Crawford Logging Co. v. M.N.R.* (1962), 29 Tax ABC 436, 62 DTC 421 (breakdown of consideration for sale of logging equipment disregarded as unrealistic); *Blackstone Hldg. Ltd. v. M.N.R.* (1966), 41 Tax ABC 224, 66 DTC 417 (valuations for hotel, land and goodwill set aside in favour of apportionment between land and building proportionate to municipal assessment values); *Can. Propane Gas & Oil Ltd. v. M.N.R.*, [1972] CTC 566, 73 DTC 5019 (F.C.T.D.) (Minister's apportionment preferred over taxpayer's in absence of any real bargaining between parties as to breakdown of price); *Clement's Drug Store (Brandon) Ltd. v. M.N.R.*, [1968] CTC 53, 68 DTC 5053 (Ex. Ct.) (in absence of sham or subterfuge, contract between arm's length parties should govern apportionment); *Klondike Helicopters Ltd. v. M.N.R.*, [1965] CTC 427, 65 DTC 5253 (Ex. Ct.) (price of $50,000 for depreciable property admittedly worth $71,300 upheld by court in absence of evidence of sham or subterfuge); *Kerim Bros. Ltd. v. M.N.R.*, [1967] Tax ABC 438, 67 DTC 326 (in arm's length sale of business, amount imputed by parties to depreciable property accepted over fair market value); *Co-op. Agricole de Granby v. M.N.R.*, [1970] Tax ABC 969, 70 DTC 1620 (consideration allotted by agreement unalterable by purchaser in light of appraisal subsequently obtained).

The general test used to determine the reasonableness of allocated values is to ask whether the building has economic value *to the seller* at the time of the sale of the property. Merely because the purchaser does not see any value in the building, and demolishes it immediately upon acquiring it, does not mean that the building does not have economic value to the seller. It means only that it has no value to the purchaser.[11] Where, however, the seller is really selling land, and does not receive any *additional* proceeds for the building, it is reasonable to allocate the entire proceeds to the land.[12]

(ii) Sale of Land Only

Where the purchaser is interested in acquiring only the land, and not the buildings situated on the land, the parties may agree to sell the property "clear of all buildings". Special rules apply, however, where buildings are demolished *prior* to their sale. In such circumstances, the proceeds of disposition of the demolished building are, in effect, determined *as if* it had been sold at its fair market value.[13] Thus, the vendor cannot avoid recapture of capital cost allowance by selling the property "clear of all buildings".

Example XXV.1

Assume that a taxpayer owns one building, to which the following data applies:

	Land	Building	Total
Adjusted cost base/capital cost	$ 200,000	$ 160,000	$ 360,000
Undepreciated capital cost (UCC)	—	$ 100,000	—
Fair market value to vendor	$ 240,000	$ 160,000	$ 400,000

---

[11] Stanley v. M.N.R., [1967] Tax ABC 1048, 67 DTC 700; affirmed [1969] CTC 430, 69 DTC 5286; affirmed [1972] CTC 34, 72 DTC 6004 (S.C.C.).

[12] *Moulds v. The Queen*, [1977] CTC 126, 77 DTC 5094; affirmed [1978] CTC 146, 78 DTC 6068 (F.C.A.); see *Mora Bldg. Corp. v. M.N.R.*, [1967] Tax ABC 365, 67 DTC 275 (proceeds of disposition may be allocated on basis of municipal assessments); *Flanders Installation Ltd. v. M.N.R.*, [1967] Tax ABC 1018, 68 DTC 9 (reasonable apportionment between land and building based on expert evidence and municipal assessment); *Coulter v. M.N.R.*, [1968] Tax ABC 369, 68 DTC 335 (in absence of allocation in deed of sale, Minister's allocation on basis of municipal assessment upheld); *Samuel-Jay Invt. Ltd. v. M.N.R.*, [1968] Tax ABC 552, 68 DTC 439 (allocation based on municipal assessment); *Hamilton v. M.N.R.*, [1969] Tax ABC 831, 69 DTC 580 (apportionment based on municipal assessment in absence of first-hand evidence of land values).

[13] Subs. 13(21.1). This rule was introduced to reverse *Malloney's Studio Ltd. v. The Queen*, [1979] CTC 206, 79 DTC 5124 (S.C.C.) (taxpayer allowed to allocate entire proceeds of disposition to land where buildings on land had been demolished prior to sale).

Example XXV.1 (continued)

The taxpayer tears down the building and sells the land for $400,000. *In the absence of the special rule* in subsection 13(21.1), the taxpayer would realize a capital gain of $200,000 and a terminal loss of $100,000. Under subsection 13(21.1), however, the proceeds of disposition of the demolished building are calculated as the *lesser* of:

(1) Aggregate proceeds of land and building		$ 400,000
Exceeds *lesser* of,		
ACB of land	$ 200,000	
FMV of land	$ 240,000	
		$ (200,000)
		$ 200,000 (1)
and		
(2) *Greater* of,		
FMV of building	$ 160,000	
UCC of building	$ 100,000	
		$ 160,000 (2)
Proceeds of disposition (lesser of (1) and (2))		$ 160,000

In effect, the taxpayer is forced to recognize his recapture of capital cost allowance of $60,000, which is the amount he would have had to recognize had he not demolished the building. The proceeds of disposition of the land are $240,000, which is also the amount fairly attributable to the land.

(f) Arm's Length Transactions

Subject to section 68, where the purchaser and the seller deal with each other at arm's length, the negotiated purchase price of assets determines the seller's proceeds of disposition and the purchaser's cost of the property. The price of each asset is usually specified in the agreement of purchase and sale. The purchaser can increase the price set out in the agreement by the amount of any transfer taxes, professional fees, commissions, finders fees, etc.[14]

(g) Non-arm's Length Transactions

Where the purchaser and the seller are not dealing with each other at arm's length, the seller's proceeds of disposition and the purchaser's acquisition costs are determined as follows:

---

[14] See IT-285R2, "Capital Cost Allowance — General Comments" (March 31, 1994).

- Where the purchaser acquires a property at an amount in *excess* of its fair market value, he or she is deemed to have acquired the property at its fair market value and not at the higher amount stipulated in the agreement of purchase and sale.[15] The seller is taxed on the basis of the actual proceeds of sale and not upon the lower figure attributed to the purchaser.

- Where a taxpayer disposes of property for *less* than its fair market value, he or she is deemed to have received proceeds of disposition equal to its fair market value.[16] The purchaser's cost of acquisition is determined by the amount actually paid for the property, and not by the seller's deemed proceeds of disposition.

(h) Accounts Receivable

(i) General Rules

In computing income from a business or property, an accrual basis taxpayer may claim a reserve for doubtful accounts receivable which have been included in his or her income.[17] An amount claimed as a reserve in one year is brought into income in the following year.[18] The taxpayer may then claim a new reserve based upon a new appraisal as to the collectability of accounts receivable.

A bad debt (as opposed to one that is merely doubtful of collection) may be written off against income.[19] A bad debt is not brought back into income in the following year *unless* it is actually recovered.[20]

Accounts receivable are usually sold at a discount from their face value. The discount reflects the difficulty and expense of collecting accounts receivable.

The sale of accounts receivable at less than their face value generally gives rise to a capital loss.[21] Thus, the vendor, who previously included sales, which gave rise to the receivables, as income can offset the discount against the sales, but only as capital losses.

The seller cannot claim a reserve in the year of sale, since no debts will be owing to him or her at the end of the year.

---

[15] Para. 69(1)(*a*).

[16] Para. 69(1)(*b*).

[17] Para. 20(1)(*l*).

[18] Para. 12(1)(*d*).

[19] Para. 20(1)(*p*).

[20] Para. 12(1)(*i*); see IT-442R, "Bad Debts and Reserves for Doubtful Debts" (September 6, 1991).

[21] *Doughty v. Comm. of Taxes*, [1927] AC 327 (P.C.) [N.Z.].

A purchaser of accounts receivable acquires a capital asset.[22] Hence, any gain or loss on subsequent collection of the accounts is considered a capital gain loss.

The purchaser cannot claim a reserve for doubtful accounts, since the receivables were not previously included in his or her income.

Thus, both the vendor and the purchaser may be prejudiced when accounts receivable are sold as part of an asset acquisition. A special rule is necessary to relieve against hardship in these circumstances.

(ii) Section 22 Election

Reference:

BULLETINS, CIRCULARS & RULINGS:

IT-188R   May 22, 1984   Sale of Accounts Receivable

Where a taxpayer who has been carrying on a business sells all, or substantially all, of the property (including accounts receivable) used in the business to a purchaser who proposes to continue the business, the seller and the purchaser can elect jointly to have the full amount of any loss on the sale of receivables deducted from the seller's income and included in the purchaser's income for the year.[23]

(A) Effect on Seller

In the absence of an election, a taxpayer who sells all of his or her accounts receivable may not claim a reserve in respect of doubtful debts in the year in which the receivables are sold. In addition, the taxpayer must bring into income any reserve for doubtful debts claimed by him or her in the preceding year.[24] Any discount on the sale of the receivables is considered a capital loss.

Where, however, the parties elect under section 22, the seller may claim a deduction from income for any discount, to the extent that the receivables have not been written off previously as a bad debt expense.[25] Thus, the effect of the election is to convert what would otherwise be a capital loss from the discount into a deduction from income.

---

[22] *Crompton v. Reynolds* (1952), 33 Tax Cas. 288 (H.L.).

[23] S. 22.

[24] Para. 12(1)(*d*).

[25] Para. 22(1)(*a*).

Example XXV.2	
Assume that a taxpayer sells his accounts receivable on the following basis:	
Face value	$ 100,000
Sale price	85,000
Bad debts written off	2,000
Reserve previously claimed	5,000
Then, assuming that the parties elect under subsection 22(1):	
Face price	$ 100,000
Sale value	$ (85,000)
Discount on sale	$ 15,000
Bad debts written off	(2,000)
Net deduction from income	$ 13,000

Thus, it is generally to the seller's advantage to elect under subsection 22(1) if the receivables are sold at a substantial discount. On the other hand, the seller will not usually benefit from the election if the receivables are sold at their face value.

(B) Effect on Purchaser

The election also requires the purchaser to include in his or her income the amount that the seller deducts from his or her income in that year.[26] In the above example, the purchaser must include $13,000 in income in the year in which he or she purchases the business assets. The overall result of the election to the purchaser and the vendor is to allow them to treat losses from accounts receivables as business losses rather than capital losses.

The advantage to the purchaser of making the election is that he or she can claim a deduction in respect of any of the receivables that later prove to be uncollectible. This is so even though the debts did not arise in the ordinary course of business.[27]

Hence, it is not usually to the purchaser's advantage to elect under section 22 if the receivables are purchased at a substantial discount, since the amount of the discount is fully taxable income.

---

[26] Para. 22(1)(b).

[27] Para. 22(1)(c).

The purchaser benefits from the election if the receivables are sold at face value, since it is possible that some of the accounts will not be collected. In such a case, the purchaser will want to claim a reserve for doubtful debts or a deduction for bad debts.

(C) Non-arm's Length Sales

Although the election under section 22 is binding upon the vendor and the purchaser, it is not binding upon the Minister if the amount paid for the receivables is at variance with their fair market value and the parties do not deal with each other at arm's length.[28]

Example XXV.3

Assume that in 1995 S sold an unincorporated business to P on the following basis:

Face value of accounts receivable not previously written off as bad debts	$ 78,000
Reserve for doubtful accounts claimed by S (1994)	$ 4,000
Bad debts written off by S (1994)	$ 2,000
Purchase price allocated to receivables	$ 70,000
Bad debts recovered by P on account of receivables purchased (1995)	$ 500
Estimated reserve for doubtful accounts from receivables purchased (1995)	$ 3,000
Bad debts written off by P (1995)	$ 200

S and P elect jointly under section 22.

Then, *effect on the seller (S)*:

Face value of receivables not previously written off as bad debts	$ 78,000
Purchase price of receivables	(70,000)
Discount deductible from income	$ 8,000
Reserve for doubtful accounts (1994)	(4,000)
Net deduction from income in 1995	$ 4,000

---

[28] Subs. 22(2).

Example XXV.3 (continued)

Effect on the purchaser (P):

Face value of receivables purchased	$ 78,000
Purchase price paid for receivables	(70,000)
Discount included in income	$ 8,000
Bad debts recovered	500
	$ 8,500
Reserve for doubtful accounts (1995)	(3,000)
Bad debts written off	(200)
Net addition to income in 1995	$ 5,300

(i) Inventory

References:

ITA:

S. 23   Sale of Inventory

BULLETINS, CIRCULARS & RULINGS:

IT-287R	July 15, 1988	Sale of Inventory
TR-25	January 26, 1976	Land Developer: Disposal of Lots *en bloc*
TR-39	October 18, 1976	Qualified Income for the Purchase of an Income-Averaging Annuity Contract

At common law, where a business disposed of its entire inventory, any gain or loss from the disposition would be considered a capital gain or loss.[29]

Section 23 of the Act provides otherwise: A taxpayer who disposes of inventory in a bulk sale upon ceasing to carry on a business is deemed to have sold the inventory in the course of business, and the proceeds are considered to be normal sales.[30] Thus, what would have been a capital gain under general legal principles is considered to be business income for tax purposes.

As noted above, subject to sections 68 and 69, a purchaser will usually find it advantageous to allocate as much as possible to the cost of inventory, in order to reduce future profits on its sale.

[29] *Doughty v. Commr. of Taxes, ante; Frankel Corp. v. M.N.R., ante; M.N.R. v. McCord Street Sites Ltd.,* [1962] CTC 387, 62 DTC 1229 (Ex. Ct.) (sand sold with sand business resulted in capital receipt).

[30] "Inventory" includes the inventory of a farmer who calculates income according to the cash method of accounting.

(j) Depreciable Property

Depreciable capital property is capital property in respect of which the owner can claim capital cost allowance ("CCA"). Depreciable capital property is divided into two broad categories: (1) Assets with a fixed term (leaseholds, patents, etc.), and (2) Assets of prescribed classes which are depreciated on a declining balance basis. There are approximately thirty-five classes of depreciable property.

(i) General Rules

The cost of depreciable properties of each class is "pooled" and CCA is claimed as a percentage of each separate pool. The amount of CCA claimed on a class in a year is deducted from the balance in the pool. The balance in a pool of assets is referred to as the undepreciated capital cost (UCC) of the class.

When an asset is sold, the UCC of the class to which the asset belonged is reduced by the amount that the taxpayer receives as net proceeds from the disposition.

Net proceeds from dispositions of depreciable property are allocated to assets, either on an asset-by-asset or on a class-by-class basis, and credited towards the undepreciated capital cost of the relevant class. Net proceeds are the proceeds of disposition less any expenses incurred for the purpose of the disposition.

The maximum amount that may be credited to a class in respect of any property is its capital cost.[31] Proceeds in excess of the capital cost of assets trigger a capital gain.

Any credit (negative) balance in the undepreciated capital cost of a class as at the *end* of the taxation year is included in income as recapture of capital cost allowance.[32] A taxpayer can reduce or eliminate the effect of recapture of capital cost allowance by purchasing assets of the *same* class prior to the end of its taxation year.

Recapture of depreciation on assets used by a Canadian-controlled private corporation in active business is eligible for the small business deduction and, where appropriate, the manufacturing and processing credit.

A debit (positive) balance remaining in the class may be deducted from income as a terminal loss, provided that the taxpayer has disposed of *all* of the property in that class.[33]

Proceeds of disposition in excess of the capital cost of the property give rise to a capital gain. A disposition of depreciable property cannot give rise to a capital loss.[34]

---

[31] Subs. 13(21) ("undepreciated capital cost") (F).

[32] Subs. 13(1).

[33] Subs. 20(16).

[34] Para. 39(1)(*b*).

The allocation of the purchase price of a business to assets is a crucial element in the negotiations leading to the acquisition. In particular, the allocation of amounts to depreciable property can have a significant effect on both the purchaser and the seller. From the purchaser's perspective, the amount allocated to depreciable property represents the basis against which future charges to income will be made. From the seller's perspective, amounts allocated to each pool of assets determine the amount of recaptured CCA capital gains.

A purchaser will generally prefer a higher proportion of the total proceeds of disposition of depreciable property to be allocated to classes with high rates of depreciation. Indeed, one of the attractive aspects of an acquisition of a business through the purchase of its assets is that it allows the purchaser to step-up the cost base of the assets for purposes of future capital cost allowance claims. The vendor generally prefers to allocate a higher percentage of the price to those classes of depreciable property that trigger the least recapture of capital cost allowance.

(ii) Land and Buildings

References:

ITA:

Subs. 13(21.1)   Disposition of a Building

BULLETINS, CIRCULARS & RULINGS:

| IT-220R2 | May 25, 1990 | Capital Cost Allowance — Proceeds of Disposition of Depreciable Property |

Where a taxpayer disposes of land and buildings together in a single transaction, the proceeds of disposition must be allocated between the two assets.[35]

The purchaser will usually want to allocate the highest amount possible to buildings, so as to be able to claim capital cost allowance on the stepped-up cost of the assets. Sometimes the very reason for the purchaser acquiring assets rather than shares is to step up the capital cost of the depreciable assets acquired.[36]

In contrast, it is usually to the seller's advantage to have as much as is reasonably possible allocated to the land and the least amount possible allocated to the buildings. This maximizes the capital gain and minimizes recapture of CCA.

A special rule applies, however, where a building is sold for less than its cost amount in order to create a tax loss.

---

[35] S. 68; but see *Golden v. The Queen*, [1983] CTC 112, 83 DTC 5138; affirmed [1986] 1 CTC 274, 86 DTC 6138 (S.C.C.).

[36] But see Reg. 1102(1)(c) (taxpayer may claim CCA only on assets required for purpose of earning income from business or property).

Where a taxpayer[37] disposes of a building for less than its cost amount and, in the same year, disposes of the land subjacent or contiguous to the building, the proceeds of disposition from the two transactions can be reallocated from the land to the building.[38] In the simplest case, subsection 13(21.1) operates to deem the proceeds of disposition of the building to equal the cost amount (usually the UCC) of the building.

A reallocation can reduce the terminal loss that might otherwise have arisen on the disposition of the building, and may even involve recapture of capital cost allowance previously claimed by the seller. Thus, the loss on the sale of the building is reduced to the extent of any gain on the sale of the land.

Example XXV.4

Assume:

The following data applies to a sale of land and a building. The building, which has a capital cost of $150,000, is demolished *prior* to its sale.

	Land	Building	Total
ACB/UCC	$ 190,000	$ 100,000	$ 290,000
Fair market value to seller	$ 230,000	$ 70,000	$ 300,000
Allocation of proceeds on sale	$ 300,000	NIL	$ 300,000

Then, effect on seller:

	General Rules	Under para. 13(21.1)(*a*)
Building		
Proceeds of disposition	NIL	$ 100,000
UCC	(100,000)	(100,000)
Terminal loss	($100,000)	NIL
Land		
Proceeds of disposition	$ 300,000	$ 200,000
ACB	(190,000)	(190,000)
Capital gain	$ 110,000	$ 10,000
Taxable capital gain	$ 82,500	$ 7,500
Net increase (decrease) in income	$ (17,500)	$ 7,500

---

[37] Or a person with whom the taxpayer is not dealing at arm's length.

[38] Subs. 13(21.1).

Example XXV.4 (continued)

In effect, paragraph 13(21.1)(*a*) applies the terminal loss attributable to the building against the capital gain attributable to the land. The terminal loss of $100,000 reduces the capital gain on the disposition of land from $110,000 to $10,000.

The cost of the land to the purchaser is $300,000, and is not affected by the reallocation of proceeds in the seller's hands.

(k) Capital Property

A disposition of capital property can trigger a capital gain or capital loss. A capital gain results if the net proceeds of disposition exceed the adjusted cost base of the property. A capital loss results to the extent that the net proceeds of disposition are less than the adjusted cost base of the property. Three-quarters of any capital gain is included in the seller's income. Three-quarters of any capital loss is deductible from income.

Allowable capital losses may be carried back three years and applied against any taxable capital gains recognized in those years. Capital losses may be carried forward indefinitely,[39] but may be offset only against future taxable capital gains. Hence, it is important for the seller to determine the allocation of the purchase price so as to trigger the optimum amount of losses utilizable (if any) against capital and income. A seller will usually favour an allocation of the purchase price so as to maximize losses on account of income rather than on account of capital.

From the purchaser's perspective, amounts allocated to capital property become the adjusted cost base of the property. These costs are recoverable by the purchaser only when he or she subsequently disposes of the property. Hence, in most cases, the purchaser usually prefers to allocate as little as possible to non-depreciable capital property since any amounts allocated to such property can only be recovered upon their eventual disposition.

(l) Eligible Capital Property

References:

BULLETINS, CIRCULARS & RULINGS:

IT-123R5	October 30, 1992	Transactions Involving Eligible Capital Property
IT-259R2	September 30, 1985	Exchanges of Property

---

[39] Para. 111(1)(*b*).

| IT-313R | October 10, 1978 | Eligible Capital Property — Ceasing to Carry on Business |
| IT-386R | October 30, 1992 | Eligible Capital Amounts |

"Eligible capital property" refers to intangible capital assets with an unlimited life, such as goodwill, perpetual franchises, customer lists, non-competition clauses and licences.[40]

Goodwill normally encompasses the following:

- Reputation;
- Employee loyalty;
- Favourable commercial contracts;
- Trademarks or trade names;
- Favourable financial relationships;
- Management performance record; and
- Protected markets.

Expenditures on account of eligible capital property are classified as "eligible capital expenditures".[41]

Where a purchaser incurs eligible capital expenditures, 75 per cent of such expenditures go into his or her cumulative eligible capital account. This account may be amortized at 7 per cent per year on a declining balance basis.[42]

A taxpayer who disposes of eligible capital property must reduce his or her cumulative eligible capital account by 75 per cent of the proceeds received in respect of such property. Any negative balance in the cumulative eligible capital account at the end of the taxation year is included in income for the year.[43]

Taxable proceeds from the sale of eligible capital property used to earn active business income qualify as "active business income" for purposes of the small business deduction.

A taxpayer who ceases to carry on a business may deduct from income any balance remaining in the cumulative eligible capital account in respect of that business.[44]

---

[40] S. 54 ("eligible capital property").

[41] Subs. 14(5) ("eligible capital expenditure").

[42] Subs. 14(5) ("cumulative eligible capital"), para. 20(1)(b) (only expenditures after 1971 qualify for amortization).

[43] Subs. 14(1).

[44] Subs. 24(1); IT-313R, "Eligible Capital Property — Ceasing to Carry on Business" (October 10, 1978) (deduction equivalent to terminal loss in respect of undepreciated balance in respect of depreciable property).

The terminal write-off of the cumulative eligible capital account may not be claimed if the terminated business is continued by the taxpayer's spouse or by a corporation controlled directly or indirectly by the taxpayer.[45] Instead, the balance in the cumulative eligible capital account is transferred to the spouse or to the corporation controlled by the taxpayer.

Where a taxpayer disposes of an eligible capital property and replaces the property within one year after the end of the year in which the proceeds of disposition become payable, he or she can elect to defer recognition of recapture of any amortization.[46] In effect, 75 per cent of the cost of the replacement eligible capital property is *retroactively* added back to the taxpayer's cumulative eligible capital account to erase the negative balance which would otherwise be included in income.

Example XXV.5

Assume that *Black Ltd.* acquires and disposes of eligible capital property in the following circumstances:

Balance in cumulative eligible capital ("CEC") 1995	$ 60,000
Proceeds from disposition of perpetual franchise (1996)	$ 200,000
Acquisition of replacement perpetual franchise (1997)	$ 240,000

Black Ltd.'s CEC is calculated as follows:

	General Rules	Subs. 14(6) Election
Opening balance in CEC (1995)	$ 60,000	$ 60,000
3/4 of proceeds of sale (1996)	(150,000)	(150,000)
3/4 of replacement property	—	180,000
Balance in CEC	$ (90,000)	$ 90,000
Recapture under subs. 14(1)	90,000	—
	NIL	$ 90,000
Maximum amortization (7%)	NIL	(6,300)
Closing balance	NIL	$ 83,700

---

[45] Subs. 24(2).

[46] Subs. 14(6). Timing problems arise where the taxpayer files a return for the year in which the property is disposed of before acquiring the replacement property.

(m) Instalment Payments

Interest expense on money borrowed to finance the acquisition of assets is deductible if the assets are acquired for the purpose of earning income from a business or property.[47] If the assets are depreciable property, the purchaser may elect to capitalize the interest expense into the capital cost of the property. Thus the purchaser can defer the immediate expense deduction and claim a larger capital cost allowance on the property.[48] Where the purchaser does elect to capitalize interest, it is necessary to allocate the portion of the interest expense that relates to the money borrowed to finance the depreciable property.

As a general rule, a taxpayer who disposes of property is neither required nor presumed to charge interest in respect of any portion of the consideration payable to him or her on an instalment basis. The determination as to whether an instalment payment is a blend of capital and interest is entirely a question of fact.

(i) Without Interest

Although it is usual in commercial dealings to charge interest on instalment sales, the absence of interest charges does not necessarily mean that the instalments represent a blend of income and capital. It is necessary to look at all of the surrounding circumstances of the transaction to determine whether there is an interest component in the instalment payments. In *Vestey*, for example, the Court said:[49]

> It is necessary to decide whether we are bound to confine our attention to the words of the agreement and the related transfer of shares, and not to have regard for any surrounding circumstances. It appears clear to us on the authorities that we are not only entitled but are bound to consider such of the surrounding circumstances as are proved and admitted in evidence; not in order to vary the legal effect of the agreement and transfer nor to decide the matter by the doctrine (now exploded) of the "substance" of the matter, but in order to ascertain the true nature of the transaction comprised in the agreement. We have to look first at the legal effect of the agreement and then at the surrounding circumstances.

(ii) Blended Payments

Reference:

BULLETINS, CIRCULARS & RULINGS:

IT-265R3   October 7, 1981   Payments of Income and Capital Combined

Where instalment payments represent a blend of interest and capital, the interest component is taxable as income from property and is not considered to be a payment on account of capital.[50] The purchaser may deduct the interest component as an

---

[47] Para. 20(1)(c).

[48] S. 21; see Chapter XI "Other Deductions".

[49] *Vestey v. I.R.C.*, [1962] Ch. 861 at 865.

[50] Subs. 16(1).

expense, provided that it relates to assets acquired for the purpose of earning income from business or property.[51]

The critical factor in determining whether a payment represents a blend of income and capital is the price paid for the property acquired. Where property is sold in an arm's length transaction at a price in excess of its fair market value, there is a strong inference that the price represents both income and capital. A persuasive argument is required to rebut the inference. As the Federal Court said:[52]

> It is well established that in similar cases the prime factor to be considered is whether or not the fair market value has been paid: if the price paid is in excess of fair market value, the excess is deemed interest; if the price reflects the fair market value, then there is no element of interest in the payment.

(n) Prepaid Expenses

A "prepaid expense" is an expenditure which is incurred in one fiscal period but relates to revenues to be realized in a subsequent period. Typical examples include amounts prepaid as rent, insurance, taxes and interest.

"Prepaid expenses" are usually considered assets under generally-accepted accounting principles.[53] As such, they should be charged against revenues in the period to which they relate. As a matter of accounting practice, however, many accountants prefer to write off prepaid expenses in the year in which they are incurred.

For tax purposes, expenses incurred for future services or in respect of specific types of periodic payments can be written off only when the services are actually rendered.[54] Thus, an amount paid by the purchaser to reimburse the vendor for prepaid expenses may be deducted by the purchaser only in the year to which the expenses relate.

From the seller's perspective, any amounts allocated to prepaid expenses are considered as on account of income.

(o) Reserves

A taxpayer who disposes of capital property in a year is entitled to claim a reserve in respect of proceeds of disposition which are not due until a subsequent year. A reserve claimed in one year must be brought into the taxpayer's income in the next

---

[51] Para. 20(1)(c).

[52] *Rodmon Const. Inc. v. The Queen*, [1975] CTC 73 at 75, 75 DTC 5038 at 5039 (F.C.T.D.); IT-265R3, "Payments of Income and Capital Combined" (October 7, 1991); see also *Groulx v. M.N.R.*, [1967] CTC 422, 67 DTC 5284 (S.C.C.) (instalment payments represented blended payments of capital and interest).

[53] See *C.I.C.A. Handbook*, s. 3040.01 ("Prepaid expenses should be classified as current assets").

[54] Subs. 18(9).

year.[55] Thus, where a taxpayer disposes of all of his or her assets, capital gains reserves claimed in the preceding year must be included in income in the year in which the assets are sold.

A taxpayer is also entitled to deduct a reasonable amount as a reserve in respect of advance payments for goods and services which will be delivered or rendered after the end of the year.[56] Here too, a reserve claimed in one year is included in the taxpayer's income in the next year.[57]

(p) Customer Lists

Reference:

BULLETINS, CIRCULARS & RULINGS:

IT-187   November 12, 1974   Customer Lists and Ledger Accounts

Customer lists acquired as part of, or ancillary to, the acquisition of a business as a going concern are considered eligible capital property, not operating expenses.

5. DETERMINATION OF PURCHASE PRICE

The valuation of a business enterprise is an uncertain exercise. This is so regardless whether one is valuing its assets or its shares. The vendor and the purchaser will almost invariably view the business differently and each will have his or her own views on its earnings potential.

The determination of the purchase price of a business is a function of many variables, including, the perception of the owners and the purchasers as to future profitability, the reasons for the purchase and sale, the method of payment, the structure of the transaction and its tax consequences.

Assuming that the acquisition price of assets is determined with the assistance of competent professionals, it is necessary to structure the transaction so as to maximize the advantages from a tax perspective.

A purchaser of assets is generally prepared to pay a higher price for the assets than in an equivalent share acquisition. This is because the purchaser can step-up the basis of the assets and thereby reduce tax through higher write-offs against future income.

Of course, the step-up in the basis of the assets that the purchaser acquires has a correlative detrimental effect on the seller, particularly if the step-up is heavily weighted towards highly depreciated property. The seller is subject to recapture of capital cost

---

[55] Para. 40(1)(*a*); subs. 40(1.1); see also Chapter XII "Computation of Taxable Income".

[56] Para. 20(1)(*m*).

[57] Para. 12(1)(*e*).

allowance, which will be taxable as ordinary income. Hence, the seller will generally demand a higher price for an asset sale than for an equivalent share sale.

An asset sale leaves the seller with a shell corporation with all of its hidden and contingent liabilities. At the same time, the seller cannot take advantage of the special rules in respect of the taxation of capital gains on shares.

The purchase price of an asset acquisition is made up of two principal components: (1) Fair market value of the specific assets, and (2) Goodwill. All assets are valued as of the closing of the transaction.

In a typical asset acquisition, the purchaser will pay an amount that exceeds the aggregate fair market value of the individual assets acquired. The excess amount represents the goodwill of the business, an asset that does not show up on the traditional historical cost balance sheet.

The agreement of purchase and sale of the assets should allocate the global purchase price to the specific assets conveyed. The allocation must be fair and the parties should be mindful of the potential application of section 68. Having said that, however, there is usually a reasonable amount of flexibility in allocating the purchase price to the various assets. Any excess that remains after allocation to the specific assets will be on account of goodwill, which will be considered an eligible capital expenditure in the hands of the purchaser.

6. PAYMENT OF PURCHASE PRICE

The purchase price of a business can be paid in several ways:

• Cash;
• Issuance of debt;
• Assumption of the seller's debt;
• Exchange of property;
• Issuance of shares; or
• Some combination of the above.

Where the purchaser assumes the seller's debt, the purchase price of the acquisition is reduced by the face value of the debt assumed. If the debt carries interest, any interest paid by the purchaser on the debt is deductible[58] as an expense incurred for the purpose of earning income from a business or property.

---

[58] Para. 20(1)(c).

(a) Deferred Payments

(i) Purchaser's Perspective

The purchaser may pay the purchase price by issuing debt (promissory note) to the seller. The debt will be payable over a period of time upon agreed conditions.

Any interest payable on the debt is deductible by the purchaser as an expense incurred to earn income from the acquired business. Blended payments must be broken down into their interest and capital components.

(ii) Reserves

Where the purchaser assumes the seller's debt, the seller will be considered to have disposed of his or her debt at its face amount.

Where the payment of the purchase price is deferred, the seller may be entitled to claim a reserve in respect of the payments to be made in the future. The amount and type of reserve depends upon the nature of the underlying asset sold.

(A) Capital Property

The seller may claim a reserve in respect of that portion of the purchase price that is allocated to capital property. The reserve claimable is limited to the *lesser* of two amounts:[59]

- A "reasonable amount"; and
- An amount determined by reference to a formula.

Revenue Canada accepts as "reasonable" a reserve that is calculated by reference to the following formula:

$$\frac{\text{Amount not payable until after the end of the year}}{\text{Total proceeds of sale}} \times \text{Capital gain}$$

In any event, regardless of what constitutes a "reasonable" reserve, the seller is required to recognize at least 20 per cent of the capital gain in each of the five consecutive years beginning with the year of sale.[60] In other words, the seller cannot claim a reserve that exceeds 80 per cent of the capital gain realized in the year that the capital property is sold.

---

[59] Subpara. 40(1)(*a*)(iii).

[60] Cl. 40(1)(*a*)(iii)(D).

(B) Inventory

A taxpayer who sells inventory is entitled to claim a reserve in respect of unpaid amounts that are not payable until some future date. In the case of inventory (other than land), the reserve may be claimed only if:[61]

- the proceeds from sale of the inventory were previously included in computing the taxpayer's income; and

- all or part of the amount payable at the end of the year is not due for at least two years after the time of sale.

In the case of land inventory the vendor may claim a reserve in respect of his or her profit from the sale of the property to the extent that the proceeds from the sale are payable after the end of the taxation year.

In either case, a reserve in respect of inventory may not be claimed in respect to the sale of property that occurred more than 36 months before the end of the year.[62]

7. EARN-OUTS

One approach to the problem of uncertain valuation of a business is to structure the transaction so that the purchase price depends on the future profitability of the business. Thus, payment of the purchase price can be based on an "earn-out" or "reverse earn-out" arrangement.

In an earn-out arrangement, the purchase price may be increased in the event that the profits of the acquired business exceed a specified amount. In a reverse earn-out, the purchase price is subject to reduction in the event that the profits of the business do not attain a specified level.

Earn-outs and reverse earn-outs can be drafted in a variety of ways to accommodate the circumstances of the acquisition. By their very nature, however, earn-out agreements are complex. The parties need to specify the manner in which profits will be determined for the purposes of triggering the earn-out, the choice of accounting principles, depreciation methods, reserves, bonuses, provisions for contingencies, etc.

Having determined the manner in which profits are calculated, the parties must also resolve whether the step-up or step-down of the purchase price will be for the full variation from the threshold amount or for only some portion thereof.

(a) Vendor's Perspective

Earn-outs have serious tax consequences for the vendor. Paragraph 12(1)(*g*) provides that an amount paid that is dependent upon "the use of or production from

---

[61] Para. 20(1)(*n*).

[62] Para. 20(8)(*b*).

property" is included in *income*, regardless whether the amount is an instalment payment on the purchase price of the property. This provision applies equally to the sale of individual assets and the sale of an entire business.[63] The vendor must include the gross amount of the earnout payment in income, rather than only the gain on the sale of the business. Thus, paragraph 12(1)(*g*) converts what may otherwise have been a capital gain or a gain on eligible capital property (both of which would be taxable at reduced rates) into fully taxable income.

Paragraph 12(1)(*g*) applies to earn-out agreements that are contingent upon future earnings of the acquired business: Only the variable portion of the purchase price is taxable as income, not the fixed component of the purchase price.

(b) Administrative Views

Revenue Canada's views are set out in IT-462 (October 27, 1980). The Department takes the position that:[64]

- Paragraph 12(1)(*g*) applies whether the sale price of the property depends upon gross income, on net income or on any other element that is related to production or use of the property.

- Where the payments under the earn-out agreement are all based on production or use, the vendor must bring into income all amounts that he or she receives under the agreement.

- Where the agreement provides for payments based upon production or use plus a fixed sum, only the former need be taken into income under paragraph 12(1)(*g*) and the fixed amount may be treated as proceeds of disposition.

- Where the agreement provides for a fixed sum but with an additional amount payable upon production or use, the fixed amount is treated as proceeds of disposition and only the additional amount, if any, is brought into income under paragraph 12(1)(*g*).

The most difficult aspect of the Department's position, however, is in respect of earn-out agreements that provide for a minimum sale price but also provide for payments based upon profitability. An earn-out agreement that provides for payments based on profitability but also stipulates that there is to be a minimum sale price will cause the payments based upon production or use to be brought into income regardless of whether they are less than or exceed the minimum sale price. In other words, the minimum sale price is not considered to be the floor of the earn-out agreement.

Paragraph 12(1)(*g*) does not apply to reverse earn-outs where the sale price of the business is originally set at a maximum amount that is equal to the fair market value

---

[63] *Gault v. M.N.R.*, [1965] CTC 261, 65 DTC 5157 (Ex. Ct.).

[64] IT-462, "Payments Based on Production or Use" (October 27, 1980).

of the assets. The portion of the fair price that is subsequently reduced if certain profitability conditions are not met is not subject to the paragraph. The entire proceeds are treated in the ordinary manner and the maximum amount is considered to be the sale price of the property. There must, however, be a reasonable expectation at the time of the disposition of the business that the profitability of the conditions will be met. If, subsequently, the conditions are not met, then an appropriate adjustment is made in the year in which the amount of the reduction in the sale price is known with certainty.

The purchaser of the business under a reverse earn-out agreement is not entitled to claim deductions in respect of the earn-out formula until such time as it is established with certainty that he or she has an absolute obligation to make the payment.[65]

8. PURCHASE OF SHARES

Where a business is operated by a corporation, a purchaser can acquire the business by buying the corporation's shares.

In most circumstances, a vendor of a business will prefer to sell the business by selling the corporation's shares. Share sales typically trigger capital gains to the vendor and only 75 per cent of capital gains are taxable as income. In contrast, an asset sale will usually trigger a mixture of ordinary income gains (recapture of depreciation, inventory) and gains that are taxable on a preferential basis (capital property and eligible capital property gains).

The determination of the share value of a corporation is a complex operation and will involve expert valuation. In a share purchase, the transaction price reflects the value of the business as a total entity, rather than the value of its individual assets. The price is usually determined by capitalizing the earnings of the business and setting as a floor the net realizable value of the business upon liquidation.

Share purchase agreements contain covenants, representations and warranties to ensure that the purchaser receives the value that he or she has bargained for and does not take on the burden of substantial undisclosed liabilities. The representations and warranties in a share purchase agreement are critical because they go to the essence of the transaction, namely, the value bargained for in the share price.

Where the business qualifies as a "small business corporation", there is an added advantage to vendors who sell its shares rather than its assets. A gain on the sale of qualified small business corporation shares will be exempt on capital gains to a maximum of $500,000.[66]

---

[65] *Mandel v. The Queen*, [1980] CTC 130, 80 DTC 6148 (S.C.C.).

[66] See subs. 110.6(2.1).

To qualify for the "super-exemption" on capital gains, the shares must satisfy three tests:[67]

1. The shares must qualify as shares of a "small business corporation" *at the time of the sale;*

2. Throughout the 24-month period prior to the sale, 50 per cent of the fair market value of the assets must be attributable to assets used in an active business carried on primarily in Canada; and

3. Throughout the 24-month period prior to the sale, the shares must not have been owned by anyone other than the vendor or a person or partnership related to the vendor.

Each of these requirements must be satisfied in order to take advantage of the exemption of capital gains.

In the event that the corporation does not qualify as a small business corporation, it can be "purified". Purification may involve a disposition of certain assets, generally through taxfree rollovers, to related corporations so as to qualify the corporation under the various percentage tests for asset use.

(a) Advantages

The advantages of share acquisitions are as follows:

- **Simplicity:**
  If the corporation to be acquired is a private corporation with a few shareholders, it is usually simpler to acquire the corporation's shares rather than its assets. The documentation required is an agreement and a transfer of the share certificates and an entry recording the transfer in the shareholder's register.[68]

- **Assignments:**
  A share acquisition involves a transfer of the entire corporate structure, with assets and liabilities intact. Thus, there are fewer problems with respect to the assignability of leases and other contracts; the consent of third parties is not usually required.

- **Speed:**
  The simplicity of the transfer of share certificates allows the acquisition to be accomplished in a short period of time.

- **Liabilities:**
  Since a corporation is a legal entity, its liabilities are not assumed directly by the purchaser. The corporate entity remains liable for its own liabilities and

---

[67] Subs. 110.6(1) ("qualifed small business corporation share").

[68] See, for example, *Canada Business Corporations Act*, R.S.C. 1985, c. C-44, subss. 50(1), 51(1).

obligations; the purchaser does not become directly obligated with respect to the corporation's liabilities.

(b) Disadvantages

The disadvantages of a share acquisition include:

- **Hidden liabilities:**
  The corporation remains liable for unknown and contingent liabilities. The purchaser cannot limit his or her liability to those specified in the acquisition contract. The purchaser may, however, obtain an indemnity for hidden and contingent liabilities.

- **Minority interests:**
  Where some shareholders of the vendor corporation refuse to sell their shares, the purchaser ends up with a corporation with outstanding minority interests.

- **Securities law:**
  An acquisition of shares may require the registration and clearance of a *prospectus* with the relevant Securities Commission.[69]

- **Compulsory acquisition of minority interests:**
  In certain jurisdictions, where a person acquires 90 per cent or more of a class of shares, the remaining shareholders of that class can require the corporation to acquire their shares.[70] This can involve a substantial cost and create cash flow problems.

(c) Timing of Acquisition

The timing of a share acquisition can be critical. The income tax status of a corporation and the tax treatment of its accounts depends sometimes upon the status of the corporation as at the *end* of the year and sometimes on its status *throughout* the year. For example:

- The small business deduction is available only to a corporation which is a Canadian-controlled private corporation *throughout* its taxation year.[71]
- The small business deduction is allocated amongst corporations that are associated with each other *at any time* in the year.[72]

---

[69] See, e.g., *Securities Act*, R.S.O. 1990, c. S.5, s. 53.

[70] See, for e.g., *Business Corporations Act*, R.S.O. 1990, c. B.16, s. 189.

[71] *Income Tax Act,* subs. 125(1).

[72] Subs. 125(3).

- The Part IV tax on intercorporate dividends is payable by a corporation that was a private corporation *at any time* in the taxation year.[73]
- Where a private corporation controlled directly or indirectly by non-resident persons becomes a Canadian-controlled private corporation, its capital dividend account is eliminated.[74]

(d) Cost Base of Shares Acquired

The adjusted cost base of the shares acquired is equal to the price paid for the shares.[75] The cost of the shares is a capital outlay and is not deductible against the future income of the corporation.

From the vendor's point of view, the sale price of the shares represents proceeds of disposition which will generally give rise to a capital gain.[76] A vendor who is not entitled to his or her entire proceeds in the year of sale may claim a reserve against any capital gain resulting from the sale.[77] The reserve allows the seller to defer recognition of the capital gain.

(e) Covenants and Warranties

Reference:

BULLETINS, CIRCULARS & RULINGS:

IT-330R   September 7, 1990   Dispositions of Capital Property Subject to Warranty, Covenant, or Other Conditional or Contingent Obligations

An agreement of purchase and sale of assets or shares is a contract between the purchaser and the vendor for the transmission of identified property at a determined or determinable price. Thus, the essence of the agreement is the proper identification of the parties, the property to be transferred, the manner in which the purchase price is determined or determinable, the method and timing of payments, and the manner in which undertakings and representations will be satisfied.

The purchase of a business implies reliance upon numerous facts, undertakings and assumptions as to the reliability of its financial and tax information. The purpose of representations, warranties and covenants is to ensure that the risk of non-compliance

---

[73] Subs. 186(1).

[74] Subs. 89(1.1).

[75] S. 54 ("adjusted cost base") (*b*).

[76] See Chapter VIII "Business and Property Income: Deductions".

[77] Para. 40(1)(*a*); see Chapter XII "Computation of Taxable Income".

or the effect of inaccurate information is properly allocated between the purchaser and the vendor. In other words: Who bears the loss when things go wrong?

To be sure, a representation, warranty or covenant is only as valuable as the financial strength and integrity of the person who makes it. It is useful in an agreement of purchase and sale, however, to anticipate where and how things can go wrong and to provide in advance for the allocation of responsibility for the essential terms of the agreement.

From a tax perspective, representations and warranties serve the same general purpose: They support the financial and tax assumptions on which the acquisition is premised and provide for an appropriate adjustment or remedy in the event of non-compliance or failure to meet contractual expectations.

Where the vendor gives a covenant or a warranty in respect of the shares sold, any amount received or receivable in respect of the covenant or warranty obligation is included in the proceeds of disposition for the shares. Thus, the full amount received or receivable is attributed to the shares sold, and is taken into account in calculating the capital gain. Any outlays or expenses incurred by the seller pursuant to the obligation, either in the year of sale or in any subsequent taxation years, are deemed to be capital losses.[78] This rule applies whether the consideration for the warranty is provided for separately from, or as part of, the consideration for the shares sold. In most cases, the warranty is made part of the agreement of purchase and sale, without any specific consideration identified in respect thereof.

(f) Interest on Borrowed Money

Interest expense incurred to finance a purchase of shares is generally deductible in computing the purchaser's income.[79]

(g) Losses

A corporation is generally entitled to carry back and carry forward its net capital losses and non-capital losses to reduce its income in other periods. Non-capital losses may be carried back for three years and forward for seven years.[80] Net capital losses incurred may be carried back three years and carried forward indefinitely.[81]

(i) Change of Control

The ability to carry forward corporate losses can be an important factor in a share acquisition. At its simplest level, the purchaser can put a profitable business into the

---

[78] S. 42.

[79] Para. 20(1)(c); see subs. 248(1) ("exempt income") (dividends on shares excluded from definition).

[80] Para. 111(1)(a) (rule applying to non-capital losses after 1982).

[81] Para. 111(1)(b).

corporation and utilize its accumulated losses to absorb the profits from the new business for the next seven years. There are, however, stringent and complex rules restricting the streaming of losses upon a change of control of a corporation. The rationale for these rules is to discourage speculative trading in "loss corporations".

(A) Timing

The timing of a share acquisition is an important determinant in the treatment of corporate losses.

Where control of a corporation changes, the corporation is deemed to end its taxation year immediately before the change of control occurs.[82] This deemed year-end rule has important consequences for the corporation because it fixes the time at which the corporation's gains and losses must be accounted for and their subsequent treatment.

The corporation is deemed to commence a new taxation year immediately after the acquisition of control. Since the corporation does not have a fiscal period before the deemed new year, it may adopt a new fiscal year-end without regard to any prior fiscal periods that may have been in effect at the time that control changed hands. The deemed change in year end rule does not apply to foreign affiliates.[83]

The control of a corporation is deemed to have been acquired at the commencement of the day on which control is acquired, regardless of the actual time at which the transaction is finally consummated.

(B) Control

The term "control" refers to *de jure* control and not *de facto* control.[84] Thus, control means the right of control that rests in ownership of such a number of shares of a corporation that ensures majority voting power. In most cases, ownership of the common shares of the corporation determines by whom the corporation is controlled. There are, however, circumstances where preferred shares may carry more votes than the common shares. In these circumstances, control may lie with the preferred shareholders and not with the common shareholders.

The loss streaming rules are triggered upon an acquisition of control "by a person or group of persons".[85] The term "person" includes an individual, trustee and another corporation.

The phrase "group of persons" is not defined for the purposes of these rules. It is, however, generally accepted by Revenue Canada that in order to constitute a "group",

---

[82] Para. 249(4)(*a*).

[83] Subss. 249(4); 95(1) ("taxation year").

[84] See IT-302R3, "Losses of a Corporation — The Effect that Acquisition of Control, Amalgamations and Windings-up Have on their Deductibility — After 1987" (February 28, 1994).

[85] Subss. 111(4) and (5).

the members must have a common link or interest, or act together to control the corporation.[86] The acquisition of a corporation through a management by-out, for example, would constitute a change of control by a group of persons because the employees would be a clearly identifiable group with a common interest.

The loss streaming provisions apply only upon an *acquisition* of control and not upon a change of control. Hence, for example, a corporation that goes public does not usually trigger the loss streaming provisions because, although there may be a divestment of control by some shareholders, there is not an acquisition of control by a new group of persons. The new shareholders in a public offering are usually total strangers to each other and do not have any common link or interest.

(C) Related Parties

Related-party transactions do not give rise to a change of control for the purposes of the loss streaming rules.[87]

(ii) Non-capital Losses

Stringent loss streaming rules apply on the change of control of a corporation. The corporation's accumulated non-capital and farm losses are deductible from income, but only if the corporation carries on its business for profit, or with a reasonable expectation of profit, *throughout* the year in which the deduction is claimed.[88]

Non-capital and farm losses may be deducted only against income from *the* business that created the loss. If the business has sold, leased or rented its properties that were previously used in the business, its non-capital and farm losses are deductible against the income derived from the sale, lease or rental of the properties, if substantially all of the income is derived from such activities.

Thus, the loss business must be identified in order to determine whether non-capital losses can be applied against the business. Whether two or more operations of an enterprise constitute a single or separate businesses depends upon the degree of their interconnection, interlacing, and interdependence.[89] One looks to factors such as:

- Manufacturing processes,
- Product lines,
- Customer groups,
- Service lines,
- Common inventory,

---

[86] See RCRT, 1988 Conference Report, 53:1-188, Question 40 and RCRT, *Report of Proceedings of the Thirty-Sixth Tax Conference,* 1984 Conference Report, 783-847, Question 42, at 816-17.

[87] Subs. 256(7).

[88] Subs. 111(5).

[89] IT-206R, "Separate Businesses" (October 29, 1979).

- Employee groups, and
- Common use of machinery, plant and equipment.

Two or more operations that use the same physical premises, share common supplies, use an interchangeable labour force and a common administration are considered a single business.

Non-capital and farm losses may also be carried back three years and applied against the income of the corporation in those years. Where, however, there has been a change of control of a corporation, its non-capital or farm loss from carrying on a business is deductible in a year preceding the change of control only if, *throughout* the taxation year in which the loss arose and in the particular taxation year, the corporation carried on its business for profit or with a reasonable expectation of profit.[90]

(iii) Net Capital Losses

The rules in respect of net capital losses upon change of control are even more stringent: Net capital losses from preceding years may not be carried forward[91] or carried back to reduce the income of taxation years subsequent or prior to the change of control.[92]

But capital losses incurred *in the year* in which control changes are not affected by this prohibition. Hence, a business should trigger capital gains in the year of change of control to utilize any capital losses. This is particularly important because accrued capital losses or non-depreciable capital property are deemed to be realized in the year of change of control.[93]

(h) Prior Years' Taxes

The purchaser of shares should determine the tax assessment status of the vendor. Revenue Canada has three years (longer, in some cases) from the date of its assessment within which it may reassess the taxpayer. The three-year period may be extended by waivers granted by the corporation. This potential liability should be taken into account in structuring the agreement of purchase and sale. The purchaser might use a right of set-off against the purchase price.

---

[90] Para. 111(5)(*b*).

[91] Para. 111(4)(*a*).

[92] Para. 111(4)(*b*).

[93] Para. 111(4)(c).

9. ANTI-AVOIDANCE RULES

(a) General

A disposition of shares that constitute capital property gives rise to proceeds of disposition. The difference between the proceeds of disposition and the adjusted cost base of the shares is a capital gain.[94] In most cases, the vendor will want to minimize the amount of the taxable capital gain.

(b) "Capital Gains Strips"

The most obvious method of reducing what might otherwise be a taxable capital gain is to convert the proceeds of disposition into a non-taxable intercorporate dividend.[95] For example, *in the absence of special anti-avoidance rules*, a corporate taxpayer that wanted to sell its shareholdings in another corporation might arrange to receive a tax-free dividend from the purchaser corporation in exchange for reducing the selling price of the shares sold by the amount of the dividend. The vendor corporation would reduce the proceeds of disposition on the sale of the shares and, as such, reduce its taxable capital gain.

Consider the following additional example. X and Y are shareholders of an operating corporation, ("Opco"). X would like to buy Y's shares; if he purchases the shares directly, Y will realize a capital gain. To avoid the gain, Y rolls over his shares to a holding corporation, ("Holdco"). Opco in turn purchases Y's shares for cancellation from Holdco. Any amount paid for the shares in excess of their paid-up capital is deemed to be a dividend. Since the dividend is paid by one corporation to another, it is non-taxable. In effect, Y would have converted what would otherwise have been a taxable capital gain on the disposition of his shares into a non-taxable intercorporate dividend.

(c) Anti-avoidance Measures

In certain circumstances, a tax-free intercorporate dividend is deemed to be a capital gain or proceeds of disposition.[96] This rule, which is directed squarely at preventing a "capital gains strip" of the type described above, applies where:[97]

- the taxpayer is a corporation resident in Canada;
- the taxpayer is in receipt of a taxable dividend in respect of which it is entitled to a deduction in respect of intercorporate dividends;[98]

---

[94] Para. 39(1)(*a*).

[95] Subs. 112(1) (such transaction referred to as "capital gains strip", which is reverse of "dividend strip").

[96] Subs. 55(2).

[97] Subs. 55(2).

[98] See subs. 112(1).

- the dividend is part of a transaction, event or series of transactions or events *one* of the purposes of which was to significantly reduce the amount of capital gain that would otherwise have been recognized; and

- the capital gain that would otherwise have been recognized is reasonably attributable to *anything* other than the corporation's post-1971 income.

In such circumstances, the dividend is deemed not to be a dividend for most tax purposes. Instead, if the shares on which the dividend was paid have been disposed of, the amount of the dividend is added to the proceeds of disposition. If the shares have not been disposed of, the dividend is deemed to be a capital gain. This rule applies only to taxable dividends, whether received or deemed to have been received; it does not apply to non-taxable dividends paid out of the capital dividend account of a corporation.

The rule can apply even where the transaction or series of transactions is business motivated and not entered into for tax avoidance. Thus, the rule applies if *one* of the purposes of the transaction, event or series of transactions was to effect a significant reduction in the amount of the capital gain that would otherwise be realized. In other words, the taxpayer must show that *none* of the purposes of the transactions was to reduce the capital gain that would otherwise be realized.

Where the taxable dividend is a deemed dividend under subsection 84(3), the rule applies if it can be shown that one of the *results* of the transaction, event or series of transactions was the reduction of the capital gain that would otherwise have been realized.

What constitutes a "significant reduction" of a capital gain is a question of fact. It may relate to the absolute dollar amount of the capital gain, or it may be determined by looking at the percentage reduction of the gain.[99]

The rule does not apply in respect of dividends paid out of post-1971 earnings, that is, out of "taxed retained earnings". This income is sometimes referred to as "safe income", and the dividend paid out of such income is referred to as a "safe dividend".

The anti-avoidance rule does not apply to rearrangements of shareholder interests where the parties are *not* related to each other[100] (for example, in typical estate planning reorganizations), or dividends received in the course of a reorganization of capital intended to "demerge" a corporation by means of a "butterfly" transaction.[101]

(d) "Butterfly" Reorganizations

A "butterfly" reorganization describes a transaction in which two or more shareholders of a corporation undertake to dissolve their business relationship in a tax-

---

[99] The Department appears to look at the absolute dollar amount of the reduction.

[100] Para. 55(3)(*a*).

[101] Para. 55(3)(*b*).

free manner, such that each shareholder (or corporation) ends up with an undivided interest in the *pro rata* share of the assets previously owned by the corporation.[102] The "butterfly" is used to divide up corporate assets amongst shareholders who cannot resolve their differences and who wish to terminate their business relationship.

Typically, a "butterfly" reorganization involves four steps which are designed to allow a corporation to divest its assets to its shareholders in such a manner that the shareholders acquire their *pro rata* share of property from the distributing corporation on a tax-free basis.

The "butterfly" reorganization is an exception to the rules in respect of "capital gains strips". The importance of this is that a deemed dividend resulting from a redemption of shares or winding-up in the course of a butterfly is not considered a capital gain. Hence, it is fully deductible as an intercorporate dividend.

Example XXV.6

Assume:

Two shareholders, A and B, each own 50 per cent of the shares of an operating company ("Opco"). They would like to "splinter" Opco in a tax-efficient manner, so that they each end up with 50 per cent of its assets within their own corporations.

Then:

  Step 1:

  A and B each incorporate a holding company, Holdco A and Holdco B, to which they transfer their respective shareholdings in Opco; they elect under subsection 85(1) so that the transfer occurs on a tax-free basis.

    Thus, Holdco A and Holdco B, each of which owns 50 per cent of Opco, become holding companies.

  Step 2:

  Opco transfers one-half of its assets to each of Holdco A and Holdco B in exchange for redeemable shares of the holding companies. Once again the transfers are executed on a tax-free basis under subsection 85(1). Typically, the redeemable shares of the holding companies have a paid-up capital that does not exceed the adjusted cost base of the shares to Opco.

---

[102] See, for example, TR-99, "Transfer of Shares to a Holding Company Followed by their Redemption" (May 23, 1980).

Example XXV.6 (continued)

Now, Holdco A and Holdco B own the assets previously owned by Opco.

Opco is reduced to a shell corporation that owns only redeemable shares in the holding companies.

Step 3:

The holding companies, Holdco A and Holdco B, redeem their shares from Opco at fair market value. The difference between the redemption price and the paid-up capital of the shares is deemed to be a dividend to Opco, and is received as a tax-free intercorporate dividend. There is no capital gain.

Now, Opco has only cash and no other assets.

Step 4:

Opco is wound up into the holding companies, Holdco A and Holdco B, and distributes its cash to the companies.

Now, each of the holding companies of the individual shareholders, A and B respectively, owns one-half of the assets formerly owned by Opco. Since A owns all of the shares of Holdco A, and B owns all of the shares of Holdco B, they have achieved their objective.

There are other variations of the butterfly, but they all involve the same techniques: a divestment of assets into one or more new corporations under the protection of subsection 85(1) in return for redeemable shares that have a low paid-up capital and a high redemption value. The redemption of the shares gives rise to a deemed dividend which is not taxable;[103] the capital gain that would otherwise have been realized on a direct divestment of the assets to the individual shareholders is thereby avoided.

In addition to ensuring that each step in a butterfly reorganization conforms to the relevant corporate law, particular care must be taken to avoid running afoul of the following provisions:

- subsection 15(1) (shareholder benefits);
- subsection 56(2) (indirect payments);
- paragraph 85(1)(e.2) (indirect gifts); and
- section 245 (GAAR).

---

[103] Subs. 84(3).

10. STATUTORY AMALGAMATIONS

Another method of acquiring a business is by way of statutory amalgamation. In an amalgamation, two or more corporations are merged to become one. All of the assets and liabilities of the merged corporations are carried over into the newly-formed corporation.[104]

(a) Advantages

There are several advantages to statutory amalgamations:

- **Simplicity of title transfers:**
  The title to the assets of an amalgamated corporation passes to the new corporation by operation of law.

- **Elimination of minority interests:**
  Minority shareholders who object to an amalgamation have the right to dissent, and can be bought out at the fair value of their shares.

- **Tax-free rollover:**
  An amalgamation that conforms to the requirements of the Act can be implemented on a tax-free basis.[105]

(b) Disadvantages

There are also some disadvantages:

- **Assumption of liabilities:**
  The new corporation continues to be liable for all the debts and obligations of the amalgamated corporations, whether such debts have been disclosed or not and whether such debts are contingent or known.

- **Shareholders' meetings:**
  An amalgamation requires two shareholders' meetings; both the buyer and the seller corporations are generally required to approve the transaction.

- **Appraisal remedy:**
  Shareholders of the amalgamating corporations who object to the amalgamation are entitled to be paid in cash for the fair value of their shares. Where there are a substantial number of dissenting shareholders, the cash outflow to purchase their shares may be a drain on the new corporation. In addition, the determination of the fair value of shares can be troublesome.

---

[104] See, e.g., *Canada Business Corporations Act*, ss. 181, 186.

[105] See s. 87; see also Chapter XXIV "Mergers and Dissolutions".

11. NON-RESIDENTS

The residence of the vendor corporation and/or its shareholders are important tax considerations in the acquisition of a business.

Where the vendor is a non-resident of Canada, there are additional income tax requirements:

- The purchaser requires a section 116 clearance certificate from the vendor (in the case of an asset acquisition) or from the vendor's shareholders (in the case of a share acquisition);

- Tax must be withheld under Part XIII on payments of certain amounts (for example, interest) to non-residents;

- Payments to non-residents may be affected by double taxation treaties between Canada and the country of the vendor's residence.

(a) Section 116 Clearance Certificate

Section 116 of the Act is intended to ensure that the vendor discharges his or her Canadian income tax obligations that may arise from the sale of property. The section contemplates two mechanisms. A non-resident vendor who *proposes* to dispose of taxable Canadian property can prepay one-third of the estimated value of the gain that will result from the proposed disposition of the property. The vendor can estimate the anticipated proceeds of disposition, determine the gain that will result from the disposition and disclose the name and address of the proposed purchaser of the property together with a description of the property itself. The Minister then issues a certificate of clearance on payment of one-third of the estimated gain or upon the deposit of acceptable security in lieu thereof.

(b) Purchaser's Liability

Obtaining a clearance certificate under section 116 is, technically speaking, an optional procedure insofar as the vendor is concerned. Where the vendor does not obtain a clearance certificate, the Act provides for an alternative mechanism to collect the vendor's tax: The purchaser of the property becomes liable to pay. The amount of the purchaser's liability depends upon the nature of the property purchased.

The purchaser's liability in respect of non-depreciable capital property purchased from a non-resident is equal to one-third of the *cost* of the property. This liability is reduced if the vendor obtains a clearance certificate in which case the purchaser is liable for one-third of the amount by which the amount of the final consideration actually paid exceeds the amount estimated for the purposes of the certificate.

The Act purportedly empowers the purchaser to recover the full amount of the tax from the non-resident vendor. This may be a difficult provision to enforce and should not be relied upon as a substitute for proper withholding. In any event, it is a dubious proposition as to how the federal tax statute confers powers upon a purchaser that fall clearly within the property and civil rights jurisdiction of the provinces.

Hence, it is clearly in the purchaser's interest to either withhold one-third of the purchase price of non-depreciable taxable Canadian property until such time as he or she obtains a clearance certificate for the proper amount. Otherwise, the purchaser becomes liable to pay the tax (or shortfall in tax) within 30 days after the end of the month in which he or she acquires the property.[106]

The purchaser's liability for tax increases to 50 percent of the purchase price in the case of depreciable taxable Canadian property.[107] The increase is justified on the basis that the tax liability on appreciated depreciable property will generally trigger not only a potential capital gain but also recapture of capital cost allowance.

Thus, the purchaser should determine the breakdown between depreciable and non-depreciable capital property in order to ascertain how much should be withheld from the proceeds. This will necessarily create some uncertainty because the allocation between depreciable and non-depreciable property and the classification of assets may be the subject of differing opinions and negotiation.

(c) Due Diligence

The purchaser is not liable to withhold any tax on behalf of the vendor if he or she is diligent and makes reasonable inquiries on the basis of which he or she comes to the conclusion that the vendor is not resident in Canada. Revenue Canada takes the view that "reasonable inquiry" requires the purchaser to at least enquire of the vendor's solicitor or agent as to the vendor's place of residence. A positive statement from the vendor that he or she is a Canadian resident is generally enough to satisfy the Department that there was a sufficiently reasonable inquiry to relieve the purchaser of any withholding tax obligations in respect of the purchase.[108]

12. THIRD PARTY LIABILITY FOR TAXES

Section 160 of the Act imposes potential liability on third parties who receive property from a person with whom they do not deal with at arm's length. The section renders the third party potentially liable for the vendor's taxes owing at the time that the property was sold. The liability is limited in amount to the shortfall between the consideration paid and the fair market value of the property purchased.

Section 160 has far reaching and enduring consequences for a non-arm's length purchaser because it can be triggered long after the date on which the property was

---

[106] Subs. 116(5).

[107] Subs. 116(5.3).

[108] IC 72-17R4, "Procedures Concerning the Disposition of Taxable Canadian Property by Non-residents of Canada — Section 116" (April 24, 1992).

purchased. The section does not have any limitation period. The Minister may reassess the vendor several years after the sale of the property and determine, retroactively, that the vendor was indeed liable for taxes at the date of the transfer of property.

Thus, the purchaser should obtain a representation that no taxes are owing by the vendor that have not been declared in the agreement of purchase and sale. The agreement should also provide for indemnification (with or without holdbacks) of the purchaser if a subsequent assessment determines that the vendor is liable for back taxes as at the date that the property was transferred.

SELECTED BIBLIOGRAPHY TO CHAPTER XXV

General

Ahmed, Firoz "Debt Forgiveness Rules and Share Purchase Transactions" (1995), 5 *Can. Current Tax* 58.

Ahmed, Firoz and Sarah Gagan, "Amalgamations after Pan Ocean", [1994] *Can. Current Tax* J71.

Albo, Wayne P., and Randal A. Henderson, *Mergers and Acquisitions of Privately Held Businesses*, 2nd ed. (Toronto: Can. Inst. of Chartered Accountants, 1989).

Bernstein, Jack, "Corporate Spin-Offs and Creditor Proofing", in *Proceedings of 39th Tax Conf.* 30:1 (Can. Tax Foundation, 1987).

Bernstein, Jack, "Sale of Businesses to Employees: The Leveraged Buy-Out", *Corp. Mgmt. Tax* Conf. 116 (Can. Tax Foundation, 1985).

Boultbee, Jack A., and Douglas S. Ewens, "The Taxation of Corporate Reorganizations" (1986) 24 *Can. Tax J.* 203.

Buying and Selling a Business — 1991 (Vancouver: Continuing Legal Education Society of British Columbia, 1991).

Cadesky, Michael, "Corporate Losses" in *Proceedings of 42nd Tax Conf.* 19:1 (Can. Tax Foundation, 1990).

Campbell, Ian R., "Valuation-related Issues: Tax Planning and Post-transaction Followups" in *Proceedings of 45th Tax Conf.* (Can. Tax Foundation, 1993).

"Case Study", *Corp. Mgmt. Tax Conf.* 157 (Can. Tax Foundation, 1972).

Colley, Geoffrey M., "Assets or Shares: What does the Purchaser Want?" (1974), 104 *CA Magazine* 54.

Colley, Geoffrey M., "Tax Planning Implications for New Business" (1980), 113 *CA Magazine* 78.

Cooke, Philip J., and Jonathan Fox, *Effective Tax Strategies for Corporate Acquisitions* (Deventer, The Netherlands: Kluver, 1986).

Corn, George, "Acquisition of Unrealized Capital Losses — Tax Avoidance" (1995), 5 *Can. Current Tax* 53.

Dalsin, Derek J., "Dispositions of Property by Non-residents: Tax Deferral by Ministerial Discretion" (1991), *Can. Tax J.* 77.

Dancey, Kevin J., "Specific Expenditures: Timing and Deductibility", *Corp. Mgmt. Tax Conf.* 116 (Can. Tax Foundation, 1981).

Dart, Robert J., and David W. Smith, "Estate Planning: A New Era", (1986), 34 *Can. Tax J.* 1.

Ewens, Douglas S., "Debt-for-Debt Exchanges" (1991), 39 *Can. Tax J.* 1615.

Ewens, Douglas S., "New Consideration In Structuring Share-for-Share Exchange Offers" (1988), 36 *Can. Tax J.* 449.

Ewens, Douglas S., "Winding-Up of Corporations Otherwise than under Section 88 (The): An Update" (1975), 23 *Can. Tax J.* 352.

Forster, David, C.A., "The Purchase and Sale of Assets of a Business: Selected Tax Aspects", *Corp. Mgmt. Tax Conf.* 2:1 (Can. Tax Foundation, 1990).

Gordon, Donald M., "Intercompany Non-Arm's Length Transactions — Income Tax Consequences", in *Proceedings of 26th Tax Conf.* 69 (Can. Tax Foundation, 1974).

Grashuk, Harry S., "The Professional Corporation in Alberta" (1977), 25 *Can. Tax J.* 109.

Haney, K.S.M., "Current Cases — Allocation of Purchase Price" (1988), 36 *Can. Tax J.* 170.

Haney, M.A., "Current Cases — Non-Arm's Length — A Question of Fact" (1987), 35 *Can. Tax J.* 1256.

Haney, M.A., "Current Cases — Sale of Shares of a Corporation Formed for Land Development — Capital Gain or Income?" (1986), 34 *Can. Tax J.* 607.

Hanson, Suzanne I.R., "Planning for a Share Sale" in *Proceedings of 44th Tax Conf.* 27:1 (Can. Tax Foundation, 1992).

Hanson, Suzanne I.R., "Tax and Estate Planning for Specific Assets", in *Proceedings of 39th Tax Conf.* 40:1 (Can. Tax Foundation, 1987).

Hogg, Roy D., C.A., "Corporate Distributions: The Proposed Part II.1 Tax", in *Proceedings of 39th Tax Conf.* 31:1 (Can. Tax Foundation, 1987).

Houle, Louis, "Acquisition Agreements: Specific Tax Clauses" (1991), 39 *Can. Tax J.* 1245.

Howick, Wallace M., "Assets Versus Shares: An Approach to the Alternatives", *Corp. Mgmt. Tax Conf.* 1:1 (Can. Tax Foundation, 1990).

Kingson, Charles I., "Liquidations, Branches, and Losses: 1986 Changes in U.S. Tax Law", in *Proceedings of 38th Tax Conf.* 30:1 (Can. Tax Foundation, 1986).

Kroft, E.G., "Tax Clauses in Acquisition Agreements", *Corp. Mgmt. Tax Conf.* 9:1 (Can. Tax Foundation, 1990).

Jones, D. Alan, "Business Equity Valuations and Real Estate Appraisals in Revenue Canada" in *Proceedings of 45th Tax Conf.* 26:1 (Can. Tax Foundation, 1993).

Laflamme, Pierre, "Acquisition Strategies" in *Proceedings of 45th Tax Conf.* 13:1 (Can. Tax Foundation, 1993).

Lahmer, Craig, C.A., "Acquisition-of-Control Rules", *Corp. Mgmt. Tax Conf.* 4:1 (Can. Tax Foundation, 1990).

Larter, Ronald W., C.A., "Capital Cost Allowance and Eligible Capital Property: Tax Reform Implications", in *Proceedings of 40th Tax Conf.* 27:1 (Can. Tax Foundation, 1988).

Loveland, Norman C., "Acquisition of a US Business by Canadians: A US Perspective", *Corp. Mgmt. Tax Conf.* 11:1 (Can. Tax Foundation, 1990).

MacDonald, Nancy, "Amalgamations Following Guaranty Properties Limited" (1991), 39 *Can. Tax J.* 1399.

Mallin, Michael G., "Organizing and Reorganizing to Ensure 'Qualified Small Business Corporation Share' Status — Part 1: Preserving Existing 'Qualified Small Business Corporation' Share Status" (1990), 38 *Can. Tax J.* 745.

Mallin, Michael G., "Organizing and Reorganizing to Ensure 'Qualified Small Business Corporation Share' Status — Part 2: The Purification Transaction" (1990), 38 *Can. Tax. J.* 1026.

Mayo, Wayne, "Interest, Exempt Income and Inter-Corporate Dividends" (1987) 4 *Australian Tax Forum* 123-42.

McCallum, J. Thomas, *Amalgamations and Wind-ups* (Vancouver: Certified General Accountants' Association of Canada, 1994).

McCrodan, Andrew, "Tackling Tax-related Troubles" (1993), *CA Magazine No. 4* 45.

McDonnell, T.F., "Current Cases — Sale of a Business as a Going Concern — Whether Vendor's Gain Is Calculated By Reference to Total Package or Individual Assets" (1986), 34 *Can. Tax J.* 398.

Meghji, Al, "Collateralized Preferred Shares" (1987), 35 *Can. Tax J.* 467.

Mida, Israel H., C.A., "Goods and Services Tax (The) and Corporate Matters", in *Proceedings of 42nd Tax Conf.*, 14:1 (Can. Tax Foundation, 1990).

Mida, Israel H., C.A., "Goods and Services Tax (The) and Corporate Reorganizations — Part 1" (1990), 38 *Can. Tax J.* 1524.

Mida, Israel H., C.A., "Goods and Services Tax (The) and Corporate Reorganizations — Part 2" (1990), 38 *Can. Tax J.* 1524.

Mida, Israel H., C.A., "More on Intragroup Transfers" (1986), 34 *Can. Tax J.* 1184.

Middleton, David W., C.A., "Common Tax Problems and Pitfalls in Effecting Reorganizations of Private Corporations", in *Proceedings of 41st Tax Conf.* 13:1 (Can. Tax Foundation, 1989).

Mitchener, Donald G., "By Gosh! The Price May Not Be Right!" (1974), 104 *CA Magazine* 69.

Moore, D.H., "Current Cases — Non-Arm's Length in Fact" (1986), 34 *Can. Tax J.* 148.

Morrow, Robert G., "Purchasing and Selling a Business" (1973), 7 *CGA Magazine* 4.

Neville, Ralph J., "Acquisition of Control and Corporate Losses" in *Proceedings of 44th Tax Conf.* 25:5 (Can. Tax Foundation, 1992).

"New Strategies for Corporate Acquisitions", *Corp. Mgmt. Tax Conf.* (Can. Tax Foundation, 1978).

Novis, Derrick A., C.A., "Provisions That Restrict or Deny Losses and Corporate Attribution", in *Proceedings of 41st Tax Conf.* 14:1 (Can. Tax Foundation, 1989).

O'Brien, "Corporate Acquisitions and Amalgamations", [1972] *Special Lectures LSUC* 319.

O'Brien, "Sale of Assets: The Vendor's Position", *Corp. Mgmt. Tax Conf.* 1 (Can. Tax Foundation, 1972).

O'Keefe, Michael J., "Surplus Stripping After Tax Reform", in *Proceedings of 40th Tax Conf.* 17:1 (Can. Tax Foundation, 1988).

Perry, F. Brenton, "Capitalization and Asset Acquisitions for New Private Corporations" in *Proceedings of 45th Tax Conf.* 22:1 (Can. Tax Foundation, 1993).

Pister, Tom, "Paragraph 88(1)(d) Bump On The Winding Up of a Subsidiary — Part 1" (1990), 38 *Can. Tax J.* 148.

Pister, Tom, "Paragraph 88(1)(d) Bump On The Winding Up of a Subsidiary — Part 2" (1990), 38 *Can. Tax J.* 426.

Promislow, Norm, "Legal and Taxation Issues Affecting Estates With Certain Business Assets", in *Proceedings of 39th Tax Conf.* 41:1 (Can. Tax Foundation, 1987).

Pullen, K.T., and Howard J. Kellough, "Tax Treatment of Intercorporate Dividends, Grandfathering Provisions, and the Use of Press Releases", *Corp. Mgmt. Tax Conf.* 3:1 (Can. Tax Foundation, 1987).

Read, Robert J.L., C.A., "Section 55: A Review of Current Issues", in *Proceedings of 40th Tax Conf.* 18:1 (Can. Tax Foundation, 1988).

Reid, Robert J., "Capital and Non-capital Losses" in *Proceedings of 42nd Tax Conf.* 20:1 (Can. Tax Foundation, 1990).

Resendes, Ray, Alan Smolal and Audrey Diamant, "Commodity Tax Implications of Corporate Reorganizations" (1989), 37 *Can. Tax J.* 171.

Richards, Gabrielle M.R., "No Relief for Revenue Canada's Carelessness: *City Centre Properties v. The Queen* Federal Court — Trial Division (1994), 4 *Can. Current Tax* J53.

Richardson, Douglas K., and Christopher H. Hanna, "US Tax Treatment of Cross-Border Acquisitive Reorganizations — Part 1" (1989), 37 *Can. Tax J.* 1074.

Richardson, Douglas K., and Christopher H. Hanna, "US Tax Treatment of Cross-Border Acquisitive Reorganizations — Part 2" (1989), 37 *Can. Tax J.* 1318.

Richardson, Elinore J., "Financing Business Acquisitions", *Corp. Mgmt. Tax Conf.* 7:1 (Can. Tax Foundation, 1990).

Richardson, Stephen R., "Purchase and Sale of a Business: Income Tax Aspects of Warranties, Price Adjustments, and Earn-outs", *Corp. Mgmt. Tax Conf.* 10:1 (Can. Tax Foundation, 1990).

Richter, Kirsten, "The Removal of Accrued Gains in Capital Stock Holdings through the Use of 'Safe Income'" (1991), 39 *Can. Tax J.* 1349.

Rohde, Richard C., "Section 85 Transfers — Limitations and Pitfalls" (1988), 36 *Can. Tax J.* 1302.

Rosenfeld, "Corporate Acquisitions", [1972] *Special Lectures LSUC* 367.

Sanderson, Anne C., "The Economics of Taxation" (1991), 39 *Can. Tax J.* 408.

Sanger, John H., "Tax Planning with Income Averaging Annuities" (1977), 110 *CA Magazine* 72.

Scace, Arthur, R.A., Q.C., "Tax Aspects of Some Takeover Defences", in *Proceedings of 38th Tax Conf.* 6:1 (Can. Tax Foundation, 1986).

Schwartz, Alan M., "Statutory Amalgamations, Arrangements, and Continuations: Tax and Corporate Law Considerations" in *Proceedings of 43rd Tax Conf.* 9:1 (Can. Tax Foundation, 1991).

Scobell, "Tax Treatment of Losses", *Corp. Mgmt. Tax Conf.* 119 (Can. Tax Foundation, 1975).

Segal, Brian D., "Disposition of Interests in and Options on Real Property and Shares by Non-residents of Canada" (1994), 42 *Can. Tax J.* 327.

"Selected Income Tax and Goods and Services Tax Aspects of the Purchase and Sale of a Business", *Corp. Mgmt. Tax Conf.* (Can. Tax Foundation, 1990).

"Shareholders' Agreements — Revisited" (1985), 33 *Can. Tax J.* 835.

Sider, Vance A., *Butterfly Reorganizations* (Don Mills, Ont.: CCH Can., 1989).

Sider, Vance A., "Corporate Restructuring Issues: Private Corporations", *Corp. Mgmt. Tax Conf.* 5:1 (Can. Tax Foundation, 1990).

Silver, "Surplus Stripping: A Practitioner's View" (1974), 21 *Can. Tax J.* 430.

Simpson, Muriel A., "Planning Around the New Paid-up Capital Restrictions" (1986), 34 *Can. Tax J.* 646.

Sinclair, B.R., "Paid-Up Capital" (1986), 34 *Can. Tax J.* 1483.

Sinclair, B.R., "Some Income Tax Aspects of Privatization" (1988), 36 *Can. Tax J.* 734.

Smith, David W., Q.C., "Corporate Restructuring Issues: Public Corporations", *Corp. Mgmt. Tax Conf.* 7:1 (Can. Tax Foundation, 1990).

Sohmer, David H., "Purchase and Sale of a Closely-Held Business (2)" (1979), 112 *CA Magazine* 70.

Spindler, Robert, "Mutual Fund Reorganizations" (1987), 35 *Can. Tax J.* 736.

Spindler, R.J., "New Part II.1 Tax (The)" (1987), 35 *Can. Tax J.* 1292.

Stacey, John A., "Transfer of Assets to and from a Corporation", in *Proceedings of 40th Tax Conf.* 14:1 (Can. Tax Foundation, 1988).

Stacey, John A., "Treatment of Losses (The)", in *Proceedings of 35th Tax Conf.* 29 (Can. Tax Foundation, 1983).

Steiss, Carl F., "Acquisition and Disposition of a Canadian Business by a Non-Resident", *Corp. Mgmt. Tax Conf.* 13:1 (Can. Tax Foundation, 1990).

Swiderski, Tony, "Transfer of US Real Property Interest in Canadian Reorganizations: Opportunities, Limitations, and Pitfalls" (1989), 37 *Can. Tax J.* 605.

Templeton, Wendy, "Anti-Avoidance and the Capital Gains Exemption: Part 2" (1986), 34 *Can Tax J.* 446.

Tillinghast, David R., "Acquisition of a US Business by Canadians: A US Perspective", *Corp. Mgmt. Tax Conf.* 12:1 (Can. Tax Foundation, 1990).

Vuketz, Michael C., "Structural Issues in Utilization of Domestic Loss Carryforward Pools" in *Proceedings of 45th Tax Conf.* 23:1 (Can. Tax Foundation, 1993).

Walker, "Acquisitions from Non-Residents: Section 116" (1972), 20 *Can. Tax J.* 131.

Ward, "Tax Considerations Relating to the Purchase of Assets of a Business", *Corp. Mgmt. Tax Conf.* 22 (Can. Tax Foundation, 1972).

Webb, "Escalator Clauses, Earn-outs and Reserves", in *Proceedings of 26th Tax Conf.* 555 (Can. Tax Foundation, 1974).

Wentzell, D.G., "Current Cases — Minister's Advantage (The) — Interest on Instalments" (1987), 35 *Can. Tax J.* 968.

Wentzell, D.G., "Current Cases — Section 68 — The Grave of a Paper Tiger" (1986), 34 *Can. Tax J.* 395.

Williamson, David M., C.A., "Checklists: Corporate Reorganizations, Amalgamations (Section 87), and Wind-Ups (Subsection 88(1))", in *Proceedings of 39th Tax Conf.* 29:1 (Can. Tax Foundation, 1987).

Williamson, Gordon W., C.A., "Recent Developments Affecting Corporate Reorganizations", in *Proceedings of 42nd Tax Conf.* 13:1 (Can. Tax Foundation, 1990).

Williamson, Gordon W., C.A., "Transfers of Assets to and from a Canadian Corporation", in *Proceedings of 38th Tax Conf.* 12:1 (Can. Tax Foundation, 1986).

Wilson, Ronald S., "Cost Adjustments in Corporate Reorganization Transactions: Policy and Practice", in *Proceedings of 38th Tax Conf.* 8:1 (Can. Tax Foundation, 1986).

Witterick on Corporate Acquisitions (Montreal: Federated Press, 1992).

Witterick, Robert G., Q.C., "Buy-Sell Agreements", in *Proceedings of 40th Tax Conf.* 16:1 (Can. Tax Foundation, 1988).

Witterick, Robert G., Q.C., "Syndicated Acquisitions and Financing of Businesses", *Corp. Mgmt. Tax Conf.* 3:1 (Can. Tax Foundation, 1990).

Woods, Judith M., "Dividend Access Shares" (1991), 39 *Can. Tax J.* 408.

Wright, J. Robert, "Remarks on Selected Securities Issues", *Corp. Mgmt. Tax Conf.* 14:1 (Can. Tax Foundation, 1990).

Butterfly Reorganizations

Ahmed, Firoz, "Proposed Rules Would Eliminate Purchase Burrerfly Transactions", [1994] *Can. Current Tax* P27.

Brown and McDonnell, "Capital Gains Strips", in *Proceedings of 32nd Tax Conf.* 51 (Can. Tax Foundation, 1980).

Dart, Robert J., F.C.A., and Howard J. Kellough, "The Butterfly Reorganization: A Descriptive Analysis", in *Proceedings of 41st Tax Conf.* 20:2 (Can. Tax Foundation, 1989).

Ewens, Douglas S., "The Capital Gains Exemption and the Butterfly" (1986), 34 *Can. Tax J.* 914.

Hiltz, Michael A., "The Butterfly Reorganization: Revenue Canada's Approach", in *Proceedings of 41st Tax Conf.* 20:32 (Can. Tax Foundation, 1989).

Lawlor, William R., "Surplus Stripping and Other Planning Opportunities with the New $500,000 Capital Gains Exemption" (1986), 34 *Can. Tax J.* 49.

Murison, Stephen R., "Transfers of Property Within a Corporate Group" (1986), 34 *Can. Tax J.* 646.

Potter, Christopher J., "Part IV Tax Complications in Butterfly Transactions" (1992), *Can. Tax J.* 992.

Richardson, Elinore, and Hillel Frankel, "Netting Canada's Elusive Cross-Border Butterfly " (1990), 2 *Int. Tax Rev.* 5.

Robertson, "Capital Gains Strips: A Revenue Canada Perspective on the Provisions of Section 55", in *Proceedings of 33rd Tax Conf.* 81 (Can. Tax Foundation, 1981).

Spindler, R.J., "Butterflies Revisited" (1989), 37 *Can. Tax J.* 605.

Storozuk, Leslie S., "An Examination of Section 55 and 1982 Proposed Amendments", *Prairie Prov. Tax Conf.* 341 (Can. Tax Foundation, 1983).

CHAPTER XXVI

ADMINISTRATION

1. GENERAL

A basic feature of the Canadian income tax system is that it relies upon taxpayers to "voluntarily" report their income for each taxation year and to estimate the tax payable thereon. Voluntary compliance and self-assessment are the foundation of the administrative structure of the Act. Of course, the tax system does not rely exclusively upon voluntary compliance. There are persuasive inducements to encourage taxpayers to disclose their income. The Minister can impose penalties, make third-party demands, garnish income, seize property, and prosecute through the criminal process. Indeed, as we see in this chapter, Revenue Canada has administrative powers that exceed those of most other government agencies and are subject to fewer legislative and judicial controls.

2. INCOME TAX RETURNS

References:

ITA:

S. 150   Tax Returns — Types, Rules
S. 151   Estimate of Tax
S. 155   Farmers and Fishers
S. 236   Execution of Documents by Corporation

BULLETINS, CIRCULARS & RULINGS:

IC 71-14R3   June 18, 1984   The Tax Audit
IC 81-11R3   March 26, 1993   Corporate Instalments

(a) Who Must File

Not all taxpayers are required to file tax returns every year: Filing requirements vary according to the taxpayer's status, type of income earned and tax credits claimed. The following are required to file income tax returns:[1]

- Corporations (other than registered charities);
- Individuals, if they are taxable in the year; and
- Individuals who have taxable capital gains or have disposed of capital property in the year.

---

[1] Subs. 150(1); IC 71-14R3, "The Tax Audit" (June 18, 1984).

In addition to income tax returns, some taxpayers also have an obligation to file various information returns that report income paid to other taxpayers.

(b) Filing Deadlines

Tax returns are filed on prescribed forms. Each return is in respect of a "taxation year"[2] in accordance with the following filing times:

Taxpayer	Time Limit	Form
Individuals	April 30 of following year	T1
Deceased persons	6 months after death	T1
Corporations (whether or not year-end tax is payable)	6 months after fiscal year end	T2
Trusts and estates (if tax is payable in respect of the year)	90 days from end of estate's or trust's taxation year	T3
Registered charities	6 months after year-end	T3010

(c) Individuals

An individual is required to file an income tax return in respect of a taxation year only if he or she is taxable in the year.[3] An individual may, however, voluntarily file a return even though he or she is not taxable in a particular year. Filing a return even if there is no tax payable will trigger the limitation period within which the individual may be reassessed in respect of the return.[4]

It is generally prudent for an individual to file annual tax returns regardless of whether or not he or she believes that tax is payable for the particular year. Otherwise the individual may be subject to penalties if it is later established that he or she was liable for tax in respect of that year.[5]

---

[2]　S. 249.

[3]　Para. 150(1)(d).

[4]　Subs. 152(4). The prescribed form for individuals is Form T1 General. Taxpayers filing simple tax returns may in certain circumstances use Form T1 Special.

[5]　S. 162.

(d) Corporations

A corporation (other than a corporation registered as a charity) is required to file an income tax return within a period of six months from the end of its taxation year.[6] The return, accompanied by financial statements and supporting schedules, must be filed whether or not the corporation is taxable.

(e) Trusts and Estates

A trust or estate is required to file a return in respect of each taxation year for *which taxes are payable* within 90 days from the end of its taxation year.[7]

A trustee in bankruptcy, liquidator, receiver or agent acting on behalf of a person who has not filed a return is required to file a return on behalf of that person within the relevant time limit.[8]

(f) Deceased Persons

The legal representative of a person who has died without filing an income tax return is required to file the deceased's return within six months from the day of death.[9]

(g) Designated Persons

Where a person who is required to file an income tax return fails to do so, the Minister may designate another person to file the return within a stipulated time.[10]

(h) Non-resident Taxpayers

A non-resident who is employed in Canada, carries on business in Canada or disposes of taxable Canadian property is taxable on income earned in Canada, and must file an income tax return in the same manner as resident taxpayers.[11] Non-resident taxpayers carrying on business in Canada are exempt from withholding tax on any income that is otherwise taxable under Part I of the Act.[12]

---

[6] Para. 150(1)(a).

[7] Para. 150(1)(c).

[8] Subs. 150(3).

[9] Para. 150(1)(b).

[10] Para. 150(1)(e).

[11] Subs. 2(3).

[12] Subs. 215(4); Reg. 805.

(i) Receipt of Documents

A document mailed by first class mail (or its equivalent) is deemed to have been received by the person to whom it was sent on the day when it was mailed.[13] Courier services are generally equivalent to first class mail service. The onus rests on the taxpayer to establish the facts, and the question may ultimately come down to the credibility of the evidence.[14]

3. AMENDED TAX RETURNS

References:

ITA:

S. 152   Assessment

BULLETINS, CIRCULARS & RULINGS:

IC 85-1R2   October 23, 1992   Voluntary Disclosures

IC 92-1   March 18, 1992   Guidelines for Accepting Late, Amended or Revoked Elections

(a) General Rule

As a general rule, a taxpayer does not have a statutory right to amend his or her tax return in respect of a taxation year. As a matter of practice, however, the Minister will usually accept a taxpayer's amended income tax return or supplementary information, and reassess the taxpayer.

(b) Voluntary Disclosure

To encourage self-assessment and voluntary disclosure of tax information, the Department accepts voluntary disclosures of undeclared income. The Department's policy in respect of voluntary disclosure is set out in its Information Circular:[15]

> If a taxpayer has never filed tax returns, and the returns are then voluntarily filed, the taxpayer will be required to pay only the tax owing on the reported incomes, with interest. If a taxpayer has given incomplete information in a return and subsequently submits the missing information, the taxpayer will be required to pay only the tax owing on the adjusted income, with interest. No prosecution will be undertaken, nor will any civil penalties, including late filing penalties, be imposed, on any amounts included in such voluntary disclosures. The identity of anyone making a voluntary disclosure will be held in confidence, as in the case with all taxpayer information.

> This policy applies to corporations and individuals making voluntary disclosures if the following requirements are met:

---

[13] Para. 248(7)(*a*).

[14] *Erroca Ent. Ltd. v. M.N.R.*, [1986] 2 CTC 2425, 86 DTC 1821 (T.C.C.).

[15] IC 85-1R2, "Voluntary Disclosures" (October 23, 1992).

(a) **Voluntary Disclosure** — The taxpayer has to initiate the voluntary disclosure. A disclosure is not considered to be voluntary if it arises when Revenue Canada, Taxation has begun audit or enforcement action.

(b) **Verification** — Each voluntary disclosure should include enough details to allow the facts to be verified.

(c) **Incomplete Disclosure** — If a disclosure is voluntary but incomplete, the disclosed information will be considered voluntary. However, the taxpayer will be subject to penalties, prosecution, or both, relating to any substantial undisclosed amounts.

(d) **Payment** — The taxpayer must pay the total amount of any taxes and interest owing, or make acceptable arrangements for paying such amounts.

(e) **Procedure** — A person can make a voluntary disclosure by contacting Revenue Canada, Taxation. That person will not need to make a detailed submission of the first contact. However, the taxpayer must do so within a period of time that is mutually agreed upon. The initial contact will be considered to be the date of the voluntary disclosure.

(c) Statutory Right to Amend Return

A taxpayer can carry back a deduction from one tax year to a preceding year and file an amended return in the following circumstances:[16]

Deduction	References
Capital losses in year of death and immediately preceding year may be carried back and deducted from other income	para. 3(e)
Three-year carryback of listed personal property losses	s. 41
Carryback of gifts made in the year of death	s. 118.1
Three-year carryback of unused foreign tax credits	subs. 126(2)
Three-year carryback of non-capital, net capital, restricted farm and farm losses	subs. 111(1)
Three-year carryback of investment tax credits to immediately preceding year	subs. 127(5)
Three-year carryback of unused Part VI tax credits	s. 125.2
Seven-year carryback of RRSP premium	para. 60(i), s. 146

---

[16] Subs. 152(6).

Deduction	References
Three-year carryback of unused Part I.3 tax credits	s. 185.3
Election upon disposition of property by legal representative of deceased taxpayer	subs. 164(6)

Taxpayers are also entitled to file amended tax returns to adjust income in a preceding taxation year where the adjustment arises as a consequence of exercising an option contract.[17]

4. WITHHOLDING TAXES

References:

ITA:

S. 153   Withholding, Payments, Remittance

S. 154   Deemed Receipt of Payment, etc.

S. 227   Withholding Taxes

REGULATION:

Reg. 202   Payments to Non-Residents

BULLETINS, CIRCULARS & RULINGS:

IT-155R3   June 16, 1989   Exemption from Non-Residents Tax on Interest Payable on Certain Bonds, Debentures, Notes, Hypothecs or Similar Obligations

IT-161R3   October 8, 1982   Non-Residents — Exemption from Tax Deductions at Source on Employment Income

---

[17] Subs. 49(4); see Chapter IX "Capital Gains".

Certain types of payments are subject to withholding taxes. For example, a person who makes a compensatory payment to a taxpayer is required to withhold an amount on account of the payee's potential tax liability.[18] Withheld taxes must be remitted to the Receiver General of Canada.[19]

A person may also be required to file an information return. For example, every person who pays a dividend or makes an interest or royalty payment to a resident taxpayer is required to file a Return of Investment Income (Form T5).[20] Similarly, a person who pays to a non-resident an amount in respect of dividends, interest, rents, royalties, management fees or alimony payments must also file an information return outlining the details of the payment.

A person who has control of or receives income, gains or profits in a fiduciary capacity is required to file a Trust Information Return.[21]

5. DEMAND TO FILE RETURN

References:

ITA:

S. 150   Tax Returns — Types, Rules

REGULATION:

Reg. 900   Delegation of Minister's Duties

The Minister can demand that a person file a tax return in prescribed form and disclose prescribed information, regardless of whether the taxpayer has already filed a return or is liable for tax.[22] The demand must be served personally on the taxpayer or sent to him or her by registered mail.[23]

---

[18] Subs. 153(1); Regs. 100–108 (withholding and remittance).

[19] See subs. 227(9) (failure to remit on time can result in penalty); *Electrocan Systems Ltd. v. M.N.R.*, [1986] 1 CTC 269, 86 DTC 6089 (*sub nom. Electrocan Systems Ltd. v. The Queen*) (F.C.T.D.) (penalty payable even if taxpayer remits arrears before assessment issued).

[20] Reg. 201.

[21] Reg. 204; Form T3.

[22] Subs. 150(2).

[23] See, generally, subs. 220(1); Reg. 900; see also subss. 244(5), (6) (procedure for proof of service).

6. FAILURE TO FILE RETURN

References:

ITA:

S. 162	Penalties
S. 163	Repeated Failures
S. 238	Offences — Failure to File Return, etc.
S. 239	Other Offences and Penalties
S. 240	Taxable Obligation and Non-taxable Obligation Defined
S. 241	Provision of Information
S. 242	Officers of Corporations
S. 243	No Power to Decrease Punishment

(a) Voluntary System

Although the income tax system relies heavily upon "voluntary" self-assessment of taxes, it also provides severe penalties for failure to voluntarily file and conform. The system is "voluntary" only in the sense that a taxpayer is required to file income tax returns without being called upon to do so by the Minister. Failure to file a return, or to respond to a demand for a return, within the time limits can trigger various penalties, interest charges and criminal prosecution.

(b) Penalties

The penalty for failure to file a tax return is two-tiered.

(i) First Offence

On the first offence, a taxpayer is subject to a penalty calculated by reference to the amount of tax unpaid at the time when the return should have been filed. This penalty is equal to the aggregate of:[24]

- 5 per cent of the tax that was unpaid at the time when the return was required to be filed; and

- 1 per cent of the unpaid tax for each complete month (not exceeding a total of 12 months) between the date on which the return was required to be filed and the date on which it was actually filed.

Thus, the maximum late-filing penalty is 17 per cent of the amount of tax unpaid at the time when the return was required to be filed.

---

[24] Subs. 162(1).

(ii) Subsequent Offences

On a second or subsequent offence, the penalty is equal to the sum of 10 per cent of the unpaid tax plus 2 per cent of the unpaid tax per month (not exceeding 20 months) of default.[25]

This penalty applies if the taxpayer, at the time of the subsequent failure to file a return, was previously assessed a penalty for failure to file within the preceding three-year period.

(iii) Criminal Sanctions

Failure to file an income tax return as required by the Act is also a criminal offence which carries a minimum fine of $1,000.[26] A taxpayer can be liable for both the civil and criminal penalties for failure to file a return but only if the civil penalty is assessed *before* the complaint giving rise to the criminal conviction is laid.[27]

(iv) Trustees

A trustee or other fiduciary who fails to file a return on behalf of a person for whom he or she is acting is liable to a penalty of $10 for each day of default,[28] subject to a maximum penalty of $50.

7. FAILURE TO PROVIDE INFORMATION

References:

ITA:

S. 162	Penalties
S. 163	Repeated Failures, False Statements
S. 233	Information Return
S. 234	Ownership Certificates
S. 237	Social Insurance Number

In addition to providing information on income tax returns, taxpayers may also have an obligation to provide further and supplementary information to the Minister. This information is used to monitor the tax system and as a check on other taxpayers. Failure to provide the supplementary information that is required of taxpayers gives rise to civil, and in some cases criminal, penalties.

---

[25] Subs. 162(2).

[26] Subs. 238(1).

[27] Subs. 238(3).

[28] Subs. 162(3).

(a) Failure to Complete Ownership Certificate

Where a non-resident person pays a Canadian resident interest or dividends by means of a bearer coupon or dividend warrant, the resident payee is under an obligation to complete an ownership certificate in prescribed form.[29]

The bank at which the coupon or dividend warrant is cashed must obtain the ownership certificate from the payee and file it with the Minister on or before the 15th day of the month following the cashing of the cheque or warrant.[30]

A taxpayer who fails to complete or deliver the ownership certificate is liable to a penalty of $50 per failure.[31]

(b) Failure to Provide Social Insurance Number

An individual must provide his or her social insurance number ("SIN") when requested to do so by a person who is required to file an information return in respect of that individual. An individual who fails to provide his or her SIN when required to do so is subject to a penalty of $100.[32]

The penalty does not apply where the individual applies for a SIN within 15 days of the request for the number and then subsequently provides the information within 15 days of its receipt.

The person who is required to supply the individual's SIN on an information return is also liable to a penalty of $100 for failure to supply the information.[33] The penalty does not apply if:

- The person made a reasonable effort to obtain the number from the individual; or
- The individual had applied for, but had not received, the number at the time when the information return was filed.

(c) Failure to File Information Returns

Taxpayers are sometimes obliged to file information returns in respect of their own and other people's affairs. A taxpayer who fails to provide the information as and when required by the Act or Regulations may be penalized.

---

[29] S. 234.

[30] Subs. 234(2); Reg. 207.

[31] Subs. 162(4).

[32] Subs. 162(6).

[33] Subs. 162(5).

The penalty depends upon the nature of the offence. Where the Act sets out a specific penalty, that penalty applies to the offence. If the Act does not specify a penalty, a general penalty equal to the *greater* of $100 and $25 per day (not exceeding 100 days) of default applies.[34]

(d) Failure to File Partnership Information

Partnerships also have an obligation to file information returns. The penalty for failure to file, which is *in addition* to the general penalty for non-compliance with the Act or Regulations, is targeted at repeat offenders. The partnership penalties apply where:[35]

- The general penalty for failure to file information has been assessed;
- A demand for the information has been made; and
- A general penalty was imposed in respect of the partnership for a similar offence in any of the three preceding fiscal years.

The penalty is $100 per member for each month (not exceeding 24 months) during which the failure continues.

(e) Tax Shelter Information

A promoter of a tax shelter is required to obtain an identification number for the shelter from the Minister prior to its sale or issuance to the general public. This number must be provided to all purchasers who acquire an interest in the tax shelter.[36] A taxpayer who purchases an interest in a tax shelter cannot claim a deduction or a credit in respect of the shelter unless the identification number is provided.

The promoter is also required to file an information return that discloses:

- The name, address and social insurance number of each person who acquires an interest in the shelter;
- The amount paid by each investor; and
- Such other information as is required by the prescribed form.

A promoter who files false or misleading information in respect of the promotion of a tax shelter is liable to a penalty.

A person who sells or accepts an investor's contribution for the purchase of a tax shelter without an officially-issued identification number is also guilty of an offence and subject to penalties. The penalty is equal to the *greater* of:

---

[34] Subs. 162(7).

[35] Subs. 162(8).

[36] Subs. 162(9); s. 237.1.

- $500; and
- 3 per cent of the aggregate interest in the tax shelter in respect of which the correct information has not been supplied or an identification number has not been obtained.

(f) Failure to Furnish Foreign-based Information

Corporations resident or carrying on business in Canada are required to file information returns for the year. The return, which must disclose prescribed information regarding transactions with non-resident, non-arm's length persons, must be filed within six months from the end of the corporation's fiscal year.[37]

A separate information return must be filed in respect of each non-resident person with whom the corporation had non-arm's length dealings at any time in the year.

A corporation that fails to provide information in respect of its non-arm's length transactions with non-resident persons within 90 days of a demand for the information is liable to a penalty. The penalty, which is in addition to any general penalty imposed under the Act, is equal to $1,000 for each month (not exceeding 24 months) during which the failure continues.

8. CALCULATION OF TAX LIABILITY

References:

ITA:

S. 151   Estimate of Tax

S. 152   Assessment

S. 161   Interest — Rules, Definitions

(a) Self-assessment Procedure

A taxpayer is responsible for determining his or her own income tax liability.[38] As already noted, there are penalties for failure to file a return or to fully disclose income. There are, however, no sanctions for incorrectly calculating the amount of tax that is payable, provided that all relevant information is fully disclosed.

(b) Interest

A taxpayer who incorrectly underestimates his or her tax liability is liable for interest on the difference between his or her estimate and the amount of tax assessed

---

[37] Subs. 162(10); s. 233.1.

[38] S. 151.

by the Minister.[39] Late payment interest charges are not deductible as an expense for tax purposes.

9. ASSESSMENTS

References:

ITA:

S. 152   Assessment

S. 244   Procedure and Evidence

(a) General Check

Income tax returns are initially computer-processed and checked for mathematical accuracy. They are also examined to ensure that information filed with the return conforms to the requirements of the Act. This process of departmental return verification and information is referred to as an "assessment".[40]

(b) Quick Assessment

The Minister is required to examine with all due dispatch all income tax returns and to assess the tax and penalties payable.[41] The Minister is also required to notify the taxpayer of his or her assessment by means of a notice sent to the address shown on the return.[42]

The initial assessment (sometimes called a "quick assessment")[43] is essentially a check of mathematical accuracy and verification of supplementary documentary evidence. It takes approximately ten weeks from the time when the return is filed to complete.

---

[39] Subs. 161(1).

[40] *Pure Spring Co. v. M.N.R.*, [1946] CTC 169, 2 DTC 844 (Ex. Ct.), *per* Thorson P. ("assessment" defined as "the summation of all the factors representing tax liability, ascertained in a variety of ways, and the fixation of the total after the necessary computations have been made").

[41] Subs. 152(1).

[42] Subs. 152(2); *Scott v. M.N.R.*, [1960] CTC 402, 60 DTC 1273 (Ex. Ct.) (notice of assessment mailed to taxpayer's solicitor not proper notice); *Charron v. The Queen*, [1984] CTC 237, 84 DTC 6241 (F.C.T.D.) (no obligation on Minister to serve assessment or send it by registered mail); see also s. 166 (effect of irregularity in complying with Act).

[43] The "quick assessment" triggers the limitation periods for reassessments under subs. 152(4).

(c) Ministerial Delay

Unfortunately, the phrase "with all due dispatch" lacks clarity and precision. As Fournier J. said in *Jolicoeur:*[44]

> There is no doubt that the Minister is bound by time limits when they are imposed by the statute, but, in my view, the words "with all due dispatch" are not to be interpreted as meaning a fixed period of time. The "with all due dispatch" time limit purports a discretion of the Minister to be exercised, for the good administration of the Act, with reason, justice and legal principles.

The courts are quite, perhaps even excessively, tolerant of Ministerial delays: up to 15 months in some cases.[45] They appear, however, to draw the line at 22 months.[46]

(d) Subsequent Changes

A "quick assessment" is valid even if it is subsequently changed by the Minister. As Thorson P. said in *Provincial Paper:*[47]

> The Minister may, therefore, properly decide to accept a taxpayer's income tax return as a correct statement of his taxable income and merely check the computations of tax in it and without any further examination or investigation fix his tax liability accordingly. If he does so it cannot be said that he has not made an assessment.

> It may happen that it will subsequently appear that an assessment so made is inaccurate and that a reassessment is desirable. But there is a vast difference between an assessment that has turned out to be erroneous and an act that is not an assessment at all. It is for the Minister to decide in each case what he shall do. Indeed, in the vast majority of cases he accepts the taxpayer's statement of taxable income as correct and fixes his liability accordingly. It would be fantastic to say that in such cases he has not made an assessment at all. In my opinion, he has plainly done so.

(e) Deemed Valid

The presumption of validity of an assessment is, perhaps, the single most significant rule for taxpayers. An assessment is *deemed* to be valid and binding on the taxpayer even if it contains an error or defect or has been incorrectly calculated or improperly issued.[48]

---

[44] *Jolicoeur v. M.N.R.*, [1961] Ex CR 85 at 99, [1960] CTC 346 at 358, 60 DTC 1254 at 1261.

[45] *Hutterian Brethren Church of Wilson v. The Queen*, [1979] CTC 1, 79 DTC 5052; affirmed [1980] CTC 1, 79 DTC 5474, 31 NR 426 (F.C.A.) (delay allowed where original assessments did not say that no tax payable; unusual circumstances; colony owed $37,000,000 in 96 actions); *Weih v. M.N.R.*, [1988] 2 CTC 2013, 88 DTC 1379 (T.C.C.) (reassessment at last possible date within four-year period allowed).

[46] *M.N.R. v. Appleby*, [1965] 1 Ex CR 244, [1964] CTC 323, 64 DTC 5199 (where misrepresentation or fraud, court will extend time limit); *J. Stollar Const. Ltd. v. M.N.R.*, [1989] 1 CTC 2171, 89 DTC 134 (T.C.C.) (delay of seven years invalidated assessment, not made with "all due dispatch").

[47] *Prov. Paper Ltd. v. M.N.R.*, [1954] CTC 367 at 374, 54 DTC 1199 at 1202 (Ex. Ct.).

[48] Subs. 152(8).

The taxpayer's only recourse to an assessment is to file a Notice of Objection to have the assessment varied by the Department or by a court.[49] The burden of proof rests squarely with the taxpayer to disprove the assessment. Thus, a taxpayer is liable to pay an assessment unless he or she can prove otherwise. This rule, from which flows the Minister's ultimate power over taxpayers, is an aberration in Anglo-Canadian law and unique to tax law.

(f) No Judicial Review

A taxpayer can appeal an assessment, but only pursuant to the procedures set out in the *Income Tax Act*.[50] The Federal Court does not have the authority to otherwise quash, review or restrain an assessment under section 18 of the *Federal Court Act*.[51]

(g) Net Worth Assessments

The Minister is not bound to accept the taxpayer's income tax return. He or she may assess the amount of tax payable using whatever method is appropriate in the circumstances.[52] The Minister may even issue an "arbitrary" or "net worth" assessment.

(i) *When Used*

The Minister generally uses an arbitrary assessment where the taxpayer refuses to file a tax return, files a return that is grossly inaccurate, or does not furnish any evidentiary support or documentation to allow verification of the return.[53] Notwithstanding that an assessment is "arbitrary", it must disclose the basis on which it is formulated.[54]

---

[49] Subs. 152(8); s. 165.

[50] See s. 169.

[51] *Federal Court Act*, R.S.C. 1985, c. F-7; *The Queen v. Parsons*, [1984] CTC 35, 84 DTC 6345 *(sub nom. M.N.R. v. Parsons)* (F.C.A.) ("legal authority" of Minister challengeable only on specific grounds of "quantum" and "liability"): *Gibbs v. M.N.R.*, [1984] CTC 434, 84 DTC 6418 (F.C.T.D.) (motion to quash assessment dismissed).

[52] Subs. 152(7); *Dezura v. M.N.R.*, [1947] CTC 375, 3 DTC 1101 (Ex. Ct.); *Commercial Hotel Ltd. v. M.N.R.*, [1948] CTC 7 (Ex. Ct.).

[53] *Johnston v. M.N.R.*, [1948] CTC 195, 3 DTC 1182 (S.C.C.).

[54] See *Kerr v. Can.*, [1989] 2 CTC 112, 89 DTC 5348 *(sub nom. Kerr v. The Queen)* (F.C.T.D.) (income from earnings as prostitute and living off avails of other prostitutes assessed on net worth basis).

(ii) Method Applied

The Minister is not statutorily constrained in the manner in which he or she arrives at an arbitrary assessment. In most cases, however, the Minister uses the "net worth" method. This method involves determining the taxpayer's worth at the beginning and at the end of the taxation years in question. Income for the period is calculated by adding the taxpayer's non-deductible expenditures to the increase in his or her "net worth" and deducting therefrom any appreciation in the value of his or her capital assets. Having determined the total increase in the taxpayer's "net worth" between two points in time, the Minister allocates, equally or otherwise, the estimated net income between the taxation years in question.

Example XXVI.1

Assume:

	19-0	19-1
Assets	$100,000	$200,000
Liabilities	$ 40,000	$ 60,000
Personal expenditures	$ 30,000	
Appreciation in capital value of assets between 19-1 and 19-0	$ 20,000	

Then:

Income = NW (19-1) − NW (19-0) + Personal expenditures − Appreciation in assets

$\qquad$ = $140,000 − 60,000 + 30,000 − 20,000

Income = $90,000

(iii) Deemed Valid

By its very nature, an arbitrary assessment is based on estimates and conjecture. The Minister assesses the taxpayer on the best evidence available. Unless the taxpayer can show that the assessment is incorrect, it is valid and binding.[55] The burden of proof in the appeal of an assessment rests with the taxpayer. This is so whether or not

---

[55] See, e.g., *Dezura v. M.N.R.*, *ante*, [1947] CTC at 380, 3 DTC at 1102 *per* Thorson P. (presumption of validity of Minister's assessment: when Minister invokes subs. 152(7), the tax so determined subject to review by court under its appellate jurisdiction; if, on appeal, court finds that amount determined by Minister is incorrect in fact, appeal must be allowed to extent of error; if court not satisfied on evidence that there has been error in amount, then appeal must be dismissed; onus of proof of error in amount of determination rests on appellant).

the Minister imposes a penalty based on the assessment.[56] As the Supreme Court of Canada said in *Anderson Logging*:[57]

> First, as to the contention of the point of onus. If, on an appeal to the judge of the Court of Revision, it appears that, on the true facts, the application of the pertinent enactment is doubtful, it would, on principle, seem that the Crown must fail. That seems to be necessarily involved in the principle according to which statutes imposing a burden upon the subject have, by inveterate practice, been interpreted and administered. But, as concerns the inquiry into the facts, the appellant is in the same position as any other appellant. He must show that the impeached assessment is an assessment which ought not to have been made; that is to say, he must establish facts upon which it can be affirmatively asserted that the assessment was not authorized by the taxing statute, or which bring the matter into such a state of doubt that, on the principles alluded to, the liability of the appellant must be negatived. The true facts may be established, of course, by direct evidence or by probable inference. The appellant may adduce facts constituting a *prima facie* case which remains unanswered; but in considering whether this has been done it is important not to forget, if it be so, that the facts are, in a special degree if not exclusively, within the appellant's cognizance, although this last is a consideration which, for obvious reasons, must not be pressed too far.

(h) Determination of Losses

A taxpayer is entitled to ask the Minister to determine the amount of the taxpayer's non-capital losses, net capital losses, restricted farm losses or farm losses for a year.[58] The Minister is required to make the calculations and send the taxpayer a notice of the determined amount. Thus, the taxpayer has an option in respect of disputes concerning his or her losses: He or she can either have the amount of the loss determined immediately or wait until such time as the amount of the loss has an effect upon his or her tax liability in another year. As we shall see, the limitation periods applicable to these two alternatives may be quite different.[59]

(i) Non-residents

Non-residents who are employed in Canada, carry on business in Canada or dispose of taxable Canadian property are taxable in Canada and are subject to the normal assessment procedures applicable to residents. Assessments arising from the withholding tax obligations and the liability for Part XIV tax on branch profits are, with appropriate modifications, also subject to the same procedures as those applicable to residents.[60]

---

[56] *The Queen v. Taylor*, [1984] CTC 436, 84 DTC 6459 (F.C.T.D.) (since burden of proof is on taxpayer, taxpayer must start by adducing evidence).

[57] *The King v. Anderson Logging Co.*, [1925] SCR 45 at 50, [1917-27] CGTC 198 at 201, 52 DTC 1209 at 1211; affirmed [1926] AC 140, [1917-27] CTC 210, 52 DTC 1215 (P.C.).

[58] Subs. 152(1.1).

[59] See subs. 152(4).

[60] Subs. 219(3).

10. REASSESSMENTS

References:

ITA:

S. 152   Assessment

S. 158   Payment of Remainder

S. 244   Procedure and Evidence

BULLETINS, CIRCULARS & RULINGS:

IT-241	August 11, 1975	Reassessments Made After the Four-Year Limit
IT-384R	January 14, 1987	Reassessment where Option Exercised in Subsequent Year
IC 75-7R3	July 9, 1984	Reassessment of a Return of Income
IC 92-3	March 18, 1992	Guidelines for Refunds Beyond the Normal Three Year Period

The Minister can also reassess a taxpayer's income. Unlike the timetable for "quick assessments", the power to reassess is subject to stringent limitation periods.

The limitation periods run from the date of *mailing* of the notice of original assessment. Within the prescribed limitation period the Minister may issue as many reassessments as the circumstances require.[61]

The limitation period depends upon two criteria:

1. Type of taxpayer; and
2. Nature of the transaction that triggers the reassessment.

(a) General Rule

Absent fraud or misrepresentation, a taxpayer may be reassessed for a particular year only within three years from the date of mailing of the notice of original assessment for the year.[62] Three years is considered to be the "normal reassessment period" for most taxpayers. During the three-year period, however, the Minister may reassess the taxpayer and reconsider *any* fact considered relevant to the calculation of the taxpayer's liability, interest or penalties.

---

[61] *Abrahams v. M.N.R.*, [1966] CTC 690, 66 DTC 5451 (Ex. Ct.).

[62] Subs. 152(4).

(b) Losses, Gifts and Tax Credits

The limitation period extends to six years in respect of claims that arise from:[63]

- An individual's death, in respect of allowable capital losses for the year immediately preceding death;
- Listed personal property losses in computing net gains from dispositions of such property for the preceding three taxation years;
- Gifts made by an individual in the year of his or her death, carried back to the preceding taxation year;
- Non-capital, net capital, restricted farm, farm and limited partnership losses that are carried back to the preceding three taxation years;
- Unused foreign tax credits to be carried back to the preceding three taxation years;
- Investment tax credits in respect of property acquired in a year that may be carried back to the preceding three taxation years;
- Deductions of unused tax credits under Part VI of the Act;
- Carrybacks arising from an election by an individual's estate to treat capital losses incurred by the estate in its first taxation year as losses deductible by the deceased taxpayer incurred in the year of death;
- Transactions involving a taxpayer and a non-resident person with whom the taxpayer was not dealing at arm's length;
- Carryback of RRSP premiums;
- Carryback of unused Part I.3 tax credits; or
- Transactions involving additional income tax payments to, or reimbursements from, the government of a foreign country.

A reassessment issued within the six-year limitation period may be made only on the basis of adjustments that may reasonably be regarded as relating to the deduction or credit that is to be carried back to a previous taxation year.

(c) Corporations

Special rules apply to corporations: The limitation period depends upon the type of corporation.

(i) Canadian-controlled Private Corporations ("CCPCs")

A CCPC can be reassessed only during the "normal reassessment period", that is, three years after the day of mailing of a Notice of an original assessment.

---

[63] Para. 152(4)(b).

(ii) *Large Corporations and Mutual Funds*

The limitation period for mutual funds and corporations other than CCCPs is extended to four years from the mailing of the original assessment.[64]

(d) Method of Giving Notice

(i) *Mail*

Most, but not all, notices of assessment and reassessment are sent by mail. A Notice of Assessment is presumed to have been mailed on the date appearing on its face. The presumption may be challenged by the submission of evidence to establish otherwise.[65] A Notice of Assessment is also deemed to have been *made* on the day when it was mailed.[66]

(ii) *Any Other Method*

The Minister is entitled to send a notice to a taxpayer by any method. For example, in the event of postal disruptions, the notice may be hand-delivered. The Act merely requires that the Minister *send* the notice of assessment within the stipulated limitation periods.[67] There is no specific requirement that the taxpayer receive the assessment. Hence, a notice properly mailed to the taxpayer's correct address is valid even if it is lost in the mail.

(e) Fraud or Misrepresentation

(i) *No Limitation*

There is no limitation period where the taxpayer makes a misrepresentation that is attributable to neglect, carelessness or wilful default, or where the taxpayer commits a fraud in connection with his or her tax return.[68]

The Minister has the onus to prove that the usual limitation period should not apply because of the taxpayer's neglect, carelessness, wilful default or fraud.

---

[64] Para. 152(3.1)(*a*).

[65] Subs. 244(14).

[66] Subs. 244(15).

[67] *Flanagan v. The Queen*, [1987] 2 CTC 167, 87 DTC 5390 (*sub nom. Flanagan v. M.N.R.*) (F.C.A.) (only dispatch required, not receipt, in this case notice of assessment not sent since retained by Revenue Canada); *Bhatti v. M.N.R.*, [1981] CTC 2555, 81 DTC 506 (*sub nom. Re Bhatti*) (F.C.T.D.) (notice sent to taxpayer's previous address invalid where taxpayer had notified Minister of change of address).

[68] Para. 152(4)(*a*).

(ii) Burden of Proof

"Fraud" means a false representation that is made knowingly or without belief in its truth, or recklessly, or without care as to whether it is true or false.[69]

If the Minister discharges the burden of proof and has the limitation period set aside, the onus reverts to the taxpayer to show that the reassessment is incorrect.[70]

Even where the Minister proves that the normal reassessment period does not apply, the reassessment may be made only in respect of amounts which the taxpayer failed to include in his or her income *as a result* of neglect, carelessness, wilful default or fraud. The Minister may not reassess any amounts which are beyond the three-year limitation period and are not attributable to the neglect, carelessness, wilful default or fraud.[71]

(iii) "Neglect, Carelessness or Wilful Default"

What constitutes neglect, carelessness or wilful default? Every error of fact is, in a sense, a misrepresentation of fact. But not every misrepresentation of fact is sufficient to set aside the statutory limitation period. The Minister must go further and show on a balance of probabilities that the misrepresentation is attributable to the taxpayer's neglect, carelessness or wilful default. Thus, the Minister must show something more than mere error: He or she must establish culpable negligence.

(A) Culpable Negligence

Culpable negligence implies fault. The "misrepresentation" does not have to be fraudulent: Innocent misrepresentation is sufficient to extend the limitation period, provided that the misrepresentation is attributable to the taxpayer's neglect, carelessness or wilful default. In *Bisson,* for example:[72]

> . . . [A]ny fraud necessarily presupposes a "misrepresentation", and if the latter word covered every type of inaccurate representation, the reference to fraud in [subpara. 152(4)(a)(i)] would be totally unnecessary. In my view, the fact that the legislator referred not only to "misrepresentation" but to "fraud" indicates that, by the first word, he meant innocent misrepresentations which, without being

---

[69] *Derry v. Peek* (1889), 14 App Cas 337 at 374 (H.L.).

[70] Subs. 152(4); IT-241, "Reassessment Made after the Four-Year Limit" (August 11, 1975); IC 75-7R3, "Reassessment of a Return of Income" (July 9, 1984); see also *M.N.R. v. Taylor*, [1961] CTC 211, 61 DTC 1139 (Ex. Ct.) (Minister must establish misrepresentation or fraud on balance of probabilities); *M.N.R. v. Foot*, [1964] CTC 317, 64 DTC 5196 (Ex. Ct.) (statutory time limit set aside where misrepresentation in reported income); *M.N.R. v. Appleby, ante*, (Minister must establish beyond a reasonable doubt that there has been a misrepresentation on the part of the taxpayer); *Roselawn Invt. Ltd. v. M.N.R.*, [1980] CTC 2316, 80 DTC 1271 (T.R.B.) (onus on Minister to establish misrepresentation or fraud in any appeal from an assessment made beyond the four-year period).

[71] Subs. 152(5).

[72] *M.N.R. v. Bisson*, [1972] CTC 446 at 454, 72 DTC 6374 at 6380 (F.C.T.D.).

fraudulent, are still culpable in the sense that they would not have been made if the person committing them had not been negligent. I therefore conclude that a taxpayer who, without any negligence on his part, commits an error in declaring his income, does not make a misrepresentation within the meaning of [subpara. 152(4)(a)(i)]. When the Minister seeks to rely on this provision to proceed with a re-assessment after four years, he must therefore not only show that the taxpayer committed an error in declaring his income but also that error is attributable to negligence on his part.

(B) Standard of Care

The test for culpability is whether the taxpayer exercised a standard of care that a wise and prudent person would in comparable circumstances. But "wisdom is not infallibility and prudence is not perfection".[73] The Minister must show more than that the taxpayer committed an error of fact. It must also be shown that the error was attributable to an unacceptable standard of care. It must be shown that the taxpayer was negligent in that he or she did not exercise reasonable care:[74]

> For the Minister to show the taxpayer has not exercised reasonable care requires, in my view, something more than simply submitting evidence that the taxpayer has made deposits to his bank accounts in amounts greater than his employment income and advising the court that he . . . does not accept the taxpayer's explanation of the source of funds. . . . It is not enough to suggest misrepresentation or fraud.

A taxpayer may be found to be negligent in the manner of misstating income because of negligence in maintaining, or failing to maintain, records. A person who does not act with sufficient care, or exercise the care of a "reasonable person", is negligent.

It is important to note, however, that a finding of "negligence" sufficient to empower the Minister to reassess beyond the normal limitation period in subsection 152(4) is not, *per se*, enough to justify the imposition of a penalty under subsection 163(2). The latter provision requires a finding of "gross negligence".

Gross negligence involves a very high degree of negligence, amounting to an indifference as to whether the law is obeyed or not.[75] In *Venne*,[76] for example:

> Gross negligence must be taken to involve greater neglect than simply a failure to use reasonable care. It must involve a high degree of negligence tantamount to intentional acting, an indifference as to whether the law is complied with or not.

(C) Burden of Proof

The onus rests initially on the Minister to establish that the taxpayer's misrepresentation is attributable to neglect, carelessness or wilful default, or that the taxpayer has

---

[73]   *Reilly v. The Queen*, [1984] CTC 21 at 42, 84 DTC 6001 at 6018 (F.C.T.D.), *per* Muldoon J.

[74]   *Markakis v. M.N.R.*, [1986] 1 CTC 2318 at 2321, 86 DTC 1237 at 1239 (T.C.C.); see also *Venne v. The Queen*, [1984] CTC 223, 84 DTC 6247 (F.C.T.D.) (taxpayer who did not read tax returns prior to signing them did not exercise reasonable care).

[75]   *Honig v. Can.*, [1991] 2 CTC 279, 91 DTC 5612 (*sub nom. Honig v. The Queen*) (F.C.T.D.).

[76]   *Venne v. The Queen, ante*, [1984] CTC at 234, 84 DTC at 6256.

committed a fraud. If the Minister successfully discharges the burden, the onus shifts to the taxpayer to establish that the reassessment is incorrect.

Where the appropriate treatment of a transaction or event is in doubt or susceptible to alternative interpretations, the taxpayer is entitled to select that interpretation which is most favourable to him or her. The taxpayer is not under any obligation to adopt the interpretation that is more favourable to the revenue authorities. This is so even if a similar or identical transaction is under dispute with the Department.[77]

(f) Waiver of Limitation Period

The Minister may ask a taxpayer to waive the normal limitation period so that the parties can adduce information or make representations in respect of a taxation year which, in the absence of the waiver, will become time-barred. Without a waiver, the Minister would feel compelled to reassess the taxpayer, who would then have to pay the tax demanded pending resolution of the dispute.[78]

The limitation period does not apply where the taxpayer files a waiver with the Department.[79] A taxpayer may, however, restrict the scope of the waiver and, by doing so, restrict the scope of matters which can be reassessed by the Minister.[80] The taxpayer can also revoke the waiver by giving the Minister six months' notice of the revocation.[81]

11. PAYMENT OF TAX

References:

ITA:

S. 152	Assessment
S. 158	Payment of Remainder
S. 220	Administration
S. 221	Regulations
S. 222	Definition of Debt

---

[77] See, e.g., *Regina Shoppers Mall Ltd. v. Can.*, [1991] 1 CTC 297, 91 DTC 5101 (*sub nom. The Queen v. Regina Shoppers Mall Ltd.*) (F.C.A.).

[78] S. 158.

[79] Subpara. 152(4)(*a*)(ii).

[80] Para. 152(5)(*c*); Form T2029.

[81] Subs. 152(4.1).

S. 223   Collection — Initiation of, Rules

S. 224   Garnishment

S. 225   Seizure

S. 226   Taxpayer Leaving Canada

S. 228   Collection Agreement

REGULATION:

Reg. 900   Delegation of Minister's Duties

BULLETINS, CIRCULARS & RULINGS:

IC 80-7   June 30, 1980   Objections and Appeals

(a) Payable When Due

A taxpayer is required to pay forthwith the full amount of assessed taxes, together with any interest and penalties thereon. The amount outstanding must be paid whether or not the taxpayer has filed a Notice of Objection to, or appeal from, the assessment.[82] The Minister may, however, accept security for payment of taxes or any other amount payable under the Act.[83]

The Minister's powers go further: He or she can demand payment of taxes even *before they are due* if he or she is suspicious that the taxpayer is about to leave Canada.[84] The Minister may not commence collection procedures, however, until 90 days after the assessment is issued.

(b) Judgment

Where a taxpayer fails to pay his or her taxes within the requisite time, the Minister may have the debt certified and registered in the Federal Court of Canada. Upon registration, the certificate can be used as a judgment under which execution can be issued for the amount unpaid.[85] The judgment may also be used to garnishee any debts due to the taxpayer by a third party,[86] or to seize the taxpayer's goods and

---

[82] S. 158; see also *Interpretation Act*, R.S.C. 1985, c. I-21, s. 26 (number of days calculated by excluding first day of notice and including last day).

[83] Subs. 220(4).

[84] Subs. 226(1).

[85] S. 223.

[86] S. 224.

chattels.[87] As already noted, the Minister may, in his or her discretion, accept security for unpaid taxes.[88]

(c) Collection Procedure

(i) Normal Procedures

As a general rule, an amount assessed against a taxpayer may not be "collected" for a period of at least 90 days after the Notice of Assessment is issued.[89] Where a taxpayer objects to a Notice of Assessment, the Minister cannot collect the tax payable until the assessment is confirmed.[90] If the taxpayer files a Notice of Appeal to a court, the Minister cannot collect any taxes under the reassessment until the court pronounces judgment.[91]

(ii) Collection in Jeopardy

The Minister may collect an account immediately where there are reasonable grounds to believe that a delay would jeopardize collection.[92] To do so, however, the Minister must make an *ex parte* application to a judge for permission to proceed.

The determination as to whether delay will jeopardize the collection of taxes from a taxpayer is made on a balance of probabilities. The Minister has the burden of proof, and must show that there is a real risk that the taxpayer's property will be dissipated if collection is delayed because of the appeal process. As McNair J. said in *Danielson:*[93]

> . . . the issue goes to the matter of collection jeopardy by reason of the delay normally attributable to the appeal process. The wording of [subs. 225.2(2)] would seem to indicate that *it is necessary to show that because of the passage of time involved to an appeal the taxpayer would become less able to pay the amount assessed.*
>
> In my opinion, the fact that the taxpayer was unable to pay the amount assessed at the time of the direction would not, by itself, be conclusive or determinative. Moreover, the mere suspicion or concern,

---

[87] S. 225; *Morgan Trust Co. v. Dellelce,* [1985] 2 CTC 370, 85 DTC 5492 (Ont. H.C.) (under *Execution Act,* R.S.O. 1980, c. 146, s. 18, sheriff can seize judgment debtor's equitable or beneficial interest in property, i.e., registered retirement savings plan); *Nat. Trust Co. v. Lorenzetti* (1983), 41 OR (2d) 772 (H.C.).

[88] Subs. 220(4).

[89] Subs. 225.1(1).

[90] Subs. 225.1(2).

[91] Subs. 225.1(3).

[92] Subs. 225.2(2).

[93] *Danielson v. Dep A.G., Can.,* [1986] 2 CTC 380 at 381, 86 DTC 6518 at 6519 (F.C.T.D.); see also *1853-9049 Que. Inc. v. The Queen,* [1987] 1 CTC 137, 87 DTC 5093 (F.C.T.D.) (mere suspicion not sufficient).

that delay may jeopardize collection would not be sufficient per se. *The test of "whether it may reasonably be considered" is susceptible of being reasonably translated into the test of whether the evidence on balance of probability is sufficient to lead to the conclusion that it is more likely than not that collection would be jeopardized by delay.* [Emphasis added.]

(d) Fleeing Taxpayer

Where the Minister suspects that a taxpayer is about to leave Canada without settling his or her tax account, the Minister may demand *immediate* payment of all amounts that are payable by the taxpayer. The demand is made by serving, either personally or by registered letter, a notice on the taxpayer demanding payment of all outstanding taxes, interest and penalties thereon for which the taxpayer is liable. In these circumstances, the Minister does not have to wait for the taxpayer to act after the notice has been served; the Minister may *immediately* seize the goods and chattels of the taxpayer by way of summary execution.[94]

12. NOTICE OF OBJECTION

References:

ITA:

S. 164	Refunds
S. 165	Objections to Assessments
S. 166.1	Application for Extension of Time to Appeal
S. 169	Appeal — Rules
S. 227	Withholding Taxes

(a) Limitation Periods

A taxpayer may appeal an income tax assessment by filing a "Notice of Objection" with the Minister. The limitation periods for filing the Notice of Objection are as follows:[95]

- Individuals and testamentary trusts: within 90 days after day of mailing of Notice of Assessment or within one year of taxpayer's "balance-due day", whichever is later.
- Other taxpayers: within 90 days after day of mailing of Notice of Assessment.

---

[94] S. 226.

[95] Subs. 165(1); Form T400A; IC 80-7, "Objections and Appeals" (June 30, 1980); see also s. 169.

(b) Procedure

The procedure for filing a Notice of Objection is straightforward: The Notice must be in writing, delivered or mailed to the Chief of Appeals in a Revenue Canada District Taxation Office, and must set out the reasons for the objection. The Minister retains discretion, however, to accept a notice that is not served in the proper manner.

A taxpayer's rights of appeal depend upon the Notice being filed within the time limit. Failure to comply with the limitation period can substantially prejudice a taxpayer's rights. Revenue Canada almost always stands on its strict and technical legal rights.[96]

Failure to meet the time limit can deprive the taxpayer of all legal rights in respect of objecting to the Notice of Assessment. A taxpayer can apply for an extension of time to file the Notice,[97] but there is no assurance that the extension will be granted.

(c) Extension of Time to File

(i) "Just and Equitable"

The Minister has discretion to extend the time for filing a Notice of Objection, but the discretion is restricted by several conditions.

The first condition is that the Minister must consider it "just and equitable" to grant the extension in the circumstances.[98] The words "just and equitable" conjure up an impression of "soft law and palm tree justice". In fact, the courts are quite reluctant to grant extensions of time. As the Chairman of the Tax Review Board said in *Savary Beach:*[99]

> This Board takes the position that the granting of an extension in time under section 166.1 will be the exception rather than the rule. Human frailty will no doubt give rise on occasion to unusual circumstances, such as those before the Board this morning, wherein it is fair and reasonable to grant such an extension. However, to simply grant such extensions and imply that all applications — where the breach is but a few days — will be granted, is to make a mockery of the period of limitations set down in the Act.

---

[96] See, e.g., *Can. Marconi Co. v. Can.*, [1989] 2 CTC 128, 89 DTC 5370; reversed [1991] 2 CTC 352, 91 DTC 5626 (*sub nom. The Queen v. Can. Marconi Co.*); leave to appeal to S.C.C. refused (1992), 90 DLR (4th) viii.

[97] Subs. 166.1.

[98] Subs. 166.1(7).

[99] *Savary Beach Lands Ltd. v. M.N.R.*, [1972] CTC 2608 at 2609, 72 DTC 1497 at 1498 (T.R.B.); but see *Thody v. M.N.R.*, [1983] CTC 2741, 83 DTC 641 (T.C.C.) (extension granted where delay explained and no "culpable negligence" on part of taxpayer); *Ramos v. M.N.R.*, [1983] CTC 2744, 83 DTC 643 (T.C.C.) (extension granted where taxpayer was out of country); *Graphic Specialties Ltd. v. M.N.R.*, [1983] CTC 2743, 83 DTC 644 (T.C.C.) (extension granted where delay attributable to taxpayer's accountants).

Therefore this Board will, in all cases, regardless of the time that passes between the limitation period in the Act and the filing of the application for extension of time, require exceptional circumstances before any such application will receive approval.

(ii) "Exceptional Circumstances"

What constitutes "exceptional circumstances" is a question of fact. The following examples illustrate some of the circumstances that are taken into account:

Extension Granted	
Bourdon v. M.N.R., [1984] CTC 2654, 84 DTC 1411 (T.C.C.)	Taxpayer's accountant filed notice 42 days late.
Caouette v. M.N.R., [1984] CTC 2447, 84 DTC 1413 (T.C.C.)	Notice of objection filed on 91st day after assessment.
The Queen v. Tohms, [1985] 2 CTC 130, 85 DTC 5286 (F.C.A.)	Taxpayer's mental and physical condition justified extension.
Batey v. M.N.R., [1986] 1 CTC 2439, 86 DTC 1294 (T.C.C.)	Mix-up caused by incorrect application and address. Court found circumstances "just and equitable" without giving any clear reasons.
Extension Denied	
Morasutti v. M.N.R., [1984] CTC 2401, 84 DTC 1374 (T.C.C.)	Taxpayer's solicitor became aware of need to file notice of objection two weeks after expiry of 90-day period.
Tanaka v. M.N.R., [1985] 1 CTC 2333, 85 DTC 305 (T.C.C.)	Notice of Objection filed late by accountant, who then appeared on behalf of client arguing that taxpayer should not be penalized for his mistake. Court commented on accountant's conflict of interest.
Harris v. M.N.R., [1985] 1 CTC 2363, 85 DTC 302 (T.C.C.)	Notice filed 14 days late. Application for extension not brought for six months. Court attributed delay to accountant's negligence.

Extension Denied	
McGill v. M.N.R., [1985] 2 CTC 209, 85 DTC 5439 (F.C.A.)	Taxpayer wholly indifferent to proper manner of exercising his legal rights. Ignorance of law may be proper excuse in certain circumstances, but not in this case.
Aspinall v. M.N.R., [1986] 1 CTC 2355, 86 DTC 1284 (T.C.C.)	Application for extension delayed for seven months; not brought as soon as circumstances permitted.
The Queen v. Pennington, [1987] 1 CTC 235, 87 DTC 5107 *(sub nom. Pennington v. M.N.R.)* (F.C.A.)	Notice of objection filed three days late and application for extension filed 359 days after expiry of limitation period. Taxpayer not acting as soon as possible in filing application, but simply passing matter on to accountant.

(iii) Additional Requirements

The Minister's discretion to dispense just and equitable relief is restricted by the following additional requirements:

- The application for the extension of time for filing the Notice must be made no later than one year after the expiry of the original time limit;[100]
- The taxpayer must have been unable to act within the limitation period or had a *bona fide* intention to object to the assessment;[101] and
- The application must be brought as soon as circumstances permit.[102]

In other words, the taxpayer must have a plausible case for objecting to the assessment and act quickly and prudently to protect his or her interests.

There are two separate requirements in respect of the time limits for an extension to file a Notice of Objection: The application must be brought "as soon as circumstances" permit *and,* at the very latest, no later than one year after the expiration

---

[100] Para. 166.1(7)(*a*).

[101] Subpara. 166.1(7)(*b*)(i); see also *Reid v. M.N.R.,* [1985] 2 CTC 2396, 85 DTC 695 (T.C.C.).

[102] Subpara. 166.1(7)(*b*)(iii).

of the original date for filing the notice. The two time periods are conjunctive and each must be satisfied independently of the other. Thus, the taxpayer should not wait to see if negotiations with Revenue Canada will prove successful and then file for an extension of time if they are not. The better course is to file the application for extension immediately upon becoming aware of the expiration of the initial deadline and to continue negotiations with Revenue Canada on a parallel track.

Pennington[103] illustrates the problems that can arise by not bringing an application for extension of time at the earliest possible opportunity. The taxpayer filed a Notice of Objection three days after the 90-day limitation period. Revenue Canada rejected the notice and sent the taxpayer a letter telling him that he could apply for an extension of time, and that the application must be made "as soon as possible and not later than one year" from the 90-day limit. The taxpayer took up the matter with his accountant and asked him to attempt to negotiate a settlement of the matter in issue. When it became clear some time later that a satisfactory settlement was unlikely, the taxpayer applied for an extension of the limitation period. The Federal Court of Appeal refused the extension on the basis that the taxpayer did not act "as soon as possible" to file his application and it was not a sufficient excuse in law that he had passed the matter on to his accountant for settlement. Thurlow C.J.F.C. said:[104]

> What the statute appears to me to require is that the taxpayer make his application as early as, under the particular circumstances, he could *reasonably be expected to get an application ready and presented.* [Emphasis added.]

The phrase "as soon as circumstances permit" is strictly construed, and should not be confused with the maximum time limit of one year prescribed in the statute.

(d) Appeal

A taxpayer can appeal the Minister's refusal to grant an extension of time to file a Notice of Objection.[105] The appeal is to the Tax Court of Canada, which has the power to grant the application on such terms as it considers just. The taxpayer must, however, satisfy all of the conditions in subsection 166.2(5), which places the same limits on the court's discretion as those placed on the Minister.[106] The courts are more willing to adopt a flexible approach to extensions upon appeals.[107]

---

[103] *The Queen v. Pennington*, [1987] 1 CTC 235, 87 DTC 5107 (F.C.A.).

[104] *The Queen v. Pennington, ante*, [1987] 1 CTC at 237, 87 DTC at 5109.

[105] S. 166.2.

[106] Subs. 166.1(7).

[107] See *Carew v. M.N.R.*, [1993] 1 CTC 1, 92 DTC 6608 (F.C.A.) (as a matter of principle, courts are loath to let procedural technicalities stand in the way of a case being decided on its merits).

(e) Disposition

The Minister is required to consider the Notice of Objection and to either confirm, vacate or vary the assessment to which objection is made.[108] Where the Minister does not confirm, vacate or vary the assessment within 90 days of service of the Notice,[109] the taxpayer may appeal to the Tax Court without further delay.[110]

(f) Refund of Taxes

A taxpayer who files a Notice of Objection or launches an appeal against his or her assessment can apply for a refund of the tax paid in respect thereof if another taxpayer has successfully challenged a similar assessment in court. The Minister is not obliged to make the refund, but may refund the tax paid if he or she is satisfied that it would be "just and equitable" to do so.[111]

13. WITHHOLDING TAXES

References:

ITA:

S. 153 Withholding, Payments, Remittance

S. 154 Deemed Receipt of Payment, etc.

REGULATION:

202   Payments to Non-Residents

BULLETINS, CIRCULARS & RULINGS:

IT-155R3	June 16, 1989	Exemption from Non-Resident Tax on Interest Payable on Certain Bonds, Debentures, Notes, Hypothecs or Similar Obligations
IT-161R3	October 8, 1982	Non-Residents — Exemption from Tax Deductions at Source on Employment Income

---

[108] Subs. 165(3).

[109] *Jolicoeur v. M.N.R.*, [1960] CTC 346, 60 DTC 1254 (Ex. Ct.) (although taxpayer may appeal to Tax Court if Minister does not respond within 90 days, no time limit imposed on Minister to reply).

[110] S. 169.

[111] Subs. 164(4.1).

Taxpayers who make certain types of payments are required to deduct tax at source. The types of payments which require withholding at source are generally payments of a compensatory nature, payments out of deferred income plans, and payments to non-residents.[112] Taxes withheld at source are to be remitted to the Receiver General of Canada. Failure to remit taxes is a strict liability offence.[113]

(a) Failure to Withhold

A person who fails to withhold taxes when required to do so may be penalized. The penalty is determined in two tiers:[114]

1. The first failure to withhold is penalized at 10 per cent of the amount not deducted or withheld; and

2. A second (or subsequent) failure made knowingly or under circumstances amounting to gross negligence in the same calendar year is penalized at 20 per cent.

The penalty applies if the tax is remitted after the due date, regardless whether the taxpayer pays the withheld taxes before the Minister issues a penalty assessment.[115]

Where a corporation fails to deduct, withhold or remit taxes in accordance with the Act, its directors may be *personally* liable for the taxes, together with interest and penalties thereon.[116] Failure to withhold taxes on account of certain payments[117] to non-residents renders the payor and the non-resident jointly and severally liable for the interest payable on the penalty.[118]

---

[112] Subs. 153(1); s. 215; Regs. 100–109.

[113] *The Queen v. Swendson*, [1987] 2 CTC 199, 87 DTC 5335 (Alta. Q.B.).

[114] Subs. 227(8).

[115] *Electrocan Systems Ltd. v. Can.*, [1989] 1 CTC 244, 89 DTC 5079 (*sub nom. Electrocan Systems Ltd. v. M.N.R.*) (F.C.A.).

[116] S. 227.1; see *Barnett v. M.N.R.*, [1985] 2 CTC 2336, 85 DTC 619 (T.C.C.) (director/sole shareholder liable for unremitted deductions); *Beutler v. M.N.R.*, [1988] 1 CTC 2414, 88 DTC 1286 (T.C.C.) (director/taxpayer did not exercise due care, skill and diligence to prevent failure to remit taxes); *Fraser Estate (Trustee) v. M.N.R.*, [1987] 1 CTC 2311, 87 DTC 250 (T.C.C.) (minority shareholder/director may be liable even if others could have prevented default).

[117] S. 215.

[118] Subs. 227(8.1).

(b) Criminal Sanctions

Where a corporation fails to remit taxes, its directors and officers become criminally liable if they acquiesced or participated in the offence. But to be criminally liable for corporate acts, the directors and officers must have the *mens rea* to participate in the offence.

14. INSTALMENT PAYMENTS

References:

ITA:

S. 153	Withholding, Payments, Remittance
S. 154	Deemed Receipt of Payment, etc.
S. 155	Farmers and Fishers
S. 156	Payment by Others, Mutual Fund Trusts
S. 157	Payment by Corporations
S. 161	Interest — Rules, Definitions
S. 227	Withholding Taxes

REGULATION:

5301   Instalment Base — Corporations

BULLETINS, CIRCULARS & RULINGS:

IC 81-11R3   March 26, 1993   Corporate Instalments

(a) General

As noted above, compensatory payments to employees are subject to withholding of tax at source. The employee is required to file an income tax return by April 30 of the year following receipt of payment and make up any deficiency in the tax payable. Where the amount withheld at source exceeds the taxpayer's liability for taxes, the employee is entitled to a refund of the excess.[119]

(b) Individuals

Individuals (other than those whose chief source of income is farming or fishing) must make tax instalments if more than 25 per cent of their income is not subject to deductions at source.[120] Instalment payments are made on a quarterly basis. Any deficiency in the amount payable is to be settled by April 30 of the following year.

---

[119] Subs. 153(1), s. 164.

[120] Subs. 156(1).

The first four instalments are payable on March 15, June 15, September 15 and December 15 in each taxation year. The amount of each instalment is 25 per cent of:

- The *estimated* tax payable for the year; or
- The taxpayer's "instalment base" for the immediately preceding taxation year.

The final instalment is payable by April 30 of the following year.

A taxpayer's "instalment base" for the immediately preceding taxation year is, in essence, the amount of tax that was payable under Part I of the Act for that preceding year.[121]

To relieve individuals from the obligation to make quarterly payments where the tax payable is insignificant, the Act exempts individuals from making instalment payments where the federal tax payable in the year, or in the preceding year, is $2,000 or less.[122] In these circumstances, the individual may pay his or her entire tax liability by April 30 of the following year.

(c) Corporations

(i) Estimated Payments

A corporation is required to make monthly instalments of its Part I tax over a 14-month period: One instalment on the last day of each month of its taxation year, and the final instalment, for the balance of the tax payable, by the last day of the second month following the end of the taxation year.[123]

A corporation's monthly instalments are determined in one of three ways:

1. Each instalment can be one-twelfth of the tax on its *estimated* taxable income for the year;
2. Each instalment can be one-twelfth of its "first instalment base"; or
3. The first two instalments can be one-twelfth of its "second instalment base" and the next ten instalments can be one-tenth of its first instalment base minus the first two payments.

A corporation's "first instalment base" is its tax payable under Part I (excluding surtax) for the immediately preceding taxation year; its "second instalment base" is its tax payable under Part I (excluding surtax) for the second preceding taxation year.[124]

---

[121] Subs. 156(3), Reg. 5300(1).

[122] Subs. 156.1(1).

[123] Subs. 157(1).

[124] Reg. 5301.

(ii) Balance Payable

The balance of any Part I tax payable is due on or before the end of the third month following its year-end, if the corporation is a Canadian-controlled private corporation that claimed the small business deduction.[125] For other corporations, the balance is payable within two months after the year-end.[126]

(iii) Exemption

A corporation is not required to pay tax instalments for a taxation year if its federal tax payable or first instalment base is $1,000 or less.[127]

(iv) Failure to Remit

Failure to remit the full amount of its instalment payments on the dates due renders the corporation liable to interest at a prescribed rate on the deficiency.[128] Hence, a corporation that makes instalment payments calculated by reference to its previous year's income may be liable for interest on deficient instalments as a consequence of a subsequent reassessment of that income.[129]

(v) Short Fiscal Periods

Special rules apply in respect of tax instalments payable by corporations with short fiscal periods. In these circumstances instalments are required only on the last day of each complete month in the short taxation year; the remainder is due on the balance due date. Note: The instalment base is calculated by grossing up the tax payable by the ratio that 365 is of the actual number of days in the year.

15. BOOKS AND RECORDS

References:

ITA:

S. 230	Books and Records
S. 238	Offences — Failure to File a Return, etc.
S. 239	Offences
S. 240	Taxable Obligation and Non-Taxable Obligation Defined

---

[125] Subpara. 157(1)(b)(i).

[126] Subpara. 157(1)(b)(ii).

[127] Subs. 157(2.1).

[128] Subs. 161(2). Interest is calculated from the date when the payment was due to the date when payment was made.

[129] *No. 384 v. M.N.R.* (1957), 16 Tax ABC 300, 57 DTC 67.

S. 241　　Provision of Information

S. 242　　Officers of Corporations

S. 243　　Power to Decrease Punishment

REGULATION:

5800　　Retention of Books and Records

(a) Form and Content

Every person who carries on a business or is obliged to pay, or withhold, taxes from payments made to others is required to keep books and records of accounts at his or her place of business or residence in Canada.[130] The books and records should be kept in a manner that allows determination of the tax payable or the tax withheld. The Minister can specify the books and records to be maintained in any particular case.

A taxpayer is not required to keep his or her accounts in any particular form or adhere to any particular bookkeeping system. The taxpayer need only maintain accounts sufficient to determine the amount of income that is taxable and the amount of tax that is owing.[131] There are, however, special rules in respect of recordkeeping requirements applicable to registered charities, amateur athletic associations and contributions to federal political parties and candidates.[132]

(b) Retention

A taxpayer is required to maintain general records, books of accounts and supporting vouchers for a period of at least six years following the taxation year to which the records and documents relate.[133] The "permanent" records of a corporation (such as minutes of directors' and shareholders' meetings, share ledgers, general ledgers and special contracts and agreements) are to be maintained for a period of at least two years after the corporation is dissolved.

Similarly, the "permanent" records of a registered charity or registered Canadian amateur athletic association must be maintained for a period of at least two years after the registration of the charity or amateur athletic association is revoked.

---

[130] S. 230. The Minister can also designate the place where the books and records are to be kept.

[131] *Labbe v. M.N.R.*, [1967] Tax ABC 697, 67 DTC 483; see also *Freitag v. M.N.R.* (1951), 5 Tax ABC 54, 51 DTC 350; *P.X. Cossette & Fils Inc. v. M.N.R.* (1959), 23 Tax ABC 65, 59 DTC 551.

[132] Subs. 230(2); s. 230.1.

[133] Reg. 5800.

Records in respect of political contributions and expenditures must be maintained for a period of at least two years following the calendar year to which the records relate.

A taxpayer who objects to or appeals from a Notice of Assessment must maintain his or her books and records until such time as the objection or appeal is resolved or the time period for a further appeal has elapsed.[134]

(c) Minister's Discretion

The statutory time periods in respect of the maintenance of books and records are all subject to the discretion of the Minister, who may require a taxpayer to maintain such books and records (together with supporting documents) for whatever length of time he or she considers necessary for the administration of the Act.[135] The taxpayer must obtain permission from the Minister to destroy any records or books of account prior to the prescribed time.[136]

Failure to comply with the requirements in respect of the maintenance of books and records is a criminal offence carrying a monetary penalty of between $1,000 and $25,000 and possible imprisonment for a term of up to 12 months.[137]

16. DIRECTORS' LIABILITY FOR CORPORATE TAXES

References:

ITA:

S. 153	Withholding, Payments, Remittance
S. 154	Deemed Receipt of Payment, etc.
S. 159	Payments on Behalf of Others
S. 227.1	Liability of Directors
S. 238	Offences — Failure to File a Return, etc.
S. 239	Offences
S. 240	Taxable Obligation and Non-Taxable Obligation Defined
S. 241	Provision of Information
S. 242	Officers of Corporations
S. 243	Power to Decrease Punishment

---

[134] Subs. 230(6).

[135] Subs. 230(7).

[136] Subs. 230(8).

[137] Subs. 238(1).

BULLETINS, CIRCULARS & RULINGS:

IC 89-2   May 1, 1989   Directors' Liability — Section 227.1 of the Income Tax Act

A corporation is a taxpayer in its own right. Thus, with few exceptions, a corporation is taxed as a separate legal entity and is responsible for the payment of its taxes. There are circumstances, however, when the Act pierces the corporate veil and holds shareholders and directors personally liable for corporate acts.

There are two categories of circumstances in which directors may be personally liable for corporate taxes: (1) Improper payment of dividends, and (2) Failure to remit withheld taxes.

(a) Improper Dividends

Directors who declare dividends that render the corporation unable to pay its taxes may be liable *to the corporation* for the amount of the improper payment.[138] Thus, directors can end up liable for the corporation's Part I tax liability.

(b) Failure to Withhold or Remit Taxes

A director may also be personally liable for corporate acts if:

- The corporation fails to withhold taxes as required or fails to remit withheld taxes;[139]

- In his or her capacity as an executor or administrator, the director fails to obtain a clearance certificate before distributing corporate property;[140] or

- The director authorizes or acquiesces in the commission of an offence by the corporation.[141]

Corporate directors are jointly and severally liable with the corporation if the corporation fails to deduct, withhold or remit income tax as required by the Act.[142]

---

[138] See, e.g., *Canada Business Corporations Act*, R.S.C. 1985, c. C-44, s. 42; para. 118(2)(*c*).

[139] *Income Tax Act*, s. 227.1.

[140] Subs. 159(3).

[141] S. 242.

[142] Subs. 227.1; *Barnett v. M.N.R.*, [1985] 2 CTC 2336, 85 DTC 619 (T.C.C.) (director liable for payroll deductions; corporation obliged to hold funds in trust for the Crown separate and apart from its own funds).

(i) Withholding Taxes

(A) On Salary, etc.

A corporation is required to withhold income tax at source when it pays salary, wages and certain other types of compensatory payments.[143] The amount to be withheld is determined in accordance with rules prescribed under Part I of the Regulations. A corporation may be civilly or criminally liable for failure to deduct or withhold income tax at source.[144]

(B) Payments to Non-residents

A resident corporation that pays or credits an amount to a non-resident person must withhold tax on behalf of the non-resident.[145] Failure to withhold renders the corporation liable for the whole amount that should have been withheld.

(C) Trust Funds

A corporation must remit all withheld taxes to the Receiver General of Canada. Pending remittance, the moneys are held in trust for the benefit of the Crown, and are not available for the satisfaction of judgment creditors.[146] The Act purports to protect from legal action any person who withholds or deducts tax at source in compliance, or *intended* compliance, with the withholding provisions.[147]

(ii) Personal Liability

The directors of a corporation that does not comply with the withholding requirements can be held personally liable for the amount due by the corporation, together with interest and penalties thereon.[148]

(iii) Limitations

A director cannot, however, be held personally liable unless:[149]

- A certificate for the amount of the corporate tax liability has been registered in the Federal Court and execution thereof has been partially or wholly unsatisfied;

---

[143] Subs. 153(1).

[144] Subs. 238(1).

[145] S. 215.

[146] Subss. 227(4), (5).

[147] Subs. 227(1). This provision raises the constitutional question as to whether the federal government has the power to withdraw a taxpayer's right of legal action.

[148] Subs. 227.1(1).

[149] Subs. 227.1(2).

- The corporation has commenced proceedings for liquidation or dissolution and a claim for the amount of the corporate tax liability is proved within six months after commencement of such proceedings; or

- The corporation has made an assignment (or had a receiving order made against it) under the *Bankruptcy and Insolvency Act* and a claim for the amount of the corporate tax liability is proved within six months after the date of the assignment or receiving order.[150]

A director of a corporation is immune from personal liability unless the Minister commences proceedings against him or her within two years from the time when he or she last ceased to be a director of the corporation.[151]

(iv) Defence of "Due Diligence"

A director of a corporation is not personally liable for the corporation's failure to withhold or remit taxes where he or she has exercised "the degree of care, diligence and skill to prevent the failure that a reasonably prudent person would have exercised in comparable circumstances".[152] What constitutes the degree of care and skill that would be exercised by a reasonably prudent person in comparable circumstances is a question of fact.

(A) Objective Test

Under the common law, a director is required to demonstrate the degree of care, skill and diligence that could reasonably be expected from him or her, *having regard to his or her knowledge and experience.*[153] The test under the Act goes one step beyond the common law: It is objective. Thus, the obligation of directors to exercise due care and skill in supervising the corporation's responsibilities to withhold and remit taxes to the Crown falls somewhere between the subjective standard applied at common law and the more stringent obligation imposed upon professionals. Corporate directors

---

[150] *Bankruptcy and Insolvency Act*, R.S.C. 1985, c. B-3.

[151] Subs. 227.1(4).

[152] Subs. 227.1(3).

[153] *Re City Equitable Fire Ins. Co.,* [1925] 1 Ch. 407 (C.A.), *per* Romer J.:

[a] director need not exhibit in the performance of his duties a greater degree of skill than may reasonably be expected from a person of his knowledge and experience. A director of a life insurance company, for instance, does not guarantee that he has the skill of an actuary or of a physician. In the words of Lindley M.R.: 'If directors act within their powers, if they act with such care as is reasonably to be expected from them, having regard to their knowledge and experience, and if they act honestly for the benefit of the company they represent, they discharge both their equitable as well as their legal duty to the company". . . . It is perhaps only another way of stating the same proposition to say that directors are not liable for mere errors of judgment.

need exercise only the degree of care, diligence and skill that a *reasonably prudent individual* would have exercised in comparable circumstances.

The rather low expectation of corporate directors is a product of the judicial perception of the qualifications necessary to become a director. The description in *Brazilian Rubber Plantations* reflects the expectations of directors:[154]

> The directors of the company, Sir Arthur Aylmer, Bart., Henry William Tugwell, Edward Barber, and Edward Henry Hancock, were all induced to become directors by Harbord or persons acting with him in the promotion of the company. Sir Arthur Aylmer was absolutely ignorant of business. He only consented to act because he was told the office would give him a little pleasant employment without his incurring any responsibility. H.W. Tugwell was partner in a firm of bankers in a good position in Bath; he was seventy-five years of age and very deaf; he was induced to join the board by representations made to him in January, 1906. Barber was a rubber broker and was told that all he would have to do would be to give an opinion as to the value of rubber when it arrived in England. Hancock was a man of business who said he was induced to join by seeing the names of Tugwell and Barber, whom he considered good men.

(B) Standard of Care

What constitutes an adequate standard of care, diligence and skill on the part of a director is a question of fact in each case. A director is not bound to give continuous attention to the affairs of the corporation.[155] It is also clear that a director is entitled to rely upon the officials of the corporation to keep him or her informed on corporate developments. In the absence of grounds for suspicion, a director is justified in trusting his or her officials to execute their duties according to corporate policies.[156]

At the very least, however, a director is expected to take positive action to ensure compliance with the remittance provisions of the Act. Passive reliance on the other directors or officers of the corporation is not sufficient to discharge the standard of care expected of directors.[157] Thus, the directors of a corporation are expected to:

- Establish corporate policies in respect of accounting for income taxes, both under Part I of the Act in respect of the corporation's own tax liabilities and in respect of withholding from employees and payments to non-residents;

- Call upon the financial officers of the corporation to report upon compliance with established corporate policies;

---

[154] *Re Brazilian Rubber Plantations & Estates Ltd.*, [1911] 1 Ch. 425 at 427; subsequent proceedings 103 LT 882 (C.A.).

[155] *Re City Equitable Fire Ins. Co.*, *ante*, at 429.

[156] *Re City Equitable Fire Ins. Co.*, *ante*, at 429.

[157] *Fraser Estate (Trustee) v. M.N.R.*, [1987] 1 CTC 2311, 87 DTC 250 (T.C.C.) (minority shareholder/director in corporation's manufacturing operations liable for failure to remit taxes); *Beutler v. M.N.R.*, [1988] 1 CTC 2414, 88 DTC 1286 (T.C.C.) (failure to deposit payroll deductions in separate trust account suggested absence of "due diligence").

- Obtain undertakings from senior corporate officials that corporate policies in respect of income tax and other financial matters have in fact been complied with during the relevant period;
- Wherever prudent, maintain a separate trust account for payroll deductions; and
- Exercise independent judgement and not simply rely on the other directors or officers of the corporation.[158]

Corporate directors cannot be expected to do much more.[159]

A director who is called upon to satisfy a claim in respect of corporate tax liabilities is entitled to claim contribution from fellow directors who are also liable under the claim.[160]

(C) Accounting Systems

Each corporate director is responsible for ensuring that the corporation uses a proper and acceptable accounting system to control the withholding and remittance of source deductions.[161] Further, the director should be aware of current practices and systems in the corporation.[162] A director is not expected to be an accounting expert

---

[158] *Fraser Estate (Trustee) v. M.N.R.*, *ante*; *Quantz v. M.N.R.*, [1988] 1 CTC 2276, 88 DTC 1201 (T.C.C.).

[159] *Re Nat. Bank of Wales Ltd.*, [1899] 2 Ch. 629 at 673 (C.A.):

Was it his duty to test the accuracy or completeness of what he was told by the general manager and the managing director? This is a question on which opinions may differ, but we are not prepared to say that he failed in his legal duty. Business cannot be carried on upon principles of distrust. Men in responsible positions must be trusted by those above them, as well as by those below them, until there is reason to distrust them. We agree that care and prudence do not involve distrust; but for a director acting honestly himself to be held legally liable for negligence, in trusting the officers under him not to conceal from what they ought to report to him, appears to us to be laying too heavy a burden on honest businessmen.;

affirmed [1901] AC 477 (*sub nom. Dovey v. Cory*) (H.L.), *per* Lord Davey:

I think the respondent was bound to give his attention to and exercise his judgment as a man of business on the matters which were brought before the board at the meetings which he attended, and it is not proved that he did not do so. But I think he was entitled to rely upon the judgment, information and advice, of the chairman and general manager, as to whose integrity, skill and competence he had no reason for suspicion.

[160] Subs. 227.1(7). It is questionable whether the *Income Tax Act* can constitutionally confer the power on a director to claim contribution from his or her fellow directors. In any event, the common law would recognize such a right.

[161] *Barnett v. M.N.R.*, *ante*; *Quantz v. M.N.R.*, *ante*; *Moore v. M.N.R.*, [1988] 2 CTC 2191, 88 DTC 1537 (T.C.C.) (director personally liable for unremitted payroll deductions as he did not exercise the required degree of care, diligence and skill); *Merson v. M.N.R.*, [1989] 1 CTC 2074, 89 DTC 22 (T.C.C.) (director not personally responsible for unremitted source deductions as he exercised the required degree of care and diligence and the corporation did not benefit).

[162] *Fraser Estate (Trustee) v. M.N.R.*, *ante*.

or a controller, and may rely upon competent professional advice and the guidance of those who are experts in accounting and control systems. A director is not expected to personally verify the collection and remittance of all source deductions, but the failure to segregate withheld deductions may indicate a lack of prudence.[163]

(D) Trust Accounts

Taxes withheld at source are trust funds. Thus, although not absolutely necessary, it is prudent to maintain a separate trust account for collecting and remitting corporate source deductions.

Although a director is a fiduciary to the corporation, he or she cannot use trust funds that belong to the government of Canada to assist the corporation in overcoming a cash shortage or financial embarrassment.[164]

(E) Passive Directors

The personal liability of directors for corporate source deductions applies equally to "passive" and "nominee" directors as to those who are actively involved in the corporation's management. As a matter of administrative practice, Revenue Canada does not distinguish between active, passive, inside and outside directors.[165]

A corporate director is not entitled to delegate his or her responsibility, and cannot claim diminished responsibility by virtue of non-involvement in the corporation's management and affairs. In this context, there is no difference between directors of large public corporations and small private corporations: They all carry the same burden of responsibility to ensure that source deductions are properly accounted for and remitted to the Receiver General.

(F) Administrative Policies

Information Circular 89-2 sets out Revenue Canada's practices in respect of assessing directors personally for source deductions:

- Revenue Canada will write to directors who may be liable to inform them that an assessment is being considered and to request an explanation of all actions taken to ensure that the corporation deducted, withheld, remitted or paid all prescribed amounts.

- A director who does not respond to Revenue Canada's information request within the time limits set out may be assessed without further notice.

---

[163] *Barnett v. M.N.R.*, *ante*; *Beutler v. M.N.R.*, *ante*.

[164] *Pilling v. M.N.R.*, [1989] 2 CTC 2037, 89 DTC 327 (T.C.C.).

[165] Revenue Canada Directive CA87-67 (October 6, 1987), obtainable under *Privacy Act*, R.S.C. 1985, c. P-21.

- Department of Justice lawyers will be consulted only where a due diligence defence has been raised by the director. Otherwise, a decision to issue the assessment against the director will be made by the Collections Division.

(c) Clearance Certificates

An assignee, liquidator, administrator or executor (other than a trustee in bankruptcy) must obtain a clearance certificate from the Minister before distributing any property under his or her control.[166] The certificate should certify that all taxes, interest and penalties chargeable against or payable out of the property that is to be distributed have been paid. This requirement does *not* extend to a director of a corporation if he or she is acting *qua* director and not *qua* executor, assignee, liquidator, or administrator.[167]

(d) Participation in Offences Committed by the Corporation

A director of a corporation may be held to be a party to, and guilty of, an offence committed by the corporation if he or she directs, authorizes, assents to, acquiesces in or participates in an offence committed by the corporation. The director can be held liable even though the corporation itself is not prosecuted or convicted for the offence.[168]

There are two elements to a director's personal liability for corporate offences:[169]

1. The corporation is guilty of an offence under the Act; and
2. The director participated in some way in the commission of the offence.

Thus, mere proof that a corporation was convicted of the offence is not sufficient by itself to convict a director; the corporation must be shown to have been guilty of, and

---

[166] Subs. 159(2).

[167] *Parsons v. M.N.R.,* [1983] CTC 321 at 330-31, 83 DTC 5329 at 5337; reversed on other grounds [1984] CTC 352 (*sub nom. The Queen v. Parsons*), 84 DTC 6345 (F.C.A.) (roles of the various fiduciaries mentioned in subs. 159(2) described by court as follows: "An assignee is a person to whom an assignment is made and assignment means that property is transferred to another. The assignee is the recipient of that property. A liquidator is a person appointed to carry out the winding up of a company whose duty is to get in and realize the property of the company, to pay its debts and to distribute the surplus (if any) among the shareholders. An executor is the person to whom the execution of a will is entrusted by a testator...an executor is bound to satisfy all claims on the estate before distributing it among the legatees and other beneficiaries. An administrator is the person to whom the property of a person dying intestate is committed for administration and whose duties with respect thereto correspond with those of an executor.").

[168] S. 242.

[169] *Hartmann v. The Queen,* [1971] CTC 396, 70 DTC 6219 (Sask. Dist. Ct.).

not merely to have been convicted of, the offence.[170] A director may be criminally convicted in his or her personal capacity only if he or she had *mens rea* to commit the offence.[171]

17. PENALTIES FOR FALSE STATEMENTS OR OMISSIONS

References:

ITA:

S. 162   Penalties

S. 163   Repeated Failures, False Statements

Subsection 163(2) of the Act authorizes the Minister to impose a penalty on a person who has either

- "knowingly", or
- "under circumstances amounting to gross negligence",

made or participated in the making of a false statement or omission in an income tax return.

(a) "Knowingly"

There are three degrees of knowledge: (1) Actual knowledge; (2) Deliberate refraining from making inquiries; and (3) Constructive knowledge.

In the first category, the taxpayer must have *actual* knowledge of the misstatement or omission on the return. The second category deals with a situation where a person *deliberately* shuts his or her eyes to an obvious means of knowledge —— in other words, deliberately refrains from making inquiries the result of which he or she might not care to know. The third category, generally referred to as "constructive knowledge", is concerned with what a taxpayer "ought to have known".[172]

(b) Gross Negligence

Negligence is a failure to use reasonable care. "Gross negligence" involves something greater or worse or more reckless than simply a failure to use reasonable care. "Gross negligence" requires a greater degree of culpability or errant behaviour on

---

[170] *The Queen v. Anisman*, [1969] 1 OR 397, 69 DTC 5199 (Ont. H.C.).

[171] *The Queen v. Swendson*, [1987] 2 CTC 199, 87 DTC 5335 (Alta. Q.B.).

[172] See *Taylor's Central Garages (Exeter) Ltd. v. Roper*, [1951] 2 TLR 284 (Div. Ct.), in particular *per* Devlin J. at 288-89.

the taxpayer's part than one might expect in a case of "ordinary" negligence. For example, in *Venne*:[173]

> . . . "gross negligence" . . . must involve a high degree of negligence tantamount to intentional acting, an indifference as to whether the law is complied with or not. . . . To be sure, the plaintiff did not exercise the care of a reasonable man, and . . . should have at least reviewed his tax returns before signing them. A reasonable man in doing so, having regard to other information available to him, would have been led to believe that something was amiss and would have pursued the matter further with his bookkeeper.

But the mere failure to exercise the care of a reasonable person is not enough to constitute *gross* negligence.

(c) "Has Made"

The penalty under subsection 163(2) can be imposed only on a taxpayer who "has made" or participated in, assented to or acquiesced in the grossly negligent misstatement or omission. In other words, a taxpayer is liable only if he or she is grossly negligent or the gross negligence of his or her agent can be directly attributed to the taxpayer. In *Udell*:[174]

> In my view the use of the verb "made" in the context in which it is used also involves a deliberate and intentional consciousness on the part of the principal to the act done. . . .

Any doubt, ambiguity or uncertainty as to whether there was deliberate or intentional consciousness on the taxpayer's part should be resolved in the taxpayer's favour:[175]

> . . . I take it to be a clear rule of construction that in the imposition of a tax or a duty, and still more of a penalty if there be any fair and reasonable doubt the statute is to be construed so as to give the party sought to be charged the benefit of the doubt.

If the words of a penal section are capable of two interpretations, one that imposes liability and one that does not inflict a penalty, the latter interpretation should prevail.[176]

Thus, subsection 163(2) applies only in two circumstances:

1. The taxpayer is grossly negligent or knowingly makes a misstatement or omission on his or her return for the year; or

2. The taxpayer's agent is grossly negligent or knowingly makes a misstatement *and* the agent's action or knowledge can be directly attributed to the taxpayer.

---

[173] *Venne v. The Queen*, [1984] CTC 223 at 234, 84 DTC 6247 at 6256 (F.C.T.D.) *per* Strayer J.

[174] *Udell v. M.N.R.*, [1969] CTC 704 at 714, 70 DTC 6019 at 6025 (Ex. Ct.) *per* Cattanach J.

[175] *Udell v. M.N.R.*, *ante*, [1969] CTC at 714, 70 DTC at 6026.

[176] *Tuck & Sons v. Priester* (1887), 19 QBD 629.

The second alternative has two separate requirements: (1) The taxpayer's advisers must be grossly negligent in the preparation of the tax return; and (2) the taxpayer must have been privy, in one of the three senses of "knowingly", to the act of gross negligence and in fact acquiesced or participated in the false statement or omission.

(d) Onus of Proof

(i) Burden

The burden of proof rests squarely on the Minister to establish that the taxpayer acted knowingly or with gross negligence in the misstatement on the income tax return. The Minister must show that the taxpayer acted in circumstances amounting to gross negligence on the particular facts.[177]

(ii) Omissions

A mere omission or misstatement of income on a return is not *in and of itself* sufficient to establish gross negligence. Subsection 163(2) requires proof of the omission or misstatement *in circumstances of conduct* that are tantamount to gross negligence. Thus, there must be an act of omission or misstatement by the taxpayer or his or her agent, and a state of mind or conduct that justifies a finding of *gross* negligence. The courts are hesitant to attribute the knowledge and conduct of accountants to their clients.[178]

18. TRANSFERS OF PROPERTY

Reference:

ITA:

S. 160   Tax Liability on Transfer of Property

(a) Tax Liability

Generally speaking, when an individual transfers property to his or her spouse or to a person under 18 years of age, the transferor and transferee become *jointly and severally* liable for any tax payable by the transferor at the time of transfer. The purpose of the joint and several liability rules is to enable the tax authorities to take their share of any tax payable to them. But the rules go further: They also apply to transfers between unrelated persons who do not deal with each other at arm's length.

---

[177] *James v. M.N.R.*, [1993] 1 CTC 2126, 93 DTC 161 (Minister failed to discharge the onus of proving that the penalties were appropriate).

[178] See, e.g., *Udell v. M.N.R., ante*; *M.N.R. v. Weeks*, [1972] CTC 60, 72 DTC 6001; affirming 70 DTC 1431 (F.C.T.D.); *Oudot v. M.N.R.*, [1970] Tax ABC 915, 70 DTC 1599; *Apex Auto-Matic Centres Ltd. v. M.N.R.*, [1971] Tax ABC 751, 71 DTC 480; *Joris v. M.N.R.*, [1981] CTC 2596, 81 DTC 470 (T.R.B.) (accountant's errors in tax returns not gross negligence on the part of the taxpayer).

The first two categories of transferees (spouses and persons under 18 years of age) are readily identifiable. Transfers to the third category (transferees not at arm's length with the transferor), however, contain hidden traps.

(b) Non-arm's Length

The Act does not define "arm's length". The question as to whether taxpayers are dealing with each other at arm's length is sometimes a question of law and sometimes a question of fact. Persons who are married or related to each other are generally considered not to be dealing with each other at arm's length. Persons may, however, also be considered not to be at arm's length with each other as a matter of fact.

Unrelated persons who do not deal with each other in an independent manner may act in concert. If they do, they are not at arm's length with each other. The question is one of fact and, as with many questions of fact, depends upon the credibility of the taxpayer's testimony.[179] The onus is on the taxpayer to establish the nature of the relationship between the parties.

The joint and several liability of the parties is equal to the shortfall between the value of the property transferred and any consideration received by the transferor. Note: Any subsequent payments by the transferor first reduce his or her personal liability in respect of his or her other tax debts. It is only when those other tax debts are fully paid that further payments reduce the joint and several liability. Hence, the non-arm's length transferee can remain liable for taxes long after the transfer of property.

19. INVESTIGATIONS

References:

ITA:

S. 230	Books and Records
S. 231.1	Inspections
S. 231.2	Requirement to Provide Documents or Information
S. 231.3	Search Warrant
S. 238	Offences — Failure to File Return, etc.
S. 239	Offences

BULLETINS, CIRCULARS & RULINGS:

IC 71-14R3	June 18, 1984	The Tax Audit

---

[179] *Lindsay v. M.N.R.*, [1990] 1 CTC 2245, 90 DTC 1085 (T.C.C.).

(a) Ministerial Powers

The income tax system relies on self-assessment. The Minister does, however, have considerable power to ensure that taxpayers do not use self-assessment to evade income taxes. The administrative requirements in respect of the maintenance of books and records, filing of tax and information returns, payments of taxes, interest and penalties are all directed towards persuading taxpayers to remain on the "straight and narrow" path.

The Department also has extensive powers to conduct investigations into a taxpayer's financial affairs. The scope of these powers is broad, sometimes frighteningly so in a free society. The powers are not, however, without limit: The Canadian *Charter of Rights and Freedoms* provides some restraint on the Minister's statutory powers.

The Department's investigative powers are intended to prevent tax evasion and fraud. The scope of the powers is, however, disproportionate to the problem. As Lord Denning M.R. said:[180]

> In the tax evasion pool, there are some big fish who do not stop at tax avoidance. They resort to frauds on a large scale. I can well see that if the legislation were confined, or could be confined, to people of that sort, it would be supported by all honest citizens. Those who defraud the Revenue in this way are parasites who suck out the life-blood of our society. The trouble is that the legislation is drawn so widely that in some hands it might be an instrument of oppression. It may be said that "honest people need not fear; that it will never be used against them; that tax inspectors can be trusted only to use it in the case of the big, bad frauds". This is an attractive argument, but I would reject it. Once great power is granted, there is a danger of it being abused. Rather than risk such abuse, it is, as I see it, the duty of the courts so to construe the statute as to see that it encroaches as little as possible on the liberties of the people. . . .

(b) Audit and Examination

(i) Business Premises

An "authorized person"[181] is entitled to audit or examine a taxpayer's books, records or property.[182] Such a person can enter into a taxpayer's business premises and, upon gaining entry, audit and examine all of the books, records, accounts, vouchers, letters, and any other documents which may, or should, relate to the amount of tax payable under the Act.

An auditor is entitled to reasonable assistance from the owner or manager of the property or business and *any* other person on the premises. He or she can demand

---

[180] *R. v. I.R.C.*, [1979] 3 All ER 385 at 399; reversed [1980] 1 All ER 80 (H.L.).

[181] S. 231 ("authorized person" is person authorized by Minister).

[182] Paras. 231.1(1)(*a*), (*b*).

written or oral answers in respect of any question relating to the audit or examination, and can require the owner or manager of the premises to attend at the premises.[183]

The auditor's right to obtain answers to questions is not restricted to questioning employees of the taxpayer. The auditor may question *any* person who is on the premises, and in certain circumstances may even question members of the taxpayer's family who are not involved in the business.

Thus, tax auditors have unfettered and unrestricted power to disrupt a business for an unlimited period of time. Other than restricting entry to a reasonable time, there are no statutory limitations on the auditor's right to scrutinize the taxpayer's books, records or documents or to question the taxpayer, his or her employees and members of the taxpayer's family.

The courts have not restrained the Minister's powers of examination. As Martland J. said in *Western Minerals:*[184]

> . . . it is not for the Court or anyone else to prescribe what the intensity of the examination of a taxpayer's return in any given case should be. That is exclusively a matter for the Minister, acting through his appropriate officers, to decide . . . There is no standard in the Act or elsewhere, either express or implied, fixing the essential requirements of an assessment. It is exclusively for the Minister to decide how he should, in any given case, ascertain and fix the liability of a taxpayer. The extent of the investigation he should make, if any, is for him to decide.

An auditor can demand entry to a taxpayer's business premises for the purpose of conducting an audit or examination, but only at a reasonable time, that is, during normal business hours. There is no limitation upon the number of times that a tax auditor can enter onto a taxpayer's premises for the purposes of the examination.

(ii) Dwelling-house

An auditor may not enter into a taxpayer's "dwelling-house"[185] without the taxpayer's consent or the authority of a search warrant.[186] A search warrant may be issued on the Minister's *ex parte* application if there are reasonable grounds for believing that entry into the dwelling-house is necessary for administrative purposes.[187]

---

[183] Para. 231.1(1)(*d*).

[184] *Western Minerals Ltd. v. M.N.R.*, [1962] CTC 270 at 273, 62 DTC 1163 at 1165 (S.C.C.), referring to the headnote of *Provincial Paper Ltd. v. M.N.R.*, [1954] CTC 367, 54 DTC 1199 (Ex. Ct.).

[185] S. 231 ("dwelling house").

[186] Subs. 231.1(2).

[187] Subs. 231.1(3).

(iii) Search Warrants

(A) Application

Section 231.3 allows the Minister to make an *ex parte* application to a judge for a search warrant to enter into a taxpayer's dwelling-house. A search warrant can also be applied for under the Criminal Code.

The judge may[188] issue the warrant if he or she is satisfied that there are reasonable grounds to believe that an offence has been committed under the Act and that evidence of the offence is likely to be found on the premises.[189]

(B) Scope

The warrant must be "reasonably specific" as to its scope, and must specify the documents to be searched for and seized.[190] Typically, a Revenue Canada investigator will prepare an Information setting out the details of a *prima facie* offence under section 239 of the Act. The auditor is, however, allowed to seize not only the documents or things referred to in the search warrant but also any other document or thing which he or she believes, on reasonable grounds, affords evidence of the commission of an offence under the Act.[191] Thus, in effect, the Minister has virtually unlimited powers[192] of search and seizure if entry is obtained on the authority of a search warrant. This is so even if the warrant is of limited scope.[193]

(C) Custody of Seized Documents

The Minister must report the list of documents seized from the taxpayer to the judge, but he or she is entitled to retain the seized items that are the subject of the investigation.[194] The Act is quite clear that the judge "shall" order retention of the seized items unless the Minister waives the right to retain the seized items. Thus, there is very limited judicial control over the Minister and his or her agents.

---

[188] The judge retains a discretion as to whether he or she will issue the warrant.

[189] Subs. 231.3(3).

[190] Subs. 231.3(4).

[191] Subs. 231.3(5).

[192] An earlier version of section 231.3, which did not give the judge any discretion over the issuance of the warrant, was ruled unconstitutional under section 8 of the Charter in *Baron v. Canada*, [1993] 1 CTC 111, 93 DTC 5018 (S.C.C.).

[193] See subs. 231.3(7) (in certain circumstances, such as non-compliance with warrant, judge may order documents returned to taxpayer).

[194] Subs. 231.3(6).

(c) Demand for Information

(i) *Minister's Power*

The Minister may demand from *any* person *any* information for *any* purpose related to the administration or enforcement of the Act. The Minister may also demand production of any books, letters, accounts, invoices, statements or other documents from any person. The person from whom the demand is made must respond within such "reasonable time" as is stipulated in the Notice of Demand.[195]

(ii) *Defences*

A taxpayer can challenge a demand for information on the basis that:

- The documents demanded are not germane or relevant to the issues between the parties;
- The Minister is on a "fishing expedition" and not on a specific inquiry as to some taxpayer's liability;
- The taxpayer has not been given a reasonable time to produce the documents; or
- The documents are privileged.

A demand for information constitutes a seizure, but not an unreasonable one within section 8 of the Charter.[196]

(iii) *Named Persons*

The Minister can make the demand only in respect of information relating to named persons and for a purpose related to the administration or enforcement of the Act.[197] The test is objective and is determined on the basis of the particular facts.

It is not necessary that the person from whom the information is sought be the person whose tax liability is under investigation. The fact that the giving of the information may disclose private transactions involving persons who are not under investigation and may not be liable for tax does not invalidate an otherwise valid demand for information.

(iv) *"Fishing Expeditions"*

The demand for information must be a genuine and serious inquiry into the tax liability of some *specific* person or persons. The Minister cannot be on a "fishing

---

[195] Subs. 231.2(1); *Joseph v. M.N.R.*, [1985] 2 CTC 164, 85 DTC 5391 (Ont. H.C.) (in case of lawyer, period of less than seven to ten days would usually not be "reasonable").

[196] *Can. v. McKinlay Tpt. Ltd.*, [1990] 2 CTC 103, 90 DTC 6243 (S.C.C.); affirming [1988] 1 CTC 426 (*sub nom. McKinlay Tpt. Ltd. v. The Queen*), 88 DTC 6314.

[197] Subs. 231.2(2).

expedition" into the affairs of an unknown group of taxpayers. For example, a taxpayer cannot be compelled to provide a random sample as a check on the general compliance of some unidentified class of taxpayers.[198]

(v) Reasonable Time to Respond

What constitutes a "reasonable time" within which information must be supplied is also a question of fact. The Minister usually stipulates a time or date in the Notice of Demand for Information. Whether the stipulated period of time is reasonable depends upon the volume and complexity of the information demanded and the ease with which the taxpayer can obtain the information. As the Federal Court observed in *Richardson:*[199]

> The purpose of the statutory provision is to ensure that the person from whom the information is required will have a reasonable time (which will vary considerably depending on the amount of information, the time required to collect and compile it, and other circumstances) to comply, and that he will comply within that reasonable time. The words "without delay" do not comply strictly with the statute, but in the sense of "within a reasonable time", which is the meaning courts have frequently held to be the correct meaning, and which in my opinion is the right meaning in the circumstances of this case, they afford the Applicant all the protection intended by the statute. A reasonable time is not exact, as is a stated period or a terminating date, but it can be ascertained for the circumstances of a particular case. If in the present case, the information is not forthcoming and legal proceedings are begun, the Minister will have to satisfy the Court that a reasonable period of time for compliance with the requirement elapsed before the proceedings were started.

(vi) Unnamed Persons

The Minister may demand information in respect of unnamed persons, but only pursuant to a court order authorizing the "fishing expedition".[200] The Minister may obtain the order on the basis of an *ex parte* application. The judge must be satisfied that:[201]

- The unnamed person or group of persons is ascertainable;
- The demand is made for the purpose of compliance with the Act;
- It is reasonable to expect that the person or group of persons will fail to supply information to comply with the Act; and
- The information is not otherwise more readily available.

---

[198] Subs. 231.2(2) (amendment to conform to decision of Supreme Court of Canada in *Richardson, post*); *James Richardson & Sons Ltd. v. M.N.R.*, [1984] CTC 345, 85 DTC 6325 (S.C.C.) (a demand can only be made for information relevant to the tax liability of a person or persons if a genuine and serious inquiry into their tax liability is being conducted).

[199] *James Richardson & Sons Ltd. v. M.N.R.*, [1981] CTC 229 at 249, 81 DTC 5232 at 5246 (F.C.T.D.); affirmed [1982] CTC 239, 82 DTC 6204 (F.C.A.); which was reversed on other grounds [1984] CTC 345, 84 DTC 6325 (S.C.C.).

[200] Subss. 231.2(2), (3).

[201] Subs. 231.2(3).

The party from whom the information is demanded may seek a review of the order within 15 days after its service.[202]

(vii) Multiple Demands

Since the purpose of the subsection is not to penalize criminal conduct but to enforce compliance with the Act, the purpose would be defeated if the Minister's power were exhausted after a single demand and conviction.[203] Thus, the Minister can make multiple demands for the same information. Failure to comply with multiple demands in respect of the same information can lead to multiple convictions.[204]

20. INQUIRY

References:

ITA:

S. 231.4   Inquiry

BULLETINS, CIRCULARS & RULINGS:

IC 73-10R3   February 13, 1987   Tax Evasion

In addition to the power to audit a taxpayer's books of account and general records, the Minister can also conduct an inquiry or private hearing into the taxpayer's affairs:[205]

> This procedure is used in Special Investigations cases where persons who are considered able to give evidence concerning transactions or practices constituting tax evasion are reluctant to furnish voluntary explanations or are so closely related to the taxpayer under examination, by family relationship or business association, that they will not, for fear of recriminations or financial loss, give information unless compelled to do so.

(a) Hearing Officer

The Minister must apply to the Tax Court for an order appointing a hearing officer to conduct the inquiry.[206] For the purposes of the inquiry, the hearing officer has all

---

[202] Subs. 231.2(5).

[203] *The Queen v. Grimwood*, [1988] 1 CTC 44, 88 DTC 6001 (S.C.C.).

[204] Subs. 238(1).

[205] S. 231.4; IC 73-10R3, "Tax Evasion" (February 13, 1987), para. 25.

[206] Subs. 231.4(2).

the powers of a commissioner under the *Inquiries Act*,[207] including the right to summon witnesses, to require evidence on oath, to compel the attendance of witnesses, to engage technical specialists (accountants, engineers, etc.) and to deputize technical advisors to inquire into matters within the scope of the commission.[208] Note: A hearing officer does not have the power to punish any person unless he or she obtains the approval of a judge of a superior court and the person to be punished is given 24 hours' notice, or such shorter time as the judge deems reasonable.[209]

(b) Exclusion From Hearing

A person whose affairs are being investigated in the course of an inquiry is entitled to be present and represented by counsel *unless* the person is excluded by the hearing officer. The basis for excluding a taxpayer and his or her counsel from an inquiry is that the taxpayer's presence would be prejudicial to the conduct of the inquiry.[210] It does not appear to matter that removing the taxpayer's legal counsel from the inquiry might be prejudicial to the taxpayer! In contrast, a person who attends as a witness in an inquiry is always entitled to be represented by legal counsel and to receive a transcript of the evidence given by him or her.[211]

21. ADVANCE RULINGS

Reference:

BULLETINS, CIRCULARS & RULINGS:

IC 70-6R2   September 28, 1990   Advance Income Tax Rulings

An advance ruling is a written statement/opinion from the Department as to how it will interpret specific provisions in the context of specific proposed transactions.

The formal advance rulings procedure was initiated in 1970. Unlike Interpretation Bulletins and Information Circulars that are issued for use by the general public, Advance Rulings are issued by Revenue Canada directly to the taxpayer who applies for the ruling. An Advance Ruling on a complex transaction provides certainty for the taxpayer, but obtaining one can be a frustrating bureaucratic process.

---

[207] *Inquiries Act*, R.S.C. 1985, c. I-11; *Income Tax Act*, subs. 231.4(3).

[208] *Income Tax Act*, subs. 231.4(3); *Inquiries Act*, R.S.C. 1985, c. I-11, s. 11.

[209] *Income Tax Act*, subs. 231.4(4).

[210] Subs. 231.4(6).

[211] Subs. 231.4(5).

(a) Procedure

A ruling is issued on the basis of specific facts set out in the taxpayer's application. Requests for income tax rulings must be forwarded in duplicate to the applicable directorate, and should identify the taxpayer and the relevant District Taxation Office.

A ruling request should contain a clear statement of relevant facts, copies of all pertinent documents, and a statement of the purpose of the transaction. It is also useful to include an interpretation of the relevant statutory provisions upon which the taxpayer is relying, citations to Interpretation Bulletins and, where relevant, any case law on point. The request should also contain a statement confirming that none of the issues are being currently considered by a District Office in respect of a return which has already been filed by the taxpayer. Revenue Canada will only rule on prospective, not completed, transactions.

(b) Fee for Service

The advance ruling mechanism is organized on the basis of a fee for service.

(c) Conference with Revenue Canada

A taxpayer may request a conference with the Department at the time that an Advance Ruling request is filed. Although the Department's official policy (IC 70-6R2) indicates that a taxpayer is entitled to only one conference as a matter of right, the Department is generally prepared to grant further conferences if the taxpayer so requests. In fact, the Department will usually accede to as many conferences as are needed in the circumstances.

(d) Rejection of Request at Initial Stage

An Advance Ruling request may be rejected on policy grounds at the time when it is filed. For example, where the request clearly falls within one of the categories listed in paragraph 14 of IC 70-6R2, the request will be returned without a ruling. Revenue Canada will not issue an Advance Ruling where:

- The central issue involves a matter that is before the courts;
- The request for a ruling contains alternative courses of action on the part of the taxpayer;
- The major issue is whether a sale or purchase of property should be viewed as of an income nature or as a capital transaction;
- The matter involved is a determination of fair market value of property;
- A ruling would require an opinion as to generally-accepted accounting or commercial practices in certain circumstances; or
- The transactions do not "clearly have a *bona fide* business purpose" or appear to be designed primarily for the improper avoidance, reduction or deferral of tax.

(e) Discretion

Revenue Canada is not bound to issue a ruling on any proposed transactions. It will issue a ruling only in circumstances when it is comfortable with the facts and the nature of the transaction that is the subject of the ruling. It is entirely in Revenue Canada's domain to determine whether it considers a proposed transaction to be "offensive" or "abusive" in the sense that it has no business purpose, is improper tax avoidance, or constitutes unlawful tax mitigation.

(f) Appeals

There is no formal appeal procedure for taxpayers who are dissatisfied with the Department's ruling. A taxpayer may, however, request a reconsideration of the ruling. The Department will entertain such a request only where the taxpayer has new information or can show that the ruling was based on a misunderstanding of the information previously submitted. In most cases, the taxpayer may meet with the Department to discuss the ruling. The Department usually contacts the taxpayer before it issues an unfavourable ruling. A taxpayer who is unable to resolve outstanding contentious issues with the Department may withdraw the ruling request prior to the issuance of an unfavourable ruling.

(g) Delayed Rulings

There is no particular timetable for the issuance of a ruling. In routine matters the ruling may be issued quite quickly (three to four months). In more contentious circumstances, however, the Department may take longer (eight to twelve months) to issue a ruling. In extreme cases the Department may simply refuse to issue a ruling even though the taxpayer's request for a ruling is based on perfectly legal grounds.

The Department will usually not issue a ruling if it is offended by the underlying tenor of the proposed transaction. This is so even if the ruling is based on perfectly legal interpretations. There is also a danger in such cases that the Department may use the delay to persuade the Department of Finance to amend the law to block transactions similar to the one proposed in the ruling request.

(h) Status of Rulings

Advance Rulings are not binding in law. They are issued at the sole discretion of Revenue Canada so that business transactions may proceed in an environment of certainty. The Advance Ruling mechanism is entirely an administrative creation, not an expression of legislative authority. A ruling has no binding effect in law. As a matter of practice, however, Revenue Canada generally considers itself to be bound in respect of both the taxpayer requesting the ruling and the issues ruled upon. The Department rarely revokes an issued ruling, but it can do so. Although it is arguable that the revocation of an issued ruling would constitute an abuse of power, it would be fairly difficult to establish.[212]

Revenue Canada does not consider itself to be bound by its rulings in the following circumstances:

- Where there is a material omission or misrepresentation in the statement of relevant facts or disclosure of purpose submitted by the taxpayer;
- Where the advanced ruling was based on an interpretation of the law which has since been changed as a result of a judicial decision;
- Where the transaction in respect of which an Advance Ruling was given has not been substantially completed within the time limits specified in the ruling; or
- Where there has been a change in the law upon which the Advance Ruling was based.

(i) Publication of Rulings

Revenue Canada publishes its Advance Rulings on a selective basis. Between June 1974 and December 8, 1980, the Department published a total of 101 rulings. In 1983 the Department announced that it would no longer publish Advance Rulings and that previously-published rulings should not be relied upon as a reflection of departmental policy.

The Department's decision to stop publishing rulings met with considerable opposition. For example, the CBA/CICA Joint Committee commented:

> It is the Committee's view that the publication of rulings was a good way to publicize Revenue Canada's position in matters affecting large numbers of taxpayers.

The Department eventually relented and began to issue a second series of Advance Tax Rulings in 1986. The Department has said that it will reissue previously issued rulings where the issues raised in the published rulings are still relevant.

The Department does not publish all of its rulings. Indeed, it is very selective in its publication of rulings, a policy that attracted adverse comment from the Auditor General in its review of Departmental procedures. Between 1985 and 1993, for example, the Department published only 58 Advance Rulings out of an estimated 4,300 that were issued. Most of the rulings were published at least two years after they were issued.

In particular, the Department is not anxious to issue rulings that endorse innovative and creative tax plans, even though such plans may be technically correct. Thus, there is an underground network among tax lawyers and accountants for unpublished rulings.

---

[212] *R. v. IRC, ex parte Matrix-Securities Ltd.*, [1994] BTC 85 (H.L.) (the revocation would need to result in clearly manifested injustice).

22. SEARCH AND SEIZURE

References:

ITA:

S. 231.3	Search Warrant
S. 232	Seizure Procedure

(a) The Power

The Minister can enter and search *any* building or place and seize therefrom *any* document or thing that *may* afford evidence as to the commission of an offence under the Act. However, the Minister's power of search and seizure can be exercised only on the basis of a search warrant issued by a superior court or Federal Court judge.[213]

(b) "Seizure"

"Seizure" is the forcible taking of possession of property. Not all seizures violate section 8 of the Charter, only unreasonable ones. Hence, the question in each case is whether there has been a "seizure" and, if so, whether it was reasonable in the circumstances.[214]

A demand for information constitutes a "seizure", but not an unreasonable one in the context of the administrative and regulatory scheme of the Act.

(c) The Warrant

(i) Ex Parte Application

The Minister may make an *ex parte* application for the issuance of a search warrant. Any document or thing that is seized pursuant to the search must be brought before the judge. The Minister's application for the search warrant must be supported by information on oath establishing the facts on which the application is based.[215]

The decision to apply for a search warrant is an administrative decision, and is not subject to judicial review.[216]

---

[213] Subs. 231.3(1).

[214] *Hunter v. Southam Inc.,* [1984] 2 SCR 145, 84 DTC 6467; *Thomson Newspapers Ltd. v. Dir. of Investigation & Research, Combines Investigation Branch* (1986), 57 OR (2d) 257 (Ont. C.A.); *The Queen v. McKinlay Tpt. Ltd.,* [1990] 2 CTC 103, 90 DTC 6243 (S.C.C.); affirming [1988] 1 CTC 426, 88 DTC 6314 (Ont. C.A.).

[215] Subs. 231.3(2).

[216] Subs. 231.3(3). *F.K. Clayton Group Ltd. v. M.N.R.,* [1989] 1 CTC 82, 89 DTC 5186 (F.C.T.D.) (Minister's decision to apply for warrant is purely a procedural step).

A judge may issue a search warrant if satisfied that there are reasonable grounds to believe that:[217]

- An income tax offence has been committed;
- A document or thing that *may* afford evidence of the commission of the offence is *likely* to be found; and
- The building or place to be searched is *likely* to contain the evidence.

(ii) Contents

The warrant must refer to the offence for which it is issued, identify the building or place to be searched and the person who allegedly committed the offence, and be reasonably specific as to the document or thing that is the object of the search.[218]

The authority of the warrant, however, extends beyond the itemized list for which it is issued. Thus, the Minister may also seize any other document or thing not specified in the warrant if he or she believes that it affords evidence of the commission of an income tax offence.[219] All documents or things that are seized by the Minister must be brought before the judge who issued the warrant or, if that judge is not available, before another judge of the same court.

(iii) Not Reviewable

A judge's decision to issue a warrant on an *ex parte* application is not reviewable by an appellate court.[220]

(d) Return of Documents

A judge may, on his or her own motion or on application by a third party, order that a document or thing seized be returned to its owner. To issue such an order for return of documents or things, the judge has to be satisfied that the document or thing:[221]

- Will not be required for an investigation or a criminal proceeding; or
- Was not seized in accordance with the warrant or the rules described in section 231.3.

---

[217] Subs. 231.3(3).

[218] Subs. 231.3(4).

[219] Subs. 231.3(5).

[220] *Knox Const. Ltd. v. The Queen*, [1989] 1 CTC 174, 89 DTC 5074 (N.B. C.A.).

[221] Subs. 231.3(7).

(e) Access to Seized Information

The person from whom the documents have been seized has the right to obtain one copy of all the seized documents.[222] The photocopies are to be supplied at the Minister's expense. In addition, the owner of the documents is entitled to have access to the documents at all reasonable times and subject to such reasonable conditions as may be imposed by the Minister. The items to be searched for and seized do not have to be described with specific particularity in the application for the warrant. Indeed, given the nature of income tax offences which lead to search and seizure, it is probably impossible to describe in detail all of the documents sought in a search.

(f) Material in "Plain View"

(i) Common Law Rule

The common law recognizes the "plain view" doctrine. Thus, where, during the course of executing a legal warrant, an officer locates anything which he or she reasonably believes is evidence of the commission of a crime, the officer has the legal power to seize it.[223] Hence, an official may seize a document without a warrant for that specific document.

(ii) Criminal Code

Revenue Canada also has the power to seize any material falling in "plain view" that affords evidence of any income tax offence. Section 489 of the Criminal Code[224] enables a person executing a warrant to seize, in addition to the material that affords evidence of an offence for which the warrant was issued, any other documentary material that he or she believes on reasonable grounds to afford evidence of any other offence under the Act. Since the Minister has the power to seize "plain view" material, the material has the same status as any other materials seized pursuant to the warrant.

The Minister's power may, however, depend upon the jurisdiction in which the warrant is obtained. In *Knox Contracting*,[225] for example, the New Brunswick court held that a warrant issued under what is now section 487 of the Criminal Code could not be used for the purpose of any other statute. Presumably, the limitation would also apply, in New Brunswick, to any "plain view" material seized under section 489.

---

[222] Subs. 231.3(8).

[223] *Ghani v. Jones*, [1970] 1 QB 693 at 706 (C.A.), *per* Lord Denning M.R.; *Chic Fashions (West Wales) Ltd. v. Jones*, [1968] 2 QB 299 at 313 (C.A.), *per* Diplock L.J.; *Reynolds v. Metro. Police Commr.*, [1984] 3 All ER 649 at 653, 659, 662 (C.A.); *The Queen v. Shea* (1983), 1 CCC (3d) 316 at 321-22 (Ont. H.C.); *Texas v. Brown*, 75 L Ed (2d) 502 (1983); *The Queen v. Longtin* (1983), 5 CCC (3d) 12 at 16 (Ont. C.A.).

[224] *Criminal Code*, R.S.C. 1985, c. C-46.

[225] *Knox Contr. v. The Queen*, [1986] 2 CTC 194, 86 DTC 6417 (N.B.Q.B.); see also *Purdy v. The Queen* (1972), 28 DLR (3d) 720 (N.B.C.A.).

(g) The Raid

The manner in which a search and seizure is carried out can be a formidable experience. The following excerpt from the reasons for judgment of Lord Denning M.R. in *I.R.C.*[226] describes the logistics of a tax raid:

It was a military style operation. It was carried out by officers of the Inland Revenue in their war against tax frauds. Zero hour was fixed for 7 am on Friday, 13th July 1979. Everything was highly secret. The other side must not be forewarned. There was a briefing session beforehand. Some 70 officers or more of the Inland Revenue attended. They were given detailed instructions. They were divided into teams each with a leader. Each team had an objective allotted to it. It was to search a particular house or office, marked, I expect, on a map: and to seize any incriminating documents found therein. Each team leader was on the day to be handed a search warrant authorising him and his team to enter the house or office. It would be empowered to use force if need be. Each team was to be accompanied by a police officer. Sometimes more than one. The role of the police was presumably to be silent witnesses: or may be to let it be known that this was all done with the authority of the law: and that the householder had better not resist — or else!

Everything went according to plan. On Thursday, 12th July, Mr. Quinlan, the senior inspector of the Inland Revenue, went to the Central Criminal Court: and put before a circuit judge, the Commons Sargeant, the suspicions which the Revenue held. The circuit judge signed the warrants. The officers made photographs of the warrants, and distributed them to the team leaders. Then in the early morning of Friday, 13th July, the next day, each team started off at first light. Each reached its objective. Some in London. Others in the Home Counties. At 7 am there was a knock on each door. One was the home in Kensington of Mr. Ronald Anthony Plummer, a chartered accountant. It was opened by his daughter aged 11. He came downstairs in his dressing-gown. The officers of the Inland Revenue were at the door accompanied by a detective inspector. The house-holder Mr. Plummer put up no resistance. He let them in. They went to his filing cabinet and removed a large number of files. They went to the safe and took building society passbooks, his children's cheque books and passports. They took his daughter's school report. They went to his bedroom, opened a suitcase, and removed a bundle of papers belonging to his mother. They searched the house. They took personal papers of his wife.

Another house was the home near Maidstone of Mr. Roy Clifford Tucker, a fellow in the Institute of Chartered Accountants. He was away on business in Guernsey. So his wife opened the door. The officers of the Inland Revenue produced the search warrant. She let them in. She did not know what to do. She telephoned her husband in Guernsey. She told him that they were going through the house taking all the documents they could find. They took envelopes addressed to students who were tenants. They went up to the attic and took papers stored there belonging to Mr. Tucker's brother. They took Mr. Tucker's passport.

The main attack was reserved for the offices at 1 Hanover Square of the Rossminster group of companies of which Mr. Plummer and Mr. Tucker were directors. They were let in by one of the employees. Many officers of the Inland Revenue went in accompanied by police officers. It was a big set of offices with many rooms full of files, papers and documents of all kinds. They took large quantities of them, pushed them into plastic bags, carried them down in the lift, and loaded them into a van. They carried them off to the offices of the Inland Revenue at Melbourne House in Aldwych. Twelve van loads. They cleared out Mr. Tucker's office completely: and other rooms too. They spent the whole day on it from 7am until 6:30 at night. They did examine some of the documents carefully, but there were so many documents and so many files that they could not examine them all. They simply put a number on each file, included it in a list, and put it into the plastic bag. Against each file they noted the time they did it. It looks as if they averaged one file a minute. They did not stop at files. They

---

[226] *The Queen v. I.R.C.*, [1979] 3 All ER 385 at 396; reversed [1980] 1 All E.R. 80 (H.L.).

took the shorthand notebooks of the typists; I do not suppose they could read them. They took some of the financial newspapers in a bundle. In one case the "top half" of a drawer was taken in the first instalment and the balance of the drawer was taken in the second.

Another set of offices was next door in St. Georges Street, I think along the same corridor. It was the office of AJR Financial Services Limited. The director Mr. Hallas was not there, of course, at 7 o'clock. He arrived at 9:10 am. He found the officers of the Inland Revenue packing the company's files into bags for removal. He said that it amounted to several hundreds of documents. Police officers were in attendance there too.

At no point did any of the householders make any resistance. They did the only thing open to them. They went off to their solicitors. They saw counsel. They acted very quickly. By the evening they had gone to a judge of the Chancery Division, Walton, J., and asked for and obtained an injunction to stop any trespassing on the premises. They telephoned the injunction through the Hanover Square at about a quarter to six at night. The officers therefore brought the search and seizure to an end. They had, however, by this time practically completed it. So the injunction made very little difference. . . .

So end the facts. As far as my knowledge of history goes, there has been no search like it, and no seizure like it, in England since that Saturday, 30 April 1763, when the Secretary of State issued a general warrant by which he authorised the King's messengers to arrest John Wilkes and seize all his books and papers. They took everything, all his manuscripts and all papers whatsoever. His pocket-book filled up the mouth of the sack. He applied to the courts. Pratt, C.J. struck down the general warrant. You will find it all set out in *R v Wilkes* [(1763), 2 Wils 151], *Huckle v Money* [(1763), 2 Wils 205] and *Entick v. Carrington* [(1763), 2 Wils 275]. Pratt CJ said:

> To enter a man's house by virtue of a nameless warrant, in order to procure evidence, is worse than the Spanish inquisition; a law under which no Englishman would wish to live an hour: it was a most daring public attack made upon the liberty of the subject [2 Wils 205 at 207].

(h) Constitutional Restrictions

(i) Section 8 of the Charter

The determination as to whether, and how, constitutionally tainted evidence may be used against a taxpayer depends upon three provisions of the Charter. There are four separate questions that need to be answered:

1. Has there been a seizure?
2. Was the seizure unreasonable?
3. Should the court provide relief against the unreasonable seizure? and
4. Should the constitutionally-tainted evidence be excluded?

Section 8 of the Charter reads as follows:

8. Everyone has the right to be secure against unreasonable search or seizure.

The operative word in section 8 is "unreasonable". There is no personal security against search and seizure *per se*. The only security is that the state's search or seizure cannot be unreasonable in the particular circumstances.[227]

---

[227] *Kourtessis v. M.N.R.*, [1989] 1 CTC 56, 89 DTC 5214 (B.C.S.C.).

A "seizure" is a forcible taking of possession of property.[228] However, not every taking is a seizure for the purposes of section 8. In Justice Grange's words:[229]

> It is not necessary to formulate a general rule as to what constitutes a seizure; it is sufficient to say that the s. 8 prohibition does not encompass an order requiring the production of documents so long as the section authorizing the order (or the law apart from that section) gives the person required to produce a reasonable opportunity to dispute the order and prevent the surrender of the documents.

The determination as to what is a "reasonable" search or seizure is made in the context of section 231.3 of the *Income Tax Act*. The judge who issues the warrant must be satisfied that the Minister has reasonable grounds to believe that an offence has been committed, and the executing officer must have reasonable grounds for believing that the documents seized afford evidence of the commission of an offence. These two safeguards render a properly executed search and seizure "reasonable" in the context of section 8 of the Charter.[230] Pratte J. explained the scope of section 8 as follows:[231]

> Searches and seizures are intrusions into the private domain of the individual. They cannot be tolerated unless circumstances justify them. A search or seizure is unreasonable if it is unjustified in the circumstance. Section 8 does not merely prohibit unreasonable searches and seizures. It goes further and guarantees the right to be secure against unreasonable search and seizure. That is to say that section 8 of the Charter will be offended, not only by an unreasonable search or seizure or by a statute authorizing expressly a search or seizure without justification, but also by a statute conferring on an authority so wide a power of search and seizure that it leaves the individual without any protection against searches and seizures.

The underlying value that is protected by section 8 of the *Charter* is the taxpayer's interest in privacy. However, section 8 provides protection from only an *unreasonable* search and seizure, not from all seizures.

What constitutes a "reasonable" search and seizure? The test is fluid: It depends upon the type of intrusion into the taxpayer's privacy (for example, demand for information vs. physical seizure of documents), the type of taxpayer (for example, individual vs. corporate), the location where the seizure is executed (for example, business premises vs. personal residence), and the context (for example, criminal vs. regulatory/administrative). As Dickson C.J.C. said in *Hunter*:[232]

---

[228] *Thomson Newspapers Ltd. v. Dir. of Investigation & Research, Combines Investigation Branch, ante,* at 267.

[229] *Thomson Newspapers Ltd. v. Dir. of Investigation & Research, Combines Investigation Branch, ante,* at 269.

[230] *Solvent Petroleums Extraction Inc. v. M.N.R.,* [1988] 1 CTC 325, 88 DTC 6224; affirmed [1989] 2 CTC 177, 89 DTC 5381 (S.C.C.).

[231] *M.N.R. v. Kruger Inc.,* [1984] CTC 506 at 512, 84 DTC 6478 at 6483 (F.C.A.).

[232] *Hunter v. Southam Inc., ante,* [1984] 2 SCR at 155, 84 DTC at 6471-72.

It is clear that the meaning of "unreasonable" cannot be determined by recourse to a dictionary, nor for that matter, by reference to the rules of statutory construction. The task of expounding a constitution is crucially different from that of construing a statute. A statute defines present rights and obligations. It is easily enacted and as easily repealed. A constitution, by contrast, is drafted with an eye to the future. Its function is to provide a continuing framework for the legitimate exercise of governmental power and, when joined by a Bill or a Charter of Rights, for the unremitting protection of individual rights and liberties.

There are essentially three tests to determine whether a search and seizure is reasonable:[233]

1. Was the search authorized by law?

2. Is the law itself reasonable? and

3. Was the manner in which the search was carried out reasonable?

If the answer to all three questions is affirmative, the seizure is reasonable and does not impugn section 8 of the Charter.

The burden of proof for adducing evidence that Charter rights have been infringed or denied depends upon the nature of the search. If the search and seizure was conducted pursuant to a warrant, the burden rests initially with the person making the allegation of infringement, namely, the taxpayer. The burden is discharged on a balance of probabilities.[234] Where, however, the search was conducted without the authority of a warrant, the onus is on the Minister to show that the search was, on a balance of probabilities, reasonable in the circumstances.[235]

(ii) Section 24 of the Charter

Prior to the Charter, the traditional remedies to protect taxpayers were sparse. Typically, and almost invariably, Canadian courts followed the English, as opposed to American, tradition, and allowed illegally obtained evidence to be used against taxpayers and citizens.[236]

If it is determined that a particular search and seizure was conducted in an "unreasonable" manner, what is to be done with any evidence that is seized as a result of the illegal search? Two provisions of the Charter bear on this question.

Subsection 24(1) provides as follows:

---

[233] *The Queen v. Collins*, [1987] 1 SCR 265.

[234] *The Queen v. Collins*, *ante*.

[235] *Hunter v. Southam Inc.*, *ante*, at 161; see also *The Queen v. Collins*, *ante*.

[236] See, e.g., *The Queen v. Wray*, [1971] SCR 272; for criticisms see Weinberg, "The Judicial Discretion to Exclude Relevant Evidence" (1975), 21 *McGill L.J.* 1, at 4-5; Sheppard, "Restricting the Discretion to Exclude Admissible Evidence: An Examination of Regina v. Wray" (1972), 14 *Cr. L.Q.* 335, at 342-47.

24.(1) Anyone whose rights or freedoms, as guaranteed by this Charter, have been infringed or denied may apply to a court of competent jurisdiction to obtain such remedy as the court considers appropriate and just in the circumstances.

This is a remedial provision which allows a court considerable, though not unlimited, latitude in devising a remedy. There is no suggestion that this provision is the exclusive remedy for Charter violations, but it appears to be the one that is most frequently invoked in tax cases.

Although subsection 24(1) of the Charter confers broad discretionary power on a court to provide relief from illegal conduct, it does not mandate the court to exclude the evidence from judicial proceedings.[237] The court *may* exclude evidence from a trial, but only if it is satisfied that the test in subsection 24(2) of the Charter is met. That subsection reads as follows:

(2) Where, in proceedings under subsection (1), a court concludes that evidence was obtained in a manner that infringed or denied any rights or freedoms guaranteed by this Charter, the evidence shall be excluded *if* it is established that, having regard to all the circumstances, the admission of it in the proceedings would bring the administration of justice into disrepute.

Unlike subsection 24(1) of the Charter, subsection 24(2) does not confer a discretion on the judge. The judge is under a duty to admit or exclude the tainted evidence.[238] Tainted evidence is *prima facie* admissible. Here too the burden of persuasion rests on the taxpayer to show that the admission of the evidence *would* bring the administration of justice into disrepute.

The focus of subsection 24(2) is on the effect that the admission of the evidence would have on the reputation of the administration of justice. The principal focus of this test is not on the misconduct of the authorities during the course of their investigative process, but on the effect that admission of the evidence would have on the administration of justice. Investigative misconduct goes to the question whether the search and seizure was "unreasonable" and contrary to section 8 of the Charter in the first place. To be sure, the nature of the misconduct may colour the decision to admit the evidence, for example, if the conduct is outrageously scandalous.

The interpretation of subsection 24(2) is complicated by the substantial difference in the language of the English and French versions of the text. The English text uses the words "*would* bring the administration of justice into disrepute". The French version provides "*est susceptible de* déconsidérer l'administration de la justice". The difference between "would" in the English text and "could" in the French text has the effect of lowering the threshold level for excluding evidence. The Supreme Court of Canada has said that the less onerous French text better serves the purpose of the Charter.[239]

---

[237] *The Queen v. Therens*, [1985] 1 SCR 613.

[238] See, *The Queen v. Collins, ante.*

[239] *The Queen v. Collins, ante.*

By what yardstick do we measure the effect of admitting or excluding evidence? By whose standards and values do we determine the likelihood that inclusion of tainted evidence could bring the administration of justice into disrepute? It is easy enough to articulate an objective "reasonable person" test. To use Professor Yves-Marie Morissette's test:[240] "Would the admission of the evidence bring the administration of justice into disrepute in the eyes of the reasonable man, dispassionate and fully apprised of the circumstances of the case?" The reasonable person test, long familiar to those who have followed the career of "the man on the Clapham omnibus", requires time for maturation before the interpretation of subsection 24(2) becomes more certain. For present purposes, the test is to be read as an objective test that involves an assessment of community views on the administration of justice.

Professor Hogg has alluded to the irony of subsection 24(2), which calls for the exclusion of evidence if its admission could taint the reputation of the administration of justice. There is some impressionistic evidence to suggest that the exclusion of incriminating evidence tends to tarnish the reputation of the administration of justice in the eyes of the community. In Professor Hogg's words:[241]

> As has been frequently pointed out, there is something irrational about allowing a guilty person to go free (usually the result when reliable evidence is excluded), because another person (usually a police officer) has committed a wrong.

It is the long-term effect of the admission of evidence on the reputation of the administration of justice that is to be weighed in determining whether to exclude tainted evidence.[242]

The difficulty with the "community values" test is that such values usually reflect the views of the majority, whereas the thrust of the Charter is to protect the minority. As the Supreme Court of Canada has said, "The Charter is designed to protect the accused from the majority, so the enforcement of the Charter must not be left to that majority."[243]

To summarize: Evidence that is constitutionally tainted as the result of an unreasonable search and seizure may be excluded if its admission *could* bring the administration of justice into disrepute. The issue is to be determined by an objective standard of the "reasonable person" in the community, but only when that community's mood is reasonable. The court is required to look at the long-term effect that the

---

[240] Yves-Marie Morissette, "The Exclusion of Evidence under the *Canadian Charter of Rights and Freedoms*: What to Do and What Not to Do" (1984), 29 *McGill L.J.* 521, at p. 538, cited with approval by the Supreme Court of Canada in *The Queen v. Collins, ante.*

[241] Hogg, *Constitutional Law of Canada*, 2nd ed. (Toronto: Carswell, 1985), at 699.

[242] *The Queen v. Collins, ante.*

[243] *The Queen v. Collins, ante.*

admission or exclusion of the evidence would have on the reputation of the justice system.

23. PRIVILEGE

References:

ITA:

S. 179   Hearings *in Camera*

S. 232   Solicitor-Client Privilege

(a) General

Certain types of communication between a taxpayer and his or her legal advisors are privileged from disclosure. At common law, communications made by a person to his or her legal counsel in counsel's professional capacity are privileged, and, subject to a few exceptions, neither counsel nor the client can be compelled to disclose the contents of such communications where they were intended to be confidential.[244]

Privilege has been described as follows:[245]

A client (whether party or stranger) cannot be compelled, and a legal adviser (whether barrister, solicitor, the clerk or intermediate agent of either, or an interpreter) will not be allowed without the express consent of his client, to disclose oral or documentary communications passing between them in professional confidence.

The claim of privilege of a communication is no longer confined to communications made in contemplation, or conduct, of litigation. Where available, it extends to all professional communications made in confidence in a professional capacity with the intent that they be kept secret.[246]

---

[244] See, generally, *Greenough v. Gaskell* (1833), 39 ER 618 (L.C.); *Clergue v. McKay* (1902), 3 OLR 478 (Ont. Div. Ct.); *Butler v. Bd. of Trade*, [1971] 1 Ch 680; *The Queen v. Bencardino* (1973), 15 CCC (2d) 342 (Ont. C.A.); *Wigmore on Evidence*, McNaughton revision, vol. 8 (Boston: Little, Brown & Co., 1961), paras. 2290-2329, at 541-641; *McCormick on Evidence*, 2nd ed. (St. Paul: West Publishing Co., 1972), at 175 *et seq.*; Radin, "The Privilege of Confidential Communication between Lawyer and Client" (1928), 16 *Calif. L. Rev.* 487; Kahrl, "The Attorney-Client Privilege" (1979), 40 *Ohio State L.J.* 699, at 701-702; Pye, "Fundamentals of the Attorney-Client Privilege" (1969), 15 *Prac. Law* 15, at 16.

[245] *Phipson on Evidence,* 10th ed. (London: Sweet & Maxwell, 1963), at 251, para. 585.

[246] *Alcan-Colony Contr. Ltd. v. M.N.R.*, [1971] 2 OR 365 (Ont. H.C.).

(b) Rationale

The rationale for holding legal communications to be privileged from disclosure is to permit legal advice to be given untrammelled by any apprehension of disclosure. As Brougham L.C. said:[247]

> The foundation of this rule is not difficult to discover. It is not (as has sometimes been said) on account of any particular importance which the law attributes to the business of legal professors, or any particular disposition to afford them protection, though certainly it may not be very easy to discover why a like privilege has been refused to others, and especially to medical advisers.
>
> But it is out of regard to the interests of justice, which cannot be upholden, and to the administration of justice, which cannot go on, without the aid of men skilled in jurisprudence. . . . If the privilege did not exist at all, every one would be thrown upon his own legal resources; deprived of all professional assistance, a man would not venture to consult any skillful person, or would only dare to tell his counsellor half his case.

Solicitor-client privilege is an evidentiary rule. The rule was stated as follows by Munroe J. in *Canada Safeway*:[248]

> This application raises a question of importance, namely, does s. 10 of the *Combines Investigation Act* abrogate the common law solicitor-and-client privilege, a privilege established three centuries ago upon grounds of public policy designed to ensure that members of the public may receive the benefit of legal assistance uninhibited by fear of any breach of their confidence. That rule as to the non-production of communications between solicitor and client says that where (as here) there has been no waiver by the client and no suggestion is made, of fraud, crime, evasion or civil wrong on his part, the client cannot be compelled and the lawyer will not be allowed without the consent of the client to disclose oral or documentary communications passing between them in professional confidence, whether or not litigation is pending.

(c) Waiver by Client

The solicitor-client privilege to withhold or conceal confidential communications belongs to the *client*. The privilege is granted to protect the interests of the client, *not* the interests of the solicitor. As such, the client can always renounce the claim for privilege. Privilege can also be waived through voluntary disclosure.[249]

(d) Statutory Definition

For tax purposes, "privilege" means the right that a person has to refuse to disclose an oral or documentary communication on the ground that the communication is one passing between client and lawyer in a professional confidence.[250]

---

[247] *Greenough v. Gaskell, ante,* at 620-21.

[248] *Dir. of Investigation & Research v. Can. Safeway Ltd.* (1972), 26 DLR (3d) 745 at 746 (B.C.S.C.).

[249] *Visser v. M.N.R.,* [1989] 1 CTC 192, 89 DTC 5172 (P.E.I. S.C.).

[250] Subs. 232(1) ("solicitor-client privilege").

In general terms, the following types of documents are covered by solicitor-client privilege:

- Correspondence between a solicitor and client;
- Opinion letters; and
- Tax plans, reorganizations, agreements of purchase and sale and other agreements.

A lawyer's accounting record (including supporting vouchers and cheques) is deemed not to be a confidential communication. A solicitor's statement of account is, however, not considered an "accounting record", and is subject to solicitor-client privilege.[251] Solicitor-client privilege is determined by reference to the law of the province in which the matter arises.[252]

A lawyer's accounting records are specifically deemed not to be confidential communications eligible for the claim of privilege. Without this exception, it would be difficult for Revenue Canada to conduct a thorough audit of the lawyer's own income tax returns.

Whether a document constitutes "an accounting record" is a question of fact. Solicitors' charge sheets[253] and statements of accounts[254] are not accounting records, and therefore may be the subject of a claim of privilege. Accounting records such as ledgers, books of accounts and supporting documents cannot be privileged. Although the matter is not free from doubt, the better view is that a lawyer's trust accounts ledger is a privileged document that is not to be revealed without the client's consent.[255]

(e) Procedure

Privilege is invoked by the solicitor on behalf of his or her client. Thus, where an official seeks to examine or seize a document *in the possession of a lawyer,* the lawyer may invoke the privilege on behalf of a *named* client.[256] Unlike the common law,

---

[251] *Mut. Life Assur. Co. of Can. v. Dep. A.G. Can.*, [1984] CTC 155, 84 DTC 6177 (Ont. H.C.).

[252] *Dep. A.G. Can. v. Brown*, [1964] CTC 483 at 486, 64 DTC 483 (S.C.C.) [B.C.] (extent of privilege depends upon law of province in which document situated); see also *In re W.W. Kask et al.*, [1966] CTC 659, 66 DTC 5374 (*sub nom. In re Kask et al. v. M.N.R.*) (B.C.S.C.) ("communication" given common law meaning); *Herman v. Dep. A.G. Can.* (1979), 79 DTC 5372 (Ont. C.A.) (decision of judge in respect of solicitor-client privilege for documents not subject to appeal).

[253] *Re Evans* (1968), 68 DTC 5277 (B.C.S.C.).

[254] *Mut. Life Assur. Co. of Can. v. Dep. A.G. Can.*, ante.

[255] *Cox v. A.G. Can.*, [1988] 2 CTC 365, 88 DTC 6494 (B.C.S.C.).

[256] Subs. 232(3).

where privilege may extend to the identity of a lawyer's clients, the Act specifically requires disclosure of the name of the client on whose behalf solicitor-client privilege is claimed.

Where a lawyer claims that a document is covered by solicitor-client privilege, the tax officer is required to place the document in a package without inspecting, examining or making copies of it. The package must be sealed and deposited either with the sheriff of the district or county in which the seizure is made or with a custodian acceptable to both parties.[257] Where the privilege is claimed in respect of a document that the tax officer is about to inspect or examine, the lawyer must place the document in a package, seal the package and retain it until the matter is adjudicated by a judge.[258]

Within 14 days from the placing of the sealed package in the custody of the sheriff (or other custodian), either the client or his or her lawyer may apply to a court to have the question of privilege adjudicated. The application to determine the existence of privilege is heard in *camera*. The judge decides the matter summarily, and will either return the document to the lawyer or give it to Revenue Canada.[259]

A lawyer who claims privilege on behalf of a client is required to disclose to the Minister the last known address of the client, so that the client can be approached and afforded the opportunity to waive the privilege.[260]

(f) Defence to Prosecution

We have seen that the Minister can examine and audit a taxpayer's business records and, where authorized, can seize any documents and records which may be required as evidence in a subsequent proceeding. Obstruction of a tax audit is a criminal offence carrying a financial penalty and the possibility of imprisonment. A lawyer who makes a good faith claim for solicitor-client privilege on behalf of a named client cannot be convicted for refusing to disclose information sought by the Minister as part of a tax audit.[261]

(g) Fraud and Crimes

Since the rationale for solicitor-client privilege is to promote the administration of justice through full and frank disclosure of all relevant information, it would be perverse to allow privilege to assist in the perpetration of a fraudulent or criminal act.

---

[257] Paras. 232(3)(*a*), (*b*).

[258] Subs. 232(3.1).

[259] Subss. 232(4), (5).

[260] Subs. 232(14).

[261] Subs. 232(2).

There is a distinction between a communication made to commit a fraud or crime and a communication made in seeking advice on the defence of past crimes or fraudulent conduct. As *McCormick on Evidence* states:[262]

> It is settled under modern authority that the privilege does not extend to communications between attorney and client where the client's purpose is the furtherance of a future intended crime or fraud. Advice secured in aid of a legitimate defence by the client against a charge of past crimes or past misconduct, even though he is guilty, stands on a different footing and such consultations are privileged. If the privilege is to be denied on the ground of unlawful purpose, the client's guilty intention is controlling, though the attorney may have acted innocently and in good faith.

Thus, privilege can be lost if it is shown that the privileged relationship exists for the purpose of perpetrating a fraud or crime.

Privilege is not set aside merely by alleging fraud. The Minister must make out a *prima facie* case of fraud and lead some evidence to support the allegation. Further, the allegation must be supported by first hand knowledge; it cannot rest solely on affidavit evidence based on information and belief of unspecified and ill-defined inquiries.[263] There must be an intelligible and specific allegation of fraud supported by sufficient evidence to establish at least a *prima facie* case.

Even where fraud is established and the privilege lost, solicitor-client privilege may be claimed in respect of communications between the solicitor and his or her client on advice given *after* the fraudulent act.[264]

(h) Third-party Communications

Third-party communications (communications by a person other than the solicitor or the client) may also be privileged in certain circumstances. Clearly, where a lawyer retains another lawyer to act as his or her agent, the communications of the agent lawyer are privileged.[265] Communications by a third party acting on behalf of a client are also privileged communications if the third party is retained as the lawyer's agent.[266] Jackett P. explained the status of third-party communications as follows:[267]

> . . . that no communication, statement or other material made or prepared by an accountant as such for a business man falls within the privilege *unless* it was prepared by the accountant as a result of a request by the business man's lawyer to be used in connection with litigation, existing or apprehended;

---

[262] *McCormick on Evidence*, 2nd ed. (St. Paul: West Publishing Co., 1972), at 199-200.

[263] *Re Romeo's Place Victoria Ltd.*, [1981] CTC 380, 81 DTC 5295 (F.C.T.D.).

[264] *Re Hoyle Indust. Ltd.*, [1980] CTC 501, 80 DTC 6363 (F.C.T.D.).

[265] *Klassen-Bronze Ltd. v. M.N.R.* (1970), 70 DTC 6361 (Ont. H.C.).

[266] *Re Sokolov*, [1968] CTC 414, 68 DTC 5266 (Man. Q.B.).

[267] *Susan Hosiery Ltd. v. M.N.R.*, [1969] CTC 353, 69 DTC 5278 at 5283 (Ex. Ct.).

and that, where an accountant is used as a representative, or one of a group of representatives, for the purpose of placing a factual situation or a problem before a lawyer to obtain legal advice or legal assistance, the fact that he is an accountant, or that he uses his knowledge and skill as an accountant in carrying out such task, does not make the communications that he makes, or participates in making, as such a representative, any the less communications from the principal, who is the client, to the lawyer and similarly, communications received by such a representative from a lawyer whose advice has been so sought are none the less communications from the lawyer to the client.

But not all third-party documents are privileged. In certain circumstances, environmental audit reports and appraisal reports have been held not to be privileged even when prepared at the solicitor's request.[268]

(i) Accountants' Communications

The general rule is that communications between an accountant and his or her client are not privileged. Thus, an accountant's audit working papers and tax files cannot be the subject of a claim for privilege. As noted above, however, where the accountant is retained as an agent of the client's solicitor, papers prepared as part of the agency contract are in effect the solicitor's papers, and are privileged communications.[269]

24. APPEALS

References:

ITA:

S. 165   Objections to Assessments

S. 167   Application for Extension of Time to Appeal

S. 168   Revocation of Registration

S. 169   Appeal — Rules

S. 170   Notice of Appeal

S. 171   Disposal of Appeal

S. 172   Appeal from Refusal to Register

S. 173   Reference to Tax Court

S. 174   Reference of Common Questions to Tax Court

S. 175   Instituting Appeal — Filing, Service

S. 176   Forwarding of Documents

---

[268] *Gregory v. M.N.R.*, [1992] 2 CTC 250, 92 DTC 6518 (F.C.T.D.).

[269] See, e.g., *Mut. Life Assur. Co. of Can. v. Dep. A.G. Can.*, [1984] CTC 155, 84 DTC 6177 (Ont. H.C.) (letter from solicitors containing professional correspondence between solicitors and chartered accountants with respect to tax matters was privileged).

BULLETINS, CIRCULARS & RULINGS:

IC 80-7   June 30, 1980   Objections and Appeals

(a) General

The income tax system operates on the basis that a taxpayer initially assesses their own tax liability in respect of a taxation year. The tax return is then examined by the Minister, who may assess, or reassess, the taxpayer in respect of his or her self-assessed liability. A taxpayer who is assessed by the Minister may appeal his or her assessment.

Once issued, the Minister's assessment may be challenged only through an appeal. It cannot be challenged by a writ of *certiorari*.[270]

(b) Notice of Objection

The first formal legal step in the appeal process is the filing of a Notice of Objection.[271] Although a taxpayer may negotiate with the Department prior to filing a Notice of Objection, *all* of the taxpayer's statutory legal rights in respect of an appeal hinge upon the timely filing of the objection — that is, within the 90-day period from the *date of mailing* of the notice of assessment or within one year of the "balance due day". The 90-day time limit is quite strictly enforced, and is extended only in exceptional circumstances.[272]

(c) Administrative Appeals

A taxpayer can discuss his or her assessment with the Department to determine whether the matters raised therein can be informally resolved. At this stage, the taxpayer may be asked to supply further information by way of explanation or supplementary documentation.

---

[270] *Federal Court Act*, R.S.C. 1985, c. F-7; see *The Queen v. Parsons*, [1984] CTC 352, 84 DTC 6345 (*sub nom. M.N.R. v. Parsons*) (F.C.A.) (Minister's assessments not to be reviewed, restrained or set aside by court in exercise of its discretion under ss. 18 and 28 of *Federal Court Act*, R.S.C. 1970, c. 10 (2nd Supp.)).

[271] S. 165.

[272] Ss. 166.1, 166.2; see, e.g., *Morasutti v. M.N.R.*, [1984] CTC 2401, 84 DTC 1374 (T.C.C.) (leave refused where taxpayer's solicitor became aware of necessity to file within two weeks of expiry of 90-day period); *Wright v. M.N.R.*, [1983] CTC 2493, 83 DTC 447 (T.R.B.) (leave refused where taxpayer missed limitation period because he would not pay his lawyer's retainer); *Horton v. M.N.R.* (1969), 69 DTC 821 (T.A.B.) (taxpayer served notice of objection 92 days after date of assessment after learning only on last day that he had to file such notice; board rejected argument and dismissed appeal); see also *Gregg v. M.N.R.*, [1969] Tax ABC 782, 69 DTC 559; *Brady-Browne v. M.N.R.* (1969), 69 DTC 797 (T.A.B.); *Grenier v. M.N.R.* (1970), 70 DTC 1299 (T.A.B.); *Vineland Quarries & Crushed Stone Ltd. v. M.N.R.*, [1971] CTC 501, 71 DTC 5269 (F.C.T.D.); varied as to costs [1971] CTC 635, 71 DTC 5372 (F.C.T.D.); *Paletta v. M.N.R.*, [1977] CTC 2285, 77 DTC 203 (T.R.B.).

Failing resolution of disputed items, the next step for the taxpayer is to proceed to the more formal administrative process before the Appeals Branch of Revenue Canada. The Appeals Branch is theoretically "independent" of the auditing and assessing sections of the Department and, therefore, takes a more objective and independent view of the disputed return. It is, however, important to bear in mind that the staff of the Appeals Branch are recruited from the audit and assessing sections of Revenue Canada and they return to their assessing responsibilities upon completion of their tour of duty with the Appeals Branch. Therefore, their approach to appeals may be influenced both by their past association with the assessing and audit divisions and the knowledge that they will return to their peers in those divisions upon completion of their assignment in Appeals.

(d) Appeal to Tax Court

An appeal lies to Tax Court where the Minister has confirmed the assessment or 90 days have elapsed from the date of service of the Notice of Objection.[273]

(i) General

The Tax Court of Canada has the sole power initially to hear appeals under the *Income Tax Act*. The court has two different tracks: Informal and General. A taxpayer can use the Informal Procedure for appeals in three circumstances:

1. Where the aggregate of all tax amounts (other than interest or provincial tax) in issue does not exceed $14,000;

2. Where the amount of the loss in issue does not exceed $24,000; or

3. Where the only amount in issue is the amount of interest assessed under the Act.

Where the disputed amounts exceed the threshold limits, the taxpayer can elect to restrict the appeal to the limits and forego any claim for the excess.

(ii) Informal Procedure

A taxpayer must elect to have the Informal Procedure apply. The limit of $14,000 for the informal track is intended to provide taxpayers with a quick and inexpensive route for the settlement of tax disputes. Since approximately 70 per cent of income tax appeals involve amounts of less than $14,000, this procedure is intended to facilitate the processing of tax disputes in an expeditious and inexpensive manner.

The following procedures apply to informal appeals:

- The appeal must be submitted in writing.
- The taxpayer can represent himself or herself or be represented by an agent. The agent may be a person other than a lawyer.

---

[273] Subs. 165(3).

- The appeal should set out the reasons for the appeal and the relevant facts.
- The Minister is generally required to submit a reply within 45 days from the time when the notice of appeal is filed.
- The appeal must be heard within 90 days of the Minister's reply.
- Judgment must be issued within 60 days of the hearing of the appeal.

Thus, it is contemplated that the entire appeal process should take approximately seven months from the time when the taxpayer files the Notice of Appeal and chooses to have the case heard through the Informal Procedure.

(iii) Formal Procedure

The formal appeal to the Tax Court of Canada is more strictly controlled by rules that are similar to the rules of the Federal Court of Canada. Generally speaking, the Formal Procedure is used where the appeal in question involves federal tax for a taxation year in excess of $14,000.

The taxpayer may represent himself or herself in a formal appeal, or may be represented by a lawyer. Agents who are not lawyers are not allowed to appear before the Tax Court of Canada in a formal appeal.

The rules of evidence apply in formal appeals in the same way as they apply in any other litigation. Decisions of the court following a formal appeal are considered precedents.

There is no particular time frame for completion of the appeal in the formal process. Thus, cases involving a formal appeal may extend over three to four years. The following chart gives a brief overview of the general and informal procedures.

	General	**Informal**
Representation	By self or lawyer	By self, lawyer or agent
Procedure	Similar to procedures now existing in most courts	No formal procedure required except for filing the appeal in writing
Evidence	Strict rules apply	Rules are flexible
Appeals	To the Federal Court of Appeal	Review by Federal Court of Appeal on questions of law and jurisdiction
Precedential value of case decisions	Yes	No

	General	**Informal**
Time frame	No mandatory time frame for completion of an appeal	Explicit time deadlines for Revenue Canada and the court Maximum of: — 45 days between filing of appeal and reply — 90 days between reply and hearing — 60 days between hearing and decision

(e) Settlements

A taxpayer who enters into a settlement with the Department is generally bound by the terms of the settlement, and may not appeal the same assessment. In *Smerchanski*,[274] the taxpayer, faced with the possibility of criminal proceedings on the grounds of income tax evasion, entered into a settlement just prior to the time when the right of prosecution would otherwise have been outlawed by the passage of time. Later, the taxpayer challenged the assessment which was the basis of the settlement on the grounds that it had been obtained by duress and threat of prosecution. The Supreme Court of Canada unanimously upheld the settlement. Laskin C.J.C. stated:[275]

> Since it is not contested that a taxpayer may validly waive his rights of appeal against a tax assessment and that no question of public policy is involved to preclude such a waiver, the only issue of importance in this appeal is whether the tax authorities, seriously contemplating prosecution, and by indictment as in the present case, are entitled to exact a waiver of rights of appeal as a binding term of settling a clear tax liability when overtures for settlement are made by the taxpayer and, in consequence, to abandon their intention to prosecute.

> The threat of prosecution underlies every tax return if a false statement is knowingly made in it and, indeed, this is inscribed on the face of the tax form. It cannot be that the tax authorities must proceed to prosecution when faced with a dispute on whether there is a wilful tax evasion rather than being amenable to a settlement, be it a compromise or an uncompromising agreement for payment of what is claimed. Here there was not even such a dispute but an acknowledgement of evasion and the taxpayer's position cannot be stronger when he is a confessed evader than when he has disputed wilful evasion.

---

[274] *Smerchanski v. M.N.R.*, [1976] CTC 488, 76 DTC 6247 (S.C.C.).

[275] *Smerchanski v. M.N.R., ante*, [1976] CTC at 494, 76 DTC at 6251.

I leave to one side situations where the tax authorities, having no substantial case against a taxpayer, nonetheless importune and harass him with the threat of prosecution in order to exact an unjustified settlement.

(f) Disposition of Appeal by Tax Court

The Tax Court can dispose of an appeal in one of four ways. It may:[276]

1. Dismiss the appeal;
2. Vacate the assessment;
3. Vary the assessment; or
4. Refer the assessment back to the Minister for further reconsideration and reassessment.

(g) Appeal to the Federal Court of Appeal

A decision of the Tax Court of Canada may be appealed to the Federal Court of Appeal.[277] The *Income Tax Act* also allows for direct appeals to the Federal Court of Appeal in certain circumstances.

(i) Procedure

An appeal to the Federal Court of Appeal must be instituted within 30 days from the pronouncement of the judgment from which the appeal is taken. The appeal is initiated by filing a Notice of Appeal in the registry of the Federal Court and by serving all parties who are directly affected by the appeal with a true copy of the notice.

Evidence of service must also be filed with the registry of the court.[278]

(ii) Direct References

The taxpayer may appeal directly to the Federal Court of Appeal where the Minister:[279]

- Refuses to grant registration as a charitable organization, private or public foundation or Canadian amateur athletic association;
- Gives notice that it is proposed to revoke the registration of one of the above-listed organizations;
- Refuses to register a retirement savings plan;
- Refuses to register a profit-sharing plan;

---

[276] Subs. 171(1).

[277] *Federal Court Act*, R.S.C. 1985, c. F-7, subs. 27(1.1).

[278] *Federal Court Act*, subss. 27(2), (3).

[279] *Income Tax Act*, subs. 172(3).

- Revokes the registration of a profit-sharing plan;
- Refuses to issue a certificate of exemption under subection 212(14) of the Act;
- Refuses to accept the registration of an education savings plan;
- Revokes the registration of an education savings plan;
- Refuses to accept the registration of a retirement income fund;
- Refuses to register a pension plan;
- Revokes the registration of a pension plan; or
- Refuses to accept an amendment to a registered pension plan.

The Minister is deemed to have refused the registration, acceptance or issuance, as the case may be, in any of the situations listed above if he or she does not notify the applicant within 180 days after the filing of the application.[280]

The appeal must be instituted within a period of 30 days from the date of the Minister's decision refusing the application for registration, issuance of a certificate of exemption, or revocation of the registration.[281] The Federal Court of Appeal may grant an extension of time beyond the 30-day period.[282]

(iii) Appeal to the Supreme Court of Canada

An appeal to the Supreme Court of Canada may be taken only with leave. The leave to appeal may be granted either by the Federal Court of Appeal or by the Supreme Court of Canada. There is no automatic right of appeal to the Supreme Court of Canada. Leave to appeal is granted only if the court is satisfied that the question being appealed involves a matter of public importance or is one which, in its opinion, it should hear for any other reason.

An appeal to the Supreme Court of Canada must be brought within 60 days from the pronouncement of the judgment, or within such further time as a judge of the Federal Court of Appeal allows.

A copy of the Notice of Appeal must be filed with the registrar of the Supreme Court, and all parties directly affected by the appeal are to be served with a copy of the Notice. Evidence of service of the Notice must also be filed with the registrar of the Supreme Court.

---

[280] Subs. 172(4).

[281] Subs. 180(1).

[282] Subs. 180(1).

SELECTED BIBLIOGRAPHY TO CHAPTER XXVI

General

Beaubier, David W., "The Tax Court of Canada: An Outline of Informal Procedure and General Procedure", in *Proceedings of 41st Tax Conf.* 41:1 (Can. Tax Foundation, 1989).

Beaufry, John, "Taxing Matters" (1991), 15 *Can. Lawyer No. 4* 23.

Brooks, Neil and Anthony N. Doob, *Making Taxpayer Compliance Easier: Preliminary Findings of a Canadian Survey* (1990).

Colley, Geoffrey M., "Tax Affairs Aren't Just an April Filing" (1989), 122 *CA Magazine* 46.

Dealing with Revenue Canada: Audits, Appeals, Instalments, Collections (Toronto: Canadian Institute, 1993).

Duncan, Deborah, "A Review of Recent Administrative Positions" in *Proceedings of 45th Tax Conf.* 47:1 (Can. Tax Foundation, 1993).

Gaignery, Gillis P., "Access to Revenue Canada Taxation Files", *Corp. Mgmt. Tax Conf.* 7:1 (Can. Tax Foundation, 1988).

Harris, Edwin C., "Curl Penalties Under the Income Tax Act", *Corp. Mgmt. Tax Conf.* 9:1 (Can. Tax Foundation, 1988).

Hickey, Paul B., "Administrative Issues Arising From Tax Reform", *Corp. Mgmt. Tax Conf.* 3:1 (Can. Tax Foundation, 1988).

Huggett, D.R., "Administration" (1985), 13 *Can. Tax News* 103.

Lefebvre, Wilfrid, and Marie-Claire Lalonde, "Recent Issues in Tax Collection", in *Proceedings of 38th Tax Conf.* (Can. Tax Foundation, 1986).

McKie, A.B., "No Accounting for Tax Audits" (1987), 2:1 *Can. Current Tax* C-1.

Nazzer, Eric G., "Section 174, Procedural Simplicity or Procedural Unfairness" (1992), 3 *Can. Current Tax* A11.

Orvoine, Alaine, "Dealing with Revenue Canada: An Accountant's Perspective" in *Proceedings of 45th Tax Conf.* 11:1 (Can. Tax Foundation, 1993).

Pitfield, Ian H., "Dealing with Revenue Canada: A Lawyer's Perspective" in *Proceedings of 45th Tax Conf.* 10:1 (Can. Tax Foundation, 1993).

Pitfield, Ian H., "Tax Collection Practices and Procedures", in *Proceedings of 37th Tax Conf.* 28:1 (Can. Tax Foundation, 1985).

Richards, Gabrielle M.R., "No Relief for Revenue Canada's Carelessness: City Centre Properties v. The Queen, Federal Court — Trial Division" (1994), 4 *Can. Current Tax* J53.

Sanford, Cedric, Michael Goldwin and Peter Hardwick, *Administrative and Compliance Costs of Taxation* (Bath: Fiscal Publications, 1989).

Scheuermann, Scott L., "Interest on Underpaid and Overpaid Amounts", *Corp. Mgmt. Tax Conf.* 10:1 (Can. Tax Foundation, 1988).

Slutsky, Samuel, *Tax Administration Reports* (Toronto: Richard De Boo, 1986).

Income Tax Returns

Tremblay, Richard G., "Information Reporting: Transactions with Non-Residents: Revenue Canada Extends its Reach" (1989), 2 *Can. Current Tax* P-57.

Withholding Taxes

Broadhurst, David G., "Issues in Withholding", *Corp. Mgmt. Tax Conf.* 11:1 (Can. Tax Foundation, 1988).

Calculation of Tax Liability

Smith, David W., "Recent Decisions Underline Taxpayers' Liabilities" (1987), 14:6 *Nat. (C.B.A.)* 28.

Assessments

Role of the Department of Justice Counsel in Tax Disputes, Audio Archives of Canada, 1984.

Reassessments

Gibson, "An Overview of Income Tax Litigation", in *Proceedings of 35th Tax Conf.* 967 (Can. Tax Foundation, 1983).

Krishna, Vern, "Reassessments Bases on Fraud or Misrepresentation" (1992), 3 *Can. Current Tax* A25.

Ledoux, Georges, "Tax Audits" in *Proceedings of 45th Tax Conf.* 47:1 (Can. Tax Foundation, 1993).

Role of the Department of Justice Counsel in Tax Disputes, Audio Archives of Canada, 1984.

Power, Mary V., "Do Statutes Have Limitations?" (1989), 122 *CA Magazine* 44.

Smith, David W., "Reassessments, Waivers: Amended Returns and Refunds", *Corp. Mgmt. Tax Conf.* 8:1 (Can. Tax Foundation, 1988).

Payment of Tax

Bartlett, R., "Judicial Review in Taxation: A Modern Perspective" (1987), *Br. Tax Rev.* 10.

Bowman, Stephen W., "Collections in the Insolvency Context", *Corp. Mgmt. Tax Conf.* 12:1 (Can. Tax Foundation, 1988).

Bowman, Stephen W., "Subsection 224(12) Supergarnishment: Constitutionality" (1992), 40 *Can. Tax J.* 395.

Lalonde, Phil and Kathleen Marta, "Revenue Canada's Super Garnishee: Secured Creditors Beware!" (1991), 8 *Nat. Bank. and Insolvency Rev.* 65.

Potvin, Jean, "'Superpriority' Garnishment Provision: Subsection 224(12)" in *Proceedings of 44th Tax Conf.* 5:54 (Can. Tax Foundation, 1992).

Robertson, Ronald N. and Edmond F.B. Lamek, "Tax Collection and Insolvency: An Update" in *Proceedings of 45th Tax Conf.* 8:1 (Can. Tax Foundation, 1993).

Skulski, B.J., "Tax Collection in Recessionary Times" in *Proceedings of 44th Tax Conf.* 9:1 (Can. Tax Foundation, 1992).

Notice of Objection

Bartlett, R., "Judicial Review in Taxation: A Modern Perspective" (1987), *Br. Tax Rev.* 10.

Dixon, Gordon D., "Just and Equitable Considerations for Applications for the Extension of Notice of Objections" (1990), 28 *Alta. L. Rev.* 762.

Krishna, Vern, "Obtaining Extension of Time to File Notice of Objection: The Palm Tree Withers" (1987), 2 *Can. Current Tax* A-1.

McDonnell, T.E., "Leave to Late File Notice of Objection Granted" (1992), 40 *Can. Tax J.* 703.

Power, Mary V., "Do Statutes Have Limitations?" (1989), 122 *CA Magazine* 44.

Instalment Payments

Carr, Brian R. and Karen Yull, "Tax on the Instalment Plan" (1994), 127 *CA Mag. No. 6* 35.

Drache, A.B.C., "Instalment Payments Clarified" (1991), 13 *Can. Taxpayer* 185.

Drache, A.B.C., "Retroactivity Upheld Still Again" (1991), 13 *Can. Taxpayer* 191.

Speiss, Terry J., "New Rules for Income Tax Instalments" (1990), 3:2 *Can. Current Tax* T-5.

Liability of Directors for Corporate Taxes

Bowman, S.W., "Director's Liability: Deficiencies in Notices of Assessments" (1991), 39 *Can. Tax J.* 1324.

Bowman, S.W., "Director's Liability — The Outsider" (1990), 38 *Can. Tax J.* 1242.

Brahmst, Oliver C., "Revenue Canada's Administration of Section 227.1 and the Application of Subsection 15(1) of the Charter" (1991), 3 *Can. Current Tax* P25.

Campbell, R. Lynn, "Director Liability for Unremitted Employee Deductions" (1992), 25 *U.B.C.L. Rev.* 211.

Fien, Cy M., "Directors' Liability and Indemnifications, Section 160 Assessments, and Ordinary Course of Business Provisions" in *Proceedings of 44th Tax Conf.* 53:1 (Can. Tax Foundation, 1992).

Fien, Cy M., "Liability of a Corporation for Acts of Corporate Officials in the Tax Field and Liability of Corporate Officials for Acts of a Corporation", *Corp. Mgmt. Tax Conf.* 177 (Can. Tax Foundation, 1983).

Fulcher, J.E., "Section 227.1 of the Income Tax Act and the Director's Duty of Care in BCA Jurisdictions: Some Lessons from the Corporate Governance Debate of the Last Twenty-five Years" (1992), 5 *Can. Petro. Tax J.* No. 1 *17*.

Gottlieb, Dan, "Corporations Have No Privilege Against Self-Incrimination" (1986), 6:13 *Lawyers Weekly* 13.

Krishna, Vern, "Liability of Shareholders for Corporate Taxes" (1993), 4 *Can. Current Tax* A11.

Krishna, Vern, "Personal Liability for Shareholders for Unpaid Corporate Taxes" (1991), 3 *Can. Current Tax* C81.

Kroft, Edwin G., "The Liability of Directors for Unpaid Canadian Taxes", in *Proceedings of 37th Tax Conf.* 30 (Can. Tax Foundation, 1985).

MacKnight, Robin J., "Indemnities for Officers and Directors: Adding Insult to Injury" (1991), 3 *Can. Current Tax* P41.

Muskowitz, Evelyn P., "Directors' Liability: An Update" in *Proceedings of 43rd Tax Conf.* 47:1 (Can. Tax Foundation, 1991).

Muskowitz, Evelyn P., "Directors' Liability Under Income Tax Legislation and Other Related Statutes" (1990), 38 *Can. Tax J.* 537.

Nicholl, John I.S., "Director's and Officer's Liability Insurance" (1985), 3 *Can. J. Ins. L.* 42.

Investigations

Corn, George, "Illegal Search and Seizure and Application of Charter of Rights and Freedoms" (1986), 1 *Can. Current Tax* J-123.

Dellinger, "Of Rights and Remedies: The Constitution as a Sword" (1972), 85 *Harvard L. Rev.* 1532.

Gauthier, E.H., "Audit Function in Revenue Canada Taxation" in *Proceedings of 44th Tax Conf.* 9:1 (Can. Tax Foundation, 1992).

Gibson, "Overview of Income Tax Litigation (An)", in *Proceedings of 35th Tax Conf.* 967 (Can. Tax Foundation, 1983).

Gibson, "Shocking the Public" (1983), 13 *Man. L.J.* 495.

Kafka, Gerald A., "Taxpayer Bill of Rights Expands Safeguards and Civil Remedies" (January 1989), 70 *J. Taxation* 4.

Kellough, Howard J., "Emerging Income Tax Issues: Section 231.2 Requirement Letters, Uses and Abuses of Trusts, and Interest Deductibility" in *Proceedings of 45th Tax Conf.* 2:1 (Can. Tax Foundation, 1993).

Krishna, Vern, "Investigative Powers Under the Income Tax Act" (1986), 1 *Can. Current Tax* 1161.

Lefebvre, Wilfrid, and Marie-Claire Lalonde, "Recent Issues in Tax Collection", in *Proceedings of 38th Tax Conf.* 41 (Can. Tax Foundation, 1986).

Levy, "The Invocation of Remedies under the Charter" (1983), 13 *Man. L.J.* 523.

Lorinc, John, "The Tax Man Cometh" (1994), 127 *CA Mag. No. 4* 28.

Martinez, Leo P., "Tax Collection and Populist Rhetoric: Shifting the Burden of Proof in Tax Cases" (1988), 39 *Hastings L.J.* 239.

McKie, A.B., "Tax Inquisitors" (1991), 3 *Can. Current Tax* C85.

McLellan and Elman, "The Enforcement of the Charter" (1983), 21 *Alta. L. Rev.* 205.

Roberts, Robert A., "Demand for Information under Section 231.1 of the Income Tax Act" (1993), 4 *Can. Current Tax* P11.

Role of the Department of Justice Counsel in Tax Disputes, Audio Archives of Canada, 1984.

Smith, David W., "Time Must be Allowed to Produce Documents" (1985), 12:11 *Nat. (C.B.A.)* 29.
"Some New Reporting Requirements and Penalties" (1988), 16 *Can. Tax News* 14.

Inquiry

Corn, George, "Illegal Search and Seizure and Application of Charter of Rights and Freedoms" (1986), 1 *Can. Current Tax* J-123.
Dellinger, "Of Rights and Remedies: The Constitution as a Sword" (1972), 85 *Harvard L. Rev.* 1532.

Search and Seizure

Butler, Alison Scott, "Making Charter Arguments in Civil Tax Cases: Can the Courts Help Taxpayers?" (1993), 41 *Can. Tax J.* 847.
Corn, George, "Illegal Search and Seizure and Application of Charter of Rights and Freedoms" (1986), 1 *Can. Current Tax* J-123.
Corr, George, "Search and Seizure: Validity of Section 231.3" (1993), 4 *Can. Current Tax* J1.
Dellinger, "Of Rights and Remedies: The Constitution as a Sword" (1972), 85 *Harvard L. Rev.* 1532.
Deschamps, J. Michel, "Crown Priorities and Tax Collection: An Overview", in *Proceedings of 37th Tax Conf.* 29:1 (Can. Tax Foundation, 1985).
Fairley, "Enforcing the Charter" (1982), 4 *S.C.L. Rev.* 217.
FISS, *The Civil Rights Injunction* (1978).
Gibson, "Determining Disrepute: Opinion Polls and the Charter" (1983), 61 *Can. Bar Rev.* 377.
Gibson, *Law of the Charter (The): General Principles* (Calgary: Carswell, 1986).
Gibson, "Overview of Income Tax Litigation (An)", in *Proceedings of 35th Tax Conf.* 967 (Can. Tax Foundation, 1983).
Gibson, "Shocking the Public" (1983), 13 *Man. L.J.* 495.
Goodman, Wolfe D., "Search and Seizure, Evasion, Records and Tax Opinions", [1986] *Special Lectures L.S.U.C.* 207.
Grossman, B.K., "Search and Seizure under the Income Tax Act: A Constitutional Assessment of the Bill C-84 Amendments to the Income Tax Act" (1987), 35 *Can. Tax J.* 1349.
Hill, "Constitutional Remedies" (1969), 69 *Columbia L. Rev.* 1109.
Kafka, Gerald A., "Taxpayer Bill of Rights Expands Safeguards and Civil Remedies" (January 1989), 70 *J. Taxation* 4.
Krishna, Vern, "Investigative Powers Under the Income Tax Act" (1986), 1 *Can. Current Tax* 1161.
Lefebvre, Wilfrid, and Marie-Claire Lalonde, "Recent Issues in Tax Collection", in *Proceedings of 38th Tax Conf.* 41 (Can. Tax Foundation, 1986).
Levy, "The Invocation of Remedies under the Charter" (1983), 13 *Man. L.J.* 523.

Martinez, Leo P., "Tax Collection and Populist Rhetoric: Shifting the Burden of Proof in Tax Cases" (1988), 39 *Hastings L.J.* 239.

McDowall, *Equity and the Constitution* (1982).

McLellan and Elman, "The Enforcement of the Charter" (1983), 21 *Alta. L. Rev.* 205.

Morisette, "The Exclusion of Evidence under the *Canadian Charter of Rights and Freedoms* — What to Do and What Not to Do" (1984), 29 *McGill L.J.* 521.

Paciocco, D., "The Proposed Canada Evidence Act and the 'Wray Formula': Perpetuating An Inadequate Discretion" (1983), 29 *McGill L.J.* 141.

Peiris, "The Admissibility of Evidence Obtained Illegally: A Comparative Analysis" (1981), 13 *Ottawa L. Rev.* 309.

Pilkington, "Damages as a Remedy for Infringement of Charter" (1984), 62 *Can. Bar Rev.* 517.

Pound, Richard W., "Audit, Inquiry, Search and Seizure", in *Proceedings of 37th Tax Conf.* 27:1 (Can. Tax Foundation, 1985).

Role of the Department of Justice Counsel in Tax Disputes, Audio Archives of Canada, 1984.

"Some New Reporting Requirements and Penalties" (1988), 16 *Can. Tax News* 14.

Templeton, W., "Search and Seizure" (1985), 13 *Can. Current Tax* 98.

Vita, Peter A., "Collection Remedies of the Crown", [1988] *Special Lectures L.S.U.C.* 411.

Ward, David A., and John M. Ulmer, "Corporate Taxation: Search and Seizure Update" (1985), 4 *Legal Alert* 142.

Watchuk, Jeanne, "Search and Seizure Provisions Contravene Charter" (1991), 39 *Can. Tax J.* 644.

Privilege

Ivankovich, Ivan F., "A Question of Privilege: Confidential Communications and the Public Accountant" (1994), 23 *Can. Bus. L. J.* 201.

MacKnight, Robin J., "Privileges of the Taxpayer" (1991), 3 *Can. Current Tax* P27.

Nathanson, David C., "The Fairness Package, the Long Reach of Section 160, and Solicitor - Client Privilege" in *Proceedings of 43rd Tax Conf.* 49:1 (Can. Tax Foundation, 1991).

Perry, John Lilburn, "The Income Tax Act: Solicitor - Client Privilege and Solicitor - Client Confidentiality" (1994), 52 *Advocate* 405.

Roberts, Robert A. and Russell W. Watson, "Solicitor - Client Privilege from a Tax Perspective" (1993), 4 *Can. Current Tax* T5.

"Some New Reporting Requirements and Penalties" (1988), 16 *Can. Tax News* 14.

Watson, Russ, "Next Case, Please: Case-by-case Privilege Offers Some Hope for Non-lawyer Advisors (1993), 4 *Can. Current Tax* P23.

Appeals

Boyle, Patrick, *Canadian Tax Objection and Appeal Procedures* (Don Mills, Ont.: CCH Canadian, 1991).

Broadhurst, David G., "Late-Filed Elections and U.K. Advance Corporation Tax Refunds" (1986), 34 *Can. Tax J.* 165.

Drache, Arthur B.C., "Hazarding an Appeal" (1995), 17 *Can. Taxpayer* 78.

Festeryga, Paul, "The Onus Issue: Who Carries the Burden of Proof in an Income Tax Appeal?" (1992), 125 *CA Mag. No. 7* 34.

Huggett, D.R., "Administration" (1985), 13 *Can. Tax News* 103.

Krishna, Vern, "Appealing Tax Assessments" (1987), 21 *CGA Magazine* 42.

Krishna, Vern, "Obtaining Extension of Time to File Notice of Objection: The Palm Tree Withers" (1987), 2 *Can. Current Tax* A-1.

Lefebvre, Wilfrid, and Deen Olsen, "The Tax Litigation Process: An Update", in *Proceedings of 39th Tax Conf.* 50:1 (Can. Tax Foundation, 1987).

McDonnell, Thomas E., "Administrative Matters and Appeals", [1986] *Special Lectures L.S.U.C.* 181.

McMechan, Robert and Gordon Bourgard, *Tax Court Practice 1995* (Scarborough, Ont.: Carswell, 1995).

Ontario Tax Appeals: Practices and Procedures (Revised) (Toronto: Ontario Ministry of Revenue, 1988).

Quigley, Michael G., "Dealing with Expert Evidence in Tax Cases" (1993), 41 *Can. Tax J.* 1071.

Smith, David W., "Time Must be Allowed to Produce Documents" (1985), 12:11 *Nat. (C.B.A.)* 29.

"Some New Reporting Requirements and Penalties" (1988), 16 *Can. Tax News* 14.

Your Right to Appeal Ontario Taxes (Revised) (Toronto: Ontario Ministry of Revenue, 1988).

Other

Bartlett, R., "Judicial Review in Taxation: A Modern Perspective" (1987), *Br. Tax Rev.* 10.

Corn, George, "Dismissal of Action for Want of Prosecution" (1993), 4 *Can. Current Tax* A1.

Corn, George, "Interpretation of the 'Fairness Package'" (1994), 4 *Can. Current Tax* A19.

Corn, George, "Restriction on Collection of Taxes and Whether Collection in Jeopardy" (1987), 2 *Can. Current Tax* A-5.

Fridman, G.H.L., "No Justice for Taxpayers: The Paucity of Restitution" (1990), 19 *Man. L. J.* 303.

Fulcher, J.E., "Is the 'New' Tax Court of Canada Absolutely Bound by Decisions of Federal Court — Trial Division? (1992), 40 *Can. Tax J.* 99.

Hsu, Berry F.C., "The Politics in the Canadian Judicial Decision Making Process: Economic Analysis of Tax Litigation" (1994), 32 *Alta. L. Rev.* 741.

King, Bruce, "A Fix for Frustration!" (1991), 124 *CA Mag. No. 4* 30.

Lanthier, Allan R., "Emerging Income Tax Issues: Public Service 2000, International Finance, and U.S. Limited Liability Companies" in *Proceedings of 45th Tax Conf.* 3:1 (Can. Tax Foundation 1993).

Lefebvre, Denis, "Recent Revenue Canada Initiatives" in *Proceedings of 45th Tax Conf.* 6:1 (Can. Tax Foundation, 1993).

McDonnell, T.E., "Ministry Refused Leave to Late File Report" (1992), 40 *Can. Tax J.* 716.

Mitchell, Robert E., "From Advisor to Business Partner" (1994), 127 *CA Mag. No. 2* 42.

Nathanson on Tax Litigation (Montreal: Federated Press, 1992).

Pateras, Bruno J., "Tax Evasion after the Charter" (1990), *Meredith Mem. Lectures* 435.

Peterson, Shirley D., "International Enforcement of Canadian and U.S. Tax Laws" in *Corp. Mgmt. Tax Conf.* (Can. Tax Foundation, 1993).

Pound, Richard, "Remedial Tax Planning: How to Fix It when It's Broke" in *Proceedings of 45th Tax Conf.* 9:1 (Can. Tax Foundation, 1993).

Read, Robert J.L., "The Income Tax Advance Rulings Service" in *Proceedings of 44th Tax Conf.* 6:1 (Can. Tax Foundation, 1992).

Roy, Robert, "The Tax Avoidance Program" in *Proceedings of 45th Tax Conf.* 7:1 (Can. Tax Foundation, 1993).

Sherman, H. Arnold and Jeffrey D. Sherman, "Income Tax Remission Orders: The Tax Planner's Least Resort or the Ultimate Weapon?" (1986), 34 *Can. Tax J.* 801.

Shultis, Elizabeth and Stephen Smith, "Valuation by Compromise in the Tax Courts: Myth or Reality?" (1992), 40 *Can. Tax J.* 1253.

Tax Litigation: Effective Preparation and Conduct (Mississauga, Ont.: Insight, 1991).

Webber, Philip B., "In the Clear with or without a Clearance Certificate: But Trustees Beware!" (1992), 40 *Can. Tax J.* 706.

Wise, Richard M., "Tax Evasion and Mens Rea Forensic Accounting" (1990), *Meredith Mem. Lectures* 405.

CHAPTER XXVII

INTERNATIONAL: GENERAL PRINCIPLES

Canadian international taxation is concerned with domestic and bilateral tax rules that apply to foreign income transactions. There is no such thing as an international law of taxation, but only a law of international taxation. Each country has sovereign jurisdiction to tax within its constitutional framework. The real parameters of the law of international taxation are neither constitutional nor jurisdictional. The important considerations are economics, commerce, international trade and enforcement. As global trade increases, the role of taxation in international commerce becomes increasingly important in business decisions.

Economic development and the attraction of foreign capital have always played an important role in the structure of Canada's international tax system. In 1966 the Carter Royal Commission on Taxation said:[1]

> [i]n the international sphere perfect tax neutrality is neither administratively feasible, nor necessarily economically desirable. The subject is therefore a challenging one and one which Canada of all countries can least afford to ignore. Canada's heavy stake in foreign trade and investment gives this country a particular interest in well-ordered international tax arrangements. Fortunately a good deal of progress has been made toward some standards of conduct for international tax behaviour by negotiation and agreement. Over the last half-century the leading trade nations, under the auspices of world organizations, have developed a few basic ground rules that eliminate the grosser inequities and economic dislocations that would otherwise arise. While these rules fall far short of the ideal of neutrality and equity, their embodiment in national taxing statutes and in international treaties gives some order and certainty where chaos could otherwise rule. The value of these arrangements has also increased with the more extensive use of income taxes by both developed and developing countries as the major source of their revenue. The direct use of income tax provisions by many countries for the achievement of domestic economic objectives, and the heightened sophistication of taxpayers in arranging their affairs to minimize their tax liabilities, will add further to the need for international tax arrangements in the future. . . .

Bilateral tax treaties play an important role in fostering international economic development. Generally speaking, most countries do not enforce foreign revenue laws. Canada neither enforces foreign revenue laws nor expects foreign jurisdictions to enforce its taxing statutes.[2] This makes it that much more important to have a comprehensive treaty network to ensure a workable international fiscal system.

---

[1] *Report of the Royal Commission on Taxation* (Ottawa: Queen's Printer, 1966) (Chair: K.M. Carter), v. 4 at 481.

[2] *Holman v. Johnson* (1975), 1 Cowp. 341.

1. JURISDICTION TO TAX

Jurisdiction or the legal authority to tax is premised on national sovereignty. Statutory assertion, whether territorial or extraterritorial, forms the initial basis of a nation's jurisdiction to tax.

A country (or a subdivision thereof) can tax as it pleases within its constitutional framework and territorial jurisdiction. Constitutional law does not require relief from double taxation of income, whether such income is derived domestically or from foreign sources. A country can also exercise extra-territorial reach over income. International law neither limits a country's jurisdiction to tax nor demands relief from double taxation. Relief, if any, is usually premised on pragmatic considerations of international economics and commerce.

The practical limits on international taxation derive from considerations of enforcement and collection. The limits are determined by the scope of power to tax effectively and efficiently. A state can exercise its power to tax by virtue of domiciliary status, in which case the power to tax is based on control of the person, or on the basis of the source of income, in which case the power is based on control of the source property. In either case the pragmatic limitation on the jurisdiction to tax is the extent of the power of the state to reach the taxpayer.

Canada exercises "extra-territorial" reach over Canadian residents: Canadian residents are subject to "full tax liability" on their world-wide income regardless of where it is earned.[3] Non-residents are subject to Canadian tax only on their Canadian source income. Thus, Canadian source international income can be subject to double taxation if another country also taxes the same income. For example, a non-resident who is temporarily employed in Canada is, subject to treaty exemptions, taxable in Canada and may also be subject to tax in his or her home country on the basis of residence in that country.

2. THE NATURE OF INTERNATIONAL INCOME

International income is income with a non-domestic component. Typically, international income is income earned in one state (the source state) but owned by a resident or national of another state (the residence state). Thus, international income can trigger double (or multiple) tax claims ("juridical double taxation") by two (or more) countries each claiming the jurisdiction to tax on the basis of different criteria. Tax claims over international income may be based upon:

- the source of the income;
- the situs of the property that gives rise to the income;
- the residence of the taxpayer who receives the income; or
- the taxpayer's nationality or citizenship.

---

[3]   Subs. 2(1); see Chapter III "Who is Taxable?"

Example XXVIII.1

Assume that NR (a U.S. citizen), an entertainer and a non-resident of Canada, performs in Canada for FC, a foreign corporation resident in Country X. NR is paid $100,000 for his performances. The amount is paid to NR from a bank account maintained in Country X. Subject to treaty relief, NR could be liable for tax in three countries: for Canadian income tax as a non-resident if he is considered to be "employed in Canada"; for tax in Country X on the basis of his residence in that country; and in the U.S. on the basis of his citizenship.

---

3. DOMESTIC RULES

References:

ITA:

Subs. 2(3)   Tax Payable by Non-Resident Persons

Subs. 20(11)   Foreign Taxes on Income From Property

S. 126   Foreign Tax Deduction

A fundamental rule of Canadian taxation is the jurisdiction to tax domestic and international income on the basis of taxpayer residence. Thus, subsection 2(1) charges Canadian residents with tax on their world-wide income regardless of where it is earned.

But Canada also claims the jurisdiction to tax non-residents based on the source of their income. Thus, a non-resident person is taxable in Canada if he or she:[4]

- is employed in Canada;
- carries on business in Canada; or
- disposes of taxable Canadian property.

Thus, the jurisdiction to tax non-residents depends upon the nexus between the taxpayer and his or her Canadian source income.

We saw in Example XXVIII.1 that tax claims based on multiple criteria, such as source of income and taxpayer residence, can create problems of juridical double taxation. These problems are aggravated because income tax (whether domestic or foreign) is not usually deductible as an expense in computing income.[5] Thus, the economic cost of juridical double taxation can be high

---

[4] Subs. 2(3).

[5] For a limited exception see subs. 20(11) (foreign taxes on income from property exceeding 15 per cent).

(a) Unilateral Relief

A country can relieve against double taxation of international income through domestic tax rules or bilateral treaties. Unilateral relief, which may take the form of exemptions,[6] credits[7] or deductions, can be either partial or complete. There are, however, financial limits to the amount of unilateral relief that a country can provide since foreign tax credits, deductions and exemptions involve a loss of revenue and a diminution of the taxable base.

Canada provides both unilateral and bilateral relief against double taxation. Resident taxpayers obtain some unilateral tax relief from double taxation through foreign tax credits and deductions.[8] Foreign tax credit relief is, however, generally limited in scope either because the credit is only partial and does not cover the full amount of the foreign tax paid or because it does not apply to the particular source of income that is subject to foreign tax.

(b) Bilateral Relief

Bilateral relief is negotiated through tax treaties. Bilateral tax treaties serve three principal purposes:

- prevention of double taxation;
- prevention of tax avoidance; and
- encouragement of international trade and commerce.

The historical focus of bilateral tax treaties has been on the prevention of juridical double taxation of income. Bilateral tax treaties generally provide relief from double taxation of international income by stipulating agreed upon source rules and maximum tax rates. Thus, tax treaties promote trade co-operation between countries by fostering an atmosphere of fiscal certainty in international transactions.

Bilateral tax treaties can be, and frequently are, used to avoid tax through treaty shopping. Taxpayers may use treaties to exploit differential tax rates between countries or to channel specific sources of income to particular jurisdictions in order to minimize withholding taxes. Thus, the instrument for the prevention of double taxation can become a vehicle for tax avoidance. There are two basic approaches to counter such avoidance: domestic legislation (such as the general anti-avoidance rule)[9] and specifically negotiated anti-avoidance or anti-shopping provisions within the treaty itself.

---

[6] See, for example, para. 149(1)(a) (employees of foreign governments).

[7] See, for example, s. 126 (foreign tax deduction).

[8] S. 126; subs. 20(11).

[9] See s. 245.

The interplay between these two mechanisms adds additional complexity to treaty interpretation.

4. TAX TREATIES

(a) Taxes Covered

Bilateral tax treaties typically cover taxes on income and on capital. There are, however, many other types of taxes that are not addressed in bilateral tax treaties. For example, consumption taxes (sales, value added, goods and services, etc.), estate taxes, payroll taxes and excise taxes are not usually covered in bilateral tax treaties. These taxes, which can have an important effect on business arrangements, should also be fully considered in planning international transactions.

(b) Double Taxation

Double taxation usually arises because of an overlap of jurisdictional connecters between source of income and residence of the taxpayer. For example, Part XIII of the Act imposes a 25 per cent withholding tax on certain types of passive income (e.g., interest) paid to non-residents of Canada. A non-resident in receipt of Canadian source passive income will be subject to double taxation if he or she is also taxable without full relief on that income in his or her country of residence.

Double taxation can also arise because of dual claims on the same person. For example, a U.S. citizen resident in Canada is subject to two tax claims: Canadian tax by virtue of residence and U.S. tax by virtue of citizenship.

Bilateral tax treaties prevent double taxation in two ways: by ceding to one jurisdiction (for example, the country of residence) the exclusive power to tax a particular type or source of income or by requiring the signatories to the treaty to provide a credit for taxes paid to the other in respect of that particular type of income.

However, the focus of bilateral treaties extends beyond the prevention of double taxation. Tax treaties also seek to prevent fiscal avoidance and evasion. Just as taxpayers are concerned with double taxation of income, governments are increasingly concerned with the complete absence of taxation of income by any jurisdiction.

It is important to note, however, that tax treaties do not impose taxes; they merely give the participating countries (usually referred to as "Contracting States") the power to impose a tax at a *maximum* stipulated rate under that country's domestic fiscal legislation. Typically, most tax treaties either exempt particular types of income from tax or stipulate a maximum rate at which a particular type of income may be taxed.

(c) General Principles

(i) Arm's Length

A fundamental principle underlying treaties directed at the prevention of double taxation is that the income of non-residents should be allocated to countries on the basis of "arm's length principles". This implies that the taxable profits of a business enterprise, whether operated in a particular country through a subsidiary or a branch, will be subject to tax as if the enterprise conducted its business independently in that country. Similarly, it is assumed for most treaty purposes that products purchased by a business enterprise from related parties (for example, by a subsidiary from its parent corporation) will be priced as if the products were purchased from an unrelated third party. Thus, both the jurisdiction to tax the business enterprise and the prices at which it is presumed to transact with related parties are premised on the notion that the enterprise operates on an arm's length and independent basis.

The arm's length principle implies that a country should assess foreigners and foreign income only in respect of income that arises in the country. Although the method by which foreign income is determined may refer to some formula, the jurisdiction to tax the taxpayer rests on the arm's length principle. The formula, if any, is merely intended to facilitate the calculation of particular types of income to most reasonably approximate the determination that would be arrived at by an arm's length approach.

(ii) The Unitary System

The unitary system of taxation is a form of the formulary approach that is intended to determine the tax base of an enterprise by reference to legal entities other than the principal taxpayer. Under this approach, the taxable income of an enterprise is determined not by reference only to the enterprise's activities but also by reference to its related taxpayers. Thus, the results of a "unitary business" are considered on the basis of all related entities within the business group. The group's income is then allocated by virtue of a formula to each jurisdiction that claims authority to tax the enterprise. For example, a country may calculate the world-wide group income of a corporation and then assess the tax due in proportion to the percentage of the group's property, payroll and sales in the particular country or subdivision thereof.

The difficulty with the unitary system of taxation is that it does not conform with generally accepted principles of international taxation as embodied in bilateral tax treaties. Hence, it is quite possible that income subject to tax under a unitary system may not receive the appropriate tax credit relief for taxes paid on a unitary basis.

It is not possible to determine in advance whether a business enterprise will benefit more or less from a system determined by reference to arm's length principles or under a unitary system of taxation. Businesses can benefit from either approach depending upon their particular circumstances. The result depends upon whether the business earns most of its profits in the place where the majority of its property and employees are based. For example, a corporation with several new overseas subsidiaries which are losing money would be taxed less under the unitary system because the losses of the subsidiaries would be counted in its world-wide income. In contrast, under an arm's length basis of determination, the corporation would be taxable as a separate and independent legal entity in the jurisdiction where it is located, without reference to its subsidiary operations.

(d) Negotiated Agreements

A tax treaty is a bilateral international agreement between two sovereign states. A "treaty" is defined as:[10]

> . . . an international agreement concluded between States in written form and governed by international law, whether embodied in a single instrument or in two or more related instruments and whatever its particular designation.

An international treaty is binding on the signatories to the treaty.[11] The *Vienna Convention* provides a comprehensive set of principles and rules that govern the law of treaties. The Convention is itself a treaty which deals with the subject of treaties, their making, observance, entry into force, amendment, suspension of operation, modification and termination.

(e) Remedy for Breach

A breach of a treaty does not *per se* give a private citizen a right of action. Canada has, however, adopted the practice of implementing its tax treaties as part of its domestic law. Thus, a taxpayer can invoke the provisions of a Canadian treaty through an action in Canadian courts. In the event of an inconsistency between the provisions of a treaty and the *Income Tax Act*, the provisions of the treaty prevail to the extent of the inconsistency. Thus, in a sense, Canada's tax treaties are both "international" and "domestic" law.

(f) Resolution of Conflicts

Reference:

BULLETINS, CIRCULARS & RULINGS:

IC 71-17R3   February 25, 1991   Mutual Agreement Procedures Requests for Competent Authority Jurisdiction

A bilateral tax treaty is a negotiated agreement between two countries. A taxpayer who considers himself or herself to be deprived of the benefits to which he or she is entitled under a tax treaty may lodge a claim with the "competent authority" in his or her own country and leave it to the authority to pursue the complaint. There is no appeal to an international court or tribunal. Canadian taxpayers may, however, litigate treaty issues in Canadian courts.

Generally speaking, a request for competent authority consideration should be made when the domestic revenue authority has developed its tax audit to a point of certainty.

---

[10] Art. 2(1)(a), the *Vienna Convention on the Law of Treaties* (the *"Vienna Convention"*), U.N. Doc. A/CONF. 39/27 (1969).

[11] Art. 26, *The Vienna Convention, ante,* "Every treaty in force is binding upon the parties to it and must be performed by them in good faith."

Although formal assessment by the revenue authority is not a prerequisite for a request for competent authority intervention, the audit itself should have developed to a stage of considerable certainty. The request for competent authority consideration should only be made after the taxpayer has presented all of the facts in support of his or her position to the revenue authorities and has given those authorities an opportunity to consider the facts. Thus, a taxpayer should request competent authority consideration only after revenue authorities fail to give satisfaction.

Canadian residents who wish to make a request for competent authority consideration can apply to the Director, Tax Avoidance and Foreign Operations Division. There is no specific form for the application; a letter is sufficient to trigger the process. The letter should give the following information:

- the taxpayers involved,
- the control and business relationship between the Canadian taxpayer and the other person,
- the taxation years or periods under review,
- the nature of the double taxation problem,
- the status or the tax liability of the taxpayer or related person in the other jurisdiction, and
- the action taken by the taxpayer to obtain a corresponding or correlative assessing adjustment and the reasons why such action was unsuccessful.

SUMMARY OF THE OECD MODEL TAX CONVENTION
TITLE AND PREAMBLE
CHAPTER I
Scope of the Convention

Art. 1   Personal scope
Art. 2   Taxes covered

CHAPTER II
Definitions

Art. 3   General definitions
Art. 4   Resident
Art. 5   Permanent establishment

CHAPTER III
Taxation of income

Art. 6   Income from immovable property
Art. 7   Business profits
Art. 8   Shipping, inland waterways transport and air transport

CHAPTER IV

Taxation of capital

CHAPTER V

Methods for elimination of double taxation

CHAPTER VI

Special provisions

CHAPTER VII

Final provisions

TITLE OF THE CONVENTION

**Convention between (State A) and (State B)
with respect to taxes on income and on capital[1]**

PREAMBLE OF THE CONVENTION[2]

---

1.   States wishing to do so may follow the widespread practice of including in the title a reference to either the elimination of double taxation or to both the elimination of double taxation and the prevention of fiscal evasion.

2.   The Preamble of the Convention shall be drafted in accordance with the constitutional procedure of both Contracting States.

CHAPTER I
SCOPE OF THE CONVENTION

Article 1
PERSONAL SCOPE

This Convention shall apply to persons who are residents of one or both of the Contracting States.

Article 2
TAXES COVERED

1.   This Convention shall apply to taxes on income and on capital imposed on behalf of a Contracting State or of its political subdivisions or local authorities, irrespective of the manner in which they are levied.

2.   There shall be regarded as taxes on income and on capital all taxes imposed on total income, on total capital, or on elements of income or of capital, including taxes on gains from the alienation of movable or immovable property, taxes on the total

amounts of wages or salaries paid by enterprises, as well as taxes on capital appreciation.

3.   The existing taxes to which the Convention shall apply are in particular:

a)   (in State A): ....

b)   (in State B): ....

4.   The Convention shall apply also to any identical or substantially similar taxes which are imposed after the date of signature of the Convention in addition to, or in place of, the existing taxes. At the end of each year, the competent authorities of the Contracting States shall notify each other of changes which have been made in their respective taxation laws.

CHAPTER II
DEFINITIONS

Article 3
GENERAL DEFINITIONS

1.   For the purposes of this Convention, unless the context otherwise requires:

a)   the term "person" includes an individual, a company and any other body of persons;

b)   the term "company" means any body corporate or any entity which is treated as a body corporate for tax purposes;

c)   the terms "enterprise of a Contracting State" and "enterprise of the other Contracting State" mean respectively an enterprise carried on by a resident of a Contracting State and an enterprise carried on by a resident of the other Contracting State;

d)   the term "international traffic" means any transport by a ship or aircraft operated by an enterprise which has its place of effective management in a Contracting State, except when the ship or aircraft is operated solely between places in the other Contracting State;

e)   the term "competent authority" means:

(i)   (in State A): ....

(ii)   (in State B): ....

f)   the term "national" means:

(i)   any individual possessing the nationality of a Contracting State;

(ii)   any legal person, partnership or association deriving its status as such from the laws in force in a Contracting State.

2. As regards the application of the Convention by a Contracting State any term not defined therein shall, unless the context otherwise requires, have the meaning which it has under the law of that State concerning the taxes to which the Convention applies.

Article 4
RESIDENT

1. For the purposes of this Convention, the term "resident of a Contracting State" means any person who, under the laws of that State, is liable to tax therein by reason of his domicile, residence, place of management or any other criterion of a similar nature. But this term does not include any person who is liable to tax in that State in respect only of income from sources in that State or capital situated therein.

2. Where by reason of the provisions of paragraph 1 an individual is a resident of both Contracting States, then his status shall be determined as follows:

   a) he shall be deemed to be a resident of the State in which he has a permanent home available to him; if he has a permanent home available to him in both States, he shall be deemed to be a resident of the State with which his personal and economic relations are closer (centre of vital interests);

   b) if the State in which he has his centre of vital interests cannot be determined, or if he has not a permanent home available to him in either State, he shall be deemed to be a resident of the State in which he has an habitual abode;

   c) if he has an habitual abode in both States or in neither of them, he shall be deemed to be a resident of the State of which he is a national;

   d) if he is a national of both States or of neither of them, the competent authorities of the Contracting States shall settle the question by mutual agreement.

3. Where by reason of the provisions of paragraph 1 a person other than an individual is a resident of both Contracting States, then it shall be deemed to be a resident of the State in which its place of effective management is situated.

Article 5
PERMANENT ESTABLISHMENT

1. For the purposes of this Convention, the term "permanent establishment" means a fixed place of business through which the business of an enterprise is wholly or partly carried on.

2. The term "permanent establishment" includes especially:

   a) a place of management;

   b) a branch;

   c) an office;

   d) a factory;

e) a workshop, and

f) a mine, an oil or gas well, a quarry or any other place of extraction of natural resources.

3. A building site or construction or installation project constitutes a permanent establishment only if it lasts more than twelve months.

4. Notwithstanding the preceding provisions of this Article, the term "permanent establishment" shall be deemed not to include:

a) the use of facilities solely for the purpose of storage, display or delivery of goods or merchandise belonging to the enterprise;

b) the maintenance of a stock of goods or merchandise belonging to the enterprise solely for the purpose of storage, display or delivery;

c) the maintenance of a stock of goods or merchandise belonging to the enterprise solely for the purpose of processing by another enterprise;

d) the maintenance of a fixed place of business solely for the purpose of purchasing goods or merchandise or of collecting information, for the enterprise;

e) the maintenance of a fixed place of business solely for the purpose of carrying on, for the enterprise, any other activity of a preparatory or auxiliary character;

f) the maintenance of a fixed place of business solely for any combination of activities mentioned in sub-paragraphs a) to e), provided that the overall activity of the fixed place of business resulting from this combination is of a preparatory or auxiliary character.

5. Notwithstanding the provisions of paragraphs 1 and 2, where a person — other than an agent of an independent status to whom paragraph 6 applies — is acting on behalf of an enterprise and has, and habitually exercises, in a Contracting State an authority to conclude contracts in the name of the enterprise, that enterprise shall be deemed to have a permanent establishment in that State in respect of any activities which that person undertakes for the enterprise, unless the activities of such person are limited to those mentioned in paragraph 4 which, if exercised through a fixed place of business, would not make this fixed place of business a permanent establishment under the provisions of that paragraph.

6. An enterprise shall not be deemed to have a permanent establishment in a Contracting State merely because it carries on business in that State through a broker, general commission agent or any other agent of an independent status, provided that such persons are acting in the ordinary course of their business.

7. The fact that a company which is a resident of a Contracting State controls or is controlled by a company which is a resident of the other Contracting State, or which carries on business in that other State (whether through a permanent establishment or otherwise), shall not of itself constitute either company a permanent establishment of the other.

CHAPTER III
TAXATION OF INCOME

Article 6
INCOME FROM IMMOVABLE PROPERTY

1.   Income derived by a resident of a Contracting State from immovable property (including income from agriculture or forestry) situated in the other Contracting State may be taxed in that other State.

2.   The term "immovable property" shall have the meaning which it has under the law of the Contracting State in which the property in question is situated. The term shall in any case include property accessory to immovable property, livestock and equipment used in agriculture and forestry, rights to which the provisions of general law respecting landed property apply, usufruct of immovable property and rights to variable or fixed payments as consideration for the working of, or the right to work, mineral deposits, sources and other natural resources; ships, boats and aircraft shall not be regarded as immovable property.

3.   The provisions of paragraph 1 shall apply to income derived from the direct use, letting, or use in any other form of immovable property.

4.   The provisions of paragraphs 1 and 3 shall also apply to the income from immovable property of an enterprise and to income from immovable property used for the performance of independent personal services.

Article 7
BUSINESS PROFITS

1.   The profits of an enterprise of a Contracting State shall be taxable only in that State unless the enterprise carries on business in the other Contracting State through a permanent establishment situated therein. If the enterprise carries on business as aforesaid, the profits of the enterprise may be taxed in the other State but only so much of them as is attributable to that permanent establishment.

2.   Subject to the provisions of paragraph 3, where an enterprise of a Contracting State carries on business in the other Contracting State through a permanent establishment situated therein, there shall in each Contracting State be attributed to that permanent establishment the profits which it might be expected to make if it were a distinct and separate enterprise engaged in the same or similar activities under the same or similar conditions and dealing wholly independently with the enterprise of which it is a permanent establishment.

3.   In determining the profits of a permanent establishment, there shall be allowed as deductions expenses which are incurred for the purposes of the permanent establishment, including executive and general administrative expenses so incurred, whether in the State in which the permanent establishment is situated or elsewhere.

4. Insofar as it has been customary in a Contracting State to determine the profits to be attributed to a permanent establishment on the basis of an apportionment of the total profits of the enterprise to its various parts, nothing in paragraph 2 shall preclude that Contracting State from determining the profits to be taxed by such an apportionment as may be customary; the method of apportionment adopted shall, however, be such that the result shall be in accordance with the principles contained in this Article.

5. No profits shall be attributed to a permanent establishment by reason of the mere purchase by that permanent establishment of goods or merchandise for the enterprise.

6. For the purposes of the preceding paragraphs, the profits to be attributed to the permanent establishment shall be determined by the same method year by year unless there is good and sufficient reason to the contrary.

7. Where profits include items of income which are dealt with separately in other Articles of this Convention, then the provisions of those Articles shall not be affected by the provisions of this Article.

Article 8

SHIPPING, INLAND WATERWAYS TRANSPORT AND AIR TRANSPORT

1. Profits from the operation of ships or aircraft in international traffic shall be taxable only in the Contracting State in which the place of effective management of the enterprise is situated.

2. Profits from the operation of boats engaged in inland waterways transport shall be taxable only in the Contracting State in which the place of effective management of the enterprise is situated.

3. If the place of effective management of a shipping enterprise or of an inland waterways transport enterprise is aboard a ship or boat, then it shall be deemed to be situated in the Contracting State in which the home harbour of the ship or boat is situated, or, if there is no such home harbour, in the Contracting State of which the operator of the ship or boat is a resident.

4. The provisions of paragraph 1 shall also apply to profits from the participation in a pool, a joint business or an international operating agency.

Article 9

ASSOCIATED ENTERPRISES

1. Where

    a) an enterprise of a Contracting State participates directly or indirectly in the management, control or capital of an enterprise of the other Contracting State, or

    b) the same persons participate directly or indirectly in the management, control or capital of an enterprise of a Contracting State and an enterprise of the other Contracting State, and in either case conditions are made or imposed between the two enterprises in their commercial or financial relations which differ from those which would be made between independent enterprises, then any profits which would, but for those conditions, have accrued to one of the enterprises, but, by reason of those conditions, have not so accrued, may be included in the profits of that enterprise and taxed accordingly.

2.   Where a Contracting State includes in the profits of an enterprise of that State—and taxes accordingly—profits on which an enterprise of the other Contracting State has been charged to tax in that other State and the profits so included are profits which would have accrued to the enterprise of the first-mentioned State if the conditions made between the two enterprises had been those which would have been made between independent enterprises, then that other State shall make an appropriate adjustment to the amount of the tax charged therein on those profits. In determining such adjustment, due regard shall be had to the other provisions of this Convention and the competent authorities of the Contracting States shall if necessary consult each other.

Article 10
DIVIDENDS

1.   Dividends paid by a company which is a resident of a Contracting State to a resident of the other Contracting State may be taxed in that other State.

2.   However, such dividends may also be taxed in the Contracting State of which the company paying the dividends is a resident and according to the laws of that State, but if the recipient is the beneficial owner of the dividends the tax so charged shall not exceed:

   a)   5 per cent of the gross amount of the dividends if the beneficial owner is a company (other than a partnership) which holds directly at least 25 per cent of the capital of the company paying the dividends;

   b)   15 per cent of the gross amount of the dividends in all other cases.

The competent authorities of the Contracting States shall by mutual agreement settle the mode of application of these limitations.

   This paragraph shall not affect the taxation of the company in respect of the profits out of which the dividends are paid.

3.   The term "dividends" as used in this Article means income from shares, "jouissance" shares or "jouissance" rights, mining shares, founders' shares or other rights, not being debt-claims, participating in profits, as well as income from other corporate rights which is subjected to the same taxation treatment as income from shares by the laws of the State of which the company making the distribution is a resident.

4.   The provisions of paragraphs 1 and 2 shall not apply if the beneficial owner of the dividends, being a resident of a Contracting State, carries on business in the other Contracting State of which the company paying the dividends is a resident, through a permanent establishment situated therein, or performs in that other State independent

personal services from a fixed base situated therein, and the holding in respect of which the dividends are paid is effectively connected with such permanent establishment or fixed base. In such case the provisions of Article 7 or Article 14, as the case may be, shall apply.

5.   Where a company which is a resident of a Contracting State derives profits or income from the other Contracting State, that other State may not impose any tax on the dividends paid by the company, except insofar as such dividends are paid to a resident of that other State or insofar as the holding in respect of which the dividends are paid is effectively connected with a permanent establishment or a fixed base situated in that other State, nor subject the company's undistributed profits to a tax on the company's undistributed profits, even if the dividends paid or the undistributed profits consist wholly or partly of profits or income arising in such other State.

Article 11

INTEREST

1.   Interest arising in a Contracting State and paid to a resident of the other Contracting State may be taxed in that other State.

2.   However, such interest may also be taxed in the Contracting State in which it arises and according to the laws of that State, but if the recipient is the beneficial owner of the interest the tax so charged shall not exceed 10 per cent of the gross amount of the interest. The competent authorities of the Contracting. States shall by mutual agreement settle the mode of application of this limitation.

3.   The term "interest" as used in this Article means income from debt-claims of every kind, whether or not secured by mortgage and whether or not carrying a right to participate in the debtor's profits, and in particular, income from government securities and income from bonds or debentures, including premiums and prizes attaching to such securities, bonds or debentures. Penalty charges for late payment shall not be regarded as interest for the purpose of this Article.

4.   The provisions of paragraphs 1 and 2 shall not apply if the beneficial owner of the interest, being a resident of a Contracting State, carries on business in the other Contracting State in which the interest arises, through a permanent establishment situated therein, or performs in that other State independent personal services from a fixed base situated therein, and the debt-claim in respect of which the interest is paid is effectively connected with such permanent establishment or fixed base. In such case the provisions of Article 7 or Article 14, as the case may be, shall apply.

5.   Interest shall be deemed to arise in a Contracting State when the payer is that State itself, a political subdivision, a local authority or a resident of that State. Where, however, the person paying the interest, whether he is a resident of a Contracting State or not, has in a Contracting State a permanent establishment or a fixed base in connection with which the indebtedness on which the interest is paid was incurred, and such interest is borne by such permanent establishment or fixed base, then such interest

shall be deemed to arise in the State in which the permanent establishment or fixed base is situated.

6. Where, by reason of a special relationship between the payer and the beneficial owner or between both of them and some other person, the amount of the interest, having regard to the debt-claim for which it is paid, exceeds the amount which would have been agreed upon by the payer and the beneficial owner in the absence of such relationship, the provisions of this Article shall apply only to the last-mentioned amount. In such case, the excess part of the payments shall remain taxable according to the laws of each Contracting State, due regard being had to the other provisions of this Convention.

Article 12
ROYALTIES

1. Royalties arising in a Contracting State and paid to a resident of the other Contracting State shall be taxable only in that other State if such resident is the beneficial owner of the royalties.

2. The term "royalties" as used in this Article means payments of any kind received as a consideration for the use of, or the right to use, any copyright of literary, artistic or scientific work including cinematograph films, any patent, trade mark, design or model, plan, secret formula or process, or for information concerning industrial, commercial or scientific experience.

3. The provisions of paragraph 1 shall not apply if the beneficial owner of the royalties, being a resident of a Contracting State, carries on business in the other Contracting State in which the royalties arise, through a permanent establishment situated therein, or performs in that other State independent personal services from a fixed base situated therein, and the right or property in respect of which the royalties are paid is effectively connected with such permanent establishment or fixed base. In such case the provisions of Article 7 or Article 14, as the case may be, shall apply.

4. Where, by reason of a special relationship between the payer and the beneficial owner or between both of them and some other person, the amount of the royalties, having regard to the use, right or information for which they are paid, exceeds the amount which would have been agreed upon by the payer and the beneficial owner in the absence of such relationship, the provisions of this Article shall apply only to the last-mentioned amount. In such case, the excess part of the payments shall remain taxable according to the laws of each Contracting State, due regard being had to the other provisions of this Convention.

Article 13
CAPITAL GAINS

1. Gains derived by a resident of a Contracting State from the alienation of immovable property referred to in Article 6 and situated in the other Contracting State may be taxed in that other State.

2. Gains from the alienation of movable property forming part of the business property of a permanent establishment which an enterprise of a Contracting State has in the other Contracting State or of movable property pertaining to a fixed base available to a resident of a Contracting State in the other Contracting State for the purpose of performing independent personal services, including such gains from the alienation of such a permanent establishment (alone or with the whole enterprise) or of such fixed base, may be taxed in that other State.

3. Gains from the alienation of ships or aircraft operated in international traffic, boats engaged in inland waterways transport or movable property pertaining to the operation of such ships, aircraft or boats, shall be taxable only in the Contracting State in which the place of effective management of the enterprise is situated.

4. Gains from the alienation of any property other than that referred to in paragraphs 1, 2 and 3, shall be taxable only in the Contracting State of which the alienator is a resident.

Article 14
INDEPENDENT PERSONAL SERVICES

1. Income derived by a resident of a Contracting State in respect of professional services or other activities of an independent character shall be taxable only in that State unless he has a fixed base regularly available to him in the other Contracting State for the purpose of performing his activities. If he has such a fixed base, the income may be taxed in the other State but only so much of it as is attributable to that fixed base.

2. The term "professional services" includes especially independent scientific, literary, artistic, educational or teaching activities as well as the independent activities of physicians, lawyers, engineers, architects, dentists and accountants.

Article 15
DEPENDENT PERSONAL SERVICES

1. Subject to the provisions of Articles 16, 18 and 19, salaries, wages and other similar remuneration derived by a resident of a Contracting State in respect of an employment shall be taxable only in that State unless the employment is exercised in the other Contracting State. If the employment is so exercised, such remuneration as is derived there from may be taxed in that other State.

2. Notwithstanding the provisions of paragraph 1, remuneration derived by a resident of a Contracting State in respect of an employment exercised in the other Contracting State shall be taxable only in the first-mentioned State if:

    a) the recipient is present in the other State for a period or periods not exceeding in the aggregate 183 days in any twelve month period commencing or ending in the fiscal year concerned, and

    b) the remuneration is paid by, or on behalf of, an employer who is not a resident of the other State, and

    c) the remuneration is not borne by a permanent establishment or a fixed base which the employer has in the other State.

3. Notwithstanding the preceding provisions of this Article, remuneration derived in respect of an employment exercised aboard a ship or aircraft operated in international traffic, or aboard a boat engaged in inland waterways transport, may be taxed in the Contracting State in which the place of effective management of the enterprise is situated.

Article 16

DIRECTORS' FEES

Directors' fees and other similar payments derived by a resident of a Contracting State in his capacity as a member of the board of directors of a company which is a resident of the other Contracting State may be taxed in that other State.

Article 17

ARTISTES AND SPORTSMEN

1. Notwithstanding the provisions of Articles 14 and 15, income derived by a resident of a Contracting State as an entertainer, such as a theatre, motion picture, radio or television artiste, or a musician, or as a sportsman, from his personal activities as such exercised in the other Contracting State, may be taxed in that other State.

2. Where income in respect of personal activities exercised by an entertainer or a sportsman in his capacity as such accrues not to the entertainer or sportsman himself but to another person, that income may, notwithstanding the provisions of Articles 7, 14 and is, be taxed in the Contracting State in which the activities of the entertainer or sportsman are exercised.

Article 18

PENSIONS

Subject to the provisions of paragraph 2 of Article 19, pensions and other similar remuneration paid to a resident of a Contracting State in consideration of past employment shall be taxable only in that State.

Article 19

GOVERNMENT SERVICE

1. a) Remuneration, other than a pension, paid by a Contracting State or a political subdivision or a local authority thereof to an individual in respect of services rendered to that State or subdivision or authority shall be taxable only in that State.

   b) However, such remuneration shall be taxable only in the other Contracting State if the services are rendered in that State and the individual is a resident of that State who:

      (i)   is a national of that State; or

      (ii)   did not become a resident of that State solely for the purpose of rendering the services.

2. a) Any pension paid by, or out of funds created by, a Contracting State or a political subdivision or a local authority thereof to an individual in respect of services rendered to that State or subdivision or authority shall be taxable only in that State.

   b) However, such pension shall be taxable only in the other Contracting State if the individual is a resident of, and a national of, that State.

3. The provisions of Articles 15, 16 and 18 shall apply to remuneration and pensions in respect of services rendered in connection with a business carried on by a Contracting State or a political subdivision or a local authority thereof.

Article 20

STUDENTS

Payments which a student or business apprentice who is or was immediately before visiting a Contracting State a resident of the other Contracting State and who is present in the first-mentioned State solely for the purpose of his education or training receives for the purpose of his maintenance, education or training shall not be taxed in that State, provided that such payments arise from sources outside that State.

Article 21

OTHER INCOME

1. Items of income of a resident of a Contracting State, wherever arising, not dealt with in the foregoing Articles of this Convention shall be taxable only in that State.

2. The provisions of paragraph 1 shall not apply to income, other than income from immovable property as defined in paragraph 2 of Article 6, if the recipient of such income, being a resident of a Contracting State, carries on business in the other Contracting State through a permanent establishment situated therein, or performs in that other State independent personal services from a fixed base situated therein, and the right or property in respect of which the income is paid is effectively connected

with such permanent establishment or fixed base. In such case the provisions of Article 7 or Article 14, as the case may be, shall apply.

CHAPTER IV
TAXATION OF CAPITAL

Article 22
CAPITAL

1. Capital represented by immovable property referred to in Article 6, owned by a resident of a Contracting State and situated in the other Contracting State, may be taxed in that other State.

2. Capital represented by movable property forming part of the business property of a permanent establishment which an enterprise of a Contracting State has in the other Contracting State or by movable property pertaining to a fixed base available to a resident of a Contracting State in the other Contracting State for the purpose of performing independent personal services, may be taxed in that other State.

3. Capital represented by ships and aircraft operated in international traffic and by boats engaged in inland waterways transport, and by movable property pertaining to the operation of such ships, aircraft and boats, shall be taxable only in the Contracting State in which the place of effective management of the enterprise is situated.

4. All other elements of capital of a resident of a Contracting State shall be taxable only in that State.

CHAPTER V
METHODS FOR ELIMINATION OF DOUBLE TAXATION

Article 23 A
EXEMPTION METHOD

1. Where a resident of a Contracting State derives income or owns capital which, in accordance with the provisions of this Convention, may be taxed in the other Contracting State, the first-mentioned State shall, subject to the provisions of paragraphs 2 and 3, exempt such income or capital from tax.

2. Where a resident of a Contracting State derives items of income which, in accordance with the provisions of Articles 10 and 11, may be taxed in the other Contracting State, the first-mentioned State shall allow as a deduction from the tax on the income of that resident an amount equal to the tax paid in that other State. Such deduction shall not, however, exceed that part of the tax, as computed before the deduction is given, which is attributable to such items of income derived from that other State.

3. Where in accordance with any provision of the Convention income derived or capital owned by a resident of a Contracting State is exempt from tax in that State, such State may nevertheless, in calculating the amount of tax on the remaining income or capital of such resident, take into account the exempted income or capital.

Article 23 B
CREDIT METHOD

1. Where a resident of a Contracting State derives income or owns capital which, in accordance with the provisions of this Convention, may be taxed in the other Contracting State, the first-mentioned State shall allow:

a) as a deduction from the tax on the income of that resident, an amount equal to the income tax paid in that other State;

b) as a deduction from the tax on the capital of that resident, an amount equal to the capital tax paid in that other State.

Such deduction in either case shall not, however, exceed that part of the income tax or capital tax, as computed before the deduction is given, which is attributable, as the case may be, to the income or the capital which may be taxed in that other State.

2. Where in accordance with any provision of the Convention income derived or capital owned by a resident of a Contracting State is exempt from tax in that State, such State may nevertheless, in calculating the amount of tax on the remaining income or capital of such resident, take into account the exempted income or capital.

CHAPTER VI
SPECIAL PROVISIONS

Article 24
NON-DISCRIMINATION

1. Nationals of a Contracting State shall not be subjected in the other Contracting State to any taxation or any requirement connected therewith, which is other or more burdensome than the taxation and connected requirements to which nationals of that other State in the same circumstances, in particular with respect to residence, are or may be subjected. This provision shall, notwithstanding the provisions of Article 1, also apply to persons who are not residents of one or both of the Contracting States.

2. Stateless persons who are residents of a Contracting State shall not be subjected in either Contracting State to any taxation or any requirement connected therewith, which is other or more burdensome than the taxation and connected requirements to which nationals of the State concerned in the same circumstances are or may be subjected.

3. The taxation on a permanent establishment which an enterprise of a Contracting State has in the other Contracting State shall not be less favourably levied in that other State than the taxation levied on enterprises of that other State carrying on the same

activities. This provision shall not be construed as obliging a Contracting State to grant to residents of the other Contracting State any personal allowances, reliefs and reductions for taxation purposes on account of civil status or family responsibilities which it grants to its own residents.

4. Except where the provisions of paragraph 1 of Article 9, paragraph 6 of Article 11, or paragraph 4 of Article 12, apply, interest, royalties and other disbursements paid by an enterprise of a Contracting State to a resident of the other Contracting State shall, for the purpose of determining the taxable profits of such enterprise, be deductible under the same conditions as if they had been paid to a resident of the first-mentioned State. Similarly, any debts of an enterprise of a Contracting State to a resident of the other Contracting State shall, for the purpose of determining the taxable capital of such enterprise, be deductible under the same conditions as if they had been contracted to a resident of the first-mentioned State.

5. Enterprises of a Contracting State, the capital of which is wholly or partly owned or controlled, directly or indirectly, by one or more residents of the other Contracting State, shall not be subjected in the first-mentioned State to any taxation or any requirement connected therewith which is other or more burdensome than the taxation and connected requirements to which other similar enterprises of the first-mentioned State are or may be subjected.

6. The provisions of this Article shall, notwithstanding the provisions of Article 2, apply to taxes of every kind and description.

Article 25
MUTUAL AGREEMENT PROCEDURE

1. Where a person considers that the actions of one or both of the Contracting States result or will result for him in taxation not in accordance with the provisions of this Convention, he may, irrespective of the remedies provided by the domestic law of those States, present his case to the competent authority of the Contracting State of which he is a resident or, if his case comes under paragraph 1 of Article 24, to that of the Contracting State of which he is a national. The case must be presented within three years from the first notification of the action resulting in taxation not in accordance with the provisions of the Convention.

2. The competent authority shall endeavour, if the objection appears to it to be justified and if it is not itself able to arrive at a satisfactory solution, to resolve the case by mutual agreement with the competent authority of the other Contracting State, with a view to the avoidance of taxation which is not in accordance with the Convention. Any agreement reached shall be implemented notwithstanding any time limits in the domestic law of the Contracting States.

3. The competent authorities of the Contracting States shall endeavour to resolve by mutual agreement any difficulties or doubts arising as to the interpretation or application of the Convention. They may also consult together for the elimination of double taxation in cases not provided for in the Convention.

4. The competent authorities of the Contracting States may communicate with each other directly for the purpose of reaching an agreement in the sense of the preceding paragraphs. When it seems advisable in order to reach agreement to have an oral exchange of opinions, such exchange may take place through a Commission consisting of representatives of the competent authorities of the Contracting States.

Article 26
EXCHANGE OF INFORMATION

1. The competent authorities of the Contracting States shall exchange such information as is necessary for carrying out the provisions of this Convention or of the domestic laws of the Contracting States concerning taxes covered by the Convention insofar as the taxation thereunder is not contrary to the Convention. The exchange of information is not restricted by Article 1. Any information received by a Contracting State shall be treated as secret in the same manner as information obtained under the domestic laws of that State and shall be disclosed only to persons or authorities (including courts and administrative bodies) involved in the assessment or collection of, the enforcement or prosecution in respect of, or the determination of appeals in relation to, the taxes covered by the Convention. Such persons or authorities shall use the information only for such purposes. They may disclose the information in public court proceedings or in judicial decisions.

2. In no case shall the provisions of paragraph 1 be construed so as to impose on a Contracting State the obligation:

   a) to carry out administrative measures at variance with the laws and administrative practice of that or of the other Contracting State;

   b) to supply information which is not obtainable under the laws or in the normal course of the administration of that or of the other Contracting State;

   c) to supply information which would disclose any trade, business, industrial, commercial or professional secret or trade process, or information, the disclosure of which would be contrary to public policy (ordre public).

Article 27
DIPLOMATIC AGENTS AND CONSULAR OFFICERS

Nothing in this Convention shall affect the fiscal privileges of diplomatic agents or consular officers under the general rules of international law or under the provisions of special agreements.

Article 28

TERRITORIAL EXTENSION[1]

1. This Convention may be extended, either in its entirety or with any necessary modifications [to any part of the territory of (State A) or of (State B) which is specifically excluded from the application of the Convention or], to any State or territory for whose international relations (State A) or (State B) is responsible, which imposes taxes substantially similar in character to those to which the Convention applies. Any such extension shall take effect from such date and subject to such modifications and conditions, including conditions as to termination, as may be specified and agreed between the Contracting States in notes to be exchanged through diplomatic channels or in any other manner in accordance with their constitutional procedures.

2. Unless otherwise agreed by both Contracting States, the termination of the Convention by one of them under Article 30 shall also terminate, in the manner provided for in that Article, the application of the Convention [to any part of the territory of (State A) or of (State B) or] to any State or territory to which it has been extended under this Article.

CHAPTER VII
FINAL PROVISIONS

Article 29

ENTRY INTO FORCE

1. This Convention shall be ratified and the instruments of ratification shall be exchanged at .... as soon as possible.

2. The Convention shall enter into force upon the exchange of instruments of ratification and its provisions shall have effect:

    a)   (in State A): ....

    b)   (in State B): ....

---

1. The words between brackets are of relevance when, by special provision, a part of the territory of a Contracting State is excluded from the application of the Convention.

Article 30

TERMINATION

This Convention shall remain in force until terminated by a Contracting State. Either Contracting State may terminate the Convention, through diplomatic channels, by giving notice of termination at least six months before the end of any calendar year after the year.......In such event, the Convention shall cease to have effect:

a) (in State A): ....

b) (in State B): ....

TERMINAL CLAUSE[1]

---

1. The terminal clause concerning the signing shall be drafted in accordance with the constitutional procedure of both Contracting States.

SELECTED BIBLIOGRAPHY TO CHAPTER XXVII

General

Adams, J.R. and Whalley, J., *The International Taxation of Multinational Enterprises in Developed Countries* (Connecticut: Greenwood Press, 1977).

Adhikaie, Ajay, et al., "Going Global" (July 1991), 124 *CA Magazine* 24.

Anthoine, Robert (ed.), *Tax Incentives for Private Investment in Developing Countries* (The Netherlands: Kluwer, 1979).

Arnold, Brian J., "Canada's Auditor-General Report Blasts Deduction of Interest on Loans to Finance Foreign Subsidiaries" (1992), 5 *Tax Notes International* 1425.

Arnold, Brian J. (ed.), *Organisation for Economic Co-operation and Development, OECD Model Tax Convention: Four Related Studies* (Paris: OECD, 1992) 101.

Bartlett, R.T., "The Making of Double Taxation Agreements" (1991), 3:4 *British Tax Review* 76.

Bischel, Jon E. and Feinschreiber, Robert, *Fundamentals of International Law* (New York City: Practising Law Institute, 1977).

Bittker, Boris I. and Lawrence Lokken, *Fundamentals of International Taxation* (New York: Warren, Gorham & Lamont, 1991).

Bracewell-Milnes, Barry, *The Economics of International Tax Avoidance — Political versus Economic Law* (The Netherlands: Kluwer, 1980).

Brean, D.J.S., "International Issues in Taxation: The Canadian Perspective", *Canadian Tax Paper No. 75* (Can. Tax Foundation, 1984).

Bryan, Greyson, "Developed Nation Tax Law and Investment in LDC's" (1978), *Columbia Journal of Transnational Law* 221.

Carroll, M.B., "International Tax Law" (1967-68) 2 *International Lawyer* 692.

Couzin, Robert, "Repatriating Canadian Capital" (1985), 14 *Tax Management Int'l Journal* 352.

"Double Taxation Treaties Between Industrialized and Developing Countries: OECD and UN Models, A Comparison: Proceedings of a Seminar Held in Stockholm in 1990 During the 44th Congress of the International Fiscal Association" (Boston: Kluwer Law and Taxation Publishers, 1992).

Eisenstein, Louis, *The Ideologies of Taxation* (New York: The Ronald Press Company, 1961).

Finch, J, "The Apportionment of Multistate and Multinational Corporate Income for Tax Purposes" (1984), 38 *Bulletin for International Fiscal Documentation* 51.

Gallagher, T. Jr., "United States Sovereignty and Principles of Transnational Taxation" (1975-1976), 2 *J. Real Estate Tax* 486.

Gammie, Malcom and Carol Lucas, "Income Tax: Some International Comparisons" (1979), 5 *British Tax Rev.* 275.

Grimwade, Nigel, *International Trade: New Patterns of Trade, Production and Investment* (London: Routledge, 1989).

Grundy, Milton, *The World of International Tax Planning* (Cambridge: Cambridge University Press, 1984).

Haufbauer, G.C., *U.S. Taxation of American Business Abroad — An Exchange of Views* (Washington, D.C.: American Enterprise Institute for Public Policy Research, 1975).

Hellawell, Robert, "United States Income Taxation and Less Developed Countries: A Critical Appraisal" (December 1986), 66 *Columbia Law Review* 1393.

Hellawell, Robert (ed.), *United States Taxation and Developing Countries* (New York: Columbia University Press, 1980).

Hepker, Michael Z, *A Modern Approach to Tax Law* (London: Heinman, 1973).

Hope, Kempe Ronald, *Economic Development in the Caribbean* (New York: Praeger Publishers, 1986).

IFA, "Rules for Determining Income and Expenses as Domestic or Foreign", Vol. 65b, *Cahiers de Droit Fiscal International*, 1980.

"International Tax Planning — Canada-U.S. Tax Issues: The Tax Treaty, Unitary Taxation, and the Future" (1984), 32 *Can. Tax J.* 547.

Johnston, D., "The Basis of Jurisdiction and the Treatment of Business Profits", in *Proceedings of 27th Tax Conf.* 303 (Can. Tax Foundation, 1975).

Kingston, Charles I, "The Coherence of International Taxation" (October 1981), 81 *Columbia Law Review* 1151.

Knechtle, A.A., *Basic Problems in International Fiscal Law* (The Netherlands: Kluwer, 1979).

Kroft, Edwin G., "Tax Avoidance Attacks Using Pre-GAAR Weapons" (1991), in *Proceedings of the 43rd Tax Conf.* 8:24.

League of Nations Economic and Financial Commission. *Report on Double Taxation* (Geneva, 1925). Report submitted to the Economic and Financial Commission by Professors Bruins, Einaudi, Seligman and Sir Joseph Stamp.

League of Nations Economic and Financial Commission. *Report and Resolutions on Double Taxation and Tax Evasion* (Geneva, 1925). Report submitted to the Economic and Financial Commission by the Technical Experts (1925) Geneva.

Martha, Rutsel Silvestre J., *The Jurisdiction to Tax in International Law: Theory and Practice of Legislative Fiscal Jurisdiction* (Deventer, The Netherlands: Kluwer, 1989).

McClure, Charles E., "International Aspects of Tax Policy for the 21st Century" (1990), 8:2 *American Journal of Tax Policy* 167.

McClure, William P. and Herman B. Bouma, "The Taxation of Foreign Income from 1909 to 1989: How a Tilted Playing Field Developed" (1989), 43:11 *Tax Notes* 1379.

McDaniel, Paul R. and Ault Hugh J., *Introduction to United States International Taxation*, 3rd ed. (Boston: Kluwer, 1989).

Morrris, D.B., "Jurisdiction to Tax: An Up-Date", in *Proceedings of 31st Tax Conf.* 414 (Can. Tax Foundation, 1979).

Musgrave, Peggy B., *United States Taxation of Foreign Investment Income: Issues and Arguments* (Cambridge: The Law School of Harvard University, 1969).

Musgrave, Richard A. and Peggy B., "Inter-nation equity" in Richard Bird and John Head (eds.) *Modern Fiscal Issues: Essays in Honor of Carl Shoup* (Toronto: University of Toronto Press, 1972).

Norr, M., "Jurisdiction to Tax and Internal Income" (1961-62), 17 *Tax Law Rev.* 431.

Palmer, Robert L., "Toward Unilateral Coherence in Determining Jurisdiction to Tax Income" (1989), 30 *Harvard Int'l. L.J.* 1.

Palmieri-Egger, N.W., "Worldwide Tax Allocation Norm v. Worldwide Combination Method of Taxation" (1983), 10 *Intertax* 390.

Perry, David B., "International Tax Comparisons, 1990" (1991), 39 *Canadian Tax Journal* 1644.

Persky, T., "Conflicts Between Source and Residence-Based Taxation" (1981), 13 *Tax Notes* 344.

Phillips, John, "Maximising the Benefits of Double Tax Treaties" (January 1986), 13 *Tax Planning International Review* 3.

Phillips, John S., *Tax Treaty Networks 1991* 1991.

Pires, Manuel, *International Juridical Double Taxation of Income* (Deventer, The Netherlands: Kluwer, 1989).

Plambeck, Charles Thelen, "International: The Taxation Implications of Global Trading" (November 1990), 44:11 *Bull. Int'l. Fisc Doc.* 527.

Postlewaite, Philip F., *International Corporate Taxation* (Colorado: Shepherds McGraw Hill, 1980).

Seligman, Edwin R.A., *Double Taxation and International Fiscal Corporation* (New York: The MacMillan Company, 1928).

Souvant, Karl P., *Trade and Foreign Investment in Data Services* (Colorado: Westview Press, Inc., 1986).

Surrey, Stanley, "United Nations Group of Experts and the Guidelines for Tax Treaties Between Developed and Developing Countries" (1978), 19 *Harvard International Law Journal* 1.

Surrey, Stanley, "Reflections on the Allocation of Income and Expenses among National Tax Jurisdictions" (1978), 10 *Law and Policy in International Business* 409.

Tillinghast, David R., "International Tax Simplification" (1990), 8:2 *American Journal of Tax Policy* 187.

van Hoorn Jr., J., "The International Tax Picture" (1977), 31 *Bull. Int'l. Fisc. Doc.* 4.

Vogel, Klaus, et al., *Klaus Vogel on Double Taxation Conventions* (Deventer, The Netherlands: Kluwer, 1991).

Wilkins, John G., "Taxation of Corporate Profits in a Global Economy" (October 7, 1991), 53 *Tax Notes* 109.

Yelpaala, Kojo, "The Efficacy of Tax Incentives Within the Framework of the Neoclassical Theory of Foreign Direct Investment: A Legislative Policy Analysis" (1984), 19 *Texas International Law Journal* 365.

CHAPTER XXVIII

IMMIGRATION

References:

BULLETINS, CIRCULARS & RULINGS:

IT-221R2   February 20, 1991   Determination of an Individual's Residence
                                     Status

FORMS:

NR74   Determination of Residency Status (Leaving Canada)

1. GENERAL

An individual who is "landed" in Canada is considered a "permanent resident" for the purposes of the *Immigration Act*.[1] A permanent resident has the right to enter and remain in Canada and may apply for Canadian citizenship upon satisfying certain conditions.

A person ceases to be a permanent resident for immigration purposes when he or she leaves Canada with the intention of abandoning Canada as his or her place of permanent residence.[2] A permanent resident who remains outside Canada for more than 183 days during any 12-month period is deemed to have abandoned permanent resident status unless he or she can satisfy the immigration authorities that he or she did not have an intention to abandon his or her status.

For tax purposes, Canadian citizens and permanent residents are taxed on the same basis, namely, "residence". The determination of residence for tax purposes is a question of fact and law.[3]

An individual who enters Canada, otherwise than as a sojourner, and establishes residential ties within Canada is considered to have become a Canadian resident on the date that he or she enters the country.[4]

---

[1]   *Immigration Act*, R.S.C. 1985, c. I-2.

[2]   *Immigration Act, ante*, subs. 24(1).

[3]   See Chapters III "Residence", XXVII "General Principles of International Tax".

[4]   Special Release to IT-221R2 "Determination of an Individual's Residence Status", para. 16 (February 20, 1991).

For example, an individual becomes a resident of Canada if:

- he or she is a refugee and establishes residential ties in Canada;
- he or she applies for landed immigrant status and establishes residential ties in Canada;
- he or she receives "Approval in Principle" from Employment and Immigration Canada to remain in Canada and he or she establishes residential ties in Canada; or
- he or she is a Canadian citizen who broke off Canadian residential ties in a prior year, but who re-establishes residential ties in Canada.

Canadian residents are generally subject to "full tax liability" on their world-wide income. In the year of arrival in Canada, however, an immigrant is considered to be a part-year resident and is taxable as two separate persons:

- as a non-resident prior to arrival in Canada, and
- as a resident after the date of arrival.

In most cases, it is better for an immigrant to establish residence in Canada rather than be considered a "sojourner" in the year of arrival: A sojourner is taxable on his or her world-wide income for the entire year; a resident is taxable on his or her world-wide income but only after arrival in Canada.

2. DEEMED ACQUISITION OF PROPERTY UPON ENTRY

Reference:

ITA:

Subs. 128.1(1)   Immigration

An immigrant is deemed to acquire his or her property at its fair market value at the time that he or she becomes a Canadian resident for tax purposes.[5] Thus, an immigrant can step-up the cost base of his or her property upon entry into Canada if it has appreciated in value. Property that has fallen in value since its acquisition is also deemed to have been acquired at its fair market value. Hence, it may be better to dispose of loss properties prior to entry into Canada if the resulting loss can be effectively offset against other gains or income.

3. TAXABLE CANADIAN PROPERTY

The deemed acquisition rules do not apply to property that is considered "taxable Canadian property".[6] Thus, there is no deemed acquisition of the following:

---

[5] *Income Tax Act*, para. 128.1(1)(*c*).

[6] Para. 115(1)(*b*).

- real property situated in Canada;
- property used in carrying on a business (other than an insurance business) in Canada;
- shares of corporations (other than public corporations) resident in Canada;
- shares of public corporations if the immigrant owned 25 per cent or more of the issued shares of any class in the five years immediately preceding;
- partnership interests where 50 per cent of the fair market value of all partnership property consists of Canadian resource properties, timber resource properties, and income interests in trusts;
- capital interests in trusts; and
- certain interests in unit and mutual fund trusts.

The deemed acquisition rules also do not apply to business inventory and eligible capital property in respect of a business.

Thus, immigrants should tax plan prior to their entry into Canada. For example, an immigrant can delay disposing of shares with accrued gains until such time as he or she takes up Canadian residence. The step-up in the cost base of the shares will eliminate recognition of the accrued gain. Shares with accumulated tax losses may be disposed of prior to entry in Canada, particularly if such losses can be used prior to the immigrant's departure from his or her home country.

4. PENSIONS

References:

ITA:

Para. 8(1)(*m*)   Employee's Registered Pension Plan Contributions

Para. 51(1)(*a*)   Pension Benefits, Unemployment Insurance Benefits

BULLETINS, CIRCULARS & RULINGS:

IT-499R   January 17, 1992   Superannuation or Pension Benefits

The general scheme for the taxation of pensions under the *Income Tax Act* is that contributions to registered superannuation or pension funds are deductible by the contributor in the year that the contribution is made.[7] Pension payments are taxable to the recipient in the year of payout.[8] Thus, insofar as Canadian residents are concerned, the scheme of deduction of contributions to, and the taxation of receipts out of, registered pension plans provides for deferred taxation of employee benefits within

---

[7]   Para. 8(1)(*m*); subs. 147.2(1).

[8]   Para. 56(1)(*a*).

stipulated limits. This is an important aspect of the Canadian tax system and provides an incentive for saving.

(a) Pension Benefits

"Superannuation or pension benefits" includes any amount received out of or under a superannuation or pension fund or plan,[9] whether or not the plan is registered for Canadian income tax purposes.[10] Pension benefits include:[11]

- pensions, supplements and spouse's allowances under the *Old Age Security Act* (and similar payments under provincial law);
- benefits under the *Canada Pension Plan* (and Quebec equivalents);
- amounts paid under prescribed provincial plans;[12] and
- payments in respect of certain foreign retirement arrangements.

A "registered pension plan" is a plan that is registered by the Minister for the purposes of the Act. The taxability of pension income does not depend upon registration of the particular plan. Registration only has the effect of allowing payments into the plan to be deductible for tax purposes.[13]

A "foreign retirement arrangement"[14] is a prescribed plan or arrangement, such as Individual Retirement Accounts (IRAs) in the United States. Payments from foreign retirement arrangements that would not be subject to income taxation if received by a recipient resident in the source country are not taxable in Canada.[15] For example, an individual who receives a return of contributions from a U.S. retirement arrangement may be entitled to exclude the amount from income if he or she was not initially entitled to a deduction for his or her contribution into the plan.

---

[9]   Subs. 248(1) ("superannuation or pension benefit").

[10]   Subs. 248(1) ("registered pension plan"); s. 147.1.

[11]   Subpara. 56(1)(*a*)(i).

[12]   Reg. 7800(1).

[13]   See Regulation 8501 *et seq.* for conditions of registration.

[14]   Subs. 248(1) ("foreign retirement arrangement"); Reg. 6803.

[15]   Cl. 56(1)(*a*)(i)(C.1).

(b) Old Age Security

Reference:

ITA:

Para. 110(1)(f)   Deductions for Payments

Old age pensions (including guaranteed monthly income supplements and spouse's allowances) paid by the federal government under the *Old Age Security Act* are initially included in income but are deductible in calculating taxable income to the extent that the payments represent a guaranteed income supplement.[16] Such payments are considered to be on account of social assistance on a means or needs test. Thus, in effect, guaranteed income supplements and spouse's allowances are not taxable. Their inclusion in income may, however, affect the amount of other deductions or tax credits (for example, the goods and services tax credit or the child tax credit) that might otherwise be available to the taxpayer on the basis of a means test.

(c) Foreign Pension Plans

Foreign superannuation and pension plans do not generally qualify for registration under the *Income Tax Act* and contributions into such plans do not usually qualify for a deduction from income for Canadian tax purposes. Nevertheless, subject to specific treaty provisions (discussed hereunder), pension income from unregistered foreign pension plans is fully taxable in the hands of Canadian residents.

(d) Employee Benefit Plans

Reference:

ITA:

Para. 6(1)(*g*)   Employee Benefit Plan Benefits

Pension receipts are taxable as income, regardless whether received as an annuity or in a single lump sum. This is so whether the receipt is from a registered or unregistered plan and even if contributions to the particular plan were not deductible for tax purposes at the time that they were made.

An unregistered pension plan may, however, be an "employee benefit plan".[17] Receipts from an employee benefit plan are also taxable to the extent that they are not a return of contributions to the planholder.[18] Thus, receipts from unregistered pension plans which constitute employee benefit plans are taxable only to the extent that the payments exceed the planholder's return of contributions into the plan.

---

[16] Para. 110(1)(*f*).

[17] Subs. 248(1) ("employee benefit plan").

[18] Para. 6(1)(*g*).

(e) OECD Model Tax Convention

The *OECD Model Convention*[19] provides that pensions in respect of private employment should be taxable only in the country where the recipient of the pension is resident.

Article 18 of the OECD Model provides as follows:

Subject to the provisions of paragraph 2 of Article 19, pensions and other similar remuneration paid to a resident of a Contracting State in consideration of past employment shall be taxable only in that State.

A special rule in Article 19 covers the taxation of pensions for government service. Article 19(2) states:

a) Any pension paid by, or out of funds created by, a Contracting State or a political subdivision or a local authority thereof to an individual in respect of services rendered to that State or subdivision or authority shall be taxable only in that State.

b) However, such pension shall be taxable only in the other Contracting State if the individual is a resident of, and a national of, that State. . . .

Article 19(2) is premised on the general principle that the State that pays the pension shall have the exclusive right to tax the payments. The OECD Committee on Fiscal Affairs is of the view, however, that the expression "shall be taxable only" does not prevent a Contracting State from taking into account the exempted pension income in determining the rate of tax that it imposes on income that its residents derive from other sources.

Article 19(2)(b) provides for an exception: Pensions in respect of government service are taxable only in the source country or country of origin, unless the recipient is a resident and national of the other country, in which case the right of taxation is transferred to the other country.

Canada reserves its position on Article 18: The Canadian position is that the country in which the pension arises should be given a limited right to tax and that this right should also extend to government pensions under Article 19. Thus, Canada reserves a limited right to tax and this policy is reflected in its bilateral tax treaties.

(f) Canada-U.S. Treaty (1980)

Article XVIII of the *Canada-U.S. Treaty*[20] deals with the taxation of pensions and annuities:

1. Pensions and annuities arising in a Contracting State and paid to a resident of the other Contracting State may be taxed in that other State, but the amount of any such pension that would be excluded from taxable income in the first-mentioned State if the recipient were a resident thereof shall be exempt from taxation in that other State.

---

[19] See Chapter XXVII ("General Principles of International Tax").

[20] *Canada-United States Income Tax Convention*, September 26, 1980, [1984] Can. T.S. No. 15.

2. However:

    (a) pensions may also be taxed in the Contracting State in which they arise and according to the laws of that State; but if a resident of the other Contracting State is the beneficial owner of a periodic pension payment, the tax so charged shall not exceed 15 per cent of the gross amount of such payment; and

    (b) annuities may also be taxed in the Contracting State in which they arise and according to the laws of that State; but if a resident of the other Contracting State is the beneficial owner of an annuity payment, the tax so charged shall not exceed 15 per cent of the portion of such payment that would not be excluded from taxable income in the first-mentioned State if the beneficial owner were a resident thereof.

3. For the purposes of this Convention, the term "pensions" includes any payment under a superannuation, pension or retirement plan, Armed Forces retirement pay, war veterans pensions and allowances and amounts paid under a sickness, accident or disability plan, but does not include payments under an income-averaging annuity contract or any benefit referred to in paragraph 5.

4. For the purposes of the Convention, the term "annuities" means a stated sum paid periodically at stated times during life or during a specified number of years, under an obligation to make the payments in return for adequate and full consideration (other than services rendered), but does not include a payment that is not a periodic payment or any annuity the cost of which was deductible for the purposes of taxation in the Contracting State in which it was acquired.

5. Benefits under the social security legislation in a Contracting State paid to a resident of the other Contracting State shall be taxable as follows:

    (a) such benefits shall be taxable only in that other State;

    (b) notwithstanding the provisions of subparagraph (a), one-half of the total amount of any such benefit paid in a taxable year shall be exempt from taxation in that other State.

Thus, a Canadian resident is taxable in Canada with respect to pensions and annuities arising in the United States. But any pension that would be exempt in the source country if the recipient had been resident in that country is also exempt in the country of residence. For example, assume that a Canadian resident receives a $10,000 pension payment from the United States, which would have exempted $5,000 of the payment had the individual been a resident of the U.S. Then, Canada will also exempt the $5,000 from tax.[21] This exemption only applies in respect of pension income and does not apply to annuities.

---

[21] Para. 110(1)(f).

The source country is also entitled to tax pensions and annuities paid to a resident of the other Contracting State but it is limited to a tax of 15 per cent of the gross amount of the pension or annuity payment. Thus, although the source country is not required to allow a deduction or exclusion for a return of capital to the pensioner, its tax rate is limited to 15 per cent of the periodic payment.

(i) Pensions

"Pension" includes, *inter alia*, payments under a "retirement plan".

A "retirement plan" includes a "Registered Retirement Savings Plan" ("RRSP") and a "Registered Retirement Income Fund" ("RRIF"). Hence, periodic payments out of RRSPs and RRIFs are generally considered as periodic pension payments and, therefore, subject to reduced withholding tax. For example, the withholding tax on RRIF payments from Canada to a U.S. resident is reduced from the normal rate of 25 per cent stipulated in paragraph 212(1)(*q*) of the Act to 15 per cent. Any amount in excess of the minimum required to be withdrawn by virtue of paragraph 146.3(1)(*b*.1) does not qualify as a periodic pension payment and is subject to the full 25 per cent withholding tax.

Article XVIII(3) defines "pensions" to include payments from the following sources:

- superannuations;
- pension or retirement plans;
- armed forces retirement pay;
- war veteran pensions and allowances; and
- amounts paid under sickness, accident or disability plans.

Thus, for the purpose of the *Canada-U.S. Treaty*, "pensions" include private pensions and public sector pensions.

(ii) Annuities

The term "annuities" means a stated sum paid periodically, at stated times during life or during a specified number of years, under an obligation to make payments in return for adequate and full consideration other than services rendered.

(iii) Social Security Benefits

Social security benefits are not taxable in the source country and are taxable only in the country of residence. The country of residence is required, however, to exempt from taxation 50 per cent of the total amount of the benefits paid to the recipient. U.S. social security benefits, for example, are generally exempt from U.S. tax. Hence, 50 per cent of such benefits are exempt from Canadian taxation if paid to a Canadian resident.

(g) Canada-U.K. Treaty

Article 17 of the *Canada-U.K. Treaty*[22] is substantially similar to the *OECD Model Tax Convention* and provides as follows:

1. Pensions arising in a Contracting State and paid to a resident of the other Contracting State who is the beneficial owner thereof shall be taxable only in that other State.

2. Annuities arising in a Contracting State and paid to a resident of the other Contracting State may be taxed in that other State. However, such annuities may also be taxed in the Contracting State in which they arise and according to the laws of that State, but if the recipient is the beneficial owner of the annuities the tax so charged shall not exceed 10 per cent of the portion thereof that is subject to tax in that State.

3. For the purposes of this Convention, the term "pension" includes any payment under a superannuation, pension or retirement plan, Armed Forces retirement pay, war veterans pensions and allowances, and any payment under a sickness, accident or disability plan, as well as any payment made under the social security legislation in a Contracting State, but does not include any payment under a superannuation, pension or retirement plan in settlement of all future entitlements under such a plan or any payment under an income-averaging annuity contract.

4. For the purposes of this Convention, the term "annuity" means a stated sum payable periodically at stated times during life or during a specified or ascertainable period of time under an obligation to make the payments in return for adequate and full consideration in money or money's worth, but does not include a pension or any payment under a superannuation, pension or retirement plan in settlement of all future entitlements under such a plan or any payment under an income-averaging annuity contract. . . .

Article 17(1) provides that pensions, whether arising by virtue of private employment or government service, are taxable only in the country where the recipient is resident. This rule necessarily implies that an individual may become taxable on previously exempt pension receipts as a result of a change of his or her residence upon retirement. In Merritt,[23] for example, the taxpayer became liable to Canadian tax on a lump sum payment that would not have been taxable had he remained resident in England.

---

[22] *Convention Between the Government of Canada and the Government of the United Kingdom of Great Britain and Northern Ireland for the Avoidance of Double Taxation and the Prevention of Fiscal Evasion with Respect to Taxes on Income and Capital Gains as amended*, 8 September 1978, [1980] Can. T.S. No. 25.

[23] *Merritt v. The Queen*, 93 DTC 978 (T.C.C.).

In contrast, purchased annuities may be taxed either in the source country or by the country in which the recipient is resident, but the maximum rate of tax chargeable by the source country is limited to 10 per cent if the recipient is the beneficial owner of the annuity.

5. MOVING EXPENSES

Reference:

ITA:

Subs. 62(1)   Moving Expenses

An immigrant will generally not be entitled to deduct moving expenses incurred in respect of a move from a residence outside Canada to a residence in Canada.[24]

6. DIVIDENDS

References:

ITA:

Subs. 82(1)   Taxable Dividends Received

Subs. 91(1)   Amounts to be Included in Respect of Share of Foreign Affiliate

Canadian residents are subject to full tax liability on their world-wide income. Dividends from domestic and foreign corporations are taxable. A resident taxpayer is generally taxable on a receipt basis on dividend income from resident corporations.[25] Dividends from offshore corporations are subject to special rules. The manner in which a Canadian resident is taxed on foreign corporate income and dividends, however, depends upon several additional factors, such as:

- the residence of the corporation;
- the size of the resident's shareholding;
- the relationship between the resident taxpayer, the corporation and the other shareholders;
- the type of income earned by the corporation;
- the jurisdiction where the corporation earns its income; and
- the timing of repatriation of the income to Canada.

There can be a substantial difference between the taxation of offshore active business income and offshore passive investment income. Generally speaking, offshore active business income is taxable only when it is received in Canada. Passive

---

[24] Subs. 62(1).

[25] Para. 82(1)(*a*).

investment income from a non-resident corporation may be taxable in Canada on an accrual basis.[26]

7. OFFSHORE TRUSTS

References:

ITA:

Subs. 104(1) Reference to Trust or Estate

Subs. 94(1) Application of Certain Provisions to Trusts Not Resident in Canada

A resident trust is taxable in Canada on its world-wide income in much the same manner as resident individuals.[27] A non-resident trust is generally taxable only on its Canadian source income.

(a) Residence

Reference:

BULLETINS, CIRCULARS & RULINGS:

IT-447 May 30, 1980 Residence of a Trust or Estate

We saw earlier that the residence of a trust is essentially a question of fact and is determined primarily by the residence of its trustees.[28] In certain circumstances, the "protector" of a trust may have sufficient power so as to be determinative of the residence of a trust. The residence of the beneficiaries of a trust is irrelevant in determining its residence.[29]

The primary considerations in determining the residence of a trust are:

- the residence of its trustees, and
- the legal capacity of the trustees to determine matters within their administration and discretion.

---

[26] Subs. 91(1).

[27] Subss. 2(1), 104(2).

[28] See generally: Chapter XXVII "General Principles of International Tax"; *Thibodeau Family Trust v. The Queen*, [1978] CTC 539, 78 DTC 6376 (F.C.T.D.) (trust's residence in Bermuda as majority of trustees resident in Bermuda and trust instrument permitted majority decision on all matters).

[29] See: *Holden v. M.N.R.* (1993), 1 DTC 243 (P.C.).

In IT-447, for example, Revenue Canada states:

> The residence of a trust or estate in Canada, or in a particular province or territory within Canada, is a question of fact to be determined according to the circumstances in each case. However, a trust is generally considered to reside where the trustee, executor, administrator, heir or other legal representative . . . who manages the trust or controls the trust assets resides.

Where there are several trustees, the Department may look to the trustee who has the so-called "management and control" of the trust. It is a dubious legal proposition, however, whether one trustee can be said to control a trust to the exclusion of its other trustees. The "protector" of a trust may, however, have sufficient power over the trustee so as to be seen as the real and effective power behind the trust. Hence, it is not prudent to have a Canadian resident act as a "protector" of an offshore trust.

Where all of the trustees have an equal say in the administration of the trust, it is considered to be resident in the jurisdiction where a majority of its trustees reside. Where a majority of the trustees are non-residents, the trust should be considered a non-resident trust. Where the trustees are equally distributed between different jurisdictions so that there is no clear indication as to where the trust is located, its residence may be determined by reference to other considerations such as the location of its meetings and effective management. Thus, the use of a corporate trustee to hold and administer the trust's assets in the jurisdiction in which it is desired to establish residency can add certainty to the determination of the trust's residence.

(b) Deemed Residence

A trust that might not otherwise be considered resident in Canada by virtue of the common law test, may, nevertheless, be deemed to be a resident trust for tax purposes.

Generally speaking, a non-resident discretionary trust with Canadian beneficial interests that acquires property from a Canadian resident is deemed to be resident in Canada.[30] This rule is intended to prevent tax minimization and tax deferral through the use of non-resident trusts. Such trusts are sometimes referred to as foreign immigration trusts because they are used by immigrants to secure their assets offshore prior to entry into Canada.

There are two basic tests to be met before a non-resident trust (whether an immigration trust or otherwise) is deemed a Canadian resident for tax purposes: (1) the "beneficiary test" and (2) the "contribution test".

(i) "Beneficiary Test"

In the context of foreign immigration trusts, the beneficiary test is generally satisfied if the immigrant (or a person related to him or her who is resident in Canada) benefits from the offshore trust. Thus, most foreign immigration trusts are caught by the "beneficiary test".

---

[30] Subs. 94(1).

The "beneficiary test" is easily met if the beneficiary is a Canadian resident. The "beneficiary test" is also satisfied when a person who is beneficially interested in the trust is:[31]

- a corporation or trust with which a resident does not deal at arm's length; or
- a controlled foreign affiliate of a resident person.

The test is satisfied if any one of the trust's beneficiaries meets any of the above conditions.

A person is considered to be beneficially interested in a trust if he or she has any right (immediate or future, absolute or contingent, conditional or unconditional) to receive any of the income or capital of the trust, whether directly from the trust itself or indirectly through another trust.[32] Thus, an immigrant who is a beneficiary of a trust is considered to have a beneficial interest in the trust.

(ii) "Contribution Test"

The "contribution test" is made up of two parts:

1. the source of the trust's property, and
2. the source of the trust's interest.

The source of property test is concerned with the source from which the trust directly acquires its property. The source of the trust interest test is concerned with indirect acquisitions of trust interests.

In the case of individuals, the "contribution test" is satisfied if the trust acquires property from a person who:[33]

- is or was a beneficiary of the trust, a person related to the beneficiary, or an uncle, aunt, nephew or niece of the beneficiary;
- was a resident in Canada at any time in the 18-month period before the end of the year in which the property was acquired; *and*
- was before the end of the particular year resident in Canada for an *aggregate period of more than 60 months.*

The test is also satisfied if the trust acquires property from another trust or corporation which in turn acquired its property from any of the above described persons with whom it did not deal at arm's length.[34]

---

[31] Para. 94(1)(*a*).

[32] Subs. 248(25).

[33] Subpara. 94(1)(*b*)(i).

[34] Cl. 94(1)(*b*)(i)(B).

Finally, the "contribution test" is met if the beneficiary acquired any or all of his or her interest in the trust directly or indirectly by way of:[35]

- a purchase;
- gift, bequest or inheritance from a related person; or
- through the exercise of the power of appointment by a related person.

(c) Discretionary Trusts

A trust is considered to be a discretionary trust if the distribution of its income or capital to any beneficiary depends upon the exercise of (or failure to exercise) a discretionary power. A discretionary trust usually gives trustees the freedom to determine who is to receive the income or capital of the trust, how much he or she is to receive, and when the distribution is to be made. The power to select, add or delete beneficiaries from a class are discretionary powers. The scope of the discretion is usually determined by the settlor or testator of the trust. It would be unusual to create an immigration trust that did not confer at least some discretionary powers on the trustee.

Non-resident discretionary trusts are generally taxable on their taxable income earned in Canada, their foreign accrual property income for the year and their share of any foreign accrual property income earned by a controlled foreign affiliate.[36] Hence, it is generally advantageous for a non-resident immigration trust to minimize its Canadian source income which would otherwise be taxable in Canada. The principal effect of the non-resident trust rules in section 94 is to subject the foreign accrual property income of such a trust to Canadian tax.

A resident trust is generally taxable on its world-wide income. The taxable income of a discretionary trust that is deemed to be resident in Canada by virtue of the "beneficiary" and "contribution" tests, however, is calculated according to special rules and is not based on its world-wide income. The taxable income for such a trust is its taxable income earned in Canada plus its foreign accrual property income for the year and its other foreign income other than active business income. Since such a trust's other income would not in any event have been taxable in Canada under the general rules applicable to non-residents, the essential focus of these rules is to render the trust taxable on its foreign accrual property income ("FAPI").

The taxable income of the trust is reduced by the portion of the trust's FAPI that may be considered to have become payable to a beneficiary of the trust.[37]

---

[35] Subpara. 94(1)(*b*)(ii).

[36] Para. 94(1)(*c*).

[37] Subs. 94(3).

(d) Non-discretionary Trusts

A non-discretionary trust is deemed to be a corporation and the beneficiary is, in effect, considered to own a portion of its outstanding shares in proportion to his or her beneficial interest in the trust. A non-discretionary foreign immigration trust is deemed to be a controlled foreign affiliate of each of its beneficiaries who have a beneficial interest of at least 10 per cent in the trust.[38] The 10 per cent is measured by reference to the aggregate fair market value of all of the beneficial interests of the trust. Thus, a Canadian resident beneficiary is taxable on a percentage share of the trust's income on an accrual basis at the time that the income is earned, regardless of when funds are remitted to the beneficiary.

8. IMMIGRATION TRUSTS

(a) Creation

A non-resident trust created and settled with property outside Canada is not resident in Canada for purposes of the Act if:

- all of its property is acquired from a non-resident settlor;
- it does not receive any financial assistance from any person resident in Canada at any time;
- its non-resident trustees constitute a majority of the trustees; and
- the non-resident trustees actively exercise their responsibilities as trustees.

If the above conditions are satisfied, section 94 of the Act does not apply and the trust is not deemed to be resident in Canada. Such a trust is not subject to Canadian tax on any of its income (including taxable capital gains) that the trustees resolve to accumulate offshore in each year. Any amounts paid to or for the benefit of a Canadian resident beneficiary (including taxable capital gains realized or deemed to be realized in any year) are taxable in the hands of the beneficiary. Distributions of capital are not subject to Canadian tax.

The creation of a foreign immigration trust requires careful planning both for tax and non-tax purposes. A professional advisor must consider the specific structure of the particular trust arrangement, the use of corporations, the source of funds for settlement of the trust, selection of an appropriate tax haven, appointment of trustees and/or a protector for the trust, and set-up and administration fees.

The following is a brief summary of the steps that would generally be required to implement a foreign immigration trust structure for Canadian income tax purposes:

- The trust would be settled in a tax haven jurisdiction by way of a gift from non-residents of Canada.

---

[38] Para. 94(1)(d).

- Non-resident trustees and protector would be appointed.
- The trust would be irrevocable and would be discretionary.
- All investment decisions in respect of the trust and meetings of the trustees would occur outside of Canada in the tax haven jurisdiction or elsewhere.
- The trust indenture would provide that the annual income of the trust be accumulated and that the trustees would have the discretionary power to make capital distributions to the beneficiaries.

The residence of the trust could be changed by changing its trustees, a power that is usually exercised through the protector of the trust.

(b) Five-year Exemption

We saw above that the "contribution test" in section 94 is satisfied if the trust acquires property (directly or indirectly) from an individual who has been resident in Canada for an aggregate period of more than 60 months. Where the trust acquires property from an individual who has been resident in Canada for less than 60 months, the "contribution test" does not apply and, therefore, the trust is not deemed to be resident in Canada. The "contribution test" is strict: even a token contribution by a relative who has been resident in Canada for more than 60 months invalidates the exemption. Thus, in order to preserve the 60-months' exemption, it is imperative that only non-residents contribute to the trust.

The five-year exemption for trusts was originally intended to allow foreign executives of multinational corporations who were temporarily transferred to Canada to leave their investments in offshore tax havens. But the exemption also allows immigrants who come to Canada on a permanent basis to structure their affairs on a tax efficient basis prior to taking up Canadian residence. The effect of the exemption in section 94 is that an immigrant can defer tax on his or her foreign accrual property income for up to 60 months. This necessarily implies that some individuals who take up Canadian residence, but who subsequently relinquish their residence in less than five years, can completely escape tax on their offshore trust income.

(c) Indefinite Exemption

The 60-month clock does not begin to tick until such time as the settlor becomes a resident of Canada provided that the beneficiary acquires the beneficial interest as a gift, bequest or inheritance.[39] But where an individual who resides outside of Canada and who does not intend to settle in Canada establishes a trust for the benefit of Canadian residents, the trust may obtain an indefinite exemption. For example, a parent of a prospective immigrant may settle a non-resident trust with the prospective immigrant as its beneficiary. Such a trust would provide its Canadian resident beneficiaries with tax-free passive investment income beyond the 60-month exemption period.

---

[39] Para. 94(1)(b).

Where a trust is settled by an individual who becomes a Canadian resident, it is in the best interests of the taxpayer to take up Canadian residence as early in the year as is possible. The offshore trust becomes taxable in the year in which the immigrant commences his or her 61st month of Canadian residency.

The 60-month exemption period commences from the time that any beneficiary (or related person) from whom the trust acquires property becomes a Canadian resident. Hence, it is important to ensure that the trust does not inadvertently acquire funds from a related person who has been resident in Canada for more than 60 months.

The 60-month period does not have to comprise consecutive days or time spent in Canada and any time previously spent in Canada as a resident is included in the calculation.

The section 94 exemption from tax for non-resident trusts with a Canadian beneficiary can extend beyond the 60-month period provided that the trust does not acquire any of its property from a Canadian resident or a person related to a Canadian resident.

(d) Funding

References:

ITA:

Subs. 75(2)   Reversionary Trusts

BULLETINS, CIRCULARS & RULINGS:

IT-369R   March 12, 1990   Attribution of Trust Income to Settlor

The income tax consequences that result from a trust depend upon various factors: the manner in which it was settled, the source of its property, the conditions on which the property is held, the powers of the trustees, and the nature of the income earned.

The funding of a trust can have important consequences for the taxation of the trust and its beneficiaries. The Act contains various rules which are intended to reduce the opportunity for income-splitting, diverting income from high marginal rate taxpayers to lower marginal rate taxpayers, and sheltering income in low tax jurisdictions or tax havens.

(i) Reversionary and Revocable Trusts

Where a trust is created on condition that property held by it may revert to the person from whom the property was received or pass through to beneficiaries to be determined subsequent to its creation, any income or loss from the property (and taxable gains and losses from the disposition thereof) are attributed to and taxable in the hands of the settlor.[40] The rules also attribute income to the settlor where he or she retains the power to restrict or direct the disposition of the property held by the trust.[41] Thus, for tax purposes, revocable trusts are treated as if their income belongs to the settlor without any transfer having been made to the trust.

Subsection 75(2) only applies to income from property and does not apply to business income.

The Department takes the view that it is the settlor of the trust who transfers property to it and to whom income is attributed under subsection 75(2). It is, however, also possible for a person other than the settlor of the trust to transfer property to it and thus be subject to the attribution rules.

Subsection 75(2) is an important limitation on the funding of offshore trusts. Clearly, where an individual is both the settlor and the beneficiary of a trust (for example, an immigrant who settles property upon himself or herself prior to arrival in Canada) and the trustee retains the power to distribute its property to the beneficiary, the trust is caught by the subsection and its income is attributed to the settlor. The subsection does not pose a problem for offshore trusts, however, where the settlor is not a Canadian resident—for example, a trust set up by a non-resident parent for his or her immigrant child. Thus, an offshore trust that is properly structured can prove to be of considerable advantage to an immigrant. The trust and its beneficiaries can escape Canadian tax on any income or capital gains that the trust generates for a period of 60 months and, in certain cases, for longer periods of time. In the event that subsection 75(2) applies, any income or capital gains from the trust would be attributed to the settlor each year which, in effect, would negate any benefit derived from the five-year immigration trust exemption.

The fact that the settlor of a trust is also a beneficiary of the trust does not by itself trigger the application of subsection 75(2).

The possibility of reversion must be a condition of the trust and not merely a possible consequence arising from a loan or sale to the trust. It is unsettled whether subsection 75(2) applies where money is loaned to a trust and is held on the condition that it revert to the person from whom it was received. In these circumstances, it is arguable that the obligation to repay the loan on the borrowed funds is a condition that calls for substituted property to revert to the creditor. But a reversion requires a transfer

---

[40] Subs. 75(2).

[41] Para. 75(2)(*b*). See also IT-369R, "Attribution of Trust Income to Settlor" (March 12, 1990).

of property and there is good law to argue that the making or repayment of a loan does not constitute a "transfer".[42]

Although subsection 75(2) only operates to attribute income to the settlor during the period in which he or she is resident in Canada, it is applicable even though the settlor was not resident in Canada at the time that the trust received the property.

(ii) Loans and Indebtedness

We saw in Chapter III "Who is Taxable" that in certain circumstances income earned by one taxpayer may be attributed to another. These rules, collectively referred to as the "attribution rules", are intended to prevent taxpayers from splitting income amongst family members in order to reduce the total tax payable.

(A) Strict Liability Rules

There are several attribution rules each of which is targeted at particular persons: Subsection 74.1(1), for example, applies to property transferred or loaned to the taxpayer's spouse; subsection 74.1(2) deals with loans and transfers of property to persons under 18 years of age. These rules apply to direct and indirect transfers and loans. They also apply to transfers and loans implemented by means of a trust.

The general attribution rules in respect of transfers and loans to spouses and persons under 18 years of age operate regardless of any intention to avoid tax through splitting income. Thus, they are strict liability rules that are automatically triggered by transfers and loans between spouses or to persons under the age of 18.

(B) Intention to Reduce Tax

There are other attribution rules which apply to a wider class of persons and which require an intention to reduce or avoid tax. Subsection 56(4.1) applies where an individual receives a loan, directly or indirectly, from another individual with whom he or she does not deal at arm's length and one of the main reasons for making the loan is to avoid or reduce tax. In these circumstances, any income derived from the loan is generally taxable in the hands of the creditor rather than the debtor. Thus, subsection 56(4.1) is considerably broader in scope than the general attribution rules in respect of spouses and minors. For example, it could apply to loans between parents and adult children and between adult brothers and sisters. It also applies to a creditor trust, that is, a trust through which another individual has, directly or indirectly, transferred property. In these circumstances, any income of the debtor is attributed to the creditor or the creditor trust as the case may be.

---

[42] *Dunkleman v. M.N.R.*, 59 DTC 1242 (Ex. Ct.). See also: *Report of Proceedings of the 38th Tax Conference*, (Can. Tax Foundation 1986) 51:1; Question 46, at 51:24. The lending of property does not constitute a "transfer of property".

Subsection 56(4.1) applies not only to loans but to all forms of indebtedness between persons who are not dealing with each other at arm's length. For example, it applies where the unpaid balance of the purchase price of property is secured by a note bearing no interest or a low rate of interest.

It is clear that a foreign immigration trust will be subject to subsection 56(4.1) only if two conditions are satisfied:

1. there is a debtor-creditor relationship between parties who do not deal with each other at arm's length; and

2. there is an intention to reduce or avoid tax.

Subsection 56(4.1) does not apply to a foreign immigration trust where the immigrant is the sole beneficiary and the creditor of the trust. There is no debtor-creditor relationship because the beneficiary of the trust and its creditor are one and the same person. Thus, a simple trust structure can be used in those circumstances where there is only one beneficiary (the immigrant) and the immigrant loans his or her property to the trust. There are, however, complications in this simple arrangement. If there are no other beneficiaries in the trust and it provides for a gift-over to the beneficiary's estate in the event of his or her death, subsection 75(2) may apply.

(iii) Corporate Attribution

Reference:

ITA:

Subs. 74.4(2)   Transfers and Loans to Corporation

Income from property transferred or loaned to a corporation may be attributed to the transferor (lender) if the transfer or loan is motivated by tax reduction.

A Canadian resident individual is deemed to receive interest based on the value of property that he or she has transferred to a corporation in circumstances where a "designated person" is a direct or indirect shareholder of the corporation and the transfer was intended to reduce the transferor's income and benefit the designated person. The corporate attribution rules apply regardless of whether or not the corporation is resident in Canada. It is also important to note that the deemed inclusion in the transferor's income by virtue of attribution applies whether or not the designated person has contemporaneously received any dividend income from the corporation. In other words, income is attributed to the transferor whether or not the property loaned or transferred to the corporation actually produces any income.

(A) Application

Where an individual transfers or loans property to a corporation (other than a small business corporation) in circumstances where one of the main purposes of the transfer is to reduce the income of the individual and benefit a "designated" person, any income generated from the transferred or loaned property is attributed to the individual.[43] For the purposes of this rule a "designated person" is:[44]

- the individual's spouse;
- a person under 18 years of age who does not deal at arm's length with the individual; or
- a nephew or niece of the individual who is under 18 years of age.

Whether one of the main purposes of a transaction is to reduce the amount of tax payable is a question of fact to be determined on an objective basis.

The amount attributed is the amount by which interest at a prescribed rate on the loan exceeds the amount actually paid on the loan[45] plus 5/4 of any taxable dividends paid on shares issued for the transfer.[46] The 5/4 factor is, in effect, the gross-up value of the dividend which takes into account an imputed corporate tax rate of 20 per cent.

The corporate attribution rules only apply where the transferor (lender) is resident in Canada during the relevant period and the corporation is not a small business corporation. The exclusion of small business corporations from the corporate attribution rules is significant and allows for income-splitting in closely-held family corporations.

(B) Exclusions

The corporate attribution rules do not apply where:[47]

- the only interest which the designated person has in the corporation is a beneficial interest in its shares held through a trust;
- the terms of the trust provide that the person may not receive (or otherwise obtain the use of) any of the income or capital of the trust while he or she is a minor or a spouse of the individual;
- the designated person does not receive or otherwise obtain the use of any of the income or capital of the trust; and
- the trust does not make any deduction in respect of amounts paid or payable to the beneficiary while he or she is the designated person in respect of the individual.

---

[43] Subs. 74.4(2).

[44] Subs. 74.5(5).

[45] Paras. 74.4(2)(d), (e).

[46] Para. 74.4(2)(f).

[47] Subs. 74.4(4).

The effect of the above is to preclude the application of the attribution rules in respect of legitimate estate plans.

The corporate attribution rules do not apply where the designated person is a child who has attained the age of majority. Nor do the rules apply where the trust provides that the transferor's spouse cannot receive or otherwise obtain the use of the income or capital of the trust whilst he or she remains a spouse of the individual.

(C) Specified Shareholders

The corporate attribution rules only apply where the designated person is a "specified shareholder" in relation to the corporation.

A "specified shareholder" is a person who owns 10 per cent or more of the shares of any class of the corporation or of any other corporation related to it.[48] A see-through rule provides that each beneficiary of a trust is deemed to own a proportion of the shares of the corporation owned by the trust.[49] Further, in the case of a discretionary trust, any beneficiary who is capable of benefitting under the trust is considered to own each share of the corporation held by the trust.[50]

(e) Trust Structures

The appropriate structure to be used to arrange an immigrant's affairs prior to his or her immigration into Canada depends upon the particular facts and circumstances of each case. The simplest structure is for the immigrant to settle a trust upon himself or herself. The immigrant would thus be the settlor and the beneficiary of the non-resident trust. As already noted, the benefits to be derived from such a trust are eradicated if the trust is considered to be a reversionary trust or is otherwise subject to subsection 75(2).

A discretionary trust is taxable, in effect, as if it was a controlled affiliate of a Canadian resident.

A non-discretionary trust is deemed to be a controlled foreign affiliate of each resident beneficiary who has at least 10 per cent interest of the aggregate fair market value of all interest in the trust. Hence, its income is taxable on an earned basis rather than on a remittance basis. Note, however, that the trust is *not* deemed to be a Canadian resident for the purposes of the Part XIII withholding tax. Any foreign accrual property income taxable to the Canadian beneficiary is deemed to be foreign source income and, hence, is eligible for foreign tax credits under section 126.

---

[48] Subs. 248(1) ("specified shareholder").

[49] Subs. 248(1) ("specified shareholder") (b).

[50] Subs. 248(1) ("specified shareholder") (e).

It is important to note that a foreign immigration trust that is subject to section 94 is taxable on its entire foreign accrual property income and not merely on that proportion of such income to which the Canadian resident beneficiary may be entitled. Thus, a foreign immigration trust's entire passive income may be subject to Canadian tax even if only one of its beneficiaries is resident in Canada. Further, in order to facilitate tax collection, the Canadian resident beneficiary is jointly and severally liable for the trust's Canadian tax.[51]

(i) Capital Distributions

A Canadian resident beneficiary of a foreign immigration trust is taxable on any income distributed to him or her in the year. Capital distributions, are not taxable to the beneficiary. Hence, a foreign immigration trust that otherwise qualifies for the 60-month (or longer) exemption period should retain its income offshore in a low tax or tax haven jurisdiction. The trust's retained income is accumulated into its capital at the beginning of its subsequent fiscal year. Distribution out of the trust's capital will not be taxable to the Canadian resident beneficiary.

This should be the result whether or not the capital distributed consists of income or taxable capital gains accumulated in previous years as long as the accumulation was a real capitalization and could not reasonably be considered to be merely a payment of income postponed until after the end of the calendar year. Thus, it is important that the trust empower its trustees to make discretionary capital distributions. The trustees should elect and clearly document that the distributions are made out of capital at the time such payments are made to the beneficiaries.

Where the settlor of the foreign immigration trust is also a beneficiary under the trust, the trust should preclude the right of the settlor to receive capital (other than accumulated investment income) from the trust. Failure to do so may trigger subsection 75(2) of the Act.

(ii) At the End of the Exemption Period

The five-year exemption period ends in the year in which the immigrant begins his or her 61st month of Canadian residency. For example, an immigrant who lands in Canada on January 1, 1995 gets five full taxation years of exemption until December 31, 2000.

An immigrant with a foreign trust will have several options available to him or her at the end of the 60-month exemption period.

In the simplest case, the trust will not be subject to Canadian tax if the immigrant (and all other contributors) ceases to be a Canadian resident upon the expiry of the 60-month period. In these circumstances, the trust will never be considered to have been resident in Canada and there will be no income tax consequences if there are no income

---

[51] Subs. 94(2).

distributions from the trust. Income payments to Canadian resident beneficiaries will be subject to tax. Distributions of capital are not taxable if the trust is considered a personal trust.[52] A "personal trust" is one in which none of the beneficiaries has paid any consideration to the trust or the settlor for his or her interest in the trust.

In the event that the individual remains a Canadian resident after the 60-month period, he or she may:

- cause the trust to become a Canadian resident trust before the end of the 60-month period and step-up the cost base of its assets;[53]

- leave the trust as a non-resident trust and begin paying tax on its annual income after the exemption period; or

- wind-up the offshore trust.

(A) Conversion to Canadian Trust

In the event that the trust becomes a Canadian resident, it can distribute its capital assets at their stepped-up cost base without attracting any immediate income tax consequences.[54] The immigrant beneficiaries of the trust will acquire the assets at their stepped-up adjusted cost base. Subsequent dispositions of capital assets at a gain may be eligible for the capital gains exemption[55] either in the trust or in the individual's hands.

A non-resident trust can be converted into a Canadian trust by replacing the non-resident trustee with a Canadian resident trustee. Upon becoming a Canadian resident trust, the trust will be deemed to have disposed of all of its property (other than taxable Canadian property, inventory, and eligible capital property of a business carried on in Canada) for proceeds of disposition equal to the fair market value of the property. Concurrently, the trust will be deemed to have reacquired each property at a cost equal to the fair market value of the property. There will be no Canadian income tax consequences from these deemed dispositions and acquisitions because they are deemed to occur immediately before the trust becomes resident in Canada.

Upon becoming a Canadian resident trust, it will be subject to the 21-year deemed disposition rules in subsection 104(4). The trust will also be eligible for the preferred beneficiary election if there is a "settlor" and a "preferred beneficiary".[56]

---

[52]   Para. 104(13)(c).

[53]   Subs. 128.1(1).

[54]   Subs. 107(2).

[55]   Capital gains exemption eliminated as of February 22, 1994.

[56]   Subs. 104(14), para. 108(1)(g); Reg. 2800.

There may be withholding tax implications if the trust has non-resident beneficiaries. Generally speaking, there is a withholding tax of 25 per cent (subject to treaty reduction) under Part XIII of the Act. There may also be Part XII.2 tax payable at the rate of 36 per cent on "designated income" if the trust has non-resident beneficiaries.[57] Generally speaking, "designated income" includes income from real property in Canada, income from businesses carried on in Canada, and taxable capital gains from dispositions of taxable Canadian property.

(B) Retain Offshore Status

We saw earlier that certain non-resident offshore trusts are taxed as if they were resident in Canada and, depending upon their structure, are subject to subsection 94(1). Both discretionary and non-discretionary offshore trusts are subject to Canadian tax on their FAPI, whether earned directly or indirectly by the trust. There would appear to be no compelling income tax reasons for maintaining the offshore trust as a non-resident. There may, however, be other business reasons for maintaining the security of a foreign trust in a tax haven jurisdiction with strong creditor-proofing laws.

(C) Winding-up Offshore Trusts

The tax consequences that result from winding-up an offshore trust will depend upon the particular trust structure. The trust can be wound-up and its capital distributed to Canadian resident beneficiaries without any income tax consequences. Timing of the wind-up may be an important consideration in order to convert the trust's income for the year into capital prior to its distribution to Canadian resident beneficiaries.

Promissory notes and debt instruments issued by the trustee may be repaid on a tax-free basis.

(f) The General Anti-Avoidance Rule

The General Anti-Avoidance Rule ("GAAR") applies to tax avoidance transactions that, inter alia, constitute an abuse or misuse of the Act read as a whole. Foreign immigration trusts are almost invariably motivated primarily for the purposes of tax minimization and avoidance. Hence, prima facie, foreign immigration trusts come within the ambit of GAAR.[58]

In the event that GAAR applies, Revenue Canada may disallow a deduction, reallocate a deduction, recharacterize a payment or ignore the tax effects that would otherwise result from the avoidance transaction. In effect, Revenue Canada can ignore the legal consequences of the avoidance transaction or arrangement and tax the trust by ignoring its otherwise legitimate structure.

---

[57] S. 210.2.

[58] See Chapter XXVI "Administration".

GAAR does not apply where it may reasonably be considered that the transaction or arrangements do not constitute "abusive" tax avoidance. An otherwise tax motivated avoidance transaction is not subject to GAAR if it can be shown that the transactions do not result directly or indirectly in a misuse of the provisions of the Act or an abuse of the Act read as a whole.

The Department takes the position that foreign immigration trusts do not constitute an abuse of the Act because they are created pursuant to the authority of specific statutory provisions which clearly contemplate the tax exemption for up to 60 months before any income is taxable under section 94. The Department's position in respect of offshore immigration trusts is that they are not generally subject to GAAR but that they are subject to other specific anti-avoidance rules such as subsections 56(4.1) and 75(2). The Department says:[59]

> The provisions of section 94 clearly indicate that where a non-resident individual, in contemplation of becoming resident in Canada, establishes and settles a non-resident trust with property that would yield foreign accrual property income, that individual may reside in Canada for up to 60 months before the income of the trust would be taxable under that section. Therefore, assuming that either the creation or the settlement of the trust is an avoidance transaction within the meaning of subsection 245(3), the transaction would not normally constitute a misuse of, or an abuse having regard to, the provisions of the Act and section 245 would not apply.

It should be noted that other provisions of the Act — for example — subsection 75(2) — may apply to the transactions in question. Where the offshore trust has been structured so as to avoid the application of such other provisions, the general anti-avoidance rule may apply.

---

[59] *Report of Proceedings of the 41st Tax Conference* (Can. Tax Foundation, 1989) 45:24, Question 42.

SELECTED BIBLIOGRAPHY TO CHAPTER XXVIII

Bissel, Thomas St. G. and Zygmund Marcinsky, "The Effects of Immigrating to North America (Canada or the United States)" (1992), 19 *Tax Planning Int'l Rev.* 10.

Drache, A.B.C., "Receiving U.S. Retirement Income" (1992), 14 *The Canadian Taxpayer* 176.

Keys, Chris, "Foreign Property: A Short Course" (1992), 40 *Canada Tax Journal* 400.

Kroft, Edwin G., "Tax Avoidance Attacks Using Pre-GAAR Weapons" (1991), in *Proceedings of the 43rd Tax Conf.* 8:24.

Lowden, John H., "Employee Transfers: Moving To or From Canada on Foreign Assignment", in *Proceedings of 41st Tax Conf.* 34:1 (Can. Tax Foundation, 1989).

Ngan, Sunny, "Foreign Trust Structures for Immigrants" (1990), 38 *Can. Tax J.* 1264.

Ngan, Sunny, "Immigration" (1990), 38 *Can. Tax J.* 688.

Raizenne, Robert J. and James Cantillon Ross, "Canadian Tax Reform: Revised Amendments of Trusts" (December 1988), 15 *Tax Planning International Review* 17.

Verchere, Bruce, "Foreign Source Income — Tax Planning Concepts", in *Proceedings of 27th Tax Conf.* 603 (Can. Tax Foundation, 1976).

CHAPTER XXIX

NON-RESIDENTS

References:

ITA:

Subs. 2(3)	Tax Payable by Non-resident Persons
S. 114	Individuals Resident in Canada for Only Part of Year
S. 115	Taxable Income Earned in Canada by Non-residents
S. 212	Tax on Income from Canada of Non-resident Persons
S. 212.1	Non-arm's Length Sale of Shares by Non-residents
S. 213	Tax Not Payable by Non-resident Person
S. 214	No Deductions
S. 215	Deduction and Payment of Tax
S. 216	Alternatives re Rents and Timber Royalties
S. 217	Election Respecting Certain Payments
S. 218	Loan to Wholly-owned Subsidiary
S. 219	Branch Tax

REGULATIONS:

2600	Income Earned in a Province by an Individual
2602	Non-residents
2603	Income from Business

BULLETINS, CIRCULARS & RULINGS:

IT-59R3	September 26, 1984	Interest on Debts Owing to Specified Non-residents (Thin Capitalization)
IT-76R2	September 3, 1982	Exempt Portion of Pension When Employee has been a Non-resident
IT-81R	May 6, 1976	Partnerships — Income of Non-resident Partners
IT-137R3	January 31, 1990	Additional Tax on Certain Corporations Carrying on Business in Canada
IT-155R3	June 16, 1989	Exemption from Non-resident Tax
IT-161R3	October 8, 1982	Non-residents — Exemption from Tax Deductions at Source on Employment Income

IT-163R2	September 19, 1985	Election by Non-resident Individuals on Certain Canadian Source Income
IT-171R2	March 30, 1992	Non-resident Individuals — Computation of Taxable Income Earned in Canada and Non-refundable Tax Credits
IT-173R2	January 30, 1989	Capital Gains Derived in Canada by Residents of the United States
IT-193SR	September 30, 1985	Taxable Income of Individuals Resident in Canada During Part of a Year
IT-221R2	February 3, 1983	Determination of an Individual's Residence Status
IT-262R	August 30, 1985	Losses of Non-residents and Part-year Residents
IT-277R	October 8, 1986	Branch Tax — Effect of Tax Treaties
IT-303	April 8, 1976	Know-how and Similar Payments to Non-residents
IT-361R2	June 16, 1989	Exemption from Tax on Interest Payments to Non-residents
IT-393R2	February 21, 1994	Election re Tax on Rents and Timber Royalties — Non-residents
IT-420R3	March 30, 1992	Non-residents — Income Earned in Canada
IT-451R	March 25, 1987	Deemed Disposition and Acquisition on Ceasing To Be or Becoming Resident in Canada
IT-465R	September 19, 1985	Non-resident Beneficiaries of Trusts
IT-468R	December 29, 1989	Management or Administration Fees Paid to Non-residents
IT-494	January 31, 1983	Hire of Ships and Aircraft from Non-residents
IC 71-17R3	February 22, 1991	Mutual Procedures — Requests for Competent Authority Consideration
IC 72-17R4	April 24, 1992	Procedures Concerning the Disposition of Taxable Canadian Property by Non-residents — Section 116
IC 76-12R4	February 19, 1988	Applicable Rate of Part XIII Tax on Amounts Paid or Credited to Persons in Treaty Countries
IC 77-16R4	May 11, 1992	Non-resident Income Tax

IC 87-2   February 27, 1987   International Transfer Pricing and Other International Transactions

The income tax consequences of investment in Canada depend upon several factors:

- the nature of the investment;
- the residence of the investor; and
- the structure of the investment.

A Canadian resident is subject to "full tax liability" on his or her world-wide income, whether from active business or from passive investments.

Non-residents may be subject to income tax under three different parts of the Act:

- under Part I on "active" Canadian-source income;
- under Part XIII on "passive" income received from Canadian residents; and
- under Part XIV for "branch tax" on non-Canadian corporations carrying on business in Canada.

A non-resident is taxable on his or her "active" Canadian source income if he or she is:[1]

- employed in Canada,
- carries on a business in Canada, or
- disposes of a taxable Canadian property

at any time in the year or in a previous year.

A non-resident is also taxable on his or her "passive" investment income. The taxation of passive investment income depends upon four principal factors:

- the type of income;
- its source;
- the nature of the recipient; and
- whether Canada has a tax treaty with the country in which the income arises.

Non-residents are liable for tax only on their Canadian-source income.[2]

A non-resident is also liable for income tax in a particular year if he or she had Canadian source earnings in a previous year. Thus, a non-resident individual who is employed in Canada cannot avoid tax simply by delaying receipt of his or her salary until a subsequent year.

Non-resident liability for income tax is computed by reference to "taxable income earned in Canada". As with residents, a non-resident's taxable base is calculated in a two-step process: Income is initially determined under the general rules of section 3; taxable income is then determined under section 115.

---

[1] Subs. 2(3).

[2] Subs. 2(3).

A taxpayer can also be a part-year resident. A part-year resident is a resident of Canada, but only for part of the year. He or she is taxable on his or her *global* income for the period of his or her Canadian residency. Deductions in computing taxable income are prorated.[3] In contrast, a non-resident is taxable only on his or her Canadian-source income net of authorized deductions.[4]

1. EMPLOYED IN CANADA

A non-resident is taxable on employment income earned in Canada.[5] The following non-resident persons are deemed to have been employed in Canada:[6]

- students in full-time attendance at post-secondary educational institutions in Canada;

- persons who in a previous year ceased to reside in Canada in order to attend or teach at a post-secondary educational institution outside Canada;

- persons who in a previous year ceased to reside in Canada in order to carry on research for which they received a research grant;[7]

- individuals who in a previous year ceased to reside in Canada but who received remuneration in the current year in respect of an office or employment from a Canadian resident; and

- individuals who received a "signing bonus" that is deductible for Canadian income tax purposes by the person who paid the bonus, if it can be shown that the payment was for services to be performed by the individuals in Canada.

A non-resident who is employed in Canada in the year is required to calculate his or her income from employment according to the usual rules:[8] salary and wages, employment benefits (including stock option benefits), taxable allowances, and directors' fees are all taxable as income. He or she may deduct related expenses.

A non-resident person who is deemed to be employed in Canada is taxable on remuneration received directly or indirectly from a Canadian resident. Canadian source scholarships, bursaries, research fellowships, education savings plan payments, and

---

[3] S. 114.

[4] Paras. 115(1)(*d*), (*d.1*), (*e*) and (*f*); IT-171R2 "Non-resident individuals — Computation of Taxable Income Earned in Canada and Non-refundable Tax Credits" (March 30, 1992).

[5] Para. 2(3)(*a*); see also subs. 248(1) ("employed"), ("employment") and ("office").

[6] Subs. 115(2); see also IT-161R3, "Non-residents — Exemption from Tax Deductions at Source on Employment Income" (October 8, 1982).

[7] Para. 56(1)(*o*).

[8] See Division B, subdivision a.

"signing bonuses" are also taxable as income.[9] But compensation for work performed outside Canada, and subject to income tax in a foreign country, and payments in connection with the selling of property, the negotiating of contracts or the rendering of services in the ordinary course of a business carried on by his employer are not Canadian-source income.[10]

(a) The OECD Model Convention

The *OECD Model Convention*[11] varies the source rule of taxation depending upon the length of an employee's stay in a country and the source of payment. Articles 15(1) and (2) of the *Model Convention* deal with the taxation of employment income other than pensions and employment income in respect of government service.

The purpose of Article 15 is to promote the mobility of qualified personnel employed by international concerns that are called upon to temporarily transfer personnel between operations in different countries. The Model Convention seeks to avoid double taxation and prevent tax avoidance through double exemptions of the same income.

Articles 15(1) and (2) read as follows:

1. Subject to the provisions of Articles 16, 18 and 19, salaries, wages and other similar remuneration derived by a resident of a Contracting State in respect of an employment shall be taxable only in that State unless the employment is exercised in the other Contracting State. If the employment is so exercised, such remuneration as is derived therefrom may be taxed in that other State.

2. Notwithstanding the provisions of paragraph 1, remuneration derived by a resident of a Contracting State in respect of an employment exercised in the other Contracting State shall be taxable only in the first-mentioned State if

a) the recipient is present in the other State for a period or periods not exceeding in the aggregate 183 days in the fiscal year concerned, and

b) the remuneration is paid by, or on behalf of, an employer who is not a resident of the other State, and

c) the remuneration is not borne by a permanent establishment or a fixed base which the employer has in the other State.

As a general rule, employment income is taxable in the source country, (that is, the country in which employment is exercised), but only if three conditions are satisfied:

- the employee is in the country for an aggregate period exceeding 183 days in any 12-month period commencing or ending in the fiscal year,

---

[9] Para. 115(2)(*e*).

[10] Subpara. 115(2)(*e*)(i); IT-161R3, "Non-residents — Exemption from Tax Deductions at Source on Employment Income" (October 8, 1982).

[11] *Model Convention for the Avoidance of Double Taxation with respect to Taxes on Income and Capital,* adopted by Organisation for Economic Co-operation and Development (OECD) on April 11, 1977, amended June 4, 1992.

- the employee is paid by, or on behalf of, an employer who is resident in the source country, and

- the income is borne by a permanent establishment or a fixed base maintained by the employer in the source country.

Thus, a resident of Country A who is sent on a temporary assignment to Country B will generally be taxed only in Country A.

The "fiscal year" referred to in Article 15(2)(a) is the fiscal year of the country in which the employment activity occurs, not the fiscal year of the country in which the employee resides.

(b) Canada-U.S. Treaty

The *Canada-U.S. Treaty* generally follows the *OECD Model Convention* but also provides for a dollar threshold limit. Articles XV (1) and (2) of the *Canada-U.S. Treaty* provide:[12]

1. Subject to the provisions of Articles XVIII (Pensions and Annuities) and XIX (Government Service), salaries, wages and other similar remuneration derived by a resident of a Contracting State in respect of an employment shall be taxable only in that State unless the employment is exercised in the other Contracting State. If the employment is so exercised, such remuneration as is derived therefrom may be taxed in that other State.

2. Notwithstanding the provisions of paragraph 1, remuneration derived by a resident of a Contracting State in respect of an employment exercised in a calendar year in the other Contracting State shall be taxable only in the first-mentioned State if:

(a) such remuneration does not exceed ten thousand dollars ($10,000) in the currency of that other State; or

(b) the recipient is present in the other Contracting State for a period or periods not exceeding in the aggregate 183 days in that year and the remuneration is not borne by an employer who is a resident of that other State or by a permanent establishment or a fixed base which the employer has in that other State.

A resident of one of the countries who receives income from employment carried out in the other country is exempt from tax in the source country if the remuneration does not exceed $10,000 (measured in the source country's dollars). Thus, the exemption in respect of taxation of employment income by the source country is limited by the dollar amount and the 183-day rule.

---

[12] Article 15 of the *Canada-UK Treaty* is similar to the *Canada-U.S. Treaty* in that the 183-day rule applies to the calendar year and not the fiscal year. The *Canada-U.K. Treaty* also provides that Article 15 applies to the remuneration of directors.

(c) Exemption from Source Country Taxation

(i) The 183-Day Rule

An employee is exempt from source country taxation only if he or she is not physically present in the source country where he or she exercises his or her employment for an aggregate period exceeding 183 days in the year.

There is an important difference in the measure of "year" between the *OECD Model Convention* and the *Canada-U.S. Treaty*: the OECD Model determines the aggregate of the days spent by the employee in any *12-month period* commencing or ending in the particular fiscal year. In contrast, the *Canada-U.S. Treaty* counts only the number of days in the particular *calendar year*. The difference between the two methods is significant. It allows employees who move between Canada and the U.S. much greater flexibility to organize their stay to fall under the 183-day limit by timing their entry and exit into and out of each country.

Example XXIX.1

Assume that X, who is ordinarily resident in the United States, is an employee of a U.S. corporation. He is temporarily assigned to his company's Canadian subsidiary from July 3, 1994 to June 30, 1995. If X stayed in Canada throughout the period, he would be physically present in Canada for 182 days in 1994 and 181 days in 1995 and would not be caught by the 183-day rule in either calendar year. He would, however, have been caught by Article 15(2)(a) of the *Model Convention* because he would be present in the source country (Canada) in which he exercises employment for more than 183 days in a 12-month period ending in June 1995.

Revenue Canada accepts the double exemption in these circumstances. Indeed, the exemption would appear to be available even if X's employment arrangement continues year after year.

The 183-day period is determined by the number of days that the employee is physically present in the source country. The following are included in the calculation of the number of days:

- part of a day,
- day of arrival,
- day of departure,
- Saturdays and Sundays,
- national holidays,
- vacation periods before, during and after the period of activity,
- training periods, strikes, lock-outs,
- days of inactivity because of delays in delivery of supplies, and
- days of sickness (whether of the individual or his family).

There is some flexibility insofar as holidays are concerned. Although holidays and vacations spent in the country of activity are normally included in the 183-day count, there appears to be some flexibility where the taxpayer can demonstrate that the holidays are clearly not related to his or her employment.[13]

Sickness in the middle of an employee's stay in the country of activity counts towards the 183 days; sickness at the end of the employee's stay does not. The rationale for the difference between the two cases is that a delay caused by sickness at the end of the employee's stay in the country of activity comes about after his or her declared intention to leave and, as such, should not count towards his or her stay in the country. In the above example, X would qualify for the exemption in 1995 even if he fell ill after June 30, 1995 and was required to spend an additional two weeks in Canada as a result of his illness.

(ii) Remuneration Not Paid by Resident of Source Country

The second condition for exemption from tax by the source country is that the employer who pays the remuneration is not a resident of the country in which the employment is exercised.[14]

The term "employer" is not defined in the *OECD Model Convention*. It is generally understood to mean the person who has the rights to the work produced and bears the risk and responsibility for its production. Substance prevails over form: Each case should be examined to see whether the functions of "employer" are exercised and, if so, by whom. Where, for example, an individual comes to Canada and carries out employment duties for a Canadian corporation and the costs are borne, directly or indirectly, by the Canadian company, the Canadian company is presumed to be the "employer". The presumption, however, is rebuttable.

Article 15(2) gives rise to abuse in international hiring-out of labour arrangements. For example, a local employer who wants to employ foreign labour for a period of less than 183 days can recruit through an intermediary corporation, established abroad, which purports to be the employer. Workers can be farmed out to the person in the country in which the employment is temporarily exercised and the employees can claim tax exempt status if they otherwise satisfy the provisions of the Article.

The determination as to whether a user of services is an "employer" is essentially a question of fact. In determining whether the real employer is the user of the labour or the foreign intermediary corporation, revenue authorities look at the following circumstances:

- Does the hirer bear the responsibility and risk for the result produced by the employee's work?

---

[13]   *OECD Commentary.*

[14]   Article 15(2)(b), *OECD Model Convention.*

- Who has the authority to provide the workers with instructions?
- Is the work performed at a place that is under the control and responsibility of the user of the services?
- Is the remuneration to the hirer calculated on the basis of the time that the employee's services are utilized?
- Are the tools and materials utilized in the employment provided by the user of the services or by the foreign hirer? and
- Are the number and qualifications of the employees determined by the hirer or the user of the services?

(iii) *Remuneration Not Borne by Permanent Establishment*

The third condition for the exemption is that the employee's remuneration is not borne by a permanent establishment or a fixed base which the employer may have in the source country where the employment is exercised. If the employer has a permanent establishment in the country in which the employment is exercised, the exemption is only available if the permanent establishment does not bear the cost of the employee's remuneration.

The terms "borne by" generally mean "allowable as a deduction in computing taxation income". For example, if a Canadian resident who is employed at the Canadian permanent establishment of a U.S. corporation performs services in the United States, his or her remuneration is not exempt from U.S. tax because the U.S. company is *entitled* to a deduction for the employee's wages in computing its taxable income. But there is some uncertainty associated with the phrase "not borne by" and the uncertainty is exacerbated by the use of the word "paid" in Article 15(2)(b) of the *OECD Model Convention* and its juxtaposition with "borne" in Article 15(2)(c). Are "borne" and "paid" intended to imply different meanings? It is also unclear what happens if an employer who is entitled to a deduction does not in fact take the deduction in the particular year.

(d) **International Transport Personnel**

Remuneration from employment exercised aboard a ship or aircraft operated in international traffic, or aboard a boat engaged in inland waterways transport, may be taxed in the country where the enterprise is effectively managed. Article 15(3) of the *OECD Model Convention* provides as follows:

> 3. Notwithstanding the preceding provisions of this Article, remuneration derived in respect of an employment exercised aboard a ship or aircraft operated in international traffic, or aboard a boat engaged in inland waterways transport, may be taxed in the Contracting State in which the place of effective management of the enterprise is situated.

In many of Canada's bilateral treaties, however, the emphasis for taxation is on the country of residence and not on the place of effective management of the enterprise provided for in the *OECD Model Convention*. For example, Article XV(3) of the *Canada-U.S. Treaty* states:

> . . . remuneration derived by a resident of a Contracting State in respect of an employment regularly exercised in more than one State on a ship, aircraft, motor vehicle or train operated by a resident of that Contracting State shall be taxable only in that State.

Thus, under the *Canada-U.S. Treaty* a resident of one of the countries is exempt from tax in the other country in respect of employment income regularly exercised on a ship, aircraft, motor vehicle or train operated by a resident of the taxpayer's country of residence.[15] The word "regularly" distinguishes crew members from other persons who are only occasionally employed on a ship, aircraft, motor vehicle, or train. It should be noted, however, that Article XV is subject to the "saving clause" of Article XXIX which allows the United States to tax its citizens regardless of their residence.

(e) Stock Options

Canadian residents are generally taxable on stock option benefits as employment source income because they are, in substance, an alternative form of cash compensation.[16] A resident individual is taxable on the value of any benefit derived from his or her employer's stock option plan if the benefit is derived in respect of, in the course of, or by virtue of his or her employment.[17]

A non-resident who exercises stock options that were granted whilst he or she was resident and employed in Canada is taxable in Canada on any benefit derived from the options. This is so regardless of whether the options are exercised within or outside Canada.

(i) The OECD Model Convention

As a general rule, most countries claim jurisdiction over stock options on the basis of where the employment is exercised. Article 15(1) of the *OECD Model Convention*, for example, establishes the rule that salaries, wages and other similar remuneration are generally taxable in the country where the taxpayer *exercises* his or her employment. This rule is subject to limited exceptions in Article 15(2).

Articles 15(1) and (2) of the *OECD Model Convention* provide as follows:

> 1. Subject to the provisions of Articles 16, 18 and 19, salaries, wages and other similar remuneration derived by a resident of a Contracting State in respect of an employment shall be taxable only in that State unless the employment is exercised in the other Contracting State. If the employment is so exercised, such remuneration as is derived therefrom may be taxed in that other State.

> 2. Notwithstanding the provisions of paragraph 1, remuneration derived by a resident of a Contracting State in respect of an employment exercised in the other Contracting State shall be taxable only in the first-mentioned State if

---

[15] See also: Article 15 in Canadian bilateral treaties with Australia, the Netherlands, Switzerland and Japan.

[16] Subs. 7(1); 7(1.1).

[17] Subs. 7(5).

a) the recipient is present in the other State for a period or periods not exceeding the fiscal year concerned, and

b) the remuneration is paid by, or on behalf of, an employer who is not a resident of the other State, and

c) the remuneration is not borne by a permanent establishment or a fixed base which the employer has in the other State.

Similarly, Article XV(1) of the *Canada-U.S. Treaty* prevents Canada from taxing the "salaries, wages and other similar remuneration" derived by a resident of the United States unless the remuneration is in respect of employment exercised in Canada.[18]

(A) Meaning of "Salaries and Wages"

The phrase "salaries, wages and other similar remuneration" is not defined in either of the *OECD Model Convention*, the *Canada-U.S.* or the *Canada-U.K. Treaties.*

Article 3(2) of the *OECD Model Convention* deals with undefined treaty terms:

As regards the application of the Convention by a Contracting State any term not defined therein shall, unless the context otherwise requires, have the meaning which it has under the law of that State concerning the taxes to which the Convention applies.

This is a general rule of treaty interpretation in respect of undefined terms.

But if there is more than one version of the domestic legislation, which one should prevail: The legislation in force when the particular Convention was signed or the version in force when the Convention is being applied to the particular circumstances? The OECD's Committee on Fiscal Affairs recommends that the version of the domestic legislation in force when the Convention is applied (that is, when the tax is imposed) should prevail.

The OECD's view accords with Canada's domestic law in respect of the interpretation of undefined treaty terms. Section 3 of the *Income Tax Conventions Interpretation Act*[19] provides that, to the extent that a convention does not define or fully define a term used in it, the term has (unless the context otherwise requires) the meaning that it has for the purposes of the *Income Tax Act, as amended from time-to-time.*

Similarly, Article III(2) of the *Canada-U.S. Treaty* provides that the domestic tax law of the contracting countries applies to undefined terms, unless the context in which the term is used requires a different definition independent of the domestic tax law. "Context" refers to the purpose and background of the provision in which the term appears. "Salary or wages" are defined in subsection 248(1) of the *Income Tax Act* as a taxpayer's income from an office or employment, including all section 7 benefits.

---

[18]   Article 15(1) of the *Canada-U.K. Treaty* contains similar provisions.

[19]   *Income Tax Conventions Interpretation Act*, R.S.C. 1985, c. I-4.

(B) Options Exercised Outside Canada

What happens if a non-resident receives stock options from his or her employment in Canada and later exercises the options when he or she has given up Canadian residence? Subsection 7(4) provides that a person who would otherwise come within the stock option rules continues to be subject to subsection 7(1) even though he or she ceases to be an employee before exercising his or her options.

In *Hale*,[20] for example, the taxpayer had been employed in Canada and received stock options during his stay in Canada. He later moved to England where he exercised his rights under the stock option plan. The taxpayer was taxable on the value of his stock option benefits by virtue of Article 15(1) of the *Canada-U.K. Treaty*. Since the taxpayer's employment was *exercised* in Canada, his benefits fell outside of the exemption in the Treaty. Tax treaties are negotiated primarily to prevent double taxation and they should be interpreted accordingly. Hale was not taxable on the value of his benefit in the United Kingdom and, consequently, was not subject to double taxation on the benefits. Giving the treaty a large and liberal construction, the taxpayer was deemed to have exercised his employment in Canada and, as such, was taxable on the value of benefits derived from the Canadian stock option plan.

Thus, Article 15(1) should be interpreted by reference to the country where the *employment*, rather than the stock option, is exercised. That, however, is not always the case. In *Tedmon*,[21] for example, the taxpayer was liable for Canadian tax for stock option benefits exercised in Canada but in respect of employment exercised in the United States for a different employer. Notwithstanding that the taxpayer received the benefit in respect of employment *exercised* in the United States, he was subject to Canadian tax because he derived the benefit while he was resident in Canada. *Tedmon* is clearly inconsistent with *Hale*. The Department has not, however, revised its view and stands by its inconsistent positions.[22]

(C) Limited Presence in Canada

There are some exceptions to the source of employment rule in Article 15(1) of the *OECD Model Convention*. Typically, an individual is not subject to Canadian tax in respect of stock option benefits exercised in Canada if he or she was not present in Canada for more than 183 days in the year and the remuneration was not borne by an employer resident in Canada or by a permanent establishment or fixed base of the employer in Canada. In the case of U.S. residents, there is a further exemption if the individual's total remuneration for employment exercised in Canada for the year in which the options were granted is less than $10,000.

---

[20] *J. Hale v. Canada*, [1992] 2 CTC 379, 92 DTC 6379 (F.C.A.).

[21] *Tedmon v. M.N.R.*, [1991] 2 CTC 2128, 91 DTC 962 (T.C.C.).

[22] Technical Interpretation (November 26, 1992).

2. CARRYING ON BUSINESS IN CANADA

Subject to treaty provisions, non-residents are liable for Canadian tax on income earned from carrying on a business in Canada.[23] There are two questions that must be answered to determine liability under this head:

- Is the non-resident person carrying on a business?
- If so, is he or she carrying on the business in Canada?

Non-residents are generally not liable to Part I tax for income from property.[24] Income from property is generally subject to withholding tax under Part XIII of the Act.

Whether income is characterized as income from a business or from property is a question of fact. Income from property represents the investment yield from property and is generally earned through a relatively passive process. In contrast, business income derives from the *use* of property, a process that generally combines labour and capital. The distinction between the two depends upon the level of activity associated with the generation of income and the distinction between a passive business and actively managed investments can be obscure.

In the case of corporate taxpayers, however, there is a rebuttable presumption that all income is business income.[25]

It is also important to distinguish between gains derived from carrying on a business and gains from dispositions of capital property. For example, under Article XIII of the *Canada-U.S. Treaty*, a gain from the alienation of property which does *not* derive its value from real property is taxable only in the country of residence of the vendor.

(a) "Business"

"Business" is defined to include "a profession, calling, trade, manufacture, or undertaking of any kind whatever and includes an adventure or concern in the nature of trade".[26] "Carrying on business in Canada" includes any activity whereby a non-resident solicits orders or offers anything for sale in Canada through an agent or servant, whether the transaction is completed inside or outside Canada.[27]

---

[23] Para. 2(3)(*b*). This rule is always subject to the provisions of a tax treaty.

[24] See, however, s. 216 which allows a non-resident to elect to pay Part I tax in respect of rental income from real property and timber royalties.

[25] See e.g., *Canadian Marconi Co. v. The Queen*, [1986] 2 CTC 465, 86 DTC 6526 (S.C.C.); reversing [1984] CTC 319, 84 DTC 6267 (F.C.A.); *Anderson Logging Co. v. The King*, 52 DTC 1209 (S.C.C.), affirmed 52 DTC 1215 (P.C.) (*raison d'etre* of a public company is to carry on business); *The Queen v. Rockmore Investments Ltd.*, [1976] CTC 291, 76 DTC 6156.

[26] Subs. 248(1) "business".

[27] Subs. 253(b).

The phrase "soliciting orders" is distinguished from an invitation to treat. As Addy, J. said[28]:

> In considering whether the Plaintiff was "soliciting orders" in Canada, I do not agree that the words can be extended to include "a mere invitation to treat". Soliciting orders means that orders must be sought and attempts made to obtain them within the jurisdiction and the word "offer", in my view, must be given its ordinary meaning in contract law, that is, a binding offer which, if accepted, would create a contract between the offeror and the offeree. This becomes all the more evident when one considers that the question at common law depended specifically on the existence of a binding contract and that the section was intended to amend the former common law to the effect that the contract need not be made within the jurisdiction.

Thus, *in the absence of treaty protection*, a non-resident is liable for Canadian tax simply by soliciting orders, or by offering goods for sale through an agent, in Canada. Canadian tax treaties, however, follow the *OECD Model Convention*, and exempt non-residents from tax on business profits unless the taxpayer carries on business in Canada through a permanent establishment.[29] A "permanent establishment" is defined as a fixed place of business, which, of course, requires that there be a place of business.[30]

(b) Real Property

The characterization of income derived from real property can be difficult. There are two questions to be answered: Does the rental income constitute income from a business or income from property? If it is business income, is the business carried on *in Canada*.

A taxpayer is generally considered to be carrying on business in Canada if he or she deals with real estate located in Canada, regardless of where any contracts in respect of the real estate are actually executed.[31] A non-resident who is a member of a partnership or a joint venture which carries on business in Canada is considered to be carrying on business in Canada through that partnership or joint venture.

---

[28] *Sudden Valley Inc. v. The Queen*, [1976] CTC 297 at 300, 76 DTC 6178 at 6180 (F.C.T.D.); affirmed [1976] CTC 775, 76 DTC 6448 (F.C.A.).

[29] See Article 7, *OECD Model Convention*.

[30] See Article 5, *OECD Model Convention* and Chapter XXXI.

[31] See generally *Loeck v. The Queen*, [1978] CTC 528, 78 DTC 6368 (F.C.T.D.); *Abed v. M.N.R.*, [1978] CTC 5, 78 DTC 6007 (F.C.T.D.); varied [1982] CTC 115, 82 DTC 6099 (sub nom. *Abed Estate v. The Queen*) (F.C.A.); *Masri v. M.N.R.*, [1973] CTC 448, 73 DTC 5367 (F.C.T.D.); *Rhodesia Metals Ltd. (liquidator) v. Commr. of Taxes*, [1940] A.C. 774 (P.C.). See also *Thea Corp. v. M.N.R.* (1967), 67 DTC 175 (T.A.B.) (non-resident individual, who purchased Montreal property through a Quebec agent, was carrying on business in Canada).

(c) Offering for Sale

A non-resident whose employees offer goods for sale in Canada is considered to be carrying on business in Canada even if the contract of purchase and sale is approved and executed outside Canada. Advertising a product for sale in Canada does not constitute an "offer" and is not, *by itself* sufficient to characterize a non-resident as carrying on business in Canada.[32]

(d) Isolated Transactions

The definition of "business" includes an "adventure or concern in the nature of trade". Thus, an isolated transaction can constitute a "business". It remains uncertain, however, whether a non-resident person who has engaged in an isolated transaction can be said to be *carrying on* a business, since the phrase "carrying on" implies continued activity. As Jackett, P. said in *Tara Exploration*:[33]

> I am of opinion that [the definition of "business" in subsection 248(1)] does not operate to make a non-resident person subject to Canadian income tax in respect of a profit from an adventure that otherwise does not amount to, and is not part of, a "business". With considerable hesitation, I have concluded that the better view is that the words "carried on" are not words that can aptly be used with the word "adventure". To carry on something involves continuity of time or operations such as is involved in the ordinary sense of a "business". An adventure is an isolated happening. One has an adventure as opposed to *carrying on* a business.

(e) Incidents of Trade

The determination of whether a taxpayer is carrying on business is a mixed question of law and fact, in which no single criterion is conclusive:[34]

> . . . the question is whether what the company do amounts to carrying on trade in the United Kingdom. There is not, I think, any principle of law which lays down what carrying on trade is. There are a multitude of things which together make up the carrying on of trade, but I know no one distinguishing incident, for it is a compound fact made up of a variety of things.

The words "carrying on business" do not have a technical meaning and should be interpreted in the context of commercial reality. The following factors should be considered:

- Where are contracts made?
- Where are goods delivered and payments made?
- Where are the business assets located?
- Is an agent or independent contractor utilized?
- Where do the operations take place from which the profits in substance arise (as opposed to where profits are realized)?

---

[32] *Sudden Valley Inc. v. The Queen*, [1976] CTC 775, 76 DTC 6448 (F.C.A.).

[33] *Tara Exploration & Dev. Co. v. M.N.R.*, [1970] CTC 557 at 567, 70 DTC 6370 at 6376, (Ex. Ct.).

[34] *Erichsen v. Last* (1881), IV T.C. 422 at 423, approved by Urie J. in *The Queen v. Gurd's Products Co.*, [1985] 2 CTC 85 at 92, 85 DTC 5314 at 5319; leave to appeal to SCC refused 64 N.R. 156.

- What is the nature of the activities/transactions?
- Where are bank accounts, listed telephone numbers and addresses located?
- Is compliance with a jurisdiction's rules and regulations business- or legally-motivated?
- Did the taxpayer intend to do business in Canada?
- Where are assets used in the business purchased?
- What is the degree of supervisory or other activity in Canada?
- What is the substance or object of the transaction?
- Is a representative or resident expert present in the country?
- Are activities in Canada merely ancillary to the main business (e.g., the business of buying, storing, selling or manufacturing the product)?
- Are there individuals in Canada who assist (or are available to assist) the taxpayer in his endeavour? and
- What is the reason for the taxpayer's existence?

The above criteria must be evaluated to determine whether the non-resident has a Canadian "centre of gravity". If he or she does, he or she is likely to be carrying on a business in Canada.

3. COMPUTATION OF INCOME

A non-resident's income from business is his or her "profit" from the business determined according to commercial principles and specific provisions of the Act.[35] Any recapture of capital cost allowance not included in the computation of business income (e.g., recapture on a rental property) is included in the determination of taxable income.[36]

A non-resident's business income is allocated to its sources. Subject to treaty provisions, business operations in Canada are subject to Canadian income tax. Where business operations are scattered amongst different countries, the Canadian portion of any business income must be determined through an appropriate allocation and, where applicable, by reference to the applicable international tax treaty. Canadian tax treaties generally provide that a non-resident is only subject to Canadian income tax on business profits attributable to his or her "permanent establishment" in Canada.[37] Business profits attributable to a permanent establishment may well be different from income from "carrying on a business in Canada" as determined under the domestic rules.[38]

---

[35] Subpara. 115(1)(a)(ii). See also subs. 9(1), ss. 18 and 20.

[36] Subpara. 115(1)(a)(iii.2).

[37] See, e.g., Article 7(1), *OECD Model Convention for Avoidance of Double Taxation with Respect to Taxes on Income and Capital*. See also, Article VII, *Canada-U.S. Income Tax Convention, 1980*, as amended.

[38] See Chapter XXXI "Outbound Investments and Foreign Income".

Business profits include incidental income from property. Thus, there is potential for double taxation where a non-resident's income from a business carried on in Canada includes *incidental* income from property. The income from property would be taxable under Part I of the Act and then again under Part XIII when remitted to the non-resident. To ensure that this does not occur, income from property that would otherwise be subject to withholding tax is included in the non-resident's business income if the amount is "reasonably attributable" to his or her Canadian business. Such income is not subject to withholding tax.[39]

4. CAPITAL GAINS

Non-residents are liable for Part I income tax on taxable capital gains (net of allowable capital losses) from dispositions of "taxable Canadian property".[40] Capital gains from other types of capital property are not subject to Canadian tax.

"Taxable Canadian property" includes the following:[41]

- real property situated in Canada;
- capital property used in carrying on a business in Canada (other than a life insurance business);
- where the non-resident is an insurer, capital property used by it in carrying on its insurance business in Canada;
- shares of resident Canadian corporations other than public corporations;
- shares in a public corporation if, at any time during the five years immediately preceding the disposition, the non-resident (or related persons) owned not less than 25 per cent of the issued shares of any class of the capital stock of the corporation;
- an interest in a partnership if, at any time during the 12 months immediately preceding the disposition, 50 per cent or more of the total fair market value of all partnership property consisted of property that is taxable Canadian property, an income interest in a trust resident in Canada, a Canadian resource property, or a timber resource property;
- a capital interest in a Canadian resident trust (other than a unit trust);
- a unit of a Canadian resident trust (other than a mutual fund trust);
- a unit of a mutual fund trust if, at any time during the five years immediately preceding the disposition, the non-resident (or related persons) owned not less than 25 per cent of the issued units of the trust; or

---

[39] Para. 214(13)(c); Regs. 805(1), (2). See *Atlas-Gest Inc. v. M.N.R.*, [1985] 2 CTC 2066, 85 DTC 430 (T.C.C.); *Twentieth Century Fox Film Corp. v. The Queen*, [1985] 2 CTC 328, 85 DTC 5513 (F.C.T.D.).

[40] Para. 2(3)(c); subpara. 115(1)(a)(iii). This rule is also subject to any exemption provided for in an international tax treaty.

[41] Para. 115(1)(b).

- any property which is deemed to be "taxable Canadian property".[42]

An interest in any of the above listed properties is also considered "taxable Canadian property".

Shares of a public corporation do not constitute "taxable Canadian property". This would appear to be the case whether the corporation issuing the shares initially qualified as a public corporation or became a public corporation after originally starting out as a private corporation.

A non-resident's capital gain for a taxation year arises from a disposition of property that qualifies as a "taxable Canadian property". Hence, the status of the property at the time of the disposition determines whether the non-resident is liable for Canadian tax.

Non-resident capital gains and losses are generally calculated according to the usual rules applicable to resident taxpayers.[43] There are, however, a few specific rules which apply only to non-residents. For example, a non-resident may not:

- deduct a reserve in calculating capital gains;[44]
- roll-over capital property to his or her spouse or to a "spouse trust";[45] or
- take full advantage of the principal residence exemption.[46]

Non-residents may deduct allowable capital losses from dispositions of taxable Canadian property against taxable capital gains.

5. TAXABLE INCOME

In computing taxable income, a non-resident is entitled to deductions in respect of:[47]

- prospectors' and grubstakers' shares;
- amounts exempt by treaty;
- workers' compensation;
- amounts repaid under unemployment insurance;
- stock option benefits from a Canadian-controlled private corporation;

---

[42] See, e.g., subsecs. 85.1(1) and 87(4).

[43] See, generally, Division B, subdivision c.

[44] Subpara. 40(2)(a)(i).

[45] Subss. 70(6), 73(1).

[46] Para. 40(2)(b).

[47] Paras. 115(1)(d), (d.1); IT-171R2, "Non-resident Individuals — Computation of Taxable Income Earned in Canada and Non-refundable Tax Credits" (March 30, 1992).

- social assistance payments that are means-tested; and
- intercorporate taxable dividends.

Within the usual limits, non-residents may also offset Canadian-source losses against Canadian-source income.[48] Thus, a non-resident may claim non-capital losses, net capital losses, restricted farm losses, and farm losses that are reasonably attributable to his or her employment in Canada, a business carried on by him or her in Canada or to the disposition of taxable Canadian property.

In addition, where "all or substantially all" of the non-resident's income for a year is derived from Canadian sources, he or she may claim such other deductions as are reasonably considered to be wholly applicable to his or her income.[49] It can be quite difficult to determine the portion of deductions that are wholly applicable to Canadian-source income. In the simplest case, however, an allocation based upon the period of time that the non-resident was employed in Canada or was carrying on business in Canada is acceptable.[50] The Department's view is that the phrase "all or substantially all" means 90 per cent or more.[51]

6. TAX PAYABLE

(a) Individuals

A non-resident individual is liable for tax on his or her taxable income earned in Canada during a taxation year. The tax payable, set out in Division E of the Act, is calculated by applying a progressive marginal rate schedule to taxable income.[52]

For provincial income tax purposes, all of a resident's income from an office or employment is attributed to the province in which he or she resides on December 31. In contrast, a non-resident's income from an office or employment is allocated to the provinces on the basis of the duties performed by him or her in each province.[53]

Business income is allocated in the same way for both residents and non-residents, i.e., by determining whether the taxpayer has a "permanent establishment" in the particular province and allocating his or her business income according to the proportion of his or her gross revenue, salaries and wages attributable to the particular province.[54]

---

[48] Para. 115(1)(e); s. 111.

[49] Para. 115(1)(f).

[50] IT-171R2, "Non-resident Individuals — Computation of Taxable Income Earned in Canada and Non-refundable Tax Credits" (March 30, 1992).

[51] See IT-171R2, "Non-resident Individuals — Computation of Taxable Income Earned in Canada and Non-refundable Tax Credits" (March 30, 1992).

[52] Subs. 117(2).

[53] Reg. 2602(1).

[54] Reg. 2603; see Reg. 2600(2) for the meaning of "permanent establishment".

(b) Corporations

A non-resident corporation is subject to tax at a flat rate of 38 per cent (1995).[55] A corporation may, however, claim a provincial tax credit equal to 10 per cent of its taxable income earned in the year in a province.[56] Corporate taxable income earned in a province is calculated by reference to its permanent establishments in Canada.

A non-resident corporation is not entitled to the small business deduction, which is only available to Canadian-controlled private corporations.[57]

7. WITHHOLDING TAX

(a) General

In addition to Part I tax on Canadian source "active" income, a non-resident is also subject to 25 per cent (subject to treaty reduction) withholding tax on "passive" income paid or credited to him or her by a Canadian resident.[58] This tax is levied under Part XIII of the Act. The tax is calculated by reference to the *gross*[59] amount paid or credited to the non-resident.[60]

Although the withholding tax is levied on the non-resident who receives Canadian-source "passive" income, the obligation to withhold the tax actually rests on the resident person who pays or credits the non-resident. Failure to withhold and remit the tax renders the resident liable for the full amount of the tax, together with interest and penalties.[61] Interest is calculated by reference to a prescribed rate.

(b) Payments Subject to Withholding

Tax at a rate of 25 per cent (reduced to 15 per cent under most Canadian treaties) is to be withheld at source[62] whenever a person resident in Canada pays or credits (or is deemed to pay or credit) a non-resident person an amount on account of one of the types of income enumerated in Part XIII of the Act.

---

[55] Subs. 123(1).

[56] Subs. 124(1).

[57] Subs. 125(1).

[58] See, generally, Part XIII, ss. 212-218.

[59] Subs. 214(1).

[60] S. 215.

[61] Subs. 215(6). See also para. 227(8)(a). In certain circumstances, the directors of a corporation may be personally liable for taxes which have not been remitted: see s. 227.1.

[62] Subs. 212(1).

(i) Management Fees

References:

BULLETINS, CIRCULARS & RULINGS:

IT-468R	December 29, 1989	Management or Administration Fees Paid to Non-residents
IC 87-2	February 27, 1987	International Transfer Pricing and Other International Transactions

A management or administration fee is an amount paid in respect of managerial services in connection with the direction or supervision of business activities. "Management and administration" includes:[63]

- planning;
- direction;
- control and coordination at a managerial level;
- accounting;
- financial and legal services;
- electronic data processing;
- employee relations;
- management consultation;
- labour negotiations; and
- tax advice.

Management fees do not include reasonable payments for services where the parties are dealing with each other at arm's length[64] and the services were rendered in the

---

[63] IT-468R, "Management or Administration Fees Paid to Non-residents" (December 29, 1989).

[64] On the meaning of arm's length see *M.N.R. v. Sheldon's Engineering Ltd.*, [1955] SCR 637, CTC 174, 55 DTC 1110, *per* Locke, J. at 643:

> The expression is one which is usually employed in cases in which transactions between trustees and cestuis que trust, guardians and wards, principals and agents or solicitors and clients are called into question. The reasons why transactions between persons standing in these relations to each other may be impeached are pointed out in the judgments of the Lord Chancellor and of Lord Blackburn in *MacPherson v. Watts* (1877), 3 App. Cas. 254.

See also *Swiss Bank Corp. v. M.N.R.*, [1971] CTC 427, 71 DTC 5235 (Ex. Ct.), *per* Thurlow, C.J., at 5240-41:

> In my view, the basic premise on which this analysis is based is that, where the "mind" by which the bargaining is directed on behalf of one party to a contract is the same "mind" that directs the bargaining on behalf of the other party, it cannot be said that the parties are dealing at arm's length. In other words where the evidence reveals that the same person was "dictating" the "terms of the bargain" on behalf of both parties, it cannot be said that the parties were dealing at arm's length.

ordinary course of the non-resident's business.[65] Reimbursed expenses actually incurred by the non-resident for services performed on behalf of the resident are not considered management fees.[66]

(ii) Interest

As a general rule, interest paid or credited to a non-resident person is subject to withholding tax of 25 per cent (reduced to 15 per cent in most Canadian treaties). There are, however, many exceptions to this rule. For example, there is no withholding tax on the following interest payments:[67]

- interest paid by a non-resident-owned (NRO) investment corporation;
- interest on certain bonds issued or guaranteed by the Government of Canada;
- interest on certain obligations payable in a foreign currency to a person with whom the resident payor is dealing at arm's length;
- interest on a bond, debenture or similar debt obligation if the interest is payable to a non-resident person who has obtained a certificate of exemption from the Minister;[68]
- interest payable by a life insurer on any obligation entered into in the course of carrying on a life insurance business in a foreign country, provided that the payor and the payee are dealing with each other at arm's length;
- interest paid by a corporation in respect of debt obligations issued after June 23, 1975 provided that the corporation and the creditor were dealing with each other at arm's length and not more than 25 per cent of the principal amount of the debt obligation was payable by the corporation within five years of the issue of the obligation;
- interest payable on a mortgage or similar obligation secured by real estate situated abroad, except to the extent that the interest payable is deductible in computing the payor's income from a business carried on by him or her in Canada or from property other than real property situated outside Canada;
- interest paid or credited in Canadian dollars by certain Canadian financial institutions in respect of Canadian dollar deposits in branches or offices outside Canada, if the depositor deals at arm's length with the Canadian financial institution;

---

[65] Para. 212(4)(a). See *Windsor Plastic Products Ltd. v. The Queen*, F.C.T.D., Doc. No. T-1943-81, 27 February, 1986, Muldoon J., (unreported).

[66] Para. 212(4)(b).

[67] Para. 212(1)(b).

[68] Subs. 212(14); the Minister can issue a certificate of exemption to a non-resident organization that would, *if* it were resident in Canada, be exempt from tax under the Act, e.g., a registered charity or a pension trust that qualifies under s. 149. Blended payments must be allocated as between principal and interest: subs. 214(2).

- interest paid to a prescribed international organization,[69] or by a prescribed financial institution on an "eligible deposit";[70] and
- interest payable under certain securities lending arrangements.

The above listed interest payments are generally exempt from withholding tax. The exemption is lost, however, if the payment of interest is contingent on some other factor, for example, revenues, profits or dividends paid to shareholders. Thus, the exemption from withholding tax is only available in respect of payments that constitute interest, both in substance and in form.

In certain cases the Act deems payments to be on account of interest and other payments not to be interest. For example, interest computed by reference to revenue, profits, cash flow, commodity prices or any other similar criteria are deemed not to be interest for certain purposes.[71]

Where a non-resident person guarantees repayment of the principal amount of a debt obligation issued by a resident of Canada, any amount paid or credited as consideration for the guarantee is deemed to be an interest payment on account of the debt. Similarly, payments by a resident to a non-resident person on account of standby fees for funds made available by the non-resident are deemed to be a payment on account of interest.[72]

(iii) Estate or Trust Income

Trust and estate income is subject to withholding tax except to the extent that it is deemed to be a non-resident's taxable capital gain from the disposition of capital property.[73] Trust or estate income *payable* to a beneficiary is generally included in his or her income whether or not it is actually paid in the year.[74] For withholding tax purposes, however, the amount *payable* to the beneficiary is deemed to have been paid or credited to him or her on the earlier of two dates:[75]

- the date of actual payment, and
- the 90th day after the end of the taxation year of the trust.

---

[69] Such as the Bank for International Settlements.

[70] Subpara. 212(1)(b)(xi); s. 33.1.

[71] See the closing words of para. 212(1)(b).

[72] Subs. 214(15).

[73] Para. 212(1)(c), subs. 104(21).

[74] Subs. 104(13).

[75] Para. 214(3)(f).

(iv) Rents and Royalties

Rents, royalties, and similar payments paid or credited to a non-resident by a resident of Canada are subject to withholding tax.[76] Payments for the use of the following types of properties are considered similar in character to rents and royalties and are also subject to withholding tax:

- inventions,
- trade names,
- patents,
- trademarks,
- designs,
- models,
- plans,
- secret formulas, and
- processes.

Note, copyright royalties on literary, dramatic, musical, or artistic works are not subject to withholding tax.[77]

"Rent" includes not only payments for the use of real property, but also leases of personal property. As Thurlow, J. said in *United Geophysical Co.*:[78]

It is, I think, apparent from the use in the section of the wording which follows the words "rent" and "royalty" that Parliament did not intend to limit the type of income referred to in the subsection to either what could strictly be called "rent" or "royalty" or to payments which had all of the strict legal characteristics of "rent" or "royalty". Nor does the scope of the section appear to be restricted to payments of that nature in respect of real property for the word "property" appears in the section and that word is defined in very broad terms in [s. 248(1), en. S.C. 1974-75-76, c. 26, subs. 125(5); am S.C. 1980-81-82-83, c. 140, subs. 128(9)] as including both real and personal property. It seems to me, therefore, that [s. 212(1)(d), as amended] includes any payment which is similar to rent but which is payable in respect of personal property. Moreover, in its ordinary usage, as opposed to its technical legal meaning, the word "rent", besides referring to returns of that nature from real property, is broad enough to include a payment for the hire of personal property. . . . Without attempting to determine just how wide the net of [s. 212(1)(d), as amended] may be, I am of the opinion that the subsection does refer to and include a fixed amount paid as rental for the use of personal property for a certain time.

Now it goes without saying that the mere use of the words "rent" and "rental" in the agreement between the [parent company] and the [subsidiary company] is not necessarily conclusive on the question whether the payment so provided for is in fact a rent or other payment of the kind referred to in [s. 212(1), as amended], but their use in the agreement, to my mind, affords some indication that the payment which was to be determined, having regard to reasonableness and the cost of each item to be "rented", was to be a payment in the nature of rent for the equipment.

---

[76] Para. 212(1)(*d*).

[77] Subpara. 212(1)(*d*)(vi). See Richard G. Tremblay, "Canada-U.S. Cross Border Computer Software 'Fees'" (1986), 1 *Cdn. Current Tax,* C163.

[78] *United Geophysical Co. v. M.N.R.*, [1961] CTC 134 at 145, 61 DTC 1099 at 1105 (Ex. Ct.). See also, *PPG Industries Can. Ltd. v. M.N.R.*, [1978] CTC 2055, 78 DTC 1062 (T.R.B.).

(v) Alimony

Reference:

BULLETINS, CIRCULARS & RULINGS:

IT-118R3   December 21, 1990   Alimony and Maintenance

As a general rule, alimony and maintenance paid for the support of a non-resident person and/or his or her dependants are subject to withholding tax.[79] In many cases, however, alimony and maintenance are paid to a person with minimal income. As such, the withholding tax payable by the non-resident could be higher than the tax that would otherwise be payable on such income under Part I. For this reason, the Act allows a non-resident to elect to pay Part I tax on alimony and maintenance instead of the withholding tax.[80] Relief under these rules may only be obtained retroactively by filing a tax return six months after the end of the taxation year. The non-resident may, however, obtain financial relief by having the withholding at source reduced.[81]

(vi) Pension Benefits

Pension and superannuation benefits are subject to withholding tax.[82] The following payments are, however, specifically excluded from the withholding tax:

- payments under the *Old Age Security Act*;
- payments under the *Canada Pension Plan* or the *Quebec Pension Plan*;
- certain exempt service pensions and allowances;
- funds "rolled over" on behalf of the non-resident person to a registered pension fund or to a registered retirement savings plan under which the non-resident is the annuitant;
- compensation payments (such as workers' compensation and social assistance) that would have been deductible in computing the non-resident person's taxable income (or that of his or spouse spouse) if he or she had been resident in Canada throughout the year;[83] and
- certain exempt payments under section 57.

---

[79] Para. 212(1)(*f*). The payments are only taxable if they would have been taxable if paid to a Canadian resident; see paras. 56(1)(*b*), (*c*) for the taxability of alimony and maintenance payments.

[80] S. 217.

[81] Subs. 215(5); Reg. 809.

[82] Para. 212(1)(*h*).

[83] Para. 110(1)(*f*) sets out the types of payments that are deductible.

Pension payments that can reasonably be regarded as being attributable to services rendered by a non-resident person when he or she was *neither* resident in Canada nor more than occasionally employed in Canada are *not* subject to withholding tax.[84]

(vii) Retiring Allowances

Generally speaking, a retiring allowance paid to a non-resident is subject to withholding tax. A payment transferred on behalf of a non-resident person to a registered pension fund or to a registered retirement savings plan under which the non-resident person is the annuitant and that would be deductible in computing his or her income if he or she were resident in Canada through the year is not subject to withholding tax.[85]

(viii) Registered Retirement Savings Plan Payments

A payment out of a registered retirement savings plan to a non-resident person is subject to withholding tax if such a payment would have been taxable to a person who was resident in Canada throughout the taxation year.[86] In other words, a non-resident is only subject to withholding tax in circumstances where a similar payment to a resident person would have been subject to Part I tax. Any portion of the registered retirement savings plan that is rolled over to another registered retirement savings plan under which the non-resident person is the annuitant is not subject to withholding tax.

(ix) Payments Out of Deferred Income Plans

A payment out of a deferred profit sharing plan,[87] registered education savings plan,[88] or a registered retirement income fund[89] to a non-resident person is subject to withholding tax *if* the payment would have been taxable had it been received by a person who was resident in Canada throughout the taxation year in which the payment is made.

---

[84] Subparas. 212(1)(*h*)(v) and (vi).

[85] Para. 212(1)(*j.1*).

[86] Para. 212(1)(*l*).

[87] Para. 212(1)(*m*); s. 147.

[88] Para. 212(1)(*r*) and s. 146.1.

[89] Para. 212(1)(*q*); s. 146.3.

(x) Dividends

A non-resident person is subject to withholding tax on dividends paid or credited, or deemed to have been paid or credited,[90] to him or her by a corporation resident in Canada that is on account of:[91]

- taxable dividends;[92] or
- capital dividends.[93]

Capital gains dividends paid by a mortgage investment corporation, a mutual fund corporation, or an NRO investment corporation are not subject to withholding tax.[94]

(A) Meaning of "Dividend"

The meaning of the term "dividend" can vary from country to country. Generally, a dividend implies an appropriation of corporate profits to the shareholder after income has been earned. Whether or not a payment constitutes a "dividend" is a matter for the domestic law of the source country.

Article 10(3) of the *OECD Model Convention* defines "dividends" as follows:

> The term "dividends" . . . means income from shares, "jouissance" shares or "jouissance" rights, mining shares, founders' shares or other rights, not being debt-claims, participating in profits as well as income from other corporate rights which is subjected to the same taxation treatment as income from shares by the laws of the State of which the company making the distribution is a resident.

The above definition is neither complete nor exhaustive. The examples do, however, illustrate the types of payments which are considered to be dividends in most OECD countries. Thus, "dividends" generally imply the distribution of profits to the shareholders of a corporation limited by shares, limited partnerships with share capital, limited liability companies or other joint stock companies. Dividends are income from capital made available to a company by its *shareholders* and do not include debt claims that participate in profits.

Partnership profit distributions are not considered to be dividends under Canadian domestic law. There are, however, certain countries in which partnerships are treated in a manner that is substantially similar to limited liability corporations.[95] Where the matter is not specifically covered by a bilateral tax treaty, the determination as to what constitutes a "dividend" is made by reference to domestic law.

---

[90] *Placements Serco Ltée v. The Queen* [1988] 1 CTC 42, 87 DTC 5425, 88 DTC 6125 (F.C.A.) ("dividend" in subs. 212(2) includes any payment deemed to be a dividend).

[91] Subs. 212(2).

[92] Subs. 89(1) "taxable dividend".

[93] Subs. 83(2). One-quarter of capital gains accumulated by a private corporation may be distributed on a tax-free basis to Canadian shareholders.

[94] By virtue of the exclusions in para. 212(2)(*a*).

[95] For example, Belgium, Portugal, Spain and certain types of distributions in France.

Economic double taxation of dividend income is an acute international economic problem. Under the classical system of taxation, dividend income is subject to taxation twice: first at the corporate level, then again at the shareholder level. The resulting tax burden on dividends can be significantly different from that on interest income depending upon the status of the payor corporation and the recipient.

An individual resident in Canada is taxable on dividends that he or she receives in the year.

Where the dividend is paid by a corporation resident in Canada, the individual is entitled to a dividend tax credit against his or her Canadian taxes.[96] Thus, the effective tax rate on Canadian source dividend income is reduced by virtue of the credit.

In contrast, foreign source dividends are fully taxable at their equivalent Canadian dollar value without any dividend tax credit for foreign corporate taxes. An individual may, however, be entitled to claim a foreign tax credit under section 126 for foreign withholding taxes.

(B) OECD Model Convention

Articles 10(1) and 10(2) of the *OECD Model Convention* provide:

1. Dividends paid by a company which is a resident of a Contracting State to a resident of the other Contracting State may be taxed in that other State.

2. However, such dividends may also be taxed in the Contracting State of which the company paying the dividends is a resident and according to the laws of that State, but if the recipient is the beneficial owner of the dividend the tax so charged shall not exceed:

    (a) 5 per cent of the gross amount of the dividend if the beneficial owner is a company (other than a partnership) which holds directly at least 25 per cent of the capital of the company paying the dividends;

    (b) 15 per cent of the gross amount of the dividend in all other cases.

The competent authorities of the Contracting States shall by mutual agreement settle the mode of application of these limitations.

This paragraph shall not affect the taxation of the company in respect of the profits out of which the dividends are paid.

Hence, dividends may be taxable both in the recipient's country of residence and in the State in which the corporation that pays the dividend is resident. The *OECD Model Convention* does not provide that dividends should be taxed exclusively either in the State of source or exclusively in the State of the shareholder's residence.

The term "paid" has a very wide meaning and implies the fulfilment of the obligation to put funds at the disposal of the shareholder in the manner required by contract or by custom.

---

[96] See para. 82(1)(*b*); s. 121.

Article 10(1) only deals with dividends that are paid by a company which is resident of a Contracting State to a resident of the other Contracting State. The Article does not apply to dividends paid by a company which is a resident of a third State. Nor does Article 10(1) apply to dividends paid by a resident company of a Contracting State which are attributable to a permanent establishment which a resident of that State has in the other Contracting State.[97]

(C) Appropriate Rate

A critical question in the context of dividends is: What is the appropriate rate of withholding tax to be applied by the source country to dividends? This question is particularly important in the context of dividends because of the different ways in which different countries tax dividends. The three basic models for the taxation of dividends are:

- the "classical" system;
- the "split rate" system; and
- the "imputation" system.

Under the "classical" system, a shareholder in a corporation suffers "economic" double taxation: the corporation pays tax on its income prior to the distribution of the income as dividends and the shareholder is taxed upon receipt of the dividend income. Thus, the rate of the withholding tax on dividends, which acts as a second tier tax, is central to the overall tax burden that is ultimately imposed on such income.

Some countries attempt to mitigate against the burden of economic double taxation by providing some relief either to the payor corporation or to the recipient shareholder. The relief generally takes one of two forms. Under a "split rate" system, undistributed profits are taxed at a higher rate than distributed earnings.

Under the "imputation" system, the tax paid by a corporation is notionally set-off against the tax liability of the recipient shareholder. This model can provide for either partial or complete relief from double taxation depending upon the rate of tax paid by the corporation and the rate at which those taxes are imputed to the recipient shareholder.

The *OECD Model Convention* allows both the payor country and the recipient's country to tax dividends; that is, dividends can be taxed by source and on the basis of residence.

Article 10(2) reserves a right to tax dividends to their source State, that is, to the State of which the corporation paying the dividends is a resident. The general rule in Article 10(2) is that the withholding tax on dividends is limited to 15 per cent of the gross value of the dividend. This is a withholding tax over and above any corporate tax which the source State might have previously imposed on the corporation that pays the dividend.

---

[97] See Article 21, *OECD Model Convention.*

Canadian tax treaties have traditionally provided for a uniform maximum withholding tax rate limit of 15 per cent on the gross amount of the dividend paid or, in some cases, for 10 per cent in the case of significant (at least 25 per cent of share capital or 10 per cent of votes) shareholdings. More recently, however, Canada has moved to negotiate a reduction in these rates. Effective January 1, 1993, for example, pursuant to a Protocol to the *Canada-Netherlands Treaty*, the withholding tax rate on dividends paid on significant shareholdings is reduced from 10 per cent to 5 per cent. The reduced rate applies from 1993 to dividends paid from the Netherlands and will be phased in over five years for dividends paid from Canada. Similarly, in the Protocol to the *Canada-U.S. Tax Convention*, the withholding tax on intercorporate dividends in the case of significant shareholdings is 5 per cent from 1997 (6 per cent in 1996 and 7 per cent in 1995).

Some countries seek to mitigate economic double taxation; others do not. A country can mitigate economic double taxation of dividend income in three principal ways:

- the corporate tax in respect of distributed profits can be charged at a lower rate than that on accumulated or retained profits (the "split rate" system);
- an individual may be allowed to offset a portion of the corporate tax paid on distributed profits against his own personal tax ("imputation" of corporate tax against personal tax); or
- distributed profits may not be taxed at all at the corporate level and only taxed at the recipient's level.

There is no consensus amongst the OECD countries as to the most appropriate method of providing relief from economic double taxation of corporate and dividend income. Canada uses the "imputation" system to provide relief for individuals who receive dividends from resident corporations.

It should be noted, however, that the Canadian method for providing relief against double taxation of dividend income is only a partial solution to the problem. The dividend tax credit is not a refundable credit and, as such, an individual does not receive any relief if the credit exceeds his or her personal tax. In this sense, the dividend tax credit is not an adjustment of the corporation's tax previously paid. Instead, it is a *notional* imputation of the corporate tax burden (whether or not the corporation actually paid the tax) to an individual resident in Canada.

SELECTED BIBLIOGRAPHY TO CHAPTER XXIX

Canadian Employment

Bacal, N. and R. Lewin, "The Taxation in Canada of Non-Resident Performing Artists and Behind-the-Camera Personnel" (1986), 34 *Can. Tax J.* 1287.

Boidman, N., "The Peripatetic Alien: His/Her Tax Problems in the U.S. and Abroad", in *Proceedings of the New York University Forty-Fourth Institute on Federal Taxation* 40-1 (New York: Matthew Bender, 1986).

Broley, J.A., "The Migrating Executive: Coming to and Transferring Within Canada", *Corp. Management Tax Conf.* 172 (Can. Tax Foundation, 1979).

Garcia, C.F. and J.H. Shividy, "Taxation of the U.S. Expatriate Living and Working in Canada" (1980), 26 *Can. Tax J.* 523.

Gray, Kerry, "U.S. Citizens Employed in Canada: An Update" (1986), 34 *Can. Tax J.* 1463.

Lowden, John H., "Employee Transfers: Moving To or From Canada on Foreign Assignment", in *Proceedings of 41st Tax Conf.* 34:1 (Can. Tax Foundation, 1989).

Miller, Donald, "Executive Transfers from the U.S. to Canada" (May 23, 1990) *Special Seminar on Current International Tax Issues* (DeBoo, 1990) 89.

Wray, D.G. and S.R. Barnard, "Taxation of Non-Resident Athletes and Entertainers Performing in Canada" (1986), 34 *Can. Tax J.* 1150.

Non-resident Investments in Canada

Boidman, N. and Bruno Ducharme, *Taxation in Canada, Implications for Foreign Investment* (Netherlands: Kluwer, 1984).

Loveland, Norman C., "Non-Resident Investment in Canada: Earning Investment Returns Exempt from Canadian Taxation", in *Proceedings of 39th Tax Conf.* 20:1 (Can. Tax Foundation, 1987).

Perry, Harvey, "Federal Income Tax: Non-Residents", *Tax Paper No. 89* (Can. Tax Foundation, 1990).

Perry, Harvey, "Federal Income Tax: Foreign Income of Residents", *Tax Paper No. 89* (Can. Tax Foundation, 1990).

Canadian Real Estate

Atlas, Michael J., *Canadian Taxation of Real Estate*, 2nd ed., (CCH Canadian, 1989).

Atlas, Michael J., "Income Tax Issues in Real Estate Leasing", *Corp. Management Tax Conf.* 3:1 (Can. Tax Foundation, 1989).

Bernstein, Jack, "Real Estate Syndications", *Corp. Management Tax Conf.* 2:1 (Can. Tax Foundation, 1989).

Boidman, N., "Non-Resident Investment in Canadian Real Estate", *Corp. Management Tax Conf.* 371 (Can. Tax Foundation, 1983).

Boidman, N., "Tax Planning for Foreign Investment in Canadian Real Estate" (1988), 15 *Tax Planning Int'l* 12.

Dalsin, Derek T., "Dispositions of Property by Non-Residents: Tax Deferral by Ministerial Discretion" (1991), 39 *Can. Tax J.* 77.

Gauthier, André, "Investment in Canadian Real Estate by Non-Residents", Corp. *Management Tax Conf.* 195 (Can. Tax Foundation, 1978).

James, Larry W., "Disposing of Real Estate", *Corp. Management Tax Conf.* 5:1 (Can. Tax Foundation, 1989).

Lambe, Hugh B., "Foreign Investment in Canadian Real Estate Through a Netherlands Corporation" (1980), 28 *Can. Tax J.* 343.

Neville, Ralph T., "Tax Considerations in Real Estate Development and Construction", *Corp. Management Tax Conf.* 7:1 (Can. Tax Foundation, 1989).

Power, Mary, "The Taxation of Non-Resident Investment in Canadian Real Estate" (1989), 37 *Can. Tax J.* 1266.

Shagrie, Alan, "Taxation of Foreign Corporations Investing in Quebec Real Estate — Recent Developments" (1987), 16 *Tax Management Int'l. J.* 336.

Silver, Sheldon, "Vehicles for Acquiring and Holding Real Estate", *Corp. Management Tax Conf.* 4:1 (Can. Tax Foundation, 1989).

Ward, David A., "Foreign Investment in Canadian Real Estate", *Corp. Management Tax Conf.* 10:1 (Can. Tax Foundation, 1989).

CHAPTER XXX

INBOUND INVESTMENTS

We saw earlier that a non-resident is taxable in Canada if he or she "carries on business" in Canada.[1] In this chapter we look at the tax implications of doing business in Canada: Structures, Financing, Reorganizations and Repatriation of Profits.

1. FORMS OF BUSINESS ORGANIZATIONS

The choice of form of business organization is usually dictated by two principal considerations: business factors and tax treatment. The most frequently used forms of business are:

- Agency;
- Branch; and
- Subsidiary.

(a) Agency

Agency is the relationship that exists between persons when one person (the "agent") is considered in law to represent the other (the "principal") so as to affect the principal's legal relations with third parties. Thus, the essence of agency is the power of an agent to affect legal relationships between his or her principal and third parties. The concept is easy to define. Unfortunately, as Lord Herschell observed, no word is more commonly and constantly abused than "agent".[2]

Agency is an attractive form of business because it is easy to set up and minimizes operating costs. An agent conducts business on behalf of his or her principal, usually with minimal investment in financial or capital assets. The disadvantage of agency is that it can deny the principal a formal presence in the country and less than complete organizational control over his or her business activities.

From a tax perspective, a non-resident person is taxable in Canada if he or she carries on business in Canada at any time in a taxation year.[3] A non-resident person who solicits orders or offers anything for sale in Canada through an agent or servant is deemed to be carrying on business in Canada in the year in respect of the activity.[4] This is so whether the contract or transaction is completed inside or outside of Canada.

---

[1] See Chapter XXIX "Non-residents".

[2] *Kennedy v. DeTrafford*, [1897] AC 180.

[3] Para. 2(3)(*b*).

[4] S. 253.

Thus, section 253 casts an extremely broad net: mere solicitation or offering of anything for sale in Canada through an agent or servant is sufficient to constitute the carrying on of a business within Canada.

The existence of an agency relationship is a mixed question of fact and law. The determinative element is whether the person who acts in a representative capacity is acting on his or her own account and behalf or on behalf of the non-resident person. An agent can be independent of, or dependent upon, the principal for whom he or she conducts business. Traditionally, the term "agent" has been used to refer to an independent agent and "servant" or "employee" to a dependent agent.

In law, a principal has the power to control his or her agent. It is a question of fact, however, whether a non-resident person has sufficient power or control over his or her representative to establish an agency relationship. One looks at various factors. For example:

- the person with whom the goods are identified;
- the manner in which the representative fills orders: from existing inventory or upon receipt of a specific order;
- the representative's degree of control over the acceptance of orders and credit terms;
- the representative's degree of control over the price of goods sold and the terms and conditions of sale;
- the method of payment for goods and the name in which payment is received;
- the mode of compensation of the representative; and
- the manner of delivery of goods and the carriage of risk on inventory.

A non-resident person carrying on business in Canada through an agency relationship is taxable on his or her net Canadian source income and on capital gains from the disposition of taxable Canadian property.

The domestic rule that a non-resident is liable for tax on his or her Canadian source income earned through an agent is subject to an important exception. Under Canada's double tax treaties, a non-resident person is not taxable in Canada unless he, she or it carries on business in Canada through a permanent establishment situated in Canada. Thus, the threshold test for subjecting a non-resident to tax in Canada is higher in respect of businesses conducted with persons resident in countries with which Canada has tax treaties.

A "permanent establishment" generally means a fixed place of business through which the non-resident person carries on its operations in Canada.[5] There are three main conditions which must be satisfied for a "permanent establishment" to exist:

---

[5] See, for example, Article 5, *OECD Model Convention.*

- there must be a place of business;
- the place of business must be fixed; and
- the business must be carried on through the fixed place of business.

A "place of business" includes any premises, facilities or installations used for the carrying on of the business. It is important to note, however, that a non-resident person may have a "place of business" even if he or she does not have premises available for carrying on the business provided that he or she has a certain amount of space available at his or her disposal. The space or premises may be owned, rented or in any other way available to him or her for the conduct of his or her activities. A place of business may even be situated in the business facilities of another enterprise.

(b) Permanent Establishment

Double taxation treaties between developed countries almost invariably predicate the taxation of the business profits of foreign enterprises on the existence of a permanent establishment in the taxing State. Thus, the existence of a "permanent establishment" determines whether a Contracting State has the right to tax the profits of an enterprise that is resident in another State.

The concept of "permanent establishment" is also relevant for the purposes of determining the source of interest and royalty payments under the provisions of the OECD Model Convention.[6]

(i) OECD Model Convention

Article 5(1) of the OECD Model Convention states the general test for a permanent establishment:

> 1. For the purposes of this Convention, the term "permanent establishment" means a fixed place of business through which the business of an enterprise is wholly or partly carried on.

The term "permanent" implies something more than a transitional or passing connection between an enterprise and a country. A "permanent establishment" requires more than transient business relations or connection between a geographical point and a place of business. There must be some fixed connection. Apart from that, however, the requirements for a fixed place of business are quite minimal. A hotel room or the living accommodation of a travelling salesman may qualify as a "permanent establishment". It is immaterial whether the premises are rented or owned by the enterprise.

The Commentary to the OECD Model Convention states:

> The place of business has to be a "fixed" one. Thus, in the normal way there has to be a link between the place of business and a specific geographical point. It is immaterial how long an enterprise of a Contracting State operates in the other Contracting State if it does not do so at a distinct place, but this does not mean that the equipment constituting the place of business has to be actually fixed to the soil on which it stands. It is enough that the equipment remains on a particular site.

---

[6] Articles 10 and 11, *OECD Model Convention*.

Although "permanent establishment" implies a certain degree of permanency, it does not necessarily mean that an establishment set up for a very short period of time cannot be a "permanent" place of business. One must also look to the duration of time in the context of the activity to determine whether it was "permanent" during its existence. Thus, a place of business that is set up at the outset for a short temporary purpose because of the nature of the enterprise's activity may, nevertheless, constitute a fixed place of business and a permanent establishment for tax purposes.

Article 5(2) of the OECD Model Convention lists some of the types of presence that constitute a permanent establishment:

> 2. The term "permanent establishment" includes especially:
>
> (a) a place of management;
>
> (b) a branch;
>
> (c) an office;
>
> (d) a factory;
>
> (e) a workshop; and
>
> (f) a mine, an oil or gas well, a quarry or any other place of extraction of natural resources.

Notwithstanding the use of the words "includes especially" in Article 5(2), the types of places listed are not deemed to be a permanent establishment. They constitute only prima facie evidence of a permanent establishment. Article 5(2) must be read in the context of Article 5(1). Thus, the types of places listed constitute permanent establishments only if they have a degree of permanence sufficient to be a fixed place of business.[7]

A special rule applies to construction projects. A building site, construction or installation project can be a permanent establishment, but only if lasts more than 12 months.

Article 5(3) of the OECD Model provides that:

> 3. A building site or construction or installation project constitutes a permanent establishment only if it lasts more than twelve months.

The 12-month requirement is the *sine qua non* for qualification as a permanent establishment. Thus, a building site, construction or installation project in which an office or a workshop is situated does not qualify as a permanent establishment if it does not satisfy the time test.

The 12-month test applies to each individual site or construction project. Thus, each site is to be considered as a self-contained project and only the time spent on that particular location counts for the purposes of determining whether or not the 12-month test is satisfied.

---

[7]   See paragraph 12, *OECD Commentary* on Article 5(2).

Certain types of facilities are deemed to be excluded from the term "permanent establishment". Article 5(4) provides:

> 4. Notwithstanding the preceding provisions of this Article, the term "permanent establishment" shall be deemed not to include:
>
> a) the use of facilities solely for the purpose of storage, display or delivery of goods or merchandise belonging to the enterprise;
>
> b) the maintenance of a stock of goods or merchandise belonging to the enterprise solely for the purpose of storage, display or delivery;
>
> c) the maintenance of a stock of goods or merchandise belonging to the enterprise solely for the purpose of processing by another enterprise;
>
> d) the maintenance of a fixed place of business solely for the purpose of purchasing goods or merchandise or of collecting information, for the enterprise;
>
> e) the maintenance of a fixed place of business solely for the purpose of carrying on, for the enterprise, any other activity of a preparatory or auxiliary character;
>
> f) the maintenance of a fixed place of business solely for any combination of activities mentioned in subparagraphs (a) to (e) provided that the overall activity of the fixed place of business resulting from this combination is of a preparatory or auxiliary character.

Article 5(4) is a deeming provision and takes precedence over Articles 5(1), (2) and (3). There can be no permanent establishment if it is determined that the presence or facility qualifies under one of the exclusions in Article 5(4). The common feature of the listed activities is that they are either preparatory or auxiliary activities. The exclusion applies even if there is a fixed place of business maintained solely for any combination of the listed activities, provided that the overall activity of the fixed place of business is of a preparatory or auxiliary character.

The exclusions of Article 5(4) are premised on two bases. First, that the economic linkage of an enterprise engaged solely in auxiliary or preparatory activities in a Contracting State is not sufficiently firm to justify the taxation of business profits by that State. Second, there is a practical problem in that it is extremely difficult to determine the business profits attributable to preparatory and auxiliary activities.

(ii) Dependent Agents

An enterprise is deemed to have a permanent establishment in a Contracting State where a dependent agent acts on its behalf in the State and the agent has, and habitually exercises, an authority to conclude contracts in the name of the enterprise. Article 5(5) of the OECD Model Convention states as follows:

> 5. Notwithstanding the provisions of paragraphs 1 and 2, where a person—other than an agent of an independent status to whom paragraph 6 applies—is acting on behalf of an enterprise and has, and habitually exercises, in a Contracting State an authority to conclude contracts in the name of the enterprise, that enterprise shall be deemed to have a permanent establishment in that State in respect of any activities which that person undertakes for the enterprise, unless the activities of such person are limited to those mentioned in paragraph 4 which, if exercised through a fixed place of business, would not make this fixed place of business a permanent establishment under the provisions of that paragraph.

Thus, dependent agents with a power to contract, other than those engaged in activities of a preparatory or auxiliary character, can cause an enterprise to have a permanent establishment in a Contracting State. The dependent agent may be an individual, corporation, or other body or persons. A subsidiary corporation can also be a dependent agent with power to contract on behalf of its parent company.

An employee is, of course, a dependent agent of his or her employer when he or she acts within the scope of his or her authority. But not all employees have or exercise the power to contract on behalf of their employers. Article 5(5) applies only if the dependent agent has an authority to conclude contracts in the name of the enterprise that he or she represents. "Authority" would appear to include "apparent" authority or authority by estoppel. Thus, it is the agent's actual behaviour that determines whether or not he or she has sufficient power to constitute a permanent establishment of his or her enterprise.

Further, it is not sufficient for the agent merely to have the authority to conclude contracts. He or she must, in fact, habitually exercise the authority on behalf of the enterprise. The term "habitually" implies a certain degree of continuity in the agent's activities.

(iii) Independent Agents

The activities of an independent agent (for example, a broker or general commission agent) on behalf of an enterprise do not constitute a permanent establishment of the enterprise if the independent agent is acting in the ordinary course of business. The independent agent must be both legally and economically independent.

Article 5(6) of the OECD Model Convention provides that:

> 6. An enterprise shall not be deemed to have a permanent establishment in a Contracting State merely because it carries on business in that State through a broker, general commission agent or any other agent of an independent status, provided that such persons are acting in the ordinary course of their business.

(iv) Parent and Subsidiaries

A controlling interest held by a parent corporation in its subsidiary does not of itself constitute either corporate entity a permanent establishment of the other. Thus, tax treaties recognize the independence and separate legal status of corporations in much the same way as private law. Similarly, a one person corporation and its sole shareholder do not constitute a permanent establishment for each other merely by virtue of the control relationship between them.

Article 5(7) of the OECD Model Convention provides as follows:

> 7. The fact that a company which is a resident of a Contracting State controls or is controlled by a company which is a resident of the other Contracting State, or which carries on business in that other State (whether through a permanent establishment or otherwise), shall not of itself constitute either company a permanent establishment of the other.

(v) Business Profits

"Business profits" constitute the single most important category of economic activity in international trade. Thus, Article 7 (Business Profits) of the OECD Model Convention (and its counterpart in international double taxation treaties) is key to the formulation of international business structures.

Article 7(1) of the OECD Model Convention states:

> 1. The profits of an enterprise of a Contracting State shall be taxable only in that State unless the enterprise carries on business in the other Contracting State through a permanent establishment situated therein. If the enterprise carries on business as aforesaid, the profits of the enterprise may be taxed in the other State but only so much of them as is attributable to that permanent establishment.

Article 7(1) states the general rule: an enterprise is taxable only in its State of residence. The exception to the general rule is that if an enterprise carries on business in another Contracting State, the other Contracting State may tax the enterprise if it is carrying on business through a permanent establishment situated therein. In that case, the enterprise's business profits may be taxed in the other Contracting State but only to the extent that the profits are attributable to that permanent establishment. Thus, Article 7 raises the threshold for subjecting a non-resident enterprise to tax from the "solicitation and offering for sale" level[8] to the much higher "permanent establishment" test. Hence, a non-resident enterprise is not taxable in a treaty country merely because it concludes therein business contracts from which it derives profits. To be taxable by that country, it must have a permanent establishment in the country.

Article 7(1) contains the four essential conditions for the taxation of a non-resident business enterprise:

- the existence of an enterprise;
- the carrying on of a business by the enterprise;
- a place of business that is fixed; and
- through which the enterprise carries on its business.

A non-resident enterprise that meets these conditions is taxable on its business profits in the State where it conducts its business, but only to the extent of the profits attributable to the permanent establishment in that State.

The rationale for confining the taxation of business profits to those attributable to a permanent establishment is that a country should not tax foreign persons until such time as the foreign person becomes closely involved in the economic affairs of the country. The OECD Commentary states as follows:[9]

> . . . it has come to be accepted in international fiscal matters that until an enterprise of one State sets up a permanent establishment in another State it should not properly be regarded as participating in the economic life of that other State to such an extent that it comes within the jurisdiction of that other State's taxing rights.

---

[8]   S. 253.

[9]   Commentary, *OECD Model Convention.*

The Model Convention's approach is also justified on administrative considerations. Multi-national business enterprises often conduct different segments of their operations through different entities which may be located in different jurisdictions. Thus, it is not unusual for one entity to manufacture in one country, another to be responsible for sales through agents in another country, and still another entity to be responsible for service and maintenance in a third jurisdiction. It would be difficult, if not impossible, to attempt to attribute the profitability of each separate segment of the business to one or other of the permanent establishments through which the entities operate. The OECD is of the view that it is not desirable to interfere with existing business organizational structures and that it would not be productive to inflict unnecessarily onerous demands for information on foreign enterprises.

This is not, however, the only view. Some jurisdictions which do not come within the scope of double taxation treaties because they are merely political subdivisions of a country have rules which extend their jurisdiction to tax beyond the confines of permanent establishments located in their jurisdiction. California, for example, has a unitary tax which extends well beyond its territorial limits. The right of political subdivisions to tax profits generated outside their boundaries is constitutionally valid in the United States and does not offend the Foreign Commerce Clause of the U.S. Constitution.[10]

(vi) Enterprise

The term "enterprise" is not defined in the OECD Model Convention. The term generally means "business". An enterprise's business activities refer to any independent activity other than the use of immovable property within the meaning of Article 6(3) and other independent personal services within the meaning of Article 14 of the Model Convention.

(vii) Business Through a Permanent Establishment

Article 7 requires that the enterprise carry on its business through a permanent establishment in the Contracting State if it is to be taxable in that State. Hence, it is necessary to look at an enterprise's activities and determine whether its activities are conducted through a particular location. Mere physical presence is not sufficient. For example, the rental of real estate located in a Contracting State does not by itself render the property a fixed place of business if the enterprise does not carry on its business on the real property.

(viii) Profits Attributable to Permanent Establishment

The State in which an enterprise has a permanent establishment is entitled to tax its business profits, but only to the extent that the profits are attributable to the permanent establishment. Thus, the application of Article 7 is contingent on the enterprise's business profits being economically connected to the permanent

---

[10] *Barclays Bank v. Franchise Tax Board of California*, (1994), 129 L E 2d 244.

establishment in the taxing State. Hence, the Article requires an allocation between profits which result from the permanent establishment's activities and those which are attributable to other centres of the enterprise, for example, its head office. This rule provides incentive for enterprises to syphon off and allocate profits and losses between countries in order to minimize their overall international tax burden. There are, however, provisions to control such abuses.[11]

(c) Branch Operations

A non-resident corporation can do business in Canada through a branch. A branch is not a separate legal entity and there are no immediate tax consequences upon its creation.

The decision to do business in Canada as a branch, rather than as a subsidiary, depends upon business and tax considerations. Since a branch is not a separate legal entity, it does not insulate the non-resident corporation from exposure to full legal liability. The debts and obligations of the branch operation are the responsibility of the non-resident corporation.

The business income of a branch is generally taxed in a manner similar to the income of domestic companies. In addition to the Part I tax, however, a branch is also liable for Part XIV tax (the "branch tax") on its net after-tax business profits to the extent that the profits are considered to have been repatriated from Canada.

The rationale of the branch tax is to ensure that business profits bear the same amount of tax regardless of the legal form of organization through which the business is conducted. However, having said that equality of taxation is the cornerstone of the branch tax mechanism, it is important to note that there can be substantial differences in the overall tax burden of a branch versus that of a subsidiary. These differences may arise as a result of differences in the timing of repatriation of profits or the manner of disposition of the branch.

(i) Tax Rationale

The advantages of setting up a business in Canada as a branch operation are as follows:

- A branch operation is generally quite easy to set up with minimal start up costs and legal requirements.
- Some of Canada's tax treaties provide for a limited branch tax exemption. The *Canada-U.S. Treaty*, for example, exempts the first $500,000 (Cdn.) of branch profits from the branch tax.
- The thin capitalization rules[12] do not apply to branches.

---

[11] See, for example, Article 9, *OECD Model Convention.*

[12] Subs. 18(4).

The disadvantages of operating a branch are as follows:

- In addition to filing returns in the home jurisdiction, the branch must also file a return with respect to its Canadian source income.
- Allocation of income and expenses between a branch and its head office may be quite difficult in certain circumstances and invite audit disputes with the revenue authorities.

Since a branch is not a separate legal entity, its profits and losses are attributable to the non-resident corporation. Branch start-up losses can be offset against the non-resident corporation's income. Thus, the desirability of a branch structure may be contingent upon the existence of sufficient income in the home country to offset losses. This advantage is reduced if the home country permits consolidated reporting of related party corporate income for tax purposes.

The thin capitalization rules do not apply to branch operations. Thus, there is considerably greater flexibility in financing branch operations through debt capital and maximizing interest deductions.

Finally, a branch's profits may be protected from the branch tax by virtue of a double tax treaty. The Canada-U.S. and the Canada-U.K. Treaties, for example, exempt the first $500,000 (Cdn.) of branch profits from tax in the source country. Thus, a branch can be used to start up a business and later incorporated into a separate subsidiary corporation upon utilization of the $500,000 exemption.

(ii) Income Earned in Canada

The profits of a non-resident corporation carrying on business in Canada are taxable in Canada.[13] Canadian double taxation treaties provide, however, that the liability for Canadian tax arises only if the non-resident is carrying on business through a permanent establishment in Canada. Where a branch constitutes a permanent establishment, it is necessary to determine the portion of the profits of the non-resident enterprise that are attributable to the permanent establishment in Canada.

Article 7 of the OECD Model Convention states the general principles by which the business profits of an enterprise are attributed to a permanent establishment. The Model Convention restricts the right to tax the business profits of a non-resident enterprise. Only business profits generated through a permanent establishment and attributable to it are taxable by the source country. This rule is premised on the principle that an enterprise should not be regarded as participating in the economic life of the source country until such time as it has a direct and intimate involvement with the country. This approach is conducive to the simple and efficient administration of tax statutes and generally follows the way in which business is organized and transacted.

---

[13] Para. 2(3)(*b*).

Article 7 of the OECD Model Convention reads as follows:

1. The profits of an enterprise of a Contracting State shall be taxable only in that State unless the enterprise carries on business in the other Contracting State through a permanent establishment situated therein. If the enterprise carries on business as aforesaid, the profits of the enterprise may be taxed in the other State but only so much of them as is attributable to that permanent establishment.

2. Subject to the provisions of paragraph 3, where an enterprise of a Contracting State carries on business in the other Contracting State through a permanent establishment situated therein, there shall in each Contracting State be attributed to that permanent establishment the profits which it might be expected to make if it were a distinct and separate enterprise engaged in the same or similar activities under the same or similar conditions and dealing wholly independently with the enterprise of which it is a permanent establishment.

3. In determining the profits of a permanent establishment, there shall be allowed as deductions expenses which are incurred for the purposes of the permanent establishment, including executive and general administrative expenses so incurred, whether in the State in which the permanent establishment is situated or elsewhere.

4. Insofar as it has been customary in a Contracting State to determine the profits to be attributed to a permanent establishment on the basis of an apportionment of the total profits of the enterprise to its various parts, nothing in paragraph 2 shall preclude that Contracting State from determining the profits to be taxed by such an apportionment as may be customary; the method of apportionment adopted shall, however, be such that the result shall be in accordance with the principles contained in this Article.

5. No profits shall be attributed to a permanent establishment by reason of the mere purchase by that permanent establishment of goods or merchandise for the enterprise.

6. For the purposes of the preceding paragraphs, the profits to be attributed to the permanent establishment shall be determined by the same method year by year unless there is good and sufficient reason to the contrary.

7. Where profits include items of income which are dealt with separately in other Articles of this Convention, then the provisions of those Articles shall not be affected by the provisions of this Article.

The determination of "business profits" is a matter for the domestic law of the State in which the permanent establishment is located. Under Canadian tax rules, income is segregated by source and income from each source in a particular place is calculated as if:[14]

- there is no income or loss except from that source;
- there are no deductions except those which are wholly applicable to that source; and
- indirect expenses are allocated on a reasonable basis as applicable to that source.

Hence, direct expenses such as the cost of goods sold, selling expenses, capital cost allowance on branch assets, and interest expense on specific borrowings for a branch asset are allocated directly to the branch. Indirect expenses such as general and administrative expenses and interest on general borrowings must be allocated to the branch on some reasonable basis.

---

[14] S. 4.

There is no set method for the allocation of indirect expenses. There are various allocation methods, all of which are somewhat arbitrary. For example, allocations may be made on the basis of sales, assets, gross income, number of employees, size of payroll or on some combination of these criteria.

Similarly, there are no hard and fast rules in respect of the sourcing of business income and expenses to a permanent establishment. The source of business income and expenses may be determined by where:

- contracts are made;
- decisions to purchase and sell are made;
- payment is made;
- delivery of goods is made;
- the goods are produced;
- services are performed;
- the profit making operation is located; or
- in the case of real estate, the property is situated.

(d) Subsidiary Corporations

A non-resident may do business in Canada either through a foreign incorporated subsidiary or a Canadian subsidiary. A Canadian subsidiary is taxable as a resident corporation on its world-wide income.[15] A foreign subsidiary corporation that is not resident in Canada is subject to tax only on its Canadian source income.

The advantages of operating through a subsidiary corporation are as follows:

- The subsidiary corporation is a separate legal entity and generally offers limited liability protection for its parent corporation.
- Since the subsidiary corporation is a separate entity, tax reporting is generally limited to its activities without disclosure of its parent corporation's operations.
- Since the subsidiary is a separate entity, it is generally much easier to account for its income and expenses and there are fewer allocational problems.
- Subsidiaries with substantial (at least 50 per cent) Canadian equity ownership may be eligible for tax incentives such as the small business deduction on the first $200,000 of active business income.
- Business reorganizations are generally easier to conduct through corporations than through other forms of organization.

---

[15] Subs. 2(1).

The disadvantages of a subsidiary corporation are as follows:

- Since a subsidiary is a separate legal entity, its losses may not be consolidated with the income of other related entities for Canadian tax purposes. Thus, a parent corporation cannot directly utilize its subsidiary's losses.

- Subsidiaries that are minimally financed with non-resident equity capital give rise to thin capitalization problems.

- Dividends from a Canadian subsidiary to a non-resident parent corporation are subject to withholding tax of 25 per cent (subject to treaty reduction).

- Subject to treaty exemptions, capital gains realized on an arm's length sale of shares of a Canadian corporation by its foreign parent are subject to taxation.

- A subsidiary corporation may be considered resident both in Canada and in its home country. This may create problems of double taxation for the subsidiary. Most Canadian double taxation treaties, however, contain "tiebreaker" rules which minimize the risk of double taxation.

- The purchase and set-up of a subsidiary corporation is generally easier than the purchase of an unincorporated business.

(e) Conversion of a Branch to Subsidiary

A branch may be converted into a subsidiary corporation by transferring its branch assets to the corporation. The theory underlying an asset transfer from a branch to a subsidiary is that the branch is considered to have disposed of its assets. In the absence of special provisions, the assets are deemed to have been disposed of at their fair market value.[16]

Section 85 permits a rollover of branch assets to a taxable Canadian corporation without triggering any immediate tax consequences. Thus, accrued gains on most assets (inventory, depreciable and non-depreciable capital property) may be deferred through appropriate elections.

Section 85 requires that the transferor receive share consideration for the assets disposed of to the taxable Canadian corporation. The parties must also jointly elect to determine the cost basis of the assets transferred to the corporation and the share consideration received in exchange. Thus, any accrued but unrealized gains from the assets disposed of will eventually be recaptured when the shares received in exchange are ultimately disposed of by the transferor.

The subsidiary corporation will ultimately be liable for tax on any accrued gains on assets that it acquires. Thus, a rollover under section 85 almost inevitably creates a potential problem of double taxation in the long run.

---

[16] S. 69.

(i) Reserves

The Act generally prohibits the deduction of reserves in computing income from business or property.[17] Reserves may be deducted only if they are specifically authorized, and then only according to specific methods.

The basic scheme for the deduction of reserves is that a reserve claimed in a year must be added back to income in the following year and a new reserve may be claimed according to the particular provision. Thus, the deduction of reserves is cyclical: Amounts deducted in one year are included in income in the following year, a new amount is claimed as a reserve, and so on.

Where a branch is converted into a subsidiary, the cycle of deductions and inclusions is broken: Reserves claimed in the penultimate year of the branch's operations are brought into its income in the final year without a corresponding deduction. This has the effect of inflating income in the final year of branch operations.

(ii) Doubtful Accounts

Section 22 is an elective provision which allows for the continuity of reserves for doubtful accounts and bad debts. An election under section 22 allows the transferor of accounts receivable to claim a deduction for the amount by which the consideration received for the receivables is less than their face value. The election is particularly useful where the transferee corporation is controlled by the person who sells the receivables, since the stop-loss rules in subsection 85(4) would ordinarily preclude the recognition of any losses on transfers of capital property to a controlled corporation.

Section 22 may be used only where the branch transfers all or substantially all of its property (including accounts receivable) used in carrying on its business to a subsidiary and the subsidiary intends to continue the business previously conducted by the branch. Thus, the section 22 election is typically only available if the Canadian branch constitutes a separate business that disposes of all or substantially all of its assets to a subsidiary corporation.

(f) Branch Tax

The principal objective of the branch tax is to remove the incentive that would otherwise exist for foreign corporations to avoid the Canadian withholding tax on dividends by carrying on their business in Canada through branch operations. Thus, the Part XIV tax is intended to equalize the tax burden between branch and subsidiary operations carrying on business in Canada. The tax base on which the Part XIV tax is imposed, however, is different from the base upon which the subsidiary operation would be subject to Part XIII withholding tax. Hence, the objective of tax equalization is not always realized.

---

[17]   Para. 18(1)(e).

Non-residents who carry on business in Canada at any time in a year through a branch operation are subject to the branch tax under Part XIV.[18] The branch tax is levied at a rate of 25 per cent (subject to treaty reduction) on the branch's Canadian net after-tax income. The Canada-U.S. Treaty exempts Canadian branches of U.S. corporations from the branch tax up to a maximum of $500,000 (Cdn.) accumulative branch profits.

The base upon which the branch tax is calculated (generally, Canadian net after-tax income) is reduced by the amount of any profits reinvested in qualifying Canadian property. The amount by which the base is reduced in one year is added to income in the following year and a new allowance may be taken if the branch was carrying on business in Canada at the end of the year. Thus, the allowance for the reduction in the branch tax base is not available to the branch in the year that it ceases to carry on business and is incorporated into a subsidiary corporation.

In limited circumstances, however, the branch tax normally payable upon a transfer of assets to a subsidiary may be deferred. The deferral is available only if the transferor receives shares of a Canadian corporation with a low paid-up capital as consideration for the transferred branch assets.[19] The requirement that the shares have a low paid-up capital ensures that the accumulated profits on which the branch tax is deferred can only be extracted from Canada as dividends subject to withholding tax and not through repatriation of share capital. The deferral is available only to the extent that qualified property is transferred to a wholly-owned subsidiary corporation.

"Qualified property" is defined as property used by the branch immediately before the transfer for the purpose of earning income from a business that it carried on in Canada. The transferee corporation must be a Canadian corporation that becomes a wholly-owned subsidiary corporation immediately after the transfer. Thus, the branch tax can be eliminated if the paid-up capital of the shares issued as consideration for qualified property does not exceed the elected amount of the qualified property less the non-share consideration in the prior year's investment allowance.

2. FINANCING

(a) General Considerations

The manner of financing a foreign operation depends upon several considerations. One has to consider the availability of funds and the cost of financing in the host and home countries, foreign exchange exposure and restrictions, debt-equity capital ratios and the anticipated cash flow from business operations to pay for borrowed capital.

Part XIII of the Act imposes a withholding tax on payments to non-residents by residents of Canada, but there are numerous exceptions and exemptions from the

---

[18] S. 219.

[19] Para. 219(1)(k).

withholding tax. The withholding tax is not generally intended to be levied on interest payments made by non-residents to other non-residents. For example, the withholding tax on interest payments by a non-resident would apply only if the non-resident:

- carried on its business principally in Canada;
- manufactured or processed goods in Canada; or
- was engaged in certain resource-related activities in Canada.

A corporation is considered to carry on its business principally in Canada if more than 50 per cent of its activities occur in Canada.

A foreign corporation can finance its Canadian operations in several ways. For example, a foreign corporation may:

- borrow and lend money to its Canadian subsidiary;
- borrow and invest in the equity of its Canadian subsidiary;
- borrow and allocate interest to its Canadian branch operations; or
- borrow and capitalize a non-resident-owned investment ("NRO") corporation which can finance the Canadian subsidiary.

Each of these options has tax consequences which need to be considered in determining the structure of the non-resident's business operations in Canada.

The thin capitalization rules disallow the deduction of interest expense on indebtedness to a non-resident related party which exceeds three times the subsidiary's equity capital. The thin capitalization rules, however, only apply to corporations that are resident in Canada. They do not apply to non-resident corporations.

(b) Debt vs. Equity Capital

One of the early decisions that a foreign business needs to make in respect of its Canadian operations is whether it will finance its business through debt or equity capital. The decision must take into account both business and tax considerations.

The advantages of financing a Canadian business through debt capital are as follows:

- There is no requirement that interest be charged on debt capital. Interest expense is, however, deductible on money borrowed and used for the purpose of earning income from a business provided that the amount claimed is reasonable and is not incurred in the pursuit of exempt income.
- Interest paid to a non-resident person by a Canadian resident is generally subject to a withholding tax at source of 25 per cent (subject to treaty reduction).[20] There are, however, extensive exemptions from the withholding tax.

---

[20] S. 212.

- Funds may be borrowed either in a foreign currency and converted to Canadian dollars or directly from a Canadian lender. There are no foreign exchange controls, but foreign exchange gains and losses can give rise to either income or capital depending upon the circumstances.

The principal disadvantage to a corporation heavily capitalized with debt capital is its exposure to the thin capitalization rules.

(c) Interest Expense

The deduction of interest expense is one of the more important deductions for businesses and investors. One starts with the simple accounting premise that interest represents the cost of the use of money over a period of time and, therefore, should be deductible as an expense if incurred for the purpose of earning income. Unfortunately, the Supreme Court of Canada decreed that interest on borrowed money is an expenditure on account of capital because a deduction on account of borrowed money would necessitate a similar deduction on account of invested capital:[21]

> It is important to remember that, in the absence of an express statutory allowance, interest payable on capital indebtedness is not deductible as an income expense. If a company has not the money capital to commence business, why should it be allowed to deduct the interest on borrowed money? The company setting up with its own contributed capital would, on such a principle, be entitled to interest on its capital before taxable income was reached, but the income statutes give no countenance to such a deduction.

Thus, in the absence of specific authority, expenditures on account of interest would not be deductible as an expense.[22]

The Act does, however, specifically authorize the deduction of interest where it:[23]

- is paid or payable in the year;
- arises from a legal obligation; and
- is payable on money borrowed used for the purpose of earning income (other than exempt income) from a business or property.

---

[21]   *Canada Safeway Ltd. v. M.N.R.*, [1957] CTC 335 at 344, 57 DTC 1239 at 1244 (S.C.C.).

[22]   Para. 18(1)(*b*).

[23]   Para. 20(1)(*c*).

These seemingly simple requirements for the deductibility of interest are, in fact, mired in technical detail which has accumulated as a result of judicial interpretation and reinterpretation over the years.[24]

(i) Definition

"Interest" is the return or consideration for the use or retention by one person, of a sum of money belonging or owed to another.[25] It represents a legal obligation calculated by reference to a principal sum of money that is owed. The obligation to pay interest may arise from an express agreement, by legal implication, or, in some cases, by statute.

Whether a payment is actually labelled as being on account of interest is totally irrelevant to its characterization.

(ii) Legal Obligation

To be deductible as an expense by the borrower, the lender must have legal rights to enforce payment of the amounts due. There is no such thing in law as gratuitous interest. The obligation to pay interest must be actual rather than contingent. There is no general requirement in law that the indebtedness must be documented to constitute a legal debt. It is, however, prudent to reduce to paper any obligations to pay interest.

(iii) Use of Money

Paragraph 20(1)(c) of the Act allows a taxpayer to deduct from income "an amount paid in the year or payable in respect of the year . . . pursuant to a legal obligation to pay interest on borrowed money used for the purpose of earning income from a business or property . . . or a reasonable amount in respect thereof, whichever is the lesser". The phrase " used for the purpose of . . ." incorporates two interrelated tests for determining the deductibility of interest expense: use and purpose. Both tests must be satisfied.

The use test is concerned with the physical flow of funds to determine the application of borrowed moneys. It is the use to which borrowed funds are actually put that determines the deductibility of interest payable on the funds.[26]

---

[24] *Interprovincial Pipeline Co. v. M.N.R.*, [1967] CTC 180, 67 DTC 5125; affirmed [1968] CTC 156, 68 DTC 5093 (S.C.C.) (total interest payments deductible in proportion to various sources of income generated by borrowed money); *Sherritt Gordon Mines Ltd. v. M.N.R.*, [1968] CTC 262, 68 DTC 5180 (Ex. Ct.) (commitment fee deductible as part of cost of borrowing capital for exploration and development of mine, plant and refinery); *Montreal Light, Heat and Power Consol. v. M.N.R.; Montreal Coke & Mfg. Co. v. M.N.R.*, [1944] CTC 94, 2 DTC 654 (P.C.) (deduction for premium, foreign exchange and discount on new bonds not permitted; financial arrangements distinct from expenditures strictly applied toward earning income).

[25] *Ref re s. 6 of Farm Security Act. 1944 of Sask.*, [1947] SCR 394 at 411 (S.C.C.); affirmed [1949] AC 110 *(sub nom. A.G. Sask. v. A.G. Can.)* (P.C.).

[26] *Bronfman Trust v. The Queen*, [1987] 1 CTC 117; 87 DTC 5059 (S.C.C.).

(A) Direct vs. Indirect Use

There are two ways in which one can look at the use of borrowed funds. Direct use can be traced by following the funds from the lender to the investment to which the funds are applied. The indirect use of funds involves their having been applied to facilitate the investment of other funds in an income producing process.

The use test is concerned with the physical flow of funds to determine the application of borrowed moneys. It is the use to which borrowed funds are actually put that generally determines the deductibility of interest payable on the funds.[27] In other words, in most cases, deductibility of interest expense is determined by the direct use test. In *Sinha v. M.N.R.*,[28] for example, a student borrowed from the Canada Student Loan Plan at a low rate of interest and reinvested the borrowed funds at a higher rate. The Board rejected the Minister's argument that the purpose of the borrowing was personal and allowed the taxpayer to deduct his interest expense since he actually utilized the borrowed money for investment purposes.

(B) Purpose of Borrowing

The second aspect of the test to determine the deductibility of interest is that the funds must be borrowed for the purpose of earning income from business or property. Thus, the taxpayer must have a bona fide intention to use the borrowed money for income earning purposes. Actual realization of income is irrelevant. The purpose test is concerned with the taxpayer's intention. Bronfman Trust considered the inter-relationship between the use and purpose tests:[29]

> Eligibility for the deduction is contingent on the use of borrowed money for the purpose of earning income. It is well established in the jurisprudence, however, that it is not the purpose of the borrowing itself which is relevant. What is relevant, rather, is the taxpayer's purpose in *using* the borrowed money in a particular manner. . . . Consequently, the focus of the inquiry must be centred on *the use to which the taxpayer put the borrowed funds.* [Emphasis added.]

For example, a taxpayer who borrows money at a given rate of interest and lends out the funds at less than his or her borrowing cost cannot be said to be borrowing for the purpose of earning income. Thus, the absence of an intention to earn income might render interest non-deductible, even when the actual use to which borrowed funds are put would otherwise qualify the payment as a deductible expense.

---

[27] *Bronfman Trust v. The Queen*, [1987] 1 CTC 117, 87 DTC 5059 (S.C.C.).

[28] *Sinha v. M.N.R.*, [1981] CTC 2599, 81 DTC 465 (T.R.B.).

[29] *Bronfman Trust v. The Queen, ante*, [1987] 1 CTC at 125, 87 DTC at 5064.

The deduction for interest expense is restricted to amounts expended for the purpose of earning income from business or property. Interest incurred to earn capital gains is not deductible against income.[30]

(C) The "Real" Purpose

The purpose of borrowing is generally determined by tracing the direct use of the borrowed money. In multi-step arrangements, however, the deductibility of interest may depend upon the real purpose of the series of transactions. In Mark Resources Inc.[31] for example, the Tax Court of Canada looked to the ultimate purpose of borrowing for an investment in the taxpayer's subsidiary.

The facts in Mark Resources Inc. were as follows:

- The taxpayer, a Canadian corporation ("Canco") borrowed funds from a bank for a predetermined period at a specified interest rate;
- Canco contributed the borrowed funds to its U.S. subsidiary ("Subco") as contributed capital;
- Subco invested the funds in a term deposit equal to the term of the loan, but at a rate of interest lower than that payable by Canco on its loan payable to the bank;
- Subco posted the term deposit with the bank as security for Canco's loan;
- The amount of the loan, its term and the purchase of the term deposit was calculated to raise income equal to Subco's accumulated losses;
- Subco's interest income from its term deposit was offset against its accumulated U.S. losses;
- Subco did not pay U.S. taxes on its interest income;
- Subco used its interest from the term deposit to pay a tax-free (net of 10 per cent withholding tax) dividend to Canco;
- Canco used its dividend income to pay the interest on its bank borrowing;
- Upon utilization of Subco's accumulated U.S. losses, the term deposit matured and the funds received were loaned back to Canco;
- Canco used the funds to repay its own loan to the bank;

---

[30] See., e.g., *Hastings v. M.N.R.*, [1988] 2 CTC 2001 (T.C.C.) (interest expense on commodities trades not deductible); *Sterling v. The Queen*, [1985] 1 CTC 275, 85 DTC 5199 (F.C.A.) (interest and safekeeping charges for purchase of gold bullion not deductible in determining capital gain); *The Queen v. Can. Pacific Ltd.*, [1977] CTC 606, 77 DTC 5383 (F.C.A.) (deduction of interest under old subsection 8(3) only where corporation subject to Part I tax); *Birmingham Corp. v. Barnes*, [1935] A.C. 292 (clarification of capital costs for laying tramway lines where expenditure contributed to by another party).

[31] *Mark Resources Inc. v. The Queen*, [1993] 2 CTC 2259, 93 DTC 1004 (T.C.C.).

- Subco was then liquidated and the inter-corporate loan and contributed capital were offset against each other;

- Canco deducted its interest expense on its bank borrowing from its income for Canadian tax purposes.

Subco had recently ceased to carry on business and was, in essence, a shell corporation whose only real value lay in its accumulated U.S. losses.

Each step in the series of transactions was properly executed:

- Canco's transactions with the bank were at arm's length and the rate of interest charged was quite reasonable in the circumstances;

- The income from the term deposits arose out of a normal commercial transaction and there was nothing improper about the payment of the dividends;

- The documentation that was necessary to implement each of the steps in the arrangement was properly prepared and executed.

Thus, the transactions were legitimate and properly executed. They were real transactions and the rights and obligations created by each step of the arrangement were those which they purported to be. The arrangement was not a sham.

The tax objective of the arrangement was to utilize Subco's accumulated U.S. losses (which would otherwise expire) and to do so on a tax efficient basis by making Canco's interest deductible for Canadian tax purposes. The essence of the scheme required four elements:

- no cost to Subco on the funds that it invested in the term deposits;

- deductible interest to Canco on its borrowing from the bank;

- tax-free interest income to Subco on the term deposit in the U.S. because of its offsetting losses; and

- tax-free dividends from Subco to its parent (Canco) by virtue of the deduction for dividends (section 113) from foreign affiliates.

The Tax Court looked to the "real purpose" of the use of the borrowed funds in the entire series of transactions and not only at the purpose of their immediate use:[32]

> Here the immediate step of investing in a subsidiary that in accordance with the scheme must necessarily pay dividends was not the real purpose of the use of the funds. The earning of interest income . . . and the payment . . . of dividends . . . were integral but subservient and incidental steps to the real objective that lay behind the implementation of the plan. . . . It is true that the overall economic result, if all the elements of the plan work, is a net gain to the appellant, but this type of gain is not from the production of income but from a reduction of taxes otherwise payable in Canada.

---

[32] *Mark Resources Inc. v. The Queen, ante,* [1993] 2 CTC at 2270, 93 DTC at 1012.

Canco was not entitled to the deduction for its interest expense because it did not satisfy the test in paragraph 20(1)(c) of the Act. The borrowed funds were not used for the purpose of earning income.

Mark Resources necessarily implies that in multi-step arrangements, the deductibility of interest expense depends upon the real purpose of the "series of transactions" and not the purpose of the immediate and direct use of the funds. There is, however, no authority for importing a series of transactions approach into paragraph 20(1)(c) of the Act. The phrase "series of transactions", which appears 41 times in the Act, is not used in paragraph 20(1)(c). Where the Act uses the phrase "series of transactions" the series is deemed to include any related transactions or events completed in contemplation of the series.[33] It is reasonable to infer from the absence of the phrase in paragraph 20(1)(c) that there was no legislative intention to import the series test into that paragraph.

Mark Resources clearly involved blatant tax avoidance: Subco's accumulated losses were about to expire, the funds were directly traceable in a series of transactions from the bank to the investment, the terms deposits, and back again to the bank; Subco was liquidated immediately after its losses were utilized. The loan from the bank, the issuance of the term deposit and its deposit with the bank as security were all done through a foreign branch of the Canadian bank. No money was ever transferred either to Canada or the U.S. or used in the operations of either Canco or Subco. Thus, the series of transactions used to implement the scheme constituted "tax avoidance" intended to utilize Subco's losses on a tax efficient basis. Today, such a scheme would need to be analyzed under the general anti-avoidance rule ("GAAR") in section 245. The rule did not apply to the assessment years under review. Prior to the enactment of GAAR, tax avoidance was not, per se, offensive, and business transactions did not require a business purpose to be valid.[34] Tax reduction was a sufficient justification.

(iv) Indirect Use

What happens if borrowed moneys are only indirectly used to earn or preserve income? Bronfman Trust[35] dealt with this point. Samuel Bronfman created a trust in favour of his daughter, under the terms of which the beneficiary was to receive annually, 50 per cent of the income from the trust property and such additional allocations as the trustees in their discretion might have decided. The capital of the trust was invested in income earning securities, some in family enterprises and others in marketable securities. The trustees, having decided to make capital allocations of $2 million to the beneficiary, chose to borrow the funds rather than liquidate trust capital to make the payment. They elected to borrow the funds because they considered it to

---

[33] Subs. 248(10).

[34] *Stubart Invt. Ltd. v. The Queen*, [1984] CTC 294, 84 DTC 6305 (S.C.C.).

[35] *Bronfman Trust v. The Queen, ante.*

be financially inexpedient to liquidate any portion of the trust's investments at that time. Was the borrowed money used for the purpose of earning income from property? By borrowing money and using the money to pay the capital allocations, the trustees had preserved intact the income yielding capacity of the trust's investments. That was not sufficient, however, to characterize the borrowed money as having been used for the purpose of earning income from property. In Chief Justice Dickson's words:[36]

> In my view, the text of the Act requires tracing the use of borrowed funds to a specific eligible use, its obviously restricted purpose being the encouragement of taxpayers to augment their income-producing potential. This, in my view, precludes the allowance of a deduction for interest paid on borrowed funds which indirectly preserve income-earning property but which are not directly "used for the purpose of earning income from . . . property".

This principle applies to all taxpayers including corporations, trusts and individuals.[37]

Deductibility depends upon the intention of the borrower at the time the funds are invested rather than upon the actual materialization of income at some later date. Provided that the funds are employed in a venture that has the potential for earning net income, the actual results of the income earning process are irrelevant to the determination of deductibility of the interest expense.[38] For example, interest on borrowed funds invested in a business venture that loses money is deductible. In this context, it is important to emphasize that the intention must be to earn income from business or property and not from capital gains. Income from capital gains is not income from property.[39] Thus, interest expenses incurred solely to earn capital gains or avoid losses are not deductible in computing income from business or property.[40]

(v) Current Use

It is quite clear that it is the current use to which borrowed funds are put that determines the deductibility of interest as an expense. As Jackett, P. said in Trans-Prairie:[41]

---

[36] *Bronfman Trust v. The Queen, ante,* [1987] 1 CTC at 129, 87 DTC at 5067.

[37] *Bronfman Trust v. The Queen, ante.*

[38] See: *Lessard v. M.N.R,* [1993] 1 CTC 2176, 93 DTC 680 (T.C.C.) (interest on funds used to acquire shares deductible even though taxpayer was sole shareholder because shares constituted a potential source of income).

[39] Subs. 9(3). See: *Ludmer v. M.N.R,* (1993) 2 CTC 2494 93 DTC 1351 (T.C.C.) affirmed; [1994] 1 CTC 368, 94 DTC 6221 (F.C.T.D.).

[40] *Bronfman Trust v. The Queen, ante.* ("The fact that the loan may have prevented capital losses cannot assist the taxpayer in obtaining a deduction from income which is limited to use of borrowed money for the purpose of earning income"). See also: *The Queen v. Mandryk,* [1992] 1 CTC 317, 92 DTC 6329 (F.C.A.) (taxpayer not entitled to deduct interest expense to honour personal guarantees of corporate indebtedness).

[41] *Trans-Prairie Pipelines Ltd. v. M.N.R.,* [1970] CTC 537, 70 DTC 6351 at 6354 (Ex. Ct.), approved by S.C.C. in *Bronfman Trust v. The Queen, ante.*

... interest should be deductible for the years in which the borrowed capital was employed in the business rather than that it should be deductible for the life of a loan as long as its first use was in the business. . . .

Similarly, in Bronfman Trust:[42]

... a taxpayer who uses or intends to use borrowed money for an ineligible purpose, but later uses the funds to earn non-exempt income from a business or property, ought not to be deprived of the deduction for the current, eligible use. . . .

Hence, if a taxpayer initially borrows money to invest in income earning property and then diverts those funds to a non-income earning purpose (for example, personal use), any interest incurred on the borrowed funds will cease to qualify for deductibility as of the date of change of use of the funds.[43] Conversely, interest on funds initially borrowed for personal purposes and later used for business purposes also qualifies for deduction as of the date of change of use. For example, a taxpayer who borrows money to purchase a residential cottage for personal use and then sells the cottage to use the proceeds for investment purposes is entitled to deduct the interest payable on the funds as of the date of the investment.

(vi) Reloaned Funds

Where an individual borrows money and then relends that money to his or her corporation, the deductibility of the interest paid by the individual depends upon that person's purpose for lending the money to the corporation. It is quite clear that funds borrowed by a taxpayer at a commercial rate of interest and reloaned at a lower rate cannot be considered to be funds used by the taxpayer for the purpose of earning income from a business or property; hence, any interest payable on the funds is *prima facie* not deductible. Revenue Canada will allow a deduction to the extent of the income actually earned.

Revenue Canada generally takes the view that interest on borrowed money is not deductible in whole or in part if the money is reloaned at a lesser rate of interest than that at which it is borrowed. It does, however, permit exceptions where a shareholder borrows and relends to his or her corporation. Revenue Canada's position is outlined in the following paragraphs:[44]

7. . . . the Department will generally permit a deduction for the full interest expense incurred when a taxpayer borrows money at interest to be loaned to a Canadian corporation of which he is a shareholder, or to its Canadian subsidiary, at less than a reasonable rate of interest, (or at no interest), if the following conditions are met:

---

[42] *Bronfman Trust v. The Queen, ante,* [1987] 1 CTC at 125, 87 at 5065.

[43] Subpara. 20(1)(c)(i).

[44] IT-445, "The Deduction of Interest on Funds Borrowed Either to be Loaned at Less Than a Reasonable Rate of Interest or to Honour a Guarantee Given for Inadequate Consideration in Non-arm's Length Circumstances" (February 23, 1981), paras. 7, 8.

(a) the proceeds of the loan are used by that corporation in its own operations to produce income from business or property which will be subject to Part I tax in Canada, or are used by that corporation to loan to its Canadian subsidiary, at less than a reasonable rate of interest (or at no interest), to be used in its operation to produce income from business or property which will be subject to Part I tax in Canada.

(b) the corporation has made every effort to borrow the necessary funds through the usual commercial money markets but cannot obtain financing, without the guarantee of the shareholder, at interest rates at which the shareholder could borrow, and

(c) the loan from the shareholder to the corporation at less than a reasonable rate of interest (or at no interest) does not result in any undue tax advantage being conferred on either the shareholder or the corporation. The Department does not consider that any undue tax advantage is conferred on either the shareholder or the corporation where the use of loans with interest at less than market rates between associated corporations is for the purpose of offsetting non-capital losses within the group of associated corporations.

8. Examples of situations where the Department considers that an undue tax advantage has been conferred on either the shareholder or the corporation are as follows:

(a) the capital cost allowance restrictions of subsection 1100(11) or (15) of the Regulations are circumvented by the corporation being able to claim capital cost allowance in excess of the maximum that would have been allowed had the corporation borrowed the money from the shareholder at a reasonable rate of interest, or

(b) provincial income tax is reduced through loans made to a corporation reporting its income in a province with a lower tax rate than that in which the shareholder who made the loan reports and it is evident that there was no other substantial business purpose for the loan.

(vii) *Exempt Income*

To be deductible, the interest expense must not have been incurred on money borrowed to acquire property, the income from which would be exempt, or to acquire a life insurance policy.[45]

(viii) *Compound Interest*

A taxpayer is entitled to deduct interest on interest, otherwise known as compound interest, if all of the other conditions of deductibility are satisfied.[46] Compound interest is only deductible when it is paid and not when it is merely payable.

Where a taxpayer makes a blended payment of capital and interest, an amount equal to the interest component may be deducted.[47]

---

[45] "Exempt income" is defined as money or property received or acquired by a person in such circumstances that it is, by reason of any provision in Part I, not included in computing income, but does not include a dividend on a share. See subs. 248(1) ("exempt income").

[46] Para. 20(1)(*d*).

[47] Subs. 16(1).

(ix) Discounts

A discount is the amount by which the face value of the debt obligation exceeds its issue or selling price. The discount can arise on issuance of the obligation or later, in accordance with market fluctuations in interest rates.

Discounts on obligations may be deductible in whole or in part in the year paid.[48] Where an obligation is issued at a price of at least 97 per cent of its principal amount and does not yield an amount in excess of 4/3 of the nominal interest rate, the entire amount of the discount is deductible in computing income. Where a bond is issued for an amount less than 97 per cent of its face amount, or its yield exceeds 4/3 of its nominal interest rate, only 3/4 of the discount is deductible in computing income.

A discount on a debt obligation which does not normally stipulate an interest rate (strip coupon bonds, for example) is considered to be interest if the discount is reasonable in the circumstances.

(x) Refinancing

Where money is borrowed to repay money previously borrowed, the second borrowing is deemed to be made for the same purposes as the original borrowing.[49] Note, however, that refinancing debt may be challenged. In Bronfman,[50] the Supreme Court indicated in dicta that such transactions may be scrutinized to determine whether they constitute a formality or a sham. In determining whether a refinancing constitutes a sham, a court will look at the interval of time between the original and refinanced loan.

(xi) Existence of Source

An essential requirement for the deduction of interest is the continued existence of the source of income to which the interest expense relates.[51] Interest on borrowed money must be traceable to an eligible use in order for the expense to be deductible. For example, a taxpayer who finances the purchase of investment securities may claim any directly related interest expense as a deduction, provided he or she continues to hold the original investment or substituted securities. This is so even if the security declines in value or becomes worthless.

---

[48] Para. 20(1)(f).

[49] Subs. 20(3); see also ATR-4 "Exchange of Interest Rates" (November 29, 1985).

[50] Bronfman Trust v. The Queen, [1987] 1 CTC 117, 87 DTC 5059 (S.C.C.).

[51] Emerson v. The Queen, [1986] 1 CTC 422, 86 DTC 6184; leave to appeal to S.C.C. refused (1986), 70 NR 160 (taxpayer not allowed to deduct interest on money used to purchase shares after selling shares at loss); see also Deschenes v. M.N.R., [1979] CTC 2690, 79 DTC 461 (T.R.B.); Alexander v. M.N.R., [1983] CTC 2516, 83 DTC 459 (T.R.B.); Lyons v. M.N.R., [1984] CTC 2690, 84 DTC 1633 (T.C.C.); McKay v. M.N.R., [1984] CTC 2804, 84 DTC 1699 (T.C.C.); Botkin v. M.N.R., [1989] 2 CTC 2110, 89 DTC 398 (T.C.C.); The Queen v. Malik, [1989] 1 CTC 316, 89 DTC 5141 (F.C.T.D.); Dockman v. M.N.R., [1990] 2 CTC 2229, 90 DTC 1804 (T.C.C.); Kornelow v. M.N.R., [1991] 1 CTC 2403, 91 DTC 431 (T.C.C.).

The deduction is not available if the investment is sold and the funds are not invested in another income earning property. Thus, a continuing obligation to pay the creditor does not necessarily imply that the funds are used for an eligible purpose.

(xii) Accrued Interest

The purchaser of a debt obligation (other than an income bond, income debenture, small business development bond, or small business bond) is allowed to deduct interest accrued but unpaid to the date of the purchase, to the extent that the amount is included as interest in computing income for the year. At the same time, the accrued interest paid to the vendor of the debt obligation is included in computing the vendor's income.[52]

(xiii) Financing Costs

A taxpayer is allowed to deduct expenses incurred in issuing shares or in borrowing money for the purpose of earning income from a business or property.[53] These financing expenses, which typically include legal and accounting fees, printing costs, commissions, etc., would otherwise be caught by the prohibition against deducting expenses not directly related to the income-earning process.[54] These expenses are deductible on a rateable basis over a five-year period.

(xiv) Capitalizing Interest

(A) General

In certain circumstances, a taxpayer may prefer not to write off interest expense against current operations. For example, there may be little advantage in taking a deduction for interest expense on money borrowed to construct an asset if the asset is not producing income. Where the deduction of interest would merely create a loss that cannot be used within the time limits allowed for carryover of losses,[55] the taxpayer may prefer to treat interest charges as part of the cost of the asset and then write off the total cost of the asset when it begins to produce income. In other words, she or he may prefer to treat interest costs as a capital expenditure rather than as a current expense.

---

[52] Subs. 20(14); IT-410R "Debt Obligations — Accrued Interest on Transfer" (September 4, 1984). This rule only operates where there has been an assignment or transfer of title; evidence of registration of title would likely be necessary. See: *Hill v. M.N.R.*, [1981] CTC 2120, 81 DTC 167 (T.R.B.) ("bond flip"; interest payment for carrying cost of bonds not deductible); *Smye v. M.N.R.*, [1980] CTC 2372 (T.R.B.) (purchase of bonds plus accrued interest; upon sale, taxpayer deducted price for accrued interest from investment yield of bond).

[53] Para. 20(1)(e).

[54] *Montreal Light, Heat & Power Consol. v. M.N.R.*, [1944] CTC 94, 2 DTC 654 (P.C.); *The Queen v. Royal Trust Corp. of Can.*, [1983] CTC 159, 83 DTC 5172 (F.C.A.) (whether or not payment constitutes "commission" is a question of fact).

[55] See para. 111(1)(a) (limitation period in respect of non-capital losses).

(B) Depreciable Property

A taxpayer who acquires depreciable property with borrowed money may elect to capitalize the interest charges.[56] Two points should be noted. First, only those costs which would otherwise have been deductible as interest expense or as an expense of borrowing money may be capitalized. Interest expense to earn exempt income is not deductible and may not be capitalized. Second, the election is available not only in respect of costs incurred in the year in which the asset is acquired, but also in respect of costs incurred in the three immediately preceding taxation years. The extension of the election to the three preceding years recognizes that large undertakings extend over many years and that money may be borrowed, and expenses incurred, prior to the period in which the money is actually used for its intended purpose of constructing a capital asset.

(C) Election

The election must be made for the taxation year in which:

- the depreciable property is acquired, or
- the money borrowed has been used for exploration, development, or the acquisition of property.

A taxpayer may not elect to capitalize interest in anticipation of the acquisition of depreciable property or the use of borrowed money for exploration or development; she or he can only elect after acquiring the property or expending the funds. When the election is made, however, it is effective for borrowing costs and interest incurred in the current year and in the three preceding years.

A taxpayer may only elect under subsection 21(1) for the taxation year in which the depreciable property is acquired. Where a building or other structure is being erected by a taxpayer, it is considered to have been "acquired" at any time to the extent of the construction costs at that time. Hence, a taxpayer must file a separate election for each taxation year in respect of the interest expense related to that year. This election is explained in Revenue Canada's IT-121R3 "Election to Capitalize Cost of Borrowed Money" dated May 6, 1988.

The election does not have to be made in respect of the full amount of the costs of borrowing; a taxpayer may elect to capitalize only part of the interest charges and deduct the remainder as a current expense.

The portion of the interest that is capitalized is added to the capital cost of the depreciable property acquired. Thus, the capitalized cost will eventually be written off through capital cost allowance. The adjusted cost base of the property will also be

---

[56] S. 21. Special restrictions on "soft costs" are discussed below; see subs. 18(3.1).

increased for the purpose of determining capital gains upon disposition of the property.[57]

(D) Reassessment

Where the taxpayer has elected to capitalize interest charges, if the election is made on interest which would otherwise have been deductible in preceding years, the Minister is required to reassess the taxpayer for those taxation years. Having made the election, the taxpayer may continue to capitalize interest in succeeding years if in each of those succeeding years, the entire amount of the interest on the property is capitalized.

(E) Compound Interest

A taxpayer is also permitted to capitalize compound interest and the expense of raising money. For example, a taxpayer may be required to pay a commitment fee to a financier before the necessary funds have been advanced to the taxpayer. The commitment fee, or standby interest, may be capitalized as part of the cost of borrowed money.[58]

(F) "Soft Costs"

"Soft costs" (such as interest expense, mortgage fees, property taxes, commitment fees, etc.) incurred in respect of the construction, renovation or alteration of a building, may not be deducted as current expenses during construction and must be added to the cost of the building.[59] Similarly, "soft costs" in respect of land subadjacent to a building under construction must be capitalized. The restriction on the deduction of these expenses only applies in respect of outlays incurred before completion of construction, renovation or alteration of the building.

The scope of the prohibition against writing off soft costs as current expenses is very broad. Included in interest expenses are expenses incurred on borrowed money used to finance working capital if it "can reasonably be considered" that the borrowed money freed up other funds for the construction of the building. In other words, "indirect financing" is caught by the prohibition.[60]

---

[57] Para. 54(*a*).

[58] *Sherritt Gordon Mines Ltd. v. M.N.R.*, [1968] CTC 262, 68 DTC 5180 (Ex. Ct.).

[59] Subs. 18(3.1). This rule does not apply to capital cost allowance, landscaping costs or scientific research expenditures.

[60] Subs. 18(3.2).

(xv) *Limitations on Deduction*

(A) Real Estate

(I) General Limitation

A taxpayer cannot deduct carrying charges (interest and property taxes) in respect of vacant land to the extent that the expenses exceed income from the land.[61] Thus, carrying charges on land are only deductible to the extent of the taxpayer's net revenues from the land. The purpose of this rule is to discourage speculation in real estate.

(II) Exceptions

Land that is used in the course of a business is exempt from the limitation in respect of carrying charges for land. However, the exemption from the rule does not apply to property developers whose business is the sale or development of land, or to land that is held, but not used, in a business.

(III) Corporations

A special rule applies to corporations whose principal business is the leasing, rental, sale or development of real property. Corporations engaged in these businesses may deduct their carrying charges on vacant land. The maximum deduction is equal to the lesser of:[62]

- the income, net of all deductions, from the land, and
- the corporation's "base level deduction" for the year.

A corporation's base level deduction for a taxation year is the amount of interest for the year in respect of $1 million of debt outstanding for the year, computed at the prescribed rate of interest.[63] Thus, the base level deduction is, in effect, the absolute maximum a corporation can deduct in a year. For example, at a prescribed rate of 10 per cent, the absolute maximum deduction for carrying charges would be $100,000.

The base level deduction of a corporation which is a member of an associated group of corporations is determined by reference to a prescribed agreement that each corporation must file. The $1 million to which the prescribed rate is applied must be allocated amongst the associated members of the group. The Minister has the power to allocate the deduction if the corporations do not file their agreements.

---

[61] Subs. 18(2).

[62] Subs. 18(2).

[63] Subs. 18(2.2).

(B) Thin Capitalization

The "thin capitalization"[64] rules limit the deduction which a corporation may claim for interest on debts owing to non-residents and persons who are related to such persons. The rules apply to limit the deductibility of interest where the corporation's debt to equity ratio in relation to the specified non-residents exceeds 3:1.

(C) Automobiles

Certain expenditures (for example, automobile expenses) incurred in the course of earning income can involve elements of both business and personal use. The Act attempts to regulate the deduction of the personal component of some of these expenditures in various ways. The rule for automobile financing is arbitrary and simple: deductible interest expense in respect of financing a passenger vehicle cannot exceed $300 times the number of months in respect of which the expense is payable.[65] Hence, the maximum deductible interest expense in respect of an automobile is $3,600 per year.

(d) Thin Capitalization

One of the principal considerations in setting up a new business operation in Canada is the choice of the form of organization through which the business will be conducted. The use of a subsidiary corporation is clearly an option. The choice of a subsidiary corporation inevitably raises the question as to whether it should be financed by way of debt capital or by way of equity capital.

The use of debt capital is frequently advantageous because of the deductibility of interest expense in the computation of income. In contrast, dividends on share capital are paid from after-tax dollars and may be subject to double taxation. Hence, it is sometimes advantageous to finance a Canadian subsidiary corporation through debt capital on which interest payments can be fully deductible for Part I tax purposes. Thus, a Canadian subsidiary corporation may benefit from the deduction and save approximately 44 per cent Part I tax and pay a withholding tax of 15 per cent (treaty rate) on interest payments to non-resident persons. If properly structured, the debt can also be set up so as to avoid withholding tax on interest paid to non-residents. To counter this type of manipulation, the Act contains special rules which deny the deduction of interest expense to a domestic corporation which is considered to be "thinly capitalized".

From the parent corporation's perspective it may be more advantageous to finance its subsidiary through equity capital rather than through debt. The return on equity capital is normally through dividends and dividends are often tax exempt to the

---

[64] Subs. 18(4)—(8); IT-59R3 "Interest on Debts Owing to Specified Non-Residents (Thin Capitalization)" (September 28, 1984).

[65] S. 67.2.

recipient corporation or, if not exempt, subject to a lower rate of tax than that applicable to interest income from debt. The ultimate structure will depend upon the consolidated effects on the parent and subsidiary corporations.

The thin capitalization rules only apply where the debtor is a corporation. They do not apply to loans made to partnerships.

(i) Alternative Approaches

There are two broad alternative approaches to attack thinly capitalized corporations: fixed formula denial of interest and anti-abuse legislation. Canada uses the fixed formula regime to control thin capitalization.

Canada relies substantially on the formulary approach. Subsection 18(4) provides that where a subsidiary corporation's debt to related party non-residents results in a debt to equity ratio in excess of 3:1, any interest on the excess portion of the loan over the maximum approved proportion is automatically disallowed for tax purposes. The formula is fixed and precise and the result is mathematically determinable.

The anti-abuse approach to thin capitalization has two principal variations. Under one variant, one looks to the circumstances to determine whether capital should be classified as debt or equity. Hence, for example, one approach is to look at the substance of the financing over its form to see if the subsidiary corporation's capital should be regarded as debt or equity.

Under the second variant of the anti-abuse approach, one applies an arm's length yardstick to determine the amount of loan that would be made in a comparable commercial transaction where the parties were dealing with each other at arm's length. Under this approach, the debt to equity ratio would constitute one, but not necessarily the determinative, factor in asserting whether a corporation was thinly capitalized.

(ii) OECD Model Convention

The interpretation of a double tax treaty generally depends upon the domestic law of the particular country concerned. The OECD Model Convention, however, has an important role to play in the interpretation of domestic law. The transfer pricing rules play a vital role in non-arm's length transactions between corporations.

Article 9 of the Model Convention concerns associated enterprises (such as parent and subsidiary corporations) under common control. The Article allows for an adjustment in the computation of taxable profits when associated enterprises do not transact with each other on an arm's length basis. The Article does not have any effect where associated enterprises transact with others on normal open market commercial terms.

Article 9 of the Model Convention reads as follows:

1. Where

   a) an enterprise of a Contracting State participates directly or indirectly in the management, control or capital of an enterprise of the other Contracting State, or

b) the same persons participate directly or indirectly in the management, control or capital of an enterprise of a Contracting State and an enterprise of the other Contracting State,

and in either case conditions are made or imposed between the two enterprises in their commercial or financial relations which differ from those which would be made between independent enterprises, then any profits which would, but for those conditions, have accrued to one of the enterprises, but, by reason of those conditions, have not so accrued, may be included in the profits of that enterprise and taxed accordingly.

2. Where a Contracting State includes in the profits of an enterprise of that State — and taxes accordingly — profits on which an enterprise of the other Contracting State has been charged to tax in that other State and the profits so included are profits which would have accrued to the enterprise of the first-mentioned State if the conditions made between the two enterprises had been those which would have been made between independent enterprises, then that other State shall make an appropriate adjustment to the amount of the tax charged therein on those profits. In determining such adjustment, due regard shall be had to the other provisions of this Convention and the competent authorities of the Contracting States shall if necessary consult each other.

The purpose of Article 9 is to prevent economic double taxation of the same income. It achieves this result through a restrictive rule that prevents treaty countries which adopt the Article from unilaterally increasing the taxable profits of an enterprise to an amount higher than that which would be determined under an equivalent arm's length commercial transaction.

An enterprise is considered to be associated with another enterprise if one participates directly or indirectly in the management, control or capital of the other enterprise. Enterprises may also be associated with each other where the same persons participate directly or indirectly in the management, control or capital of the other enterprise.

The OECD Committee on Fiscal Affairs' Report on Thin Capitalization was of the view that the Article is relevant in the determination of whether the rate of interest in a loan contract is an arm's length rate. It is also pertinent to the determination as to whether capital is considered as debt or as equity.

The general rule is that an enterprise's profits are taxable only by the Contracting State in which the enterprise has its residence. Profits are determined according to the domestic law of the Contracting State. For example, the thin capitalization rules apply to determine the amount of interest that is deductible for Canadian tax purposes. Article 9 permits an adjustment of the profits determined in accordance with domestic rules where associated enterprises do not transact with each other on an arm's length basis.

The application of the thin capitalization rules to a particular enterprise should not have the effect of increasing its taxable profits to more than the arm's length equivalent that would have been earned had it been transacting under normal commercial conditions. The application of a rigid statutory formula for the disallowance of interest in a thinly capitalized corporation may result in an increase in taxable income beyond the amount that would have been determined in an arm's length transaction. In these circumstances, the domestic rule would conflict with Article 9 of the OECD Model Convention.

The legal basis for making interest deduction adjustments to thinly capitalized corporations lies in domestic Canadian law, specifically, subsections 18(4) to (8) of the Income Tax Act. Article 9 of the OECD Model Convention (and its equivalents in double tax treaties) does not, by itself, permit a taxing authority to make an adjustment to the taxable profits of an enterprise. The adjustment must be authorized by domestic law. Article 9 merely restricts the power of the domestic taxing authority so that it cannot make adjustments beyond the amounts that would be earned in equivalent arm's length commercial transactions.

Article 9 focuses on business enterprises that are factually and legally separate entities, but are in some way associated with each other. The underlying rationale of the Article is to prevent the manipulation of profits through transactions that artificially lower prices through the use of distorted "transfer pricing" techniques. Hence, the basic thrust of the Article is to adjust taxable profits to a level comparable to those that would have been achieved in open market transactions.

Article 9(2) deals with economic double taxation that may result from an upward adjustment of taxable profits in one country without an appropriate readjustment in the other country. In essence, the Article provides that where the taxable profits of a subsidiary are revised upwards in one Contracting State, the other Contracting State in which the artificially higher profits will have been earned should provide appropriate relief in order to avoid economic double taxation.

(iii) Canada-U.S. Treaty

Article IX of the Canada-U.S. Treaty, which is substantially similar to the Model Convention, reads as follows:

1. Where a person in a Contracting State and a person in the other Contracting State are related and where the arrangements between them differ from those which would be made between unrelated persons, each State may adjust the amount of the income, loss or tax payable to reflect the income, deductions, credits or allowances which would, but for those arrangements, have been taken into account in computing such income, loss or tax.

2. For the purposes of this Article, a person shall be deemed to be related to another person if either person participates directly or indirectly in the management or control of the other, or if any third person or persons participate directly or indirectly in the management or control of both.

3. Where an adjustment is made or to be made by a Contracting State in accordance with paragraph 1, the other Contracting State shall (notwithstanding any time or procedural limitations in the domestic law of that other State) make a corresponding adjustment to the income, loss or tax of the related person in that other State if:

(a) it agrees with the first-mentioned adjustment; and

(b) within six years from the end of the taxable year to which the first-mentioned adjustment relates, the competent authority of the other State has been notified of the first-mentioned adjustment.

4. In the event that the notification referred to in paragraph 3 is not given within the time period referred to therein, and if the person to whom the first-mentioned adjustment relates has not received, at least six months prior to the expiration of such time period, notification of such adjustment from the Contracting State which has made or is to make such adjustment that State shall, notwithstanding the

provisions of paragraph 1, not make the first-mentioned adjustment to the extent that such adjustment would give rise to double taxation.

5. The provisions of paragraphs 3 and 4 shall not apply in the case of fraud, wilful default or neglect or gross negligence.

The term "person" encompasses a company resident in a third State with, for example, a permanent establishment in either Canada or the United States.

For the purposes of Article IX(2) only, a person is deemed to be related to another person if either participates directly or indirectly in the management or control of the other or if any third person or persons participate directly or indirectly in the management or control of both. Thus, if a resident of any State controls directly or indirectly a company resident in Canada and a company resident in the United States, the Canadian and U.S. company are deemed to be related persons. Thus, Article IX(2) may encompass situations that would not be covered by provisions in the domestic law.[66]

Article IX(3) contains a limitation period for the adjustment to taxable profits. An adjustment of income cannot be made after six years from the end of the taxation year to which the adjustment relates. The adjustment is predicated upon notification within a period of six months to the competent authorities of the other Contracting State. The adjustments to income do not apply in the case of fraud, wilful default, neglect or gross negligence on the part of the taxpayer or any related person.

(iv) Disallowance of Interest Expense

The Act does not provide for a formal recharacterization of debt as equity. This is so even where the amount of non-arm's length debt exceeds the amount that could ordinarily be borrowed at commercial rates from arm's length lenders. The Act does, however, provide for a disallowance of interest expense to the extent that the amount claimed is unreasonable.[67]

Subsection 18(4) of the Income Tax Act disallows a deduction for interest expense paid to specified non-residents on that portion of debt that exceeds three times the borrowing company's equity. For the purposes of this rule, debt means the greatest amount of interest-bearing debt that was outstanding to specified non-residents during the fiscal period.

The greatest amount of outstanding debt during a fiscal period is determined by aggregating all debts outstanding to specified non-residents. Similarly, total interest expense payable for the year is determined by aggregating all interest payable to specified non-residents. The restrictions on interest deductibility apply if the 3:1 ratio of debt to equity is exceeded at any time in the year. Thus, in the extreme case, interest

---

[66] See Technical Explanation to *Canada-U.S. Treaty.*

[67] S. 245.

bearing debt that is outstanding for a period of even one day can result in a substantial restriction on the deductibility of interest expense for the year.

In contrast, the borrower corporation's equity is the amount of its equity at the beginning of the year plus any increases in its paid-up capital during the year.

More specifically, where the amount of "outstanding debts to specified non-residents"[68] exceeds three times the "equity"[69] of the Canadian resident corporation, a pro rata portion of the interest paid or payable in the year to the non-residents may not be deducted in computing the income of the Canadian resident corporation. The formula for determining the non-deductible portion of interest is as follows:

$$
\begin{array}{l}
\text{Interest otherwise} \\
\text{deductible on} \\
\text{outstanding debts} \\
\text{to specified non-} \\
\text{residents}
\end{array}
\quad \times \quad
\frac{
\begin{array}{l}
\text{greatest amount of debts out-} \\
\text{standing to specified non-} \\
\text{residents during year less} \\
\text{3 times equity of corporation}
\end{array}
}{
\begin{array}{l}
\text{greatest amount of debts out-} \\
\text{standing to specified non-} \\
\text{residents during year}
\end{array}
}
$$

The phrase "outstanding debts to specified non-residents" means debts, on which interest expense would otherwise be deductible, owing to a creditor who is a non-resident if the creditor and/or any other person with whom the creditor does not deal at arm's length owns 25 per cent or more of the issued shares of any class of the Canadian resident corporation.

Further, where the lender is a shareholder of the borrower corporation, any excess interest may be taxable as a dividend if it is considered to be an appropriation of profits. The dividend would be subject to withholding tax. The net effect of this approach may be the same as recharacterization of debt as equity for tax purposes.

Revenue Canada is of the view that Canada's double taxation treaties do not modify the thin capitalization rules in subsection 18(4). Since double tax treaties are intended to protect the revenue base of signatory countries and thwart artificial transfers of profits through the manipulation of transfer prices, the thin capitalization rules do not violate the non-discrimination clauses in Canada's treaties. Indeed, it is arguable that the thin capitalization rules support the general principle encountered in double tax treaties that related parties should deal with each other at arm's length.

---

[68] Para. 20(1)(*c*).

[69] Para. 18(5)(*a*).

(v) Anti-avoidance Rule

Apart from the General Anti-Avoidance Rule ("GAAR"),[70] there is a specific rule to prevent taxpayers from avoiding the thin capitalization rules by funnelling loans through third parties. Subsection 18(6) provides that where a specified non-resident loans money to a third party on the condition that the third party lend money to a Canadian corporation, any interest paid to the third party falls within the thin capitalization rules and is treated as if it had been paid directly by the Canadian corporation to a specified non-resident.

Subsection 18(6) covers only back-to-back loan arrangements and does not extend to guarantees or letters of credit from a specified non-resident to a third-party lender. Thus, a Canadian subsidiary corporation may be thinly capitalized through the use of third-party loans guaranteed by the subsidiary's non-resident parent corporation. In these circumstances, however, GAAR may apply if the transaction is viewed as an avoidance transaction that constitutes a misuse of subsection 18(6).

---

[70] Subpara. 18(4)(*a*)(ii).

SELECTED BIBLIOGRAPHY TO CHAPTER XXX

Non-resident Business Operations in Canada

Baker, Samuel R., "Carrying on Business Through a Branch and Disposing of Taxable Canadian Property", in *Proceedings of 27th Tax Conf. 84* (Can. Tax Foundation, 1975).

Boidman, N., "Taxation of Foreign Investment and Business Start-Ups in Canada" (1986), 14 *Int'l. Business Lawyer* 23.

Chan, William C., Clara Ip and Jenny Goh, "Tax Implications of Joint Projects in Canada Between Singaporean and Canadian Companies" (1990), 38 *Can. Tax J.* 96.

Cochrane, E. Cal, "A Review of the New Branch Tax Regulations" (1975), 23 *Can. Tax J.* 142.

Deaves, Brian M., "Advising Non-Residents on Taking Care of Canadian Business" (July 1986), 119 *CA Magazine* 52.

Frommel, S.N., Taxation of Branches and Subsidiaries in Western Europe, Canada and the U.S.A., 2nd ed. (London: Kluwer, 1978).

Goodison, Don, "Fit for Business" (November 1989), 23 *CGA Magazine* 19.

Gordon, M.J., The Taxation of Canadian Subsidiaries of Foreign Corporations, Occasional Paper No. 3 (Ottawa: Canadian Institute for Economic Policy, 1984).

Gordon, Richard A., "The Tax Reform Act of 1986: Impact on U.S. Parent Corporations with Canadian Subsidiaries", in *Proceedings of 38th Tax Conf.* 31:1 (Can. Tax Foundation, 1986).

Hirsch, Morley P., "Canadian Tax Considerations in Structuring Foreign Investment in Canada", in *1984 Prairie Provinces Tax Conf.* 45 (Can. Tax Foundation, 1984).

"Host Country Business Operations: Branch or Subsidiary?" (1986), 7 *Tax Management Int'l. Forum* 1:7.

Humphreys, Brenda, "Hands Across the Border" (May 1989), 63 *CMA* 22.

Krishna, S.S., "Ontario Taxation of Foreign Corporations" (1990), 38 *Can. Tax J.* 601.

Krishna, Vern, "Deducting Non-Capital Losses" (October 1987), 21 *CGA Magazine* 49.

Lindsay, Robert F., "Canadian Subsidiaries and Non-Resident Parent Corporations: Selected Tax Issues", in *Proceedings of 37th Tax Conf.* 21:1 (Can. Tax Foundation, 1985).

Lindsay, Robert F., "Financing of a Canadian Subsidiary by a Non-resident Parent Corporation", *Corporate Management Tax Conf.* 48 (Can. Tax Foundation, 1986).

Lindsay, Robert F., "Purchase and Sale of a Canadian Business by a Non-Resident of Canada", *Corporate Management Tax Conf.* 305 (Can. Tax Foundation, 1984).

Loveland, N.C., "Income Tax Impediments to Foreign Investment in Canada", in *Proceedings of 34th Tax Conf.* 666 (Can. Tax Foundation, 1982).

McLean, Bruce M., "Sourcing of Business Income", *Corporate Management Tax Conf.* 9:1 (Can. Tax Foundation, 1987).

Pennal, Sue, "Canadian Taxation of Non-Resident Insurers" (1989), 37 *Can. Tax J.* 1035.

Perry, Harvey, "Federal Income Tax: Foreign Income of Residents", *Tax Paper No. 89* (Can. Tax Foundation, 1990).

Perry, Harvey, "Federal Income Tax: Non-Residents", *Tax Paper No. 89* (Can. Tax Foundation, 1990).

Silver, Sheldon, "U.S. Business Operations in Canada" (1966), 14 *Can. Tax J.* 368.

Singer, Paul B., "Branch Tax Planning", in *Proceedings of 41st Tax Conf.* 21:1 (Can. Tax Foundation, 1989).

Stacey, J.A. and W.J. Strain, "Investment in Canada" (1989), 43:2 *Bull. Int'l. Fisc. Doc.* 55.

Steiss, Carl F., "Acquisition and Disposition of a Canadian Business by a Non-Resident", *Corporate Management Tax Conf.* 13:1 (Can. Tax Foundation, 1990).

Tremblay, Richard G., "Permanent Establishments in Canada", in *Proceedings of 41st Tax Conf.* 38:1 (Can. Tax Foundation, 1989).

CHAPTER XXXI

OUTBOUND INVESTMENTS AND FOREIGN INCOME

References:

ITA:

S. 90	Dividends Received from Non-resident Corporation
S. 91	Amounts to be Included in respect of Share of Foreign Affiliate
S. 95	Definitions — Shareholders of Non-resident Corporations
S. 113	Deduction in respect of Dividend from Foreign Affiliate
S. 126	Foreign Tax Deduction

REGULATIONS:

5900	Dividends Out of Exempt, Taxable, and Pre-acquisition Surplus
5901	Order of Surplus Distributions
5904	Participating Percentage
5907	Interpretation

BULLETINS, CIRCULARS & RULINGS:

IT-64R3	March 9, 1992	Corporations: Association and Control — After 1988
IT-73R4	February 13, 1989	The Small Business Deduction — Income from an Active Business, a Specified Investment Business and a Personal Services Business
IT-90	February 19, 1973	What is a Partnership?
IT-270R2	February 11, 1991	Foreign Tax Credit
IT-302R3	February 28, 1994	Losses of a Corporation — The Effect that Acquisitions of Control, Amalgamations, and Windings-up have on their Deductibility — After January 15, 1987
IT-343R	September 28, 1994	Meaning of the Term "Corporation"
IT-388	August 15, 1977	Income Bonds Issued by Foreign Corporations
IT-506	January 5, 1977	Foreign Income Taxes as a Deduction from Income
IC 77-9R	June 22, 1983	Books, Records and Other Requirements for Taxpayers Having Foreign Affiliates

1. INTRODUCTION

As Canada increasingly encourages foreign investment and international trade, it has had to adapt its tax policy to meet new needs. Thus, it has a sophisticated structure for the taxation of both direct and indirect foreign investments. To be sure, trade and non-tax factors play a dominant role in the determination of business activities by multinational corporations. But tax rates and the structure of the taxation of direct and indirect foreign investments also play a vital role in the structure of international business transactions and the direction of capital flows. As the OECD said:[1]

> As economic integration in the OECD area proceeds, the economic, technological, and institutional barriers to cross-border investment continue to wane. The pattern of international investment in corporate assets is therefore likely to become increasingly sensitive to cross-country differences in corporate tax rules. In particular, tax differentials may come to exert an important impact on international portfolio investment in shares. Moreover, even though non-tax factors will probably remain the dominant determinant of foreign direct investment in most cases, the influence of tax differentials on the location decisions of multi-national enterprises may also be expected to become stronger. The increasing international mobility of capital therefore may increase the need for international co-ordination of taxes on corporate-source income.

Canada's international tax regime is particularly sensitive to its dependence on international trade and, in particular, trade with its principal trading partner, the United States. But direct investment into the U.S. is only one of the options available to Canadian businesses and individuals. Indirect investments through intermediate holding companies in attractive offshore jurisdictions and treaty havens are now routine and must also be carefully considered in the context of planning for international business transactions. To quote the OECD:[2]

> The removal of non-tax barriers . . . to international capital flows and the globalization of financial markets, has focused attention on the effect of taxation on foreign direct investment. Governments and others are concerned about how taxation may influence inward and outward direct investment flows and the ways in which these investments are financed. They are also concerned with the ways in which the revenues from international transactions are shared between countries and the new avenues opened up by globalization for the avoidance of tax.

But just as governments are concerned about undue tax avoidance and the manipulation of capital flows to take advantage of opportunities offered in low tax jurisdictions, Canadian policy-makers are also concerned about the potential for double taxation of income and the harmful results that flow from such a system. Thus, the tax system attempts to chart a course through these different policy parameters. The resulting complexity is a direct reflection of the underlying conflict between the different interests that are served.

---

[1] Organization for Economic Co-operation and Development, *Taxing Profits in a Global Economy Domestic and International Issues* (Paris: Organization for Economic Co-operation and Development 1991), at 21.

[2] Ibid

"Residence" is the primary basis for taxation in Canada.[3] Canadian residents are subject to tax in respect of their global income.[4] Resident taxpayers may, however, claim a credit against their Canadian tax payable for foreign taxes.[5]

Non-residents are generally subject to Canadian tax only on their Canadian-source income.[6] What constitutes Canadian-source income is a mixed question of fact and law.

Thus, as in the domestic arena, there are two fundamental questions to be answered in the context of foreign operations: (1) Who is taxable? and, (2) What is the basis of taxation?

The income tax consequences of foreign business operations of Canadian taxpayers depend upon four principal factors:

1. the business structure used;
2. the method of financing the structure;
3. the nature of the foreign income earned; and
4. the manner in which profits are repatriated to Canada.

2. STRUCTURES

The form of organization selected to do business or invest is a critical element in determining both the Canadian tax consequences of foreign operations and the tax treatment accorded in the foreign jurisdiction. The choice of structure depends upon local and foreign law. Taxpayers can usually conduct foreign operations as individuals, partnerships (including limited partnerships and joint ventures), or through corporations. The method selected depends in large measure upon the combined effect of the law applicable in the particular foreign jurisdiction and Canadian tax law.

(a) Individuals

Individuals are taxpayers in their own right and are taxable on their global income regardless of where it is earned. An individual is taxable on any dividends that he or she receives in the year from a non-resident corporation.[7] Business and property income from foreign sources is generally taxable on a "net profit" basis subject to a credit for foreign taxes paid.[8]

---

[3]   See Chapters III "Who is Taxable?" and XXVIII "Immigration".

[4]   Subs. 2(1).

[5]   S. 126. See Chapter XIII "Computation of Tax Payable".

[6]   Subs. 2(3); see Chapter XXIX, "Non-residents".

[7]   S. 90, para. 12(1)(k).

[8]   S. 126.

It is not generally advantageous for an individual resident in Canada to directly own shares of a foreign corporation. Dividends from non-resident corporations are taxable without the benefit of the dividend tax credit[9] or deductions available to Canadian holding corporations.[10] Hence, the net tax burden of foreign dividends is usually higher than it would be for dividends from Canadian corporations.

(b) Corporations

Canadian corporations are also subject to tax on their world-wide income. Canadian corporations have a choice, however, as to the manner in which they conduct their foreign operations. A Canadian corporation may operate through a foreign branch or a foreign subsidiary. In certain jurisdictions, for example the United States, a Canadian corporation may also conduct its operations through a "limited liability company" that may be taxable as a partnership.

(i) Branch Operations

The income of a foreign branch of a Canadian resident corporation is taxable in Canada. Whether the branch is taxable in the foreign jurisdiction depends upon the rules applicable to that jurisdiction. Canadian branch operations in countries with which Canada has double taxation treaties are generally subject to tax in the foreign country, but only if they have a "permanent establishment" therein.[11]

Foreign branch profits of a Canadian resident corporation are subject to federal tax (including surtaxes) at the prevailing rate.[12] But branch profits of a permanent establishment are not subject to provincial taxes and, therefore, are not eligible for provincial tax abatements and credits. A resident corporation is entitled to a foreign tax credit for business income taxes paid to the foreign jurisdiction in respect of its branch operations.[13]

Branch profits that are not attributable to a foreign permanent establishment are subject to both federal and provincial taxes in Canada.

(A) Start-up Losses

A branch operation is generally the preferable method to start up a foreign business. This is particularly so if the Canadian resident corporation expects its branch to incur net losses during the start-up period so that the losses can be offset against the corporation's profits. In certain circumstances, corporations can also take advantage of

---

[9] S. 121.

[10] S. 113.

[11] See, generally, Articles 5 and 7, *OECD Model Convention*.

[12] Subs. 123(1), s. 123.2.

[13] Subs. 126(2).

the branch tax exemption in double taxation treaties. The Canada-U.S. Treaty, for example, exempts the first $500,000 of branch profits from tax.

(B) Status of Canadian Corporation

The effect that a foreign branch will have on the tax status of a Canadian corporation has an important bearing on corporate structures. The nature and size of the foreign branch operations will determine whether the Canadian corporation qualifies as a small business corporation ("SBC"). A SBC is a Canadian-controlled private corporation ("CCPC") that carries on an active business primarily in Canada.[14] Shareholders who dispose of shares of a qualified SBC[15] are entitled to a special capital gains exemption of up to $500,000 on the disposition.[16] Shareholders may also realize an allowable business investment loss on the disposition of the shares or debt of a SBC.

A Canadian-controlled private corporation can only qualify as a SBC if all or substantially all (at least 90 per cent) of the fair market value of its assets are attributable to assets used primarily in an active business in Canada. In addition, the corporation is required to derive more than 50 per cent of the fair market value of its assets from active Canadian business assets for a period of 24 months preceding the disposition of the shares. Thus, the existence of a foreign branch operation can be an important determinant in characterizing the tax status of a Canadian corporation as a SBC.

Where a Canadian corporation owns shares of a foreign subsidiary, one of the factors to be considered in determining SBC status is the percentage that the foreign subsidiary's shares represent of the parent's total assets. Where a foreign subsidiary is likely to contaminate its parent corporation's SBC status, it may be preferable to have the foreign subsidiary owned by a sister Canadian corporation.

(C) Small Business Deduction

A CCPC is entitled to claim the small business deduction on its active business income earned in Canada.[17] Active business income of a foreign branch operation is not eligible for the small business deduction. Foreign active business income does not, however, contaminate a Canadian corporation's small business deduction in respect of its domestic business operations.

The profits of a foreign branch must be calculated in Canadian dollars. Foreign exchange gains and losses must be characterized as being on account of income or capital.

---

[14] Subs. 248(1) "small business corporation".

[15] Subs. 110.6(1) "qualified small business corporation share".

[16] Subs. 110.6(2.1).

[17] Subs. 125(1).

(D) Foreign Tax Credits

Foreign branch profits are taxable as they are earned. A resident corporation may, however, claim a federal tax credit for business income taxes paid in respect of its foreign branch.[18] The foreign tax credit in respect of "business income tax" and "non-business income tax" is determined separately in respect of each foreign country.

Generally speaking, the foreign tax credit is limited to the lesser of the income or profits tax paid to the foreign country and the equivalent Canadian tax that would otherwise have been payable if the foreign income had in fact been earned in Canada. Thus, a resident corporation ends up paying the higher of the Canadian or the foreign tax on its foreign source income from branch operations.

Example XXX1.1

Assume:

A Canadian corporation with a foreign branch earns $1000 from its domestic operations and $100 from its foreign branch. The branch is taxed at 34 per cent. Canadian tax is levied at 39.14 per cent.

Then:

Canadian business income	$ 1,000
Foreign branch business income	100
Taxable income	$ 1,100
Foreign tax paid	$ 34
Business foreign tax credit is least of:	
1. Foreign tax paid	$ 34
2. Canadian tax otherwise payable ("CTOP") ($1,100 × 39.14%)	$430
3. CTOP	
Attributable to foreign branch	
$\dfrac{100}{1,100} \times 430$	$ 39
Foreign business tax credit	$ 34

---

[18] Subs. 126(2).

An income or profits tax paid to any foreign tax jurisdiction qualifies as a business-income tax in respect of businesses carried on in the particular country. To qualify for foreign tax credit purposes, the income or profits tax must be paid to the government of a foreign country or to a political subdivision (state, province, etc.) thereof.

The test to determine whether a foreign tax qualifies as an "income or profits tax" is to compare it with its Canadian equivalent. If the basis of the foreign tax is substantially similar to an equivalent Canadian tax, it is considered an income or profits tax for purposes of the foreign tax credit. Foreign taxes that are levied on net income or profits are generally considered to be "substantially similar" to their Canadian equivalent. The following taxes do not qualify as income or profits taxes:

- withholding taxes on gross income;
- sales, commodity, consumption or turnover taxes;
- succession duties or inheritance taxes;
- property or real estate taxes;
- franchise or business taxes;
- customs or import duties;
- excise taxes or duties; and
- gift taxes.

A Canadian corporation is also entitled to a foreign tax credit in respect of foreign non-business income taxes paid. The deduction is equal to the lesser of:

- the foreign non-business income tax paid; and
- the proportion of Canadian tax otherwise payable that is attributable to the non-business income from the particular country.

Non-business foreign tax credits may not be carried over. Thus, unutilized foreign non-business taxes should be deducted under subsection 20(12) of the Act. Alternatively, the Canadian corporation can increase its taxable income through a section 110.5 election in order to fully utilize the foreign taxes.

(E) Determination of Branch Income

The foreign tax credit for a corporation with a foreign branch is limited to that portion of its Canadian tax otherwise payable ("CTOP") that is attributable to the business income of the branch. The limitation is expressed as follows:

$$\text{CTOP} \times \frac{\text{Taxable Income from Foreign Branch Business}}{\text{Taxable Income}}$$

Thus, it is necessary to determine the taxable income of the foreign branch in order to measure its proportion of the resident corporation's taxable income. Unused business foreign tax credits may be carried back for three years or carried forward for seven years.

A foreign branch operation's net income is determined by deducting expenses that specifically relate to the branch or that may be considered to be a reasonable allocation of common or shared expenses from its gross income.

Inventory profits are only recognized upon transfers or sale of inventory to a third party. No profit is recognized on transfers of inventory between a Canadian corporation and its foreign branch operation.

Because of differences in the methods of calculating taxable income between countries, it is possible that the effective rate of foreign tax on a branch may be different than the effective Canadian rate on the income of the branch. This may restrict the resident corporation's ability to fully claim its foreign tax credits.

A Canadian corporation can elect to reduce its excess foreign tax credits. It may, for example, elect under section 110.5 to increase its taxable income by an amount sufficient to utilize the excess foreign tax credit. Any amount added to its taxable income under this election is also added to its non-capital loss carry-over. Non-capital losses may be carried forward only for seven years, but they are not restricted in their application to foreign-source income.

(F) Provincial Abatement

The 10 per cent provincial abatement is not applicable to income allocated to a foreign branch that constitutes a permanent establishment. This is because the income of the foreign permanent establishment is not subject to provincial tax. Thus, the Canadian tax on foreign branch income is 39.14 per cent (including surtaxes). Where the foreign branch does not constitute a permanent establishment, the provincial abatement applies and provincial taxes are imposed on income from a foreign branch.

The definition of a "permanent establishment" in the Regulations, which applies for provincial tax purposes, differs from the definition generally used in Canada's tax treaties. For example, a warehouse in the U.S. would constitute a permanent establishment under the Regulations but would not be so considered under the Canada-U.S. Treaty.[19]

(G) Disposition of Branch Assets

A Canadian corporation that carries on more than one business is required to maintain separate capital cost allowance and cumulative eligible capital cost pools in respect of each of its businesses. Whether or not a Canadian corporation is carrying on two or more separate businesses depends upon the degree of interconnection, interlacing or interdependence of its various operations. In determining the interconnection,

---

[19] See Article V(6), *Canada-U.S. Treaty.*

interlacing or interdependence between business operations, Revenue Canada generally looks at the following:

- the extent to which the two operations have common factors, such as:
  — processes,
  — products,
  — customers,
  — services offered to customers,
  — types of inventories,
  — employees,
  — machinery and equipment;
- whether the operations are carried on in the same premises or in distinct locations;
- whether one operation exists primarily to supply the other and is an integral part of the business that it supplies;
- whether the operations have different fiscal year ends; and
- whether the accounting systems for the businesses are integrated and considered to be the records of one economic entity.

Thus, the disposition of foreign branch assets may have significant Canadian tax consequences. A foreign branch that is considered to be a separate business from the Canadian corporation may be exposed to recapture of capital cost allowance or terminal losses on the disposition of its depreciable property. Similarly, there may be a disposition of eligible capital property in the event that the foreign branch is terminated.

(ii) Incorporation of a Foreign Branch

There is no tax deferral available upon the incorporation of a foreign branch into a foreign subsidiary corporation. Subsection 85(1) permits a rollover only upon the disposition of assets to a taxable Canadian corporation. The rollover is not available in respect of dispositions to foreign corporations. Hence, the incorporation of a foreign branch into a foreign subsidiary generally triggers fully taxable gains and losses in respect of its assets. Any realized gains are subject to full tax liability on a current basis. Losses, however, are deemed to be nil. Thus capital losses and any losses in respect of cumulative eligible capital may not be claimed.

Given the lack of a tax deferred rollover upon the incorporation of a foreign branch, Canadian corporations may consider two options: (1) leasing or licensing branch assets to a foreign subsidiary, or (2) transfer of branch assets to a taxable Canadian corporation followed by corporate emigration.

A lease can be used to defer the gain that would otherwise arise from a disposition of assets. There are, however, withholding tax considerations. For example, payments by the foreign subsidiary to the Canadian corporation in respect of the leased branch assets may be subject to foreign withholding taxes.

(iii) Foreign Subsidiary

A foreign subsidiary of a Canadian corporation is considered to be a separate taxpayer in its own right. The Canadian income tax treatment of income earned by the foreign subsidiary depends upon two factors: the type of income earned and the jurisdiction where it is earned. As a general rule, the active business income of a foreign subsidiary is not taxable to its Canadian parent corporation until such time as it is remitted to the parent. There are, however, different rules in respect of passive income of foreign subsidiaries.

(c) U.S. Business Structures

For the purposes of U.S. federal tax law, organizations are classified either as associations, trusts or partnerships. Associations are taxable as corporations.

Under the Internal Revenue Code ("IRC") a "trust" refers to an arrangement created by will or by an inter vivos declaration whereby trustees take title to property for the purpose of protecting or conserving it for certain beneficiaries under the ordinary rules of equity.[20] Such arrangements are referred to as "ordinary trusts" and are distinguished for tax purposes from "business or commercial trusts".

The concept of a "partnership" for tax purposes is broader in scope than the common law notion of partnership. The term "partnership" includes an unincorporated organization in which two or more persons engage in any business, financial operation, or venture for profit and which is not a corporation, trust or estate for tax purposes.[21]

A "partnership" includes a syndicate, group, pool, joint venture, or other unincorporated organization, through or by means of which any business, financial operation, or venture is carried on, and which is not a trust or state or a corporation.[22] Thus, a partnership is a form of residual business organization that does not fit into either of the other classifications of entities or relationships.

A corporation is a legal entity: an association formed by individuals, trusts, partnerships or other corporations. Corporations are governed by state law. There is no such thing as a "federal corporation" under U.S. law. There are, however, numerous federal laws which govern the conduct of corporations in respect of securities, anti-trust activities and taxation.

The procedures and formalities that create a business corporation are dictated by the relevant state law. Thus, the legal requirements to form or dissolve a corporation and the rules in respect of corporate relationships between directors, shareholders and third parties may vary between jurisdictions. Many states have, however, adopted the Model Business Corporations Act and there is some degree of consistency between the different states.

---

[20] Section 301.7701-4, IRC.

[21] Section 301.7701-3, IRC.

[22] Regulation 301.7701-3.

(i) Tax Status

Under U.S. tax law, a corporation is a taxpayer in its own right and is generally taxed separately from its shareholders. A corporation is taxable on its net business earnings. Its shareholders are also taxable when it pays out dividends, but the shareholders do not receive any credit or deduction for the corporation's taxes. This system of double taxation of corporate income (referred to as the "classical system") applies at both the federal and state levels.

There are some special provisions to relieve the burden of double taxation of corporate income. For example, a special type of corporation (known as the "S Corporation") can elect to eliminate its corporate tax liability and pass through its tax directly to its shareholders. The S Corporation election, however, is limited to corporations that do not have more than 35 shareholders who are all U.S. residents or citizens. As such, the election is limited to closely-held family corporations owned entirely by U.S. residents.

(ii) Shareholders

U.S. shareholders are taxable on dividend income at both the federal and state level. Non-U.S. shareholders, however, are taxable on dividends only at the federal level through the withholding tax system. The general withholding rate is 30 per cent. This rate is reduced to 10 or 15 per cent (depending on the degree of share ownership) by the Canada-U.S. Tax Treaty.[23] U.S. tax treaties apply to corporations formed under the law of any U.S. state. The Canada-U.S. Treaty Protocol signed in 1994 will reduce the withholding tax rate on certain dividends from 10 per cent to 5 per cent. The reduction is to be phased in as follows:

> 1995 — 7 per cent
> 1996 — 6 per cent
> 1997 — 5 per cent

(iii) Formation of Corporations

The procedure for incorporating a U.S. corporation is similar to the process used for a federal incorporation in Canada. The incorporators must select a name that is approved by the state of incorporation and the name must include some reference (for example, "Corp.", "Company", or "Inc.") to indicate corporate status. The incorporators prepare Articles of Incorporation in accordance with the relevant state law (some states have minimum capital requirements). The Articles name at least one incorporator, an initial director, officers and a local registered agent for service of process. The Articles are filed with the Secretary of State together with incorporation fees and capital tax. In most states, the corporation is considered to come into existence as of the date of filing of its Articles.

---

[23] Article X, *Canada-U.S. Income Tax Convention* (1980).

A corporation will have by-laws, appoint a board of directors and issue shares to shareholders. Shares must be in registered form, but nominees are usually permitted. A corporation is required to file annual corporate reports with the Secretary of State in the jurisdiction in which it is incorporated. The report must name current directors and officers, set out the current corporate address, tax identification number, etc. The corporation's annual report is considered a public document and as such is accessible to the public.

(iv) Limited Liability Companies ("LLCs")

The double taxation of corporate income under the classical system is a serious disadvantage of the corporate form of business. It provides an incentive to seek alternative ways to reduce the burden of tax through the use of "pass through" business structures. The S Corporation election is one such alternative, but it does not satisfactorily address the problem because the election is limited to corporations with not more than 35 shareholders. Enter the LLC: a hybrid entity that offers investors the advantages of limited personal liability with the "pass-through" tax features of a partnership.

Many states allow for the formation of LLCs and others are jumping on the bandwagon. Wyoming was the first to enact LLC legislation in 1977. The concept of the LLC, however, did not gain momentum until the Internal Revenue Service ("IRS") ruled that LLCs may in certain circumstances be treated for tax purposes as if they were partnerships. The ability to treat LLCs as "pass through" entities captured the imagination of promoters and investors and the recognition of such companies under Delaware law opened up the market.

(A) Nature of an LLC

An LLC is a legal entity in its own right. It is formed under state law by filing "Articles of Organization" with the relevant state authorities. Since each state has its own rules in respect of the process for forming LLCs, there is no uniformity or consistency between the various states. Generally speaking, however, the common theme under state statutes is that an LLC is an unincorporated association with limited liability: The members of an LLC are not liable for its debts and obligations. It is this marriage between an "unincorporated association" and limited liability that makes the LLC an attractive investment structure for tax purposes.

(B) Formation

Typically, an LLC is formed by having two or more persons subscribe to Articles of Organization which are filed with the relevant state authority. The Articles of Organization require the same information as corporate and partnership registrations: name (including some indication of limited liability status), duration of existence, and registered office. There is, however, less consistency in respect of the formation of LLCs than there is for business corporations. LLCs are comparatively new entities and there is no model statute for the states to follow in enacting their legislation.

(C) Classification for Tax Purposes

For tax purposes "organizations" are considered as associations (which are taxable as corporations), partnerships or trusts.[24]

The major characteristics of an organization are that it has:[25]

1. associates;
2. an objective to carry on business and to divide the gains therefrom;
3. continuity of life;
4. centralization of management;
5. liability for corporate debts limited to corporate property; and
6. free transferability of its interests.

These characteristics determine the nature of the organization and whether it is classified as a partnership or as an association taxable as a corporation. Thus, an LLC may be taxable either as a corporation or as a partnership.

The primary attraction of an LLC is the pass through nature of the entity which allows its profits to flow through directly to its members who are then taxed on the income at their personal rates. This avoids the double taxation problem that is intrinsic in the traditional corporate tax structure.

An organization is considered to be an association taxable as a corporation if its corporate characteristics are such that it more nearly resembles a corporation than a partnership or trust.[26]

Since both corporations and partnerships have associates, carry on business for profit and divide their gains therefrom amongst their members, the determination as to whether an organization should be considered a partnership or a corporation really depends upon the last four characteristics: continuity of life, centralized management, limited liability and free transferability of interests. These four characteristics are sometimes referred to as the "flexible characteristics" to distinguish them from the first two (associates and profit objective) that are common to both corporations and partnerships.

Thus, characterization of LLCs is a process of balancing the entity's features: An unincorporated organization that possesses more corporate characteristics than non-corporate characteristics is taxable as a corporation.[27] Conversely, an organization that has more non-corporate features than corporate is considered a partnership. The

---

[24]　Regulation 301.7701-1.

[25]　Regulation 301.7701-2.

[26]　*Morrissey v. Commissioner* (1935), 296 U.S. 344.

[27]　Regulation 301.7701-2(a)(3).

IRS interprets this rule to mean an organization must have more than two of the four flexible characteristics to be taxable as a corporation. Otherwise, the organization is taxable as a partnership. Each of the four flexible characteristics — continuity of life, centralization of management, limited liability and free transferability of interests — has equal weight in the characterization process.[28]

(D) Continuity of Life

An organization has continuity of life if the death, insanity, bankruptcy, retirement, resignation, or expulsion of any member from the organization does not cause its dissolution.[29]

Dissolution of an organization means an alteration of its identity by reason of a change in the relationship between its members. For example, the resignation of a partner from a general partnership destroys the mutual agency that exists between the partner and his or her co-partners. This alters the personal relationships between the partners. Hence, the resignation of a partner is considered to dissolve a partnership.

In contrast, a corporation has a continuing identity that is separate and apart from that of its stockholders. The death, insanity or bankruptcy of a shareholder or the sale of a shareholder's interest has no effect upon the identity of the corporation and, therefore, does not cause its dissolution.

By agreement, an organization may establish that its business will be continued by the remaining members in the event of the death or withdrawal of any member. Such an agreement does not, per se, establish continuity of life for tax purposes if under local law the organization is considered to dissolve upon the death or withdrawal of any member. Thus, an organization may be dissolved and, therefore, not have continuity of life even though its remaining members carry on its business.

(E) Centralization of Management

An organization has centralized management if any person (or any group of persons) has continuing exclusive authority to make the management decisions necessary to conduct its business.[30] The powers and functions of persons with such authority resemble the directors of a business corporation. Centralized management may come about by virtue of election to office or by any other means that has the effect of giving any group continuing exclusive authority to make management decisions.

Centralized management implies a concentration of continuing exclusive authority to make independent business decisions on behalf of the organization. The managers must have the sole authority to make such decisions. Authority merely to perform

---

[28] *Larson v. C.I.R.* (1976), 66 TC 159.

[29] Regulation 301.7701-2(b).

[30] Regulation 301.7701-2(c).

ministerial acts as an agent at the direction of a principal does not constitute centralized management.

(F) Limited Liability

An organization has limited liability if under local law there is no member who is personally liable for its debts.[31] Personal liability means that a creditor of an organization may seek personal satisfaction from a member of the organization to the extent that the assets of the organization are insufficient to satisfy the creditor's claims.

A member of an organization who is personally liable for its obligation may make an agreement under which another person assumes his or her liability or agrees to indemnify him or her from any such liability. In these circumstances, however, notwithstanding the indemnity agreement the member continues to be personally liable to creditors.

(G) Free Transferability of Interests

An organization is considered to have free transferability of interests if each of its members (or those members who own substantially all of the interests in the organization) have the power to replace themselves in the organization with a person who is not a member of the organization.[32] This power of substitution exists where a member can, without the consent of other members, confer upon his or her substitute all of the attributes of his or her interest in the organization. It does not exist where the member can only confer or assign a portion of his or her rights (for example the right to share in profits) but without assigning, for example, the right to participate in the management of the organization.

(H) Classification of Foreign Unincorporated Business Organizations

A foreign unincorporated organization is classified for U.S. tax purposes on the basis of the six tests described above to determine whether it is a corporation, partnership or a trust. It is important to note, however, that although the tests used to classify foreign organizations are determined under the IRC, it is the local law of the foreign jurisdiction that determines the legal relationships of the members of the organization among themselves and with the public at large.[33]

(v) The Delaware LLC

Delaware is quite clearly the state of choice of incorporation for most business corporations. Delaware corporate law is known, established and well settled. Also, Delaware does not have a state income tax.

---

[31] Regulation 301.7701-2(d).

[32] Regulation 301.7701-2(e).

[33] Regulation 301.7701-1(c). See also Revenue Ruling 73-254.

An LLC may be created under the Delaware Limited Liability Company Act (the "Delaware Act"). Section 18-402 of the Delaware Act provides that unless otherwise provided in a limited liability company agreement, the management of an LLC is vested in its members in proportion to their current percentage interest in the profits of the LLC. An LLC agreement may, however, provide for the management, in whole or in part, of an LLC by a manager who is chosen by its members. Thus, a Delaware LLC may be managed either by an elected manager or by its members.

Section 18-303 of the Delaware Act provides that except as otherwise provided in the Act, the debts, obligations and liabilities of an LLC, whether arising in contract, tort or otherwise, are solely the debts, obligations, and liabilities of the LLC; no member or manager is obligated personally for any debt, obligation or liability of the LLC solely by reason of being a member or acting as a manager of the LLC.

Section 18-701 of the Delaware Act provides that an LLC interest is personal property. An LLC interest is assignable in whole or in part except as provided in an LLC agreement. The assignee of a member's LLC interest has no right to participate in its management and affairs except as provided in the LLC agreement.

Section 18-801 of the Delaware Act provides that an LLC is dissolved upon the first of the following events:

- at the time specified in the LLC agreement or 30 years from the date of its formation if no time is set forth in the agreement;

- upon the happening of events specified in the LLC agreement;

- by the written consent of all members;

- by the death, retirement, resignation, expulsion, bankruptcy, or dissolution of a member or the occurrence of any other event that terminates the continued membership of a member in the LLC unless the business of the LLC is continued either by the consent of all the remaining members within 90 days following the occurrence of any terminating event; or

- by the entry of a decree of judicial dissolution under the Act.

Thus, the Delaware Act contains numerous provisions that can be modified by agreement. Hence, it is possible to structure an LLC organization under Delaware law and have it qualify either as a corporation or as a partnership for federal U.S. tax purposes.[34] That, in essence, is what makes the LLC an attractive form of business organization.

(vi) Cross-border LLCs

The Canadian income tax system does not have a comparable concept of an "association taxable as a corporation". For Canadian tax purposes, business organizations are classified either as partnerships (whether general or limited) or

---

[34] See, for example, Revenue Ruling 93-38, 1993-21 IRC.

corporations. Revenue Canada takes the view that a corporation is a limited liability entity distinct from its members or shareholders.[35] Thus, Revenue Canada does not at this time recognize LLCs as anything other than corporations.

In the absence of a comprehensive statutory definition, in the Income Tax Act however, it is difficult to reconcile Revenue Canada's position on the basis of the principles of conflicts of laws. The definition of a "corporation" for Canadian tax purposes includes "an incorporated company" (which is self evident). This definition does not, however, address the central issue: What is the status of a U.S. unincorporated association with a preponderance of non-corporate characteristics that causes it to be classified as a "partnership" under U.S. federal tax rules?

For the purpose of the definition of a "foreign affiliate",[36] Revenue Canada defines a "corporation" as:[37]

... an entity created by law having a legal personality and existence separate and distinct from the personality and existence of those who caused its creation or those who own it. . . . [and as having] its own capacity to acquire rights and to assume liabilities. . . .

Thus, as long as an entity has separate identity and existence, the Department considers the entity to be a corporation even though under some circumstances or for some purposes the law may ignore some facet of its separate existence or identity.

LLCs may be used with advantage in Canadian-U.S. joint venture arrangements. The Canadian parent company will be taxable in the U.S. on its percentage share of its LLC's earnings. The American LLC, however, will be considered a corporation for Canadian income tax purposes and, therefore its earnings will not be taxable to its Canadian parent corporation. Since the American LLC is considered to be a corporation for Canadian tax purposes, dividends paid from its active business income to the Canadian parent corporation should be exempt from Canadian tax.[38]

3. FINANCING SUBSIDIARY OPERATIONS

(a) Debt

(i) Deduction of Interest

The deductibility of interest expense on borrowed money depends upon the purpose for which the funds are used and whether there is a reasonable expectation of profit. Interest on money borrowed by a Canadian corporation and invested directly in its foreign subsidiary is deductible if the funds are borrowed for the purpose of earning income from the investment. Canada uses a direct tracing method to determine the use

---

[35] IT-343R "Meaning of the Term 'Corporation'" (September 26, 1977).

[36] Para. 95(1)(d).

[37] IT-343R "Meaning of the Term 'Corporation'" (September 26, 1977), para. 2.

[38] S. 113.

of borrowed funds and the deductibility of interest expense. In addition, there is some jurisprudence to the effect that courts may look to the real purpose of an investment to determine whether it is intended to earn income.[39]

It is generally advantageous for a Canadian parent corporation to finance its foreign subsidiary by borrowing in Canada and investing the funds in the foreign corporation. This allows the parent corporation to obtain a deduction for its interest expense on the borrowed money. There are no Canadian withholding tax considerations unless the creditor is a non-resident of Canada.

There is generally no concern if funds are borrowed to purchase common shares, regardless whether the shares currently pay dividends. Money invested to purchase preferred shares that do not carry a dividend greater than the borrowing costs may result in some portion of the interest not being deductible. Revenue Canada generally permits a deduction to the full extent of the dividend entitlement on the preferred shares, but excess interest costs may not be deductible. Excess interest expense may be carried over to the following year and deducted to the extent of any dividend income earned in the later year.[40]

(ii) Low Interest Loans

A Canadian corporation may loan money, with or without interest, to its foreign subsidiary. A low-cost loan without reasonable interest will trigger imputed interest income for the resident corporation if the loan is outstanding for more than one year.[41] There is no imputed interest on a loan to a "subsidiary controlled corporation" if the money loaned is used by the subsidiary for the purpose of gaining or producing income.[42] A corporation is considered to be a "subsidiary controlled corporation" if its parent corporation owns more than 50 per cent of its full voting issued shares.[43]

Where a Canadian corporation borrows money to loan to its subsidiary at a higher rate of interest than it pays on its borrowing, its interest expense is fully deductible. This route may, however, create another problem: The Canadian parent corporation may not be able to fully utilize its non-business foreign tax credit in respect of foreign withholding taxes on interest payments to Canada. Withholding taxes are generally payable on the gross amount of interest paid, whereas the foreign tax credit is calculated on the net amount of foreign source non-business income. Thus, Canadian interest income on the loan after deduction of applicable interest expenses will be less than the amount on which the foreign tax credit can be fully utilized.

---

[39] *Mark Resources Inc. v. The Queen*, [1993] 2 CTC 2258, 93 DTC 1004 (T.C.C.).

[40] Proposed para. 20(1)(*qq*) (interest on share purchase).

[41] Subs. 17(1); *Upper Lakes Shipping Ltd. v. M.N.R.*, [1993] 1 CTC 2011, 92 DTC 2381 (T.C.C.).

[42] Subs. 17(3); *Massey-Ferguson Ltd. v. The Queen*, [1977] CTC 6, 77 DTC 398 (F.C.A.).

[43] Subs. 248(1) ("subsidiary wholly-owned corporation").

4. DISPOSITION OF FOREIGN SUBSIDIARY

Where a Canadian corporation disposes of its shares in its foreign subsidiary, it can elect under section 93 to treat all or a portion of the proceeds of sale as a dividend rather than as proceeds of disposition. This allows the Canadian parent corporation to receive the deemed dividends on a tax-free basis to the extent that the foreign subsidiary has a pool of active business income from which it can pay dividends. Thus, the subsidiary's exempt surplus pools and its underlying foreign taxes may be fully utilized by converting what would otherwise be a capital gain into a dividend. In certain cases, this election also allows the Canadian parent corporation to avoid foreign withholding taxes that might otherwise be payable on a dividend paid out of foreign profits before the sale of the shares.

Where a parent corporation disposes of its shares in its foreign subsidiary to a taxable Canadian corporation, it can defer the Canadian tax payable on any gain on the shares if it takes back share consideration as part of the purchase price.[44]

Where the sale is to a foreign corporation, a rollover may be available under section 85.1. This rollover is also only available if the Canadian parent corporation takes back shares from the purchaser corporation as consideration for the disposition.

5. FOREIGN SOURCE INCOME

The rules in respect of the taxation of foreign-source income reflect three underlying policies: (1) They are intended to facilitate foreign investment by Canadian taxpayers; (2) They are intended to prevent Canadian taxpayers from taking advantage of lower tax rates in certain countries by placing their investments abroad;[45] and (3) They are designed to provide relief against double taxation of income.

Corporations are legal entities and taxpayers in their own right. Thus, in the absence of special rules, a Canadian resident could avoid Canadian income tax by placing his or her investments in a non-resident corporation situated in a low-tax jurisdiction. Under the general rules, Canadian tax would only be payable when the foreign corporation remitted dividends to the Canadian resident. Meanwhile, however,

---

[44] S. 85.

[45] Prior to 1971, foreign corporations, trusts and partnerships were used to reduce Canadian tax on business and investment income earned outside Canada. By locating business investment operations in tax haven jurisdictions, Canadian taxpayers could substantially reduce, sometimes completely eliminate, and at other times indefinitely postpone, taxes that might otherwise have been payable in Canada. The foreign affiliate rules are the direct product of Revenue Canada's frustrations in policing the foreign operations of resident Canadian taxpayers. In his Budget Speech on June 18, 1971, introducing the tax reform proposals, the Minister of Finance stated:

> [a] number of foreign countries impose taxes substantially lower than those in Canada, and investment income has been diverted to these countries to avoid Canadian tax. Rules...will tax the investment income of foreign affiliates to the same extent as if it had been received in Canada.

the foreign corporation could be used to defer tax for the resident taxpayer and result in a corresponding loss for domestic treasuries.

There are detailed and complex rules dealing with the taxation of foreign-source income earned by Canadian corporations. The purpose of these rules is to counter undue tax deferral and avoidance schemes. To describe these rules as "detailed and complex" is to underestimate their character. Their principal thrust is simple enough: prevention of tax avoidance (whether by way of tax deferral or reduction) through the use of offshore non-resident corporations. The language of the rules and regulations, however is excruciatingly complicated.

The statutory provisions are complex because they serve three different policies: foreign investment compatible with international trade agreements, prevention of undue tax avoidance, and prevention of double taxation of Canadian enterprises. Complexity is inevitable if the provisions are to be both effective in curtailing abuse and yet fair in their application to multinational corporations based in Canada.

The taxation of foreign-source income depends upon four principal factors:

1. type of income earned;
2. relationship between the foreign taxpayer and the Canadian resident;
3. manner and timing of repatriation of foreign earnings to Canada; and
4. existence of a Canadian double taxation treaty with the source jurisdiction.

Foreign-source income is classified into three broad categories:

1. investment income;
2. business income; and
3. capital gains.

Investment income is of two types: (1) "portfolio" dividends and (2) passive property income from "foreign affiliates".

(a) Portfolio Investments

The term "portfolio dividends" is not defined in the Act but is used to describe dividends from investments that constitute less than 10 per cent of the payor corporation's shareholdings.

A resident taxpayer is taxable on any "portfolio" dividends that he or she receives in the year from a non-resident corporation.[46]

Depending upon the type of income and its source, a taxpayer may be entitled to a deduction or credit in respect of foreign taxes paid on such income. In the case of individuals, the credit in respect of foreign withholding tax on dividends is limited to

---

[46] S. 90 and para. 12(1)(k). See para. 12(1)(j) and subs. 82(1).

a maximum of 15 per cent of the dividend.[47] In addition, however, individuals may also claim any foreign taxes in excess of 15 per cent as a deduction from income.[48]

The rules in respect of corporations are more complex and depend upon additional considerations described hereunder.

(b) Foreign Affiliates

(i) General

A "foreign affiliate" is defined in terms of the percentage ownership of corporate shares. A "foreign affiliate" is a non-resident corporation in which a resident taxpayer owns 10 per cent or more of any class of its shares.[49] A foreign affiliate that is controlled by Canadian residents is a "controlled foreign affiliate".[50]

The distinction between a "foreign affiliate" and a "controlled foreign affiliate" is crucial to the structure of the taxation of business income and passive property income. Income from a controlled foreign affiliate may be taxed in Canada either on a remittance or an accrual basis depending upon whether it is active or passive.

A Canadian resident is required to recognize "passive" investment income from a "controlled foreign affiliate"[51] in the year the income is earned, regardless whether he or she actually receives the income in the year.[52] This requirement of "accrual basis" accounting prevents any tax deferral that might otherwise be possible by delaying remittance of the income to Canada.

A Canadian resident is required to include in income his or her "participating percentage"[53] of the foreign accrual property income ("FAPI") of every share that he or she owns in a controlled foreign affiliate.[54] FAPI is generally non-active business income and gains from the disposition of assets other than those used in an active

---

[47] Subs. 126(1). The 15 per cent limitation is contained in the definition of "non-business-income tax" in subs. 126(7)(c).

[48] Subs. 20(11).

[49] Para. 95(1)(*d*) ("foreign affiliate").

[50] Subs. 95(1)(a) ("controlled foreign affiliate"). See *infra* for a detailed definition of "controlled foreign affiliate".

[51] Para. 95(10)(*a*).

[52] Subs. 91(1).

[53] Para. 95(1)(*e*).

[54] Subs. 91(1).

business.[55] The resident may claim a deduction for any underlying foreign and withholding taxes in respect of the amount included in his or her income.[56]

A resident taxpayer who receives a dividend from a controlled foreign affiliate's retained earnings that was previously included in his or her income may deduct the amount of the dividend.[57] This avoids double taxation of the same amount.

The adjusted cost base of the shares of a controlled foreign affiliate is recalculated each time there is an inclusion in, or deduction from, income.[58] These adjustments also prevent double taxation.

In contrast, active business income is not taxed until it is actually received in Canada. The tax treatment upon receipt depends upon the status of the country in which income was earned. Generally speaking, active business income earned in a "listed" country (that is, a country with which Canada has a tax treaty in force) is not taxable in Canada to a Canadian corporate shareholder.

Active business income earned in an unlisted country and remitted to Canada is included in income, but is eligible for tax credits. Thus, such income is potentially taxable only when it is actually received by a resident taxpayer, and then only to the extent that the Canadian tax applicable to such income exceeds any foreign tax paid on it.

(ii) Meaning of "Foreign Affiliate"

The concept of "foreign affiliate" is central to the scheme for the taxation of foreign-source investment income. A "foreign affiliate" is a non-resident corporation (other than a non-resident-owned investment corporation) in which the taxpayer has an "equity percentage"[59] of not less than 10 per cent.[60] Thus, there are two steps to determine whether a non-resident entity is a foreign affiliate of a Canadian resident taxpayer: (1) determine whether the foreign entity is a "corporation", and (2) calculate the resident's "equity percentage" in the non-resident corporation.

---

[55] Para. 95(1)(b) ("foreign accrual property income").

[56] Subs. 91(4).

[57] Subs. 91(5).

[58] Subs. 92(1).

[59] Para. 95(4)(b).

[60] Para. 95(1)(d).

(iii) Meaning of "Corporation"

(A) Canadian Entities

The definition of "foreign affiliate" is cast in terms of the relationship between a non-resident corporation and a taxpayer resident in Canada.[61] Under Canadian law, a corporation is a legal entity created under the authority of a statute. It has a legal existence that is separate and distinct from those who create or own it. Thus, a corporation is a legal person that has the capacity to acquire rights and to assume liabilities on its own behalf. In most circumstances, the rights and liabilities of a corporation are distinct from the rights and liabilities of those who have an ownership interest in the corporation.[62]

(B) Foreign Entities

The status of a corporation in other legal systems depends upon the relevant law. Common law jurisdictions generally recognize a corporation as a separate legal entity. Other legal systems may have different interpretations.

For the purpose of the foreign affiliate rules, Revenue Canada interprets "corporation" to include not only "joint stock" and "limited liability companies" as known to Canadian law, but also comparable entities organized under the laws of foreign jurisdictions.[63] Thus, for tax purposes, the Department considers the following types of foreign associations as equivalent to a corporation:

Aksjeselskap (A/S or A.S.) (Norway)
Aktieselskab (A/S) (Denmark)
Aktiebolag (Sweden)
Aktiengesellschaft (A.G.)
Anpartsselskab (ApS) (Denmark)
Anstalt (Liechtenstein)
Besloten Vennootschap met beperkte aansprakelijkheid
   (B.V.) (Netherlands and possessions)
Compania Anonima
Gesellschaft mit beschrankter Haftung (G.m.b.H. or Ges m.b.H.)
Kabushiki Kaisha (K.K.) (Japan)
Limitada (Sociedade por quotas) (Portugal)
Naamloze Vennootschap (N.V.) (Netherlands and possessions)
Sharikat Al-Mossahamah (Saudi Arabia)
Sharikat Mussahama
Sherkat Sahami Aam (Iran)

---

[61] Para. 95(4)(*b*).

[62] See, e.g., *Canada Business Corporations Act*, R.S.C. 1985, c. C.44, subs. 15(1); *Business Corporations Act*, R.S.O. 1990, c. B.16, s. 15.

[63] IT-343R "Meaning of the Term 'Corporation'" (September 26, 1977).

Sherkat Sahami Khas (Iran)
Sociedad(e)(s) anoniam(s) (S.A.)
Sociedad(e)(s) (anonima) de responsabilid(e) (ad) limitada (por quotas)
     (S.L.)(S.A.R.L.)(SRL)
Société anonyme
Société de personnes à responsabilité limitée
Société à responsabilité limitée
Societa per Azioni (Italy)
Yugen Kaisha (Japan)

The critical common characteristic of these entities is that they have a separate identity and existence for most purposes.

(C) Partnerships

The characterization of foreign partnerships is more difficult than the characterization of foreign "corporations". Under Canadian law, a partnership is not a separate legal entity. Rather, a partnership is a relationship between persons carrying on business in common with a view to profit.[64] The members of a partnership have joint and unlimited liability in respect of its debts and obligations. An interest in a partnership is a property right in and of itself and is distinguishable from the partnership's assets.

There is also a special type of partnership called a "limited partnership". A limited partnership is created under statutory authority[65] in which some, but not all, of the partners have limited liability. Generally speaking, the limited partners are liable for the debts and obligations of the partnership, but only to the extent of their capital contributions to the partnership.[66] A limited partnership must have at least one general partner who has unlimited liability for partnership debts. Thus, a limited partnership stands somewhere between a general partnership with unlimited liability and a corporation with limited liability.

Under Canadian law, a partnership is not a separate legal entity. Some foreign jurisdictions[67] do, however, recognize partnerships as separate legal personalities. A foreign partnership that is considered to be a separate legal entity in its home jurisdiction may be considered a "corporation" for the purposes of the foreign affiliate rules. Thus, a foreign partnership may be a foreign affiliate of a Canadian resident taxpayer.

---

[64] See, e.g., *Partnerships Act*, R.S.O. 1990, c. P.5, s. 2.

[65] See, e.g., *Limited Partnerships Act*, R.S.O. 1990, c. L.16.

[66] See, e.g., *Limited Partnerships Act*, R.S.O. 1990, c. L.16, s. 9.

[67] For example, Scotland and France recognize partnerships as separate legal personalities.

(D) Trusts

The rules in respect of the taxation of foreign affiliates also apply to certain non-resident trusts. A discretionary trust may be deemed to be a person resident in Canada and subject to Canadian tax on its FAPI.[68] A non-discretionary trust's FAPI may be imputed to its Canadian resident beneficiaries by treating the trust as a corporation.[69]

(iv) Equity Percentage

A resident's "equity percentage" in a non-resident corporation is determined by adding his or her direct and indirect interests in the corporation.[70]

A resident's direct interest in a non-resident corporation (referred to as "direct equity percentage")[71] is his or her highest percentage ownership of any class of shares issued by the non-resident corporation.

Example XXXI.2

Assume:

A Ltd., a Canadian resident corporation, owns the following percentages of shares in two non-resident corporations, NR1 and NR2:

NR1	—	9%	Class A shares
		12%	Class B shares
NR2	—	7%	Class C shares
		8%	Class D shares

Then:

A Ltd.'s "direct equity percentage" in NR1 is 12%; and in NR2 is 8%.

A taxpayer has an indirect equity interest when he or she owns shares in one corporation which in turn owns shares in other corporations. The indirect equity interest is calculated by multiplying the taxpayer's direct equity percentage in the first corporation by the first corporation's direct equity percentage in the second corporation, and so on.[72] Thus, a person's equity percentage in a particular corporation is his or her

---

[68] Para. 94(1)(c).

[69] Para. 94(1)(d).

[70] Para. 95(4)(b) ("equity percentage").

[71] Para. 95(4)(a) ("direct equity percentage").

[72] Subpara. 95(4)(b)(ii).

direct equity percentage in the corporation plus the product obtained when his or her equity percentage in any other corporation is multiplied by that corporation's direct equity percentage in the particular corporation.

Example XXXI.3

Assume:

- A Ltd., a resident corporation, owns 30% of the issued shares of NR1 and 5% of the issued shares of NR2;
- NR1 owns 40% of the issued shares of NR2;
- NR2 owns 20% of the issued shares of NR3.
- NR1, NR2 and NR3 are all non-resident corporations.

A Ltd.'s equity percentage (being the sum of its direct and indirect interests) in NR1, NR2 and NR3 is calculated as follows:

In NR1
Direct equity percentage   30%

In NR2
Direct equity percentage   5%
Indirect interests (30% × 40%)   12%
                                             17%

In NR3
Indirect interests (17% × 20%)   3.4%

Assuming that these are all of the relevant interests held, NR1 and NR2 are foreign affiliates of A Ltd.; NR3 is not a foreign affiliate of A Ltd.

For the purpose of determining foreign affiliate status, it is irrelevant whether the shares on the basis of which equity percentages are calculated are voting or non-voting. Note also, for the purposes of the foreign affiliate rules, an income bond or debenture[73] issued by a non-resident corporation is deemed to be a share unless the interest payable on the bond or debenture is deductible under the tax laws of the country in which the corporation is resident.[74]

---

[73] Subs. 248(1) "income bond".

[74] Subs. 95(5); IT-388, "Income Bonds Issued by Foreign Corporations" (August 15, 1977).

(c) Anti-avoidance Rules

There are two anti-avoidance rules that are intended to prevent taxpayers from manipulating their equity percentages in non-resident corporations for the purpose of avoiding the foreign affiliate rules. The first rule deals with options and rights to acquire shares: Where a taxpayer has a contractual right or option to acquire shares and one of his or her main reasons for the existence of the option or rights may reasonably be considered to be the reduction or deferral of tax that might otherwise be payable, the rights or options are deemed to be shares owned by the taxpayer.[75] The test is objective and the Minister's discretion is reviewable in a judicial proceeding.

The second rule deals with the motive for the issuance of shares by a non-resident corporation: Where a taxpayer's foreign affiliate or a non-resident corporation controlled by the taxpayer issues shares and one of the main reasons for the issuance of the shares may reasonably be considered to be either a reduction in, or deferral of, tax that would otherwise be payable, the shares are deemed never to have been issued.[76] The control test applied to the taxpayer may be de jure or de facto, direct or indirect, and may rest in the taxpayer alone, or in a group related to the taxpayer.[77]

(d) Dividends

(i) General

Canadian residents are generally required to include dividends from non-resident corporations in income on a receipt basis.[78] This rule applies to both individual and corporate taxpayers regardless of the status of the non-resident corporation. There are, however, special rules for dividends from foreign affiliates.

The tax treatment of dividends from foreign affiliates depends upon two factors: (1) the type of income earned by the payor corporation, and (2) the jurisdiction in which the payor conducts its activities.

Dividends from a foreign affiliate that is resident, and carrying on an active business, in a "listed" country are generally fully deductible in computing the resident corporation's income. A "listed" country is one with which Canada has a tax treaty in force. In other cases, the deduction available in respect of dividends from a foreign affiliate depends upon the amount of foreign tax paid by the foreign affiliate in respect of its income (known as the "underlying foreign tax") and the amount of tax withheld on the dividend.

---

[75] Para. 95(6)(a).

[76] Para. 95(6)(b).

[77] Subs. 256(5.1).

[78] S. 90.

(ii) Surplus Account Deductions

The technical mechanism for allowing a deduction for foreign taxes is quite complex and depends upon a detailed analysis of the payor corporation's surplus accounts. There are three categories of surplus accounts: exempt surplus, taxable surplus and pre-acquisition surplus. The deduction available depends upon the surplus pool from which the dividend is paid.

A Canadian resident corporation that receives a dividend from its foreign affiliate is entitled to a deduction in computing its taxable income on the following basis:[79]

- the full amount of any dividend paid out of the foreign affiliate's "exempt surplus";

- an amount in respect of any portion of the dividend paid out of the foreign affiliate's "taxable surplus" that represents its underlying foreign corporate tax and foreign withholding tax; and

- the amount of the dividend paid out of the foreign affiliate's "pre-acquisition surplus".

Thus, dividends from a foreign affiliate may be entirely tax-free or included in income and subject to a credit for foreign taxes paid on the underlying income. The distinction between the exemption and credit methods of accounting for dividends from foreign affiliates depends upon the type of income earned by the affiliate and its country of origin.

A Canadian resident corporation in receipt of a dividend from its foreign affiliate's exempt surplus must include the dividend in its income.[80] It may, however, deduct an equivalent amount in computing its taxable income.[81] Thus, in effect, dividends out of exempt surplus are completely tax-free. In contrast, dividends from taxable surplus are eligible for a tax credit.

(A) Exempt Surplus

Generally speaking, an affiliate's "exempt surplus" is its active business earnings from businesses carried on in a "listed" country.[82] The "listed" countries are countries with which Canada has signed a treaty that is in force.[83] The rationale for exempting dividends paid out of exempt surplus from Canadian tax is that the underlying income from which these dividends are paid is assumed to have already borne tax in one of the listed countries at rates that are approximately equivalent to Canadian tax rates. This

---

[79] Subs. 113(1).

[80] S. 90.

[81] Para. 113(1)(a).

[82] Reg. 5907(1)(d).

[83] Reg. 5907(11).

assumption is generally valid because Canada does not enter into tax treaties with tax havens. It is, however, not always valid because some "treaty haven" countries[84] levy very low rates of tax on business income.

(B) Taxable Surplus

Generally speaking, a foreign affiliate's "taxable surplus" comprises its active business income earned in a non-listed country, that is, a country with which Canada does not have a tax treaty.

A Canadian resident corporation in receipt of a dividend from its foreign affiliate's taxable surplus must also include the dividend in income. The corporation may, however, claim a deduction for foreign income taxes that the foreign affiliate paid on its income and for any tax withheld on the dividends.[85] The deduction is equal to the grossed-up amount of the underlying foreign income and withholding taxes paid to the foreign country. The grossed-up amount of underlying foreign income taxes is determined by multiplying the foreign income tax paid by the affiliate by the result of the "relevant tax factor" minus 1. The grossed-up amount of the withholding tax is determined by multiplying the withholding tax by the relevant tax factor.

(C) Relevant Tax Factor

The "relevant tax factor" ("RTF") is a mathematical formula designed to permit a deduction for the grossed-up value of the foreign tax paid on foreign-source income. The RTF is the reciprocal of the tax rate applicable to the taxpayer.[86]

The RTF for individuals is 2, which is premised on a marginal tax rate of 50 per cent.

The reciprocal of the corporate tax rate at 38 per cent is 2.63158. The RTF is reduced by 1 to calculate the deduction for underlying foreign taxes levied on income paid out of taxable surplus of a foreign affiliate. Hence, the factor applied to determine the underlying corporate foreign taxes is 1.63158.

---

[84] See, for example, the Cyprus, Malta, Ireland, and Barbados treaties with Canada.

[85] Paras. 113(1)(*b*), 113(1)(*c*).

[86] Para. 95(1)(*f*) ("relevant tax factor").

Example XXXI.4

Assume that FA, a foreign affiliate, earns $10,000 in an unlisted country, pays foreign corporate tax of $3,800 and remits $6,200 out of its taxable surplus to a Canadian resident corporation. Assume that there is no withholding tax.

Then:

A. *Foreign affiliate (FA)*

Taxable income	$ 10,000
Tax @ 38%	3,800
Net available (paid as dividend)	$ 6,200

B. *Resident corporation*

Dividend income	$ 6,200
Less: 1.63 × $3,800	6,200
Amount taxable in Canada	NIL

The factor of "minus 1" in the formula simply adjusts for the fact that the resident corporation has already included its foreign affiliate's after-tax earnings in income and that the foreign affiliate deducted 1 times the tax rate ($3,800 in the above example) in arriving at the amount that went into its taxable surplus account. No such adjustment is required in the case of withholding taxes on dividends from a foreign affiliate because the resident corporation includes the gross amount of the dividend, without any reduction for withholding tax, in its income. The rationale for these mathematical rules in respect of taxable surplus dividends is to ensure that foreign earnings repatriated to Canada from non-treaty countries bear tax at a rate that is at least equal to the prevailing Canadian federal corporate tax rate.

(D) Pre-acquisition Surplus Deduction

A dividend from a foreign affiliate in excess of its exempt and taxable surpluses is presumed to come out of its "pre-acquisition surplus".[87] A foreign affiliate's pre-acquisition surplus is only a notional account. Dividends are presumed to be paid out of pre-acquisition surplus only when an affiliate's exempt surplus and taxable surplus are exhausted.

A dividend from a foreign affiliate's pre-acquisition surplus is also deductible in computing taxable income,[88] but the cost base of the foreign affiliate's shares is reduced by the amount of the dividend less any withholding tax.[89] The resident

---

[87] Reg. 5901.

[88] Para. 113(1)(*d*).

[89] Subs. 92(2).

corporation is deemed to have realized a capital gain, if the adjusted cost base of its foreign affiliate's shares becomes a negative amount.[90]

(iii) Computation of Surplus Accounts

A foreign affiliate is presumed to pay dividends in the following order: first out of its exempt surplus (net of any taxable deficit); next, out of its taxable surplus (net of any exempt deficit); and, finally, out of pre-acquisition surplus.[91] It may, however, elect to reverse the order of the payments as between exempt surplus and taxable surplus.[92] This may be advantageous, for example, if the resident corporation needs to use up its loss carryovers or deductions.

The taxation of dividends from a foreign affiliate to a Canadian resident corporation depends upon the surplus pot from which the dividend is paid. This necessitates a complex system of accounting for each foreign affiliate's surplus pots.[93] The system is further complicated by the requirement to maintain separate accounts for each foreign affiliate and for each Canadian corporation in respect of which the foreign corporation is a foreign affiliate. The surplus accounts are to be computed by reference to the foreign affiliate's taxation year for local tax purposes and in the currency of the country in which it is resident or in such other foreign currency as is reasonable in the circumstances.[94]

(A) Exempt Surplus

In general terms, the exempt surplus of a foreign affiliate resident in a listed country is the sum of:

- its pre-1976 earnings from an active business carried on anywhere; and
- its post-1975 earnings from an active business carried on in any listed country.

The affiliate's earnings are determined according to the tax laws of the country in which the affiliate is resident if that country requires computation of income according to its laws. If the country of residence does not specify the method of determining income, it is calculated according to the tax laws of the country in which the affiliate carries on its business. If neither foreign country specifies a method of computation, earnings are calculated according to Canadian tax rules.

More specifically, a foreign affiliate's exempt surplus is its exempt earnings (losses) for prior completed taxation years and dividends received from other foreign

---

[90] Subs. 40(3).

[91] Reg. 5901.

[92] Reg. 5900(2).

[93] The detailed rules are provided in Part LIX of the Income Tax Regulations; see also Information Circular 77-9R "Books, Records and Other Requirements for Taxpayers Having Foreign Affiliates" (June 22, 1983).

[94] Reg. 5907(6).

affiliates of the resident corporation that were paid out of the exempt surplus of such affiliates less any dividends paid out by it from its exempt surplus.[95] That is, a foreign affiliate's exempt surplus is the amount by which the aggregate of:

- its opening surplus balance determined under Regulation 5905;
- its "exempt earnings"[96] for each taxation year ending in the period of computation;
- dividends received in the period of computation that have been paid out of the exempt surplus of another foreign affiliate of the Canadian resident corporation;
- refunds of tax received in respect of dividends received from another foreign affiliate out of its exempt surplus (unless such a refund is applied to reduce the tax liability of the foreign affiliate); and
- taxable dividends received from taxable Canadian corporations or corporations carrying on business in Canada to the extent that they would have been deductible under section 112 if the recipient had been a corporation resident in Canada,

exceeds the aggregate of:

- its opening exempt deficit of the affiliate as determined under Regulation 5905;
- its exempt losses for any of its taxation years ending in the period;
- any income or profit taxes paid on the receipt of dividends that are prescribed to have been paid out of the exempt surplus of another affiliate;
- any income or profit taxes paid on refunds of tax in respect of dividends out of the exempt surplus of another foreign affiliate;
- any income or profit taxes on dividends that would have been deductible under section 112 if the recipient had been a corporation resident in Canada;
- any dividends paid out of its own exempt surplus; and
- dividends deemed to have been paid out of its exempt surplus.[97]

An "exempt deficit" arises when the deductions in the above list exceed the inclusions.

A foreign affiliate's "exempt earnings" are calculated for each taxation year of the affiliate. Note, however, that only the exempt earnings (losses) of completed taxation years are taken into account in calculating the affiliate's exempt surplus or deficit at any particular time.

---

[95] Reg. 5907(1)(d).

[96] Reg. 5907(1)(b).

[97] Reg. 5905(8) and subs. 93(1).

The calculation of exempt earnings (losses) takes into account four elements:[98]

1. capital gains and losses;
2. active business earnings carried on in listed (treaty) countries;
3. pre-1975 earnings and losses; and
4. earnings that qualify for tax-sparing because of an investment made or undertaken prior to 1976.

Post-1975 net earnings from an active business are included in exempt earnings only if the affiliate is resident in a listed country and the active business is carried on in a listed country or in Canada, or if a tax-sparing provision applies.[99]

One of the principal determinants in the calculation of "exempt earnings" is "net earnings" for the year from an active business. "Net earnings" generally represent "earnings" net of applicable taxes.[100]

A foreign affiliate's "earnings" for a taxation year from an active business are:[101]

- its income or profit from the business for the year computed in accordance with the income tax law of the country in which it is resident if it is required by such law to compute that profit or income;

- its income or profit for the year computed in accordance with the income tax law of the country in which the business is carried on if it is required to calculate that income or profit according to such law; or

- in any other case, its income or profit for the year computed in accordance with the Canadian Income Tax Act on the assumption that the business was carried on in Canada and it was resident in Canada.

Thus, Canadian tax rules in respect of calculating earnings apply only if neither the foreign affiliate's country of residence nor the country in which it carries on business provide specific computational rules.

(B) Taxable Surplus

A foreign affiliate's income from active business is included in its "taxable surplus" unless:[102]

- it is resident in a listed country; and
- the income is earned from an active business that it carries on either in Canada or in a listed country.

---

[98] Reg. 5907(1)(b).

[99] Reg. 5907(10).

[100] Reg. 5907(1)(f).

[101] Reg. 5907(1)(a)(i).

[102] Reg. 5907(1)(k).

The rationale for the rules in respect of the taxation of dividends out of "taxable surplus" is to step-up the level of tax on foreign earnings to bring it into line with Canadian tax rates.

A foreign affiliate's taxable surplus at any particular time is the amount by which the aggregate of:[103]

- its opening taxable surplus determined under Regulation 5905;

- its taxable earnings for each taxation year ending in the period of computation; and

- the portion of all dividends received in the period of computation that have been paid out of the taxable surplus of another foreign affiliate of the Canadian corporation;

exceeds the aggregate of:

- its opening taxable deficit determined under Regulation 5905;

- its taxable losses for each taxation year ending in the period of computation;

- the portion of dividends paid in the period of computation from its taxable surplus;

- the portion of dividends that would otherwise have been deemed to have been paid out of exempt surplus but that are deemed by Regulation 5901(3) to be paid out of taxable surplus rather than exempt surplus;

- any reductions required in the period of computation in respect of certain dispositions of shares of the affiliate in respect of which an election has been made under subsection 93(1); and

- the amount of income or profit taxes paid on dividends received by the affiliate to the government of a country.

(iv) Dividends Out of Taxable Surplus

As already noted, a resident Canadian corporation in receipt of a dividend from its foreign affiliate must include the full amount of the dividend in its income.[104] It may, however, deduct an amount on account of:[105]

- any underlying foreign tax prescribed to be applicable to the dividend; and

- any non-business income tax paid by the corporation in respect of the dividend.

---

[103] Reg. 5907(1)(k).

[104] S. 90.

[105] Paras. 113(1)(b) and (c).

These two deductions reflect the foreign tax and non-business income tax applicable to the dividend and, in effect, equate the net tax payable with the amount of tax that would have been payable under a full foreign tax credit system.

$$\text{Underlying foreign tax prescribed to be applicable to dividend paid out of taxable surplus} \times \frac{1}{\text{Corporate tax rate}} - 1$$

The deduction in respect of the underlying foreign tax paid on a dividend is calculated according to the following formula:

Thus, the deduction is equal to the amount of the foreign tax that is attributable to the dividend paid out of taxable surplus multiplied by the result of the corporation's "relevant tax factor"[106] less 1. Given a basic Canadian federal corporate tax rate of 38 per cent, the multiplier is 1.63158. The deduction cannot exceed the amount of the dividend included in the resident corporation's income.

Example XXXI.5

Assume:

Alpha Ltd., a resident corporation, received a dividend of $16,000 in 1995 out of the taxable surplus of its foreign affiliate, Beta Ltd. Beta Ltd. paid foreign tax of $4,000; in addition, Beta Ltd. was subject to a withholding tax of 15 per cent on the dividend.

The tax payable on the dividend is calculated as follows:

Dividend income [s. 90]		$ 16,000
Less:		
Underlying foreign tax [para. 113(1)(b)] $4,000 \times [(1/0.38) - 1]$	$ 6,526	
Withholding tax [para. 113(1)(c)] $2,400 \times (1/0.38)$	6,316	(12,842)
Amount taxable		$ 3,158
Tax thereon at 38%		$ 1,200

---

[106] The "relevant tax factor" is defined in para. 95(1)(f). For a corporate taxpayer, the factor is derived by dividing one by the corporate tax rate.

Example XXXI.5 (continued)

The tax payable under the credit system is equal to the tax that would have been payable on an equivalent amount of income under a system of full foreign tax credits.

Dividend income		$ 16,000
Add: underlying foreign tax		4,000
Amount taxable		$ 20,000
Tax thereon at 38%		$ 7,600
Less: foreign tax	$ 4,000	
withholding tax	2,400	(6,400)
Net tax		$ 1,200

The system in fact overcredits foreign tax because effective Canadian tax rates are higher than 38 per cent.

The deduction for non-business income taxes is calculated by multiplying the non-business tax paid by the corporation by its relevant tax factor.[107] This factor is currently 2.63158.

(v) Holding Companies

An individual who invests directly in a foreign business will be personally taxable on any dividends that he or she receives from the foreign corporation. Foreign dividends are not eligible for the dividend tax credit and, as such, will be taxable at the full personal rate. The personal rate varies between provinces. At the top end of income brackets, the highest marginal rate in Ontario in 1994 was 53.19 per cent on dividend income not eligible for the dividend tax credit. The corresponding rate in Alberta was 46.07 per cent; British Columbia 54.16 per cent; Nova Scotia 53.75 per cent.

In the event that a Canadian resident taxpayer wishes to invest in a treaty country, it is generally advantageous to invest through a Canadian holding company rather than directly. The following example illustrates the comparative tax consequences of a direct investment in the U.S. versus an indirect investment through the use of a holding company.

---

[107] Para. 113(1)(c).

Example XXXI.6

Assume:

An individual resident in Ontario with a marginal rate of 53.19 per cent invests in the U.S. either directly in a U.S. corporation ("U.S. Co") or through a Canadian holding company ("HOLDCO"). U.S. Co is engaged in a business and remits its after-tax income to the individual or HOLDCO, as the case may be.

	Direct investment by Canadian individual in U.S. Co.	Investment by Canadian individual in U.S. Co. through Canadian Holdco
HOST COUNTRY TAX		
Net income earned by U.S. Co.	$ 100.00	$ 100.00
Host country tax	34.00	34.00
Net income after tax	$ 66.00	$ 66.00
Dividend from U.S. Co.	$ 66.00	$ 66.00
Withholding tax (15% or 10%)	9.90	6.60
Net dividend to Canadian investor	$ 56.10	$ 59.40
CANADIAN TAX		
Canadian corporate tax on dividend	N/A	NIL (exempt surplus)
Canadian personal tax:		
Foreign source dividend	$ 35.11	
Domestic source dividend		$ 21.34
Foreign non-business tax credit	(9.90)	N/A
Net Canadian personal tax	$ 25.21	$ 21.34
Total Canadian and foreign tax	$ 69.11	$ 61.94
Net cash retained by Canadian investor	$ 30.89	$ 38.06
Percentage increase in investment yield		7.17%

6. FOREIGN ACCRUAL PROPERTY INCOME (FAPI)

(a) General

As already noted, the taxation of foreign-source income depends upon the type of income, its country of origin, and the relationship between the recipient corporation and the payor corporation. Dividends from portfolio investments are taxable on receipt.[108] Dividends from foreign affiliates are also taxed upon receipt, but are eligible for deductions that depend upon the source of the income from which the dividends are paid.[109]

In contrast, Canadian residents are taxable on passive investment income earned by a "controlled foreign affiliate"[110] on an accrual basis.[111] A resident taxpayer is taxable on a current basis on his or her share of any foreign accrual property income ("FAPI") earned by his or her controlled foreign affiliates.[112] There is no imputation of income to a Canadian shareholder where the FAPI of a foreign affiliate is less than $5,000 in a particular year.[113]

The FAPI rules apply to resident taxpayers who own shares in a "controlled foreign affiliate", regardless whether the affiliate was incorporated, or is resident, in a treaty or non-treaty country. The primary thrust of the FAPI rules is to prevent what is perceived as "unfair" tax avoidance. The rules probably do not contribute much to Canadian government revenue.

Two points warrant emphasis. First, FAPI is only attributed to a resident taxpayer if he or she has direct share ownership in a controlled foreign affiliate.[114] Thus, although indirect shareholdings are taken into account to determine foreign affiliate status,[115] imputation of FAPI depends upon the taxpayer's direct shareholding in the controlled foreign affiliate.

Second, where a resident taxpayer owns shares in a controlled foreign affiliate, he or she must include in income not only any FAPI from that particular controlled foreign affiliate, but also from any other controlled foreign affiliate to the extent of the first affiliate's interest in the second affiliate, and so on down the various tiers of share

---

[108] S. 90.

[109] S. 113.

[110] Para. 95(1) ("controlled foreign affiliate") (a).

[111] Subs. 91(1).

[112] Subs. 91(1).

[113] See subpara. 95(1)(e)(i).

[114] Subs. 91(1).

[115] Paras. 95(4)(a), (b), 95(1)(d).

ownership.[116] Thus, shareholdings in a first tier controlled foreign affiliate may result in attribution of FAPI from a second or third tier controlled foreign affiliate.[117]

Example XXXI.7

Assume:

X, a resident individual, owns 100 per cent of NR1 (non-resident); NR1 owns 100 per cent of NR2 (non-resident); NR2 owns 55 per cent of NR3 (non-resident).

Then:

NR1, NR2 and NR3 are all controlled foreign affiliates of X. The FAPI of NR2 and NR3 is attributable to X. X's shares in NR1 have a participating percentage of 100 in NR2 and 55 in NR3. The participating percentage determines the amount of FAPI to be reported.

FAPI is included in income for the year in which it is earned, regardless of whether it is actually repatriated to Canada as a dividend.[118] A resident taxpayer may, however, deduct any income taxes ("foreign accrual taxes") paid by the affiliate (or by another affiliate of the taxpayer) that may reasonably be considered applicable to his or her FAPI.[119] This deduction is similar to the foreign tax credit system. The deduction for foreign income tax is equivalent to the Canadian tax rate that would have been applied to such income if it had been earned in Canada.[120] The taxpayer may also increase the cost base of his or her shares by the net amount of FAPI included in his or her income.[121]

---

[116] Para. 95(1)(e).

[117] Subs. 91(1).

[118] Subs. 91(1).

[119] Subs. 91(4).

[120] *The Queen v. Bank of N.S.*, [1981] CTC 162, 81 DTC 5115 (F.C.A.).

[121] Subs. 92(1).

Example XXXI.8

Assume:

X, a resident individual, owns 100 per cent of the shares of NR Ltd., a non-resident corporation. The following data applies to X and NR Ltd.:

FAPI	$ 20,000
Foreign accrual tax paid in same year	$ 4,000

Then:

Amount of FAPI included in X's income		$ 20,000
Deduct, lesser of:		
• foreign accrual tax times RTF* ($4,000 × 2) and	$ 8,000	
• income amount minus previous year's deductions ($20,000 − 0)	$ 20,000	
Lesser amount		(8,000)
Taxable amount		$ 12,000

*The RTF for individuals is 2.

When a resident taxpayer actually receives a dividend from FAPI on which he or she previously paid tax, he or she may deduct an amount that is calculated by reference to the previous adjustment made to the cost base of the shares at the time that he or she included the FAPI in income.[122]

(b) "Controlled Foreign Affiliate"

The characterization of the status of a non-resident corporation as a foreign affiliate or a controlled foreign affiliate is critical. A Canadian resident corporation will generally find it advantageous to have the foreign corporation in which it holds shares qualify as its foreign affiliate. This is because a resident corporation receives favourable tax treatment, either by way of exemption or credit, on any dividends that it receives from a non-resident corporation.[123] In contrast, it is generally disadvantageous to have

---

[122] Subs. 91(5).

[123] S. 113.

a controlled foreign affiliate because the affiliate's FAPI is imputed to the resident regardless of actual repatriation of funds.[124]

For a resident individual, however, it makes little difference whether or not a foreign corporation is characterized as his or her foreign affiliate, since individuals may not deduct any underlying foreign taxes paid by their foreign affiliates. To have a foreign corporation characterized as a controlled foreign affiliate of a resident individual, however, is a definite disadvantage because of the attribution of FAPI.

There are two separate tests that must be satisfied in order to constitute a corporation a "controlled foreign affiliate": the requisite degree of share ownership in a non-resident corporation to qualify as a "foreign affiliate" and control of that corporation.

A "controlled foreign affiliate" is a foreign affiliate of a resident taxpayer that is controlled by:[125]

- the taxpayer;
- the taxpayer and not more than four other persons resident in Canada;
- not more than four persons (other than the taxpayer) resident in Canada;
- a person or persons with whom the taxpayer does not deal at arm's length; or
- the taxpayer and a person or persons with whom the taxpayer does not deal at arm's length.

(i) "Control"

There is no specific definition of the term "control" for the purposes of the foreign affiliate rules. It means de jure rather than de facto control.[126] Thus, "control" of a corporation generally contemplates the right of control that rests in the ownership of a sufficient number of shares that carries the power to elect a majority of the board of directors. As Jackett, P. said:[127]

Many approaches might conceivably be adopted in applying the word "control" in a statute such as the Income Tax Act to a corporation. It might, for example, refer to control by "management", where management and the Board of Directors are separate, or it might refer to control by the Board of Directors. The kind of control exercised by management officials or the Board of Directors is, however, clearly not intended by [s. 256] when it contemplates control of one corporation by another as well as control of a corporation by individuals . . . . The word "control" might conceivably refer to de facto control by one or more shareholders whether or not they hold a majority of shares. I am of the view, however, that in section [256] of the Income Tax Act, the word "controlled" contemplates the right of control that rests in ownership of such a number of shares as carries with it the right to a majority of

---

[124] S. 91.

[125] Para. 95(1)(a).

[126] Subs. 256(5.1) does not apply.

[127] *Buckerfield's Ltd. v. M.N.R.*, [1964] CTC 504 at 507, 64 DTC 5301 at 5303 (Ex. Ct.).

the votes in the election of the Board of Directors. See British American Tobacco Co v. I.R.C.,[128] . . . where Viscount Simon, L.C...says:

> The owners of the majority of the voting power in a company are the persons who are in effective control of its affairs and fortunes.

This aspect of corporate "control" hinges on the legal power to elect the board of directors and not on the number of shares owned.[129] In most cases, ownership of more than 50 per cent of the issued voting shares of a corporation constitutes control. There are, however, circumstances in which ownership of less than 50 per cent of the issued shares of a corporation may confer the power to elect its board of directors. For example, where an escrow agreement prevents the majority shareholder from voting all of his shares, control of the corporation, in the sense of having the power to elect a majority of its board of directors, may rest with a person who owns less than 50 per cent of its issued voting shares.

Where voting power is equally distributed amongst two or more persons, control may be determined by reference to factors other than the power to elect directors. For example, the power to wind-up a corporation and appropriate the corporation's property can constitute "control" of the corporation.[130]

For the purpose of determining "controlled foreign affiliate" status, one of the tests is whether control rests with the resident taxpayer and not more than four other persons resident in Canada.[131] The important point to observe is that the test does not require the taxpayer and the other Canadian residents to deal at non-arm's length with each other. It is enough if the resident taxpayer and the other Canadian residents together control the foreign affiliate, and taxpayers at arm's length with each other can satisfy the test. The anti-avoidance provisions discussed previously in the context of the determination of foreign affiliate status also apply to the determination of "controlled foreign affiliate" status.[132]

(ii) "FAPI"

(A) General

In general terms, FAPI is income from property and passive business income. Thus, FAPI generally means passive investment income including net taxable gains and

---

[128] *British American Tobacco Co v. I.R.C.*, [1943] 1 All E.R. 13 at 15.

[129] *International Mercantile Factors Ltd. v. The Queen*, [1990] 2 CTC 137, 90 DTC 6390 (F.C.T.D.).

[130] *The Queen v. Imperial Gen. Properties Ltd.*, [1985] 2 CTC 299, 85 DTC 5500 (S.C.C.).

[131] Para. 95(1) ("controlled foreign affiliate") (*a*).

[132] Para. 95(6)(*b*).

excludes active business income.[133] There are, however, several technical adjustments to this general understanding of FAPI.[134]

Since FAPI generally represents passive investment income and does not include active business income, it is important to determine the meaning of "active business" for the purpose of the foreign affiliate rules. The distinction is also important in the context of determining "exempt surplus" that a foreign affiliate can pay out as tax-free dividends. The definition of "active business" in paragraph 125(7)(a) is not relevant for the purposes of the foreign affiliate rules since that definition is limited to use in section 125.[135]

What constitutes an active business is a question of fact having regard to all of the surrounding circumstances. The determination is made in the context of the corporation's activities and course of conduct over an extended period of time.[136] Some courts have said that any quantum of business activity that gives rise to income in a year is sufficient to characterize it as income from an active business.[137] The courts have not laid down general rules of law as to the meaning of active business. Instead, they have left the determination of whether income constitutes income from an active or inactive business as a question of fact to be determined in each case. This necessarily adds uncertainty to the determination of a central question in the taxation of foreign source income.[138]

(B) Meaning of "Active Business Income"

The words "active business" are not defined for the purposes of the foreign affiliate rules. The general definition of "active business" in subsection 248(1) only applies to resident taxpayers and does not apply to foreign affiliates. The definition of "active

---

[133] Para. 95(1) ("foreign accrual property income") (*b*).

[134] See, e.g., para. 95(2)(*a*).

[135] Reg. 5907(1)(a) also provides little assistance.

[136] *Cdn. Marconi Co. v. The Queen*, [1986] 2 CTC 465, 86 DTC 6526 (S.C.C.) (rebuttable presumption that corporate income is income from a business if earned pursuant to the corporation's constating documents); *Burri v. The Queen*, [1985] 2 CTC 42, 85 DTC 5287 (F.C.T.D.) (presumption that corporate income is business income rebutted on the facts); *The Queen v. Marsh & McLennan, Ltd.*, [1983] CTC 231, 83 DTC 5180 (F.C.A.) (income from short-term investments characterized as income from property held in the course of carrying on business); re leave to appeal to S.C.C. refused (1983), 52 N.R. 231; *M.R.T. Investments Ltd. et al. v. The Queen*, [1975] CTC 354, 75 DTC 5224 (F.C.T.D.); aff'd [1976] CTC 294, 76 DTC 6158 (F.C.A.); *The Queen v. Rockmore Investments Ltd.*, [1976] CTC 294, 76 DTC 6156 (F.C.A.) (income from mortgage loans constituted active business income).

[137] See *The Queen v. Cadboro Bay Holdings Ltd.*, [1977] CTC 186, 77 DTC 5115 (F.C.T.D.).

[138] In *King George Hotels Ltd. v. The Queen*, [1981] CTC 87, 81 DTC 5082 (F.C.A.), the Federal Court of Appeal said that ". . . The quantum of activity may well vary from case to case but it is still necessary for the Court to weigh all the evidence to characterize the quality of the particular business".

business carried on by a corporation" in paragraph 125(7)(a) only applies for the purposes of the small business deduction and not for other parts of the Act.

The expression "active business" should be read in light of the jurisprudence dealing with the meaning of the words "business" and "active". "Business" is described in subsection 248(1) "to include a profession, calling, trade, manufacture or undertaking of any kind whatever . . .". It is obvious, however, that every business cannot be considered to be an "active" business. Since FAPI explicitly includes income from an active business,[139] the phrase "active business" must have a meaning that is narrower than the meaning of "business" in general.

There is a long line of cases dealing with the meaning of active business in the context of personal corporations under the old Act and under section 125 of the current Act prior to the 1979 amendments. The following propositions are extracted from these decisions:

- In determining whether an operation constitutes an "active business", each case should be decided on its own facts and in the context of the entities' operations over some extended period of time.

- The general tendency of the courts has been to give an expansive interpretation to the meaning of "active". For example: "any quantum of business activity that gives rise to income in a taxation year for a private corporation in Canada is sufficient to characterize of such income as income from an 'active' business carried on in Canada".[140]

- Businesses engaged in the lending of money under security of mortgages, investing in securities and the renting of property have been held to qualify as active businesses for the purposes of the rules in sections 125 and 129.

The general thrust of the jurisprudence dealing with the concept of "active business" is towards a broad, liberal and generous understanding of "active". The concept does, however, imply some level of activity. In Rockmore Investments, for example, Jackett, C.J. said:[141]

> In considering whether there is an "active business" for the purposes of Part I, the first step is to decide whether there is a "business" within the meaning of that word. . . . Apart from these provisions [section 248 and paragraph 3(a)], I know of no special considerations to be taken into account from a legal point of view in deciding whether an activity or situation constitutes the carrying on of a business for the purposes of Part I of the Income Tax Act. Subject thereto, as I understand it, each problem that arises as to whether a business is or was being carried on must be solved as a question of fact having regard to the circumstances of the particular case.

---

[139] Para. 95(1) ("foreign accrual property income") (b).

[140] *The Queen v. Cadboro Bay Holdings*, [1977] CTC 186 at 199, 77 DTC 5115 at 5123 (F.C.T.D.).

[141] In *The Queen v. Rockmore Investments Ltd.*, [1976] CTC 291 at 293, 76 DTC 6156 at 6157 (F.C.A.).

... the second question to be answered is whether the business that was being carried on was an "active" business. . . . Obviously, the concept of "active" business is not used to exclude a business that is in an absolute state of suspension because [subparagraph] 125(1)(a)(i) is dealing with "income . . . from an active business" and it must be assumed that the word "active" was used to exclude some businesses having sufficient activity in the year to give rise to income.

In Canadian Marconi[142] the Supreme Court of Canada held that there is a rebuttable presumption in favour of corporations that their income derives from business. In Madam Justice Wilson's words:

> It is frequently stated in both the English and Canadian case law that there is in the case of a corporate taxpayer a rebuttable presumption that income received from or generated by an activity done in pursuit of an object set out in the corporation's constating documents is income from a business. (at C.T.C. 468)

> The question whether particular income is income from business or property remains a question of fact in every case. However, the fact that a particular taxpayer is a corporation is a very relevant matter to be considered because of the existence of the presumption and its implications in terms of the evidentiary burden resting on the appellant. (at C.T.C. 470)

The presumption[143] that income earned by a corporation is "business" income coupled with broad judicial interpretation of "active" makes it easier to structure offshore operations to qualify under the "exempt surplus rules" and to avoid the FAPI rules.

(C) Method of Calculation

The Act is silent on the method to be used and the appropriate law to be applied in calculating FAPI. This is in contrast with the rules in respect of the earnings of a foreign affiliate from an active business.[144] In the absence of specific rules, it is reasonable to assume that the domestic rules apply. Support for this view is found in subsection 9(1) which specifies that income from a business or property is the profit therefrom for the year. Presumably, the use of the word "income" in the definition of FAPI implies that the general rules of the Act apply in this context. On one point,

---

[142] *Cdn. Marconi v. The Queen*, [1986] 2 CTC 465 (S.C.C.).

[143] See, however, *Ensite Limited v. The Queen*, [1986] 2 CTC 459, 86 DTC 6521 (S.C.C.), where Wilson J. states that the presumption cannot be used to dissolve the distinction between income from property and business. See also, IT-73R4, "The Small Business Deduction—Income From An Active Business, a Specified Business and a Personal Services Business" (February 13, 1989). See generally, *Cosmopolitan Investments Co. v. M.N.R.*, [1974] CTC 2335, 74 DTC 1252 (T.R.B.); *Lazare Investments Corp. v. M.N.R.*, [1975] CTC 2036, 75 DTC 26 (T.R.B.); *Parico Ltée v. M.N.R.*, [1975] CTC 2234, 75 DTC 173 (T.R.B.); *M.R.T. Investments Ltd. v. The Queen, ante.* But see, *L&F Holdings Ltd. v. M.N.R.*, [1975] CTC 2192, 75 DTC 150 (T.R.B.) (reversed on consent); *Marlee Investments Ltd. v. M.N.R.*, [1975] CTC 2189, 75 DTC 153 (T.R.B.); *The Queen v. Cadboro Bay Holdings Ltd., ante*; *Farlan Investments Ltd. v. M.N.R.*, [1975] CTC 2016, 75 DTC 12 (T.R.B.); *Baramy Investments Ltd. v. M.N.R.*, [1977] CTC 2558, 77 DTC 400 (T.R.B.); *Smithers Plaza Ltd. v. M.N.R.*, [1975] CTC 2171, 75 DTC 137 (T.R.B.); *Income Tax Commr. v. Hanover Agencies Ltd.*, [1967] 1 AC 681 (P.C.); *SBI Properties Ltd. v. M.N.R.*, [1981] CTC 2288, 81 DTC 263 (T.R.B.) (rental income held to be income from active business even though management of properties was done by related company).

[144] Reg. 5907(1)(a).

however, the Act is quite specific: The calculation of capital gains and losses must be made in accordance with the Income Tax Act, specifically subdivision c of Division B.[145]

(iii) "Participating Percentage"

The amount of FAPI attributable to a resident taxpayer in respect of his or her controlled foreign affiliate is determined by the "participating percentage"[146] of each share of the first tier foreign corporation through which the controlled foreign affiliate is held.[147] The determination is made on a per share basis as at the end of each taxation year of the controlled foreign affiliate, regardless of any changes in shareholdings during the course of the year. Note, "participating percentage" is not synonymous with "equity percentage".

The "participating percentage" of a resident taxpayer in the capital stock of his or her controlled foreign affiliate is determined by one of two rules.[148] The general thrust of these rules is to determine the portion of the foreign income for the year that would have been received by the resident taxpayer if all of such income had been distributed (whether through a chain of corporations or otherwise) as at the end of the year. Where the controlled foreign affiliate has only one class of issued shares at the end of its taxation year and where all other corporations relevant to the calculation have only one class of shares, the taxpayer's participating percentage is the same as his or her equity percentage in the affiliate but calculated on a per share basis. Thus, in the simplest case, where a controlled foreign affiliate has only one class of shares with 100 shares outstanding at the end of a taxation year and the resident taxpayer holds all of the shares, the resident's equity percentage is 100 per cent and his or her participating percentage per share is 1 per cent.

Where more than one non-resident corporation is involved, it is necessary to calculate the resident taxpayer's equity percentage through a chain of corporations and then state that percentage on a per share basis to determine his or her participating percentage. Where the non-resident corporation has issued more than one class of shares, the calculation of the participating percentage is considerably more complicated.[149]

Note, however, in either case, there is no attribution where FAPI is $5,000 or less.[150]

---

[145] Para. 95(1)(b).

[146] Para. 95(1) ("participating percentage") (e).

[147] Subs. 91(1).

[148] Para. 95(1) ("participating percentage") (e).

[149] Reg. 5904.

[150] Subpara. 95(1)(e)(i).

Example XXXI.9

Assume:

NR Corp. (a non-resident corporation) has issued only 100 shares of a single class.

These shares are held by:

CR Ltd. (resident)	70 shares
NX Ltd. (non-resident)	30 shares
	100 shares

NX Ltd. has issued 1,000 shares of which 90 are owned by CR Ltd. CR Ltd.'s equity percentage in NR Ltd. is determined as follows:

Direct interest	70.0%
Indirect interest	2.7%
	72.7%

Therefore, the participating percentage per share of NR and NX Ltd. is 0.727 per cent.

---

7. DIVIDENDS FROM CONTROLLED FOREIGN AFFILIATES

A resident taxpayer must include FAPI in income as it is earned by his or her controlled foreign affiliates,[151] but he or she may deduct the amount of dividends received from previously taxed FAPI. The deduction is limited to the lesser of that portion of the dividend which remains after the deduction for underlying foreign tax[152] and the net adjustment to the adjusted cost base of the shares in the foreign affiliate.[153]

Example XXXI.10

Assume:

X Ltd. (a resident corporation) has a 100 per cent controlled foreign affiliate, Y Ltd. In 19-1, X Ltd.'s FAPI in Y Ltd. was $20,000 on which foreign tax of 20 per cent was paid. In 19-2, Y Ltd. pays a dividend of $16,000 out of its taxable surplus; there is withholding tax of $2,400.

---

[151] Subs. 91(1).

[152] Para. 113(1)(*b*).

[153] Subs. 91(5).

Example XXXI.10 (continued)

Then:

In 19-1

Earned FAPI	$ 20,000
Less:	
Foreign accrual tax deduction ($4,000 × 2.6315)	(10,526)
Taxable amount	$ 9,474
Tax thereon at 38%	$ 3,600

The total tax of $7,600 ($4,000 foreign and $3,600 domestic) is equal to the amount of tax that would have been payable had the same amount of income been earned in Canada and taxed at Canadian tax rates ($20,000 × 38% = $7,600).

In 19-2

Dividend received		$ 16,000
Less:		
Previously taxed FAPI		(9,474)
Income		$ 6,526
Less:		
Underlying foreign tax paid* ($4,000 × 1.6315)	$ 6,526	
Withholding tax** ($2,400 × 2.6315)	6,316	(12,842)
Loss		$ (6,316)
Tax saving thereon at 38%		$ (2,400)

Reconciliation of taxes paid:

Total taxes paid:

Foreign income tax	$ 4,000
Foreign withholding tax	2,400
Canadian income tax (19-1)	3,600
Canadian income tax (19-2)	(2,400)
	$ 7,600

   * Para. 113(1)(b)
  ** Para. 113(1)(c)

8. DISPOSITION OF SHARES OF FOREIGN AFFILIATE

A taxpayer may roll over his or her shares of a foreign affiliate to a corporation that qualifies as his or her foreign affiliate. More specifically, a taxpayer who disposes of his or her shares in a foreign affiliate to a corporation, that qualifies as his foreign affiliate immediately after the disposition, in exchange for consideration that includes shares of the acquiring foreign affiliate, may defer any capital gain or loss that might otherwise arise by virtue of the disposition.[154] The rollover is subject to anti-avoidance rules (discussed below).[155]

The rollover, which is available without election, works as follows: the vendor of the shares is deemed to receive proceeds of disposition equal to the deemed cost to him or her of all of the consideration that he or she receives in exchange for his or her shares.[156] Thus, he or she defers the recognition of any capital gains and losses that have accrued on the shares.

Non-share consideration is valued at its fair market value.[157] The cost of share consideration received from the acquiring affiliate is simply the difference between the adjusted cost base of the shares disposed of by the vendor and the fair market value of non-share consideration received in exchange from the acquiring affiliate.[158] Thus, non-share consideration in excess of the adjusted cost base of the shares disposed of will trigger an immediate capital gain.

The affiliate acquires the vendor's shares at an amount equal to the vendor's deemed proceeds of disposition.[159] In effect, for tax purposes, the acquiring affiliate steps into the shoes of the vendor.

---

[154] Subs. 85.1(3).

[155] Subs. 85.1(4).

[156] Para. 85.1(3)(c).

[157] Para. 85.1(3)(a).

[158] Para. 85.1(3)(b).

[159] Para. 85.1(3)(d).

Example XXXI.11

Assume:

CR Ltd. (a Canadian corporation) has two foreign affiliates: NR1 Ltd. and NR2 Ltd. The adjusted cost base of NR1 Ltd.'s shares is $800. CR Ltd. reorganizes its shareholdings and sells its shares in NR1 Ltd. to NR2 Ltd. in exchange for the following consideration:

	Case A	Case B	Case C
Debt (FMV)	NIL	$ 200	$1,000
Shares of NR2 Ltd.	?	?	?
Then:			
ACB of shares sold	$ 800	$ 800	$ 800
FMV of debt	—	(200)	(1,000)
ACB of new shares of NR2 Ltd.	$ 800	$ 600	NIL
Deemed POD	$ 800	$ 800	$1,000
ACB of shares sold	(800)	(800)	(800)
Capital gain	NIL	NIL	$ 200
Cost of NR1 Ltd.'s shares to NR2 Ltd.:	$ 800	$ 800	1,000

A rollover is also available where a taxpayer's foreign affiliate disposes of shares of another foreign affiliate of the taxpayer to a corporation which, immediately following the disposition, is also a foreign affiliate of the taxpayer.[160]

(a) Election to Treat Proceeds as Dividends

Where a Canadian resident corporation disposes of its shares of a foreign affiliate, it can elect to treat all, or any part, of its proceeds as a dividend rather than as proceeds of disposition.[161] The election is also available when a foreign affiliate of a Canadian resident corporation disposes of its shares of another of the resident corporation's foreign affiliates.

The purpose of this election is to allow Canadian resident corporations to take advantage of the deductions available in respect of dividends received from foreign

[160] Para. 95(2)(c).

[161] Subs. 93(1).

affiliates without having to actually pay a dividend and incur foreign tax.[162] As noted earlier, where a Canadian resident corporation receives a dividend from the exempt surplus of its foreign affiliates, the dividend is exempt from tax.[163] The election allows the resident corporation to take advantage of this rule if its foreign affiliate has accumulated an exempt surplus balance.

Where a foreign affiliate of a resident corporation disposes of shares of another foreign affiliate of the corporation and the shares are "excluded property",[164] the resident corporation is deemed to have made the election in respect of each share disposed of and to have designated the prescribed amount.[165]

"Excluded property" means shares in the capital of the other foreign affiliate where substantially all of the property of the affiliate is used or held in an active business.[166]

The amount that is deemed to have been designated is the lesser of:[167]

- the capital gain otherwise determined in respect of the particular disposition; and
- the amount that would have been received on the share if the affiliate had paid dividends in an amount equal to its net surplus.

The amount elected is deducted from the corporation's proceeds of disposition. Thus, the corporation's capital gain is reduced by a corresponding amount.

Example XXXI.12

Assume:

CR Ltd. (a resident corporation) has a wholly-owned foreign affiliate, FA Ltd. The adjusted cost base of FA Ltd.'s shares to CR Ltd. is $50,000.

CR Ltd. sells its shares in FA Ltd. for $10,000. The following data applies to FA Ltd.:

Exempt surplus	$ 20,000
Taxable surplus	$ 30,000
Underlying foreign tax	$ 10,000

---

[162] See subs. 113(1).

[163] Para. 113(1)(*a*).

[164] Para. 95(1)(*a.1*).

[165] Subs. 93(1.1), see the Example XXXII.11.

[166] Para. 95(1)(*a.1*).

[167] Reg. 5902(6).

Example XXXI.12 (continued)

Then:

	Without election	With $50,000 Subsec. 93(1) election
Proceeds of disposition	$ 100,000	$ 50,000
ACB	(50,000)	(50,000)
Capital gain	$ 50,000	NIL
Deemed dividend		$ 50,000
Less, aggregate of:		
(i) exempt surplus [para. 113(1)(a)]		(20,000)
(ii) underlying foreign tax × 1.6315 [para. 113(1)(b)]		(16,315)
Increase in taxable income	$ 37,500	$ 13,685

Special rules limit the amount of a capital loss that can be recognized on the disposition of shares of a foreign affiliate. The capital loss determined according to usual rules[168] is reduced by the amount of exempt dividends paid on the shares prior to their disposition.[169]

(b) Loss Limitation Rules

Where a resident taxpayer acquires shares in a foreign affiliate as a result of a disposition of his or her shares in another of his or her foreign affiliates, any capital loss resulting from the disposition is deemed to be nil and is added to the adjusted cost base of his or her newly acquired shares.[170]

---

[168] Subdivision c of Division B of the *Income Tax Act*.

[169] Subs. 93(2).

[170] Subs. 93(4).

(c) Anti-avoidance Rules

The rollover available to resident taxpayers who dispose of shares of one foreign affiliate to another foreign affiliate[171] is subject to an anti-avoidance rule. The rollover does not apply to dispositions of shares of foreign affiliates if:[172]

- all or substantially all of the affiliate's property is used to produce active business income; and

- the disposition is part of a transaction or series of transactions for the purpose of disposing of the shares to a person with whom the taxpayer is at arm's length.

---

[171] Subs. 85.1(3).

[172] Subs. 85.1(4).

SELECTED BIBLIOGRAPHY TO CHAPTER XXXI

Foreign Business Operations

Albeseder, Werner, "East Europe: Joint Venture Developments in Eastern Europe — Survey Over the Last Two Years" (1989), 29 *European Taxation* 270.

Andrews, Joseph R., "U.S. Tax Considerations in Financing Foreign Subsidiaries" (1990), 68 *Taxes* 683.

Ansley, et al., "Taxation Considerations With Respect to Transactions in China" (1987), 35 *Can. Tax J.* 433.

Arnold, Brian J., "An Analysis of the Amendments to the FAPI and Foreign Affiliate Rules" (1983), 31 *Can. Tax J.* 183.

Arnold, Brian J., "Partnerships and the Foreign Affiliate Rules" (1983), 31 *Can. Tax J.* 353.

Arnold, Brian J., "The Taxation of Controlled Foreign Corporations: An International Comparison", *Canadian Tax Paper No. 78/237* (Can. Tax Foundation, 1986).

Arnold, Brian J., "The Taxation of Controlled Foreign Corporations: Defining and Designing Tax Havens" (1985), 33 *Can. Tax J.* 445.

Bird, Richard. "International Aspects of Integration." (1975) 28 *National Tax Journal* 302.

Blessing, Peter H., "The Branch Tax in the U.S." (1986), 3 *The Journal of Strategy in Int'l. Taxation* 64.

Boidman, N., "Canada's Administrative Guidelines for Multinational Transactions: Information Circular No. 87-2" (1987), 40 *The Tax Executive* 35.

Boidman, N., "Canadian Tax Proposals — Cross Border Effects (Part II)" (November 9, 1990), 19 *Tax Management Int'l. J.* 485.

Boidman, N., "The Canadian Approach to Offshore International Transactions" (1988), 40 *The Tax Executive* 283.

Boidman, N., The Foreign Affiliate System: Canadian Taxation After 1982: A Structured Overview (Don Mills, Ontario: CCH Canadian Ltd., 1983).

Boidman, N. and Gary Carter, "Canada/U.S. Tax Reforms and Cross-Border Acquisitions" (July 1989), *Int'l. Tax Report* 1.

Boidman, N. and Gary Carter, "Tax Effective Strategies for Canada/U.S. Cross-Border Deals" (March 1989), *Int'l. Tax Report* 5.

Bradley, J. Douglas, "Financing Foreign Affiliates", *Corporate Management Tax Conf.* 411 (Can. Tax Foundation, 1986).

Broadhurst, D., "Recent Developments Here and There in Taxing International Income" (1979), 27 *Can. Tax J.* 201.

Broadhurst, D., "Revised Foreign Affiliate Regulations" (1985), 33 *Can. Tax J.* 344.

Broadhurst, D., "The All New 1983 Foreign Affiliate Regulations" (1982), 30 *Can. Tax J.* 891.

Broadhurst, D., "The All New 1983 Foreign Affiliate Regulations — Part II" (1983), 31 *Can. Tax J.* 61.

Brown, Robert D., "Taxation of Business Investment in the Federal Republic of Germany" (1988), 36 *Can. Tax J.* 177.

Cinnamon, Alan, "Why Foreign Investment in the U.K. Can Be Worthwhile" (January 1978), *Accountancy* 82.

Conley, Terrance W. and Paul W. Beamish, "Joint Ventures in China: Legal Implications" (November 1986), 51 *Business Quarterly* 39.

Dalsin, Derek, "Canada-U.S. Dual Resident Corporation: Tax Planning Restricted" (1986), 34 *Can. Tax J.* 621.

Dancey, K.J., R.A. Friesen and D.Y. Timbrell, Canadian Taxation of Foreign Affiliates, 4th ed. (Don Mills, Ont.: CCH Canadian Ltd., 1986).

Daniels, T. H.M., "Inbound Investments in the Netherlands: Supreme Court Rules on Abuse of Law" (1989), 10 *Intertax* 422.

Dart, Robert J., et al., "The 1982 Amendments: Implications for International Taxation", in *Proceedings of 34th Tax Conf.* 199 (Can. Tax Foundation, 1983).

Dart, Robert J., and David G. Broadhurst, "The Draft Technical Amendments" (1990), 38 *Can. Tax J.* 949.

Desjobert, Tatiana, "Legal and Tax Environment of Joint Ventures in the U.S.S.R." (1990), 1 *Int'l. Business Law J.* 557.

Dewhurst, J.R., Migration United Kingdom, 2nd ed., (Deventer, the Netherlands: Kluwer, 1986).

Dolan, D. Kevin, "A Primer on 'General Utilities' Issues in International Acquisitions, Dispositions and Restructurings" (1989), 10 *Intertax* 399.

Dolan, D. Kevin and Carolyn M. Dupuy, "Engaged in U.S. Business — Permanent Establishment", American Law Institute — American Bar Association Course of Study Materials: International Taxation 67-90 (October 26-27, 1989, New York, New York).

Easson, A.J. and Li Jinyan, Taxation of Foreign Investments in the People's Republic of China (Deventer, the Netherlands: Kluwer, 1989).

Ensslin, Dankwart, "Taxation of Business Investment in the Federal Republic of Germany" (1988), 36 *Can. Tax J.* 176.

Feingold, Fred and Mark E. Berg, "Whither the Branches?" (1989), 44 *Tax Law Review* 205.

Feingold, Fred and David M. Rozen, "Branch Level Taxation — A Second Level of Concern" (1986), 34 *Can. Tax J.* 1192.

Fisher, Arthur L. and Aaron A. Rubenstein, "The Branch Level Taxes of the Tax Reform Act of 1986 — One Step Towards Equality of Treatment for Branches and Subsidiaries" (1987), *The Tax Adviser* 634.

Fiszer, Janusz, "Poland: Taxation of Foreign Investment and Income Tax Treaties", [1991] 4 *Intertax* 221.

Freisen, Robert A., "Financing Foreign Affiliates", *Corporate Management Tax Conf.* 330 (Can. Tax Foundation, 1980).

Frommel, S.N., Taxation of Branches and Subsidiaries in Western Europe, Canada and the U.S.A., 2nd ed. (London: Kluwer, 1978).

Gibson, Roger, "Doing Business in Australia: A Tax Perspective" (1987), 35 *Can. Tax J.* 1263.

Glicklich, Peter A., "Acquisitions of U.S. Businesses by Foreign Persons", American Law Institute — American Bar Association Course of Study Materials: International Taxation 273 (October 26-27, 1989, New York, New York).

Glover, Paul, "Basic Tax Reform in the U.S." (November/December 1986), 60 *CMA* 44.

Goldberg, ". . . ultinational Analysis" (1986), 39 *The Tax Executive* 5.

Gordon, Richard A., Andrew C. Newman and Rodney W. Burton, "International Examination Issues — A Survey of Various Countries" (1986), 38:3 *The Tax Executive* 213.

Halphen, Christine, "The Proposed Branch Tax and Foreign Investment in U.S. Real Estate" (1986), 15 *Tax Management Int'l J.* 126.

Halphen, Christine and N. Boidman, "Interaction Between the U.S. Branch Tax, FIRPTA and Investments by Canadian Corporations" (1986), 15 *Tax Management Int'l. J.* 487.

Hammer, Richard M., "Canadian Acquisition of a U.S. Business: A U.S. Perspective", *Corporate Management Tax Conf.* 274 (Can. Tax Foundation, 1984).

Harris, E., "Recent Canadian Income Tax Amendments: International Aspects" (1981), 35 Bull. Int'l. Fisc. Doc. 368.

Hart, John C., "Foreign Investment . . . Acquisitions" (1988), 40 *The Tax Executive* 261.

Hausman, J., "International Tax Developments", in *Proceedings of 33rd Tax Conf.* 893 (Can. Tax Foundation, 1981).

Howick, Wallace M., "Expansion into the United States: Selected Tax Considerations", in *Proceedings of 41st Tax Conf.* 16:1 (Can. Tax Foundation, 1989).

"Host Country Business Operations: Branch or Subsidiary?" (1986), 7 *Tax Management Int'l. Forum* 1:7.

Howick, Wallace M., "Expansion into the U.S.: Selected Tax Considerations", in *Proceedings of 41st Tax Conf.* 16:1 (Can. Tax Foundation, 1989).

Hudson, Robert F. Jr., "Post-1988 Tax Planning for Foreign Direct Investment in the United States" (January 13, 1989), 18:1 *Tax Management Int'l. J.* 3.

Huggett, Donald R., "U.S. Update" (1990), XVII *Can. Tax News* 74.

Jacobsen, Richard A., "An Introduction to Foreign Investment in the United States After the Tax Reform Act of 1986" (1987), 65 *Taxes* 339.

Johnson, Thomas E., "Structuring Joint Ventures in Eastern Europe" (March 1991), 18:3 *Tax Planning Int'l. Rev.* 25.

Kinoshita, Ray, "Tax Issues for Canadian Companies with U.S. Operations" (December/January 1991), 64 *CMA Magazine* 31.

Kutzin, Michael S., "Canadian Limited Partner in U.S. Partnership has a U.S. Permanent Establishment Under Canada-U.S. Tax Treaty" (1990), 38 *Can. Tax J.* 1053.

Lam, Bill and Kaushal Tikku, "Tax Implications of Doing Business in Hong Kong" (1987), 35 *Can. Tax J.* 1467.

Lanthier, Allan R., "Canada: Tough Times Ahead for Multinationals?" (1989), 41 *The Tax Executive* 123.

Lanthier, Allan R., "Liquidations of Foreign Affiliates Under Subsection 88(3)" (1985), 33 *Can. Tax J.* 245.

Levey, Marc M. ed., Foreign Investment in the United States: Law, Taxation, Finance (New York: John Wiley & Sons, 1989).

Li, Jinyan. "The Concept of Permanent Establishment in China's Tax Treaties." (1989) 7:120 *International Tax and Business Lawyer* 120.

Loveland, Norman C., "Acquisition of a U.S. Business by Canadians: A Canadian Perspective", *Corporate Management Tax Conf.* 11:1 (Can. Tax Foundation, 1990).

McDaniel, Paul R. and Miriam V. Sheehan, "Investing and Doing Business in the U.S.A." (1988), 10 *Intertax* 336.

McDaniel, Paul R. and Miriam V. Sheehan, "Investing and Doing Business in the U.S.A." (1988), 12 *Intertax* 435.

McLure, Charles E. Jr., "Economic Integration and European Taxation of Corporate Income — Some Lessons from the U.S. Experience" (1989), 29 *European Taxation* 243.

Mizuno, Tadatsune. "The Basic Concepts of International Taxation and their Application to Japanese Law." (1988) 22 *University of British Columbia Law Review* 159.

Moser, Michael J. and Winston K. Zee, China Tax Guide (Oxford: Oxford University Press, 1987).

Nitikman, Joel, "The Meaning of 'Permanent Establishment' in the 1981 U.S. Model Income Tax Treaty: Part I" (1989), 15 *Int'l. Tax J.* 159.

Nitikman, Joel, "The Meaning of 'Permanent Establishment' in the 1981 U.S. Model Income Tax Treaty: Part 2" (1989), 15 *Int'l. Tax J.* 257.

Peter, C.M., "Taxation of Foreign Investments in Tanzania: An Overview" (1989), 4 *Intertax* 136.

Richardson, E., "International Developments in Canadian Income Tax Laws" (1983), 11 *Int'l. Bus. Law* 81.

Rohrer, William D. and Richard M. Hammer, "U.S. Branch Taxation: A Venture into the Unknown" (1987), 41 *Bull. Int'l. Fisc. Doc.* 3.

Rolt, Sidney C. and Hamed Talib, "Income Taxation in the Asean Countries, Singapore, Asian-Pacific", Tax & Investment Research Centre, 1986.

Rosenbloom, H. David, "Foreign Banks Operating in the United States", American Law Institute — American Bar Association Course of Study Materials: International Taxation 147 (October 26-27, 1989, New York, New York).

Rosenbloom, H. David, "The New U.S. Tax Treatment of Branches" (1986), 18 *Investment/U.S.A.* 3.

Schwartz, Alan M., "Tax-Free Reorganizations of Foreign Affiliates" (1984), 32 *Can. Tax J.* 1039.

Silbergleit, Kenneth R., "Structuring or Restructuring Canadian Investment in U.S. Assets" (1988), 36 *Can. Tax J.* 1584.

Silbergleit, Kenneth R., "Structuring or Restructuring Canadian Investment in U.S. Assets (Particularly Real Property): A Primer on FIRPTA, the BPT and Other Relevant U.S. Tax Provisions — Part 2" (1989), 37 *Can. Tax J.* 517.

Singer, Paul B., "Branch Tax Planning", in *Proceedings of 39th Tax Conf.* 21:1 (Can. Tax Foundation, 1987).

Stikeman, Heward H., "Taxation of Offshore Income and the Canadian Treaty Network" (1982), 36 *Bull. Int'l. Fisc. Doc.* 351.

"Third Country Investment in Home Country Through the Use of Home Country Treaty With Tax Havens" (1987), 8 *Tax Management Int'l. Forum* 1.

Tremblay, Richard G., "'Active Business' Income in the FAPI Context: Recent Developments" (1987), 2:2 *Canadian Current Tax* C-4.

Ulmer, John M., "Canadian Acquisition of a Foreign Business: A Canadian Perspective", *Corporate Management Tax Conf.* 245 (Can. Tax Foundation, 1984).

Verchere, B., "Foreign Source Income-Tax Planning Concepts", in *Proceedings of 27th Tax Conf.* 603 (Can. Tax Foundation, 1976).

Ward, David A., "Taxation of Income of Foreign Affiliates", in Ward's Tax Law and Planning, Chapter 20 (Toronto: Carswell, 1983).

Webb, Gary J., "Structuring and Financing U.S. Operations: A Current Canadian Perspective" (May 23, 1990) Special Seminar on Current International Tax Issues (DeBoo, 1990) 159.

Webb, Gary J., "Tax Factors Affecting the Choice Between a U.S. Branch and a U.S. Subsidiary", in *Proceedings of 40th Tax Conf.* 45:1 (Can. Tax Foundation, 1988).

Wenehed, Lars Erik and Willem G. Kuiper, "High Tax Countries: An Alternative for Tax Havens?" (1988), 28 *European Taxation* 103.

Williams, Robert L., "Permanent Establishments in the United States" (1976), 29 Tax Lawyer 277.

Worrell, DeLisle, "The Tax System of Barbados" (1989), 43 *Bull. Int'l. Fisc. Doc.* 457.

Yam, Stephen, "Accounting for Joint Ventures in China" (July/August 1986), 60 *CMA* 24.

Zbigniew, Czubinski, "Poland — New Joint Venture Legislation" (1989), 29:4 *European Taxation* 132.

Zheng, Henry R. "The Sino-U.S. Income Tax Treaty and its Effect on Chinese Taxation of American Economic Interests" (Spring 1987), 40 *Tax Law* 733.

Foreign Real Estate

Barnicke, Paul L., "U.S. Vacation Property" (1989), 37 *Can. Tax J.* 763.

Boidman, N., "Canadian Investment in U.S. Real Estate", in *Proceedings of 33rd Tax Conf.* 454 (Can. Tax Foundation, 1981).

Boidman, N., "Canadian Investment in U.S. Real Estate — Impact of the New Canada-U.S. Tax Convention and the Foreign Investment in Real Property Tax Act of 1980, May 1981 and June 1981", *Tax Management Int'l. J.*

Boidman, N. and Gary J. Gartner, "Reorganizing Canadian Investments in U.S. Real Estate — Proposed FIRPTA Regulations" (January 13, 1989), 18:1 *Tax Management Int'l. J.* 28.

Boidman, N. and Richard M. Hammer, "Canadian Investment in U.S. Real Estate: Canada and U.S. Perspectives", *Corporate Management Tax Conf.* 9:1 (Can. Tax Foundation, 1989).

Cohen, S.J., "Canadian Investment in U.S. Real Property", in *Proceedings of 38th Tax Conf.* 29:1 (Can. Tax Foundation, 1986).

Fijolek, Richard M. and Timothy E. Powers, "Complying With FIRPTA: A Manual of Forms", 1989 American Bar Association Real Property, Probate and Trust Law Section, Committee on Foreign Investment in U.S. Real Estate.

Forst, Robert C., "Federal Income Taxation of Foreign Investment in the United States" (1979), 3 British Tax Rev. 145.

Goldberg, S.H. and M. Kirschfeld, "Reporting Requirements for Foreign Investments in U.S. Realty" (1983), 31 *Can. Tax J.* 95.

Goldberg, S.H. and M. Kirschfeld, "Reporting Requirements for Foreign Investment in U.S. Realty — Recent Highlights" (1983), 31 *Can. Tax J.* 256.

Gunkel, Manfred and Heinz-Klaus Kroppen, "Taxation of Investments in German Real Estate by Foreign Corporate Investors" (1991), 6-7 *Intertax* 325.

Halphen, Christine, "The Proposed Branch Tax and Foreign Investment in U.S. Real Estate" (1986), 15 *Tax Management Int'l J.* 126.

Hammer, Richard M., "Tax Rules on Foreign Investment in Real Estate", in *Proceedings of 33rd Tax Conf.* 420 (Can. Tax Foundation, 1981).

Hausman, James S., "The Canada-U.S. Tax Convention: New Rules for Canadians Investing in U.S. Real Estate", in *Proceedings of 36th Tax Conf.* 257 (Can. Tax Foundation, 1984).

Hudson, Robert F., "Planning for Foreign Investment in U.S. Real Estate After the Tax Reform Act of 1986" (1987), 16 *Tax Management Int'l. J.* 3.

Hudson, Robert F., Stephen A. Nauheim and Stanley L. Blend, "Use of Split-Interest Partnerships for Foreign Investment in U.S. Real Estate" (1988), 17 *Tax Management Int'l. J.* 275.

Knight, Donald, "Investment in U.S. Real Estate Through Netherlands Antilles Corporations: Effect of the U.S. Tax Reform Act of 1986 and New U.S.-Netherlands Antilles Tax Treaty" (1986), 8 *Investment/U.S.A.* 2.

Morris, Ronald A., Larry S. Wolf and Carolyn J.L. Ichel, Federal Taxation of Real Estate (New York: Practising Law Institute, 1989).

Nauheim, Stephen A., "Foreign Acquisition of U.S. Real Estate", American Law Institute — American Bar Association Course of Study Materials: International Taxation 91 (October 26-27, 1989, New York, New York).

Nauheim, Stephen A. and Hugh H. Jacobsen, "Proposed United States-Netherlands Antilles Income Tax Treaty: New Opportunities for Foreign Investment in U.S. Real Estate" (1986), 15 *Tax Management Int'l J.* 462.

Saunders, M. Roy, Structuring International Real Estate Transactions (London: Sweet & Maxwell Ltd., 1991).

Silbergleit, Kenneth R., "Structuring or Restructuring Canadian Investment in U.S. Assets" (1988), 36 *Can. Tax J.* 1584.

Silbergleit, Kenneth R., "Structuring or Restructuring Canadian Investment in U.S. Assets (Particularly Real Property): A Primer on FIRPTA, the BPT and Other Relevant U.S. Tax Provisions — Part 2" (1989), 37 *Can. Tax J.* 517.

Smith, David C., "Canadian Investment in U.S. Real Estate: A U.S. Perspective", *Corporate Management Tax Conf.* 341 (Can. Tax Foundation, 1983).

Swiderski, Tony, "Transfers of U.S. Real Property Interests in Canadian Reorganizations: Opportunities, Limitations, and Pitfalls" (1989), 37 *Can. Tax J.* 605.

Walker, Marlan C. and Eric M. Casper, "United States Real Estate and Foreign Corporate Investors: Maximizing Tax Benefits from Real Estate Carrying Charges by Passive Foreign Corporate Investors" (1987), *Journal of Real Estate Taxation* 137.

Ward, David A., "Canadian Investment in U.S. Real Estate: A Canadian Perspective", *Corporate Management Tax Conf.* 311 (Can. Tax Foundation, 1983).

CHAPTER XXXII

EMIGRATION

We saw earlier that a Canadian resident is subject to tax on his or her world-wide income. A Canadian resident who gives up his or her Canadian residence is subject to tax on global income earned up to the date of his or her departure. Thereafter, he is taxed as a non-resident of Canada.

1. INDIVIDUALS

Whether an individual has given up his or her Canadian residence is a question of fact in each case. Generally speaking, giving up Canadian residence involves severing physical, financial, family, social and business ties with Canada to a sufficient degree so that one does not have a continued nexus with the country. The Department's view is that a Canadian resident generally becomes a non-resident on the latest of dates following:

- the day of his or her departure from Canada;
- the day his or her spouse/or dependants leave Canada; and
- the date that he or she becomes a resident of the country to which he or she is emigrating.

These indicia are not absolute and much depends upon the taxpayer's life profile. Generally speaking, an individual who was previously resident in another country and who returns to that country will find it easier to give up his Canadian residence than an individual who has always been a Canadian resident.

(a) Departure Tax

An individual who gives up his or her Canadian residence is subject to a "departure tax" in respect of certain properties. A taxpayer who ceases to be resident in Canada is considered to have disposed of his or her property immediately before he gives up his or her Canadian residence. Subject to certain exceptions, a taxpayer is deemed to dispose of each of the following properties at their fair market value immediately prior to the cessation of residence. The deemed disposition rules do not apply to certain types of property such as:

- taxable Canadian property;
- capital property which the taxpayer elects to treat as "taxable Canadian property";
- inventory used in a business carried on in Canada;
- right to receive certain payments; and
- eligible capital property.

The above list of exempt properties is justified on the basis that Canada can expect to tax any gain realized on their disposition at a later time.

(b) Taxable Canadian Property

An individual is not subject to the departure tax on his or her taxable Canadian property. Taxable Canadian property is only subject to tax upon its actual disposition by the non-resident or upon its deemed disposition for Canadian income tax purposes, such as, upon the death of the taxpayer.

Paragraph 115(1)(b) defines the taxpayer's "taxable Canadian property" to include the following:

- real estate in Canada;
- capital property used by the taxpayer in carrying on a business (other than an insurance business) in Canada;
- shares of a private corporation resident in Canada;
- shares of a public corporation if at any time in the five-year period immediately preceding his or her departure the taxpayer (or a person with whom he or she did not deal at arm's length) owned not less than 25 per cent of the issued shares of any class;
- partnership interest in which at least 50 per cent of the fair market value of the assets consist of Canadian resource properties, timber resource properties, income interests in trusts resident in Canada or any other "taxable Canadian properties";
- capital interests in trusts (other than unit trusts) resident in Canada;
- units of certain unit trusts resident in Canada;
- units of Canadian mutual fund trusts if at any time in the five-year period immediately preceding departure the taxpayer (or persons with whom he or she did not deal at arm's length) owned not less than 25 per cent of its issued units;
- any other properties deemed by the Act to be "taxable Canadian properties";
- Canadian resource properties;
- timber resource properties;
- income interests in resident trusts;
- retiring partner's income rights under certain partnership agreements; and
- life insurance policies in Canada (see extended definition in proposed changes to subsection 248(1)).

The above properties are not subject to the deemed disposition rules that are triggered by an individual's giving up his or her Canadian residence.

(i) Election to Trigger Tax

An individual (other than the trust) may elect to have his or her taxable Canadian property made subject to the departure tax rules. The taxpayer must file the elections no later than the time that he or she would file the income tax return for the year of departure. It should be noted, however, that the taxpayer's ability to use the election to trigger losses is limited: the taxpayer's losses may not exceed his or her income or gains realized from his or her deemed dispositions.

Thus, capital property that is generally subject to the deemed disposition and departure tax rules includes the following:

* portfolio investments in public corporations;
* shares in non-resident corporations;
* foreign real estate;
* capital interests in foreign trusts;
* capital property that is not used in carrying on a business in Canada;
* certain partnership interests;
* personal use property; and
* listed personal property.

(ii) Election to Defer Tax

An individual (other than the trust) may elect not to have the departure tax rules apply to the deemed disposition of his or her capital property. In these circumstances, however, the individual must provide the Department with adequate security for any tax foregone as a result of the election. Property covered by the election is considered to be "taxable Canadian property" until such time as the taxpayer disposes of it or the taxpayer again becomes resident in Canada. This election must also be made in a prescribed manner by the taxpayer's balance-due day for the taxation year in which he or she becomes a non-resident. The taxpayer's ability to create a loss through the use of the election is also limited.

(iii) Resident in Canada for Less Than Five Years

A taxpayer who has been resident in Canada for less than an aggregate period of 60 months in the ten years immediately preceding his or her departure is not subject to the departure tax in respect of any property that he or she owned at the time that he or she last became a Canadian resident or that he or she acquired during Canadian residency by inheritance or bequest.

Recaptured depreciation resulting from a deemed disposition of depreciable capital property is subject to the departure tax.

Real estate inventory outside of Canada is subject to the departure tax.

A taxpayer who might otherwise be subject to the departure tax can elect to have his or her capital property treated as "taxable Canadian property". Such an election allows the taxpayer to defer any tax that might be payable on accrued capital gains until such time as he or she actually disposes of the property or is deemed to have disposed of the property.

The election must be made by April 30 of the year following the year of departure from Canada. In the event that the non-resident becomes subject to tax in another country on the capital gain, the taxpayer may reduce his or her Canadian Part I tax that would otherwise be payable by the amount of his or her foreign tax liability. The foreign tax credit is subject to certain limits.[1]

The Department will usually accept as security a charge on the property, a guarantee from another person or a declaration of trust from a financial institution.

The loss limitation rules on the election are intended to prevent a taxpayer from deferring tax on accrued capital gains and realizing losses at the same time.

The decision to elect treatment of capital property as "taxable Canadian property" will depend upon individual circumstances, including, any anticipated increase in the value of the property, availability of losses, and the ability to pay tax at the particular time. Generally speaking, it is advantageous to make the election to avoid potential double taxation problems. In the event that an individual does not make an election and pays the departure tax, a subsequent gain on the property calculated by reference to the historic cost of the property may result in double taxation without any offsetting tax credit.

An individual who wants to give up his or her Canadian residence for tax purposes should consider the following:

- Sell Canadian home: continued ownership of a home in Canada may be construed as a strong link with Canada for tax purposes. In the event that it is not possible to sell the home, it is generally desirable to lease it for a period of at least one or, preferably, two years. An individual who leaves Canada but maintains a dwelling place suitable for year round occupancy would not generally be considered to have severed residential ties with Canada.

- Terminate Canadian lease: residential leases should be cancelled or the premises should be sublet on a long-term (one or two years) lease.

- Family members should depart Canada: dependent children should not remain in Canada and certainly not in the family home. In the event that the children are to continue their education in Canada, they should either live in independent quarters or in a boarding school.

---

[1] Subs. 126(2.2).

- Cancellation of club and professional memberships: the individual should cancel all Canadian club memberships, and, wherever practicable, obtain non-resident membership status.
- Sale of automobiles, boats, etc.: the registration of all automobiles and boats, etc. should be changed to reflect the individual's new residence.
- Cancellation of credit cards: it is generally preferable for the individual to cancel all of his Canadian credit cards and take out new credit cards in his new country.
- Closure of bank accounts: all Canadian bank accounts should be closed. In the event that it is necessary to maintain a Canadian account, it should be maintained on a non-resident basis with a non-resident address and appropriate withholding taxes should be paid on any investment income earned.

(iv) Principal Residence

The sale or deemed disposition of an individual's principal residence does not usually trigger tax liability in Canada provided that the property has been owner-occupied during the relevant period. A principal residence in Canada would be considered to be taxable Canadian property and, therefore, would be exempt from the departure tax. When the non-resident subsequently disposes of the property, he will be liable for tax on the portion of the gain that is accrued subsequent to his or her departure from Canada. Any gain accrued during his or her residence in Canada would be tax exempt if the property was owner-occupied during the period of time.

Where a departing resident rents out his or her home, the resulting change in use of the property is considered a deemed disposition for tax purposes. The taxpayer is deemed to have disposed of his or her residence for proceeds equal to the fair market value of the property and to have reacquired it immediately thereafter at a cost equal to its fair market value.

An individual may elect to have his or her residence to continue to qualify as a principal residence even though he or she has changed its use to a rental property. The election allows the non-resident individual to designate the Canadian residence as the principal residence for a period of up to four years while the election remains in force.

If the non-resident disposes of the property within the four-year period, it will be exempt from Canadian tax for the period during which he or she was resident in Canada plus one year if the home is designated as a principal residence during that period of time.

An individual who plans to give up Canadian residency will generally find it advantageous to dispose of his or her principal residence while still a Canadian resident. This will maximize the tax exempt capital gain and minimize foreign tax complications.

In the event that the residence is sold after a taxpayer becomes a non-resident, the capital gain on the disposition will have to be determined according to the rules of the taxpayer's new country of residence.

The principal residence that is outside of Canada is subject to departure tax. Such a residence may, however, be designated as a principal residence in order to avoid the departure tax.

(c) Residence for U.S. Income Tax

Residence is the primary basis of U.S. jurisdiction to tax income. "Resident aliens" are taxable on their world-wide income; "non-resident aliens" are generally taxable on their U.S. source income. Domicile, which is a broader concept than residence, is used as the jurisdictional basis to tax estates on death.

An individual is a "resident alien" if, and only if, he or she:[2]

- is a lawful permanent resident of the U.S. *at any time* during the calendar year ("green card" test);
- has a "substantial presence" in the U.S.; or
- elects to be treated as a resident.

An individual is considered a non-resident alien if he is neither a citizen nor a resident of the U.S.

(i) "Green Card" Test

An individual is considered a lawful permanent resident of the U.S. if he or she has a "green card" (the original colour of the registration card) issued by the U.S. Immigration and Naturalization Service to foreign nationals with permanent residence status. This is a bright line test that clearly establishes whether or not an individual is a resident alien for U.S. tax purposes. The Immigration and Naturalization Service automatically notifies the Internal Revenue Service of a foreign national's arrival in the U.S.

(ii) "Substantial Presence" Test

An individual can also be considered a resident alien through a "substantial presence" in the U.S. Substantial presence is determined by a weighted average formula that looks at the number of days of physical presence in the U.S. in the current year and the previous two years.

An individual is considered to have a substantial presence with respect to any calendar year if:[3]

- he or she was present in the U.S. on at least 31 days during the year, *and*
- the number of days spent in the U.S. during the year in question, plus one-third of the number of days in the preceding year, plus one-sixth of the number of days in the second preceding year, exceeds 182 days.

---

[2]   Subs. 7701(b) IRC.

[3]   Subs. 7701(b)(3) IRC.

Thus, an individual who spends 183 days or more in a calendar year in the U.S. is automatically a resident alien for U.S. tax purposes. An individual who spends less than 31 days in the U.S. is not a resident alien even if the weighted average of his presence in the U.S. in the past two years exceeds 183 days.

Example XXXII.1

Assume that an individual spends 120 days of each year in the U.S. The individual would not have a "substantial presence" in the U.S. because the composite of his or her stays in the U.S. in the three-year period would only amount to 182 days.

YEAR	NUMBER OF DAYS	MULTIPLIER	COMPOSITE
1994	120	1	120
1993	120	1/3	40
1992	120	1/6	20
		TOTAL	180

If, however, the individual spent 123 days in 1994 in the U.S., he or she would have a "substantial presence" in the U.S. in 1994 and be deemed a resident alien for income tax purposes. Assuming that the individual spent the remainder of his or her time in Canada, he or she would also be considered a Canadian resident.[4]

In computing the weighted average of days, fractional days of presence in the U.S. are considered as whole days. When dividing by the one-third or one-sixth factors for preceding years, however, any resultant fractions are ignored.

Example XXXII.2

YEAR	NUMBER OF DAYS	MULTIPLIER	COMPOSITE
1994	122	1	122
1993	122	1/3	40 2/3
1992	122	1/6	20 1/3
		TOTAL	182

Foreign nationals with a substantial presence in the U.S. are considered resident aliens from the first day of the year that they are physically present in the U.S. The last day of residency is generally the date on which the foreign national physically departs the U.S.

---

[4] Subs. 250(1).

(iii) Presence in the U.S.

Although physical presence in the U.S. is a question of fact, there are special exceptions and rules for certain individuals. An individual is not considered to be present in the U.S. on any day if his or her presence in the country is attributable to his or her inability to leave because of a medical condition which arose while he or she was present in the U.S. There are also exemptions in respect of diplomats, public international organization employees, teachers, trainees, students, professional athletes temporarily in the U.S. to compete in charitable events, commuters from Canada and Mexico, and the immediate family of any of these persons.

(iv) "Closer Connection" with Another Country

An individual who otherwise meets the substantial presence test in a year may, nevertheless, claim not to be a resident of the U.S. if:

- he or she is present in the U.S. for less than 183 days in the year,
- he or she has a "tax home"[5] in another country, and
- he or she has a "closer connection" to that country.

Example XXXII.3

Assume that an individual was present in the U.S. for 180 days in 1994, 21 days in 1993 and 18 days in 1992.

YEAR	NUMBER OF DAYS	MULTIPLIER	COMPOSITE
1994	180	1	180
1993	21	1/3	7
1992	18	1/6	3
		TOTAL	190

In these circumstances, the individual would generally be considered to have a "substantial presence" in the U.S.[6] If, however, the individual has a tax home in another country and a "closer connection" to that country than to the U.S., he or she is not considered to have a substantial presence in the U.S. Thus, there can be a significant difference in the U.S. tax status of an individual who spends 183 days in a year in the U.S. and an individual who spends less than 183 days.

---

[5] Subs. 911(d)(3) IRC.

[6] Subs. 911(d)(3) IRC.

(v) Filing Requirements

A U.S. resident is required to file an income tax return (Form 1040) for each calendar year. Thus, an individual who meets the substantial presence test is normally expected to file a U.S. income tax return unless he or she can establish that he or she is not required to do so by virtue of a treaty.

Individuals who claim to have a closer connection to another country are required to file a statement to that effect with the Internal Revenue Service. Failure to file the statement on a timely basis precludes the individual from claiming the "closer connection" exemption.

(vi) "Closer Connection" Statement

An individual's closer connection with another country is a question of fact determined by his or her family, social and business connections and contacts. An individual who claims a "closer connection" with another country should file a statement with the Internal Revenue Service and disclose the following:

- number of days present in the U.S. in the current year and in each of the immediately preceding two years;
- the address of any permanent furnished residence outside of the U.S.;
- name and address of the authorities to whom property and school taxes are paid;
- disclosure information on driver's licence;
- disclosure information as to club memberships, affiliations with churches, congregations, etc.;
- disclosure as to personal banking facilities and maintenance of investment accounts with foreign financial institutions;
- disclosure of registration as a voter in the foreign country;
- disclosure of the dollar value of gross income from the conduct of business in the U.S.; and
- a statement that no steps have been taken to secure permanent resident status in the U.S. and that there is no application pending for such status before the U.S. authorities.

(vii) Canada-U.S. Treaty

Article IV of the *Canada-U.S. Treaty* is as follows:

1. For the purposes of this Convention, the term "resident of a Contracting State" means any person who, under the laws of that State, is liable to tax therein by reason of his domicile, residence, place of management, place of incorporation or any other criterion of a similar nature, but in the case of an estate or trust, only to the extent that income derived by such estate or trust is liable to tax in that State, either in its hands or in the hands of its beneficiaries.

2. Where by reason of the provisions of paragraph 1 an individual is a resident of both Contracting States, then his status shall be determined as follows:

(a) he shall be deemed to be a resident of the Contracting State in which he has a permanent home available to him; if he has a permanent home available to him in both States or in neither State, he shall be deemed to be a resident of the Contracting State with which his personal and economic relations are closer (centre of vital interests);

(b) if the Contracting State in which he has his centre of vital interests cannot be determined, he shall be deemed to be a resident of the Contracting State in which he has an habitual abode;

(c) if he has an habitual abode in both States or in neither State, he shall be deemed to be a resident of the Contracting State of which he is a citizen; and

(d) if he is a citizen of both States or of neither of them, the competent authorities of the Contracting States shall settle the question by mutual agreement.

. . .

4. Where by reason of the provisions of paragraph 1 an estate, trust or other person (other than an individual or a company) is a resident of both Contracting States, the competent authorities of the States shall by mutual agreement endeavour to settle the question and to determine the mode of application of the Convention to such person.

5. Notwithstanding the provisions of the preceding paragraphs, an individual shall be deemed to be a resident of a Contracting State if:

(a) the individual is an employee of that State or of a political subdivision, local authority or instrumentality thereof rendering services in the discharge of functions of a governmental nature in the other Contracting State or in a third State; and

(b) the individual is subjected in the first-mentioned State to similar obligations in respect of taxes on income as are residents of the first-mentioned State.

The spouse and dependent children residing with such an individual and meeting the requirements of subparagraph (b) above shall also be deemed to be residents of the first-mentioned State.

Article IV generally follows the *OECD Model Convention*, but the term "national" is not used in either the Canadian or U.S. domestic fiscal statutes. Instead, both countries refer to "citizens" and this is reflected in the *Canada-U.S. Treaty* to resolve cases of dual residence.[7]

The phrase "any other criterion of a similar nature" includes, for U.S. purposes, an election to be treated as a resident under the Code.

An estate or trust is considered to be a resident of a Contracting State only to the extent that income derived by the estate or trust is liable to tax in that State either in its hands or in the hands of its beneficiaries. To the extent that an estate or trust is considered a resident of a Contracting State, it can be a "beneficial owner" of specific types of income that may be specified in other articles of the Convention, for example, under Article X(2) (Dividends).[8]

Article IV(5) of the *Canada-U.S. Treaty* deems an individual to be resident in a Contracting State if:

---

[7] Article IV(2)(c).

[8] See: Technical Explanation.

- he or she is employed directly by that State or a sub-division of its government; and

- he or she is subjected in his or her home State to similar tax obligations as its own residents.

The individual's spouse and dependent children who reside with him or her (and are subject to tax on a basis similar to other residents in the home State) are also deemed to be residents of their home States. This rule overrides the normal tie-breaker rules in Article IV(2).

A U.S. citizen or resident who is an employee of the U.S. government in a foreign country or who is a spouse or dependant of such employee is considered to be subject in the U.S. to "similar obligations" in respect of taxes on income as those imposed on other residents of the U.S. Thus, a U.S. citizen who is an employee of the U.S. government is not considered a Canadian resident.

(viii) Dual Residence

A U.S. "dual resident" is an individual who qualifies as a resident alien under Section 7701 IRC but is also a resident of another country, either as a result of that country's domestic law or because of a treaty between the two countries.

An individual who claims dual residence is required to disclose his or her filing position to the Internal Revenue Service. Section 6114 *IRC* requires the taxpayer to:

- specify the Internal Revenue Code provisions overruled or modified;

- specify the provisions of the limitation on benefits article (if any) and the treaty that the taxpayer relies on to prevent application of that article;

- explain the treaty-based return position taken together with a brief summary of the facts on which it is based; and

- list the nature and amount (or a reasonable estimate) of gross receipts, each separate gross payment and each separate gross income item for which the treaty benefit is claimed. A separate form is required for each treaty-based return position taken by the taxpayer.

A Canadian resident who cannot claim the closer connection exemption under IRC 7701(b)(3)(B) because he or she has crossed the threshold of having spent more than 182 days in the U.S. may, nevertheless, be able to claim the exemption from U.S. tax by virtue of the *Canada-U.S. Treaty.*

There is an important difference, however, between the status of an individual who claims the "closer connection" exemption and an individual who claims treaty protection as a "dual resident": the closer connection exemption deems qualifying individuals to be non-residents of the U.S.; the treaty exemption only exempts dual residents from paying tax but they are still considered to be resident in the U.S. under domestic law. Thus, dual residents claiming treaty exemption are required to disclose their world-wide income to the Internal Revenue Service and to file U.S. forms and disclosure reports.

For example, they would be required to provide details of their shareholdings or interests in foreign private corporations, partnerships or trusts.

(A) First Year of Residency

Residency generally begins on the foreign national's first day in the U.S. in the relevant year. For green card holders, it is the first day in the US with a green card. Green card holders will continue their residency in the U.S. until such time as they formally abandon their permanent residence status.

Where, however, an individual satisfies the substantial presence test with respect to any calendar year, his or her residency starting date is the first day during the year that he is present in the U.S.

(B) Last Year of Residency

Generally, an individual is considered to give up his or her residence on the last day of the calendar year prior to the year in which he or she is no longer considered a resident. This rule only applies, however, if the individual has a closer connection to a foreign country than to the U.S. and he or she is not a resident of the U.S. at any time during the next calendar year.

CHAPTER XXXIII

TAX AVOIDANCE

Lawyers use the law as shoemakers use leather: rubbing it, pressing it, and stretching it with their teeth, all to the end of making it fit for their purposes.

Louis XII of France

1. INTRODUCTION

It is a fundamental principle of Anglo-Canadian tax law that a taxpayer is *entitled* to arrange his or her affairs to minimize tax. Tax avoidance implies the reduction of tax payable by lawful means. Thus, we start with the premise that the avoidance of tax is perfectly legitimate.

As world economies become interlinked and cross-border transactions increase, tax planning assumes greater importance and governments focus on methods to curtail tax avoidance. The response of the major industrialized countries to tax avoidance varies: Some enact highly specific domestic legislative provisions, others resort to broad anti-avoidance rules. Canada has both.

On the international front, there is no rule of law that forbids double taxation — the imposition of taxes in two jurisdictions on the same taxpayer in respect of the same income. But since double taxation is harmful to economic growth, countries attempt to promote the exchange of goods and services and the movement of capital and persons by eliminating international double taxation through double tax treaties. Tax treaties are, however, bilateral in nature and their terms must be individually negotiated. Tax treaties are also sometimes used for tax avoidance through "treaty shopping" and the search for for a form of convenience.

Having said that tax avoidance is legitimate, one needs to distinguish in law between acceptable tax mitigation and "abusive" tax avoidance. The fact that tax avoidance is legal does not necessarily imply that it is always successful. Success depends upon whether the avoidance transactions achieve their desired goal of tax minimization.

Tax avoidance falls into two categories: (1) Tax mitigation[1] and (2) Abusive avoidance. In the former case, transactions achieve the desired result of tax minimization and, therefore, are effective. In the latter case, abusive transactions may be ignored for tax purposes and do not achieve the desired goal of tax minimization. What is not always clear, however, is the line between the two: When does lawful tax mitigation cross over and become abusive tax avoidance? How far may a taxpayer go

---

[1] See, *C.I.R. v. Challenge Corporation Ltd.*, [1986] NZTC 5219 (P.C.).

in reducing tax before Revenue Canada intervenes to disallow the benefits of tax planning? How innovative and creative can one be in arranging or rearranging one's affairs to reduce taxes? What types of measures are available to Revenue Canada in restraining tax avoidance? Is tax planning subject to the general principles of natural justice and constitutional doctrines, or is it subject to different rules and, if so, why?

The short history of Canadian taxation is replete with statutory measures and judicial doctrines intended to control and curtail tax avoidance. The history is one of a tug-of-war between the taxpayer, anxious to preserve his or her earnings, and Revenue Canada, with its apparently insatiable appetite for revenues to support public sector spending.

The measures to control tax avoidance vary in scope and intensity. Some are narrow and specific to certain types of transactions, others are broad and stated as general principles. At the apex of all the anti-avoidance measures sits the General Anti-Avoidance Rule ("GAAR"), a vague and broadly stated statement of principle and statutory construction that affects domestic and international tax planning.

How did we arrive at GAAR? In reviewing the legislative history of a provision, it is always difficult to identify with absolute certainty the single event that resulted in, or directly dictated its ultimate form. It is not any easier with GAAR. The rule is a deceptively complex piece of legislation tucked away in one small, self- contained section at the tail end of the *Income Tax Act*. But the Supreme Court's decision in *Stubart*,[2] that the validity of tax arrangements does not depend upon the existence of an underlying business purpose was, probably, the straw that ultimately broke the camel's back and provided the impetus for the enactment of a statutory rule such as GAAR.

Tax professionals hailed *Stubart* as striking a blow for the rights of taxpayers. Some read *Stubart* as an open invitation to aggressive tax planning. Lawyers and accountants arranged transactions solely for tax advantages. Indeed, the tax advantage was often the *raison d'être* for many business arrangements. Commercial considerations were often secondary and, sometimes, even marginal. Thus, *Stubart* created a breach in the Canadian tax system, one that required repair if the integrity of the system was to be preserved. GAAR was enacted as the legislative solution to *Stubart*.

But did GAAR go too far? The rule shifted fiscal control away from the judicial process to the hidden and discretionary administrative processes of Revenue Canada. Commercial transactions and tax planning now depend more than ever before on administrative advance rulings, that are issued on a discretionary basis. Thus, GAAR places taxpayers at the mercy of administrative discretion.

---

[2] *Stubart Invt. Ltd. v. The Queen*, [1984] CTC 294, 84 DTC 6305 (S.C.C.) (transaction cannot be disregarded for tax purposes solely on the basis that it was entered into without a *bona fide* business purpose).

GAAR is a fertile source for tax opinions and rulings. The rule gives Revenue Canada the ultimate weapon with which to control tax avoidance: Administrative discretion that can be applied behind closed doors. By exercising its discretion to issue or withhold advance rulings on specific transactions and through its statements in circulars and public pronouncements, Revenue Canada's administrative practices shape the application of the rule. Thus, the rule shifts the power base of control into the hands of governmental administrators and bureaucrats not directly accountable to taxpayers.

The law says that no person is under any legal obligation to abstain from arranging his or her affairs to reduce the tax bite. To be sure, a person is *entitled* to arrange his or her affairs so as to reduce tax. This right, however, is subject to a proviso: The arrangement must constitute lawful tax mitigation. Thus, the question becomes: What constitutes lawful tax mitigation? The answer to this seemingly simple question is fraught with uncertainty. By definition, all tax planning involves tax minimization. But at what point does one cross over from acceptable tax mitigation to unacceptable tax avoidance?

Tax mitigation that is not subject to GAAR is "lawful" avoidance. Tax avoidance that is caught by GAAR is considered "unlawful" in the sense that it is not in accordance with the law as it is subsequently determined. The distinction, however, between what is "lawful" and "unlawful" depends upon the purpose of the transaction, the rationale of the particular provision(s) and the "object and spirit" of the Act read as a whole. Thus, the tax adviser must exercise judgement and distinguish between minimization schemes that will withstand GAAR and tax avoidance arrangements that will not. That is not always an easy task. How far can one go in tax planning without running into GAAR? What are the limits of the rule? The answer is that the boundaries are not marked: Proceed with caution. To employ the analogy of Mr. Justice Brandeis:[3]

> If you are walking along a precipice, no human being can tell you how near you can go to that precipice without falling over, because you may stumble on a loose stone, you may slip, and go over; but anybody can tell you where you can walk perfectly safely within convenient distance of that precipice.

GAAR is a loose stone that lies near the thin line between lawful tax mitigation and unlawful tax avoidance. Revenue will rule on "perfectly safe" tax plans. The tax adviser's task is to give legal opinions on whether GAAR applies to arrangements that are closer to the precipice and more vulnerable to loose stones.

2. JUDICIAL DOCTRINES TO CONTROL TAX AVOIDANCE

> Over and over again courts have said that there is nothing sinister in so arranging one's affairs as to keep taxes as low as possible. Everybody does so, rich or poor; and all do right, for nobody owes any public duty to pay more than the law demands: taxes are enforced exactions, not voluntary contributions. To demand more in the name of morals is mere cant.
> Justice Learned Hand
> *C.I.R. v. Newman*, 159 Fed. (2d) 848, at 850-851 (1947).

---

[3] Brandeis, Mason, *A Free Man's Life* (1946), p. 352.

Tax planning is not a new phenomenon: It is as old as civilization itself and has always provided stimulus for innovative and creative schemes. It showed up 6,000 years ago in Mesopotamia when a king was forced to impose a fine on his citizens who swam across the local river to avoid the toll tax on the local ferry.

The containment of tax planning within acceptable boundaries is both a legislative and judicial function. Thus, some control mechanisms have been developed judicially, others are built into the Act. Although GAAR falls into the latter category, its design and structure are best understood in the context of older judge-made doctrines.

(a) Taxpayers' Rights

It is well settled that one is entitled to arrange one's affairs so as to attract the minimum amount of tax. This principle is usually identified with the decision of the House of Lords in *I.R.C. v. Duke of Westminster* in which Lord Tomlin said:[4]

> . . . Every man is entitled, if he can, to order his affairs so that the tax attaching under the appropriate Acts is less than it otherwise would be. If he succeeds in ordering them so as to secure this result . . . he cannot be compelled to pay an increased tax.

Similarly, in *Fisher's Executors*:[5]

> [M]y Lords, the highest authorities have always recognized that the subject is entitled so to arrange his affairs as not to attract tax imposed by the Crown, so far as he can do so within the law, and that he may legitimately claim the advantage of any express terms or any omissions that he can find in his favour in taxing Acts. In so doing he neither comes under liability nor incurs blame.

And, again, in *Ayrshire Pullman Motor Service v. C.I.R.*,[6]

> . . . [N]o man in this country is under the smallest obligation, moral or other, so to arrange his legal relations to his business or to his property as to enable the Inland Revenue to put the largest possible shovel into his stores. The Inland Revenue is not slow — and quite rightly — to take every advantage which is open to it under the taxing statutes for the purpose of depleting the taxpayer's pocket. And the taxpayer is, in like manner, entitled to be astute to prevent, so far as he honestly can, the depletion of his means by the Revenue. . . .

The *Westminster* principle is also well entrenched in American tax jurisprudence. As Mr. Justice Holmes said:[7]

> We do not speak of evasion, because, when the law draws a line, a case is on one side of it or the other, and if on the safe side is none the worse legally than a party that has availed himself to the full of what the law permits. When an act is condemned as an evasion, what is meant is that it is on the wrong side of the line indicated by the policy if not by the mere letter of the law.

---

[4] *I.R.C. v. Duke of Westminster*, [1936] AC 1 at 19-20, 19 TC 490 at 520 (H.L.).

[5] *I.R.C. v. Fisher's Executors*, [1926] AC 395 at 412 (H.L.) (taxpayer may reduce taxes by distributing profits to shareholders in the form of debenture stocks).

[6] *Ayrshire Pullman Motor Service v. C.I.R.* (1929), 14 Tax Cas. 754 at 763-64 (Scot.) (taxpayer may arrange his/her affairs so as to reduce taxes, however, the transaction is not effectual prior to the dates on which it was executed).

[7] *Bullen v. Wisconsin*, 240 USR 625 at 630-31 (1916).

These speeches reflect the high water mark of judicial tolerance towards tax planning. The phrase ". . . every man is entitled to arrange his affairs to minimize tax . . ." is probably the best known and most frequently cited maxim of tax law. Taken at its face level, however, the maxim is deceptive. How far can a taxpayer go in arranging affairs so as to minimize tax? What are the acceptable outer limits of tax planning?

(i) Tax Mitigation

The danger with the *Westminster* principle, as with any maxim, is that blanket reliance upon it can mislead taxpayers into believing that their tax plans are sound. The maxim invites taxpayers to believe that they need attend only to the specific words of the Act without concern for the underlying policies of tax law.

To be sure, a taxpayer is entitled to arrange his or her affairs so as to mitigate tax if it is done in an acceptable and lawful manner. Thus, tax planning is not an open arena: It is circumscribed by several judicial doctrines and legislative restraints. Tax arrangements must withstand the scrutiny of judicial and legislative anti-avoidance doctrines that constrain the freedom to tax plan.

Four judicial doctrines warrant close attention:

1. The "sham transactions" doctrine;

2. The "ineffectual transactions" doctrine;

3. The "substance over form" doctrine; and

4. The "business purpose" test.

These doctrines hover over all tax planning and need to be taken into careful consideration when structuring tax arrangements.

(ii) Judicial Attitudes

Judicial attitudes towards tax planning tend to shift to reflect the social, political and economic values. We see the ebb and flow of judicial tolerance towards tax avoidance reflected in the case law: The tolerance of the *Westminster* principle in the heyday of *laissez-faire* economics; the hardening of attitudes after the Second World War and a lessening tolerance towards tax arrangements that threaten to curtail public revenues. We see, for example, the beginning of the change in sentiment towards tax avoidance in Lord Greene's speech in *Lord Howard de Walden v. C.I.R.*:[8]

> For years a battle of manoeuvre has been waged between the Legislature and those who are minded to throw the burden of taxation off their own shoulders on to those of their fellow-subjects. In that battle the Legislature has often been worsted by the skill, determination and resourcefulness of its opponents, of whom the present appellant has not been the least successful. It would not shock us in the least to find that the Legislature has determined to put an end to the struggle by imposing the severest of penalties. It scarcely lies in the mouth of the taxpayer who plays with fire to complain of burnt fingers.

---

[8] *Lord Howard de Walden v. C.I.R.*, [1942] 1 KB 389 at 397 (C.A.) (taxpayer who transferred assets to a foreign Canadian company liable for income tax and surtax as he had the "power to enjoy" these assets within the meaning of the *Finance Act*).

And in Viscount Simon's speech in *Latilla*:[9]

> [T]here is, of course, no doubt that they are within their legal rights, but that is no reason why their efforts, or those of the professional gentlemen who assist them in the matter, should be regarded as a commendable exercise of ingenuity or as a discharge of the duties of good citizenship.

And, later, in Lord Denning's characteristically terse admonition: "The avoidance of tax may be lawful, but it is not yet a virtue".[10]

(b) Evasion, Avoidance and Mitigation

The law distinguishes between evasion, avoidance and lawful tax mitigation. The distinction between these three concepts lies at the core of effective tax planning, both from a substantive and an evidentiary perspective.

Tax evasion is the commission of an act knowingly *with the intent to deceive* so that the tax reported by the taxpayer is less than the tax payable under the law. This may occur through a deliberate omission of revenue, the fraudulent claiming of expenses or allowances, or the deliberate misrepresentation, concealment or withholding of material facts.[11]

Tax evasion is a *mens rea* criminal offence: The Crown carries the burden to prove the offence beyond a reasonable doubt. Similarly, the prosecution of tax evasion is governed by the procedural rules of criminal law.

Tax avoidance is concerned with the minimization of tax. It can be "lawful" or "unlawful" either because of the manner or the motive with which it is executed.

Lawful tax planning is the mitigation of taxes that would otherwise be payable in the absence of the plan.

Tax avoidance is unlawful, but only where it offends established judicial doctrines or prescriptive legislation such as GAAR. Otherwise, it is lawful. In a civil tax dispute the taxpayer has the burden to prove, on a balance of probabilities, that the Minister's assessment is incorrect. An assessment is presumed to be valid until the taxpayer demonstrates otherwise.

---

[9]   *Latilla v. I.R.C.*, [1943] AC 377 at 381 (H.L.) (taxpayer unsuccessfully attempted to reduce British income tax by transferring profit to capital; transaction within s. 18 of the *Finance Act*).

[10]   *Re Weston's Settlements; Weston v. Weston*, [1969] 1 Ch. 223 at 245 (C.A.) (in making a determination whether to vary trusts for the purpose of avoiding or reducing tax, court may consider the expediency of such a scheme and the interests of the beneficiaries).

[11]   See IC 73-10R3, "Tax Evasion" (February 13, 1987); see also *The Queen v. Myers*, [1977] CTC 507, 77 DTC 5278 (Alta. Dist. Ct.); *The Queen v. Baker* (1973), 6 NSR (2d) 38 (Co. Ct.); *The Queen v. Paveley*, [1976] CTC 477, 76 DTC 6415 (Sask. C.A.); *The Queen v. Nicholson* (1974), 75 DTC 5095 (Ont. Prov. Ct.); *The Queen v. Thistle*, [1974] CTC 798, 74 DTC 6632 (*sub nom. Thistle v. The Queen*) (Ont. Co. Ct.); *The Queen v. Regehr*, [1968] CTC 122, 68 DTC 5078 (Y.T. C.A.); *Branch v. The Queen*, [1976] CTC 193, 76 DTC 6112 (Alta. Dist. Ct.).

(c) Motive

It used to be the general rule that the motive with which a taxpayer entered into an avoidance transaction was irrelevant to the legitimacy of the transaction. As Viscount Dilhorne said:[12]

... [A] trading transaction does not cease to be such merely because it is entered into in the confident hope that ... some fiscal advantage will result.

Similarly, *per* Justice Learned Hand:[13]

... [T]he rights resulting from a legal transaction otherwise valid, are not different vis-a-vis taxation, because it has been undertaken to escape taxation. That is a doctrine essential to industry and commerce in a society like our own, in which, and so far as possible, business is always shaped to the form best suited to keep down taxes.

Now, however, motive is an important component of the rules to control tax avoidance. Motive determines whether a transaction constitutes an "avoidance transaction" under GAAR.

(d) Sham Transactions

The legal effect of an arrangement is determined by the rights and obligations that it *actually* creates and not merely by the wording of documentation. An arrangement that does not, in fact, create the legal rights and obligations that it purports to create is a "sham" and may be ignored for the purposes of determining its tax consequences.

(i) Meaning of "Sham"

A "sham" is a fiction: An apparition of rights and obligations that do not really exist.[14] A sham transaction is one in which acts committed or documents executed by the parties to the transaction attempt to give to third parties the appearance of having created between the parties, legal rights and obligations that are different from those

---

[12] *F.A. & A.B. Ltd. v. Lupton*, [1972] AC 635 at 655 (H.L.) (transactions of the taxpayers clearly joint ventures guised as share-dealing transactions intended to result in tax minimization; transactions fail).

[13] *C.I.R. v. Nat. Carbide Corp.*, 167 Fed. (2d) 304 at 306 (1948) (creation of wholly-owned subsidiaries not necessarily invalid due to underlying motive to avoid taxation).

[14] *Snook v. London & West Riding Invt. Ltd.*, [1967] 2 QB 786 (C.A.) (to have a sham transaction all parties must be in common agreement that the acts and documents do not create the legal rights and obligations that they appear to create); see also *C.I.R. v. Challenge Corp.*, [1986] STC 548 (P.C.) ("sham is transaction constructed to create false impression in eyes of tax authority"); *Susan Hosiery Ltd. v. M.N.R.*, [1969] CTC 533, 69 DTC 5346 (Ex. Ct.); *M.N.R. v. Cameron*, [1972] CTC 380, 72 DTC 6325 (S.C.C.); *Richardson Terminals Ltd. v. M.N.R.*, [1971] CTC 42, 71 DTC 5028; affirmed [1972] CTC 528, 72 DTC 6431 (S.C.C.); *Malka v. The Queen*, [1978] CTC 219, 78 DTC 6144 (F.C.T.D.); *Dom. Bridge Co. v. The Queen*, [1975] CTC 263, 75 DTC 5150; affirmed [1977] CTC 554, 77 DTC 5367 (F.C.A.).

which the parties actually intended to create.[15] The definition implies that the parties to the transaction have deliberately set out to misrepresent the actual state of affairs.

A sham may exist despite documentary appearance.[16] Sham requires an intention that the rights and obligations created by the documentary evidence be different from the actual rights and obligations contemplated by the parties to the transaction. In the words of Lord Diplock:[17]

> I apprehend that, if it has any meaning in law, it means acts done or documents executed by the parties to the "sham" which are intended by them to give to third parties or to the court the appearance of creating between the parties legal rights and obligations different from the actual legal rights and obligations (if any) which the parties intend to create. One thing I think, however, is clear in legal principle, morality and the authorities . . . that for acts or documents to be a "sham," with whatever legal consequences follow from this, all the parties thereto must have a common intention that the acts or documents are not to create the legal rights and obligations which they give the appearance of creating. No unexpressed intentions of a "shammer" affect the rights of a party whom he deceived.

(ii) Development of Doctrine

(A) Uncertainty

The term "sham", however, is sometimes also used to attack transactions on the basis of the general aroma (the "smell test") of a scheme that cannot otherwise be struck down on other grounds.[18]

At other times, the doctrine is confused with the "ineffectual transactions" doctrine and the "business purpose" test. In *Spur Oil*,[19] for example, the court said that sham transactions ". . . appear to be transactions in which the taxpayer has used various technicalities or devices for the purpose of tax avoidance".[20] This argument is circular and not at all helpful: Tax avoidance is lawful if the arrangement is not a sham and does not otherwise offend GAAR.

---

[15] This definition was adopted by the Supreme Court of Canada in *M.N.R. v. Cameron*, 72 DTC 6325 (S.C.C.).

[16] *The Queen v. Redpath Industries*, [1984] CTC 483, 84 DTC 6349 (Que. C.S.P.) (must be *prima facie* evidence that tax was undisputably payable before the court will decide tax has been eroded and a sham has occurred).

[17] *Snook v. London & West Riding Invt. Ltd.*, [1967] 1 All ER 518 at 528 (C.A.).

[18] See, for example, *Stubart Invt. Ltd. v. The Queen, ante.*

[19] *Spur Oil Ltd. v. R.*, [1980] CTC 170, 80 DTC 6105 (F.C.T.D.); reversed [1981] CTC 336, 81 DTC 5168 (F.C.A.); leave to appeal to S.C.C. refused 39 NR 406 (purchase of oil from an offshore affiliated company at a price below market value not a sham despite the fact that the oil could have been obtained for less).

[20] *Spur Oil Ltd. v. R.*, [1980] CTC 170 at 186 (F.C.T.D.); reversed [1981] CTC 336 (F.C.A.).

(B) Clarification

The decision of the Supreme Court of Canada in *Stubart*[21] removed some of the confusion previously associated with the sham transactions doctrine by substantially limiting its application to the circumstances contemplated by Lord Diplock in *Snook*.[22] As Mr. Justice Estey said:[23]

> . . . sham transaction: This expression comes to us from decisions in the United Kingdom, and it has been generally taken to mean (but not without ambiguity) a transaction conducted with an element of deceit so as to create an illusion calculated to lead the tax collector away from the taxpayer or the true nature of the transaction; or, simple deception whereby the taxpayer creates a façade of reality quite different from the disguised reality. . . . With respect to the courts below, it seems to me that there may have been an unwitting confusion between the incomplete transaction test and the sham test. . . . The courts have thus far not extended the concept of sham to a transaction otherwise valid but entered into between parties not at arm's length. The reversibility of the transaction by reason of common ownership likewise has never been found, in any case drawn to the Court's attention, to be an element qualifying or disqualifying the transaction as a sham.

Did Mr. Justice Estey's use of the word "deceit" in his description of "sham" narrow Lord Diplock's interpretation of the doctrine? Probably not. A transaction that purports to put forward the appearance of legal rights and obligations which are different from those actually created is "deceitful" according to the common understanding of that term. Any more technical or legal interpretation of "deceit" that involves a significant redefinition of an established doctrine would require a more explicit judicial statement.

(C) More Uncertainty

But only three years after *Stubart*, the Supreme Court clouded the doctrine again. In *Bronfman Trust*,[24] the taxpayer financed a capital payment through a bank loan. Revenue Canada disallowed a deduction for the interest expense on the loan on the basis that it was a payment on account of capital. The taxpayer argued that the expense would have been deductible if it had restructured the borrowing to make the interest payable on account of business income. For example, the trust could have:

- Sold its portfolio securities to raise cash;
- Made its capital expenditure with the cash;
- Borrowed an equal amount from the bank; and
- Used the borrowed funds to repurchase the portfolio of securities.

Had the trust executed each of these four steps in sequence, it would *actually* have created the legal rights and obligations that it purported to create, namely, borrowing

---

[21] *Stubart Invt. Ltd. v. The Queen, ante.*

[22] *Snook v. London & West Riding Invt. Ltd., ante.*

[23] *Stubart Invt. Ltd. v. The Queen, ante,* [1984] CTC at 298 and 313, 84 DTC at 6308 and 6320.

[24] *The Queen v. Bronfman Trust,* [1987] 1 CTC 117, 87 DTC 5059 (S.C.C.).

to purchase income bearing securities. Each of the individual steps would have been a legitimate and valid commercial transaction and, hence, outside of the definition of "sham". The Supreme Court, however, albeit only in *obiter*, observed that the restructured arrangement *might* be considered a sham. The Chief Justice said:[25]

> If, for example, the trust had sold a particular income-producing asset, made the capital allocation to the beneficiary and repurchased the same asset, all within a brief interval of time, the courts might well consider the sale and repurchase to constitute a formality or a sham designed to conceal the essence of the transaction, namely that money was borrowed and used to fund a capital allocation to the beneficiary.

The Court's statement has restored some of the uncertainty associated with the sham transactions doctrine.

(e) Ineffectual Transactions

A taxpayer is entitled to arrange his or her affairs to minimize tax. To be effective, however, the plan must be completely and fully implemented according to the relevant law. Tax reduction schemes in particular tend to attract close scrutiny and should be meticulously documented.[26] In *Atinco Paper Prod. v. The Queen*, for example, Urie J. cautioned:[27]

> I do not think that I should leave this appeal without expressing my views on the general question of transactions undertaken purportedly for the purpose of estate planning and tax avoidance. It is trite law to say that every taxpayer is entitled to so arrange his affairs as to minimize his tax liability. No one has ever suggested that this is contrary to public policy. It is equally true that this court is not the watch dog of the Minister of National Revenue. Nonetheless, it is the duty of the Court to carefully scrutinize everything that a taxpayer has done to ensure that everything which appears to have been done, in fact, has been done in accordance with applicable law. It is not sufficient to employ devices to achieve a desired result without ensuring that those devices are not simply cosmetically correct, that is correct in form, but, in fact, are in all respects legally correct, real transactions. . . . The only course for the Court to take is to apply the law as the Court sees it to the facts as found in the particular transaction. If the transaction can withstand that scrutiny, then it will, of course, be supported. If it cannot, it will fall.

---

[25] *The Queen v. Bronfman Trust, ante,* [1987] SCR 55, [1987] 1 CTC 129-130.

[26] See, for example, *The Queen v. Daly,* [1981] CTC 270 at 279, 81 DTC 5179 at 5204 (F.C.A.):
In a case of this kind, where it is acknowledged that what is sought by a certain course of action is a tax advantage, it is the duty of the court to examine all of the evidence relating to the transaction in order to satisfy itself that what was done resulted in a valid, completed transaction.
See also *Kingsdale Securities Co. v. M.N.R.,* [1975] CTC 10, 74 DTC 6674 (F.C.A.); *Richardson Terminals Ltd. v. M.N.R.,* [1971] CTC 42, 71 DTC 5028; affirmed [1972] CTC 528, 72 DTC 6431 (S.C.C.).

[27] *Atinco Paper Prod. v. The Queen,* [1978] CTC 566 at 577-78 (F.C.A.); leave to appeal to S.C.C. refused 25 NR 603 (ineffectual trust; only legal partners to the business were corporations; unsuccessful attempt to income split).

Thus, tax mitigation arrangements should be *bona fide* and properly executed. They must be real. As Viscount Simon said in *I.R.C. v. Wesleyan & Gen. Assur. Soc.:*[28]

> [I]t may be well to repeat two propositions which are well established in the application of the law relating to Income Tax. First, the name given to a transaction by the parties concerned does not necessarily decide the nature of the transaction.... The question always is what is the real character of the payment, not what the parties call it. Secondly, a transaction which, on its true construction, is of a kind that would escape tax, is not taxable on the ground that the same result could be brought about by a transaction in another form which would attract tax.

(f) Substance vs. Form

It is sometimes said that the substance of a transaction determines its legal and tax consequences. This doctrine has intuitive appeal and is easy to state. It is not, however, quite so easy to define.

The difficulty with the doctrine is that, despite its intuitive appeal, it does not offer any objective criteria or parameters by which particular facts may be measured against particular facts. Hence, it is an unpredictable doctrine of varying scope. Lord Tomlin referred to it as the "so-called doctrine" in *I.R.C. v. Duke of Westminster:*[29]

> . . . it is said that in revenue cases there is a doctrine that the Court may ignore the legal position and regard what is called "the substance of the matter". . . . This supposed doctrine (upon which the Commissioners apparently acted) seems to rest for its support upon a misunderstanding of language used in some earlier cases. The sooner this misunderstanding is dispelled, and the supposed doctrine given its quietus, the better it will be for all concerned, for the doctrine seems to involve substituting "the incertain and crooked cord of discretion" for "the golden and streight metwand of the law". . . . Every man is entitled if he can to order his affairs so as that the tax attaching under the appropriate Acts is less than it otherwise would be. . . . This so-called doctrine of "the substance" seems to me to be nothing more than an attempt to make a man pay and notwithstanding that he has so ordered his affairs that the amount of tax sought from him is not legally claimable.

The doctrine of substance over form is often used to attack tax plans that are perceived to be "offensive" in some vague and unarticulated sense but that are otherwise in technical compliance with the Act. Used in this manner, the doctrine becomes a camouflage for applying a motive test to tax mitigation arrangements.

3. BACKGROUND OF GAAR

> Kings and government ought to shear, not skin their sheep.
> Robert Herrick.

---

[28] *I.R.C. v. Wesleyan & Gen. Assur. Soc.* (1948), 30 Tax Cas. 11 at 25 (H.L.) (taxpayer not taxable on amount given to employee on account of a loan).

[29] *I.R.C. v. Duke of Westminster*, [1936] AC 1 at 19-20 (H.L.) (employer's annual payments, under covenant, to servants not payments of salary and wages; taxpayer may arrange his affairs so as to minimize taxes).

(a) The Business purpose Test

The *Westminster* principle allows taxpayers to mitigate their taxes by arranging their affairs in any lawful manner. Prior to the enactment of GAAR, tax transactions and arrangements did not need to be supported by a business or economic purpose. A tax saving was, in and of itself, sufficient justification to structure a transaction in a particular manner. As Mr. Justice Noel said:[30]

> There is indeed no provision in the *Income Tax Act* which provides that, where it appears that the main purpose, or one of the purposes for which any transaction or transactions was or were effected was the avoidance or reduction of liability to income tax, the court may, if it thinks fit, direct that such adjustments shall be made as respects liability to income tax, as it considers appropriate so as to counteract the avoidance or reduction of liability to income tax which would otherwise be effected by the transaction or transactions.

Although otherwise lawful transactions did not require a business purpose, some courts saw the absence of such a purpose as suggestive that the transaction was a "sham".[31] The absence of a business purpose in an arrangement has sometimes prompted courts to ignore the arrangement under some other doctrine, for example, substance over form. Thus, the business-purpose test has played, both directly and indirectly, an important role as an anti-avoidance mechanism in Canadian tax law.

The first judicial reference to the requirement that a transaction should have a "business purpose" appeared in 1967. In *Smythe v. M.N.R.*,[32] the Exchequer Court held that the transaction was not *bona fide* because it had no legitimate business purpose. The doctrine emerged again in *Dom. Bridge Co. v. The Queen*,[33] where the Federal Court looked at the absence of a business purpose to determine whether the taxpayer's arrangements constituted a sham.

In *M.N.R. v. Leon*,[34] the Federal Court of Appeal held that the interposition of management companies between employer and employees had no *bona fide* business purpose and, therefore, was a "sham" whose sole purpose was to save income tax. The services provided by the management company could just as easily have been provided by the employees without the company's intervention. In the circumstances, the existence of the management companies amounted to ". . . a sham pure and simple, the sole purpose of which was to avoid payment of tax".

---

[30] *Foreign Power Securities Corp. Ltd. v. M.N.R.*, 66 DTC 5012 at 5027 (Ex. Ct.) (profits from the sale of shares was capital gain rather then business income, despite parent company's involvement).

[31] See, for e.g., *Massey-Ferguson Ltd. v. The Queen*, [1977] CTC 6, 77 DTC 5013 (F.C.A.) (creation of subsidiary intended to lend funds through was part of the legitimate business practices of the corporation, not a sham).

[32] *Smythe v. M.N.R.*, [1967] CTC 498, 67 DTC 533 (Ex. Ct.); affirmed [1969] CTC 558 (S.C.C.).

[33] *Dom. Bridge Co. v. The Queen*, [1975] CTC 263, 75 DTC 5150 (F.C.T.D.).

[34] *M.N.R. v. Leon*, [1976] CTC 532, 76 DTC 6299 (F.C.A.).

The business purpose doctrine continued to gather momentum in the late seventies. In *Lipper v. The Queen*, for example, the Federal Court disallowed the taxpayer's claim for capital cost allowance on motion picture films because of an absence of business purpose:[35]

> As to the limited partnership relationship itself it does have a business purpose and is an ideal vehicle for encouraging *bona fide* investment, but it is also an ideal vehicle for tax shelter purposes. A question can arise, as in the present case, as to whether the essential or fundamental purpose of a contract into which the limited partners enter is to obtain a tax advantage rather than to engage upon a *bona fide* business venture, which might at the same time and quite legitimately involve certain tax advantages which would minimize the possible losses and, therefore, render the venture considerably more attractive.

In *Agar v. R.*,[36] the Federal Court held that there was a complete absence of any *bona fide* business purpose in the interposition of a corporation to render personal services to a construction business. The Court characterized the entire arrangement as a sham.

By 1980, business purpose had become the *sine qua non* of tax planning.

The doctrine eventually surfaced before the Supreme Court of Canada in *Stubart*.[37] The facts were simple. The taxpayer's profitable business was transferred to a sister corporation with accumulated tax losses. The *sole* objective of the arrangement was to marry the profits and the losses. The taxpayer continued to operate the business, but now as an agent of its sister corporation. The transfer had no business purpose. Tax mitigation through the utilization of tax losses in the sister corporation was the sole purpose of the transaction.

The question put to the Court was simple: Was the arrangement invalid because it lacked a business purpose? The Court rejected the necessity of a business purpose test as a *judicial* device to control tax avoidance:[38]

> I would therefore reject the proposition that a transaction may be disregarded for tax purposes solely on the basis that it was entered into by a taxpayer without an independent or *bona fide* business purpose.

The Court reasoned that reading a business purpose test into Canadian tax law might deter taxpayers from participating in the very activities which the Act sought to promote:[39]

---

[35] *Lipper v. The Queen*, [1979] CTC 316, 79 DTC 5246 (F.C.T.D.) taxpayer's claim for capital cost allowance on motion picture films disallowed; venture intended to obtain a tax advantage rather then a financial gain).

[36] *Agar v. R.*, [1980] CTC 397, 80 DTC 6311 (F.C.T.D.) (court pierced the corporate veil; no *bona fide* business purpose for the interposition of the corporation except to reduce income tax).

[37] *Stubart Invt. Ltd. v. The Queen, ante.*

[38] *Id.*, per Estey J., at 575 (SCR), 314 (CTC).

[39] *Id.*, per Estey J., at 576 (SCR), 315 (CTC).

> Without the inducement offered by the statute, the activity may not be undertaken by the taxpayer for whom the induced action would otherwise have no *bona fide* business purpose. Thus, by imposing a positive requirement that there be such a *bona fide* business purpose, a taxpayer might be barred from undertaking the very activity Parliament wishes to encourage. At minimum, a business purpose requirement might inhibit the taxpayer from undertaking the specified activity which Parliament has invited in order to attain economic and perhaps social policy goals.

Thus, by 1984, the business purpose test had ceased to exist as a separate judicial doctrine to control tax avoidance.

(b) Interpretational Guidelines

But having rejected the business purpose test as the *sine qua non* of tax planning, the Supreme Court did not abandon all judicial control of tax avoidance. The Court prescribed some interpretive guidelines. The most significant of these guidelines was the admonition that the formal validity of a transaction may not be enough to sustain it if it was offensive to the "object and spirit" of the Act:[40]

> . . . the formal validity of the transaction may also be insufficient where:

>> . . . "the object and spirit" of the allowance or benefit provision is defeated by the procedures blatantly adopted by the taxpayer to synthesize a loss, delay or other tax saving device. . . . This may be illustrated where the taxpayer, in order to qualify for an "allowance" or a "benefit", takes steps which the terms of the allowance provisions of the Act may, when taken in isolation and read narrowly, be stretched to support. However, when the allowance provision is read in the context of the whole statute, and with the "object and spirit" and purpose of the allowance provision in mind, the accounting result produced by the taxpayer's actions would not, by itself, avail him of the benefit of the allowance.

Thus, Revenue Canada could attack a tax plan if it involved steps that violated the "object and spirit" of specific statutory provisions.

The interpretive guidelines, however, were not enough to allay the concerns of the Department of Finance. The Department saw the guidelines as uncertain new ideas that would take many years to distill into a concrete doctrine capable of curbing the flood of tax avoidance schemes that followed the demise of the business purpose test.

(c) Inadequacy of Specific Avoidance Rules

It is clear that the specific statutory provisions in place prior to the introduction of GAAR were not sufficient to counter the proliferation of tax schemes that spawned each year. The frenzy of legislative activity between 1972 and 1987 was directed in substantial measure at the ever expanding inventory of tax planning schemes. As quickly as the Legislature blocked one avenue of fiscal escape, innovative tax planners burrowed another hole in the statutory patchwork. Predictably, particularization of the statute bred more, not less, avoidance. The frustration of the Department of Finance is reflected in its testimony before the House Committee on Finance and Economic

---

[40] *Id.*, at 579-80 (SCR), 316-17 (CTC).

Affairs: ". . . we no sooner get the stuff out and the ink gets dry than there is a new way to beat the rules".[41] Canadian legislators began to realize, as their American counterparts had done much earlier,[42] that when they closed the dike in one place, they often opened up a hole right next to it.

(i) Anti-avoidance Measures 1984-1989

The following is a summary of some of the more significant anti-avoidance measures introduced between 1984 and 1989.

Oct. 1984   Moratorium on quick-flip scientific research tax credit investments.

May 1985   1985 Budget introduced the following tightening amendments:

- The minimum tax on individuals;
- Tighter attribution rules, including an extension of the rules to tax income from property acquired from the proceeds of loans;
- New rules ensuring the taxability of inducement payments;
- Elimination of the scientific research tax credit (SRTC); and
- Elimination of tax shelter schemes involving yachts, houseboats and hotels.

July 1985   Measures to prevent tax avoidance through the use of oil and gas carve-out arrangements.

Nov. 1985   New rules to prevent the use of trusts to market securities issued in such a way that income and capital returns to investors were distributed tax-free.

Dec. 1985   New rules to end the use of partnerships in corporate takeovers to increase tax deductions through the so-called "partnership step-up" rules and to tighten rules so that pension plans could not avoid the limits on foreign property investments.

Feb. 1986   1986 Budget introduced the following tightening amendments:

- Introduction of "at-risk" rules for limited and certain other partnerships which restricted the amount of investment tax credits and business losses that may be flowed out to limited partners to the amount of their investment at risk in the partnership;
- Introduction of provisions to remove the tax advantage of salary deferral arrangements; and
- General corporate tax restructuring measures in the February 1986 budget included the reduction in or elimination of investment tax credits and the removal of the inventory allowance.

---

[41] Minutes of the Commons Standing Committee on Finance and Economic Affairs, June 29, 1987, *per* Jim Wilson.

[42] *Gregory v. Helvering, C.I.R.*, 293 US 465 (1935), 69 F (2d) 809.

Oct. 1986	New rule to limit the flow-through of investment tax credits earned by a trust for its beneficiaries to investment tax credits earned by a testamentary trust.
Nov. 1986	Special tax announced to be paid by those corporations which distribute their surplus as proceeds of disposition of shares rather than as taxable dividends.
	Deduction of intercorporate dividends on collateralized preferred shares denied.
Jan. 1987	Amendments to prevent trading in tax losses through acquisitions of corporate control and other means.
	New rules for share-for-share exchanges under which the tax cost to the purchaser corporation of shares acquired on a share-for-share exchange to which section 85.1 applies was limited to the lesser of the fair market value of the shares and their paid-up capital immediately before the exchange.
	New restrictions in the share-for-share exchange rules to allow the rule to apply only where the purchaser corporation issues shares not previously issued in exchange for the shares of the acquired corporation, and to provide that the increase in paid-up capital of the purchaser corporation's shares issued on the exchange may not exceed the paid-up capital of the shares acquired.
Feb. 1987	New rules to prevent the use of commercial trusts to avoid tax.
June 1987	Phase One of Tax Reform, in addition to general base broadening, proposed a number of measures to curb tax avoidance and the transfer of tax losses. Some major provisions were:

- The imposition of a tax on dividends on preferred shares closed a major route for the transfer of tax losses;
- The extension of the limited partnership at-risk to resource expenses.

Sept. 1987	Press release to stop tax avoidance involving capital dividend account strips.
Dec. 1987	Detailed tax reform documents introduced two new tightening measures:

- Rules restricting the R&D tax incentives to R&D related to a taxpayer's business; and
- A creditable capital tax was imposed on large financial institutions to ensure that they paid a minimum level of tax.

Feb. 1988	Budget introduced the following tightening amendments:

- The associated corporation rules tightened to prevent multiplication of entitlements to the small business deduction;

- Rules preventing the tax-free receipt of social assistance payments by professionals;
- Rules preventing tax shelter syndications of the accelerated capital cost allowance available in respect of energy conservation equipment; and
- Rules preventing the use of non-resident owned investment corporations to convert a corporation's surplus into interest bearing debt.

May 1988   New rules to prevent the use of limited partnerships to avoid the attribution rules.

April 1989   Budget introduced the following tightening amendments:

- Comprehensive rules to prevent the use of leasing as an after-tax financing vehicle; and
- Rules curbing the use of dividend rentals.

(ii) Creative Tax Avoidance

Tax avoidance is an international game unrestricted by geographical boundaries. Indeed, tax avoidance often provides as much of an impetus towards the global economy as any other single direct economic stimulus. The source of the impetus can vary, but the incentive to reduce tax is always present in international business transactions.

In Britain, the impetus for tax avoidance schemes came from real estate: The property boom in Southern England, followed by the collapse of the real estate market in 1973-74. Paper losses had to be generated to offset gains. One company alone (The Rossminster Group) is estimated to have sold tax schemes between 1970 and 1979 that saved taxpayers £746 million.

(A) A Game

The British experience reveals the artistic creativity of the minds that play the tax planning game. A fairly typical British scheme was as follows: A taxpayer who owned shares that had substantially appreciated in value might wish to dispose of the shares and realize the profit. If the shares were held by a wholly-owned holding company (A) and the shares were sold directly, the gain would be subject to capital gains tax. To avoid the tax, the taxpayer could incorporate a new company (B) (perhaps in a tax haven) and A would exchange the appreciated shares with B in return for B's shares — a share-for-share exchange. B would then sell the appreciated shares to C for cash and realize the gain. The substance of the transaction was that the economic gain would be realized on the first transaction, the share-for-share exchange between A and B. The disposition from B to C would not trigger any economic gain since it occurred immediately after the first transaction without any further increase in value. If, as the British statute provided, the first gain was exempt from tax by virtue of a specific provision and the second transaction did not trigger a gain, then all of the potential tax on the appreciated shares would disappear when A exchanged the shares with B and sold the shares to C.

It was all a game: An expensive one for the Treasury but a profitable one for the taxpayer and his or her advisers. Lord Templeton used the language of theatre to describe the game in *Ramsey*:[43]

> The game is recognizable by four rules. First, the play is devised and scripted prior to performance. Secondly, real money and real documents are circulated and exchanged. Thirdly, the money is returned by the end of the performance. Fourthly, the financial position of the actors is the same at the end as it was in the beginning save that the taxpayer in the course of the performance pays the hired actors for their services. The object of the performance is to create the illusion that something has happened, that Hamlet has been killed and that Bottom did don an asses head so that tax advantages can be claimed as if something had happened.

> The audience are informed that the actors reserve the right to walk out in the middle of the performance but in fact they are creatures of the consultant who has sold, and the taxpayer who has bought, the play; the actors are never in a position to make a profit and there is no chance that they will go on strike. The critics are mistakenly informed that the play is based on a classic masterpiece called "The Duke of Westminster" but in that piece the old retainer entered the theatre with his salary and left with a genuine entitlement to his salary and to an additional annuity.

Ramsey is estimated to have netted the U.K. Treasury approximately £1,000 million in tax settlements from pending litigation.

(B) Judicial Intervention

The game was exciting but short-lived. The House of Lords salvaged the U.K. Treasury from fiscal ruin by developing an antidote: The step transactions doctrine.

The step transactions doctrine may be summarized as follows: The fiscal consequences of a preordained series of transactions, intended to operate as such, are generally to be ascertained by considering the result of the series as a whole, and not by dissecting the scheme and considering each individual transaction separately.[44]

(d) The Artificial Transactions Doctrine

The income tax system relies in varying degrees on specific statutory anti-avoidance provisions targeted at "offensive" tax activities or transactions. Some of these anti-avoidance rules are detailed and specific and apply only to a particular provision or type of transaction; others are of a more general nature and apply to a wider area, for example, the computation of capital gains.[45] The number of specific anti-avoidance provisions has increased in proportion to the size of the Act. Particularization of the statute breeds loopholes; loopholes invite ever more detailed provisions to block avenues of escape; detail causes complexity, and complexity provides the tax planner with the opportunity to ferret out more loopholes and slip through gaps in the legislation.

---

[43] *W.T. Ramsay Ltd. v. I.R.C.*, [1979] 3 All ER 213 at 214-15; affirmed [1982] AC 300 (H.L.).

[44] *Furniss (Inspector of Taxes) v. Dawson*, [1984] 1 All ER 530 at 543 (H.L.).

[45] See, e.g., subss. 110.6(6), (7) and (8) which govern the capital gains exemption.

Prior to the introduction of GAAR, the Act contained a broad rule that was intended to curb "artificial" transactions. Subsection 245(1) (prior to September 13, 1988) read as follows:

> In computing income for the purposes of this Act, no deduction may be made in respect of a disbursement or expense made or incurred in respect of a transaction or operation that, if allowed, would unduly or artificially reduce the income.

The artificial transactions doctrine was initially introduced in the *Income War Tax Act*. Despite its long history, the doctrine did not serve the tax collector particularly well. The subsection was of limited scope: It only applied to transactions that unduly or artificially reduced *income*; it did not apply to transactions that reduced taxable income or tax payable. Second, the courts tended to apply the section only in cases involving the most outrageous and flagrant tax avoidance schemes. Tax avoidance schemes devised with any degree of sophistication and finesse usually escaped.[46] Third, it was never quite clear whether the terms "disbursements" and "expenses" included non-cash outlays such as capital cost allowance.[47]

The specific anti-avoidance rules did not work well and were unpredictable. They did little to contain the growth in tax-avoidance. As the General Counsel of the Department of Finance said to the Commons Standing Committee on Finance and Economic Affairs:[48]

> It is apparent, from looking at the kind of activity that gave rise to very specific anti-avoidance rules over the last couple of years, that taxpayers are becoming a bit more aggressive than they have been historically. And that is reflected, I think in a number of ways. Obviously the proliferation of fairly well publicized tax-avoidance schemes is evidence, I think, of the willingness of taxpayers and their advisers to undertake fairly aggressive tax planning. They do that because they examine, presumably, as advisers do, the limits that exist on tax avoidance, statutory or judicial, and they feel comfortable that within those limits they can still advise taxpayers to proceed. The result of that I think has been the proliferation of legislation, which we have seen over the last couple of years, to deal with it on a case-by-case or specific basis.

The Department of Finance saw three difficulties with the specific anti-avoidance rules. First, specific rules targeted at specific transactions close the barn door only after the horses have bolted. Moreover, in most cases, newly introduced specific rules that

---

[46] See, e.g., *Shulman v. M.N.R.*, [1961] CTC 385 (Ex. Ct.); *Murphy v. M.N.R.*, [1968] CTC 248 (Ex. Ct.); *Edwards v. M.N.R.*, [1969] Tax ABC 1069; *Mendels v. The Queen*, [1978] CTC 404, 78 DTC 6267 (F.C.T.D.); *Parsons v. M.N.R.*, [1984] CTC 352, 84 DTC 6345 (F.C.A.); *Susan Hosiery Ltd. v. M.N.R.*, [1969] CTC 533, 69 DTC 5346 (Ex. Ct.); *Cattermole-Tretheway Contr. Ltd. v. M.N.R.*, [1970] CTC 619, 71 DTC 5010 (Ex. Ct.); *Produits LDG Prod. Inc. v. M.N.R.*, [1973] CTC 273, 73 DTC 5222; reversed [1976] CTC 591, 76 DTC 6344 (F.C.A.); *Montgomery v. M.N.R.*, [1987] 2 CTC 2023, 87 DTC 355 (T.C.C.).

[47] See *Harris v. M.N.R.*, [1966] CTC 226 (S.C.C.); *McKee v. The Queen*, [1977] CTC 490, 77 DTC 5345 (F.C.T.D.).

[48] Minutes of the Commons Standing Committee on Finance and Economic Affairs, June 29, 1987, *per* Jim Wilson.

address a particular abuse usually exempt any completed or partially completed transactions. Thus, the most innovative and aggressive tax planners usually escape.

Second, specific provisions add tremendous complexity to the statute by attempting to anticipate every conceivable permutation and combination of potential tax abuse that might arise in commercial transactions.

Third, the tax avoidance industry is far more productive, both in terms of intellectual energy and efficiency, than tax collectors and policy advisors. Given the formidable intellectual talent that is engaged in the tax avoidance industry in Canada's legal and accounting firms, the Department of Finance felt it needed a more powerful weapon to equalize the battle against an increasingly aggressive group of tax lawyers and accountants.

The Department's testimony before the House Committee captures its frustration:[49]

> You could wait until [the] courts develop more sophisticated judicial limits along the lines of what the courts have done in the United States. The difficulty with that, though, is that the Supreme Court of Canada, in one case at least [the *Stubart* decision], looked at the existing Canadian Act, looked at the question of whether there should be a judicially introduced tax-avoidance test, and said no, there exists in the Canadian *Income Tax Act* already a general anti-avoidance rule and it is therefore inappropriate for the courts to develop such a rule.

> In reviewing the existing provisions of the Act, particularly the one referred to by the Supreme Court, our view is that it is not of broad enough application, as I think has been amply demonstrated over the last couple of years. If taxpayers thought the rule was that effective, we would not have had nearly the need for the kind of legislation we have introduced over the last couple of years. Obviously taxpayers are not intimidated. . . .

The Department looked at other doctrines to contain tax avoidance, the business-purpose test in the United States and the step transactions doctrine in the United Kingdom, and constructed GAAR as an amalgam of the two. Thus, GAAR is a statutory business purpose test that looks through all of the steps of a transaction or series of transactions. The rule fills the vacuum created by *Stubart*.[50] Unlike its American and British counterparts, however, GAAR depends heavily upon the exercise of administrative discretion. Once invoked, the taxpayer carries the onus to establish the "object and spirit" of the impugned provision or the Act read as a whole.

4. THE GENERAL ANTI-AVOIDANCE RULE

> If not the taxpaying public or the fisc, who ultimately benefits from this approach? The only unequivocal beneficiary is the tax bar. The heavier the layers of judicial divination superimposed on the Internal Revenue Code, the richer tax lawyers are apt to get. The development of an exquisite set of intuitions about what kinds of transactions the courts "like" and "don't like" has become a large part of what tax lawyers sell.

> Joseph Isenbergh, "Musings on Form and Substance in Taxation" (1982), 49 *Univ. of Chicago LR* 859 at 883.

---

[49] Ibid.

[50] *Stubart Invt. Ltd. v. The Queen, ante.*

References:

ITA:

S. 152	Assessment
S. 245	General Anti-Avoidance Rule

BULLETINS, CIRCULARS & RULINGS:

IC 73-10R3	February 13, 1987	Tax Evasion
IC 88-2	October 21, 1988	General Anti-Avoidance Rule — Section 245 of the Income Tax Act
IC 88-2	July 31, 1990	Supplement 1
ATR-22R	April 14, 1989	Estate Freeze Using Share Exchange
ATR-36	November 4, 1988	Estate Freeze
ATR-42	December 13, 1991	Transfer of Shares
ATR-44	February 17, 1992	Utilization of Deductions within a Related Corporate Group
ATR-47	February 24, 1992	Transfer of Assets to Realtyco
ATR-53	April 8, 1993	Purification of a Small Business Corporation
ATR-54	April 8, 1993	Reduction of Paid-Up Capital
ATR-55	April 8, 1993	Amalgamation Followed by Sale of Shares
ATR-56	April 8, 1993	Purification of a Family Farm
ATR-57	May 28, 1993	Transfer of Property for Estate Planning Purposes
ATR-58	June 11, 1993	Divisive Reorganization

(a) Purpose

GAAR is intended to prevent "abusive" tax avoidance transactions or arrangements. The rule is extremely broad and general and supplements the multitude of specific anti-avoidance rules in the Act. It is intended to restrain what the specific and detailed statutory rules and judicial doctrines fail to curtail.

The rule is an amalgam of three different influences: (1) The American business purpose test; (2) The British step transactions doctrine; and (3) The Canadian "object and spirit" test.

The Technical Notes (June 30, 1988) explain the rationale of GAAR as follows:

> . . . [S]ection 245 of the Act is a general anti-avoidance rule which is intended to prevent abusive tax avoidance transactions or arrangements but at the same time is not intended to interfere with legitimate commercial and family transactions. Consequently, the new rule seeks to distinguish between legitimate tax planning and abusive tax avoidance and to establish a reasonable balance between the protection of the tax base and the need for certainty for taxpayers in planning their affairs.

Thus, GAAR is a supplementary rule that is intended to catch abusive tax avoidance where the other, more specific, anti-avoidance rules fail. In fact, however, GAAR has a life and force of its own and should be considered independently of any specific anti-avoidance rules.

The key question is: What is the distinction between lawful tax mitigation and "abusive" tax planning? Transactions that comply with the policy of statutory provisions in the context of the Act read as a whole are not caught by the General Anti-Avoidance Rule. The Technical Notes focus on the "object and spirit" of the Act:

> Transactions that comply with the object and spirit of other provisions of the Act read as a whole will not be affected by the application of this general anti-avoidance rule. For example, a transaction that qualifies for a tax-free rollover under an explicit provision of the Act, and that is carried out in accordance, not only with the letter of that provision but also with the spirit of the Act read as a whole, will not be subject to new section 245. However, where the transaction is part of a series of transactions designed to avoid tax and results in a misuse or abuse of the provision that allows a tax-free rollover, the rule may apply. If for example, a taxpayer, for the purpose of converting an income gain on a sale of property into a capital gain, transfers the property on a rollover basis to a shell corporation in exchange for shares in a situation where new section 54.2 of the Act does not apply and subsequently sells the shares, the new section could be expected to apply.

Revenue Canada uses the Minister's Technical Notes and Parliamentary debates to determine the legislative intention underlying provisions of the Act.[51] Thus, the starting point in the determination as to whether a transaction or arrangement constitutes lawful tax mitigation or tax avoidance is to ascertain the purpose of the statutory provisions used to implement the tax plan. But, as we shall see, the purpose of individual provisions must be read in the context of the Act read as a whole.

(b) The Charging Provision

Subsection 245(2) reads as follows:

> Where a transaction is an avoidance transaction, the tax consequences to a person shall be determined as is reasonable in the circumstances in order to deny a tax benefit that, but for this section, would result, directly or indirectly, from that transaction or from a series of transactions that includes that transaction.

The key terms in the charging provision are: "tax benefit", "tax consequences" and "transaction". These terms are defined in subsection 245(1):

- "Tax benefits" means a reduction, avoidance or deferral of tax or other amount payable under this Act or an increase in a refund of tax or other amount under this Act;

- "Tax consequences" to a person means the amount of income, taxable income, or taxable income earned in Canada, of tax or other amount payable by, or refundable to the person under this Act, or any other amount that is relevant for the purposes of computing that amount; and

- "Transaction" includes an arrangement or event.

---

[51] See, e.g., Technical Interpretation (October 24, 1990).

(i) Legislative Intention

The Technical Notes explain the scope of the rule as follows:

> Generally, for the purposes of section 245, a transaction, to be an avoidance transaction, must result in a "tax benefit". This expression is defined as a reduction, avoidance or deferral of tax or other amount payable under the Act or an increase in a refund of tax or other amount under the Act. The references in this definition to "other amount payable under this Act" and "other amount under this Act" are intended to cover interest, penalties, the remittance of source deductions, and other amounts that do not constitute tax.

> Where a transaction is an avoidance transaction, new subsection 245(2) provides that the tax consequences to any person shall be determined as is reasonable in the circumstances in order to deny the tax benefit that would otherwise result from that transaction. The expression "tax consequences" is defined in such a way as to permit an adjustment to the income, taxable income, or taxable income earned in Canada of, tax or other amount payable by, or amount refundable to, any person under the Act as well as any other amount, such as the adjusted cost base of a property or the paid-up capital of a share, that is relevant for the purposes of the computation of the income or other above-mentioned amount.

> The term "transaction" is defined to include an arrangement or event.

(ii) Recharacterization of Transactions

A taxpayer is entitled to mitigate his or her taxes provided that the mitigation does not result in tax avoidance.

The tax consequences of an "avoidance transaction" may be recharacterized by ignoring any tax benefits derived from the particular transaction. In other words, the tax consequences of an avoidance transaction may be redetermined "as is reasonable in the circumstances". An abusive transaction can be ignored for tax purposes and the taxpayer's liability recalculated on some other "reasonable" basis. According to the Technical Notes:

> Subsection 245(2) of the Act provides that where a transaction is an avoidance transaction, the tax consequences to a person...are to be determined as is reasonable in the circumstances in order to deny the tax benefit of that transaction....

> Where subsection 245(2) applies, the tax consequences to a person are to be determined so as to deny the tax benefit on a basis that is reasonable in the circumstances. New subsection 245(5) provides a non-exhaustive list of what may be done to achieve that result. In many cases the manner in which this should be accomplished will be obvious or will be provided for in the Act. However, the "reasonable basis" approach adopted in subsection 245(2) recognizes that it is not possible to exhaustively prescribe the appropriate tax consequences for the range of avoidance transactions to which the rule might apply.

Therein lies the formidable power of GAAR: The rule empowers the Minister to ignore and set aside a taxpayer's arrangements and substitute an alternative tax cost in lieu thereof.

It is important to note, however, that the Minister does *not* have the power to recharacterize a transaction for the purpose of determining that it is an "avoidance transaction". The Minister can only recharacterize the consequences of a transaction *after* it is determined that it constitutes an "avoidance transaction". Thus, within the parameters of the rule, a taxpayer may still arrange his or her affairs to mitigate tax. The Technical Notes explain as follows:

> Subsection 245(3) does not permit the "recharacterization" of a transaction for the purposes of determining whether or not it is an avoidance transaction. In other words, it does not permit a transaction to be considered to be an avoidance transaction because some alternative transaction that might have achieved an equivalent result would have resulted in higher taxes. It is recognized that tax planning — arranging one's affairs so as to attract the least amount of tax — is a legitimate and accepted part of Canadian tax law. If a taxpayer selects a transaction that minimizes his tax liability and this transaction is not carried out primarily to obtain a tax benefit, he should not be taxed as if he had engaged in other transactions that would have resulted in higher taxes.

Thus, in the face of a GAAR assessment, a taxpayer must demonstrate that his or her tax plan or arrangement is lawful tax mitigation in the sense that it constitutes avoidance, but avoidance that is not "abusive" of the Act read as a whole. The taxpayer carries the burden to show that his or her plan does not offend the underlying policy of the statute.

(iii) "Reasonable in the Circumstances"

What is "reasonable in the circumstances" is a question of fact. The language is broad enough to allow the Minister to keep open the list of transactions that he or she may consider abusive in the future, and allows Revenue Canada considerable administrative flexibility in coping with new circumstances as they arise. Revenue Canada can ignore the offensive component or steps of an avoidance transaction and determine its tax consequences as if that component or step had not occurred.

GAAR is a modified statutory version of the *Furniss v. Dawson* doctrine:[52]

> [T]he fiscal consequences of a preordained series of transactions, intended to operate as such, are generally to be ascertained by considering the result of the series as a whole, and not by dissecting the scheme and considering each individual transaction separately.

Thus, in effect, the rule legislatively implements what the House of Lords did judicially in *Furniss v. Dawson*: It empowers the Minister to ignore certain steps in a series of commercial transactions and recalculate the resulting tax liability without regard to those steps.

In a sense, however, GAAR goes further than the step transactions doctrine in *Furniss v. Dawson*: It looks at the "object and spirit" of the Act read as a whole. Thus, its potential reach is longer than that of its English counterpart.

(iv) Immunity from GAAR

GAAR does not apply to *any* transaction (whether an avoidance transaction or otherwise) that does not misuse the provisions of the Act or abuse the provisions of the

---

[52] *Furniss (Inspector of Taxes) v. Dawson*, [1984] 1 All ER 530 at 532, *per* Lord Fraser of Tullybelton (H.L.).

Act when read as a whole.[53] This limitation is the only significant constraint on what would otherwise be a boundless rule.

(c) Avoidance Transactions

Reference:

ITA:

Subs. 245(3)   Avoidance Transaction

An "avoidance transaction" is:[54]

. . .any transaction

(a)   that . . . would result, directly or indirectly, in a tax benefit, unless the transaction may reasonably be considered to have been undertaken or arranged primarily for bona fide purposes other than to obtain the tax benefit; or

(b)   that is part of a series of transactions, which . . . would result, directly or indirectly, in a tax benefit, unless the transaction may reasonably be considered to have been undertaken or arranged primarily for bona fide purposes other than to obtain the tax benefit.

Thus, an "avoidance transaction" is any transaction, or series of transactions, that gives rise to *any* tax benefit unless the transaction may reasonably be considered to have been undertaken *primarily* for *bona fide* purposes other than obtaining the tax benefit. In order for a transaction not to be considered an "avoidance transaction", it must be supported by substantial reasons other than the tax benefit or savings that result from the transaction.

Given the broad definition of "tax benefit", however, it is difficult to characterize any financial transaction as other than tax driven. The tax benefit of the transaction does *not* have to be "significant". *Any* tax benefit is sufficient. This allows Revenue Canada virtually unlimited discretionary latitude to apply the rule as it sees fit. As a matter of practice, Revenue Canada only applies the rule to transactions of substance that involve tax savings in excess of $500,000 or that are otherwise odious.

(i) Legislative Intention

The June 30, 1988 Technical Explanatory Notes explain the meaning of an "avoidance transaction" as follows:

. . . if a transaction is an avoidance transaction, the tax consequences to any person are determined as is reasonable in the circumstances in order to deny the tax benefit resulting from the circumstances in order to deny the tax benefit resulting from that transaction.

. . . a transaction that, but for section 245, would result, directly or indirectly, in a tax benefit is considered to be an avoidance transaction unless the transaction may reasonably be considered to have

---

[53] Subs. 245(4).

[54] Subs. 245(3).

been undertaken or arranged primarily for bona fide purposes other than for the purposes of obtaining the tax benefit.

New paragraph 245(3)(*a*) refers to "bona fide purpose other than to obtain the tax benefit" rather than to "bona fide business purposes" as originally proposed, because the latter expression might be found not to apply to transactions which are not carried out in the context of a business, narrowly construed. The vast majority of business family or investment transactions will not be affected by proposed section 245 since they will have bona fide non-tax purposes.

Where a transaction is carried out for a combination of bona fide non-tax purposes and tax avoidance, the primary purposes of the transaction must be determined. This will likely involve weighing and balancing the tax and non-tax purposes of the transaction. If, having regard to the circumstances, a transaction is determined to meet this non-tax purposes test, it will not be considered to be an avoidance transaction. Thus a transaction will not be considered to be an avoidance transaction because, incidentally, it results in a tax benefit or because tax considerations were a significant, but not the primary, purpose for carrying out the transaction.

Ordinarily, transitory arrangements would not be considered to have been carried out primarily for bona fide purposes other than the obtaining of a tax benefit. Such transitory arrangements might include an issue of shares that are immediately redeemed or the establishment of an entity, such as a corporation or a partnership, followed within a short period by its elimination.

New paragraph 245(3)(*b*) recognizes that one step in a series of transactions may not by itself result in a tax benefit. Thus, where a taxpayer, in carrying out a series of transactions, inserts a transaction that is not carried out primarily for bona fide non-tax purposes and the series results in a tax benefit, that tax benefit may be denied under subsection 245(2). This is accomplished by expressly defining an avoidance transaction in paragraph 245(3)(*b*) as including a step transaction (a step transaction being one that is part of a series of transactions) in a series that, but for new section 245, would result directly or indirectly in a tax benefit, unless that transaction has primary non-tax purposes. For that purpose, reference may be made to existing subsection 248(10) of the Act which provides that a series of transactions includes any related transactions or events completed in contemplation of the series.

Thus, where a series of transactions would result in a tax benefit, that tax benefit will be denied unless the primary objective of each transaction in the series is to achieve some legitimate non-tax purposes. Therefore, in order not to fall within the definition of "avoidance transaction" in subsection 245(3), each step in such a series must be carried out primarily for bona fide non-tax purposes.

(ii) Business Purpose

A transaction need not satisfy a business purpose test. An arrangement without a business purpose is a valid transaction for tax purposes if it is undertaken *primarily* for *bona fide* purposes *other than* obtaining a tax benefit or saving. Thus, non-business reasons can support a commercial transaction. For example, family and financial security reasons can be used to justify the structure of transactions.

(iii) Contextual Interpretation

An arrangement must be seen in its entire context in order to determine whether it constitutes an avoidance transaction for tax purposes. Where an arrangement is implemented through a series of transactions or steps, one should look at the entire series to determine whether or not the resulting transactions constitute tax avoidance.

(iv) *Summary*

The scope of GAAR may be summarized as follows:

- An avoidance transaction is one that is entered into for the purposes of obtaining a tax benefit or advantage;
- An arrangement predicated primarily on *bona fide* non-tax purposes is not an avoidance transaction;
- GAAR applies only to "abusive" tax avoidance; it does *not* apply to lawful tax mitigation;
- Lawful tax mitigation does not misuse specific provisions of the Act or abuse the provisions of the Act read as a whole;
- In determining whether an arrangement or event is an avoidance transaction or lawful tax mitigation, the Minister may take into account not only the transaction itself, but also all other transactions that are part of the same series of transactions or events;
- The Minister may recharacterize the tax consequences of an "abusive" avoidance transaction in any reasonable manner.

(d) Purpose of Transaction

Subsection 245(3) exculpates a transaction (or series of transactions) if it may reasonably be considered to have been undertaken or arranged primarily for *bona fide* purposes other than to obtain a tax benefit. How do we determine a taxpayer's "purpose" in undertaking a transaction or series of transactions?

Is the taxpayer's purpose to be determined objectively or subjectively? What is the difference between the two methods? The words "reasonably be considered" are not particularly helpful in the analysis of a taxpayer's purpose. It would be quite unusual for any statute to require that the determination of anything, let alone anything as important as the determination of a taxpayer's "purpose", should be done in anything other than a reasonable manner.

The words "reasonably be considered" simply mean that the determination of purpose is tested against the circumstances surrounding the transaction and the nature of the evidence. A taxpayer's "purpose" is his or her intention in, or reason for, engaging in a transaction or series of transactions. The law cannot enter into a taxpayer's mind to determine his or her purpose or intention. It can, however, evaluate assertions of intention and purpose in an objective manner to determine whether the asserted purpose is plausible in the circumstances.

In the absence of any other external evidence to support a transaction, the taxpayer's credibility may be the only basis for explanation of the transaction. Thus, uncorroborated but credible testimony can be sufficient proof of taxpayer intention.

(i) Primary Purpose

An "avoidance transaction" is one that is undertaken for tax purposes. A transaction or series of transactions undertaken *primarily* for non-tax purposes is not an avoidance transaction.

A transaction undertaken for both tax and non-tax reasons must be carefully scrutinized to determine its *primary* purpose. This is not an easy task and requires careful evaluation of both tax and non-tax considerations to determine which dominates the transaction.

GAAR does not apply if the *primary* purpose of a transaction is to obtain non-tax benefits. But what if the tax and non-tax reasons are equal considerations. The taxpayer loses because she or he would not have discharged the burden of proof.

(e) Immunity from GAAR

GAAR applies to all avoidance transactions except those which do not misuse or abuse the Act. Subsection 245(4) provides that GAAR:

> . . . does not apply to a transaction where it may reasonably be considered that the transaction would not result directly or indirectly in a misuse of the provisions of this Act or an abuse having regard to the provisions of this Act, other than this section, read as a whole.

GAAR does not apply to a tax driven transaction if the transaction does not result in a "misuse" of the Act or an "abuse of the Act read as a whole". Thus, tax-driven transactions constitute lawful tax mitigation if they do not violate the underlying policy of the *Income Tax Act*. This subsection, which is probably the most obscure and obtuse aspect of GAAR, is also the single most significant limitation on the Rule.

(i) Legislative Intention

The Technical Notes explain subsection 245(4) as follows:

> Even where a transaction results, directly or indirectly, in a tax benefit and has been carried out primarily for tax purposes, section 245 will not apply if it may reasonably be considered that the transaction would not result directly or indirectly in a misuse of the provisions of the Act or an abuse having regard to the provisions of the Act read as a whole. This measure is intended to apply where a taxpayer establishes that a transaction carried out primarily for tax purposes does not, nonetheless, constitute an abuse of the Act.
>
> Subsection 245(4) recognizes that the provisions of the Act are intended to apply to transactions with real economic substance, not to transactions intended to exploit, misuse or frustrate the Act to avoid tax. It also recognizes, however, that a number of provisions of the Act either contemplate or encourage transactions that may seem to be primarily tax-motivated. The so-called "butterfly" reorganization is a good example of such transactions. It is not intended that section 245 will apply to deny the tax benefits that results from these transactions as long as they are carried out within the object and spirit of the provisions of the Act read as a whole. Nor is it intended that tax incentives expressly provided for in the legislation would be neutralized by this section.
>
> Where a taxpayer carries out transactions primarily in order to obtain, through the application of specific provisions of the Act, a tax benefit that is not intended by such provisions and by the Act read as a whole, section 245 should apply. This would be the case even though the strict words of the relevant specific provisions may support the tax result sought by the taxpayer. Thus, where applicable, section 245 will override other provisions of the Act since, otherwise, its object and purpose would be defeated.

Subsection 245(4) draws on the doctrine of "abuse of rights" which applies in some jurisdictions to defeat schemes intended to abuse the tax legislation. It refers to an abuse having regard to the provisions of the Act read as a whole as well as to a misuse of some specific provisions. For instance, a transaction structured to take advantage of technical provisions of the Act but which would be inconsistent with the overall purpose of these provisions would be seen as a misuse of these provisions. On the other hand, a transaction may be abusive having regard to the Act read as a whole even where it might be argued, on a narrow interpretation, that it does not constitute a misuse of a specific provision. Thus, in reading the Act as a whole, specific provisions will be read in the context of and in harmony with the other provisions of the Act in order to achieve a result which is consistent with the general scheme of the Act.

Therefore, the application of new subsection 245 must be determined by reference to the facts in a particular case in the context of the scheme of the Act. For example, the attribution provisions of the Act set out detailed rules that seek to prevent a taxpayer from transferring property by way of a gift and thereby transferring income to a spouse or minor children. A review of the scheme of these provisions indicates that income splitting is of concern in relation to gifts of property only where the transfer is to a spouse or child under 18 years of age. The attribution rules are not intended to apply to gifts to adult children. This can be discerned from a review of the scheme of the Act, its relevant provisions and permissible extrinsic aids. Thus a straightforward gift from a parent to his adult child will not be within the scope of section 245 either because it is made primarily for non-tax purposes or because it may reasonably be regarded as not being an abuse of the provisions of the Act. If however, the gift is made so that the adult child acquires an investment and, through a series of transactions, disposes of it and subsequently transfers the proceeds, including any income therefrom, to the parent, proposed section 245 should apply where the purpose of the transaction is the reduction, avoidance or deferral of tax. As another example, "estate freezing" transactions whereby a taxpayer transfers future growth in the value of assets to his children or grandchildren will not ordinarily be avoidance transactions to which the proposed rules would apply despite the fact that they may result in a deferral, avoidance or reduction of tax. Apart from the fact that many of these transactions may be considered to be primarily motivated by non-tax considerations, it would be reasonable to consider that such transactions do not ordinarily result in a misuse or abuse given the scheme of the Act and the recent enactment of subsection 74.4(4) of the Act to accommodate estate freezes.

Another example involves the transfer of income or deductions within a related group of corporations. There are a number of provisions in the Act that limit the claim by a taxpayer of losses, deductions and credits incurred or earned by unrelated taxpayers, particularly corporations. The loss limitation rules contained in subsections 111(4) to (5.2) of the Act that apply on a change of control of a corporation represent an important example. These rules are generally restricted to the claiming of losses, deductions and other amounts by unrelated parties. There are explicit exceptions intended to apply with respect to transactions that would allow losses, deductions or credits earned by one corporation to be claimed by related Canadian corporations. In fact, the scheme of the Act as a whole, and the expressed object and spirit of the corporate loss limitation rules, clearly permit such transactions between related corporations where these transactions are otherwise legally effective and comply with the letter and spirit of these exceptions. Therefore, even if these transactions may appear to be primarily tax-motivated, they ordinarily do not fall within the scope of section 245 since they usually do not result in a misuse or abuse.

However, not all inter-company transactions within a related corporate group will necessarily be outside the scope of the anti-avoidance rule. There may be circumstances where new section 245 would apply, for example:

- where the transaction results in the deduction of the same amount twice,
- where the transactions are entered into to make two or more corporations related only for the purpose of avoiding a loss limitation, or
- where the transaction otherwise attempts to abuse the loss limitation rules.

(ii) Abuse of the Act

As noted above, GAAR does not apply to any transaction which does not misuse or abuse the Act. What constitutes a "misuse" of the Act depends upon the object and spirit of the particular provision under scrutiny. What constitutes an "abuse" of the Act as a whole is a broader question that requires contextual examination of the inter-relationship of the relevant statutory provisions.

The determination as to whether or not a particular provision of the Act has been misused, or whether the Act read as a whole has been abused, is made by reference to the purpose ("object and spirit") of the particular provision or scheme of provisions. In other words, it is not sufficient merely to rely on the technical language of the particular provision or scheme of provisions to determine whether there has been a misuse of the Act or an abuse of the Act read as a whole. This is quite clear in the Ministerial Technical Notes:

> Where a taxpayer carries out transactions primarily in order to obtain, through the application of specific provisions of the Act, a tax benefit that is not *intended* by such provisions and by the Act read as a whole, section 245 should apply. This would be the case even though the strict words of the relevant specific provisions may support the tax result sought by the taxpayer. Thus, where applicable, section 245 will override other provisions of the Act since, otherwise, its object and purpose would be defeated.

One must dig deep and ferret out the "object and spirit" of provisions of the Act and understand the interrelated scheme of the statute. One can do so by referring to the Technical Notes, speeches in the House, academic writings and any other relevant material. Although, traditionally, Canadian courts have not made extensive use of extrinsic aids in determining the purpose of legislation, GAAR is a clear mandate that they should do so in the future.

The terms "misuse" and "abuse" essentially refer to the legislative rationale that underlies specific or interrelated provisions of the Act. The Department of Finance explains these terms as follows:[55]

> . . . the application of subsection 245(4) should involve an analysis of the object and spirit of the provisions of the Act read as a whole in the context of each particular case. An attempt to define the object and spirit of the provisions, far from being a 'meaningless platitude', as once suggested, will be the key to a coherent solution of those cases where it is uncertain whether the proposed rule will apply.

(A) Misuse of a Provision

An avoidance transaction that offends the underlying *purpose* of a *specific* rule is a misuse of the rule that attracts GAAR. An avoidance transaction that does not misuse a provision used to implement it may, nevertheless, be caught by GAAR if it is part of a transaction that abuses the Act as a whole.

---

[55] David A. Dodge, "A New More Coherent Approach to Tax Avoidance" (1988), 36 *Can. Tax J.* 1-22 at 21; see also IC 88-2, "General Anti-Avoidance Rule — Section 245 of the *Income Tax Act*" (October 21, 1988), para. 5.

It is important to distinguish between the *purpose* of a particular provision and its effect. A taxpayer can use a provision to mitigate taxes (the *Westminster* principle) if he or she does not offend *its purpose*. A transaction that is expressly permitted by the Act cannot, *in and of itself*, constitute misuse of the Act. For example, a transaction that takes advantage of a specific authorization to claim a deduction or offset a loss is not normally subject to GAAR.

The exclusionary rule requires an examination of the "object and spirit" of the provision under review to determine whether its purpose has been misused in the particular circumstances. Thus, in a sense, the rule implicitly applies the *Stubart* guidelines to test the validity of tax-driven transactions.

Example XXXIII.1

A corporation that holds publicly traded shares with unrealized gains rolls over the shares at cost (under section 85) to its wholly-owned subsidiary. The shares are then immediately repurchased by the corporation at their fair market value. The subsidiary has sufficient deductions available to offset the gain from the sale of the shares to its parent corporation.

The Department says that it will *not* apply GAAR in these circumstances.[56] Section 85 specifically allows a taxpayer to rollover property at its cost amount and the cumulative effect of the series of transaction does not offend the underlying premise of the provision. Query: Is the effective result of the series of transactions to allow a consolidation of income and losses between associated corporations? What if the subsidiary had losses, which were about to expire, that were used to offset the gain from the sale of the shares?

The "misuse" test in subsection 245(4) is essentially the same as the "object and spirit" test prior to the introduction of GAAR. Hence, a transaction that was not offensive or abusive of the object and spirit of a particular provision before GAAR is not considered a misuse of the provision after the enactment of GAAR. The Department has stated that:[57]

> Since the principles of statutory interpretation that Revenue Canada will follow will be similar to those followed to date, transactions that before the enactment of the general anti-avoidance rule were seen to comply with the Act in the sense mentioned will not now be seen to constitute a misuse of the provisions of the Act or an abuse of the Act read as a whole. Therefore the vast majority of transactions

---

[56] Memorandum dated February 23, 1990, Financial Industries Division; see also IC 88-2, "General Anti-Avoidance Rule — Section 245 of the *Income Tax Act*" (October 21, 1988), examples 8 and 9.

[57] Michael Hiltz, "Section 245 of the *Income Tax Act*", in Proceedings of 40th Tax Conf. 7:1, (Can. Tax Foundation, 1988), at 7:3.

undertaken primarily to obtain a tax benefit that were seen to be consistent with the intention of Parliament before the amendment of section 245 will continue to be acceptable.

But, as we see below, the misuse test is not as clearcut as the Department suggests. They also say that:[58]

> ... transactions that rely on specific provisions, whether incentive provisions or otherwise, for their tax consequences, or on general rules of the Act can be negated if these consequences are *so inconsistent* with the general scheme of the Act that they cannot have been within the contemplation of Parliament.

How do we determine the object and spirit of a provision? Through the use of extrinsic evidence, including legislative history and Ministerial technical notes:[59]

> In determining the intention of Parliament, Revenue Canada will take into account the words and context of any relevant provisions of the Act and the scheme of the Act read as a whole and any legislative history including the comments and examples contained in the Explanatory Notes to Legislation Relating to Income Tax issued by the Minister of Finance on June 30, 1988.

The Department does not usually invoke GAAR where a transaction or series of transactions clearly comes within the technical ambit of clearly specific provisions.[60]

Example XXXIII.2

A taxpayer disposes of a capital property to trigger a capital loss to offset realized capital gains. The taxpayer then reacquires an identical property 31 days after the disposition. The acquisition of the property on the 31st day after its disposition is intended to avoid the "superficial loss" rules in subparagraph $40(2)(g)(i)$ [acquisition prior to 31 days would deem the loss to be nil].

The sale and reacquisition of the property clearly constitute avoidance transactions. They are not caught by GAAR, however, because they clearly fall outside of a definite and stipulated time limit.[61] Thus, the transactions circumvent GAAR because they do not misuse subparagraph $40(2)(g)(i)$.

---

[58] IC 88-2, "General Anti-Avoidance Rule — Section 245 of the *Income Tax Act*" (October 21, 1988), para. 5.

[59] Michael Hiltz, "Section 245 of the *Income Tax Act*", in *Proceedings of 40th Tax Conf.* 7:1 (Can. Tax Foundation, 1988), at 7:3.

[60] See, e.g. ATR-57, "Transfer of Property for Estate Planning Purposes" (May 28, 1993).

[61] Revenue Canada Round Table, in *Proceedings of 41st Tax Conf.* (Can. Tax Foundation, 1989), Question 41 45:24.

Example XXXIII.3

An individual (who has utilized her capital gains exemption) gives shares of a family farm corporation to her children. Subsection 73(4) allows the taxpayer to rollover the shares without triggering a capital gain. Immediately thereafter, the children sell the shares in an arm's length transaction and claim a capital gains exemption of $500,000. The purpose of the transactions is to multiply the capital gains exemption.

Revenue Canada states that GAAR does not apply to the transaction because:

- Subsection 73(4) specifically provides for a rollover in the circumstances; and
- Subsection 110.6(2) allows for the capital gains exemption for shares of a family farm corporation without stipulating a minimum holding period for the shares.[62]

Since both provisions are permissive, the series of transactions does not misuse either. The Act allows each individual a capital gains exemption of $500,000 in respect of farm property. The transactions merely take advantage of specifically permitted deductions.

Example XXXIII.4

An individual, concerned that the exemption of $500,000 in respect of capital gains on QSBC shares might be reduced or eliminated, transfers his shares in an operating company ("Opco") to his holding company ("Holdco") in exchange for new shares. The aggregate paid-up capital of the new shares is equal to the paid-up capital of his old shares in Opco. By electing an appropriate amount under subsection 85(1), the individual triggers a capital gain of $500,000 on the Opco shares. The gain is eligible for the exemption under subsection 110.6(2.1) and the adjusted cost base of the Opco shares is increased by the amount of the capital gain. Holdco acquires the Opco shares at a stepped-up cost base, which will, in effect, reduce the ultimate capital gain on a subsequent disposition of the shares. Thus, the individual has crystallized his accrued capital gain in the Opco shares and is protected from any subsequent elimination or reduction of the exemption.

---

[62] Revenue Canada Round Table, in *Proceedings of 41st Tax Conf.* (Can. Tax Foundation, 1989), Question 44 at 45:26.

Example XXXIII.4 (continued)

GAAR does not apply to the crystallization transaction even though it is clearly intended to avoid tax.[63] Section 85 specifically allows a taxpayer to elect an amount as proceeds of disposition and to trigger or defer a gain as appropriate in the circumstances. Subsection 110.6(2.1) specifically exempts from tax certain amounts of capital gains from the disposition of QSBC shares. The combined effect of the two transactions does not offend the object and spirit of either provision, individually or collectively. The transactions come within the *Westminster* principle of lawful tax mitigation.

The above examples illustrate that Revenue is currently interpreting "misuse of the Act" in a fairly narrow and technical manner. The Department does not, however, have any philosophical commitment to its interpretative techniques: Each case is decided on its own facts and is subject to the exercise of administrative discretion. Thus, the Department's view can change without notice.

Example XXXIII.5

X, an individual who sojourned in Canada for 190 days in 1995, owns a controlling interest in Alpha Ltd., a Canadian private corporation. Under Article IV of the *Canada-U.S. Tax Convention*, X is deemed to be a U.S. resident for tax purposes. Alpha Ltd. qualifies as a CCPC for the purposes of the small business deduction by virtue of X's deemed residence in Canada under paragraph 250(1)(a), *unless* his sojourn in Canada was arranged for the purpose of qualifying Alpha Ltd. for the deduction, in which case GAAR might apply![64]

(B) Abuse of the Act

GAAR does not apply to avoidance transactions consummated primarily for tax purposes if the transaction does not constitute an abuse of the Act read as a whole. "Abuse of law", essentially a civil law concept incorporated into GAAR, can be used to defeat an otherwise lawful tax arrangement that is considered offensive in policy terms.

---

[63] Revenue Canada Round Table, in *Proceedings of 41st Tax Conf.* (Can. Tax Foundation, 1989), at 53:9.

[64] Technical Interpretation (September 11, 1992).

Immunity from GAAR is only available if the avoidance transaction does not fall within *either* the "misuse" and "abuse" tests.[65] A transaction which misuses a particular provision but does not abuse the Act read as a whole is caught by GAAR. Conversely, a transaction which complies with the literal and technical words of particular statutory provisions may, nevertheless, be subject to GAAR if its composite effect abuses the Act as a whole.

The abuse test in subsection 245(4) is probably the most controversial aspect of GAAR. A taxpayer must evaluate the statutory purpose of several, sometimes conflicting, provisions with no clear-cut or articulated rationale. This aspect of the Rule also gives the Department its broadest discretionary power, particularly in the context of its advance rulings procedures. Since Revenue does not rule on questions of fact, it can squash virtually any GAAR ruling request by refusing to rule. The only small comfort that one can derive is from the Department's public pronouncement: ". . . Transactions that before the enactment of the general anti-avoidance rule were seen to comply with the Act . . . will not now be seen to constitute a misuse of the provisions of the Act or an abuse of the Act read as a whole".[66] Apart from this statement, however, the Department does not provide any interpretational guidance to taxpayers. Thus, one obtains guidance as to the scope of subsection 245(4) by deducing its meaning from *ad hoc* advance rulings, which are infrequently published on an entirely discretionary basis.

Example XXXIII.6

Partnership A owns a depreciable asset. On the last day of A's fiscal year, Partnership B acquires a 99.9 per cent interest in A. In calculating its income, A deducts the maximum allowable CCA for that fiscal year. The following day A is dissolved and pursuant to subsection 98(3) of the Act, B becomes the owner of a 99.9 per cent undivided interest in the asset. In calculating its income for its fiscal year of 365 days ending two days following the end of A's fiscal year, B also deducts the maximum allowable CCA regarding the asset. The primary purpose of the series of transactions is to double the amount of CCA allowable for the same asset for the investors in Partnership B and to avoid the application of subparagraph 13(21)(*f*)(iv) of the Act.

GAAR applies to the series of transactions. The purchase of the interest in A by B, and the subsequent dissolution of A, are undertaken to avoid the restriction on the CCA allowable for the asset for the year and the consequences of a straightforward disposition of the asset.

---

[65] Subs. 245(4).

[66] Michael Hiltz, "Section 245 of the *Income Tax Act*", in *Proceedings of 40th Tax Conf.* 7:1 (Can. Tax Foundation, 1988), at 7:3.

(C) Burden of Proof

Subsection 245(4) clearly excludes certain types of transactions from the category of "abusive" avoidance. Since the subsection derogates from the thrust of the charging provision, it is, in effect, a relieving provision. At least that was the intention of the Department of Finance that tabled the legislation. As David A. Dodge, Senior Assistant Deputy Minister, said:[67]

> Subsection 245(4) is intended to be a relieving provision. Where a transaction does not have primarily non-tax purposes, it nonetheless escapes the application of the proposed section 245 if, on a normal construction of the Act read as a whole, it may reasonably be concluded that the transaction does not represent a misuse of the provisions of the Act or an abuse of the Act read as a whole.

The taxpayer carries the burden of proof to show that the Minister's assessment is incorrect. The burden is discharged on a balance of probabilities.

A taxpayer who relies on subsection 245(4) carries the burden of establishing that the transactions in question do not offend the underlying policy of particular provision or involve an abuse of the Act read as a whole. This is not an easy task. In many, if not most, cases it is quite difficult to obtain an authoritative reading of the "object and spirit" of particular provisions. The Canadian tradition of tabling Technical Notes to explain income tax amendments commenced only in 1982. It is that much more difficult to determine what constitutes an abuse of the Act "read as a whole".

In this context, it is important to distinguish between the rule of statutory construction that requires an ambiguous provision to be interpreted according to its "object and spirit" (the purpose rule) and the application of subsection 245(4), which limits the scope of GAAR to avoidance transactions that do not offend the policy of the Act. The general rule of statutory construction is that clear and unequivocal words are to be given their ordinary, grammatical meaning in the context in which they appear. Thus, it is not necessary to determine the object and spirit of a clear and unequivocal statutory provision. The statute is read as it is written.

Subsection 245(4), however, exempts an "avoidance transaction" from GAAR if it does not result in a misuse of the particular provision or an abuse of the Act read as a whole. Thus, compliance with the literal language of the Act, even where that language is clear and unequivocal, is not sufficient to immunize a transaction from GAAR. The Technical Notes (June 30, 1988) make this quite clear:

> . . . a transaction structured to take advantage of technical provisions of the Act but which would be inconsistent with the overall purpose of these provisions would be seen as a misuse of these provisions. On the other hand, a transaction may be abusive having regard to the Act read as a whole even where it might be argued, on a narrow interpretation, that it does not constitute a misuse of a specific provision. Thus, in reading the Act as a whole, specific provisions will be read in the context of and in harmony with the other provisions of the Act in order to achieve a result which is consistent with the general scheme of the Act.

---

[67] David A. Dodge, "A New and More Coherent Approach to Tax Avoidance" (1988), 36 *Can. Tax J.* 1.

To summarize, there are only two types of transactions that are safe from attack by GAAR:

1. Transactions arranged *primarily* for *bona fide* non-tax purposes; and

2. Avoidance transactions that are carried out primarily for tax purposes but that do not result, directly or indirectly, in a misuse of specific provisions of the Act or an abuse of the provisions of the Act read as a whole.

All other transactions are caught by GAAR if Revenue exercises its administrative discretion to invoke the rule.

The only judicial decision on the application of GAAR to date,[68] is under section 274 of the *Excise Tax Act*[69], a provision that is virtually identical with its counterpart in the *Income Tax Act*.[70] Michelin Tires Canada Ltd. ("Michelin"), a Canadian corporation engaged in the business of manufacturing and distributing motor vehicle tires, sold its inventory of imported tires to Uniroyal Goodrich ("Goodrich"), an affiliated Canadian corporation in the same business

Michelin imported tires and remitted FST at the applicable rate of 13.5 per cent but, as a result of the transition from the FST to the GST, licensed manufacturers were granted inventory rebates of only 8.1 per cent. This meant that Michelin would not obtain the full refund of FST paid on the purchase of its imported tires.

Having committed itself to its customers that it would be reducing its prices following the introduction of the GST, Michelin entered into an agreement to sell its entire inventory of imported tires to Uniroyal in the expectation that such a transaction would entitle it to a full 13.5 per cent refund rather than the 8.1 per cent inventory rebate. The transaction resulted in a tax benefit of approximately $800,000.

To implement the scheme, Uniroyal expanded its manufacturer's license to be considered the manufacturer of tires marketed under Michelin's brand name and to be able to import or purchase these tires on an FST-exempt basis. In consideration of $30,000 a week, the imported tires were held at Michelin's warehouses.

Uniroyal then entered into another agreement with Michelin and sold the imported tires back to Michelin as of the opening of business on January 2, 1991. Uniroyal and Michelin filed a joint election under subsection 156(2) of the *Excise Tax Act* and the taxable supply made between them was deemed to have been made for no consideration. Hence, no GST was collected on the sale of the imported tires from Uniroyal to Michelin.

---

[68] As of July 4, 1995.

[69] R.S.C. 1985, c. E-15.

[70] *Michelin v. Canada*, [1995] GSTC 17.

The sole purpose of the transactions was to allow Michelin to obtain a full refund of the FST paid on the imported tires. There was absolutely no *bona fide* business purpose to the transactions. The Minister refused the refund.

The transactions lacked economic substance other than the benefit to be derived from the refund. The only question was whether Michelin could get out from under GAAR by using the escape hatch in subsection 274(4): Did the impugned transactions misuse the provisions of the *Excise Tax Act* or in any other way abuse the statute read as a whole?

The burden of proof in challenging the Minister's assessment generally rests upon the taxpayer.[71] The Minister typically bases his or her assessment on assumptions derived from the facts of the underlying transaction. Then, it is up to the taxpayer to rebut the assumptions of fact. Thus, typically, the taxpayer carries the burden of proof to establish that the Minister's assessment is incorrect and should be set aside or amended.

Section 68.2 of the *Excise Tax Act* was intended to permit refunds of the FST in order to avoid the duplication of taxes that would otherwise have transpired with the introduction of the GST. The section provided for refunds where a manufacturer, wholesaler or importer, who had paid the FST on the purchase of certain goods, subsequently sold those goods under tax-exempt circumstances.

It was quite clear that the transaction constituted a misuse of section 68.2 of the *Excise Tax Act* and an abuse of the Act. The impugned transactions were abusive of the underlying policy of the legislation.

(f) Interpretation of GAAR

(i) Extrinsic Evidence

Extrinsic evidence is admissible to determine the "object and spirit" of specific tax provisions. Indeed, *Stubart* requires ambiguous provisions to be determined according to their "object and spirit" and this can only be done through the admission of extrinsic evidence to determine the purpose of tax provisions.

(A) The Initial Proposal

The first version of GAAR (December 16, 1987) would have admitted, as evidence of the legislative intention underlying the rule, extrinsic evidence in the form of the Minister's technical notes . Subsection 245(10) (as originally proposed) lent support to the new judicial tendency to admit extrinsic evidence in tax cases. The proposed subsection specifically authorized the introduction of certain forms of extrinsic evidence in the interpretation of GAAR. For example, in applying the purpose, scope and application of GAAR to a particular set of circumstances, a court would have been allowed to take into account the explanatory notes published in the *Canada Gazette*.

---

[71] *Assessment Commissioner v. Mennonite Home Association*, [1973] SCR 189.

Subsection 245(10) (as proposed) would not, in effect, have substantially changed the rules of statutory interpretation. The specific authorization to admit a particular source of extrinsic evidence would not, *per se*, have precluded the admission of other sources of extrinsic evidence in the interpretation of GAAR. The subsection would merely have reinforced the evidentiary rule that all *relevant* extrinsic evidence is admissible in interpreting the Act.

The importance of the subsection lay not in what it would have admitted as evidence of abusive tax avoidance, but in what it would have precluded from the ambit of GAAR. For example, the Technical Notes say that the rule will not ordinarily apply to "estate freezing" transactions in which a taxpayer transfers future growth in the value of any assets to his or her children. This explanation permits a certain degree of certainty in arranging family transactions. Subsection 245(10) (as proposed) would have permitted the introduction of such statements to immunize certain routine tax driven transactions from attack by GAAR.

Subsection 245(10) was, however, vehemently opposed by the Joint Committee of the Canadian Bar and the Canadian Institute of Chartered Accountants (CBA/CICA). The Department of Finance retreated, as it is inclined to do in the face of opposition from the CBA/CICA, and dropped the subsection.

It is arguable that the withdrawal of subsection 245(10) as proposed reflected a legislative intention to preclude the admission of extrinsic evidence in the interpretation of GAAR. Any such argument should, however, be rejected. The intervention of the CBA/CICA Joint Committee was not intended to preclude extrinsic evidence or stem the new trend of legislative interpretation. It was merely a narrow and technical response driven more by a sense of panic than by analysis of the extrinsic evidence rule.

(B) Documentation of Transactions

The importance of proper documentation in implementing business transactions cannot be overemphasized. A taxpayer should be prepared to carry the full burden of proving that the primary purpose of a transaction, or series of transactions, was *bona fide* and not primarily tax-driven.

In the event that a transaction is tax motivated, the taxpayer must establish that the transaction does not offend the object and spirit of the specific provisions used in its implementation *and* that it does not offend the object and spirit of the provisions of the Act read as a whole. Thus, tax plans must not only be technically sound, but must also comply with the purpose and philosophy of the provisions used and the general structure of the Act. According to the Technical Notes (June 30, 1988):

> Transactions that comply with the object and spirit of other provisions of the Act read as a whole will not be affected by the application of this general anti-avoidance rule. For example, a transaction that qualifies for a tax-free rollover under an explicit provision of the Act, and that is carried out in accordance not only with the letter of that provision but also with the spirit of the Act read as a whole, will not be subject to new section 245. However, where the transaction is part of a series of transactions

designed to avoid tax and result in a misuse or abuse of the provision that allows a tax-free rollover, the rule may apply. If, for example, a taxpayer, for the purpose of converting an income gain on a sale of property into a capital gain, transfers the property to a shell corporation in exchange for shares and subsequently sells the shares, the proposed section would ordinarily apply.

(g) Redetermination of Tax Liability

Subsection 245(5) allows the Minister to ignore the tax benefits of a transaction to which GAAR applies. The subsection reads as follows:

Without restricting the generality of subsection (2),

(a) any deduction in computing income, taxable income, taxable income earned in Canada or tax payable or any part thereof may be allowed or disallowed in whole or in part,

(b) any such deduction, any income, loss or other amount or part thereof may be allocated to any person,

(c) the nature of any payment or other amount may be recharacterized, and

(d) the tax effects that would otherwise result from the application of other provisions of this Act may be ignored

in determining the tax consequences to a person as is reasonable in the circumstances in order to deny a tax benefit that would, but for this section, result, directly or indirectly, from an avoidance transaction.

(i) Legislative History

Subsection 245(5) is explained in the Technical Notes as follows:

Where new subsection 245(2) applies, the tax consequences to a person are to be determined so as to deny the tax benefit on a basis that is reasonable in the circumstances. For that purpose, by virtue of new subsection 245(5), among other things:

• all or part of any deduction in computing income, taxable income, taxable income earned in Canada or tax payable may be disallowed,

• all or part of any deduction, income, loss or other amount may be allocated to any person,

• a payment or other amount may be recharacterized, or

• the tax effects that would otherwise result from the application of other provisions of the Act may be ignored.

For example, payments under an agreement that are, in legal form, a lease may be characterized as proceeds of disposition of property where, having regard to the agreement as a whole, it would be reasonable to establish the tax results of that transaction as if it were a sale.

As another example, assume that, in contemplation of an arm's length sale, an asset is transferred on a tax-free basis, under a rollover provision of the Act, to a related corporation, the shares of which are subsequently sold. New subsection 245(2) could be applied if the sale to the related corporation is found to be an avoidance transaction. The appropriate tax treatment might be to treat the taxpayer as having sold the property *directly* to the ultimate purchaser. Further, it might be appropriate in this situation for the Minister to approve, through a determination under subsection 152(1.11), an increase in the cost base of the shares of the related corporation in order to prevent the double taxation of the sale proceeds, once when the property is sold and again when the taxpayer disposes of the shares. Thus, the effect of the rollover provision would be ignored in order to allow this increased cost base.

A taxpayer has the right to dispute, through the ordinary notice of objection and appeal procedures, not only a Ministerial determination that a transaction is an avoidance transaction, but also the reasonable determination of the appropriate tax consequences.

(ii) Reasonable Redetermination

A taxpayer's liability under GAAR can be redetermined "as is reasonable in the circumstances" in order to deny him or her the tax benefits of the avoidance transaction. What is "reasonable in the circumstances" is a question of fact in each case. Among other things, the Minister may:

- Disallow all or part of any deduction in computing income, taxable income, taxable income earned in Canada or tax payable; or

- Allocate all or part of any deduction, income, loss or other amount to any person, recharacterize a payment or other amount, or ignore the tax effects that would otherwise result from the application of other provisions of the Act.

The taxpayer is then liable for the redetermined tax payable after the recharacterization of the offensive payments, deductions, etc. The taxpayer may dispute the reconstruction of his or her tax liability in accordance with the usual objection and appeal procedures.

(h) Third Parties

Where the reconstruction of a taxpayer's income tax liability affects a third part, the third party may request an adjustment to his or her tax liability, taking into account the amended and redetermined amounts. Subsection 245(6) reads as follows:

Where with respect to a transaction

(a) a notice of assessment, reassessment or additional assessment involving the application of subsection (2) with respect to the transaction has been sent to a person, or

(b) a notice of determination pursuant to subsection 152(1.11) has been sent to a person with respect to the transaction

any person (other than a person referred to in paragraph (a) or (b)) shall be entitled, within 180 days after the day of mailing of the notice, to request in writing that the Minister make an assessment, reassessment or additional assessment applying subsection (2) or make a determination applying subsection 152(1.11) with respect to that transaction.

(i) Legislative History

The Technical Notes explain the structure of subsection 245(6):

Under new subsection 245(6), where proposed subsection 245(2) applies with respect to a transaction and, consequently, a taxpayer has been assessed or reassessed or a determination has been made under proposed subsection 152(1.11) with respect to that person, another person is entitled to request that the Minister apply subsection 245(2) in his case in order to make adjustments of a relieving nature with respect to the same transaction.

A request for adjustment may be made by that other person within 180 days after the day of mailing to the taxpayer of a notice of assessment, reassessment or determination, as the case may be.

Amendments to section 245 of the Act allow that other person to make an application to the Tax Court of Canada for a time extension in the circumstances considered in existing subsection 267(5).

Subsection 245(6) does not apply to a taxpayer who has already been assessed or in respect of whom a determination pursuant to subsection 152(1.11) has been made by the Minister of National Revenue under section 245, because this taxpayer is in a position to request the appropriate adjustments through the objection and appeal mechanisms provided by other provisions of the Act.

The request for adjustments must be made within 180 days after the day of mailing to the taxpayer of the notice of assessment, reassessment or redetermination.

(ii) Redetermination vs. Recharacterization

It is important to distinguish between redetermination of the taxpayer's liability in the light of adjustments made because of an avoidance transaction and recharacterization of a transaction for the purposes of determining whether or not it is an avoidance transaction. Subsection 245(3) does not permit Revenue Canada to recharacterize a transaction to determine whether it is an avoidance transaction. Either the transaction is an avoidance transaction or it is not. Merely because the taxpayer could have rearranged his or her affairs to achieve an equivalent result at a higher tax cost does not mean that the transaction is *per se* an avoidance transaction. A taxpayer is entitled to mitigate his or her taxes if tax mitigation is not the primary motivation for the transaction or the Act is not misused or abused in the process of the taxpayer's planning.

5. SERIES OF TRANSACTIONS

I am at one with those of your Lordships who find the complicated and stylised antics of the tax avoidance industry both unedifying and unattractive but I entirely dissent from the proposition that because there is present...the element of a desire to mitigate or postpone the respondents' tax burdens, this fact alone demands from your Lordships a predisposition to expand the scope of the doctrine of *Ramsey* and of *Furniss v. Dawson* beyond its rational basis in order to strike down a transaction which would not otherwise realistically fall within it.

Lord Oliver
Craven. v. White, [1988] 3 WLR 423 at 463-64.

(a) General

An "avoidance transaction" includes arrangements that are part of a series of transactions undertaken for the purpose of obtaining a tax benefit.[72] When do events or transactions constitute "a series of transactions"?

The word "series" is defined in the *Shorter Oxford English Dictionary* as "a number of things of one kind following one another in temporal succession...". In the context of GAAR, it is clear that the term "series" cannot merely mean a sequence of

---

[72] See subss. 245(2) and (3).

events in a temporal sense. It is trite to observe that all events occur in a sequence. As Lord Oliver said in *Craven v. White:*[73]

> . . . a series means no more than a succession of related matters — a description that applies to virtually every human activity embarked upon with a view to producing any rational result.

What constitutes a "series of transactions" for the purposes of GAAR? In determining the "legitimacy" of a taxpayer's arrangements or transactions, when can the Minister treat the interrelated steps of an integrated transaction as a composite whole? How do we define and identify a single composite transaction from two or more transactions which are independent of each other? What are the parameters of the "step transactions doctrine"?

"Series of transactions" refers to the integration of individual and separate steps into a composite transaction. The linkage of the separate steps into a "series" results from their interdependence and the manner in which the transactions are structured. Thus, the question to be determined is: When is a sequence of events (e.g., A to B, then B to C) considered a single composite transaction, such as A to C?

(b) *Floor v. Davis*

The origins of the step transactions doctrine in the U.K. can be traced to the dissenting judgment of Eveleigh L.J., in *Floor v. Davis.*[74] The taxpayers, who were shareholders in a corporation (A), agreed in principle to sell their shares to another corporation (B). With a view to reducing or avoiding capital gains tax that would otherwise be payable on a direct sale of the shares, the taxpayers incorporated a new corporation, (C), with which they exchanged their shares in A. Corporation C, now the owner of the A shares, then sold the shares for cash to the ultimate purchaser, Corporation B. C, the new corporation, was then wound up. As a result of the reorganization of its capital, C passed on the cash that it received from B to an offshore corporation. The taxpayers would not be liable for capital gains tax if it could be shown that they had not disposed of their shares directly for cash to the ultimate purchaser of the shares.

The majority of the Court of Appeal held that each step in the sequence of transactions was properly executed and represented a genuine transaction. Eveleigh L.J. dissented: The taxpayer had, in effect, directly disposed of his shares to the ultimate purchaser even though they were transmitted through the medium of an intermediary corporation. His Lordship considered the series of events as one composite transaction.

---

[73] *Craven. v. White*, [1988] 3 WLR 423 at 452 (H.L.).

[74] *Floor v. Davis*, [1980] AC 695; affirming [1978] 1 Ch 295.

(c) The *Ramsey* Principle

In *Ramsey*,[75] the taxpayer, a farming corporation, realized a substantial capital gain on the sale of farmland which would have been subject to capital gains tax. To avoid the tax that would otherwise have been payable, the taxpayer embarked upon a "scheme" to create a paper capital loss to offset the capital gain on the farmland. The essence of the capital loss scheme was as follows:

- The taxpayer purchased the shares of a company and loaned it two equal amounts at a rate of 11 per cent;

- The loans were made on the basis that the interest on one loan could be increased provided that there was a corresponding decrease in the interest rate charged on the other loan;

- The taxpayer reduced the interest rate on one loan to zero and increased the interest rate on the other loan to 22 per cent;

- The zero interest loan was then paid in full and, as a result, the taxpayer sustained a loss in the value of the shares of the corporation;

- The loss was equal to the gain realized on the other loan.

Thus, the decreasing asset was sold to create a loss; the increasing asset was sold to create a tax-exempt gain. The scheme had neither commercial justification nor business purpose: The sole purpose was to produce a paper loss equal in amount to the capital gain that the taxpayer realized.

(i) Circular Transactions

Ramsey involved a circular transaction. The arrangements were, in Lord Oliver's words:[76]

> An artificially contrived concatenation of individual transactions linked together for the purpose of producing an end result entirely different from that which, on the face of it, would have been achieved by each successive link. . . .

The entire arrangement constituted two transactions of a self-cancelling nature which returned the taxpayer to his starting position. In the process, however, the taxable capital gain was eliminated by offsetting it against a paper capital loss. Lord Wilberforce described the scheme as follows:[77]

> . . . In each case two assets appear, like "particles" in a gas chamber with opposite charges, one of which is used to create the loss, the other of which gives rise to an equivalent gain which prevents the taxpayer from supporting any real loss, and which gain is intended not to be taxable. Like the particles, these assets have a very short life. Having served their purpose they cancel each other out and disappear. At the end of the series of operations, the taxpayer's financial position is precisely as it was at the beginning, except that he has paid a fee, and certain expenses, to the promoter of the scheme.

---

[75] *W.T. Ramsey v. I.R.C.*, [1981] WLR 449 (H.L.).

[76] *Craven v. White*, [1988] 3 WLR 423 at 452 (H.L.).

[77] *W.T. Ramsey v. I. R. C.*, [1982] AC 300 at 322 (H.L.).

Every step of the transactions was genuinely carried through and every transaction was exactly what it purported to be: No part of the scheme was a sham. Although there was no binding arrangement that each step would be followed by the next planned step, it was *well understood* that the entire sequence of events would be carried through to completion. Otherwise the scheme had no value.

The composite effect of the two transactions was that the taxpayer made neither a gain nor a loss. The transactions *taken together* were nothing more than a scheme to avoid taxes and the House of Lords treated it as such. Lord Wilberforce said:[78]

> To force the courts to adopt, in relation to closely integrated situations, a step by step, dissecting, approach which the parties themselves may have negated, would be a denial rather than an affirmation of the true judicial process.

(ii) Effect on Westminster Principle

Ramsey does not overrule the *Westminster* principle: It merely limits it to genuine cases of tax mitigation. The principle does not apply where it is plain that a particular transaction is but one step in a connected series of interdependent steps designed to produce a *single* composite overall result. Lord Wilberforce said of the principle:[79]

> While obliging the court to accept documents or transactions, found to be genuine, as such, it does not compel the court to look at a document or a transaction in blinkers, isolated from any context to which it properly belongs. If it can be seen that a document or transaction was intended to have effect as part of a nexus or series of transactions, or as an ingredient of a wider transaction intended as a whole, there is nothing in the doctrine to prevent it being so regarded; to do so is not to prefer form to substance, or substance to form. It is the task of the court to ascertain the legal nature of any transaction to which it is sought to attach a tax or a tax consequence and if that emerges from a series or a combination of transactions, intended to operate as such, it is that series or combination which may be regarded.

(iii) Integrated Transactions

In what circumstances can one aggregate separate transactions into a composite transaction? What, in effect, constitutes a "series of transactions"? The facts in *Ramsey* provide a clue to the answer: The transactions were circular, could not stand alone, were not intended to do so, and it was well understood that all of the steps had to be completed in order for the tax plan to work. In Lord Oliver's words:[80]

> But the fact was, as was plain to see, that those transactions not only were not intended to be interrupted or to stand in isolation but could not in fact have done so in the real world. They were totally dependent upon and integrated with other transactions whose purpose, and whose only purpose, was to nullify their effects and to leave the taxpayer in exactly the same position as they were before. In the one case there was actually a contractual obligation to carry the steps through to the end; in the other there was the confident expectation that they would be carried through to the end and no likelihood whatever that they would not.

---

[78] *W.T. Ramsey Ltd. v. I.R.C., ante*, at 326.

[79] *W.T. Ramsey v. I.R.C.*, [1982] AC 300 at 323.

[80] *Craven v. White*, [1988] 3 WLR 423 at 454 (H.L.).

But *Ramsey* did not imply that all sequential steps must necessarily be aggregated into a composite transaction. A sequence is only a "series" if the component transactions cannot have an independent existence and are not intended to do so. As Lord Oliver said:[81]

> What the case does demonstrate, as it seems to me, is that the underlying problem is simply one of the construction of the relevant statute and an analysis of the transaction or transactions which are claimed to give rise to the liability or the tax exemption. But it does not follow that because the court, when confronted with a number of factually separate but sequential steps, is not compelled, in the face of the facts, to treat them as if each of them had been effected in isolation, that all sequential steps must invariably be treated as integrated, interdependent and without individual legal effect.

(d) *Burmah Oil*

The House of Lords reaffirmed the *Ramsey* principle in *Burmah Oil*,[82] and clarified the *Westminster* doctrine. Lord Diplock said:[83]

> It would be disingenuous to suggest, and dangerous on the part of those who advise on elaborate tax avoidance schemes to assume, that *Ramsey*'s case did not mark a significant change in the approach adopted by this House in its judicial role to a preordained series of transactions (whether or not they include the achievement of a legitimate commercial end) into which there are inserted steps that have no commercial purpose apart from the avoidance of a liability to tax which in the absence of those particular steps would have been payable. The difference is in approach. It does not necessitate the overruling of any earlier decisions of this House; but it does involve recognizing that Lord Tomlin's oft quoted dictum in *I.R.C. v. Duke of Westminster* . . ." Every man is entitled, if he can, to order his affairs so that the tax attaching under the appropriate Acts is less than it otherwise would be", tells us little or nothing as to what methods of ordering one's affairs will be recognized by the courts as effective to lessen the tax that would attach to them if business transactions were conducted in a straightforward way.

Lord Scarman went even further:[84]

> First, it is of the utmost importance that the business community (and others, including their advisers) should appreciate . . . that *Ramsey*'s case marks "a significant change in the approach adopted by this House in its judicial role" towards tax avoidance schemes. Secondly, it is now crucial when considering any such scheme to take the analysis far enough to determine where the profit, gain or loss is really to be found.

Thus, "circular" tax planning schemes solely intended to produce self-cancelling consequences do not constitute legitimate tax mitigation. But what of schemes that are not self-cancelling but have enduring consequences?

---

[81] Ibid.

[82] *I.R.C. v. Burmah Oil Co. Ltd.* (1981), 82 BTC 56 (H.L.).

[83] *I.R.C. v. Burmah Oil Co. Ltd., ante*, at 58.

[84] *I.R.C. v. Burmah Oil Co. Ltd., ante*, at 64-65.

(e) *Furniss v. Dawson*

Furniss v. Dawson[85] involved a tax scheme intended to mitigate the capital gains tax that would have been payable by the taxpayer had he disposed of the shares of his corporation in an open-market transaction directly to the intended ultimate purchaser. To avoid the capital gains tax, the taxpayer exchanged his shares for shares of an offshore investment corporation that he owned. The offshore investment corporation then sold the shares to the ultimate purchaser, who was unconnected to the taxpayer. Under the U.K. *Finance Act*, 1965, the first disposition by way of share exchange to the offshore investment corporation was not a disposition or acquisition for capital gains tax purposes. Further, there would be no capital gains tax liability on the sale of the shares by the offshore investment corporation until such time as the taxpayers disposed of their shares in the investment corporation. Thus *Furniss* involved a "linear" as opposed to a "circular" transaction.

The House of Lords applied the *Ramsey* principle, not only to self-cancelling transactions, but also to those which have "enduring legal consequences". (The offshore investment corporation was not wound up after it had disposed of the corporation's shares to the ultimate purchaser, but continued in existence.) Lord Brightman's speech captures the essence of the decision:[86]

> My Lords, in my opinion the rationale of the new approach is this: in a pre-planned tax-saving scheme, no distinction is to be drawn for fiscal purposes, because none exists in reality, between (i) a series of steps which are followed through by virtue of an arrangement which falls short of a binding contract, and (ii) a like series of steps which are followed through because the participants are contractually bound to take each step *seriatim*. In a contractual case the fiscal consequences will naturally fall to be assessed in the light of the contractually agreed results. . . . The day is not saved for the taxpayer because the arrangement is unsigned or contains the words 'this is not a binding contract'.
>
> . . . *Burmah* expresses the limitations of the *Ramsey* principle. First, there must be a preordained series of transactions, or, if one likes, one single composite transaction. This composite transaction may or may not include the achievement of a legitimate commercial (i.e. business) end. . . . Secondly, there must be steps inserted which have no commercial (business) *purpose* apart from the avoidance of a liability to tax, not "no business *effect*". If those two ingredients exist, the inserted steps are to be disregarded for fiscal purposes. The court must then look at the end result. Precisely how the end result will be taxed will depend on the terms of the taxing statute sought to be applied.

Thus, a series of transactions constitutes a composite whole when its individual components are linked or glued together through "firm" arrangements or understandings that each component will be completed. In other words, it is "well understood" that the entire sequence will be carried to completion.

(i) *Preordained Transactions*

How "firm" does the understanding have to be in order to provide the linkage between individual transactions? Must the arrangements be "preordained" in a legal

---

[85] *Furniss (Inspector of Taxes) v. Dawson*, [1984] 1 All ER 530 (H.L.).

[86] *Furniss (Inspector of Taxes) v. Dawson*, [1984] 1 All ER 530 at 542-43 (H.L.).

sense in order to constitute a series of transactions? The answer is clearly "No". There is no distinction between tax schemes comprised of a series of steps that are followed through by virtue of an arrangement that falls short of a binding contract and schemes that are followed through because the participants are contractually bound to take each step *seriatim*. Preordination does not depend upon strict contractual rights, but on a practical certainty that transactions will be completed as planned.

Whether a series of transactions constitutes a composite linear transaction depends upon two principal factors: (1) The purpose of the transactions and (2) The manner in which they are structured.

A sequence of transactions is considered a "series" if, at the time when the intermediate transaction is entered into:[87]

- The sequence is preordained to produce a given result;
- The transaction has no other purpose than tax mitigation;
- There is no practical likelihood that the preplanned events will not take place in the order ordained, so that the intermediate transaction is not even contemplated practically as having an independent life; and
- The pre-ordained events do in fact take place.

In these circumstances, the first transaction can be linked to the last and the linked group is considered a single composite whole.

A preordained series of transactions implies, at the very least, an orchestrated sequence with a degree of certainty and control over the end result at the time that the intermediate steps are taken. It does not require absolute certainty as to every detail, but there should be no practical or substantial likelihood or risk that the transaction will not take place. Thus, a series of transactions is preordained, so as to constitute a single composite transaction, if there is a practical certainty when the first transaction takes place that the subsequent transactions will also take place.[88]

(ii) Composite Transactions

A composite transaction is one in which, when the first transaction is implemented, all of the *essential features* (not just the general nature) of the second transaction are determined by persons who have the firm *intention and ability* to implement the second transaction. For example: In a sale from A to B and from B to C, at the time that A sells to B, C is identified as a prospective purchaser and *all the main terms* of the sale are agreed to in principle. There does not have to be a pre-existing contract when the scheme begins: It is sufficient that there is a practical certainty that all the steps of the various transactions will be carried through to completion.

---

[87] *Craven v. White*, [1988] 3 WLR 423 at 462-63 (H.L.).

[88] *Hatton v. I.R.C.*, [1992] BTC 8024 (Ch. Div.).

(iii) The Westminster Principle

Where does the series of transactions doctrine leave the dictum in the *Duke of Westminster*? The dictum is accurate so far as tax mitigation is concerned. It does not apply to abusive tax avoidance, whether implemented through a single transaction or a series of transactions.[89] As Lord Diplock candidly put it in *Burmah Oil Co.*, the principle that every taxpayer is entitled to order his or her affairs to minimize tax ". . . tells us little or nothing as to what methods of ordering one's affairs will be recognized by the courts . . . ".[90]

Tax arrangements that are not shams or artificial and that are effectively implemented can be structured to mitigate tax. Tax mitigation, in and of itself, is neither abusive nor offensive. The manner in which it is executed, however, determines whether it is effective. As Lord Oliver put it:[91]

> I am at one with those of your Lordships who find the complicated and stylised antics of the tax avoidance industry both unedifying and unattractive but I entirely dissent from the proposition that because there is present . . . the element of a desire to mitigate or postpone the respondents' tax burden, this fact alone demands from your Lordships a predisposition to expand the scope of the doctrine of *Ramsey* and of *Furniss v. Dawson* beyond its rational basis in order to strike down a transaction which would not otherwise realistically fall within it.

His Lordship distanced himself, however, from Lord Scarman's suggestion that abusive tax avoidance schemes constitute "tax evasion":[92]

> . . . [T]here appears to be introduced in the speech of Lord Scarman at least, a moral dimension by which the court is to identify what he described as "unacceptable tax evasion". On the face of it this might be taken to suggest that the long accepted distinction between tax avoidance and tax evasion is to be elided and that the fiscal effect of a transaction is no longer to be judged, as *Ramsay* and *Burmah*, by the criterion of what the taxpayer has actually done, but by whether what he has done is "acceptable". It may be doubted whether this was indeed what Lord Scarman intended to suggest, but if it was, he was, I think, alone in expressing this view.

---

[89] *Ensign Tankers (Leasing) Ltd. v. Stokes (Inspector of Taxes)*, [1992] STC 226 (H.L.).

[90] *I.R.C. v. Burmah Oil Co. Ltd.*, ante, at 64-65.

[91] *Craven v. White*, [1988] 3 WLR 423 at 463-64.

[92] *Craven v. White, ante*, at 467-68.

6. ADMINISTRATION

References:

BULLETINS, CIRCULARS & RULINGS:

IC 88-2	October 21, 1988	General Anti-Avoidance Rule — Section 245 of the Income Tax Act
IC 88-2 Supp.	July 13, 1990	Supplement

The administrative responsibility for GAAR lies with Revenue Canada. Unlike other income tax matters, however, where tax returns and assessments are administered by the District Offices of Revenue Canada through normal audit procedures, the administration of GAAR is centered in Ottawa. Income tax assessments that might invoke the Rule are cleared through the GAAR Committee in Ottawa so as to provide a more consistent basis of application.

(a) Assessments

The assessment and appeal procedure in respect of GAAR is, with one exception, essentially the same as that which applies to other income tax assessments under section 152 of the Act. Subsection 245(7) provides as follows:

> Notwithstanding any other provision of this Act, the tax consequences to any person, following the application of this section, shall only be determined through a Notice of Assessment, reassessment, additional assessment or determination pursuant to subsection 152(1.11) involving the application of this section.

Thus, notwithstanding the application of GAAR to a taxpayer's income tax return, the usual assessment procedures of section 152 apply.[93]

> The purpose of subsection 245(7) is explained in the Technical Notes as follows:

> New subsection 245(7) of the Act provides that a person may not rely on subsection 245(2) in order to determine his income, taxable income, or taxable income earned in Canada of, tax or other amount payable by, or amount refundable to, any person under the Act as well as any other amount under the Act which is relevant for the purposes of the computation of the foregoing, except through a request for adjustment under subsection 245(6). This prevents a person from using the provisions of subsection 245(2) in order to adjust his income, or any of the above-mentioned amounts, without requesting that adjustment following the procedure set out in subsection 245(6).

(b) Request for Adjustment

Where the rule is used to assess a taxpayer and that assessment has consequential effects on another taxpayer, the second taxpayer may request an adjustment to his or her return. The request for the adjustment must be made within a period of 180 days after the Notice of Assessment or Reassessment has been mailed.

---

[93] *Michelin Tire v. Canada*, [1995] GSTC 17.

Where a taxpayer asks the Minister to adjust his or her income tax liability because of another taxpayer's assessment under GAAR, the Minister is required to make the necessary adjustments. Subsection 245(8) provides as follows:

> Upon receipt of a request by a person under subsection (6), the Minister shall, with all due dispatch, consider the request *and notwithstanding subsection 152(4)* assess, reassess or make an additional assessment or determination pursuant to subsection 152(1.11) with respect to that person, except that an assessment, additional assessment or determination may be made under this subsection only to the extent that it may reasonably be regarded as relating to the transaction referred to in subsection (6). [Emphasis added.]

The Minister's obligation to reassess or make the necessary adjustments only extends to matters that may reasonably be regarded as relating to transactions affected by subsection 245(6).

Where a taxpayer makes a request in respect of a matter raised pursuant to a third-party assessment, the Minister must consider the request and is obliged to assess the taxpayer even though the relevant statutory limitation period may have expired. Note, however, that the Minister's obligation to make an adjustment or issue a reassessment only extends to matters that may reasonably be regarded as relating to a transaction under subsection 245(6). In the event that the Minister rejects the request, he or she must notify the taxpayer by registered mail.

Subsection 152(1.11) allows the Minister to readjust or reassess amounts affected because of the application of GAAR. For example, the application of GAAR to one taxpayer may well affect the adjusted cost base of property or the paid-up capital of shares of another taxpayer. The Minister's authority to make a determination under subsection 152(1.11) is restricted to those cases where there has been a request for an adjustment of amounts under subsection 245(6). In the absence of such a request, the Minister is entitled to wait until he or she can assess a person to determine that individual's tax circumstances under subsection 245(2). For example, an avoidance transaction can result in an inappropriate increase in the capital cost of a depreciable property. In these circumstances, the Minister has two options:

1. If a request for an adjustment has been made, the Minister can rely on subsection 152(1.11) to make a determination of the undepreciated capital cost of the class of property to which that property belongs; or

2. If no request for a determination has been made, the Minister can wait until capital cost allowance is claimed in respect of the class and issue an assessment either denying all or a part of that claim.

(c) Administrative Structure

Assessments involving GAAR are reviewed by the head office of Revenue Canada in Ottawa. The head office has an informal committee (the "GAAR Committee"), which is made up of officials from the Rulings and Audit Divisions of Revenue Canada and representatives from the Departments of Justice and Finance. The Committee reviews files that are referred to it from the Audit and Rulings function. It also handles any relevant GAAR matters that are referred to it from the various district offices.

The GAAR Committee has enormous administrative power, both in respect of its power to issue GAAR related assessments and its power to issue or deny requests for advance rulings. The administrative perception of what is "abusive" or "offensive" determines the disposition of most proposed transactions. Although, in theory, the power of the Committee is neither greater nor less than the power of the Rulings Division to "bless or kill" proposed transactions, it actually has a far greater influence in respect of GAAR. A Committee decision to turn down a request for a GAAR ruling has a chilling effect on the proposed transaction. As IC 88-2 states:[94]

> Transactions that rely on specific provisions, whether incentive provisions or otherwise, for their tax consequences, or on general rules of the Act can be negated if these consequences are so inconsistent with the general scheme of the Act that they cannot have been within the contemplation of Parliament. On the other hand, a transaction that is consistent with the object and spirit of provisions of the Act is not to be affected. Revenue Canada will follow this principle in interpreting section 245 of the Act.

The "object and spirit" of a provision or of a series of provisions can result in the application of GAAR and put the burden of proof on the taxpayer to establish that the transaction is not "offensive".

7. ADMINISTRATIVE INTERPRETATION

We have seen that a taxpayer's right to arrange his or her affairs to mitigate taxes is not an unfettered right. Section 245 of the Act curtails the *Westminster* principle: a taxpayer is only entitled to arrange affairs in a tax efficient manner if his or her arrangements are not "abusive" or "offensive" to the underlying purpose of the Act.

(a) Discretionary Power

The explanatory notes to GAAR are the foundation upon which Revenue Canada administratively interprets the rule. In the Department of Finance's words:[95]

> It is recognized that the introduction of the new Rule will inevitably carry with it a degree of uncertainty that in some cases can only be clarified through judicial interpretation of specific cases. To minimize this uncertainty to the maximum extent possible, the detailed explanatory notes . . . describe the rule in some detail and how it is intended to deal with artificial tax avoidance arrangements.

Although useful as explanatory policy statements, the Technical Notes are of limited value in applying the rule to specific situations. To be sure, expository statements that the rule is not intended to apply to certain types of transactions provide tax practitioners with some comfort in arranging business transactions. The Notes are, however, qualified by several *caveats* and, as such, need to be read closely if they are to be relied upon. The Technical Notes explain:

---

[94] IC 88-2, "General Anti-Avoidance Rule — Section 245 of the *Income Tax Act*" (October 21, 1988).

[95] Canada, Department of Finance, *Tax Reform 1987: Income Tax Reform* (Ottawa: June 18, 1987), at 130.

. . . transactions that comply with the object and spirit of other provisions of the Act read as a whole will not be affected by the application of this General Anti-Avoidance Rule. For example, a transaction that qualifies for a tax-free rollover under an explicit provision of the Act, *and that is carried out in accordance not only with the letter of that provision but also with the spirit of the Act read as a whole, will not be subject to new section 245.* [Emphasis added.]

Revenue Canada is responsible for administering the *Income Tax Act* and it assumes the primary role in the interpretation of GAAR. Although Revenue's role in administering the rule is not, at least in theory, any different from its general administrative responsibility for the Act, it has a substantially enhanced role to play in the context of the rule. The rule depends upon two factors: (1) The taxpayer's primary motive in undertaking a transaction, and (2) an interpretation as to what constitutes an "abusive" or "offensive" transaction. The determination of both of these elements requires the exercise of administrative discretion.

The potential for abuse of discretionary power concerned the Joint Committee of the CBA/CICA:

The potential for abuse of power, while inherent in the administration by government of any legislation, is writ large in the context of GAAR because of the breadth of section 245. We therefore applaud the sensitivity to this problem displayed by the Department of National Revenue, Taxation, in deciding, as indicated in Information Circular No. 88-2, to review proposed assessments involving GAAR at Head Office in order to ensure application of GAAR in a consistent manner. . . . For so long as GAAR remains with us, much administrative effort will have to be expended with a view to making it work from a practical point of view. . . . If nothing else, the Circular illustrates the extent to which the whole exercise of interpreting and applying GAAR is fact-oriented and involves subjective elements.

Information Circular 88-2 is of interest, but of limited value, to tax practitioners. The circular does very little, if anything, to contribute to an understanding of the development of policy in the interpretation of the rule. Indeed, it is somewhat of a paradox that the circular, which focuses on the "object and spirit" of the Act, does very little to contribute to the development of principles or the interpretation of tax policy. The circular is little more than an aggregation of factual examples supplemented by terse, sometimes single sentence, statements that the rule does or does not apply to particular facts. The circular may be helpful to those who have transactions involving factual circumstances that are virtually identical to those described, but it is of limited value to those who must base their professional advice on facts that are not "on all fours" with those described in the circular.

(b) Purposive Approach

The purpose underlying GAAR is set out in the testimony of Mr. Jim Wilson (General Counsel/General Director, Department of Finance) speaking on the need for an anti-avoidance rule in Canada and the experience of other jurisdictions in similar matters:

The main rule we saw when we looked at the United States experience was the business-purpose doctrine. . . . They do have a business-purpose test. They have had one for 50 years. It was developed by the courts, and it is a very simple doctrine and one that is quite compelling. Their courts looked at the tax code in the States and they said it is drafted to deal with business or commercial transactions;

therefore, when you have in front of you a transaction that lacks any business purpose whatsoever, it is not unreasonable to treat it differently from transactions that have a business purpose and come within the general intention or purpose of the tax code. So we looked at the U.S. experience.

We also looked at the U.K. experience, and they recently, like Canada, took a very strict or literalistic approach to tax interpretation. . . . Recently, however, the U.K. courts looked at the U.S. experience and struck down a number of transactions that had no business purpose, that were effectively step transactions designed to create paper losses. The Courts looked at them, looked at the U.S. experience and I think, frankly, said enough is enough; the strict literal approach to tax interpretation is no longer appropriate.

With the proposed General Anti-Avoidance Rule the underlying premises are really two. First, specific rules do not work in every case . . . second — and I think the second premise is as important — Canada is out of line with other jurisdictions and it is time it was brought into line.
. . .

I think the rule is aimed at transactions that use provisions of the Act inappropriately or avoid provisions of the Act inappropriately. [Emphasis added.]

The clear inference is that the interpretation of what constitutes an "avoidance transaction" must be made in the context of the policy rationale of the Act as a whole to determine whether its provisions have been used appropriately or inappropriately.

The purposive approach to statutory interpretation is simple to state: Since legislation has a purpose, it should be interpreted in such a manner as best enhances the attainment of that purpose. As Justice Frankfurter said:[96]

Legislation has an aim; it seeks to obviate some mischief, to supply an inadequacy, to effect a change of policy, to formulate a plan of government. That aim, that policy is not drawn, like nitrogen, out of the air; it is evinced in the language of the statute, as read in the light of other external manifestations of purpose.

The question is: How do we get at the purpose, "object and spirit" or intention of particular statutory provisions or of the Act as a whole. The answer to this question is of as much, if not more, concern to tax planners as it is to litigation counsel.

If the courts are to apply the purposive approach to statutory construction, they must admit all relevant evidence in determining the legislative intention underlying particular provisions. There is no useful purpose to be served by setting up *a priori* rules of exclusion. The trier of fact can always assess the reliability of the evidence and the weight that should be attached to it:[97]

Unhappily, there is no table of logarithms for statutory construction. No item of evidence has a fixed or even average weight. One or another may be decisive in one set of circumstances, while of little value elsewhere. A painstaking, detailed report by a Senate Committee bearing directly on the immediate question may settle the matter. A loose statement even by a chairman of a committee, made impromptu in the heat of debate, less informing in cold type than when heard on the floor, will hardly be accorded the weight of an encyclical.

---

[96] Felix Frankfurter, "Some Reflections on the Reading of Statutes" (1947), 47:4 *Columbia L. R.* 527 at 538-539.

[97] Felix Frankfurter, "Some Reflections on the Reading of Statutes" (1947), 47:4 *Columbia L. R.* 527 at 543.

(c) Avoidance Transactions

An avoidance transaction is a single transaction carried out *primarily* to obtain a tax benefit. A "tax benefit" means a reduction, avoidance or deferral of tax or any other amount payable or an increase in a refund of tax or any other amount under the Act.

An "avoidance transaction" includes a transaction that is primarily tax-motivated but forms part of a series of transactions carried out primarily for non-tax purposes. In Revenue's view, the fact that the *series* of transactions has *bona fide* non-tax purposes does not preclude one of its components from being considered an avoidance transaction. Hence, in effect, a single tax-motivated transaction can upset a multi-part scheme or business arrangement that is not *per se* tax driven.

(i) Determination of Purpose

A taxpayer's purpose for undertaking a transaction in a particular manner is to be determined, not only from the taxpayer's statement of intention, but also from all of the circumstances that surround the transaction(s). The taxpayer's declared statement of intention is not necessarily determinative in any case.

It is important to distinguish between the purpose and the effect of a transaction. An "avoidance transaction" is one that is carried out primarily for tax purposes. Thus, even though a transaction has a business, investment, family or other non-tax effect, it may nevertheless be an "avoidance transaction" if its *primary* purpose is to obtain a tax benefit.

(ii) Misuse or Abuse of the Act

A tax motivated transaction that complies with the specific provisions of the Act may, nevertheless, be considered to be an "avoidance transaction" if it results in consequences that ". . . are so inconsistent with the general scheme of the Act that they cannot have been within the contemplation of Parliament".[98]

Thus, in respect of the determination of both the purpose of a transaction and whether the transaction offends the general scheme of the Act, the taxpayer, in effect, carries the burden of proof to show that the transaction is not an avoidance transaction.

Determining whether a particular provision of the Act has been misused, or whether the Act read as a whole has been abused, requires an examination of the purpose ("object and spirit") of the particular provision or scheme of provisions. It is not sufficient merely to rely on the technical language of the particular provision or scheme of provisions to determine whether there has been a misuse of the Act or an abuse of the Act read as a whole. This is quite clear in the Technical Notes:

> Where a taxpayer carries out transactions primarily in order to obtain, through the application of specific provisions of the Act, a tax benefit that is not *intended* by such provisions and by the Act read as a whole, section 245 should apply. This would be the case even though the strict words of the relevant

---

[98] IC 88-2, "General Anti-Avoidance Rule — Section 245 of the *Income Tax Act*", para. 5.

specific provisions may support the tax result sought by the taxpayer. Thus, where applicable, section 245 will override other provisions of the Act since, otherwise, its object and purpose would be defeated. [Emphasis added.]

8. INTERPRETATIONS AND RULINGS

The general theme running through Revenue Canada's Information Circular 88-2 is that a taxpayer is not entitled to arrange his or her affairs to reduce tax if such an arrangement permits him or her to do indirectly what the spirit of the Act would not permit directly. Time and again, Revenue Canada indicates in its Circular that it will apply the General Anti-Avoidance Rule in circumstances where the taxpayer implements an arrangement or transaction by utilizing two or more provisions of the Act to circumvent a specific provision. We see this in the examples discussed below. Where the Act contains, whether specifically or by inference, a prohibition against a deduction or characterization of a receipt, a multiple-step arrangement that bypasses the prohibition can trigger GAAR. Thus, the concept of "abuse of the Act read as a whole" is very wide indeed and, probably, more extensive in its reach than comparable anti-avoidance doctrines in other jurisdictions.

(a) Form of Business Organization

The choice of form of a business organization can depend upon several factors: legal restrictions, considerations of limiting legal liability, sources of financing, and income tax considerations. Most small businesses face a real choice at the time that the business is started. This choice is usually between a sole proprietorship and a limited liability corporation.

If it is anticipated that a business will suffer losses in its start-up period, it is generally preferable to conduct a business as a sole proprietorship so that the owner's business losses can be offset against income from other sources. Later, when the business becomes successful, the sole proprietorship can be converted, on a tax-free basis, into a limited liability corporation. It is generally preferable to conduct a successful business through a Canadian-controlled private corporation because of the low income tax rate chargeable on active business income earned by such corporations.

Revenue Canada's view is that there is nothing offensive about incorporating a sole proprietorship through a transfer of business assets on a tax-free basis under section 85. Even though the incorporation of the proprietorship may be motivated by income tax considerations, the rollover of the business does not offend the scheme of the Act in general and is not contrary to the object and spirit of any particular provisions. The Act clearly contemplates a choice of form of business organization. Hence, the incorporation of a sole proprietorship is not subject to the Rule.[99]

---

[99] IC 88-2, "General Anti-Avoidance Rule — Section 245 of the *Income Tax Act*" (October 21, 1988), para. 11.

(b) Consolidation of Profits and Losses in a Corporate Group

A corporation is a separate legal entity and a taxpayer in its own right. A related group of corporations cannot consolidate the group's income for tax purposes. Each separate corporation within a related group of corporations must file an income tax return based on its own income or loss for its fiscal period.

A corporation may, however, transfer property that it uses in its business to a related corporation so that the transferee corporation can deduct its non-capital losses against the income generated from the property. Thus, related corporations can sometimes obtain the economic effect of consolidated tax returns by transferring assets within the group in order to offset income from profitable assets against accumulated business losses.

Revenue Canada does not consider a transfer of property between related corporations to be an abusive "avoidance transaction" where all of the shares of the transferor and transferee corporations have been owned by the same taxpayer during the period in which the losses where incurred. Such a transfer is considered to be "consistent with the scheme of the Act". Therefore, subsection 245(2) will not be applied.

A transfer of property between related corporations may, however, be considered to be "abusive" where there has been a change of control by an arm's length person. If the transfer of property is undertaken to avoid a specific rule, such as a rule designed to preclude the deduction of losses after the acquisition of control of a corporation by an arm's length person, the transfer would constitute a misuse of the provisions of the Act and, therefore, be subject to GAAR.

(c) Purifying a Corporation

Where a taxpayer disposes of shares of a "qualified small business corporation" ("QSBC") as defined in subsection 110.6(1), any capital gain resulting from the disposition of the shares may be eligible for the capital gains exemption of $500,000. Thus, there is a substantial tax advantage to a QSBC. One of the requirements to qualify is that *all or substantially all* of the assets of the corporation are used in an active business carried on primarily in Canada. A corporation that is off-side this requirement can, however, be reorganized and "purified" for the purposes of the capital gains exemption.

A fairly typical scheme to "purify" a corporation is to have the shareholders of the non-qualifying corporation ("Opco") incorporate a corporation ("Newco"). The shareholders can transfer to Newco sufficient shares of Opco with a fair market value equal to the market of the assets that are not used in the active business of Opco. Opco can then purchase its common shares from Newco and pay for the shares by transferring its non-business assets to Newco.

Revenue Canada does not consider the formation of Newco and the transfer of Opco's shares to it to be an abuse of the Act. Section 85 specifically permits a transfer of capital property to a taxable Canadian corporation on a tax-free basis. Nor does Revenue Canada consider the distribution of Opco's non-business assets prior to the sale of its shares to constitute an abuse of the Act read as a whole. The definition of a small business corporation does not require that all or substantially all of the assets of the corporation be used in carrying on an active business in Canada for a particular period of time prior to the sale of the shares. Hence, the series of transactions to "purify" Opco are in accordance with the scheme of the Act and, as such, do not constitute an abusive "avoidance transaction" under GAAR. (Note, however, that the transactions described may generate a tax liability to Opco when it disposes of its non-business assets to Newco, and that Newco may be subject to subsection 55(2) if the gain on the purchased shares is attributable to something other than income earned or realized by Opco.)

(d) Services Rendered to a Corporation

Where an individual renders services to a corporation, the manner of payment for the services can depend upon the relationship between the individual and the corporation.

(i) Non-payment of Salary

Where an individual provides services to a corporation with which he or she does not deal at arm's length, the parties may agree that the corporation is not under an obligation to pay the individual a salary for services rendered because payment of a salary would increase the corporation's loss for the year. Since there is no provision in the Act requiring payment of a salary for services rendered, the failure to do so is not considered to be contrary to the scheme of the Act read as a whole. Hence, Revenue Canada will not apply subsection 245(2) to deem a salary to have been paid by the corporation to the individual. Note, however, that the situation would be different if there were a legal obligation to pay the salary and if the individual were to waive payment of the amount.

(ii) Salary/Bonus Mix

A Canadian-controlled private corporation is taxable at a special low rate on the first $200,000 of its active business income earned in a year. Hence, where an owner/manager of a Canadian-controlled private corporation is taxable at a higher rate than the corporation, it is usually advantageous to reduce the corporation's income to $200,000 for the year through, for example, payment of a salary/bonus to the owner/manager. Provided that the amount of the salary/bonus is not in excess of a reasonable amount, Revenue Canada will not use GAAR to deny a deduction for the payment since the Act permits the deductibility of reasonable business expenses.

(iii) Unpaid Amounts

Where a corporation owes an amount for services rendered to it, any amount accrued for payment is deductible to the corporation in the year in which the service is rendered. If the amount accrued is not paid, however, the person who renders the services is not taxable on the accrued amount. This misalignment between the deduction to the corporation and the non-inclusion to the individual allows the corporate taxpayer the advantage of the deduction and the individual the benefit of tax deferral until receipt.

To prevent taxpayers from taking undue advantage of this imbalance between deduction and inclusion, section 78 provides that either the corporation or the individual entitled to the payment must include the amount in income in the third taxation year following the year in which the expense is incurred. Thus, the Act specifically contemplates that limited tax deferral is acceptable: The "object and spirit" of subsection 78(1) is to permit such a deferral. Hence, subsection 245(2) does not apply in these circumstances, even though the arrangement is patently tax motivated.

(e) Conversion of Salary into Capital Gain

Salaries and bonuses are taxable as employment income and, as such, are potentially subject to higher rates of tax. In contrast, a capital gain may either be completely non-taxable or, if taxable, subject to a low effective rate of tax. Hence, it is usually to an employee's benefit to be compensated through capital gains rather than through salary or bonus payments. Thus, it will usually be advantageous to convert potential salary payments into capital gains.

Where an employee of a private corporation wishes to receive a portion of a salary or bonus as a capital gain, she or he can subscribe for the employer's preferred shares, redeemable at a premium that reflects the relevant portion of the employee's annual salary or bonus payment. Prior to the redemption of the preferred shares, the shares can be purchased by a corporation related to the employer corporation, thereby allowing the employee to receive a distribution of surplus as a capital gain. In these circumstances, since the acquisition of the preferred shares is part of an arrangement designed to avoid tax that would otherwise have been paid had the income been received as a salary or bonus, the transactions would be considered to be "avoidance transactions". In Revenue Canada's view, the transaction results in an abuse of the Act as a whole.

Presumably, if the initial arrangement with the employee was structured so that she or he would be compensated on the basis of salary/bonus and equity participation in preferred shares *and* the arrangement was primarily driven by non-tax considerations, the arrangement would not constitute an "avoidance transaction" and the question of abuse of the Act as a whole would not arise. In other words, where an arrangement does not constitute an "avoidance transaction" in that it is undertaken *primarily* for non-tax purposes, it does not matter that the arrangement may circumvent specific provisions of the Act or be tantamount to an abuse of the Act read as a whole.

Provided that an arrangement has been sanctified by having been undertaken primarily for non-tax purposes, it does not matter that it runs counter to the "object and spirit" of the Act. Non-tax motivated transactions need only comply with the technical requirements of the Act. Hence, the principal focus of tax planning should be to ensure that business and family transactions are undertaken primarily for non-tax purposes. It is only if transactions are undertaken primarily for tax purposes that it is necessary to ensure they do not offend either the scheme of the Act read as a whole or any particular provisions.

(f) Interest Expense

Paragraph 20(1)(c) limits the deductibility of interest expenses to, *inter alia*, borrowing incurred for the purpose of gaining or producing income from business or property. This restriction on the deductibility of interest can cause difficulties for a related group of corporations where one of the corporations is profitable and the other sustains losses and needs additional capital to carry on its operations. In these circumstances, although the unprofitable corporation can borrow money, it cannot use the tax saving by deducting its interest expense. If the profitable corporation borrows the money from its bank and subscribes for common shares in the non-profitable corporation, it can reduce its net income by deducting the interest expense. The non-profitable corporation can use the money received from the sale of shares to gain or produce income from its business. The borrowing by the profitable corporation is for the purpose of gaining or producing income and, therefore, subsection 245(2) would not apply.

The above example illustrates the vulnerability of taxpayers to the administrative discretion of Revenue Canada. The Department issues terse statements that an arrangement is or is not an "avoidance transaction" or that it does or does not abuse the Act read as a whole. In this case, compliance with paragraph 20(1)(c) of the Act is considered sufficient reason not to classify the transaction as an "avoidance transaction". In other circumstances, however, compliance with the technical statutory requirements of a provision(s) may not *per se* be sufficient to avoid characterizing a transaction as an "avoidance transaction".

Without explanation or elaboration, the Department has stated that borrowing by one corporation for the purposes of financing the business activities of another related corporation is deductible because the transaction conforms with the technical wording of the statute.[100]

The statement provides comfort for the particular transaction described. It is, however, quite dangerous to extrapolate from this statement that technical compliance with the requirements of the statute will, in all cases, be sufficient to avoid the rule. Clearly this is not the case.

---

[100] IC 88-2, "General Anti-Avoidance Rule — Section 245 of the *Income Tax Act*" (October 21, 1988), para. 19:

The borrowing by the parent corporation is for the purpose of gaining or producing income as required by para. 20(1)(c) of the Act, and subs. 245(2) would, therefore, not apply.

Similarly, Revenue Canada has indicated that borrowing from one corporation to finance the purchase of shares of another corporation, followed by an amalgamation of the purchaser with its subsidiary will not trigger the rule in respect of the deductibility of interest expense. For example, where a taxable Canadian corporation has agreed to purchase all of the shares of an operating corporation, which is also a taxable Canadian corporation, the purchaser can incorporate a holding corporation (Holdco) which borrows the purchase price and pays the vendor for the shares. Holdco and the operating corporation amalgamate so that the interest payable on the monies borrowed to acquire the shares can be deducted in computing the income from the business of the amalgamated corporation. The Department's position is that the borrowing by the holding corporation and the amalgamation are not abusive and that subsection 245(2) does not apply to the borrowing by the holding corporation.

(g) Section 85 Rollover to Related Corporations

Suppose an individual has property with an unrealized capital gain that she or he wishes to sell to a third party. The individual also has a related corporation with net capital loss. If she or he sold the property directly to a third party, she or he would realize a capital gain. To avoid the gain, the property is transferred to the individual's related corporation on a tax-deferred basis under subsection 85(1). The related corporation then sells the property to the third party and offsets the resulting taxable capital gain against its net capital loss.

It is clear that such a transaction is tax motivated and, without more, would be an avoidance transaction. Revenue Canada does not, however, consider a transfer of property to a *related* corporation on a tax-deferred basis to contravene the object and spirit of the Act. Since subsection 69(11) does not permit a person to transfer property to an *unrelated* corporation on a tax-deferred basis where it is intended that the unrelated corporation will sell the property and reduce the amount of the gain by amounts of losses or similar deductions which it may claim, the Department reasons that ". . . by implication, the subsection does permit a transfer to a *related* corporation on a tax-deferred basis".

The Department does not address the broader question of whether the grouping of income and losses of a related corporate group is within the general scheme of the Act with respect to consolidated income reporting for tax purposes. This may suggest that in applying GAAR, Revenue Canada is less likely to be concerned with the general scheme of the Act read as a whole and more concerned with the misuse of specific statutory provisions.

(h) Estate Freezes

Generally speaking, estate freezing is a technique whereby an individual organizes or, more usually, reorganizes property with a view to "freezing" the value of that property for the purposes of minimizing the tax payable on accrued capital gains at death. Subsection 70(5) deems a taxpayer to have disposed of all capital property immediately before his or her death. Hence, where a taxpayer dies with unrealized capital gains, this subsection will trigger the capital gains by deeming the property to have been disposed of at fair market value. To curtail the amount of gain that may be realized on a deemed disposition of property, a taxpayer may rearrange his or her affairs and freeze the value of the estate. Most, if not all, estate freezes are tax motivated transactions.

(i) Holding Company Freeze

A typical estate freeze might operate as follows: a parent who owns shares of an operating company ("Opco") which have appreciated in value, may transfer the shares to a newly formed corporation ("Holdco") in exchange for Holdco's shares and/or debt. The transfer can be made under subsection 85(1) on a tax-deferred basis so that the parent does not realize any capital gain on the transfer of Opco's shares to Holdco. The consideration for the transfer is usually made up of preferred shares that are retractable at the option of the parent for an amount equal to the fair market value of the Opco shares transferred. The preference shares carry voting control. A trust for the parent's minor children can subscribe for Holdco's common shares for a nominal amount. Properly executed, the value of the preferred shares taken back by the parent should be frozen at their value as at the date of the reorganization.

Revenue Canada's position on estate freezes is that, *generally speaking*, they will not ordinarily result in a misuse or abuse of the Act. The Technical Notes state:

> . . . "Estate freezing" transactions whereby a taxpayer transfers future growth in the value of assets to his children or grandchildren will not ordinarily be avoidance transactions to which the proposed rules would apply despite the fact that they may result in a deferral, avoidance or reduction of tax. Apart from the fact that many of these transactions may be considered to be primarily motivated by non-tax considerations, it would be reasonable to consider that such transactions do not ordinarily result in a misuse or abuse given the scheme of the Act and the recent enactment of subsection 74.4(4) of the Act to accommodate estate freezes.

(ii) Income Splitting

Section 74.4 deals with income splitting and may apply to estate freeze transactions. Under this section, an amount may be deemed to be received as interest by an individual who loans or transfers property to a corporation where one of the main purposes of such a loan or transfer may reasonably be considered the reduction in income of the individual, and the benefit of a designated person.

A designated person is the individual's spouse, or a person under 18 who does not deal with the individual at arm's length, or who is the individual's niece or nephew.

There are several exceptions to the attribution rules, for example: they do not apply in respect of loans or transfers of property to a small business corporation; and they do not apply where the only interest which the designated person has in the corporation is a beneficial interest in the shares of the corporation which are held through a trust, and the terms of the trust provide that that person may not obtain the use of any income or capital of the trust while he or she is the designated person.[101]

These rules and their exceptions are intended to facilitate estate freezing transactions. The Department's view is that subsection 245(2) does not apply to a transfer of shares to a corporation where subsection 74.4(2) applies to deem the parent to receive an amount as interest. Similarly, subsection 245(2) does not apply where subsection 74.4(2) does not apply to deem the parent to receive an amount as interest.

(iii) Reorganization of Capital

Similar considerations apply to an estate freeze executed under section 86 of the Act, which allows a corporation to reorganize its capital.[102] For example, a taxpayer may wish to dispose of the common shares of an operating company in exchange for shares that are structured so as to freeze their value at their fair market value as of the date of reorganization. In Advance Income Tax Ruling ATR-22R, "Estate Freeze Using Share Exchange" (April 14, 1989) the Department confirmed that it would not apply subsection 245(2) to an estate freeze using a share exchange under subsection 86(1).

(i) Avoidance of Part IV Tax on Taxable Dividends

The Part IV tax applies to private corporations.[103] It is a special tax intended to prevent tax deferral through the use of holding companies. The tax is also used to integrate personal and corporate taxes insofar as private corporations are concerned. The Part IV tax places an individual who owns portfolio investments through a holding company in the same position as a person who holds portfolio investments directly.

The critical factor in determining the liability of a corporation for the Part IV tax is its relationship with the corporation from which it receives a dividend. If the payor and recipient corporations are not connected with each other, the recipient is liable for the tax on taxable dividends it receives from the payor. If the corporations are connected, the recipient is only liable for the tax if the payor corporation obtains a refund by paying the dividend. Thus, in certain circumstances, there is an incentive to connect corporations which might otherwise not be connected.

For example, assume that each of two private corporations owns less than 10 per cent of the common shares of a payor corporation required to pay a substantial taxable dividend which would otherwise be subject to Part IV tax, and that none of the corporations are related to each other. The payor corporation will not be entitled to a dividend refund on the payment of the dividend. To avoid the Part IV tax, each of the two corporations then transfers its shareholdings to a new holding corporation

---

[101] Subs. 74.4(4).

[102] See Chapter XXIII "Share-for-share Exchanges".

[103] See Chapter XVI "Private Corporations: Investment Income".

("Newco") in exchange for common shares of Newco. The parties elect under subsection 85(1) to execute the transfer on a tax-deferred basis. Following the transfer of the payor corporation's shares to Newco, it will be connected with the payor corporation. The dividend is then paid. Since the corporations are now connected to each other, the dividend can flow through Newco to the two private corporations without any Part IV tax liability. Newco then pays the same amount to the private corporations as a dividend, also free of Part IV tax. The primary purpose for the transfer of the shares is to avoid the Part IV tax which would otherwise be payable if the dividend was paid directly to the private corporations.

Revenue Canada has indicated that in these circumstances, the transfer of the shares to Newco would be an "avoidance transaction". The Department has also indicated, but without elaboration or explanation, that ". . . the transfer of the shares would be a misuse of a provision of the Act *or* an abuse of the Act as a whole . . .".[104] Whether the transactions constitute a misuse of the specific Part IV provisions *or* an abuse of the Act as a whole is not clarified in the circular.

(j) Change of Fiscal Periods

Generally speaking, a corporation is entitled to select its fiscal year end, provided that the fiscal period of the corporation is not more than 53 weeks. A corporation cannot change its usual and accepted fiscal period without the concurrence of the Minister.

Where a corporation amalgamates with another corporation to form a new corporation, the taxation year of the "old" corporation is deemed to end immediately before the amalgamation, and the newly created amalgamated corporation commences its fiscal period.[105]

Where an operating corporation amalgamates with a shell corporation pursuant to subsection 87(1), and the merger is undertaken solely for the purpose of terminating the taxation year of the operating company immediately before the amalgamation, the transaction is considered an "avoidance transaction" to which GAAR applies.

(k) Indirect Transfer of Land Inventory

Subsection 85(1) allows a taxpayer to transfer property to a taxable Canadian corporation on a tax-deferred basis. An important exception to this rule is that a taxpayer is not permitted to transfer land inventory on a tax-deferred basis to a corporation. There is, however, no explicit prohibition against transferring land inventory on a tax-deferred basis to a Canadian partnership. Hence, where a taxpayer wants to transfer land inventory to a corporation on a tax-deferred basis, he or she can

---

[104] IC 88-2, "General Anti-Avoidance Rule — Section 245 of the *Income Tax Act*" (October 28, 1988), para. 13.

[105] Para. 87(2)(*a*).

proceed in two stages. First, the taxpayer can form a partnership with the prospective purchaser of the property and transfer the land to the partnership, electing under subsection 97(2) to defer the gain on the transfer. The purchaser can contribute a nominal amount of cash for the partnership interest. Second, the vendor can transfer his or her partnership interest to the purchaser corporation in consideration for shares with a fair market value equal to the value of the partnership interest, and the parties may then elect under subsection 85(1) in respect of the transfer. On the acquisition by the purchaser corporation of the taxpayer's partnership interest, the partnership ceases to exist and subsection 98(5) applies to deem the purchaser to have acquired the land at an amount equal to the taxpayer's cost amount for the land.

As a consequence of this two-step arrangement, the purchaser corporation acquires the land inventory and the taxpayer avoids the recognition of any gain on the transfer of the property. The purpose of the transactions is to circumvent the prohibition in subsection 85(1) against the transfer of land inventory to a taxable Canadian corporation. Hence, the transactions misuse the subsection and GAAR applies: the transfer of the land to the partnership is contrary to the scheme of the Act read as a whole.

In other words, Revenue Canada appears to take the position that it will invoke section 245 where a taxpayer does indirectly what he or she cannot do directly. Stated another way, a taxpayer does not have *carte blanche* to arrange his or her affairs so as to minimize a tax burden through technically correct arrangements. A taxpayer is only entitled to mitigate tax if the arrangements undertaken in this respect comply with the spirit of the *Act read as a whole.*

(l) Indirect Disposition of Property Through a Partnership

Generally speaking, the disposition of a property triggers an income gain (loss) or a capital gain (loss). But a taxpayer who owns property which, if it were disposed of in a straightforward manner, would result in the immediate realization of an income or capital gain, may proceed by a more circuitous route. For example, the taxpayer and the prospective purchaser of the property can form a partnership. The taxpayer can then transfer the property into the partnership and elect under subsection 97(2) to defer recognition of any gain which would otherwise arise. The purchaser may contribute cash into the partnership in an amount equal to the fair market value of the property. The taxpayer then withdraws all of the cash from the partnership and, because of such withdrawal, his or her share of the income and loss of the partnership is correspondingly reduced. The partnership continues to carry on business and the purchaser, in effect, acquires the property. Revenue Canada considers such an arrangement as an attempt to circumvent provisions which provide that the proceeds of disposition of property are to be accounted for at the time of their receipt. Hence, it views the entire arrangement as one that is ". . . contrary to the scheme of the Act read as a whole . . ." and will apply GAAR to such arrangements.

(m) Conversion of Income Gains into Dividends

Generally, where a taxpayer disposes of depreciable property, any proceeds of disposition over and above the undepreciated capital cost of the property are included in income as recapture of capital cost allowance. Recaptured capital cost allowance is taxable as ordinary income.

A corporation that is resident in Canada and that owns depreciable property, may wish to circumvent the potential recapture of capital cost allowance as follows:

- The taxpayer can sell the property to an arm's length taxable Canadian corporation in consideration for redeemable shares having a redemption amount equal to the fair market value of the property sold.

- The taxpayer and the purchaser can elect under subsection 85(1), in respect of the property, to defer recognition of the profit which would otherwise have been realized on a direct sale of the property.

- The shares have a paid-up capital equal to the amount elected so that, on their redemption, the amount received in excess of paid-up capital is characterized as a taxable dividend deductible under subsection 112(1) of the Act.

Revenue Canada has stated that it will apply GAAR to this type of transaction. Since the taxpayer would normally have been taxable on the excess of the proceeds of disposition over the undepreciated capital cost of the property as ordinary income, the two-step transaction converting ordinary income into a non-taxable dividend is offensive in that it circumvents the scheme of the Act. The taxpayer's right, then, to arrange his or her affairs to mitigate tax, is curtailed by GAAR.

(n) Reserves for Future Proceeds

Generally speaking, where a taxpayer realizes a gain on the sale of property, the amount of the gain must be taken into income in the year of disposition. Where, however, a taxpayer does not receive the full amount of the proceeds of disposition, he or she is entitled to claim a reserve in respect of proceeds to be received at a later date. Hence, subject to certain limiting rules, a taxpayer is entitled to defer recognition of a gain on the disposition of property to the extent that the proceeds of disposition from its sale have not been realized.

A taxpayer who does not wish to recognize sale proceeds from a cash sale to an arm's length purchaser may sell the property to an intermediary corporation and defer receipt of the proceeds of disposition for more than two years after the date of the sale. The intermediary corporation can then sell the property to the arm's length purchaser for cash. The vendor can receive interest from the intermediary corporation in respect of the moneys received by the corporation from the third party purchaser.

Revenue Canada's view is that if the interposition of the intermediary is made solely to enable the owner of the property to defer recognition of the gain from the sale of the real property, the transaction is subject to GAAR. Although the Department does not give any explicit reason for applying the rule, it appears reasonable to presume that they interpret the transaction as contravening the general rule that a reserve may only be claimed in respect of proceeds that have not actually been received. Thus, in the above example, Revenue Canada, by inference, considers the owner of the real property and any intermediary corporation to be, in effect, one taxpayer for the purposes of the reserve rules.

(o) Conversion of Dividend Income into Capital Gains

As a general rule, the effective income tax rate on dividend income is approximately equal to that on capital gains for taxpayers in the highest marginal tax bracket. There is, however, one important difference between the tax burden on dividend income and capital gains: an individual is entitled to receive a certain amount ($100,000 or $500,000 depending upon the type of property sold) of capital gains on a tax-free basis. This makes it attractive for taxpayers to utilize their capital gains exemption instead of receiving taxable dividends.

Where a private corporation wishes to provide an annual dividend payment to its individual shareholders as tax-free capital gains, it may arrange to pay a stock dividend instead of a cash dividend. The shares received as part of a stock dividend have a low paid-up capital and a high fair market value. As a part of the same arrangement, the shares are purchased by a corporation related to the issuing corporation (or by a third party broker or dealer) and the purchase price of the shares is funded by the issuing corporation. Since the payment and the repurchase of the stock dividend shares is part of an arrangement to avoid the shareholder tax which would normally be required to be paid on taxable cash dividends, the payment and repurchase of the shares is considered to be a misuse of a provision of the Act *or* an abuse of the Act as a whole, and GAAR applies.

SELECTED BIBLIOGRAPHY TO CHAPTER XXXIII

Canada

Adams, L.D., "Craven v. White: U.K. Step-Transaction Doctrine Evolves — Canadian Planners Beware" (1988), 2:13 *Can. Current Tax* C-57.

Adamson, Edith and Jane McEwan, *For Conscience Sake* (Victoria, B.C.: Conscience Canada, 1991).

Ahmed, Firoz, "Certain Guesses as to the Application of GAAR", in *Ontario Tax Conf.* Tab 13 (Toronto: Canadian Tax Foundation, 1988).

Allgood and Ahmed, "The Modified General Anti-Avoidance Rule", in *Recent Tax Changes Including the Tax Reform Proposals: Proceedings of a Conference of the Law Society of Upper Canada and the Canadian Bar Association — Ontario* (Toronto: Department of Education, Law Society of Upper Canada and Canadian Bar Association — Ontario, 1988) C-1.

"Anti-Avoidance" (1987), 15:6 *Can. Tax News* 100.

"Anti-Avoidance Proposal Goes Too Far" (1987), 9:16 *Can. Taxpayer* 121.

"Anti-Avoidance Remains Central Theme of Tax Legislation" (1988), 10:9 *Can. Taxpayer* 65.

"Anti-Avoidance Rule Guidelines" (1988), 16:4 *Can. Tax News* 46.

"Anti-Avoidance Rules" (1987), 15:2 *Can. Tax News* 22.

Armstrong, George H., *Hart System of Effective Tax Avoidance* (Winnipeg: A & A Pub., 1990).

Arnold, Brian J., "In Praise of the Business Purpose Test", in *Proceedings of 39th Tax Conf.* 10:1 (Can. Tax Foundation, 1987).

Arnold, Brian J., and James R. Wilson, "The General Anti-Avoidance Rule — Part 1" (1988), 36 *Can. Tax J.* 829.

Arnold, Brian J. and James R. Wilson, "The General Anti-Avoidance Rule — Part II" (1988), 36 *Can. Tax J.* 1123.

Arnold, Brian J., and James R. Wilson, "The General Anti-Avoidance Rule — Part III" (1988), 36 *Can. Tax J.* 1369.

Avey, T., and M. Quigley, "A Case of Tax Evasion: An Accountant's Day in Court" (1984), 117:9 *CA Magazine* 58.

Baille, W.J., "Form or Substance — Where Are We?" (1980), 18 *Alta. L. Rev.* 237.

Barbeau, "Tax Opinions: The Dilemma" (1963), 6 *Can. B.J.* 328.

Beach, Don, "Anti-Avoidance Rules are an End Run Around the Courts" (1987), *Financial Times* 25.

Bergh, Colin S., *Effective Tax Avoidance* (Toronto: Carswell, 1965).

Bergh, Colin S., "Handling Tax Fraud Cases" (1963), 82 *Can. Chart. Acc.* 54.

Birnie, David A.G., "Living with GAAR: The Effect on Tax Practice", *Corporate Management Tax Conf.* 5:1 (Can. Tax Foundation, 1988).

Boultbee, J.A., "Minimizing the Taxation Effects of Dividends", in *Proceedings of 37th Tax Conf.* 7:1 (Can. Tax Foundation, 1985).

Bouvet, Y., "Analyse des mesures anti-evitement relatives a l'exoneration du gain en capital", 9 *RPFS* 357.

Bowman, Stephen W., "Collections under the Income Tax Act" in *Proceedings of 42nd Tax Conf.* 22:1 (Can. Tax Found., 1990).

Bowman, S.W., "Wilful Evasion — Nature of Offence — Relevance of Sham Arguments — Use of Offshore Companies [Case Comment: *R. v. Redpath Industries Ltd.*, [1984] CTC 483, 84 DTC 6349 (Que. S.C.)]" (1984), 32 *Can. Tax J.* 906.

Boyd, C.W., "The Enforcement of Tax Compliance: Some Theoretical Issues" (1986), 34 *Can. Tax J.* 588.

Brown, Robert D., "Revenue Canada's New View of Tax Avoidance Activities" in *Proceedings of 44th Tax Conf.* 5:2 (Can. Tax Found., 1992).

Brown, Robert D., et al., "GAAR and Tax Practice: More Questions Than Answers", in *Proceedings of 41st Tax Conf.* 11:1 (Can. Tax Foundation, 1989).

CICA, *General Anti-Avoidance Rules*, August 1989.

Cameron, D.B., "Tax Evasion by Non-payment of Assessments", [1969] *Pitblado Lect.* 101.

Canada, Department of Finance, "Explanatory Notes to Legislation Relating to Income Tax", in *Can. Tax Reports*, Special Report No. 851, extra ed. (Don Mills, Ont.: CCH Canadian, June 30, 1988) 315.

Canada, Department of Finance, "Supplementary Information Relating to Tax Reform Measures" (Ottawa: The Department, December 16, 1987).

Canada, Department of Finance, "Tax Reform 1987: Income Tax Reform" (Ottawa: the Department, June 18, 1987).

Canada, Department of Finance, "Tax Reform 1987: Proposed Legislative and Regulatory Amendments" (Ottawa: the Department, December 16, 1987).

Canada, House of Commons, "The Standing Committee on Finance and Economic Affairs, Report of the White Paper on Tax Reform (Stage I)" (Ottawa: Queen's Printer, November 1987).

Canada, "Report of the Royal Commission on Taxation," Vol. 3 (Ottawa: Queen's Printer, 1966), 537.

Carlyle, W.M., "Section 138A Should Be Repealed" (1968), 11 *Can. Bar J.* 212.

Chisholm, Patricia, "U.S. Tax Doesn't Affect Evasion Here" (1985), 4:23 *Ont. Lawyers Weekly* 6.

Clow, John M., "The Great GAAR Guessing Game" (1989), 63 *CMA* 58.

Colley, Geoffrey M., "Anti-Avoidance Rules Under Tax Reform Too Broad" (1987), 120 *CA Magazine* 44.

Colley, Geoffrey M., "What You See is What You Get: Or Is It? (New Anti-Avoidance Income Tax Provisions)" (1989), 122:1 *CA Magazine* 50.

Corn, G., "Disposition of Economic Interests and Attribution of Income on Issuance of Treasury Shares" (1991), 3 *Can. Current Tax* J-101.

Corn, G., "Right to Arrange One's Affairs to Avoid Taxation — Lack of Business Purpose — Sham Transactions" (1984), 1 *Can. Current Tax* 131.

Corporate Crime in Canada (Toronto: Law Society of Upper Canada, Dpt. of Education, 1988).

Creighton, G.D., *"Stubart Investments Ltd. v. The Queen,* [1984] CTC 294; 84 DTC 6305" (1984), 1 *Business and Law* 42.

Cullity, M.C., "Trusts and Estates" (1981), *Can. Taxation* 773.

Dodge, David A., "A New and More Coherent Approach to Tax Avoidance" (1988), 36 *Can. Tax J.* 1.

Dodge, David A., "Tax Reform and the Anti-Avoidance Proposal", in *B. C. Tax Conf.* Tab 4 (Can. Tax Foundation, 1987).

Drache, A.B.C., "Anti-avoidance Proposal Goes Too Far" (1987), 9 *Can. Taxpayer* 121.

Duval, G., "Acquisition et disposition d'une entreprise canadienne par un non-resident" (1987), 9 *RPFS* 413.

Dymond, A. Christopher, Robert J. Reid, and Michael A. Cutran, *Income Tax Administration, Avoidance and Evasion* (Toronto: Butterworths, 1981).

Edwards, Stanley E., "Planning After the Stubart Decision", in *Proceedings of 36th Tax Conf.* 78 (Can. Tax Foundation, 1984).

Forgie, Jeremy, "Series of Acquisitions and Dispositions Found not to Constitute Tax Avoidance" (1993), 1 *RRSP Plan.* 13.

Fraser, Rodney, "Tax-Planning Strategies in the World According To GAAR", (January 9, 1989) *Financial Times* 17.

Fraser, Rodney, "You Can Still Do the Splits, But..." (1989), *Financial Times* 19.

Freisen, R.A. and D.Y. Timbrell, "Shams and Simulacra II — The Capital Gains Aspect" (1979), 27 *Can. Tax J.* 135.

Fryers, Clifford H., "Tax Planning and the New General Anti-Avoidance Rule", in *Prairie Provinces Tax Conf.* Tab 10 (Can. Tax Foundation, 1989).

Fuke, J.M. "Can Tax Advisers Successfully Serve Two Masters? Les conseillers fiscaux peuvent-ils servir deux maîtres à la fois?" (1985), 118:3 *CA Magazine* 32.

"GAAR Circular Released" (1988), 10:21 *Can. Taxpayer* 161.

"GAAR Supplement Issued" (1990), 12:17 *Can. Taxpayer* 130.

"General Anti-Avoidance Provisions Promised" (1987), 9:11 *Can. Taxpayer* 82.

"General Anti-Avoidance Rule", *Can. Tax Handbook 1988-89* (Toronto: Carswell, 1989) 8.

"General Anti-Avoidance Rule" (1988), 17:2 *Tax Profile* 113.

Glover, Paul, "The General Anti-Avoidance Provisions" (September 1988), 62 *CMA Magazine* 44.

Gideon, Kenneth W., and Ruth E. Kent, "Mrs. Gregory's Northern Tour: Canadian Proposals to Adopt the Business Purpose Rule and the Step Transaction Doctrine", in *Proceedings of 39th Tax Conf.* 7:1 (Can. Tax Foundation, 1987).

Goodlet, W.E., "Tax Minimization: Avoidance or Planning" (1971), 98 *Can. Chart. Acc.* 195.

Goodman, W.D., "The Impact of Tax Reform on Estate Planning" (1988), 8 *Estates and Trusts Quarterly* 281.

Goodman, W.D., "Search and Seizure, Evasion, Records and Tax Opinions", [1986] *Special Lectures LSUC* 207.

Goodman, W.D., "What has Canada to Gain from the Proposed General Anti-Avoidance Rule?", *Insight: Tax Reform 1987 — The New Regime*, L'hotel (Toronto), July 22, 1987, Tab VI.

Gourlay, J.L., "Tax Abuse — a View From Revenue Canada" (1980), 87 *Can. Taxation* 82.

Gourlay, J.L., "Enforcement Provisions: Offences and Tax Avoidance" [1968] *Pitblado Lect.* 110.

Gourlay, J.L., "Tax Planning or Tax Evasion" (1969), 95 *Can. Chart. Acc.* 250.

Greenspan, Edward L., "Tax Evasion is a Crime!", *Corporate Management Tax Conf.* 1:1 (Can. Tax Foundation, 1988).

Hanly, K.S.M., "Management Companies — Business Purpose Test [Case Comment: *R. v. Parsons*, [1984] CTC 354, 84 DTC 6447; *R. v. Vivian* (1984), 84 DTC 6452 (Fed. CA)" (1984), 32 *Can. Tax J.* 891.

Harris, D.C., "Nonfiling and Underreporting of Income Taxes in the United States" (1980), 2 *Can. Taxation* 88.

Harris, E.C., "Intercompany Cross-Border Transactions: A Growing Concern for Revenue Canada/Les operations intersociétés menées par délà les frontières inquiétent Revenu Canada" (1985), 118:6 *CA Magazine* 22.

Harris, R.G., "Tax Planning: The Practitioner's Viewpoint" (1970), 96 *Can. Chart. Acc.* 156.

Hartkorn, D.N., "Income Splitting: the New Rules" (1985), 33 *Can. Tax J.* 1226.

Hasson, R., "Tax Evasion and Social Security Abuse — Some Tentative Observations" (1980), 2 *Can. Taxation* 98.

Hellerstein, Jerome R., "Judicial Approaches to Tax Avoidance", in *Proceedings of 18th Tax Conf.* 62 (Can. Tax Foundation, 1964).

Hiltz, Michael, "Section 245 of the ITA", in *Proceedings of 40th Tax Conf.* 7:1 (Can. Tax Foundation, 1988).

Hiltz, Michael, "Subsection 247(1) and the 1985 Amendments to the Income Tax Act", in *Proceedings of 39th Tax Conf.* 7:1 (Can. Tax Foundation, 1987).

Hobson, William J.A., "New Guidelines from the Supreme Court of Canada and Other Canadian Courts: A Broad Interpretation of Subsection 245(1), the Interpretation Test, and Clearer Lines of Demarcation for Tax Avoidance and Tax Evasion", in *Proceedings of 36th Tax Conf.* 148 (Can. Tax Foundation, 1984).

Huggett, Donald R., "With Cap in Hand" (1988), 16 *Can. Tax News* 9.

Huggett, Donald R., "Foul Balls" (1979), 7 *Can. Tax News* 17.

Huggett, Donald R., "Tax Avoidance — Recent Developments", in *Proceedings of 21st Tax Conf.* 452 (Can. Tax Foundation, 1968).

Ilersic, A.R., "Tax Havens and Residence" (1982), 30 *Can. Tax J.* 52.

Innes, W.I., *Tax Evasion in Canada* (Toronto: Carswell, 1987).

International Fiscal Association, "Seminar on Recent International Developments to Counter Tax Avoidance and Evasion: Texts of Seminar Papers Presented February 18, 1982" (Don Mills, Ontario: Richard De Boo, 1982).

"International Tax Planning — Stubart: What the Courts Did Next" (1987), 35 *Can. Tax J.* 155.

Jacques, Harold, "A Practical Overview of GAAR and the Parts IV.1 and VI.1 Dividend Taxes", in *Prairie Provinces Tax Conf.* Tab 13 (Can. Tax Foundation, 1988).

Kellough, H.J., "A Discussion of the White Paper's Proposed General Anti-Avoidance Rule", in *B. C. Tax Conf.* Tab 6 (Can. Tax Foundation, 1987).

Kellough, Howard J., "A Review and Analysis of the Redrafted General Anti-Avoidance Rule" (1988), 36 *Can. Tax J.* 23.

Kellough, Howard J., "The Legal Efficacy of Unwinding or Negating a Transaction in Whole or in Part", in *Proceedings of 37th Tax Conf.* 9:1 (Can. Tax Foundation, 1985).

Kellough, H.J., "The Pre White Paper Anti-Avoidance Regime", *Insight: Tax Reform 1987 — The New Regime*, L'hotel (Toronto), July 22, 1987, Tab VII.

Krishna, Vern, "Deductibility of Legal and Accounting Fees in Defending Tax Evasion Charges (IT-99R3)" (1986), 1 *Can. Current Tax* C-129.

Krishna, Vern, "The Demise of the Business Purpose Test?" (1984), 1 *Can. Current Tax* C-43.

Krishna, Vern, "GAAR: The Ultimate Tax Avoidance Weapon" (1988), 2:16 *Can. Current Tax* C-75.

Krishna, Vern, "GAAR and the Purification of Corporations for the Capital Gains Exemption (Part 1) (1993), 4 *Can. Current Tax* A7.

Krishna, Vern, "General Anti-Avoidance Rule: An Attempt to Control Tax Abuses" (1988), *CGA Magazine* 16.

Krishna, Vern, "Step Transactions and the General Anti-Avoidance Rule — Part I" (July 1990), 24 *CGA Magazine* 34.

Krishna, Vern, "Step Transactions and the General Anti-Avoidance Rule — Part II" (August 1990), 24 *CGA Magazine* 25.

Krishna, Vern, "Step Transactions: An Emerging Doctrine or an Extension of the Business Purpose Test?" (1984), 1 *Can. Current Tax* C-15.

Krishna, Vern, *Tax Avoidance: The General Anti-Aviodance Rule* (Toronto: Carswell, 1990).

Labrie, F.E., "Fraudulent Tax Transactions" (1964), 3 *Western L. Rev.* 48.

Labrie, F.E., "The Role of the Courts in Tax Avoidance" (1955), 3 *Can. Tax. J.* 326; (1955-56) 11 *UTLJ* 128.

Labrie, F.E., "The Uncertainties of Tax Planning" (1960), 9 *Chitty's L.J.* 114; 146; 177.

Latimer, W.R., H.E. Crate and Jacques Barbeau, "Crimes under the Income Tax", in *Proceedings of 14th Tax Conf.* 53 (Can. Tax Foundation, 1961).

Lavery, J. Michael and Karen Watson, "Is It or Is It Not, Canadian Tax Reform?" (1987), 3 *The Journal of Strategy in Int'l. Taxation* 264.

Lawlor, William R.G., "Surplus Stripping and Other Planning Opportunities With the New $500,000 Capital Gains Exemption", in *Proceedings of 37th Tax Conf.* 8:1 (Can. Tax Foundation, 1985).

Lefebvre, Wilfrid, "Tax Avoidance: An Update", [1990] *Meredith Mem. Lectures* 389.

Lemon, K.W., "Artificial Transactions: Business Purpose" (1978), 43 *Bus. Q.* 4:5.

Lindsay, Robert F., "The General Anti-Avoidance Rule: Points to Consider", in *Proceedings of 40th Tax Conf.* 5:1 (Can. Tax Foundation, 1989).

McBarnet, Doreen, "Legitimate Rackets: Tax Evasion, Tax Avoidance, and the Boundaries of Legality" (1992), 3 *J. of Hum. Justice No. 2* 56.

McCracken, Gerald H., "Preventing Tax Evasion Through Enforcement: The Government Perspective", *Corp. Management Tax Conference* 2:1 (Can. Tax Foundation, 1988).

McDonnell, Thomas E., "Legislative Anti-Avoidance: The Interaction of the New General Rule and Representative Specific Rules", in *Proceedings of 40th Tax Conf.* 6:1 (Can. Tax Foundation, 1988).

McDonnell, Thomas E., "Developments Relating to Sham, Benefits and Business Purpose", in *Proceedings of 29th Tax Conf.* 89 (Can. Tax Foundation, 1977).

McDonnell, Thomas E., "Professional Responsibility and Tax Practice", in *Proceedings of 27th Tax Conf.* 953 (Can. Tax. Foundation, 1975).

McDonnell, Thomas E., "Tax Avoidance: Section 137(2) as a Charging Section" (1968), 16 *Can. Tax. J.* 281.

McDonnell, T.E., "Tax Avoidance: Splitting Decision" (1991), 39 *Can. Tax J.* 637.

McDonnell, Thomas E., and R.B. Thomas, "GAAR and Pre-September 13, 1988 Tax Planning: Part 2 — The Commodity Straddles Issue" (1989), 37 *Can. Tax J.* 728.

McDonnell, Thomas E., and R.B. Thomas, "The Supreme Court and Business Purpose: Is There Life After Stubart [*Stubart Investments Ltd. v. The Queen,* 84 DTC 6305]?" (1984), 32 *Can. Tax. J.* 853.

McGregor, G., "Dividend Stripping: The Business Purpose Test" (1968), 16 *Can. Tax J.* 16.

McGregor, G., "The Business Purpose Test" (1984), 6 *Can. Taxpayer* 5.

McKie, A.B., "Compliance — A Fine (or penalty) State of Affairs" (1988), 2 *Can. Current Tax* C-69.

McKie, A.B., "Tax Havens — Health Bulletin" (1982), 89:1 *Can. Bank* 62.

McKie, A.B., "Tax Tellers" (1982), 89:2 *Can. Bank* 28.

McKie, A.B., "Info-Intertax" (1980), 87 *Can. Bank* 69.

McKie, A.B., "Offshore Banking — or Laundering?" (1983), 90:5 *Can. Bank* 18.

McKie, A.B., "Oversight of Tax Havens" (1980), 87:3 *Can. Bank* 50.

McKie, A.B., "Tax Sparing — Some Thoughts" (1985), 1:1 *Can. Bank* 62.

McKie, A.B., "Tax Avoidance, Handle with Care" (1978), 85:4 *Can. Bank* 37.

McNair, Arnold, et al., ed., *Materials on Canadian Income Tax*, 8th ed. (Don Mills, Ontario: DeBoo Publishers, 1989) 148.

Morgan, Vivien, "Stubart: What the Courts Did Next" (1987), 35 *Can. Tax J.* 155.

"Most Attacked Tax Proposals" (1987), 9:20 *Can. Taxpayer* 153.

Nathanson, David C., "The Proposed General Anti-Avoidance Rule", in *Proceedings of 39th Tax Conf.* 9:1 (Can. Tax Foundation, 1987).

Nathanson, David C., "General Anti-Avoidance Rule and Tax Reform: The Business Purpose Test — Proposed Section 245", Paper Presented at Insight Conference, November 14, 1988.

Nathanson, David C., "The Reach for Information", in *Proceedings of 30th Tax Conf.* 299 (Can. Tax Foundation, 1978).

Nichols, Neil W., "Tax Planning After Stubart: Consolidated Bathurst and Other Interpretations", in *Proceedings of 37th Tax Conf.* 39:1 (Can. Tax Foundation, 1985).

Nitikman, Joel, "Is GAAR Void for Vagueness?" (1989), 37 *Can. Tax J.* 1409.

"No, We're Not Happy", 9:14 *Can. Taxpayer* 101.

Noble, W.R., "Some Tax Avoidance Aspects of Non-Resident Trusts" (1979), 5 *EJQ* 81.

O'Keefe, M.J., "The Business Purpose Test — Who Needs It?" (1977), 25 *Can. Tax J.* 139.

Pateras, Bruno J., "Tax Evasion after the Charter" [1990] *Meredith Mem. Lect.* 435.

Pitfield, I.H., "Search and Seizure and the Income Tax Act" (1981), 29 *Can. Tax J.* 30.

Potvin, Jean, "Tax Evasion in Canada" (1977), 25 *Can. Tax J.* 229.

"Reflections on the Legal Duty to Avoid Taxes", *Can. Tax Letter* (February 19, 1988) 1.

Revenue Canada Panel, "Section 245", *Corporate Management Tax Conf.* 8:17 (Can. Tax Foundation, 1989).

Robertson, J.R., "The Use of Tax Evasion and Tax Avoidance by Multinational Companies: A Canadian View" (1977), 25 *Can. Tax J.* 513.

Robison, I. Michael, "Personal Services Corporations: New Opportunities and Old Concerns" in *Corporate Management Tax Conf.* 165 (Can. Tax Foundation, 1985).

Roseman, Ellen, "Anti-Avoidance Law Irks Tax Planners," *The Globe and Mail* (November 28, 1988) B1.

Rossiter, J., "The Application of Part 13 Non-Resident Withholding Tax to Deemed Payments" (1986), 34 *Can. Tax J.* 511.

Rochon, M., "Évasion fiscale" (1978), 9 *R. Gen.* 438.

Roy, J.P., "L'interprétation des lois fiscales dans la foulée de l'arrêt Stubart" (1986), 9 *RPFS* 207.

Roy, Robert, "The Tax Avoidance Program" in *Proceedings of 45th Tax Conf.* 7:1 (Can. Tax Found., 1993).

Sasseville, J., "Implementation of the Anti-Avoidance Rule", *Corporate Management Tax Conf.* 4:1 (Can. Tax Foundation, 1988).

Sasseville, J., "La règle générale anti-évitement" (1988), 10 *RPFS* 221.

Savage, H.B., *Tax Saving* (Montreal: 1952).

Schmitz, Cristin, "Lawyers Find Flaws with Proposed Tax Avoidance Rule" (July 17, 1987), 7:12 *Lawyers Weekly* 12.

Schwartz, Alan M., "Tax Avoidance", in *Proceedings of 33rd Tax Conf.* 922 (Can. Tax Foundation, 1981).

Shafer, J., "Furniss v. Dawson, [1984] 1 All ER 530" (1984), *Inc. Tax Aspects* 47.

Sherbaniuk, "Tax Avoidance — Recent Developments", in *Proceedings of 21st Tax Conf.* 430 (Can. Tax Foundation, 1968).

Sherman, H.A., "How to Kill a Mouse With an Elephant Gun, or, Foreign Accrual Property Income: Some Problem Areas" (1972), 20 *Can. Tax J.* 397.

Silver, S., "Surplus Stripping: A Practitioner's View" (1974), 22 *Can. Tax J.* 430.

Sossin, Lorne, "Welfare State Crime in Canada: The Politics of Tax Evasion in the 1980s" (1992), 12 *Windsor Y.B. Access Justice* 98.

Stacey, John A., "Revenue Canada's Administration of the General Anti-Avoidance rule", in *Proceedings of 42nd Tax Conf.* 4:2 (Can. Tax Foundation, 1990).

Stanley, Edward, "Planning After the Stubart Decision", in *Proceedings of 36th Tax Conf.* 78 (Can. Tax Foundation, 1984).

Stikeman, Elliott, *Tax Reform '87: An Analysis* (Toronto: DeBoo, July 17, 1987).

Stikeman, H., "Furniss v. Dawson: The Canadian Approach" (1986), 7 *Fiscal Studies* 82.

Stikeman, H., "Is the Business Purpose Test Dead? Its Life After Stubart" (1985), *Cambridge Lect.* 197.

Stikeman, H., "Tax Reform '87 — An Analysis", (July 17, 1987) *Can. Tax Service* 231.

Strother, Robert C., "Avoidance and Evasion: The World Beyond Stubart", in *Proceedings of 36th Tax Conf.* 89 (Can. Tax Foundation, 1984).

Sturrock, Craig, C., "Tax Reform and the Anti-Avoidance Proposals", in *B. C. Tax Conf.* Tab 7 (Can. Tax Foundation, 1987).

"Tax and Social Security Abuse: Panel Discussion" (1980), 2 *Can. Taxation* 109.

"Tax Legislation: The Latest Media Event", *Can. Tax Letter* (February 27, 1987) 1.

"Tax Reform", *Explanatory Notes for April 13th Draft Income Tax Amendments Special Release* (April 21, 1988) 240.

"Tax Reform '87 — An Analysis" (July 9, 1987), *Can. Tax Reports* 106.

"Tax Reform — Some Comments" (August/September 1988), 16:3 *Can. Tax News* 31.

Templeton, Wendy, "Anti-Avoidance and the Capital Gains Exemption" (1986), 34 *Can. Tax. J.* 203.

Templeton, Wendy, "Anti-Avoidance and the Capital Gains Exemption: Part Two" (1986), 34 *Can. Tax. J.* 446.

"The Proposed Anti-Avoidance Provision: Mark II" (1988), 10:2 *Can. Taxpayer* 9.

Thomas, R.B., "The Business Purpose Test — Not in Canada, Thank You! (Case Comment) *Stubart Investments Ltd. v. R.*, [1984] CTC 294 (SCC)", 32 *Can. Tax. J.* 529.

Thorsteinsson, P.M., "Precautionary Considerations on Tax Haven Companies" (1966), 2 *UBC Law Rev.* 491.

Tiley, John, "Series of Transactions", in *Proceedings of 40th Tax Conf.* 8:1 (Can. Tax Foundation, 1988).

Timbrell, D.Y., "Of Shams and Simulacra" (1973), 21 *Can. Tax J.* 529.

Timbrell, D.Y., "Planning after the Stubart Decision: The Business Purpose Test", in *Proceedings of 36th Tax Conf.* 89 (Can. Tax Foundation, 1984).

Vercheres, B., "Tax Havens: Myth or Reality", [1969] *RJT* 23.

Ward, David A., "Tax Avoidance and Compliance", *Insight: Tax Reform 1987 — The New Regime*, L'hotel (Toronto), July 22, 1987, Tab VIII.

Ward, David A., "Tax Avoidance: Judicial and Legislative Approaches in Other Jurisdictions", in *Proceedings of 39th Tax Conf.* 45:1 (Can. Tax Foundation, 1987).

Ward, David A., "Has Revenue Canada Become 'Big Brother'?/Revenu Canada, est-il tout-puissant?" (1984), 117:4 *CA Magazine* 22.

Ward, David A., "The Judicial Approach to Tax Avoidance", in *Proceedings of 25th Tax Conf.* 408 (Can. Tax Foundation, 1973).

Ward, David A. and Maurice C. Cullity, "Abuse of Rights and the Business Purpose Test as Applied to Taxing Statutes" (1981), 29 *Can. Tax. J.* 451.

Ware, "The Business Purpose Test and Sham Transactions", in *Proceedings of 28th Tax Conf.* 602 (Can. Tax Foundation, 1976).

Watson, Russ, "GAAR (General Anti-avoidance Rule)" (1992), 3 *Can. Current Tax* P51.

"Whither GAAR?" (1990), 12:9 *Can. Taxpayer* 70.

Wilkie, "The Stubart Decision: An Act of Reason", in *Can. Tax Letter* (1985), No. 351 (De Boo, 1985).

Wise, Richard M., "Tax Evasion and Mens Rea in Forensic Accounting", [1990] *Meredith Mem. Lectures* 405.

"With Cap in Hand" (June/July 1988), 16:2 *Can. Tax News* 9.

World According to GAAR (Toronto: Canadian Bar Association — Ontario, Continuing Legal Education, 1990).

Yaksich, M.M., "Captive Insurance Company — *Stubart Investments Ltd.* Applied [Case Comment: *Consolidated Bathurst Ltd. v. R.*, [1985] 1 CTC 142 (Fed. TD)]" (1985), 33 *Can. Tax. J.* 333.

Zylberberg, Frank, "GAAR and Estate Planning", in *Proceedings of 42nd Tax Conf.* 38:1 (Can. Tax Foundation, 1990).

Australia

A.P.M., "*Gerard v. C.I.R.*, 75 ATC 6020 [Family Trusts]" (1973), *NZLJ* 152.

A.P.M., "*Wheelans v. C.I.R.*: *Ashton v. C.I.R.*, 73 ATC 6030 [Family Trusts]" (1973), *NZLJ* 151.

Avery Jones, J.F., "Nothing Either Good or Bad, But Thinking Makes It So — The Mental Element in Anti-Avoidance Legislation — I", [1983] 1 *British Tax Rev.* 9.

Avery Jones, J.F., "Nothing Either Good or Bad, But Thinking Makes It So — The Mental Element in Anti-Avoidance Legislation — II", [1983] 2 *British Tax Rev.* 113.

Azzi, John, "Assignments of Partnership Income" (1989), 18 *Aust. Tax Rev.* 262 at 268.

Bassett, J.G., "Estate Plans and Arrangements to Avoid Income Tax" (1978), 9 *Victoria University of Wellington L. Rev.* 217.

Baxt, R., "The New Anti-Avoidance Provisions" (1981), 9 *Aust. Bus. Rev.* 284.

Beattie, C.N., "*Furniss v. Dawson* — The *Duke of Westminster* Doctrine and Lord Tomlin's Dictum" (March 2, 1984), 128 *Solic. J.* 139.

Binetter, Michael T.R., "A Reflection on Part IVA" (1987), 21 *Tax. in Aust.* 404.

Boucher, Trevor, "Section 260/Part IVA — The Doctors' Cases (1986), 20 *Tax. in Aust.* 633.

Briggs, Peter, "John v. Federal Commissioner of Taxation: The Uneasy Death of Curran (1989) ATC 1" (March 1990), 12 *Syd. L.R.* 584.

Burgess, P., "Lessons from the Bottom of the Harbour" (1984), *NZLJ* 16.

Challoner, N.E., "Section 260 — How Far Will the Resurgence Extend?" (June 1985), 55 *Chartered Acc.* 59.

Challoner, N.E., "Income Splitting — S. 260 and Part IVA" (September 1986), 57 *Chartered Acc.* 69.

Challoner, N.E., "Section 260 Now Clarified — Or Is It? (March 1986), 55 *Chartered Acc.* 64; (April 1986), 56 *Chartered Acc.* 57.

Challoner, N.E., "The Taxpayer: Contract, Agreement or Arrangement Within s. 260" (March 1987), 57 *Chartered Acc.* 65.

Cooke, M.I., "Practical Issues Arising From the Gulland, Watson and Pincus Cases" (1986), 20 *Tax. in Aust.* 680.

Cooper, Graeme S., Richard E. Krever and Richard J. Vann, *Income Taxation: Commentary and Materials* (Sydney: The Law Book Company, 1989).

"Correspondence — Part IVA" (1981), 15 *Tax. in Aust.* 387.

Dabner, Justin, "The First Part IVA Cases and Rulings — The Worst Fears Realized" (1990), 24 *Tax. in Aust.* 665.

Dabner, Justin, "Tax Planning for Professional People — What Remains After the Unholy Trinity" (1987), 21 *Tax. in Aust.* 568.

Dalton, D.J., "Avoidance of Taxation: Section 260 of the Income Tax Assessment Act", 9 *MULR* 95.

Davies, J.D., "'Purpose' in Section 26(A) and in Section 260" (1977), 6 *Aust. Tax Rev.* 32.

"Dr. Gulland, Pincus and Watson" (January 22, 1986), 7 *Leg. Rep.* 1.

"Editorial" (1986), 14 *Aust. Business Law Rep.* 61.

Edstein, John V., "Superannuation: Anti-Avoidance Provisions and Judicial Approaches" (1989), 23 *Tax. in Aust.* 524.

Fayle, R.D., "Tax Planning and Current Thinking" (1983), 17 *Tax. in Aust.* 704.

Ferrers, A.O., "Does Fiscal Nullity Apply in Australia?" (1988), 17 *Aust. Tax Rev.* 104.

Ferrers, A.O., "Fair is Foul and Foul is Fair" (1989), 18 *Aust. Tax Rev.* 93.

Ferrers, A.O., "Fiscal Nullity in the Nether World: The *Ramsay* Doctrine in Australia" (1988), *NZLJ* 315.

Ferrers, A.O., "Tax Avoidance — What's in a Name? (1982), *NZLJ* 412.

Forsyth, N.H.M., "The General Structure of Part IVA" (1981), 10 *Aust. Tax Rev.* 133.

Forsyth, N.H.M., "Morality and Tax Avoidance", 7 *Brief* 74-79, 82-87.

Gotterson, Alan, "That Ruling" (February 1985), 55 *Chartered Acc.* 22.

Grantham, R.B., "Fiscal Nullity Reconsidered" (1988), *NZLJ* 311.

Grantham, R.B., "John v. FCT: A New Direction in the Judicial Response to Tax Avoidance" (1989), 33:7 *NZ Current Tax* 161.

Greenwood, J.M., "Taxation Notes: New Zealand — Avoidance of Tax [*Haliwell v. C.I.R.*, (1977) 3 NZTC 61208]", 30 *Chartered Sec.* 38.

"*The Gregrhon Investments Pty. Ltd.* Appeal" (1988), 17 *Aust. Tax Rev.* 1.

Grbich, Y., "Anti-Avoidance Discretions: The Continuing Battle to Control Tax Avoidance", 4 *UNSWLJ* 17.

Grbich, Y., "Problems of Tax Avoidance in Australia", *Taxation Issues of the 1980's* (Australian Tax Research Foundation: Sydney, 1983) 413.

Grbich, Y., "Section 260 Re-Examined: Posing Critical Questions About Tax Avoidance" (1975), 1 *UNSWLJ* 211.

Guild, W.G., "Fiscal Nullities and the Overruling of Curran's Case", [1989] *AT* 36017.

Guild, W.G., "Shams, Fiscal Nullities and Section 260 of the Income Tax Assessment Act 1936 (Cth)", [1985] *AT* 36036.

Guild, W.G., "Tax Avoidance Schemes and Losses and Outgoings", [1984] *AT* 36083.

Halkyard, Andrew, "Hong Kong: A Tax Haven Enacts Anti-Avoidance Legislation" (1986), 15 *Aust. Tax Rev.* 170.

Hambly, J.C., "The High Court's Decision in John's Case" (1989), 18 *Aust. Tax Rev.* 69 at 72.

Harley, G.J., "Structural Inequities and Concepts of Tax Avoidance" (1983), 13 *Victoria University of Wellington L. Rev.* 38.

Hill, D.G., "A New Interpretation of s. 260 and Its Implications for Part IVA", *Tax Institute of Australia 7th National Convention Papers* 3.

"The House of Lords and Tax Avoidance [*W.T.Ramsey Ltd. v. I.R.C.*, [1981] 2 WLR 449]" (1981), 55 *ALJ* 315.

Hulme, S.E.K., "The Place of Part IVA in the Income Tax Assessment Act" (1981), 10 *Aust. Tax Rev.* 121.

"I Can Get It For You Tax Free! — The Ethics of Tax Avoidance", 11 *Q. Law Soc. J.* 144.

Jenkin, P.J.H., "Tax Avoidance, Politics and Privy Councillors or: How Does One Mitigate the *Challenge* Decision?" (1988), *NZLJ* 305.

Kinross, Jeremy, "Applicability of 'Fiscal Nullity' Doctrine" (March 1988), *CLQ* 7.

Krever, Richard, ed., *Australian Taxation: Principles and Practice*, (Melbourne: Longman, 1987).

Krever, Richard, "*Furniss v. Dawson* — Tax Jurisprudence Re-Enters the Real World" (1984), 18 *Tax. in Aust.* 1057.

Krever, Richard E., "Tax Avoidance and Tax Reform: Who's to Blame and Who's to Repair?" (September 1987), 14 *Brief* 22.

Krever, Richard, "Tax Reform in Australia: Base-Broadening Down Under" (1986), 34 *Can. Tax. J.* 346.

MacDonald, J.H.S., "The Principle of Certainty", 9:3 *Brief* 10.

MacLean, D.M., "Recent Developments in Fiscal Nullity" (1987), 16 *Aust. Tax Rev.* 166.

MacLean, D.M., "Section 260 and Tupicoff's Case", (1985) 14 *Aust. Tax Rev.* 5.

Madden, Bryan, "The Revival of Section 260: Implications for Part IVA" (1985), 19 *Tax. in Aust.* 709.

Maher, L.W., "Lawyers' Ethics and Tax Avoidance", 56 *LIJ* 515.

Mannix, E.F., "*Ramsay* in Australia", [1984] *AT* 36017.

McKay, L., "Section 108 and the Issue of Legislative Propriety" (1976), *NZLJ* 238.

McLaughlin, D.W., "Section 108: Further Problems for the Commissioner", 5 *NZULR* 72.

Molloy, A.P., "Fiscal Fantasy" (1974), *NZLJ* 297.

Myers, A.J., "Federal Court Decides for Commissioner in Gregrhon Investments Case" (1988), 1 *BWT Bull.* 2.

Myers, A.J., "The Federal Court Decision in the Gregrhon Investments Pty. Ltd. Case" (1988), 17 *Aust. Tax Rev.* 4.

"The New Approach by the High Court on Section 260" (1986), 15 *Aust. Tax Rev.* 1.

New Zealand, Commissioner of Inland Revenue, "Policy Statement on Sec. 99" (June 1990), 44 *Bull. Int'l. Fisc. Doc.* 288.

Norman, Peter J., "Gulland, Watson and Pincus in the High Court" (1986), 20 *Tax. in Aust.* 639.

O'Connor, R.K., "Analysis and Implications of the Gulland, Watson and Pincus Cases on s. 260" (January 21, 1986), 3 *BWT Bull.* 16.

O'Connor, R.K., "Income-Splitting by Professionals" (1986), 20 *Tax. in Aust.* 87.

Pane, Tony, "The Relevance of Fiscal Nullity After John's Case" (1989), 1 *J. Aust. Tax* 34.

Prebble, J., "Tax Avoiding Arrangements that Comply With Section 104, Income Tax Act 1976", 8 *NZULR* 70.

Reicher, H., "Taxation" (1982), 10 *Aust. Bus. Rev.* 68.

Reicher, H., "Taxation [Tax Avoidance Schemes and the New Legislation]", 6 *Aust. Bus. Rev.* 177.

Reicher, H., "Tax Avoidance in 1977: The Decline and Fall of Section 260" (1978), 12 *Tax. in Aust.* 680.

Richardson, I.L.M., "Appellate Court Responsibilities and Tax Avoidance", 2:1 *ATF* 3.

Richardson, Jim, "Splitting Personal Income" (1990), 60 *Aust. Acc.* 43.

Richardson, R.J. and M. Ferrier, "Commissioner's Views on Section 260 and Part IVA" (August/September 1986), 38 *Prof. Admin.* 40.

Russell, D.G., "Bury the Great Duke" (1984), 19 *Tax. in Aust.* 250.

Slater, A.H., "A Ruse by Any Other Name Would Smell as Sweet [*FC of T. v. K. Porter & Co. Pty. Ltd.*]" (1974), 45:1 *Chartered Acc.* 30-1.

Somers, T.C., "Income Tax — Anti-Avoidance Provisions New Developments in Relation to S. 260 and Part IVA of the Income Tax Assessment Act 1936 (as amended)" (1987), 17 *Q. Law Soc. J.* 417.

Speed, Robin, "The High Court and Part IVA" (1986), 15 *Aust. Tax Rev.* 156.

Spry, I.C.F., "A Further Decision on Section 260" (1978), 7 *Aust. Tax Rev.* 9.

Spry, I.C.F., "A Recent Privy Council Decision on Tax Avoidance" (1975), 4 *Aust. Tax Rev.* 220.

Spry, I.C.F., *Arrangements for the Avoidance of Taxation* (Melbourne: Law Book Co., 1971).

Spry, I.C.F., "Arrangements for the Avoidance of Taxation", 46 *LIJ* 344-45.

Spry, I.C.F., "Discretionary Trusts and Section 260" (1971), 1 *Aust. Tax Rev.* 265.

Spry, I.C.F., "Fiscal Nullity in Australia" (1984), 13 *Aust. Tax Rev.* 150.

Spry, I.C.F., "Recent Decisions Concerning Section 260 [*Gerard v. C.I.R.*; *Wheelans v. C.I.R.*]" (1973), 2 *Aust. Tax Rev.* 170.

Spry, I.C.F., "Section 260 and Choices Presented to Taxpayers" (1971), 1 *Aust. Tax Rev.* 54.

Spry, I.C.F., "Section 260 of the Income Tax Assessment Act" (1984), 13 *Aust. Tax Rev.* 236.

Spry, I.C.F., "The Use of Tax Shelters" (1981), 10 *Aust. Tax Rev.* 4.

Stone, Philippa, and K. Powrie, "Taxation: The Fiscal Nullity Doctrine" (1989), 63 *ALJ* 622.

Sweeney, C.A., ed., "Revenue Note" (1988), 62 *ALJ* 470.

Sweeney, C.A., ed., "Revenue Note — Curran's Case Confined to Its Own Facts" (1987), 61 *ALJ* 742.

Sweeney, C.A., ed., "Revenue Note — Revised Legislative Provisions Against Avoidance of Income Tax" (1981), 55 *ALJ* 887.

Sweeney, C.A., ed., "Revenue Note — Section 260 Finds New Life" (1986), 60 *ALJ* 302.

Sweeney, C.A., ed., "Revenue Note" (1985), 59 *ALJ* 346.

Sweeney, C.A., ed., "Revenue Note" (1987), 61 *ALJ* 148.

Sweidan, Andre, "Section 260 of the Income Tax Assessment Act 1936 (Cth) Vendor Shareholders" (1988), 22 *Tax. in Aust.* 113.

"Tax Avoidance: Is Part IVA Really Necessary?" (August 1984), 54 *Aust. Acc.* 566.

"Tax Avoidance Reform?", [January 1980] 17 *Reform* 107.

"Tax Avoidance: The Gulland and Watson Cases" (October 1984), 54 *Aust. Acc.* 756.

"Tax Avoidance: The Pursuit of Scapegoats" (1987), 16 *Aust. Tax Rev.* 3.

Trebilcock, M.J., "Arrangements for the Avoidance of Taxation", 4 *Adelaide L.R.* 491.

Trebilcock, M.J., "Section 260: A Critical Examination" (1964), 38 *ALJ* 237.

Voumard, L.C., "Arrangements for the Avoidance of Taxation", 10 *Law Soc. J.* 131.

Voumard, L.C., "New Zealand's Section 108 Again [*Gerard v. C.I.R.*; *Whelan and Ashton v. C.I.R.*]", 48 *LIJ* 434.

Voumard, L.C., "New Zealand's Section 260 [*Gerard v. C.I.R.*; *Wheelans v. C.I.R.*]", 47 *LIJ* 230.

Wallace, E.W., "Government Moves on Stamp Duty Avoidance — Stamp Duties Amendment Act 1980", 3:1 *Law Soc. Bull.* 1.

Wallace, E.W., "Stamp Duty Amendments — Proposed Abolition of Death Duty and Sixth Schedule Rates, Anti-Avoidance" (1981), 19 *Law Soc. J.* 223.

Wallschutzky, I., "A Further Decision on Section 260" (1978), 7 *Aust. Tax Rev.* 79.

Wallschutzky, I., "Results of a Survey on Some Aspects of Tax Avoidance" (1983), 17 *Tax. in Aust.* 282.

Wallschutsky, I., "Towards a Definition of the Term Tax Avoidance" (1985), 14 *Aust. Tax Rev.* 48.

United Kingdom

Adams, L.D., "*Craven v. White*: U.K. Step-Transaction Doctrine Evolves — Canadian Planners Beware" (1988), 2:13 *Can. Current Tax* C-75.

Archambault, P., "La nouvelle disposition générale anti-envitement et l'expérience jurisprudentielle anglaise récente" (1987), 9 *RPFS* 501.

Ashton, R.K., "The Ramsay and Burmah Decisions — A Reappraisal" (1983), 4 *British Tax Rev.* 221.

Avery Jones, J.F., "The New Approach in U.K. Tax Law — Where Do We Stand?" (October 1987), *Asian-Pacific Tax and Investment Bull.* 414.

Avery Jones, J.F., "Nothing Either Good or Bad, But Thinking Makes It So — The Mental Element in Anti-Avoidance Legislation — I" (1983), 1 *British Tax Rev.* 9.

Avery Jones, J.F., "Nothing Either Good or Bad, But Thinking Makes It So — The Mental Element in Anti-Avoidance Legislation — II" (1983), 2 *British Tax Rev.* 113.

Avery Jones, J.F., ed., *Tax Havens and Measures Against Tax Evasion and Avoidance in the EEC* (London: Associated Business Programmes, 1974)

Bartlett, R.T., "The Constitutionality of the Ramsay Principle" (1985), 6 *British Tax Rev.* 338.

Beattie, C.N., "*Furniss v. Dawson* — I: The Duke of Westminster Doctrine and Lord Tomlin's Dictum" (1984), 128 *Solic. J.* 139.

Beattie, C.N., "Notes of Cases — *Furniss v. Dawson*" (1984), 2 *British Tax Rev.* 109.

Bretten, G.R., and Fay Stockton, "The Ramsay Doctrine: An Interim Review" (1987), 8 *British Tax Rev.* 280.

"The Boundaries of Ramsay" (1985), 4 *British Tax Rev.* 197.

Cane, L., "*Furniss v. Dawson*, [[1984] 2 WLR 226]: Where Do We Go From Here?" (1984) *New L.J.* 597.

Chopin, L.F., "Taxation of Unremitted Partnership Income: A Vestige of Unchecked Tax Abuse" (1979), 42 *Modern L. Rev.* 342.

"Current Notes: Bringing Forth More Mice" (1988), 10 *British Tax Rev.* 401.

"Current Notes: Taking Stock of the New Approach" (1988), 6 *British Tax Rev.* 209.

Deane, K.D., "Law, Morality and Tax Evasion" (1984), 13:1 *Anglo-Am. L. Rev.* 1.

"Development Land Tax: Tax Avoidance Scheme — Application of Ramsay Principle" (1986), 130 *Solic. J.* 15.

Farnsworth, A., "Legal Evasion of Taxation" (1942), 6 *Modern L. Rev.* 243.

Ferrier, Ian, "The Meaning of the Statute: Mansfield on Tax Avoidance" (1981), *British Tax Rev.* 303.

Flanagan, T., "Tax Avoidance and the Legal Personality", [1979] 43 *Conv.* 195.

Gammie, M.J., "After Dawson" (1984), 5:3 *Fiscal Studies* 23.

Gammie, M.J., "The Implications of *Furniss v. Dawson*" (1985), 6:3 *Fiscal Studies* 51.

Gammie, M.J., "Revenue Practice — A Suitable Case for Treatment" (1980), *British Tax Rev.* 304.

Goldberg, D., "Mete Wands: How Gold and Straight?" (1981), *British Tax Rev.* 233.

Goldberg, D., "O Brave New World That Hath Such Decisions in It: And Herein of the Separation of Powers" (1982), *British Tax Rev.* 13.

Goldsworth, John, "United Kingdom: Anti-Avoidance Cases Examined" (1989), 1 *Tax Notes Int'l.* 180.

Goldsworth, John, "United Kingdom: The Fiscal Motive — Not Enough to Invoke the Ramsay Principle" (1989), 1 *Tax Notes Int'l.* 294.

Hayton, D., "The Revenue's Trump Card Against Tax Avoidance" (1984), 43 *Cambridge L.J.* 259.

Kay, J.A., "The Economics of Tax Avoidance" (1979), 6 *British Tax. Rev.* 354.

Kessler, James, "Notes of Cases: *Craven v. White*" (1987), 7 *British Tax Rev.* 266.

Kessler, James, "Note of Case: *Kwok Chi Leung Karl v. Commissioner of Estate Duty*" (1989), 4 *British Tax Rev.* 130.

Lawton, P., "The Ramsay Doctrine" (April 1982), *Taxation Practitioner* 88.

MacDonald, E., "Reflections on Recent Leading Tax Cases" (1985), 129 *Solic. J.* 307.

MacDonald, G., "*Coates (Inspector of Taxes) v. Arndale Properties Ltd.* [[1982] STC 573] — Tax Avoidance, Trading Stock and Motive" (1982), *British Tax Rev.* 382.

Mansfield, Graham, "The 'New Approach' to Tax Avoidance: First Circular, Then Linear, Now Narrower" (1989), 1 *British Tax Rev.* 5.

Marsh, I.A., " *Magnavox Electronics Co. Ltd. (in liqidation) v. Hall* [[1985] STC 260]" (1985), *British Tax Rev.* 313.

Millett, Peter J., "A New Approach to Tax Avoidance Schemes" (1982), 98 *Law Quarterly Rev.* 209.

Millett, Peter J., "Artificial Tax Avoidance: The English and American Approaches" (1986), 6 *British Tax Rev.* 327.

Monroe, H. H., "Fiscal Finesse: Tax Avoidance and the Duke of Westminster" (1982), *British Tax Rev.* 200.

Morse, G.K., "New Mythology of Tax Avoidance", [1983] 47 *Conv.* 11.

Morse, G.K., "Tax Avoidance: Mythology as Fact", [1984] 48 *Conv.* 296.

Nicoll, David, "Notes of Cases: *IRC v. Challenge Corporation Ltd.* — Tax Mitigation" (1987), 3 *British Tax Rev.* 134.

Oliver, J.D.B., "Current Note: *Sherdley v. Sherdley* or *Furniss v. Dawson* Again" (1986), *British Tax Rev.* 249.

Oliver, J.D.B., "The Boundaries of Ramsay" (1985), 4 *British Tax Rev.* 197.

Oliver, Stephen, "The Ramsay/Dawson Doctrine — The Quest for the Relevant Transaction", in *Recent Tax Problems: Current Legal Problems* 1 (Stevens & Sons: London, 1985).

Potter, D.C., "Retrospective Anti-Avoidance Legislation" (1978), *British Tax Rev.* 133.

Ray, R.P., "Deeds of Covenant — Revisited" (1984), 134 *New L.J.* 63.

Ray, R.P., "Revenue Suffers Further Anti-Avoidance Setback" (June 30, 1989), *Taxes* 1.

Shipwright, J., "Is Tax Planning Dead? — Burmah: A Case Note" (1982), 126 *Solic. J.* 144.

Shipwright, J., "Play Based on the Duke of Westminster? The Ramsay and Rawling Cases" (1981), 125 *Solic. J.* 227.

Stary, Erica, "*Furniss v. Dawson*: Revenue Guidelines" (1985), *British Tax Rev.* 1015.
"Tax Avoidance" (1988), 38 *New L.J.* 527.
Tax Havens and Measures Against Tax Evasion and Avoidance in the EEC, ed., J.F. Avery Jones (London: Associated Business Programmes, 1974).
Tax Law After Furniss v. Dawson (London: The Law Society of England and Wales, 1988).
Tax Law in the Melting Pot (London: The Law Society of England and Wales, 1985).
Taylor, T.P.D., "Tax Planning and Tax Avoidance after Ramsay" (1982), *Taxation* 494.
Thompson, A., "Some Thoughts on Tax Avoidance" (1978), 128 *New L.J.* 629.
Tiley, John, "An Academic Perspective on the Ramsay/Dawson Doctrine", in *Recent Tax Problems: Current Legal Problems* 19 (London: Stevens & Sons, 1985).
Tiley, John, *Butterworth's U.K. Tax Guide 1989-90* (8th Ed.), (London: Butterworth, 1989) 4-17, 862-900.
Tiley, John, "Judicial Anti-Avoidance Doctrines: Corporations and Conclusions" (1988), 4 *British Tax Rev.* 108.
Tiley, John, "Judicial Anti-Avoidance Doctrines: Some Problem Areas" (1988), 3 *British Tax Rev.* 63.
Tiley, John, "Judicial Anti-Avoidance Doctrines: The U.S. Alternatives — Part I" (1987), 5 *British Tax Rev.* 180.
Tiley, John, "Judicial Anti-Avoidance Doctrines: The U.S. Alternatives — Part II" (1987), 6 *British Tax Rev.* 220.
Tiley, John, "Note of Case" (1989), 1 *British Tax Rev.* 20.
Tiley, John, "Tax Avoidance — A Change in the Rules" (1982), 41 *Cambridge L.J.* 50.
Tiley, John, "Tax Enforcement, Avoidance and Evasion" (1985), *Cambridge Lect.* 211.
Ward, David A., et al., "The Business Purpose Test and Abuse of Rights" (1985), 2 *British Tax Rev.* 68.
Wheatcroft, G.S.A., "The Attitude of the Legislature and the Courts to Tax Avoidance" (1955), 18 *Modern L.R.* 209.
White, Roger, "The New Approach and the Views of the Law Society" (1986), 1 *British Tax Rev.* 18.
Whitehorse, Chris, "Reopening the Door to Tax Avoidance" (1988), 138 *New L.J.* 540.

United States

Aidinoff, M.B., "*Furniss v. Dawson*: The U.S. Experience" (1985), 6:4 *Fiscal Studies* 76.
Angell, Mongomery B., "Tax Evasion and Tax Avoidance" (1938), 38 *Colum. L. Rev.* 80.
Bittker, Boris I., *Federal Taxation of Income and Gifts*, 5th ed. (New York: Warren, Gorham & Lamont, 1985) 4:29.
Bittker, Boris I., "Pervasive Judicial Doctrines in the Construction of the Internal Revenue Code" (1978), 21 *Howard L.J.* 693, 714.
Bittker, Boris I., "What is 'Business Purpose' in Reorganizations?" (1950), in *New York University's 8th Annual Institute on Federal Taxation* 134.

Blum, Walter J., "Knetsch v. U.S.: A Pronouncement on Tax Avoidance" (1962), 40 *Taxes* 296.

Blum, Walter J., "Motive, Intent and Purpose in Federal Income Taxation" (1967), 34 *University of Chicago Law Rev.* 485.

Carr Kelly, David, "Tax Motivated Divorce and the Sham Transaction Doctrine — *Boyter v. Commissioner* [668 F. 2d 1382] (1982), 18 *Wake Forest L. Rev.* 881.

The Carter Commission Report, 3 *Report of the Royal Commission on Taxation: Taxation of Income* (Canada, 1966) 537.

Chirelstein, Marvin A., "Learned Hand's Contribution to the Law of Tax Avoidance" (1968), 77 *Yale L.J.* 440.

Cohen, Edwin S., "Tax Avoidance Purpose as a Statutory Test in Tax Legislation" (1960), in *Proceedings of the Ninth Annual Tulane Tax Institute* 229.

Ditkoff, J.H., "Intercorporate Dividends and Legitimate Tax Avoidance" (1977), 4 *J. Corporate Taxation* 5.

Falcone, Angelo C. and David G. Mann, "Tax Avoidance and the Anti-Avoidance Proposals: The U.S. Experience with the Business Purpose Doctrine", in *1987 B. C. Tax Conf.* (Can. Tax Foundation, 1987).

Fuller, Hoffman F., "Business Purpose, Sham Transactions and the Relation of Private Law to the Law of Taxation" (1963), 37 *Tul. L. Rev.* 355.

Gideon, Kenneth W. and Ruth E. Kent, "Mrs. Gregory's Northern Tour: Canadian Proposals to Adopt the Business Purpose Rule and the Step Transaction Doctrine", in *Proceedings of 39th Tax Conf.* 7:1 (Can. Tax Foundation, 1987).

Gissel, L.H., "Income Shifting Devices — What's Left?" (1986) 20 *Inst. of Est. Plan.* 14.1.

Greiner, R.G., P.L. Behling and J.D. Moffett, "Assumption of Liabilities and the Improper Purpose — A Re-examination of Section 357(b)", (1978) 32 *Tax Lawyer* 111.

Griesel, L.W. and D. Beail, "Tax Planning: Problem or Solution?" (1984), 38 *Wash. St. B. News* 23.

Gunn, A., "Tax Avoidance" (1978), 76 *Mich. L. Rev.* 733.

Gunn, A., "The Hatian Vacation: The Applicability of Sham Doctrines to Year-End Divorces" (1979), 77 *Mich. L. Rev.* 1332.

Hobbet, "The Step Transaction Doctrine and Its Effect on Corporate Transactions" (1970), 19 *Tul. Tax Inst.* 102.

Isenbergh, "Musings on Form and Substance in Taxation" (1982), 49 *University of Chicago L. Rev.* 859.

McMahon, "Defining the 'Aquisition' in B Reorganizations Through the Step Transaction Doctrine" (1981), 67 *Iowa Law Rev.* 31.

Millett, Peter, "Artificial Tax Avoidance: The English and American Approach" (1986), 6 *British Tax Rev.* 327.

Mintz, S.S. and W.T. Plumb Jr., "Step Transactions in Corporate Reorganizations", in *Proceedings of New York University's 12th Annual Institute on Federal Taxation*, November 4-13, 1953 (New York: Matthew Bender, 1954) 247.

Moore, S.M., "Form v. Substance: When Will Courts Respect the Form of a Transaction?" (1987), 66 *J. Taxation* 66.

Murray Jr., Oliver C., "Step Transactions" (1969), 24 *University of Miami Law Rev.* 60.

Note, "Evolution of the Step Transaction Doctrine" (1971), 11 *Washburn Law J.* 84.

Paul, Randolph E., "Restatement of the Law of Tax Avoidance" (1937), in *Selected Studies in Federal Taxation* 9.

Paul, Randolph E. and Philip Zimet, "Step Transactions", in *Selected Studies in Federal Taxation* (2nd series, 1938) 200.

Rice, Ralph S., "Judicial Techniques in Combatting Tax Avoidance" (1953), 51 *Mich. L. Rev.* 1021.

Rosenberg, Joshua D., "Tax Avoidance and Income Measurement" (November 1988), 87 *Michigan Law Rev.* 365.

Schneider, D.M., "Internal Revenue Code Section 306 and Tax Avoidance" (1985), 4 *Va. Rev.* 287.

Steele, T.H., "Sham in Substance: The Tax Court's Emerging Standard for Testing Sale-Leasebacks" (1986), 14 *J. Real Est. Taxation* 3.

"Step Transactions" (1969), 24 *U. Miami L. Rev.* 60,66.

Summers, Robert S., "A Critique of the Business Purpose Doctrine" (1961), 41 *Or. L. Rev.* 38.

Tiley, John, "Judicial Anti-Avoidance Doctrines: The U.S. Alternatives — Part I" (1987), 5 *British Tax Rev.* 180.

Tiley, John, "Judicial Anti-Avoidance Doctrines: The U.S. Alternatives — Part II" (1987), 6 *British Tax Rev.* 220.

Waizer, Harry, "The Business Purpose Doctrine: The Effect of Motive on Federal Income Tax Liability" (1981), 49 *Fordham L. Rev.* 1078.

Warren, A.C., "Requirement of Economic Profit in Tax Motivated Transactions" (1981), 59 *Taxes* 985.

Weinstein, W.J., "Pay the Taxes, Dammit" (1980), 59 *Mich. B.J.* 686.

Whitmire, R.L., "Bailing Out of Tax Shelters: Selected Techniques" (1978), 30 *So. Calif. Tax Inst.* 503.

Wolfman, Bernard, "The Supreme Court in the *Lyon's* Den: A Failure of Judicial Process" (1981), 66 *Cornell L. Rev.* 1075.

Ireland

Judge, Norman E., ed., *Tax Law: Principles and Practice* (Butterworth & Co. (Publishers) Ltd.)

Other

Bracewell-Milnes, Barry, *The Economics of International Tax Avoidance* (Deventer, the Netherlands: Kluwer).

Edwards, P.S.A., "Anti-Avoidance Provisions in Hong Kong" (1987), 3 *The Journal of Strategy in Int'l. Taxation* 247.

Garde, H.S., *Swedish National Reporter Tax Avoidance and Tax Evasion* (London: Sweet & Maxwell, 1982).

Halkyard, Andrew, "Hong Kong: A Tax Haven Enacts Anti-Avoidance Legislation" (1986), 15 *Australian Tax Rev.* 170.

OECD, "International Tax Avoidance and Evasion", 31 *Bull. Int'l. Fisc. Doc.* 11.

OECD, *International Tax Avoidance and Evasion, Four Related Studies* (Paris: OECD, 1987).

OECD, "Work on Tax Avoidance and Evasion" (1980-81), *Intertax* 11.

Van Hoorn, J., "Problems, Possibilities and Limitations With Respect to Measures Against International Tax Avoidance and Evasion" (1978), 8 *Ga. J. Int'l. & Comp. L.* 763.

Ward, David A., "Tax Avoidance: Judicial and Legislative Approaches in Other Jurisdictions", in *Proceedings of 39th Tax Conf.* 8:1 (Can. Tax Foundation, 1987).

Wisselink, M.A. and Barry Bracewell-Milnes, *International Tax Avoidance — Volume A*, pp. 128-134, 198-214 (Deventer, the Netherlands: Kluwer, 1979).

INDEX TO INCOME TAX

All references are to page numbers.

Charities, 578-581, 583, 584

Charter of Rights and Freedoms, 1137-1142

Child care expenses, 372, 557-560

Classical system, 804, 805, 1249

Clearance certificates
- generally, 1118
- section 116 certificates, 1066, 1067
- winding-up, 1015

Closer connection statement, 1361

Collateralized preferred shares, 814

Collection procedure, 1099

Common law spouse, principal residence, 496

Competent authority consideration, 1170

Completed contract method of accounting, 296

Compound interest, 390, 394, 1277, 1281

Compulsory offer clause, 863

Computation of tax payable. *See* Tax payable

Concessions, 420

Conformity of accounting methods, 305-308

Connected corporations, 747-749, 939

Constitutional background, 4-7

Constitutional limits, 50

Constructive receipt of income, 526

Contingent arrangements, 218

Contingent liability, 374

Contract of service vs contract for services, 187-193

Contractors, 298

Contribution test, 1205

Control, 595, 596. *See also* Corporate control

Control test, 188, 189

Controlled corporation, dispositions to, 489, 593

Controlled foreign affiliate, 1332-1339

Convention expenses, 430, 431

Convertible debt, 723-725

Corporate attribution rules, 919, 1212-1214, 1237

Corporate control
- *de facto* control, 789, 790
- *de jure* control, 784-789

Corporate emigration, 1015-1017

Corporate partnerships, 775, 776

Corporate reorganization. *See* Section 85 reorganization

Corporate shares, situs, 139-141

Corporations. *See also* Shareholders, Shares
- acquisition of own shares, 690, 692, 697
- advantages, 674-676
- capital gains, 755-757
- carrying charges on vacant land, 395, 1282
- convention expenses, 431
- creditor's rights, 694
- discretionary dividends, 529
- distribution of profits, 803
- double taxation. *See* Double taxation
- equity financing. *See* Equity financing
  - exemption from tax (Indian), 136
- funding, sources of, 681
- income splitting, 528-530, 675
- information returns, 1086
- instalment payments, 1108, 1109
- integration. *See* Tax integration
- intra-company meetings, 431
- large corporations capital tax, 638
- non-resident, 1240
- piercing corporate veil, 656-659
- private. *See* Private corporations
- reassessments, 1093, 194
- reorganization. *See* Section 85 reorganization
- residence. *See* Residence — corporations
- rollovers. *See* Rollovers
- separate legal entity, 653-656
- short fiscal periods, 1109
- structure of corporate taxation, 660-668
- surplus stripping. *See* Non-arm's length share transfers